D0041216

# Scotland

Neil Wilson
Alan Murphy

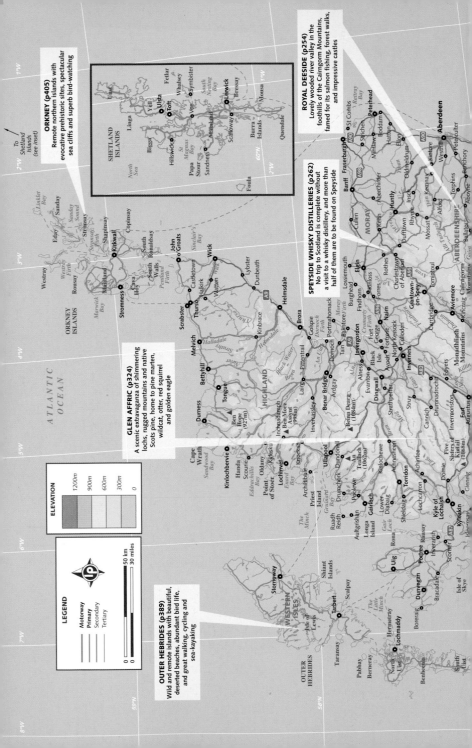

**OUTER HEBRIDES (p389)**
Wild and remote islands with beautiful, deserted beaches, abundant bird life, and great walking, cycling and sea-kayaking

**GLEN AFFRIC (p324)**
A scenic extravaganza of shimmering lochs, rugged mountains and native Scots pine, home to pine marten, wildcat, otter, red squirrel and golden eagle

**ORKNEY (p405)**
Remote northern islands with evocative prehistoric sites, spectacular sea cliffs and superb bird-watching

**ROYAL DEESIDE (p254)**
Lovely wooded river valley in the foothills of the Cairngorm Mountains, famed for its salmon fishing, forest walks, and impressive castles

**SPEYSIDE WHISKY DISTILLERIES (p262)**
No trip to Scotland is complete without a visit to a whisky distillery, and more than half of them are to be found on Speyside

**LEGEND**

Motorway
Primary
Secondary
Tertiary

**ELEVATION**

1200m
900m
600m
300m
0

To Shetland Islands (see inset)

SHETLAND ISLANDS

North Sea

Fethaland
Hillswick
Papa Stour
Sandness
Fodla
Bigga
Yell
Ulsta
Toft
Whalsay
Vidlin
Symbister
Voe
Linga
Vaila
St Magnus Bay
Mainland
Scalloway
Lerwick
Burra Islands
Bressay
Mousa
Quendale
South Nesting Bay

ATLANTIC OCEAN

Linklet Bay
Sanday
Sanday Sound
Eday
Westray
Stronsay
Shapinsay
Copinsay
Rousay
Mainland
ORKNEY ISLANDS
Kirkwall
Stromsay
Marwick Bay
Sandwood Bay
Scapa Flow
Hoy
South Walls
Pentland Firth
John O'Groats
South Ronaldsay
Sinclair's Bay
Wick

Cape Wrath
Durness
Kinlochbervie
Scourie
Handa
Eddrachillis Bay
Point of Stoer
Lochinver
Knockan
Ullapool
Dundonnell
Aultbea
Poolewe
Gairloch
Longa Island
Raadh Reidh
Gruinard Bay
Priest Island
Summer Isles
Little Loch Broom
Loch Maree
Kinlochewe
Torridon
Lower Diabaig
Shieldaig
Applecross
Lochcarron
Achintee
Kyle of Lochalsh
Kyleakin
Dornie
Five Sisters of Kintail (1068m)
Glenelg
Arnisdale
Loch Hourn

Melvich
Bettyhill
Tongue
Durness
Ben Hope (927m)
Halladale
Strath Naver
Strathy
Strath More
Bonar Bridge
Lairg
Inchnadamph
Ben More Assynt (998m)
Invershin
Ardgay
Beinn Dearg (1084m)
Strath Oykel
Garve
Strathpeffer
Dingwall
Struy
Cannich
Drumnadrochit
Invermoriston
Foyers
Fort Augustus

HIGHLAND

Scrabster
Thurso
Halkirk
Watten
Castletown
Dunbeath
Lybster
Latheron
Helmsdale
Brora
Golspie
Dunrobin
Dornoch
Portmahomack
Tain
Invergordon
Alness
Evanton
Fortrose
Fort George
Cromarty
North Kessock
Inverness
Culloden
Black Isle
Avoch
Moray Firth
Dornoch Firth

Kinbrace
An Teallach (1062m)
Black Water

MORAY

ABERDEENSHIRE

Lossiemouth
Burghead
Findhorn
Forres
Elgin
Rothes
Charlestown of Aberlour
Dufftown
Keith
Cullen
Buckie
Fochabers
Rhynie
Huntly
Insch
Inverurie
Alford
Mossat
Tomintoul
Grantown-on-Spey
Aviemore
Carrbridge
Monadhliath Mountains
Cairngorm Mountains
Ballater
Braemar
Tomnavoulin
Cairn Gorm (1245m)

Banff
Fraserburgh
St Combs
Rattray Head
Peterhead
Mintlaw
Strichen
Boddam
Hatton
New Pitsligo
Turriff
Oldmeldrum
Ellon
Kintore
Westhill
Aberdeen
Peterculter
Torphins
Aboyne
Banchory

WESTERN ISLES

Isle of Lewis
Stornoway
Taransay
Tarbert
Pabbay
Berneray
Scalpay
Shiant Islands
Borreraig
North Uist
Lochmaddy
Benbecula
Uig
Portree
Raasay
Dunvegan
Bracadale
Isle of Skye
Sconser
Inverarish
Kyleakin
Broadford
The Minch
The Little Minch
Spuir List

**OUTER HEBRIDES**

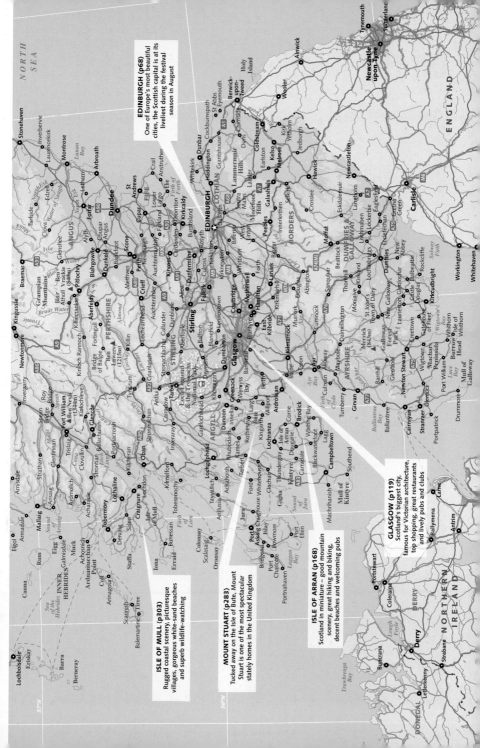

**EDINBURGH (p68)**
One of Europe's most beautiful cities, the Scottish capital is at its liveliest during the festival season in August

**GLASGOW (p119)**
Scotland's biggest city, famous for Victorian architecture, top shopping, great restaurants and lively pubs and clubs

**ISLE OF MULL (p303)**
Rugged coastal scenery, picturesque villages, gorgeous white-sand beaches and superb wildlife-watching

**MOUNT STUART (p283)**
Tucked away on the Isle of Bute, Mount Stuart is one of the most spectacular stately homes in the United Kingdom

**ISLE OF ARRAN (p168)**
Scotland in miniature – good mountain scenery, great hiking and biking, decent beaches and welcoming pubs

# On the Road

## NEIL WILSON

'To the ends of the earth'…well, to the ends of Scotland, at least. This is Bosta, on the northern tip of Great Bernera (p396) in the Outer Hebrides, about as far away from my home in Edinburgh as you can get without leaving the country; next stop over the horizon is Canada. It's a wild and beautiful spot, with a superb sandy beach, and a totally unexpected bonus – a reconstruction of an Iron Age house, complete with strips of mutton smoking over the peat fire. Well worth the long journey.

## ALAN MURPHY

The northwest Highlands (p364) are simply magical and driving the single-track roads between the mighty Munros is always breathtaking. Although there are often dark rain clouds and mist swirling around the rocky peaks looming over Glen Torridon, when a sunny day strikes, the mountains themselves become crystal clear, save the long afternoon shadows cast by legions of fluffy white clouds. No matter the conditions, this area never fails to make me want to strap on my boots and head straight up the nearest one.

*See full author bios page 462*

# SCOTLAND

Scotland is where Europe kicks off its shoes, wriggles its toes in the Atlantic surf, and gets back to the basics – inspiring landscapes, fascinating cities, spectacular wildlife, and hospitable, down-to-earth inhabitants. It's where glaciers and storms have conspired to sculpt some of the UK's most astounding scenery; where crag-top castles and ancient stone circles speak of a rich and turbulent past; where eagles glide above jagged peaks, otters tumble in the kelp along rocky shores, and dolphins break the waves amid sparkling seas. And where, after a day of hiking the high summits, you can swap tales of your experiences over a whisky or three.

# Edinburgh, Glasgow & Southern Scotland

One cultured and cosmopolitan, the other commercial and cutting-edge, Edinburgh and Glasgow are forever facing off in friendly rivalry. But both offer a wealth of inspiring architecture, great museums and galleries, rave-review restaurants and party-on pubs and clubs. And both are within easy reach of southern Scotland, a region often overlooked by visitors but home to a range of under-appreciated delights, from the dramatic ruined abbeys of Melrose and Jedburgh to the jagged peaks and picturesque villages of the Isle of Arran.

### ❶ Edinburgh Castle
Perched on a brooding black crag overlooking the city centre, Edinburgh Castle (p80) has played a pivotal role in Scottish history.

### ❷ Rosslyn Chapel
Rosslyn Chapel (p115), of *Da Vinci Code* fame, is Scotland's most beautiful and enigmatic church, its ornately carved interior a monument to the stonemason's art.

### ❸ Glasgow Pubs
Some of Scotland's liveliest nightlife is to be found in the din and roar of Glasgow's drinking dens (p140), from the many traditional Victorian-era pubs to the city's famed style bars.

### ❹ Isle of Arran
Often described as Scotland in miniature, the enchanting Isle of Arran (p168) is a treasure house of scenic delights within easy reach of Glasgow.

### ❺ Kelvingrove Art Gallery & Museum
A grand Victorian cathedral of culture, Kelvingrove (p129) is one of Scotland's best museums, recently reopened after an enormous refurbishment programme.

# Central & Northeast Scotland

Curled around the southern and eastern fringes of the Highlands, this region is famous for its whisky distilleries, but there's plenty more to enjoy – from imposing Baronial castles, cosy country-house hotels and quaint little fishing villages, to championship golf courses, salmon-rich rivers and long walks among heather-clad hills. Pull up an armchair, put another log on the fire and settle down with a warming dram of single malt.

**3**

### ❶ Stirling
With its winding cobblestone streets, medieval architecture, and dramatic, crag-top castle, Stirling (p193) rivals Edinburgh for historical attractions and atmosphere.

### ❷ St Andrews Old Course
Scotland is the home of golf, and the Old Course at St Andrews (p211) – the oldest golf course in the world – is on every golfer's wish list.

### ❸ Glen Clova
The longest and loveliest of the Angus Glens, Glen Clova (p243) is surrounded by steep, heather-clad Highland hills that offer scenic and challenging hiking territory.

### ❹ Royal Deeside
The valley of the River Dee – often called Royal Deeside (p254) because of the royal family's long association with the area – is famed for its salmon fishing, forest walks, and grandiose castles, including the Queen's holiday home at Balmoral.

### ❺ Speyside Distilleries
No trip to Scotland is complete without a visit to a whisky distillery, and the Speyside region, around Dufftown (p262) in Moray, has one of the highest concentrations in the country.

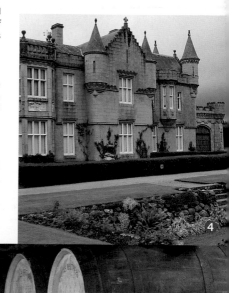

**4**

**5**

# Highlands & Islands

The big skies and lonely landscapes of the Highlands and islands are the very essence of Scotland, a wilderness of sea and mountains that remains one of Europe's most unspoilt regions. From the sylvan shores of Loch Lomond and the sub-Arctic plateau of the Cairngorms, to the rocky mountains of Sutherland and the dazzling beaches of the Hebrides, Scotland's Highlands and islands are one huge adventure playground, offering countless challenges to hikers, bikers, climbers and kayakers, and providing the chance to see some of the UK's most spectacular wildlife.

### ❶ Glen Affric

Beautiful Glen Affric (p324) is a walkers' wonderland, a scenic extravaganza of shimmering lochs, rugged mountains and native Scots pine, home to pine marten, wildcat, otter, red squirrel and golden eagle.

### ❷ Lewis & Harris

The remote beaches of Lewis (p391; pictured) and Harris (p396) are a revelation, flaunting their golden sands and turquoise waters like Caribbean impostors.

### ❸ Isle of Mull

From the rugged ridges of Ben More to the rose-pink granite and emerald waters of the Ross, Mull (p303) can lay claim to some of the finest and most varied scenery in Scotland, and the waters off its west coast provide some of the best whale-spotting opportunities in the country.

### ❹ Isle of Eigg

Dominated by its own mini-mountain, the Sgurr of Eigg, this delightful island (p351) is a haven of peace, offering good walking, lots of wildlife, singing sands and a haunted cave.

### ❺ Mount Stuart

Home to the marquess of Bute, Mount Stuart (p283) is the grandest neo-Gothic stately home in Scotland, a kaleidoscopic confection of polished marble, polychrome painting, glittering crystal and colourful stained glass.

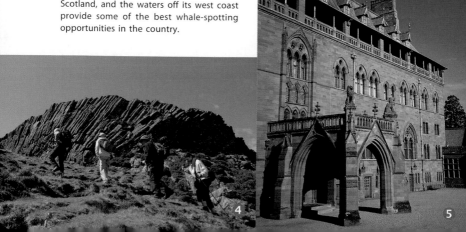

# Orkney & Shetland Islands

Even further away from it all than the rest of the country, Scotland's northern isles are scattered among stormy waters where the Atlantic crashes into the North Sea. Possessed of a desolate beauty, these treeless, cliff-bound islands have a fascinating Viking heritage, harbour a unique collection of prehistoric villages, tombs and stone circles, and are home to some of Europe's largest colonies of nesting sea birds.

### ❶ Skara Brae

Predating Stonehenge and the pyramids of Egypt, Skara Brae (p417) is the best-preserved prehistoric village in northern Europe, complete with Stone Age furniture.

### ❷ Unst

Scotland's northernmost inhabited island, Unst (p434) is about as remote as you can get, a wild and windswept outpost of rugged beauty, and home to thousands of nesting seabirds.

### ❸ Shetland Museum

An impressive collection covering 5000 years' worth of culture and landscape, Shetland Museum (p426) houses a smorgasbord of island treasures.

# Contents

# Regional Map Contents

See Inset

Shetland Islands (p424)

Orkney Islands (p406)

Northern Highlands & Islands (p354)

Central & Western Highlands (p317)

Northeast Scotland (p233)

Southern Highlands & Islands (p267)

Central Scotland (p192)

Glasgow (p121)

Edinburgh (p71)

Southern Scotland (pp150–1)

# Destination Scotland

As an old Scots saying has it, 'guid gear comes in sma' bouk' (good things come in small packages). And despite its small size, Scotland certainly has many treasures crammed into its compact territory. There's something for all tastes, from sophisticated cities, fine food and malt whisky to wild mountain scenery and sparkling, island-studded seas. Wildlife watchers will find otters, eagles, whales and dolphins, while hill walkers have almost 300 Munros to bag. There's turbulent history and fascinating genealogy, castles and country pubs, canoeing and caber-tossing, golfing and fishing and all-round good *craic* (lively conversation).

Although an integral part of Great Britain since 1707, Scotland has maintained a separate and distinct identity throughout the last 300 years. The return of a devolved Scottish parliament to Edinburgh in 1999 marked a growing confidence and sense of pride in the nation's achievements.

The new Scottish parliament building (p85) was officially opened in 2004. The project was dogged with controversy, costing 10 times the original budget and running three years over schedule, and reaction to the building has been mixed, to say the least. Experts have acclaimed it as a masterpiece, and it has won half a dozen major international architectural awards, but the general public has been less appreciative.

Now the fuss has died down, more attention is being focused on what's happening inside the building. The Scottish parliamentary elections of 2007 saw the Labour party lose control of Scottish politics for the first time since their rise to dominance in the 1960s. The Scottish Nationalist Party (SNP), whose central platform is independence for Scotland, won by just one seat and Alex Salmond, the SNP leader, became first minister. But with only 47 out of 129 seats, it is very much a minority administration.

The first decade of devolution has seen Scottish politics diverge significantly from the Westminster way. Distinctive policies that have been applied in Scotland but not in the rest of the UK include free long-term care for the elderly, the abolition of tuition fees for university students, and higher pay for teachers. The SNP has committed itself to holding a referendum on whether Scotland should have full independence, but opinion polls show that most Scots are happy with the status quo.

Ask them what they do worry about, and the Scots come up with much the same answers as the rest of the UK – the health service, education, crime, immigration, soaring property prices and the war in Iraq. Press them on distinctly Scottish problems, however, and – beyond moaning about the utter uselessness of Holyrood politicians – their list will probably mention things such as sectarianism and traffic congestion.

Sectarianism – the bitter hatred that exists between sections of the country's Protestant and Catholic communities – has been called Scotland's 'secret shame'. At its worst in Glasgow, where 'religiously aggravated offences' (a category introduced in 2003) are 60 times more common than in the rest of the country, sectarianism's most public face appears in football matches between Rangers and Celtic. The issue has come to the fore in debates about state funding of 'faith schools' (schools run by a religious body). Many Scots feel that having separate schools for Roman Catholics simply entrenches the sectarian divide, and that the state should not be providing financial support for them.

If you're unfortunate enough to find yourself driving into one of Scotland's larger cities during the weekday rush hour, you'll soon find that traffic

## FAST FACTS

Population: 5.1 million

Area: 78,722 sq km

Number of seats in Scottish parliament: 129

First Minister: Alex Salmond (Scottish National Party)

GDP (per head): £16,332 (2004)

Inflation: 2.5% (2007)

Unemployment: 4.8% (2007)

Amount of whisky exported annually: 1 billion bottles

Value of haggis sold for Burns Night: £1.2 million

Number of times Scotland has won the football World Cup: 0

congestion is one of the country's curses. Edinburgh has led the way in trying to discourage car use with popular measures like cycle routes, dedicated bus lanes and park-and-rides schemes, and unpopular ones like increased parking charges and fines, and a small army of parking 'enforcers'. Construction work has begun on a scheme to reintroduce trams to the city by 2011.

One of the worst traffic bottlenecks in the country is the Forth Road Bridge, with southbound tailbacks several miles long on weekday mornings. Controversial plans have been proposed for a second road bridge across the Firth of Forth, which would allow Edinburgh's new tram network to be extended as far as Dunfermline. These have been lent a new urgency by the discovery of serious corrosion problems with the existing bridge; already carrying close to double its planned capacity of 30,000 vehicles a day, it may have to be closed to heavy goods traffic by 2013, and possibly closed completely by 2020.

These are mainly metropolitan concerns, however, and north of the Highland line other talking points dominate debate. One of the first laws to be passed in the new Scottish parliament gave the Gaelic language official status. Opinion in Scotland is deeply divided between those who believe Gaelic should receive state support in the form of bilingual signage, a dedicated Gaelic TV channel and school classes taught in Gaelic, and those who feel that Gaelic is irrelevant to modern Scotland and should be allowed to die a natural death if it cannot survive without external funding.

The Gaelic Language Act (2005) recognises Gaelic as an official language in Scotland and requires the creation of a national plan for the future development of the language. This is quite a turnaround from an attitude that began with an act passed by the old Scottish parliament in 1616 ruling that Gaelic be 'abolishit and removit' from Scotland. State persecution of Gaelic language and culture intensified following the Jacobite rebellion of 1745, and this attitude persisted well into the 20th century; indeed, there are people still alive today who can recall being beaten for speaking Gaelic in school.

Crofting and land ownership are important issues in the Gaelic-speaking areas of northwest Scotland. A headline-grabbing clause in the Land Reform (Scotland) Act (2003) allowed crofting communities to buy out the land that they live on with the aid of taxpayers' money, in the hope of halting or even reversing the gradual depopulation of the Highlands and islands. Several estates have followed the likes of Eigg, Gigha, Knoydart and North Harris into community ownership. The Isle of Gigha, which underwent a community buyout in 2002, has seen its population increase by 50% and several new businesses start up. In 2006 South Uist saw the biggest community buyout yet, with plans for a world-class golf course, a wind farm and a new pier and marina complex at Lochboisdale.

Scotland may be small but as you can see even from this brief overview, there's a lot going on. Take a little time to look behind the latest news headlines when you arrive and you'll find your experience of the country to be that much richer and more memorable.

# Getting Started

Scotland is the sort of place you can arrive in without a plan, and have a great time just wandering around and following your whims. But planning your trip is half the fun, and essential if your time is limited or if there is something in particular that you want to see or do.

## WHEN TO GO

Any time is a good time to visit Scotland, but your choice of when to go will depend on what you want to do.

The main tourist period is April to September, and the height of the season is during the school holidays in July and August when accommodation, be it camping grounds, B&Bs or luxury hotels, is at a premium. Edinburgh in particular becomes impossibly crowded during the festival period in August, so book well ahead if you plan to visit then (a year ahead is not too early!).

In winter public transport is less frequent and travel to the islands can be a problem if high winds disrupt the ferries. Outside the main cities, some tourist attractions are closed from November to March.

Considering how far north it lies – Edinburgh is on the same latitude as Labrador in Canada – you might expect Scotland to have a colder climate, but the breezes from the Atlantic are warmed by the Gulf Stream, a warm ocean current that flows from the southeast coast of the USA and bathes the western shores of the British Isles.

See Climate Charts (p439) for more information.

The east coast tends to be drier than the west – rainfall averages around 650mm – and it is often warmer in summer and colder in winter. Temperatures rarely drop below 0°C on the coast, although a wind blowing off the North Sea will make you shiver any time of year. The west coast is milder and wetter, with more than 1500mm of rain and average summer highs of 19°C. The western Highlands around Fort William are the wettest place in Britain, with annual rainfall as high as 3000mm.

Statistically, your best chances of fine weather are in May, June and September; July and August are usually warm, but may be wet too. In summer, daylight hours are long; the midsummer sun sets around 11pm in the Shetland Islands and even Edinburgh evenings seem to last forever in June and July. Conversely, in December the sun doesn't show its face until after 9am, and it's dark again by 4pm.

In April and May Scotland's glorious scenery is set off by snow lingering on the mountains and colourful displays of wildflowers in the bluebell woods of southern Scotland and the machair (grass- and wildflower-covered dunes) of the Western Isles. June brings a pink haze of rhododendron blossoms to the Highland glens, but it's not until August that the hill sides put on their famous show of purple heather.

October sees the forests of Perthshire and the Trossachs alight with a blaze of glorious autumn colours. Midwinter can be dreich (a wonderfully descriptive Scots word meaning 'dull and miserable'), but if you get a clear spell of hard frost and sunshine the scenery can be every bit as stunning as in summer.

The many seabird colonies around the Scottish coast are at their most spectacular during the nesting season (April to July), while coastal nature reserves see huge flocks of migrating ducks, geese and waders in spring and autumn. You can see seals, dolphins and porpoises almost all year round, but the whale-watching season peaks in July and August. One seasonal species you should definitely be aware of is the dreaded midge (p458). They are usually around from June to September, but are at their worst in July and August.

## COSTS & MONEY

The strength of the pound sterling makes Scotland an expensive destination for non-Europeans. Food, accommodation and transport are all fairly pricey, and more so in Edinburgh, Glasgow and Aberdeen than in the rest of the country; the only real bargains are the many excellent museums and galleries that you can visit for free.

A realistic daily budget for two people sharing a double room, staying in B&Bs and guesthouses and eating in midrange restaurants is around £40 to £50 per person per day. Backpackers using hostels and cooking their own meals can get by on £25 to £30 a day, not including transport.

If you're travelling in your own car you'll probably average a further £12 to £20 per day on petrol and parking; car rental will add a minimum of £23 a day.

If you're travelling as a family, be aware that many hotels and guesthouses have family rooms, usually with a double bed and one or two singles, plus a folding bed, which can save a fair bit of money. Most tourist attractions with admission fees also offer discounted family tickets – a major saving at places such as Edinburgh Castle, which charges £11 for one adult.

Students, young people (under 26) and seniors (over 60) can get discounts on transport (see p456), and admission fees.

The price of food and fuel rises quite steeply in remote parts of the Highlands and islands where delivery costs are higher. Petrol can cost 10% to 15% more in the Outer Hebrides than in the Central Lowlands.

Surprisingly, Scotland is one of the most expensive places to buy Scotch whisky. If your travels will be taking you to mainland Europe, you'll find you can buy whisky there for about 60% of the price charged in Scottish shops.

**HOW MUCH?**

*Scotsman* newspaper 65p

Fish and chips £4.80

Cinema ticket £6

Bottle of malt whisky £25-35

Car hire per day from £23

See also Lonely Planet Index, inside front cover.

## TRAVEL LITERATURE

Two of the greatest Scottish travelogues date from the 18th century. *A Journey to the Western Isles of Scotland* (1759) and *Journal of a Tour to the Hebrides* (1785) by James Boswell are vivid accounts of two journeys made by the author in the company of the famous lexicographer Samuel Johnson. Boswell writes engagingly of their travails and encounters with the local people, from lairds to crofters, and paints a vivid picture of Highland life in the late 18th century.

A much more recent travelogue is *Raw Spirit* (2004) by novelist Iain Banks (see the boxed text, p46), an immensely enjoyable jaunt around Scotland supposedly in search of the perfect single malt whisky. Although half the book has nothing to do with whisky, and reads more like an extended pub conversation, Banks makes an entertaining companion as he regales you with his opinions on cars (he owns several), tales of driving on Scottish roads and hilarious anecdotes from his youth.

Another travel tale with a twist is recounted in *Adrift in Caledonia* (2006) by Nick Thorpe, an entertaining and insightful tale of travelling around Scotland by hitching rides on a variety of vessels, from canal barge and rowing boat to steam puffer and square-rigged sailing ship.

The full text of Boswell's *Journal of a Tour to the Hebrides* is available online for free at www .gutenberg.org.

---

**DON'T LEAVE HOME WITHOUT...**

- a copy of your travel insurance policy details (p443)
- a pair of binoculars for whale- and dolphin-spotting
- insect repellent (p458)
- waterproofs, patience and a sense of adventure

# TOP 10

## TOP TENS

### Favourite Festivals & Events

Scots always enjoy a good party, and will find some reason to celebrate at almost any time of the year. The following list is our Top 10, but for comprehensive listings of festivals and events, see the Directory, p441.

1 Up-Helly-Aa (Shetland), January (p426)

2 Melrose Rugby Sevens Match (Melrose), April (p158)

3 Feis Ile (Islay Festival; Isle of Islay), May (p290)

4 Burns an' a' That (Ayr), May (p173)

5 Royal Highland Show (Edinburgh), June (p97)

6 Jethart Callant Festival (Jedburgh), July (p161)

7 Edinburgh Festival & Fringe (Edinburgh), August (see boxed text, p97)

8 Edinburgh Military Tattoo (Edinburgh), August (see boxed text, p97)

9 Braemar Gathering (Braemar), September (see boxed text, p256)

10 Edinburgh's Hogmanay (Edinburgh), December (see boxed text, p96)

## Natural Wonders

Scotland's stunning scenery has many awe-inspiring natural features, including spectacular sea stacks and rock formations, thundering waterfalls, impressive gorges and swirling whirlpools. Here are our 10 favourites:

1 Corryvreckan Whirlpool (boxed text, p294)

2 Fingal's Cave (p310)

3 Carsaig Arches (boxed text, p307)

4 Falls of Lora (p314)

5 Sgurr of Eigg (p351)

6 Smoo Cave (p368)

7 Stac Pollaidh (p371)

8 Falls of Measach (p374)

9 The Quiraing (p388)

10 Old Man of Hoy (p418)

## Must-See Films

Head down to the local video store or browse www.amazon.com to pick up our choice of Scotland's 10 best films. All are set in Scotland and many were directed by Scots. See the Culture chapter, p46, for more on Scottish cinema.

1 *Whisky Galore!* (1949), Director: Alexander Mackendrick

2 *Tunes of Glory* (1960), Director: Ronald Neame

3 *Gregory's Girl* (1981), Director: Bill Forsyth

4 *Local Hero* (1983), Director: Bill Forsyth

5 *Rob Roy* (1995), Director: Michael Caton-Jones

6 *Trainspotting* (1996), Director: Danny Boyle

7 *Small Faces* (1996), Director: Gillies Mackinnon

8 *Sweet Sixteen* (2002), Director: Ken Loach

9 *Young Adam* (2003), Director: David MacKenzie

10 *Red Road* (2006), Director: Andrea Arnold

*Stone Voices: The Search for Scotland* (2002), by respected Scots journalist Neal Ascherson, is a highly readable and very personal exploration of Scottish history and culture, filled with fascinating insights and some contentious conclusions that will provide the starting point for some lively bar-room conversations.

Anyone with an interest in the Scottish hills should seek out *Always A Little Further* (1939) by Alastair Borthwick and *Mountaineering in Scotland* (1947) by WH Murray. Both are classic accounts, beautifully written, of camping, hiking and rock climbing in Scotland in the 1930s, when just getting to Glen Coe was an adventure in itself and the most advanced ice-climbing equipment was a slater's pick.

## INTERNET RESOURCES

**Internet Guide to Scotland** (www.scotland-info.co.uk) The best of several online tourist guides to Scotland.

**Lonely Planet** (www.lonelyplanet.com) Get started with summaries on Scotland, the popular Thorn Tree bulletin board and links to Scotland-related sites.

**ScotchWhisky.net** (www.scotchwhisky.net) Everything you wanted to know about Scotch whisky.

**Scotland's People** (www.scotlandspeople.gov.uk) A comprehensive online resource for exploring your Scottish ancestry.

**Traveline** (www.travelinescotland.com) Public transport timetables and journey planner for all of Scotland.

**VisitScotland** (www.visitscotland.com) The official Scottish Tourist Board site, with an online accommodation-booking service.

# Itineraries
## CLASSIC ROUTES

### A HIGHLAND FLING
**Two Weeks / Edinburgh to Inverness**

This route takes you through the magnificent mountain scenery of the western Highlands. From **Edinburgh** (p68) head northwest to see Scotland's other great castle at **Stirling** (p193), then on to the **Trossachs** (p199) for your first taste of Highland scenery. As you continue north, the mountain scenery becomes more impressive, culminating in the grandeur of **Glen Coe** (p337).

Keen hill walkers will pause at **Fort William** (p340) to climb **Ben Nevis** (p345), or you can view it from **Corpach** (p345) at the start of the Road to the Isles. Head on to glorious **Glenfinnan** (p347) and the **Silver Sands of Morar** (p348), then **Mallaig** (p348); stop for lunch or overnight here and dine at one of its seafood restaurants.

From Mallaig take the ferry to the **Isle of Skye** (p378), and spend a day or two here exploring the island. Cross the Skye Bridge back to the mainland, and head north via the pretty village of **Plockton** (p377) to the magnificent mountain scenery of **Glen Torridon** (p375). Follow the A832 alongside lovely **Loch Maree** (p375) and continue north into the big-sky wilderness of western Sutherland, beneath the towering pinnacles of **An Teallach** (p374), before heading back east to the fleshpots of **Inverness** (p318).

In theory you could cover this spectacular 475-mile route in two days, but allowing time to stop and enjoy the scenery and the seafood makes two weeks a more realistic estimate.

## CASTLES & WHISKY          Two Weeks / Edinburgh to Edinburgh

From **Edinburgh** (p68) head west to Queensferry to visit stately **Hopetoun House** (p115), then go north across the Forth Road Bridge to Fife and turn east along the coastal road through the delightful fishing villages of **East Neuk** (p214) to the home of golf, **St Andrews** (p208). Continue north across the Tay Bridge to **Dundee** (p234) and **Glamis Castle** (p239) before heading into the Grampian Mountains to reach **Braemar** (p255).

A feast of castles lies ahead as you travel east along Deeside, passing royal residence **Balmoral Castle** (p255) and fairy-tale **Crathes Castle** (p254) on your way to the granite city of **Aberdeen** (p245). Try to get a table at the **Silver Darling restaurant** (p251) here.

Now strike west again along the A944, making small detours to visit **Castle Fraser** (p254), **Craigievar Castle** (p258) and **Kildrummy Castle** (p258) before turning north to **Huntly** (p260) and west again to **Dufftown** (p262) in the heart of the Spey valley. Base yourself here for at least a day to explore the many whisky distilleries nearby.

Go northwest to **Elgin** (p260), then west on the A96, visiting **Brodie Castle** (p324), **Fort George** (p323), **Cawdor Castle** (p324) and **Culloden** (p323) on the way to **Inverness** (p318).

Whisky fans (see the boxed text, p55) can make the short trip north to the **Glenmorangie Distillery** (p356) at Tain before returning south to Edinburgh on the A9 and M9, stopping off at **Blair Castle** (p230), **Dunkeld** (p226) and **Scone Palace** (p218).

This journey through the heart of Scotland is a 475-mile round-trip, starting and finishing in Edinburgh, with a total driving time of around 10 to 12 hours. Tain is an extra 50-mile round-trip north of Inverness.

# ROADS LESS TRAVELLED

### BORDER RAID                                    Eight Days / Edinburgh to Glasgow

From **Edinburgh** (p68) the majority of tourists head north, which is a very good reason to head south, into the Borders…

Your first objective should be a traipse around the beautiful Border abbeys of **Melrose** (p158) and **Jedburgh** (p160); Melrose is a charming place to stay the night. Then head southwest to **Selkirk** (p160) and along the A708 to **Moffat** (p190). Continue to **Dumfries** (p178) and make a short side-trip to see spectacular **Caerlaverock Castle** (p180).

Push on southwest around the Galloway coast to **Newton Stewart** (p185), and detour south to visit the bookshops of **Wigtown** (p185) and the holy site of **Whithorn** (p186). From Newton Stewart head back east along the A712 to **New Galloway** (p184), via the lovely Galloway Forest Park, and then north on the A713 towards Ayr and Burns country.

At **Alloway** (p175) allow at least a day to visit Robert Burns' birthplace and other Burns-related sites, then go on to **Ayr** (p173) and head north to **Ardrossan** (p168). Take the ferry here across to the lovely **Isle of Arran** (p168) for a spot of hill walking, fishing or relaxing at one of the island's pubs.

Back on the mainland, head north to **Wemyss Bay** (p148) and take the ferry to **Rothesay** (p282) on the Isle of Bute, where you can visit stunning Mount Stuart, one of Scotland's most impressive stately homes. Return to the mainland again and head east to **Glasgow** (p119).

You could cover this 430-mile arc through the Southern Uplands in two long days, or spin it out to two weeks, but eight days is comfortable.

## ISLES AT THE EDGE OF THE SEA
**Two Weeks / Oban to Thurso**

This route can be done by car, but it also makes a brilliant cycle tour taking three to four weeks. Both start and finish are accessible by rail.

From **Oban** (p297) make the long ferry crossing to **Barra** (p401). After a look at romantic Kisimul Castle and a circuit of the island take the ferry to **South Uist** (p400); if you've brought your fishing rod, look forward to a bit of sport on the island's many trout lochs. Keep your binoculars handy as you follow the road north through **Benbecula** (p400) and **North Uist** (p399), as this is prime bird-watching country; then, take another ferry to **Harris** (p396).

Pray for sun, as the road along Harris' west coast has some of the most spectacular beaches in Scotland. The road continues north through the rugged Harris hills to **Lewis** (p391).

Turn west to make a circuit past the **Callanish Standing Stones** (p395), **Dun Carloway** (p395) broch and **Arnol Blackhouse museum** (p395) – the highlights of the Western Isles – and if you have time detour west to the beautiful beaches around **Miavaig** (p396).

From bustling **Stornoway** (p392) take the ferry to **Ullapool** (p371), where you have the choice of heading direct to **Inverness** (p318), or continuing north around the mainland coast through the jaw-dropping wilderness of **Inverpolly Nature Reserve** (p371), **Cape Wrath** (p369) and **Durness** (p368) to **Thurso** (p364), where the ferry to the **Orkney Islands** (p405) awaits.

CalMac's Island Hopscotch ticket No 8 (p453) includes all the ferries needed for the Outer Hebrides part of this route.

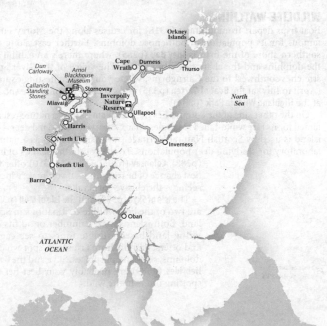

**This trip involves 290 miles between Oban and Thurso, plus 10 hours of ferry crossings. You could drive it in four days at a push, but two weeks is more enjoyable. Touring Orkney would add another 60 or 70 miles, plus four hours on the ferry.**

# TAILORED TRIPS

## THE BONNIE PRINCE CHARLIE TRAIL

Many visitors to Scotland are captivated by the romanticised legend of Bonnie Prince Charlie (p34), who in 1745 tried to recapture the British throne for the Stuart dynasty. The Young Pretender first set foot on Scottish soil at **Prince's Strand** (p401) on the island of Eriskay, and raised his standard at **Glenfinnan** (p347) before leading his army of Highlanders south as far as Derby in England. He was harried in retreat all the way to final defeat at **Culloden** (p323) in 1746, stopping briefly at **Linlithgow Palace** (p117) on the way, after which he was on the run in the **Isle of Skye** (p388) and the **Outer Hebrides** (p400). He finally departed Scotland for the last time from a point in Arisaig marked by the **Prince's Cairn** (p348).

Museums that have exhibits relating to Bonnie Prince Charlie and other places associated with his campaign include Kingussie's **Ruthven Barracks** (p336), the **West Highland Museum** (p341) in Fort William, the **Seven Men of Moidart** (p347), Achnacarry's **Clan Cameron Museum** (p345), and on Skye, the **Museum of the Isles** (p382) in Armadale and **Dunvegan Castle** (p387) in Dunvegan. Sir Walter Scott's house at **Abbotsford** (p159) displays a lock of the prince's hair.

## WILDLIFE-WATCHING

Boat trips depart from **Inverness** (p318) for cruises along the Moray Firth, famous for its population of bottlenose dolphins. Further east along the southern shore of the firth is **Spey Bay** (p265), where there's an exhibit on the dolphins and the chance of seeing seals. The valley of the River Spey stretches southwest to the Cairngorms, where you can see nesting ospreys (April to July) at the **Boat of Garten** (p335) and get close to some rare species at the **Highland Wildlife Park** (p334).

On the other side of the country lies the **Isle of Rum** (p350), a nature reserve famed for its rare white-tailed sea eagles, Manx shearwaters and red deer – the island is used by Scottish Natural Heritage (www.snh.org.uk) as a natural laboratory for studying deer populations. To the south, the islands of **Islay** (p288), **Colonsay** (p295) and **Coll** (p310) offer the best chance of hearing and – if you're very lucky, seeing – the elusive corncrake.

The **Isle of Skye** (p378) and the **Isle of Mull** (p303) are two of the best wildlife destinations in Scotland. Both islands have a number of outfits offering land-based wildlife tours to see eagles and otters, and offshore cruises to spot whales, dolphins, seals and porpoises. Skye and the **Outer Hebrides** (p389) are probably your best bet for spotting otters in the wild.

# History

Scottish history is a compelling interwoven web, laced with heroic figures and defining battles. Events in the relatively recent past are well documented, but Scotland's history stretches far back into the mists of times where myth and legend take precedence over sketchy facts and scant archaeological records.

In order to pull apart the historical threads that piece together modern Scotland, this chapter is divided into two sections: the timeline chronologically sets out the major events in Scottish history; the text fleshes out the major events in the timeline, and, although following a roughly chronological ordering of Scottish history, it focuses on themes such as religion, a defining battle or the immortal figures, some heavily romanticised, who've made their mark on the country's extraordinary history.

## EARLY DAYS

Hunters and gatherers have left remains of shells and animal bones, providing fragments of evidence of the earliest human habitation in Scotland. These early people came in waves from northern Europe and Ireland as the glaciers retreated in the wake of the last Ice Age around 10,000 BC.

Early Neolithic farming people moved into Scotland from mainland Europe and left behind an astonishing diary of human development including the incredibly well-preserved Neolithic village of Skara Brae (p417), dating from around 3100 BC, and extraordinary chambered cairns such as Maes Howe (p416), which indicate they had a belief in the afterlife. Today, the islands of Orkney are the best place to see such prehistoric sites, boasting Europe's greatest concentration. Kilmartin Glen (p285) also has many prehistoric sites, including extensive rock carvings.

Next came the Beaker people who were responsible for leaving behind standing stones, such as those at Callanish (p395 in Lewis; it is one of the most evocative sites in Scotland and testament to the advanced culture that had taken root by 3000 BC.

## ROMANS & PICTS

The Roman invasion of Britain by Emperor Claudius began in AD 43, almost a century after Julius Caesar first invaded. However, the Roman onslaught ground to a halt in the north, not far beyond the present-day Scottish border. Between AD 78 and 84, the Roman Governor Agricola marched northwards and spent several years trying to subdue the wild tribes the Romans called the Picts (from the Latin *pictus,* meaning painted). Little is know about the Picts who inhabited northern and eastern Scotland. The only material evidence of

*A Traveller's History of Scotland* by Andrew Fisher is a concise account of Scottish history that relates historical events to places you can visit. It covers events from Scotland's first people right up to Devolution.

## TIMELINE

| 4500 BC | 3000 BC | AD 43 |
|---|---|---|
| Neolithic farmers move to Scotland from mainland Europe; prehistoric sites from these ancient days dot today's countryside with the best concentrated in Orkney. | Beaker people come to Scotland bringing with them the Bronze Age which produces the sword and shield, making warfare more popular. They also erect the mystifying stone circles, hill forts and crannogs. | Emperor Claudius begins the Roman conquest of Britain, almost a century after Julius Caesar first invaded. By AD 80 a string of forts is built from the Clyde to the Forth. |

their culture is their unique carved symbol stones. These boulders, engraved with the mysterious symbols of an otherwise unknown culture, can be found in many parts of eastern Scotland (p231).

By the 2nd century Emperor Hadrian, tired of fighting the tribes in the north, decided to cut his losses and built the wall (AD 122–28) that bears his name across northern England between Carlisle and Newcastle. Two decades later Hadrian's successor, Antoninus Pius, invaded Scotland again and built a turf rampart, the Antonine Wall, between the Firth of Forth and the River Clyde. The Roman fort at Cramond (p90) marked its eastern end. In northern Britain, the Romans found they had met their match.

## CHRISTIANITY

Scots History (www
.scotshistoryonline.co.uk)
gives a useful window
into Scotland's past and
its people going back
8000 years. It's especially
good for images of
historic sites.

Eventually the Romans left Britain and at this time there were at least two indigenous peoples in the northern region of the British Isles: the Picts in the north and east, and the Celtic Britons in the south.

St Ninian conducted the first missionary work among the Picts. He remains a mysterious figure shrouded in myth, but there is little doubt that his influence was profound.

St Columba, Scotland's most famous missionary, resumed St Ninian's work. After fleeing Ireland in 563 he established a monastery on Iona (p309), and Christianity became popular with pagan kings as it seemed to offer them supernatural powers.

According to legend, Columba was a scholar and a soldier-priest who went into exile after involvement in a bloody battle. After arriving on Iona he promptly set about banishing women and cows as he believed 'where there is a cow there is a woman, and where there is a woman there is mischief'. His manner of living was austere – he was said to sleep on the bare floor with a stone for a pillow. After his death he was credited with miraculous feats such as defeating what is today known as the Loch Ness monster. A visit to this holy island today to see the reconstructed 13th-century abbey and the many fine stone carvings is a highlight of the Inner Hebrides.

## MACALPIN & CANMORE DYNASTIES

Stone of Destiny by Pat
Gerber is an intriguing
investigation into the
history of Scotland's most
famous lump of stone.
Is the one in Edinburgh
Castle a fake, with the
real stone waiting to be
rescued from its medieval
hiding place?

The Picts and Scots were drawn together by the threat of a Norse invasion and by the combination of political and spiritual power from their common Christianity. One story has it that Kenneth MacAlpin, the first king of a united Scotland, achieved power at a 'black dinner' by setting traps underneath the benches of Pictish nobles. He made Scone his capital, and brought to it the sacred Stone of Destiny (see the boxed text, p81), used in the coronation of Scottish kings.

Nearly two centuries later, Kenneth MacAlpin's great-great-great-grand-son, Malcolm II (r 1005–18), defeated the Northumbrian Angles led by King Canute at the Battle of Carham (1018) near Roxburgh on the River Tweed.

| AD 142 | AD 397 | 5th century |
| --- | --- | --- |
| Building of Antonine Wall marks northern limit of Roman Empire. It is patrolled for about 40 years, but after this the Romans decide northern Britain, with its treacherous terrain, is too difficult to conquer. | The first Christian mission beyond Hadrian's Wall, in Whithorn, is initiated by St Ninian. The earliest recorded church in Scotland is built here to house his remains. | Roman soldiers stationed in Britain are recalled to Rome as the Empire faces attack from many different barbarian tribes. Eventually the last Romans depart and Emperor Honorious tells Britons to fend for themselves. |

## THE CLAN WHO WOULD BE KING

In medieval times, when overland travel through the Scottish Highlands was slow, difficult and dangerous, the sea lochs, firths, kyles and sounds of the west coast were the motorways of their time. Cut off from the rest of Scotland, but united by these sea roads, the west coast and islands were a world – and a kingdom – unto themselves.

Descended from the legendary Somerled – a half-Gaelic, half-Norse warrior of the 12th century, himself descended from the Irish king Conn of the 100 Battles – the chiefs of Clan Donald claimed sovereignty over this watery kingdom. It was John Macdonald of Islay who first styled himself Dominus Insularum (Lord of the Isles) in 1353. He and his descendants ruled their vast territory from their headquarters at Finlaggan (p293) in Islay, backed up by fleets of swift *birlinns* and *nyvaigs* (Hebridean galleys), an intimate knowledge of the sea routes of the west and a network of coastal castles that included Skipness (p287), Dunstaffnage (p314), Duart (p304), Stalker (p315), Dunvegan (p387) and Kisimul (p402).

Clan Donald held sway over the isles, often in defiance of the Scottish king, from 1350 to 1493. At its greatest extent, in the second half of the 15th century, the Lordship of the Isles included all the islands on the west coast of Scotland, the west-coast mainland from Kintyre to Ross-shire, and the Antrim coast of northern Ireland. But in challenging the Scottish king for territory, and siding with the English king against him, Clan Donald finally pushed its luck too far.

Following a failed rebellion in 1493, the Lordship was forfeited to King James IV of Scotland, and the title has remained in possession of the Scottish, and later British, royal family ever since. Lord of the Isles is one of the many titles held today by Prince Charles, heir to the British throne.

---

This victory brought Edinburgh and Lothian under Scottish control and extended Scottish territory as far south as the Tweed.

With his Saxon queen, Margaret, Malcolm III Canmore (r 1058–93) – whose father Duncan was murdered by Macbeth (as described in Shakespeare's eponymous play) – founded a dynasty of able Scottish rulers. They introduced new Anglo-Norman systems of government and religious foundations.

Malcolm's son David I (r 1124-53) imported monks to found the great Border abbeys; their fiery remains are major attractions in Melrose (p158), Jedburgh (p160) and Dryburgh (p159). He increased his power by adopting the Norman feudal system, granting land to noble Norman families in return for military service.

But the Highland clans, inaccessible in their glens, remained a law unto themselves for another 600 years. The exploits of Rob Roy, especially his daring raids into the Lowlands and reputation as a champion of the poor, typified the romantic notion of these wild clans. A cultural and linguistic divide grew up between the Gaelic-speaking Highlanders and Lowlanders who spoke the Scots tongue (p459).

A well-presented and easily absorbed introduction to Scottish history is at www.bbc .co.uk/history/scottishhis tory. The accompanying images of historical sites help to bring it to life.

| Early 6th century | 6th century | 780 |
|---|---|---|
| A Celtic tribe, the Scots, cross the sea from northern Ireland and establish a kingdom in Argyll called Dalriada. | St Columba establishes a Christian mission on Iona. By the late 8th century the mission is responsible for the conversion of most of pagan Scotland. | From the 780s onwards, Norsemen in longboats from Scandinavia begin to pillage the Scottish coast and islands, eventually taking control of Orkney, Shetland and the Western Isles. |

## THE DECLARATION OF ARBROATH

During the Wars of Independence, a group of Scottish nobles sent a letter to Pope John XXII requesting support for the cause of Scottish independence. Bearing the seals of eight earls and 31 barons, and written in Latin by the abbot of Arbroath in 1320, it is the earliest document that seeks to place limits on the power of a king.

Having railed against the tyranny of Edward I of England and having sung the praises of Robert the Bruce, the declaration famously concludes:

Yet even the same Robert, should he turn aside from the task and yield Scotland or us to the English king or people, him we should cast out as the enemy of us all, and choose another king to defend our freedom; for so long as a hundred of us remain alive, we will yield in no least way to English dominion. For we fight, not for glory nor for riches nor for honour, but only and alone for freedom, which no good man surrenders but with his life.

## ROBERT THE BRUCE & WILLIAM WALLACE

When Alexander III fell to his death over a coastal cliff in Fife in 1286, there followed a dispute over the succession to the throne. There were no less than 13 claimants, but in the end it came down to a choice of two: Robert de Brus, lord of Annandale, and John Balliol, lord of Galloway. Edward I of England, as the greatest feudal lord in Britain, was asked to arbitrate. He chose Balliol, whom he thought he could manipulate more easily.

Seeking to tighten his feudal grip on Scotland, Edward – known as the 'Hammer of the Scots' – treated the Scots king as his vassal rather than his equal. The humiliated Balliol finally turned against him and allied Scotland with France in 1295, thus beginning the enduring 'Auld Alliance' and ushering in the Wars of Independence.

Edward's response was bloody. In 1296 he invaded Scotland and Balliol was incarcerated in the Tower of London; in a final blow to Scots pride, Edward I removed the Stone of Destiny from Scone and took it back to London.

Enter arguably Scotland's most tragic hero, William Wallace (see p195). Bands of rebels were attacking the English occupiers and one such band, led by William Wallace, defeated the English army at the Battle of Stirling Bridge in 1297. Wallace was knighted and proclaimed Guardian of Scotland in 1298. However, he lost a major battle at Falkirk, resigned as guardian and went into hiding in Europe – on his return to Scotland, he was betrayed, caught and executed in 1305. This betrayal was largely put down to the fickle loyalties of the Scottish nobility who sided with Edward.

After William Wallace was executed, Robert the Bruce, grandson of the lord of Annandale, saw his chance, defied Edward (whom he had previously aligned himself with), murdered his rival John Comyn and had himself crowned king of Scotland at Scone in 1306. Bruce mounted a campaign to drive the English out of Scotland but suffered repeated defeats. According to

| 843 | 872 | 1263 |
| --- | --- | --- |
| Kenneth MacAlpin, the king of Dalriada, takes advantage of the Picts' custom of matrilineal succession to take over the Pictish throne, thus uniting Scotland north of the Firth of Forth into a single kingdom. | The King of Norway creates an earldom in Orkney, and Shetland is also governed from here – these island groups become a vital Viking base for raids and colonisation down the west of Scotland. | Norse power, which controlled the entire western seaboard, is finally broken at the Battle of Largs, which marks the retreat of Viking influence and eventually the handing back of the western isles to Scotland. |

legend, while Bruce was on the run he was inspired to renew his efforts by a spider's persistence in spinning its web. And the inspiration was not in vain – he went on to secure an illustrious victory over the English at Bannockburn. The exploits of this famous battle are enshrined in Scottish legend as one of the finest moments in the country's young history.

## THE STEWART DYNASTY & THE RENAISSANCE

After the death of Robert the Bruce in 1329 – he's buried at Dunfermline (see p208), although his heart is buried in Melrose Abbey (p158) – the country was ravaged by civil disputes and continuing wars with England. Edinburgh was occupied several times by English armies and in 1385 the Kirk of St Giles was burned to the ground.

James IV (r 1488–1513) married the daughter of Henry VII of England, the first of the Tudor monarchs, thereby linking the two royal families through 'the Marriage of the Thistle and the Rose'. This didn't prevent the French from persuading James to go to war with his in-laws, and he was killed at the Battle of Flodden in 1513, along with 10,000 of his subjects.

Renaissance ideas flourished during James IV's reign. Scottish poetry thrived, created by *makars* (makers of verses) such as William Dunbar, the court poet of James IV, and Gavin Douglas. Much graceful Scottish architecture is from this period, and examples of Renaissance style can be seen in alterations to palaces at Holyrood (p83), Stirling (p193), Linlithgow (p117) and Falkland (p207).

## MARY, QUEEN OF SCOTS & THE REFORMATION

No figure in Scottish history has had a more turbulent and troublesome history than Mary, Queen of Scots (r 1542–67).

In 1542 King James V, childless, lay on his deathbed brokenhearted, it is said, after his defeat by the English at Solway Moss. On 8 December a messenger brought word that his wife had given birth to a baby girl at the Palace of Linlithgow. Fearing the end of the Stewart dynasty, and recalling its origin through Robert the Bruce's daughter, James sighed, 'It cam' wi' a lass, and it will gang wi' a lass'. He died a few days later, leaving his week-old daughter, Mary, to inherit the throne as Queen of Scots.

She was sent to France at an early age and Scotland was ruled by regents, who rejected overtures from Henry VIII of England urging them to wed the infant queen to his son. Henry was furious, and sent his armies to take vengeance on the Scots. The 'Rough Wooing', as it was called, failed to persuade the Scots of the error of their ways. In 1558 Mary was married to the French dauphin and became queen of France as well as Scotland.

While Mary was in France, being raised as a Roman Catholic, the Reformation tore through Scotland. The wealthy Catholic Church was riddled with corruption, and the preachings of John Knox, a pupil of the Swiss reformer Calvin, found sympathetic ears. To give you an idea of this influential man, Knox, concerned with the sway that political rulers wielded over the church,

*Mary Queen of Scots* by Antonia Fraser is the classic biography of Scotland's ill-starred queen, digging deep behind the myths to discover the real woman caught up in the labyrinthine politics of the period.

| **1296** | **1298–1305** | **1314** |
| --- | --- | --- |
| King Edward 1 marches on Scotland with an army of 30,000 men, razing ports, butchering citizens, and capturing the castles of Berwick, Edinburgh, Roxburgh and Stirling. | William Wallace is proclaimed Guardian of Scotland in March 1298. After Edward's force defeats the Scots at the Battle of Falkirk, Wallace resigns as guardian and goes into hiding, but is fatally betrayed after his return in 1305. | Robert the Bruce wins a famous victory over the English at the Battle of Bannockburn – a victory which would turn the tide in favour of the Scots for the next 400 years. |

wrote *The First Blast of the Trumpet Against the Monstrous Regiment of Women*. It was an attack on three women rulers calling the shots in Scotland, England and France and linked his name to a hatred of women ever since.

Following the death of her sickly husband, the 18-year-old Mary returned to Scotland in 1561. She was formally welcomed to her capital city and held a famous audience at Holyrood Palace with John Knox. The great reformer harangued the young queen and she later agreed to protect the budding Protestant Church in Scotland while continuing to hear Mass in private.

She married Henry Stewart, Lord Darnley, in the Chapel Royal at Holyrood and gave birth to a son (later James VI) in Edinburgh Castle in 1565. Any domestic bliss was short-lived and, in a scarcely believable train of events, Darnley was involved in the murder of Mary's Italian secretary Rizzio (rumoured to be her lover), before he himself was murdered, probably by Mary's new lover and second-husband-to-be, the earl of Bothwell!

'The Scots had had enough – Mary's enemies finally confronted her at Carberry Hill and Mary was forced to abdicate in 1567'

The Scots had had enough – Mary's enemies finally confronted her at Carberry Hill, just east of Edinburgh, and Mary was forced to abdicate in 1567. Her son, the infant James VI (r 1567–1625), was crowned at Stirling, and a series of regents ruled in his place. Meanwhile in England, Queen Elizabeth I of England died childless, and the English, desperate for a male monarch, soon turned their attention north. James VI of Scotland became James I of Great Britain and moved his court to London and, for the most part, the Stewarts ignored Scotland from then on. Indeed, when Charles I (r 1625–49) succeeded James, he couldn't be bothered to travel north to Edinburgh to be formally crowned as king of Scotland until 1633.

## COVENANTERS & CIVIL WAR

Civil war was to strangle Scotland and England in the 17th century. The arrogant attempts by Charles I to impose episcopacy (the rule of bishops) and an English liturgy on the Presbyterian Scottish Church set off public riots in Edinburgh. The Presbyterians believed in a personal bond with God that had no need of mediation through priests, popes and kings. On 28 February 1638 hundreds gathered in Greyfriars Kirkyard (p85) to sign a National Covenant affirming their rights and beliefs. Scotland was divided between the Covenanters and those who supported the king.

In the 1640s civil war raged in England between the Royalists and Oliver Cromwell's Parliamentarians. Although there was an alliance between the Covenanters and the English parliament against Charles I, the Scots were appalled when the Parliamentarians executed the king in 1649. They offered his son the Scottish Crown provided he signed the Covenant and renounced his father, which he did. Charles II (r 1649–85) was crowned at Scone on 1 January 1651 but was soon forced into exile by Cromwell, who invaded Scotland and captured Edinburgh.

After Charles II's restoration in 1660, he reneged on the Covenant; episcopacy was reinstated and hardline Presbyterian ministers were deprived

| 1328 | 1371 | 1468–69 |
|---|---|---|
| Continuing raids on northern England force Edward II to sue for peace and the Treaty of Northampton gives Scotland its independence, with Robert I, the Bruce, as king. | The last of the Bruce dynasty dies to be succeeded by the Stewards (Stewarts), who are to rule Scotland and Britain for the next three centuries. | Orkney and then Shetland are mortgaged to Scotland as part of a dowry from Danish King Christian I, whose daughter is to marry the future King James III of Scotland. |

of their churches. Charles' brother and successor, the Catholic James VII/II (r 1685–89), made worshipping as a Covenanter a capital offence.

James' daughter, Mary, and her husband William of Orange (1689–1702) restored the Presbyterian structure in the church and kicked out the bishops, but the political and legal functions of the church were subject to parliamentary control. And so Scotland's turbulent reformation came to an end.

## UNION WITH ENGLAND

The civil wars left the country and its economy ruined. During the 1690s famine killed up to a third of the population in some areas. Anti-English feeling ran high: William was at war with France and was using Scottish soldiers and taxes – many Scots, sympathetic to the French, disapproved. This feeling was exacerbated by the failure of an investment venture in Panama (the so-called Darien Scheme), which resulted in widespread bankruptcy in Scotland.

The failure of the Darien Scheme made it clear to the wealthy Scottish merchants and stockholders that the only way they could gain access to the lucrative markets of developing colonies was through union with England. The English parliament favoured union through fear of Jacobite sympathies in Scotland being exploited by its enemies, the French.

On receiving the Act of Union in Edinburgh, the chancellor of Scotland, Lord Seafield – leader of the parliament that the Act of Union abolished – is said to have murmured under his breath, 'Now there's an end to an auld sang'. Robert Burns later castigated the wealthy politicians who engineered the Union in characteristically stronger language: 'We're bought and sold for English gold – such a parcel of rogues in a nation!'

## THE JACOBITES

The Jacobite rebellions of the 18th century sought to displace the Hanoverian monarchy (chosen by the English parliament in 1701 to succeed the house of Orange) and restore a Catholic Stuart king to the British throne.

James Edward Stuart, known as the Old Pretender, was the son of James VII/II. With French support he arrived in the Firth of Forth with a fleet of ships in 1708, causing panic in Edinburgh, but was seen off by English men-of-war.

The earl of Mar led another Jacobite rebellion in 1715 but proved an ineffectual leader better at propaganda than warfare. Once again the Old Pretender made his way to Scotland and Mar, who met him, demonstrated his propaganda skills by sending news to encourage his army and the people: 'Withouth any complements to him and to do him nothing but justice, set aside his being a Prince, he really is the finest gentleman I ever knew…and has the sweetest temper in the world.' His campaign fizzled out soon after the inconclusive Battle of Sheriffmuir.

Jacobite is a Latin term derived from 'James', which is used to describe the political movement committed to the return of the Stuart kings to the thrones of England and Scotland.

The Old Pretender's son, Charles Edward Stuart, better known as Bonnie Prince Charlie or the Young Pretender, landed in Scotland for the final uprising. He had little military experience, didn't speak Gaelic and had a shaky grasp of English. Nevertheless, supported by an army of Highlanders, he marched southwards and captured Edinburgh, except for the castle, in September 1745. He got as far south as Derby in England, but success was short-lived; a Hanoverian army led by the duke of Cumberland harried him all the way back to the Highlands, where Jacobite dreams were finally extinguished at the Battle of Culloden in 1746 (p323).

Although a heavily romanticised figure, Bonnie Prince Charlie was partly responsible for the annihilation of Highland culture, given the crackdown and subsequent clearances following his doomed attempt to recapture the crown. After returning to France he gained a reputation for mistreating his subsequent mistresses and at the age of 52 married a young princess, but she fled his drunken violence and he never got the heir he wanted.

## THE HIGHLAND CLEARANCES

In the aftermath of the Jacobite rebellions, Highland dress, the bearing of arms and the bagpipes were outlawed. The Highlands were effectively put under military control and private armies were banned. The relationship of Highland chief to clansman changed dramatically and landowners were tempted by the easy profits to be made from sheep farming.

John Prebble's wonderfully written book *The Highland Clearances* tells the terrible story of how the Highlanders were driven out of their homes and forced into emigration.

The clansmen, no longer of any use as soldiers and uneconomical as tenants, were evicted from their homes and farms to make way for the flocks – in Easter Ross the year 1792 was known for decades afterwards as the Year of the Sheep. A few stayed to work the sheep farms; many more were forced to seek work in the cities, or to eke a living from crofts (small holdings) on poor coastal land (see p360). And many thousands emigrated – some willingly, some under duress – to the developing colonies of North America, Australia and New Zealand.

If you do much walking in the Highlands and islands, you are almost certain to come across a ruckle of stones among the bracken, all that remains of a house or cottage. Look around and you'll find another, and another, and soon you'll realise that this was once a crofting settlement. It's one of the saddest sights you'll see in Scotland – this emptiness, where once there was a thriving community. The Mull of Oa on the island of Islay, for example, once supported a population of 4000, but today there are barely 40 people living there.

## THE SCOTTISH ENLIGHTENMENT

During the period known as the Scottish Enlightenment (roughly 1740–1830) Edinburgh became known as 'a hotbed of genius'. The philosophers David Hume and Adam Smith and the sociologist Adam Ferguson emerged as influential thinkers, nourished on generations of theological debate. Medic

| 1707 | 1745–46 | 1740s–1830s |
| --- | --- | --- |
| Despite popular opposition, the Act of Union, which brings England and Scotland under one parliament, one sovereign and one flag, takes effect on 1 May 1707. | The culmination of the Jacobite rebellions sees Bonnie Prince Charlie land in Scotland, gather an army and march southwards – however, he is eventually defeated at the Battle of Culloden. | Following the loss of the Scottish parliament in 1707, Edinburgh declines in political importance, but its cultural and intellectual life flourishes during a period known as the Scottish Enlightenment. |

William Cullen produced the first modern pharmacopoeia, chemist Joseph Black advanced the science of thermodynamics and geologist James Hutton challenged long-held beliefs about the age of the Earth.

After centuries of bloodshed and religious fanaticism, people applied themselves with the same energy and piety to the making of money and the enjoyment of leisure. There was a revival of interest in Scottish history and literature. The writings of Sir Walter Scott (see p159) and the poetry of Robert Burns (see p176), a true man of the people, achieved lasting popularity.

Most clan tartans are in fact a 19th-century creation (long after the demise of the clan system) inspired by the brilliance of wordsmith Sir Walter Scott.

## THE INDUSTRIAL REVOLUTION

The development of the steam engine ushered in the Industrial Revolution. The Carron Ironworks near Falkirk, established in 1759, became the largest ironworks and gun factory in Britain, and the growth of the textile

### RADICALS & REDS

Scotland, and especially Glasgow, has a long history of radical politics. These were founded on the emergence of a well-educated, literate and articulate working class in the late 18th century, and the long-held belief in self-improvement.

James Keir Hardie (1856–1915) first went down the mines at the age of 10, but was an avid reader and self-improver. By the age of 22 he had become an active campaigner for better wages and working conditions, and was blacklisted by the mine owners. He founded the Scottish Labour Party in 1888 and its successor, the Independent Labour Party, in 1893, specifically to represent the interests of the working classes in parliament.

By the early years of the 20th century, Scotland had a fully fledged alternative political culture. The Independent Labour Party was joined by Marxist organisations such as the Social Democratic Federation and the Socialist Labour Party, who advocated class war and direct action. The Glasgow schoolteacher and socialist revolutionary John Maclean (1879–1923) delivered lectures on Marxist theory to audiences of thousands. Maclean was appointed 'Bolshevik consul in Scotland' by Lenin following the Russian Revolution of 1917, and was an outspoken critic of Britain's involvement in WWI; he was arrested for sedition on half a dozen occasions.

The most notorious event in the history of Scottish radicalism was the Bloody Friday Riot of 1919. Fearing mass unemployment after WWI, the Clyde Workers Committee called a strike in support of a shorter working week. Strikers demonstrating in Glasgow's George Sq began a riot and fearing a Bolshevik-style revolution, the government sent in tanks, a howitzer and machine-gunners; fortunately, no-one was hurt.

Glasgow and the west of Scotland's socialist sympathies earned it the nickname of 'Red Clydeside'. Backed by the influx of Clydeside Reds at Westminster following the 1922 election, Lossiemouth-born James Ramsay Macdonald (1866–1937) was elected leader of the Labour Party and became Britain's first Labour prime minister in 1924.

Keir Hardie would barely recognise his party's present incarnation, the centre-left New Labour, which took power in Westminster in 1997.

| Late 18th century | 1914–1932 | 1941–45 |
|---|---|---|
| Scottish industry flourishes during the Industrial Revolution and Scotland becomes a world leader in the production of textiles, iron, steel and coal, and above all in shipbuilding and marine engineering. | Scottish industry slumps during WWI, and collapses in its aftermath in the face of new Eastern production and a contraction in world trade culminating in the Great Depression. About 400,000 Scots emigrate between 1921 and 1931. | Clydebank is blitzed by German bombers in 1941 with 1200 deaths; and by 1945 one out of four males in the workforce is employed in heavy industries to support the war effort. |

industry saw the construction of huge weaving mills in Lanarkshire (see p164), Dundee, Angus and Aberdeenshire. The world's first steamboat, the *Charlotte Dundas,* sailed along the newly opened Forth and Clyde Canal in 1802, and the world's first sea-going steamship, the *Comet,* was launched on the Clyde in 1812.

Glasgow, deprived of its lucrative tobacco trade following the American War of Independence (1776–83), developed into an industrial powerhouse, the 'second city' of the British Empire (after London). Cotton mills, iron and steelworks, chemical works, shipbuilding yards and heavy-engineering works proliferated along the River Clyde in the 19th century, powered by the coal mines of Lanarkshire, Ayrshire, Fife and Midlothian.

## WAR & PEACE

Scotland largely escaped the trauma and devastation wrought by WWII on the industrial cities of England. Indeed, the war brought a measure of renewed

### EXPLORING YOUR SCOTTISH ROOTS

Genealogy is a hugely popular pastime, and many visitors to Scotland take the opportunity to do some detective work on their Scottish ancestry.

One of the best guides is *Tracing Your Scottish Ancestry* by Kathleen B Cory, and there are many useful websites; **GenUKI** (www.genuki.org.uk) is a good starting point.

At the **Scotland's People Website** (www.scotlandspeople.gov.uk) you can search the indexes to the Old Parish Registers and Statutory Registers up to 100 years ago (75 years ago for deaths), and the indexes to the 1881, 1891 and 1901 census returns, on a pay-per-view basis. The **International Genealogical Index** (www.familysearch.com), compiled by the Mormon Church, includes freely searchable records of Scottish baptisms and marriages from 1553 to 1875.

The following places in Edinburgh can help out:

**General Register Office for Scotland** ( ☎ 0131-314 4433; www.gro-scotland.gov.uk; New Register House, 3 West Register St, Edinburgh EH1 3YT; per full-/half-day £17/10; ☽ 9am-4.30pm Mon-Fri) The main records used in Scottish genealogical research – the Statutory Registers of births, marriages and deaths (1855 to the present), the Old Parish Registers (1533–1854) and the 10-yearly census returns from 1841 to 1901 – are held here. The registration of births, marriages and deaths became compulsory in Scotland on 1 January 1855; before that date, the ministers of the Church of Scotland kept registers of baptisms and marriages. The oldest surviving parish registers date back to 1553, but these records are far from complete, and many births and marriages before 1855 went unrecorded.

**National Archives of Scotland** ( ☎ 0131-535 1334; www.nas.gov.uk; Register House, 2 Princes St, Edinburgh EH1 3YY; admission free; ☽ 9am-4.45pm Mon-Fri) You will need to ask for a reader's ticket (free) – bring some form of ID bearing your name and signature (eg passport, driving licence, bank card). Use of the Historical Search Room is free, and is first come, first served.

**Scottish Genealogy Society Library & Family History Centre** ( ☎ 0131-220 3677; www.scotsgeneal ogy.com; 15 Victoria Tce, Edinburgh EH1 2JL; ☽ 10.30am-5.30pm Mon, Tue & Thu, to 8.30pm Wed, 10am-5pm Sat) Maintains the world's largest library of Scottish gravestone inscriptions. Entry is free for society members, £5 for nonmembers.

| 1970s | 1999–2004 | 2007 |
|---|---|---|
| The discovery of oil and gas in the North Sea brings new prosperity to Aberdeen and the surrounding area, and also to the Shetland Islands. | Scottish parliament is convened for the first time on 12 May 1999. After plenty of scandal and huge sums of money, a stunning new parliament building is opened by Queen Elizabeth II in October 2004 at Holyrood in Edinburgh. | Scottish National Party wins the third general election of the devolved Scottish parliament. This victory means the issue of Scottish independence is once again back on the political agenda. |

prosperity to Scotland as the shipyards and engineering works geared up to supply the war effort. But the postwar period saw the collapse of shipbuilding and heavy industry, on which Scotland had become over-reliant.

After the discovery of North Sea oil, revenues were siphoned off to England and this, along with takeovers of Scots companies by English ones (which then closed the Scots operation, asset-stripped and transferred jobs to England), fuelled increasing nationalist sentiment in Scotland. The Scottish Nationalist Party (SNP) developed into a third force in Scottish politics, taking 30% of the popular vote in the 1974 general election.

Between 1904 and 1931 around a million people emigrated from Scotland to begin a new life in North America and Australia.

## DEVOLUTION

In 1979 a referendum was held on whether to set up a directly elected Scottish Assembly. Fifty-two per cent of those who voted said 'yes' to devolution, but the Labour prime minister James Callaghan decided that everyone who didn't vote should be counted as a 'no'. By this devious reasoning, only 33% of the electorate had voted 'yes', so the Scottish Assembly was rejected.

From 1979 to 1997 Scotland was ruled by a Conservative government in London for which the majority of Scots hadn't voted. Separatist feelings, always present, grew stronger. Following the landslide victory of the Labour Party in May 1997, another referendum was held on the creation of a Scottish parliament. This time the result was overwhelmingly and unambiguously in favour.

Elections to the new parliament took place on 6 May 1999 and the Scottish parliament convened for the first time on 12 May in Edinburgh; Donald Dewar (1937–2000), formerly the Secretary of State for Scotland, was nominated as first minister (the Scottish parliament's equivalent of prime minister).

The Scottish National Party recently won power in Scotland's third election and wants full independence from England. It is making plans for a referendum on the issue which will also give voters an option of more devolved powers from London (such as control over North Sea oil and gas revenues).

# The Culture

## THE NATIONAL PSYCHE

Having lived next door to a large and powerful neighbour for so long, it is hardly surprising that a considerable part of the Scottish national identity lies in simply not being English. Throughout history England – still regularly referred to as 'the Auld Enemy' – was often seen as standing for power, greed, arrogance and oppression, and in reaction to that Scots have regarded themselves, collectively, as the plucky underdog, a freedom-loving David to England's imperialist Goliath.

Historically, the Scottish character has been shaped by the harsh climate, the Protestant work ethic and a strong sense of social justice. A good, broad-based education has always been part of a Scots upbringing – Scotland introduced tax-subsidised education for all as long ago as 1696, resulting in one of the most literate and best-educated populations in 18th-century Europe – and doing well at school and university is still much admired.

This background has created a people who are shrewd, meritocratic and outward looking, with a sceptical, inquiring nature – it's no accident of history that Scots have been responsible for many of the Western world's most important inventions and innovations (see boxed text, p50). The flipside of the national character is a deep-seated sense of insecurity that occasionally sees Scots talk themselves down rather than celebrate their successes.

Robert Louis Stevenson wrote that the mark of a Scot is that 'there burns alive in him a sense of identity with the dead even to the twentieth generation'. Scotland's unofficial anthem – 'Flower of Scotland', written by the late Roy Williamson and sung with gusto at football and rugby matches – harks back to the Battle of Bannockburn in 1314 when the Scots, outnumbered 10 to one, defeated the English; in the words of the song, they 'stood against him, proud Edward's army, and sent him homewards to think again'.

This historical baggage weighs heavily on the Scots, and has led to a long-standing resentment of English cultural and political domination. This reached a peak during the Thatcher government (1979–90), when a Conservative administration used the Scots as guinea pigs for the hugely unpopular poll tax, imposing it on Scotland a full year before it was extended to England and Wales – so much for a United Kingdom.

Although much of the resentment has dissipated since 1997, when a Labour government replaced the Conservatives, it still simmers under the surface. Just let a TV commentator once refer to a Scot as English, as occasionally happens when Scottish sportsmen and women are doing well in international competitions, and you can guarantee that a hundred hands will be reaching for the phone to complain to the BBC, while the next day's papers will be spluttering with outrage.

Today the Scotland–England rivalry is generally good-natured, and the conflict has long since moved from battlefield to sports stadium. A Scottish win over England at football or rugby is often seen as more important than winning an entire competition. There are few things Scots sports fans enjoy as much as an England team getting a good hiding, no matter who they are playing against.

But the rivalry runs both ways. Asked whether he would support the Scottish football team if England were eliminated from the World Cup, an English fan replied: 'I have no problem at all in supporting the Scottish team. By doing so I am showing support for my fellow Britons and building on our common historical and cultural ties. Also, it really annoys them.'

It is illegal to import haggis into the USA, as the US government has declared that sheep lungs are unfit for human consumption.

In June Shetland enjoys four hours more daylight each day than London.

## LIFESTYLE

Scotland consistently rates highly in quality-of-life surveys. It's an attractive place to live, with excellent social, cultural and leisure amenities. There is still a strong sense of community in rural areas, and even in parts of the big cities. Like many places in the UK, the Scottish social scene often centres upon the local pub.

Just as the Eskimos are supposed to have 40 different words for snow, it seems as if the Scots have 40 different words for drunk – bevvied, blootered, hammered, guttered, fleein', fou, steamin', stotious, paralytic, plastered and just plain pished, to name but a few.

There's no denying that, like most northern Europeans, the Scots enjoy a drink. For the vast majority that means a few pints of beer down the pub or a few glasses of wine with a meal, but for a significant minority the attitude is: if a thing's worth doing, it's worth overdoing. As a result, the level of alcohol-related deaths in Scotland is twice the UK average (27.4 deaths per 100,000 people in Scotland in 2002–04, compared with 12.8 for the UK as a whole).

Things ain't much better when you look at the Scottish diet. Favourite foods such as chips, pies, sweets and fizzy drinks have resulted in obesity levels that are the second highest in the developed world (after the USA), and death rates from heart disease that are higher than in the rest of the UK and Western Europe.

On the positive side, the ban on smoking in enclosed public spaces (including pubs) that came into force in March 2006 appears to be having an effect – in the year following the ban there were 17% fewer hospital admissions for heart attacks. Apart from a few forlorn smokers puffing away in the rain outside pub doors, the ban has been overwhelmingly popular and its success has caused several European countries to think about following suit.

Since 2006 smoking has been banned in all enclosed public places in Scotland; see www .clearingtheairscotland .com.

## ECONOMY

Scotland once led the world in shipbuilding, steel-making and engineering, but its days as a centre of heavy industry are long gone. In 2007, as the country celebrated the 40th anniversary of the launch of the QE2 – the last great ship to be built on the River Clyde – most of Scotland's coal mines and all of its steel works had closed, and the shipbuilding industry hung by a thread.

They have been replaced by energy, finance, services, life sciences, and hi-tech engineering and electronics. The service sector now accounts for around 67% of the Scottish economy, manufacturing 22%, construction 6%, agriculture, fishing and forestry 3% and mining a mere 2%.

Financial and business services have provided more new jobs in Scotland than electronics and North Sea oil combined, and Edinburgh is the fifth-largest financial centre in Europe. Tourism is one of the most important contributors to the Scottish economy, injecting £4 billion annually and employing one in 15 of the workforce. The biggest single employer in Scotland, however, is the government – almost one in four Scots works in the public sector.

The majority of Scotland's manufacturing output is accounted for by electronics, textiles, clothing (especially woollen knitwear), and food and drink – Scotch whisky is one of the country's most lucrative exports. Some traditional cottage industries, like the weaving of Harris Tweed, survive and thrive on a small scale.

In the Highlands some sheep and cattle farming continues, boosted by salmon and shellfish farming on the west coast, but tourism is the main income provider here.

## TARTANALIA TOP FIVE

Here's a quick guide to the top five icons of Scottish culture.

### Bagpipes

Highland soldiers were traditionally accompanied into battle by the skirl of the pipes, and the Scottish Highland bagpipe is unique in being the only musical instrument ever to be classed as a weapon. The playing of the pipes was banned – under pain of death – by the British government in 1747 as part of a scheme to suppress Highland culture in the wake of the Jacobite uprising of 1745 (p33). The pipes were revived when the Highland regiments were drafted into the British Army towards the end of the 18th century.

The bagpipe consists of a leather bag held under the arm, kept inflated by blowing through the blowstick; the piper forces air through the pipes by squeezing the bag with the forearm. Three of the pipes, known as drones, play a constant note (one bass, two tenor) in the background. The fourth pipe, the chanter, plays the melody.

### Ceilidh

The Gaelic word *ceilidh* (pronounced *kay*-lay) means 'visit'. A *ceilidh* was originally a social gathering in the house after the day's work was over, enlivened with storytelling, music and song. These days, a *ceilidh* means an evening of traditional Scottish entertainment including music, song and dance.

### Tartan

The oldest surviving piece of tartan – a patterned woollen textile now made into everything from kilts to key rings – dates back to the Roman period. Today tartan is popular the world over, and beyond – astronaut Al Bean took his MacBean tartan to the moon and back. Particular setts (tartan patterns) didn't come to be associated with particular clans until the 17th century, although today every clan, and indeed every Scottish football team, has one or more distinctive tartans.

### Kilt

The original Scottish Highland dress was not the kilt but the plaid – a long length of tartan cloth wrapped around the body and over the shoulder. The wearing of Highland dress was banned after the Jacobite rebellions but revived under royal patronage in the 19th century. George IV and his English courtiers donned kilts for their visit to Scotland in 1822. During the same century Sir Walter Scott, novelist, poet and dedicated patriot, did much to rekindle interest in Scottish ways. By then, however, many of the old setts had been forgotten, and as a result some tartans are actually Victorian creations. The modern kilt only appeared in the 18th century and was reputedly invented by Thomas Rawlinson, an Englishman!

Kilts don't have pockets, so kilted Scotsmen keep their beer money in a sporran, a pouch made of leather or animal skin that hangs in front of the kilt, suspended from a chain around the waist.

### Scottish Flag

Scottish football and rugby supporters can never seem to make up their minds which flag to wave, the Saltire or the Lion Rampant. The Saltire or St Andrew's Cross – a diagonal white cross on a blue ground – is one of the oldest national flags in the world, dating from at least the 12th century. Originally a religious emblem – St Andrew was crucified on a diagonal cross – it became a national emblem in the 14th century. According to legend, white clouds in the form of a saltire appeared in a blue sky during the battle of Nechtansmere between Scots and Saxons, urging the Scots to victory. It was incorporated in the Union Flag of the UK following the Act of Union in 1707.

The Lion Rampant – a red lion on a golden-yellow ground – is the Royal Banner of Scotland. It is thought to derive from the arms of King William I the Lion (r 1143–1214), and strictly speaking should only be used by a Scottish monarch. It is incorporated in the British Royal Standard, quartered with the three lions of England and the harp of Ireland.

Unemployment is fairly low (4.8% in September 2007) and average income is reasonable (around £24,000 a year, about 92% of the UK average). However, Scotland shares in the UK's culture of long working hours: a third of people work more than 48 hours a week, and one in six works more than 60 hours. The EU average is 40.3 hours.

## POPULATION

The internationally recognised image of Scotland is of crofts and castles and wild mountain scenery, but the country's population of 5.1 million is in fact overwhelmingly urban, with 80% living in the cities and towns of the Central Lowlands.

The Highland region is one of Europe's most sparsely populated areas, with an average of only nine people per square kilometre – a mere one-thirtieth of the UK average. A major problem since WWII has been the depopulation of the rural Highlands and, especially, the Western Isles, as younger people leave to find jobs. This movement of people from rural to urban areas, which began in the 18th century, is still going on – the population of the Outer Hebrides has fallen by 8% in the last decade.

Scotland's total population has increased slightly in recent years, due mainly to people moving from other parts of the UK and overseas (there are an estimated 86,000 Poles living in Scotland, having moved after Poland joined the EU in 2004). The age profile of the Scottish population is getting older (more than half of Scots are aged 40 or over), mainly as a result of a decreasing birth rate.

There are an estimated 60 million people around the world who claim Scottish ancestry.

## SPORT
### Football

Football (soccer) in Scotland is not so much a sport as a religion, with thousands turning out to worship their local teams on Wednesdays and weekends throughout the season (August to May). Sacred rites include standing in the freezing cold of a February day, drinking hot Bovril and eating a Scotch pie as you watch your team getting gubbed.

Scotland's top 10 clubs play in the **Scottish Premier League** (www.scotprem.com), but two teams – Glasgow Rangers and Glasgow Celtic – dominate the competition. On only 18 occasions since 1890 has a team other than Rangers or Celtic won the league; the last time was when Aberdeen won in 1985. Celtic was Premier League champion in 2006 and 2007.

Glasgow Celtic was the first British team to win the European Cup (1967) and, so far, the only Scottish club to have done so. The team that won back then was made up entirely of Scots players from the Glasgow area. In comparison, Rangers made history in 2000 by being the first to field a team composed entirely of non-Scottish players, and today half the players in the Premier League are of non-Scottish origin, a situation that angers many grassroots supporters and bodes ill for the future of the national team.

If supporting local teams is like a religion, supporting the Scottish national team is more like a penance. The beginning of each European Championship and World Cup is filled with hope, but usually ends in despair.

Despite their team's often poor results, Scotland fans – known as the Tartan Army – are famed for their friendliness and good behaviour abroad, to the extent that some English and French football fans have joined them. The non-Scottish contingent has been dubbed the 'Sporran Legion'.

### Rugby Union

Traditionally, football was the sport of Scotland's urban working classes, while rugby union (www.scottishrugby.org) was the preserve of agricultural workers from the Borders and middle-class university graduates. Although this distinction is breaking down – rugby's popularity soared after the 1999 World Cup was staged in the UK, and the middle classes have invaded the football terraces – it persists to some extent.

Each year, starting in January, Scotland takes part in the Six Nations Rugby Union Championship. The most important fixture is the clash against England for the Calcutta Cup – it's always an emotive event, though Scotland has only won once in the last 12 years.

At club level, the season runs from September to May, and among the better teams are those from the Borders such as Hawick, Kelso and Melrose. At the end of the season, teams play a rugby sevens (seven-a-side) variation of the 15-player competition.

## Golf

Scotland is the home of golf (www.scottishgolfunion.org). The game was probably invented here in the 12th century, and the world's oldest documentary evidence of a game being played (dating from 1456) was on Bruntsfield Links in Edinburgh.

Although St Andrews claims seniority in having the oldest golf course in the world, it was at Edinburgh's Leith Links in 1744 that the first official rules of the game were formulated by the Honorable Company of Edinburgh Golfers (now the famous Muirfield Golf Club). Rule number 9 gives some insight into the 18th-century game – 'If a ball be stop'd by any person, Horse, Dog or anything else, the Ball so stop'd must be played where it lyes'.

Today, there are more than 550 golf courses in Scotland – that's more per capita than in any other country. The sport is hugely popular and much more egalitarian than in other countries, with lots of affordable, council-owned courses. There are many world-famous championship courses too, from Muirfield in East Lothian and Turnberry and Troon in Ayrshire, to Carnoustie in Angus and St Andrews' Old Course in Fife.

In the realm of professional golf, Colin Montgomerie has been Scotland's top golfer for over a decade, consistently finishing in the top five in international tournaments. In the 2005 British Open Championship at St Andrews, Montgomerie was runner-up to Tiger Woods, and he lost the 2006 US Open by a single shot – he's widely regarded as the best golfer never to have won a major tournament.

## Highland Games

Highland games are held in Scotland throughout the summer, and not just in the Highlands. You can find dates and details of Highland games held all over the country on the website **VisitScotland** (www.visitscotland.com/libr ary/highlandgamescalendar).

The traditional sporting events are accompanied by piping and dancing competitions, and attract locals and tourists alike. Some events are peculiarly Scottish, particularly those that involve trials of strength: tossing the caber (heaving a tree trunk into the air), throwing the hammer and putting the stone. Major Highland games are staged at Dunoon (p281), Oban (p299) and Braemar (p256).

## Shinty

Shinty (*camanachd* in Gaelic) is a fast and physical ball-and-stick sport similar to Ireland's hurling, with more than a little resemblance to clan warfare. It's an indigenous Scottish game played mainly in the Highlands, and the most prized trophy is the Camanachd Cup. The cup final, held in September, is a great Gaelic get-together. The Kingussie team has dominated in recent times, winning the cup every year from 1997 to 2003, then again in

You can search for your own clan tartan at www .tartansauthority.com.

For more information on shinty, see www .shinty.com.

2006, though Inveraray broke their winning streak in 2004 and Fort William won in 2005 and 2007.

Each year in October there's an international match between Scotland and Ireland, played under composite shinty/hurling rules, and held alternately in Ireland and Scotland.

## Curling

Curling, a winter sport which involves propelling a 19kg granite stone along the ice towards a target, was probably invented in Scotland in medieval times. Though traditionally Scottish, it was very much a minority sport in Scotland until it got an enormous publicity boost when the British women's team (all Scots) won the gold medal in the 2002 Winter Olympics. Scottish teams took the Men's World Curling Championships in 2006, and came third in the Women's World Curling Championships in 2007.

For more information on curling, see www .royalcaledoniancurling club.org.

## MEDIA

Although London dominates the UK media industry, Scotland has a flourishing media sector of its own, the legacy of a long tradition of Scottish publishing. The *Herald* (formerly the *Glasgow Herald*), established in 1783, is one of the oldest English-language newspapers in the world.

BBC Scotland, with its headquarters in a shiny new building next to the Science Centre in Glasgow, is the Scottish arm of the UK's public-service TV and radio broadcaster. It produces and broadcasts programmes that reflect Scotland's distinctive cultural identity. Funded by an annual TV licence, the BBC doesn't carry advertising.

There are two Scottish-based commercial TV broadcasters. Scottish Television (STV) covers southern Scotland and some of the western Highlands, while STV North transmits to the Highlands from Perth to the Western Isles and Shetland. All three broadcasters produce some Gaelic-language programming.

The Falkirk Tartan is a piece of cream and brown cloth that was found with a hoard of Roman coins dating from around AD 320. It is now in the Museum of Scotland in Edinburgh.

There's a healthy newspaper sector too. Sales figures for Scotland (excluding the rest of the UK) show that the highest-selling dailies are the tabloids the *Sun* (a Scottish edition of the London-based paper) and the home-grown *Daily Record*, based in Glasgow. The three main, home-published quality newspapers – the *Scotsman, Herald* and *Press & Journal* – easily outsell all five London-produced quality dailies (*Telegraph, Times, Guardian, Independent* and *Financial Times*).

## RELIGION

Although the Christian church has played a hugely important role in Scottish history, religious observance in Scotland has been in decline since the 20th century. Today only 6.5% of the population regularly attend church on Sunday. Church attendance is highest in the Outer Hebrides (almost 40%) and lowest in the cities. For more on religion in the Outer Hebrides, see the boxed text, p392.

For news stories and information on religion in Scotland, check out the Hot Topics list on the *Scotsman* website (http://news.scotsman .com/topics.cfm), and click on Religious Issues.

The two largest religious denominations are the Presbyterian Church of Scotland (47%) and the Roman Catholic Church (16%), with 28% claiming no religious affiliation at all. Non-Christian religions account for only 2% of the population, mostly small communities of Muslims, Hindus, Sikhs and Jews.

## ARTS
### Literature

Scotland has a long and distinguished literary history, from the days of the medieval makars ('makers' of verses, ie poets) to the modern 'brat pack' of Iain Banks, Irvine Welsh, Ian Rankin and Christopher Brookmyre.

## BURNS & SCOTT

Scotland's best-loved and most famous literary figure is, of course, Robert Burns (1759–96). His works have been translated into dozens of languages and are known and admired the world over (see the boxed text, p176).

In 1787 Burns was introduced to a 16-year-old boy at a social gathering in the house of an Edinburgh professor. The boy grew up to be Sir Walter Scott (1771–1832), Scotland's greatest and most prolific novelist. The son of an Edinburgh lawyer, Scott was born in Guthrie St (off Chambers St; the house no longer exists) and lived at various New Town addresses before moving to his country house at Abbotsford (p159). Scott's early works were rhyming ballads, such as *The Lady of the Lake*, and his first historical novels – Scott effectively invented the genre – were published anonymously. He almost single-handedly revived interest in Scottish history and legend in the early 19th century, and was largely responsible for organising King George IV's visit to Scotland in 1822. Plagued by debt in later life, he wrote obsessively – to the detriment of his health – in order to make money, but will always be

---

### ESSENTIAL SCOTTISH READS

- *Waverley* (1814, Sir Walter Scott) English literature's first historical novel, a romantic account of a Scottish soldier caught up in the 1745 Jacobite rebellion. Hard to get into but worth the effort.

- *Kidnapped!* (1886, Robert Louis Stevenson) A rip-roaring adventure tale for all ages, following 16-year-old Davie Balfour as he escapes through the Highlands with Jacobite rebel Allan Breck Stuart.

- *The Silver Darlings* (1941, Neil M Gunn) A moving and mystical novel set in 19th-century Caithness, following the attempts by Highlanders dispossessed by the Clearances to wrest a living from the herring fishery.

- *A Scot's Quair* (1946, Lewis Grassic Gibbon) A trilogy set in rural northeast Scotland that follows heroine Chris Guthrie as she tries to resolve the conflict between her love of the land and her desire to escape a constricting peasant culture.

- *Para Handy Tales* (1955, Neil Munro) A much-loved collection of humorous stories about the crew of a steampuffer as it cruises the sea lochs of Argyllshire and the Crinan Canal.

- *The Prime of Miss Jean Brodie* (1962, Muriel Spark) The story of a charismatic teacher in a 1930s Edinburgh girls school who leads her chosen girls – her *crème de la crème* – in the pursuit of truth and beauty, with devastating consequences.

- *Greenvoe* (1972, George Mackay Brown) A vivid evocation of life in an Orkney fishing village in the 1960s; it is warm, funny, poetic and ultimately very, very moving.

- *Laidlaw* (1977, William McIlvanney) A gritty detective story set in the mean streets of 1970s Glasgow, following in the footsteps of unorthodox policeman-cum-philosopher Jack Laidlaw.

- *Trainspotting* (1993, Irvine Welsh) A disturbing and darkly humorous journey through Edinburgh's junkie underworld, pulling no punches as it charts hero Renton's descent into heroin addiction.

- *Black & Blue* (1997, Ian Rankin) Stars hard-drinking detective John Rebus, Edinburgh's answer to Laidlaw, as he re-examines the notorious Bible John murders of the late 1960s. Gripping noir-style writing.

- *The Trick Is to Keep Breathing* (1999, Janice Galloway) Follows a young drama teacher, ironically named Joy, as she slips over the edge into depression and madness. Fluent, witty writing and comic minor characters keep the pages turning.

- *Indelible Acts* (2003, AL Kennedy) A collection of mesmerising short stories on the theme of love and longing by a master (or rather mistress) of the form writing at the very top of her game.

best remembered for classic tales such as *Waverley, The Antiquary, The Heart of Midlothian, Ivanhoe, Redgauntlet* and *Castle Dangerous.*

## THE 19TH CENTURY

Along with Scott, Robert Louis Stevenson (1850–94) ranks as Scotland's best-known novelist. Born at 8 Howard Pl in Edinburgh into a family of famous lighthouse engineers, Stevenson studied law at Edinburgh University but was always intent on pursuing the life of a writer. An inveterate traveller, but dogged by ill-health, he finally settled in Samoa in 1889, where he was revered by the natives as 'Tusitala' – the teller of tales. Stevenson is known and loved around the world for those tales: *Kidnapped, Catriona, Treasure Island, The Master of Ballantrae* and *The Strange Case of Dr Jekyll and Mr Hyde.* The Writers' Museum (p82) in Edinburgh celebrates the work of Burns, Scott and Stevenson.

Sir Arthur Conan Doyle (1859–1930), the creator of Sherlock Holmes, was born in Edinburgh and studied medicine at Edinburgh University. He based the character of Holmes on one of his lecturers, the surgeon Dr Joseph Bell, who had employed his forensic skills and powers of deduction on several murder cases in Edinburgh. There's a fascinating exhibit on Dr Bell in Edinburgh's Surgeons' Hall Museums (p95).

## THE 20TH CENTURY

Scotland's finest modern poet was Hugh MacDiarmid (born Christopher Murray Grieve; 1892–1978). Originally from Dumfriesshire, he moved to Edinburgh in 1908, where he trained as a teacher and a journalist, but spent most of his life in Montrose, Shetland, Glasgow and Biggar. His masterpiece is 'A Drunk Man Looks at the Thistle', a 2685-line Joycean monologue.

Born in Edinburgh, Norman MacCaig (1910–96) is widely regarded as the greatest Scottish poet of his generation. A primary school teacher for almost 40 years, MacCaig wrote poetry that is witty, adventurous, moving and filled with sharp observation; poems such as 'November Night, Edinburgh' vividly capture the atmosphere of his home city.

The poet and storyteller George Mackay Brown (1921–96) was born in Stromness in the Orkney Islands, and lived there almost all his life. Although his poems and novels are rooted in Orkney, his work, like that of Burns, transcends local and national boundaries. His novel *Greenvoe* is a warm, witty and poetic evocation of everyday life in an Orkney community.

Lewis Grassic Gibbon (born James Leslie Mitchell; 1901–35) is another Scots writer whose novels vividly capture a sense of place – in this case the rural northeast of Kincardineshire and Aberdeenshire. His most famous work is the trilogy of novels called *A Scot's Quair.*

Dame Muriel Spark (1918–2006) was born in Edinburgh and educated at James Gillespie's High School for Girls, an experience that provided material for perhaps her best-known novel, *The Prime of Miss Jean Brodie,* a shrewd portrait of 1930s Edinburgh. Dame Muriel was a prolific writer; her last novel, *The Finishing School,* published in 2004, was her 22nd.

## CONTEMPORARY SCENE

The most widely known Scots writers today include the award-winning James Kelman (1946–), Iain Banks (see the boxed text, p46), Irvine Welsh (1961–) and Ian Rankin (1960–). The grim realities of modern Glasgow are vividly conjured up in Kelman's short story collection *Not Not While the Giro;* his controversial novel *How Late It Was, How Late* won the 1994 Booker Prize.

The novels of Irvine Welsh, who grew up in Edinburgh's working-class district of Muirhouse, describe a very different world from that inhabited

'The grim realities of modern Glasgow are vividly conjured up in James Kelman's short story collection *Not Not While the Giro*'

## AUTHOR PROFILE: IAIN BANKS

One of Scotland's most successful contemporary authors, Iain Banks (1954–) is also one of its most prolific. He has published 21 novels since 1984, 10 of them science fiction written under 'the world's most penetrable pseudonym', Iain M Banks.

Hailed as one of the most imaginative writers of his generation, Banks burst on the Scottish literary scene with his dazzling debut novel *The Wasp Factory* (1984), a macabre but utterly compelling exploration of the inner world of Frank, a strange and deeply disturbed teenager. Though violent and unsettling, its dark humour and sharp dialogue keep the pages turning right to the bitter (and twisted) end.

Banks' most recent novel, *The Steep Approach to Garbadale* (2007), is a tale of lost love with a none-too-subtle subtext that is highly critical of US imperialism. Though enjoyable, it has a hard time living up to the impossibly high standard set by earlier books such as *Complicity* (1993), a gruesome and often hilarious thriller-cum-satire on the greed and corruption of the Thatcher years, and the immensely likable *The Crow Road* (1992), a warm, witty and moving family saga based in the fictional Argyllshire town of Gallanach (a thinly disguised Oban transplanted to the shores of Loch Crinan). The latter provides one of Scottish fiction's most memorable opening sentences: 'It was the day my grandmother exploded.'

Despite dodgy Scottish accents from Liam Neeson and Jessica Lange, *Rob Roy* is a witty and moving cinematic version of Sir Walter Scott's tale of the outlaw MacGregor.

by Miss Jean Brodie – the modern city's underworld of drugs, drink, despair and violence. Best known for his debut novel *Trainspotting*, Welsh's most accomplished work is probably *Marabou Stork Nightmares*, in which a soccer hooligan, paralysed and in a coma, reviews his violent and brutal life.

Ian Rankin's Edinburgh-based crime novels, featuring the hard-drinking, introspective Detective Inspector John Rebus, are sinister, engrossing mysteries that explore the darker side of Scotland's capital city. Rankin's novels are filled with sharp dialogue, telling detail and three-dimensional characters; he attracts a growing international following (his books have been translated into 22 languages). Rankin seems to improve with every book – his latest, *Exit Music* (2007), is one of his best.

### Cinema

Scotland has never really had its own film industry, but in recent years the government-funded agency **Scottish Screen** (www.scottishscreen.com) has been created to nurture native talent and promote and develop all aspects of film, TV and new media in Scotland. Despite criticism from within the industry, in recent years its backing has helped to create award-winning films such as *Red Road* (2006), *The Last King of Scotland* (2006) and *Hallam Foe* (2007).

Perthshire-born John Grierson (1898–1972) is acknowledged around the world as the father of the documentary film. His legacy includes the classic *Drifters* (about the Scottish herring fishery) and *Seaward the Great Ships* (about Clyde shipbuilding). Filmmaker Bill Douglas (1934–91), the director of an award-winning trilogy of films documenting his childhood and early adult life, was born in the former mining village of Newcraighall just south of Edinburgh.

Glasgow-born writer-director Bill Forsyth (1946–) is best known for *Local Hero* (1983), a gentle comedy about an oil magnate seduced by the beauty of the Highlands, and *Gregory's Girl* (1980), about an awkward, teenage schoolboy's romantic exploits. The directing credits of Gillies MacKinnon (1948–), another Glasgow native, include *Small Faces* (1996), *Regeneration* (1997) and *Hideous Kinky* (1998). Michael Caton-Jones (1958–), director of *Memphis Belle* (1990) and *Rob Roy* (1995), was born in West Lothian and is a graduate of Edinburgh University.

In the 1990s the rise of the director-producer-writer team of Danny Boyle (English), Andrew Macdonald and John Hodge (both Scottish) – who wrote the scripts for *Shallow Grave* (1994), *Trainspotting* (1996) and *A Life Less Ordinary* (1997) – marked the beginnings of what might be described as a home-grown Scottish film industry. Writer and director David McKenzie hit the headlines in recent years with *Young Adam* (2003), which starred Ewan McGregor and Tilda Swinton, and won BAFTAs for best actor, best actress, best director and best film. McKenzie recently gave us *Hallam Foe* (2007).

Other Scottish directorial talent includes Kevin Macdonald who made *Touching the Void* (2003), *The Last King of Scotland* (2006) and *State of Play* (2008), and Andrea Arnold who directed *Red Road* (2006).

Scotland's most famous actor is, of course, Sir Sean Connery (1930–), the original and best James Bond, and star of dozens of other hit films including *Highlander* (1986), *The Name of the Rose* (1986), *Indiana Jones and the Last Crusade* (1989), *The Hunt for Red October* (1990) and *The League of Extraordinary Gentlemen* (2003). Connery started life as 'Big Tam' Connery, sometime milkman and brickie, born in a tenement in Fountainbridge, Edinburgh.

Other Scottish actors who have achieved international recognition include Robert Carlyle, who starred in *Trainspotting* (1996), *The Full Monty* (1997) – the UK's most commercially successful film – *The World Is Not Enough* (1999) and *28 Weeks Later* (2007); and Ewan McGregor, who appeared in *Trainspotting, Moulin Rouge* (2001) and the most recent Star Wars films.

It's less widely known that Scotland produced some of the stars of silent film, including Eric Campbell (the big, bearded villain in Charlie Chaplin's films) and Jimmy Finlayson (the cross-eyed character in Laurel and Hardy films); in fact English-born Stan Laurel grew up and made his acting debut in Glasgow.

> For a guide to Scottish film locations check out www.scotlandthemovie.com.

## Music
### FOLK MUSIC
Scotland has always had a strong folk tradition. In the 1960s and 1970s Robin Hall and Jimmy MacGregor, the Corries and the hugely talented Ewan McColl worked the pubs and clubs up and down the country. The Boys of the Lough, headed by Shetland fiddler Aly Bain, was one of the first professional bands to promote the traditional Celtic music of Scotland and Ireland. It has been followed by the Battlefield Band, Runrig (who writes songs in Gaelic), Alba, Capercaillie and others.

The Scots folk songs that you will often hear sung in pubs and at *ceilidhs* draw on Scotland's rich history. A huge number of them relate to the Jacobite rebellions in the 18th century and, in particular, to Bonnie Prince Charlie – *Hey Johnnie Cope,* the *Skye Boat Song* and *Will Ye No Come Back Again,* for example – while others relate to the Covenanters and the Highland Clearances.

### ROCK & POP
It would take an entire book to list all the Scottish artists and bands that have made it big in the world of rock and pop. From Glasgow-born King of Skiffle, Lonnie Donegan, in the 1950s, to the Glasgow-bred kings of guitar-pop Franz Ferdinand today, the roll call is long and impressive.

The 1960s saw Lulu shout her way into the charts, alongside Donovan and the Incredible String Band, while the 70s produced the Average White Band, Nazareth, the Sensational Alex Harvey Band, John Martyn and – God help us – the Bay City Rollers, a global phenomenon whose allure remains a mystery to all except those who were teenage girls in the early 1970s.

The punk era produced the short-lived but superb Rezillos, plus the more durable Big Country, followed by a long roll call of other chart-toppers in the 80s – Simple Minds, the Waterboys, Primal Scream, Jesus and Mary Chain, Blue Nile, Lloyd Cole and the Commotions, Aztec Camera, the Associates,

Deacon Blue, the Cocteau Twins, the Proclaimers, Wet Wet Wet, Texas, Hue and Cry, Runrig, the Bluebells – where do you stop?

The 90s saw the emergence of three bands that took the top three places in a vote for the best Scottish band of all time – melodic indie-pop songsters Belle and Sebastian, like-Oasis-only-better Brit-rock band Travis, and indie rockers Idlewild, who opened for the Rolling Stones in 2003 – as well as the Delgados, Trashcan Sinatras and Teenage Fanclub.

Scottish artists who have made an impression in the last five years include Dogs Die in Hot Cars, whose bouncy, melodic, 80s-style pop is reminiscent of XTC and Dexy's Midnight Runners; Mylo, a DJ from the Isle of Skye; and the latest darlings of indie rock, the View. The bespectacled twin brothers Craig and Charlie Reid from Auchtermuchty in Fife, better known as the Proclaimers, produced a new album in 2005 (Restless Soul), which is as passionate and invigorating as the songs that first made them famous back in the late 80s, 'Letter From America', and 'I'm Gonna Be (500 Miles)'; there was yet another new album in the pipeline at the time of research.

The airwaves have been awash with female singer-songwriters in recent years, but few are as gutsy and versatile as Edinburgh-born, St Andrews–raised KT Tunstall. Although she's been writing and singing for the last 10 years, it was her 2005 debut album Eye to the Telescope that introduced her to a wider audience. And then there's Glasgow-born Angela McCluskey, whose husky vocals have been compared to Billie Holiday and Cerys Matthews.

## Painting

If asked to think of a Scottish painting, most people probably picture Monarch of the Glen, a romanticised portrait of a magnificent Highland red deer stag by Sir Edwin Landseer (1802–73). Landseer was not a Scot but a Londoner, though he did spend a lot of time in Scotland, leasing a cottage in Glen Feshie and visiting the young Queen Victoria at Balmoral to tutor her in drawing and etching.

Perhaps the most famous Scottish painting is the portrait Reverend Robert Walker Skating on Duddingston Loch by Sir Henry Raeburn (1756–1823), in the National Gallery of Scotland (p88). This image of a Presbyterian minister at play beneath Arthur's Seat, with all the poise of a ballerina and the hint of a smile on his lips, is a symbol of Enlightenment Edinburgh, the triumph of reason over wild nature.

Scottish portraiture reached its peak during the Scottish Enlightenment in the second half of the 18th century with the paintings of Raeburn and his contemporary Allan Ramsay (1713–84). You can see many fine examples of their work in the Scottish National Portrait Gallery (p89). At the same time, Alexander Nasmyth (1758–1840) emerged as an important landscape painter whose work had an immense influence on the 19th century. One of the greatest artists of the 19th century was Sir David Wilkie (1785–1841), whose genre paintings depicted rustic scenes of rural Highland life.

In the early 20th century the Scottish painters most widely acclaimed outside of the country were the group known as the Scottish Colourists – SJ Peploe, Francis Cadell, Leslie Hunter and JD Fergusson – whose striking paintings drew on French postimpressionist and Fauvist influences. Peploe and Cadell, active in the 1920s and 1930s, often spent the summer painting together on the Isle of Iona, and reproductions of their beautiful landscapes and seascapes appear on many a print and postcard. Aberdeen Art Gallery (p248), Kirkcaldy Museum & Art Gallery (p207) and the JD Fergusson Gallery in Perth (p219) all have good examples of their work.

In the 1930s a group of modernist landscape artists called themselves the Edinburgh School. Chief among them were William Gillies (1898–1978),

*The Living Tradition* is a bimonthly magazine covering the folk and traditional music of Scotland and the British Isles, as well as Celtic music, with features and reviews of albums and live gigs. See also www .folkmusic.net.

Sir William MacTaggart (1903–81) and Anne Redpath (1895–1965). Following WWII, artists such as Alan Davie (1920–) and Sir Eduardo Paolozzi (1924–2005) gained international reputations in abstract expressionism and pop art. The Dean Gallery (p90) in Edinburgh has a large collection of Paolozzi's work.

Among contemporary Scottish artists the most famous – or rather notorious – are Peter Howson and Jack Vettriano. Howson (1958–), best known for his grim portraits of Glasgow down-and-outs and muscular workers, hit the headlines when he went to Bosnia as an official war artist in 1993 and produced some disturbing and controversial works. *Croatian and Muslim,* an uncompromising rape scene, sparked a debate about what was acceptable in a public exhibition of art. More recently his nude portraits of Madonna – the pop icon, not the religious one – garnered even more column inches in the press. His work is much sought after and collected by celebrities such as David Bowie and Madonna herself. You can see examples of Howson's work at Aberdeen Art Gallery (p248) and Glasgow's Gallery of Modern Art (p125).

Jack Vettriano (1954–) was formerly a mining engineer, but now ranks as one of Scotland's most commercially successful artists. An entirely self-taught painter, his work – realistic, voyeuristic, occasionally sinister and often carrying a powerful erotic charge – has been compared to that of the American painters Edward Hopper and Walter Sickert. You can see reproductions of his work in coffee-table books and posters, but not in any Scottish art gallery. The Scottish art establishment looks down its nose at him, despite – or perhaps because of – the enormous popularity of his work.

## ARCHITECTURE

There are interesting buildings all over Scotland, but Edinburgh has a particularly rich heritage of 18th- and early-19th-century architecture, and Glasgow is noted for its superb Victorian buildings.

### Prehistoric

The northern islands of Scotland have some of the best surviving examples of prehistoric buildings in Europe. The best known are the stone villages of Skara Brae (from 3100 BC) in Orkney (p417) and Jarlshof (from 1500 BC) in Shetland (p431). The characteristic stone defensive towers known as brochs that can be seen in the north and west, including Glenelg (south of Kyle of Lochalsh; p378), Dun Carloway (Lewis; p395) and Mousa (Shetland; p430), are thought to date from the Iron Age (2nd century BC to 1st century AD).

### Romanesque (12th Century)

The Romanesque style – with its characteristic round arches and chevron decoration – was introduced to Scotland via the monasteries that were founded during the reign of David I (1124–53). Good examples survive in Dunfermline Abbey (see the boxed text, p208), and St Magnus Cathedral in Kirkwall (p408).

### Gothic (12th to 16th Centuries)

The more elaborate Gothic style, with its tall, pointed arches, ornate window tracery and ribbed vaulting, was brought to Scotland and adapted by the monastic orders. Examples of Early Gothic architecture can be seen in the ruins of the great Border abbeys of Jedburgh (p160) and Dryburgh (p159), at Holyrood Abbey in Edinburgh (p84) and in Glasgow Cathedral (p128). The more decorative Middle and Late Gothic styles appear in Melrose Abbey (p158), the cathedrals of Dunkeld (p226) and Elgin (p260), and the parish churches of Haddington (St Mary's; p116) and Stirling (Church of the Holy Rude; p194).

'The northern islands of Scotland have some of the best surviving examples of prehistoric buildings in Europe'

## SCOTTISH INVENTIONS & DISCOVERIES

The Scots have made a contribution to modern civilisation that is disproportionate to the size of their country. Although Scotland accounts for only 10% of Britain's population, it has produced more than 20% of leading British scientists, philosophers, engineers and inventors. Scots established the modern disciplines of economics, sociology, geology, electromagnetic theory, anaesthesiology and antibiotics, and pioneered the steam engine, the pneumatic tyre, the telephone and the TV.

Given the weather in Scotland perhaps it's not surprising that it was a Scot – the chemist Charles Macintosh (1766–1843) – who invented the waterproof material for the raincoat that still bears his name.

James Watt (1736–1819) didn't invent the steam engine (that was done by an Englishman, Thomas Newcomen), but it was Watt's modifications and improvements – notably the separate condenser – that led to its widespread usefulness in industry.

The chemical engineer James Young (1811–83), known as 'Paraffin' Young, developed the process of refining crude oil and established the world's first oil industry, based on extracting oil from the oil shales of West Lothian.

Not only did John Logie Baird (1888–1946) from Helensburgh invent TV, but it was his own company that produced (with the BBC) the world's first TV broadcast, the first broadcast with sound and the first outside broadcast. He also developed the concept of colour TV and took out a patent on fibre optics.

Alexander Graham Bell (1847–1922) was born in Edinburgh and emigrated to Canada and the USA, where he made a series of inventions, the most famous being the telephone in 1876.

In 1996 a team of Scottish embryologists working at the Roslin Institute near Edinburgh scored a first when they successfully cloned a sheep, Dolly, from the breast cell of an adult sheep. They added to this success when Dolly was mated naturally with a Welsh ram; in April 1998 she gave birth to a healthy lamb, Bonnie.

The list of famous Scots goes on and on: James Gregory (1638–75), inventor of the reflecting telescope; John McAdam (1756–1836), who developed road-building and surfacing techniques; Thomas Telford (1757–1834), one of the greatest civil engineers of his time; Robert William Thomson (1822–73), who patented the pneumatic tyre in 1845; John Boyd Dunlop (1840–1921), who reinvented the pneumatic tyre in 1888; and Sir Robert Watson-Watt (1892–1973), a direct descendant of James Watt, who developed the radar system that helped Britain to victory in WWII.

Other Scottish inventions and discoveries:

- antiseptic
- bicycle
- breech-loading rifle
- carbon dioxide
- colour photography
- decimal point
- electric light
- fire alarm
- gas mask
- golf
- grand piano
- iron and steel ships
- iron plough
- kaleidoscope
- lawnmower
- logarithm
- marmalade
- morphine
- postage stamp (adhesive)
- refrigeration
- speedometer
- steam-powered ship
- telescope
- ultrasound
- vacuum flask
- water softener

Scotland has also produced a significant number of Nobel Prize winners. Sir William Ramsay (1852–1916), whose work helped in the development of the nuclear industry, received the chemistry prize in 1904. Sir Alexander Fleming (1881–1955), codiscoverer of penicillin, received the prize for medicine in 1945. Other prize winners include Charles Wilson, John Orr, Alexander Robertus Todd and Sir James Black.

## Post-Reformation (16th & 17th Centuries)

After the Reformation many abbeys and cathedrals were damaged or destroyed, as the new religion frowned on ceremony and ornament.

During this period the old style of castle, with its central keep and curtain wall such as Dirleton Castle (p117), was superseded by the tower house. Good examples include Castle Campbell (p205), Loch Leven Castle (p217) and Neidpath Castle (p163). The Renaissance style was introduced in the royal palaces of Linlithgow (p117) and Falkland (p207).

## Georgian (18th & Early 19th Centuries)

The leading Scottish architects of the 18th century were William Adam (1684–1748) and his son Robert Adam (1728–92), whose revival of classical Greek and Roman forms influenced architects throughout Europe. Among the many neoclassical buildings they designed are Hopetoun House (p115), Culzean Castle (p176) and Edinburgh's Charlotte Sq (p88), possibly the finest example of Georgian architecture anywhere.

The New Town of Edinburgh, and other planned towns such as Inveraray (Argyll) and Blair Atholl (Perthshire), are characterised by their elegant Georgian architecture.

## Victorian (Mid- to Late 19th Century)

Alexander 'Greek' Thomson (1817–75) changed the face of 19th-century Glasgow with his neoclassical designs. Masterpieces such as the Egyptian Halls and Caledonia Road Church in Glasgow combine Egyptian and Hindu motifs with Greek and Roman forms.

In Edinburgh, William Henry Playfair (1790–1857) continued Robert Adam's neoclassical tradition in the Greek temples of the National Monument (p89) on Calton Hill, the Royal Scottish Academy (p87) and the National Gallery of Scotland (p88), before moving on to the neo-Gothic style in Edinburgh University's New College on The Mound.

The 19th-century boom in country-house building was led by architects William Burn (1789–1870) and David Bryce (1803–76). The resurgence of interest in Scottish history and identity, led by writers such as Sir Walter Scott, saw architects turn to the towers, pointed turrets and crow-stepped gables of the 16th century for inspiration. The Victorian revival of the Scottish Baronial style, which first made an appearance in 16th-century buildings such as Craigievar Castle (p258), produced many fanciful abodes such as Balmoral Castle (p255), Scone Palace (p218) and Abbotsford (p159).

*Scotland's Castles* by Chris Tabraham is an excellent companion for anyone touring Scottish castles – a readable, illustrated history detailing how and why they were built.

## The 20th Century

Scotland's best known 20th-century architect and designer is Charles Rennie Mackintosh (1868–1928), one of the most influential exponents of the Art Nouveau style. His finest building is the Glasgow School of Art (1896; p126), which still looks modern more than a century after it was built. For more on Charles Rennie Mackintosh, see the boxed text, p128. The Art Deco style of the 1930s made little impact in Scotland; the few examples include St Andrews House in Edinburgh and the beautifully restored Luma Tower in Glasgow.

During the 1960s Scotland's larger towns and cities suffered badly under the onslaught of the motor car and the unsympathetic impact of large-scale, concrete building developments. However, modern architecture discovered a new confidence in the 1980s and 1990s, exemplified by the impressive gallery housing the Burrell Collection (p130) in Glasgow and the stunning modern buildings lining the banks of Glasgow's River Clyde (p123).

Scotland's most controversial new structure is the Scottish parliament building in Edinburgh (see boxed text, p85).

# Food & Drink

Traditional Scottish cookery is all about basic comfort food: solid, nourishing fare, often high in fat, that would keep you warm on a winter's day spent in the fields or out fishing, and sweet treats to come home to in the evening.

But a new culinary style known as Modern Scottish has emerged over the last two decades. It's a style that should be familiar to fans of Californian Cuisine and Mod Oz. Chefs take top-quality Scottish produce – from Highland venison, Aberdeen Angus beef and freshly landed seafood, to root vegetables, raspberries and Ayrshire cheeses – and prepare it simply, in a way that enhances the natural flavours, often adding a French, Italian or Asian twist.

Scotland's traditional drinks – whisky and beer – have also found a new lease of life in recent years, with single malts being marketed like fine wines, and a new breed of micro-breweries springing up all over the country.

*A Caledonian Feast* by Annette Hope is a fascinating and readable history of Scottish cuisine, providing a wealth of historical and sociological background.

## STAPLES & SPECIALITIES

Haggis may be the national dish that Scotland is most famous for, but when it comes to what Scottish people actually cook and eat most often, the hands-down winner has to be mince and tatties (potatoes). Minced beef, browned in the pan and then stewed slowly with onion, carrot and gravy, is served with mashed potatoes (with a splash of milk and a knob of butter added during the mashing) – it's tasty, warming and you don't even have to chew.

### Breakfast

Surprisingly few Scots eat porridge for breakfast – these days a cappuccino and a croissant is just as likely – and even fewer eat it in the traditional way; that is, with salt to taste, but no sugar. The breakfast offered in a B&B or hotel usually consists of fruit juice and cereal or muesli, followed by a choice of bacon, sausage, black pudding (a type of sausage made from dried blood), grilled tomato, mushrooms and a fried egg or two.

Fish for breakfast may sound strange, but was not unusual in crofting and fishing communities where seafood was a staple; many hotels still offer grilled kippers (smoked herrings) or smoked haddock (poached in milk and served with a poached egg) for breakfast – delicious with lots of buttered toast.

---

### HAGGIS – SCOTLAND'S NATIONAL DISH

Scotland's national dish is often ridiculed by foreigners because of its ingredients, which admittedly don't sound promising – the finely chopped lungs, heart and liver of a sheep, mixed with oatmeal and onion and stuffed into a sheep's stomach bag. However, it actually tastes surprisingly good.

Haggis should be served with *champit tatties* and *bashed neeps* (mashed potatoes and turnips), with a generous dollop of butter and a good sprinkling of black pepper.

Although it's eaten year-round, haggis is central to the celebrations of 25 January, in honour of Scotland's national poet, Robert Burns. Scots worldwide unite on Burns Night to revel in their Scottishness. A piper announces the arrival of the haggis and Burns' poem *Address to a Haggis* is recited to this 'Great chieftan o' the puddin-race'. The bulging haggis is then lanced with a dirk (dagger) to reveal the steaming offal within, 'warm, reekin, rich'.

Vegetarians (and quite a few carnivores, no doubt) will be relieved to know that veggie haggis is available in some restaurants.

## Soups

Scotch broth, made with mutton stock, barley, lentils and peas, is nutritious and tasty, while cock-a-leekie is a hearty soup made with chicken and leeks. Warming vegetable soups include leek and potato soup, and lentil soup (traditionally made using ham stock – vegetarians beware!).

Seafood soups include the delicious *Cullen skink*, made with smoked haddock, potato, onion and milk, and *partan bree* (crab soup).

Popular Scottish TV chef Nick Nairn's book *Wild Harvest* contains over 100 recipes based on the use of fresh, seasonal Scottish produce.

## Meat & Game

Steak eaters will enjoy a thick fillet of world-famous Aberdeen Angus beef, and beef from Highland cattle is much sought after. Venison, from the red deer, is leaner and appears on many menus. Both may be served with a wine-based or creamy whisky sauce. Then there's haggis, Scotland's much-maligned national dish...

## Fish & Seafood

Scottish salmon is famous worldwide, but there's a big difference between the now-ubiquitous farmed salmon and the leaner, more expensive, wild fish. Also, there are concerns over the environmental impact of salmon farms on the marine environment.

Smoked salmon is traditionally dressed with a squeeze of lemon juice and eaten with fresh brown bread and butter. Trout, salmon's smaller cousin –

---

### SSSSSSMOKIN'!

Scotland is famous for its smoked salmon, but there are many other varieties of smoked fish – plus smoked meats and cheeses – to enjoy. Smoking food to preserve it is an ancient art that has recently undergone a revival, but this time it's more about flavour than preservation.

There are two parts to the process – first the cure, which involves covering the fish in a mixture of salt and molasses sugar, or soaking it in brine; and then the smoke, which can be either cold smoking (at less than 34°C), which results in a raw product, or hot smoking (at more than 60°C), which cooks it. Cold-smoked products include traditional smoked salmon, kippers and Finnan haddies. Hot-smoked products include *bradan rost* ('flaky' smoked salmon) and Arbroath smokies.

Arbroath smokies are haddock that have been gutted, beheaded and cleaned, then salted and dried overnight, tied together at the tail in pairs, and hot-smoked over oak or beech chippings for 45 to 90 minutes. Finnan haddies (named after the fishing village of Findon in Aberdeenshire) are also haddock, but these are split down the middle like kippers, and cold-smoked.

Kippers (smoked herring) were invented in Northumberland, in northern England, in the mid-19th century, but Scotland soon picked up the technique, and both Loch Fyne and Mallaig were famous for their kippers.

There are dozens of modern smokehouses scattered all over Scotland, many of which offer a mail-order service as well as an on-site shop; here are a few recommended ones:

**Hebridean Smokehouse** ( ☎ 01876-580209; www.hebrideansmokehouse.com; Cladach, North Uist, Outer Hebrides; ☗ 8am-5.30pm Mon-Fri, 9am-5pm Sat) Peat-smoked salmon and seatrout.

**Inverawe Smokehouse & Fishery** ( ☎ 01866-822274; www.smokedsalmon.co.uk; Inverawe, Dalmally, Argyllshire; ☗ 8am-5.30pm Mar-Oct) Delicate smoked salmon, plump juicy kippers.

**Marrbury Smokehouse** ( ☎ 01671-840241; www.visitmarrbury.co.uk; Carsluith Castle, Creetown, Dumfries & Galloway; ☗ 11am-4pm Thu & Fri, 10am-2pm Sat) Supplier to Gleneagles Hotel and other top restaurants.

**Salar Smokehouse** ( ☎ 01870-610324; www.salar.co.uk; Lochcarnan, South Uist, Outer Hebrides; ☗ 9am-5pm Mon-Fri) Famous for its flaky, hot-smoked salmon.

**Spey Valley Smokehouse** ( ☎ 01479-873078; www.speyvalleysmokedsalmon.com; Achnagonalin, Grantown-on-Spey, Inverness-shire; ☗ 9am-5pm Mon-Fri, plus 10am-1pm Sat & Sun Easter-Oct) Established 1888; now owned by Ian Anderson, lead singer of rock group Jethro Tull.

whether wild, rod-caught brown trout or farmed rainbow trout – is delicious fried in oatmeal.

As an alternative to kippers (smoked herrings) you may be offered Arbroath smokies (lightly smoked fresh haddock), traditionally eaten cold. Herring fillets fried in oatmeal are good, if you don't mind picking out a few bones. Mackerel pâté and smoked or peppered mackerel (both served cold) are also popular.

Juicy langoustines (also known as Dublin Bay prawns), crabs, lobsters, oysters, mussels and scallops are also widely available throughout Scotland.

### Puddings

Traditional Scottish puddings are irresistibly creamy, high-calorie concoctions. *Cranachan* is whipped cream flavoured with whisky, and mixed with toasted oatmeal and raspberries. *Atholl brose* is a mixture of cream, whisky and honey, flavoured with oatmeal. *Clootie dumpling* is a rich steamed pudding filled with currants and raisins.

## VEGETARIANS & VEGANS

Scotland has the same proportion of vegetarians as the rest of the UK – around 8% to 10% of the population – and vegetarianism has moved away from the hippie-student image of a few decades ago and is now firmly in the mainstream. Even the most remote Highland pub usually has at least one vegetarian dish on the menu, and there are many dedicated vegetarian restaurants in the cities. If you get stuck, there's almost always an Italian or Indian restaurant where you can get meat-free pizza, pasta or curry. Vegans, though, may find the options a bit limited outside of Edinburgh and Glasgow.

One thing to keep in mind is that lentil soup, a seemingly vegetarian staple of Scottish pub and restaurant menus, is traditionally made with ham stock.

## EATING WITH KIDS

Sadly, the majority of Scotland's eating places make no effort to welcome children, and many are actively hostile. In a recent survey nine out of 10 families thought the majority of UK restaurants were not family friendly. There's no way of gauging restaurant attitudes other than by asking.

This situation is changing, albeit slowly, especially in the cities and more popular tourist towns where several restaurants and pubs now have family rooms and/or play areas. However, in many smaller towns and country areas kids will still get a frosty reception.

You should be aware that children under the age of 14 are not allowed into the majority of Scottish pubs, even those that serve bar meals; even in family-friendly pubs (those in possession of a Children's Certificate), under-14s are only allowed in between 11am and 8pm, and must be accompanied by an adult aged 18 or above.

## COOKERY COURSES

There are two principal places that offer courses in Scottish cookery:

**Kinloch Lodge Hotel** ( ☎ 01471-833333; www.claire-macdonald.com; Kinloch Lodge, Isle of Skye IV43 8QY) Cookery demonstrations using fresh, seasonal Scottish produce given by Lady Claire Macdonald, author of *Scottish Highland Hospitality* and *Celebrations*.

**Nairns Cook School** ( ☎ 01877-389900; www.nairnscookschool.com; Port of Menteith, Stirling FK8 3JZ) Two-day courses in modern Scottish cooking at the school owned by Scotland's top TV chef Nick Nairn, author of *Wild Harvest* and *Island Harvest*.

---

The classic work on traditional Scottish cooking is *The Scots Kitchen* by F Marian McNeill, first published in 1929 but still going strong in various reprints.

The most ever paid for a bottle of whisky was US$75,000 for a 1926 Macallan (bought by a South Korean collector in 2005). But high prices reflect rarity rather than quality – that Macallan probably tastes no better than the distillery's more recent bottlings.

## HOW TO BE A MALT WHISKY BUFF

'Love makes the world go round? Not at all! Whisky makes it go round twice as fast.'

*From* Whisky Galore *by Compton Mackenzie (1883–1972)*

Whisky-tasting today is almost as popular as wine-tasting was in the yuppie heyday of the late 1980s. Being able to tell your Ardbeg from your Edradour is *de rigueur* among the whisky-nosing set, so here are some pointers to help you impress your friends.

### What's the difference between malt and grain whiskies?

Malts are distilled from malted barley – that is, barley that has been soaked in water, then allowed to germinate for around 10 days until the starch has turned into sugar – while grain whiskies are distilled from other cereals, usually wheat, corn or unmalted barley.

### So what is a single malt?

A single malt is a whisky that has been distilled from malted barley and is the product of a single distillery. A pure (vatted) malt is a mixture of single malts from several distilleries, and a blended whisky is a mixture of various grain whiskies (about 60%) and malt whiskies (about 40%) from many different distilleries.

### Why are single malts more desirable than blends?

A single malt, like a fine wine, somehow captures the essence of the place where it was made and matured – a combination of the water, the barley, the peat smoke, the oak barrels in which it was aged, and (in the case of certain coastal distilleries) the sea air and salt spray. Each distillation varies from the one before, like different vintages from the same vineyard.

### How should a single malt be drunk?

Either neat, or preferably with a little water added. To appreciate the aroma and flavour to the utmost, a measure of malt whisky should be cut (diluted) with one-third to two-thirds as much spring water (still, bottled spring water will do). Ice, tap water and (God forbid) mixers are for philistines. Would you add lemonade or ice to a glass of Chablis?

### Give me some tasting tips!

Go into a bar and order a Lagavulin (Islay) and a Glenfiddich (Speyside). Cut each one with half as much again of still, bottled spring water. Taking each one in turn, hold the glass up to the light to check the colour. Then stick your nose in the glass and take two or three short, sharp sniffs. By now, everyone in the pub will be giving you funny looks, but never mind.

For the Lagavulin you should be thinking: amber colour, peat smoke, iodine, seaweed. For the Glenfiddich: pale white-wine colour, malt, pear drops, acetone, citrus. Then taste them. Then try some others. Either you'll be hooked, or you'll never touch whisky again.

### Where's the cheapest place to buy Scotch whisky?

A French supermarket, unfortunately. In the UK, where a bottle of single malt typically costs £25 to £35, taxes account for around 72% of the price, making Scotland one of the most expensive places in Europe to enjoy its own national drink.

### Where can I learn more?

If you're serious about spirits, the **Scotch Malt Whisky Society** ( ☎ 0131-554 3451; www.smws .com) has branches all round the world. Membership of the society costs from £70 per year and includes use of members' rooms in Edinburgh and London.

See the boxed text, p263, for our 10 favourite single malts.

## DRINKS

The website www
.scottishbrewing.com has
a comprehensive list of
Scottish breweries, both
large and small.

Scotland's most famous soft drink is Barr's Irn Bru: a sweet fizzy drink, radioactive orange in colour, that smells like bubble gum and almost strips the enamel from your teeth. Many Scots swear by its restorative effects as a cure for a hangover.

Scotch whisky (always spelt without an 'e' – whiskey with an 'e' is Irish or American) is Scotland's best-known product and biggest export. The spirit has been distilled in Scotland at least since the 15th century. See the boxed texts, p55 and p263 for more information.

As well as whiskies, there are whisky-based liqueurs such as Drambuie. If you must mix your whisky with anything other than water, try a whisky-mac (whisky with ginger wine). After a long walk in the rain there's nothing better to put a warm glow in your belly.

At a bar, older Scots may order a 'half' or 'nip' of whisky as a chaser to a pint or half-pint of beer (a 'hauf and a hauf'). Only tourists ask for 'Scotch' – what else would you be served in Scotland? The standard measure in pubs is either 25mL or 35mL.

In the early 1900s
Edinburgh was a major
beer-brewing centre
with no fewer than 28
breweries. As recently as
the 1960s the city still
had 18 breweries, but
today there is only one.
Fortunately it produces
one of Scotland's finest
beers: Deuchar's IPA.

Scottish breweries produce a wide range of beers. The market is dominated by multinational brewers such as Scottish & Newcastle, but smaller local breweries generally create tastier brews, some of them very strong. The aptly named Skullsplitter from Orkney is a good example, at 8.5% alcohol by volume.

Many Scottish beers use old-fashioned shilling categories to indicate strength (the number of shillings was originally the price per barrel; the stronger the beer, the higher the price). The usual range is from 60 to 80 shillings (written 80/-). You'll also see IPA, which stands for India Pale Ale, a strong, hoppy beer first brewed in the early 19th century for export to India (the extra alcohol meant that it kept better on the long sea voyage).

Draught beer is served in pints (usually costing from £2 to £3) or half-pints; alcoholic content generally ranges from 3% to 6%. What the English call bitter, Scots call heavy, or export – Caledonian 80/-, Maclays 80/- and Belhaven 80/- are all worth trying, but Deuchar's IPA from Edinburgh's Caledonian Brewery is our favourite.

---

### SCOTTISH ALES

The increasing popularity of real ales and a backlash against the bland conformity of globalised multinational brewing conglomerates has seen a huge rise in the number of specialist brewers and microbreweries springing up all over Scotland. They take pride in using only natural ingredients, and many try to revive ancient recipes, such as heather- and seaweed-flavoured ales.

These beers are sold in pubs, off-licences and delicatessens. Here are a few of our favourites to look out for:

**Black Isle Brewery** ( ☎ 01463-811871; www.blackislebrewery.com; Old Allangrance, Munlochy, Ross-shire) Range of organic beers.

**Colonsay Brewery** ( ☎ 01951-200190; www.colonsaybrewery.co.uk; Scalasaig, Isle of Colonsay) Produces lager, 80/- and IPA.

**Islay Ales** ( ☎ 01496-810014; www.islayales.com; Islay House Sq, Bridgend, Isle of Islay) Refreshing and citrusy Saligo Ale.

**Isle of Skye Brewery** ( ☎ 01470-542477; www.skyebrewery.co.uk; The Pier, Uig) Distinctive Hebridean Gold ale, brewed with porridge oats.

**Traquair House Brewery** ( ☎ 01896-830323; www.traquair.co.uk/brewery.html; Traquair House, Innerleithen, Peeblesshire) Traquair House Ale, at 7.2% alcohol, is rich, dark and strong.

**Williams Bros** ( ☎ 01259-725511; www.fraoch.com; New Alloa Brewery, Alloa) Produces historic beers flavoured with heather flowers, seaweed, Scots pine and elderberries.

# Outdoor Activities

Scotland is a brilliant place for outdoor recreation and has something to offer everyone, from those who enjoy a short stroll to full-on adrenaline junkies. Although hiking, golf, fishing and cycling are the most popular activities, there is an astonishing variety of things to do.

Most activities are well organised and have clubs and associations that can give visitors invaluable information and, sometimes, substantial discounts. **VisitScotland** (www.visitscotland.com) and **VisitBritain** (www.visitbritain.com) have brochures on most activities.

Detailed information can be found in the regional chapters throughout this guide.

## WALKING

Scotland's wild, dramatic scenery and varied landscape has made walking a hugely popular pastime for locals and tourists alike. There really is something for everyone, from after-breakfast strolls to the popular sport of Munro bagging (p62).

The best time of year for hill walking is usually May to September, although snow can fall on the highest summits even in midsummer. Winter walking on the higher hills of Scotland is for experienced mountaineers only, requiring the use of ice axe and crampons.

Highland hikers should be properly equipped, and cautious, as the weather can become vicious at any time of year. After rain, peaty soil can become boggy; always wear stout shoes or boots and carry a map and compass, waterproof clothing, a head-torch, whistle, bivouac bag, and extra food and drink – many unsuspecting walkers have had to survive an unplanned night in the open. On longer hill walks, always make sure that someone knows where you are going, and when you expect to return – don't depend on mobile phones (although carrying one with you is a good idea, and can be a life-saver if you can get a signal). If necessary, leave a note of your route and expected time of return in the windscreen of your car.

There is a tradition of relatively free access to open country in Scotland, especially on mountains and moorlands. You should, however, avoid areas where you might disrupt or disturb wildlife, lambing (generally mid-April

You can buy walking maps of Scotland online from the Ordnance Survey website (www .ordnancesurvey.co.uk) – click on the Map Shop link.

The ultimate guidebooks for Scottish hill-walkers are the six district guides produced by the Scottish Mountaineering Club, which cover the Scottish hills in great detail – see www.smc.org.uk for further information.

---

### SCOTTISH OUTDOOR ACCESS CODE

Access to the countryside has been a thorny issue in Scotland for many years. In Victorian times, belligerent landowners attempted to prevent walkers from using well-established trails. Moves to counter this led to successful legislation for the walkers and the formation of what later became the Scottish Rights of Way & Access Society.

In January 2003, the Scottish parliament formalised access to the countryside and passed the Land Reform (Scotland) Bill, creating statutory rights of access to land in Scotland for the first time. Basically, the Scottish Outdoor Access Code states that everyone has the right to be on most land and inland water providing they act responsibly. As far as wild camping goes, this means that you can pitch a tent almost anywhere that doesn't cause inconvenience to others or damage to property, as long as you stay no longer than two or three nights in any one spot, take all litter away with you, and keep well away from houses and roads. Full details can be found at www.outdooraccess-scotland.com.

More information on rights of way can be obtained from the **Scottish Rights of Way & Access Society** ( ☎ 0131-558 1222; www.scotways.com; 24 Annandale St, Edinburgh EH7 4AN).

to the end of May), grouse shooting (from 12 August to the third week in October) or deer stalking (1 July to 15 February, but the peak period is August to October). You can get up-to-date information on deer stalking in various areas through the **Hillphone** (www.hillphones.info) service.

VisitScotland's website dedicated to walking is http://walking.visitscotland.com.

Rights of way exist but local authorities aren't required to list and map them so they're not shown on Ordnance Survey (OS) maps of Scotland, as they are in England and Wales. However, the Scottish Rights of Way & Access Society (see boxed text, p57) keeps records of these routes, provides and maintains signposting, and publicises them in its guidebook, *Scottish Hill Tracks*.

Some official long-distance footpaths:

| Walk | Distance | Features | Duration | Difficulty | Page |
|---|---|---|---|---|---|
| Fife Coastal Path | 78 miles | Firth of Forth, undulating country | 5-6 days | easy | p210 |
| Great Glen Way | 73 miles | Loch Ness, canal paths, forest tracks | 4 days | easy | p327 |
| Pilgrims Way | 25 miles | Machars peninsula, standing stones, burial mounds | 2-3 days | easy | boxed text, p152 |
| St Cuthbert's Way | 62 miles | follows life of famous saint | 6-7 days | medium | boxed text, p152 |
| Southern Upland Way | 212 miles | remote hills & moorlands | 9-14 days | medium-hard | boxed text, p152 |
| Speyside Way | 66 miles | follows river, whisky distilleries | 3-4 days | easy-medium | boxed text, opposite |
| West Highland Way | 95 miles | spectacular scenery, mountains & lochs | 6-8 days | medium | boxed text, p280 |

Every tourist office has leaflets (free or for a nominal charge) of suggested walks that take in local points of interest. Lonely Planet's *Walking in Scotland* is a comprehensive resource, covering short walks and long-distance paths; its *Walking in Britain* guide covers Scottish walks too. For general advice, VisitScotland produces a *Walking Scotland* brochure, describing numerous routes in various parts of the country, plus safety tips and other information.

Other useful sources:

**Mountaineering Council of Scotland** ( ☎ 01738-638227; www.mountaineering-scotland .org.uk; The Old Granary, West Mill St, Perth PH1 5QP)

**Ramblers' Association Scotland** ( ☎ 01577-861222; www.ramblers.org.uk/scotland; Kingfisher House, Auld Mart Business Park, Milnathort, Kinross KY13 9DA)

# GOLF

VisitScotland's website dedicated to golf (http://golf.visitscotland.com) has a course directory and online booking.

Scotland is the home of golf. The game has been played in Scotland for centuries and there are more courses per head of population here than in any other country. Most clubs are open to visitors – details can be found on the web at www.scotlands-golf-courses.com.

St Andrews is the headquarters of the game's governing body, the Royal and Ancient Golf Club, and the location of the world's most famous golf course, the Old Course (see boxed text, p211). There are several major championship courses around the country including those at Royal Troon (p176) and Turnberry (p177).

VisitScotland publishes the *Official Guide to Golf in Scotland,* a free annual brochure listing course details, costs and clubs with information on where

---

**THE SPEYSIDE WAY**

This long-distance footpath follows the course of the River Spey, one of Scotland's most famous salmon-fishing rivers. It starts at Buckie and first follows the coast to Spey Bay, east of Elgin, then runs inland along the river to Aviemore in the Cairngorms (with branches to Tomintoul and Dufftown). At only 66 miles, the main walk can be done in three or four days, although including the branch trails to Dufftown and Tomintoul will push the total walking distance to 102 miles (allow seven days).

This route has also been dubbed the 'Whisky Trail' as it passes near a number of distilleries, including Glenlivet and Glenfiddich, which are open to the public. If you stop at them all, the walk may take considerably longer than the usual three or four days!

*The Speyside Way* guidebook by Jacquetta Megarry and Jim Strachan describes the route in detail; there's also a *Speyside Way* leaflet produced by the **Speyside Way Ranger Service** ( ☎ 01340-881266). Check out the route at www.speysideway.org.

---

to stay. Some regions offer a **Golf Pass** (http://golf.visitscotland.com/golf-passes), costing between £50 and £100 for five days (Monday to Friday), which allows play on a range of courses.

## FISHING

Fishing – coarse, sea and game – is enormously popular in Scotland, whose lochs and rivers are filled with salmon, trout (sea, brown and rainbow), pike, arctic char and many other species. Fly-fishing in particular is a joy in Scotland's many lochs and rivers – it's a tricky but very rewarding form of fishing, closer to an art form than a sport.

For wild brown trout the close season is early October to mid March. The close season for salmon and sea trout varies between districts; it's generally from early November to early February.

Fishing rights to most waters are privately owned and you must obtain a permit to fish in them – these are often readily available at the local fishing-tackle shop or hotel. Permits cost from around £15 per day but some salmon rivers – notably the Tweed, the Tay and the Spey – can be much more expensive.

There are numerous fish farms throughout Scotland with stocked ponds where you can hire equipment and have a couple of lessons; they are a particularly good option for the kids. Examples include the Orchill Loch Trout Fishery (p221) and Inverawe Smokehouse & Fishery (p314).

The VisitScotland booklet *Fish Scotland* is a good introduction and is available from tourist offices. Other organisations that can provide information include the following:

**Scottish Anglers National Association** ( ☎ 01577-861116; www.sana.org.uk; The National Game Angling Academy, The Pier, Loch Leven, Kinross KY13 8UF)

**Scottish Federation of Sea Anglers** ( ☎ 01592 657520; sfsasec@sfsacu.com; Unit 62, Evans Business Centre, Mitchelston Drive, Mitchelston Industrial Estate, Kirkcaldy, Fife KY1 3NB)

## CYCLING

Cycling is an excellent way to explore Scotland. There are hundreds of miles of forest trails and quiet minor roads, and dedicated cycle routes along canal towpaths and disused railway tracks. Depending on your energy and enthusiasm you can take a leisurely trip through idyllic farm country, stopping at the numerous pubs along the way, or head off-road for some serious, mud-spattered trail-riding. Cyclists in search of the wild and remote will enjoy northwestern Scotland and the Outer Hebrides, which offer peaceful pedalling through breathtaking landscapes. The beautiful forests, lochs, glens and

The UK record for a rod-caught salmon is 29kg, caught by a Miss Ballantyne in 1922 on the River Tay in Perthshire.

hills in the central and southern areas of Scotland are more easily accessible and, like the gentle, undulating countryside in the beautiful Borders region, make for excellent cycling country.

Hardcore mountain-bikers will also find plenty of challenges, from long off-road routes such as the Great Glen Mountain Bike Trail (p327) to world-class downhill courses such as those at Laggan Wolftrax (p337) and Nevis Range (p344). The latter hosts the **UCI Mountain Bike World Cup Finals** (www .fortwilliamwo rldchamps.co.uk).

VisitScotland publishes a useful free booklet, *Cycle Scotland,* and has a dedicated website (www.cyclingscotland.com). Many regional tourist offices have information on local cycling routes and places to hire bikes. They also stock cycling guides and books.

For up-to-date, detailed information on Scotland's cycle-route network contact **Sustrans** ( ☎ 0845 113 0065, 0131-539 8122; www.sustrans.org.uk; 16a Randolph Cres, Edinburgh EH3 7TT).

**Cyclists' Touring Club** (CTC; ☎ 0870 873 0060; www.ctc.org.uk; Cotterell House, 69 Meadrow, Godalming, Surrey GU7 3HS) is a membership organisation offering comprehensive information about cycling in Britain.

> It was a Scotsman, John Boyd Dunlop (1840-1921), who in 1888 patented the first successful pneumatic tyre for bicycles.

## BIRD-WATCHING

Scotland is a bird-watcher's paradise. There are more than 80 ornithologically important nature reserves managed by **Scottish Natural Heritage** (SNH; www .snh.org.uk), the **Royal Society for the Protection of Birds** (RSPB; www.rspb.org.uk) and the **Scottish Wildlife Trust** (SWT; www.swt. org.uk).

Scotland is the best place in the British Isles (and in some cases the only place) to spot bird species such as the golden eagle, white-tailed sea eagle, osprey, corncrake, capercaillie, crested tit and ptarmigan, and the country's coast and islands are some of Europe's most important seabird nesting grounds.

Further information can be obtained from the **Scottish Ornithologists Club** ( ☎ 01875-871330; www.the-soc.org.uk; Waterson House, Aberlady, East Lothian EH32 0PY).

## HORSE RIDING & PONY TREKKING

Seeing the country from the saddle is highly recommended, even if you're not an experienced rider. There are riding schools catering to all levels of proficiency throughout the country.

For more information:

**British Horse Society** ( ☎ 08701-202244; www.bhs.org.uk; British Equestrian Centre, Stoneleigh Park, Kenilworth, Warwickshire CV8 2XZ)

**Trekking & Riding Society of Scotland** ( ☎ 01567-820909; www.ridinginscotland.com; Bruach na h'Abhainne, Maragowan, Killin, Perthshire FK21 8TN)

## ROCK CLIMBING

Scotland has a long history of rock climbing and mountaineering, with many of the classic routes on Ben Nevis and Glen Coe having been pioneered in the 19th century. The country's main rock-climbing areas include Ben Nevis (p345), with routes up to 400m in length, Glen Coe, the Cairngorms, the Cuillin Hills of Skye (p379), Arrochar and the Isle of Arran (see p170), but there are also hundreds of smaller crags situated all over the country. One unusual feature of Scotland's rock-climbing scene is the sea stacks found around the coast, the most famous of these being the 140m-high Old Man of Hoy (p418).

*Rock Climbing in Scotland,* by Kevin Howett, and the Scottish Mountaineering Club's regional *Rock & Ice Climbs* guides are excellent guidebooks that cover the whole country.

> There's lots of useful information on rock climbing at www .ukclimbing.com.

More information:
**Mountaineering Council of Scotland** ( ☎ 01738-638227; www.mountaineering-scotland
.org.uk; The Old Granary, West Mill St, Perth PH1 5QP)
**Scottish Mountaineering Club** (www.smc.org.uk)

## SKIING & SNOWBOARDING

There are five ski centres in Scotland, offering downhill skiing and
snowboarding:

**Cairngorm Mountain** ( ☎ 01479-861261; www.cairngormmountain.com) 1097m; has almost
30 runs spread over an extensive area; see p332.

**Glencoe** ( ☎ 01855-851226; www.ski-glencoe.co.uk) 1108m; has only five tows and two
chairlifts; see p338.

**Glenshee** ( ☎ 01339-741320; www.ski-glenshee.co.uk) 920m; situated on the A93 road between
Perth and Braemar; offers the largest network of lifts and the widest range of runs in all of
Scotland; see p230.

**Lecht** ( ☎ 01975-651440; www.lecht.co.uk) 793m; the smallest and most remote centre, on the
A939 between Ballater and Grantown-on-Spey; see p258.

**Nevis Range** ( ☎ 01397-705825; www.nevisrange.co.uk) 1221m; near Fort William; offers the
highest ski runs, the grandest setting and some of the best off-piste potential in Scotland; see p344.

The high season is from January to April but it's sometimes possible to ski
from as early as November to as late as May. It's easy to turn up at the slopes,
hire some kit, buy a day pass and off you go.

VisitScotland's *Ski Scotland* brochure is useful and includes a list of accommodation options. General information can be obtained from **Snowsport
Scotland** ( ☎ 0131-445 4151; www.snsc.demon.co.uk; Hillend, Biggar Rd, Edinburgh EH10 7EF).

For the latest weather and snow condition reports phone your resort or
check the websites www.ski-scotland.com and www.winterhighland.info.

## WATER SPORTS
### Canoeing

Scotland, with its islands, sea lochs and indented coastline, is ideal for
sea-kayaking, while its inland lochs and Highland rivers are great for both
Canadian and white-water canoeing.

For information contact the **Scottish Canoe Association** ( ☎ 0131-317 7314; www.canoes
cotland.com; Caledonia House, South Gyle, Edinburgh EH12 9DQ). It publishes coastal navigation
sheets as well as organising tours, including introductory ones for beginners.

### Diving

It may lack coral reefs and warm, limpid waters but Scotland offers some
of the most spectacular and challenging scuba diving in Europe, if not the
world. The sea bed around St Abbs (p152) is Scotland's first voluntary
marine nature-reserve.

There are also hundreds of fascinating shipwrecks, the most famous of
which are the seven remaining hulks of the WWI German High Seas Fleet,
scuttled in 1919, which lie on the bed of Scapa Flow in the Orkney Islands
(see boxed text, p412).

For more information on the country's diving options contact the **Scot-
tish Sub Aqua Club** ( ☎ 0141-425 1021; www.scotsac.com; The Cockburn Centre, 40 Bogmoor Place,
Glasgow G51 4TQ).

### Sailing

The west coast of Scotland, with its myriad islands, superb scenery and
challenging winds and tides, is widely acknowledged to be one of the finest
yachting areas in the world.

'with its
islands, sea
lochs and
indented
coastline,
Scotland is
ideal for sea-
kayaking'

Experienced skippers with suitable qualifications can charter a yacht from one of dozens of agencies; prices for bareboat charter start at around £1500 a week in high season for a six-berth yacht; hiring a skipper to sail the boat for you will cost £120 a day or £700 a week. Sailing dinghies can be rented from many places for around £50 a day.

Beginners can take a Royal Yachting Association training course in yachting or dinghy sailing at many sailing schools around the coast; for details of charter agencies, sailing schools and water-sports centres, get hold of VisitScotland's *Sail Scotland* brochure, or check out the website www.sailscotland.co.uk.

## Surfing

Even with a wetsuit on you definitely have to be hardy to enjoy surfing in Scottish waters. That said, the country does have some of the best surfing breaks in Europe.

The tidal range is large, which means there is often a completely different set of breaks at low and high tides. It's the north and west coasts, particularly around Thurso (p365) and in the Outer Hebrides, which have outstanding, world-class surf. Indeed, Lewis has the best and most consistent surf in Britain, with around 120 recorded breaks and waves up to 5m. For more information contact **Hebridean Surf** ( ☎ 01851-705862; www.hebrideansurf.co.uk; 28 Francis St, Stornoway, Lewis HS1 2ND).

## HANG GLIDING & PARAGLIDING

There's a well-established hang-gliding and paragliding scene in Scotland. The Highlands offer many impressive flying spots, complete with stunning scenery and challenging conditions. For information and details on clubs and training schools contact the **British Hang Gliding & Paragliding Association** (www.bhpa .co.uk).

---

**THE ANCIENT ART OF MUNRO BAGGING**

At the end of the 19th century an eager hill walker, Sir Hugh Munro, published a list of 545 Scottish mountains measuring over 3000ft (914m) – a height at which he believed they gained a special significance. Of these summits he classified 277 as mountains in their own right (new surveys have since revised this to a total of 284), the rest being satellites of lesser consequence (known as 'tops'). Sir Hugh couldn't have realised that his name would one day be used to describe any Scottish mountain over the magical 3000ft mark. Many keen hill-walkers now set themselves the target of reaching the summit of (or bagging) all 284 Munros.

The peculiar practice of Munro bagging started soon after the list was published – by 1901 the Reverend AE Robertson had become the first person to bag the lot. Between 1901 and 1981, only 250 people managed to climb all the Munros, but the huge increase in the popularity of hill walking from the 1980s onward saw the number of officially declared 'Munroists' soar to 4000 (see www.smc.org.uk/Munros) by 2007. Many people have completed the round more than once; the record for single-minded Munro bagging is held by Edinburgh's Steven Fallon, who was halfway through his 14th round in 2007.

To the uninitiated it may seem odd that Munro baggers see a day (or longer) spent plodding around in mist, cloud and driving rain to the point of exhaustion as time well spent. However, for those who can add one or more ticks to their list, the vagaries of the weather are part of the enjoyment, at least in retrospect. Munro bagging is, of course, more than merely ticking names on a list – it takes you to some of the wildest, most beautiful parts of Scotland.

Once you've bagged all the Munros you can move onto the Corbetts – hills over 2500ft (700m), with a drop of at least 500ft (150m) on all sides – and the Donalds, lowland hills over 2000ft (610m). And for connoisseurs of the diminutive, there are the McPhies: 'eminences in excess of 300ft (90m)'.

## CANAL BOATING

Scotland's canal network is pretty limited compared with England's or Ireland's, but still offers interesting cruising opportunities.

The Millennium Link project (completed in 2002) restored the 35-mile Forth and Clyde Canal (running between Grangemouth in the east and Bowling near Dumbarton in the west) and the 31-mile Union Canal (joining central Edinburgh with Falkirk) to full working order, and linked the two by means of the mighty Falkirk Wheel (see the boxed text, p206). The Linlithgow Canal Centre (p118) rents out day boats on the Union Canal. Holiday narrow boats can be hired by the week from **Capercaillie Cruisers** ( ☎ 0131-449 3288; www .capercailliecruisers.co.uk; 2 Lanark Rd West, Currie, Midlothian EH14 5ER).

The 60-mile Caledonian Canal, which slices through the Great Glen from Fort William to Inverness, has a mixture of canal reaches, open lochs and stunning scenery, making it fully geared to boating holidays. The main operator here is **Caley Cruisers** ( ☎ 01463-236328; www.caleycruisers.com; Canal Rd, Inverness IV3 8NF), which has a fleet of 40 motor cruisers ranging from two to eight berths available for hire from March to October.

Scotland's canals are owned and operated by the **British Waterways Board** ( ☎ 0141-332 6936; www.scottishcanals.co.uk; Canal House, 1 Applecross St, Glasgow G4 9SP), which publishes the free *Skippers' Guides* to all the canals (available online). It also publishes a list of boat-hire and canal-holiday companies.

'The 60-mile Caledonian Canal has a mixture of canal reaches, open lochs and stunning scenery'

# Environment

Scotland's environment is a major attraction of the country. Visitors from all over the world revel in the solitude and dramatic scenery encompassing much of the country. Soaring peaks with veins of snow trickling down their summits, steely blue lochs, deep inlets, forgotten beaches and surging peninsulas are a taste of the astonishing natural diversity. The best wildlife in Britain – from the mighty osprey to the red deer, its bellow reverberating among large strands of native forest – is found throughout the wild places of Scotland. Large chunks of land moored just offshore or miles out into the raging northern Atlantic Ocean, offer environmental gems for those with the inkling to explore island life.

## THE LAND

The Scottish mainland can be neatly divided into three parts – the Southern Uplands, the Central Lowlands and the Highlands.

The Southern Uplands, a range of rounded hills covered with grass and heather, bounded by fertile coastal plains, form the southern boundary to the Central Lowlands. The geological divide – the Southern Uplands Fault – runs in a line from Girvan in Ayrshire to Dunbar in East Lothian.

The Central Lowlands lie in a broad band stretching from Glasgow and Ayr in the west to Edinburgh and Dundee in the east. This area is underlaid by sedimentary rocks, including the beds of coal and oil shale that fuelled Scotland's industrial revolution. Most of the country's industry, its two largest cities and 80% of the population are concentrated here.

Another great geological divide – the Highland Boundary Fault – runs from Helensburgh in the west to Stonehaven on the east coast, and marks the southern edge of the Scottish Highlands. These Highland hills – most of their summits reach to around the 900m to 1000m mark – were deeply dissected by glaciers during the last Ice Age, creating a series of deep, U-shaped valleys: the long, narrow sea lochs that today are such a feature of Highland scenery.

Remember that, for all their pristine beauty, the wild, empty landscapes of the western and northern Highlands are artificial wildernesses. Before the Highland Clearances (see the boxed text, p360) many of these empty corners of Scotland supported sizable populations.

> Scotland accounts for one third of the British mainland's surface area, but it has a massive 80% of Britain's coastline and only 10% of its population.

## WILDLIFE

Scotland's wildlife is one of its big attractions and an organised safari (p224) geared towards wildlife-watching can be the best way to see it. Many species that have disappeared from, or are rare in, the rest of Britain survive here, including red deer, golden eagles, otters, wildcats and ospreys.

Scotland's flowering plants are an attractive feature of the landscape, especially for walkers, and its precious areas of native forest a highlight for visitors.

### Animals

Red deer are in large numbers in Scotland, but the reindeer (apart from a herd of introduced domestic reindeer living in a semiwild state in the Cairngorms), beaver and aurochs (wild ox) are all long extinct; the last wolf was shot in Sutherland in 1700. In mid-2007 the Scottish government signalled plans to reintroduce the beaver on a trial basis, probably in Argyll. A small population of wildcats survives in parts of the Highlands but they are extremely shy and rarely seen in the wild.

Otters are found in most parts of Scotland, around the coast and along salmon and trout rivers. The best places to spot them are in the northwest, especially in

> One of the best-loved pieces of Scottish wildlife writing is *Ring of Bright Water* by Gavin Maxwell, in which the author describes life on the remote Glenelg peninsula with his two pet otters in the 1950s.

Skye and the Outer Hebrides. The piers at Kyle of Lochalsh and Portree are otter 'hot spots', as the otters have learned to scavenge from fishing boats.

Bred for their quality beef, Highland cattle are Scotland's most distinctive bovine breed. They are fierce looking (with their horns) but docile-natured, with long reddish-brown coats.

The blue mountain hare dwells in high mountain environments, and swaps a grey-brown summer coat for a pure white winter one.

The waters off Scotland's west coast are rich in marine mammals, including whales. Dolphins and porpoises are fairly common, and in summer minke whales are regular visitors. Growing up to 10m long, they make an impressive sight when they breach through a shoal of herring fry. (Minke whales have also been spotted around the Isle of May in the Firth of Forth.) Both the Atlantic grey (identified by its roman nose) and the common seal (with a face like a dog) can be seen along the coast of Scotland, including Arran's shoreline (p169).

## BIRDS

Scotland has an immense variety of bird species and this is one of its premier wildlife attractions. For bird-watchers, the Shetland Islands (see p432) are paradise. Twenty-one of the British Isles' 24 seabird species are found here and being entertained by the clownish antics of the puffin is a highlight for visitors.

Large numbers of grouse – a popular game bird – graze the heather on the moors. The ptarmigan (a type of grouse) is a native of the hills, seldom seen below 700m, with the unusual feature of having feathered feet. It is the only British bird that plays the Arctic trick of changing its plumage from mottled brown in summer to dazzling white in winter, the better to blend in with the snowfields. In heavily forested areas you may see a capercaillie, a black, turkey-like bird and the largest member of the grouse family. Birds of prey, such as the golden eagle, osprey, peregrine falcon and hen harrier, are protected. Millions of greylag geese winter on Lowland stubble fields.

*A beautifully written book about Scotland's wildlife, penned by a man who lived and breathed alongside the country's critters in a remote part of the Highlands, is* A Last Wild Place *by Mike Tomkies.*

## ENDANGERED SPECIES

Scotland is home to many endangered mammals and birds that are constantly threatened by the changing environment.

The habitat of the once common corncrake, for example, was almost completely wiped out by modern farming methods. Farmers now receive a subsidy for mowing in a corncrake-friendly fashion and there are good prospects for the bird's survival. Listen for their distinctive call – like a thumbnail drawn along the teeth of a comb – on the Isle of Coll (p310) and at Loch Gruinart Nature Reserve on Islay (p292).

In early 2007 the squirrelpox virus, spread by the introduced grey squirrel, was found in Lockerbie. Grey squirrels are unaffected by the disease, but red squirrels die about 15 days after infection; Scotland is home to 75% of Britain's red squirrel population and if this deadly disease is allowed to spread it could wipe out the country's remaining red squirrels.

On a more optimistic note, wildlife species that were slaughtered to the point of extermination in the 19th century – golden eagles, buzzards, pine martens, polecats and wildcats among them – are now protected by law and are slowly recovering. Both the red kite and the white-tailed sea eagle, absent from Scotland since the 19th century, have been successfully reintroduced.

The majestic osprey (absent for most of the 20th century) nests in Scotland from mid-March through to September, after migrating from West Africa. There are around 200 breeding pairs and you can see nesting sites throughout the country, including at Loch Garten (p335) and Loch of the Lowes (p227). White-tailed sea eagles, the fourth largest eagle in the world and distinguishable by their yellow beak and talons, are found along the

*Scottish Natural Heritage (www.snh.org.uk) is the government agency responsible for the conservation of Scotland's wildlife, habitats and landscapes. A key initiative is to reverse biodiversity loss.*

west coast and in the Hebrides – visitors can see them (via closed-circuit TV cameras at a secret nesting site) at the Aros Experience on Skye (p384). Galloway Forest Park (p184) is a good place to spot red kites.

## Plants

Although the thistle is commonly associated with Scotland, the national flower is the Scottish bluebell, which carpets the floor of native woodlands in spring. Heather, whose tiny pink and purple flowers emerge in August, covers much of the hills and moors. Other conspicuous flowering plants include the introduced vivid pink rhododendrons – which grow vigorously but tend to displace native trees and shrubs – and bright yellow gorse (or whin), which both flower in May and June. Only 1% of Scotland's ancient woodlands survive, but regeneration forests are slowly covering more of the landscape – especially in the Highlands. Perthshire (p216) is home to many woodlands (and a 5000-year-old yew tree; p225) and forest walks.

## NATIONAL PARKS

Scotland has two national parks – **Loch Lomond & the Trossachs National Park** (www.lochlomond-trossachs.org) and the **Cairngorms National Park** (www.cairngorms.co.uk). Plans for the country's first national marine park were shelved by the Scottish Executive in 2007. Instead, priority is being given to a dedicated Marine Bill with a focus on sustainability to manage Scotland's coastlines and seas.

## ENVIRONMENTAL ISSUES

Wind farms and the use of alternative power sources for electricity generation are hot topics on Scotland's environmental front. Essentially concentrations of giant, electricity-generating windmills, wind farms are a key element of the government's commitment to cutting greenhouse gas emissions and meeting climate-change targets. The Scottish Executive has set a target of generating 40% of electricity in Scotland from renewable sources by 2020.

Although this involves a mix of green sources – plans to build a wave farm on Orkney are back on track after setbacks in 2005 – it appears wind is top of the list. The problem is, although everyone agrees that wind power is clean and economical, there's a powerful NIMBY (not in my back yard) element who don't want the windmills spoiling their view. There are also concerns that wind farms could have a detrimental effect on tourism, birdlife and nearby airport radar stations.

Small community wind farms are seen as a way forward. The island of Gigha was the first community wind farm in Scotland, its three turbines supplying all the power the island needs and selling its surplus to the National Grid. However, the escalating cost, and increased global demand for turbines has made them difficult to acquire. Communities in Westray, Tiree, North Harris and Melness in Sutherland are all waiting for turbines.

But for large scale commercial farms it's full steam ahead: there are large-scale wind farms around the country in, for example, Orkney and Braes Doune in Stirlingshire. Currently the most controversial large-scale project is a proposed wind farm on the Isle of Lewis. The massive 181-turbine proposal is under heavy fire from local crofters with a decision pending from the Scottish Executive.

There has been much debate in government and community circles on whether to increase reliance on nuclear power for electricity generation. Although the British Prime Minister Gordon Brown has signalled his government's intent to build a new generation of nuclear power stations to help cut greenhouse gas emissions, the SNP-led Scottish Executive has ruled out the construction of new nuclear power stations in Scotland.

Friends of the Earth Scotland (www.foe-scotland.org.uk), a voluntary organisation campaigning on all kinds of environmental issues, has about 10 local groups based around the country.

Scottish Environment LINK (www.scotlink.org), the umbrella body for Scotland's voluntary environmental organisations, includes 36 bodies committed to environmental sustainability.

When Braes of Doune wind farm recently came online it made the UK one of only seven countries able to produce more than two gigawatts of power from wind.

## PROTECTED AREAS

| Park | Features | Activities | Best time to visit | Page |
| --- | --- | --- | --- | --- |
| Balranald Nature Reserve | lochan (small lochs), moor & marsh: corncrakes, red-necked phalaropes | bird-watching | Apr-Aug | p399 |
| Caenlochan National Nature Reserve | mountain & glen: rare alpine flora | hill walking | Jul & Aug | p243 |
| Cairngorms National Park | subarctic mountain plateau, native pine forests: ospreys, ptarmigans, pine martens | hill walking, climbing, skiing | Aug | p329 |
| Craigellachie Nature Reserve | pine forest, crags: capercaillies, peregrine falcons | walking | May-Sep | p331 |
| Galloway Forest Park | hills, forests, lochs: red deer, red kites | walking, mountain biking | Oct | p184 |
| Glen Affric National Nature Reserve | mountain, loch, native pine forest: golden eagles, red deer, pine martens, wildcats | hill walking | Jul-Oct | p324 |
| Hermaness Nature Reserve | coastal cliffs: puffins | bird-watching | Apr-Aug | p434 |
| Inverpolly Nature Reserve | mountain, loch & moorland: red deer, wildcats, otters, golden eagles, peregrine falcons, red-throated divers | walking | Apr-Oct | p371 |
| Isle of Rum National Nature Reserve | dramatic rocky mountains & coast: red deer, wild goats, golden eagles, white-tailed sea eagles, Manx shearwaters | walking, hill walking, bird-watching | Apr-Oct | p350 |
| Loch Druidibeg National Nature Reserve | freshwater loch, farmland, machair: dunlins, redshanks, ringed plovers, greylag geese, corncrakes | bird-watching, walking | Apr-Oct | p400 |
| Loch Gruinart Nature Reserve | farmland, tidal flats: corncrakes, migrating geese & waders | bird-watching | Apr-Oct | p292 |
| Loch Lomond & the Trossachs National Park | scenic lochs, forests, hills | hill walking, angling, water sports | Sep-Nov | p267 |
| Noss National Nature Reserve | spectacular coastal cliffs: nesting seabirds | bird-watching | May-Aug | p428 |
| St Abb's Head National Nature Reserve | coastal cliffs: nesting seabirds | walking, bird-watching | Apr & May | p152 |

In Caithness, the Dounreay nuclear-waste-reprocessing plant (p367) had a poor safety record over several decades. Following a series of accidents and disclosures about errors and cover-ups – around 170kg of weapons-grade uranium remains unaccounted for – the British government decided to close it down in 1998. However cleaning up the site and storing the waste safely will take until 2036 and cost £2.7 billion; after that it'll take until 2095 to dismantle the plant safely and encase the remains in concrete.

With rapidly declining fish stocks, especially cod, the viability of Scotland's fishing industry is in doubt and strict quotas imposed by the EU to sustain the industry are controversial. The new Scottish Executive is trying to find ways of sustaining the fishing industry by the introduction of the Marine Bill (see opposite); and by considering a proposal involving voluntary real-time closures of sea areas, instigated by skippers at sea when juvenile cod are encountered.

Sustainable Scotland (www.sustainable-scotland.net/climatechange) is a local government initiative to combat climate change and address sustainability in Scotland. Learn about community efforts to tackle a global problem.

# Edinburgh

Edinburgh is a city that just begs to be explored. From the vaults and wynds that riddle the Old Town to the picturesque urban villages of Stockbridge and Cramond, it's filled with quirky, come-hither nooks that tempt you to walk just that little bit further. And every corner turned reveals sudden views and unexpected vistas – green sunlit hills, a glimpse of rust-red crags, a blue flash of distant sea. It's a place to put the guidebook away for a bit, and just wander.

Not only is Edinburgh one of the most beautiful cities in Europe, it also enjoys one of Europe's most beautiful settings. It's a town entangled in its landscape, where the rocky battlements of Salisbury Crags overlook one end of the Old Town and the leafy corridor of the Water of Leith snakes along only yards from the elegant Georgian terraces of the New Town. Fingers of greenery insinuate themselves among streets and suburbs everywhere, and you can walk or cycle across the city from the Firth of Forth to the Pentland Hills almost without touching a tarmac road.

But there's more to Edinburgh than just sightseeing – there are top shops, world-class restaurants and a bacchanalia of bars to enjoy. This is a city of pub crawls and impromptu music sessions, mad-for-it clubbing and all-night parties, overindulgence, late nights and wandering home through cobbled streets at dawn.

All these superlatives come together in August at festival time, when it seems as if half the world descends on Edinburgh for one enormous party. If you can possibly manage it, join them.

---

## HIGHLIGHTS

- Taking in the views from the battlements of **Edinburgh Castle** (p80)
- Feasting on steak and oysters at the **Tower Restaurant** (p104) as the sun sets over the city
- Nosing around the Queen's private quarters on the former **Royal Yacht Britannia** (p90) at Leith
- Listening to live folk music at **Sandy Bell's** (p109)
- Trying to decipher the Da Vinci Code at mysterious **Rosslyn Chapel** (p115)

Royal Yacht Britannia • Edinburgh Castle ★ ★ Tower Restaurant ★ Sandy Bell's • Rosslyn Chapel ★

---

| ■ TELEPHONE CODE: 0131 | ■ POPULATION: 430,000 | ■ AREA: 116 SQ KM |

# HISTORY

Edinburgh owes its existence to the Castle Rock, the glacier-worn stump of a long-extinct volcano that provided a near-perfect defensive position guarding the coastal route from northeast England into central Scotland.

Back in the 7th century the Castle Rock was called Dun Eiden (meaning 'Fort on the Hill Slope'). When it was captured by invaders from the kingdom of Northumbria in northeast England in 638, they took the existing Gaelic name 'Eiden' and tacked it onto their own Old English word for fort, 'burh', to create the name Edinburgh.

Originally a purely defensive site, Edinburgh began to expand in the 12th century when King David I held court at the castle and founded the abbey at Holyrood. The royal court came to prefer Edinburgh to Dunfermline and, as parliament followed the king, Edinburgh became Scotland's capital. The city's first effective town wall was constructed around 1450, enclosing the Old Town as far east as Netherbow and south to the Grassmarket. This overcrowded area – by then the most populous town in Scotland – became a medieval Manhattan, forcing its densely packed inhabitants to build upwards instead of outwards, creating tenements five and six storeys high.

The capital played an important role in the Reformation (1560–1690), led by the Calvinist firebrand John Knox. Mary, Queen of Scots held court in the Palace of Holyroodhouse for six brief years, but when her son James VI succeeded to the English throne in 1603 he moved his court to London. The Act of Union in 1707 further reduced Edinburgh's importance, but its cultural and intellectual life flourished.

In the second half of the 18th century a planned new town was created across the valley to the north of the Old Town. During the Scottish Enlightenment (roughly 1740–1830), Edinburgh became known as 'a hotbed of genius', inhabited by leading scientists and philosophers such as David Hume and Adam Smith.

In the 19th century the population quadrupled to 400,000, not much less than today's, and the Old Town's tenements were taken over by refugees from the Irish famines. A new ring of crescents and circuses was built to the north of New Town, and grey Victorian terraces spread south of the Old Town.

In the 1920s the city's borders expanded again to encompass Leith in the north, Cramond in the west and the Pentland Hills in the south. Following WWII, the city's cultural life blossomed, stimulated by the Edinburgh

## EDINBURGH IN...

### Two Days

Kick off with coffee at the **Elephant House** (see the boxed text, p103) – choose a window table with a view of the castle – then head uphill to **Edinburgh Castle** (p80) to do the touristy bit. Afterwards, begin strolling down the **Royal Mile** (p81) and think about where to have lunch; **Café Marlayne** (p102) is temptingly close by. Once you've eaten, continue to the foot of the Royal Mile to see the new **Scottish parliament building** (p85), then work up an appetite by climbing **Arthur's Seat** (p84), or ogling the designer shoes in **Harvey Nichols** (p112). Satisfy your hunger with dinner at **Oloroso** (p105), while you watch the sun set over the Firth of Forth.

On day two spend the morning soaking up some history in the **Museum of Scotland** (p86) and in the afternoon catch the bus to Leith for a visit to the **Royal Yacht Britannia** (p90). In the evening have an early dinner at **Daniel's Bistro** (see the boxed text, p105), then scare yourself silly on a guided ghost tour with **Black Hart Storytellers** (p96).

### Four Days

A third day calls for a morning stroll around the **Royal Botanic Garden** (p91) then lunch at the **Old Chain Pier** (see the boxed text, p105) and a trip to the seaside village of **Cramond** (p90). Take binoculars (for bird-watching and yacht-spotting) and a book (to read in the sun). Dinner at the **Café Royal Oyster Bar** (p105) could be before or after your sunset walk to the summit of **Calton Hill** (p89).

On day four head out to the pretty harbour village of **Queensferry** (p114), nestled beneath the Forth Bridges, or take a day trip to the enigmatic and beautiful **Rosslyn Chapel** (p115).

International Festival and its fellow traveller the Fringe, both held for the first time in 1947 and now recognised as world-class arts festivals.

Edinburgh entered a new era following the 1997 referendum vote in favour of a devolved Scottish parliament, which first convened in July 1999. The parliament is housed in a controversial new building at the foot of the Royal Mile, where the 2007 elections saw the Scottish National Party – whose long-term aim is independence for Scotland – take power for the first time.

## ORIENTATION

The city's most prominent landmarks are Edinburgh Castle, at the western end of the Old Town, and Arthur's Seat (251m), the rocky peak that rises above the eastern end of the Old Town. The Royal Mile (Lawnmarket, High St and Canongate) is the Old Town's main street and runs along the crest of a ridge from the castle to the Palace of Holyroodhouse at the foot of Arthur's Seat.

New Town lies to the north of the Old Town, separated by a dip containing Princes Street Gardens and Waverley train station. The city's main shopping street, Princes St, runs along the northern side of the gardens. At its eastern end rises Calton Hill, which is crowned by several monuments.

The Edinburgh & Scotland Information Centre (ESIC) lies between Waverley train station and Princes St, above Princes Mall. The bus station is nearby in New Town at the northeastern corner of St Andrew Sq, north of the eastern end of Princes St.

Long streets may be known by different names along their length. For example, the southern end of Leith Walk is variously called Union Pl and Antigua St on one side, Elm Row and Greenside Pl on the other.

## Maps

The maps in this guide will help you find your way around the city. For coverage of the whole city in more detail, the best maps are Nicolson's *Edinburgh Citymap* and the Ordnance Survey's (OS) *Edinburgh Street Atlas*. You can buy these at the Edinburgh & Scotland Information Centre, bookshops and newsagents.

The OS's 1:50,000 Landranger map *Edinburgh, Penicuik & North Berwick* (Sheet No 66) covers the city and the surrounding region

to the south and east at a scale of 1.25 inches to one mile; it's useful for walking in the Pentland Hills and exploring East Lothian.

## INFORMATION
### Bookshops

**Blackwell's Bookshop** (Map pp76–7; ☎ 622 8222; 53-62 South Bridge; ☺ 9am-8pm Mon & Wed-Fri, 9.30am-8pm Tue, 9am-6pm Sat, noon-6pm Sun) The city's principal bookstore; big selection of academic books.

**TSO Bookshop** (Map pp76–7; ☎ 606 5566; 71 Lothian Rd; ☺ 9am-5pm Mon-Fri, 10am-5pm Sat) Has the widest range of OS maps in town.

**Waterstone's** East End (Map pp76–7; ☎ 556 3034; 13 Princes St; ☺ 9am-8pm Mon-Fri, to 7.30pm Sat, 10am-7pm Sun); George St (Map pp76–7; ☎ 225 3436; 83 George St; ☺ 9.30am-9pm Mon-Fri, to 8pm Sat, 11am-6pm Sun); West End (Map pp76–7; ☎ 226 2666; 128 Princes St; ☺ 8.30am-8pm Mon-Sat, 10.30am-7pm Sun) The West End branch has an in-store café with great views.

**Word Power** Map pp76–7; ☎ 662 9112; 43 West Nicolson St; ☺ 10am-6pm Mon-Fri, 10.30am-6pm Sat, noon-5pm Sun) Radical, independent bookshop with wide range of political, gay and feminist literature.

### Cultural Centres

**Institut Français d'Écosse** (Map pp72–3; ☎ 225 5366; www.ifecosse.org.uk; 13 Randolph Cres; ☺ 9.30am-6.30pm Mon-Fri, 9.30am-2pm Sat) Runs courses in French and has a French-language library.

**Italian Cultural Institute** (Map pp76–7; ☎ 668 2232; www.iicedimburgo.esteri.it; 82 Nicolson St; ☺ 9am-1pm & 2-5pm Mon-Fri)

### Emergency

In an emergency, dial ☎ 999 or ☎ 112 (free from public phones) and ask for police, ambulance, fire brigade or coastguard.

**Edinburgh Rape Crisis Centre** ( ☎ 556 9437; www .rapecrisisscotland.org.uk)

**Lothian & Borders Police HQ** (Map pp72–3; ☎ 311 3131; www.lbp.police.uk; Fettes Ave)

**Lothian & Borders Police Information Centre** (Map pp76–7; ☎ 226 6966; 188 High St; ☺ 10am-7.30pm Mar-Oct, 10am-6pm Nov-Feb) Report a crime or make lost property inquiries here.

### Internet Access

There are internet cafés spread around the city. Some convenient ones:

**connect@edinburgh** (Map pp76–7; ☎ 473 3800; Princes Mall, 3 Princes St; per 15min 50p) See Edinburgh & Scotland Information Centre (p79) for hours.

*(Continued on page 78)*

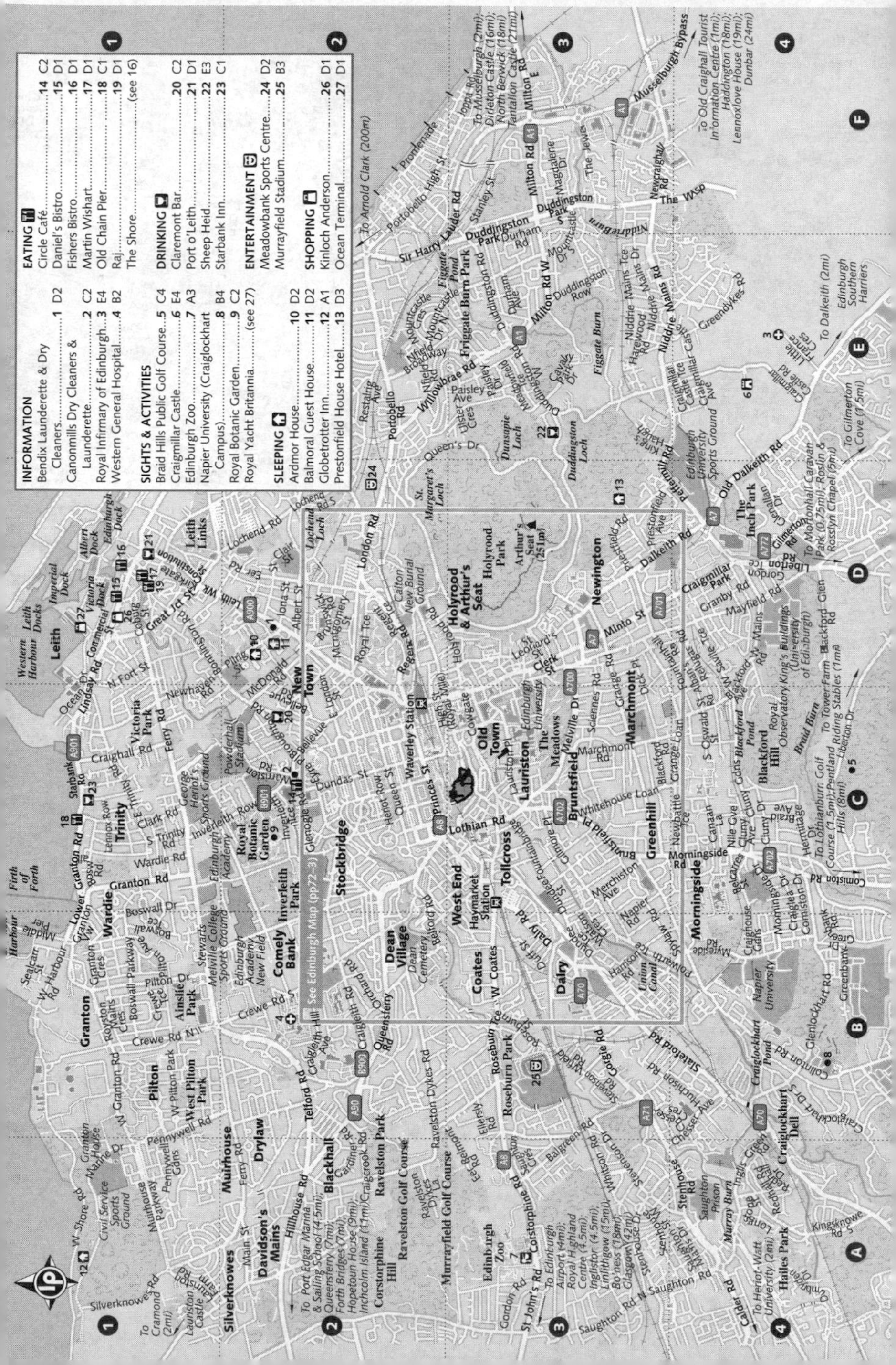

0 — 2 km
0 — 1 mile

## INFORMATION
Bendix Launderette & Dry Cleaners..................1 D2
Canonmills Dry Cleaners & Launderette...........2 C2
Royal Infirmary of Edinburgh.......3 E4
Western General Hospital.......4 B2

## SIGHTS & ACTIVITIES
Braid Hills Public Golf Course.....5 C4
Craigmillar Castle.......6 E4
Edinburgh Zoo.......7 A3
Napier University (Craiglockhart Campus).......8 B4
Royal Botanic Garden.......9 C2
Royal Yacht Britannia.......(see 27)

## SLEEPING
Ardmor House.......10 D2
Balmoral Guest House.......11 D2
Globetrotter Inn.......12 A1
Prestonfield House Hotel.......13 D3

## EATING
Circle Café.......14 C2
Daniel's Bistro.......15 D1
Fishers Bistro.......16 D1
Martin Wishart.......17 D1
Old Chain Pier.......18 C1
Raj.......19 D1
The Shore.......(see 16)

## DRINKING
Claremont Bar.......20 C2
Port o' Leith.......21 D1
Sheep Heid.......22 E3
Starbank Inn.......23 C1

## ENTERTAINMENT
Meadowbank Sports Centre.......24 D2
Murrayfield Stadium.......25 B3

## SHOPPING
Kinloch Anderson.......26 D1
Ocean Terminal.......27 D1

See Edinburgh Map (pp72–3)

**A**  **B**  **C**  **D**

Inverleith Park

Inverleith Pond

**1**

Western General Hospital
Carrington Rd
Craigleith Hill Ave

Craigleith Rd

Royal Victoria Hospital

Comely Bank Cemetery

7

Fette Ave

**Stockbridge**

Edinburgh Academy Sports Ground

Glenogle Rd

Grange Cricket Ground

71

**British Philatelic Bureau**

28

**King George V Park**

Eyre

Comely Bank Rd
Raeburn Pl

Henderson Row
Henderson Pl La

70

Fettes Row
Cumberland St
Dundas St
Great King St

Northumberland

**2**

Orchard Brae
Orchard Gdns
Orchard Rd

Orchard Tce
Orchard Cres

Queensferry Rd

Belford Gdns
Belford Ave

Orchard Rd

Learmonth Gdns
S Learmonth Gdns
Learmonth Tce La
Buckingham Tce
Clarendon Cres
Eton

Dean Park Mews

Dean Park

Oxford Tce
Lennox St
Ann St

St Bernard's Cres
Leslie Pl

Danube St

13

Dean Bridge

Queen Street Gardens

Heriot Row

Queen St
Thistle St

Ravelston Dykes Rd

Dean Cemetery

**Dean Village**

14

Ravelston Park

22

Belgrave Cres
Belgrave Cres

**Dean Gardens**

Dean Path
Bell's Brae

Eton Tce

Moray Pl

Young St

Rose St

**Princes St**

**3**

Coltbridge Gdns
Wer Coates Gdns

Ravelston Tce

Belford Rd
Belford Pl

Water of Leith

27

Rothesay Mws
Rothesay Tce

Chester St

Palmerston Pl

Lynedoch Pl
Glencairn Cres
Melville St

Glencairn Cres

52

6

1

William St

**West End**

Coates Cres

Shandwick Pl
Atholl Cres

Rutland Sq

Queensferry St

Charlotte Sq

**West Princes Street Gardens**

King's Stables Rd

Castle Tce

Johnston Tce

**4**

Roseburn Tce
W Coates

Donaldson's College for the Deaf

**Coates**

Magdala Cres
Coates Gdns

Douglas Cres

Grosvenor Cres
Lansdowne Cres

Haymarket Tce

Torphichen St
Dewar Pl La

Edinburgh International Conference Centre

Morrison St

Bread St

**Tollcross**

King's Stables La
W Port

Lauriston Pl

Russell Gdns
Roseburn Mains
W Catherine Pl
Balbirnie Pl

W Coates

Stanhope St
Suther

Distillery La

Haymarket Station

Dalry Rd

Cathcart Pl

48

Caledonian Rd

Upper Gro
Crown Pl

31

Upper Gve

W Approach Rd

**Fountain-Bridge**

Fountainbridge

Gardner's Cres

Morrison St

Earl Grey

W Tollcross

60

Home

50

10

Lochrin Pl

73

66

55

Panmure Pl

Brougham Pl
Lonsdale Tce

Muricston Cres

Fountainpark Leisure Centre

62

Dundee St

Gilmore Pl

Gilmore Pl

Upper Gilmore Pl

25

Glengyle Tce

Barclay Pl

46

Gillespie Cres

**Bruntsfield Links**

**Bruntsfield**

Warrender Par

Warrender

**5**

**Gorgie Rd**

69

White

North Merchiston Cemetery

Slateford Rd

Henderson Tce

54

Angle Park Tce

Dundee St

Watson Cres

Yeaman Pl

Temple Park Cres

Polwarth Gdns

Dorset Pl
Merchiston Mws

Merchiston Pl

**Merchiston**

38

40

35

24

Montpelier Park
Montpelier

Whitehouse

Viewforth

51

Warrender

**Bruntsfield**

Greenhill Tce

**Greenhill**

Clinton Rd

**6**

Shandon Cres
Myrtle Tce

Union Canal

**Harrison Park**

Harrison Rd

Polwarth Tce

Merchiston Cres

Merchiston Ave

Forbes Rd

Bruntsfield Cres
Greenhill Gdns

Chamberlain Rd

Greenhill Park

Strathearn Pl

Hope Tce

Hollybank Tce
Ashley Tce
Cowan Rd
Almondbank Tce
Brashank Tce
Ashley Gdns
Ashley Dve

Polwarth Tce

W Castle Rd

Napier Rd

Napier University

8

Church Hill

Morningside Rd

**Greenhill**

Clinton Rd

Thirlestane

Strathearn Rd

Spylaw Rd

Gillsland Rd

Colinton Rd

Albert Tce

Newbattle Tce

**Morningside**

Stable La

**Shandon**

LP

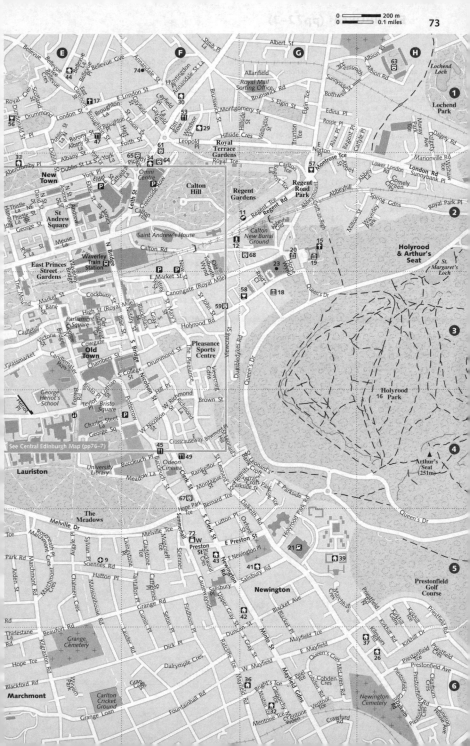

0 — 200 m
0 — 0.1 miles

**E** **F** **G** **H**

Albert St

Shrub Pl

Bellevue  Bellevue
Bellevue Cres
Annandale St
Huntingdon
Annandale St La
Allanfield
Royal Mail
Sorting Office
Brunswick Rd
Albion Pl
63
Albion Rd
Harrismith
Sunnyside
**1**
Lochend
Loch

Lochend
Park

44
Scotland
East  Clarendon
Cayfield
30
E London St
74
Brunswick St
Montgomery St
Elgin Tce
Elgin St
Bothwell
Edina Pl
Rossie Pl
Moray
Park
Ave
Marionville Rd
Dalgety Rd
Wishaw Tce

56
Royal
Drummond
Pl
Drummond
56
London St
12
N St
Broughton
Broughton
La
E Union St
53
Windsor
Row
Hillside St
Wellington
Brunton
Tce
E Norton Abbey
Montrose Tce
Aya Pl
Regent Pl
Carlyle Pl
London Rd
Sunnybank Pl
Comely
Green
Lower London
Rd
Royal Park Tce
**2**

33
N St  Barony St
Albany St
Albany La
47
Forth St
29
Leopold
Hillside Cres
Royal
Terrace
Gardens
Royal Tce
57
Montrose Tce
Abbey
Spring Gdns
Waverley
Park
Milton

Abercromby Pl
33
Dublin St La S
York  Eldon
65
Picardy
34
61
64
Regent Gardens
11
Regent Tce
Regent Rd
Abbeyhill
Carlton Tce
Regent
Road
Park
Abbeymount
Croft-an-Righ
Holyrood &
Arthur's
Seat
St
Margaret's
Loch

**New
Town**
York St
N St David St
St
Andrew
Square
George St
Rose St
Thistle St NE
Leith St
Calton
Omni
Centre
P
Greenside Row
Greenside Pl
**Calton
Hill**
Saint Andrew's House
Calton Rd
12
68
Calton
New Burial
Ground
20
23
15
19
Queen's Dr
**3**
**Holyrood &
Arthur's Seat**

St
Andrew
Square
Meuse La
Rose St
Thistle St
George St

**East Princes
Street
Gardens**
Waverley
Train
Station
Waverley
Bridge
Waverley
Bridge
E Market St
P
P
Cockburn
N Bank St
Market St
High St (Royal Mile)
Jeffrey St
Old
Tolbooth
Wynd
Canongate (Royal Mile)
58
18
Queen's Dr
**Holyrood
16 Park**

**The Mound**
Castlehill
Victoria
St
Parliament
Square
Bank
St
Blair St
Niddry St
St Mary's
59
Holyrood Rd
Dumbiedykes Rd
Viewcraig
Viewcraig Gdns

**Old
Town**
Cowgate
Chambers St
S Bridge
Drummond St
**Pleasance
Sports
Centre**
Brown St

Grassmarket
Candlemaker Row
George Heriot's
School
Forrest Rd
Lauriston Pl
Bristo
Bristol
Bristo
Square
Teviot
Pl
Chambers St
Potterow
Nicolson St
Hill St
W Richmond
St
W Nicolson St
Crosscauseway
Bowmont Pl
**Arthur's
Seat
(251m)**
**4**
Queen's Dr

**See Central Edinburgh Map (pp76-7)**
**Lauriston**
George Sq
45
**University
Library**
Buccleuch Pl
49
Buccleuch St
Odeon
Cinema
Meadow La
Rankeillor St
St Leonard's
Bank
Leonard's
Hill
St Leonard's
Hermits Croft
East
Croft
Parkside Tce
E Parkside

**The
Meadows**
Melville Dr
Melville Dr
Sylvan Pl
Livingstone
Gladstone
Tce
Summerhall
67
Hope Park
Tce
Bernard Tce
Lutton Pl
S Clerk St
Oxford St
Dalkeith Rd
Holyrood Park Rd
21
39
**5**
**Prestonfield
Golf
Course**

9
Scienne Rd
Hatton Pl
Chalmers Cres
Tantallon Pl
Marchmont
Cres
72
43
Preston St
E Preston St
E Newington Pl
41
Salisbury Rd
**Newington**
Marchhall
Cres
Prestonfield

**Marchmont**
Park Rd
Arden St
Thirlestane
La
Beaufort Rd
**Grange
Cemetery**
Kilgraston
Rd
**Carlton
Cricket
Ground**
Grange Loan
Lauder Rd
Dick Pl
Dalrymple Cres
Blackwood
Salisbury
Upper Gray St
Duncan St
Minto St
42
Blacket Ave
Blacket Pl
Mayfield Tce
E Mayfield
Queen's Cres
W Mayfield
Mayfield Gdns
Real
Cobden
Cres
Cobden Rd
McLaren Rd
37
26
Kirkhill Rd
Kirkhill Tce
Kirkhill Dr
Prestonfield Cres
Prestonfield Ave
Prestonfield Rd
**6**

Blackford Rd
Hope Tce
Wyvern
Park
Blackford Rd
Fountainhall Rd
36
Churchhill
Mentone Tce
Crentone
Mayfield Rd
32
Ventnor Pl
Crawfurd
**Newington
Cemetery**

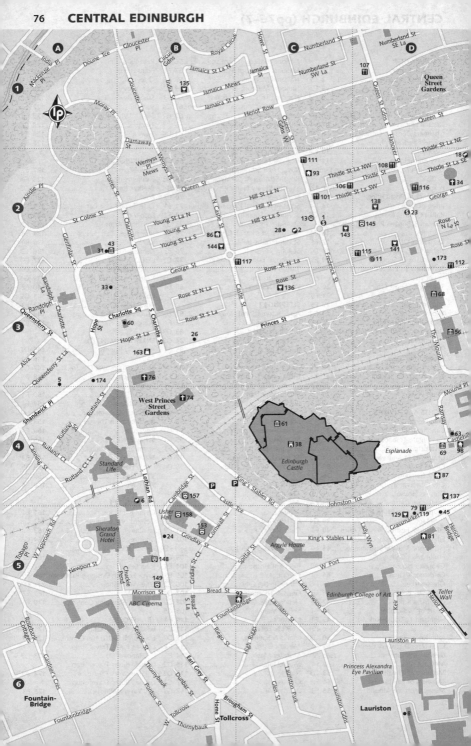

0    200 m
0    0.1 miles

**E**    **F**    **G**    **H**

Abercromby Pl

Dublin St La S    Picardy Pl

New Town    York Pl    159    Greenside Row

121    Elder St E    Cathedral La    Omni Centre    Regent Gardens    1
156    James    Little King St    Calton Hill
71    171    17    167    The Edinburgh Experience
Edinburgh Bus Station    126    170    St James Shopping Centre    37    58
165    19    Leith St    62
St Andrew Square    72    131    66    Calton Hill    Dugald Stewart's Monument
120    36    88    133    140    Regent Bridge Waterloo Pl    Regent Rd    67    2
127    27    73
166    82    Calton Rd
70    12 169 9    29    Waverley Train Station    Old Tolbooth Wynd    32    64
East Princes Street Gardens    172    E Market St    54    3
Jeffrey St    New St    Canongate (Royal Mile)
175 78    Carlton Highland Hotel    84    50    118
96    142    35    95    94    164    83    162    53
132    Cockburn St    89    St Mary's St    Boyd's Entry
55    City Chambers    High St (Royal Mile)    39    97    20    103
N Bank St    St Giles    65    36    40    Hunter Sq    Niddry St    Blackfriars St    New St    Skinner's Cl    S Gray's Cl    Gullan's    Holyrood Rd
80    161    51 99    91    160    10    128    90    High School Yards    St John's Hill
134 44    48    52 16    Blair St    St John's Rd
Lawnmarket    75    102    146    Pleasance Sports Centre
49    Parliament Square    Tron    Dickson's Cl    Robertson's Cl    Infirmary St    Holyrood & Arthur's Seat
113    Signet Library    57    Old Town    Sq    Cowgate    154    152
130    High Courts    150    Drummond St    New Arthur Pl    Viewcraig Gdns
14    7    Sheriff Court    Guthrie    4    S Bridge    Roxburgh Pl    Brown St
85    Merchant    Chambers St    Edinburgh University Old College    25    122    W Adam St    E Adam St    Baliks    5
104    125    National Museum of Scotland    59    S College St    77    Hill Pl    Richmond Pl
168    46    Bristo Port    147    109    Carnegie St
Greyfriars Kirkyard    47    Brighton St    Nicolson Sq    15    124
George Heriot's School    155    114    Lothian St    Charlesfield    Marshall St    Nicolson St    W Richmond St    Richmond La    Gilmour    Hardwell Cl
21    105    Forrest Hill    Potterrow    100    30    W Nicolson St    David St    Simon Sq    Bowmont Pl
22    Teviot Pl    Bristo Square    123    139    Crosscauseway    Forbes St
Edinburgh University    41    Charles Street La    Crichton St    W Crosscauseway    Cowen's    New John's
George Sq    Chapel St    W Crosscauseway

EDINBURGH

(Continued from page 70)

**easyInternetcafé** (Map pp76-7; ☎ 220 3580; www.easy
-everything.com; 58 Rose St; per hr £1; ☺ 7.30am-10.30pm)
**e-corner** (Map pp76-7; ☎ 558 7858; www.e-corner
.co.uk; 55 Blackfriars St; per 20min £1; ☺ 7.30am-9pm
Mon-Fri, 8am-9pm Sat & Sun)
**Internet Café** (Map pp76-7; ☎ 226 5400; 98 West Bow;
per 30min £1; ☺ 10am-11pm)

There are several internet-enabled telephone
boxes (10p a minute, 50p minimum) scattered
around the city centre, and countless wi-fi hot
spots – search on www.jiwire.com.

## Internet Resources

**City of Edinburgh Council** (www.edinburgh.gov.uk)
The city council's official site, with a useful events guide.
**City of Edinburgh Museums & Galleries** (www
.cac.org.uk) Details of events and exhibitions in the city
council's museums and galleries.
**Edinburgh Architecture** (www.edinburgharchitecture
.co.uk) Informative site dedicated to the city's modern
architecture.
**Edinburgh & Lothians Tourist Board** (www
.edinburgh.org) Official tourist-board site, with listings of
accommodation, sights, activities and events.
**Your Edinburgh** (www.youredinburgh.info) Comprehensive directory of Edinburgh-related websites.

## Laundry

Most of Edinburgh's backpacker hostels will
wash and dry a load of laundry for you for
around £4; some have self-service, coin-
operated washing machines where you do the
laundry yourself. There are self-service laun-
dries all over the city – expect to pay around
£4 for a wash and dry. Check the *Yellow Pages*
under Launderettes to find the nearest.
**Bendix Launderette & Dry Cleaners** (Map p71;
☎ 554 2180; 342 Leith Walk; ☺ 8am-8pm Mon-Fri, to
5pm Sat, 9am-4pm Sun)
**Canonmills Dry Cleaners & Launderette** (Map p71;
☎ 556 3199; 7 Huntly St; ☺ 8am-8pm Mon-Fri, to 4pm
Sat, 9am-4pm Sun)
**Tarvit Launderette** (Map pp72-3; ☎ 229 6382; 7-9
Tarvit St; ☺ 8am-8pm Mon-Fri, 9am-4pm Sat & Sun)

## Left Luggage

**Edinburgh airport left-luggage office** (per item per
4hr/24hr £5/6; ☺ 5.15am-10.45pm) On the ground floor
between check-in and international arrivals.
**St Andrew Sq bus and coach station lockers** (Map
pp76-7; small/medium/large locker per 24hr £3/4/5;
☺ 6am-midnight)

**Waverley train station left-luggage office** (Map
pp76-7; per item per 24hr £6; ☺ 7am-11pm) Beside
platform 1.

## Libraries

**Central Library** (Map pp76-7; ☎ 242 8020; George
IV Bridge; ☺ 10am-8pm Mon-Thu, 10am-5pm Fri,
9am-1pm Sat) General lending library with a room
devoted to Edinburgh (one floor down), another to all
things Scottish (in the basement), and a reference room
on the top floor.
**National Library of Scotland** (Map pp76-7; ☎ 226
4531; www.nls.uk; George IV Bridge; ☺ 9.30am-8.30pm
Mon, Tue, Thu & Fri, 10am-8.30pm Wed, 9.30am-1pm Sat)
Copyright library with a reference-only reading room; you'll
need ID (passport or driving licence) to get admission.

## Media

Edinburgh's home-grown daily newspapers
include the *Scotsman* (www.scotsman.com),
a quality daily covering Scottish, UK and international news, sport and current affairs,
and the *Edinburgh Evening News* (www.edin
burghnews.com), covering news and entertainment in the city and its environs; *Scotland
on Sunday* is the weekend newspaper from the
same publisher.

## Medical Services

Chemists (pharmacists) can advise you on
minor ailments. At least one local chemist remains open round the clock – its location will
be displayed in the windows of other chemists.
For urgent medical advice you can call the **NHS
24 Helpline** ( ☎ 08454 24 24 24; www.nhs24.com).

For urgent dental treatment you can visit
the walk-in **Chalmers Dental Centre** (Map pp76-7;
3 Chalmers St; ☺ 9am-4.45pm Mon-Thu, 9am-4.15pm Fri).
In the case of a dental emergency in the evenings or at weekends, call **Lothian Dental Advice
Line** ( ☎ 536 4800).
**Boots** (Map pp76-7; ☎ 225 6757; 48 Shandwick Pl;
☺ 8am-9pm Mon-Fri, 8am-6pm Sat, 10.30am-4.30pm
Sun) Chemist open longer hours than most.
**Royal Hospital for Sick Children** (Map pp72-3;
☎ 536 0000; 9 Sciennes Rd) Casualty department for
children aged under 13 years; located in Marchmont.
**Royal Infirmary of Edinburgh** (Map p71; ☎ 536
1000; 51 Little France Cres, Old Dalkeith Rd) Edinburgh's
main general hospital; has 24-hour accident and emer-
gency department.
**Western General Hospital** (Map p71; ☎ 537 1330;
Crewe Rd South; ☺ 9am-9pm) For non-life-threatening
injuries and ailments, you can attend the Minor Injuries
Unit without having to make an appointment.

## Money

There are banks and ATMs all over the city. You can change currency and travellers cheques at bureaus de change scattered throughout the city centre, and in banks, post offices and travel agencies. Banks generally offer the best rates.

**American Express** (Map pp76-7; ☎ 718 2501; 69 George St; ◷ 9am-5.30pm Mon-Fri, 9am-4pm Sat) Charges no commission on Amex travellers cheques, 2% on cash and generally offers a good rate of exchange.

**Bank of Scotland** (Map pp76-7; ☎ 465 3900; 38 St Andrew Sq; ◷ 9am-5pm Mon, Tue, Thu, Fri, 10am-5pm Wed)

**Fexco** (Map pp76-7; ☎ 557 3953; Princes Mall, 3 Princes St) Convenient location inside the Edinburgh & Scotland Information Centre (below); charges no commission on cash, but has a poor exchange rate.

**Royal Bank of Scotland** (Map pp76-7; ☎ 556 8555; 36 St Andrew Sq; ◷ 9.15am-4.45pm Mon, Tue, Thu & Fri, 10am-4.45pm Wed, 10am-2pm Sat)

**Thomas Cook** (Map pp76-7; ☎ 226 5500; 52 Hanover St; ◷ 9am-5.30pm Mon, Tue & Thu-Sat, 10am-5.30pm Wed) Charges 2% commission (minimum £3) on both cash and travellers cheques.

## Post

**Frederick St post office** (Map pp76-7; 40 Frederick St) In New Town.

**Main post office** (Map pp76-7; ☎ 0845 722 3344; St James Centre, Leith St; ◷ 8.30am-5.30pm Mon-Fri, to 6pm Sat) Items addressed to poste restante can be picked up here.

**St Mary's St post office** (Map pp76-7; 46 St Mary's St) In Old Town.

## Telephone

There are telephone booths scattered all over the city; see also the Directory, p446.

## Tourist Information

**Edinburgh & Scotland Information Centre** (ESIC; Map pp76-7; ☎ 0845 225 5121; info@visitscotland.com; Princes Mall, 3 Princes St; ◷ 9am-9pm Mon-Sat, 10am-8pm Sun Jul & Aug, 9am-7pm Mon-Sat, 10am-7pm Sun May, Jun & Sep, 9am-5pm Mon-Wed, 9am-6pm Thu-Sun Oct-Apr) Includes an accommodation booking service, currency exchange, gift and bookshop, internet access, and counters selling tickets for Edinburgh city tours and Scottish Citylink bus services.

**Old Craighall tourist office** (☎ 653 6172; Old Craighall Junction, A1) In a service area on the main A1 road, about 5 miles east of the city centre.

**Tourist & Airport Information Desk** (☎ 0845 225 5121) At Edinburgh airport.

## Travel Agencies

There are hundreds of travel agencies all over the city. Two agencies that specialise in budget and student travel:

**STA Travel** (Map pp76-7; ☎ 0871 468 0617; www.statravel.co.uk; 27 Forrest Rd; ◷ 10am-6pm Mon-Wed & Fri, 10am-7pm Thu, 10am-5pm Sat)

**Student Flights** (Map pp76-7; ☎ 226 6868; www.studentflight.co.uk; 53 Forrest Rd; ◷ 9.30am-6pm Mon-Fri, 11am-5pm Sat)

## Universities

Edinburgh has three universities. The oldest, biggest and most prestigious is the University of Edinburgh, with more than 15,000 undergraduates.

**Heriot-Watt University** (☎ 449 5111; www.hw.ac.uk) The main campus is southwest of the city at Riccarton, near Currie.

**Napier University** (☎ 444 2266; www.napier.ac.uk) Craiglockhart campus (Map p71; 219 Colinton Rd); Merchiston campus (Map pp72-3; 10 Colinton Rd)

**University of Edinburgh Information Centre** (Map pp76-7; ☎ 650 1000; www.ed.ac.uk; 7-11 Nicolson St; ◷ 9.15am-5pm Mon-Fri) Provides details of short-term courses.

# DANGERS & ANNOYANCES

Edinburgh is safer than most cities of a similar size, but it has its share of crime so all of the normal big-city precautions apply here.

Lothian Rd, Dalry Rd, Rose St and the western end of Princes St, at the junction with Shandwick Pl and Queensferry and Hope Sts, can get a bit rowdy on Friday and Saturday nights after the pubs close. Calton Hill offers good views during the day but is best avoided at night. Women on their own should avoid walking across the Meadows after dark and walking in the red-light district between Salamander St and Leith Links, in Leith.

# SIGHTS

Edinburgh's main attractions are concentrated in the city centre – on and around the Old Town's Royal Mile between the castle and Holyrood, and in New Town. A major exception is the Royal Yacht *Britannia*, which is in the redeveloped docklands district of Leith, 2 miles northeast of the centre.

If you tire of sightseeing, good areas for aimless wandering include the posh suburbs of Stockbridge and Morningside, the pretty riverside village of Cramond, and the winding footpaths of Calton Hill and Arthur's Seat.

**EDINBURGH**

## Old Town

Edinburgh's Old Town stretches along a ridge to the east of the castle, and tumbles down Victoria St to the broad expanse of the Grassmarket. It's a jagged and jumbled maze of masonry riddled with closes (alleys) and wynds (narrow lanes), stairs and vaults, and cleft along its spine by the cobbled ravine of the Royal Mile.

Until the founding of New Town in the 18th century, old Edinburgh was an overcrowded and insanitary hive of humanity squeezed between the boggy ground of the Nor' Loch (North Loch, now drained and occupied by Princes Street Gardens) to the north and the city walls to the south and east. The only way for the town to expand was upwards, and the five- and six-storey tenements that were raised along the Royal Mile in the 16th and 17th centuries were the skyscrapers of their day, remarked upon with wonder by visiting writers such as Daniel Defoe. All classes of society, from beggars to magistrates, lived cheek by jowl in these urban ants' nests, the wealthy occupying the middle floors – high enough to be above the noise and stink of the streets, but not so high that climbing the stairs would be too tiring – while the poor squeezed into attics, basements, cellars and vaults amid the rats, rubbish and raw sewage.

The renovated Old Town tenements still support a thriving city-centre community, and today the street level is crammed with cafés, restaurants, bars, backpacker hostels and tacky souvenir shops. Few visitors wander beyond the main drag of the Royal Mile, but it's worth taking time to explore the countless closes that lead off the street into quiet courtyards, often with unexpected views of city, sea and hills.

### EDINBURGH CASTLE

The brooding, black crags of Castle Rock rising above the western end of Princes St are the very reason for Edinburgh's existence. This rocky hill was the most easily defended hill-top on the invasion route between England and central Scotland, a route followed by countless armies from the Roman legions of the 1st and 2nd centuries AD to the Jacobite troops of Bonnie Prince Charlie in 1745.

**Edinburgh Castle** (Map pp76-7; ☎ 225 9846; Castle Hill; adult/concession/child incl audio guide £11/9/5.50; ☼ 9.30am-6pm Apr-Sep, 9.30am-5pm Oct-Mar, last admission 45min before closing) has played a pivotal role in Scottish history, both as a royal residence – King Malcolm Canmore (r 1058–93) and Queen Margaret first made their home here in the 11th century – and as a military stronghold. The castle last saw military action in 1745; from then until the 1920s it served as the British army's main base in Scotland. Today it is one of Scotland's most atmospheric, most popular – and most expensive – tourist attractions.

The **Entrance Gateway**, flanked by statues of Robert the Bruce and William Wallace, opens to a cobbled lane that leads up beneath the 16th-century **Portcullis Gate** to the cannon ranged along the Argyle and Mills Mount batteries. The battlements here have great views over New Town to the Firth of Forth.

At the far end of Mills Mount Battery is the famous **One O'Clock Gun**, where crowds gather to watch a gleaming WWII 25-pounder fire an ear-splitting time signal at exactly 1pm (every day except Sundays, Christmas Day and Good Friday).

At the western end of the castle, to the left of the castle restaurant, a road leads down to the **National War Museum of Scotland** (Map pp76-7; ☎ 247 4413; admission incl in Edinburgh Castle ticket; ☼ 9.45am-5.45pm Apr-Oct, 9.45am-4.45pm Nov-Mar), which brings Scotland's military history vividly to life. The exhibits have been personalised by telling the stories of the original owners of the objects on display, making it easier to empathise with the experiences of war than any dry display of dusty weaponry ever could.

South of Mills Mount, the road curls up leftwards through **Foog's Gate** to the highest part of Castle Rock, crowned by the tiny, Romanesque **St Margaret's Chapel**, the oldest surviving building in Edinburgh. It was probably built by David I or Alexander I in memory of their mother, Queen Margaret, sometime around 1130 (she was canonised in 1250). Beside the chapel stands **Mons Meg**, a giant 15th-century siege gun built at Mons (in what is now Belgium) in 1449.

The main group of buildings on the summit of Castle Rock are ranged around Crown Sq, dominated by the shrine of the **Scottish National War Memorial**. Opposite is the **Great Hall**, built for James IV (r 1488–1513) as a ceremonial hall and used as a meeting place for the Scottish parliament until 1639. Its most remarkable feature is the original, 16th-century hammer-beam roof.

On the eastern side of the square is the **Royal Palace**, built during the 15th and 16th centuries, where a series of historical tableaux leads to the highlight of the castle – a strongroom housing the **Honours of Scotland** (the Scottish crown jewels), the oldest surviving crown jewels in Europe. Locked away in a chest following the Act of Union in 1707, the crown (made in 1540 from the gold of Robert the Bruce's 14th-century coronet), sword and sceptre lay forgotten until they were unearthed at the instigation of the novelist Sir Walter Scott in 1818. Also on display here is the **Stone of Destiny** (see the boxed text, below).

Among the neighbouring **Royal Apartments** is the bedchamber where Mary, Queen of Scots gave birth to her son James VI, who was to unite the crowns of Scotland and England in 1603.

The **Castle Vaults** beneath the Great Hall (entered from Crown Sq via the Prisons of War exhibit) were used variously as storerooms, bakeries and prison. The vaults have been done up to resemble 18th- and early-19th-century prisons, where graffiti carved by French and American prisoners can be seen on the ancient wooden doors.

## THE ROYAL MILE

This mile-long street earned its regal nickname in the 16th century when it was used by the king to travel between the castle and the Palace of Holyroodhouse. There are four sections – Castlehill, Lawnmarket, High St and Canongate – whose names reflect their historical origins. Allow at least half a day to wander down the Mile, taking time to visit the attractions.

### Castlehill

A short distance downhill from the Castle Esplanade, a former school houses the **Scotch Whisky Heritage Centre** (Map pp76–7; ☎ 220 0441; 354 Castlehill; adult/child incl tour & tasting £9.25/4.95; ☷ 9.30am-6.30pm Jun-Aug, 10am-5pm Sep-May; ☖ ). The centre explains the making of whisky from barley to bottle, in a series of exhibits that combine sight, sound and smell; look out for the distillery cat! There's also a restaurant that serves traditional Scottish dishes with, where possible, a dash of whisky thrown in.

The quaint building across the street is the **Outlook Tower & Camera Obscura** (Map pp76–7; ☎ 226 3709; Castlehill; adult/child £7.50/5; ☷ 9.30am-7.30pm Jul & Aug, 9.30am-6pm Apr-Jun, Sep & Oct, 10am-5pm Nov-Mar). The 'camera obscura' itself is a curious

---

## THE STONE OF DESTINY

On St Andrew's Day 1996 a block of sandstone – 26½ inches by 16½ inches by 11 inches in size, with rusted iron hoops at either end – was installed with much pomp and ceremony in Edinburgh Castle. For the previous 700 years it had lain in London, beneath the Coronation Chair in Westminster Abbey. Almost all English, and later British, monarchs from Edward II in 1307 to Elizabeth II in 1953 have parked their backsides firmly over this stone during their coronation ceremony.

The legendary Stone of Destiny – said to have originated in the Holy Land, and on which Scottish kings placed their feet during their coronation (not their bums; the English got that bit wrong) – was stolen from Scone Abbey near Perth by King Edward I of England in 1296. It was taken to London and there it remained for seven centuries – except for a brief removal to Gloucester during WWII air raids, and a three-month sojourn in Scotland after it was stolen by Scottish Nationalist students at Christmas in 1950 – an enduring symbol of Scotland's subjugation by England.

The Stone of Destiny returned to the political limelight in 1996, when the then Scottish Secretary and Conservative Party MP, Michael Forsyth, arranged for the return of the sandstone block to Scotland. A blatant attempt to boost the flagging popularity of the Conservative Party in Scotland prior to a general election, Forsyth's publicity stunt failed miserably. The Scots said thanks very much for the stone and then, in May 1997, voted every Conservative MP in Scotland into oblivion.

Many people, however, believe that Edward I was fobbed off with a shoddy imitation in 1296 and that the true Stone of Destiny remains safely hidden somewhere in Scotland. This is not impossible – some descriptions of the original state that it was made of black marble and decorated with elaborate carvings. Interested parties should read *Stone of Destiny* (1997) by Pat Gerber, which details the history of Scotland's most famous lump of rock.

19th-century device – in constant use since 1853 – that uses lenses and mirrors to throw a live image of the city onto a large horizontal screen. The accompanying commentary is entertaining and the whole experience has a quirky charm. Stairs lead up through various displays on optics to the Outlook Tower, which offers great views over the city.

With Edinburgh's tallest spire (71.7m), the **Highland Tolbooth Kirk** (Map pp76–7) is a prominent feature of the Old Town's skyline. The interior has been refurbished and it now houses the **Hub** (Map pp76-7; ☎ 473 2000; www.thehub-edinburgh.com; Castlehill; admission free; ⏰ 10am-7pm), the ticket office and information centre for the Edinburgh Festival. There's also a good café here.

### Lawnmarket

Lawnmarket (a corruption of 'Landmarket', a market selling goods from the land outside the city) takes its name from the large cloth market that flourished here until the 18th century. This was the poshest part of the Old Town, where many of its most distinguished citizens made their homes.

One of these was the merchant Thomas Gledstanes, who in 1617 purchased the tenement later known as **Gladstone's Land** (NTS; Map pp76-7; ☎ 226 5856; 477 Lawnmarket; adult/child £5/4; ⏰ 10am-7pm Jul & Aug, 10am-5pm Apr-Jun, Sep & Oct). It contains fine painted ceilings, walls and beams, and some splendid furniture from the 17th and 18th centuries. The volunteer guides provide a wealth of anecdotes and a detailed history.

Tucked down a close just east of Gladstone's Land you'll find the **Writers' Museum** (Map pp76-7; ☎ 529 4901; Lady Stair's Close, Lawnmarket; admission free; ⏰ 10am-5pm Mon-Sat year-round, and 2-5pm Sun during Edinburgh Festival). Located in Lady Stair's House (1622), the museum contains manuscripts and memorabilia belonging to Robert Burns, Sir Walter Scott and Robert Louis Stevenson.

### High St

High St, which stretches from George IV Bridge down to the Netherbow at St Mary's St, is the heart and soul of the Old Town, home to the city's main church, the Law Courts, the city council and – until 1707 – the Scottish parliament.

Dominating High St is the great grey bulk of **St Giles Cathedral** (Map pp76-7; ☎ 225 9442; High St;

admission free, £3 donation suggested; ⏰ 9am-7pm Mon-Fri, 9am-5pm Sat, 1-5pm Sun May-Sep, 9am-5pm Mon-Sat, 1-5pm Sun Oct-Apr). Properly called the High Kirk of Edinburgh (it was only a true cathedral – the seat of a bishop – from 1633 to 1638 and from 1661 to 1689), St Giles Cathedral was named after the patron saint of cripples and beggars. A Norman-style church was built here in 1126 but was destroyed by English invaders in 1385; the only substantial remains are the central piers that support the tower.

The present church dates largely from the 15th century – the beautiful crown spire was completed in 1495 – but much of it was restored in the 19th century. The interior lacks grandeur but is rich in history: St Giles was at the heart of the Scottish Reformation, and John Knox served as minister here from 1559 to 1572. One of the most interesting corners of the kirk is the **Thistle Chapel**, built in 1911 for the Knights of the Most Ancient & Most Noble Order of the Thistle. The elaborately carved Gothic-style stalls have canopies topped with the helms and arms of the 16 knights – look out for the bagpipe-playing angel amid the vaulting.

By the side of the street, outside the western door of St Giles, is a cobblestone **Heart of Midlothian** (Map pp76–7) set into the paving. This marks the site of the Tolbooth. Built in the 15th century and demolished in the early 19th century, the Tolbooth served variously as a meeting place for parliament, the town council and the General Assembly of the Reformed Kirk, before becoming law courts and, finally, a notorious prison and place of execution. Passers-by traditionally spit on the heart for luck (don't stand downwind!).

At the other end of St Giles is the **Mercat Cross** (Map pp76–7), a 19th-century copy of the 1365 original, where merchants and traders met to transact business and royal proclamations were read.

Next to the Mercat Cross is the **Loch Ness Discovery Centre** (Map pp76-7; ☎ 225 2290; 1 Parliament Sq; adult/child £4.95/3.95; ⏰ 9.30am-10pm Jul & Aug, 9.30am-8pm Apr-Jun, Sep & Oct, 10am-5pm Nov-Mar), which explores the legend of the Loch Ness Monster (for more on Nessie, see the boxed text, p328) by means of various photographic displays and a 3-D movie. Plus, of course, a gift shop crammed with cheekily priced cuddly toys in the form of Nessie…

Across from the Cross is the **City Chambers** (Map pp76–7), originally built by John Adam (brother of Robert) between 1753 and 1761 to serve as the Royal Exchange – a covered meeting place for city merchants. However, the merchants preferred their old stamping grounds in the street and the building became the city council offices in 1811.

Part of the Royal Exchange was built over the sealed-off remains of Mary King's Close, and the lower levels of this medieval Old Town alley have survived almost unchanged in the foundations of the City Chambers for 250 years. Now open to the public as the **Real Mary King's Close** (Map pp76-7; ☎ 0870 243 0160; 2 Warriston's Close, Writers Ct, High St; adult/child £9.50/6; ☿ 10am-9pm Apr-Oct, 10am-4pm Sun-Fri, 10am-9pm Sat Nov-Mar), this spooky, subterranean labyrinth is a fascinating insight into the daily life of 16th- and 17th-century Edinburgh. Costumed characters give tours through a 16th-century town house and the plague-stricken home of a 17th-century gravedigger. Tours must be booked in advance.

Halfway down the next block is 'the noisiest museum in the world' – the **Museum of Childhood** (Map pp76-7; ☎ 529 4142; 42 High St; admission free; ☿ 10am-5pm Mon-Sat, 2-5pm Sun). Often filled with the chatter of excited children, it covers serious issues related to childhood – health, education, upbringing and so on – but also has an enormous collection of toys, dolls, games and books. (Note – it may be closed on Sundays from 2008; phone to check.)

The Royal Mile narrows at the foot of High St beside the jutting façade of **John Knox House** (Map pp76-7; ☎ 556 9579; 43-45 High St; adult/child £3.50/2.75; ☿ 10am-6pm Mon-Sat year-round, plus noon-6pm Sun Jul & Aug). This is the oldest surviving tenement in Edinburgh, dating from around 1490; John Knox, an influential church reformer and leader of the Protestant Reformation in Scotland, is thought to have lived here from 1561 to 1572. The labyrinthine interior has some beautiful painted-timber ceilings and an interesting display on Knox' life and work.

### Canongate

Canongate, the stretch of the Royal Mile from Netherbow to Holyrood, takes its name from the Augustinian canons (monks) of Holyrood Abbey. From the 16th century it was home to aristocrats attracted to the Palace of Holyroodhouse. Originally governed by the monks, Canongate was an independent burgh separate from Edinburgh until 1856.

One of the surviving symbols of Canongate's former independence is the **Canongate Tolbooth** (Map pp76-7). Built in 1591, it served successively as a collection point for tolls (taxes), a council house, a courtroom and a jail. With its picturesque turrets and projecting clock, it's an interesting example of 16th-century architecture, and now houses a fascinating museum called the **People's Story** (Map pp76-7; ☎ 529 4057; 163 Canongate; admission free; ☿ 10am-5pm Mon-Sat year-round, 2-5pm Sun Aug), which covers the life, work and pastimes of ordinary Edinburgh folk from the 18th century to the present day.

Across the street from the Tolbooth is Huntly House. Built in 1570, it now houses the **Museum of Edinburgh** (Map pp76-7; ☎ 529 4143; 142 Canongate; admission free; ☿ 10am-5pm Mon-Sat year-round, plus 2-5pm Sun Aug). It covers the history of the city from prehistory to the present. Exhibits of national importance include an original copy of the National Covenant of 1638, but the big crowd pleaser is the dog collar and feeding bowl that once belonged to Greyfriars Bobby, the city's most famous canine citizen (see p85).

Downhill on the left is the attractive curved gable of the **Canongate Kirk** (Map pp76-7), built in 1688. The kirkyard contains the graves of several famous people, including the economist Adam Smith (1723–90), author of *The Wealth of Nations*, Mrs Agnes MacLehose (the 'Clarinda' of Robert Burns' love poems), and the 18th-century poet Robert Fergusson (1750–74). Fergusson was much admired by Robert Burns, who paid for the gravestone and penned the epitaph – take a look at the inscription on the back.

### HOLYROOD

The **Palace of Holyroodhouse** (Map pp72-3; ☎ 556 5100; www.royal.gov.uk; Canongate; adult/child £9.50/5.50; ☿ 9.30am-6pm Apr-Oct, 9.30am-4.30pm Nov-Mar) is the royal family's official residence in Scotland, but is most famous as the 16th-century home of the ill-fated Mary, Queen of Scots. The palace developed from a guesthouse attached to Holyrood Abbey, which was extended by King James IV in 1501. The oldest surviving part of the building, the northwestern tower, was built in 1529 as a royal apartment for James V and his wife, Mary of Guise. Mary, Queen of Scots spent six turbulent years here, during which time she debated with John Knox, married both her first and second husbands, and witnessed the murder of her secretary Rizzio. The palace is closed to the public when the royal family is visiting and during state functions (usually in mid-May, and mid-June to early July; check the website for exact dates).

The guided tour leads you through a series of impressive royal apartments, ending in the **Great Gallery**. The 89 portraits of Scottish kings were commissioned by Charles II and supposedly record his unbroken lineage from Scota, the Egyptian pharaoh's daughter who discovered the infant Moses in a reed basket on the banks of the Nile.

But the highlight of the tour is **Mary, Queen of Scots' Bed Chamber**, home to the unfortunate Mary from 1561 to 1567, and connected by a secret stairway to her husband's bedchamber. It was here that her jealous first husband, Lord Darnley, restrained the pregnant queen while his henchmen murdered her secretary – and favourite – David Rizzio. A plaque in the neighbouring room marks the spot where he bled to death.

The exit from the palace leads into the ruins of **Holyrood Abbey** (Map pp72–3). King David I founded the abbey here in the shadow of Salisbury Crags in 1128. It was probably named after a fragment of the True Cross (rood is an old Scots word for cross), said to have been brought to Scotland by his mother, St Margaret. Most of the surviving ruins date from the 12th and 13th centuries, although a doorway in the far southeastern corner has survived from the original Norman church.

The **Queen's Gallery** (Map pp72-3; adult/child £5/3, joint ticket incl admission to palace £13/7.50; 9.30am-6pm Apr-Oct, 9.30am-4.30pm Nov-Mar), beside the palace ticket office, is a showcase for a range of changing exhibitions of art from the Royal Collections.

The modernistic white marquee pitched beneath Salisbury Crags marks **Our Dynamic Earth** (Map pp72-3; 550 7800; Holyrood Rd; adult/child £8.95/5.75; 10am-6pm Jul & Aug, 10am-5pm Apr-Jun, Sep & Oct, 10am-5pm Wed-Sun Nov-Mar, last admission 70min before closing), billed as an interactive, multimedia journey of discovery through Earth's history from the Big Bang to the present day. Hugely popular with kids of all ages, it's a slick extravaganza of whizz-bang special effects cleverly designed to fire up young minds with curiosity about all things geological and environmental. Its true purpose, of course, is to disgorge you into a gift shop where you can buy model dinosaurs and souvenir T-shirts.

In **Holyrood Park** (Map pp72–3), Edinburgh is blessed by having a little bit of wilderness in the heart of the city. The former hunting ground of Scottish monarchs, the park covers 263 hectares of varied landscape, including crags, moorland and loch. The highest point is the 251m summit of **Arthur's Seat** (Map p71), the deeply eroded remnant of a long-extinct volcano. Holyrood park can be circumnavigated by car or bike along Queen's Dr (it is closed to motorised traffic on Sunday), and you can hike from Holyrood to the summit in 45 minutes.

### NORTH OF THE ROYAL MILE

**Cockburn St**, lined with trendy fashion, jewellery and music shops, leads down from the Royal Mile to Waverley Bridge. A right turn into Market St leads to the **Fruitmarket Gallery** (Map pp76-7; 225 2383; www.fruitmarket.co.uk; 45 Market St; admission free; 11am-6pm Mon-Sat, noon-5pm Sun). One of Edinburgh's most innovative and popular galleries, the Fruitmarket showcases contemporary Scottish and international artists, and also has an excellent arts bookshop and café.

Across the street is the **City Art Centre** (Map pp76-7; 529 3993; www.cac.org.uk; 2 Market St; admission free except for temporary exhibitions; 10am-5pm Mon-Sat, noon-5pm Sun), comprising six floors of exhibitions with a variety of themes, including an extensive collection of Scottish art. (Note – it may be closed Sundays from 2008.)

### SOUTH OF THE ROYAL MILE

The site of a cattle market from the 15th century until the start of the 20th, the **Grassmarket** (Map pp76–7) has always been a focal point of the Old Town. It was also the city's main place of execution, and over 100 martyred Covenanters are commemorated by a monument at the eastern end, where the gallows used to stand. The notorious murderers Burke and Hare operated from a now-vanished close off the western end. In 1827 they enticed at least 18 victims to their boarding house, suffocated them and sold the bodies to Edinburgh's medical schools. The law finally caught up with Burke and Hare – the latter turned King's evidence and testified against Burke, who was hanged outside St Giles in 1828. In an ironic twist, his corpse was donated to the anatomy school for public dissection, and a pocket book was made from his flayed skin (now on display in the Surgeons' Hall Museums, p95).

## SCOTTISH PARLIAMENT BUILDING

The new **Scottish parliament building** (Map pp72-3; ☎ 348 5200; www.scottish.parliament.uk; admission free; ☉ 9am-7pm Tue-Thu, 10am-6pm Mon & Fri in session, 10am-6pm Mon-Fri in recess Apr-Oct, 10am-4pm in recess Nov-Mar; ⓰ ), built on the site of a former brewery close to the Palace of Holyroodhouse, was officially opened by HM the Queen in October 2005.

The public areas of the parliament building – the Main Hall, where there is an exhibition, a shop and café, and the public gallery in the Debating Chamber – are open to visitors; alternatively you can pay for a guided tour (adult/child £5/3) which includes a visit to the Debating Chamber, a committee room, the Garden Lobby and, if possible, the office of an MSP (Member of the Scottish Parliament). If you want to see the parliament in session, check in advance that it will be sitting – business days are normally Tuesday to Thursday year-round.

Enric Miralles (1955–2000), the architect who conceived the Scottish parliament building, believed that a building could be a work of art. However, the weird concrete confection that has sprouted at the foot of Salisbury Crags has left the good people of Edinburgh staring and scratching their heads in confusion. What does it all mean? The strange forms of the exterior are all symbolic in some way, from the oddly shaped windows on the west wall (inspired by the silhouette of the *Reverend Robert Walker Skating on Duddingston Loch,* one of Scotland's most famous paintings), to the ground plan of the whole complex, which represents a 'flower of democracy rooted in Scottish soil' (best seen looking down from Salisbury Crags).

The Main Hall, inside the public entrance, has a low, triple-arched ceiling of polished concrete, like a cave, or cellar, or castle vault. It is a dimly lit space, the starting point for a metaphorical journey from this relative darkness up to the Debating Chamber (sitting directly above the Main Hall), which is, in contrast, a palace of light – the light of democracy. This magnificent chamber is the centrepiece of the parliament, designed not to glorify but to humble the politicians who sit within it. The windows face Calton Hill, allowing MSPs to look up to its monuments (reminders of the Scottish Enlightenment), while the massive, pointed oak beams of the roof are suspended by steel threads above the MSPs' heads like so many Damoclean swords.

Nowadays the broad, open square, edged by tall tenements and dominated by the looming castle, has many lively pubs and restaurants, including the **White Hart Inn** (Map pp76–7), which was once patronised by Robert Burns. **Cowgate** – the long, dark ravine leading eastwards from the Grassmarket – was once the road along which cattle were driven from the pastures around Arthur's Seat to the safety of the city walls. Today it is the heart of Edinburgh's nightlife, with around two dozen clubs and bars within five minutes' walk of each other.

Candlemaker Row leads from the eastern end of the Grassmarket towards one of Edinburgh's most famous churches. **Greyfriars Kirk** (Map pp76–7) was built on the site of a Franciscan friary and opened for worship on Christmas Day 1620. In 1638 the National Covenant was signed here, rejecting Charles I's attempts to impose episcopacy and a new English prayer book, and affirming the independence of the Scottish Church. Many who signed were later executed at the Grassmarket and, in 1679, 1200 Covenanters were held

prisoner in terrible conditions in the southwestern corner of the kirkyard. There's a small exhibition inside the church.

Hemmed in by high walls and overlooked by the brooding presence of the castle, **Greyfriars Kirkyard** is one of Edinburgh's most evocative cemeteries, a peaceful green oasis dotted with elaborate monuments. Many famous Edinburgh names are buried here, including the poet Allan Ramsay (1686–1758), architect William Adam (1689–1748) and William Smellie (1740–95), the editor of the first edition of the *Encyclopedia Britannica*. If you want to experience the graveyard at its scariest – inside a burial vault, in the dark, at night – go on one of Black Hart Storytellers' guided tours (see p96).

However, the memorial that draws the biggest crowds is the tiny **Greyfriars Bobby statue** (Map pp76–7), in front of the pub beside the kirkyard gate. Bobby was a Skye terrier who, from 1858 to 1872, maintained a vigil over the grave of his master, an Edinburgh police officer. The story was immortalised (and romanticised) in a novel by Eleanor Atkinson

**EDINBURGH**

in 1912, and in 1963 was made into a movie by – who else? – Walt Disney. Bobby's own grave, marked by a small, pink granite stone, is just inside the entrance to the kirkyard. You can see his original collar and bowl in the Museum of Edinburgh (p83).

### CHAMBERS STREET

The broad, elegant Chambers St stretches eastwards from Greyfriars Bobby, dominated by the long façade of the **National Museum of Scotland** (Map pp76-7; ☎ 247 4422; www.nms.ac.uk; Chambers St; admission free, special exhibitions extra; 🕐 10am-5pm). The collections are spread between two buildings, one modern, one Victorian.

The golden stone and striking modern architecture of the **Museum of Scotland** building, opened in 1998, is one of the city's most distinctive landmarks. The five floors of the museum trace the history of Scotland from geological beginnings to the 1990s, with many imaginative and stimulating exhibits – audio guides are available in several languages. Highlights include the Monymusk Reliquary, a tiny silver casket dating from AD 750, which is said to have been carried into battle with Robert the Bruce at Bannockburn in 1314, and a set of charming 12th-century chess pieces made from walrus ivory. Don't forget to take the lift to the roof terrace for a fantastic view of the castle.

The Museum of Scotland connects with the Victorian **Royal Museum** building, dating from 1861, whose stolid, grey exterior gives way to a bright and airy, glass-roofed entrance hall. The museum houses an eclectic collection covering natural history, archaeology, scientific and industrial technology, and the decorative arts of ancient Egypt, Islam, China, Japan, Korea and the West.

## New Town

Edinburgh's New Town lies north of the Old Town, on a ridge running parallel to the Royal Mile and separated from it by the valley of Princes Street Gardens. Its regular grid of elegant, Georgian terraces is a complete contrast to the chaotic tangle of tenements and wynds that characterise the Old Town.

Between the end of the 14th century and the start of the 18th, the population of Edinburgh – still confined within the walls of the Old Town – increased from 2000 to 50,000. The tottering tenements were unsafe and occasionally collapsed, fire was an ever-present danger, and the overcrowding and squalor became unbearable.

When the Act of Union in 1707 brought the prospect of long-term stability, the upper classes were keen to find healthier, more spacious living quarters, and in 1766 the lord provost of Edinburgh announced an architectural competition to design an extension to the city. It was won by an unknown 23-year-old, James Craig, a self-taught architect whose simple and elegant plan envisaged the main axis being George St, with grand squares at either end, and with building restricted to one side only of Princes and Queen Sts so that the houses enjoyed views over the Firth of Forth to the north and to the castle and Old Town to the south.

During the 18th and 19th centuries New Town continued to sprout squares, circuses, parks and terraces, with some of its finest neoclassical architecture designed by Robert Adam. Today Edinburgh's New Town remains the world's most complete and unspoilt example of Georgian architecture and town planning. Along with the Old Town, it was declared a Unesco World Heritage site in 1995.

### PRINCES STREET

Princes St is one of the world's most spectacular shopping streets. Built up on the north side only, it catches the sun in summer and allows expansive views across Princes Street Gardens to the castle and the crowded skyline of the Old Town.

The western end of Princes St is dominated by the red-sandstone edifice of the Caledonian Hilton Hotel, and the tower of **St John's Church** (Map pp76-7), worth visiting for its fine Gothic Revival interior. It overlooks **St Cuthbert's Parish Church** (Map pp76-7), built in the 1890s on a site of great antiquity – there has been a church here since at least the 12th century, and perhaps since the 7th century. There is a circular **watchtower** in the graveyard – a reminder of the Burke and Hare days when graves had to be guarded against robbers.

At the eastern end is the prominent clock tower – traditionally three minutes fast so that you don't miss your train – of the **Balmoral Hotel** (p102), and the beautiful 1788 **Register House** (Map pp76-7), designed by Robert Adam, with a statue of the duke of Wellington on horseback in front. It houses the National Archives of Scotland.

**Princes Street Gardens** (Map pp76–7) lie in a valley that was once occupied by the Nor' Loch, a boggy depression that was drained in the early 19th century. The gardens are split in the middle by **The Mound**, which was created by around two million cart-loads of earth excavated from the foundations of New Town being dumped here to provide a road link across the valley to the Old Town. It was completed in 1830.

The eastern half of the gardens is dominated by the massive Gothic spire of the **Scott Monument** (Map pp76-7; ☎ 529 4068; East Princes Street Gardens; admission £3; ☼ 9am-6pm Mon-Sat, 10am-6pm Sun Apr-Sep, 9am-3pm Mon-Sat, 10am-3pm Sun Oct-Mar), built by public subscription in memory of the novelist Sir Walter Scott after his death in 1832. Inside you can see an exhibition on Scott's life, and climb the 287 steps to the top for a superb view of the city.

## ROYAL SCOTTISH ACADEMY

The distinguished Greek Doric temple at the corner of The Mound and Princes St, its northern pediment crowned by a seated figure of Queen Victoria, is the home of the **Royal Scottish Academy** (RSA; Map pp76-7; ☎ 225 6671; www.royalscottishacademy.org; The Mound; admission free, fee for special exhibitions; ☼ 10am-5pm Mon-Sat, 2-5pm Sun; &). Designed by William Playfair and built between 1823 and 1836, it was originally called the Royal Institution; the RSA took over the building in 1910. The galleries display a collection of paintings, sculptures and architectural drawings by academy members dating from 1831, and they also host temporary exhibitions throughout the year.

The RSA and the National Gallery of Scotland are linked via an underground mall – the Weston Link – which gives them twice the

---

## UNDERGROUND EDINBURGH

As Edinburgh expanded in the late 18th and early 19th centuries, many old tenements were demolished and new bridges were built to link the Old Town to the newly built areas to its north and south. South Bridge (built between 1785 and 1788) and George IV Bridge (built between 1829 and 1834) lead southwards from the Royal Mile over the deep valley of Cowgate, but so many buildings have been built closely around them that you can hardly tell they are bridges – George IV Bridge has a total of nine arches but only two are visible; South Bridge has no less than 18 hidden arches.

These subterranean vaults were originally used as storerooms, workshops and drinking dens. But as early-19th-century Edinburgh's population was swelled by an influx of penniless Highlanders cleared from their lands, and Irish refugees from the potato famine, the dark, dripping chambers were given over to slum accommodation and abandoned to poverty, filth and crime.

The vaults were eventually cleared in the late 19th century, then lay forgotten until 1994 when the South Bridge vaults were opened to guided tours (see Mercat Tours, p96). Certain chambers are said to be haunted and one particular vault was investigated by paranormal researchers in 2001.

Nevertheless, the most ghoulish aspect of Edinburgh's hidden history dates from much earlier – from the plague that struck the city in 1645. Legend has it that the disease-ridden inhabitants of Mary King's Close (a lane on the northern side of the Royal Mile on the site of the City Chambers – you can still see its blocked-off northern end from Cockburn St) were walled up in their houses and left to perish. When the lifeless bodies were eventually cleared from the houses, they were so stiff that workmen had to hack off limbs to get them through the small doorways and narrow, twisting stairs.

From that day on, the close was said to be haunted by the spirits of the plague victims. The few people who were prepared to live there reported seeing apparitions of severed heads and limbs, and the largely abandoned close fell into ruin. When the Royal Exchange (now the City Chambers) was constructed between 1753 and 1761, it was built over the lower levels of Mary King's Close, which were left intact and sealed off beneath the building.

Interest in the close revived in the 20th century when Edinburgh's city council began to allow occasional guided tours to enter. Visitors have reported many supernatural experiences – the most famous ghost is 'Sarah', a little girl whose sad tale has prompted people to leave gifts of dolls in a corner of one of the rooms. In 2003 the close was opened to the public as the Real Mary King's Close (see p83).

EDINBURGH

temporary exhibition space of the Prado in Madrid and three times that of the Royal Academy in London, as well as housing cloakrooms, a lecture theatre and a restaurant. The galleries have become famous in recent years for 'blockbuster' exhibitions such as 'Monet: The Seine and the Sea', and 'The Age of Titian'.

## NATIONAL GALLERY OF SCOTLAND

Immediately south of the RSA is the **National Gallery of Scotland** (Map pp76-7; ☎ 624 6200; www .nationalgalleries.org; The Mound; admission free, special exhibitions extra; ☒ 10am-5pm daily, to 7pm Thu; ☒ ). Also designed by William Playfair, this imposing classical building with its Ionic porticoes dates from the 1850s. Its octagonal rooms, lit by skylights, have been restored to their original Victorian décor of deep-green carpets and dark-red walls.

The gallery houses an important collection of European art from the Renaissance to postimpressionism, with works by Verrocchio (Leonardo da Vinci's teacher), Tintoretto, Titian, Holbein, Rubens, Van Dyck, Vermeer, El Greco, Poussin, Rembrandt, Gainsborough, Turner, Constable, Monet, Pissaro, Gauguin and Cézanne; each year in January the gallery exhibits its collection of Turner watercolours, bequeathed by Henry Vaughan in 1900.

Room XII is graced by Antonio Canova's white marble sculpture, *The Three Graces*; it is owned jointly with London's Victoria & Albert Museum, to which it will return in late 2008.

The upstairs galleries house portraits by Sir Joshua Reynolds and Sir Henry Raeburn, and a clutch of Impressionists including Monet's luminous *Haystacks*, Van Gogh's demonic *Olive Trees* and Gauguin's hallucinatory *Vision After the Sermon*. But the painting that really catches your eye is the gorgeous portrait of *Lady Agnew of Lochnaw* by John Singer Sargent.

The basement galleries dedicated to Scottish art include glowing portraits by Allan Ramsay and Sir Henry Raeburn, rural scenes by Sir David Wilkie and impressionistic landscapes by William MacTaggart. Look out for Raeburn's iconic *Reverend Robert Walker Skating on Duddingston Loch*, and Sir George Harvey's hugely entertaining *A Schule Skailin* (A School Emptying) – a stern dominie (teacher) looks on as the boys stampede for the classroom door, one reaching for a spinning top confiscated earlier. Kids

will love the fantasy paintings of Sir Joseph Noel Paton in Room B5, incredibly detailed canvases crammed with hundreds of tiny fairies, goblins and elves.

## GEORGE STREET & CHARLOTTE SQUARE

Until the 1990s George St – the major axis of New Town – was the centre of Edinburgh's financial industry, and Scotland's equivalent of Wall St. Now many of the big financial firms have moved to premises in the Exchange office district west of Lothian Rd, and George St's former banks and offices house upmarket shops, pubs and restaurants.

At the western end of George St is **Charlotte Square** (Map pp76-7), the architectural jewel of New Town, designed by Robert Adam shortly before his death in 1791. The northern side of the square is Adam's masterpiece and one of the finest examples of Georgian architecture anywhere. **Bute House** (Map pp76-7), in the centre at No 6, is the official residence of Scotland's first minister.

Next door is the **Georgian House** (Map pp76-7; ☎ 226 2160; 7 Charlotte Sq; adult/child £5/4; ☒ 10am-7pm Jul & Aug, 10am-5pm Apr-Jun, Sep & Oct, 11am-3pm Mar & Nov), which has been beautifully restored and furnished to show how Edinburgh's wealthy elite lived at the end of the 18th century. The walls are decorated with paintings by Allan Ramsay, Sir Henry Raeburn and Sir Joshua Reynolds.

The headquarters of the **National Trust for Scotland** (NTS; Map pp76-7; ☎ 243 9300; www.nts.org.uk; 28 Charlotte Sq; admission free; ☒ 9.30am-5pm Mon-Sat) is on the southern side of the square. As well as a shop, café and information desk, the building contains a restored 1820s **drawing room** ( ☒ 11am-3pm Mon-Fri) with Regency furniture and a collection of 20th-century Scottish paintings.

## ST ANDREW SQUARE

Not as architecturally distinguished as its sister at the opposite end of George St, **St Andrew Square** (Map pp76-7) is dominated by the fluted column of the **Melville Monument** (Map pp76-7), commemorating Henry Dundas, 1st Viscount Melville (1742–1811). Dundas was the most powerful Scottish politician of his time, often referred to when alive as 'Harry IX, the Uncrowned King of Scotland'. The impressive Palladian mansion of **Dundas House** (Map pp76-7), built between 1772 and 1774, on the eastern side of the square, was built for Sir Laurence Dundas (1712–81) – no relation to

Viscount Melville. It has been the head office of the Royal Bank of Scotland since 1825 and has a spectacular domed banking hall dating from 1857 (you can nip inside for a look).

A short distance along George St is the **Church of St Andrew & St George** (Map pp76–7), built in 1784 with an unusual oval nave. It was the scene of the Disruption of 1843, when 451 dissenting ministers left the Church of Scotland to form the Free Church.

Just north of the square at the junction with Queen St is the Venetian Gothic palace of the **Scottish National Portrait Gallery** (Map pp76-7; ☎ 624 6200; www.nationalgalleries.org; 1 Queen St; admission free; ☺ 10am-5pm daily, to 7pm Thu). Its galleries illustrate Scottish history through portraits and sculptures of famous Scottish personalities, from Robert Burns and Bonnie Prince Charlie to Sean Connery and Billy Connolly. Opening hours are extended during the Edinburgh Festival.

## Calton Hill

Calton Hill (100m), rising dramatically above the eastern end of Princes St, is Edinburgh's acropolis, its summit scattered with grandiose memorials mostly dating from the first half of the 19th century. It is also one of the best viewpoints in Edinburgh, with a panorama that takes in the castle, Holyrood, Arthur's Seat, the Firth of Forth, New Town and the full length of Princes St.

On the southern side of the hill, on Regent Rd, is the modernist façade of **St Andrew's House** (Map pp76–7), built between 1936 and 1939, which housed the civil servants of the Westminster government's Scottish Office until they were moved to the new Scottish Executive building in Leith in 1996.

Just beyond St Andrew's House and on the opposite side of the road is the imposing **Royal High School** (Map pp76–7) building, dating from 1829 and modelled on the Temple of Theseus in Athens. Former pupils include Robert Adam, Alexander Graham Bell and Sir Walter Scott. It now stands empty. To its east, on the other side of Regent Rd, is the 1830 **Burns Monument** (Map pp72–3), a Greek-style memorial to Robert Burns.

You can reach the summit of Calton Hill via the road beside the Royal High School or by the stairs at the eastern end of Waterloo Pl. The largest structure on the summit is the **National Monument** (Map pp76–7), an over-ambitious attempt to replicate the Parthenon

and intended to honour Scotland's dead in the Napoleonic Wars. Construction – paid for by public subscription – began in 1822, but funds ran dry when only 12 columns were complete.

Looking a bit like an upturned telescope – the similarity is intentional – and offering even better views, the **Nelson Monument** (Map pp76-7; ☎ 556 2716; Calton Hill; admission £3; ☺ 1-6pm Mon, 10am-6pm Tue-Sat Apr-Sep, 10am-3pm Mon-Sat Oct-Mar) was built to commemorate Admiral Lord Nelson's victory at Trafalgar in 1805.

The design of the **City Observatory** (Map pp76–7), built in 1818, was based on the ancient Greek Temple of the Winds in Athens. Its original function was to provide a precise, astronomical time-keeping service for marine navigators, but smoke from Waverley train station forced the astronomers to move to Blackford Hill in the south of Edinburgh in 1895.

## Dean Village

If you follow Queensferry St northwards from the western end of Princes St, you come to **Dean Bridge** (Map pp72–3), designed by Thomas Telford and built between 1829 and 1832. Down in the valley just west of the bridge is Dean Village (from 'dene', a Scots word for valley). It was founded as a milling community by the canons of Holyrood Abbey in the 12th century and by 1700 there were 11 water mills here operated by the Incorporation of Baxters (the bakers' trade guild). One of the old mill buildings has been converted into flats, and the village is now an attractive residential area.

### SCOTTISH NATIONAL GALLERY OF MODERN ART & DEAN GALLERY

Set in an impressive neoclassical building surrounded by a landscaped sculpture park some 500m west of Dean Village is the **Scottish National Gallery of Modern Art** (Map pp72-3; ☎ 624 6200; www.nationalgalleries.org; 75 Belford Rd; admission free, fee for special exhibitions; ☺ 10am-5pm). The collection concentrates on 20th-century art, with various European movements represented by the likes of Matisse, Picasso, Kirchner, Magritte, Miró, Mondrian and Giacometti. American and English artists are also represented, but most space is given to Scottish painters – from the Scottish colourists of the early 20th century to contemporary artists such as Peter Howson and Ken Currie. There's an excellent café downstairs, and the surrounding park features sculptures by Henry Moore, Rachel Whiteread and Barbara Hepworth among others, as well as a 'landform artwork' by Charles Jencks.

Directly across Belford Rd from the National Gallery of Modern Art, another neoclassical mansion houses its annexe, the **Dean Gallery** (Map pp72-3; ☎ 624 6200; 73 Belford Rd; admission free, special exhibitions extra; ♥ 10am-5pm). The Dean holds the Gallery of Modern Art's collection of Dada and surrealist art, including works by Dali, Giacometti and Picasso, and a large collection of sculpture and graphic art created by the Edinburgh-born sculptor Sir Eduardo Paolozzi.

## Leith

Two miles northeast of the city centre, Leith (Map p71) has been Edinburgh's seaport since the 14th century and remained an independent burgh with its own town council until it was incorporated by the city in the 1920s. Like many of Britain's dockland areas, it fell into decay in the decades following WWII but has been undergoing a revival since the late 1980s. Old warehouses have been turned into luxury flats, and a lush crop of trendy bars and restaurants has sprouted along the waterfront. The area was given an additional boost in the late 1990s when the Scottish Executive (a government department) moved to a new building on Leith docks. The city council has now formulated a major redevelopment plan for the entire Edinburgh waterfront from Leith to Granton, the first phase of which is **Ocean Terminal** (Map p71), a shopping and leisure complex that includes the former Royal Yacht *Britannia* and a berth for visiting cruise liners. Parts of Leith are still a bit rough but it's a distinctive corner of the city and well worth exploring.

One of Scotland's biggest tourist attractions is the former **Royal Yacht Britannia** (Map p71; ☎ 555 5566; www.royalyachtbritannia.co.uk; Ocean Terminal, Leith; adult/child £9.50/5.50; ♥ 9.30am-6pm Apr-Sep, 10am-5pm Oct-Mar, last admission 1½hr before closing; ⚐ ). She was the British royal family's floating home during their foreign travels from the time of her launch in 1953 until her decommissioning in 1997, and is now moored permanently in front of Ocean Terminal.

The tour, which you take at your own pace with an audio guide (available in 20 languages), gives an intriguing insight into the Queen's private tastes – *Britannia* was one of the few places where the royal family could enjoy true privacy. The entire ship is a monument to 1950s' décor and technology, and the accommodation reveals Her Majesty's preference for simple, unfussy surroundings – the Queen's own bed is surprisingly tiny and plain.

There was nothing simple or unfussy, however, about the running of the ship. When the Queen travelled, along with her went 45 members of the royal household, five tons of luggage and a Rolls-Royce that was carefully squeezed into a specially built garage on the deck. The ship's company consisted of an admiral, 20 officers and 220 yachtsmen. The decks (of Burmese teak) were scrubbed daily, but all work near the royal accommodation was carried out in complete silence and had to be finished by 8am. A thermometer was kept in the Queen's bathroom to make sure that the water was the correct temperature, and when in harbour one yachtsman was charged with ensuring that the angle of the gangway never exceeded 12 degrees. And note the mahogany windbreak that was added to the balcony deck in front of the bridge. It was put there to stop wayward breezes from blowing up skirts and inadvertently revealing the royal undies.

The Majestic Tour bus (see p96) runs from Waverley Bridge to *Britannia* during opening times. Alternatively, take Lothian Bus 1, 11, 22, 34, 35 or 36 to Ocean Terminal.

## Greater Edinburgh
### CRAIGMILLAR CASTLE

If you want to explore a Scottish fortress away from the crowds that throng Edinburgh Castle, try **Craigmillar Castle** (Map p71; ☎ 661 4445; Craigmillar Castle Rd; adult/child £4/2; ♥ 9.30am-5.30pm Apr-Sep, 9.30am-4.30pm Sat-Wed Oct-Mar). Dating from the 15th century, the tower house rises above two sets of machicolated curtain walls. Mary, Queen of Scots took refuge here after the murder of Rizzio; it was here too that plans to murder her husband Darnley were laid. Look for the prison cell complete with built-in sanitation, something some 'modern' British prisons only finally managed in 1996.

The castle is 2.5 miles southeast of the city centre. Take bus 33 eastbound from Princes St to Old Dalkeith Rd and walk 500m up Craigmillar Castle Rd.

### CRAMOND

With its moored yachts, stately swans and whitewashed houses spilling down the hill side at the mouth of the River Almond, Cramond is the most picturesque corner of Edinburgh. It is also rich in history. The Romans built a fort here in the 2nd century AD (the village's name comes from Caer Amon, 'the fort on the River Almond'), but recent archaeological excavations have revealed evidence of a Bronze Age settlement dating from 8500 BC, the oldest known site in the whole of Scotland.

Cramond, which was originally a mill village, has a historic 17th-century church and a 15th-century tower house, as well as some rather unimpressive Roman remains, but most people come to enjoy the walks along the river to the ruined mills and to stroll along the seafront. On the riverside, opposite the cottage on the far bank, is the **Maltings** ( ☎ 312 6034; Cramond Village; admission free; ☷ 2-5pm Sat & Sun Jun-Sep, daily during Edinburgh Festival), which hosts an interesting exhibition on Cramond's history.

Cramond is 5 miles northwest of the city centre; take bus 41 from The Mound, Princes St (west bound) or Queensferry St to Cramond Glebe Rd, then walk north for 400m.

### EDINBURGH ZOO

Opened in 1913, **Edinburgh Zoo** (Map p71; ☎ 334 9171; www.edinburghzoo.org.uk; 134 Corstorphine Rd; adult/ child £10.50/7.50; ☷ 9am-6pm Apr-Sep, 9am-5pm Oct & Mar, 9am-4.30pm Nov-Feb; ☖ ) is one of the world's leading conservation zoos. Edinburgh's captive breeding programme has saved many endangered species, including Siberian tigers, pygmy hippos and red pandas. The main attractions are the penguins (kept in the world's biggest penguin pool), the sea lion and red panda feeding times (check the website for details), the animal-handling sessions and the Lifelinks 'hands-on' zoology centre.

The zoo is 2.5 miles west of the city centre; take Lothian Bus 12, 26 or 31, First Bus 16, 18, 80 or 86, or the Airlink Bus 100 westbound from Princes St.

### ROYAL BOTANIC GARDEN

Just north of Stockbridge is the lovely **Royal Botanic Garden** (Map p71; ☎ 552 7171; www.rbge.org.uk; 20a Inverleith Row; admission to gardens free, to glasshouses £3.50; ☷ 10am-7pm Apr-Sep, 10am-6pm Mar & Oct, 10am-4pm Nov-Feb). Twenty-eight beautifully landscaped hectares include splendid Victorian palm houses, colourful swathes of rhododendron and azalea, and a world-famous rock garden. The Terrace Café offers good views towards the city centre. Take Lothian Bus 8, 17, 23 or 27 to the East Gate, or the Majestic Tour bus (see p96).

## ACTIVITIES
### Walking

Edinburgh is lucky to have several good walking areas within the city boundary, including Arthur's Seat, Calton Hill, Blackford Hill, Hermitage of Braid, Corstorphine Hill, and the coast and river at Cramond. The **Pentland Hills**, which rise to over 500m, stretch southwest from the city for 15 miles, offering excellent high- and low-level walking.

You can follow the **Water of Leith Walkway** from the city centre to Balerno (8 miles), and continue across the Pentlands to Silverburn (6.5 miles) or Carlops (8 miles), and return to Edinburgh by bus. Another good walk is along the towpath of the **Union Canal**, which begins in Fountainbridge and runs all the way to Falkirk (31 miles). You can return to Edinburgh by bus at Ratho (8.5 miles) or Broxburn (12 miles), and by bus or train from Linlithgow (21 miles).

### Cycling

Edinburgh and its surroundings offer many excellent opportunities for cycling. The main off-road routes from the city centre out to the countryside follow the Union Canal towpath and the Water of Leith Walkway from Tollcross southwestwards to Balerno (7.5 miles) on the edge of the Pentland Hills, and the Innocent Railway Cycle Path from the southern side of Arthur's Seat eastwards to Musselburgh (5 miles) and on to Ormiston and Pencaitland. There are several routes through the Pentland Hills that are suitable for mountain bikes. For details ask at any bike shop or contact the **Pentland Hills Ranger Service** ( ☎ 445 3383). The *Edinburgh City Bike Map* (available from cycle shops) shows all the city's cycle routes.

The friendly and helpful folk at **Edinburgh Cycle Hire & Scottish Cycle Safaris** (Map pp76-7; ☎ 556 5560; www.cyclescotland.co.uk; 29 Blackfriars St; per day £10-15, per week £50-70; ☷ 10am-6pm Mon-Sat) rent out top-quality bikes; rates include helmet, lock and repair kit. You can hire tents and touring equipment too. The company also organises cycle tours in Edinburgh and all over Scotland – check the website for details.

### Golf

There are no fewer than 19 golf courses in Edinburgh – the following are two of the best city courses.

**Braid Hills Public Golf Course** ( ☎ 447 6666; Braid Hills Approach; green fees weekday/weekend £18.50/23) A scenic but challenging course to the south of the city centre.

**EDINBURGH**

**Lothianburn Golf Course** ( ☎ 445 2288; 106a Biggar Rd, Fairmilehead; green fees weekday/weekend £20/25) Enjoys a scenic setting at the foot of the Pentland Hills, south of the city.

## Swimming

The Firth of Forth is a bit on the chilly side for enjoyable swimming, but there are several indoor alternatives. The **Royal Commonwealth Pool** (Map pp72-3; ☎ 667 7211; 21 Dalkeith Rd; adult/child £4.20/1.80; ⏰ 6am-9.30pm Mon-Fri, 10am-4.30pm Sat & Sun, closed 9-10am Wed) is Edinburgh's main facility, with a 50m pool, diving pool, children's pool, flumes and fitness centre.

## Water Sports

The sheltered waters of the Firth of Forth host all kinds of water sports. **Port Edgar Marina & Sailing School** ( ☎ 331 3330; www.edinburghleisure.co.uk; Shore Rd, Queensferry; ⏰ 9am-7.30pm Apr-Oct, 9am-4.30pm Nov-Mar) offers a wide range of courses in sailing, canoeing and power-boating.

## Horse Riding

There are many scenic bridle paths suitable for horse riding in the countryside around Edinburgh, and a number of riding schools offer two- and three-hour treks as well as tuition, including **Tower Farm Riding Stables** ( ☎ 664 3375; www.towerfarm.org; 85 Liberton Dr; per hr £23) in the south of the city.

## WALKING TOUR

Edinburgh's Old Town stretches along the Royal Mile to the east of the castle and south to the Grassmarket and Cowgate. This walk explores a few of the many interesting nooks and crannies around the upper part of the Royal Mile, and involves a fair bit of climbing up and down steep stairs and closes. Allow one to two hours.

Begin at Castlehill and the start of the Royal Mile. The 17th-century house on the right, above the steps of North Castle Wynd, is known as **Cannonball House (1)** because of the iron ball lodged in the wall (look between,

---

**WALK FACTS**

**Distance:** 0.75 miles
**Duration:** one to two hours

---

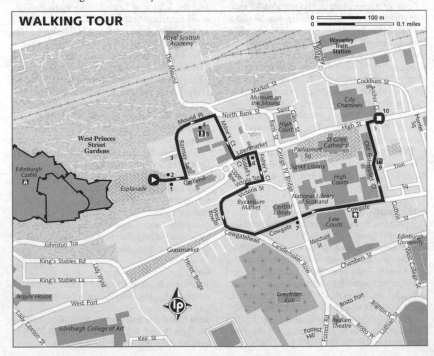

## WALKING TOUR

and slightly below, the two largest windows). It was not fired in anger, but instead marks the gravitation height to which water would flow naturally from the city's first piped water supply.

The low, rectangular building across the street (now a touristy tartan-weaving mill) was originally the reservoir that held the Old Town's water supply. On its west wall is the **Witches Well (2)**, where a modern bronze fountain commemorates around 4000 people (mostly women) who were burned or strangled in Edinburgh between 1479 and 1722 for suspicion of witchcraft.

Go past the reservoir and turn left down Ramsay Lanc, and take a look at **Ramsay Garden (3)** – one of the most desirable addresses in Edinburgh – where late-19th-century apartments were built around the nucleus of the octagonal Ramsay Lodge, once home to poet Allan Ramsay. The cobbled street continues around to the right below student residences, to the twin towers of the **New College (4)** – home to Edinburgh University's Faculty of Divinity. Nip into the courtyard to see the **statue of John Knox (5)**.

Just past New College turn right and climb up the stairs into Milne's Ct, a student residence. Exit into Lawnmarket, cross the street (bearing slightly left) and duck into **Riddell's Court (6)** at No 322–328, a typical Old Town close. You'll find yourself in a small courtyard, but the house in front of you (built in 1590) was originally the edge of the street (the building you just walked under was added in 1726; check the doorway on the right). The arch with the inscription *Vivendo discimus* ('we live and learn') leads into the original 16th-century courtyard.

Go back into the street, turn right, and then right again down Fisher's Close, which ejects you onto the delightful Victoria Terrace, poised above the cobbled curve of Victoria St. Wander right, enjoying the view, then descend the stairs at the foot of Upper Bow and continue downhill to the Grassmarket. Turn left along the gloomy defile of the Cowgate. The first bridge you come to is **George IV Bridge (7**; built 1829–34). Although you can see only one arch here, there are nine in total – one more is visible a block south at Merchant St, but the rest are hidden beneath and between the surrounding buildings, as are the haunted vaults of South Bridge, further west along Cowgate.

Pass under George IV Bridge. The buildings to your right are the new Law Courts, while high up to the left you can see the complex of buildings behind Parliament Sq. Past the courts and on the right is **Tailors Hall (8**; built 1621, extended 1757), now a hotel and bar, but formerly the meeting place of the 'Companie of Tailzeours' (Tailors' Guild).

Turn left and climb up Old Fishmarket Close, and perhaps stop for lunch at the brasserie **Café Marlayne (9**; p102). Emerge once more into the Royal Mile. Across the street and slightly downhill on the left is **Anchor Close (10)**, named for a tavern that once stood there. It hosted the Crochallan Fencibles, an 18th-century drinking club that provided its patrons with an agreeable blend of intellectual debate and intoxicating liquor. The club was founded by William Smellie, editor of the first edition of the *Encyclopedia Britannica;* its best-known member was Robert Burns, the poet.

Should you wish to wet your own whistle, more than a dozen hostelries lie between here and Holyrood. And it's downhill all the way…

## EDINBURGH FOR CHILDREN
Edinburgh has a multitude of attractions for children, and most things to see and do are child-friendly. Kids under five travel for free on Edinburgh buses, and five- to 15-year-olds pay a flat fare of 60p. However, you should be aware that the majority of Scottish pubs, even those that serve bar meals, are forbidden by law to admit children under the age of 14; even in the family-friendly pubs (ie those in possession of a Children's Certificate), under-14s are only admitted between the hours of 11am and 8pm, and only when accompanied by an adult aged 18 or over.

The Edinburgh & Scotland Information Centre (p79) has lots of info on children's events, and the handy guidebook *Edinburgh for Under Fives* can be found in most bookshops. The *List* magazine (www.list.co.uk) has a special Kids section listing children's activities and events in and around Edinburgh. The week-long **Children's International Theatre Festival** ( ☎ 225 8050; www.imaginate.org.uk) takes place each year in late May/early June.

There are good, safe **playgrounds** in most Edinburgh parks, including Princes Street Gardens West, Inverleith Park (opposite the Royal Botanic Garden), George V Park (New Town), the Meadows and Bruntsfield Links.

## A VOICE FROM THE GRAVE

Adam Lyal (deceased) – aka Andrew Henderson – is the ghost of an Edinburgh highwayman who was hanged at the Tolbooth in 1811, and a tour leader with Cadies & Witchery Tours (p96).

**Edinburgh is famous for its grisly past. What makes the city such a good place for a ghost to, er, live?** I would have to say it's the tremendous richness of history in this city. The stories alone are impressive, but the physical presence of the past is overwhelming. There are buildings in Edinburgh which are 400 to 500 years old, still standing in their original forms! You can walk around the Old Town and get a feel for a real medieval city with its narrow alleyways and wynds. On the other hand, you could pop over to the New Town and enjoy the more 'modern' Georgian world (it's only 300 years old, so there aren't quite so many ghosts there!). History is everywhere you look in Edinburgh, so it's pretty easy to understand why it would be so thoroughly haunted!

**Where are you most likely to meet a ghost (apart from one of your tours)?** Historically speaking, the largest number of hauntings is concentrated in just one street, the West Bow (which is now part of Victoria St, near the Grassmarket). Even more remarkably, they're all down to just one man, the Wizard of the West Bow, Major Thomas Weir. He was a self-confessed sorcerer, whose evil was apparently so intense that after his death the area around his home was the site of regular (sometimes nightly) supernatural occurrences for over 250 years! It's a little quieter now, but overall, it's still the best place to look!

**What are Edinburgh's spookiest places?** My favourite spooky places in Edinburgh are probably the graveyards, though I would hesitate to recommend that anyone go to visit them at night! The best are probably those around St John's and St Cuthbert's churches on the corner of Lothian Rd and Princes St, though the spookiest by far is undoubtedly the Old Calton Burial Ground on Waterloo Rd, home to such departed notables as philosopher David Hume.

**Where would a hard-working ghoul go to slake his thirst at the end (or beginning) of an evening's haunting?** It might be expected that we'd be found in one of those expensive theme pubs where they hang rubber skeletons on the walls and spray you with cobwebs when you enter, but no! We at the Cadies still subscribe to the ancient and unofficial motto of our trade: 'Poor but Honest' (or at least the former, if not the latter). Therefore we tend to do our carousing in some of the Old Town's marvellous little howffs, such as the Jolly Judge (p107) or the Last Drop (p107), named after the nearby gallows in the Grassmarket. Of course, when we've been walking the streets all night proximity is a virtue, and we can often be found in the Bow Bar (p107) just two doors up from our shop, which is very cosy, extremely friendly and stocks a greater array of whiskies than you could hope to find anywhere else!

**Can you recommend any good 'off-the-beaten-track' place to go/things to do in Edinburgh?** The wonderful thing about Edinburgh's Old Town is that so much of it is 'off the beaten track'! One of my favourite venues would have to be Whistle Binkie's (p109). It's quite hard to spot, being located under the actual street with only a doorway on the pavement leading down, but it's well worth finding. Of course, there are other tours in Edinburgh, and the one I'd recommend to anyone is the Literary Pub Tour (p96). Booze, history and Scottish literature? It's a work of genius!

Some more ideas for outdoor activities include exploring the **Royal Botanic Garden** (p91), going to see the animals at **Edinburgh Zoo** (p91), visiting the statue of **Greyfriars Bobby** (p85) and feeding the swans and playing on the beach at **Cramond** (p90). During the Edinburgh and Fringe Festivals there is also plenty of street theatre for kids, especially on the High St and at the foot of The Mound, and in December there's an open-air ice rink and fairground rides in Princes Street Gardens.

If it's raining, you can visit the Discovery Centre, a hands-on activity zone on Level 3 of the **Museum of Scotland** (p86), play on the flumes at the **Royal Commonwealth Pool** (p92), try out the earthquake simulator at **Our Dynamic Earth** (p84), or take a tour of the haunted **Real Mary King's Close** (p83).

## Childminding Services

For full listings of government-approved childminding services, check out **Childcare Link** (www.childcarelink.gov.uk), or **City of Edinburgh Childcare Information Service** ( ☎ 0800 032 0323). The following are reliable Edinburgh agencies that charge from £6 an hour for babysitting:

**Family Circle Care** ( ☎ 554 9500; www.familycircles .org; 22 Tower St, Leith)

**Panda's Nanny Agency** ( ☎ 663 3967; www.pandas nannyagency.co.uk; 22 Durham Pl, Bonnyrigg)

## QUIRKY EDINBURGH

Edinburgh is full of unusual attractions and out-of-the-way corners that most visitors never see – even though they may be standing just a few metres away. Here are a few of the city's less mainstream attractions.

In complete contrast to the austerity of most of Edinburgh's religious buildings, the 19th-century, neo-Romanesque **Mansfield Place Church** (Map pp72-3; ☎ 474 8033; www.mansfieldtraquair .uk; Mansfield Pl; ⊗ 1-4pm 2nd Sun of the month, 11am-1pm Sun-Thu during Edinburgh Festival Fringe) at the foot of Broughton St contains a remarkable series of Renaissance-style frescoes painted in the 1890s by Irish-born artist Phoebe Anna Traquair (1852–1936). Now undergoing restoration, the murals are on view to the public at certain times (check the website for any changes).

The **Museum on the Mound** (Map pp76-7; ☎ 529 1288; The Mound; admission free; ⊗ 10am-5pm Tue-Fri, 1-5pm Sat & Sun), housed in the Bank of Scotland's splendid Georgian HQ, is a treasure trove of gold coins, bullion chests, safes, banknotes, forgeries, cartoons and lots of fascinating old documents and photographs charting the history of Scotland's oldest bank.

Musicians will enjoy the **Edinburgh University Collection of Historic Musical Instruments** (Map pp76-7; ☎ 650 2423; Reid Concert Hall, Teviot Pl; admission free; ⊗ 3-5pm Wed, 10am-1pm Sat year-round, 2-5pm Mon-Fri during Edinburgh Festival), which contains more than 1000 instruments ranging from a 400-year-old lute to a 1959 synthesiser.

Further off the beaten track are the **Surgeons' Hall Museums** (Map pp76-7; ☎ 527 1649; www.rcsed

.ac.uk; Nicolson St; adult/child £5/3; ⊗ noon-4pm Mon-Fri). The **History of Surgery Museum** is a fascinating look at surgery in Scotland from the 15th century – when barbers supplemented their income with blood-letting, amputations and other surgical procedures – to the present day. The highlight is the exhibit on Burke and Hare, which includes Burke's death mask and a pocket book bound in his skin. Covering dentistry, with its wince-inducing collections of extraction tools, is the adjacent **Menzies Campbell Dental Museum**. The **Pathology Museum** houses a gruesome but compelling 19th-century collection of diseased organs and massive tumours pickled in formaldehyde.

While ghost tours of Edinburgh's underground vaults and haunted graveyards have become a mainstream attraction, few tourists have yet explored **Gilmerton Cove** ( ☎ 557 6464; www.gilmertoncove.org.uk; 16 Drum St, Gilmerton; adult/ child £5/3; ⊗ tours 10am-5pm Sat, 7pm Wed, Sat & Sun). Hidden in the southern suburbs, the mysterious cove is a series of manmade subterranean caverns hacked out of the rock, their origin and function unknown. Book through Mercat Tours (see p96).

Another refreshing alternative to the mainstream walking tours is offered by **Celtic Trails** ( ☎ 448 2869; www.celtictrails.co.uk; tours £25-49), whose knowledgeable owner Jackie Queally leads guided tours of Edinburgh's ancient and sacred sites, covering subjects such as Celtic mythology, geomancy, sacred geometry and the Knights Templar.

And finally, if you're in Edinburgh on the first Friday of August, head west to the village of Queensferry (p114) to see the bizarre **Burry Man**. As part of the village gala day, a local man spends nine hours roaming the streets wearing a woolly suit, which has been laboriously covered from head to toe in big, green, prickly burrs. One glance at his costume – he looks like a child's drawing of a Martian, with added prickles – would make you think he's suffering a medieval punishment, but it's actually a great honour to be selected.

## TOURS
### Bus Tours

Open-topped buses leave from Waverley Bridge outside the main train station and offer hop-on, hop-off tours of the main sights, taking in New Town, the Grassmarket and the Royal Mile. They're a good way to get your bearings, although with a bus map and a Day Saver bus ticket (£2.50) you could do much the same thing but without the commentary. Tours run daily, year-round, except for 24 and 25 December.

Tickets for the following three tours remain valid for 24 hours.

**Edinburgh Tour** ( ☎ 555 6363; adult/child £9/3) Lothian Buses' bright red buses depart every 20 minutes from Waverley Bridge.

**Mac Tours** ( ☎ 220 0770; adult/child £9/3) Offers similar tours to Edinburgh Tour, but in a vintage bus.

**Majestic Tour** ( ☎ 220 0770; adult/child £9/3) Runs every 30 minutes (every 20 minutes in July and August) from Waverley Bridge to the Royal Yacht *Britannia* at Ocean Terminal via the Royal Botanic Garden and Newhaven, returning via Leith Walk, Holyrood and the Royal Mile.

## Walking Tours

There are plenty of organised walks around Edinburgh, many of them related to ghosts, murders and witches. For starting times of individual walks, phone or check the following websites:

**Black Hart Storytellers** ( ☎ 225 9044; www.blackhart .uk.com; adult/concession £8.50/6.50) Not suitable for young children. The 'City of the Dead' tour of Greyfriars Kirkyard is probably the best of Edinburgh's 'ghost' tours. Many people have reported encounters with the 'McKenzie Poltergeist'.

**Cadies & Witchery Tours** ( ☎ 225 6745; www .witcherytours.com; adult/child £7.50/5) The becloaked and pasty-faced Adam Lyal (deceased) leads a 'Murder & Mystery' tour of the Old Town's darker corners. These tours are famous for their 'jumper-ooters' – costumed actors who 'jump oot' when you least expect it. Ooooh, scary.

**Edinburgh Literary Pub Tour** ( ☎ 226 6665; www .edinburghliterarypubtour.co.uk; adult/student £9/7) An enlightening two-hour trawl through Edinburgh's literary history – and its associated howffs – in the entertaining company of Messrs Clart and McBrain. One of the best of Edinburgh's walking tours.

**Mercat Tours** ( ☎ 557 6464; www.mercattours .com; adult/child £8.50/5) Mercat offers a wide range of fascinating tours including history walks in the Old Town and Leith, 'Ghosts & Ghouls' tours and visits to haunted underground vaults.

**Trainspotting Tours** ( ☎ 555 2500; www.leithwalks .co.uk; per person £7) A tour of locations from Irvine Welsh's notorious novel *Trainspotting*, delivered with wit and enthusiasm.

## FESTIVALS & EVENTS

Edinburgh hosts an amazing number of festivals throughout the year, notably the Edinburgh International Festival, the Edinburgh Festival Fringe and the Military Tattoo, which are all held around the same time in August (see the boxed text, opposite). Hogmanay, Scottish New Year's celebrations, is also a peak party time; see the boxed text, below.

### April

**Edinburgh International Science Festival** ( ☎ 558 7666; www.sciencefestival.co.uk) First held in 1987, it hosts a wide range of events, including talks, lectures, exhibitions, demonstrations, guided tours and interactive experiments designed to stimulate, inspire and challenge. From dinosaurs to ghosts to alien life forms, there's something to interest everyone. The festival runs over 10 days at the beginning of April.

### May

**Scottish International Children's Festival** ( ☎ 225 6440; www.imaginate.org.uk) This is Britain's biggest festival of performing arts for children, with events suitable for kids from three to 12. Groups from around the world perform classic tales like *Hansel and Gretel* as well as new material written specially for children. The festival takes place annually in the last week of May.

---

### EDINBURGH'S HOGMANAY

Traditionally, the New Year has always been a more important celebration for Scots than Christmas. In towns, cities and villages all over the country, people fill the streets at midnight on 31 December to wish each other a Guid New Year and, yes, to knock back a dram or six to keep the cold at bay.

In 1993 Edinburgh's city council had the excellent idea of spicing up Hogmanay by organising some events, laying on some live music in Princes St and issuing an open invitation to the rest of the world. Most of them turned up, or so it seemed, and had such a good time that they told all their pals and came back again the next year. Now **Edinburgh's Hogmanay** ( ☎ 529 3914; www.edinburghshogmanay.com) is the biggest winter festival in Europe, regularly pulling in more than 250,000 partying punters. Events run from 29 December to 1 January, and include a torchlight procession, huge street party and a New Year's Day triathlon. To get into the main party area in the city centre after 8pm on 31 December you'll need a ticket – book well in advance.

## FESTIVAL CITY

August in Edinburgh sees a frenzy of festivals, with half a dozen world-class events running at the same time.

The month kicks off with the **Edinburgh Military Tattoo** (Map pp76–7; ☎ 0870 755 5118; www .edintattoo.co.uk; Tattoo Office, 32 Market St), a spectacular display of military marching bands, massed pipes and drums, acrobats, cheerleaders and motorcycle display teams, all played out in front of the magnificent backdrop of the floodlit castle. Each show traditionally finishes with a lone piper, dramatically lit, playing a lament on the battlements. The Tattoo takes place over the first three weeks of August (from a Friday to a Saturday); there's one show at 9pm Monday to Friday and two (at 7.30pm and 10.30pm) on Saturday, but no performance on Sunday.

First held in 1947 to mark a return to peace after the ordeal of WWII, the **Edinburgh International Festival** ( ☎ 473 2099; www.eif.co.uk) is festooned with superlatives – the oldest, the biggest, the most famous, the best in the world. The original was a modest affair, but today hundreds of the world's top musicians and performers congregate in Edinburgh for three weeks of diverse and inspirational music, opera, theatre and dance.

Tickets for popular events – especially music and opera – sell out quickly, so it's best to book as far in advance as possible. You can buy tickets in person at the Hub (Map pp76–7), or by phone, fax or internet. Edinburgh's annual culture-fest takes place over the three weeks ending on the first Saturday in September; the programme is usually available from April.

When the first Edinburgh Festival was held in 1947, there were eight theatre companies who didn't make it onto the main programme. Undeterred, they grouped together and held their own minifestival, on the fringe, and an Edinburgh institution was born. Today the **Edinburgh Festival Fringe** (Map pp76–7; ☎ 226 0026; www.edfringe.com; Edinburgh Festival Fringe Office, 180 High St) is *the* biggest festival of the performing arts anywhere in the world.

Since 1990 the Fringe has been dominated by stand-up comedy, but the sheer variety of shows on offer is staggering – everything from chain-saw juggling to performance poetry to Tibetan yak-milk gargling. So how do you decide what to see? There are daily reviews in the *Scotsman* newspaper – one good *Scotsman* review and a show sells out in hours – but the best recommendation is word of mouth. If you have the time, go to at least one unknown show – it may be crap, but at least you'll have your obligatory 'worst show I ever saw' story.

The big names play at the megavenues like the **Assembly Rooms** ( ☎ 220 4348; www.assembly roomsedinburgh.co.uk; 54 George St) and the **Pleasance** ( ☎ 556 6550; www.pleasance.co.uk/edinburgh; 60 Pleasance), and charge megaprices (£10 a ticket and more, with one famous comic notoriously charging £37.50 in 2007), but there are plenty of good shows in the £5 to £7 range and, best of all, lots of free stuff. Fringe Sunday – usually the second Sunday – is a smorgasbord of free performances, staged in the Meadows park to the south of the city centre.

The Fringe take place over 3½ weeks in August, the last two weeks overlapping with the first two of the Edinburgh International Festival.

Held in a little village of marquees in the middle of Charlotte Sq, the **Edinburgh International Book Festival** ( ☎ 228 5444; www.edbookfest.co.uk) is a fun fortnight of talks, readings, debates, lectures, book signings and meet-the-author events, with a café and tented bookshop thrown in. The festival lasts for two weeks in August (usually the first two weeks of the Edinburgh International Festival).

## June

**Scottish Traditional Beer Festival** (www.camra.org .uk; Assembly Rooms, 54 George St) A celebration of all things fermented and yeasty, Scotland's biggest beer-fest gives you the opportunity to sample a wide range of traditionally brewed beers from Scotland and around the world. Froth-topped bliss. The festival is held on the second weekend in June.

**Royal Highland Show** ( ☎ 335 6200; www.royal highlandshow.org; Royal Highland Centre, Ingliston)

Scotland's hugely popular national agricultural show is a four-day feast of all things rural, with everything from show-jumping and tractor-driving to sheep-shearing and falconry. Countless pens are filled with coiffed show-cattle and pedicured prize-ewes. The show is held over a long weekend (Thursday to Sunday) in late June.

**Edinburgh International Film Festival** ( ☎ 229 2550; www.edfilmfest.org.uk) One of the original Edinburgh Festival trinity, having first been staged in 1947 along with the International Festival and the Fringe, the two-week film festival moved its dates from August to June starting in 2008. It is a major international event, serving as a showcase for new British and European films, and staging the European premieres of one or two Hollywood blockbusters.

## July
**Edinburgh International Jazz & Blues Festival**
( ☎ 467 5200; www.edinburghjazzfestival.co.uk) Held annually since 1978, the Jazz & Blues Festival pulls in top talent from all over the world. The festival runs for nine days, beginning on the last Friday in July (the week before the Fringe and Tattoo begin). The first weekend sees a Mardi Gras street parade on Saturday from the City Chambers, up the Royal Mile and down Victoria St into the Grassmarket, for an afternoon of free, open-air music. On the Sunday there's a series of free concerts at the Ross Bandstand in Princes Street Gardens.

## August
See the boxed text, p97, for details of August's festivals.

## December
**Edinburgh's Christmas** ( ☎ 529 3914; www.edin burghschristmas.com) The newest of the Scottish capital's festivals, first held in 2000, the Christmas bash includes a big street parade, a fairground and Ferris wheel, and an open-air ice rink in Princes Street Gardens. The celebrations are held over the three weeks before Christmas.
**Edinburgh's Hogmanay** See boxed text, p96.

# SLEEPING
A boom in hotel building has seen Edinburgh's tourist capacity swell significantly in the last decade, but you can guarantee that the city will still be packed to the gills during the festival period (August) and over Hogmanay (New Year). If you want a room during these periods, book as far in advance as possible – a year ahead if possible. In general, it's best to book ahead for accommodation at Easter and from mid-May to mid-September.

Hotels and backpacker hostels are found throughout the Old and New Towns, while midrange B&Bs and guesthouses are concentrated outside the centre in the suburbs of Tollcross, Bruntsfield, Newington and Pilrig.

If you're driving, don't even think about staying in the city centre unless your hotel has its own private car park – parking in the centre is a nightmare. Instead, look for somewhere in a suburb like Newington, where there's a chance of finding free, on-street parking (even then, don't bet on getting a parking space

outside the front door). Alternatively, stay outside the city and travel in by bus or train.

Edinburgh accommodation is slightly more expensive than in the rest of Scotland, so the price breakdown in these listings is different from that described on p436 – budget is less than £30, midrange £30 to £60, and top end is more than £60, based on the cost per person for bed and breakfast (B&B), sharing a double room (or for a single dorm bed in a hostel).

## Accommodation Agencies
If you arrive in Edinburgh without a room, the Edinburgh & Scotland Information Centre (p79) booking service will try to find a room to suit you (and will charge a £5 fee if successful). If you have the time, pick up the tourist office's accommodation brochure and ring around yourself.

You can also try VisitScotland's **Booking Hotline** ( ☎ 0845 225 5121), which has a £3 surcharge; or search for accommodation on the **Edinburgh & Lothians Tourist Board** (www.edinburgh .org/accom) website.

## Budget
There are plenty of independent backpacker hostels in Edinburgh, many of them right in the centre of town. Most have 24-hour access and no curfew.

### OLD TOWN & AROUND
**Brodies Hostel** ( ☎ 556 2223; www.brodieshostels.co.uk; Brodies Hostel 1 Map pp76-7; 12 High St; dm £9-22; 🖳 ); Brodies Hostel 2 (Map pp76-7; 93 High St; dm £9-22, d £35-62; 🖳 ) Brodies 1 is a small (50-bed), friendly place with four dorms (three mixed and one women-only) and seriously comfy hotel-quality mattresses and duvets. It has a kitchen and a cosy lounge area with a fireplace and no TV, which makes for good socialising. The newer Brodies 2, up the hill at 93 High St, offers double and family rooms too. Both have top locations bang in the middle of the Royal Mile, and don't accept stag-night groups.

**Castle Rock Hostel** (Map pp76-7; ☎ 225 9666; www .scotlands-top-hostels.com; 15 Johnston Tce; dm £13-15, d £40-55; 🖳 ) With its bright, spacious, single-sex dorms, superb views and friendly staff, the 200-bed Castle Rock has prompted plenty of positive feedback from travellers. It has a great location – the only way to get closer to the castle would be to pitch a tent on the esplanade – a games room, reading lounge and big-screen video nights.

**Edinburgh Backpackers Hostel** (Map pp76-7; ☎ 220 2200; www.hoppo.com; 65 Cockburn St; dm £14-18.50; 💻) Just a short walk from the train station, Edinburgh Backpackers is clean, bright and friendly, with a lively bistro-bar on the ground floor. It's right in the heart of Edinburgh's pub culture, which makes it great for partying but not so good for a peaceful night's sleep.

**St Christopher's Inn** (Map pp76-7; ☎ 226 1446; www.st-christophers.co.uk; 9-13 Market St; dm £9.50-21, d £50-60; 💻 ♿) The 108-bed St Christopher's is just across the street from the Market St entrance to Waverley train station, with accommodation in four- to 14-bed dorms, each with a toilet and power shower. It's a real party joint, with two bars (one chilled, one pumping) and a good-value restaurant, and it accepts stag and hen nights, so don't expect to catch up on your beauty sleep. There's a minumum two-night stay at weekends.

Other recommendations:

**Budget Backpackers Hostel** (Map pp76-7; ☎ 226 6351; www.budgetbackpackers.com; 37-39 Cowgate; dm £12.50-16, tw £48; 💻) Big, colourful, party place.

**Edinburgh Metro** (SYHA; Map pp76-7; ☎ 0870 004 1115; 11/2 Robertson's Close, Cowgate; s £18.50-23; ⊙ Jul & Aug) Summer only, all single rooms.

**Royal Mile Backpackers** (Map pp76-7; ☎ 557 6120; www.scotlands-top-hostels.com; 105 High St; dm £13-15) Small, cosy and quaint.

### NEW TOWN & AROUND

**City Centre Tourist Hostel** (Map pp76-7; ☎ 441 6628; www.citycentrehostel.com; 3rd fl, 5 West Register St; dm £10-20) The City Centre is a small (around 40 beds), clean and relatively quiet hostel, with pine-wood bunks and comfy mattresses in four-, six-, eight- and 10-bed dorms. There's a small kitchen and TV lounge, and a laundry. The location is great – just two minutes' walk from train and bus stations. Don't confuse it with Princes St Backpackers, which shares the entrance.

**Belford Hostel** (Map pp72-3; ☎ 220 2200; www.hoppo.com; 6/8 Douglas Gardens; dm £14-18.50, d £45-65; 💻) An unusual hostel housed in a converted church, the Belford is under the same management as Edinburgh Backpackers. Although some people complain about noise – there are only thin partitions between dorms, and no ceilings – it's cheerful and well run with good facilities. This hostel is about 20 minutes' walk west of Waverley train station. If you're arriving by train from Glasgow or the north,

get off at Haymarket station, which is much closer.

**Edinburgh Central Youth Hostel** (SYHA; Map pp72-3; ☎ 0870 155 3255; www.edinburghcentral.org; 9 Haddington Pl, Leith Walk; dm £17-24.50, s/tw from £33/49; 💻 ♿) This brand new hostel, located about a half-mile north of Waverley train station, is a big (300 beds), flashy, five-star establishment with its own café-bistro as well as self-catering kitchen, smart and comfortable eight-bed dorms and private rooms, and mod cons including key-card entry and plasma-screen TVs.

### OUTSIDE THE CENTRE

**Mortonhall Caravan Park** ( ☎ 664 1533; www.meadowhead.co.uk/mortonhall; 38 Mortonhall Gate, Frogston Rd East; tent sites incl 1 car & 2 people £18, tent & 1 person only £8; ⊙ Mar-Oct) Located in attractive parkland 5 miles southeast of the centre, Mortonhall has an onsite shop, bar and restaurant. Note – the one-person tent rate is not available during the Edinburgh International Festival. Take bus 11 from Princes St (westbound).

**Globetrotter Inn** (Map p71; ☎ 336 1030; www.globetrotterinns.com; 46 Marine Dr; dm £15-19, d & tw £46; 💻) A large and comfortable hostel with luxury bunks, TV lounges, sauna and gym. Good value, but can occasionally be plagued by noisy stag-party groups. It's close to the waterfront and about 20 minutes by a shuttle bus from the city centre (£2.50 return, pick-up from Waterloo Place).

**Menzies Guest House** (Map pp72-3; ☎ 229 4629; www.menzies-guesthouse.co.uk; 33 Leamington Tce; s £47, d £40-60) This is a clean, friendly and well-run place, with seven spacious, high-ceilinged Victorian rooms spread over three floors. The cheaper rooms, with shared bathroom, are small but offer excellent value.

## Midrange

### OLD TOWN

Most of the midrange accommodation in the Old Town is in chain hotels.

**Travelodge Edinburgh Central** (Map pp76-7; ☎ 0871 984 6137; www.travelodge.co.uk; 33 St Mary's St; r £71) Another centrally located chain hotel, convenient for the Royal Mile; twin rooms accommodate up to two adults and two kids.

**Ibis Hotel** (Map pp76-7; ☎ 240 7000; www.ibishotel.com; 6 Hunter Sq; r £89) The Ibis is a spruce, modern, chain hotel, with a superb location just off the Royal Mile. The flat room rate does not include breakfast.

## NEW TOWN

**Dene Guest House** (Map pp72-3; ☎ 556 2700; www .deneguesthouse.com; 7 Eyre Pl; s £20-40, d £40-80; ⚲) The Dene is a friendly and informal place, set in a charming Georgian town house, with a welcoming owner and spacious bedrooms. The inexpensive single rooms make it ideal for solo travellers.

**Castle Guest House** (Map pp76-7; ☎ 225 1975; www .castleguesthouse.com; 38 North Castle St; r per person £30-45) The bedrooms in this lovely traditionally decorated Georgian house – deep red walls and polished wood – are a little spartan, but at these prices and with this location it seems churlish to moan.

**Stuart Guest House** (Map p71; ☎ 557 9030; www .stuartguesthouse.com; 12 East Claremont St; r per person £38-55) A readers' favourite, the Stuart is a welcoming late-Georgian town house with many period features, including staircase, fireplaces and cornices.

**Gerald's Place** (Map pp72-3; ☎ 558 7017; www .geraldsplace.com; 21b Abercromby Pl; d £75-120; ▣) Gerald is an unfailingly charming and helpful host, and his lovely Georgian garden flat has a great location across from a peaceful park and is just an easy stroll from the city centre.

**rick's** (Map pp76-7; ☎ 622 7800; www.ricksedinburgh .co.uk; 55a Frederick St; r £118) One of the first boutique hotels to appear in Edinburgh, rick's offers sharp styling and a laid-back atmosphere. The bedrooms boast walnut headboards and designer fabrics, with fluffy bathrobes, well-stocked minibars and Molton Brown toiletries.

## TOLLCROSS

Tollcross is half a mile south of the western end of Princes St, along Lothian Rd.

**Edinburgh City B&B** (Map pp72-3; ☎ 622 0144; www .edinburghcityguesthouse.co.uk; 31 Grove St; d £50-70) This bright and cheerful four-bedroomed B&B, set in a Georgian-style terrace, boasts a superb location only 10 minutes' walk from the castle, and only 400m from Haymarket train station.

**Amaryllis Guest House** (Map pp72-3; ☎ 229 3293; www.amaryllisguesthouse.com; 21 Upper Gilmore Pl; s £30-40, d £50-80; ℗) The Amaryllis is a cute little Georgian town house on a quiet back street. There are five bedrooms, including a spacious family room that can take two adults and up to four kids. Princes St is only 10 minutes' walk away.

## BRUNTSFIELD

Another half-mile south from Tollcross is Bruntsfield.

**Robertson Guest House** (Map pp72-3; ☎ 229 2652; www.robertson-guesthouse.com; 5 Hartington Gardens; s £35-60, d £58-76; ⚲) Yet another homely Victorian house tucked away in this quiet back street, the Robertson offers a warm welcome and a range of healthy breakfast food, including yogurt, fruit and a vegetarian fry-up.

**Albyn Townhouse** (Map pp72-3; ☎ 229 6459; www .albyntownhouse.co.uk; 16 Hartington Gardens; s £59-79, d £60-90; ⚲) Located at the end of a quiet, tree-lined cul-de-sac, the Albyn is a large Victorian villa whose hospitable owners will make you feel more than welcome. The 10 spacious, high-ceiling bedrooms, brightly done up in shades of pale yellow and green, include three family rooms (sleeping up to four people), with a baby cot available on request.

**Greenhouse** (Map pp72-3; ☎ 622 7634; www.greenhouse -edinburgh.com; 14 Hartington Gardens; s £65-80, d £70-90) The award-winning Greenhouse is a wholly vegetarian and vegan guesthouse, which uses organic and genetically modified-free foods as much as possible – the breakfast menu includes homemade veggie sausages, scrambled tofu, and pancakes with maple syrup – and even the soap and shampoo are free of animal products.

## NEWINGTON

There are lots of guesthouses on and around Minto St and Mayfield Gardens (the continuation of North Bridge and Nicolson St) in Newington. This is the main traffic artery from the south and a main bus route into the city centre.

**Fairholme Guest House** (Map pp72-3; ☎ 667 8645; www.fairholme.co.uk; 13 Moston Tce; r per person £25-45) A pleasant, quiet Victorian villa with five rooms (four with en-suite bathroom), the gay- and vegetarian-friendly Fairholme has been recommended by several travellers. It's on a quiet street close to a main bus route into the city centre.

**Hopetoun** (Map pp72-3; ☎ 667 7691; www.hopetoun .com; 15 Mayfield Rd; s £25-45, d £50-90) The Hopetoun is a homely Victorian terrace about 10 minutes by bus from the city centre. There are two bedrooms, both decorated in bright and cheerful modern shades, with colourful paintings on the walls – no tartan kitschery here – and the landlady is a fount of knowledge about local history and traditional Scottish music.

**Aonach Mor Guest House** (Map pp72-3; ☎ 667 8694; www.aonachmor.com; 14 Kilmaurs Tce; r per person £27-70; 🖳 ) This elegant Victorian terraced house is located on a quiet back street and has seven bedrooms, beautifully decorated, with many original period features. Our favourite is the four-poster bedroom with polished mahogany furniture and period fireplace.

**Pollock Halls of Residence** (Map pp72-3; ☎ 0800 028 7118; www.edinburghfirst.com; 18 Holyrood Park Rd; s £29-39, d £75-84; **P** ) This is a modern student complex belonging to the University of Edinburgh, with 1200 rooms (500 with en-suite bathroom). It's busy and often noisy, but close to the city centre and with Arthur's Seat as a backdrop. Available during Easter and summer vacations.

**Southside Guest House** (Map pp72-3; ☎ 668 4422; www.southsideguesthouse.co.uk; 8 Newington Rd; s £50-65, d £64-130) Though set in a typical Victorian terrace, the Southside transcends the traditional guesthouse category and feels more like a modern boutique hotel. Its eight stylish rooms just ooze interior design, standing out from other Newington B&Bs through the clever use of bold colours and modern furniture.

Other recommendations:

**Kenvie Guest House** (Map pp72-3; ☎ 668 1964; www .kenvie.co.uk; 16 Kilmaurs Rd; r per person £25-40) Situated in a quiet side street but close to a main bus route.

**Salisbury Hotel** (Map pp72-3; ☎ 667 1264; www.the -salisbury.co.uk; 45 Salisbury Rd; s £50-70, d £60-110; **P** ) Boutique-style guesthouse in quiet, comfortable Georgian villa with large garden.

**Sherwood Guest House** (Map pp72-3; ☎ 667 1200; www.sherwood-edinburgh.com; 42 Minto St; s £35-65, d £45-80; **P** ) Clean, comfortable and convenient.

### PILRIG

Northeast of the New Town and west of Leith Walk, Pilrig St has lots of guesthouses, all within about a mile of the centre. To get there, take bus 11 from Princes St.

**Balmoral Guest House** (Map p71; ☎ 554 1857; www .balmoralguesthouse.co.uk; 32 Pilrig St; r per person £22-40) Travellers have recommended this comfortable, five-room B&B located in an elegant, flower-bedecked, Victorian terraced house with lots of period features.

**Ardmor House** (Map p71; ☎ 554 4944; www.ardmor house.com; 74 Pilrig St; s £50-65, d £65-110) The 'gay-owned, straight-friendly' Ardmor is a stylishly renovated Victorian house with five en-suite bedrooms, and all those little touches that

make a place special – an open fire, thick towels, crisp white bed linen and free newspapers at breakfast.

## Top End
### OLD TOWN

**Apex International Hotel** (Map pp76-7; ☎ 300 3456; www .apexhotels.co.uk; 31-35 Grassmarket; r £99-244; **P** ) Centrally located and with good business facilities, the 171-room Apex has stylish, modern décor, large, luxurious bedrooms, a rooftop restaurant and great views of the castle.

**Point Hotel** (Map pp76-7; ☎ 221 5555; www.point-hotel .co.uk; 34 Bread St; s/d from £135/155) Love it or hate it, there's no denying that the cutting-edge design of the Point Hotel is a talking point. For some, its stark minimalism and bold use of colour epitomise the best of contemporary design; for others, it's just plain odd. The superior bedrooms (known as Executive rooms) and the four Jacuzzi-equipped suites are spacious, stylish, and equipped with chic black leather sofas and fantastic views of Edinburgh Castle.

**Witchery by the Castle** (Map pp76-7; ☎ 225 5613; www .thewitchery.com; Castlehill, Royal Mile; ste £295) Set in a 16th-century Old Town house in the shadow of Edinburgh Castle, the Witchery's seven lavish suites are extravagantly furnished with antiques, oak panelling, tapestries, open fires and roll-top baths, and supplied with flowers, chocolates and complimentary champagne. Overwhelmingly popular – you'll have to book several months in advance to be sure of getting a room.

### NEW TOWN

**Dukes of Windsor Street** (Map pp72-3; ☎ 556 6046; www .dukesofwindsor.com; 17 Windsor St; r £80-160) A relaxing eight-bedroom Georgian town house set on a quiet side street, only a few paces from Princes St, Dukes offers an appealing blend of modern sophistication and period atmosphere.

**Scotsman Hotel** (Map pp76-7; ☎ 556 5565; www.thescots manhotelgroup.co.uk; 20 North Bridge; r £270-350; 🖳 🖀 ) The former offices of the *Scotsman* newspaper – opened in 1904 and hailed as 'the most magnificent newspaper building in the world' – are now home to this luxury hotel. Rooms on the northern side enjoy superb views over the New Town and Calton Hill, while the Penthouse Suite (£1200) has its own library and sauna.

**Glasshouse** (Map pp72-3; ☎ 525 8200; www.theeton collection.com; 2 Greenside Pl; r £275. ste £400; **P** ) A palace of cutting-edge design perched atop the Omni Centre at the foot of Calton Hill, and entered through the preserved façade of a 19th-century church, the Glasshouse sports luxury rooms with floor-to-ceiling windows, leather sofas, marble bathrooms and a rooftop garden.

**Balmoral Hotel** (Map pp76-7; ☎ 556 2414; www.the balmoralhotel.com; 1 Princes St; s £290-450, d £345-510; P ⊠) The sumptuous Balmoral – a prominent landmark at the eastern end of Princes St – offers some of the best accommodation in Edinburgh, including suites with 18th-century décor and some superb views over the city.

### OUTSIDE THE CENTRE

**our pick Prestonfield House Hotel** (Map p71; ☎ 668 3346; www.prestonfield.com; Priestfield Rd; r £225-275; ⊡ P) If the blonde wood, brown leather and brushed steel of modern boutique hotels leave you cold, then this is the place for you. A 17th-century mansion set in 20 acres of parkland (complete with peacocks and Highland cattle), Prestonfield House is draped in damask, packed with antiques and decorated in red, black and gold – look out for original tapestries, 17th-century embossed-leather panels, and £500-a-roll hand-painted wallpaper. The hotel's 30 rooms are supplied with all mod cons, including internet access, Bose sound systems, DVD players and flat-screen TVs.

## EATING

In the last decade there has been a boom in the number of restaurants in Edinburgh – the city now has more restaurants per head of population than London. Eating out has become a commonplace event rather than something reserved for special occasions, and the choice of eateries ranges from stylish but inexpensive bistros and cafés to gourmet restaurants.

In addition, most pubs serve food, offering either bar meals or a more formal restaurant or both, but be aware that pubs without a Children's Certificate are not allowed to serve children under the age of 14.

If you want more listings than we can provide here, the excellent *Edinburgh & Glasgow Eating & Drinking Guide* (www.list.co.uk/eating-and-drinking), published annually by *The List* magazine, contains reviews of around 800 restaurants, cafés and bars.

## Old Town & Around
### BUDGET

**Kebab Mahal** (Map pp76-7; ☎ 667 5214; 7 Nicolson Sq; kebabs £4-7; ⏰ noon-midnight Sun-Thu, noon-2am Fri & Sat) Sophisticated it ain't, but this is the Holy Grail of kebab shops – quality shish kebab and tandoori dishes washed down with chilled lassi for less than a fiver. It's a basic cafeteria-style place with a stainless-steel counter and glaring fluorescent lights, but the menu is 100% halal (the Edinburgh Mosque is just 100m along the road) and the kebabs and curries are authentic and delicious.

**Always Sunday** (Map pp76-7; ☎ 622 0667; 170 High St, Royal Mile; mains £4-8; ⏰ 8am-6pm Mon-Fri, 9am-6pm Sat & Sun) If the thought of a greasy fry-up is enough to put you off your breakfast, head instead for this bright and breezy café which dishes up hearty but healthy grub such as fresh fruit smoothies, crisp salads, homemade soups and speciality sandwiches, washed down with Fairtrade coffee or herbal tea.

**our pick Monster Mash** (Map pp76-7; ☎ 225 7069; 4a Forrest Rd; mains £5-7; ⏰ 8am-10pm Mon-Fri, 9am-10pm Sat, 10am-10pm Sun) Classic British grub of the 1950s – bangers and mash, shepherd's pie, fish and chips – is the mainstay of the menu at this nostalgia-fuelled café. But there's a twist – the food is all top-quality nosh freshly prepared from local produce, including Crombie's gourmet sausages. And there's even a wine list!

**Favorit** (Map pp76-7; ☎ 220 6880; 19-20 Teviot Pl; mains £6-8; ⏰ 8am-3am) A stylish café-bar with a retro vibe, Favorit caters for everyone – workers grabbing breakfast on the way to the office, coffee-slurping students skiving off afternoon lectures and late-night clubbers with an attack of the munchies. It also does excellent bacon *butties* (sandwiches).

### MIDRANGE

**Café Marlayne** (Map pp76-7; ☎ 225 3838; 7 Old Fishmarket Close, High St; mains £7-15; ⏰ noon-2pm & 6-10pm Tue-Sat) The second branch of the New Town French bistro (see above) is a hidden gem, down a steep cobbled alley off the Royal Mile, with a changed-daily menu of market-fresh produce and a lovely little lunchtime sun-trap of an outdoor terrace.

**our pick Apartment** (Map pp72-3; ☎ 228 6456; 7-13 Barclay Pl; mains £8-12; ⏰ noon-3pm & 5-11pm Mon-Fri, noon-11pm Sat & Sun) Effortlessly cool, classy and almost always full, the Apartment is famed for fantastic bistro food and a buzzy, busy at-

## TOP FIVE EDINBURGH CAFÉS

Café culture is firmly ensconced in Edinburgh, and it is as easy to get your daily caffeine fix here as it is in New York or Paris. Most cafés offer some kind of food, from cakes and sandwiches to full-on meals.

**Ndebele** (Map pp72-3; ☎ 221 1141; 57 Home St; mains £4-7; ⊕ 9am-6pm Mon-Sat, noon-5pm Sun) This South African café is hidden deep in darkest Tollcross, but is worth seeking out for the changing menu of unusual African dishes (including at least one veggie option) and delicious African coffees and teas. Try a *boerewors* sandwich (sausage made with beef and coriander) with tomato and onion relish.

**Circle Cafe** (Map p71; ☎ 624 4666; 1 Brandon Tce; mains £5-8; ⊕ 8.30am-5pm Mon-Sat, 9am-4.30pm Sun) A great place for breakfast or a good value lunch, Circle is a bustling neighbourhood café serving great coffee and cakes, and fresh, tasty lunch dishes ranging from chunky, home-baked quiches to prawn and chilli salad.

**Elephant House** (Map pp76-7; ☎ 220 5355; 21 George IV Bridge; mains £5-8; ⊕ 9am-10pm) Here you'll find counters at the front, tables and views of the castle at the back, and little effigies and images of elephants everywhere. Excellent coffee and tasty, homemade food – pizzas, quiches, pies, sandwiches and cakes – at reasonable prices make Elephant House deservedly popular with local students, shoppers and office workers.

**Glass & Thompson** (Map pp76-7; ☎ 557 0909; 2 Dundas St; mains £7-9; ⊕ 8am-6pm Mon-Sat, 10.30am-4.30pm Sun) Grab a table in this spick and span New Town deli and sip a double espresso as you ogle the cheeses in the cold counter or watch the world go by through the floor-to-ceiling windows. Munchies include tasty platters such as dolmati and falafel, or parma ham and parmesan.

**Valvona & Crolla Caffè Bar** (Map pp72-3; ☎ 556 6066; 19 Elm Row, Leith Walk; mains £10-15; ⊕ 8am-6pm Mon-Sat, 10.30am-4.30pm Sun) Try breakfast with an Italian flavour – full *paesano* (meat) or *verdure* (veggie) fry-ups, or deliciously light and crisp *panettone* in *carrozza* (sweet brioche dipped in egg and fried) – or choose from almond croissants, muesli, yogurt and fruit, freshly squeezed orange juice and perfect Italian coffee. There's also a tasty lunch menu of classic Italian dishes.

mosphere; book in advance – by at least three weeks, preferably – and don't be surprised if you still have to wait. But it's worth being patient for treats such as marinated lamb meatballs with merguez and basil-wrapped goat's cheese.

**Maxie's Bistro** (Map pp76-7; ☎ 226 7770; 5b Johnston Tce; mains £8-13; ⊕ 11am-11pm) Maxie's candle-lit bistro, with its cushion-lined nooks set amid stone walls and wooden beams is a pleasant enough setting for a cosy dinner, but at summer lunchtimes people queue for the outdoor tables on Victoria Tce, with great views over Victoria St. The food is dependable – Maxie's has been in the food business for more than 20 years – ranging from pastas, steaks and stir-fries to superb seafood platters and daily specials, and there's an excellent selection of wines.

**Buffalo Grill** (Map pp76-7; ☎ 667 7427; 12-14 Chapel St; mains £8-17; ⊕ noon-2pm & 6-10.30pm Mon-Fri, 6-10.30pm Sat, 5-10.15pm Sun) The Buffalo Grill is cramped, noisy, fun and always busy, so book ahead. An American-style menu offers burgers, steaks and side orders of fries and onion rings, along

with fish and chicken dishes, prawn tempura and a vegetarian burger, but steaks are the main event. You can buy booze in the restaurant, or bring your own wine (£1 corkage per bottle).

**Khushi's** (Map pp76-7; ☎ 220 0057; 9 Victoria St; mains £9-13; ⊕ noon-11pm Mon-Sat, noon-10pm Sun) Established in 1947, Khushi's is something of an Edinburgh institution despite having moved from its original canteenlike home to bigger and brighter premises. Its speciality is basic Punjabi dishes cooked in the traditional way (listed on the menu as plain lamb, chicken or fish curry), but there are also several good vegetarian dishes. It's not licensed, but you can bring your own booze (no corkage).

**Pancho Villa's** (Map pp76-7; ☎ 557 4416; 240 Canongate; mains £9-13; ⊕ noon-10pm Mon-Sat, 5-10pm Sun) With a Mexican-born owner and lots of Latin American and Spanish staff, it's not surprising that this colourful and lively restaurant is one of the most authentic-feeling Mexican places in town. The dinner menu includes delicious steak fajitas and great vegetarian spinach enchiladas. It's often busy, so book ahead.

**Suruchi** (Map pp76-7; ☎ 556 6583; 14a Nicolson St; mains £9-14; noon-2pm & 5.30-11.30pm) A laid-back Indian eatery with handmade turquoise tiles, lazy ceiling fans and chilled-out jazz guitar, Suruchi offers a range of exotic dishes as well as the traditional tandoori standards, many with a Scottish twist. An amusing touch is provided by menu descriptions translated into broad Scots ('*a beezer o' a curry this…gey nippie oan the tongue*').

**Amber** (Map pp76-7; ☎ 477 8477; 354 Castlehill; mains £12-18; noon-3.45pm daily, 7-9pm Tue-Sat) Located in the Scotch Whisky Heritage Centre, this whisky-themed restaurant manages to avoid the tourist clichés and create genuinely interesting and flavoursome dishes such as fillet of pork with whisky and apple chutney, or vegetarian haggis in filo pastry with whisky cream sauce.

**Point Hotel** (Map pp76-7; ☎ 221 5555; 34 Bread St; 2-course dinner £20; noon-2pm & 6-10pm Mon-Fri, 6-10pm Sat, 6-9pm Sun) The legendary set menus and reasonably priced wine list at the Point Hotel offer exceptional value – delicious Scottish/international cuisine served in an elegant room with crisp, white linen and attentive service. Reservations are strongly recommended.

### TOP END

**Tower** (Map pp76-7; ☎ 225 3003; Museum of Scotland, Chambers St; mains £16-25; noon-11pm) Chic and sleek, with a great view of the castle, Tower is set atop the Museum of Scotland building. It offers a menu of quality Scottish food, simply prepared – try half a dozen Loch Fyne oysters followed by a chargrilled Aberdeen Angus steak. A two-course pretheatre menu (£13) is available from 5pm to 6.30pm.

**Atrium** (Map pp76-7; ☎ 228 8882; 10 Cambridge St; mains £20-24; noon-2pm & 6-10pm Mon-Fri, 6-10pm Sat) Elegantly draped in cream linen and candlelight, the Atrium is one of Edinburgh's most fashionable restaurants, counting Mick Jagger and Jack Nicholson among its past guests. The cuisine is modern Scottish with a Mediterranean twist, with the emphasis on the finest of fresh, seasonal produce – carpaccio of Aberdeen Angus beef with truffled potato salad, or rump of Perthshire lamb with dauphinoise potatoes.

## New Town & Around

### BUDGET

**Queen St Café** (Map pp76-7; ☎ 557 2844; 1 Queen St; mains £5-7; 10am-4.30pm Mon-Sat, 11am-4.30pm Sun) The ever-popular café in the Scottish National Portrait Gallery bakes its own range of tempting cakes and scones, and serves a lunch menu (noon to 2.30pm) of hearty homemade soups (such as roast red pepper and sweet potato, or more traditional leek and potato), salads and sandwiches.

**Blue Moon Café** (Map pp72-3; ☎ 556 2788; 1 Barony St; mains £6-8; 11am-10pm Mon-Fri, 10am-10pm Sat & Sun) The Blue Moon is the focus of Broughton St's gay social life, always busy, always friendly, and serving up delicious nachos, salads, sandwiches and baked potatoes. It's famous for its homemade hamburgers (and beanburgers), which come plain or topped with cheese, chillis or salsa, and delicious daily specials.

### MIDRANGE

**Songkran** (Map pp72-3; ☎ 225 7889; 24a Stafford St; mains £9-13; noon-2.30pm & 5.30-11pm Mon-Sat) You'd better book a table – and be prepared for a squeeze – to get in to this tiny New Town basement. The reason for the crush is some of the best Thai food in Edinburgh. Try the tender *yang* (marinated and barbecued beef, chicken or prawn), the crisp and tart orange chicken, or the chilli-loaded warm beef salad. A two-course lunch is £9.

our pick **Valvona & Crolla VinCaffè** (Map pp76-7; ☎ 557 0088; 11 Multrees Walk, St Andrew Sq; mains £9-18; 10am-late Mon-Sat, 11am-5.30pm Sun) Foodie colours dominate the décor at this delightful Italian bistro – bottle-green pillars and banquettes, chocolate-and-cream coloured walls, espresso-black tables – a perfect backdrop for VinCaffè's superb antipasto (£18 for two), washed down with a bottle of pink Pinot Grigio. Live jazz from 7pm on Wednesdays.

**Nargile** (Map pp76-7; ☎ 225 5755; 73 Hanover St; mains £10-15; noon-2pm & 5.30-10.30pm Mon-Thu, noon-2pm & 5.30-11pm Fri & Sat) Throw away any preconceptions about boring kebabs – this glitzy Turkish restaurant is a class act. Enjoy a spread of delicious *mezeler* (think Turkish tapas) followed by meltingly sweet, marinated lamb char-grilled to crispy perfection. Finish off with *baklava* (nut-filled pastry soaked in honey) and a Turkish coffee.

**Café Marlayne** (Map pp76-7; ☎ 226 2230; 76 Thistle St; mains £12-16; noon-2pm & 6-10pm) All weathered wood and warm yellow walls, little Café Marlayne is a cosy nook offering French farmhouse cooking – *escargots* with garlic and parsley, oysters with lemon and Tabasco, roast quail, *boudin noir* (black pudding) with sautéed apples – at very reasonable prices. There's another branch in the Old Town (see p102).

## TOP FIVE LUNCH SPOTS

Many restaurants in Edinburgh offer good-value lunches. Here are a few suggestions from various parts of the city.

**Old Chain Pier** (Map p71; ☎ 552 1233; 1 Trinity Cres; mains £5-10; ☺ food served noon-9pm Mon-Sat, 12.30-8pm Sun) The Old Chain Pier is a lovely little pub overlooking – nay, over*hanging* – the Firth of Forth on the waterfront near Granton Harbour. The excellent bar menu includes soup of the day, a creamy and filling seafood chowder, and a succulent steak-and-onion baguette with chips. The menu of real ales is no less enticing than the food.

**First Coast** (Map pp72-3; ☎ 313 4404; 99-101 Dalry Rd; mains £9-15; ☺ noon-2pm & 5-10.30pm Mon-Sat) Our favourite neighbourhood bistro, First Coast has a striking main dining area with pale grey-wood panelling, stripped stone walls and Victorian cornices, and a short and simple menu offering hearty comfort food such as whitefish fillet with crispy pancetta and peas, char-grilled lemon chicken, and pan-fried herb gnocchi. At lunch, and from 5pm to 6.30pm, you can have an excellent two-course meal for £10.

**Daniel's Bistro** (Map p71; ☎ 553 5933; 88 Commercial St; mains £11-15; ☺ 10am-10pm) Daniel comes from Alsace, and his all-French kitchen staff combine top Scottish and French produce with Gallic know-how to create a wide range of delicious dishes. The fish soup is excellent, and main courses range from slow-cooked knuckle of pork to Alpine *tartiflette* (French dish of cheese, potato, ham or pork, and cream). A seriously filling three-course lunch is £9.

**La P'tite Folie** (Map pp76-7; ☎ 225 7983; 61 Frederick St; mains £11-15; ☺ noon-3pm & 6-11pm Mon-Sat, 6-11pm Sun) This is a delightful little restaurant with a Breton owner whose menu includes French classics – onion soup, *moules marinières* – alongside steaks, seafood and a range of *plats du jour*. The two-/three-course lunch is a bargain at £7.50/9.

**Petit Paris** (Map pp76-7; ☎ 226 2442; 38-40 Grassmarket; mains £13-16; ☺ noon-3pm & 5.30-11pm, closed Mon Oct-Mar) Like the name says, this is a little piece of Paris, complete with checked tablecloths, friendly waiters and good-value grub – the *moules-frites* (mussels and chips) are excellent. There's a lunch deal offering the *plat du jour* and a coffee for £7; add a starter and it's £10.

**Mussel Inn** (Map pp76-7; ☎ 225 5979; 61-65 Rose St; mains £13-16; ☺ noon-3pm & 6-10pm Mon-Thu, noon-10pm Fri & Sat, 5-10pm Sun) Owned by west-coast shellfish farmers, the Mussel Inn provides a direct outlet for fresh Scottish seafood. The busy restaurant, decorated with bright beech wood indoors, spills out onto the pavement in summer. A kilogram pot of mussels with a choice of sauces – try leek, horseradish, cider and cream – costs £10.50.

**Stac Polly** (Map pp76-7; ☎ 556 2231; 29-33 Dublin St; mains £18-20; ☺ noon-2pm Mon-Fri, 6-10pm Mon-Sat) Named after a mountain in northwestern Scotland, Stac Polly's kitchen adds sophisticated twists to fresh Highland produce. Dishes such as loin of venison with redcurrant and rosemary jus keep the punters coming back for more.

### TOP END

**Café Royal Oyster Bar** (Map pp76-7; ☎ 556 4124; 17a West Register St; mains £16-20; ☺ noon-2pm & 7-10pm) Pass through the revolving doors on the corner of West Register St and you're transported back to Victorian times – a palace of glinting mahogany, polished brass, marble floors, stained glass, Doulton tiles, gilded cornices and starched table linen so thick that it creaks when you fold it. The menu is mostly classic seafood, from oysters on ice to *Coquilles St Jacques Parisienne* and lobster thermidor, augmented by a handful of beef and game dishes.

**Oloroso** (Map pp76-7; ☎ 226 7614; 33 Castle St; mains £16-24; ☺ restaurant noon-2.30pm & 7-10.30pm, bar 11am-1am) Oloroso is one of Edinburgh's most stylish restaurants, perched on a glass-encased New Town rooftop with views across a Mary Poppins' chimney-scape to the Firth of Forth and Fife hills. Swathed in sophisticated cream linen and charcoal upholstery enlivened with splashes of deep yellow, the dining room serves top-notch Scottish produce with Asian and Mediterranean touches.

## Leith
### MIDRANGE

**ourpick** **Fishers Bistro** (Map p71; ☎ 554 5666; 1 The Shore; mains £9-22; ☺ noon-10.30pm) This cosy little bar-turned-restaurant, tucked beneath a 17th-century signal tower, is one of the city's best seafood places. Fishers' fish cakes are

## TOP FIVE VEGETARIAN RESTAURANTS

Many Edinburgh restaurants offer vegetarian options on the menu, some good, some bad, some indifferent. The places listed here are all 100% veggie and all fall into the 'good' category.

**David Bann** (Map pp76-7; ☎ 556 5888; 56-58 St Mary's St; mains £8-12; ⏰ 11am-10pm Sun-Thu, 11am-10.30pm Fri & Sat) If you want to convince a carnivorous friend that cuisine à la veg can be as tasty and inventive as a meat-muncher's menu, take them to David Bann's stylish restaurant – dishes such as Thai-spiced fritters of tofu and peas with mango chutney, and tart of braised fennel, spinach and goat's-cheese curd are guaranteed to win converts.

**Ann Purna** (Map pp72-3; ☎ 662 1807; 45 St Patrick's Sq; mains £5-9; ⏰ noon-2pm & 5.30-11pm Mon-Fri, 5.30-11pm Sat & Sun) This little gem of an Indian restaurant serves exclusively vegetarian dishes from southern India, served with a smile by the family team who run the place. If you're new to this kind of food, opt for a *thali* – a self-contained platter that has about half a dozen different dishes, including a dessert. You can get a light lunch for £5.

**Susie's Wholefood Diner** (Map pp76-7; ☎ 667 8729; 51-53 West Nicolson St; mains £4-7; ⏰ noon-8pm Mon, noon-9pm Tue-Sat, 1-8pm Sun) Susie's is a down-to-earth, self-service, vegetarian cafeteria with scrubbed-wood tables, rickety chairs and a friendly atmosphere. The menu changes daily but includes things such as tofu, aubergine and pepper casserole, stuffed roast tomatoes and Susie's famous falafel plates – reputedly 'the best falafel in the Western world'. BYOB, or try a bottle of organic wine.

**Henderson's** (Map pp76-7; ☎ 225 2131; 94 Hanover St; mains £5-8; ⏰ 8am-10.45pm Mon-Sat) Established in 1962, Henderson's is the grandmother of Edinburgh's vegetarian restaurants. The food is mostly organic and guaranteed genetically modified-free, and special dietary requirements can be catered for. The self-service restaurant still has something of a 1970s cafeteria feel to it (but in a good way), and the daily salads and hot dishes are as popular as ever. Three-course set lunch is £9.

**Kalpna** (Map pp72-3; ☎ 667 9890; 2-3 St Patrick Sq; mains £5-11; ⏰ noon-2pm & 5.30-10.30pm Mon-Sat year-round, plus 6-10.30pm Sun May-Sep) Another long-standing Edinburgh favourite, Kalpna is one of the best Indian restaurants in the country, vegetarian or otherwise. The cuisine is mostly Gujarati, with a smattering of dishes from other parts of India – try the *khumb masala* (spiced mushrooms in a coconut milk, tomato, garlic and coriander sauce).

---

an Edinburgh institution, and the rest of the handwritten menu (you might need a calligrapher to decipher it) rarely disappoints. Booking is recommended.

**The Shore** (Map p71; ☎ 553 5080; 3-4 The Shore; mains £13-17; ⏰ noon-2.30pm & 6.30-10pm Mon-Fri, noon-3pm & 6.30-10pm Sat & Sun) The atmospheric dining room next door to the popular Shore Bar is a haven of wood-panelled peace, with old photographs, nautical knick-knacks, fresh flowers and an open fire adding to the romantic theme. The menu is small, and specialises in Scottish seafood and game.

**Raj** (Map p71; ☎ 553 3980; 91 Henderson St, The Shore; mains £8-15; ⏰ noon-2.30pm & 5.30-11.30pm Sun-Thu, to midnight Fri & Sat) Run by celebrity chef Tommy Miah (author of *True Taste of Asia*), the Raj is an atmospheric curry house overlooking the Water of Leith and serving Indian (including Goan) and Bangladeshi cuisine. Specialities include the tongue-tingling green Bengal chicken (marinated with lime juice, mint and chilli) and spicy Goan lamb garam fry.

If you can't get a table at Fishers Bistro, try the New Town branch, **Fishers in the City** (Map pp76-7; ☎ 225 5109; 58 Thistle St).

### TOP END

**Martin Wishart** (Map p71; ☎ 553 3557; 54 The Shore; 3-course lunch/dinner £23/50; ⏰ noon-2pm & 7-10pm Tue-Sat) In 2001 this restaurant became the first in Edinburgh to win a Michelin star. The eponymous chef has worked with Albert Roux, Marco Pierre White and Nick Nairn, and brings a modern French approach to the best Scottish produce, from lobster and smoked haddock soufflé to braised saddle of lamb.

## Self-Catering

There are grocery stores and food shops all over the city, many of them open 9am to 10pm daily. Many petrol stations also have late-opening shops that sell groceries.

There are several large supermarkets spread throughout the city such as **Sainsbury's** (Map pp76-7; ☎ 225 8400; 9-10 St Andrew Sq; ⏰ 7am-10pm

Mon-Sat, 9am-8pm Sun) and **Tesco** (Map pp76-7; ☎ 456 2400; 94 Nicolson St; ⏲ 7am-midnight Mon-Sat, 9am-10pm Sun). The food hall in **Marks & Spencer** (Map pp76-7; ☎ 225 2301; 54 Princes St; ⏲ 9am-6pm Mon-Wed, Fri & Sat, 9am-8pm Thu, 11am-6pm Sun) sells high-quality ready-cooked meals.

Good delis for buying picnic goodies include **Valvona & Crolla** (Map pp72-3; ☎ 556 6066; 19 Elm Row, Leith Walk; ⏲ 8am-6.30pm Mon-Sat, 11am-5pm Sun), **Peckham's** (Map pp72-3; ☎ 229 7054; 155-159 Bruntsfield Pl; ⏲ 8am-midnight Mon-Sat, 9am-11pm Sun) and the food hall in Jenners (p112).

# DRINKING

Edinburgh has more than 700 bars, which are as varied as the population – everything from Victorian palaces to rough-and-ready drinking dens, and from bearded, real-ale howffs (pubs) to trendy cocktail bars.

## Royal Mile & Around

**Jolly Judge** (Map pp76-7; ☎ 225 2669; 7a James Crt) A snug little howff tucked away down a close, the Judge exudes a cosy 17th-century atmosphere (low, timber-beamed painted ceilings) and has the added attraction of a cheering open fire in cold weather. No music or gaming machines, just the buzz of conversation.

**Ecco Vino** (Map pp76-7; ☎ 225 1441; 19 Cockburn St) With outdoor tables on sunny afternoons, and cosy candle-lit intimacy in the evenings, this comfortably cramped Tuscan-style wine bar offers a tempting range of Italian wines, though only a few are available by the glass – best to share a bottle.

**Royal Mile Tavern** (Map pp76-7; ☎ 557 9681; 127 High St) An elegant, traditional bar lined with polished wood, mirrors and brass, Royal Mile serves real ale, good wines and fine food – *moules marinières* (mussels) and crusty bread is a lunchtime speciality.

**The Tun** (Map pp72-3; ☎ 557 9297; The Tun Bldg, Holyrood Rd) Set among the glass-and-steel architecture of the redeveloped Holyrood district, the Tun is a funky fish-tank of a place, with chunky leather sofas and steel bar stools. It's popular with political types and media people from the neighbouring BBC studios and the *Scotsman* newspaper offices just across the road.

## Grassmarket & Around

The pubs in the Grassmarket have outdoor tables on sunny summer afternoons, but in the evenings are favoured by boozed-up lads on the pull, so steer clear if that's not your thing.

The Cowgate – the Grassmarket's extension to the east – is Edinburgh's clubland.

**Last Drop** (Map pp76-7; ☎ 225 4851; 74 Grassmarket) The name commemorates the gallows that used to stand nearby, but the only swingers today are the pub's partying clientele, largely students and backpackers.

**Bow Bar** (Map pp76-7; ☎ 226 7667; 80 West Bow) One of the city's best traditional-style pubs (it's not as old as it looks) serving a range of excellent real ales and a vast selection of malt whiskies, the Bow Bar often has standing room only on Friday and Saturday evenings.

**Beehive Inn** (Map pp76-7; ☎ 225 7171; 18-20 Grassmarket) The historic Beehive – a former coaching inn – is a big, buzzing party-pub, with a range of real ales, but the main attraction is sitting out the back in the Grassmarket's only beer garden, with views up to the castle.

**Bannerman's** (Map pp76-7; ☎ 556 3254; 212 Cowgate) A long-established favourite, Bannerman's straggles through a warren of old vaults and pulls in crowds of students, locals and backpackers with live rock, punk and indie bands.

**Pear Tree House** (Map pp76-7; ☎ 667 7533; 38 West Nicolson St) The Pear Tree is another student favourite, with comfy sofas and board games inside, plus the city's biggest and most popular beer garden in summer.

## Rose Street & Around

Rose St was once a famous pub crawl, where generations of students, sailors and rugby fans would try to visit every pub on the street (around 17 of them) and down a pint of beer in each one.

**Kenilworth** (Map pp76-7; ☎ 226 4385; 152-154 Rose St) A gorgeous, Edwardian drinking palace, complete with original fittings – from the tile floors, mahogany circle bar and gantry, to the ornate mirrors and gas lamps – the Kenilworth was Edinburgh's original gay bar back in the 1970s. Today it attracts a mixed crowd of all ages, and serves a good range of real ales and malt whiskies.

**Robertsons 37 Bar** (Map pp76-7; ☎ 225 6185; 37 Rose St) No 37 is to malt whisky connoisseurs what the Diggers (now called the Athletic Arms) once was to real-ale fans. Its long gantry sports a choice of more than 100 single malts and the bar provides a quiet and elegant environment in which to sample them.

**Guildford Arms** (Map pp76-7; ☎ 556 4312; 1 West Register St) Located next door to the Café Royal Circle

EDINBURGH

## TOP FIVE TRADITIONAL PUBS

Edinburgh is blessed with a large number of traditional 19th- and early-20th-century pubs, which have preserved much of their original Victorian or Edwardian decoration and serve cask-conditioned real ales and a staggering range of malt whiskies.

**Athletic Arms** (Diggers; Map pp72-3; ☎ 337 3822; 1-3 Angle Park Tce) Named after the cemetery across the street – the grave-diggers used to nip in and slake their thirst after a hard day's interring – the Diggers dates from the 1890s. It's still staunchly traditional – the décor has barely changed in 100 years – and has recently attempted to revive its reputation as a real-ale drinker's mecca by serving locally brewed Diggers' 80-shilling ale. Packed to the gills with football and rugby fans on match days.

**Abbotsford** (Map pp76-7; ☎ 225 5276; 3 Rose St) One of the few pubs in Rose St that has retained its Edwardian splendour, the Abbotsford has long been a hang-out for writers, actors, journalists and media people, and has many loyal regulars. Dating from 1902, and named after Sir Walter Scott's country house, the pub's centrepiece is a splendid, mahogany island bar. Good selection of Scottish and English real ales.

**Bennet's Bar** (Map pp72-3; ☎ 229 5143; 8 Leven St) Situated beside the King's Theatre, Bennet's has managed to hang on to almost all of its beautiful Victorian fittings, from the leaded, stained-glass windows and ornate mirrors to the wooden gantry and the brass water taps on the bar (for your whisky – there are over 100 malts to choose from).

**Café Royal Circle Bar** (Map pp76-7; ☎ 556 1884; 17 West Register St) Perhaps the classic Edinburgh bar, the Café Royal's main claims to fame are its magnificent oval bar and the series of Doulton tile portraits of famous Victorian inventors. Check out the bottles on the gantry – staff line them up to look like there's a mirror there, and many a drink-befuddled customer has been seen squinting and wondering why he can't see his reflection.

**Sheep Heid** (Map p71; ☎ 656 6951; 43-45 The Causeway, Duddingston) Possibly the oldest inn in Edinburgh – with a licence dating back to 1360 – the Sheep Heid feels more like a country pub than an Edinburgh bar. Set in the semirural shadow of Arthur's Seat, it's famous for its 19th-century skittles alley and the lovely little beer garden.

Bar, the Guildford is another classic Victorian pub full of polished mahogany, brass and ornate cornices. The bar lunches are good – try to get a table in the unusual upstairs gallery, with a view over the sea of drinkers down below.

## New Town & Broughton Street

**Cumberland Bar** (Map pp72-3; ☎ 558 3134; 1-3 Cumberland St) Immortalised as the stereotypical New Town pub in Alexander McCall-Smith's serialised novel *44 Scotland Street*, the Cumberland has an authentic, traditional wood-brass-and-mirrors look (despite being relatively new), and serves well-looked-after, cask-conditioned ales and a wide range of malt whiskies. There's also a pleasant little beer garden outside.

**Opal Lounge** (Map pp76-7; ☎ 226 2275; 51 George St; ☻ noon-3am) The Opal Lounge is jammed at weekends with affluent twenty-somethings who've spent £200 and two hours in front of a mirror to achieve that artlessly scruffy look. During the week, when the air-kissing, cocktail-sipping crowds thin out, it's a good

place to relax with a fruit smoothie (or an expensive but expertly mixed cocktail) and sample the tasty Asian food. Expect to queue on weekend evenings.

**Kay's Bar** (Map pp76-7; ☎ 225 1858; 39 Jamaica St) Housed in a former wine-merchant's office, tiny Kay's Bar is a cosy haven with a coal fire and a fine range of real ales. Good food is served in the back room at lunchtime, but you'll have to book a table – Kay's is a popular spot.

**Pivo Caffé** (Map pp76-7; ☎ 557 2925; 2-6 Calton Rd) Aiming to add a little taste of Bohemia to Edinburgh's bar scene, Pivo (the Czech word for beer) serves bottled Czech beers, Budvar-Budweiser on draught and two-pint cocktails, and has DJs on the decks from 10pm on.

**Standing Order** (Map pp76-7; ☎ 225 4460; 62-66 George St) One of several converted banks on George St, Standing Order is a cavernous beer hall with a fantastic vaulted ceiling and some cosy rooms off to the right – look for the one with the original 27-tonne safe. Despite its size, it can be standing-room only at weekends.

**Tonic** (Map pp76-7; ☎ 225 6431; 34a North Castle St) As cool and classy as a perfectly mixed martini, from the chic décor to the Phillipe Starck bar stools, Tonic prides itself on the authenticity of its cocktails, of which there are many – the menu goes on forever.

## Leith & Granton

**Port O'Leith** (Map p71; ☎ 554 3568; 58 Constitution St) This is a good, old-fashioned, friendly local boozer. The Port is swathed with flags and cap bands left behind by visiting sailors – the harbour is just down the road. Pop in for a pint and you'll probably stay until closing time.

**Starbank Inn** (Map p71; ☎ 552 4141; 64 Laverockbank Rd) Along with the Old Chain Pier (see the Top Five Lunch Spots boxed text, p105), the Starbank is an oasis of fine ales and good, homemade food on Edinburgh's windswept waterfront. In summer there's a sunny conservatory, and in winter a blazing fire to toast your toes in front of.

## ENTERTAINMENT

Edinburgh has a number of fine theatres and concert halls, and there are independent art-house cinemas as well as mainstream movie theatres. Many pubs offer entertainment ranging from live Scottish folk music to pop, rock and jazz as well as karaoke and quiz nights, while a range of stylish modern bars purvey house, dance and hip-hop to the preclubbing crowd.

The comprehensive source for what's-on info is the *List* (www.list.co.uk), an excellent listings magazine covering both Edinburgh and Glasgow. It's available from most newsagents, and is published fortnightly on a Thursday.

## Live Music

Check out the *List* and the *Gig Guide* (www.gigguide.co.uk), a free leaflet available in bars and music venues, to see who's playing where.

### JAZZ, BLUES & ROCK

**Henry's Cellar Bar** (Map pp76-7; ☎ 538 7385; 8a Morrison St) One of Edinburgh's best live-music venues, Henry's has something going on every night of the week, from rock and indie to jazz and blues, funk to hip-hop to hardcore, staging both local bands and acts from around the world. Open till 3am at weekends.

**Liquid Room** (Map pp76-7; ☎ 225 2564; www.liquidroom .com; 9c Victoria St) The Liquid Room (see also Clubs) stages all kinds of gigs from local rock bands to tribute bands to the Average White Band. Check the programme on the website.

**Whistle Binkie's** (Map pp76-7; ☎ 557 5114; www .whistlebinkies.com; 4-6 South Bridge; ☯ 7pm-3am) This crowded cellar-bar just off the Royal Mile has live music every night till 3am, from rock and blues to folk and jazz. Open mic night on Monday and breaking bands on Tuesday are showcases for new talent.

**Jazz Bar** (Map pp76-7; ☎ 220 4298; www.thejazzbar .co.uk; 1a Chambers St) This atmospheric cellar bar, with its polished parquet floors, bare stone walls, candle-lit tables and stylish steel-framed chairs is owned and operated by jazz musicians. There's live music every night from 8.30pm to 3am, and on Saturday from 3.30pm.

### TRADITIONAL

The capital is a great place to hear traditional Scottish (and Irish) folk music, with a mix of regular spots and impromptu sessions.

**Royal Oak** (Map pp76-7; ☎ 557 2976; www.royal-oak-folk .com; 1 Infirmary St) This popular folk pub is tiny, so get there early (9pm start) if you want to be sure of a place. Sundays from 4pm to 8pm is open-session – bring your own instruments (or a good singing voice).

**Sandy Bell's** (Map pp76-7; ☎ 225 2751; 25 Forrest Rd) This unassuming bar has been a stalwart of the traditional-music scene since the Corrs were in nappies. There's music almost every evening at 9pm, and also at 3.30pm and 8pm on Sunday.

**Pleasance Cabaret Bar** (Map pp76-7; ☎ 650 2349; 60 The Pleasance; admission £7) The Pleasance is home to the Edinburgh Folk Club, which runs a programme of visiting bands and singers at 8pm on Wednesday nights.

## Clubs

Edinburgh's club scene has some fine DJ talent and is well worth exploring; there are club-night listings in the *List*. Most of the venues are concentrated in and around the twin sumps of Cowgate and Calton Rd – so it's downhill all the way…

**Bongo Club** (Map pp72-3; ☎ 558 7604; www.thebongo club.com; Moray House, Paterson's Land, 37 Holyrood Rd) The weird and wonderful Bongo Club is famous for its long-running hip-hop, funk and breakbeat club night Headspin (admission £6 to £12; first or second Saturday of the month from 11pm). Also worth checking out is the booming bass of roots and dub reggae night Messenger Sound System (admission £8; held third Saturday of the month from 11pm). The club is open as a café and exhibition space during the day.

**Liquid Room** (Map pp76-7; ☎ 225 2564; www.liquid room.com; 9c Victoria St) Set in a subterranean vault deep beneath Victoria St, the Liquid Room is a superb club venue with a thundering sound system. There are regular club nights Wednesday to Saturday as well as live bands. The long-running Evol (admission £5; Friday from 10.30pm) is an Edinburgh institution catering to the indie-kid crowd, and is regularly voted as Scotland's top club night out.

**Studio 24** (Map pp72-3; ☎ 558 3758; www.studio24 edinburgh.co.uk; 24 Calton Rd) Studio 24 is the dark heart of Edinburgh's underground music scene, with a programme that covers all bases, from house to nu metal via punk, ska, reggae, crossover, tribal, electro, techno and dance. Retribution (admission £5; Saturday from 11pm) is the city's classic rock, metal and alt night (with Sanctuary, an alcohol-free club for 14- to 18-year-olds, running 6pm to 10pm the same evening).

**Ego** (Map pp72-3; ☎ 478 7434; www.clubego.co.uk; 14 Picardy Pl) A glitzy two-floor venue housed in a former casino, with huge Renaissance-style wall paintings, gay-friendly Ego dishes up everything from the dance classics of Fever (admission £10; second Saturday of the month from 11pm) to the hard house and trance of Nuklear Puppy (admission £12; second Friday of the month from 10.30pm).

**Cabaret Voltaire** (Map pp76-7; ☎ 220 6176; www.thecab aretvoltaire.com; 36 Blair St) An atmospheric warren of stone-lined vaults houses Edinburgh's most 'alternative' club, which eschews huge dance floors and egotistical DJ-worship in favour of a 'creative crucible' hosting an eclectic mix of DJs, live acts, comedy, theatre, visual arts and the spoken word. Well worth a look.

## Cinema

Film buffs will find plenty to keep them happy in Edinburgh's art-house cinemas, while popcorn munchers can choose from a range of multiplexes.

**Cameo** (Map pp72-3; ☎ 228 2800; 38 Home St; tickets £6.10) The three-screen, independently owned Cameo is a good, old-fashioned cinema showing an imaginative mix of mainstream and art-house movies. There is a good programme of

midnight movies and Sunday matinees, and the seats in Screen 1 are big enough to get lost in.

**Filmhouse** (Map pp76-7; ☎ 228 2688; 88 Lothian Rd; tickets £6; &) The Filmhouse is the main venue for the annual Edinburgh International Film Festival and screens a full programme of arthouse, classic, foreign and second-run films, with lots of themes, retrospectives and 70mm screenings. It has wheelchair access to all three screens.

**Cineworld Fountainpark** (Map pp72-3; ☎ 0871 200 2000; Fountainpark Complex, Dundee St; tickets £6.30) The Cineworld is a massive 12-screen multiplex complete with café-bar, movie-poster shop and frighteningly overpriced popcorn.

**VUE Cinema** (Map pp76-7; ☎ 08712 240 240; Omni Centre, Greenside Pl; tickets £6.50) Another 12-screen multiplex, with three 'Gold Class' screens where you can watch from a luxurious leather reclining seat complete with side table for your drink and complimentary snacks (£9).

## Classical Music, Opera & Ballet

The following are the main venues for classical music.

**Edinburgh Festival Theatre** (Map pp76-7; ☎ 529 6000; www.eft.co.uk; 13-29 Nicolson St; ☯ box office 10am-6pm Mon-Sat, to 8pm show nights, 4pm-showtime Sun) A beautifully restored Art Deco theatre with a modern frontage, the Festival is the city's main venue for opera, dance and ballet, but also stages musicals, concerts, drama and children's shows.

**Usher Hall** (Map pp76-7; ☎ 228 1155; www.usherhall .co.uk; Lothian Rd; ☯ box office 10.30am-5.30pm, to 8pm show nights) The architecturally impressive Usher Hall hosts concerts by the Royal Scottish National Orchestra (RSNO) and performances of popular music. Closed for renovations until the start of the Edinburgh International Festival 2008.

**St Giles Cathedral** (Map pp76-7; ☎ 225 9442; www .stgiles.net; High St) The big kirk on the Royal Mile plays host to a regular and varied programme of classical music, including popular lunchtime and evening concerts and organ recitals. The cathedral choir sings at the 10am and 11.30am Sunday services.

**Queen's Hall** (Map pp72-3; ☎ 668 2019; www.thequeens hall.net; Clerk St; ☯ box office 10am-5.30pm Mon-Sat, or till 15min after show begins) The home of the Scottish Chamber Orchestra also stages jazz, blues, folk, rock and comedy.

## Sport

Edinburgh is home to two rival football teams playing in the Scottish Premier League – Heart of Midlothian (aka Hearts) and Hibernian (aka Hibs). The domestic football season lasts from August to May, and most matches are played at 3pm on Saturday or 7.30pm on Tuesday or Wednesday.

Hearts has its home ground at **Tynecastle Stadium** (Map pp72-3; ☎ 200 7200; www.heartsfc.co.uk; Gorgie Rd), southwest of the city centre in Gorgie. Hibernian's home ground is northeast of the city centre at **Easter Road Stadium** (Map pp72-3; ☎ 661 2159; www.hibs.co.uk; 12 Albion Pl).

Each year, from January to March, Scotland's national rugby team takes part in the Six Nations Rugby Union Championship. The most important fixture is the clash against England for the Calcutta Cup. At club level the season runs from September to May. **Murrayfield Stadium** (Map p71; ☎ 346 5000; www.scottishrugby.org; 112 Roseburn St), about 1.5 miles west of the city centre, is the venue for international matches.

Most other sporting events, including athletics and cycling, are held at **Meadowbank Sports Centre** (Map p71; ☎ 661 5351; 139 London Rd), Scotland's main sports arena.

Horse-racing enthusiasts should head 6 miles east to **Musselburgh Racecourse** ( ☎ 665 2859; www.musselburgh-racecourse.co.uk; Linkfield Rd, Musselburgh; admission £15-20), Scotland's oldest racecourse (founded 1816), where meetings are held throughout the year.

## Theatre, Musicals & Comedy

The cost of theatre tickets is in the £10 to £30 range.

**Royal Lyceum Theatre** (Map pp76-7; ☎ 248 4848; www.lyceum.org.uk; 30b Grindlay St; ☽ box office 10am-6pm Mon-Sat, to 8pm show nights) A grand Victorian theatre located beside the Usher Hall, the Lyceum stages drama, concerts, musicals and ballet.

**Traverse Theatre** (Map pp76-7; ☎ 228 1404; www.traverse.co.uk; 10 Cambridge St; ☽ box office 10am-6pm Mon-Sat, till 8pm on show nights) The Traverse is the main focus for new Scottish writing and stages an adventurous programme of contemporary drama and dance. The box office is only open on Sunday (from 4pm) when there's a show on.

---

### GAY & LESBIAN EDINBURGH

Edinburgh has a small – but perfectly formed – gay and lesbian scene, centred on the area around Broughton St (known affectionately as the 'Pink Triangle') at the eastern end of New Town. Blue Moon Café (see p104) at the foot of Broughton St is a friendly G&L caff offering good food and good company. It's also a good place to pick up on what's happening on the local scene.

*Scotsgay* (www.scotsgay.co.uk) is the local monthly magazine covering gay and lesbian issues, with listings of gay-friendly pubs and clubs.

Useful contacts:

**Edinburgh LGBT Centre** ( ☎ 478 7069; 58-60 Broughton St; ☽ 11am-11pm Mon-Fri, 10am-11pm Sat & Sun)
**Lothian Gay & Lesbian Switchboard** ( ☎ 556 4049; www.lgls.co.uk; ☽ 7.30-10pm)
**Lothian Lesbian Line** ( ☎ 557 0751; ☽ 7.30-10pm Mon & Thu)

#### Pubs & Clubs

Edinburgh's most popular gay club nights are the long-running **Taste** (www.taste-clubs.com), currently hosted by Cabaret Voltaire (see Clubs), and **Fever** at Ego (see Clubs).

**CC Blooms** (Map pp72-3; ☎ 556 9331; 23 Greenside Pl, Leith Walk; admission free; ☽ 6pm-3am Mon-Sat, 7pm-3am Sun) The raddled old queen of the Edinburgh gay scene, CC's offers two floors of deafening dance and disco. It's a bit overpriced and overcrowded but worth a visit – go early, or sample the wild karaoke on Thursday and Sunday nights.

**Regent** (Map pp72-3; ☎ 661 8198; 2 Montrose Tce; ☽ 11am-1am Mon-Sat, 12.30pm-1am Sun) This is a pleasant, gay local with a relaxed atmosphere (no loud music), serving coffee and croissants as well as excellent real ales, including Deuchars IPA and Caledonian 80/-. Meeting place for the Lesbian and Gay Real Ale Drinkers club (first Monday of month, 9pm).

**Claremont Bar** (Map p71; ☎ 556 5662; 133-135 East Claremont St; ☽ 11am-midnight Mon-Thu, to 1am Fri & Sat, 12.30pm-midnight Sun) Scotland's only sci-fi theme pub (no, you have to see it), Claremont is a friendly, gay-owned bar and restaurant. Saturday nights are men-only nights, when leather, kilts, skinheads and bears are the order of the evening.

**King's Theatre** (Map pp72-3; ☎ 529 6000; www.eft .co.uk; 2 Leven St, Bruntsfield; ⏰ box office open 1hr before show) King's is a traditional theatre with a pro-gramme of musicals, drama, comedy and its famous Christmas pantomime.

**Edinburgh Playhouse** (Map pp72-3; ☎ 524 3301, bookings ☎ 0870 606 3424; www.edinburgh-playhouse.co.uk; 18-22 Greenside Pl; ⏰ box office 10am-6pm Mon-Sat, to 8pm show nights) This restored theatre at the top of Leith Walk stages Broadway musicals, dance shows, opera and popular-music concerts.

**Stand Comedy Club** (Map pp76-7; ☎ 558 7272; www.the stand.co.uk; 5 York Pl; tickets £2-12) The Stand, founded in 1995, is Edinburgh's main comedy venue. It's an intimate cabaret bar with performances every night and a free Sunday lunchtime show.

## SHOPPING

Princes St is Edinburgh's principal shopping street, lined with all the big high-street stores, with many smaller shops along pedestrianised Rose St, and more expensive designer bou-tiques on George St. There are also two big shopping centres in the New Town – **Princes Mall** (Map pp76-7), at the eastern end of Princes St, and the nearby **St James Centre** (Map pp76-7) at the top of Leith St, plus a designer shopping complex with a flagship Harvey Ni-chols store on the eastern side of St Andrew Sq. The huge **Ocean Terminal** (Map p71) in Leith is the biggest shopping centre in the city.

For more off-beat shopping – including fashion, music, crafts, gifts and jewellery – head for the cobbled lanes of Cockburn, Vic-toria and St Mary's Sts, all near the Royal Mile in the Old Town, William St in the western part of New Town, and the Stockbridge dis-trict, immediately north of the New Town.

### Cashmere & Wool

Woollen textiles and knitwear are one of Scot-land's classic exports. Scottish cashmere – a fine, soft wool from young goats and lambs – provides the most luxurious and expensive knitwear and has been seen gracing the tor-sos of pop star Robbie Williams and England footballer David Beckham.

**Designs On Cashmere** (Map pp76-7; ☎ 556 6394; 28 High St) and the **Cashmere Store** (Map pp76-7; ☎ 226 1577; 2 St Giles St) are good places to start, with a wide range of traditional and modern knitwear, while the colourful designs at **Joyce Forsyth De-signer Knitwear** (Map pp76-7; ☎ 220 4112; 42 Candlemaker Row; ⏰ closed Sun & Mon) will drag your ideas about woollens firmly into the 21st century.

**Edinburgh Woollen Mill** (Map pp76-7; ☎ 226 3840; 139 Princes St) is an old stalwart of the tourist trade, with a good selection of traditional jer-seys, cardigans, scarves, shawls and rugs.

### Crafts & Gifts

The **One World Shop** (Map pp76-7; ☎ 229 4541; St John's Church, Princes St) stocks a wide range of hand-made crafts from developing countries, in-cluding paper goods, rugs, textiles, jewellery, ceramics, accessories, food and drink, all from accredited Fair Trade suppliers. During the Festival period (when the shop stays open till 6pm) there's a crafts fair in the churchyard outside.

**Meadows Pottery** (Map pp72-3; ☎ 662 4064; 11a Summerhall Pl) sells colourful stoneware, all hand-thrown on the premises, and the **Adam Pottery** (Map pp72-3; ☎ 557 3978; 76 Henderson Row) produces its own ceramics, mostly decorative, in a wide range of styles.

**Galerie Mirages** (Map pp72-3; ☎ 315 2603; 46a Rae-burn Pl) is an Aladdin's Cave packed with jew-ellery, textiles and handicrafts from all over the world, best known for its silver, amber and gemstone jewellery in both ethnic and contemporary designs.

### Department Stores

**Jenners** (Map pp76-7; ☎ 225 2442; 48 Princes St) Founded in 1838, Jenners is the *grande dame* of Scottish department stores. It stocks a wide range of quality goods, both classic and contemporary.

**John Lewis** (Map pp76-7; ☎ 556 9121; St James Centre) The place to go for good-value clothes and household goods.

**Harvey Nichols** (Map pp76-7; ☎ 524 8388; 30-34 St An-drew Sq) The jewel in the crown of Edinburgh's shopping scene has four floors of designer labels and eye-popping price tags.

### Tartan & Highland Dress

There are dozens of shops along the Royal Mile and Princes St where you can buy kilts and tartan goods.

**Kinloch Anderson** (Map p71; ☎ 555 1390; 4 Dock St, Leith) One of the best, this was founded in 1868 and is still family-run. Kinloch Anderson is a supplier of kilts and Highland dress to the royal family.

**Geoffrey (Tailor) Inc** (Map pp76-7; ☎ 557 0256; 57-59 High St) Can fit you out in traditional Highland dress, or run up a kilt in your own clan tartan. Its offshoot, 21st Century Kilts, offers modern fashion kilts in a variety of fabrics.

## GETTING THERE & AWAY
### Air
**Edinburgh Airport** ( ☎ 333 1000; www.edinburghairport
.com), 8 miles west of the city, has numerous
flights to other parts of Scotland and the UK,
Ireland and mainland Europe. See p449 for
details of flights to Edinburgh from outside
Scotland. **British Airways/Loganair** ( ☎ 0845 773
3377) operates daily flights to Inverness, Wick,
Orkney, Shetland and Stornoway.

### Bus
**Edinburgh Bus Station** (Map pp76–7) is at the
northeast corner of St Andrew Sq, with
pedestrian entrances from the square and
from Elder St. For timetable information,
call **Traveline** ( ☎ 0871 200 22 33; www.travelinescot
land.com).

    **Scottish Citylink** ( ☎ 0870 550 5050; www.citylink
.co.uk) buses connect Edinburgh with all of
Scotland's cities and major towns. The following are sample one-way fares departing
from Edinburgh.

| Destination | Fare | Duration | Frequency |
| --- | --- | --- | --- |
| Aberdeen | £20 | 3¼hr | 3 daily |
| Dundee | £11 | 1¾hr | hourly |
| Fort William | £23 | 4–5hr | 7 daily |
| Glasgow | £5 | 1¼hr | 15min |
| Inverness | £20 | 4½hr | 3 daily |
| Portree | £35 | 8hr | 2 daily |
| Stirling | £5 | 1hr | hourly |

Bus service 900 runs frequently between Edinburgh and Glasgow (£5, 1¼ hours, every
15 minutes).

    It's also worth checking with **Megabus**
( ☎ 0900 160 0900; www.megabus.com) for cheap
intercity bus fares (from as little as £1.50)
from Edinburgh to Aberdeen, Dundee, Glasgow, Inverness and Perth.

    See the Transport chapter, p451, for details
of buses to Edinburgh from London and the
rest of the UK.

### Car & Motorcycle
Arriving in or leaving Edinburgh by car during the morning and evening rush hours
(7.30am to 9.30am and 4.30pm to 6.30pm
Monday to Friday) is an experience you can
live without. Try to time your journey to avoid
these periods. In particular, there can be huge
tailbacks on the A90 between Edinburgh and
the Forth Road Bridge.

### Train
The main terminus in Edinburgh is Waverley train station (Map pp76–7), located in
the heart of the city. Trains arriving from,
and departing for, the west also stop at Haymarket station (Map pp72–3), which is more
convenient for the West End. You can buy
tickets, make reservations and get travel information at the **Edinburgh Rail Travel Centre** (Map
pp76–7; ☽ 4.45am-12.30am Mon-Sat, 7am-12.30am Sun)
in Waverley station. For fare and timetable
information, phone the **National Rail Enquiry
Service** ( ☎ 08457 48 49 50; www.nationalrail.co.uk) or
use the Journey Planner on the website.

    First ScotRail operates a regular shuttle
service between Edinburgh and Glasgow
(£10.30, 50 minutes, every 15 minutes), and
frequent daily services to all Scottish cities
including Aberdeen (£37, 2½ hours), Dundee (£19, 1½ hours) and Inverness (£37, 3¼
hours).

    See the Transport chapter, p451, for details
of trains to Edinburgh from London.

## GETTING AROUND
### To/From the Airport
The Lothian Buses **Airlink** (www.flybybus.com)
service 100 runs from Waverley Bridge, located just outside the train station, to the
airport (£3/5 one way/return, 30 minutes,
every 10 to 15 minutes) via the West End
and Haymarket.

    An airport taxi to the city centre costs
around £14 and takes about 20 minutes. Both
buses and taxis depart from outside the arrivals hall; go out through the main doors
and turn left.

### Bicycle
Thanks to the efforts of local cycling campaign group Spokes and a bike-friendly city
council, Edinburgh is well equipped with bike
lanes and dedicated cycle tracks. You can buy
a map of the city's cycle routes from most
bike shops.

    **Biketrax** (Map pp72-3; ☎ 228 6633; www.biketrax
.co.uk; 11 Lochrin Pl; ☽ 9.30am-6pm Mon-Fri, to 5.30pm Sat,
noon-5pm Sun) rents out a wide range of cycles
and equipment, including kids' bikes, tan-
dems, recumbents, pannier bags, child seats –
even unicycles! A mountain bike costs £16 for
24 hours, £12 for extra days, and £70 for one
week. You'll need a £100 cash or credit-card
deposit and some form of ID.

    For more on cycling, see p59.

## Car & Motorcycle

Though useful for day trips beyond the city, a car in central Edinburgh is more of a liability than a convenience. There is restricted access on Princes St, George St and Charlotte Sq, many streets are one way and finding a parking place in the city centre is like striking gold. Queen's Dr around Holyrood Park is closed to motorised traffic on Sunday.

### PARKING

There's no parking on main roads into the city from 7.30am to 6.30pm Monday to Saturday. Also, parking in the city centre can be a nightmare. On-street parking is controlled by self-service ticket machines from 8.30am to 6.30pm Monday to Saturday, and costs £1.80 per hour, with a two-hour maximum. If you break the rules, you'll get a fine, often within minutes of your ticket expiring – Edinburgh's parking wardens are both numerous and notorious. The fine is £60, reduced to £30 if you pay up within 14 days. Cars parked illegally will be towed away. There are large, long-stay car parks at the St James Centre, Greenside Pl, New St, Castle Tce and Morrison St. Motorcycles can be parked free at designated areas in the city centre.

### CAR RENTAL

All the big, international car-rental agencies have offices in Edinburgh (see p454).

There are many smaller, local agencies that offer better rates. One of the best is **Arnold Clark** (Map p71; ☎ 657 9120; www.arnoldclarkrental.co.uk; 20 Seafield Rd East) near Portobello, which charges from £23 a day, or £110 a week for a small car, including VAT and insurance. The daily rate includes 250 miles a day; excess is charged at 4p a mile. For periods of four days and more, mileage is unlimited.

## Public Transport

Edinburgh's public transport system consists entirely of buses; the main operators are **Lothian Buses** (www.lothianbuses.co.uk) and **First-Edinburgh** (www.firstedinburgh.co.uk); for timetable information contact **Traveline** ( ☎ 0871 200 22 33; www.travelinescotland.com).

Bus timetables, route maps and fare guides are posted at all main bus stops, and you can pick up a copy of the free *Lothian Buses Route Map* from **Lothian Buses Travelshop** Hanover St (Map pp76-7; ☺ 8.15am-6pm Mon-Sat); Shandwick Pl (Map pp76-7; ☺ 8.15am-6pm Mon-Sat); Waverley Bridge

(Map pp76-7; ☎ 555 6363; ☺ 8.15am-6pm Mon-Sat, 9.30am-5pm Sun).

Adult fares are £1; children aged under five travel free and those aged five to 15 pay a flat fare of 60p. On Lothian Buses you must pay the driver the exact fare, but First Edinburgh buses will give change. Lothian Bus drivers also sell a Daysaver ticket (£2.50) that gives unlimited travel (on Lothian Buses only, excluding night buses) for a day. Night-service buses (www.nightbuses.com), which run hourly between midnight and 5am, charge a flat fare of £2.50.

You can also buy a Ridacard (from Travelshops; not available from bus drivers) that gives unlimited travel for one week for £13.

The **Lothian Buses lost property office** (Map pp72-3; ☎ 558 8858; lostproperty@lothianbuses.co.uk; Main Depot, Annadale St; ☺ 10am-1.30pm Mon-Fri) is located north of the city centre.

## Taxi

Edinburgh's black taxis can be hailed in the street, ordered by phone (extra 60p charge), or picked up at one of the many central ranks. The minimum charge is £1.50 (£2.50 at night) for the first 450m, then 25p for every subsequent 225m or 45 seconds – a typical 2-mile trip across the city centre will cost around £5. Tipping is up to you – because of the high fares local people rarely tip on short journeys, but occasionally round up to the nearest 50p on longer ones. Some taxi companies:

**Central Taxis** ( ☎ 229 2468)
**City Cabs** ( ☎ 228 1211)
**ComCab** ( ☎ 272 8000)

# AROUND EDINBURGH

Edinburgh is small enough that, when you need a break from the city, the beautiful surrounding countryside isn't far away and is easily accessible by public transport, or even by bike. The old counties around Edinburgh are called Midlothian, West Lothian and East Lothian, often referred to collectively as 'the Lothians'.

## MIDLOTHIAN
### Queensferry
☎ 0131

Queensferry is located at the narrowest part of the Firth of Forth, where ferries have sailed to Fife from the earliest times. The village takes its name from Queen Margaret (1046–93), who gave pilgrims free passage across the firth on their way to St Andrews. Ferries continued to operate until 1964 when the graceful **Forth Road Bridge** – now Europe's fifth longest – was opened.

Predating the road bridge by 74 years, the magnificent **Forth Bridge** – only outsiders ever call it the Forth Rail Bridge – is one of the finest engineering achievements of the 19th century. Completed in 1890 after seven years' work, its three huge cantilevers span 1447m and took 59,000 tonnes of steel, eight million rivets and the lives of 58 men to build.

In the pretty, terraced High St in Queensferry is the small **Queensferry Museum** ( ☎ 331 5545; 53 High St; admission free; ◷ 10am-1pm & 2.15-5pm Mon & Thu-Sat, noon-5pm Sun). It contains some interesting background information on the bridges, and a fascinating exhibit on the 'Burry Man', part of the village's summer gala festivities (see p95).

There are several good places to eat and drink along the High St, including the stylish **Orocco Pier** ( ☎ 331 1298; www.oroccopier.co.uk; 17 High St; mains £12-23; ◷ 9am-10pm), which has a modern dining area and outdoor terrace with a stunning view of the Forth Bridge.

The atmospheric **Hawes Inn** ( ☎ 331 1990; Newhalls Rd; mains £6-12; ◷ food served noon-10pm), famously mentioned in Robert Louis Stevenson's novel *Kidnapped*, serves excellent pub grub; it's opposite the Inchcolm ferry, right beside the railway bridge.

**GETTING THERE & AWAY**

Queensferry lies on the southern bank of the Firth of Forth, 8 miles west of Edinburgh city centre. To get there, take First Edinburgh bus 43 (£2.20, 30 minutes, three hourly) westbound from St Andrew Sq. It's a 10-minute walk from the bus stop to the Hawes Inn and the Inchcolm ferry.

Trains go from Edinburgh's Waverley and Haymarket stations to Dalmeny station (£3.20, 15 minutes, two to four hourly). From the station exit, the Hawes Inn is five minutes' walk along a footpath (across the road, behind the bus stop) that leads north beside the railway and then downhill under the bridge.

**Inchcolm**

The island of Inchcolm lies east of the Forth bridges, less than a mile off the coast of Fife. Only 800m long, it is home to the ruins of

**Inchcolm Abbey** ( ☎ 01383-823332; Inchcolm, Fife; adult/child £4.50/2.25; ◷ 9.30am-5.30pm Apr-Sep), one of Scotland's best-preserved medieval abbeys, founded by Augustinian priors in 1123.

The ferry boat **Maid of the Forth** ( ☎ 0131-331 4857; www.maidoftheforth.co.uk) sails to Inchcolm from Hawes Pier in Queensferry. There are one to four sailings most days from May to October. The return fare is £13.50/5.25 per adult/child, including admission to Inchcolm Abbey. It's a half-hour sail to Inchcolm and you get 1½ hours ashore. As well as the abbey, the trip gives you the chance to see the island's grey seals, puffins and other seabirds.

**Sea.fari** ( ☎ 331 4857; www.seafari.co.uk) runs high-speed boat trips to Inchcolm from Newhaven harbour near Leith, in Edinburgh (adult/child £20/16), giving you 50 minutes ashore on the island.

## Hopetoun House
☎ 0131

**Hopetoun House** ( ☎ 331 2451; www.hopetounhouse .com; adult/child £8/4.25; ◷ 10.30am-5pm Easter-Sep, last admission 4pm) is one of Scotland's finest stately homes, with a superb location in lovely grounds beside the Firth of Forth. There are two parts – the older built to Sir William Bruce's plans between 1699 and 1702 and dominated by a splendid stairwell with (modern) trompe l'oeil paintings; and the newer designed between 1720 and 1750 by three members of the Adam family, William and sons Robert and John. The highlights are the red and yellow Adam drawing rooms, lined in silk damask, and the view from the roof terrace.

Britain's most elegant equine accommodation – where the marquis once housed his pampered racehorses – is now the stylish **Stables Tearoom** ( ☎ 331 3661; mains £5-8; ◷ 10am-5.30pm Easter-Sep), a delightful spot for lunch.

Hopetoun House is 2 miles west of Queensferry along the coast road. Driving from Edinburgh, turn off the A90 onto the A904 just before the Forth Bridge and follow the signs.

## Rosslyn Chapel
☎ 0131

The success of Dan Brown's novel *The Da Vinci Code* and the subsequent Hollywood film has seen a flood of visitors descend on Scotland's most beautiful and enigmatic church – **Rosslyn Chapel** (Collegiate Church of St Matthew;

☎ 440 2159; www.rosslynchapel.com; Roslin; adult/child £7/free; ☉ 9.30am-6pm Mon-Sat, noon-4.45pm Sun Apr-Sep, 9.30am-5pm Mon-Sat, noon-4.45pm Sun Oct-Mar). The chapel was built in the mid-15th century for William St Clair, third earl of Orkney, and the ornately carved interior – at odds with the architectural fashion of its time – is a monument to the mason's art, rich in symbolic imagery. As well as flowers, vines, angels and biblical figures, the carved stones include many examples of the pagan 'Green Man'; other figures are associated with Freemasonry and the Knights Templar. Intriguingly, there are also carvings of plants from the Americas that predate Columbus' voyage of discovery. The symbolism of these images has led some researchers to conclude that Rosslyn is some kind of secret Templar repository, and it has been claimed that hidden vaults beneath the chapel could conceal anything from the Holy Grail or the head of John the Baptist to the body of Christ himself. The chapel is owned by the Episcopal Church of Scotland and services are still held here on Sunday mornings.

The chapel is on the eastern edge of the village of Roslin, 7 miles south of Edinburgh's centre. Lothian Bus 15 (not 15A) runs from St Andrew Sq in Edinburgh to Roslin (£1, 30 minutes, every 30 minutes).

**Celtic Trails** ( ☎ 448 2869; www.celtictrails.co.uk) offers half-/whole-day tours of the chapel and surrounding area for £32/49 per person, including admission fees.

### Pentland Hills

Rising on the southern edge of Edinburgh, the Pentland Hills stretch 16 miles southwest to near Carnwath in Lanarkshire. The hills rise to 579m at their highest point and offer excellent, not-too-strenuous walking with great views. There are several access points along the A702 road on the southern side of the hills. MacEwan's bus 100 runs four times daily along the A702 from Princes St in Edinburgh to Biggar.

## EAST LOTHIAN

Beyond the former coalfields of Dalkeith and Musselburgh, the fertile farmland of East Lothian stretches eastwards along the coast to the seaside resort of North Berwick and the fishing harbour of Dunbar. In the middle lies the prosperous market town of Haddington.

### Haddington & Around

☎ 01620 / pop 8850

Haddington, straddling the River Tyne 18 miles east of Edinburgh, was made a royal burgh by David I in the 12th century. Most of the modern town, however, dates from the 17th to 19th centuries during the period of prosperity after the Agricultural Revolution. The prettiest part of town is the tree-lined Court St, with its wide pavement and grand 18th- and 19th-century buildings.

Church St leads from the eastern end of High St to **St Mary's Parish Church** ( ☎ 823109; Sidegate; admission free; ☉ 11am-4pm Mon-Sat, 2-4.30pm Sun Apr-Sep). Built in 1462, it's the largest parish church in Scotland and one of the finest pre-Reformation churches in the country.

A mile south of Haddington is **Lennoxlove House** ( ☎ 823720; Lennoxlove Estate; adult/child £5/3; ☉ guided tours 1.30-4pm Wed, Thu & Sun Apr-Oct), a hidden gem of a country house dating originally from around 1345, with major extensions and renovations from the 17th to the early 20th centuries. It contains fine furniture and paintings, and memorabilia relating to Mary, Queen of Scots. Chief among these are her death mask and a silver casket given to her by Francis II of France, her first husband. The house has been the seat of the duke of Hamilton since 1947.

First Edinburgh buses X6 and X8 run between Edinburgh and Haddington every 30 minutes. The nearest train station is at Drem, 3 miles to the north.

### North Berwick

☎ 01620 / pop 6220

North Berwick is an attractive Victorian seaside resort with long sandy beaches, three golf courses and a small harbour. The **tourist office** ( ☎ 892197; Quality St; ☉ 9am-6pm Mon-Sat, 11am-4pm Sun Jun-Sep, 9am-6pm Mon-Sat Apr & May, 9am-5pm Mon-Sat Oct-Mar) is two blocks inland from the harbour.

#### SIGHTS & ACTIVITIES

Top marks to the bright spark who came up with the idea for the **Scottish Seabird Centre** ( ☎ 890202; www.seabird.org; The Harbour; adult/child £6.95/4.50; ☉ 10am-6pm Apr-Sep, 10am-5pm Mon-Fri, 10am-5.30pm Sat & Sun Feb, Mar & Oct, 10am-4pm Mon-Fri, 10am-5.30pm Sat & Sun Nov-Jan), an ornithologist's paradise that uses remote-control video cameras sited on the Bass Rock and other islands to relay live images of nesting gannets and other seabirds – you can control the cameras yourself, and zoom in on scenes of cosy gannet domesticity.

Off High St, a short steep path climbs up **North Berwick Law** (184m), a conical hill that dominates the town. When the weather's fine there are great views to spectacular **Bass Rock**, iced white in spring and summer with guano from thousands of nesting gannets. The **Sula II** ( ☎ 892838) runs boat trips (adult/child £8.50/4, 1¼ hours, daily April to September) around Bass Rock and Fidra Island, departing from North Berwick's harbour.

Two miles west of North Berwick is **Dirleton Castle** (HS; ☎ 850330; Dirleton; adult/child £4.50/2.25; ☉ 9.30am-5.30pm Apr-Sep, 9.30am-4.30pm Oct-Mar), an impressive medieval fortress with massive round towers, a drawbridge and a horrific pit dungeon, surrounded rather incongruously by beautiful, manicured gardens.

Perched on a cliff 3 miles east of North Berwick is the spectacular ruin of **Tantallon Castle** (HS; ☎ 892727; adult/child £4.50/2.25; ☉ 9.30am-5.30pm Apr-Sep, 9.30am-4.30pm Sat-Wed Oct-Mar). Built around 1350, it was the fortress residence of the Douglas earls of Angus (the 'Red Douglases'), defended on one side by a series of ditches and on the other by an almost sheer drop into the sea.

### SLEEPING & EATING

North Berwick has plenty of places to stay, though they can fill up quickly at weekends when golfers are in town. Recommended B&Bs include **Glebe House** ( ☎ 892608; www .glebehouse-nb.co.uk; Law Rd; r per person £40-45; **P** ), a beautiful Georgian country house with three spacious bedrooms, and homely **Beach Lodge** ( ☎ 892257; www.beachlodge.co.uk; 5 Beach Rd; r per person from £40), which offers sea views and vegetarian breakfasts.

The top eating places in the area are the **Grange** ( ☎ 893344; 35 High St; 3-course lunch £10, mains £12-19; ☉ lunch & dinner) in the centre of town, and the delightful **Deveau's Brasserie** ( ☎ 850241; Open Arms Hotel, Dirleton; mains £11-17; ☉ lunch & dinner) in the village of Dirleton.

### GETTING THERE & AWAY

North Berwick is 24 miles east of Edinburgh. First Edinburgh bus 124 runs between Edinburgh and North Berwick (1¼ hours, every 20 minutes). There are frequent trains between North Berwick and Edinburgh (£4.60, 35 minutes, hourly).

## Dunbar

☎ 01368 / pop 6350

Dunbar was an important Scottish fortress town in the Middle Ages, but little remains of its past save for the tottering ruins of **Dunbar Castle** overlooking the harbour. Today the town survives as a fishing port and seaside resort, famed in the USA as the birthplace of John Muir (1838–1914), pioneer conservationist and father of the US national park system.

The **tourist office** ( ☎ 863353; 143 High St; ☉ 9am-5pm Mon-Sat, 11am-4pm Sun Jun-Sep, 9am-5pm Mon-Sat Apr, May & Oct) is near the town hall.

The slightly down-at-heel town centre is home to **John Muir House** ( ☎ 862595; 128 High St; admission free; ☉ 10am-5pm Mon-Sat, 1-5pm Sun Apr-Oct, 10am-5pm Wed-Sat, 1-5pm Sun Nov-Mar), the birthplace and childhood home of the great man himself. The nearby **Dunbar Town House Museum** ( ☎ 863734; High St; admission free; ☉ 12.30-4.30pm Apr-Oct, 2-4.30pm Sat & Sun Nov-Mar) provides an introduction to local history and archaeology.

From the castle, a scenic 2-mile cliff-top trail follows the coastline west to the sands of Belhaven Bay and **John Muir Country Park**.

First Edinburgh bus X6 (one hour, hourly) runs between Edinburgh and Dunbar. Trains from Edinburgh's Waverley train station serve Dunbar (£8, 20 minutes) every hour or so.

# WEST LOTHIAN
## Linlithgow

☎ 01506 / pop 13,400

This ancient royal burgh is one of Scotland's oldest towns, though much of it 'only' dates from the 15th to 17th centuries. Its centre retains a certain charm, despite some ugly modern buildings and occasional traffic congestion, and the town makes an excellent day trip from Edinburgh.

The **tourist office** ( ☎ 844600; ☉ 10am-5pm Apr-Oct) is in the Burgh Halls at the Cross.

### SIGHTS & ACTIVITIES

The town's main attraction is the magnificent **Linlithgow Palace** (HS; ☎ 842896; Church Peel; adult/child £5/2.50; ☉ 9.30am-5.30pm Apr-Sep, 9.30am-4.30pm Oct-Mar), begun by James I in 1425. The building of the palace continued for over a century and it became a favourite royal residence – James V was born here in 1512, as was his daughter Mary (later Queen of Scots) in 1542, and Bonnie Prince Charlie visited briefly in 1745. The elaborately carved **King's Fountain**, the centrepiece of the palace courtyard, flowed with wine during Charlie's stay. The fountain, commissioned by James V in 1537, is the oldest in Britain, and was restored to full working order in 2005.

Beside the palace is the Gothic **St Michael's Church** ( ☎ 842188; Church Peel; admission free; ◷ 10.30am-4pm Mon-Sat, 12.30-4.30pm Sun May-Sep, 10.30am-1pm Mon-Fri Oct-Apr). Built between the 1420s and 1530s, it is topped by a controversial aluminium spire that was added in 1964. The church is said to be haunted by a ghost that foretold King James IV of his impending defeat at Flodden in 1513.

The **Linlithgow Story** ( ☎ 670677; Annet House, 143 High St; adult/child £1.50/1, Sun free; ◷ 11am-5pm Mon-Sat & 1-4pm Sun Apr-Oct) is a small museum that tells the story of the Stewart monarchy and the history of the town.

Just 150m south of the town centre lies the Union Canal and the pretty **Linlithgow Canal Centre** ( ☎ 671215; www.lucs.org.uk; Manse Rd Canal Basin; admission free; ◷ 2-5pm Sat & Sun Easter-Oct, plus 2-5pm Mon-Fri Jul & Aug), where a little museum records the history of the canal.

The centre runs three-hour **canal boat trips** (adult/child £6/3) west to the Avon Aqueduct departing at 2pm Saturday and Sunday, Easter to September, and occasionally to the **Falkirk Wheel** (see the boxed text, p206). Shorter 20-minute cruises (adult/child £2.50/1.50) leave every half hour during the centre's opening times.

### EATING & DRINKING

Linlithgow has several good pubs and restaurants. The **Four Marys** ( ☎ 842171; 65-76 High St; mains £5-10; ◷ food served noon-3pm & 5-9pm Mon-Fri, noon-9pm Sat & Sun) is an attractive traditional pub (opposite the palace entrance) that serves real ales and excellent pub grub, including haggis, neeps and tatties (haggis, mashed turnip and mashed potato). A few doors along the street is **Marynka** ( ☎ 840123; 57 High St; lunch mains £6-10; ◷ noon-2pm & 6-10pm Tue-Sat), a pleasant little gourmet restaurant (two-/three-course dinner £22/26).

The rustic **Champany Inn** ( ☎ 834532; Champany; mains £15-25; ◷ 12.30-2pm & 7-10pm Mon-Fri, 7-10pm Sat) is a trencherman's delight, famous for its excellent Aberdeen Angus steaks and Scottish lobsters. The neighbouring **Chop & Ale House** (mains £8-16) is a less expensive alternative to the main dining room, offering delicious homemade burgers and steaks. The inn is 2 miles northeast of Linlithgow on the A803/A904 road towards Bo'ness and Queensferry.

### GETTING THERE & AWAY

Linlithgow is 15 miles west of Edinburgh, and is served by frequent trains from the capital (£3.70, 20 minutes, four every hour); the train station is 250m east of the town centre.

You can also cycle from Edinburgh to Linlithgow along the Union Canal towpath (21 miles); allow 1½ to two hours.

# Glasgow

Glasgow is regenerating and evolving at a dizzying pace – style cats beware, this city is edgy, modish and downright ballsy. Its Victorian architectural legacy is now swamped with cutting-edge style bars, world-class venues to tickle your taste buds, and a hedonistic club culture that will bring out your nocturnal instincts. Best of all, though, is Glasgow's pounding live-music scene which is one of the best in Britain, and accessible through countless venues dedicated to homegrown beats.

The city is going through a long-term transformation, evident along the revitalised River Clyde, where visitors can explore Glasgow's mighty maritime heritage along riverfront walkways. Museums and galleries abound and the city's resume has been made even more impressive with the reopening of the colossal Kelvingrove Art Gallery & Museum – which, in typical Glaswegian fashion, strips the city of any false pretences and tells it like it is – both the inspiring and the infuriating aspects of life here.

Glasgow combines urban mayhem and black humour and is so friendly, it's sometimes downright unnerving – throw off the shackles of urban restraint and immerse yourself in a down-to-earth metropolis that is all about fun. And besides, where else in the world can you land in the middle of a city in a seaplane?

Glaswegians are proud of their working class background and leftist traditions. Their rivalry with Edinburgh is fierce and folk are full of contempt for what they see as a prissy, right-wing establishment on the east coast, full of toffs with clipped accents and, infuriatingly, holding the title of capital city. However Glaswegians remind themselves that Edinburgh may be the capital, but Glasgow has the capital.

---

## HIGHLIGHTS

- Rediscovering the colossal **Kelvingrove Art Gallery & Museum** (p129), open again after a huge refurbishment programme
- Cruising along the **River Clyde** (p123) where evidence of the city's remarkable regeneration is evident in the city's maritime heritage
- Wandering the vast, medieval **Glasgow Cathedral** (p128), a shining example of pre-Reformation Gothic architecture
- Showing the locals your latest dance moves among Glasgow's plethora of **nightclubs** (p142) where the country's best DJs strut their stuff
- Nursing a pint of local brew in the **perfect watering hole** (p140) – from traditional Victorian-era pubs to the city's famed style bars along Bath St

Kelvingrove Art Gallery & Museum
★ ★ Glasgow Cathedral
River Clyde

---

■ TELEPHONE CODE: 0141    ■ POPULATION: 630,000    ■ AREA: 176 SQ KM

## HISTORY

Glasgow grew up around the cathedral founded by St Mungo in the 6th century, and in 1451 the city became the site of the University of Glasgow, the second university to be founded in Scotland after St Andrews.

In the 18th century much of the tobacco trade between Europe and the USA was routed through Glasgow and provided a great source of wealth. Even after the tobacco trade declined in the 19th century, the city continued to prosper as a centre of textile manufacturing, shipbuilding, and the coal and steel industries.

The industries created a huge demand for labour, and peasants poured in from Ireland and the Highlands to crowd the tenements. The outward appearance of prosperity, however, was tempered by dire working conditions in the factories, particularly for women and children. In the second half of the 19th century, life expectancy was only 30 years.

While the workers suffered, the textile barons and shipping magnates prospered, and Glasgow could justifiably call itself the second city of the empire. In the first half of the 20th century, Glasgow was the centre of Britain's munitions industry, supplying arms and ships for the two world wars. After those boom years, however, the port and heavy industries began to decline, and by the early 1970s the city looked doomed. Glasgow has always been proud of its predominantly working-class nature but, unlike middle-class Edinburgh with its varied service industries, it had few alternatives when recession hit and unemployment spiralled.

In the late 20th and early 21st centuries there has been increasing confidence in the city as it determinedly sets about an enormous campaign of regeneration. Glasgow won the 1990 European City of Culture award, and followed this up by serving as the UK's City of Architecture & Design in 1999. But, behind all the optimism, the general standard of living remains relatively low, and life is tough for those affected by the comparatively high unemployment and inadequate housing

## ORIENTATION

The city centre is built on a grid system on the northern side of the River Clyde. The two train stations (Central and Queen St), the Buchanan bus station and the tourist office are all on or within a couple of blocks of George Sq, the main city square. Merchant City is the city's main commercial and entertainment district, east of George Sq.

Motorways bore through the suburbs and the M8 sweeps round the northern and western edges of the city centre, passing the airport 10 miles west.

### Maps

The Automobile Association's *Glasgow Street by Street* (£5.99) is a handy, easy-to-read street guide, available in bookshops. Glasgow City Council publishes the excellent *Fit for Life* map (free from the tourist office) showing cycle and walking routes around the city.

## INFORMATION

The *List* (£2.20; www.list.co.uk), available from newsagents, is Glasgow and Edinburgh's invaluable fortnightly guide to films, theatre, cabaret, music, clubs – the works. The excellent *Eating & Drinking Guide* (£5.95), published by the *List* every April, covers Glasgow and Edinburgh.

### Bookshops

**Borders** (Map p126; ☎ 222 7700; 98 Buchanan St; ☾ 8.30am-10pm Mon-Sat, 10am-8pm Sun) A browsing bonanza, also sells CDs and international newspapers and magazines.
**Waterstone's** (Map p126; ☎ 332 9105; 153 Sauchiehall St; ☾ 8.30am-7pm Mon, Tue, Wed & Fri, 8.30am-8pm Thu, 9am-7pm Sat, 10am-6pm Sun) A major bookshop, also sells guidebooks and street maps of Glasgow.

### Emergency

**Ambulance, Fire, Police, Mountain rescue or Coastguard** (☎ 999, 112)

### Internet Access

**easyInternet** (Map p126; ☎ 222 2364; www.easy -everything.com; 57 St Vincent St; charges vary; ☾ 7am-9pm Mon-Fri, 8am-9pm Sat, 9am-7pm Sun) Consider buying a cheaper four-hour pass.
**Gallery of Modern Art** (Map p126; ☎ 229 1996; Royal Exchange Sq, Queen St; ☾ 10am-5pm Mon-Wed & Sat, 10am-8pm Thu, 11am-5pm Fri & Sun) Basement library; free internet access. Bookings recommended. See also p125.
**ICafe** (Map p124; cnr Great Western Rd & Dunearn St; per hr £3; ☾ 10am-11pm) Sip a coffee and munch on a pastry while you check your emails on superfast connections.
**Mitchell Library** (Map p124; ☎ 287 2999; North St; ☾ 9am-8pm Mon-Thu, to 5pm Fri & Sat) Offers free internet access; bookings recommended.

GLASGOW

# GREATER GLASGOW

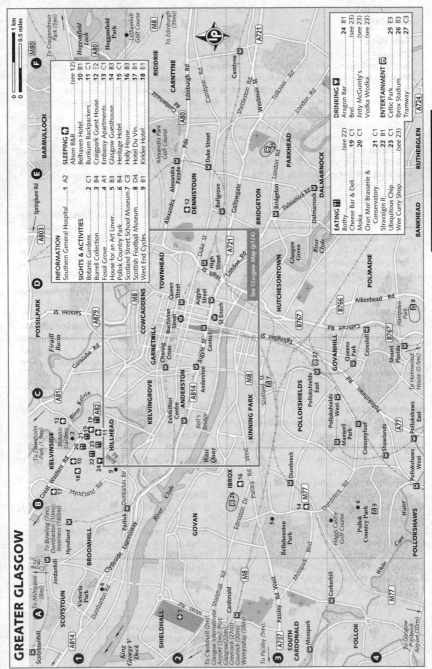

**INFORMATION**
Southern General Hospital..........1 A2

**SIGHTS & ACTIVITIES**
Botanic Gardens.........................2 C1
Burrell Collection.......................3 B4
Fossil Grove.............................4 A1
House for an Art Lover..................5 B3
Pollok Country Park.....................6 B4
Scotland Street School Museum.....7 C3
Scottish Football Museum.............8 D4
West End Cycles.........................9 B1

**SLEEPING** 🛏
Alison B&B.........................(see 12)
Belhaven Hotel........................10 B1
Bunkum Backpackers.................11 C1
Craigpark Guest House...............12 E2
Embassy Apartments.................13 C1
Glasgow Guesthouse.................14 B3
Heritage Hotel........................15 C1
Holly House..........................16 B3
Hotel Du Vin.........................17 B1
Kirklee Hotel........................18 B1

**EATING** 🍴
Bothy.................................(see 22)
Cheese Bar & Deli....................19 C1
Moka.................................20 C1
Oran Mor Brasserie & 
  Conservatory......................21 C1
Stravaigin II........................22 B1
Ubiquitous Chip......................23 C1
Wee Curry Shop....................(see 23)

**DRINKING** 🍷
Aragon Bar..........................24 B1
Brel...............................(see 23)
Jinty McGuinty's...................(see 23)
Vodka Wodka........................(see 23)

**ENTERTAINMENT** 🎭
Celtic Park..........................25 E3
Ibrox Stadium.......................26 B3
Tramway............................27 C3

## GLASGOW IN...

### Two Days

Start your day with breakfast and a spot of people-watching in the trendy **Merchant City** (p137). Take a stroll around the leafy cathedral precinct in the **East End** (p127), popping your head into **Glasgow Cathedral** (p128) and **St Mungo's Museum of Religious Life & Art** (p128). Treat yourself to a fine German brew and a schnitzel at **West Brewing Company** (p138), swoon to traditional jazz at the plush **Drum & Monkey** (p140) and then dedicate the night to **Arches** (p141), one of Glasgow's premier pubs/clubs.

A visit to the wonderful **Burrell Collection** (p130) is a must on your second day, and while in the area check out the **Scottish Football Museum** (p130). If you're here on a weekend, don't miss the **Barras** (p131), Glasgow's flea market and, some would say, its heart and soul. At night, head to Bath St for unpretentious style bars and fine dining along the city centre's trendiest strip. Drop into **King Tut's Wah Wah Hut** (p143) to hear some of Glasgow's freshest live-music talent.

### Four Days

Follow the two-day itinerary, then on your third day add a trip to the bohemian **West End** (p129); some of the city's best cafés and restaurants are here. Don't miss the fabulous **Kelvingrove Art Gallery & Museum** (p129) and be sure to check out the **Hunterian Museum** (p129) and **Hunterian Art Gallery** (p129). On the fourth day stroll along the **Clyde Walkway** (p132) and discover the rejuvenation on Glasgow's waterfront. Learn about the city's unique heritage by taking a boat trip down the **River Clyde** (p125), visiting the **Clydebuilt** (p125) museum and **Tall Ship** (opposite) en route – then catch a 3-D flick at the **Glasgow Science Centre** (opposite).

### One Week

Follow the four-day itinerary and then spend a day discovering what all the **Mackintoshania** (p128) fuss is about. Drop into the **Glasgow School of Art** (p126), **Willow Tea Rooms** (p126) and **The Mackintosh Church** (p131). Finish up with a couple of day trips out of the city: head to **Paisley** (p147) and marvel at its magnificent abbey, and take a wander around the revitalised waterfront at **Greenock** (p147), popping into the **HM Customs & Excise Museum** (p147).

## Internet Resources

**Glasgow City Council** (www.glasgow.gov.uk) Has a particularly good daily 'What's On' section.

**Glasgow Disability Access Guide** (www.glasgow accesspanel.org.uk) An online guide for people with disabilities.

**Glasgow Museums** (www.glasgowmuseums.com) A very useful guide to the city's superb museums.

**The Guide** (www.glasgowlife.com) An online city guide particularly good for eating and entertainment.

## Left Luggage

**Buchanan bus station** (Map p126; ☎ 333 3708; Killermont St; per 2 hr/day £2.50/3.50)

**Queen Street station** (Map p126; ☎ 0845 601 5929; North Hanover St; small/medium/large piece of luggage per 24hr £5/6/7)

## Medical Services

To see a doctor, visit the outpatients department at any general hospital. Recommended hospitals:

**Glasgow Dental Hospital** (Map p126; ☎ 211 9600; 378 Sauchiehall St)

**Glasgow Royal Infirmary** (Map p124; ☎ 211 4000; 84 Castle St)

**Southern General Hospital** (Map p121; ☎ 201 1100; Govan Rd)

## Money

The post office and the tourist office have a bureau de change.

**American Express** (Amex; Map p126; ☎ 222 1405; 115 Hope St; ⏰ 9am-5.30pm Mon, Tue, Thu & Fri, 9.30am-5.30pm Wed, 9am-noon Sat)

**Clydesdale Bank** (Map p126; 7 St Enoch Sq) Has four 24-hour ATMs.

## Post

There are post offices in some supermarkets; the larger ones are open Sunday as well.

**Main post office** (Map p126; 47 St Vincent St; ⏰ 8.30am-5.45pm Mon-Fri, 9am-5.30pm Sat) Passport photos available.

## Tourist Information

**Glasgow tourist office** (Map p126; ☎ 204 4400; www.seeglasgow.com; 11 George Sq; ⏰ 9am-6pm Mon-Sat Oct-Jan & Easter-May, 9am-7pm Mon-Sat Jun & Sep, 9am-8pm Mon-Sat Jul-Aug, 10am-6pm Sun Easter-Sep) Excellent tourist office; makes local and national accommodation bookings (£3).

**St Enoch Square Travel Centre** (Map p126; St Enoch Sq; ⏰ 8.30am-5.30pm Mon-Sat) Travel information only.

**Tourist office branch** ( ☎ 848 4440; Glasgow International Airport; ⏰ 7.30am-5pm Easter-Sep, 7.30am-5pm Mon-Sat, 8am-3.30pm Sun Oct-Easter)

## Travel Agencies

**Glasgow Flight Centre** (Map p126; ☎ 353 1351; www.flightcentre.co.uk; 280 Sauchiehall St)

## DANGERS & ANNOYANCES

Glasgow, like any big city, has its share of crime, some violent and much alcohol or drug fuelled. The usual precautions apply. Stick to well-lit areas at night, catch a taxi if you're going into a part of the city you're unfamiliar with and don't wander around by yourself along nightclub/late night bar precincts such as Sauchiehall St late at night. Women should avoid walking alone at night in the red-light district situated around Anderston/Blythswood Sq.

Keep clear of Orange marches, which are exhibitions of solidarity with the Protestant Northern Irish cause; violence can result when Catholics try to 'break the ranks'. These events aren't for tourists.

Glasgow is very friendly though and very few visitors encounter problems – most of the violent crime is underworld-related, which rarely affects tourists. For more information, see also Dangers and Annoyances (p440) in the Directory.

## SIGHTS

Glasgow's major sights are fairly evenly dispersed around the city, with many found along the Clyde – the focus of a long-term regeneration programme – the leafy cathedral precinct in the East End and the museum-rich South Side. The city centre itself also contains a variety of attractions, particularly Mackintoshania. The trendy West End swarms with students during term time, but it's quieter during the holidays.

### The Clyde

The tide has turned for the Clyde. In the last decade Glasgow has been returning to its roots

with a major campaign to rejuvenate the riverfront and celebrate the city's unique industrial heritage. Included in this strategy is a 10-year plan to redevelop Glasgow Harbour, involving the conversion of former docklands into shops and public areas, and rebuilding seven Art-Nouveau Mackintosh-designed tearooms. It's also expected that access to almost 2 miles of formerly inaccessible waterfront will be made available – to find out more about this project see www.glasgowharbour.com.

A new museum, **The Riverside Museum**, is the latest development on Glasgow Harbour with construction beginning in 2007 – it may be open by the time you read this. The museum will replace the **Museum of Transport** (see p130) showcasing Glasgow's transport and technology collections and linking with its maritime heritage. Ask at the tourist office for further information.

### GLASGOW SCIENCE CENTRE

Scotland's flagship millennium project, the superb, ultramodern **Glasgow Science Centre** (Map p124; ☎ 420 5000; 50 Pacific Quay; Science Mall adult/child £6.95/4.95, IMAX £6.95/4.95, combined ticket £9.95/7.95; ⏰ 10am-6pm; ♿ 🅿 ) will keep the kids entertained for hours (that's middle-aged kids, too!). It brings science and technology alive through hundreds of interactive exhibits on four floors. Look out for the illusions (like rearranging your features through a 3-D headscan) and the cloud chamber, showing tracks of natural radiation. It consists of an egg-shaped titanium-covered **IMAX** theatre (phone for current screenings) and an interactive **Science Mall** with floor-to-ceiling windows – a bounty of discovery for young, inquisitive minds. There's also a rotating **observation tower**, 127m high. And check out the planetarium, where the **Scottish Power Space Theatre** brings the night sky to life and a **Virtual Science Theatre** treats visitors to a 3-D molecular journey. To get here take Arriva bus 24 from Renfield St or First Glasgow bus 89 or 90 from Union St.

### TALL SHIP & PUMPHOUSE

Across the Clyde from the science centre, via Bell's Bridge, is the magnificent **Tall Ship** (Glenlee; Map p124; ☎ 222 2513; 100 Stobcross Rd, Glasgow Harbour; adult £4.95, 1 child free, then per child £2.50; ⏰ 10am-5pm Mar-Oct, to 4pm Nov-Feb; 🅿 ), one of five sailing ships built on the Clyde still afloat. The *Glenlee* was launched in December 1896. The sheer size of this three-masted ship is

GLASGOW

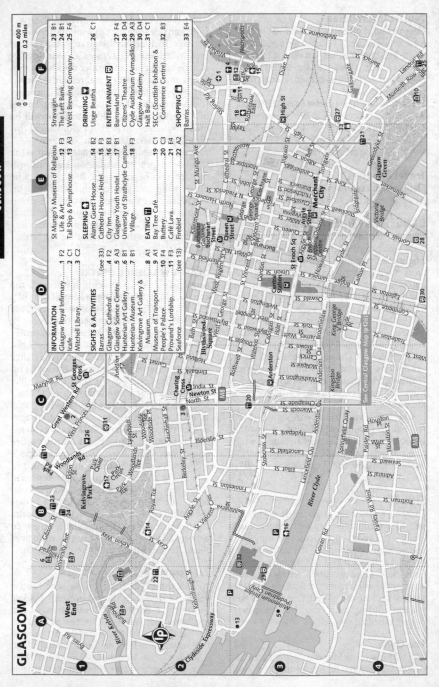

**INFORMATION**
Glasgow Royal Infirmary............1 F2
Icafe......................................2 C1
Mitchell Library......................3 C2

**SIGHTS & ACTIVITIES**
Barras....................................(see 33)
Glasgow Cathedral...................4 F2
Glasgow Science Centre...........5 A3
Hunterian Art Gallery..............6 B1
Hunterian Museum..................7 B1
Kelvingrove Art Gallery &
  Museum................................8 A1
Museum of Transport..............9 A1
People's Palace.......................10 F4
Provand's Lordship.................11 F3
Seaforce...............................(see 13)

St Mungo's Museum of Religious
  Life & Art............................12 F3
Tall Ship & Pumphouse...........13 A3

**SLEEPING**
Alamo Guest House.................14 B2
Cathedral House Hotel.............15 F3
City Inn..................................16 B3
Glasgow Youth Hostel.............17 B1
University of Strathclyde Campus
  Village..................................18 F3

**EATING**
Bay Tree Café.........................19 C1
Buttery..................................20 C3
Café Lava..............................21 E4
Firebird.................................22 A2

Stravaigin..............................23 B1
The Left Bank.........................24 B1
West Brewing Company...........25 F4

**DRINKING**
Uisge Beatha.........................26 C1

**ENTERTAINMENT**
Barrowland.............................27 F4
Citizens' Theatre.....................28 D4
Clyde Auditorium (Armadillo)...29 A3
Glasgow Academy...................30 D4
Halt Bar................................31 C1
SECC (Scottish Exhibition &
  Conference Centre)...............32 B3

**SHOPPING**
Barras....................................33 E4

**GETTING AROUND ON THE CLYDE**

**Pride o' the Clyde** (Map p126; ☎ 07711 250 969; Central Station Bridge) is a waterbus linking Glasgow city centre with Braehead, home of the Clydebuilt museum. It's a terrific way to witness the progress of the Clyde's regeneration and to avoid city congestion. A single/return ticket costs £4.25/7.50; there are five to six sailings daily.

**Seaforce** (Map p124; ☎ 221 1070; Tall Ship, 100 Stobcross Rd, Glasgow Harbour) offers speedy powerboat jaunts along the Clyde. There's a variety of trips (tickets £10 to £50), including a half-hour ride around central Glasgow, an hour trip to the Erskine Bridge or four-hour rides to local wildlife hot spots.

The **Waverley** (☎ 0845 130 4647; www.waverleyexcursions.co.uk; Anderston Quay), the world's last ocean-going paddle steamer (built in 1947), cruises the Firth of Clyde from April to September (tickets £10 to £30); the website details days of departure. It serves several towns and the islands of Bute, Great Cumbrae and Arran. It departs from Glasgow Science Centre (see p123).

impressive, and there are displays about her history, restoration and life on board in the early 20th century.

Inside the nearby old **Pumphouse**, now a visitor centre, a captivating exhibit unfurls the interwoven stories of Glasgow and the Clyde, including the amazing dredging work carried out to enable the big ships to sail into Glasgow.

Check upcoming events here, as there's often good stuff on offer for the kids over summer.

### CLYDEBUILT

If immersing yourself in a city's heritage floats your boat, a visit to **Clydebuilt** (☎ 886 1013; Kings Inch Rd, Braehead; adult/child £4.25/2.50; 10am-5.30pm Mon-Sat, 11am-5pm Sun) will get you paddlin'. It's a superb collection of model ships, industrial displays and narrative, vividly painting the history of the Clyde, the fate of which has been inextricably linked with Glasgow and its people. It's a cleverly designed museum, with twists and turns that offer something new around every corner. Getting here via the Pride o' the Clyde (see the boxed text, above) is half the fun. Outside you can board *Kyles*, a typical 1872 vessel. Moored on the empty shores of the Clyde, with only the crying gulls above breaking the silence, it's a perfect place to contemplate the defunct shipyards that formed the cornerstone of Glasgow's industrial heritage.

## City Centre

The grid layout of the city centre makes it easy to get around, and there are many cafés and pubs that make a good pit stop between attractions.

### CITY CHAMBERS

The grand **City Chambers** (Map p126; ☎ 287 4018; George Sq; admission free), the seat of local government, were built in the 1880s at the high point of the city's wealth. Its interior is even more extravagant than the exterior. Guided tours are held at 10.30am and 2.30pm Monday to Friday.

### GALLERY OF MODERN ART

Scotland's most popular contemporary **art gallery** (Map p126; ☎ 229 1996; Royal Exchange Sq, Queen St; admission free; 10am-5pm Mon-Wed & Sat, to 8pm Thu, 11am-5pm Fri & Sun) features modern works from artists worldwide in a graceful neoclassical building. The original interior is used to make a daring, inventive art display. Social issues are a focal point of the museum and if you're interested in seeing some thought-provoking artistic interpretations of the more marginalised people in today's society, you should definitely swing by this museum.

### TENEMENT HOUSE

For a time-capsule experience, visit the small apartment in the **Tenement House** (NTS; Map p126; ☎ 333 0183; 145 Buccleuch St; adult/child £5/4; 1-5pm Mar-Oct). It gives a vivid insight into middle-class city life at the turn of the 20th century, with box-beds, the original kitchen range, and all the fixtures and fittings of the family who lived here for more than 50 years.

The house is an interesting place, but surely the Toward family wouldn't have kept it quite as squeaky clean and orderly as the National Trust for Scotland (NTS) manages to do now. Despite the additional exhibition area in the ground-floor flat, it can get crowded.

GLASGOW

## ROYAL HIGHLAND FUSILIERS MUSEUM

Visitors with an interest in Scotland's proud military history should duck into the commendable **Royal Highland Fusiliers Museum** (Map p126; ☎ 332 5639; 518 Sauchiehall St; admission free; ⏱ 8am-4pm Mon-Fri). It charts the history of this and previous regiments from 1678 to the present. The walls are dripping with exhibits, including uniforms, medals, pictures and other militaria. Wrought ironwork in the museum was designed by Mackintosh.

## GLASGOW SCHOOL OF ART

Widely recognised as Mackintosh's greatest building, the **Glasgow School of Art** (Map p126; ☎ 353 4526; 167 Renfrew St; adult/child £6.50/4.80) still houses the educational institution. It's hard not to be impressed by the thoroughness of the design; the architect's pencil seems to have shaped everything inside and outside the building. The interior design is strikingly austere, with simple colour combinations (often just black and cream) and those uncomfortable-looking high-backed chairs for which Mackintosh is famous. The library, designed as an addition in 1907, is a masterpiece. To view the school, you must take a guided tour – times vary, usually seven daily April to September and two daily October to March. There may be interruptions to tours as a major renovation's pending.

## WILLOW TEA ROOMS

Admirers of the great Mackintosh will love the **Willow Tea Rooms** (Map p126; ☎ 332 0521; 217

CENTRAL GLASGOW

Sauchiehall St; admission free; ⊙ 9am-5pm Mon-Sat, 11am-
5pm Sun), an authentic reconstruction of the
tearoom Mackintosh designed and furnished
in 1904 for restaurateur Kate Cranston. Relive the original splendour of this unique
tearoom and admire the architect's stroke in
just about everything. He had a free rein and
even the teaspoons were given his distinctive
touch. Reconstruction took two years and the
Willow opened as a tearoom again in 1980
(having been closed since 1926). The street
name Sauchiehall means 'lane of willows',
hence the choice of a stylised willow motif.
See also p138.

### THE LIGHTHOUSE

If you've been admiring Glasgow's architecture, make sure you check out the **Lighthouse**
(Map p126; ☎ 221 6362; 11 Mitchell Lane; adult/child £3/1;
⊙ 10.30am-5pm Mon & Wed-Sat, 11am-5pm Tue, noon-
5pm Sun), one of Glasgow's hidden treasures.

Tucked away in a small lane, in the former
*Glasgow Herald* building, it serves as **Scotland's
Centre for Architecture & Design**, giving an insight into modern architectural feats. It was
designed by Mackintosh in 1893, and also
features the **Mackintosh Interpretation Centre**.
Learn more about this extraordinary man,
see exhibitions of avant-garde furniture and
drink in great rooftop views from the former
water tower. It's also worth dropping into the
Doocot Cafe & Bar here for a different kind
of drink – it's a good place to rest weary legs
and minds.

## East End

The oldest part of the city, given a facelift in
the 1990s, is concentrated around Glasgow
Cathedral, to the east of the modern centre.
The crumbling tombs of the city's rich and
famous crowd the necropolis, located behind
the cathedral.

**GLASGOW**

| INFORMATION | | | | | |
|---|---|---|---|---|---|
| American Express | 1 B3 | Pipers Tryst Hotel | 32 C1 | Revolver | 63 D3 |
| Borders | 2 B3 | Quality Hotel | 33 B3 | Scotia | 64 C4 |
| Clydesdale Bank | 3 C3 | Rab Ha's | 34 D3 | The Butterfly & The Pig | 65 C4 |
| easyInternet | 4 C3 | Victorian House | 35 A1 | Waterloo Bar | 66 B3 |
| Glasgow Dental Hospital | 5 A2 | | | Waxy O'Connors | 67 C3 |
| Glasgow Flight Centre | 6 B2 | EATING 🍴 | | | |
| Glasgow Tourise Office | 7 C3 | Arisaig | 36 B3 | ENTERTAINMENT 🎭 | |
| Main Post Office | 8 C3 | Bar 91 | 37 D3 | 13th Note Cafe | 68 D4 |
| Spa 19 | 9 C4 | Bar Soba | (see 16) | ABC | 69 B2 |
| St Enoch Square Travel Centre | 10 C4 | Brutti Ma Buoni | (see 26) | Arches | 70 B3 |
| Waterstone's | 11 B2 | Café Gandolfi | 38 D3 | Art School | (see 14) |
| | | Dakhin | (see 37) | Barfly | 71 C4 |
| SIGHTS & ACTIVITIES | | Lily's Coffee Shop | 39 D3 | Bennet's | 72 D3 |
| City Chambers | 12 D3 | Loon Fung | 40 A2 | Brunswick Cellars | 73 B2 |
| Gallery of Modern Art | 13 C3 | Mono | 41 D4 | Cathouse | 74 B3 |
| Glasgow School of Art | 14 B2 | Noodle Bar | 42 A1 | Centre for Contemporary Arts | 75 A2 |
| Hutcheson's Hall | 15 D3 | Red Onion | 43 B2 | Glasgow Film Theatre | 76 B2 |
| Jelly Club | (see 89) | Wagamama | 44 C3 | Glasgow Royal Concert Hall | 77 C2 |
| Lighthouse | 16 C3 | Wee Curry Shop | 45 B1 | King Tut's Wah Wah Hut | 78 A2 |
| Pride o' the Clyde | 17 B4 | West Regent Street Bistro | 46 C2 | King's Theatre | 79 A2 |
| Royal Highland Fusiliers | | Where the Monkey Sleeps | 47 B2 | Mono | (see 41) |
| Museum | 18 A1 | Willow Tea Rooms | 48 B2 | Odeon City Centre | 80 C2 |
| Sharmanka Kinetic Gallery & | | Willow Tea Rooms | 49 C3 | Sub Club | 81 B3 |
| Theatre | 19 D4 | | | Theatre Royal | 82 C2 |
| Tenement House | 20 A1 | DRINKING 🍺 🍸 | | Tron Theatre | 83 D4 |
| Tobacco Exchange | 21 C3 | Artá | 50 D3 | Tunnel | 84 C3 |
| Trades Hall | 22 D3 | Babbity Bowster | (see 25) | | |
| Willow Tea Rooms | (see 48) | Bar 10 | 51 C3 | SHOPPING 🛍 | |
| | | Blackfriars | 52 D4 | Adventure 1 | 85 C2 |
| SLEEPING 🛏 | | Corinthian | 53 D3 | Argyll Arcade | 86 C3 |
| Adelaide's | 23 B2 | Delmonica's | 54 D3 | Buchanan Galleries | 87 C2 |
| Artto | 24 B3 | Drum & Monkey | 55 C3 | Catherine Shaw | (see 86) |
| Babbity Bowster | 25 D3 | Firewater | 56 A2 | Princes Square | 88 C3 |
| Brunswick Hotel | 26 D3 | Horse Shoe | 57 C3 | St Enoch Shopping Centre | 89 C4 |
| Euro Hostel | 27 B4 | Moda | (see 54) | Tiso's | 90 C3 |
| Malmaison | 28 A2 | Mojama | 58 A2 | | |
| Merchant Lodge | 29 D3 | Moskito | 59 B2 | TRANSPORT | |
| Millennium Hotel | 30 C3 | Nice 'n' Sleazy | 60 A2 | Buchanan St Bus Station | 91 C2 |
| Old School House | 31 A1 | Pivo Pivo | 61 B3 | Queen Street Station | 92 C2 |
| | | Polo Lounge | 62 D3 | | |

GLASGOW

It takes 15 to 20 minutes to walk from George Sq, but numerous buses pass nearby, including buses 11, 12, 36, 37, 38 and 42.

## GLASGOW CATHEDRAL

An attraction that shouldn't be missed, **Glasgow Cathedral** (HS; Map p124; ☎ 552 6891; Cathedral Sq; admission free; ☺ 9.30am-5.30pm Mon-Sat, 1-5pm Sun Apr-Sep, 9.30am-4pm Mon-Sat, 1-4pm Sun Oct-Mar) has a rare timelessness. The dark, imposing interior conjures up medieval might and can send a shiver down the spine. It's a shining example of pre-Reformation Gothic architecture, and the only mainland Scottish cathedral to have survived the Reformation. Most of the current building dates from the 15th century, and only the western towers were destroyed in the turmoil.

The entry is through a side door into the **nave**, which is hung with some regimental colours. The wooden roof above has been restored many times since its original construction, but some of the timber dates from the 14th century; note the impressive shields. Many of the cathedral's stunning, narrow windows of stained glass are modern and, to your left, is Francis Spear's 1958 work *The Creation*, which fills the west window.

The cathedral, divided by a late-5th-century stone choir screen, is decorated with seven pairs of figures to represent the Seven Deadly Sins. Beyond is the **choir**. The four stained-glass panels of the east window, depicting the apostles and also by Francis Spear, are particularly effective. At the northeastern corner is the entrance to the 15th-century **upper chapter house**, where Glasgow University was founded. It's now used as a sacristy.

The most interesting part of the cathedral, the **lower church**, is reached by a stairway. Its forest of pillars creates a powerful atmosphere around St Mungo's tomb (St Mungo founded a monastic community here in the 5th century), the focus of a famous medieval pilgrimage that was believed to be as meritorious as a visit to Rome.

Sunday services are at 11am and 6.30pm.

## ST MUNGO'S MUSEUM OF RELIGIOUS LIFE & ART

A startling achievement, **St Mungo's Museum** (Map p124; ☎ 553 2557; 2 Castle St; admission free; ☺ 10am-5pm Mon-Thu & Sat, 11am-5pm Fri & Sun) is an audacious attempt to capture the world's major religions in an artistic nutshell. The result is commendable. The attraction is twofold: firstly, impressive art that blurs the lines between religion and culture; and secondly, the opportunity to delve into different faiths, an experience that can be as deep or shallow as

---

### THE GENIUS OF CHARLES RENNIE MACKINTOSH

Great cities have great artists, designers and architects contributing to the cultural and historical roots of their urban environment while expressing its soul and individuality. Charles Rennie Mackintosh was all of these. The quirky, linear and geometric designs of this famous Scottish architect and designer have had almost as much influence on the city as have Gaudí's on Barcelona. Many of the buildings Mackintosh designed in Glasgow are open to the public, and you'll see his tall, thin, Art-Nouveau typeface repeatedly reproduced.

Born in 1868, Mackintosh studied at the Glasgow School of Art. In 1896, when he was aged only 27, he won a competition for his design of the School of Art's new building. The first section was opened in 1899 and is considered to be the earliest example of Art Nouveau in Britain, as well as Mackintosh's supreme architectural achievement. This building demonstrates his skill in combining function and style.

Although Mackintosh's genius was quickly recognised on the Continent, he did not receive the same encouragement in Scotland. His architectural career here lasted only until 1914, when he moved to England to concentrate on furniture design. He died in 1928, and it is only since the last decades of the 20th century that Mackintosh's genius has been widely recognised. For more about the man and his work, contact the **Charles Rennie Mackintosh Society** ( ☎ 946 6600; www.crmsociety.com; The Mackintosh Church, Queen's Cross, 870 Garscube Rd, Glasgow G20 7EL). From April to October the society runs weekend tours (Thursday night to Sunday) of his buildings (once or twice a month); the cost is £460/800 for one/two people, including dinner, B&B for three nights, lunches, coach, guide and admission.

See Helensburgh (p279) for information on Hill House, perhaps Mackintosh's finest creation.

you wish. There are three galleries, representing religion as art, religious life and, on the top floor, religion in Scotland. Britain's only Zen garden is outside.

## PROVAND'S LORDSHIP

Across the road from St Mungo's Museum is **Provand's Lordship** (Map p126; ☎ 552 8819; 3 Castle St; admission free; ☺ 10am-5pm Mon-Thu & Sat, 11am-5pm Fri & Sun), the oldest house in Glasgow. A rare example of 15th-century domestic Scottish architecture, it was built in 1471 as a manse for the chaplain of St Nicholas Hospital. The ceilings and doorways are low, and the rooms are sparsely furnished with period artefacts, except for an upstairs room, which has been furnished to reflect the living space of an early-16th-century chaplain. The building's best feature is its authentic feel – if you ignore the tacky imitation-stone linoleum covering the ground floor.

## West End

With its expectant buzz, trendy bars and cafés and nonchalant swagger, the West End is probably the most engaging area of Glasgow – it's great for people-watching, and is as close as Glasgow gets to bohemian.

## HUNTERIAN MUSEUM & ART GALLERY

Part of the university and housed in two separate buildings on either side of University Ave, the Hunterian contains the collection of William Hunter (1718–83), famous physician, medical teacher and one-time student of the university.

Don't forget to drag your eyes down to the exhibits in the **Hunterian Museum** (Map p124; ☎ 330 4221; University Ave; admission free; ☺ 9.30am-5pm Mon-Sat), which can be difficult as the university building itself is quite breathtaking.

The museum has had a recent makeover after an extensive refurbishment and changes include a permanent exhibition dedicated to William Hunter. There's also a new display called Weird & Wonderful which shows a quirky side to the collection and is worth lingering over.

The Main Hall has much improved displays and themes with a highlight being the 1674 'Map of the Whole World' in the World Culture section.

Across the road, the Scottish Colourists (Samuel Peploe, Francis Cadell, JD Fergusson) are well represented in the **Hunterian Art Gallery** (Map p124; ☎ 330 5431; 82 Hillhead St; admission free; ☺ 9.30am-5pm Mon-Sat). There are also Sir William MacTaggart's impressionistic Scottish landscapes, and a gem by Thomas Millie Dow. There's a special collection of James McNeill Whistler's limpid prints, drawings and paintings. The **Mackintosh House** (☎ 330 5431; 82 Hillhead St; admission £3, after 2pm Wed free; ☺ 9.30am-12.30pm & 1.30-5pm Mon-Sat) is the final section in the gallery. Set up as a reconstruction of Charles Rennie Mackintosh's Glasgow home (which had to be demolished), the Mackintosh House is startling even today. You ascend from the gallery's sombre ground floor into the cool, white, austere drawing-room. There's something otherworldly about the very mannered style of the beaten silver panels, the long-backed chairs and the surface decorations echoing Celtic manuscript illuminations. Buses 11 and 44 pass this way from the city centre (Hope St).

## BOTANIC GARDENS

The best thing about walking into these beautiful **gardens** (Map p121; ☎ 334 2422; 730 Great Western Rd; ☺ daily, closes 10pm in summer, glasshouse 10am-4.45pm, visitor centre 11am-4pm) is the noise of Great Western Rd quickly receding into the background. Amazingly, the lush grounds don't seem that popular with locals (except on sunny weekends) and away from the entrance you may just about have the place to yourself. The wooded gardens follow the riverbank of the River Kelvin and there's plenty of tropical species to discover. Check out the herb garden, too, with its medicinal species. The gorgeous hilly grounds make the perfect place for a picnic lunch. There are also organised walks and concerts in summer – have a look at the noticeboard near the entrance to see what's on.

**Kibble Palace**, an impressive Victorian iron and glass structure dating from 1873, is one of the largest glasshouses in Britain, and recently reopened after an extensive renovation. It's inside the gardens.

## KELVINGROVE ART GALLERY & MUSEUM

In a magnificent Edwardian building, this grand Victorian cathedral of culture is one of Glasgow's best, particularly its collection of Scottish and European art, and is the most visited museum in the UK outside of London. The **Kelvingrove** (Map p124; ☎ 276 9599; Argyle St; admission free; 10am-5pm Mon-Thu & Sat, 11am-5pm Fri, Sun; ♿) recently reopened after an enormous refurbishment programme. You could spend

GLASGOW

days in here…literally. The museum is provocative because it poses many questions of relevance in relation to daily life. There are many different sections to browse including natural history exhibits; a full-size Spitfire plane from WWII; a Glasgow Stories Exhibit which tells how the city inspires and infuriates; a display of swinging heads all wringing out a different expression (which we found kinda scary); and plenty on Scottish history including Viking influence. For such a large place there is a real intimacy here. Other highlights include Salvador Dali's *Christ of St John of the Cross*. There's also a plethora of quality art from across Europe, including the Glasgow Boys and the Scottish Colourists.

### MUSEUM OF TRANSPORT

Across Argyle St from the Hunterian Museum & Art Gallery is the surprisingly interesting and very comprehensive, but badly signposted, **Museum of Transport** (Map p124; ☎ 287 2720; 1 Bunhouse Rd; admission free; ☺ 10am-5pm Mon-Thu & Sat, 11am-5pm Fri & Sun). Not convinced? It's actually a very fine museum with exhibits including a reproduction of a 1938 Glasgow street scene, a display of cars made in Scotland, plus assorted railway locos, trams, bikes (including the world's first pedal-powered bicycle from 1847) and model ships. There's a room dedicated to the Clyde shipyards. It's like peeping through a porthole at the not-too-distant past. Note that the museum is due to be incorporated into a new Riverside Museum down at Glasgow Harbour, sometime in 2008 (p123). By train it's a 15-minute walk from Partick station. First Glasgow buses 9, 16, 18, 42, 62 and 64 all stop nearby.

### FOSSIL GROVE

With sections of 350-million-year-old fossilised trees lying as they were found, **Fossil Grove** (Map p121; ☎ 950 1448; Victoria Park, Dumbarton Rd; admission free; ☺ 10am-5pm Mon, Thu-Sun, Apr-Sep) is an intriguing site. This Site of Special Scientific Interest (SSSI) feels quite spooky and makes you realise you're but a blip on the earth's timeline. To get here, take bus 44 from the city centre to Victoria Park Dr North, or bus 9 or 62 to Dumbarton Rd.

## South Side

The south side is a tangled web of busy roads with a few oases giving relief from the urban congestion. It does, however, contain some of Glasgow's best museums.

### BURRELL COLLECTION

One of Glasgow's top attractions is the **Burrell Collection** (Map p121; ☎ 287 2550; Pollok Country Park; admission free, parking £1.50; ☺ 10am-5pm Mon-Thu & Sat, 11am-5pm Fri & Sun). Amassed by wealthy industrialist Sir William Burrell before being donated to the city, it is housed in an outstanding museum, 3 miles south of the city centre. This idiosyncratic collection of treasure includes everything from Chinese porcelain and medieval furniture to paintings by Renoir and Cézanne. It's not so big as to be overwhelming, and the stamp of the collector lends an intriguing coherence.

Visitors will find their own favourite part of this museum, but the exquisite tapestry galleries are outstanding. Intricate stories capturing life in Europe are woven into staggering, wall-size pieces dating from the 13th century. The huge *Triumph of the Virgin* exemplifies the complexity in nature and theme of this medium, while posing the serious question: 'how long must this have taken?'

Within the spectacular interior, carved-stone Romanesque doorways are incorporated into the structure so you actually walk through them. Floor-to-ceiling windows admit a flood of light, and enable the surrounding landscape outside to enhance the effect of the exhibits. It feels like you're wandering in a huge tranquil greenhouse.

There are occasional guided tours. Many buses pass the park gates (including buses 45, 47, 48 and 57 from the city centre), and there's a twice-hourly bus service between the gallery and the gates (a pleasant 10-minute walk). Alternatively catch a train to Pollokshaws West from Central station (four per hour; you want the second station on the line for East Kilbride or Kilmarnock).

### SCOTTISH FOOTBALL MUSEUM

Football fans will just love the **Scottish Football Museum** (Map p121; ☎ 616 6139; Hampden Park; adult/child £5.50/2.75; ☺ 10am-5pm Mon-Sat, 11am-5pm Sun), which features exhibits on the history of the game in Scotland and the influence of Scots on the world game. Football inspires an incredible passion in Scotland and the museum is crammed full of impressive memorabilia, including a cap and match ticket from the very first international football game (which took place in 1872 between Scotland and England, and ended with a score of 0-0). The museum's engrossing exhibits give insight into the players, the fans, the media

### THE GLASGOW BOYS

The great rivalry between Glasgow and Edinburgh goes back a long way. In the late 19th century a group of Glaswegian painters challenged the domineering artistic establishment in Edinburgh. Up to this point, paintings were largely confined to historical scenes and sentimental visions of the Highlands. These painters – including Sir James Guthrie, EA Hornel, George Henry and Joseph Crawhall – experimented with colour and themes of rural life, shocking Edinburgh's artistic society. Like Charles Rennie Mackintosh, the Glasgow Boys achieved success on the Continent, where their work met with admiration and artistic recognition.

The Glasgow Boys had an enormous influence on the Scottish art world, inspiring the next generation of Scottish painters – the Colourists. The Glasgow Boys' works can be seen in various Scottish collections, including the Burrell Collection (opposite) and Broughton House, Kirkcudbright (p182).

and the way the game has changed over the last 130 years. The museum's location is at Hampden Park, off Aikenhead Rd. To get there, take a train to Mount Florida station or take bus 5, 31, 37 or 75 from Stockwell St.

### THE BARRAS

Glasgow's flea market, the **Barras on Gallowgate** (Map p124; London Rd; 9am-5pm Sat & Sun), is the living, breathing heart of this city in many respects. It has almost a thousand stalls and people come here just for a wander as much as for shopping, which gives the place a holiday air. The Barras is notorious for designer frauds, so be cautious. Watch your wallet, too.

### THE PEOPLE'S PALACE

The city's oldest park, on Glasgow Green, is the **People's Palace** (Map p124; 271 2962; Glasgow Green; admission free; 10am-5pm Mon-Thu & Sat, 11am-5pm Fri & Sun). It is an impressive museum of social history, telling the story of the city from 1750 to the present. It has creative, inventive displays, which are great for families – the kids will love the re-creation of a WWII air raid. The Palace was built in the late 19th century as a cultural centre for Glasgow's East End. Drop into the Winter Gardens next door for a coffee.

### SCOTLAND STREET SCHOOL MUSEUM

An impressive Mackintosh building, the **Scotland Street School Museum** (Map p121; 287 0500; 225 Scotland St; admission free; 10am-5pm Mon-Thu & Sat, 11am-5pm Fri & Sun, Apr-Sep) is dominated by two glass towers. It's a fascinating museum of education, with reconstructions of classrooms from Victorian times and the 1940s to the 1960s. The place evokes childhood memories for just about everyone – don't be surprised if you hear a few titters from elderly visitors as they pass the headmaster's office.

### HOUSE FOR AN ART LOVER

Although designed in 1901 as an entry to a competition run by a German magazine, the **House for an Art Lover** (Map p121; 353 4770; Bellahouston Park, 10 Dumbreck Rd; adult/child £3.50/2.50; 10am-4pm Mon-Wed, 10am-1pm Thu-Sun Apr-Sep, 10am-1pm Sat & Sun Oct-Mar) was not completed until 1996. Mackintosh worked closely with his wife on the design and her influence is evident, especially in the rose motif. The overall result of this brilliant architect's design is one of space and light. Buses 3, 9, 54, 55 and 56 all run here from the city centre.

### HOLMWOOD HOUSE

An interesting building designed by Alexander 'Greek' Thomson, **Holmwood House** ( 637 2129; 61-63 Netherlee Rd, Cathcart; adult/child £5/4; noon-5pm Thu-Mon Apr-Oct) dates from 1857. Despite constant ongoing renovations, it's well worth a visit. Look for sun symbols downstairs and stars upstairs in this attractive house with its adaptation of classical Greek architecture. To get to Cathcart train station, take a 'Cathcart Circle' train via Queen's Park or a train to Neilston. Otherwise, take bus 44, 44A, 44D or 66 from the city centre. Follow Rhannan Rd for about 800m to Holmwood House.

## North Side

The north side doesn't have much of interest for visitors, apart from a unique church that also happens to be the headquarters of the Rennie Mackintosh Society.

### THE MACKINTOSH CHURCH

Now the headquarters of the Charles Rennie Mackintosh Society, the **Church** (Map p121; 946 6600; 870 Garscube Rd; adult/child £2/free; 10am-5pm Mon-Fri 2-5pm Sun Mar-Oct) is the only one of Mackintosh's church designs to be built. It has excellent stained glass and relief carvings, and the wonderful simplicity and grace of the barrel-shaped design is particularly inspiring.

## ACTIVITIES

There are numerous green spaces within the city. **Pollok Country Park** (Map p121) surrounds the Burrell Collection and has several woodland trails. Nearer the centre of the city, the **Kelvin Walkway** follows the River Kelvin through Kelvingrove Park (Map p124), the Botanic Gardens and on to Dawsholm Park.

The tourist office has a range of maps and leaflets detailing these jaunts, and the long-distance routes described under Walking & Cycling (see below), most of which start from Bell's Bridge (Map p126; by the SECC). It also stocks the *Fit for Life* map detailing walking and cycling routes around the city.

### Walking & Cycling

It is possible to walk 9 miles of the Clyde through Glasgow. An outstanding section lies between the Victoria Bridge and the SECC, taking in 150 years of bridge engineering and a chunk of Glasgow's shipbuilding heritage. The **Clyde Walkway** extends from Glasgow to Strathclyde Park, between Motherwell and Hamilton, and will eventually continue to the Falls of Clyde in Lanark (p164). It should be about 40 miles long when completed.

The well-trodden, long-distance footpath called the **West Highland Way** begins in Milngavie, 8 miles north of Glasgow (you can walk to Milngavie from Glasgow along the River Klein), and runs for 95 spectacular miles to Fort William.

There are several long-distance pedestrian/cycle routes that begin in Glasgow and follow off-road routes for most of the way.

The **Glasgow–Loch Lomond route** traverses residential and industrial areas, following a disused railway to Clydebank, the Forth and Clyde canal towpath to Bowling, then a disused railway to Dumbarton, reaching Loch Lomond via the towpath by the River Leven. This route continues to Inverness, from Balloch via Aberfoyle, Loch Vennachar, Callander and Strathyre to link with the Glen Ogle Trail, Killin, Pitlochry and Aviemore.

The **Glasgow–Greenock/Gourock route** runs via Paisley, the first section partly on roads. From Johnstone to Greenock the route follows a disused railway line, and the final section to Gourock has also been built. Sculpture from the Sustrans public arts project brightens parts of the way.

The **Glasgow–Irvine, Ardrossan & West Kilbride Cycle Way** runs via Paisley, then off-road to Glengarnock. From here to Kilwinning it follows minor roads, then the route is partly off-road. Ferries to the Isle of Arran, popular with cyclists, leave from Ardrossan. An extension via Ayr, Maybole and Glentrool leads to the Solway coast and Carlisle.

The **Glasgow–Edinburgh Cycle Way** partly follows the Clyde Walkway and a disused railway line. It skirts south Lanarkshire and continues through Uddingston, Airdrie, Bathgate and onto Edinburgh.

Hire a bike at **West End Cycles** (Map p121; ☎ 357 1344; 16 Chancellor St) at the southern end of Byres Rd. It hires 24-speed mountain bikes for £15/85 per day/week. You need ID, and a £100 deposit or a credit card.

## WALKING TOUR

This absorbing stroll will take you from George Sq to Glasgow Cathedral through the trendy Merchant City, a planned 18th-century civic development, and home to many fine pubs and restaurants.

The tourist office on **George Sq (1)** is a good starting point for exploring the city. The square is surrounded by imposing Victorian architecture, including the old post office, the Bank of Scotland and the grandiose **City Chambers (2**; p125). There are statues of Robert Burns, James Watt, Lord Clyde and, atop a 24m-high Doric column, Sir Walter Scott.

Once you've ogled the City Chambers, cross George Sq and walk one block south down Queen St to the **Gallery of Modern Art (3**; p125). This striking, four-floor, colonnaded building, built in 1827, was once the Royal Exchange. Pop in for a look at some of the country's best contemporary art displays.

The gallery faces Ingram St, which you should cross and then follow east for four blocks to **Hutchesons' Hall (4)**. Built in 1805 to a design by David Hamilton, this elegant building is now maintained by the NTS. On your way, duck into the former Court House cells now housing the ornate, dazzling **Corinthian (5**; p141) pub/club for a glimpse of the extravagant interior (and perhaps a cheeky half!). Retrace your steps one block and continue south down Glassford St past **Trades Hall (6)**, designed by Robert Adam in 1791 to house the trades guild. This is the only surviving

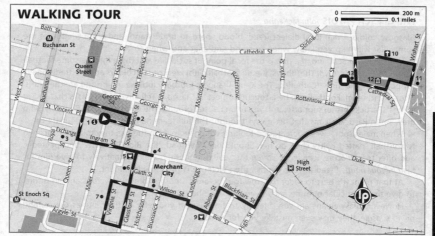

## WALKING TOUR

**Distance:** just over 1.25 miles
**Duration:** approximately 1½ hours

building in Glasgow by this famous Scottish architect; the exterior is best viewed from Garth St. Turn right into Wilson St and first left along Virginia St, which is lined with the old warehouses of the Tobacco Lords; many of these have been converted into flats for the upwardly mobile. The **Tobacco Exchange (7)** became the Sugar Exchange in 1820, but it's now in poor condition.

Back on Wilson St, the bulky **Sheriff Court House (8)** fills a whole block. This arresting building was originally Glasgow's town hall, but has been developed as luxury apartments. Continue east on Wilson St into Bell St and take a break at the excellent **Blackfriars pub (9**; p140), where you can people-watch while sipping a cask ale. Turn left into Albion St, then first right into Blackfriars St. Emerging onto High St, turn left and follow High St up to the **Cathedral (10**; p128). Behind the cathedral wind your way up through the noble, crumbling tombs of the **Necropolis (11)**, with great city views. On your way back you can check out the free and fabulous **St Mungo's Museum of Religious Life & Art (12**; p128) and **Provand's Lordship (13**; p129).

## GLASGOW FOR CHILDREN

Although Glasgow is a bigger, busier city that Edinburgh, it's an easy city to travel around with children due to its extensive public transport system and friendly locals. The city boasts excellent family attractions, including the **Glasgow Science Centre** (p123) and **Sharmanka Kinetic Gallery & Theatre** (see below), which both vie for Glasgow's top child-friendly attraction. The **People's Palace** (p131) and **Museum of Transport** (p130) are also recommended. A boat trip along the Clyde can be a lot of fun for kids.

For suggestions of short-term child-care agencies, get in touch with the council-run **Glasgow Childcare Information Service** ( ☎ 287 5223; EducationChis@glasgow.gov.uk; Wheatley House, 25 Cochrane St).

Parks in Glasgow often have playgrounds for children; call ☎ 287 5064 for information. We recommend two indoor playgrounds (far more practical). The crèche at **Buchanan Galleries** ( ☎ 332 4353; www.buchanangalleries.co.uk; Royal Exchange Sq) shopping centre is available for children aged two to eight and staffed by qualified nursery assistants. The **Jelly Club** ( ☎ 248 6800; www.jellyclub.co.uk; St Enoch shopping centre; child from £4; ⏰ 10.30am-6.30pm) encourages physical activity by providing imaginative exercises to stimulate the mind and body (for children under 13).

## QUIRKY GLASGOW

For those up to their eyeballs in museums and galleries, check out a show at the extraordinary **Sharmanka Kinetic Gallery & Theatre** (Map p126; ☎ 552 7080; 64 Osbourne St; adult/child £4/free; ♿ ). Originally from St Petersburg, this mechanical theatre brings inanimate objects to

---

**THE GLESCA PATOIS** *John McKenna*

Glasgow enjoys a rich local dialect (read: bloody hard to understand) and a knowledge of the vernacular will help you know when to stand and chat and when to run.

Unusually, for Scotland, the pub is the focal point of social life and there may be some football supporters in the crowd. The 'Bhoys' (Celtic football club) wear green colours and are traditionally supported by the 'Tims' (Catholics). The 'Gers' (Rangers football club) wear blue and are the 'Huns' (Protestant) team. Football can be a touchy subject in Glasgow. Tell anyone who asks that you're a 'Jags' (Partick Thistle) supporter and you're on neutral ground. The comedian Billy Connolly, who grew up in Partick, claims that he always thought the full team name was 'Partick Thistle Nil'.

When males spot a *wee stoater* (good-looking young woman) in the bar, they might be inclined to try their 'patter' (witty chat) on her. Should her boyfriend, 'the Big Yin', arrive unexpectedly, and offer to *mollocate, wanner* or *stiffen* the would-be Lothario, or alternatively to give him his *heid in your hauns* (head in your hands), then violence is probably imminent.

At that point it's best to *shoot the crow* (go) before a *stooshie* (brawl) develops and, in future, to give that particular pub the *body swerve* (a wide berth).

However, Glaswegians are very friendly to travellers. If you refer to their city as *Glesca*, and never *Glasgie*, they may even mistake you for a local.

---

life; sculptured pieces of old scrap and tiny carved figures perform humorous and tragic stories of the human spirit to haunting music. It's joyful, ironic theatre: inspirational one moment and macabre the next, but always colourful, clever and thought provoking. It's art for reflection – and lots of fun! Full performances are at 7pm Thursday and Sunday, and a matinee for families is at 3pm Sunday. The gallery is also open from noon to 7pm Monday to Thursday and from noon to 3pm Friday for visits by appointment only; short performance included.

## TOURS

From April to October **City Sightseeing** ( ☎ 204 0444) runs tourist buses every 15 minutes (9.30am to 5pm) along the main sight-seeing routes, starting at George Sq. You get on and off as you wish. A day ticket per adult/child costs £9/3; if you buy a day ticket you get the next day's travel for free (buy from the driver or the tourist office). All buses have wheelchair access.

## FESTIVALS & EVENTS

Not to be outdone by Edinburgh, Glasgow has some kicking festivals of its own.

**Celtic Connections** ( ☎ 353 8000; www.grch.com) Two-week music festival held in January.

**Glasgow Jazz Festival** ( ☎ 552 3552; www.jazzfest .co.uk) Excellent festival held in June; George Sq is a good place for free jazz at this time.

**Indian Summer** (www.indiansummerglasgow.com) A boutique music festival held in mid-July in Victoria

Park (West End). An intimate outdoor event with a picnic atmosphere.

**RSNO Proms** ( ☎ 353 8000; www.grch.com) Classical music in June.

**West End Festival** ( ☎ 341 0844; www.westend festival.co.uk) This music and the arts event is Glasgow's biggest festival, running for two weeks in June.

**World Pipe Band Championships** ( ☎ 221 5414; tickets £7) Around 200 pipe bands; held in mid-August.

## SLEEPING

Finding somewhere decent in July and August can be difficult. Finding accommodation in Glasgow on weekends can be dicey at any time of year – it's wise to book ahead.

### Budget

CITY CENTRE

**our pick Glasgow Youth Hostel** (Map p124; ☎ 0870 004 1119; www.syha.org.uk; 8 Park Tce; dm £14-19) Perched on a hill overlooking Kelvingrove Park in a charming town house, this place is simply fabulous and one of Scotland's best official hostels. Dorms are mostly four to six beds and all have their own en suite – very posh. The common rooms are spacious, plush and good for lounging about.

**Euro Hostel** (Map p126; ☎ 222 2828; www.euro-hostels .com; 318 Clyde St; per person £15-40; 🖳 ) A mammoth hostel, Euro does not inspire warmth or a community feel, but it does provide high-quality budget accommodation in a central location. The dorms range in size from twin rooms through to 14 beds. Common areas are small, especially the kitchen. It's ideal for groups and has a rockin' bar onsite.

**University of Strathclyde Campus Village** (Map p124; ☎ 553 4148; www.rescat.strath.ac.uk; Rottenrow East; 4-/6-bed flats weekly £340/370, B&B per person £27, with en suite £33, bed only £22; ☼ mid-Jun–mid-Sep) The uni opens its halls of residence to tourists over summer. The Campus Village, opposite Glasgow Cathedral, offers accommodation in shared, single-sex, self-catering flats on a weekly basis, or good-value B&B.

### WEST END

**Bunkum Backpackers** (Map p121; ☎ /fax 581 4481; www.bunkumglasgow.co.uk; 26 Hillhead St; dm/tw £12/32) This is a backpackers with a great vibe in a terrific house with no curfew. One very big plus is the space – in an old Victorian terrace, the common rooms are large and the well-kept, six-bed dorms are also a pretty good size. It's very close to Glasgow University and the hot spots on Byres Rd; most of the partying is done outside the hostel.

### CAMPING

**Craigendmuir Park** ( ☎ 779 4159; www.craigendmuir.co.uk; Campsie View, Stepps; tent sites for 2 from £13.50) The nearest camping ground to town, this is about 800m from Stepps station. It has sites for caravans and tents, and there are a few well-equipped chalets and holiday homes.

## Midrange

### CITY CENTRE

There are some fantastic options around the city centre. If you're driving, watch out for parking inspectors around here.

**Adelaide's** (Map p126; ☎ 248 4970; www.adelaides.co.uk; 209 Bath St; s £32, s/d with en suite £45/54, family r per person £25) Eight-room Adelaide's is ideal for folk who want to stay in Glasgow's vibrant centre. It's an unusual place – a simple, friendly (and relatively cheap) guesthouse on prestigious Bath St set in an historic church conversion. Tariffs are room only and families are very welcome (there are two family rooms sleeping four or six).

**Old School House** (Map p126; ☎ 332 7600; www.schoolhousehotelglasgow.co.uk; 194 Renfrew St; s/d £40/60) The classiest guesthouse on this city-centre accommodation strip, The Old School House is a small exclusive detached villa with heaps of character. Rooms have had a major makeover and now exude a debonair, urban cool with earthy tones.

**Babbity Bowster** (Map p126; ☎ 552 5055; babbity bowster@gofornet.co.uk; 16-18 Blackfriars St; s/d £45/60)

Smack bang in the heart of the trendy Merchant City, this lively bar has rooms with sleek furnishings and a minimalist design (No 3 is a good one). Staying here is an excellent Glaswegian experience – the building's design is attributed to Robert Adam. Unusually, room rates do not include breakfast – but that helps keep prices down.

**Pipers Tryst Hotel** (Map p126; ☎ 353 5551; www.thepipingcentre.co.uk; 30-34 McPhater St; s/d £50/65) An alternative to some of the blander, bigger hotels, Pipers Tryst is intimate, cosy and very Scottish. Cheery staff, great value and a prime city centre location (especially for the Theatre Royal across the road) make this a cut above other places. Of the eight well-appointed rooms, Nos 6 and 7 are our faves; you won't have far to migrate after a night of Celtic music and fine single malts in the snug bar-restaurant downstairs.

**Artto** (Map p126; ☎ 248 2480; www.arttohotel.com; 37 Hope St; s/d £70/90) Everything is squeaky clean and gleaming in this fashionable hotel. Rooms have light subtle tones combined with earthy, darkish maroons giving them modish appeal. High ceilings and slick, sparkling en suites with power showers complete the happy picture. Remember when booking that rooms at the rear are much quieter.

**our pick Rab Ha's** (Map p126; ☎ 572 0400; 83 Hutcheson St; r £75-95) This Merchant City favourite is an atmospheric pub-restaurant with four stylish upstairs rooms. Each is a good size with a dark polished wood theme and a spotless en suite. It's the personal touches, such as fresh flowers in the rooms, and designer photographic prints on the walls, which make you feel special. Breakfast can be delivered to your room and you can come and go as you please, long after the bar downstairs has closed.

Other recommendations:

**Brunswick Hotel** (Map p126; ☎ 552 0001; www.brunswickhotel.co.uk; 106-108 Brunswick St; r £65-95) Stylish, inner-city hotel retaining its down-to-earth, friendly character.

**Merchant Lodge** (Map p126; ☎ 552 2424; 52 Virginia St; s/d £40/62) In the heart of the Merchant City. Simply furnished rooms feature pine fittings and polished wooden floors. Rooms on the 2nd and 3rd floors have the better outlook. Recommended for gay and lesbian travellers for its proximity to gay venues.

**Victorian House** (Map p126; ☎ 332 0129; www.thevictorian.co.uk; 212 Renfrew St; s/d £32/46, with bathroom £39/60) Solid old refurbished guesthouse, offering value for money.

**GLASGOW**

## EAST END

**Alison B&B** (Map p121; ☎ /fax 556 1431; 26 Circus Dr; s £25-30, d £38-54) This is an informal guesthouse where you're made to feel right at home by the chatty hosts – some people just enjoy their work. There's a great room for singles in the attic, as long as you don't mind a climb up a ladder; once there, you'll have plenty of room to yourself. The communal dining table encourages breakfast conversation.

**Craigpark Guest House** (Map p121; ☎ 554 4160; www .craigparkguesthouse.com; 33 Circus Dr; s £25-30, d £50-54) Sometimes a B&B just feels good. A classy guesthouse in a top East End location, this large, airy house has modern furnishings and a rustic feel. The meticulous interior reflects the owner's quiet efficiency. Country furniture complements the radiant rooms (particularly No 3), which share bathrooms, although one double has an en-suite shower.

**our pick Cathedral House Hotel** (Map p124; ☎ 552 3519; www.cathedralhouse.com; 28-32 Cathedral Sq; s/d £60/90) In the heart of the leafy, dignified East End is a very special property. A 19th-century Scottish Baronial–style hotel, complete with turrets and eight individual and beautifully furnished rooms, it's hotels like this (an antithesis to chain hotels) that give Glasgow such a classy edge. Room Nos 4 or 7 – very spacious corner rooms that include sumptuous king-size beds – are our faves.

## WEST END

**Alamo Guest House** (Map p124; ☎ 339 2395; www.alamo guesthouse.com; 46 Gray St; r per person £24-32) The Alamo may sound forbidding, but that couldn't be further from the truth. It's a great place to stay in a leafy spot overlooking Kelvingrove Park, and oozes warmth and sumptuous living. You feel miles from the city at this strategically located place, and yet the city centre and the West End are both a walk away.

**Heritage Hotel** (Map p121; ☎ 339 6955; bookings@ heritagehotel.fsbusiness.co.uk; 4 Alfred Tce, Great Western Rd; s/d £38/58) A stone's throw from all the action of the West End, this friendly hotel has a very open, airy and bright feel. Generally, the rooms on the 1st and 2nd floors are a bit more spacious (No 21 is best of the doubles) and have a better outlook. Rooms are kitted out with pine furniture, and a speck of dirt would feel lonely in the spotless en suites. Fresh fruit for brekky.

**Belhaven Hotel** (Map p121; ☎ 339 3222; www .belhavenhotel.com; 15 Belhaven Tce; s £45-50, d £60-70) Consistently friendly and blessed with some fantastically large rooms, Belhaven's rooms are lush little oases. A stylish Art-Nouveau red pervades with subtle lighting, a hint of decadence and, in some rooms, almost floor-to-ceiling windows. Make sure you try a pint of the delicious Kingfisher lager in the inhouse bar before you head out.

**Kirklee Hotel** (Map p121; ☎ 334 5555; kirklee@clara .net; 11 Kensington Gate; s/d £55/72) Want to spoil someone special? In a leafy neighbourhood, Kirklee is a quiet little gem that combines the luxury of a classy hotel with the warmth of staying in someone's home. The rooms are simply gorgeous, beautifully furnished and mostly looking onto lush gardens. For families there is an excellent downstairs room with enormous en suite.

**Embassy Apartments** (Map p121; ☎ 946 6698; www .glasgowhotelsandapartments.co.uk; 8 Kelvin Dr; 1/2/3/4/5/6/7 person flat per week £357/448/560/588/735/810/1015) If you're after a self-catering option, it's hard to go past this elegant place both for facilities and location. Situated in the leafy West End on a quiet, exclusive street right on the edge of the Botanical Gardens, it sleeps one to seven in studio-style apartments that have fully-equipped kitchens and are sparkling clean. Particularly good option for couples and families with older kids.

## SOUTH SIDE

**Holly House** (Map p121; ☎ 427 5609; www.thehollyhouse .co.uk; 54 Ibrox Tce; r per person £25-27) If you're seeing a football game at Ibrox (Rangers home ground), this friendly place is very handy. It's an excellent, homely B&B: inside there are four rooms – one double, one family and two singles. All are a very good size and the family room, which is also let out to couples, is simply huge.

**Glasgow Guest House** (Map p121; ☎ 427 0129; glasgowguesthouse@hotmail.com; 56 Dumbreck Rd; s/d/f £32/50/75) The large, en-suite bedrooms are tastefully furnished with polished wood, and the crisp white linen betrays the cleanliness regime. Guests may use the kitchen to prepare evening meals. There's a fair bit of noise – it's literally on a junction of the M77 motorway – although once inside this graceful property, the traffic seems to melt away.

## Top End
### THE CLYDE

**City Inn** (Map p124; ☎ 240 1002; www.cityinn.com/glasgow; Finnieston Quay; r £170; (P)) Popular with business travellers and ideally located for attractions along the riverfront, rooms are very modern, compact and chock-a-block full of gadgetry (modern conveniences), although not all that spacious, reflecting their functional nature. The better rooms are river facing; call in advance for the best rate.

### CITY CENTRE
**Malmaison** (Map p126; ☎ 572 1000; www.malmaison.com; 278 West George St; standard r Fri-Sun £99, standard r Mon-Thu £135, ste £195) Heavenly Malmaison is just so… now daaaahling. Cutting-edge urban living at its best, this sassy sister of hospitality is super slinky and a cornerstone of faith in Glaswegian accommodation. Stylish rooms with their moody lighting have a dark, brooding tone, plush furnishings and a designer touch.

**Quality Hotel** (Map p126; ☎ 221 9680; enquiries@quality-hotels-glasgow.com; 99 Gordon St; s £110, standard/premier d £120/140; **P**) The Quality Hotel is a down-to-earth, charismatic option right on Central station. Inside, everything is in huge proportion, the corridors are endless and the chandeliers baroque. Standard rooms are quite adequate, but only slightly more expensive premier rooms are enormous. And here's the bit for the trainspotter – you can get a room that actually overlooks the main passenger area of Central station!

**Millennium Hotel** (Map p126; ☎ 332 6711; www.millenniumhotels.com; George Sq; standard/club room £175/200, ste £235; **P** &) You want central? This is central. Overlooking George Sq, the massive Victorian building constructed for the Tobacco Lords is now a top luxury hotel blessed with helpful and attentive staff. Rooms that overlook George Sq with their floor-to-ceiling windows are best, but if you find that a bit noisy (although windows do have double glazing) rooms towards the rear of the hotel are much quieter. Book through the website for better prices.

An elegant new five-star hotel, **Blythswood Square Hotel**, with all the trimmings, is due to open right in the heart of the city centre in mid 2008. There will be 88 luxury bedrooms to choose from, along with suites, in a luxury Georgian building overlooking the square.

### WEST END
**Hotel Du Vin** (Map p121; ☎ 339 2001; www.hotelduvin.com; 1 Devonshire Gardens; r from £140, mews ste £950; **P**) Now under new management, this is the favoured hotel for the rich and famous, and the patriarch of sophistication and comfort. A study in elegance, it's sumptuously decorated and occupies three classical terrace houses. There are 35 rooms, all individually furnished, and two fine restaurants are on-site with a wine selection exceeding 600 varieties.

## EATING
Glasgow is the best place to eat in Scotland, with an excellent range of eateries. The West End is the culinary centre of the city. Many Glasgow restaurants post offers on the internet (changing daily) at **5pm.co.uk** (www.5pm.co.uk). Note also that pubs and bars are always a good lunchtime option.

### City Centre
#### BUDGET
**ourpick** **Lily's Coffee Shop** (Map p126; ☎ 552 8788; 103 Ingram St; mains £5; 9.30am-5pm Mon-Sat) Don't be put off by the slightly sterile feel, this is a top lunch spot fusing a creative blend of east and west. It's a unique cross between a Chinese bistro and chic café with made-to-order Chinese food (such as dumpling buns and mandarin duck wraps) and standards like burgers and baked potatoes that are tarted up almost beyond recognition. The Chinese food is outstanding – fresh, lively and served with fruits and salad.

**Mono** (Map p126; ☎ 553 2400; 12 Kings Crt, King St; mains £3-7; lunch, dinner) Combining vegetarian food with music, Mono is one of Glasgow's few vegan eateries. Monorail is in the same premises which means you can browse through an indie record shop while waiting for your food to be prepared. The all-day bar-menu provides classics such as the breakfast fry-up while the main menu has a touch of flair demonstrating a Mediterranean influence. The lasagne is well worth ploughing through.

**Café Lava** (Map p124; ☎ 553 1123; 24 St Andrew's St; dishes £2-6; 8am-6pm Mon-Fri, 10am-5pm Sat & Sun; ) Everyone wants to live next door to a café like this. The understated menu here delivers delicious home cooking. Try the Stornaway black pudding and eggs Benedict. The coffee is some of the best around town, and the carrot cake the best in Scotland: we know, we tried it from Dumfries to Shetland.

**Where the Monkey Sleeps** (Map p126; ☎ 226 3406; 182 West Regent St; dishes £4-6; 7am-5pm Mon-Fri, 10am-6pm Sat) This funky little number in the middle of the business district is just what you need to get away from the ubiquitous coffee chains. Laid-back and a little hippy, the bagels and *paninis*, with names like maverick or renegade, are highlights as are some very inventive dishes, such as the 'nuclear' beans, dripping with cayenne and Tabasco.

**Wee Curry Shop** (Map p126; ☎ 353 0777; 7 Buccleuch St; 2-course lunch £5, dinner mains £8; ☺ lunch Mon-Sat, dinner daily) Some of the best home-cooked curries you're likely to taste outside India can be found here. It's wise to book – it's a snug place with a big reputation, a limited menu and a sensational-value two-course lunch.

Also recommended:

**Willow Tea Rooms** Sauchiehall St (Map p126; ☎ 332 0521; 217 Sauchiehall St; light meals £4-7; ☺ 9am-4.30pm Mon-Sat, 11am-4.30pm Sun); Buchanan St (Map p126; ☎ 204 5242; 97 Buchanan St) Designed by Charles Rennie Mackintosh in 1904; at lunch and tea-time the queues can extend into the shop downstairs at the Sauchiehall St branch.

**Noodle Bar** (Map p126; ☎ 333 1883; 482 Sauchiehall St; dishes £4-6; ☺ noon-4am) For large doses of late-night noodles with oodles of different combinations.

### MIDRANGE

our pick **Brutti Ma Buoni** (Map p126; ☎ 552 0001; 106 Brunswick St; mains £6-10; ☺ noon-9pm Mon-Sat, to 8pm Sun) If you like dining in a place that has a sense of fun, Brutti delivers – it's the antithesis of some of the pretentious places around the Merchant City. With dishes such as 'ugly but good' pizza and 'angry or peaceful' prawns, Brutti's menu draws a smile for its quirkiness and its prices. The Italian and Spanish influences give rise to tapas-like servings or full-blown meals, which are imaginative, fresh and frankly delicious.

**West Brewing Company** (Map p124; ☎ 550 0135; Binnie Pl, Glasgow Green; starters £4, mains £8; ☺ lunch, dinner) A cavernous room with an airy, industrial feel on the edge of Glasgow Green, this brewery churns out four German beers brewed in strict accordance with Reinheitsgebot – German purity law. Which basically means it's bloody good. Excellent German dishes accompany the amber fluid, such as bratwurst sausages, sauerkraut and schnitzels; good ole pasta dishes are also available. Migrate to the beer garden overlooking the People's Palace in summer.

**Bar Soba** (Map p126; ☎ 204 2404; 11 Mitchell Lane; mains £7-10; ☺ lunch & dinner) With seating around the edges of the room and candles flickering in windows there's a certain sense of intimacy in

---

**TOP FIVE EATS**

**Cafe Lava** (p137)
**Bar Soba** (left)
**The Left Bank** (opposite)
**Cheese Bar & Deli** (opposite)
**Stravaigin** (p140)

---

this stylish and very friendly bar. You can eat in the plush downstairs restaurant, or in the bar. The food is Asian fusion and the laksas go down a treat – followed up of course with an irresistible chocolate brownie. Background beats are perfect for chilling and it can be a good spot to escape Friday evening crowds.

**Bar 91** (Map p126; ☎ 552 5211; 91 Candleriggs; mains £6-7; ☺ noon-9pm Mon-Thu, to 6pm Fri-Sun, bar until midnight daily) By day this happy, buzzy bar serves excellent meals, far better than average pub food. Salads, pasta and burgers are among the many tasty offerings, and in summer tables spill out onto the sidewalk – ideal for some people-watching of the bold and the beautiful variety.

**Dakhin** (Map p126; ☎ 553 2585; 89 Candleriggs; dosas £8-12, 2-course lunch £10; ☺ lunch, dinner) This south Indian restaurant breathes some fresh air into the city's curry scene. Dishes are from all over the south, but we recommend that you try a dosa (a thin crispy crepe full of yummy stuff) or a thali (if you're really hungry – which is basically Indian tapas. South Indian cooking is fragrant and noted for its use of coconut.

**West Regent Street Bistro** (Map p126; ☎ 331 0303; 48 West Regent St; starters £4.75, mains £8-12; ☺ noon-10pm) Chic, stylishly laid-back and sleek in design, this bistro serves big wholesome portions of food at very reasonable prices. Popular with the after-work crowd (come later) it does a good mix of down-to-earth pub food tarted up and more inventive cuisine. Try the lamb shank slowly braised in red wine, orange, thyme and redcurrant jelly.

**Café Gandolfi** (Map p126; ☎ 552 6813; 64 Albion St; mains £8-14; ☺ 9am-11.30pm Mon-Sat, noon-11.30pm Sun) In the fashionable Merchant City, this café was once part of the old cheese market. It's been pulling in the punters for years, and packs an interesting clientele: die-hard Gandolfers, the upwardly mobile and tourists. It's an excellent, friendly bistro and upmarket coffee shop – very much the place to be seen. Book a Tim Stead-designed, medieval-looking table in advance for well-prepared Scottish and Continental food.

**Arisaig** (Map p126; ☎ 204 5399; 140 St Vincent St; starters £6-8, mains £11-17; ☺ lunch & dinner) Candlelight, crisp linen, an open kitchen and calming landscape pictures on the walls combine to create a soothing, relaxed dining atmosphere in this classy, airy restaurant. Dishes are divided into The Sea and The Land and are sourced from around the country, like grilled Shetland monkfish or Ayrshire lamb cutlets. This place is also highly regarded for its inventive vegetarian dishes that include roast pepper and red onion sausages.

Also recommended:

**Wagamama** (Map p126; ☎ 229 1468; 97 West George St; mains £6.50-9; ☺ noon-11pm Mon-Sat, 12.30-10pm Sun) Classy noodle restaurant with communal tables that is perpetually busy for its quality, well-priced food.

**Loon Fung** (Map p126; ☎ 332 1240; 417 Sauchiehall St; mains £9-13; ☺ lunch & dinner) One of the best Chinese restaurants in town; pretheatre 2-course meal is £9.

**Red Onion** (Map p126; ☎ 221 6000; 257 West Campbell St; starters £7, mains £9-12; ☺ lunch, dinner) An eclectic, French and Asian-influenced menu drives the dining at this impressive restaurant run by a well-renowned chef.

## West End

Just off Byres Rd, on the east side, Ashton Lane is packed with places to eat, including some of Glasgow's best restaurants.

### BUDGET

**Moka** (Map p121; ☎ 337 1642; 219 Byres Rd; lunch £3.50-4.50; ☺ 7.15am-9pm Mon-Sat, 9am-9pm Sun) If you're looking for lunch in the West End, drop into Moka where you can sit in or take away (to the nearby Botanic Gardens, for example). Sarnies, *paninis*, baguettes and salads are all on offer, and fillings are fresh and inventive. It's also good for vegetarians, and there are freshly squeezed juices available. For brekky you can't go past the pancakes.

### MIDRANGE

On the west side of Byres Rd, directly across from Ashton Lane, is Ruthven Lane. Here and nearby are a number of fine places to eat. Those staying in the vicinity of Kelvingrove Park will find a scattering of good restaurants on or around Gibson St and Great Western Rd.

**our pick** **The Left Bank** (Map p124; ☎ 339 5969; 33 Gibson St; mains £8-12; ☺ lunch, dinner) Huge windows fronting the street greet patrons to this outstanding new eatery specialising in gastronomic delights and lazy afternoons. There are lots of little spaces filled with couches and chunky tables reflecting a sense of intimacy. The large starter-menu can be treated like tapas making it good for sharing plates. There are lots of delightful creations that use seasonal and local produce. Try the garlic masala fried fish on a Goan seafood curry with malabar fish chip pickle – it's outstanding.

**Oran Mor Brasserie & Conservatory** (Map p121; ☎ 357 6200; cnr Byres & Great Western Rds; brasserie mains £10-15, conservatory mains £6-9; ☺ lunch & dinner) This temple to Scottish dining and drinking is a superb venue in an old church. Giving new meaning to the word 'conversion', the brasserie pumps out high-quality meals in a dark, Mackintosh-inspired space. There are also cheaper bistro-style meals, such as *Cullen skink* (soup made with smoked haddock, potato, onion and milk) or vegetarian haggis served with Arran mustard sauce, and more relaxed dining in the conservatory, adjoining the main bar (see p142).

**Firebird** (Map p124; ☎ 334 0594; 1321 Argyle St; mains £8-13; ☺ lunch, dinner) A combined bar and bistro with a cheery feel, Firebird has zany artwork on its bright walls and, more importantly, quality nosh whisked under the noses of its patrons. Local flavours and Mediterranean highlights (mainly Italian and Spanish) are evident and organic produce is used wherever possible. Taste sensations range from wood-fired pizzas to a Moroccan chicken and chickpea salad.

**Cheese Bar & Deli** (Map p121; ☎ 337 2282; 61 Otago St; mains £7-10; ☺ lunch, dinner) If you've a hankering to gorge on dairy get here quick-sticks – mouth-watering cheeseboards have fine accompaniments too such as walnut bread and red wine poached pear. Heavenly. Fondue features but there are plenty of rustic noncheese dishes too, notably Lebanese pizza and hand-rolled venison sausages. Dining is unfussy in simple surrounds and service is prompt.

**Wee Curry Shop** (Map p121; ☎ 357 5280; 29 Ashton Lane; dinner mains £9; ☺ lunch & dinner) A bit classier and more pricey than its city-centre cousin, Wee Curry, upstairs at Jinty McGuintys, is very big on quality home-cooked Indian food. The curries are exceptional and a window seat gives you people-watching potential over Ashton Lane. Indian tapas-style dishes are available at lunchtime.

**Stravaigin II** (Map p121; ☎ 334 7165; 8 Ruthven Lane; starters £5, mains £8-13; ☺ lunch & dinner) Clinking wine glasses and cracking mussel shells greet patrons at this refined eatery. There are a range of inventive taste-trips, such as skewered Dumfriesshire lamb fillet satay, cumin and lemon-roasted corn-fed chicken breast or organic wild-boar sausages. Two-course, lunch and pretheatre meals are great value at £12.

**Bay Tree Café** (Map p126; ☎ 334 5898; 403 Great Western Rd; mains £6-10; ☺ 9am-10pm Mon-Sat, to 9pm Sun) This mostly vegetarian café is excellent value. It has smiling staff, filling mains (mostly Middle Eastern and Greek), generous salads and a good range of hot drinks. The café is famous for its all-day Sunday brunch, including vegetarian burger, tattie scone, mushrooms, beans and tomato. It also serves a vegan breakfast. Good people-watching potential, too.

**Bothy** (Map p121; ☎ 334 4040; 11 Ruthven Lane; dinner mains £9-16, 3-course lunch £13.50; ☺ lunch, dinner) A bothy is not normally the most comfortable of abodes, but this West End player pays little heed to this tradition boasting a combo of modern design and comfy retro furnishings. It also blows apart the myth that Scottish food is stodgy and uninteresting. The Bothy dishes out traditional, uniquely Scottish, home-style fare – such as stoved howtodie wi' drappit eggs: translation, pot-roast chicken stuffed with white pudding, served with spinach and a poached egg.

### TOP END

**Ubiquitous Chip** (Map p121; ☎ 334 5007; 12 Ashton Lane; 2-/3-course dinner £35/40; ☺ lunch & dinner) The original champion of Scottish produce, this restaurant has won lots of awards for its unparalleled Scottish cuisine, and for its lengthy wine list. Just reading the ever-changing menu will induce worship from your tastebuds. Set among potted plants of arboreal proportions, this is an ideal place to treat that someone special. There's a cheaper restaurant here, **Upstairs at the Chip** (mains £10), where the menu follows in the tradition of creativity and top-notch ingredients.

**Buttery** (Map p124; ☎ 221 8188; 652 Argyle St; 2-/3-course dinner £35/40; ☺ lunch Tue-Fri, dinner Tue-Sat) This well-respected, elegant restaurant is just west of the M8. Although it's surrounded by grim, grey, tower-block flats (get a taxi here or drive), it's a top, Victorian-era restaurant offering fine dining among crisp tablecloths and oak panelling, with a classy clientele to match. The menu is a combination of seasonal Scottish and British organic produce.

**Stravaigin** (Map p124; ☎ 334 2665; 28 Gibson St; 2-course dinner £25; ☺ lunch, dinner) Stravaigin is a serious foodie's delight, with a menu constantly pushing the boundaries of originality and offering creative culinary excellence. There's a buzzing bar upstairs (open daily and offering simpler food) and a cool contemporary dining space in the basement with booth seating, and helpful, laid-back waiting-staff to assist in deciphering the audacious menu.

## DRINKING

Some of Scotland's best nightlife is found in the din and sometimes roar of Glasgow's pubs and bars. There are as many different styles of bar as there are punters to guzzle in them; a month of solid drinking wouldn't get you past the halfway mark.

### City Centre

#### TRADITIONAL PUBS

Glasgow is simply laden with traditional pubs exuding an old-world character.

**our pick Drum & Monkey** (Map p126; ☎ 221 6636; 93-95 St Vincent St) Jazz fans can get their fix on Sunday afternoon; the rest of the week jazz records accompany the dark wood and marble columns of this attractive drinking emporium, peppered with church pews and leather lounge chairs. Its cosy and relaxing vibe makes you want to curl up in an armchair with a pint for the afternoon.

**Horse Shoe** (Map p126; ☎ 221 3051; 17 Drury St) This legendary city pub and popular meeting place dates from the late 19th century and is largely unchanged. It has the longest continuous bar in the UK, but its main attraction is what's served over it – real ale and good food. Upstairs in the lounge are the best-value three-course lunches (£3.45) in town.

**Scotia** (Map p126; ☎ 552 8681; 112 Stockwell St) Drinks have been poured down throats at Scotia, Glasgow's oldest pub, since 1792. And while the last good airing feels like it happened back in the mid-1850s, Scotia's cheery charm outweighs the grungy atmosphere.

**Blackfriars** (Map p126; ☎ 552 5924; 36 Bell St) Merchant City's most relaxed and atmospheric pub, Blackfriars' friendly staff and chilled-out house make it special. Importantly, you don't have to ask – it's a cask. There's a seating area with large windows that are great for people-watching.

**Babbity Bowster** (Map p126; ☎ 552 5055; 16-18 Blackfriars St) Babbity Bowster has a Continental feel and is perfect for a quiet daytime drink, particularly in the adjoining beer garden. There's also accommodation here (see p135). The interior has a classy vibe, with a suit crowd to match on weekday evenings. There's music on Saturday night, usually of the folky-fiddler variety.

## BARS

**ourpick The Butterfly & the Pig** (Map p126; ☎ 221 7711; 153 Bath St) A breath of fresh air along trendy Bath St, the piggery is a little offbeat, a little zany and makes you feel comfortable as soon as you plunge into its basement depths. The décor is an eclectic bunch with a retro feel and this adds to its familiarity. You get the feeling that servicing this place regularly would be rewarded with your favourite pint being poured just as you enter the doorway.

**Artá** (Map p126; ☎ 552 2101; 13-19 Walls St; ☯ until 3am) Very much a beloved destination, this extraordinary hacienda-style place has to be seen to be believed. As its door slides open, Artá's opulent, cavernous candle-lit interior is exposed. Floor-to-ceiling velvet, red curtains reveal a staircase to the tapas bar and restaurant above in a show of decadence that the Romans would have appreciated. This mock baroque-cum-Mediterranean showpiece has a relaxed, chilled vibe and a mixed crowd. Get a woowoo cocktail into ya.

**Corinthian** (Map p126; ☎ 552 1101; 191 Ingram St) A breathtaking, domed ceiling and majestic chandeliers make Corinthian an awesome venue. Originally a bank and later Glasgow's High Court, this regal building also houses a plush club, downstairs in old court cells, which pumps out funk and club classics on Fridays and Saturdays. It also has Glasgow's only late-night piano bar, open until 3am nightly.

**Bar 10** (Map p126; ☎ 572 1448; 10 Mitchell Lane) A tiny city treasure that will cause the canny Glasgow drinker to give you a knowing glance if you mention its name. As laid-back as you could ask in a hip city bar, the friendly, tuned-in staff complete the happy picture. It transforms from a quiet daytime bar to a happening weekend pub on Friday and Saturday nights.

**Nice 'n' Sleazy** (Map p126; ☎ 333 9637; 421 Sauchiehall St) Close to the Glasgow School of Art, students come here to discuss primers, Duchamp and Nietzsche over some of Glasgow's cheapest drinks. With 1970s retro décor, a relaxed atmosphere and great menu for under a fiver, it's a top spot to kick back and relish the tunes of the city's freshest live music.

**Firewater** (Map p126; ☎ 354 0350; 341 Sauchiehall St; ☯ until 3am) A large venue constantly mobbed, Firewater is a good honest servant of Sauchiehall St. It's always lively and there are usually some pretty good bands plying their trade. Huge American pool tables, drink offers and club passes means it's a good place to get connected.

**Pivo Pivo** (Map p126; ☎ 564 8100; 15 Waterloo St) A cavernous downstairs beer hall with beers aplenty – 100 from 32 different countries to be exact. Add to that an impressive array of vodka and schnapps, and it may be a while before you see daylight. Buy any two drinks between 5pm and 7pm Monday to Thursday and get a free pizza – bargain.

**Arches** (Map p126; ☎ 565 1035; 253 Argyle St) A one-stop culture/entertainment fix, this place doubles as a theatre showing contemporary, avant-garde productions and there's also a club (p142). The hotel-like entrance belies the deep interior, which make you feel as though you've discovered Hades' bohemian underworld. The crowd is mixed – hiking boots are as welcome as Versace.

**Waxy O'Connors** (Map p126; ☎ 354 5154; 46 West George St) If you've been trying to avoid those acid flashbacks, steer clear of Waxy O'Connors. This labyrinthine maze of six bars on three levels (you may not emerge for days), including the inspiringly named Murphy's Bar, is an Escher drawing brought to life. Sadly, it's also an Irish-themed bar, but even that doesn't ruin the surreal fun.

**Moskito** (Map p126; ☎ 331 1777; 200 Bath St) A classic Bath St basement bar, Moskito is just the place to kick back and get boozed up. Let the inhouse DJs mellow you out with their deep beats and electronica. Grab the pool table if all this lying about drinking is getting too much.

**Mojama** (Map p126; ☎ 332 4760; Sauchiehall St) Very retro and very futuristic at the same time, it's worth popping your head into this *Jetsons*-like place to curl up nursing a drink in the blood-red interior. On Monday it's wannabee DJs who spin their own tracks.

## West End
### TRADITIONAL PUBS

**Uisge Beatha** (Map p124; ☎ 564 1596; 232-246 Woodlands Rd) If you enjoy a drink among dead things, you'll love Uisge Beatha (Gaelic for whisky, literally 'water of life'). This mishmash of church pews, stuffed animal heads and portraits of

GLASGOW

depressed nobility (the Maggie mannequin is our favourite) is patrolled by Andy Capp-like characters during the day and students at night. With 100 whiskies and four quirky rooms to choose from, this unique pub is one of Glasgow's best – an antidote to style bars.

**Aragon Bar** (Map p121; 131 Byers Rd) A traditional bar located in this trendy part of town, with changing guest ales and board games behind the bar for those lazy afternoons. There's also a decent wine selection.

## BARS

**our pick** **Oran Mor Brasserie & Conservatory** (Map p121; ☎ 357 6200; cnr Byres & Great Western Rds) Now some may be a little uncomfortable with the thought of drinking in a church. But we say – the lord giveth. Praise be and let's give thanks – a converted church and an almighty one at that is now a bar, eating venue (see p139) and club venue. The bar feels like it's been here for years – all wood and thick, exposed stone giving it warmth and a celestial air. There's an excellent array of whiskies. The only thing missing is holy water on your way in.

**Jinty McGuinty's** (Map p121; ☎ 339 0747; 23-29 Ashton Lane) This is a popular Irish theme pub with unusual booth seating and a literary hall of fame. There's also a spacious and popular beer garden that often spills into secluded Ashton Lane in summer. Its Guinness is brewed in Ireland.

**Brel** (Map p121; ☎ 342 4966; 39 Ashton Lane) A popular watering-hole on Ashton Lane, the name may be pretentious (it's named after a famous – famous in Belgium – musician), as are the Belgian beers, but fortunately Brel's clientele – mainly students – keeps it down to earth and informal. There's a conservatory out the back so you can pretend you're sitting outside when it's raining, and when the sun does peek through there's a beer garden.

**Vodka Wodka** (Map p121; ☎ 341 0669; 31 Ashton Lane) This watering hole is every vodka drinker's dream, with more varieties of the stealthy poison than you could possibly conquer in one sitting. Its brushed metal bar dishes out the liquid fire to students during the day and groups of mid-20s in the evening.

## ENTERTAINMENT

Glasgow is Scotland's entertainment city, from classical music, fine theatres and ballet, to cracking nightclubs pumping out cheesy chart tunes or the latest dance-music phe-nomenon, and contemporary Scottish bands at the cutting edge of modern music.

To tap into your scene, check out the *List* (www.list.co.uk), an invaluable fortnightly events-guide available at newsagents and bookshops. If you plan to spend any time in the city, pick up a copy of *Itchy* (£3.50), a handy pocket-sized entertainment guide, available at bookshops. The *Herald* and the *Evening Times* newspapers list events happening around the city. Pick up a copy of the *Gig Guide* (www.gigguide.co.uk), published monthly and available free in most pubs and venues for the latest on music gigs.

For theatre tickets book directly with the venue. For concerts, a useful booking centre is **Tickets Scotland** ( ☎ 204 5151, 0870 220 1116; www .tickets-scotland.com; 239 Argyle St).

## Clubs

Glasgow has one of Britain's biggest clubbing scenes attracting style-cats from afar. Glaswegians usually hit clubs after the pubs have closed, so many clubs offer discounted admission and cheaper drinks if you go before 10.30pm. Entry costs £4 to £7 (up to £25 for big events), although bars often hand out free passes. Most clubs close around 3am.

**Arches** (Map p126; ☎ 0870 240 7528; 253 Argyle St) R-e-s-p-e-c-t is the mantra with the Arches. The Godfather of Glaswegian clubs, it has a design based around hundreds of arches slammed together, and is a must for funk and hip-hop freaks. It is one of the city's biggest clubs pulling top DJs, and you'll also hear some of the UK's up-and-coming turntable spinners. It's located off Jamaica St.

**Cathouse** (Map p126; ☎ 332 1067; 15 Union St; ☺ Thu-Sun) Don the ghostly war paint, dust off the steel caps and rejoin your Goth brethren at the three-level Cathouse, Glasgow's top indie and alternative venue. A recent makeover hasn't changed the make-up of the punters. There are two dance floors: upstairs is pretty intense with lots of metal and hard rock, downstairs is a little less scary if you're not keen on moshing.

**Tunnel** (Map p126; ☎ 204 1000; 84 Mitchell St; Wed-Sun) This is a good venue for young clubbers or those new to the scene with plenty of cheap drink promos and a variety of beats. Wednesday (Allure) and Thursday (Kinky Pinky) are big gay nights (see p144), Friday is for house, hip-hop and soul-rock worshippers, while Saturday is devoted to RnB, funky tunes and disco – something for everyone.

**Sub Club** (; ☎ 248 4600; 22 Jamaica St) Offering up hardcore beats (not for those with sensitive hearing) to a student crowd, Sub Club, with its claustrophobic, last-one-in vibe, is not for those faint of heart. This is serious clubbing and it's all about your moves and the odd head-case on the dance floor.

**ABC** (p126; ☎ 332 2232; www.abcglasgow.com; 300 Sauchiehall St) A beautiful creature of the clubbing world, ABC has gorgeous bars, punters who scrub up pretty darn good and a varied music selection. It attracts heaps of students and is a good all-round venue. Indie lovers should check out Thursday nights.

**Art School** (p126; ☎ 353 4530; 167 Renfrew St) An impressive venue in the Glasgow School of Art (would CRM have approved?), this is where the style-cats of the student world hang out in force. It's a welcoming place and the dance nights are legendary. Cheap booze and a good selection of DJs rounds off the happy picture.

## Live Music

Glasgow has long been regarded as the centre of Scotland's live-music scene. Year after year, touring musicians, artists and travellers alike name Glasgow as one of their favourite cities in the world to enjoy live music. As much of Glasgow's character is encapsulated within the soul and humour of its inhabitants, the main reason for the city's musical success lies within its audience and the musical community it has bred and nurtured for years. On any given night you may find your breath taken by a wave of voices as the audience spontaneously harmonises with an artist on a chorus, a song or even, on special nights, an entire show.

One of the city's premier live-music pub venues, the excellent **King Tut's Wah Wah Hut** (Map p126; ☎ 221 5279; www.kingtuts.co.uk; 272a St Vincent St) hosts bands every night of the week. Oasis were signed after playing here.

Two bars to see the best, and worst, of Glasgow's newest bands are **Brunswick Cellars** (Map p126; ☎ 332 9329; 239 Sauchiehall St) and the **Halt Bar** (Map p124; ☎ 352 9996; 160 Woodlands Rd), which is a popular university pub that hasn't been tarted up.

Other recommendations:

**13th Note Cafe** (Map p126; ☎ 553 1638; www.13thnote.co.uk; 50-60 King St)

**ABC** (Map p126; ☎ 0870 4000 818; www.abcglasgow .com; 300 Sauchiehall St) Former cinema, new venue; medium- to large-size acts.

**Barfly** (Map p126; ☎ 0870 907 0999; www.barflyclub .com; 260 Clyde St)

**Barrowland** (Map p124; ☎ 552 4601; www.glasgow -barrowland.com; 244 Gallowgate) An exceptional old dancehall catering for some of the larger acts that visit the city.

**Clyde Auditorium** (Map p124; ☎ 0870 040 4000; www.secc.co.uk) Also known as the Armadillo because of its bizarre shape, adjoins SECC, and caters for big national and international acts.

**Glasgow Academy** (Map p124; ☎ 418 3000; www .glasgow-academy.co.uk; 121 Eglinton St)

**Mono** (Map p126; ☎ 553 2400; 12 Kings Crt, King St) Smaller acts, vegan food, great bar.

**Nice 'n' Sleazy** (Map p126; ☎ 333 0900; 421 Sauchiehall St) Nurturing much of Glasgow's alternative music scene.

**SECC** (Map p126; ☎ 0870 040 4000; www.secc.co.uk; Finnieston Quay) Adjoins Clyde Auditorium, and hosts major national and international acts.

## Cinemas

**Glasgow Film Theatre** (Map p126; ☎ 332 8128; www .gft.org.uk; 12 Rose St; adult/concession £5/4) The two-screen Glasgow Film Theatre, off Sauchiehall St, screens arthouse cinema and classics.

**Odeon Renfield Street** (Map p126; ☎ 0870 505 0007; 56 Renfield St; adult/concession £6/4) The nine-screen Odeon Renfield Street shows mainstream films.

## Theatres & Concert Halls

**Theatre Royal** (Map p126; ☎ 332 3321; www.the ambassadors.com/theatreroyalglasgow; 282 Hope St) This is the home of Scottish Opera, and the Scottish Ballet often has performances here. Ask about standby tickets if you'll be in town for a few days.

**Glasgow Royal Concert Hall** (Map p126; ☎ 353 8080; www.grch.com; 2 Sauchiehall St) A feast of classical music is showcased at this concert hall, the modern home of the Royal Scottish National Orchestra.

**King's Theatre** (Map p126; ☎ 0870 060 6648; www .kings-glasgow.co.uk; 297 Bath St) This theatre hosts mainly musicals; on rare occasions there are variety shows, pantomimes and comedies.

**Citizens' Theatre** (Map p124; ☎ 429 0022; www.citz .co.uk; 119 Gorbals St) This is one of the top theatres in Scotland and it's well worth trying to catch a performance here.

**Tron Theatre** (Map p126; ☎ 552 4267; www.tron.co.uk; 63 Trongate) Tron Theatre stages contemporary Scottish and international performances. There's also a good café.

**Centre for Contemporary Arts** (Map p126; ☎ 352 4900; www.cca-glasgow.com; 350 Sauchiehall St) This is

GLASGOW

a shmick venue making terrific use of space and light. It showcases the visual and performing arts, including movies, talks and galleries.

**Tramway** (Map p121; ☎ 0845 330 3501; 25 Albert Dr) This theatre and exhibition space attracts cutting-edge theatrical groups, the visual and performing arts, and a varied range of artistic exhibitions.

## Sport

Two football clubs dominate the sporting scene in Scotland, having vastly more resources than other clubs and a long history (and rivalry). This rivalry is also along partisan lines, with Rangers representing Protestant supporters, and Celtic, of course, Catholic.

**Celtic Football Club** (Map p121; ☎ 0871 226 1888; www.celticfc.co.uk; Celtic Park, Parkhead) Has a 60,832-seat stadium.

**Rangers Football Club** ( ☎ 0871 702 1972; www .rangers.co.uk; Ibrox Stadium, 150 Edmiston Dr) Tours of the stadium and trophy room run three times daily Monday and Friday, once on Saturday (tours £7/5 per adult/child). Rangers' stadium holds 50,500 seats.

---

### GAY & LESBIAN GLASGOW

Glasgow has a vibrant gay scene, with the gay quarter found in and around the Merchant City (particularly Virginia, Wilson and Glassford Sts). The city's gay community has a reputation for being very friendly.

To get the lowdown, the best contact for gay and lesbian travellers is the **Glasgow LGBT Centre** (Map p126; ☎ 0141-552-4958; www.glgbt.org.uk; 84 Bell St; ⏰ 11am-midnight; ♿ ). It has a bulletin board with information about activities and events, as well as personal ads; there's also a café-bar here. For confidential advice or help try the **Gay & Lesbian switchboard** ( ☎ 332 8372). See also the Gay & Lesbian section (p442) in the Directory.

**Spa 19** (Map p126; ☎ 572 0347; 2nd fl, 19 Dixon St; admission £10; ⏰ noon-10pm Sun-Fri, to 4am Sat) is an excellent gay health centre, with a small gym, sauna and Jacuzzi, TV lounge, café and cyber centre for firing off emails.

To tap into the scene, check out *The List,* the free *Scots Gay* magazine and the **GayScotland website** (www.gayscotland.com/glasgow/glasgow_index.htm).

Many straight clubs and bars have gay and lesbian nights, such as **Utter Gutter @ The Riverside Club** ( ☎ 248 3144; 33 Fox St; admission £10; ⏰ 10.30pm-3am) on the first Saturday monthly. Everyone's welcome at this friendly night – one of Glasgow's best.

The following are just a selection of gay and lesbian pubs and clubs in the city.

**Bennet's** (Map p126; ☎ 552 5761; www.bennets.co.uk; 90 Glassford St) Glasgow's longest-running gay club is slightly seedy and stuck in the 1980s. It cranks out tunes from hard house to cheesy chart faves from Wednesday to Sunday.

**Delmonica's** (Map p126; ☎ 552 4803; 68 Virginia St; ⏰ noon-midnight) Metres from the Polo Lounge, Delmonica's is a world away, with its predatorial feeling of people on the pull. It's packed on weekday evenings. Friday night is glam night with chart tunes and Sunday is a karaoke free-for-all.

**Moda** (Map p126; ☎ 553 2553; cnr Virginia & Wilson Sts; ⏰ 5pm-midnight Mon, Tue & Thu, until 3am rest of the week) Blonde wood, fake tans and fluffy pink cocktails are the chief attributes of Moda, a place where beautiful folk strike a pose over daytime drinks, or recuperate before returning to the Polo Lounge next door or going downmarket at Delmonica's.

**Polo Lounge** (Map p126; ☎ 553 1221; 84 Wilson St; ⏰ 5pm-1am Mon-Thu, to 3am Fri-Sun) Staff claim 'the city's best talent' is found here; a quick glance at the many glamour pusses – male and female – proves their claim. The downstairs club is packed on weekends; just the main bars open on other nights.

**Revolver** (Map p126; ☎ 553 2456; 6a John St) Hip little Revolver, downstairs on cosmopolitan John St, sports a relaxed crowd and, crucially, a free jukebox.

**Waterloo Bar** (Map p126; ☎ 229 5891; 306 Argyle St) This is a traditional place and Scotland's oldest gay bar. It attracts punters of all ages. It's very friendly and, with a large group of regulars, a good place to meet people.

If you're in Glasgow in autumn check out **Glasgay** ( ☎ 334 7126; www.glasgay.co.uk), a gay performing arts festival, held around October/November each year.

## SHOPPING

Boasting the UK's largest retail contingency outside London, Glasgow is a shopaholic's paradise.

Fashion junkies can procure relief at **Versace** ( ☎ 552 6510) and **Armani** ( ☎ 552 2277) in the stylish **Italian Centre** (Map p126; John St). Alternatively, **Designer Exchange** (Map p126; ☎ 221 6898; 3 Royal Exchange Ct) stocks cheaper samples and resale designer labels. Trendy traders litter the pedestrian malls of Sauchiehall and Buchanan Sts. Try **Buchanan Galleries** ( ☎ 332 4353; www.buchanangalleries.co.uk; Royal Exchange Sq) and the exquisite **Princes Sq** (Map p126), which is set in a magnificent 1841 renovated square.

Munro baggers and other outdoor enthusiasts can go berserk at **Tiso's** (Map p126; ☎ 248 4877; 129 Buchanan St; ☯ 9.30am-5.30pm Mon-Wed, Fri & Sat, to 7pm Thu, 11am-5pm Sun) and **Adventure 1** (Map p126; ☎ 353 3788; 38 Dundas St), which is an excellent place to buy hiking boots.

Institutions include Buchanan St's splendid, jewellery-laden **Argyll Arcade** (Map p126), where you'll find **Catherine Shaw** (Map p126; ☎ 221 9038; www.carrick-jewellery.co.uk) for distinct pieces transcending mass production, and the **Barras** (Map p124; ☎ 552 4601; London Rd), a burgeoning flea market open every weekend.

## GETTING THERE & AWAY

Glasgow is 42 miles from Edinburgh and 166 miles from Inverness.

### Air

Ten miles west of the city, **Glasgow International Airport** ( ☎ 887 1111; www.baa.co.uk/glasgow) handles domestic traffic and international flights. Glasgow Prestwick airport, 30 miles southwest of Glasgow, handles some of the cheap, no-frills airlines, and has many European flights. There are direct flights from many European cities, including Amsterdam, Brussels, Prague and Dublin. **Ryanair** ( ☎ 0871 246 0000; www.ryanair.com) flies to Glasgow Prestwick airport from London Stansted airport (1¼ hours, frequent) for around £25 plus taxes, but check its website for ridiculously cheap specials.

Ever thought about getting to, or departing from, Glasgow in a seaplane? Probably not – but it's not a bad way to make an entry. **Loch Lomond Seaplanes** ( ☎ 0870 242 1457; www.lochlomondseaplanes.com; Clyde River, Glasgow Science Centre) flies regularly from the Clyde to Oban on Scotland's west coast (once or twice daily), but keep an eye on its website as services will be expanding to other destinations. See p453 for more information.

### Bus

All long-distance buses arrive and depart from **Buchanan bus station** (Map p126; ☎ 333 3708; Killermont St).

Buses from London are very competitive. **Megabus** ( ☎ 0900 160 0900; www.megabus.com) should be your first port of call if you're looking for the cheapest fare. It has one-way fares for around £10; check the website for your date of departure.

**Silver Choice** ( ☎ 01355-230403; www.silverchoicetravel.co.uk) also has great deals (advance-purchase return ticket £24, 8½ hours). It departs at 10pm daily from both London Victoria coach station and Buchanan bus station in Glasgow. The service is very popular, so you'll need to book well in advance.

**National Express** ( ☎ 0870 580 8080; www.nationalexpress.com) leaves from the same bus stations (single £31, nine hours, at least four daily). There's a daily direct overnight bus from Heathrow Airport, usually departing at 11.05pm.

National Express also has numerous links with other English cities. Direct services and single tickets include: up to five daily buses from Birmingham (£44, seven hours); at least four from Manchester (£25, five hours); one from Newcastle (£27, four hours); and one from York (£32, seven hours).

**Scottish Citylink** ( ☎ 0870 550 5050; www.citylink.co.uk) has buses to most major towns in Scotland. There are very frequent services to Edinburgh (£5, 1¼ hours), every 20 minutes during the day. Frequent buses also run to Stirling (£5, 45 minutes), Inverness (£19, four hours) and Aberdeen (£20, 3¼ to four hours). Regular long-distance services to/from Glasgow include Oban (£15, three hours, four direct daily), Fort William (£16, three hours, seven daily) and Portree on Skye (£29, 6¼ to seven hours, three daily).

There's a twice-daily service via Stranraer, connecting with the ferry, to Belfast in Northern Ireland (single/return £23/39, six hours).

Walkers should check out **First Glasgow** ( ☎ 423 6600), which runs buses every hour or two to Milngavie (30 minutes), the start of the West Highland Way.

### Car & Motorcycle

There are numerous car-rental companies; the big names have offices at Glasgow

International Airport. Companies include the following:

**Arnold Clark** ( ☎ 423 9559; www.arnoldclarkrental.co.uk; 43 Allison St) Rates per day/week from £17/85.
**Avis** ( ☎ 0870 608 6339, 221 2827; www.avis.co.uk; 70 Lancefield St)

## Train

As a general rule, Glasgow Central station serves southern Scotland, England and Wales, and Queen St station serves the north and east. There are buses every 10 minutes between them. There are direct trains from London's King's Cross and Euston stations; they're much quicker (from £18, five hours, nine direct daily) and more comfortable than the bus.

**First ScotRail** ( ☎ 0845 755 0033; www.firstgroup.com/scotrail/index.php) runs the West Highland line heading north to Oban and Fort William, and other direct links to Dundee (£21), Aberdeen (£37) and Inverness (£37). There are trains every 15 to 30 minutes to/from Edinburgh (£10.50, 50 minutes).

## GETTING AROUND
### To/From the Airport

There are buses every 10 or 15 minutes from Glasgow International Airport to Buchanan bus station (single/return £4/6). A taxi costs about £20.

## Car & Motorcycle

The most difficult thing about driving in Glasgow, as with most Scottish urban centres, is the confusing one-way system. If you miss a turn-off, you can end up a long way from your destination, particularly if you get spat out on the motorway encircling the city centre – likely. For short-term parking (30 minutes to two hours) you've a decent chance of finding something on the street, especially away from the city centre (around the centre it's very expensive – 30p for 10 minutes). Otherwise, multistorey car parks are probably your best bet – the St Enoch Centre in the city has free parking. Note that the West End generally, and Great Western Rd in particular, are very busy during the day and bumper to bumper during peak hour (8am to 9.30am and 4pm to 6pm).

## Public Transport

Glasgow has an excellent public transport system, especially the rail network. The Roundabout Glasgow ticket (adult/child £4.50/2.25) covers all underground and train transport in the city for a day.

**First Glasgow** ( ☎ 423 6600; www.firstglasgow.com) has a FirstDay ticket that allows hop-on/off travel on all its buses; it can be bought from drivers for £3 and is valid until 1am. It also covers unlimited travel in the Greater Glasgow area as far as East Kilbride or Paisley.

### BUS

City bus services are frequent. You can buy tickets when you board buses, but on most you must have the exact change. First Glasgow publishes the complicated but useful *Glasgow Mapmate* (£1), which shows all local First Glasgow bus routes. Trips around the city cost on average £1. Pick up a copy of the First Glasgow *Night Network* brochure to find out about services running through until the wee hours.

### TAXI

There's no shortage of taxis, and if you want to know anything about Glasgow, striking up a conversation with a cabbie is a good place to start.

You can pay by credit card with **Glasgow Taxis** ( ☎ 429 7070) if you order by phone; most of its taxis are wheelchair accessible.

### TRAIN & SUBWAY

There's an extensive suburban network of trains in and around Glasgow; tickets should be bought before travel if the station is staffed, or from the conductor if it isn't.

There's also an underground line that serves 15 stations in the centre, west and south of the city (single £1). The rail network connects with the Underground at Buchanan St station. The Discovery Ticket (£1.90) gives unlimited travel after 9.30am on the Underground system for a day.

# AROUND GLASGOW

There are some wonderful sights in the urban centres around Glasgow, although it's best to visit this grim hinterland of postindustrial communities via a day trip. It's like finding diamonds in a coal mine – well worth looking, but you wouldn't want to spend the night there. Paisley's abbey should head your itinerary – it's a stupendous sight and a marvellous architectural achievement. If you're interested

**WORTH THE TRIP**

Effectively a suburb about 5 miles west of Glasgow, the reason for visiting **Paisley** is to see its timeless abbey – one of the finest in southern Scotland. Overlooking the river like a giant sentinel, **Paisley Abbey** ( ☎ 0141-889 7654; www.paisleyabbey.org.uk; Abbey Close; admission free; ☻ 10am-3.30pm Mon-Sat) is an awesome sight. Inside, the stonework gives a chilly embrace and you feel as though you've passed through a portal to another age – the scruffy town outside seems a world away.

The abbey was founded in 1163 by Walter Fitzallan, the first high steward of Scotland and ancestor of the Stuart dynasty. It was damaged by fire during the Wars of Independence in 1306, but rebuilt soon after. Most of the nave is 14th or 15th century. The building was a ruin from the 16th century until the 19th-century restoration, not completed until 1928. There are two royal tombs in the abbey, excellent stained-glass windows and the 10th-century Celtic **Barochan Cross**.

If you've time, at the western end of the High St, there's the **University of Paisley** and the **Museum & Art Gallery** ( ☎ 0141-889 3151; High St; admission free; ☻ 10am-5pm Tue-Sat, 2-5pm Sun), which features Paisley psychedelia! There are some marvellous exhibits, including contemporary displays of children in the modern world – it's worth at least a couple of hours. It also has collections of local and natural history, ceramics and 19th-century Scottish art.

There are frequent buses from Central Rd. Trains leave Glasgow's Central station for Paisley's Gilmour St station (off-peak/day return £3.50/4.50, 15 minutes, eight per hour).

---

in Clyde shipbuilding and its spectacular fall from economic grace, Greenock is a must.

## INVERCLYDE

The ghostly remains of once-great shipyards still line the banks of the Clyde west of Glasgow.

The only place worth stopping along the coast west of the city is Greenock, although there are a couple of items of interest in the otherwise unprepossessing town of **Port Glasgow**, including the fine 16th-century **Newark Castle** (HS; ☎ 01475-741858; adult/child £3.50/1.75; ☻ 9.30am-5.30pm Apr-Sep), which is still largely intact.

## Greenock

☎ 01475 / pop 46,000

Greenock has a lovely, revitalised waterfront area by the James Watt College, which is very pleasant to wander around. Other parts of town are a little scrappy and can be confusing to navigate.

An enjoyable walk up to Lyle Hill, above Gourock Bay, leads to the Free French memorial, commemorating sailors who lost their lives in the Battle of the Atlantic during WWII, and a great view over the Firth of Clyde.

### SIGHTS

**McLean Museum & Art Gallery** ( ☎ 715624; 15 Kelly St; admission free; ☻ 10am-5pm Mon-Sat) is well worth checking out. It's quite an extensive collection, with displays charting the history of steam power and Clyde shipping. There's also a pictorial history of Greenock through the ages, while upstairs there are very good temporary exhibitions and small displays from China, Japan and Egypt. The natural history section highlights the sad reality of species extinction in the modern world.

**HM Customs & Excise Museum** ( ☎ 881300; Custom House Quay; admission free; ☻ 10am-4pm Mon-Fri) is intriguing in parts, and good for killing an hour or so. You can also learn a thing or two about searches and smuggling techniques. You have to feel sorry for the customs officers who searched an Airbus from the West Indies and found more than 5kg of marijuana in the aircraft toilet tanks! The search took 4½ hours.

### SLEEPING & EATING

**James Watt College** ( ☎ 731360; enquiries@jameswatt .ac.uk; Halls of Residence, Custom House Way; r per person from £22; ☒ ) Fairly central and down on the waterfront, this residence hall has 164 single rooms, many with en suite. It's good value, and the management only ask that you leave the place as you found it. Fair enough.

**Tontine Hotel** ( ☎/fax 723316; www.tontinehotel.co.uk; 6 Ardgowan Sq; s £65-90, d £80-95) This grand hotel with well-appointed rooms, each with en suite, is genteel and well worth the pounds. The premier rooms in the old wing are more luxurious and spacious. Book early for stays over summer – ask about room-only rates, too.

GLASGOW

## SHIPBUILDING ON THE CLYDE

One of the earliest permanent Lower Clyde shipyards was established in 1711 by John Scott at Greenock. Initial construction was for small-scale local trade but, by the end of the 18th century, large ocean-going vessels were being built. As the market expanded, shipyards also opened at Dumbarton and Port Glasgow.

The *Comet*, Europe's first steamship, was launched at Port Glasgow in 1812. By the 1830s and 1840s the Clyde had secured its position as the world leader in shipbuilding. Steel hulls came into use by the 1880s, allowing construction of larger ships with the latest and best engines.

In 1899 John Brown & Co, a Sheffield steelmaker, took over a Clydebank yard and by 1907 had become part of the world's largest shipbuilding conglomerate, producing ocean-going liners. Output from the Clyde shipyards steadily increased up to WWI and, with the advent of the war, there was huge demand for new shipping from both the Royal Navy and Merchant Navy.

During and after the war many small companies disappeared and shipbuilding giants, such as Lithgows Ltd, took their place. The depression years of the 1920s and 1930s saw many yards mothballed or closed. Another boom followed during WWII but these were to be the twilight years.

Many yards went into liquidation in the 1960s, and in 1972 Upper Clyde Shipbuilders was liquidated, causing complete chaos, a sit-in and a bad headache for Ted Heath's government.

Now the great shipyards of the Clyde are mostly derelict and empty. The remains of a once-mighty industry include just a handful of companies still operating along the Clyde.

**Port & Harbour** ( ☎ 730370; Custom House Pl; mains £11-17; ☹ lunch & dinner) On the waterfront next to the HM Customs & Excise Museum, this fine restaurant offers candle-lit dining, specialising in local seafood, lamb and venison dishes. The surroundings are suitably dark and cosy, perfect for blustery nights.

### GETTING THERE & AWAY

Greenock is 27 miles west of Glasgow. The Glasgow–Greenock/Gourock pedestrian/cycle route (p132) follows an old railway track for 10 miles. There are trains from Glasgow Central station (£6 off-peak return, 45 minutes, three per hour) and hourly buses.

## Gourock

☎ 01475 / pop 11,511
Gourock is a seaside resort situated 3 miles west of Greenock. Although the small central area is run-down, the town's location is wonderful and it is an important hub for transport.

For accommodation, you'd best head for Glasgow or Dunoon, though there are options in Gourock.

**Spinnaker Hotel** ( ☎ 633107; www.spinnakerhotel .co.uk; 121 Albert Rd; s/d from £30/60, mains £8) is an excellent pub. Rooms (with either en suite or shared bathroom) have country-pine décor, are clean and spacious, and have large screen TVs. Downstairs the comfy bar is laid-back and has guest ales on tap. Pretty basic pub grub is also on offer.

**CalMac** ( ☎ 650100) ferries leave daily for Dunoon (passenger/car £3.25/8, 25 minutes, hourly) on Argyll's Cowal peninsula.

There's a council-operated, passenger-only ferry service to Kilcreggan (£1.90, 12 minutes, 12 daily Monday to Saturday, three Sunday) and Helensburgh (£1.90, 40 minutes, three or four daily); buy tickets on board.

**Western Ferries** ( ☎ 01369-704452) has a service to Dunoon (passenger/car £3.40/9.60, 20 minutes, two to three hourly) from McInroy's Point, 2 miles from the train station; Scottish Citylink buses run to here.

Gourock train station is next to the CalMac terminal; there are trains to/from Glasgow Central station (£5, 45 minutes, three per hour).

## Wemyss Bay

☎ 01475 / pop 2466
Eight miles south of Gourock is Wemyss Bay (pronounced weemz), where you can jump off a train and onto a ferry for Rothesay on the Isle of Bute (p281). There are trains from Glasgow (£5.50, 50 minutes, hourly). **CalMac** ( ☎ 520521) ferries to Rothesay connect with most trains and cost £3.80/15.25 per passenger/car.

# Southern Scotland

An enchanting region of Scotland that seems to slip off the radar for many international visitors, southern Scotland is often missed by the hordes scrambling to destinations further north. A shame – but also a wonderful part of its attraction. Crowd-free castles to ramble around, miles of open countryside and small traffic-free roads along which to explore it all – it takes no time to stumble across a pocket of country you'll have all to yourself.

Stretching from the Scottish Borders, with the fiery remnants of the great Border abbeys to the floating paradise of Arran, southern Scotland is one big trail of treasures and pleasures. Unlike its cousin, central Scotland, a bit further north, the attractions aren't quite so jam packed, there's room to breathe down here. But the stately mansions, picture-perfect countryside and smoking ruins that encapsulate centuries of conflict with England are worth the time and effort to discover.

Woodland areas such as the exhilarating and remote Galloway Forest are a relief from Britain's naked landscape and there are many ways to enjoy them, including mountain-bike trails that criss-cross the region. Important wildlife survives in these lush valleys and undulating hills, with the bellow of the red deer reverberating in remote forests. The stunning Isle of Arran is a jewel of the Hebridean isles with easy access, historical sights, an excellent walking and cycling route around its perimeter and gourmet produce infused into its delectable cuisine.

This is an area that ignites the imagination – Sir Walter Scott and Robert Burns, Scotland's two great literary sons, romanticised the region. After a short time here it's easy to see why.

**SOUTHERN SCOTLAND**

---

## HIGHLIGHTS

- Tumbling around lush Border country and roaming the hulking burnt-out shells of the **great Border abbeys** (p150)

- Getting snug by an open fire, local brew in hand, at one of the many fine pubs on **Isle of Arran** (p168), a walking and cycling paradise

- Admiring the architectural genius of the 18th century at **Culzean Castle** (p176), perched on wild sea cliffs

- Discovering some of Scotland's best wildlife at **Galloway Forest Park** (p184), a taste of the Highlands in the Lowlands

- Exploring the charming, dignified **Kirkcudbright** (p182), and the creative flair of its inhabitants

Isle of Arran ★

★ Great Border Abbeys

Culzean Castle ★

Galloway ★ Forest Park

Kirkcudbright ★

---

| ■ POPULATION: 1,246,000 | ■ AREA: 16,769 SQ KM |
|---|---|

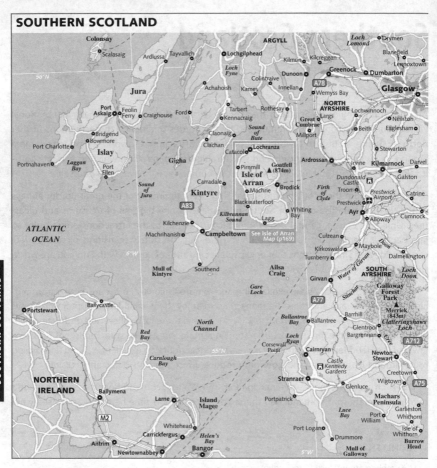

SOUTHERN SCOTLAND

## Getting Around

Call **Traveline** ( ☎ 0871 200 22 33) for public-transport information. Bus transport is excellent around Ayrshire (p166), the Borders (opposite) and Lothians, and reasonable on the main north–south routes and the A75 to Stranraer, but limited elsewhere in Dumfries & Galloway. Various explorer tickets, which can be bought from bus drivers or at bus stations, are usually your best-value option.

Train services are limited. There are stations at Berwick-upon-Tweed (in Northumberland on the English side of the border, but the jumping-off point for the Tweed Valley) on the main east-coast line; at Dumfries on the main west-coast line; and at Stranraer and Ayr, which are linked to Glasgow. For time-

tables and fares, call the **National Rail Enquiry Service** ( ☎ 0845 748 4950; www.nationalrail.co.uk).

# BORDERS REGION

Domestic tourists grease the wheel of the Borders' economy – they flock here from north and south of the border, eager to explore links to the country's medieval past. It's a distinctive region – centuries of war and plunder have left a battle-scarred landscape, encapsulated by the remnants of the great Border abbeys. They were an irresistible magnet during the Border wars, and were destroyed and rebuilt numerous times. The monasteries met their scorched end in the 16th century and were

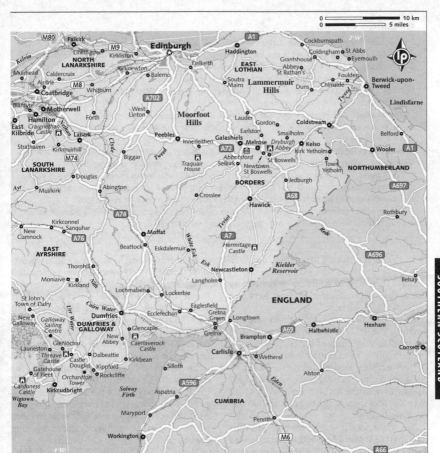

never rebuilt. Today these massive stone shells are the region's finest attraction.

But there's also much more to this captivating area. Welcoming villages with ancient traditions pepper the countryside, one of the best cold-water diving sites in Europe is off the coast, and grandiose mansions all await exploration. It's fine walking and cycling country too, the gentle hills lush with an artist's palette of innumerable shades of green. And whatever you do, don't miss Hermitage Castle; nothing encapsulates the region's turbulent history like this spooky stronghold.

### Getting Around

There's a good network of local buses. **First** ( ☎ 0870 872 7271) operates between most of the border towns and connects the larger towns with Edinburgh. Local bus companies serving border towns also include **Munro's of Jedburgh** ( ☎ 01835-862253) and **Buskers** ( ☎ 01896-755808). Tourist offices stock excellent public-transport booklets to local areas.

## COCKBURNSPATH

The 16th-century Mercat Cross in Cockburnspath village square, about a mile inland from the coast, is the official eastern-end start of the Southern Upland Way.

## COLDINGHAM BAY & ST ABB'S HEAD

Coldingham and St Abbs are the two most popular places for tourists on this section of Scotland's east coast, a short distance north

### WALKING & CYCLING

The region's most famous walk is the challenging 212-mile **Southern Upland Way**. If you want a sample, one of the best bits is the two-day section from St John's Town of Dalry to Beattock. Another long-distance walk is the 62-mile **St Cuthbert's Way**, inspired by the travels of St Cuthbert (a 7th-century saint who worked in Melrose Abbey), which crosses some superb scenery between Melrose and Lindisfarne (in England). In Galloway the **Pilgrims Way** follows a 25-mile trail from Glenluce Abbey to the Isle of Whithorn.

The **Borders Abbeys Way** links all the great Border abbeys in a 65-mile circuit. For shorter walks and especially circular loops in the hills, the towns of Melrose, Jedburgh and Kelso all make ideal bases.

With the exception of the main north–south A roads and the A75 to Stranraer, traffic is sparse, which, along with the beauty of the countryside, makes this ideal cycling country.

The **Tweed Cycle Way** is a waymarked route running 62 miles along the beautiful Tweed Valley following minor roads from Biggar to Peebles (13 miles), Melrose (16 miles), Coldstream (19 miles) and Berwick-upon-Tweed (14 miles). Jedburgh tourist office has details (see p160).

For an island tour, the **Isle of Arran** offers excellent cycling opportunities. The 50-mile coast-road circuit is stunning and is worth splitting into two or three days.



of the English border. This picturesque area is fantastic for those who love the great outdoors – there's loads to do, as evidenced by the anglers, scuba divers, bird-watchers and walkers who flock here.

From the village of Coldingham, with its twisting streets, take the B6438 downhill to the small fishing village of St Abbs, a gorgeous, peaceful little community with a picture-perfect harbour nestled below the cliffs. St Abbs is a great place for walking – head for the car park at the harbour and have a stroll over the rocky sea walls to get a feel of this fabulous location.

The clear, clean waters around St Abbs form part of **St Abbs & Eyemouth Voluntary Marine Reserve** (☎ 018907-71443; www.marine-reserve.co.uk; Rangers Cottage, Northfield, St Abbs), one of the best cold-water diving sites in Europe. The reserve is home to a variety of marine life, including grey seals and porpoises. Visibility is about 7m to 8m but has been recorded at 24m.

Drop by the **St Abbs Dive Centre** (☎ 018907-71237; 🕑 8am-4pm Mon, 8am-4.30pm Tue, Thu & Fri, 8am-1pm Wed, 8.30am-3.30pm Sat, 8.30am-3pm Sun) at the post office; these folk provide plenty of advice on diving in the area. They also sell and repair (no charge) equipment, and nothing seems to be too much trouble. Knock on the door outside of hours if you've a problem with your diving equipment, and come here if you're having difficulty finding accommodation.

Divers can charter boats from **Paul Crowe** (☎ 018907-71945, 07710-961050) or **Billy Aitchison** (☎ 018907-71288).

Back in Coldingham you could try **Scoutscroft** (☎ 018907-71669; www.scoutscroft.co.uk; Scoutscroft Holiday Centre, St Abbs Rd, Coldingham) for pointers on the best places to dive in the area and what you'll likely see. You can also hire equipment here (£40) and organise a boat dive (£10: note that combined equipment hire and dive is cheaper). Bike (£12 for half day) and fishing-gear hire is also available.

In Coldingham, a signposted turn-off to the east leads 0.75 miles down to away-from-it-all Coldingham Bay, which has a sandy beach and a cliff-top walking trail to Eyemouth (3 miles). At St Vedas Hotel (opposite) is **St Vedas Surf Shop** where you can hire surfboards and snorkelling gear. Surfing lessons are also available.

North of St Abbs, the 78-hectare **St Abb's Head National Nature Reserve** (NTS; ☎ 018907-71443; Rangers Cottage, Northfield St, St Abbs) is an ornithologist's wonderland, with large colonies of guillemots, kittiwakes, herring gulls, fulmars, razorbills and some puffins. You get to the reserve by following the trail that begins beside the Northfield Farm car park (£2) and Smiddy café, on the road just west of St Abbs. The cliff-top walks here are spectacular, especially on sunny days.

## Sleeping & Eating

**our pick** **Springbank Cottage** (☎ 018907-71477; www.springbankcottage.co.uk; The Harbour, St Abbs; s/d £30/56) Down at the harbour, you'd be hard pressed to find friendlier folk in Scotland than the crew here. Cottage-style, en-suite rooms are wee but have magic views over the harbour and are super snug (especially when the rain is lashing outside). Watch out for the narrowest staircase in Britain and the low ceilings – especially in the twin room. There's homecooking in the onsite outdoor café and fresh crab is the speciality.

**Castle Rock Guest House** ( ☎ 018907-71715; www .castlerockbandb.co.uk; Murrayfield St, St Abbs; s/d £30/60) If you want to stay at the place with the best views and a prime cliff-top location close to the town centre – look no further. There are sea views from all rooms, which have en suite and satellite TV.

**St Vedas Hotel** ( ☎ 018907-71679; www.stvedas .co.uk; Coldingham Bay; s £35, d £70-80) Just opposite the path down to the beach, St Veda's is a cheery, British beach resort-style hotel. It has a touch of faded grandeur, and is very popular at weekends over summer. Rooms are plain but neat and tidy – No 1 is a good double with seaviews and en suite. Meals are available at the restaurant (mains £6 to £9).

Also recommended:

**Coldingham Sands Youth Hostel** (SYHA; ☎ 0870 004 1111; The Mount; dm adult/child £13/9.25; ⏰ Apr-Sep) On the cliff above the southern side of the bay. A grand old property with a slightly school-holiday-camp feel.

**Old Smiddy** ( ☎ 018907-71707; St Abbs Rd; lunch £6; ⏰ 11am-4pm daily, dinner Fri & Sat; ♿ ) Seafood dominates the menu (try the smoked-fish chowder or a St Abbs crab baguette).

## Getting There & Away

Bus 253 between Edinburgh and Berwick-upon-Tweed (six daily Monday to Saturday, three Sunday) stops in Coldingham and St Abbs, as does bus 235, which runs at least hourly from Eyemouth.

## EYEMOUTH

☎ 018907 / pop 3400

Eyemouth is a busy fishing port and popular domestic holiday destination. The harbour itself is very atmospheric – you may even spot seals frolicking in the water, and tourists frolicking around the boats, snapping pics of old fishing nets.

The community here suffered its greatest catastrophe in October 1881, when a storm destroyed the coastal fishing fleet, killing 189 fishermen, 129 of whom were locals.

## Information

The Bank of Scotland and the Royal Bank of Scotland have ATMs.

**Laundrette** (Church St; ⏰ 9am-12.30pm & 2-4pm Mon-Fri, 9am-12.30pm Sat)

**Tourist office** ( ☎ 0870 608 0404; Manse Rd; ⏰ 10am-5pm Mon-Sat Apr-Oct, 10am-1pm Sun Apr-Jun & Sep, 10am-2pm Sun Jul & Aug) Very helpful; it's in Eyemouth Museum near the harbour.

## Sights

Captivating **Eyemouth Museum** ( ☎ 50678; Auld Kirk, Manse Rd; adult/child £2.50/free; ⏰ 10am-5pm Mon-Sat Apr-Oct, 10am-1pm Sun Apr-Jun & Sep, 10am-2pm Sun Jul & Aug) has local-history displays, particularly relating to the town's fishing heritage. Its centrepiece is the tapestry commemorating the 1881 fishing disaster.

Situated right on Eyemouth's working fishing harbour, which lends it an air of authenticity, the **Eyemouth Maritime Centre** ( ☎ 751020; Harbour Rd; adults/kids £2.50/2; ⏰ 10.30am-6pm) is shaped like an old 18th-century frigate. It feels like a vast hangar inside and there are lots of interesting model ships, a changing exhibition, and film and slide shows.

## Sleeping & Eating

**Bantry** (Mackays; ☎ 51900; joanne@mackaysofeyemouth .co.uk; 20 High St; s £28.50, d per person £28.50-35) Plonked on top of the restaurant of the same name on the main drag, this place has redecorated and refurbished rooms with muted tones and a luxurious, modern feel, positioned right on the waterfront. Try to get No 3, if you're after a double, as it's the only one with sea-facing views. Whip £5 off the price if you only require a continental breakfast.

**Churches** ( ☎ 50401; www.churcheshotel.co.uk; Albert Rd; s/d £80/105) This is a very stylish place set in an 18th-century building, with rooms exuding a cool demeanour and a classical look. Each room has a different theme but No 4 with four-poster bed and No 6 with huge windows overlooking the harbour are our favourites. The menu (mains £12 to £17) is blessed with the day's catch from the harbour – it's the best spot in town for fresh seafood.

**Obló** ( ☎ 52527; 20 Harbour St; mains £10-15; ⏰ from 10am daily) For a meal pretty much anytime find your way upstairs to this modern bar-bistro with its comfy seating and modish interior. It's urban, it's trendy, it's just down from the tourist office. Try the Eyemouth langoustines on a bed of tarragon-flavoured carrots.

The pubs along the quay have suitably nautical names – the **Contented Sole** ( ☎ 50268; 3 Old Quay, Harbour Rd) and the **Ship Hotel** ( ☎ 50224;

Harbour Rd) – and serve freshly caught seafood for about £8 for a main dish.

### Getting There & Away

Eyemouth is 5 miles north of the Scotland-England border. Bus C4 runs to/from Kelso via Duns (1½ hours, once daily Monday to Friday); buses 235, 236 go south to Berwick-upon-Tweed (15 minutes, frequent), which has the nearest train station. Bus 253 from Berwick to Edinburgh (£4.50, 1¾ hours, six daily Monday to Saturday, three Sunday) also passes through Eyemouth.

## SOUTH OF EYEMOUTH

Further south, beyond the village of Foulden and about 3 miles west of the A1 along the B6461, is **Paxton House** ( ☎ 01289-386291; adult/child £6/3; ☼ 11am-5pm Apr-Oct, grounds 10am-sunset Apr-Oct; ♿ ). It's beside the River Tweed and surrounded by over 32 hectares of parkland and gardens. It was built in 1758 by Patrick Home for his intended wife, the daughter of Prussia's Frederick the Great. Unfortunately, she stood him up, but it was her loss; designed by the Adam family – brothers John, James and Robert – it's acknowledged as one of the finest 18th-century Palladian houses in Britain. It contains a large collection of Chippendale and Regency furniture, and its picture gallery houses paintings from the national galleries of Scotland. The nursery is a new feature designed to provide insight into a child's 18th-century life.

In the grounds are walking trails and a riverside museum on salmon fishing.

## DUNS & AROUND

☎ 01361 / pop 2300

Duns is a peaceful market town in the centre of Berwickshire, with some pleasant walks. You can get to **Duns Law** (218m) in Duns Castle Estate by following Castle St up from the square. The summit offers great views of the Merse and Lammermuir Hills. The Covenanter's Stone marks the spot where the Covenanting armies camped in 1639; a copy of the Covenant was later signed at Duns Castle.

On the northern side of the main square, **White Swan Hotel** ( ☎ 883338; 31-32 Market Sq; s £30-40, d £50-70) is a solid old place with decent-sized rooms – the refurbished ones have en suites.

Buses running between Galashiels and Berwick-upon-Tweed (six to nine daily) stop at Duns.

## LAMMERMUIR HILLS

North of Duns, the low-lying Lammermuir Hills, with their extensive grouse moors, rolling farmland and wooded valleys, run east–west along the border with East Lothian. The hills are popular with walkers and there are numerous trails, including a section of the **Southern Upland Way**.

To the west, the Way can be accessed at **Lauder**, where it passes through the grounds of **Thirlestane Castle** ( ☎ 01578-722430; castle & grounds adult/child £7/5, grounds only £3/1.50; ☼ 10am-4pm Wed, Thu & Sun mid Apr-Jun & Sep, Sun-Thu Jul & Aug). The narcissism and folly of the aristocracy is evident here perhaps more than in most 'great homes'. Notice how many of the family portraits adorning the walls look similar? The extensive assemblage here is the result of the common practice of mass production used at the time. Many of the family have almost identical features, as the same bodies were used for their portraits with different clothes, faces and hands superimposed.

Thirlestane is also home to some of the finest plasterwork ceilings in Europe, and don't miss Henry the Ram (a snuff box) in the dining room – kitsch beyond kitsch.

Thirlestane is just outside town, off the A68, beside Leader Water. Munro's buses 29 and 30, running between Kelso and Edinburgh, pass by.

You're able to get onto the Southern Upland Way from the tiny village of **Abbey St Bathan's** in the secluded, bucolic Whiteadder Valley, off the B6355. From here, the final 10-mile section of the trail heads northeast to Cockburnspath beside the coast.

## COLDSTREAM

☎ 01890 / pop 1800

On a sweeping bend of the River Tweed, which forms the border with England, Coldstream is small and relatively hidden from the well-trodden Borders tourist beat. It can be a handy base when nearby Kelso is overflowing with visitors and accommodation options are sparse.

The proud history of the Coldstream Guards is covered in the **Coldstream Museum** ( ☎ 882630; 12 Market Sq; admission free; ☼ 10am-4pm Mon-Sat, 2-4pm Sun Apr-Sep, 10am-4pm Mon-Sat Oct), including recent missions in the 1990s. The Coldstream Guards were formed in 1650 in Berwick-upon-Tweed for duty in Scotland as part of Oliver Cromwell's New Model Army.

The regiment took its present name from the town where it was stationed in 1659. It played a significant part in the restoration of the monarchy in 1660 and saw service at Waterloo against Napoleon, at Sebastopol during the Crimean War, in the Boer War, at the Somme and Ypres in WWI, and at Dunkirk and Tobruk in WWII. It remains the oldest regiment in continuous existence in the British army and is the only one directly descended from the New Model Army.

## Sleeping

**Garth House B&B** ( ☎ 882477; 7 Market St; r per person £20-23) This old bastion is cheap and comfy with no frills attached. It's a basic, old-fashioned B&B – personable, good value and friendly – but nothing flash. If you want value for money – here it is.

**ourpick Eastbraes B&B** ( ☎ 883949; www.eastbraes .co.uk; 100C High St; s/d £35/60) Eastbraes is full of personality and good vibes. A double and twin share a bathroom and there's one en-suite double, which is simply enormous, and comes with separate sitting area. This family-run place is in a gorgeous building with stupendous views and plenty of walking opportunities literally on the doorstep.

**Calico House** ( ☎ 885870; www.calicohouse.net; 44 High St; r 1/2 nights £60/50) Set behind a shop that churns out high-quality interior designs, this is a superb B&B with sumptuous rooms blessed with great views and attention to detail. Cleanliness is next to godliness could easily be the mantra. Privacy from your hosts and value for money are two very strong points in this excellent accommodation option.

## Getting There & Away

Coldstream is on the busy A697 road that links Newcastle upon Tyne in Northumberland, England, with Edinburgh. There are about six buses daily Monday to Saturday (three on Sunday) between Kelso (20 minutes) and Berwick-upon-Tweed (45 minutes) via Coldstream.

# KELSO

☎ 01573 / pop 5200

Kelso, a prosperous market town with a broad, cobbled square flanked by Georgian buildings, has a French feel to it and an historic appeal. During the day it's a busy little place, but after 8pm you'll have the streets to yourself. The town has a lovely site at the junction of the Rivers Tweed and Teviot, and is one of the most enjoyable places in the Borders.

## Information

**Border Books** ( ☎ 225861; Horsemarket; ☒ 10.30am-4pm Mon, Tue & Thu-Sat) Great range of books, especially out of date and antiquarian.

**Kelso Hospital** ( ☎ 223441; Inch Rd)

**Kelso Library** ( ☎ 223171; Bowmont St; ☒ 10am-1pm & 2-5pm Mon, Tue, Thu & Fri, plus 5.30-7pm Tue & Thu, 10am-1pm Wed, 9.30am-12.30pm Sat) Free internet access.

**Tourist office** ( ☎ 0870 608 0404; www.visitscottish borders.com; Town House, The Square; ☒ daily Apr-Nov, Mon-Sat Dec-Mar)

## Sights & Activities

### KELSO ABBEY

Once one of the richest abbeys in southern Scotland, **Kelso Abbey** (HS; admission free; Bridge St; ☒ 9.30am-6.30pm Mon-Sat, 2-6pm Sun Apr-Dec) was built by the Tironensians, an order founded at Tiron in Picardy and brought to the Borders around 1113 by David I. English raids in the 16th century reduced it to ruins, though what remains today is some of the finest surviving Romanesque architecture in Scotland.

Nearby, the rare, octagonal **Kelso Old Parish Church** (The Butts; ☒ 10am-4pm Mon-Fri May-Sep), built in 1773, is intriguing.

### FLOORS CASTLE

Grandiose **Floors Castle** ( ☎ 223333; adult/child £6.50/3.50; ☒ 11am-5pm Easter-Oct) is Scotland's largest inhabited mansion and overlooks the Tweed about a mile west of Kelso. Built by William Adam in the 1720s, the original Georgian simplicity was 'improved' in the 1840s with the addition of rather ridiculous battlements and turrets. Inside, view the vivid colours of the 17th-century Brussels tapestries in the drawing room and the intricate oak carvings in the ornate ballroom. Palatial windows reveal a ribbon of green countryside extending well beyond the estate. Unfortunately, there's also a rather questionable collection of stuffed birds, easily interpreted as bad taste. Floors is unashamedly in the tourism business – you walk past the restaurant to enter and past the gift shop to leave.

### WALKING

The **Pennine Way**, which starts its long journey at Edale in the Peak district, ends at Kirk Yetholm Youth Hostel, about 7 miles southeast of Kelso on the B6352.

SOUTHERN SCOTLAND

The **Borders Abbeys Way** links the great abbeys of Kelso, Jedburgh, Melrose and Dryburgh to create a 65-mile circuit. The Kelso–Jedburgh section (12 miles) is a fairly easy walk, largely following the River Teviot between the towns. The tourist office has a free leaflet with a map and description of the route.

Less-ambitious walkers should leave the Square by Roxburgh St and take the sign-posted alley to **Cobby Riverside Walk**, a pleasant ramble along the river to Floors Castle (although you have to rejoin Roxburgh St to gain admission to the castle).

## Sleeping

**Duncan House** ( ☎ 225682; Chalkheugh Tce; s/d £40/65) This elderly resident in the hospitality industry is a lovely Georgian house with views over the Rivers Tweed and Teviot. It has elegantly kitted-out rooms with Victorian furnishings, freestanding bathtubs and a whole lotta TLC.

**our pick** **The Old Priory** ( ☎ 223030; www.theoldpriorykelso.com; 33 Woodmarket St; s/d £45/70) The doubles in this atmospheric place are fantastic and the family room has to be seen to be believed;

rooms are both sumptuous and debonair with gorgeous dark polished wood pieces. The good news extends to the garden – perfect for a coffee in the morning, and there's off-street parking. The huge windows are another feature, flooding the rooms with natural light. Special diets are catered for.

**Ednam House Hotel** ( ☎ 224168; www.ednamhouse .com; Bridge St; s/d from £77/100; 🖳 ) The genteel, Georgian Ednam House, touched with a quiet dignity, contains many of its original features and is the top place in town, with fine gardens overlooking the river and the excellent Ednam House Restaurant. It's very popular with fisher folk and during salmon season, from the end of August until November when a permit can cost £1000, the hotel is very busy.

Also recommended:

**Craignethan B&B** ( ☎ 224818; Jedburgh Rd; s/d £25/50) Welcoming, laid-back family home. Upstairs double has the best view – you can see over the whole town and Floors Castle. Old-fashioned hospitality.

**Inglestone House** ( ☎ 225800; www.inglestonehouse .co.uk; Abbey Row; s/d £40/60; 🖳 ) Wedged between the Square and abbey; well-run guesthouse that's great for families or couples.

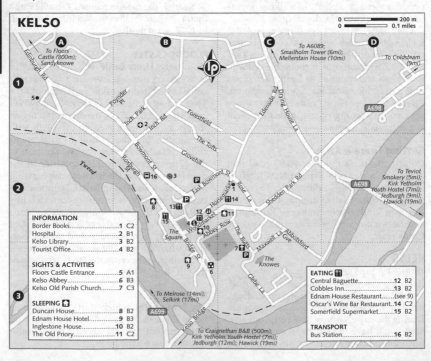

### KELSO

0 ────── 200 m
0 ────── 0.1 miles

To Floors Castle (800m); Sandyknowe
To A6089; Smailholm Tower (6mi); Mellerstain House (10mi)
To Coldstream (9mi)
To Teviot Smokery (5mi); Kirk Yetholm Youth Hostel (7mi); Jedburgh (9mi); Hawick (19mi)
To Melrose (14mi); Selkirk (17mi)
To Craignethan B&B (500m); Kirk Yetholm Youth Hostel (7mi); Jedburgh (12mi); Hawick (19mi)

Edinburgh Rd
Poynder Pl
Inch Park
Inch Rd
Forrestfield
The Tofts
Grovehill
Bowmont St
Roxburgh St
East Bowmont St
Rose La
Horsemarket
Edenside Rd
Drying House La
Shedden Park Rd
Abbotsford
Maxwell La Gve
The Butts
Woodmarket
Abbey Row
Bridge St
The Square
The Knowes
Glebe La
Kelso Bridge
A698
A699
Tweed

**INFORMATION**
Border Books........................1 C2
Hospital..............................2 B1
Kelso Library........................3 B2
Tourist Office........................4 B2

**SIGHTS & ACTIVITIES**
Floors Castle Entrance..........5 A1
Kelso Abbey.........................6 B3
Kelso Old Parish Church........7 C3

**SLEEPING**
Duncan House.......................8 B2
Ednam House Hotel...............9 B3
Inglestone House.................10 B2
The Old Priory.....................11 C2

**EATING**
Central Baguette..................12 B2
Cobbles Inn........................13 B2
Ednam House Restaurant......(see 9)
Oscar's Wine Bar Restaurant..14 C2
Somerfield Supermarket........15 B2

**TRANSPORT**
Bus Station........................16 B2

## Eating

**Cobbles Inn** ( ☎ 223548; 7 Bowmont St; mains £10-15; ☺ lunch & dinner Tue-Sat, lunch Sun) The new owners of this traditional pub, up an alley north of the main square, were finding their feet when we passed through. It was being refurbished and cask ales are a new feature. The sandwiches are ordinary but the game pie – a cauldron of game meats and mushrooms in red-wine sauce – looked delicious.

**our pick** **Oscar's Wine Bar Restaurant** ( ☎ 224008; 33 Horsemarket; starters £5, mains £10-16; ☺ dinner) If you enjoy a glass of wine with your dinner in a Mediterranean-theme setting, this is the place for you. Dishes on the extensive and varied menu are simple and well prepared. Try the roast monkfish with a fresh herb and almond crust or the crispy black pudding with a fresh mango salsa. Dessert portions are small.

For self-caterers there is a Somerfield supermarket located on the corner of the main square.

Also recommended:

**Central Baguette** ( ☎ 228853; 52 The Square; baguettes £1.50-2.50; ☺ breakfast & lunch Mon-Sat) Baguette fillings feature everything from hot haggis to Cajun chicken.

**Ednam House Restaurant** ( ☎ 224168; Bridge St; 2-/3-course dinner £19/25; ☺ lunch & dinner) Turns out delectable dinners and is the perfect place for a treat.

## Getting There & Away

See Coldstream transport information (p155) for details on the bus service to Berwick-upon-Tweed. Munro's bus 20 runs to/from Jedburgh (25 minutes, up to 11 daily Monday to Saturday, five Sunday) and Hawick (one hour, seven daily Monday to Saturday, four

---

**SMOKEY DELIGHTS**

If you're into smoked foods you will love **Teviot Smokery** ( ☎ 850253; Kirkbank House; light meals & mains £6-9; ☺ lunch). The restaurant at this shop/gardens churns out some delicious smoked numbers such as smoked salmon and asparagus tartlets. The adjoining shop also sells some excellent real ales and you can buy smoked salmon to take home if you haven't gorged on it enough for lunch. There are also satisfying riverside rambles to work off your meal. The smokery is located five miles southwest of Kelso on the A698.

---

Sunday). There are also frequent services to Galashiels (55 minutes), and from there to Edinburgh.

## AROUND KELSO
### Smailholm Tower

Perched on a rocky knoll above a small lake, the narrow, stone **Smailholm Tower** (HS; ☎ 01573-460365; Sandyknowe Farm, Smailholm; adult/child £3.50/1.75; ☺ 9.30am-5.30pm Apr-Sep, 9.30am-4.30pm Sat-Wed Oct, 9.30am-4.30pm Sat & Sun Nov-Mar) provides one of the most evocative sights in the Borders and keeps the bloody uncertainties of its history alive. Although the displays inside are sparse, the panoramic view from the top is worth the climb.

The nearby farm, **Sandyknowe**, was owned by Sir Walter Scott's grandfather. As Scott himself recognised, his imagination was fired by the ballads and stories he heard as a child at Sandyknowe, and by the ruined tower a stone's throw away.

The tower is 6 miles west of Kelso, a mile south of Smailholm village on the B6397. You pass through the farmyard to get to the tower. Munro's bus 65 between Melrose and Kelso stops in Smailholm village.

### Mellerstain House

Finished in 1778, **Mellerstain House** ( ☎ 01573-410225; Gordon; adult/child £6/free; ☺ 12.30-5pm Sun, Wed & Bank Hol Mon May, Jun & Sep, 12.30-5pm Easter, 12.30-5pm Sun, Mon, Wed & Thu Jul & Aug, plus Sun Oct) is considered to be Scotland's finest Robert Adam–designed mansion. It is famous for its classic elegance, ornate interiors and plaster ceilings; the library in particular is outstanding. Give the garish upstairs bedrooms a miss, but have a peek at the bizarre puppet-and-doll collection in the gallery.

It's about 10 miles northwest of Kelso near Gordon. Munro's bus 65 between Melrose and Kelso passes about a mile from Mellerstain House.

### Town Yetholm & Kirk Yetholm

The twin villages of Town Yetholm and Kirk Yetholm, separated by Bowmont Water, are close to the English border, about 6 miles southeast of Kelso. Hill-walking centres, they lie at the northern end of the **Pennine Way** and on **St Cuthbert's Way** between Melrose and Lindisfarne (Holy Island) in Northumberland.

As the last stop on the Pennine Way, **Kirk Yetholm Youth Hostel** (SYHA; ☎ 0870 004 1132; Kirk

Yetholm, Kelso; dm adult/child £12.50/9.50; ⊗ Apr-Sep) is often busy – there's a twin room and two dorms (six and eight beds); book well in advance. Bus 81 from Kelso runs up to seven times a day Monday to Saturday (three times on Sunday).

# MELROSE

☎ 01896 / pop 1700

Tiny, charming Melrose is a polished village running on the well-greased wheels of tourism. This little enclave is a complete contrast with overbearing Galashiels, whose urban sprawl laps at its western edges. Sitting at the feet of the three heather-covered Eildon Hills, Melrose has a classic market square and its most famous resident is one of the great abbey ruins.

## Information

**Melrose Library** ( ☎ 823052; 18 Market Sq; ⊗ 10am-1pm & 2.30-5pm Mon & Wed, 2.30-5pm & 5.30-7pm Fri) Free internet access.

**Post office** (Buccleuch St)

**Tourist office** ( ☎ 0870 608 0404; Abbey House, Abbey St; ⊗ 10am-5pm Mon-Sat, 10am-2pm Sun Apr & May, 9.30am-5pm Mon-Sat, 10am-2pm Sun Jun & Sep, 9.30am-5.30pm Mon-Sat, 10am-4pm Sun Jul & Aug, 10am-4pm Mon-Sat, 10am-2pm Sun Oct, 10am-2pm Mon-Sat, noon-4pm Sun Nov-Mar)

## Sights

Perhaps the most interesting of all the great Border abbeys, the red-sandstone **Melrose Abbey** (HS; ☎ 822562; adult/child £5/2.50; ⊗ 9.30am-5.30pm Apr-Sep, 9.30am-4.30pm Oct-Mar) was repeatedly destroyed by the English in the 14th century. The remaining broken shell is pure Gothic and the ruins are famous for their decorative stonework – see if you can glimpse the pig gargoyle playing the bagpipes on the roof. You can climb to the top for tremendous views. The abbey was founded by David I in 1136 for Cistercian monks from Rievaulx in Yorkshire. It was rebuilt by Robert the Bruce, whose heart is buried here. The ruins date from the 14th and 15th centuries, and were repaired by Sir Walter Scott in the 19th century.

The adjoining **museum** (free for abbey ticket holders) has many fine examples of 12th- to 15th-century stonework and pottery found in the area. Note the impressive remains of the 'great drain' outside – a medieval sewerage system.

The **Melrose Rugby Heritage Centre** ( ☎ 822993; The Greenyards; admission free; ⊗ 11am-3pm Mon, Wed & Fri) will appeal to rugby fans – it offers an insight into Rugby Sevens, which was founded here in the late 19th century.

## Activities

There are many attractive walks in the **Eildon Hills**, accessible via a footpath off Dingleton Rd (the B6359) south of the town, or via the trail along the River Tweed. Grab a copy of the *Walks Around Melrose* booklet (£1) for local guidance.

The **St Cuthbert's Way** long-distance path starts in Melrose, while the coast-to-coast **Southern Upland Way** passes through town. You can do a day's walk along St Cuthbert's Way as far as Harestanes (16 miles), on the A68 near Jedburgh, and return to Melrose on the hourly Jedburgh–Galashiels bus. The **Tweed Cycle Way** also passes through Melrose.

## Festivals & Events

In mid-April rugby followers fill the town to see the week-long **Melrose Rugby Sevens** competition. A popular event on the festivals calendar is the **Borders Book Festival** (www.bordersbookfestival.org), stretching over four days in late June.

## Sleeping

Melrose B&Bs and hotels aren't cheap by Scottish standards, but they are of a high standard; this would make a great place to treat yourself.

**Melrose Youth Hostel** (SYHA; ☎ 0870 004 1141; Priorwood; dm adult/child £14/11; ⊗ late-Mar–Oct; ⌨ ) Housed in a large Georgian mansion on the edge of town, these spick-and-span dorms are complemented by a big garden and barbecue area. Not a party house, this hostel is mainly used by walkers looking to turn in early. From Market Sq, follow the signposts to the A68.

**Braidwood** ( ☎ 822488; enquiries@braidwoodmelrose.co.uk; Buccleuch St; r per person £25-30) Mr and Mrs Dalgetty's popular town house near the abbey is an excellent place, with high-quality facilities and a warm welcome. The sparkling rooms are finely decorated and the twin has great views. Note, singles not available in summer.

**Burts Hotel** ( ☎ 822285; www.burtshotel.co.uk; Market Sq; s/d £60/112) Set in an early-18th-century house, and with an enviable reputation, Burts retains much of its period charm and has been run by the same couple for over 30 years. It would suit older visitors or families. Room No 5 is the best.

**Townhouse** ( ☎ 822645; www.thetownhousemelrose .co.uk; Market Sq; s/d £70/100, superior r £120) The classy Townhouse, exuding warmth and professionalism, has some of the best rooms in town – tastefully furnished with attention to detail. There are two superior rooms that are enormous in size with lavish furnishings; the one on the ground floor in particular has an excellent en suite, which includes a Jacuzzi. It's well worth the price.

## Eating

**The Cellar** ( ☎ 823224; 17 Market Sq; mains £4-7; ⏱ 10am-5pm) Drop into The Cellar for a caffeine hit. It's also good for a glass of wine on the town square, food platters and speciality cheeses.

**Russell's Restaurant** ( ☎ 822335; Market Sq; dishes £5-7; ⏱ 9.30am-4.30pm Tue-Thu, 9.30am-5pm Fri & Sat, noon-5pm Sun) Russell's is a stylish little tearoom/restaurant with a large range of snacks and more substantial offerings, such as a ploughman's lunch.

**Marmion's Brasserie** ( ☎ 822245; 5 Buccleuch St; starters £6, mains £10-13; ⏱ lunch & dinner Mon-Sat) This atmospheric, oak-panelled niche serves snacks all day, but the lunch and dinner menus include gastronomic delights, such as roast quail, braised lamb, or pan-seared cod with a king prawn red-curry sauce. For lunch the focaccias with creative fillings are a good choice.

**Townhouse** ( ☎ 822645; Market Sq; mains £12, 3-course dinner £24; ⏱ lunch & dinner) The gourmet cuisine here is the best in town. Dishes are exquisitely prepared, and your stomach will thank you for weeks should you treat yourself to a three-course dinner. Desserts such as a peach-and-ginger tart served with sweet, pickled rhubarb are exquisite.

## Getting There & Away

There are First buses to/from Galashiels (20 minutes, frequent), Jedburgh (30 minutes, at least hourly Monday to Saturday), Peebles (1¼ hours, at least hourly Monday to Saturday) and Edinburgh (£5.50, 2¼ hours, half-hourly Monday to Saturday).

## AROUND MELROSE
### Dryburgh Abbey

The most beautiful, complete Border abbey is **Dryburgh Abbey** (HS; ☎ 01835-822381; adult/child £4.50/2.25; ⏱ 9.30am-5.30pm Apr-Sep, 9.30am-4.30pm Oct-Mar), partly because the neighbouring town of Dryburgh no longer exists (another victim of the wars) and partly because it has a lovely site in a sheltered valley by the River Tweed, accompanied only by a symphony of birdsong. The abbey conjures up images of 12th-century monastic life more successfully than its counterparts in nearby towns. Dating from about 1150, it belonged to the Premonstratensians, a religious order founded in France. The pink-hued stone ruins were chosen as the burial place for Sir Walter Scott.

The abbey is 5 miles southeast of Melrose on the B6404, which passes famous **Scott's View** overlooking the valley. You can hike there along the southern bank of the River Tweed, or take a bus to the nearby village of Newtown St Boswells.

### Abbotsford

Fans of Sir Walter Scott should visit his former residence, **Abbotsford** ( ☎ 01896-752043; adult/child £6/3; ⏱ 9.30am-5pm late-Mar–Oct, 2-5pm Sun Mar-May & Oct). Probably drawing inspiration from the surrounding 'wild' countryside, he created an extraordinary collection of works. These

---

### SIR WALTER SCOTT (1771–1832)

Sir Walter Scott is one of Scotland's greatest literary figures. It was here, rambling around the Borders countryside as a child, that he developed a passion for historical ballads and Scottish heroes.

The Lay of the Last Minstrel (1805) was an early critical success. Further works earning him an international reputation included The Lady of the Lake (1810), set around Loch Katrine and the Trossachs. He later turned his hand to novels and virtually invented the historical genre. Waverley (1814), which dealt with the 1745 Jacobite rebellion, set the classical pattern of the historical novel. Other works included Guy Mannering (1815) and Rob Roy (1817). In Guy Mannering he wrote about Border farmer Dandie Dinmont and his pack of dogs, which became so popular that they became known as Dandie Dinmont Terriers, the only breed of dog named after a literary character.

Later in life Scott wrote obsessively to stave off bankruptcy. His works virtually single-handedly revived interest in Scottish history and legend in the early 19th century. Tourist offices stock a Sir Walter Scott Trail booklet, guiding you to many places associated with his life in the Borders.

are on display, as are many other personal possessions.

The mansion is about 2 miles west of Melrose between the River Tweed and the B6360. Frequent buses run between Galashiels and Melrose; alight at the Tweed bank roundabout and follow the signposts (it's a 15-minute walk). You can also walk from Melrose to Abbotsford in an hour along the southern bank of the Tweed.

## GALASHIELS
☎ 01896 / pop 14,500

Galashiels has little to recommend it – during the day it's uninviting and in the evening it carries an air of menace, but it's an important transport hub for the Scottish Borders. Fortunately, the charming town of Melrose is just 3 miles east.

The unmanned tourist office is in the **Lochcarron Cashmere & Wool Centre** ( ☎ 751100; Waverley Mill, Huddersfield St; 9am-5pm Mon-Sat year-round, plus noon-5pm Sun Jun-Sep), which also houses a museum on Galashiels history. Tours are available (adult/child £3.50/free).

There are frequent buses to/from Edinburgh (1¼hr, half hourly), Melrose (15 minutes, hourly), Hawick (40 minutes, half hourly), Kelso (one hour, hourly), and Peebles (45 minutes, half hourly).

## SELKIRK
☎ 01750 / pop 5800

Selkirk is a serene little town that climbs a steep ridge above the Ettrick Water, a tributary of the Tweed. Mills came to the area in the early 1800s, but today it's a quiet place with a couple of great attractions.

The helpful **tourist office** ( ☎ 20054; Halliwell's Close; Apr-Oct) is tucked away off Market Sq. Inside is **Halliwell's House Museum** ( ☎ 20096; Halliwell's Close; admission free; 10am-5pm Mon-Sat, to noon Sun late-Mar–Sep, except 10am-1pm Sun Jul & Aug, 10am-4pm Mon-Sat, to noon Sun Oct), the oldest building (1712) in Selkirk. The museum charts local history with an engrossing exhibition, and the Robson Gallery has changing exhibitions.

Drop into **Sir Walter Scott's Court Room** ( ☎ 20096; Market Sq; admission free; 10am-4pm Mon-Fri, to 2pm Sat Apr-Sep, plus 10am-2pm Sun May-Aug, 1-4pm Mon-Sat Oct; ), where the great man served as Selkirk County's sheriff. There's an exhibition on his life and writings, plus a fascinating account of the courageous explorer Mungo Park (born near Selkirk) and his search for the River Niger.

You're better off staying overnight in Melrose or Jedburgh, or try the **County Hotel** ( ☎ 721233; www.countyhotelselkirk.co.uk; Market Sq; s/d £40/75), which has comfortable rooms with small couches and is popular with golfers. It also serves good bar meals (£8).

First bus 95 and express bus X95 run halfhourly or hourly between Hawick, Selkirk, Galashiels and Edinburgh. Selkirk to Edinburgh costs £5 (two hours).

## JEDBURGH
☎ 01835 / pop 4100

The most popular of the Border towns, attractive Jedburgh is a lush, compact oasis, where many old buildings and wynds (narrow alleys) have been intelligently restored, inviting exploration by foot. It's constantly busy with domestic tourists, but wander into some of the pretty side streets and you won't hear a pin drop.

## Information
**Library** (Castlegate; 10am-1pm & 2-5pm Mon-Fri, 5.30-7pm Mon & Fri) Free internet access.
**Post office** (High St)
**Tourist office** ( ☎ 863170; Murray's Green; 9.15am-5pm Mon-Sat, 10am-5pm Sun Apr, May & Oct, 9am-6pm Mon-Sat, 10am-5pm Sun Jun-Jul & Sep, 9am-7pm Mon-Sat, 10am-6pm Sun Aug, 9.30am-4.30pm Mon-Sat Nov-Mar) Best tourist office in the Borders. Historic guided walks (£3) of Jedburgh leave from the tourist office at 6pm Monday and Friday, plus 2.30pm on Wednesday in summer.

## Sights
### JEDBURGH ABBEY
Dominating the town skyline, **Jedburgh Abbey** (HS; ☎ 863925; Abbey Bridge End; adult/child £5/2.50; 9.30am-5.30pm Apr-Sep, 9.30am-4.30pm Oct-Mar) was the first great Border abbey to be passed into state care, and it shows – audio and visual presentations telling the abbey's story are scattered throughout the carefully preserved ruins (good for the kids or if it's raining). The red-sandstone ruins are roofless but relatively intact, and the ingenuity of the master mason can be seen in some of the rich (if somewhat faded) stone carvings in the nave (be careful of the staircase in the nave – it's slippery when wet). The abbey was founded in 1138 by David I as a priory for Augustinian canons.

### MARY QUEEN OF SCOTS HOUSE
Mary stayed at this beautiful 16th-century **tower house** ( ☎ 863331; Queen St; adult/child £3/free;

10am-4.30pm Mon-Sat, 11am-4.30pm Sun Mar-Nov) in 1566 after her famous ride to visit the injured earl of Bothwell, her future husband, at Hermitage Castle (p162). The interesting displays evoke the sad saga of Mary's life.

## Activities

The tourist office sells some handy walking booklets, including *Walks around Jedburgh* (£1), which has 1.5-mile to 5.5-mile walks, good route descriptions and small maps. Those looking to really stretch the legs can take on small sections of the Southern Upland Way – grab a copy of *Short Walks* (£2.50). The *Borders Abbeys Way Circular Walking Route* is an excellent booklet (£2); simple maps included. For information about the **Borders Abbeys Way**, see p156.

## Festivals & Events

For two weeks in late June/early July the **Jethart Callant Festival** marks the perilous time when people rode out on horseback checking for English incursions (see the boxed text, right).

## Sleeping

**Jedburgh Camping & Caravanning Club Site** ( ☎ 863393; Elliot Park, A68; tent sites £9.30; late-Apr–Oct) About a mile north of the town centre, opposite Jedburgh Woollen Mill, this site is set on the banks of Jed Water and is quiet and convenient, particularly if you're interested in fishing.

**Maplebank** ( ☎ 862051; 3 Smiths Wynd; s/d £20/36) There are not many B&Bs left like this one. It's a very old-fashioned place (you really are staying in someone's home) and one word sums it up: clutter. It's slightly grotty as well, but the shared bathroom sparkles and the rooms are very comfy – large and definitely homely. The owner is just lovely and the breakfast (particularly if you like fruit, homemade yogurts and a selection of everything) is better than you'll get at a posh guesthouse. This is Scottish eccentricity at its best.

**Willow Court** ( ☎ 863702; www.willowcourtjedburgh .co.uk; The Friars; r per person £22) With superb views over Jedburgh from the conservatory, where you are served a three-meals-in-one breakfast, Willow Court is a traditional B&B with homespun décor, smiling hosts and a large garden. Ask about the self-catering cottage just out of town.

**Glenfriars Guest House** ( ☎ 862000; glenfriars@ edenroad.demon.co.uk; The Friars; s/d £35/70) We really

### RIDING OF THE MARCHES

The Riding of the Marches, or Common Riding, takes place in early summer in the major Border towns. Like many Scottish festivals it has ancient traditions, dating back to the Middle Ages, when riders would be sent to the town boundary to check on the common lands. The colourful event normally involves extravagant convoys of horse riders following the town flag or standard as it's taken on a well-worn route. Festivities vary between towns but usually involve lots of singing, sport, pageants, concerts and a screaming good time! If you want to zero in on the oldest and largest of the Ridings, head to Selkirk for the Jethart Callant Festival.

like this place. Glenfriars is a classy Georgian affair being slowly, lovingly refurbished. All rooms have en suites and Nos 4 and 6 are excellent, especially the old drawing room (No 4), which has stupendous views. Four-poster beds, laid-back hosts and plenty of space make this stylish, ramshackle hotel a favourite.

Also recommended:

**Mrs Elliot** (Akaso Uram; ☎ 862482; 7 Queen St; s/d £20/36) Musty and fusty, sure, but one of the cheapest digs in town.

**Craigowen** ( ☎ 862604; duggleby21@hotmail.com; 30 High St; s/d £30/50) B&B with terrific, central location and huge rooms.

## Eating

**The Sunrise** ( ☎ 863503; 51 High St; mains £6-9; lunch & dinner) You'll pay slightly higher prices for the dishes at this curry house but it's well worth it. Featuring aromatic south Indian cooking, there's plenty on offer for vegetarians, including delicious homemade samosas stuffed with goodies, plus succulent, spicy tandoori chicken and generous side dishes.

**Carters Rest** ( ☎ 864745; Abbey Pl; mains £8-10; lunch & dinner) Upmarket pub dining that would suit families or older couples. The dinner menu is much better than lunch, featuring dishes such as grilled fillet of sea bass served over a smoked haddock mash and drizzled with fresh pesto. It also makes a good pit stop for a cold drink after an exploration of the abbey – it's practically on its doorstep.

**Nightjar** ( ☎ 862552; 1 Abbey Close; mains £12.50-14.50; dinner Tue-Sat) A highly commended restaurant dishing out a mix of creative meals (try the salad of warm quail with chorizo and grapefruit), including seafood and Thai cuisine. The real highlight is if you're lucky enough to be here on the last Tuesday of the month when a special Thai menu is revealed; locals rave about this night.

### Getting There & Away

Jedburgh has good bus connections to Hawick (25 minutes, roughly hourly), Melrose (30 minutes, at least hourly Monday to Saturday) and Kelso (25 minutes, at least hourly Monday to Saturday, four Sunday). Munro's runs from Edinburgh to Jedburgh (£5.60, two hours, at least hourly Monday to Saturday, five Sunday).

## HAWICK

☎ 01450 / pop 15,000

Straddling the River Teviot, Hawick is the largest town in the Borders and has long been a major production centre for knitwear. Most people come to Hawick to shop: it's a bargain-hunter's paradise with numerous factory outlets, including **Pringle** ( ☎ 377644; Commercial Rd); a full list is available from the **tourist office** ( ☎ 372547; 1 Tower Knowe; 10am-5pm Mon-Sat, noon-3pm Sun Apr-Sep, 10am-5pm Mon-Sat Oct), at the western end of High St.

In the same building is **Drumlanrig's Tower Visitor Centre** ( ☎ 377615; 1 Tower Knowe; adult/child £2.50/free; 10am-5pm Mon-Sat late-Mar–Oct, noon-3pm Sun late-Mar–Sep), which tells the story of cross-border warfare from the 16th century.

Across the river, **Hawick Museum & Scott Art Gallery** ( ☎ 373457; Wilton Lodge Park; admission free; 10am-noon & 1-5pm Mon-Fri, 2-5pm Sat & Sun Apr-Sep, 1-4pm Mon-Fri, 2-4pm Sun Oct-Mar; ) has an interesting collection of mostly 19th-century manufacturing and domestic memorabilia.

If you've ever had the urge to trace your Scottish heritage, or are a fanatical fan of Border sons such as Walter Scott, then the state-of-the-art **Heritage Hub** ( ☎ 433743; Towerdykeside; 10am-4.45pm Mon, Fri & Sat, 10am-7.45pm Tue & Thu) is for you. It's just behind the tourist office.

You'll be met with a cheery welcome at the amiable **Bridgehouse B&B** ( ☎ 370701; sergioshawick@aol.com; Sandbed; s/d £30/44). Functional rooms, in a former stables dating back to 1760, are brightly decorated and as neat as a pin, although en suites can be pokey. There's a café and a bar overlooking the river, but if you feel like something more substantial, pop

into **Sergio's** ( ☎ 370094; mains £8; lunch & dinner) next door for pizza and pasta dishes.

The half-hourly First buses 95 and X95 connect Hawick with Galashiels, Selkirk and Edinburgh (£5.50, two hours).

## HERMITAGE CASTLE

A massive collection of stone, with a heavy cubist beauty, **Hermitage Castle** (HS; ☎ 01387-376222; adult/child £3.50/1.75; 9.30am-5.30pm Apr-Sep) sits isolated beside a rushing stream surrounded by bleak, empty moorland. Dating from the 13th century, but substantially rebuilt in the 15th, it embodies the brutal history of the Borders; the stones themselves almost speak of the past. Sir Walter Scott's favourite castle, it is probably best known as the home of the earl of Bothwell and the place to which Mary, Queen of Scots, rode in 1566 to see him after he had been wounded in a border raid.

It's also where, in 1338, Sir William Douglas imprisoned his enemy Sir Alexander Ramsay in a pit and deliberately starved him to death. Ramsay survived for 17 days by eating grain that trickled into his pit (which can still be seen) from the granary above. The castle is said to be haunted and it certainly has a slightly spooky feel, especially when dark clouds gather. If you have the place to yourself, a visit can be quite magical – it's one of the best castles to visit in southern Scotland.

The castle is about 12 miles south of Hawick on the B6357.

## PEEBLES

☎ 01721 / pop 8100

Prosperous Peebles sits smugly on the banks of the River Tweed, content in the knowledge that it has a prime Borders location, set among rolling, wooded hills. Its agreeable and picturesque ambience will happily entice you to linger for a couple of days. The helpful **tourist office** ( ☎ 720138; High St; daily Apr-Dec, Mon-Sat Jan-Mar) will chase down accommodation for you.

### Sights & Activities

The small gallery at **Beltane Studios** ( ☎ 724888; www.beltanestudios.com; 2 Soonhope Farm Holdings) is quite superb with plenty of high-quality artwork: the highlight is also the speciality – bronze wax casting. There are huge windows looking into the workshop where you can see the masters at work. Beltane is outside of Peebles, on the road to Galashiels, just past the Hydro Hotel turn-off.

If it's sunny, the **riverside walk** along the River Tweed has plenty of grassed areas ideal for a picnic, and there's a children's playground (near the main road bridge). You could even walk to **Neidpath Castle** ( ☎ 702333; adult/child £3/1; ☼ 10.30am-5pm Wed-Sat, 12.30-5pm Sun May-Sep), a tower house perched on a bluff above the River Tweed. It's in a lovely spot, a mile west of the town centre, with good views from the parapets.

## Sleeping & Eating

**Rosetta Caravan & Camping Park** ( ☎ 720770; www .rosettacaravanpark.com; Rosetta Rd; tent site & 2 people £15; ☼ Apr-Oct) This award-winning camping ground, about 800m north of the town centre, has an exquisite green setting. There are plenty of amusements for the kids, such as a bowling green and a games room.

**Cross Keys Hotel** ( ☎ 724222; www.crosskeyspeebles .co.uk; 24 Northgate; dm/s/d/f £22/35/60/75) The Cross Keys is a renovated 17th-century coaching inn, and the current owners have maintained the tradition of fine hospitality. Some rooms are very large, though all are neat and well presented. Kings Orchard Brasserie here knocks together good pub grub (mains £7 to £10), and there's a bar with real ales and live music at weekends.

**Rowanbrae** ( ☎ 721630; john@rowanbrae.freeserve .co.uk, 103 Northgate; s £30-35, d £50) This is a classy B&B in a quiet cul-de-sac, a short walk from the town centre. The personable owners have been doing B&B here for almost 30 years and it shows with little touches such as fresh flowers in the rooms. There are three upstairs bedrooms, two with en suite, and an excellent guest lounge for relaxation.

**Cringletie House Hotel & Restaurant** ( ☎ 725750; www.cringletie.com; s/d from £165/220; ☖ ) This elegant Baronial mansion, 2 miles north of Peebles on the A703, calls itself a house, but that's being coy – it's a mansion. A very luxurious, Baronial mansion, in fact, set in lush, wooded grounds with an excellent restaurant (three-course dinner £40). If you enjoy pampering, genteel elegance and linen so soft you could wrap a newborn in it, this is the place for you.

**Sunflower Restaurant** ( ☎ 722420; 4 Bridgegate; starters £6, mains £10-15; ☼ lunch Mon-Sat, dinner Thu-Sat) The Sunflower, with its warm yellow dining room, is in a quiet spot off the main drag. It serves good salads for lunch and has an admirable menu in the evenings, with dishes such as wild-boar sausages or prawn, spring onion and lemongrass fishcakes with lemon and chive dip.

## Getting There & Away

The bus stop is beside the post office on Eastgate. First bus 62 runs half hourly to Edinburgh (£4, 1¼ hours), Galashiels (45 minutes) and Melrose (1¼ hours).

# AROUND PEEBLES
## Traquair House

One of Scotland's great country houses, **Traquair House** ( ☎ 01896-830323; www.traquair .co.uk; Innerleithen; adult/child £6.30/3.40; ☼ 10.30am-5pm Jun-Aug, noon-5pm Apr-May & Sep, 11am-4pm Oct, 11am-3pm Sat & Sun Nov; ☖ ) has a powerful ethereal beauty, and an exploration here is like time travel. Odd, sloping floors and a musty odour bestow a genuine feel, and parts of the building are believed to have been constructed long before the first official record of its existence in 1107. The massive tower house was gradually expanded over the next 500 years but has remained virtually unchanged since 1642.

Since the 15th century the house has belonged to various branches of the Stuart family, and the family's unwavering Catholicism and loyalty to the Stuart cause are largely why development ceased when it did. The family's estate, wealth and influence were gradually whittled down after the Reformation, and there was neither the opportunity nor, one suspects, the will to make any changes.

One of its most interesting places is the concealed room where priests secretly lived and performed Mass – up until 1829 when the Catholic Emancipation Act was finally passed. Other beautiful, time-worn rooms hold fascinating relics, including the cradle used by Mary for her son, James VI of Scotland (who also became James I of England), and many letters written by the Stuart pretenders to their supporters.

In addition to the house, there's a **garden maze**, an **art gallery**, a small **brewery** producing the tasty Bear Ale, and an active craft community. The **Scottish Beer Festival** takes place here in late May and there's the **Traquair Fair** in early August.

Traquair is 1.5 miles south of Innerleithen, about 6 miles southeast of Peebles. Bus C1 departs from Peebles at 10.15am for Traquair daily and returns at 3.05pm.

SOUTHERN SCOTLAND

# SOUTH LANARKSHIRE

South Lanarkshire is an area of contrasts. It combines a highly urbanised area south of Glasgow with scenically gorgeous country around the Falls of Clyde and the World Heritage-listed area of New Lanark, by far the biggest drawcard of the region. If you're roaring up to Scotland on the M74, there are some fine places to break your journey.

South and east of Glasgow are the large satellite towns of **East Kilbride**, **Hamilton**, **Motherwell** and **Coatbridge**. These are, for the most part, urban nightmares, and day trips only from Glasgow are recommended. Note also that you're far better off on public transport, given the plethora of roundabouts and one-way streets in these towns.

## BLANTYRE
☎ 01698

Blantyre's most famous son is David Livingstone, epitome of the Victorian missionary-explorer, who opened up central Africa to European religion. Visitors with an interest in Africa shouldn't miss the absorbing **David Livingstone Centre** (NTS; ☎ 823140; 165 Station Rd; adult/child £5/4; ☼ 10am-5pm Mon-Sat, 12.30-5pm Sun Easter-Dec; ☒ ), which tells the story of his life. In 30 years it's estimated he travelled 29,000 miles, mostly on foot – the sheer tenacity of the man was incredible. The centre is just downhill from Blantyre train station.

It's a 30-minute walk along the river to **Bothwell Castle** (HS; ☎ 816894; adult/child £3.50/1.75; ☼ 9.30am-5.30pm Apr-Sep, 9.30am-4.30pm Sat-Wed Oct-Mar), regarded as the finest 13th-century castle in Scotland. The stark, roofless, red-sandstone ruins are substantial and, largely due to their beautiful green setting, romantic. The castle is very popular with wedding parties.

Trains run from Glasgow Central station to Blantyre (£4.25/3.25 peak/off-peak return, 20 minutes, three hourly).

## LANARK & NEW LANARK
☎ 01555 / pop 8300

Below the market town of Lanark, in an attractive gorge by the River Clyde, is the World Heritage site of **New Lanark** – an intriguing collection of restored mill buildings and warehouses.

Once the largest cotton-spinning complex in Britain, it was better known for the pioneering social experiments of Robert Owen, who managed the mill from 1800. New Lanark is really a memorial to this enlightened capitalist. He provided his workers with housing, a cooperative store (the inspiration for the modern cooperative movement), the world's first nursery school for children, a school with adult-education classes, a sick-pay fund for workers and a social centre he called the New Institute for the Formation of Character. You'll need at least half a day to explore this site, as there's plenty to see.

### Information
There are two banks with ATMs on High St.
**Lanark Health Centre** ( ☎ 665522)
**Post office** (St Leonards St)
**Tourist office** ( ☎ 661661; Horsemarket, Ladyacre Rd, Lanark; ☼ 10am-5pm Easter-Oct, 10am-5pm Mon-Sat Nov-Easter) Close to the bus and train stations.

### Sights & Activities
#### NEW LANARK
The best way to get the feel of New Lanark is to wander round the outside of this impressive place. What must once have been a thriving, noisy, grimy industrial village, pumping out enough cotton to wrap the planet, is now a peaceful oasis with only the swishing of trees and the rushing of the River Clyde to be heard.

At the **New Lanark Visitor Centre** ( ☎ 661345; www.newlanark.org; New Lanark Mills; adult/child/family £6/5/18; ☼ 11am-5pm Sep-May, 10.30am-5pm Jun-Aug) you need to buy a ticket to enter the main attractions. These include the **Historic Schoolhouse**, which contains an innovative, hi-tech journey to New Lanark's past via a 3-D hologram of the spirit of Annie McLeod, a 10-year-old mill girl who describes life here in 1820. The kids will love it as it's very realistic, although the 'do good for all mankind' theme is a little overbearing.

Also included in your admission is a **millworker's house**, Robert Owen's **home** and exhibitions on 'saving New Lanark'. There's also a 1920s-style **village store**.

#### FALLS OF CLYDE
After you have viewed New Lanark you can then walk up to the **Falls of Clyde** (one hour) through the beautiful nature reserve managed by the Scottish Wildlife Trust. But before you go, drop into the **Falls of Clyde Wildlife Centre** ( ☎ 665262; adult/child £2/1; ☼ 11am-5pm Mar-Dec, noon-

4pm Jan & Feb) by the river in New Lanark. This place has undergone major refurbishment that includes interactive displays focused on badgers, bats, peregrines and other prominent species. There's also a bee tree where you can see golden honeycomb being created before your eyes.

### CRAIGNETHAN CASTLE
This **castle** (HS; ☎ 860364; Tillietudlem; adult/child £3.50/1.75; ☒ 9.30am-5.30pm Apr-Sep, 9.30am-4.30pm Sat-Wed Oct, 9.30am-4.30pm Sat & Sun Nov-Mar) has a very authentic feel – it hasn't been restored beyond recognition – and is in a stunning, tranquil spot, too. You'll feel miles from anywhere, so bring a picnic and make a day of it.

With a commanding position above the River Nethan, this extensive ruin includes a virtually intact tower house and a **caponier** (unique in the UK) – a small gun emplacement with holes in the wall so men with handguns could pick off attackers. The chilly chambers under the tower house are quite eerie.

Craignethan is 5 miles northwest of Lanark. If you don't have your own transport, take an hourly Lanark–Hamilton bus to Crossford, then follow the footpath along the northern bank of the River Nethan (20 minutes).

### WALKING
You can organise bat walks (£5) or badger-watching (£7) at the Falls of Clyde Wildlife Centre (opposite). From the centre there's also a 2.5-mile walk along a riverside path to the beautiful **Cora Linn** (waterfalls that inspired both Turner and Wordsworth) and beyond them to **Bonnington Linn**, a smaller waterfall of about 12 metres along the same river.

## Sleeping
**New Lanark Youth Hostel** (SYHA; ☎ 0870 004 1143; Wee Row, Rosedale St, New Lanark; dm adult/child £14.50/10.75, tw £30; ☒ Apr-Oct; ☐ ) This hostel has a great location in an old mill building by the River Clyde. There are mainly four-bed dorms with attached bathroom and one twin room. It makes a great base for exploring this fascinating World Heritage site.

**Mrs Berkley** ( ☎ 665487; mary@martinberkley.com; 159 Hyndford Rd; r per person £22-28) A green oasis next to the thumping A73, Mrs Berkley provides simple, traditional accommodation on a lovely property.

**Summerlea** ( ☎ 664889; 32 Hyndford Rd; s/d £25/50) Just up from the tourist office, this modern

guesthouse is one of the more central choices available. It has all the comforts of home and mainly twin rooms. The huge single is a great choice as long as you don't mind the colour lavender.

**New Lanark Mill Hotel** ( ☎ 667200; hotel@newlanark .org; Mill One, New Lanark; s/d from £70/110, cottages per week from £270; ☒ ) Cleverly converted from an 18th-century mill, this hotel is full of character and is a stone's throw from the major attractions. It has luxury rooms (£25 extra for a spacious suite and added decadence) or self-catering accommodation in cottages. The hotel also serves meals.

## Eating
**Prego** ( ☎ 666300; 3 High St; mains £8-13; ☒ lunch & dinner) This perpetually busy Italian restaurant manages to create a modern ambience in a traditional setting. It dishes up excellent pasta, pizza and fillet steak at very reasonable prices, and the service matches the cuisine.

**Crown Tavern** ( ☎ 664639; 17 Hope St; lunch £7, dinner mains £10-13; ☒ lunch & dinner) Off the main street, the Crowny is a local favourite. It's a highly regarded place that does good bar meals and even better food (pasta, seafood and vegetarian dishes) in the evenings in its restaurant. Try the local trout or the Highlander chicken.

Also recommended:

**Cafe Espresso** (Bannatyne St; light meals under £5; ☒ 8am-4pm Mon-Sat) Pull up a pew by the window and watch Lanark life tick by.

**New Lanark Mill Hotel** ( ☎ 667200; hotel@newlanark .org; Mill One, New Lanark; bar meals £9, 2-course dinner £19) Creative and tasty bar meals. Mediterranean-influenced restaurant with excellent wine list.

## Getting There & Around
Lanark is 25 miles southeast of Glasgow. Express buses from Glasgow, run by Irvine's Coaches, make the hourly run from Monday to Saturday (£4.75, one hour).

Trains also run daily between Glasgow Central station and Lanark (£5, 55 minutes, every 30 minutes).

There's a half-hourly bus service from the train station (daily) to/from New Lanark. If you need a taxi, call **Clydewide** ( ☎ 663221).

## BIGGAR
☎ 01899 / pop 2100
Biggar is a pleasant town in a rural setting dominated by Tinto Hill (712m). The town is well worth a visit – it probably has more

**SOUTHERN SCOTLAND**

museums and attractions per inhabitant than anywhere else its size.

## Information

**Health Centre** ( ☎ 220383; South Croft Rd)
**Post office** (High St)
**Royal Bank ATM** (High St)
**Tourist office** ( ☎ 221066; 155 High St; ✆ 10am-5pm Mon-Sat, noon-5pm Sun Easter-Sep)

## Sights

The Biggar Museums Trust looks after four major museums in the town.

**Moat Park Heritage Centre** ( ☎ 221050; Kirkstyle; adult/child £2/1; ✆ 11am-4.30pm Mon-Sat, 2-4.30pm Sun May-Sep), in a renovated church, covers the history of the area with geological and archaeological displays.

**Greenhill Covenanter's House** ( ☎ 221050; Burnbrae; adult/child £1/50p; ✆ 2-5pm Sat & Sun May-Sep) is an intelligently reconstructed farmhouse, with 17th-century furnishings and artefacts relating to the fascinating story of the local Covenanters, who valiantly defied their king to protect their religious beliefs.

**Gladstone Court** ( ☎ 221050; North Back Rd; adult/child £2/1; ✆ 11am-4.30pm Mon-Sat, 2-4.30pm Sun May-Sep) is an indoor street museum with historic nook-and-cranny shops that you can pop into to steal a glimpse of the past. Don't miss the old printing press and the Albion A2 Dogcart, one of the oldest British cars still around.

**Biggar Puppet Theatre** ( ☎ 220631; 8 Broughton Rd; all seats £6.50; ✆ 11am-4.30pm Tue-Sat; ♿ ) has miniature Victorian puppets and bizarre modern ones over 1m high that glow in the dark. There are several ultraviolet displays, but you shouldn't need your sunglasses. Different shows are suitable for varying age groups, so inquire before you take along the kids. Guided tours cost £2.50/2 per adult/child.

**Tinto Hill** dominates the town. The hill is a straightforward 4.5-mile ascent by its northern ridge from the car park just off the A73 by Thankerton Crossroads. Look out for the Stone Age fort on your way up.

## Sleeping & Eating

**School Green Cottage** ( ☎ 220388; isobel.burness@virgin.net; 1 Kirkstyle; r per person £25) There's a double and a twin available in this conveniently located cottage. The neat rooms are well kitted out with New Zealand oak furnishings. Expect homespun hospitality, but be warned – there's no puffin' on the premises.

**Cornhill House** ( ☎ 220001; www.cornhillhousehotel .com; Cornhill Rd, Coulter; s/d £60/80) This is a well-appointed place, complete with turrets, and is situated in a peaceful setting 2 miles southwest of Biggar. The rooms are good value, particularly those that have been refurbished, and a three-course breakfast is included. Its excellent restaurant (mains £17) serves local produce.

## Getting There & Away

Biggar is 33 miles southeast of Glasgow. McEwan's bus 100 runs to/from Edinburgh (£4, 1¼ hours, hourly Monday to Saturday, three Sunday). HAD Coaches bus 191 runs hourly to/from Lanark (30 minutes).

# AYRSHIRE

Ayrshire is synonymous with golf and with Robert Burns – and there's plenty on offer here to satisfy both of these pursuits. Troon has six golf courses for starters, and plenty of yachties, and there's enough Burns memorabilia in the region to satisfy his most fanatic admirers.

This region's main drawcard though is the irresistible Isle of Arran. With a gourmet culinary scene, atmospheric watering holes (and some of the best beer gardens in the country), and the most varied and scenic countryside of the southern Hebridean islands, this easily accessible island shouldn't be missed.

Back on the mainland, retro holiday towns by the seaside, such as Largs, give Ayrshire a unique flavour, while towns such as Irvine provide a link to the region's maritime heritage. There's also spectacular coastal scenery, best admired at Culzean Castle, one of the finest stately homes in the country.

## Getting There & Around

Call **Traveline** ( ☎ 0871 200 22 33) for public-transport information. **Stagecoach Western** ( ☎ 01292-613500) is the main bus operator on the mainland. On Arran, **Western** ( ☎ 01770-302000) and **Royal Mail** ( ☎ 01463-256200) buses whiz you around the island, while **CalMac** ( ☎ 01770-302166) ferries will get you there from the mainland.

## NORTH AYRSHIRE
### Largs
☎ 01475 / pop 11,300
Largs has a kitsch, resort-style waterfront that is loads of fun. You need to approach

the amusements, old-fashioned eateries and bouncing castle with the right attitude – on a sunny day buy an ice cream and go for a stroll to check out this slice of retro Scotland.

There's a **tourist office** ( ☎ 689962; ☺ 9am-5pm Mon-Sat Easter-Oct) at the train station. The **post office** (Aitken St) is just off Main St.

The main attraction in Largs is the award-winning **Vikingar!** ( ☎ 689777; Greenock Rd; adult/child £4.20/3.20; ☺ 10.30am-5.30pm Apr-Sep, 10.30am-3.30pm Oct & Mar, 10.30am-3.30pm Sat & Sun Nov & Feb). This multimedia exhibition describes Viking influence in Scotland until its demise at the Battle of Largs in 1263. Tours with staff in Viking outfits run every half-hour. There's also a theatre, cinema, café, shop, swimming pool and leisure centre. To get here, follow the A78 coast road north from the tourist office. You can't miss it, as it's the only place with a longship outside.

Largs hosts a **Viking festival** during the first week in September. The festival celebrates the Battle of Largs and the end of Viking political domination in Scotland. In early June the **Largs Jazz Festival** (www.largsjazzfestival.org.uk) gets cranked up.

### SLEEPING

**Glendarroch** ( ☎ 676305; 24 Irvine Rd; r per person £23) This B&B typifies Scottish hospitality – the rooms are well kept and the owner is friendly without being intrusive. If it's full, staff will probably ring around to try and find you something else.

**Brisbane House Hotel** ( ☎ 687700; www.brisbane househotel.com; 14 Greenock Rd, Esplanade; s/d from £75/90) A genteel place standing proudly on the foreshore, the refined Brisbane House is set in lovely gardens and has luxury rooms, some with spas and sea views. Children under five stay for free and cots are available.

Two solid guesthouses in a street full of 'em are **Glenroy Guest House** ( ☎ 674220; 3 Charles St; r per person £23), which doesn't bother locking the doors – always a good sign, and **Haven House** ( ☎ 676389; 18 Charles St; r per person £20), where you'll be greeted with a smile. They're typical of the friendliness of this town and are a short walk to the ferry. Rooms share a bathroom, but are comfortable, clean and a good size.

### GETTING THERE & AWAY

Largs is 32 miles west of Glasgow by road. Buses run to Greenock (45 minutes, frequent), and roughly one or two hourly to Ardros-san (30 minutes), Irvine (55 minutes) and Ayr (1¼ hours). There are trains to Largs from Glasgow Central station (£6, one hour, hourly).

## Isle of Great Cumbrae
☎ 01475 / pop 1200

Walking or cycling is the best way to explore this accessible, hilly island (it's only 4 miles long), ideal for a day trip from Largs. **Millport** is the only town, strung out a long way around the bay overlooking neighbouring Little Cumbrae. With the frequent ferry service, the place buzzes with day-trippers and families (there's heaps of stuff for kids to do, such as crazy golf and a funfair). Walking around the bay admiring the views is one of the most pleasurable things to do in town, where you'll find a post office, supermarket, bank (with ATM) and your choice of chippies.

The town boasts Europe's smallest cathedral, the lovely **Cathedral of the Isles** ( ☎ 530353; College St; admission free; ☺ daylight hours), which was completed in 1851. Inside it's quite ornate with a lattice woodwork ceiling and fragments of early Christian carved stones.

Just east of town is the interesting **Robertson Museum & Aquarium** ( ☎ 530581; adult/child £1.50/1; ☺ 8.45am-12.15pm & 1.45-4.15pm Mon-Fri year-round, plus Sat Jun-Sep). A short way along the coast from the aquarium is a remarkable rock feature, the **Lion**.

Rural parts of the island are pleasant for **cycling**; the narrow Inner Circle Rd is a particularly good cycle route. There are several bike-hire places in Millport, including **Mapes** ( ☎ 530444; 3-5 Guildford St; per 1/6 hr £2/4.50).

If you're staying overnight on the island, try the unusual **College of the Holy Spirit** ( ☎ 530353; tccumbrae@argyll.anglican.org; College St; s £33-50, d £60-70), next to the cathedral; there's a refectory-style dining room and a library.

The **Dancing Midgie** ( ☎ 531278; 24 Glasgow St; snacks £2-5; ☺ 9am-4pm) is a cheerful café on the seafront providing some healthy, tasty alternatives to the chippies in town, as well as an ideal spot for a read of the newspaper. Food is freshly prepared (sandwiches, salads, soups) and the coffee freshly brewed.

A very frequent 15-minute CalMac ferry ride links Largs with Great Cumbrae (passenger/car £4.20/18.40) daily. Buses meet the ferries for the 3.5-mile journey to Millport (£2.30 return).

## Ardrossan

☎ 01294 / pop 11,000

The main reason – OK the *only* reason – for coming here is to catch a CalMac ferry to Arran. Trains leave Glasgow Central station (£5.45, one hour, half-hourly) to connect with ferries.

Although the port area is receiving a much needed facelift, Ardrossan is very run down, and if you're hungry you're better off saving your appetite for more palatable surrounds, which beckon just across the bay.

If you need a B&B, **Edenmore Guest House** ( ☎ 462306; fax 604016; 47 Parkhouse Rd; s/d £30/50) is the saving grace of this ramshackle town. It's very friendly, and offers small, spotless rooms and a hearty welcome – nothing seems too much trouble for the owner. Room No 4 is the best double. The guesthouse is just off the main A78 and offers evening meals (thank goodness!).

## ISLE OF ARRAN

☎ 01770 / pop 4800

Enchanting Arran is a jewel in Scotland's tourism crown. Strangely undiscovered by foreign tourists, the island is a visual feast, and boasts culinary delights, cosy pubs (including its own brewery) and stacks of accommodation. The variations in Scotland's dramatic landscape can all be experienced on this one small island, best explored by pulling on the hiking boots or jumping on a bicycle. Arran offers some challenging walks in the mountainous north, often compared to the Highlands, while the island's circular road is very popular with cyclists.

Arran's many watering holes are legendary, and over summer most have regular live-music sessions.

## Orientation & Information

The ferry from Ardrossan docks at Brodick, the island's main town. To the south, Lamlash is actually the capital and, like nearby Whiting Bay, a popular seaside resort. From the village of Lochranza in the north there's a ferry link to Claonaig on the Kintyre peninsula.

In Brodick there are banks with ATMs.

**Arran Library** ( ☎ 302835; Brodick Hall; 10am-5pm Tue, 10am-7.30pm Thu & Fri, 10am-1pm Sat) Free internet access.

**Hospital** ( ☎ 600777; Lamlash)

**Internet resources** (www.ayrshire-arran.com, www.arrantourism.com)

**Kildonan Hotel** ( ☎ 820207; Kildonan) Internet access £1 per hour. Also has wireless internet.

**Tourist office** ( ☎ 303774/6; arran@visitscotland.com; 9am-7.30pm Mon-Sat, 10am-5pm Sun Jun-Sep, 9am-5pm Mon-Thu, 9am-7.30pm Fri, 10am-5pm Sat Oct-May, also 10am-5pm Sun May only) Efficient; near Brodick pier.

## Sights

### BRODICK

Most visitors arrive in Brodick, the heartbeat of the island, and congregate along the coastal road to admire the town's long curving bay.

**Brodick Castle & Park** (NTS; ☎ 302202; adult/child castle & park £10/7, park only £5/4; castle 11am-4.30pm Apr-Oct, park 9.30am-sunset) is 2.5 miles north of Brodick. The first impression is that of an animal morgue as you enter via the hunting gallery, wallpapered with prized deer heads. On your way to the formal dining room (with its peculiar table furnishings), note the intricacy of the fireplace in the library. The castle has more of a lived-in feel than some NTS properties. Only a small portion is open to visitors. The extensive grounds, now a country

---

**WORTH THE TRIP**

Boat lovers should check out the **Scottish Maritime Museum** ( ☎ 278283; Gottries Rd, Harbourside; family/adult/child £7/3/2; 10am-5pm Apr-Oct) in Irvine. In the massive Linthouse Engine Shop – an old hangar with a cast-iron framework – is an absorbing collection of boats and machinery. A ticket also gives admission to the boat shop, with its wonderful works of art and huge kids activity area. Free guided tours leave from the boat shop – guides will take you down to the pontoons where you can clamber over various ships and visitors can also see a shipyard worker's restored flat.

If you're feeling peckish, drop into the wonderful **Ship Inn** ( ☎ 279722; 120 Harbour St; mains £7-10; lunch & dinner). It's the oldest pub in Irvine (1597), serves tasty bar meals and has bucket loads of character.

Irvine is 26 miles from Glasgow. There are frequent buses from Ayr (30 minutes) and Largs (45 minutes). Trains run to/from Glasgow Central station (£5.35, 35 minutes, half-hourly); the other way they go to Ayr.

ISLE OF ARRAN

local artist Marvin Elliot. After **Sannox**, with a sandy beach and great views of the mountains, the road cuts inland. Heading to the very north, on the island's main road, visitors weave through lush glens flanked by Arran's towering mountain splendour.

## LOCHRANZA

The village of Lochranza is in a stunning location in a small bay at the north of the island. On a promontory stand the ruins of the 13th-century **Lochranza Castle** (HS; admission free; always open), said to be the inspiration for the castle in *The Black Island*, Hergé's Tintin adventure. It's basically a draughty shell inside, with interpretive signs to help you decipher the layout.

Also in Lochranza is **Isle of Arran Distillers** ( 830264; 10am-6pm mid-Mar–Oct), which has innovative tours (adult/child £4/free), including an obligatory dram.

## WEST COAST

On the western side of the island, reached by String Rd across the centre (or the coast road), is the **Machrie Moor Stone Circle**, upright sandstone slabs erected around 6000 years ago. It's an eerie place, and these are the most impressive of the six stone circles on the island. There's another group at nearby **Auchagallon**, surrounding a Bronze Age burial cairn.

**Blackwaterfoot** is the largest village on the west coast; it has a shop/post office and two hotels. You can walk to **King's Cave** from here, via Drumadoon Farm – Arran is one of several islands that lay claim to a cave where Robert the Bruce had his famous arachnid encounter (p30). This walk could be combined with a visit to the Machrie stones.

## SOUTH COAST

The landscape in the southern part of the island is much gentler; the road drops into little wooded valleys, and it's particularly lovely around **Lagg**. There's a 10-minute walk from Lagg post office to **Torrylinn Cairn**, a chambered tomb over 4000 years old where at least eight bodies were found. **Kildonan** has pleasant sandy beaches, a gorgeous water outlook, two hotels, a campground and an ivy-clad ruined castle.

In **Whiting Bay** you'll find small sandy beaches, a village shop, a post office and **Arran Art Gallery** ( 700250; www.arranartgallery.com; Shore Rd), which has exquisite landscape portraits of Arran.

park with various trails among the rhododendrons, justify the steep entry fee.

As you follow the coast along Brodick Bay, look out for **seals**, often seen on the rocks around Merkland Point. Two types live in these waters, the Atlantic grey seal and the common seal. They're actually quite easy to tell apart – the common seal has a face like a dog; the Atlantic grey seal has a Roman nose.

## CLADACH

As well as a shop where you can purchase every imaginable thing related to beer (and many you can't), there's an excellent self-guided brewery tour at **Isle of Arran Brewery** ( 302353; www.arranbrewery.com; Cladach; 10am-5pm Mon-Sat, 12.30-5pm Sun) for £2, which includes tastings in the shop. Arran beers are pure quality. Warning: Arran Dark is highly addictive.

## CORRIE TO LOCHRANZA

The coast road continues north to the small, pretty village of Corrie, where there's a shop and hotel, and one of the tracks up **Goatfell** (the island's tallest peak) starts here. Corrie Village Shop sells wonderful sculptures by

SOUTHERN SCOTLAND

**LAMLASH**

Lamlash is an upmarket town (even the streets feel wider here) in a dazzling setting, strung along the beachfront. The bay was used as a safe anchorage by the navy during WWI and WWII.

Just off the coast is **Holy Island**, owned by the Samye Ling Tibetan Centre and used as a retreat, but day visits are allowed. The **ferry** ( ☎ 600998) makes eight trips a day (£10, 15 minutes) from Lamlash and runs between May and September. No dogs, alcohol or fires are allowed on the island. There's a good walk to the top of the hill (314m), taking two or three hours return. It is possible to stay on the island in accommodation belonging to the grandiose-named **Holy Island Centre for World Peace & Health** ( ☎ 601100; www.holyisland.org; dm/s/d £25/45/65). Although designed more for groups doing yoga and meditation courses at the centre, individuals are welcome. There's also a dining room and library for guests.

## Activities

Drop into the tourist office for plenty of walking and cycling suggestions around the island. The handy *Selection of Arran Walks* (£3) is a selection of leaflets covering Arran's best-known walks. There are also plenty of maps available.

The walk up and down **Goatfell** takes up to eight hours return, starting in Brodick and finishing in the grounds of Brodick Castle. If the weather's fine, there are superb views to Ben Lomond and the coast of Northern Ireland. It can, however, be very cold and windy up there; take the appropriate maps (available at the tourist office), waterproof gear and a compass.

More moderate walks here include the trail through **Glen Sannox**, which goes from the village of Sannox up the burn, a two-hour return trip. From Whiting Bay Youth Hostel there are easy one-hour walks through the forest to the **Giant's Graves** and **Glenashdale Falls**, and back – keep an eye out for golden eagles and other birds of prey.

The 50-mile circuit on the coastal road is popular with cyclists and has few serious hills – more in the south than to the north.

The **Arran Adventure Company** ( ☎ 302244; www.arranadventure.com; Shore Rd, Brodick) has loads of activities on offer and runs a different one each day (such as gorge walking, kayaking, climbing, abseiling and mountain biking). All activities run for about three hours and cost around £35/20 for adults/kids. Drop in to see what's available while you're around.

## Festivals & Events

The week-long **Arran Folk Festival** ( ☎ 302623; www.arranfolkfestival.org) takes place in early June. There are also local village festivals from June to September.

## Sleeping
### BUDGET

Camping isn't allowed without permission from the landowner, but there are several camping grounds (open April to October).

**Glen Rosa Farm** ( ☎ 302380; camp sites per person £3.50) In a lush glen by a river, 2 miles from Brodick, this large place has plenty of nooks and crannies to pitch a tent. It's remote camping with cold water and toilets only. To get there from Brodick head north, take String Rd, then turn right almost immediately on the road signed to Glen Rosa. After 400m, on the left is a white house where you book in; the campground is further down the road.

**Seal Shore Camping Site** ( ☎ 820320; mdeighton@ sealshore.fsnet.co.uk; Kildonan; camp sites per person/tent £6/1) This campground is by the sea, and the breeze keeps the midges away. It has a manicured grassed area and is right next to the Kildonan Hotel.

**Lochranza Youth Hostel** (SYHA; ☎ 0870 004 1140; Lochranza; dm adult/child £13/10; ☉ May-Oct) In the north of the island, this hostel has clean, spacious dorms, helpful owners and buckets of information about Arran. Its worn furnishings are offset by the lovely views.

### MIDRANGE
### Brodick

**our pick** **Fellview** ( ☎ 302153; fellviewarran@yahoo.co.uk; 6 Strathwhillan Rd; r per person £25, bunkhouse per person £15) This lovely house is an excellent place to stay and rooms are imbued with personable touches. It's a bit pokey inside and there's not much parking, but the owner is warm, friendly and encapsulates Scottish hospitality. The snug bunkhouse out the back is wee with just two bunks and you need to use the bathroom inside the house. The owner doesn't charge a supplement for singles (because, in her words – 'it's not their fault'). To get here, head north out of Brodick and take the left-hand turn to Strathwhillan. Fellview is just up on the right.

**Belvedere Guest House** ( ☎ 302397; belvedere@vision -unlimited.co.uk; Alma Rd; s £25-30, d £60-80) Imperiously overlooking the town, bay and surrounding mountains, Belvedere has well-presented rooms and seems perpetually busy: book early.

**McLaren Hotel** ( ☎ 302226; mclaren@arran-hotels .co.uk; Shore Rd; r per person £35) The McLaren is a creaking, ageing servant of hospitality on the Brodick seafront. It's a bit grotty and rooms are dated, but it's quirky too. The modern décor helps to freshen the old furnishings in the rooms, which feature some unusual layouts. We like it. Besides, you won't have far to wander after an evening's boozing in the huge beer garden out the front.

**Rosaburn Lodge** ( ☎ /fax 302383; d £60; 🅖 ) By the River Rosa, 800m from the centre of Brodick, this very friendly lodge gets heaps of natural light. The Rosa suite overlooks the river via its bay window and is closer to an apartment than a bedroom. Note that there are no singles.

### Corrie

**Corrie Hotel** ( ☎ 810273; corriehotel@btinternet.com; r per person £25, with en suite £30) The traditional stone Corrie Hotel offers quaint, slightly ram-shackle, but comfy, loft-style rooms – No 6 is a good option for three people. Singles are very small and plain, although some have good views of the Holy Island. Its wonderful beer garden scrapes the water's edge.

### Lochranza

**Lochranza Hotel** ( ☎ /fax 830223; hotel@lochranza.co.uk; s/d £52/84) The Lochranza, a bastion of Arran hospitality, has some rooms with outrageous pink floral décor, but they're a good size, sort of homely, and the double and twin at the front (room Nos 1 and 10) have views you can't buy. Rooms are a bit expensive, but they get cheaper if you stay more than one night.

**Apple Lodge** ( ☎ /fax 830229; Lochranza; d £70-78; 🅖 ) Lavish Apple Lodge, the finest place to stay in Lochranza, has beautifully, individually furnished rooms, one with a four-poster bed, and a guest lounge perfect for curling up with a good book. It makes all the difference when your hosts love their job.

### Whiting Bay

**Viewbank House** ( ☎ 700326; www.viewbank-arran .co.uk; s £25-28, d £56-70) Appropriately named, it does indeed have tremendous views from its vantage point above Whiting Bay. Rooms are tastefully furnished and well kept. The real pull of this wonderful B&B, however, is its friendly hosts – expect a good dose of Arran hospitality. There's also a great lawn at the front to stretch out on during those shimmering sunny Arran days.

**our pick** **Royal Arran Hotel** ( ☎ 700286; www.royal arran.co.uk; s £42.50, d £42.50-47.50; 🅖 ) This place has had a major refurbishment and the results are magnificent. It's a personalised, intimate hotel with just four rooms. The double upstairs is our idea of accommodation heaven – four-poster bed, big heavy linen, a huge room and gorgeous water views. Room No 1 downstairs is a great size and has a private patio. The hosts couldn't be more welcoming.

**Argentine House** ( ☎ 700662; www.argentinearran .co.uk; Shore Rd; s/d from £55/70; 🖳 ) Swiss hospitality in very modish, minimalist rooms is what you can expect at this small hotel. Of the five stylish rooms, the 'Firth of Clyde' is by far the best with smashing views and heaps of space. The owners speak French, German, Italian and Spanish. If you don't enjoy your stay here you really *are* fussy. Note that prices increase for a sea facing room but decrease with multiple-night stays.

**Eden Lodge Hotel** ( ☎ 700357; www.edenlodgehotel .co.uk; r without/with bathroom £60/80; 🅖 ) This new kid on the block injects a bit of flair into the local accommodation scene. Rooms are very modern with a minimalist bent and a hint of TLC in the air. If you want to spoil yourself try the Jacuzzi room at £90. The dishes downstairs use lots of local Arran produce and there's a good range of salads.

### Lamlash

**Lilybank Guest House** ( ☎ 600230; www.lilybank-arran .co.uk; Shore Rd, Lamlash; r per person £25-30) Built in the 17th century, Lilybank retains its heritage but has been refurbished for 21st-century needs. Rooms are slightly frilly, but clean and comfortable. Breakfast includes oak-smoked kippers and Arran goodies. It's right next to the Glenisle Hotel.

### TOP END

**Lagg Inn** ( ☎ 870255; www.lagghotel.com; Lagg; s/d from £60/80) An 18th-century coach house, this inn has a beautiful location and is the perfect place for a romantic weekend. Grab a superior room with garden views. There's also a cracking beer garden and a fine restaurant.

**Kildonan Hotel** ( ☎ 820207; www.kildonanhotel.com; Kildonan; standard/superior r £60/90; 🖵 ) The Kildonan offers stylish, upmarket B&B in light and airy rooms with a minimalist bent. The grassed area in the front of this classy hotel has been landscaped into a beautiful garden providing a fantastic seating area overlooking the water. Bar meals are available all day and the restaurant, in a lovely conservatory, specialises in fresh, local seafood – the menu changes daily depending on the catch.

**Kilmichael Country House Hotel** ( ☎ 302219; www .kilmichael.com; Glen Cloy; s/d from £100/150) The island's best hotel, the Kilmichael is also the oldest building – it has a glass window dating from 1650. The hotel is a luxurious, tastefully decorated hideaway, a mile outside Brodick, with eight rooms and an excellent restaurant.

## Eating & Drinking

**Island Cheese Co** (Home Farm, Duchess Ct) Anyone with a fetish for cheese should stop by this place, where you can stock up on the famed local cheeses and watch the masters at work. There are free samples.

**our pick Catacol Bay Hotel** ( ☎ 830231; Catacol; bar mains £6-9; 🕑 lunch & dinner) Two miles from Lochranza, this bar does great food. The Sunday buffet for £10 (over 60s – £7) is famous, and the cheery service makes you feel like a local. With its snug bar, sunny beer garden, frequent live music and great beers on tap, it's the best pub on the island.

**Drift Inn** ( ☎ 600656; Shore Rd, Lamlash; mains £5.50-12; 🕑 lunch & dinner; 👶 ) There are few better places to be on the island on a sunny day than the beer garden at this child-friendly hotel, ploughing your way through an excellent bar meal while gazing over to the Holy Island. There are pub faves and genuine Angus beef burgers, with generous portions all round.

**Ormidale Hotel** ( ☎ 302293; Glen Cloy; mains £8-10; 🕑 lunch & dinner) This hotel has decent bar food. Vegetarians should try the mushroom and stilton lasagne, while carnivores can dig into braised steak and onions in Arran ale, or a cold Kintyre salmon salad. Arran beers are on tap.

**Breadalbane Hotel** ( ☎ 820284; Kildonan; mains £8-10; 🕑 lunch & dinner) Good home-cooked food is served here, and you can dine by the fire on blustery nights or on the decking overlooking the water if the sun is shining. If you want to drown out the sound of your chomping, give the jukebox a whirl.

**Brodick Bar & Brasserie** ( ☎ 302169; Alma Rd, Brodick; mains £8-15; 🕑 lunch Mon-Sat, dinner daily; 👶 ) By the post office, this is a good choice for families (high chairs are available) and the older crowd, particularly if you like tucking into pizzas.

**our pick Creelers Seafood Restaurant** ( ☎ 302810; Duchess Ct; lunch £8, dinner mains £15-17; 🕑 closed Mon) This award-winning restaurant, 1.5 miles north of Brodick, offers formal but unpretentious dining and is religious about seafood, sourcing all of its delicacies from Arran and the Western Isles. Try the seafood salad with avocado and lime dressing. The Smokehouse next door sells seafood over the counter.

**Lighthouse Tearoom & Bunkhouse** ( ☎ 850240; Pirnmill; mains £9-13; 🕑 lunch & dinner) Calling itself a tearoom is being coy! The restaurant here has an extensive menu, great desserts and outdoor seating, all in a very, very blue lighthouse theme. It's getting quite a name for its excellent dishes (such as baked whole seabass stuffed with lime and coriander) using seasonal produce. Book in advance for dinner.

**Joshua's** ( ☎ 700308; Shore Rd, Whiting Bay; starters £4, mains £9-14; 🕑 10am-8.30pm Mon-Sat, 11am-4pm Sun) This funky place decked out in suave red tones and with a sun-drenched conservatory on the water's edge serves grills, seafood and salads in the evening, with lighter offerings during the day.

Other recommendations:

**Corrie Hotel** ( ☎ 810273; Corrie; mains £7-10; 🕑 lunch & dinner) Substantial bar meals; delicious Banoffee pie.

**Glenisle Hotel** ( ☎ 600559; Shore Rd, Lamlash; starters £4.50, mains £9-12; 🕑 lunch & dinner) Excellent pub food; serves Scottish faves such as *Cullen skink* (soup made with smoked haddock, potato, onion and milk). Good wine list.

## Getting There & Away

CalMac runs a car ferry between Ardrossan and Brodick (passenger/car return £8.75/53, 55 minutes, four to eight daily), and from April to late October runs services between Claonaig and Lochranza (passenger/car return £7.85/35.50, 30 minutes, seven to nine daily).

## Getting Around

### BICYCLE

Several places hire out bicycles in Brodick, including **Arran Adventure Company** ( ☎ 302244; Shore Rd; day/week £15/50) and the **Boathouse** ( ☎ 302868; Brodick Beach; day/week £12.50/45). Other bike-hire places around the island include **Blackwaterfoot Garage** ( ☎ 860277; Blackwaterfoot; day/week £8/20).

## CAR & MOTORCYCLE
At the service station near the ferry pier, **Arran Transport** ( ☎ 302121; Brodick) hires cars from around £28 per day. Note that it also hires cars for part days at a pro-rata rate. Child seats are available.

## PUBLIC TRANSPORT
There are frequent bus services on the island. Five or six buses daily go from Brodick pier to Lochranza (45 minutes, Monday to Saturday), and three to 10 daily go from Brodick to Lamlash and Whiting Bay (30 minutes). Pick up a timetable from the tourist office. An Arran Rural Rover ticket costs £4.20 and permits travel anywhere on the island for a day (buy it from the driver). For a taxi, call ☎ 302274 in Brodick or ☎ 600903 in Lamlash.

# EAST AYRSHIRE
In **Kilmarnock**, where Johnnie Walker whisky has been blended since 1820, is **Dean Castle** ( ☎ 01563-522702; www.deancastle.com; Dean Rd; admission free; ☉ 11am-5pm Wed-Sun), a 15-minute walk from the bus and train stations. The castle, restored in the first half of the 20th century, has a virtually windowless keep (dating from 1350) and an adjacent palace (1468), with a superb collection of medieval arms, armour, tapestries and musical instruments. The grounds, an 81-hectare park, are a good place for a picnic, or you can eat at the visitor centre's tearoom, where snacks and light meals cost under £5. Free guided tours are available. From Ayr there are frequent buses throughout the day.

# SOUTH AYRSHIRE
## Ayr
☎ 01292 / pop 46,500
Ayr is a large, bustling town and a convenient base for a tour of Burns territory. The town's long sandy beach has made it a popular family seaside resort since Victorian times. There are many fine Georgian and Victorian buildings, although some areas of town show signs of neglect.

## INFORMATION
Banks with ATMs are on High St and Sandgate. The post office is also on Sandgate.
**Ayr Hospital** ( ☎ 610555) South of town, by the Dalmellington road.
**Carnegie Library** ( ☎ 286385; 12 Main St; ☉ 10am-7.30pm Mon, Tue, Thu & Fri, 10am-5pm Wed & Sat) Offers fast, free internet access.

**Tourist office** ( ☎ 0845 225 5121; 22 Sandgate; ☉ 9am-5pm Mon-Sat Apr-Jun & Sep-Mar, 11am-4pm Sun Sep, 9am-6pm Mon-Sat, 10am-5pm Sun Jul & Aug)

## SIGHTS
Most things to see in Ayr are Burns-related. The bard was baptised in the **Auld Kirk** (Old Church; ☎ 262938) off High St. The atmospheric cemetery here overlooks the river and is good for a stroll, offering an escape from the bustle of High St. Several of his poems are set here in Ayr; in *Twa Brigs*, Ayr's old and new bridges argue with one another. The **Auld Brig** (Old Bridge) was built in 1491 and spans the river just north of the church. In Burns' poem *Tam o'Shanter*, Tam spends a boozy evening in the **pub** that now bears his name, at 230 High St.

**St John's Tower** ( ☎ 286385; Eglinton Tce; admission free; ☉ by arrangement) is the only remnant of a church where a parliament was held in 1315, the year after the celebrated victory at Bannockburn. John Knox's son-in-law was the minister here, and Mary, Queen of Scots, stayed overnight in 1563.

## ACTIVITIES
With only a few steep hills, the area is well suited to cyclists. From Ayr, you could cycle to Alloway and spend a couple of hours seeing the Burns sights before continuing to Culzean via Maybole. You could either camp here, after seeing Culzean Castle, or cycle back along the coast road to Ayr, a return trip of about 22 miles. **AMG Cycles** ( ☎ 287580; 55 Dalblair Rd; day/weekend/week £12.50/15/35) hires out bikes.

The beachfront is good for a walk in sunny weather, especially at low tide when a huge sandy beach is revealed. The silhouettes of Arrans peaks in the bay form an impressive backdrop.

## FESTIVALS & EVENTS
The **Burns an' a' That** festival, held in Ayr in May, has been running for only a few years, but looks set to become a major event on Scotland's cultural calendar.

## SLEEPING
**Heads of Ayr Caravan Park** ( ☎ 442269; tent site & 2 people £16-18, chalets per week from £200; ☉ Mar-Oct) This caravan park is in a lovely, quiet location close to the beach. From Ayr take the A719 south for about 5 miles.

**SOUTHERN SCOTLAND**

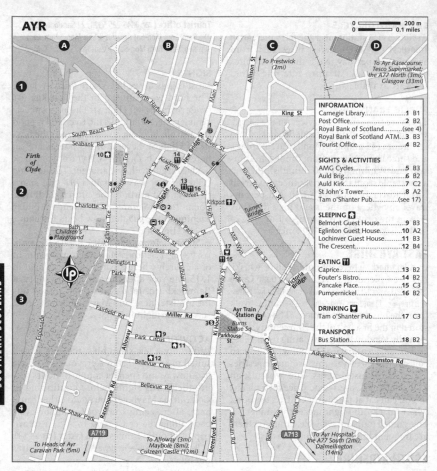

AYR

0 _____ 200 m
0 _____ 0.1 miles

INFORMATION
Carnegie Library...................1 B1
Post Office...........................2 B2
Royal Bank of Scotland.........(see 4)
Royal Bank of Scotland ATM...3 B3
Tourist Office.......................4 B2

SIGHTS & ACTIVITIES
AMG Cycles.........................5 B3
Auld Brig............................6 B2
Auld Kirk............................7 C2
St John's Tower...................8 A2
Tam o'Shanter Pub..............(see 17)

SLEEPING
Belmont Guest House............9 B3
Eglinton Guest House..........10 A2
Lochinver Guest House........11 B3
The Crescent......................12 B4

EATING
Caprice.............................13 B2
Fouter's Bistro....................14 B2
Pancake Place.....................15 C3
Pumpernickel......................16 B2

DRINKING
Tam o'Shanter Pub..............17 C3

TRANSPORT
Bus Station.........................18 B2

**Eglinton Guest House** ( ☎ /fax 264623; 23 Eglinton Tce; r per person £24) A short walk west of the bus station, this family-run Georgian property is in a quiet cul-de-sac and has a range of traditional, tidy rooms. The location is brilliant – between the beach and the town.

**Lochinver Guest House** ( ☎ /fax 265086; young .lochinver@talk21.com; 32 Park Circus; s/d £25/50) Though a little faded, Lochinver is a solid old guesthouse that is particularly good value for singles. Most rooms are well sized in this towering old Victorian terrace house and some have renovated bathrooms. It's a good place if you like your distance from the owners as it's not very personable.

**Belmont Guest House** ( ☎ 265588; www.belmont guesthouse.co.uk; 15 Park Circus; s/d £29/54) There's a relaxing lounge and library for guests in this comfortable Victorian town house. It's a little deceptive inside, with the '70s décor punctuated by pictures of wildlife staring hungrily down at diners, but the rooms with Victorian furnishings are clean and mostly of a good size. Chocolates on your pillow give a romantic feel to the rooms. Note that over busy periods it doesn't accommodate singles.

**The Crescent** ( ☎ 287329; www.26crescent.freeserve .co.uk; 26 Bellevue Cres; s £45, d £60-70) If you want to move up a couple of rungs on the luxury and comfort scale, consider this outstanding small hotel. There are five opulent, individually furnished rooms, including a four-poster suite fit for royalty and a room with French doors opening onto the garden.

## EATING & DRINKING

**Pumpernickel** ( ☎ 263830; 32 Newmarket St; snacks £4-6; ☺ breakfast & lunch Mon-Sat) Continental-style toasties and other delicious snacks are dished out at this deli-café. Dine indoors among the cheeses, meats and preserves or at outdoor tables on the pedestrianised street. It's a good spot for a glass of wine in the afternoon, too. If the weather's right, go for a gelato (£6).

**Caprice** ( ☎ 610916; 48 Newmarket St; mains £8-12; ☺ lunch & dinner daily, breakfast Mon-Fri) This French bistro-style bar-café provides dining among imported beers and well-to-do locals. Stained-glass windows, plenty of natural light, booth seating and a long bar gives Caprice a warm and intimate setting. There are great early meal deals too such as pizza, pasta or risotto for £5, from 5pm to 6.30pm Sunday to Thursday.

**Fouter's Bistro** ( ☎ 261391; 2a Academy St; 2-/3-course lunch £10/13, dinner starters £6, mains £14-17; ☺ lunch & dinner Tue-Sat) The best place to eat in town, Fouter's is a class act set in a former bank vault opposite the town hall. It's an ideal place to splash out on a top-class dinner without breaking the budget. It specialises in Ayrshire produce (such as new season local lamb with pine nut, garlic and herb crust) and Mediterranean-style seafood.

If you are after a supermarket for self-catering, there's a huge **Tesco** (Whitletts Rd) by Ayr Racecourse, and there's an **Asda** (Wallace St) near the river.

Also recommended:

**Pancake Place** ( ☎ 288666; 231 High St; mains £5-7; ☺ 9.30am-6pm Mon-Sat, 11am-5pm Sun) Serves sweet and savoury pancakes (with fillings such as Mexican chilli or toffee apple) and all-day breakfasts.

**Tam 'o' Shanter** ( ☎ 611684; 230 High St; mains £7; ☺ lunch & dinner) Atmospheric old pub with traditional pub grub.

## GETTING THERE & AROUND

Ayr is 33 miles from Glasgow and is Ayrshire's major transport hub. The main bus operator in the area is **Stagecoach Western** ( ☎ 613500) – its very frequent X77 service (Monday to Saturday) from Glasgow to Ayr costs £4.50 (one hour). It also runs buses from Ayr to Stranraer (£6.50, two hours, four to eight daily), Greenock (£6.40, 1¾ hours, every 20 minutes Monday to Saturday, two Sunday), Largs (£4.80, 1¼ hours, every 20 minutes Monday to Saturday, two Sunday) and Dumfries (£5.30, 2¼ hours, five to seven daily).

The Ayr Dayrider (£3.40) allows one day's unlimited travel in and around Ayr, including Alloway, from 9am.

There are at least two trains an hour that run from Glasgow Central station to Ayr (£6.20, 50 minutes), and some trains continue south from Ayr to Stranraer (£11.70, 1½ hours).

For a taxi, call **Central Taxis** ( ☎ 267655).

## Alloway

☎ 01292

The pretty, lush town of Alloway (3 miles south of Ayr) should be on the itinerary of every Robert Burns fan – he was born here on 25 January 1759. Even if you haven't been seduced by Burns mania, it's still well worth a visit since the Burns-related exhibitions give a good impression of life in Ayrshire in the late 18th century. The sights are within easy walking distance of each other and come under the umbrella title **Burns National Heritage Park** (www.burnsheritagepark.com). Rumours of major renovations to these Burns attractions are flying around, so things may have changed (for the better) by the time you read this.

The **Burns Cottage & Museum** ( ☎ 441215; adult/child £4/2.50; ☺ 10am-5.30pm Apr-Sep, 10am-5pm Oct-Mar) is situated next to the main road from Ayr. A 10-minute video introduces you to Burns, his family and the cottage. Born in the little box bed in this cramped thatched dwelling, the poet spent the first seven years of his life here. A fascinating museum of Burnsiana next to the cottage exhibits some fabulous artwork, and many of his songs and letters.

The nearby **Tam o'Shanter Experience** ( ☎ 443700; Murdoch's Lane; adult/child £2/1.25; ☺ 10am-5.30pm Apr-Oct, 10am-5pm Nov-Mar) has a clever audiovisual display of the famous poem, although an understanding of Burns' 18th-century Lowland Scots dialect would greatly enhance appreciation.

From here, you can visit the ruins of **Alloway Auld Kirk**, the setting for part of *Tam o'Shanter*. Burns' father, William Burnes (his son dropped the 'e' from his name), is buried in the kirkyard.

The **Burns Monument & Gardens** ( ☺ 9am-5pm) are nearby. The monument was built in 1823 and affords a view of the 13th-century **Brig o'Doon** (see p176). There are also statues of Burns' drinking cronies in the gardens.

SOUTHERN SCOTLAND

### ROBERT BURNS (1759–96)

Best remembered for penning the words of *Auld Lang Syne*, Robert Burns is Scotland's most famous poet and a popular hero whose birthday (25 January) is celebrated as Burns Night by Scots around the world. The Scottish executive hopes to turn Burns Night into a national celebration to rival Ireland's St Patrick's Day.

Burns was born in 1759 in Alloway. At school he soon showed an aptitude for literature and a fondness for the folk song. He later began to write his own songs and satires. When the problems of his arduous farming life were compounded by the threat of prosecution from the father of Jean Armour, with whom he'd had an affair, he decided to emigrate to Jamaica. He gave up his share of the family farm and published his poems to raise money for the journey.

The poems were so well reviewed in Edinburgh that Burns decided to remain in Scotland and devote himself to writing. He went to Edinburgh in 1787 to publish a second edition, but the financial rewards were not enough to live on and he had to take a job as a customs officer in Dumfriesshire. He contributed many songs to collections published by Johnson and Thomson in Edinburgh, and a 3rd edition of his poems was published in 1793. To give an idea of the prodigious writings of the man, Robert Burns composed more than 28,000 lines of verse over 22 years. Burns died of rheumatic fever in Dumfries in 1796, aged 37.

Burns wrote in Lallans, the Scottish Lowland dialect of English that is not very accessible to the Sassenach (Englishman), or foreigner; perhaps this is part of his appeal. He was also very much a man of the people, satirising the upper classes and the church for their hypocrisy.

Many of the local landmarks mentioned in the verse-tale *Tam o'Shanter* can still be visited. Farmer Tam, riding home after a hard night's drinking in a pub in Ayr, sees witches dancing in Alloway churchyard. He calls out to the one pretty witch, but is pursued by them all and has to reach the other side of the River Doon to be safe. He just manages to cross the Brig o'Doon, but his mare loses her tail to the witches.

The Burns connection in southern Scotland is milked for all it's worth and tourist offices have a *Burns Heritage Trail* leaflet leading you to every place that can claim some link with the bard. Burns fans should have a look at www.robertburns.org.

### GETTING THERE & AWAY

Stagecoach Western bus 57 operates hourly between Alloway and Ayr from 8.45am to 3.45pm Monday to Saturday (10 minutes). Otherwise, rent a bike and cycle here.

## Troon

☎ 01292 / pop 14,800

Troon, a major sailing centre on the coast 7 miles north of Ayr, has excellent sandy beaches and six golf courses. The demanding championship course **Royal Troon** ( ☎ 311555; www.royaltroon.co.uk; Craigend Rd) offers two rounds of golf for £220, including lunch in the clubhouse (caddie hire is £35 extra).

**Dundonald Castle** ( ☎ 01563-851489; Dundonald; adult/child £2.50/1.50; ❤ 10am-5pm Apr-Oct) commands impressive views and has one of the finest barrel-vaulted ceilings in Scotland. The compulsory guided tour can be tiresome, but inside you can still see the original mason's signature on the stones. It was the first home of the Stuart kings, built by Robert II in 1371, and reckoned to be the third most important castle in Scotland, after Edinburgh and Stirling. The visitor centre has a useful timeline of settlements here starting from 1500 BC. There are also models of the castle's development starting with a Dark Age fort from about 500AD.

### GETTING THERE & AWAY

Dundonald Castle is 4 miles northeast of Troon. Stagecoach Western runs hourly buses (Monday to Saturday) between Troon and Kilmarnock, via Dundonald village.

There are half-hourly trains to Ayr (£2.30, 11 minutes) and Glasgow (£5.60, 45 minutes).

**P&O** ( ☎ 0870 242 4777; www.poirishsea.com) sails twice daily to Larne in Northern Ireland (£20 for passengers, £50 to £60 for a car and driver, two hours).

## Culzean Castle & Country Park

The Scottish National Trust's flagship property, magnificent **Culzean** (NTS; cull-ane; ☎ 01655-884400; www.culzeanexperience.org; adult/child/family £12/8/30, park only adult/child £8/5; ❤ castle 10.30am-5pm

Apr-Oct, park 9.30am-sunset year round) is one of the most impressive of Scotland's great stately homes. The entrance to Culzean is a converted viaduct, and on approach the castle appears like a mirage, floating into view. Designed by Robert Adam, who was encouraged to exercise his romantic genius in its design, this 18th-century mansion is perched dramatically on the edge of the cliffs. Robert Adam was the most influential architect of his time, renowned for his meticulous attention to detail and the elegant classical embellishments with which he decorated his ceilings and fireplaces.

The beautiful oval staircase here is regarded as one of his finest achievements. On the 1st floor, the opulence of the circular saloon contrasts violently with the views of the wild sea below. Lord Cassillis' bedroom is said to be haunted by a lady in green, mourning for a lost baby. Even the bathrooms are palatial, the dressing room beside the state bedroom being equipped with a Victorian state-of-the-art shower.

There are also two ice houses, a swan pond, a pagoda, a re-creation of a Victorian vinery, an orangery, a deer park and an aviary. Wildlife in the area includes otters.

If you really want to experience the magic of this place, it's possible to stay in the **castle** (culzean@nts.org.uk; s/d from £140/225, Eisenhower ste £250/375) from April to October. If you're not in that league there's a **Camping & Caravanning Club** ( ☎ 01655-760627; tent sites members/nonmembers £8/14) with good facilities in the park.

**GETTING THERE & AWAY**

Culzean is 12 miles south of Ayr; Maybole is the nearest train station, but since it's 4 miles away it's best to come by bus from Ayr (30 minutes, 11 daily, Monday to Saturday). Buses pass the park gates, from where it's a 20-minute walk through the grounds to the castle.

## Turnberry

☎ 01655 / pop 200

Visitors playing the world-famous golf course here usually stay at the luxurious **Westin Turnberry Resort** ( ☎ 331000; www.turnberry.co.uk; r from £270), where they're able to land their private aircraft or helicopter. If you can afford the price of accommodation, a six-course dinner in the award-winning restaurant is a snip at £50.

## Kirkoswald

☎ 01655 / pop 500

Just 2 miles east of Kirkoswald, by the A77, **Crossraguel Abbey** (HS; ☎ 883113; adult/child £3.50/1.75; ⓨ 9.30am-5.30pm Apr-Sep) is a substantial ruin dating back to the 13th century that's good fun to explore. The recently renovated 16th-century gatehouse is the best part – you'll find decorative stonework and superb views from the top. Inside, if you have the place to yourself, you'll hear only the whistling wind – an apt reflection of the abbey's long-deceased monastic tradition. Don't miss the echo in the chilly sacristy.

Stagecoach Western runs Ayr to Girvan buses via Crossraguel Abbey and Kirkoswald (35 minutes, hourly Monday to Saturday, every two hours Sunday).

## Ailsa Craig

The curiously shaped island of Ailsa Craig can be seen from much of southern Ayrshire. While its unusual blue-tinted granite has been used by geologists to trace the movements of the great Ice Age ice sheet, bird-watchers know Ailsa Craig as the world's second-largest gannet colony – around 10,000 pairs breed annually on the island's sheer cliffs.

To see the island close up you can take a cruise from Girvan on the **MV Glorious** ( ☎ 01465-713219; bookings at 7 Harbour St). It's possible to land if the sea is reasonably calm; a four-hour trip costs £17/12 per adult/child (an extra £5 if you want to do a spot of fishing). A minimum of eight people and one week's notice are required.

Trains going to Girvan run approximately hourly (with only three trains Sunday) from Ayr (£4, 30 minutes).

---

**WORTH THE TRIP**

In mid-2007 a Palladian mansion, designed in the 1750s by the Adam brothers, was saved from being privately sold off. Prince Charles intervened in the break up and sale of **Dumfries House** and its contents by the Marquess of Bute. The house has been described as an architectural jewel and its preservation, dating to the 1750s, is said to be unique. It also contains an extraordinarily well-preserved collection of Thomas Chippendale furniture. Dumfries House should be open to the public in 2008 and is located 13 miles east of Ayr, near Cumnock. For information about its opening, contact the Ayr tourist office.

# DUMFRIES & GALLOWAY

Some of the region's finest attractions lie in the gentle hills and lush valleys of Dumfries & Galloway. Ideal for families, there's plenty on offer for the kids and, happily, restaurants, B&Bs and guesthouses that are very used to children. Galloway Forest is a highlight, with its sublime views, mountain-biking and walking trails, red deer, kites and other wildlife, as are the dream-like ruins of Caerlaverock Castle.

Adding to the appeal of this enticing region is a string of southern Scotland's most idyllic towns. Although they are devoid of the tourist crush, domestic day-trippers flood pretty Castle Douglas and other hotspots when the sun shines. And shine it does. Warmed by the Gulf Stream, this is the mildest region in Scotland, a phenomenon that has allowed the development of some famous gardens.

## Getting There & Around

Buses between London and Belfast, via Birmingham, Manchester, Carlisle, the towns along the A75 (including Dumfries and Newton Stewart) and Stranraer are available with **Eurolines/National Express** ( ☎ 0870 514 3219).

Local bus operators frequently change, although routes (and bus numbers) rarely alter. The main operators are **Stagecoach Western** ( ☎ 01776-704484) and **MacEwan's** ( ☎ 01387-256533). The Day Discoverer (adult/child £5/2) is a useful day ticket valid on most buses in the region and on Stagecoach Cumberland in Cumbria.

Two train lines from Carlisle to Glasgow cross the region, via Dumfries and Moffat respectively. The line from Glasgow to Stranraer runs via Ayr.

## DUMFRIES

☎ 01387 / pop 31,500

Despite having several important Burns-related museums, Dumfries has escaped mass tourism. Lovely, red-hued sandstone bridges connect the sprawling town, which is bisected by the wide River Nith, and there are pleasant grassed areas along the river bank.

Historically, Dumfries held a strategic position in the path of vengeful English armies. Consequently, although it has existed since Roman times, the oldest standing building dates from the 17th century.

## Information

There is a Royal Bank of Scotland with ATMs near the tourist office.

**Ewart library cyber centre** ( ☎ 253820; Catherine St; ☺ 9.15am-7.30pm Mon-Wed & Fri, 9.15am-5pm Thu & Sat) Free internet access at this library's excellent cyber centre.

**Laundrette** ( ☎ 252295; 26 Annan Rd; ☺ 9am-5pm Mon-Fri, 9am-4pm Sat) Wash and dry from £8.

**Tourist office** ( ☎ 253862; dumfriestic@visitscotland .com; 64 Whitesands; ☺ 9.30am-5pm Mon-Sat Apr-Jun, 9am-6pm Mon-Sat, 10.30am-4.30pm Sun Jul-Aug, 9am-5.30pm Mon-Sat, 10.30am-4.30pm Sun Sep, 9.30am-5pm Mon-Sat, 10.30am-4pm Sun Oct, 9am-5pm Mon-Sat, 9am-4pm Sun Nov, 9.30am-5pm Mon-Fri Dec-Mar) A very good tourist office with plenty of information on the region. You can book Eurolines and Scottish Citylink buses here.

## Sights

The red-sandstone bridges arching over the River Nith are the most attractive features of the town, and Devorgilla Bridge (1431) is one of the oldest bridges in Scotland.

**Burns House** ( ☎ 255297; Burns St; admission free; ☺ 10am-5pm Mon-Sat, 2-5pm Sun Apr-Sep, 10am-1pm & 2-5pm Tue-Sat Oct-Mar) is a place of pilgrimage for Burns enthusiasts. It's here that the poet spent the last years of his life, and there are some interesting relics, original letters and manuscripts.

**Robert Burns Centre** ( ☎ 264808; Mill Rd; admission free, audiovisual presentation £1.60/80p; ☺ 10am-8pm Mon-Sat, 2-5pm Sun Apr-Sep, 10am-1pm & 2-5pm Tue-Sat Oct-Mar) is an award-winning museum in an old mill on the banks of the River Nith. It tells the story of Burns and Dumfries in the 1790s. The audiovisual presentation explains the exhibition's contents, and there are original Burns manuscripts. Also check out the photographic exhibition, which includes local wildlife and some beautiful shots of the Solway coast.

Burns' **mausoleum** is in the graveyard at **St Michael's Kirk**. At the top of High St is a **statue** of the bard; take a close look at the sheepdog at his feet.

## Sleeping

**The Merlin B&B** ( ☎ 261002; 2 Kenmure Tce; r per person £25) The folks here have been doing B&B a long time and they know their stuff. The whole setup is impressive and effortless. There are three rooms – the best is No 2, which has

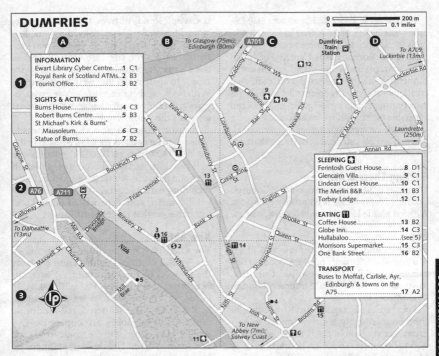

DUMFRIES

| INFORMATION | |
| --- | --- |
| Ewart Library Cyber Centre.....**1** | C1 |
| Royal Bank of Scotland ATMs...**2** | B3 |
| Tourist Office.........................**3** | B2 |

| SIGHTS & ACTIVITIES | |
| --- | --- |
| Burns House..........................**4** | C3 |
| Robert Burns Centre...............**5** | B3 |
| St Michael's Kirk & Burns' | |
| Mausoleum......................**6** | C3 |
| Statue of Burns.....................**7** | B2 |

| SLEEPING | |
| --- | --- |
| Ferintosh Guest House..............**8** | D1 |
| Glencairn Villa........................**9** | C1 |
| Lindean Guest House..............**10** | C1 |
| The Merlin B&B.....................**11** | B3 |
| Torbay Lodge........................**12** | C1 |

| EATING | |
| --- | --- |
| Coffee House........................**13** | B2 |
| Globe Inn............................**14** | C3 |
| Hullabaloo.......................(see **5**) | |
| Morrisons Supermarket...........**15** | C3 |
| One Bank Street....................**16** | B2 |

| TRANSPORT | |
| --- | --- |
| Buses to Moffat, Carlisle, Ayr, | |
| Edinburgh & towns on the | |
| A75...............................**17** | A2 |

superb river and town vistas. Little touches like homemade choccies and fresh milk in the rooms sets this place apart. Right on the river bank and next to a pedestrian bridge, it has the best location in Dumfries.

**Torbay Lodge** ( ☎ 253922; www.torbaylodge.co.uk; 31 Lovers Walk; r per person £28) New owners have breathed a bit of life into rooms that were already at a high standard at this guesthouse. There are six beautifully presented bedrooms with generously sized en suites and the good vibe is topped off with an excellent breakfast.

**Ferintosh Guest House** ( ☎ 252262; www.ferintosh .net; 30 Lovers Walk; s £30-45, d £50-56) A Victorian villa, opposite the train station, Ferintosh has sumptuous rooms done in individual themes. The whisky room is our fave – no matter which you choose, there'll probably be a free dram awaiting you on arrival. These people have the right attitude towards hospitality. The owner's original artwork complements the décor and mountain bikers are welcomed with a shed out the back for bikes.

Two B&Bs, opposite each other, that excel in the B&B trade are **Glencairn Villa** ( ☎ /fax 262467; info@glencairnvilla.co.uk; 45 Rae St; s/d from £22/48) – room No 3 is a great double – and efficiently run **Lindean Guest House** ( ☎ 251888; 50 Rae St; s/d £22/50).

## Eating

**Coffee House** ( ☎ 251771; 148 High St; snacks £2.50-3.50; ☷ 8am-6pm Mon-Sat, 11am-4.30pm Sun; ☐ ) For a relaxing pit stop smack bang in the middle of High St, check out this cheeky little number bringing a bit of caffeine snobbery to Dumfries. Grab the paper, your favourite tea or coffee and watch the world tick by.

**One Bank St** ( ☎ 279754; 1 Bank St; lunch £3.50-5.50; ☷ lunch Mon-Sat) This wee room upstairs around the corner from the tourist office (look for sign on the street) does gourmet rolls and baked potatoes, but gets even more adventurous with wraps like roast veg and humus or smoked chicken and raspberry. You can also scoff a bagel or ploughman's lunch. Roll fillings include brie and grape, or stilton and pear.

**our pick** **Globe Inn** ( ☎ 252335; 56 High St; bar mains £5.50-6.50; ☷ lunch & dinner) A traditional, rickety old nook-and-cranny pub, said to be Burns' favourite watering hole, serving great home-cooked bar meals. The Globe is atmospheric, warm and welcoming.

**Hullabaloo** ( ☎ 259679; Mill Rd; lunch mains £4.50-8.50, dinner mains £10-14; ☺ lunch daily, dinner Tue-Sat) At weekends locals flock to this contemporary restaurant at the Robert Burns Centre. For lunch there's wraps, melts and ciabattas, but come dinner time it's inventive angles on traditional creations – try butterfly bream fillet stuffed with king prawns, courgette and garlic, or Moroccan vegetable tagine with spicy couscous.

For self-caterers looking for a supermarket, you can buy all you need at the huge **Morrisons** (Brooms Rd).

## Getting There & Away
Dumfries is 80 miles southwest of Edinburgh on the A76. Stranraer is 68 miles west on the A75, via Castle Douglas and Newton Stewart.

### BUS
Eurolines and National Express run buses 920 and 921 twice daily between London/Birmingham and Belfast, via Carlisle, Dumfries, towns along the A75 and Stranraer; London to Dumfries is £29.

Local buses run regularly to Kirkcudbright (one hour, roughly hourly Monday to Saturday, six on Sunday) and towns along the A75 to Stranraer (£6.50, 2¼ hours, nine daily Monday to Saturday, three on Sunday).

Bus 100/101 runs to/from Edinburgh (£6, 2¾ hours, six daily), via Moffat and Biggar.

### TRAIN
There are trains between Carlisle and Dumfries (£7.70, 35 minutes, every hour or two, Monday to Saturday), and direct trains between Dumfries and Glasgow (£11.60, 1¾ hours, eight daily Monday to Saturday); there's a reduced service on Sunday.

## Getting Around
Bikes are available for hire from **Grierson & Graham** (Shed; ☎ 270275; The Steading, Mabie Forest; per 24hr from £16; ☺ 10am-6pm Mon-Sat) near Dumfries and close to mountain-biking terrain, but don't forget to bring photo ID and cash for your deposit. For a taxi call **Dixon's Taxis** ( ☎ 720900).

## SOUTH OF DUMFRIES
### Caerlaverock
The ruins of **Caerlaverock Castle** (HS; ☎ 01387-770244; adult/child £5/2.50; ☺ 9.30am-5.30pm Apr-Sep, 9.30am-4.30pm Oct-Mar), by Glencaple on a beautiful stretch of the Solway coast, are among the loveliest in Britain. Surrounded by a moat, lawns and stands of trees, the unusual pink-stoned triangular castle looks impregnable – in fact, it fell several times. The current castle dates from the late 13th century. Inside, there's an extraordinary Scottish Renaissance façade to apartments that were built in 1634. With nooks and crannies to explore, passageways and remnants of fireplaces, this castle is great for the whole family.

It's worth combining a visit to the castle with one to **Caerlaverock Wildlife & Wetlands Centre** ( ☎ 01387-770200; adult/child £5.50/2.75; ☺ 10am-5pm), a mile east. It protects 546 hectares of salt marsh and mud flats, the habitat for numerous birds, including barnacle geese. There's free, daily wildlife safaris with experienced rangers and a coffee shop that serves organic food.

### New Abbey
The small, picturesque village of New Abbey lies 7 miles south of Dumfries and contains the remains of the 13th-century Cistercian **Sweetheart Abbey** (HS; ☎ 01387-850397; adult/child £3/1.50; ☺ 9.30am-5.30pm Apr-Sep, 9.30am-4.30pm Sat-Wed Oct-Mar). The shattered, red-sandstone remnants of the abbey are impressive and stand in stark contrast to the manicured lawns surrounding them. The abbey was founded by Devorgilla de Balliol in honour of her dead husband (with whom she had founded Balliol College, Oxford). On his death, she had his heart embalmed and carried it with her until she died 22 years later. She and the heart are buried in the presbytery – hence the name.

**Mabie Farm Park** ( ☎ 01387-259666; www.mabiefarm park.co.uk; family/adult/child £18/5/4.50; ☺ 10am-5pm daily Apr-Oct, Sat & Sun Mar-Nov; ⚹ ) Kids complaining? Has your trip been all castles, historic sights, the odd pub and Robert Burns? Pack up the clan and get down to this park, 4 miles north of New Abbey off the A710. There's plenty of animals and activities for kids, including petting and feeding sessions, donkey rides, go-karting, hacking around in dirt buggies, slides, a soft play area, picnic areas…the list goes on – put a full day aside.

Staying in New Abbey is a good alternative to Dumfries and the **Abbey Arms** ( ☎ 01387-850489; www.abbeyarms.com; The Square; s/d £30/56) is a fine old inn with comfy rooms (nothing flash though and a bit leaky when it rains) and a good dose of homespun hospitality. The food is home-cooked (mains £8) and dishes include some Czech specials such as goulash. The Black Sheep bitter on tap is superb.

## Dalbeattie

Off the B794, 2 miles north of Dalbeattie, the **Motte of Urr** (admission free; 24hr) is one of Scotland's largest 12th-century Norman motte-and-bailey castles. About 4 miles south is the 15th-century **Orchardton Tower** (HS; Palnackie; admission free; 9.30am-5.30pm Apr-Sep, 9.30am-4.30pm Oct-Mar), the only circular tower house in Scotland; the keyholder lives in the nearby cottage.

From Dalbeattie, you can either follow the scenic coast road to Kirkcudbright or head inland on the A745 to Castle Douglas.

### Getting There & Away

From Dumfries, Stagecoach Western bus 371 runs nine times a day Monday to Saturday (twice Sunday) to Caerlaverock Castle. By car take the B725 south.

Bus 372 from Dumfries stops in New Abbey, Kirkbean, Rockcliffe, Kippford and Dalbeattie; from there bus 505 continues to Kirkcudbright (but not on Sunday).

## CASTLE DOUGLAS & AROUND

☎ 01556 / pop 3671

Castle Douglas attracts a lot of day-trippers but hasn't been 'spruced up' for tourism. It's an open, attractive, well-cared-for town. There are some remarkably beautiful areas close to the centre, such as the small **Carlingwark Loch**. The town was laid out in the 18th century by Sir William Douglas, who had made a fortune in the Americas.

The **tourist office** ( 502611; Market Hill, King St; daily Easter-Sep, Mon-Sat Oct) is in a small park on King St. The **library** ( 502643; Market Hill, King St; 10am-7.30pm Mon-Wed & Fri, 10am-5pm Thu & Sat) has free internet access.

### Sights & Activities

#### SULWATH BREWERY

You can see traditional brewing processes at **Sulwath Brewery** ( 504525; 209 King St; adult/child £3.50/free; 10am-4pm Mon-Sat). Admission includes a half-pint of Galloway real ale (tea or coffee is also available). Recommended is the Criffel, an original pale ale, and Knockendoch, a dark brew with a delicious taste of roasted malt.

#### THREAVE CASTLE

Two miles further west, **Threave Castle** (HS; 07711-223101; adult/child incl ferry £4/2; 9.30am-5.30pm Apr-Sep) is an impressive tower on a small island in the River Dee. Built in the late 14th century, it became a principal stronghold

---

**TOP FIVE DISTRACTIONS FOR KIDS IN DUMFRIES & GALLOWAY**

**Mabie Farm Park** (opposite)
**Galloway Wildlife Conservation Park** (p182)
**Cream o' Galloway** (p183)
**Galloway Forest Park** (p184)
**Caerlaverock Castle** (opposite)

---

of the Black Douglases. It's now basically a shell, having been badly damaged by the Covenanters in the 1640s, but it's a romantic ruin nonetheless.

It's a 10-minute walk from the car park to the ferry landing, where you ring a bell for the custodian to take you across to the island in a small boat.

#### LOCH KEN

Stretching for 9 miles northwest of Castle Douglas beside the A713, Loch Ken is a popular outdoor recreational area. The range of water sports includes windsurfing, sailing, canoeing, power-boating and kayaking. Back on land, off-road buggies can also be hired. **Galloway Sailing Centre** ( 01644-420626; www.lochken.co.uk; Apr-Oct), on the eastern bank north of Parton village, provides equipment, training and accommodation. Activities cost £21/42/54 for 1½, three or six hours. There are also walking trails and a rich variety of bird life. The Royal Society for the Protection of Birds (RSPB) has a **nature reserve** ( 01671-402861) on the western bank, north of Glenlochar.

### Sleeping & Eating

**Lochside Caravan & Camping Site** ( /fax 502949; Lochside Park; tent sites £10.50-12.60; Easter-Oct) This is an attractive spot beside Carlingwark Loch; there's plenty of grass and fine trees providing shade. With over 50 pitches available, booking isn't necessary.

**The Craig** ( 504840; www.thecraigcastledouglas .co.uk; 44 Abercromby Rd; s/d £25/50) This solid old property is a fine B&B with a conscientious owner, large rooms and fresh fruit served up for breakfast. It's old-fashioned hospitality – genuine and very comfortable. Would suit older visitors. It's out on the road to St John's Town of Dalry and New Galloway.

**Douglas House** ( 503262; www.douglas-house .com; 63 Queen St; s £30-35, d £75-80; ) New owners are doing away with the frill and the lace (thank god) at this well-regarded place. Instead, most rooms are sleek and contemporary with en suites that are something to behold. The two upstairs doubles are the best, although the downstairs double is huge and has a king-size bed – you could sleep four in it…if you're into that kinda thing. It's a luxury guesthouse well worth the extra coin.

**Douglas Arms Hotel** ( ☎ 502231; www.douglasarms hotel.com; 206 King St; s/d/f £50/80/90) Smack bang in the middle of town, Douglas Arms was originally a coaching inn, but these days all the mod cons comfort the weary traveller. Rooms are slowly being upgraded and No 19 is a stunner – it has a four-poster bed and views over the main drag from a collage of windows. The lively bar serves scrummy food (bar meals £8 to £12), although the atmosphere is a bit staid. The steak-and-ale pie made with Galloway beef is recommended.

**Kings Arms Hotel** ( ☎ 502626; cnr Queen & St Andrew Sts; mains £6.50-13; ☺ lunch & dinner) This traditional pub sells very traditional pub meals – and it does them pretty well. It's recommended by locals, and there are plenty of them in here scoffing the tempting morsels.

Also recommended:

**Galloway Sailing Centre** ( ☎ /fax 01644-420626; Loch Ken; dm £13.50) Year-round backpacker accommodation 6 miles north of Castle Douglas.

**Deli 173** ( ☎ 504880; 173 King St; baguette or panini £2.50; ☺ lunch) For a truly awesome baguette drop into this fine-foods deli. We recommend 'the Godfather'.

**Simply Delicious** ( ☎ 503718; 134 King St; mains £2-5; ☺ breakfast, lunch Mon-Sat) Great café serving all-day brekky (£5), luxury melts and freshly ground coffee.

## Getting There & Away

McEwan's buses 501 and 502 pass through Castle Douglas roughly hourly en route to Dumfries (45 minutes) and Kirkcudbright (20 minutes). Buses 520 and S2 along the A713 connect Castle Douglas with New Galloway (30 minutes, six daily Monday to Saturday, one Sunday) and Ayr (£6, 2¼ hours, two or three daily Monday to Saturday, one Sunday).

## KIRKCUDBRIGHT

☎ 01557 / pop 3500

Kirkcudbright (kirk-*coo*-bree), with its dignified streets of 17th- and 18th-century merchants' houses and its appealing harbour, is the ideal base from which to explore the south coast. This delightful town has one of

the most beautifully restored high streets in Dumfries & Galloway. Look out for the nook-and-cranny wynds in the elbow of High St. With its architecture and setting, it's easy to see why Kirkcudbright has been an artists' colony since the late 19th century.

## Information

There's a handy **tourist office** ( ☎ 330494; kirkcud brighttic@visitscotland.com; Harbour Sq; ☺ daily mid-Feb–Nov) with useful brochures detailing walks and road tours in the surrounding district. You'll find a bank with an ATM on St Mary St. Check out www.kirkcudbright.co.uk and www.kirk cudbrightartiststown.co.uk for heaps of information on the town.

## Sights & Activities

Kirkcudbright is a great town for a wander and it won't be long before you stumble across its charming sights.

**MacLellan's Castle** (HS; ☎ 331856; Castle St; adult/child £3.50/1.75; ☺ 9.30am-5.30pm Apr-Sep), near the harbour, is a large, atmospheric ruin built in 1577 by Thomas MacLellan, then provost of Kirkcudbright, as his town residence. Inside look for the 'lairds' lug', a 16th-century hidey hole designed for the laird to eavesdrop on his guests.

**Tolbooth Arts Centre** ( ☎ 331556; High St; admission free; ☺ 11am-5pm Mon-Sat May, Jun & Sep, 10am-5pm Mon-Sat Jul-Aug, 11am-4pm Mon-Sat Oct-Apr, 2-5pm Sun May-Oct), as well as catering for today's local artists, has an exhibition on the history of the town's artistic development. The place is as interesting for the building itself as for the artistic works on display. It's one of the oldest and best-preserved tolbooths in Scotland and interpretive signboards reveal its past.

Nearby, the 18th-century **Broughton House** (NTS; ☎ 330437; 12 High St; adult/child £8/5; ☺ noon-5pm Jul & Aug, noon-5pm Thu-Mon Apr-Jun, Sep & Oct) displays paintings by EA Hornel (he lived and worked here), one of the Glasgow Boys group of painters (p131). Behind the house is a lovely Japanese-style garden. The library with its wood panelling and stone carvings is probably the most impressive room. You need to be very interested in this style of art to justify the hefty entry fee.

**Galloway Wildlife Conservation Park** ( ☎ 331645; Lochfergus Plantation; adult/child £5/3; ☺ 10am-dusk Feb-Nov; ☺ ), a mile from Kirkcudbright on the B727, makes an easy walk from town, and you'll see red pandas, wolves, monkeys, kangaroos, Scottish wildcats and many more creatures in a beautiful setting. An important role of the park is the conservation of rare and threatened species.

## Sleeping & Eating

**Silvercraigs Caravan & Camping Site** ( ☎ /fax 330123; Silvercraigs Rd; car & tent £10.50-13) There are brilliant views from this campground; you feel like you're sleeping on top of the town. Great stargazing on clear nights. The campground has good facilities, too, including a laundry.

**Parkview** ( ☎ 330056; kathmac@talk21.com; 22 Millburn St; s/d £25/46) A small, blue-painted, traditional guesthouse off St Cuthbert St, Parkview is a great choice. Rooms are tidy and well kept. Be careful if you scale the steep staircase under the influence.

**Toadhall** ( ☎ 330204; toadh16@aol.com; 16 Castle St; d £45) This is a wonderfully eccentric house with artefacts from the owners' travels and general bric-a-brac dripping from the walls. It's very friendly, and rooms are terrific value and an excellent size (the upstairs double has a four-poster bed). It's possibly the best option in town, considering its central location, welcoming hosts and stonking breakfasts.

**Gordon House Hotel** ( ☎ /fax 330670; www.gordon -house-hotel.co.uk; 116 High St; s/d £40/70) The small, laid-back hotel rooms are in good shape, but they vary a bit, so have a look at a few. No 2 is probably the best of the doubles. You can dine in the restaurant (mains £11 to £13), which serves posh nosh like pan-seared breast of guinea fowl with tarragon and grain mustard, or the lounge bar, and there's a beer garden for sunny afternoons.

**The Castle Restaurant** ( ☎ 330569; 5 Castle St; starters £5, mains £15; ☼ dinner; 亀 ) The Castle Restaurant is the best place to eat in town and uses organic produce where possible. It covers a few bases with a chicken, beef and seafood dish on offer as well as tempting morsels for vegetarians. Try the prosciutto-wrapped monk fish with saffron-infused, roasted-red-pepper sauce. Families are welcome.

Also recommended:

**Anchorlee** ( ☎ 330197; www.anchorlee.co.uk; 95 St Mary St; r £57) Top-floor rooms are a bit frilly but very spacious and neat as a pin. All have en suites except for one.

**Selkirk Arms Hotel** ( ☎ 330402; www.selkirkarmshotel .co.uk; High St; s/d from £70/100; 亀 ) Superior rooms are excellent – wood furnishings and views over the back garden give them a rustic appeal. Try No 20. Meals are also available (mains £9 to £14, 2-/3-course dinner £18/24).

## Getting There & Away

Kirkcudbright is 28 miles southwest of Dumfries. Buses 501 and 505 run hourly to Dumfries (one hour) via Castle Douglas and Dalbeattie respectively. To get to Stranraer (about £5.80), take bus 501 to Gatehouse of Fleet (two to five daily) and change to bus 500 or X75.

## GATEHOUSE OF FLEET

☎ 01557 / pop 900

Gatehouse of Fleet is an attractive little town stretched along a sloping main street, in the middle of which sits an unusual castellated clock tower. The town lies on the banks of the Water of Fleet, completely off the beaten track, and is surrounded by partly wooded hills. There's a **tourist office** ( ☎ 814212; High St; ☼ daily Jul-Sep, Mon-Sat Easter-Jun & Oct).

One mile southwest on the A75, the well-preserved **Cardoness Castle** (HS; ☎ 814427; adult/child £3.50/1.75; ☼ 9.30am-5.30pm Apr-Sep, closed Thu & Fri Oct, to 4.30pm Sat & Sun Nov-Mar) was the home of the McCulloch clan. It's a classic 15th-century tower house with great views from the top. Back in town, **Mill on the Fleet Museum** ( ☎ 814099; High St; admission free; ☼ 10.30am-5pm Apr-Oct; 亀 ), in a converted 18th-century cotton mill, traces the history of the local industry. The town was originally planned as workers' accommodation. Check out the magnificent *View over Gatehouse* painting, and the fantastic jumbled bookshop and small gallery in the loft.

**Bobbin Guest House** ( ☎ 814229; 36 High St; s/d/f £35/50/70), situated right in the middle of town, is a homely, child-friendly place with well-appointed rooms.

The friendly, family-run **Bank of Fleet Hotel** ( ☎ 814302; www.bankoffleet.co.uk; 47 High St; s/d from £28/60) has bright rooms with a blue décor that gives them a cool, contemporary feel. Live entertainment's on offer, plus good bar meals (mains £8 to £12) – try the grilled Galloway trout.

Buses X75 and 500 between Dumfries (one hour) and Stranraer (1¼ hours) stop here eight times daily (three on Sunday). Bus 501 from Dumfries (one hour, eight daily), via Castle Douglas, terminates in the village.

## AROUND GATEHOUSE

Ideal for families, **Cream o' Galloway** ( ☎ 814040; Rainton; adult/child for visitor centre £2/4; ☼ 10am-4pm Feb & Mar, 10am-6pm Easter-Aug, 10am-5pm Sep & Oct; 亀 亀 ) has taken off big time. It offers a plethora of activities and events at the home of that delicious ice cream you'll see around the region. There are 4 miles of nature trails, an adventure playground for all ages, a 3-D maze, wildlife-watching, a farm to explore and plenty of ice cream to taste. Try the daily Ready, Steady, Freeze event (£5.50), when you get ingredients to create your own ice cream (the kids will love it!). It's about 4 miles from Gatehouse off the A75 – signposted all the way. You can also hire bikes from here.

## NEW GALLOWAY & AROUND
☎ 01644 / pop 290

New Galloway lies in the Glenkens district, north of Loch Ken. The unremarkable village is surrounded by some magnificent countryside in which you feel as if you're on a high plateau, surrounded by tumbling, short-pitched hills. This great swath of wooded landscape is unique in southern Scotland.

### Galloway Forest Park
South and northwest of town is the 300-sq-mile Galloway Forest Park, with numerous lochs and great whale-backed, heather- and pine-covered mountains. The highest point is **Merrick** (843m). The park is crisscrossed by some superb signposted walking trails, from gentle strolls to long-distance paths, including the **Southern Upland Way** (see boxed text, p152).

The 19-mile A712 (Queen's Way) between New Galloway and Newton Stewart slices through the southern section of the park.

On the shore of Clatteringshaws Loch, 6 miles west of New Galloway, is **Clatteringshaws Visitor Centre** ( ☎ for info 402420; admission free, car-park fee £1; ☑ 10.30am-5.30pm Apr-Sep), with an exhibition on the area's flora and fauna. Pick up a copy of the *Galloway Kite Trail* leaflet here, which details a circular route through impressive scenery that offers a good chance to spot one of the majestic birds. From the visitor centre you can walk to a replica of a Romano-British homestead, and to Bruce's Stone, where Robert the Bruce is said to have rested after defeating the English at the Battle of Rapploch Moss (1307).

Near the loch there are ranger-guided walks of the **Galloway Red Deer Range** ( ☎ 07771-748400; adult/child £3.50/1.50). During rutting season in autumn it's a bit like watching a bullfight as snorting, charging stags compete for the harem. Walks take place at 11am and 2pm

**MOUNTAIN-BIKING HEAVEN**

A brilliant way to experience southern Scotland's forests is by pedal power. The **7stanes** (stones) are seven mountain-biking centres around the region with trails through some of the finest forest scenery you'll find in the country. Glentrool is one of these centres and the Blue Route here is 5.6 miles in length and a lovely ride climbing up to Green Torr Ridge overlooking Loch Trool. If you've more serious intentions, the Big Country Route is 36 miles of challenging ascents and descents that afford magnificent views of the Galloway Forest. It takes a full day and is not for wimps. For more information on routes see www.7stanes .gov.uk or www.7stanes.com.

Tuesday and Thursday, and at 2.30pm Sunday from mid-June to mid-September.

Walkers and cyclists head for **Glentrool** in the park's west, accessed by the forest road east from Bargrennan off the A714, north of Newton Stewart. Located just over a mile from Bargrennan is the **Glentrool Visitor Centre** ( ☎ 01671-840302; admission free; ☑ 10.30am-4.30pm late-Mar–early May & Sep-Oct, 10.30am-5.30pm May-Aug), which stocks information on activities, including mountain biking, in the area. There is a coffee shop with snacks to replenish those weary legs. The road then winds and climbs up to Loch Trool, where there are magnificent views.

### St John's Town of Dalry
St John's Town of Dalry is a charming village, distinctly more pleasant than New Galloway, hugging the hill-side about 3 miles north on the A713. It's on the Water of Ken and gives access to the Southern Upland Way.

### Sleeping
**Kendoon Youth Hostel** (SYHA; ☎ 0870 004 1130; St John's Town of Dalry; dm adult/child £12.50/9.50; ☑ May-early Sep) This hostel, popular with walkers, is about 5 miles north of St John's on the B7000. Bus 520 stops about a mile away.

**Leamington House Hotel** ( ☎ 420327; www.leamington-hotel.com; High St, New Galloway; s/d from £25/55; ⌖ ) The Leamington has a range of rooms, with and without bathroom. The congenial owner prides herself on guest comfort and wouldn't let a fly in the bedrooms. The split-level family room would suit three people.

**The Lodgings** ( ☎ 430015; www.thelodgings.co.uk; St John's Town of Dalry; r per person £27.50) This classy little affair has just two very good rooms, one sleeping three and the other a family room sleeping five. Its advantage over other B&Bs in the town is privacy – the owners live off-site. Groups can book the whole place out. Very well located on Main St, just up from the Clachan Inn.

**Lochinvar Hotel** ( ☎ 430107; St John's Town of Dalry; s/d £40/60, with bathroom £45/70) The vine-engulfed Lochinvar, an old hunting lodge built in the 1750s with a stately interior, is a fine place to stay. It has a new set of owners and new renovation plans. Rooms vary a lot so ask to see a few. Front-facing rooms have the best views. Some of the old-fashioned en suites are 'a bit funky' but that is likely to change by the time you read this.

## Getting There & Away

Bus 521 runs once or twice daily (except Sunday) to Dumfries (55 minutes). Bus 520/S2 connects New Galloway with Castle Douglas (30 minutes, three daily Monday to Saturday, one Sunday); one to three services continue north to Ayr (1¼ to 1¾ hours).

## NEWTON STEWART

☎ 01671 / pop 3600

On the banks of the sparkling River Cree, Newton Stewart is at the heart of some beautiful countryside, and is popular with hikers and anglers. On the eastern bank, across the bridge, is the older and smaller settlement of Minnigaff. It's worth dropping into the **tourist office** ( ☎ 402431; newtonstewarttic@visitscotland .com; Dashwood Sq; ☯ 10am-3pm Mon-Sat Easter-Jun & Oct, 9.30am-4.30pm Mon-Sat, 10am-2pm Sun Jul-Sep).

For advice on landing the big one, fishing gear and permits drop into **Galloway Angling Centre** ( ☎ 401333; 1 Queen St). Also see the very useful site at www.fishgalloway.co.uk.

## Sleeping & Eating

**Minnigaff Youth Hostel** (SYHA; ☎ 0870 004 1142; Minnigaff; dm adult/child £12.50/9.50; ☯ Apr-Sep) This converted school is a well-equipped hostel with eight-bed dorms in a tranquil spot 800m north of the bridge on the eastern bank. Although it's popular with outdoor enthusiasts, you may just about have the place to yourself.

**Flowerbank Guest House** ( ☎ 402629; www.flower bankgh.com; Millcroft Rd, Minnigaff; s/d £27/58) This dignified 18th-century house is set in a magnificent landscaped garden on the banks of the River Cree. The two elegantly furnished rooms at the front of the house are slightly more expensive, but are spacious and have lovely garden views. Two-course dinners are £11.

**Galloway Arms Hotel** ( ☎ 402653; 54 Victoria St; r per person £35) A traditional refurbished hotel offering excellent-value accommodation, with good-sized, well-furnished rooms and sparkling renovated en suites. Try No 11 if you're after a double. The restaurant churns out value fare specialising in local produce and burgers (try the pork and apple burger). The New Toll House bar is both a clever and quirky renovation.

**Creebridge House Hotel** ( ☎ 402121; www.creebridge .co.uk; Minnigaff; s/d from £55/110) This is a magnificent refurbished 18th-century mansion built for the earl of Galloway. A maze inside, the tastefully decorated rooms have modern furnishings and loads of character. Try to get a room overlooking the garden (No 7 is a good one).

**Bruce Hotel** ( ☎ 402294; 88 Queen St; mains £8-15; ☯ lunch & dinner) Situated in the quieter part of town, the filling bar meals here include local seafood, venison, salmon and lamb. It's a good place to try Galloway beef (steaks £18).

## Getting There & Away

Buses stop in Newton Stewart (Dashwood Sq) on their way to Stranraer (45 minutes) and Dumfries (1½ hours), including buses 920 and 921 (Eurolines/National Express) and buses X75 and 500 (various operators, three to eight daily). Frequent buses also run south to the Isle of Whithorn.

## THE MACHARS

South of Newton Stewart, the Galloway Hills give way to the softly rolling pastures of the triangular peninsula known as the Machars. The south has many early Christian sites and the loping 25-mile **Pilgrims Way**.

Bus 415 runs every hour or two between Newton Stewart and the Isle of Whithorn (one hour) via Wigtown (15 minutes).

### Wigtown

☎ 01988 / pop 1000

Wigtown is a huge success story. Economically run down for many years, the town's revival began in 1998 when it became Scotland's National Book Town. Today 24 bookshops offer the widest selection of books in Scotland and give book enthusiasts the opportunity to get lost here for days (check out www.wig town-booktown.co.uk).

The **Book Shop** ( ☎ 402499; 17 North Main St; ☺ 9am-5pm Mon-Sat) claims to be Scotland's largest secondhand bookshop, and has a great collection of Scottish and regional titles. **Readinglasses Bookshop Café** ( ☎ 403266; 17 South Main St; ☺ 10am-5pm Mon-Sat, noon-5pm Sun) sells caffeine to prolong your reading time. It specialises in books on the social sciences and women's studies.

Folk in this town love their resident ospreys. It's a good conversation starter and if you'd like to learn a bit more about the majestic birds and see a live CCTV link to a nearby nest, drop by the **Wigtown County Buildings** (Market Sq; admission free; ☺ 10am-5pm Mon, Thu & Sat, 10am-7.30pm Tue, Wed & Fri, 2-5pm Sun) for its osprey exhibition.

Four miles west of Wigtown, off the B733, the well-preserved recumbent **Torhouse Stone Circle** dates from the 2nd millennium BC.

Wow! That's what we said when we saw the rooms in **Hillcrest House** ( ☎ 402018; www.hillcrest-wigtown.co.uk; Maidland Pl, Station Rd; s £30, d £50-66). Spend the extra and get a superior room, which have stupendous views. The colour schemes are…well, questionable, but who cares when you stay in huge, airy rooms overlooking rolling green hills and the sea beyond. This is all complemented by a ripper breakfast involving fresh local produce. Dinner also available.

Pop into the bright dining room at **Café Rendezvous** ( ☎ 402074; 2 Agnew Cres; dishes £3-6; ☺ breakfast & lunch Mon-Sat) for fresh, home-cooked paninis and filled crepes. There's also decent coffee, gooey treats and outdoor seating.

## Garlieston

You can't get more off the beaten track than Garlieston, which has a neat little harbour with a ring of 18th-century cottages behind a bowling green. A coastal path leads south to the ruins of **Cruggleton Castle**.

Drop into the **Harbour Inn** ( ☎ 01988-600685; 18 South Cres; mains £5-10; ☺ lunch & dinner) for great views and tasty pub grub.

## Whithorn

☎ 01988 / pop 900

Whithorn has a broad, attractive High St virtually closed at both ends – designed to enclose a medieval market. There are few facilities in town, but it's worth visiting because of its fascinating history.

In 397, while the Romans were still in Britain, St Ninian established the first Christian mission beyond Hadrian's Wall in Whithorn (predating St Columba on Iona by 166 years). After his death, Whithorn Priory, the earliest recorded church in Scotland, was built to house his remains, and Whithorn became the focus of an important medieval pilgrimage.

Today the priory's substantial ruins are the centre point of the **Whithorn Trust Discovery Centre** ( ☎ 500508; 45 George St; adult/child £3/1.50; ☺ 10.30am-5pm Apr-Oct), with absorbing exhibitions and an audiovisual display. The considerable remains of the old monastic settlement are being excavated and you'll see some important finds. There's also a museum with some fascinating early Christian stone sculptures, including the Latinus Stone (c 450), reputedly Scotland's oldest Christian artefact. Learn about the influences their carvers drew from around the British Isles and beyond.

## Isle of Whithorn

☎ 01988 / pop 400

The Isle of Whithorn, once an island but now linked to the mainland by a causeway, is a curious place with an attractive natural harbour and colourful houses. The roofless 13th-century **St Ninian's Chapel**, probably built for pilgrims who landed nearby, is on the windswept, evocative rocky headland. Around Burrow Head, to the southwest but accessed from a path off the A747 before you enter the Isle of Whithorn, is **St Ninian's Cave**, where the saint went to pray.

The 300-year-old **Dunbar House** ( ☎ 500336; pompeylewis@aol.com; Tonderghie Rd; s/d £22/36) overlooking the harbour has large, bright rooms. You can admire the view while tucking into your breakfast in the dining room.

The quayside **Steam Packet Inn** ( ☎ 500334; www.steampacketinn.com; Harbour Row; r per person £30-40) is a popular pub with real ales, scrumptious bar meals (mains £5 to £10), a snug bar and comfy lodgings. Try to get a room to the front of the building as they have lovely views over the little harbour (No 2 is a good one).

## STRANRAER

☎ 01776 / pop 11,000

Though a little ramshackle, Stranraer is more pleasant than the average ferry port and perhaps about to get better. There is a major waterfront development sett to take place. Stena Line is moving its Northern Ireland–bound ferry service from Stranraer harbour to Cairnryan down the road. The Stranraer waterfront in turn is undergoing a huge development to turn it into a marina. Folk in Stranraer are worried their buzzing little settlement will turn into a ghost town once Stena Line moves to Cairnryan, but as there's not much in the way of accommodation in Cairnryan, that's unlikely.

## Orientation & Information

The bus stops, train station, accommodation and tourist office are close to the new marina.

**Clydesdale Bank** (Bridge St) Has ATM.

**Stranraer library** ( ☎ 707400; North Strand St; 🕑 9.15am-7.30pm Mon-Wed & Fri, 9.15am-5pm Thu & Sat) Free internet access.

**Tourist office** ( ☎ 888143; stranraertic@visitscotland .com; 28 Harbour St; 🕑 Mon-Sat Sep–mid-Jun, daily mid-Jun–Aug) Efficient and friendly.

## Sights

Worth a quick visit, **St John's Castle** ( ☎ 705544; George St; admission free; 🕑 10am-1pm & 2-5pm Mon-Sat Easter–mid-Sep) was built in 1510 by the Adairs of Kihilt, a powerful local family. The old stone cells carry a distinctly musty smell. There are displays and a couple of videos that trace its history and, from the top of the castle, superb views of Loch Ryan and the ferries chugging out to Ireland.

**Stranraer Museum** ( ☎ 705088; 55 George St; admission free; 🕑 10am-5pm Mon-Fri, 10am-1pm & 2-5pm Sat) houses exhibits on local history and you can learn about Stranraer's polar explorers. The highlight is the carved stone pipe from Madagascar.

## Sleeping

**Aird Donald Caravan Park** ( ☎ 702025; www.aird-donald .co.uk; London Rd; tent sites for 2 £11.50) The nearest tent-friendly campground is 1 mile east of the town centre. It has manicured lawns, plenty of trees and countless bunnies.

**ourpick** **Balyett Farm Hostel & B&B** ( ☎ /fax 703395; www.balyettbb.co.uk; Cairnryan Rd; dm/s/d £15/35/50) A mile north of town on the A77, Balyett provides tranquil accommodation in its tidy hostel section, which accommodates six people and has a kitchen/living area. The relaxed B&B at the nearby ivy-covered farmhouse could be the best deal in town. The rooms are light, bright and clean as a whistle. Room No 2 is our fave but all are beautifully furnished and come with lovely aspects over the surrounding country. The real bargain are the two caravans out the front (£15 per person). They sleep up to six, and the bedrooms are very pokey, but

the living areas are excellent. It's very private, and there's a million-dollar view over the bay. The owner will let out the caravans to couples, so book ahead.

**Ivy House** ( ☎ 704176; www.ivyplace.worldonline.co.uk; 3 Ivy Pl; r per person £22-28) This is a great guesthouse and does Scottish hospitality proud, with excellent facilities, personable hosts, tidy rooms and a smashing breakfast. Nothing is too much trouble for the hosts, who always have a smile for their guests.

**North West Castle Hotel** ( ☎ 704413; www.north westcastle.co.uk; Port Rodie; s/d from £75/110; 🏊 ) Elegant and old fashioned, this is the most luxurious hotel in Stranraer and was formerly the home of Arctic explorer Sir John Ross. It's a little fussy and, although an interior designer

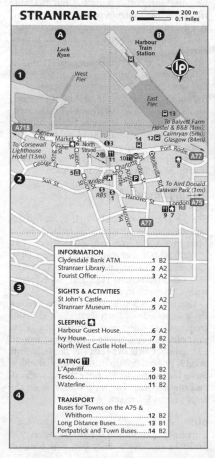

**STRANRAER**

SOUTHERN SCOTLAND

would tut tut over the busy designs and clash of colours, the rooms are sumptuous indeed. Try to get a front-facing room for seaviews. But here's the real puller: it was the first hotel in the world to have an indoor curling rink.

Also recommended:

**Harbour Guest House** ( ☎ 704626; www.harbour guesthousestranraer.co.uk; 11 Market St; B&B per person £25-30) On the harbour front, near the town centre.

**Corsewall Lighthouse Hotel** ( ☎ 853220; www .lighthousehotel.co.uk; Kirkcolm; r per person £80-135; ⓖ ) Thirteen miles northwest of Stranraer at Corsewall Point. Single occupancy is the same rate minus £20.

## Eating

**Waterline** ( ☎ 889727; North Strand St; mains £5.50-8; ⓥ lunch & dinner Mon-Sat) This chain pub across from the tourist office is soulless, but it's family friendly, close to the ferry and, for Stranraer, is a decent option for a meal or quiet drink. Good-value burgers, baguettes, pasta dishes, curries and pub faves are dished out all day.

**L'Aperitif** ( ☎ 702991; London Rd; mains £11.50-13.50; ⓥ lunch & dinner Mon-Sat) With its extensive menu, fine wines and delectable food, this is the best restaurant in town by a long shot. It's famous for its pasta, with dishes from £7.50. The service is also excellent. If you're feeling hungry, a set three-course dinner (£14.50) is available from 5.30pm to 7pm.

If you're after a supermarket for self-catering, there's a **Tesco** (Charlotte St) in town.

## Getting There & Away

### BOAT

See the Transport chapter (p452) for full details on services to Northern Ireland. From Stranraer there are two alternatives: **P&O** ( ☎ 0870 242 4777; www.poirishsea.com) ferries from Cairnryan to Larne, and **Stena Line** ( ☎ 0870 570 7070; www.stenaline.co.uk) HSS and Superferries from Cairnryan to Belfast.

Cairnryan is 5 miles north of Stranraer on the eastern side of Loch Ryan. Bus 358 runs frequently to Cairnryan (terminating at the post office). For a taxi to Cairnryan (around £7), contact **McLean's Taxis** ( ☎ 703343; 21 North Strand St; ⓥ 24hr), just up from the tourist office. Stena Line ferries for Belfast connect with rail and bus services. The train station is on the ferry pier in Stranraer.

### BUS

Eurolines and National Express buses 920 and 921 run twice daily between London and Belfast, via the towns along the A75 and Stranraer.

Scottish Citylink buses run to Glasgow (£14, 2½ hours, twice daily) and Edinburgh (£16, 3¾ hours, twice daily).

There are also several daily local buses to Kirkcudbright and the towns along the A75, such as Newton Stewart (45 minutes, at least hourly) and Dumfries (£5.80, 2¼ hours, nine daily Monday to Saturday, three on Sunday).

### TRAIN

First Scotrail runs to/from Glasgow (£17.50, 2½ hours, two to seven trains daily); it may be necessary to change at Ayr.

## AROUND STRANRAER

Magnificent **Castle Kennedy Gardens** ( ☎ 01776-702024; www.castlekennedygardens.co.uk; Rephad; adult/child £4/1; ⓥ 10am-5pm Apr-Sep, Sat & Sun Feb-Mar), 3 miles east of Stranraer, are among the most famous in Scotland. They cover 30 hectares and are set on an isthmus between two lochs and two castles (Castle Kennedy, burnt in 1716, and Lochinch Castle, built in 1864). The landscaping was undertaken in 1730 by the earl of Stair, who used unoccupied soldiers to do the work. Buses 430 (hourly) and 500 from Stranraer stop here.

## PORTPATRICK

☎ 01776 / pop 600

Portpatrick is a charming port on the rugged west coast of the Rhinns (or Rhins) of the Galloway peninsula. Until the mid-19th century it was the main port for Northern Ireland, so it's quite substantial. It's now a coastguard station and a quiet holiday resort.

It is also a good base from which to explore the south of the peninsula, and it's the starting point for the **Southern Upland Way**. You can follow part of the Way to Stranraer (9 miles). It's a cliff-top walk, followed by sections of farmland and heather moor. Start at the Way's information shelter at the northern end of the harbour. The walk is waymarked until 800m south of Stranraer, where you get the first good views of the village.

**Harbour House Hotel** ( ☎ 810456; www.theharbour househotel.co.uk; 53 Main St; s/d from £37.50/75) was formerly the customs house but is now a popular, solid old pub. Some of the tastefully furnished rooms have brilliant views over the harbour. The tariff is an extra £5 if you bring your pooch. The hotel is also a warm nook for a traditional bar meal (£7 to £10). You may have trouble dragging yourself outside again, given the delicious real ales on tap, including Kilkellan.

For total luxury, check out the **Portpatrick Hotel** (☎ 810333; www.shearingsholidays.com; Heugh Rd; r from £60) perched high above town and gazing imperiously over the harbour and out to sea. It's part of a chain, but the location is unrivalled.

Buses 358 and 367 run to Stranraer (20 minutes, eight Monday to Saturday, three Sunday).

## SOUTH OF PORTPATRICK

From Portpatrick, the road south to the Mull of Galloway passes coastal scenery that includes rugged cliffs, tiny harbours and sandy beaches. The warm waters of the Gulf Stream give the peninsula the mildest climate in Scotland.

This mildness is demonstrated at **Logan Botanic Garden** (☎ 01776-860231; www.rbge.org.uk; adult/child £3.50/1; 10am-5pm Mar & Oct, 10am-6pm Apr-Sep), a mile north of Port Logan, where an array of subtropical flora includes tree ferns and cabbage palms. The garden is an outpost of the Royal Botanic Garden in Edinburgh.

Further south, **Drummore** is a fishing village on the east coast. From here it's another 5 miles to the **Mull of Galloway**, Scotland's most southerly point. It's a rocky, bleak and windy headland. The 26m-high **lighthouse** (adults/child £2/1; tours every 30 min, 10am-3.30pm Sat & Sun Apr-Sep) here was built by Robert Stevenson in 1826. The Mull of Galloway RSPB nature reserve, home to thousands of sea birds, has a **visitor centre** (☎ 01776-830682; admission free; 10am-4pm Apr-Oct) with plenty of information on local species, including where to see them.

## ANNANDALE & ESKDALE

These valleys, in Dumfries & Galloway's east, form part of two major routes that cut across Scotland's south. Away from the highways, the roads are quiet and there are some interesting places to visit, especially if you're looking to break a road trip.

### Gretna & Gretna Green

☎ 01461 / pop 2700

This is one eccentric place, and it's worth dropping by just to experience the tourist hordes. Many people are drawn to Gretna and Gretna Green by its romantic associations (see the boxed text, below). Today's Gretna Green, on the northwestern edge of Gretna, is very touristy and very tacky – but the place has a real buzz. Such is the power of the name that about 5000 weddings are performed here annually.

The very helpful **tourist office** (☎ 337834; gretnagreen@dgtb.visitscotland.com; Gretna Gateway village, Gretna; 10am-6pm Apr-Oct, 10am-4.30pm Mon-Sat, 10am-4pm Sun Nov-Mar) is able to assist with most inquiries.

The commercialised **Old Blacksmith's Shop** (☎ 338441; Gretna Green; adult/child £3/2; 9am-7pm Jun-Sep, 9am-6pm Oct & Nov, 9am-5pm Dec-May) has an exhibition on Gretna Green's history, a sculpture park and a coach museum (there's even an anvil marriage room!).

**Hazeldene Hotel** (☎ 338292; www.hotels-gretnagreen.co.uk; Gretna Green; s/d from £40/60, honeymoon ste £120), a small hotel near the Old Blacksmith's Shop, has eight modern, comfortable rooms. The honeymoon suite has a four-poster bed, a sauna and a complimentary bottle of champagne.

Bus 79 runs between Gretna and Dumfries (one hour, hourly Monday to Saturday, every two hours Sunday). Trains run from Gretna Green to Dumfries (£6.20, 25 minutes, every hour or two, five Sunday) and Carlisle (£3.50, 11 minutes).

SOUTHERN SCOTLAND

### TYING THE KNOT IN GRETNA GREEN

From the mid-18th century, eloping couples south of the border realised that under Scottish law people could (and still can) tie the knot at the age of 16 without parental consent (in England and Wales the legal age was 21). Gretna Green's location close to the border made it the most popular venue.

At one time anyone could perform a legal marriage ceremony, but in Gretna Green it was usually the local blacksmith, who became known as the 'Anvil Priest'. In 1940 the 'anvil weddings' were outlawed, but eloping couples still got married in the church or registry office.

Today many people make or reaffirm their marriage vows in the village. If you want to get married over the famous anvil in the Old Blacksmith's Shop at Gretna Green, check out **Gretna Green Weddings** (www.gretnaweddings.com).

## Lockerbie

☎ 01576 / pop 4000

Red-sandstone buildings line the main street of this small country town. Its peace was shattered in 1988 when pieces from a Pan-Am passenger jet fell on the town after a bomb blew up the aircraft; 207 people were killed, including 11 townsfolk. In 2001 a Libyan intelligence agent was convicted of the bombing and sentenced to life imprisonment. A second Libyan was acquitted. However, in 2007 the jailed Libyan agent was granted a right of appeal. The Scottish criminal cases review commission found six instances where a miscarriage of justice may have occurred in the original case. In 2003 Libya agreed to set up a US$2.7 billion fund for the families of people killed in the bombing, admitting 'civil responsibility' for the tragedy. Little evidence of the event remains, but the townspeople have created a small garden of remembrance in **Dryfesdale Cemetery**, about a mile west on the Dumfries road.

For traditional accommodation, grab a room in the **Kings Arms Hotel** ( ☎ 202410; www .kingsarmshotel.co.uk; High St; s/d £45/75) overlooking High St and follow in the footsteps of luminaries such as Bonnie Prince Charlie and Sir Walter Scott. If you're after pampering, go for the Special Occasion package for £120, which includes breakfast in bed.

Bus 382 runs to/from Moffat (30 minutes, hourly).

## Moffat

☎ 01683 / pop 2200

Moffat lies in wild, hilly country near the upper reaches of Annandale. It's really enjoyed by the older brigade and is a popular tourist-coach spot. The former spa town is a centre for the local wool industry, symbolised by the bronze ram statue on High St. The **tourist office** ( ☎ 220620; Churchgate; ⏰ 10am-5pm Mon-Sat Apr-Jun, 9.30am-5.30pm Mon-Sat, 11am-5pm Sun Jul-Sep, 10am-4.30pm Mon-Sat, 11am-4pm Sun Oct) is well organised.

At **Moffat Woollen Mill** ( ☎ 220134; Ladyknowe; admission free; ⏰ 9am-5pm), near the tourist office, you can see a working weaving exhibition. This place is a retail bonanza – if that's your thing, you're going to love it here.

The flower-decked **Buchan Guest House** ( ☎ 220378; www.buchanguesthouse.co.uk; Beechgrove; s/d £30/56) is in a quiet street just a short walk north of the town centre. Room No 5 is a good choice, as it has a lovely outlook over nearby fields.

**ourpick Groom's Cottage** ( ☎ 220049; The Lodge, Beattock Rd; cottage per person £30) is a beautifully presented, cosy wee nook with everything you could want for a comfortable stay. There are self-catering facilities (but breakfast is included). It has good privacy from the owner's residence, views over green fields and even an orthopaedic bed. It's a stylish job and very reasonably priced – weekly deals are available too. Look for 'The Lodge' sign coming in from the M74 – it's on your left before you hit the town centre. This option is ideally suited to couples.

There are several daily buses to Edinburgh (buses 100 and X100), Glasgow (Scottish Citylink bus 974) and Dumfries (buses 100 and 114). Bus 382 runs hourly to Gretna Green (1¼ hours) and Carlisle (two hours), via Lockerbie (half an hour).

## Langholm

☎ 013873 / pop 2300

The waters of three rivers – the Esk, Ewes and Wauchope – meet at Langholm, a gracious old town at the centre of Scotland's tweed industry. Most people come for **fishing** and **walking** in the surrounding moors and woodlands; check out the **Langholm Walks website** (www.langholmwalks.co.uk) for details.

**Border House** ( ☎ 80376; High St; r per person £30) is an excellent central accommodation option with large rooms (the downstairs double in particular), a lovely hostess and big sink-in-and-smile beds.

Bus 124/112 has up to five daily connections with Eskdalemuir (no Sunday service).

## Eskdalemuir

Surrounded by wooded hills, Eskdalemuir is a remote settlement 13 miles northwest of Langholm. About 1.5 miles further north is the **Samye Ling Tibetan Centre** ( ☎ 013873-73232), the first Tibetan Buddhist monastery built in the West (1968). The colourful prayer flags and the red and gold of the temple itself are a striking contrast to the stark grey and green landscape. The centre offers meditation courses, including weekend workshops (£62) for which basic food and board is available (dorm beds £23, single £35, twin £56, breakfast £2.50 and lunch £5).

Those staying here are asked to give two hours a day to help in the kitchen, garden and farm. The temple opens to casual visitors (9am to 5pm), for whom there's also a small café.

Buses A1 and 112 from Langholm/Lockerbie stop at the centre.

# Central Scotland

The country's historical roots are deeply embedded in the sandy soils of Central Scotland. Significant ruins and castles that chronicle the region's charismatic history pepper the landscape. Key battlegrounds shaped the country's fortunes around Stirling, and Perth is the former capital where kings were crowned on the Stone of Destiny.

Arriving from the cities of Glasgow and Edinburgh, visitors begin to get a sense of the country further north as the lowland belt gives way to Highland splendour. It is here that the majesty of Scotland's landscape unfolds in deep, dark steely blue lochs that hold the shimmering silhouettes of soaring, sentinel-like craggy peaks on a still day.

This part of Scotland is big-tree country, with pockets of ancient woodlands thriving side by side with regrowth forests, some planted by visionary landowners 300 years ago. Opportunities to enjoy the landscape abound and walking, cycling, mountaineering and wildlife safaris are all easy possibilities. Capping off the exhaustingly fresh outdoors are some of the country's best pubs and eateries, which greet weary visitors at the end of the day.

It's also the variety in the region that pulls the punters – learn all about crannogs, have a drink in an ancient pub that holds scrawlings from Robert Burns, throw a line into a picture-perfect loch and explore one of the country's most stunning wooded glens all in a day.

The coastline along the 'kingdom' of Fife offers quaint fishing villages along East Neuk and one of Scotland's most enjoyable towns – St Andrews. The township, touched with a gentle dignity, has a medieval shell that belies the sophistication and dynamism of a student population drawn from around the globe.

## HIGHLIGHTS

- Walking the eerie fields of Bannockburn and rambling through the imperious castle lording it over the city in **Stirling** (p193)
- Mixing history, nostalgia and, of course, golf on the hallowed fairways of **St Andrews Old Course** (p211)
- Bagging magnificent **Ben Lawers** (p224), and keeping an eye out for Neolithic rock art on the way
- Whizzing down the slopes of **Glenshee** (p230), one of the country's largest ski runs
- Nursing a pint of Ale of Atholl and toasting the toes by a roaring log fire at the **Moulin Inn** (p229), a pub dripping with Scottish character.

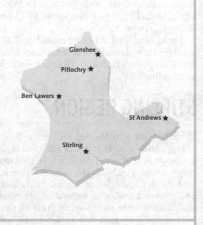

Glenshee

Pitlochry

Ben Lawers

St Andrews

Stirling

- POPULATION: 764,000
- AREA: 9254 SQ KM

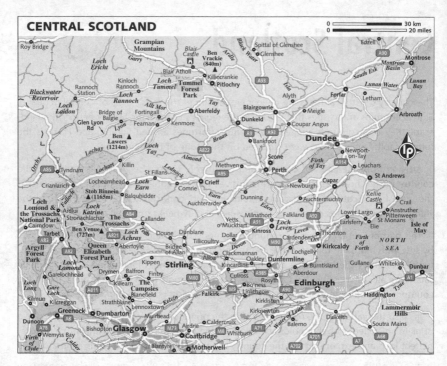

CENTRAL SCOTLAND

## Getting Around

For public-transport info, call **Traveline** ( ☎ 0871 200 2233). **Scottish Citylink** ( ☎ 0870 550 5050) connects the main towns in the area, and Perth is a major hub for its services. **Royal Mail postbuses** ( ☎ 01246-546329) serve many remote communities, such as those in West Perthshire, charging on average £2 to £5 for single journeys.

The Central Scotland Rover rail ticket (£30), valid for three days out of seven, allows train travel between Edinburgh, Glasgow, Falkirk and Stirling.

# STIRLING REGION

Stirling is one of those regions central Scotland specialises in. It provides a taste of both lowlands and Highlands; has a staggering share of landmark battlegrounds; is peppered with castles and tales of legendary figures; and contains a slice of natural beauty that will literally leave you gasping. And all that packed cheek by jowl into such a small and delightful area.

The capital, also named Stirling, controlled the main route into the Highlands and its strategic location meant it was the stage for some of Scotland's crucial battles of independence against the repressive English. The region was home to Rob Roy, and the legendary exploits of this champion of the poor still echo around the southern border of the Highlands.

The region has lured walkers and climbers since Victorian times, and the forests and wildlife in this unique environment are protected as part of the Loch Lomond & the Trossachs National Park (p267).

## Getting Around

For local transport information in the Stirling region, phone ☎ 01786-442707. The main bus operator is **First** ( ☎ 0870 872 7271). Its First-Day ticket (£5) gives one day's travel on all its services in the central Scotland region and through to Edinburgh or Glasgow.

From late May (although sometimes delayed until June or July) to early October the vintage **Trossachs Trundler** ( ☎ 01786-442707) is a useful bus service circling Aberfoyle, Callander and Trossachs Pier on Loch Katrine.

A day ticket per adult/child is £8/2.80. The bus is wheelchair accessible and can carry two bikes. It runs four times daily except Wednesday. Stirling town is the rail hub, but the lines only skirt the rest of the region.

## STIRLING

☎ 01786 / pop 45,500

Stirling lies at one of Scotland's most strategic sites and has been at the heart of many conflicts. There's a hustle and bustle on the streets and footpaths during the day, but at night it all disappears and a twilight walk of the old town can be magical. In the right light and away from the buzz of the retail calamity in the centre, there's something a bit fairytale-like about Stirling. For visitors the city rivals Edinburgh (but on a smaller scale) for historical attractions and the atmosphere of its old town.

Replete with winding cobblestone streets, the old town clings to the slopes beneath the castle and the fascinating remnants divulge tales of Stirling's historical development, stretching over a 500-year period. Another parallel with Edinburgh is the magnificent castle, perched high on a rocky outcrop gazing over the city. The old town slopes up from the train and bus stations to the castle, which sits 75m above the plain atop the plug of an extinct volcano.

## Information

**Post office** (Barnton St)
**Royal Bank of Scotland** (Barnton St) Has an ATM.
**Stirling Library** (Corn Exchange Rd; ☾ 9.30am-5.30pm Mon, Wed & Fri, to 7pm Tue & Thu, to 5pm Sat) Free internet access.
**Stirling Royal Infirmary** ( ☎ 434000; Livilands Rd) Hospital; south of the town centre.
**Tourist office** ( ☎ 0870 720 0620; info@stirling .visitscotland.com; 41 Dumbarton Rd; ☾ Mon-Sat year-round, plus Sun Jun–mid-Sep; ☐ ) Plenty of brochures about Stirling's attractions and the region, but service from staff is patchy.

## Sights

### STIRLING CASTLE & ARGYLL'S LODGING

Hold Stirling and you control the whole country. This simple strategy has ensured that a **castle** (HS; ☎ 450000; adult/child incl Argyll's Lodging £9/4.50; ☾ 9.30am-6pm Apr-Sep, to 5pm Oct-Mar; ☐ ) has existed here since prehistoric times. The superb views it commands mean you cannot help drawing parallels with Edinburgh Castle – but Stirling is better. Location, architecture and historical significance combine to make it one of the grandest of all Scottish castles.

There has been a fortress of some kind here for several thousand years, but the current building dates from the late 14th to the 16th century, when it was a residence of the Stuart monarchs. The Great Hall and Gatehouse were built by James IV; observe the hammer-beam roof and huge fireplaces in the largest medieval hall in Scotland and the result of 35 years' worth of restoration.

The spectacular palace was constructed in the reign of James V (1513–42); however, the Royal Lodgings may be temporarily closed to visitors as they are part of the last phase of the castle's massive restoration project.

James VI (r 1567–1625) remodelled the Chapel Royal and was the last king of Scots to live here.

In the King's Old Building is the **museum of the Argyll & Sutherland Highlanders** (admission free, donations encouraged), which traces the history of this famous regiment from 1794 to the present day. It has a great collection of ornately decorated dirks (daggers).

The **Royal Burgh of Stirling Visitor Centre** ( ☎ 479901; Castle Esplanade; admission free; ☾ 9.30am-6pm Apr-Oct, to 5pm Nov-Mar) has an audiovisual presentation and exhibition about Stirling, including the history and architecture of the castle.

There's a car park next to the castle (£2 for two hours).

Complete with turrets, spectacular **Argyll's Lodging** is the most impressive 17th-century town house in Scotland and you'll find it by the castle, at the top of Castle Wynd. It's the former home of William Alexander, Earl of Stirling and noted literary figure. It has been tastefully restored and gives an insight into lavish, 17th-century aristocratic life.

### OLD TOWN

Below the castle, the old town has a remarkably different feel to modern Stirling, its cobblestone streets packed with fine examples of 15th- to 17th-century architectural gems. Its growth began when Stirling became a royal burgh, about 1124, and in the 15th and 16th centuries rich merchants built their houses here. The steep slopes ensure visitors will enjoy recuperation in a nearby coffee shop or pub after exploring for a couple of hours.

**CENTRAL SCOTLAND**

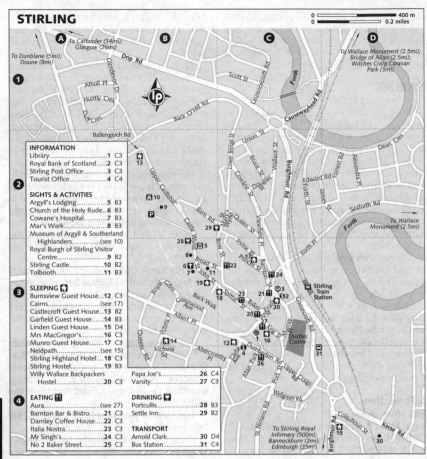

**STIRLING**

| INFORMATION | |
|---|---|
| Library.......................1 | C3 |
| Royal Bank of Scotland.........2 | C3 |
| Stirling Post Office...........3 | C3 |
| Tourist Office.................4 | C4 |

| SIGHTS & ACTIVITIES | |
|---|---|
| Argyll's Lodging...............5 | B3 |
| Church of the Holy Rude....6 | B3 |
| Cowane's Hospital..............7 | B3 |
| Mar's Wark.....................8 | B3 |
| Museum of Argyll & Southerland Highlanders...............(see 10) | |
| Royal Burgh of Stirling Visitor Centre......................9 | B2 |
| Stirling Castle...............10 | B2 |
| Tolbooth.....................11 | B3 |

| SLEEPING | |
|---|---|
| Burnsview Guest House....12 | C3 |
| Cairns...................(see 17) | |
| Castlecroft Guest House....13 | B2 |
| Garfield Guest House......14 | B3 |
| Linden Guest House.......15 | D4 |
| Mrs MacGregor's...........16 | C3 |
| Munro Guest House........17 | C3 |
| Neidpath..................(see 15) | |
| Stirling Highland Hotel....18 | C3 |
| Stirling Hostel...........19 | B3 |
| Willy Wallace Backpackers Hostel.....................20 | C3 |

| EATING | |
|---|---|
| Aura......................(see 27) | |
| Barnton Bar & Bistro......21 | C3 |
| Darnley Coffee House......22 | C3 |
| Italia Nostra.............23 | B3 |
| Mr Singh's................24 | C3 |
| No 2 Baker Street.........25 | C3 |

| | |
|---|---|
| Papa Joe's................26 | C4 |
| Varsity..................27 | C3 |

| DRINKING | |
|---|---|
| Portcullis.................28 | B3 |
| Settle Inn................29 | B2 |

| TRANSPORT | |
|---|---|
| Arnold Clark..............30 | D4 |
| Bus Station...............31 | C4 |

Stirling has the best surviving town wall in Scotland. It was built around 1547 when Henry VIII of England began the 'Rough Wooing' – attacking the town in order to force Mary, Queen of Scots to marry his son so that the two kingdoms could be united. The wall can be explored on the **Back Walk**, which follows the line of the wall from Dumbarton Rd (near the tourist office) to the castle, continuing around Castle Rock and back to the old town.

**Mar's Wark**, on Castle Wynd at the head of the old town, is the ornate façade of what was once a Renaissance-style town house commissioned in 1569 by the wealthy earl of Mar, regent of Scotland during James VI's minority.

The **Church of the Holy Rude** (St John St; admission free; 11am-4pm Easter-Sep) has been the town's

parish church for 600 years and James VI was crowned here in 1567. The nave and tower date from 1456, and the church has one of the few surviving medieval open-timber roofs. It's the only remaining church in Scotland that's seen a coronation. Stunning stained-glass windows and huge stone pillars create a powerful effect.

Behind the church is **Cowane's hospital** ( 472247; 49 St John St; admission free; no set hr). Built as an almshouse in 1637 by the merchant John Cowane, its medicinal methods now include hosting *ceilidhs* (evenings of traditional Scottish entertainment), banquets and exhibitions. There's a family-tree database where you can search for your ancestry if they were born around this area.

The **Mercat Cross**, in Broad St, is topped with a unicorn and was once surrounded by a bustling market. Nearby is the **Tolbooth**, built in 1705 as the town's administrative centre. A courthouse and jail were added in the following century, and it was renovated in 2001 to become the city's premier arts and music venue.

### BANNOCKBURN

On 24 June 1314, the greatest victory in the history of Scotland's struggle to remain independent took place at the Battle of Bannockburn. Robert the Bruce overcame superior numbers and sent Edward II's English force running for their lives. In the long and bitter struggle against the threat of English domination, this victory turned the tide of fortune sufficiently in favour of the Scots for the following 400 years.

**Bannockburn Heritage Centre** (NTS; ☎ 812664; Glasgow Rd; adult/child £5/4; ☑ 10am-5.30pm Apr-Oct, 10.30am-4pm Mar) tells the story of the battle in a simple and eloquent exhibition, including a 12-minute audiovisual display that stirs the imagination, helping to bring the historic battle to life. There are also interesting dioramas about medieval Scotland and the Battle of Stirling Bridge. Outside is the eerie Borestone site, said to have been Robert the Bruce's command post before the battle. Check out his grim-looking statue, dressed in full battle gear and mounted on a charger. The battle site itself never closes. Bannockburn is located 2 miles south of Stirling.

### WALLACE MONUMENT

Two and a half miles north of Stirling is Scotland's impressive Victorian **monument** ( ☎ 472140; Abbey Craig, Hillfoots Rd, Causewayhead; adult/child/family £6.50/4/15; ☑ 10am-5pm Mar-May & Oct, to 6pm Jun, 9am-6pm Jul & Aug, 9.30am-5.30pm Sep, 10.30am-4pm Nov-Feb) to Sir William Wallace, who was hung, drawn and quartered by the English in 1305. The view from the top, of no less than seven battlegrounds, is as breathtaking as the 67m climb up to it. The monument contains interesting displays, including a parade of other Scottish heroes and Wallace's mighty two-handed sword. Clearly, the man was no weakling.

## Tours

From April to October, **City Sightseeing** ( ☎ 446611; www.citysightseeing.co.uk) runs an open-top, hop-on, hop-off bus tour daily, departing every 45 minutes (hourly November to March). It runs between the castle and the Wallace Monument via Bridge of Allan. A day ticket costs £7.50/3 per adult/child.

## Sleeping

### BUDGET

**Willy Wallace Backpackers Hostel** ( ☎ 446773; www .willywallacehostel.com; 77 Murray Pl; dm £10-14, d £35) This is a friendly, grungy hostel in the middle of town, and the focal point of the traveller's scene. There are mixed, male and female dorms (quite cramped) generally accommodating six to 12 beds. The lounge area has comfy chairs and great views.

**Stirling Hostel** (SYHA; ☎ 0870 004 1149; St John St; dm adult/child £15.50/12; ☐ ) The façade of an 18th-century church conceals this place, which is in a perfect location in the old part of town. It's a superb, modern hostel with 126 beds in four-to six-bed dorms. A less attractive annexe in Union St opens in summer only.

**Witches Craig Caravan Park** ( ☎ 474947; www.witches craig.co.uk; Blairlogie; tent sites £12-16; ☑ Apr-Oct) In a

---

**WILLIAM WALLACE, SCOTTISH PATRIOT**

William Wallace is one of Scotland's most endearing heroes and a patriot whose exploits helped revive interest in Scottish history. Born in 1270, he was catapulted into fame and a place in history as a highly successful guerrilla commander who harassed the English invaders for many years.

Wallace was knighted by Robert the Bruce and proclaimed Guardian of Scotland in March 1298. However, it was only a short time before English military superiority and the fickle nature of the nobility's loyalties would turn against the defender of Scottish independence.

Disaster struck in July of that year when King Edward's force defeated the Scots at the Battle of Falkirk. Wallace resigned as guardian, went into hiding, and travelled throughout Europe to drum up support for the Scottish cause. Many of the Scots nobility were prepared to side with Edward, and Wallace was betrayed after his return to Scotland in 1305.

Sir William Wallace was tried for treason at Westminster, and he was hanged, beheaded and disembowelled at Smithfield, London.

brilliant spot right at the foot of the Ochil Hills, which are begging to be walked, Witches Craig is 3 miles east of Stirling by the A91. It's a former 'national loo of the year' winner.

### MIDRANGE

**Burnsview Guest House** ( ☎ 451002; www.burnsview -guesthouse.com; 1 Albert Pl; d per person £20-26) Burnsview has four renovated rooms, two with en-suite facilities. The breakfast has been recommended, as has the high standard of hospitality. It's not for party animals, though – the thoughtful owners enjoy hosting discerning guests.

**Mrs MacGregor's** ( ☎ /fax 471082; www.sruighlea.com; 27 King St; d £40-50) This place feels like a secret hideaway, but it's conveniently located smack bang in the centre of town. You'll feel like a local staying here, and there are eating and drinking places practically on the doorstep. It's a B&B that welcomes guests with the kind of warmth that keeps them returning.

**Garfield Guest House** ( ☎ 473730; 12 Victoria Sq; s £26-56, d £50-60) This grand old Victorian dame has seen better days, but once a stunner always a stunner. Inside is detailed cornice work, floor to ceiling mirrors and, of course, floral carpets – it wouldn't be a guesthouse without them. The very comfy rooms are mostly palatial in size, and enormous bay windows overlooking the square opposite open onto lovely green views. It's a magnificent property in a peaceful, leafy area of town.

Two high-quality guesthouses sit side by side in a great central location about 10 minutes from the castle. **Munro Guest House** ( ☎ 472685; www.munroguesthouse.co.uk; 14 Princes St; s £28-40, d £46-54) is a family-run place with five en-suite rooms all bordering on luxurious, and friendly **Cairns** ( ☎ 479228; 12 Princes St; s £25, d & tw £50) next door has a double and a twin, both with en suite, and two single rooms. You can take a room here without breakfast.

Other recommendations:

**Neidpath** ( ☎ 469017; www.neidpath-stirling.co.uk; 24 Linden Ave; s/d £35/48) Spotless rooms and a filling breakfast.

**Linden Guest House** ( ☎ /fax 448850; www.linden guesthouse.co.uk; 22 Linden Ave; s £45, d £50-58) For those who like their creature comforts. High-standard accommodation.

**Castlecroft Guest House** ( ☎ 474933; www.castle croft-uk.com; Ballengeich Rd; s/d/f £50/55/68) Brilliant location, nestled just under the castle and blessed with panoramic views of the countryside. Couples should go

or the family room; it's worth the extra coin for the stupendous views.

### TOP END

**Stirling Highland Hotel** ( ☎ 272727; stirling@paramount -hotels.co.uk; Spittal St; r from £100; 🖳 ) The smartest hotel in town, Stirling Highland Hotel is a sympathetic refurbishment of the old high school. It's very convenient for the castle and old town and the rooms are deluxe, although staying in an old school may not generate good memories for everyone.

## Eating

**Barnton Bar & Bistro** ( ☎ 461698; 312 Barnton St; mains £3.50-5.50; 🕙 daily until late) Opposite the post office, this is a very popular, grungy hang-out serving excellent all-day breakfasts, chilli, homemade lasagne and burgers. It is a great place to eat or drink, and there's something on most weeknights, including a Friday night disco. Good options for vegetarians, too.

**Varsity** ( ☎ 461041; 1 Corn Exchange Rd; mains £5; 🕙 lunch & dinner) Attracting the town's style-cats, this trendy, nouveau bar-café serves cheap food. The décor and furnishings are young at heart, as is the pop music on large TV screens. Pub mains plus hot melts and salads tickle the tastebuds.

**Darnley Coffee House** ( ☎ 474468; 18 Bow St; snacks £3.50-5; 🕙 breakfast & lunch) Just down the hill from the castle, beyond the end of Broad St, Darnley Coffee House is a good pit stop for home baking and speciality coffees during a walk around the old town.

**No 2 Baker Street** (2 Baker St; mains £5-8; 🕙 lunch & dinner) Great pub options with a few innovations, such as wild mushroom Wellington (veggie option) or a Caerphilly cheese and leek burger, or crab and coldwater prawn salad. Excellent selection of real ales on tap.

**Aura** ( ☎ 470333; 51 King St; lunch mains £7-9, dinner mains £10-16; 🕙 breakfast weekends, lunch daily, dinner Tue-Sat) Aura is an interesting mix – American deli by day dishing out giant sandwiches, and wine bar and restaurant day and night. Muted tones entice diners into its soft, relaxing environment, ideal for a wonderful meal. The early evening dinner special means small mains are only £7, including Moroccan beef or mussels in garlic sauce. There's plenty for vegetarians, too. On our visit the amateurish service was a letdown.

**Italia Nostra** ( ☎ 473208; 25 Baker St; pizza & pasta £11-16; 🕙 lunch & dinner; 🚼 ) The Nostra is a busy

Italian place popular with families. It has a warm, friendly atmosphere and is also good for women or solo travellers. There's a large menu, including delicious *gelato*, and it does takeaways.

Also recommended:

**Papa Joe's** ( ☎ 446414; 21 Dumbarton Rd; lunch mains £5.50, dinner mains £7-14; ☒ lunch Sat, dinner daily) Dine on excellent pizzas, pasta and some Tex-Mex dishes among an eclectic collection of antiques, musical instruments and sporting paraphernalia. Good wine list. Friendly, efficient service.

**Mr Singh's** ( ☎ 472137; 16-18 Barnton St; starters £4, mains £6-8; ☒ lunch & dinner Mon-Sat, dinner Sun) Fine curry house with a terrific-value buffet lunch (£6). Four-course buffet dinner is £12 on Sunday, Tuesday and Thursday nights. Dishes from all over India, including Goanese, Punjabi and Biryani dishes.

## Drinking

**Portcullis** ( ☎ 472290; Castle Wynd) With a friendly atmosphere and a great location just below the castle, this is the best pub in Stirling. Excellent bar meals are served all day and there's a large range of malt whiskies, too.

**Settle Inn** ( ☎ 474609; 91 St Mary's Wynd) Established in 1733, the Settle Inn is the oldest pub in Stirling and is a good place to rest weary legs and enjoy a cosy drink, especially when the rain is lashing outside.

Barnton Bar & Bistro (opposite) is another popular place for a drink.

## Getting There & Away

### BUS

Scottish Citylink runs frequent buses to/from Glasgow (£5, 45 minutes). Some buses continue to Aberdeen (£20, 3½ hours) via Perth (£6) and Dundee (£10); others go to Inverness. For buses to Inverness (£16, 3½ hours) you'll usually have to change at Perth. A four-times-daily service from Edinburgh to Fort William goes via Stirling once a day (with connections to Oban or Skye); fares to Edinburgh, Oban, Fort William and Portree are £5, £17, £17.50 and £30, respectively. All buses go from the bus station on Goosecroft Rd.

First runs local buses (to Callander, Aberfoyle – both £3.50 – for example) and operates an express service to Edinburgh (£4.50, one hour, hourly Monday to Saturday).

### TRAIN

First ScotRail has services to/from Edinburgh (£6.20, 55 minutes, at least twice hourly Mon-

day to Saturday, hourly Sunday). Services run at least twice an hour from Glasgow (£6.50, 40 minutes, every two hours or so on Sunday), and there are regular services to Perth (£9.30, 35 minutes), Dundee (£14.30, 55 minutes) and Aberdeen (£35, 2¼ hours).

## Getting Around

It's easy enough to walk around the central part of the town.

If you want wheels, you can hire a car from **Arnold Clark** ( ☎ 478686; www.arnoldclarkrental.co.uk; Kerse Rd). The cheapest deal is for an economy car at around £20 per day.

# AROUND STIRLING
## Bridge of Allan
☎ 01786 / pop 4600

This upbeat former spa town, just 2.5 miles north of Stirling, has an open street plan, giving it a laid-back sense of space. It's a good alternative to staying in Stirling.

At the **Bridge of Allan Brewery** ( ☎ 834555; Queen's Lane; admission free; ☒ noon-5pm daily Jul-Sep, noon-5pm Sat & Sun Oct-Jun), just off Henderson St, you can learn about the microbrewing techniques behind traditional Scottish ales. This is a great spot to taste local beers – it's very friendly and the genuine quality microbrews are recommended, particularly the Wallace Monument (tastings are free).

### SLEEPING & EATING

**our pick** **Inverallan Lodge** ( ☎ 832791; david .thursby@tesco.net; 116 Henderson St; s/d/f £30/50/60) This is the best guesthouse in town and a travellers' favourite. Down to earth, perpetually friendly (but not overbearing) and good value, the lodge has decent-sized rooms, some with huge bay windows drawing in lots of light.

**Anam Cara** ( ☎ 832030; caringclown@hotmail.com; 107 Henderson St; s/d £35/50) A simple B&B with a double and a twin room, the attraction here is your host – she's a laughter therapist. If everything is a bit grey outside and your time in Scotland is getting you down, this may be just the place for you. Make sure you knock on the door of No 107 around the side of the house (No 109 is not the smiley place).

**Queen's Hotel** ( ☎ 833268; www.queenshotelscotland .com; 24 Henderson St; s/d £100/160) Gorgeous, modern, plush rooms here have a dark and fuzzy décor that makes you want to get naked and have a good roll around. All rooms have car-wash showers, but only some come with bath.

The rooms are different sizes, so ask to see a selection and ask about weekend specials. Even if you're not staying, drop in for lunch or dinner and taste the contemporary cooking in the bar; mains are £7 to £10.

**Clive Ramsay Café** (☎ 831616; Henderson St; mains £8-12; ⏰ breakfast, lunch & dinner) With a claim to 'sexy food', this little show pony also has a wonderful deli next door selling fresh local produce. The café has a very trendy vibe and somehow seems the centre of the town's universe. Thai fish cakes with Asian-style coleslaw or Catalan-style paella won't break your budget.

**Jekyll's Restaurant** (☎ 833268; www.queenshotelscotland.com; 24 Henderson St; 2/3 courses £24/29; ⏰ dinner) For serious foodies, this restaurant attached to the Queen's Hotel does delightful and imaginative things with Scottish produce.

### GETTING THERE & AWAY

You can walk to Bridge of Allan from Stirling in just over an hour. Frequent local buses from Stirling stop in Henderson St. Trains to Dunblane, Stirling, Glasgow and Edinburgh depart frequently from the station at the western end of Henderson St.

## Dunblane

**☎ 01786 / pop 8000**

Dunblane is a very enjoyable town to wander, although the name will always be associated with the horrific massacre in which 16 children and a teacher were murdered in the local primary school in March 1996.

The main attraction is the fabulous **Dunblane Cathedral** (HS; ☎ 823388; Cathedral Sq; admission free; ⏰ 9.30am-5.30pm Mon-Sat, 2-5.30pm Sun Apr-Sep, 9.30am-4.30pm Mon-Sat, 2-4.30pm Sun Oct-Mar), which is well worth a detour. It's a superb, elegant sandstone building – a fine example of Gothic style. The lower parts of the walls date from Norman times, the rest mainly 13th to 15th century. There is a sculpted Pictish stone on display (found on the site), suggesting that it was used as a centre of worship well before the current structure existed.

The musty old **Leighton Library** (☎ 822296; 61 High St; admission free; ⏰ 10am-12.30pm & 2-4.30pm Wed-Fri May-Oct), dating from 1684, is the oldest private library in Scotland. There are 4500 books in 90 languages.

You can walk to Bridge of Allan from Dunblane along Darn Rd, an ancient path used by monks, in about an hour. Alternatively, Scottish Citylink buses run to Stirling, Glasgow and Perth once every hour or two. Trains to Stirling and Glasgow or Edinburgh are more frequent – roughly three per hour, fewer on Sunday.

# THE CAMPSIES & STRATHBLANE

The beautiful Campsie Fells, commonly called the Campsies, reach nearly 600m and lie 10 miles north of Glasgow. The plain of the River Forth lies to the north; Strathblane and Loch Lomond lie to the west.

One of several villages around the Campsies, attractive **Killearn** is known for its 31m-high obelisk, raised in honour of George Buchanan, James VI's tutor. Eight miles to the east, **Fintry** has carved itself a gorgeous spot deep in the Campsies on the banks of Endrick Water, which has an impressive 28m waterfall, the **Loup of Fintry**. Six miles north of Fintry, **Kippen** has a very attractive **parish church** (⏰ 9.30am-5pm). In the west (on the West Highland Way) is **Drymen**, a pretty village with lots of character, which is popular due to its close proximity to Loch Lomond.

## Activities

One of the best walks in the area is the ascent of spectacular Dumgoyne hill (427m) from Glengoyne distillery, about 2 miles south of

CENTRAL SCOTLAND

### WORTH THE TRIP

**Doune Castle** (HS; ☎ 01786-841742; Castle Rd, Doune; adult/child £4/2; ⏰ 9.30am-5.30pm Apr-Sep, to 4.30pm Sat-Wed Oct-Mar) is one of the best-preserved 14th-century castles in Scotland, having remained largely unchanged since it was built for the duke of Albany. It was a favourite royal hunting lodge, but was also of great strategic importance because it controlled the route between the Lowlands and Highlands, and Mary, Queen of Scots stayed here. The inner hall was restored in 1883. There are great views from the castle walls, and the lofty gatehouse is very impressive, rising nearly 30m. If you're a Monty Python fan, you may recognise the castle from the *Holy Grail*.

Doune is 7 miles northwest of Stirling. First buses run every hour or two to Doune from Stirling (30 minutes), less frequently on Sunday.

Killearn. Allow at least one hour for the ascent of Dumgoyne. It will take another hour to Earl's Seat, and 1½ hours to return from there to the distillery. The tourist office in Drymen and other local offices have detailed route information.

## Sleeping & Eating

**Elmbank B&B** ( ☎ 01360-661016; Stirling Rd, Drymen; s £28, d £23-27) Just off the square, this substantial property offers a variety of rooms and has a very friendly owner. The recommended rooms include the large double with en suite downstairs and the smallish double upstairs with king-size bed. The owner will happily do deals for singles and groups.

**Culcreuch Castle** ( ☎ 01360-860555; Fintry; r per person £60-90) Fancy a night in a 700-year-old castle? Culcreuch dates to 1296 and is a remarkably well-preserved historic building. The 14 rooms are individually styled with Victorian décor. Most rooms are sumptuous and look out onto the collage of greenery engulfing the surrounding estate. A little dowdy perhaps, and popular with groups, but this place, with its period furnishings, has real character. The castle is signposted from the village and is 600m off the B822 coming into Fintry.

**Black Bull Hotel** ( ☎ 01360-550215; www.blackbull hotel.com; 2 The Square, Killearn; s/d £75/110; ) The 15 rooms at this stylish, modern hotel are in a historic shell with plenty of character. It's a small, intimate family-run place. The excellent service and top-notch facilities ensure most visitors are repeat clientele.

**Clachan Inn** ( ☎ 01360-660824; The Square, Drymen; mains £7-18;  lunch & dinner) The best place to eat in the area is the cosy Clachan Inn (opened in 1734). The extensive menu includes steaks, burgers, salads and vegetarian dishes. Try the seafood salad for lunch, washed down beautifully with a pint of St Andrews Ale.

Also recommended:

**Fintry Inn** ( ☎ 01360-860224; www.thefintryinn.com; 23 Main St, Fintry; r per person £25) Above the inn is a self-catering flat sleeping up to six. Continental breakfast only.

**Lander B&B** ( ☎ 01360-660273; www.bandb.labbs.com; 17 Stirling Rd, Drymen; s/d £25/40) Simple B&B lodgings, private access to guest rooms – very homely.

## Getting There & Away

First bus 10 runs from Glasgow to Killearn and Balfron every hour or two; change at Balfron for Aberfoyle (£4.50 from Glasgow). There are frequent daily services (except Sunday) between Balfron and Drymen on First bus 8. A Royal Mail postbus runs twice on weekdays between Balfron and Fintry, once on Saturday.

## THE TROSSACHS

The Trossachs has been a major tourist draw since the early 19th century when Sir Walter Scott's historical novel *Rob Roy* brought eager visitors to the region. In the 21st century its natural beauty, variety of wildlife and fragile environment have been recognised with the establishment of the Loch Lomond & the Trossachs National Park (p267).

The narrow glen between Loch Katrine and Loch Achray is actually named the Trossachs, but the term is now used to describe a wider scenic area around the southern border of the Highlands.

### Aberfoyle & Around
☎ 01877

Crawling with visitors most weekends and dominated by a huge car park, Aberfoyle (population 576) is a hit with domestic tourists as it provides a convenient base to explore the beautiful Trossachs. It's a fairly uninteresting place though, easily overwhelmed by daytrippers and we'd recommend staying in Callander or other Trossach towns.

The **tourist office** ( ☎ 0870 720 0604, 382352; Main St;  10am-5pm Apr-Jun & Sep-Oct, 9.30am-6pm Jul-Aug, 10am-4pm Sat & Sun Nov-Mar;  ) is in the Trossachs Discovery Centre, which details a history of the Trossachs and provides a soft play area for kids.

Three miles east is the Lake of Menteith. A ferry takes visitors from Port of Menteith village (on the lake) to the substantial ruins of **Inchmahome Priory** (HS; ☎ 385294; Inchmahome Island; adult/child incl ferry ride £4.50/2.25;  9.30am-5.30pm Apr-Sep). Mary, Queen of Scots was kept safe here as a child during Henry VIII's 'Rough Wooing' (p31).

Half a mile north of Aberfoyle, on the A821, is the **David Marshall Lodge Visitor Centre** ( ☎ 382258; admission free, car-park fee £1;  daily Mar-Jun & Sep-Dec, 10am-6pm Jul-Aug, 10am-5pm Sat & Sun Feb; ) in the **Queen Elizabeth Forest Park**, which has info about the many walks and cycle routes in and around the park (many departing from the visitor centre). The Royal Society for the Protection of Birds (RSPB) has a display here on local bird life, the highlight being a live video link to the resident osprey family. The centre is worth visiting solely for the views.

CENTRAL SCOTLAND

## ACTIVITIES

Waymarked walking trails start from the David Marshall Lodge Visitor Centre on the hills above the town; the tourist office has a booklet for £1.

There's an excellent 20-mile circular cycle route that links up with the **Sir Walter Scott Steamship** ( ☎ 376316) along Loch Katrine. Following the southern shore of Loch Achray, you reach the pier on Loch Katrine; departures are at 10.30am daily April to October, as well as afternoon departures at 2.30pm on Wednesday, Saturday and Sunday. The ferry should drop you at Stronachlachar (adult/child one way £6/4.50) at the western end. From Stronachlachar, follow the B829 via Loch Ard to Aberfoyle.

### SLEEPING & EATING

**Mayfield Guest House** ( ☎ 382962; randmhooks@btopenworld.com; Main St; s/d £30/50) Nothing is too much trouble for the friendly hosts at this guesthouse. There's a double and two twin rooms, all very well kept, and a garage at the back for bikes. Pets welcome.

**Crannaig House** ( ☎ 382276; www.crannaighouse.com; s/d £40/70; &) An opulent Victorian house, Crannaig provides excellent B&B in four family rooms, a single and a twin room. Being a grandiose Victorian affair, all the rooms are a good size. The upstairs family room, with bay window and couch, is the pick of the bunch. There's a cot for youngsters and there are discounts for kids.

**Forth Inn** ( ☎ 382372; www.forthinn.com; Main St; bar meals £7, dinner mains £14; lunch & dinner; &) In the middle of the village, the solid Forth Inn seems to be the lifeblood of the town, with locals and visitors alike queuing up for good honest pub fare. The tasty bar meals are the best in town. It also provides shelter and beer, with drinkers spilling outside into the sunny courtyard. Single/double rooms are available at the inn for £45/70.

### GETTING THERE & AWAY

First has up to four daily buses from Stirling (£5) and connecting services from Glasgow (£4.50) via Balfron.

A postbus does a return trip, Monday to Saturday, from Aberfoyle to Inversnaid Hotel on Loch Lomond, giving access to the West Highland Way long-distance footpath.

The Trossachs Trundler does a circuit starting from Stirling that includes Aberfoyle, Port of Menteith, Trossachs Pier on Loch Katrine and Callander; a day ticket per adult/child is £8/2.80. It's wheelchair accessible and can carry two bikes. The bus runs daily (except Wednesdays) from late May to early October.

### GETTING AROUND

Bicycles can be hired from **Trossachs Cycle Hire** ( ☎ 382614; Trossachs Holiday Park; half-/full day £9/15).

## Callander

☎ 01877 / pop 3000

Callander has been pulling in the tourists for over 150 years, and has a laid-back ambience along its main thoroughfare. It's a far better place than Aberfoyle to spend time in, quickly lulling visitors into lazy pottering. There's also an excellent array of accommodation options.

### INFORMATION

**Bank of Scotland** (Main St) Has ATM.

**Loch Lomond & the Trossachs National Park Visitor Centre** ( ☎ 722126; www.lochlomond-trossachs .org; 52 Main St; 9.30am-3.30pm Mon-Fri) This place is a useful centre for specific information on the park and its inhabitants. Not for accommodation though – see Rob Roy & Trossachs Visitor Centre (below) for this.

**Post office** (Main St)

**Rob Roy & Trossachs Visitor Centre** ( ☎ 0845 225 5121; Ancaster Sq; audiovisual show on Rob Roy & the Trossachs £1.50; 10am-5pm Mar-Jun & Sep-Oct, 10am-6pm Jul-Aug, 10am-4pm Nov-Feb; ) This helpful centre has heaps of info on the area and runs an audiovisual show about the great man.

**Royal Bank of Scotland** (Main St) Has ATM.

### ACTIVITIES

The impressive **Bracklinn Falls** are reached by track and footpath from Bracklinn Rd (30 minutes each way from the car park). Also off Bracklinn Rd, a woodland trail leads up to Callander Crags, with great views over the surroundings; a return trip is about 4 miles from the car park. Note that at the time of research the bridge at the falls had been washed away, due to flooding, making the round trip back to Callander closed – you need to retrace your steps.

The Trossachs is a lovely area to cycle around. **Cycle Hire Callander** (Mounter Bikes; ☎ 331052; Ancaster Sq) rents bikes for £6 for two hours or £12 for a full day. Child seats are £3. It's right next to the visitor centre.

## SLEEPING & EATING

**Trossachs Tryst Hostel** ( ☎ /fax 331200; info@scottish -hostel.com; Invertrossachs Rd; dm/f £15/70) This backpackers is in a beautifully isolated spot. To get there, take Bridge St off Main St, then turn right onto Invertrossachs Rd and follow the road, which runs on the southern side of the river draining Loch Vennachar, for a mile. The excellent dorms are very spacious with eight beds and their own bathroom. Rates include sheets.

**Callander Meadows** ( ☎ 330181; www.callander meadows.co.uk; 24 Main St; r per person £28-30) Rooms are tastefully decorated here and have the best of modern convenience in Victorian elegance. Room 1 has a great view of the River Teith, while room 2 is a grandiose four-poster bed affair. The restaurant is small and personal, providing sophisticated dining, beautifully presented food and faultless service. A two-course lunch is £8, mains are £13 to £16 and it's open for lunch and dinner Thursday to Monday.

**Roman Camp Hotel** ( ☎ 330003; www.roman-camp -hotel.co.uk; s/d £85/135) Indulgent Roman Camp is the spot to spoil yourself. It's magnificently located by the River Teith and dates from 1625. There is complimentary sherry upon arrival, a first-class restaurant (reservations required) where you can indulge in a five-course dinner (£44) or à la carte mains (£25), and even a tiny chapel for weddings.

**Deli Ecosse** (10 Ancaster Sq; mains £2.50-5; ⏱ 8am-5.30pm) Top spot for brekky or lunch, it dishes out paninis and baguettes. Lots of yummy condiments on sale, too, such as Arran cheeses and plump green olives to sustain yourself walking up surrounding peaks.

**Cafe Circa Doune** ( ☎ 01786-841683; Buchany; lunch £8.50, 2/3-course dinner £16/20; ⏱ lunch daily, dinner Sat) Worth the 6 mile drive/cycle from Callander (towards Doune) along the A84, this place, at the Scottish Antiques and Arts Centre, is gaining a reputation for fine Scottish dining using local produce and a touch of creativity. Try the roast loin or Rannoch Moor pork. Refined dining, it would suit couples or small groups.

Along Main St you'll find a Co-op supermarket and lots of places offering meals and snacks for under £5.

Also recommended:

**Linley Guest House** ( ☎ 330087; www.linleyguest house.co.uk; 139 Main St; r per person £17-22) A spick-and-span B&B with bright rooms and helpful owners. The double en suite is worth the extra. It's beautifully appointed with a large window drawing in lots of natural light.

**Arden House** ( ☎ /fax 330235; www.ardenhouse.org .uk; Bracklinn Rd; r per person £32.50-37.50; ⏱ Apr-Oct) A wonderful place for grown-ups (no kids allowed) drowning in a deluge of red and purple flowers in summer. Guests are well looked after in luxury rooms.

## GETTING THERE & AWAY

First operates buses from Stirling (45 minutes, every two hours Monday to Saturday) and Killin (45 minutes, three to six daily Monday to Saturday). There's also a daily Scottish Citylink bus from Edinburgh to Fort William

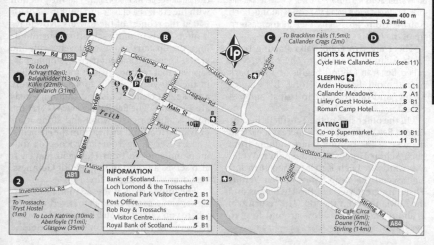

**CALLANDER**

0 — 400 m
0 — 0.2 miles

To Bracklinn Falls (1.5mi);
Callander Crags (2mi)

Leny Rd A84

Glenartney Rd

Ancaster Rd

Craigard Rd

Main St

Pearl St

Teith

Murdiston Ave

Montana Cres

Stirling Rd A84

To Loch Achray (10mi);
Balquhidder (13mi);
Killin (22mi);
Crianlarich (31mi)

To Loch Katrine (10mi);
Aberfoyle (11mi);
Glasgow (35mi)

To Trossachs Tryst Hostel (1mi)

Invertrossachs Rd

A81

Mansefield La

Bridgend

To Cafe Circa
Doune (6mi);
Doune (7mi);
Stirling (14mi)

**SIGHTS & ACTIVITIES**
Cycle Hire Callander............(see 11)

**SLEEPING**
Arden House.......................**6** C1
Callander Meadows.............**7** A1
Linley Guest House.............**8** B1
Roman Camp Hotel.............**9** C2

**EATING**
Co-op Supermarket............**10** B1
Deli Ecosse......................**11** B1

**INFORMATION**
Bank of Scotland.........................**1** B1
Loch Lomond & the Trossachs
  National Park Visitor Centre**2** B1
Post Office...................................**3** C2
Rob Roy & Trossachs
  Visitor Centre............................**4** B1
Royal Bank of Scotland............**5** B1

## LOCH LUBNAIG

When tracking north from Callander along the A84 towards Crianlarich, you'll skirt past the shores of gorgeous Loch Lubnaig. Not as famous as some of its cousins, it's still well worth a detour. Look for parking spots on the eastern shores of the loch, and go and have a chat to some of the local fishermen. If it's a sunny day there are bound to be some rods in the water and a few locals lunching by the water's edge. The surrounding views of forested mountains are sublime.

via Callander (£10.50, 1¾ hours) with connections to Oban and Skye.

Royal Mail runs a postbus from Callander to Trossachs Pier linking with the sailing of the SS *Sir Walter Scott* on Loch Katrine (see below).

The Trossachs Trundler calls at Callander (p200) and reaches the pier on Loch Katrine 26 minutes later four times daily, except Wednesday. A trip covering just the Trossachs area is £5/1.80 per adult/child.

Aberfoyle Coaches runs between Callander and Aberfoyle (half-hour, four times daily Monday to Saturday).

### Loch Katrine & Loch Achray

This rugged area, 6 miles north of Aberfoyle and 10 miles west of Callander, is the heart of the Trossachs. From April to October the **SS Sir Walter Scott** ( ☎ 01877-376315/6; www.lochkatrine .com; adult/child return from £7/5) chugs along Loch Katrine from Trossachs Pier at the eastern tip of the loch.

There are two good **walks** starting from Loch Achray. The path to the rocky cone called **Ben A'an** (460m) begins at a car park near the old Trossachs Hotel. It's easy to follow, and the return trip is just under 4 miles.

On the other side of the Trossachs lies the rugged **Ben Venue** (727m) – there is a path all the way to the summit. Start walking from Loch Achray Hotel, follow the Achray Water westwards to Loch Katrine, then turn left and ascend the steep flanks of Ben Venue. There are great views of the Highlands and the Lowlands from the top. The return trip is about 5.5 miles – allow around four to five hours.

## BALQUHIDDER & AROUND

Steeped in clan history, this mountainous and sparsely populated area is in the northern part of the Stirling administrative region. There are a few villages and lots of good hill walks.

### Balquhidder

☎ 01567 / pop 50

In this small village (pronounced balwhidder), 2 miles off the A84, there's a churchyard with **Rob Roy's grave** (which has the words 'Despite Them' defiantly etched onto the headstone) – it's an appropriately beautiful spot in a deep, winding glen in big-sky country. There are some other interesting headstones in the graveyard, and a plaque on the old kirk wall helps unravel their origins. Rob Roy's wife and two of his sons are also interred here. In the church are the 8th-century **St Angus' stone**, probably a marker to the original tomb of St Angus, an 8th-century monk who built the first church here, a 17th-century church bell, and a free leaflet giving details on notable gravestones, artefacts and people of the area.

Four miles on from Rob Roy's grave is **Monachyle Mhor Hotel** ( ☎ 01877-384622; www .monachylemhor.com; r from £95), a luxury hideaway. The restaurant here is something special with ingredients sourced locally – including from the hotel's organic garden. Rooms are sumptuous and combine contemporary furnishings in a traditional setting.

**our pick** **Kings House Hotel** ( ☎ 01877-384646; www .kingshouse-scotland.co.uk; Balquhidder; s/d £33/55, self-catering cottage per wk £180-425; ♿ ), at the junction with the A84, is a classic inn built in 1779 for £40 at the request of the drovers. Nowadays it offers B&B in more salubrious surroundings; the upstairs rooms are lovely, with fine views. There's an ancient narrow, sloping passageway that reminds visitors they're treading in the 200-year-old-plus footsteps of many a passing traveller. Cots and children's beds are available. The **Rob Roy Bar** (mains £4-8) at the hotel is a tiny, rickety wood-and-stone affair providing food and shelter from the elements. There's everything from sandwiches to a rollmop and smoked trout Highland platter. It also serves an outstanding pint of Guinness, best drunk by the open fire.

The minor road at the A84 junction continues along pretty **Loch Voil** to Inverlochlarig, where you can climb **Stob Binnein** (1165m) by its southern ridge. Stob Binnein is one of the

CENTRAL SCOTLAND

highest mountains in the area, and it has a most unusual shape, like a cone with its top chopped off.

### GETTING THERE & AWAY
Buses between Callander and Killin stop at the Kings House Hotel. On weekdays a postbus operates from Killin to Callander; it also stops at the Kings House Hotel. The daily Scottish Citylink bus from Edinburgh to Fort William stops here at 11.09am.

## Crianlarich & Tyndrum
☎ 01838 / combined pop 350

In good tramping country, and on the West Highland Way, these villages are little more than service junctions on the main A82 road, just north of the Loch Lomond & the Trossachs National Park. There's a train station at Crianlarich. Tiny Tyndrum, just 5 miles along the road, is blessed with two stations and a very flash **tourist office** ( ☎ 400246; info@tyndrum .visitscotland.co.uk; ⏰ 10am–5pm Apr–Jun, 10am–6pm Jul & Aug, 10.30am–5pm Sep–Oct), which has piles of information and a bureau de change. Ask here about day walks along the West Highland Way and ascents of popular An Caisteal (995m), Ben More (1174m) and magnificent Ben Lui (1130m). The tourist office stocks the well-regarded Ordnance Survey (OS) maps from the British Mapping Agency and has detailed route information.

The **Green Welly Stop** ( ☎ 400271; www.thegreen wellystop.co.uk; Tyndrum; hot meals £7) is a shrine to tourism. This little shopping complex has a very good (if slightly pricey) outdoor store, ideal if you're looking for supplies before you grapple with your Munro. It's also a good fuel stop, with hot meals served all day.

### SLEEPING & EATING
**Crianlarich Youth Hostel** (SYHA; ☎ 0870 004 1112; Station Rd; dm adult/child £14/10; 🖳 ) This hostel is a modern bungalow with six-bed dorms. It has a good Highland setup – large kitchen, clean dining area and warm, comfy lounge. There's bike hire (£12 per day) and it's the best budget option (B&Bs tend to be expensive in Crianlarich).

**Auchtertyre Farm** (Strathfillan Wigwams; ☎ 400 251; www.sac.ac.uk/wigwams; Tyndrum; camp sites per person £5, small/large wigwam & 2 adults £25/30, lodge per week £190-320) This charismatic place, 3 miles from Crianlarich (and 2 miles from Tyndrum), is off the A82 and has 16 heated wigwams – essentially wooden A-frame cabins. They're a little squashy (each has five beds) but great value. Auchtertyre Farm also has camping with access to all facilities and a self-contained lodge, ideal for families.

**Tyndrum Lodge Hotel** ( ☎ 400219; Tyndrum; s/d £25/60) In Tyndrum you'll get quality homespun accommodation and good cheer in this well-run, refurbished hotel. Walkers should head for rooms 1 to 12, which are towards the back and a bit quieter, ensuring a decent night's shuteye. Bar meals are available for £7 for both guests and nonguests.

### GETTING THERE & AWAY
Scottish Citylink runs several buses daily to Glasgow, Oban and Skye from both villages. A postbus service links Crianlarich, Tyndrum and Killin twice on each weekday (with connections to Callander) and once on Saturday.

First ScotRail runs train services from Tyndrum and Crianlarich to Fort William (£13.50, 1¾ hours, four daily Monday to

---

### ROB ROY

As all the tourist literature repeatedly informs you, this is Rob Roy country. Rob Roy Macgregor (1671–1734) was the wild leader of one of the wildest of Scotland's clans, Clan Gregor. Although he claimed direct descent from a 10th-century king of Scots and rights to the lands the clan occupied, these Macgregor lands stood between powerful neighbours. Rob Roy became notorious for his daring raids into the Lowlands to carry off cattle and sheep – hence the clan's sobriquet, 'Children of the Mist' – and led to the outlawing of the clan.

He was eventually captured and sentenced to transportation, but was pardoned and he lived out the rest of his life in Balquhidder. Although he achieved a 'Robin Hood'–type reputation as a champion of the poor and his life has been heavily romanticised, he was undoubtedly an infamous bandit and blackmailer. The tale of Rob Roy highlights the confrontation between the dying clan culture of the Highlands and the feudal culture of the lowland Scots. Rob Roy is buried in the churchyard at Balquhidder, by Loch Voil.

Saturday, two on Sunday), Oban (£8, one hour, three daily Monday to Saturday) and Glasgow (£14.60, two hours, three or four daily).

## Killin

☎ 01567 / pop 700

Tumbling through the centre of this charming little village are the frothy **Falls of Dochart**. The canny locals have made the best of their unusual water feature, pulling in many a passing tourist coach. Killin is in the northeastern corner of the Stirling region and is a handy base for exploring the mighty mountains and glens that surround it.

### INFORMATION

The village has a post office and a Bank of Scotland ATM, both on Main St.

**Outdoor Centre** ( ☎ 820652; Main St) Hires out all sorts of equipment, including canoes (£40 per day), kayaks (£30 per day) and mountain bikes (£11/15 per half-/full day). Note that a child's seat is complimentary when two bikes are hired.

**Tourist office** ( ☎ 0870 720 0627; ☼ 10am-5pm Apr-Jun & Sep-Oct, 10am-5.30pm Jul & Aug) In the Breadalbane Folklore Centre, by the River Dochart.

### SIGHTS

Bringing ancient magic and miracles to life is the **Breadalbane Folklore Centre** ( ☎ 820254; adult/child £2.75/1.80; ☼ 10am-5pm Apr-Jun & Sep-Oct, 10am-5.30pm Jul & Aug), in an old water mill overlooking the falls. There is an audiovisual presentation about St Fillan, a local saint whose religious teachings are said to have helped unite the ancient kingdoms of the Scots and the Picts in the 8th century. Robert the Bruce carried a relic of the saint into battle at Bannockburn some 600 years later, which he used to inspire his followers. There are displays about local and clan history, including the Macgregors and MacNabs.

The **Clan MacNab burial ground** lies on an island in the river, crossed by the main road and just downstream from the falls; ask at the tourist office for the gate key.

### ACTIVITIES

Killin is at the northern end of the **Lochs and Glens cycle route** from Glasgow, which follows forest trails, small roads and disused rail routes via the Trossachs – the tourist office has detailed information.

Seven miles northeast of Killin, **Ben Lawers** (1214m) rises above Loch Tay. There's an NTS visitor centre here and trails lead to the summit (see p224).

Glen Lochay runs westwards from Killin into the hills of Mamlorn. You can take a **mountain bike** for about 11 miles up the glen to just beyond Batavaime. The scenery is impressive and the hills aren't too difficult to climb. It's possible, on a nice summer day, to climb over the top of **Ben Challum** (1025m) and descend to Crianlarich, but it's hard work.

For more information, pick up a copy of the *Walks Around Killin* leaflet (30p) from the tourist office.

### SLEEPING & EATING

**High Creagan** ( ☎ 820449; Aberfeldy Rd; camp sites per person £5) This place has a well-kept, sheltered camping site with plenty of grass set high on the slopes overlooking sparkling Loch Tay, just outside Killin. No children.

**Killin Youth Hostel** (SYHA; ☎ 0870 004 1131; dm adult/child from £13.50/10; ☼ Apr-Oct) At the northern end of the village, this lovely Victorian mansion has one family room and well-kept four- to 12-bed dorms. Dorms are an excellent size and most (such as dorm 3) have bay windows drawing in plenty of light. Common areas, including the kitchen, are very clean.

**Drumfin Guest House** ( ☎ 820900; www.drumfinn .co.uk; Manse Rd; s/d from £35/56) This top guesthouse boasts pristine facilities. Two rooms share a bathroom while three rooms have en suites. Have a look at a couple of rooms, as the view varies, although all are light and bright. But it's the friendly, enthusiastic owners who set this place apart. Besides, anyone who has frog musicians in the garden gets our vote – the garden gnome has met its match.

**Falls of Dochart Inn** ( ☎ 820270; Falls of Dochart; s/d £45/60) Overlooking the falls, the Dochart Inn has smallish, pristine upstairs rooms – try to request one with a view of the falls (such as room 2). Rooms at the back are quiet but have no real view. Downstairs is a very snug, atmospheric space with a roaring fire, a good beer and wine selection, and creative takes on traditional Scottish dishes; mains £10 to £15. The impressive service is friendly and efficient.

You'll find supermarkets along Main St, including Costcutter and Co-op.

### GETTING THERE & AWAY

First runs a service from Stirling (£5.50, 1¾ hours, once or twice daily Monday to Friday, once on Saturday) via Callander. There's a postbus to Crianlarich and Tyndrum twice on weekdays and once on Saturday. There's a postbus service between Aberfeldy and Killin (1¾ hours to Aberfeldy, Monday to Saturday). A Scottish Citylink bus leaves for Oban twice a day (1½ hours).

# CLACKMANNANSHIRE

Inviting Clackmannanshire has some great attractions that are worth a detour if you're in the Stirling region. The tiny district is a top spot for day trips from the city of Stirling.

## DOLLAR

☎ 01259 / pop 2900

About 11 miles east of Stirling, in the lower Ochil Hills, is the charming town of Dollar. **Castle Campbell** (HS; ☎ 742408; Dollar Glen; adult/child £4.50/2.25; ⏱ 9.30am-5.30pm Apr-Sep, to 4.30pm Sat-Wed Oct-Mar) is a 20-minute walk up **Dollar Glen**, into the wooded hills above the town. It's a spooky old stronghold of the dukes of Argyll and stands between two ravines; you can clearly see why it was known as Castle Gloom. There's been a fortress of some kind on this site from the 11th century, but the present structure dates from the 15th century. The castle was sacked by Cromwell in 1654, but the tower is well preserved. There's a great ramble with sweeping views over Castle Campbell and the surrounding country from the little car park near the castle. Note that it can get boggy if it's been raining.

There are regular First buses to Dollar from Stirling; other services run from Alloa (every two hours Monday to Friday).

## CLACKMANNAN

☎ 01259 / pop 3500

This quiet village (you really could hear a pin drop) lies 2 miles southeast of Alloa and has several interesting sights. **Clackmannan Stone** (Main St) sits on top of a large shaft – it's sacred to the pagan deity Mannan and predates Christian times.

Next to the stone is a 17th-century **cross** engraved with the Bruce coat of arms; the lower part is heavily worn, due to prisoners' chains. Also adjacent is the striking **Tolbooth**, built in 1592 for £284, which served as court and prison. **Clackmannan Tower**, uphill from the church and about 450m from Main St, was a residence of the Bruce family from 1365

to 1772. In 1787, the widow of the last laird knighted Robert Burns in the tower with the sword of Robert the Bruce. The five-storey tower has structural problems due to subsidence and it isn't open to the public, but the exterior is well worth a look. The idyllic views aren't bad either.

First buses run to/from Stirling (40 minutes, about every 20 minutes) and frequently to Alloa.

# FALKIRK REGION

The little administrative district of Falkirk contains one of Scotland's modern marvels of engineering – the Falkirk Wheel. The region also covers some interesting areas to the east, including Bo'ness. If you're here in early May, check out **Big in Falkirk** (www.biginfalkirk.com), a free street art festival.

## FALKIRK

☎ 01324 / pop 32,500

Falkirk, a large town about 10 miles southeast of Stirling, is home to the famous Falkirk Wheel – an astounding achievement of modern engineering. Watching it spin its boat-bound occupants around has become a major tourist attraction. Drop into the **tourist office** ( ☎ 0870 720 0614; 2 Glebe St; ⏱ Mon-Sat year-round) for more information, and see the boxed text, p206.

First runs regular buses to Stirling and Edinburgh. Trains go to Stirling, Dunblane, Perth, Glasgow (£5.50) and Edinburgh (£5) from Falkirk Grahamston station. Glasgow–Edinburgh express trains stop at Falkirk High station every 15 to 30 minutes.

## BO'NESS & KINNEIL RAILWAY

The town of Bo'ness on the Firth of Forth is best known for the steam train that shuttles to and fro on the **Bo'ness & Kinneil Railway** ( ☎ 01506-822298; Bo'ness Station, Union St; adult/child return £5/2.50). The train runs from April to October, with three or four departures each weekend. In July and August the train runs during the week as well. Tickets costing £8/4.50 per adult/child include admission to the **Birkhill Fireclay Mine**, 130 steps down in the Avon gorge; guided tours run in conjunction with train arrivals. There's also a free **railway exhibition** at the station in Bo'ness.

Direct buses to Bo'ness from Glasgow, Edinburgh, Falkirk and Stirling are run by First.

## MODERN MARVELS

The Union Canal, linking central Edinburgh to the Forth and Clyde Canal at Falkirk, was completed in 1822, allowing cheap coal from the mines of western-central Scotland to be carried by barge to the Scottish capital. Slate and stone for Edinburgh's New Town were also carried via the canal. However, the expansion of the railways in the mid-19th century rendered the canals obsolete and they fell into disuse.

A £84.5-million Millennium Link Project has restored the Forth and Clyde Canal, and Union Canal to full working order, linking Edinburgh with west and central Scotland. The centrepiece is the Falkirk Wheel, a unique engineering structure designed to replace the flight of locks that once linked the two canals at Falkirk. It is the world's first rotating boat lift, raising vessels (plus almost 300 tonnes of water) 35m in one steel caisson, while descending boats are carried down in the second caisson on the opposite side of the wheel.

Visitors can take boat trips on the **Falkirk Wheel** ( ☎ 0870 050 0208; www.thefalkirkwheel.co.uk; adult/child/family £8/4.25/21.50, car-park fee £2; ☼ 9.30am-6pm Apr-Jul & Sep-Oct, until 7pm Sat & Sun Aug), spinning around on its giant gondolas. Boats leave every half-hour (hourly in winter) and travel from the visitor centre into the wheel, getting delivered to the Union Canal, high above. Boats then go through Roughcastle Tunnel before the descent on the wheel and return trip to the visitor centre. Anyone with an interest in engineering marvels should not miss this boat ride – it's great for kids, too. The nearby visitor centre explains the workings of the mighty wheel – it only takes the power of about eight toasters for a full rotation!

# FIFE

A chubby finger of land jutting out into the icy North Sea, Fife, or 'the kingdom of Fife', as it likes to be known – it was home to Scottish kings for 500 years – is a treasure-trove of attractions waiting to be explored. Highlights include a string of delightful fishing villages perched on the East Neuk coast, and, further north, one of the most appealing towns in the country: St Andrews. Despite integration with the rest of Scotland, Fife has held onto its unique Lowland identity. Many people enter 'the kingdom' via the Forth Road or Tay Bridges – perhaps traversing these enormous gateways adds to the sense of entering a new realm. The Fife Coastal Path links these two bridges along 80 miles of glorious coastal scenery, and the laid-back, serene countryside with its rolling, lush farmland invites exploration.

## Getting Around

Fife Council produces a useful transport map, *Getting Around Fife,* available from tourist offices – good links for public-transport information can be found at www.fifedirect .org.uk. The main bus operator is **Stagecoach Fife** ( ☎ 01334-474238). For £5.50 you can buy a Fifedayrider ticket, which gives unlimited travel around Fife on Stagecoach buses.

If you are driving from the Forth Road Bridge to St Andrews, a slower but much more scenic route than the M90/A91 is along the signposted **Fife Coastal Tourist Route**.

Note that at the time of writing a trial hovercraft service was operating from Portobello to Kirkcaldy (£4.50 return, 20 minutes, departs hourly). If successful this might be a permanent service by the time you read this.

## CULROSS

☎ 01383 / pop 500

A thicket of forest above the town wedges Culross (pronounced coo-*ross*) between the firth and wooded slopes. An enchanting little town, it's Scotland's best-preserved example of a 17th-century Scottish burgh, and the NTS owns 20 of the buildings, including the palace. Small, red-tiled, whitewashed buildings line the cobbled streets, and the winding Back Causeway to the abbey is embellished with whimsical stone cottages.

## Sights

You can visit **Culross Palace** (NTS; ☎ 880359; palace, town house & study adult/child £8/5; ☼ noon-5pm Thu-Mon Apr-May & Sep, noon-5pm daily Jun-Aug, noon-4pm Thu-Mon Oct), more a large house than a palace, which features extraordinary decorative painted woodwork, barrel-vaulted ceilings and an interior largely unchanged since the early 17th century. It's dark and spooky inside on an overcast day. The **town house** (visitor centre downstairs) and the **study**, also completed in the early 17th century, are open to the public, but the other NTS properties can only be viewed from the outside.

Ruined **Culross Abbey** (admission free; ☑ 9am-7pm Easter-Aug, other times by arrangement), founded by the Cistercians in 1217, is on the hill in a lovely peaceful spot with vistas of the firth; the choir of the abbey church is now the parish church. In the northeastern corner of the north transept there's an unusual sight – statues of eight children kneeling in front of their parents' memorial.

### Sleeping

**Burnbank Cottage** ( ☎ 880240; Blairburn, Low Causeway; r per person £20) This cottage has one double and one twin, both with shared bathroom. It's home-grown Scottish hospitality at its best, and the cosy private living room for guests is great for an evening snuggle.

### Getting There & Away

Culross is 12 miles west of the Forth Road Bridge. Stagecoach Fife buses run roughly hourly between Stirling (one hour) and Dunfermline (20 minutes), less often on weekends, via Culross.

## ABERDOUR

☎ 01383 / pop 1700

It's worth stopping in this popular seaside town to ramble around impressive **Aberdour Castle** (HS; ☎ 860519; adult/child £4/2; ☑ 9.30am-5.30pm Apr-Sep, 9.30am-4.30pm Sat-Wed Oct-Mar, closed Thu & Fri). The castle was built by the Douglas family in 1342, but by the 18th century it was partly in ruins and abandoned by its owners. There's an interesting account of James Douglas, the forth earl of Morton, giving an insight into treachery among the nobility. **St Fillan's Church**, by the castle, was founded in 1123, but the current building is mostly 17th century. It's believed to have been visited by Robert the Bruce and there's certainly a sense of the ancient inside, where harsh grey stone walls contrast vividly with stunning stained-glass windows.

With real ales and good vegetarian choices on the menu, the family-run **Aberdour Hotel** ( ☎ 860325; www.aberdourhotel.co.uk; 38 High St; s/d £52/75) is not only a good place to stay, but also the best place to eat in town. Mains are £7 and there is an emphasis on hearty home-cooked food.

There are trains to Edinburgh (£4.30, one hour, at least hourly weekdays, every two hours on Sunday).

## KIRKCALDY

☎ 01592 / pop 47,000

Kirkcaldy (kir-kod-ay) sprawls along the edge of the sea for several miles and has a rather shabby promenade with spectacular pounding surf on windy days. It's worth stopping in town to visit the excellent museum.

The **tourist office** ( ☎ 267775; kirkcaldy@visitfife.com; Merchant House, 339 High St; ☑ 9.30am-5.30pm Mon-Sat, 11am-4pm Sun Apr-Sep, 9.30am-5pm Mon-Sat Oct-Mar) is at the eastern end of High St.

Just a short walk east from the train and bus stations, in the War Memorial Gardens, you'll find the **Kirkcaldy Museum & Art Gallery** ( ☎ 412860; War Memorial Gardens; admission free; ☑ 10.30am-5pm Mon-Sat, 2-5pm Sun; ⊛ ⊛ ), which combines historical accounts with contemporary exhibits. The kids will have a ball as there are plenty of hands-on attractions. There's also an impressive collection of Scottish paintings from the 18th to the 20th century, including work from the Scottish Colourists and the Glasgow Boys.

You're better off staying in Edinburgh, East Neuk or St Andrews, but you could try **Ashgrove B&B** ( ☎ 561354; www.ashgrovebnb.co.uk; 213 Nicol St; s/d £38/58; ⊛ ). The bustling, likeable Scot who runs this joint is as quirky as the layout of the rabbit warren inside. Rooms are smallish but well setup and exude a comforting homely warmth. Book in advance over summer.

Frequent buses (usually hourly) run from Hill St bus station to St Andrews (one hour), Anstruther (one hour 15 minutes) and Edinburgh (one hour). Kirkcaldy is on the main railway line between Edinburgh (£5.60, 45 minutes) and Dundee (£9.50, 40 minutes); there are two to four trains an hour.

## FALKLAND

☎ 01337 / pop 1200

Below the soft ridges of the Lomond Hills in the centre of Fife is the charming village of Falkland. Although overrun with tourists in summer, it's a captivating town and there are many heritage-listed conservation buildings.

Rising majestically out of the town centre and dominating the skyline is the outstanding 16th-century **Falkland Palace** (NTS; ☎ 857397; adult/child £10/7; ☑ 10am-5pm Mon-Sat, 1-5pm Sun Mar-Oct), a country residence of the Stuart monarchs.

**CENTRAL SCOTLAND**

---

**WORTH THE TRIP**

Dunfermline is an unappealing large regional town with a couple of great attractions reflecting its historical importance.

Queen Margaret founded a Benedictine priory on the hill here in the 11th century, and later her son King David I built **Dunfermline Abbey** (HS; ☎ 739026; St Margaret St; adult/child £3.50/1.75; ☷ 9.30am-5.30pm Apr-Sep, 9.30am-4.30pm Mon-Wed & Sat, to 12.30pm Thu & 2-4.30pm Sun Oct-Mar) in a commanding but sheltered position on the site. Six Scottish kings are buried at Dunfermline Abbey. You can explore the wonderful Norman nave with its ornate columns and superb stained-glass windows. Note the picture of Robert the Bruce standing over the devil (England perhaps?). The Bruce is buried under the pulpit.

Next to the abbey are the ruins of **Dunfermline Palace**, rebuilt from the abbey guesthouse in the 16th century for James VI. If it's quiet you'll get a guided tour from staff, which is well worthwhile as their commentary brings a previously wealthy and thriving royal court to life.

The award-winning **Abbot House Heritage Centre** ( ☎ 733266; Maygate; adult/child £4/free; ☷ 10am-5pm), near the abbey, dates from the 15th century. History buffs could get lost for hours among the absorbing displays about the history of Scotland, the abbey and Dunfermline.

Dunfermline is easy to visit on a day trip from Edinburgh (40 minutes) or St Andrews (1¼ hours), with frequent buses at least hourly. There are also trains to/from Edinburgh (£4, 30 minutes, at least hourly Monday to Saturday, less frequently Sunday).

---

Mary, Queen of Scots is said to have spent the happiest days of her life 'playing the country girl in the woods and parks' at Falkland. The palace was built between 1501 and 1541 to replace a castle dating from the 12th century; French and Scottish craftspeople were employed to create a masterpiece of Scottish Gothic architecture. The king's bedchamber and the chapel, with its beautiful painted ceiling, have both been restored. Don't miss the prodigious 17th-century Flemish hunting tapestries in the hall. One feature of the royal leisure centre still exists: the oldest royal tennis court in Britain, built in 1539 for James V. It's in the grounds and still in use.

Opposite the palace, the very cosy little **Hunting Lodge** ( ☎ 857226; timlees@huntinglodge.fsbusiness.co.uk; High St; s/d from £27.50/45) dates back to 1607. The homely rooms, exuding warmth and character, are upstairs, while pints and chattering locals furnish the downstairs area.

An 18th-century coaching inn, on the square opposite the palace, **Covenanter Hotel** ( ☎ 857224; www.covenanterhotel.co.uk; The Square; s/d/ste £46/64/72) is a snug, classy little abode with fine rooms that are often discounted when things are quiet (it's worth asking!). The three-person suite is the best.

Falkland is 11 miles north of Kirkcaldy. There are Stagecoach Fife buses roughly hourly Monday to Saturday to/from Perth (one hour) and Cupar (30 minutes).

## ST ANDREWS
☎ 01334 / pop 14,500

Anyone who's belted a little white ball around a fairway will probably have heard of St Andrews. Apart from its historical links with golf though, this is one of Scotland's most charming and enjoyable towns to explore. Walking around The Scores, with the wide sweep of St Andrews Bay set against the surprisingly intact medieval layout and dramatic ruins of the town, evokes a feeling of being on a film set – it's all so picture perfect. The town is blessed with a thriving café and pub/bar scene and many fine restaurants, no doubt due to its burgeoning student population, which injects the streets with a real energy. You'll hear just as many English accents around town as you will Scottish; it's also home to an ancient university where wealthy English undergraduates rub shoulders with Scottish theology students.

### History

St Andrews is said to have been founded by St Regulus, who arrived from Greece in the 4th century bringing the bones of St Andrew – Scotland's patron saint. The town soon grew into a major pilgrimage centre and St Andrews developed into the ecclesiastical capital of the country. The university was founded in 1410, the first in Scotland. By the mid-16th century there were three colleges, St Salvator's, St Leonard's and St Mary's.

St Andrews is perhaps most famous for its historical links to golf. It's the headquarters of golf's governing body, the Royal and Ancient Golf Club. It's also the location of the world's most famous golf course, the Old Course. The British Open Championship has taken place regularly at St Andrews since 1873.

## Orientation

St Andrews preserves its medieval plan of parallel streets with small closes (alleys) leading off them. The most important parts of the old town, lying to the east of the bus station, are easily explored on foot. Like Cambridge and Oxford, St Andrews has no campus – most university buildings are integrated into the central part of the town. There's a small harbour near the cathedral, and two sandy beaches: East Sands extends south from the harbour and the wider West Sands is north of the town.

## Information

Parking in the central area requires a voucher (60p per hour), which is on sale in many shops and at the tourist office.

**Bank of Scotland** (South St) Has ATM.

**J&G Innes** ( ☎ 472174; 107 South St) Plenty of local-interest books, such as Fife's history of burning witches.

**Library** (Church Sq; ☼ 9.30am-5pm Mon, Fri & Sat, to 7pm Tue-Thu) Free internet access – drop-in only; no bookings.

**Royal Bank of Scotland** (South St)

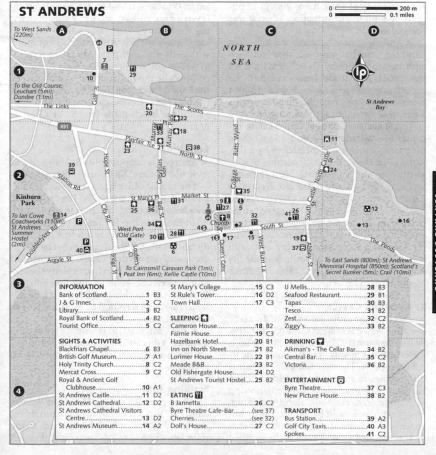

**ST ANDREWS**

CENTRAL SCOTLAND

**St Andrews Memorial Hospital** ( ☎ 472327; Abbey Walk) Minor injuries only; located south of Abbey St.
**Tourist office** ( ☎ 472021; www.visit-standrews.co.uk; 70 Market St; ⌚ 9.15am-5pm Mon-Sat, 11am-4pm Sun Apr-Jun & Sep–mid-Oct, 9.15am-7pm Mon-Sat, 10am-5pm Sun Jul & Aug, 9.30am-5pm Mon-Sat mid-Oct–Mar) Helpful staff with good knowledge of St Andrews and Fife.

## Sights

### ST ANDREWS CATHEDRAL

Situated at the eastern end of North St is the ruined western end of **St Andrews Cathedral** (HS; ☎ 472563; The Pends; adult/child £4/2, incl St Andrews Castle £7/3.50; ⌚ 9.30am-5.30pm Apr-Sep, to 4.30pm Oct-Mar; ♿ ), once the largest and one of the most magnificent cathedrals in Britain; the striking ruins convey a sense of its immensity. Although it was founded in 1160, it wasn't consecrated until 1318. It was a focus of pilgrimage until the Reformation, when it was pillaged in 1559.

St Andrew's bones lie under the high altar. Until the cathedral was built, they had been enshrined in the nearby Church of St Rule. All that remains is the **St Rule's Tower** – well worth the climb for the view across St Andrews and a great place for taking photographs. In the same area are parts of the ruined 13th-century priory.

The **St Andrews Cathedral Visitors Centre** includes the **calefactory**, the only room where the monks could warm themselves by a fire; masons' marks on the red sandstone blocks, identifying who shaped each block, can still be clearly seen. There's also a collection of Celtic crosses and gravestones that were found on the site. The highlight is the carved stone **sarcophagus**. It was carved in the 8th century and the detail is simply amazing. What survives is mainly a woodland hunting scene with the animals seemingly about to leap off the stone. Although it's Pictish, it shows definite Mediterranean influence.

### ST ANDREWS CASTLE

Not far from the cathedral and with dramatic coastline views, **St Andrews Castle** (HS; ☎ 477196; The Scores; adult/child £5/2.50; ⌚ 9.30am-5.30pm Apr-Sep, to 4.30pm Oct-Mar) is mainly in ruins, but the site itself is evocative. The most intriguing feature is the complex of siege tunnels, said to be the best surviving example of siege engineering in Europe. You can walk along the damp, mossy tunnels, now lit by electric light – but be warned, it helps if you're short. The castle was founded around 1200 as the fortified

home of the bishop. A visitor centre gives a good audiovisual introduction and also has a small collection of Pictish stones.

### ST ANDREWS MUSEUM

Near the bus station, **St Andrews Museum** ( ☎ 412690; Kinburn Park, Doubledykes Rd; admission free; ⌚ 10am-5pm Apr-Sep, 10.30am-4pm Mon-Fri, 12.30-5pm Sat & Sun Oct-Mar) has interesting displays that chart the history of the town from its founding by St Regulus to its growth as an ecclesiastical, academic and sporting centre. Local preservation work is a focal point of the museum.

### BRITISH GOLF MUSEUM

Golfers shouldn't miss the **British Golf Museum** ( ☎ 460046; Bruce Embankment; adult/child £5.25/2.90; ⌚ 10am-4pm Jan-Mar, 9.30am-5.30pm Mon-Sat, 10am-5pm Sun Apr-Oct, 10am-4pm Nov-Feb; ♿ ), an interesting (even for nongolfers), modern museum charting the history of the game and its intimate association with St Andrews. It's equipped with audiovisual displays and touch screens, as well as golf memorabilia.

Opposite the museum is the clubhouse of the **Royal & Ancient Golf Club**. Outside the club is the **Old Course**, and beside it stretch the West Sands, the beach made famous by *Chariots of Fire*.

## Activities

St Andrews is famous for its links to golf and its world famous Old Course – see opposite.

The tourist office has a list of local walks and also sells OS maps. The **Fife Coastal Path** (www.fifecoastalpath.com), stretching from the Forth Road Bridge to the Tay Bridge (Dundee) – a distance of 78 miles – is a wonderful long-distance walk, but the section between St Andrews and just north of Crail is recommended for experienced walkers (particularly the section between St Andrews and Boarhills), as the path is not as clearly defined and includes tidal and rough terrain. The tourist office has a detailed map.

Kellie Castle (p215) is within easy cycling distance. You can also cycle north to the forest, beach and nature trail at Tentsmuirs Sands (8 miles).

## Walking Tour

The best place to start is **St Andrews Museum** (above). Turn left out of the museum driveway and follow Doubledykes Rd back to the roundabout on City Rd. Turn right, then left

## PLAY THE OLD COURSE

Golf has been played at St Andrews since the 15th century, and by 1457 it was apparently so popular that James II had to ban it because it was interfering with his troops' archery practice. Few people realise that anyone can play the Old Course, the world's most famous golf course. Although it lies beside the exclusive, all-male Royal & Ancient Golf Club, the Old Course is a public course and is not owned by the club.

Getting a tee-off time is – literally – something of a lottery. Unless you book months in advance, the only chance you have of playing here is by entering a ballot before 2pm on the day before you wish to play. Be warned that applications by ballot are normally heavily oversubscribed, and green fees are a mere £125. There's no play on Sunday.

If your number doesn't come up, there are five other public courses in the area, none with quite the cachet of the Old Course but all significantly cheaper. Their fees are: New £65, Jubilee £65, Eden £35, Strathtyrum £24 and Balgove £12. See the tourist office for more information on playing these courses.

Bookings for the Old Course can be made online or by letter, fax or email to the **Reservations Office, St Andrews Links Trust** ( ☎ 466666; www.standrews.org.uk; Pilmour House, St Andrews, Fife KY16 9SF). A booking form is on the website.

onto South St. You'll pass through **West Port**, formerly Southgait Port, the main entrance to the old town. Built in 1589, it was based on Netherbow Port in Edinburgh. Walking east along South St, you pass **Louden's Close** on the right, a good example of the closes built according to the city's medieval street plan. Continue along South St to see the apse of the 16th-century **Blackfriars Chapel**, which stands in front of Madras College.

Further along South St, opposite the Victorian **town hall**, is **Holy Trinity Church**, the town's parish church, built in 1410. Positioned on the same side of the street as the town hall is **St Mary's College**, founded in 1537; beside it is the university library. The oak tree in the courtyard is over 250 years old.

Go left along Church St to cobbled Market St. Street markets are held around the **Mercat Cross**, although the cross is now a fountain. The tourist office is nearby at 70 Market St.

### Tours

There is a **Witches Tour** ( ☎ 655057; adult/child £7/5) that recounts the history and folklore of the town in an unusual fashion, with tales of ghosts and witches enlivened by theatrical stunts. It starts at 8pm (7.30pm September to April) on Friday (also Sunday in June, July and August and Thursday in July and August). Meet outside Greyfriars Hotel on North St.

### Festivals & Events

The Royal and Ancient Golf Club is the body that organises the annual **Open Golf Champion-** ship, which takes place in July. However, the tournament venue changes from year to year, and the Open only comes to St Andrews itself every five or six years – the venue for future championships can be found on the Open's official website (www.opengolf.com).

**St Andrews Highland Games** ( ☎ 476305) are held on the North Haugh on the last Sunday in July.

**St Andrews Week** is five days of festivities held around St Andrews Day (30 November), the feast day of Scotland's patron saint. The celebrations include a festival of Scottish food and drink, and various arts events.

### Sleeping

Bear in mind that St Andrews accommodation is often heavily booked year-round (especially in summer), so you're well advised to book in advance.

### BUDGET

**St Andrews Tourist Hostel** ( ☎ 479911; www.standrews hostel.com; Inchcape House, St Mary's Pl; dm £12-14) This place has had a thorough refurbishment injecting some much needed TLC into four- to eight-bed dorms. It's not particularly cheery, but it is the only year-round hostel in town and has a good, modern kitchen and a large lounge ideal for flopping around.

**Cairnsmill Caravan Park** ( ☎ 473604; cairnsmill@aol .com; Largo Rd; tent sites for 2 from £14; ⊙ Apr-Oct; ☲ ) About a mile west of St Andrews on the A915, this camping ground is on a crest with brilliant views over the town. There's not much space between sites – they pack 'em in. Fly-fishing reservoir on site.

**St Andrews Summer Hostel** (SYHA; ☎ 476726; reservations@syha.org.uk; David Russell Apartments, Buchanan Gardens; s/d £25/38) This very good hostel is unfortunately only open in July and August. It provides accommodation in shared apartments, each with five en-suite double rooms, lounge and kitchen.

### MIDRANGE
Note that single rooms are extremely hard to come by and should be booked in advance. Almost every house on Murray Park and Murray Pl is a guesthouse. The area couldn't be more convenient, but prices are on the high side.

[our pick] **Meade B&B** (☎ 477350; annmeade10@hotmail.com; 5 Albany Pl on Playfair Tce; r per person £25-27.50; 👶) This family home has two rooms on offer – one red and one yellow – and they're absolute bargains. The red room is the best – large and airy. It's in a great location and has free parking just across the road. Children are very welcome – under 16s are charged £17.50; under fours are free. Single supplement £10.

**Lorimer House** (☎ /fax 476599; www.lorimerhouse.com; 19 Murray Park; r per person £25-45; 👶 👶) This well-run, cheerful, spick-and-span place has cosy, well-furnished rooms, most admitting a flood of natural light. There are two larger doubles (see if one of those is available first), spacious family rooms, and single rooms. Wi-fi is available.

**Fairnie House** (☎ 474094; www.fairniehouse.com; 10 Abbey St; r per person £28-38) A relaxed and friendly B&B in a Georgian town house near the Byre Theatre, Fairnie House has one double and two twin rooms. Although it has recently modernised its furnishings, giving rooms a classy look, there's still a very homely feel to this place, and the communal dining room encourages conversation.

**Cameron House** (☎ 472306; www.cameronhouse-sta.co.uk; 11 Murray Park; r per person £35-45) Cameron House is a soft and cuddly place (with a cheery owner) that makes you feel right at home, especially with the teddy bears hanging off the bedposts. Single rooms are available.

[our pick] **Old Fishergate House** (☎ 470874; www.oldfishergatehouse.co.uk; North Castle St; d £90) This historic 17th-century town house, furnished with period pieces, is in a great location – the oldest part of town – close to the cathedral and castle. The two twin rooms are very spacious and even have their own sitting room

and cushioned ledges on their window sills. On a scale of one to 10 for quaintness, we'd rate it about a 9½.

### TOP END
**Inn on North Street** (☎ 473387; relax@theinnonnorthstreet.com; 127 North St; s/d £80/120) If you want to eat, drink and sleep in the same stylish place then this classy inn could be for you. Effortlessly dashing with a Gaelic twist, rooms 1 to 3 come with Jacuzzi and more space, while all rooms have DVD player, crisp white linen and large windows giving them an airy feel. The Oak room is the place for breakfast and a read of the paper, the bar is perfect for a snug tipple, and the Lizard Lounge in the basement is a late-night bar that gets cranked with live gigs and regular DJs.

**Hazelbank Hotel** (☎ /fax 472466; www.hazelbank.com; 28 The Scores; s/d £90/140) The elegant Hazelbank is a small (10 rooms) but comfy family-run hotel in a fine 1898 Victorian town house. Every room is different at this affable place – room 7 has stupendous views, while 3 also has fine views and is huge. Book ahead, as it's very popular.

## Eating
### BUDGET
**B Jannetta** (☎ 473285; 31 South St; 1-3 dip cone £1-3) This is a St Andrews institution. On a hot weekend there's a constant stream of people outside the place feverishly licking a delicious cone before it becomes a puddle. You can choose from 52 varieties of ice cream. The most popular flavour? Vanilla. The weirdest? Irn Bru!

**Cherries** (91 South St; baguette £2.50-3.50; 🕐 lunch) Best place for a roll or a baguette in town. The creative combinations give a fresh injection to lunchtimes and there are good options for vegetarians.

**Zest** (95 South St; dishes £2-4; 🕐 breakfast & lunch) Serving toasties, paninis and filled rolls along with a good coffee selection, this slick place is popular with students. The French doors opening onto the street make it a great spot for people-watching on a breezy summer day. Specialises in smoothies and juices.

Some self-catering options:

**Tesco** (138 Market St) A good centrally located supermarket.

**IJ Mellis** (149 South St) Traditional cheesemonger.

### MIDRANGE
**Byre Theatre Cafe-Bar** (☎ 468720; Abbey St; lunch mains £5, dinner mains £7-10; 🕐 10am-8.45pm) A happy,

buzzy spot with comfy couches, works of art on the wall and a well-developed menu that encompasses some delicious fusion cooking. Sandwiches at lunch come with interesting fillings, such as hummus and red pepper. Dinner gets more sophisticated, featuring dishes such as seared tuna steak on sultana and nutmeg couscous with smoked tomato dressing.

**Tapas** ( ☎ 471111; 177 South St; tapas £6-10, paella for 2 £25; ☾ lunch & dinner) Now who doesn't like tapas? This place dishes out some terrific little tidbits and it makes a cosy spot for dinner.

**Ziggy's** ( ☎ 473686; 6 Murray Pl; mains £6-14; ☾ lunch & dinner; ⚇ ) This small, darkened restaurant has an offbeat recording-studio theme. There's an open kitchen and a menu that does a bit of everything, including pizza, burgers, a range of steaks, and Mexican, seafood and veggie dishes. Good kids menu.

**Doll's House** ( ☎ 477422; 3 Church Sq; mains £11-14; ☾ lunch & dinner) With its high-backed chairs, bright colours and creaky wooden floor, the Doll's House tries to be rustic and modern at the same time. The result is a surprising warmth and no pretensions. The menu makes the most of local fish and other Scottish produce. The two-course lunch for £6.95 is unbeatable value, and the early-evening two-course deal for £12.95 isn't bad either.

**TOP END**

**Peat Inn** ( ☎ 840206; 3-course lunch/dinner £16/32; ☾ lunch & dinner Tue-Sat) The Peat Inn is one of the best restaurants in Scotland. Housed in a rustic country inn about 6 miles west of St Andrews, its award-winning menu is culinary heaven and demonstrates a French influence. To get there, head west on the A915 then turn right on the B940.

**Seafood Restaurant** ( ☎ 479475; The Scores; 3-course dinner £35; ☾ lunch & dinner) The Seafood Restaurant occupies a stylish glass-walled room, built out over the sea, with plush navy carpet, crisp white linen, an open kitchen and panoramic views of St Andrews Bay. It offers top seafood and an excellent wine list, and has won a clutch of awards. Look out for its special winter menu – three-course lunch for £15, weekdays only.

## Drinking

**Central Bar** (Market St) The Central Bar is all polished brass and polished accents, full of students from south of the border, tourists and locals. This is the most popular pub in town with an impressive array of beers.

**Victoria** ( ☎ 476964; 1 St Mary's Pl; ☾ closes midnight Sun-Wed, 1am Thu-Sat) Upstairs at the Victoria is popular with all types of students and serves good bar meals. There's a grungy café-bar with plenty of natural light or a classier lounge bar where you can sink into a sofa. Check out the jazz on Sunday night.

**our pick Aikman's – The Cellar Bar** ( ☎ 477425; 32 Bell St) Want to get away from clipped accents and enjoy a real beer or two? Any bar that has spent 19 years in the CAMRA (Campaign for Real Ale) *Good Beer Guide* is all right by us. Here you'll find the best selection of real ales in town and a dimly lit cellar bar to enjoy them in. It's worn around the edges (and in the middle too), but geez the beer is good. An antithesis to the more prissy bars in town.

## Entertainment

Check the local *What's On* guide, published weekly and available from the tourist office or its website (www.visit-standrews.co.uk).

**Byre Theatre** ( ☎ 475000; www.byretheatre.com; Abbey St) This theatre company started life in a converted cow byre in the 1930s, and is now in a flashy premises making clever use of light and space. Contact the tourist office or check the website for details of performances.

**New Picture House** ( ☎ 473509; North St; tickets £3.50-5.50) This two-screen cinema shows current films.

## Getting There & Away

St Andrews is 55 miles north of Edinburgh and 13 miles south of Dundee.

**BUS**

Stagecoach Fife operates a bus service from Edinburgh to St Andrews via Kirkcaldy (£7, two hours, hourly). Buses to Dundee (30 minutes, three hourly) also run frequently. Bus 23 runs to Stirling (£6, two hours, five daily Monday to Saturday). Frequent services to East Neuk destinations include Crail (30 minutes) and Anstruther (40 minutes). All buses leave from the bus station on Station Rd.

**TRAIN**

There is no train station in St Andrews itself, but you can take a train from Edinburgh (try to get a seat on the right-hand side of the carriage for great firth views) to Leuchars, 5 miles to the northwest (£10, one hour, hourly), and then a bus (£2) or taxi into town.

CENTRAL SCOTLAND

From Leuchars, buses 94, 96 and 99 leave every 20 minutes during the day (hourly in the evening) for St Andrews.

## Getting Around

**Ian Cowe Coachworks** (ICC Rentals; ☎ 472543; carhire@iccrentals.com; 76 Argyle St) hires out small cars for £25 per day with unlimited mileage.

There are taxi ranks at the bus station and at Holy Trinity Church on South St. To order a cab, call **Golf City Taxis** ( ☎ 477788; Argyle St). **Town & Country** ( ☎ 840444) has taxis with wheelchair access. A taxi between Leuchars train station and the town centre costs around £10.

**Spokes** ( ☎ 477835; 37 South St) hires out mountain bikes for £6.50/10.50 per half-/full day.

## EAST NEUK

The section of the southern Fife coast that stretches from Crail westwards to Largo Bay is known as East Neuk (neuk means 'corner' in Scots). There are several picturesque fishing villages and some good coastal walks in the area.

## Crail

☎ 01333 / pop 1700

One of the prettiest East Neuk villages and a favourite with artists, Crail has a much-photographed and painted harbour ringed by stone cottages with red-pantiled roofs.

The helpful **tourist office** ( ☎ 450869; 62 Marketgate; ☼ 10am-1pm & 2-5pm Mon-Sat, noon-5pm Sun Easter-early Oct) is at the museum.

There are far fewer fishing boats here now than there once were, but you can still buy fresh lobster (£20 per kilogram) and crab (£3 per serving) from a **kiosk** ( ☼ usually noon-4pm Sat & Sun) at the harbour.

The village's history and involvement with the fishing industry is outlined in the **Crail Museum** ( ☎ 450869; 62 Marketgate; admission free; ☼ 10am-1pm & 2-5pm Mon-Sat, 2-5pm Sun Jun-Sep, 2-5pm Sat & Sun Apr & May).

**Crail Gallery** ( ☎ 450316; www.crailgallery.com; 22 High St; ☼ 10am-5pm Easter-Oct) is a local gallery with some terrific artists' impressions of Crail and East Neuk and framed prints of St Andrews.

The 18th-century **Selcraig House** ( ☎ 450697; www.selcraighouse.co.uk; 47 Nethergate; s/d £30/60) is a gold mine for antiquaries and very friendly. Some of the rooms are just fantastic, especially on the 1st floor, where you get a four-poster, bucketloads of space and beautiful furnishings.

The **Marine Hotel** ( ☎ 450207; marinerosebery@tiscali .co.uk; 54 Nethergate South; s/d £30/55) is a cracking small hotel overlooking the sea. Rooms are neat and furnished to a high standard, although en suites are old fashioned and could do with some work. The bistro here specialises in fine seafood creations (lobster and crab from Crail harbour); mains cost between £10 and £14. Best of all, the large garden area overlooking the sea provides the perfect place for a cold drink on a summer afternoon.

Crail is 10 miles southeast of St Andrews. Stagecoach Fife bus 95 between Leven, Anstruther, Crail and St Andrews passes through Crail hourly every day (30 minutes to St Andrews).

## Anstruther

☎ 01333 / pop 3500

Anstruther is a vivacious former fishing village with lots of twisting streets, interesting wynds (lanes) and knick-knack shops lining Rodger and High Sts. The waterfront is popular in summer with tourists and locals chomping down on fish and chips while enjoying the sunshine.

The **tourist office** ( ☎ 311073; Fisheries Museum, St Ayles, Harbourhead; ☼ 10am-5pm Mon-Sat, 11am-4pm Sun Easter-Oct) is the best in East Neuk. There are banks with ATMs in the town centre.

### SIGHTS

The displays at the excellent **Scottish Fisheries Museum** ( ☎ 310628; www.scotfishmuseum.org; St Ayles, Harbourhead; adult/child £5/free; ☼ 10am-5.30pm Mon-Sat, 11am-5pm Sun Apr-Sep, 10am-4.30pm Mon-Sat, noon-4.30pm Sun Oct-Mar; ﴾ﻸ﴿ ) include the Zulu Gallery, which houses the huge, partly restored hull of a traditional Zulu-class fishing boat, redolent with the scent of tar and timber. Afloat in the harbour outside the museum lies the *Reaper*, a fully restored Fifie-class fishing boat, built in 1902.

The mile-long **Isle of May**, 6 miles southeast of Anstruther, is a stunning nature reserve. Between April and July the intimidating cliffs are packed with breeding kittiwakes, razorbills, guillemots, shags and around 40,000 puffins. Minke whales have also been spotted around the island in early summer. Inland are the remains of the 12th-century **St Adrian's Chapel**, dedicated to a monk who was murdered on the island by the Danes in 875.

The five-hour trip to the island on the **May Princess** ( ☎ 310103; www.isleofmayferry.com; adult/child £16/8), including two to three hours ashore, sails from three to seven times weekly (weather permitting) from mid-April to September (daily July to September). You can make reservations and buy tickets at the harbour kiosk near the museum at least an hour before departure. Departure times vary depending on the tide – check times for the coming week or so by calling, or check the website.

### SLEEPING & EATING

Finding reasonably priced B&B accommodation in Anstruther is difficult – for solo travellers almost impossible.

**Sheiling** ( ☎ 310697; 32 Glenogil Gardens; r per person £20-25) This place offers two genteel, elegantly furnished rooms with shared bathroom and a homespun vibe. It also has an excellent breakfast menu. Good for solo travellers.

**Middlemarch B&B** ( ☎ 311140; www.middlemarch bandb.co.uk; Crail Rd; r per person £30-35) With two double bedrooms awash with fabrics, cushions and exotic memorabilia, Middlemarch is a pretty special place. Couples looking for a romantic break will enjoy indulging here – nothing is too much trouble for the friendly hosts.

**Spindrift** ( ☎ /fax 310573; www.thespindrift.co.uk; Pittenweem Rd; s/d £45/70; 🖳 ) This is a top place to spoil yourself – it's a luxury, licensed small hotel in a 19th-century sea-captain's house. Couples should go for the captain's room on the top floor. The hosts ensure you'll enjoy their sumptuous accommodation, which is a cut above the other guesthouses on this street.

**our pick** **Dreel Tavern** ( ☎ 310727; 16 High St West; mains £9; 🕑 lunch & dinner) This charming old pub on the banks of the Dreel Burn has bucketloads of character and serves excellent bar meals (try the smoked-fish pie); chow down in the outdoor beer garden in summer. There are also some top-quality cask ales here.

**Cellar Restaurant** ( ☎ 310378; 24 East Green; 3-course set dinner £39; 🕑 lunch Wed-Sat, dinner Mon-Sat) Tucked away in an alley behind the museum, the Cellar is famous for its seafood – try the prime east coast halibut with greens, pinenuts, bacon and hollandaise – and fine wines. Inside it's elegant and upmarket. Advance bookings are essential.

**Anstruther Fish Bar** ( ☎ 310518; www.anstruther fishbar.co.uk; 44 Shore St, fish & chips £6.50) Renowned chippie selling classy takes on an old favourite, such as organic Shetland cod, or grilled rainbow trout – with chips, of course.

There's a fresh-seafood kiosk situated on the waterfront selling dressed crab (£2.70 per serving), mussels and jellied eel.

### GETTING THERE & AWAY

Anstruther is located 9 miles south of St Andrews. Stagecoach Fife bus 95 runs daily from Leven (more departures from St Monans) to Anstruther and on to St Andrews (40 minutes, hourly) via Crail.

## Around Anstruther

A magnificent example of Lowland Scottish domestic architecture, **Kellie Castle** (NTS; ☎ 01333-720271; adult/child £8/5; 🕑 castle 1-5pm Apr-Oct, garden 9.30am-5.30pm year-round) has creaky floors, crooked little doorways and some marvellous works of art, giving it an air of authenticity. It's set in a beautiful garden, and many rooms contain superb plasterwork, the Vine room being the most exquisite. The original part of the building dates from 1360; it was enlarged to its present dimensions around 1606.

The castle is 3 miles west of Anstruther on the B9171. Stagecoach bus 95A runs from Anstruther to Grangemuir (two daily Monday to Saturday); from here it's about a 1.5 mile walk to the castle.

Three miles north of Anstruther, off the B9131 to St Andrews, is **Scotland's Secret Bunker** ( ☎ 01333-310301; www.secretbunker.co.uk; Troy Wood; adult/child £9/5; 🕑 10am-6pm Apr-Oct; 🖳 ). This fascinating Cold War relic was to be one of Britain's underground command centres and a home for Scots leaders in the event of nuclear war. Hidden 30m underground and surrounded by nearly 5m of reinforced concrete are the austere operation rooms, communication centre and dormitories. It's very authentic and uses artefacts of the period, which make for an absorbing exploration. The Scottish Campaign for Nuclear Disarmament (CND) has an exhibit, bringing home the realities of Britain's current nuclear Trident policy. The bunker is a gripping experience and highly recommended.

Take Stagecoach bus X26, which goes from Anstruther to St Andrews, jump off at the Drumrack crossroads and walk east for about 1.5 miles along the B940 to reach the bunker.

## Pittenweem

☎ 01333 / pop 1650

This is now the main fishing port on the East Neuk coast, and there are lively fish sales at the harbour from 8am. On a sunny day, buy an ice cream and stroll the short, breezy promenade, admiring the picturesque waterfront.

The village name means 'place of the cave', referring to **St Fillan's cave** in Cove Wynd, which was used as a chapel by a 7th-century missionary. The saint reputedly possessed miraculous powers – apparently, when he wrote his sermons in the dark cave, his arm would throw light on his work by emitting a luminous glow. The cave is protected by a locked gate, but a key is available from a nearby house (see sign on gate).

**Harbour Guest House** ( ☎ 311273, 312937; 14 Mid Shore; s/d £30/60) has en-suite rooms overlooking the harbour. Prices depend on time of year and how many nights you stay.

Drop into **Heron Gallery & Bistro** ( ☎ 311014; 15a High St; mains £5-7; ☻ 10.30am-4pm Thu-Tue, to 2pm Wed) for a snack or meal. Dressed crab and homemade smoked mackerel pâté feature on the menu, and you dine among local works of art that inject some real colour into this pretty harbour town – it's good for a browse and everything is for sale. Bus details are as for Anstruther.

## St Monans
☎ 01333 / pop 1450
This ancient fishing village is just over a mile west of Pittenweem and is named after a local cave-dwelling saint who was probably killed by pirates.

The **parish church**, at the western end of the village, was built in 1362 on the orders of a grateful King David II, who was rescued by villagers from a shipwreck in the Firth of Forth. A model of a full-rigged ship, dating from 1800, hangs above the altar. The church commands sweeping views of the firth, and the past echoes inside its cold, whitewashed walls.

**St Monans Heritage Collection** (5 West Shore; admission free; ☻ 11am-1pm & 2-4pm Tue, Thu, Sat & Sun Easter-Oct), on the harbour, is a wonderful small gallery devoted to the history of the St Monans' fishing industry through a collection of 20th-century B&W photos and several artefacts. Most of the photos were taken by a local photographer and the collection changes monthly.

You're better off staying in Anstruther as there is little accommodation in St Monans.

**Harbour Howff Café** ( ☎ 730901; 6 Station Rd; light meals £3-4; ☻ 10am-4pm Wed-Sun; ▣ ) is a community-run café promoting healthy eating and serving excellent sandwiches and fresh cakes.

**ourpick** **Seafood Restaurant** ( ☎ 730327; 16 West End; 3-course lunch/dinner £24/35; ☻ lunch & dinner, winter closed Mon & Tue) is an outstanding restaurant just west of the harbour and within salt-spray distance of the sea. It commands sweeping harbour views and has been highly commended for its delectable seafood (try the spiced collops of monkfish). In winter a three-course lunch is available for £15.

Stagecoach Fife bus 95 runs daily from St Monans to St Andrews (50 minutes, at least hourly), via Anstruther.

## Elie & Earlsferry
☎ 01333 / pop 1500
These two attractive villages mark the southwestern end of East Neuk. There are great sandy beaches and good walks along the coast.

**Elie Watersports** ( ☎ 330962; www.eliewatersports .com), on the harbour at Elie, hires out windsurfers (£30 for two hours), sailing dinghies (Lasers £15 per hour, Wayfarers £20 per hour), canoes (£9 an hour) and mountain bikes (£12 a day), and provides instruction as well.

**Ship Inn** ( ☎ 330246; The Toft, Elie; mains £9-15; ☻ lunch & dinner; ♿ ), down by Elie harbour, is a pleasant and popular place for a bar lunch. Seafood and Asian dishes feature on the menu and, on a sunny day, you can tuck in at an outside table overlooking the wide sweep of the bay.

# PERTHSHIRE & KINROSS

Perthshire and Kinross is the living, breathing heart of Scotland in more ways than one: the region is the former home of the Stone of Destiny, Aberfeldy is the geographical centre of the country and Perth is the former capital of Scotland.

The region is a joy to explore with its hulking castles, historic roots, medieval cathedrals and – perhaps its greatest drawcard – stunning countryside. Scenically, Perthshire and Kinross contain, in miniature, as many variations in terrain as Scotland itself. In an area that has a thriving logging industry, Perthshire is also home to big-tree country too, where ancient woodlands survive among younger, prosperous regeneration forests. Loch Tay in western Perthshire is a highlight with picture-perfect Kenmore at its eastern head, Ben Lawers (1214m) standing guard over its northern bank and remote, magical Glen Lyon on the other side of the strapping Ben Lawers.

## Getting Around

Perth and Kinross Council produces a useful public-transport map showing all services in the region; it's available at tourist offices. The major bus operators in the region:

**Aberfeldy postbus** ( ☎ 01887-820400) Serves remote west Perthshire.
**Scottish Citylink** ( ☎ 0870 550 5050)
**Stagecoach Fife** ( ☎ 01383-511911)
**Stagecoach Perth** ( ☎ 01738-629339)
**Strathtay Scottish** ( ☎ 01382-227201)

Trains run alongside the A9, destined for Aviemore and Inverness. The other main line connects Perth with Stirling (in the south) and Dundee and Arbroath (in the east).

## KINROSS & LOCH LEVEN

☎ 01577 / pop 4700

Kinross is best known as the access point for Loch Leven Castle, a quintessential Scottish treasure – a castle that sits on a small island.

The helpful **Heart of Scotland tourist office** ( ☎ 863680; kinrosstic@perthshire.co.uk; 9.30am-5pm Mon-Sat Apr-Jun & Sep-Oct, to 6pm Jul & Aug, 11am-4pm Sun Apr-Oct), by junction 6 of the M90, has an exhibition on the area.

Evocative **Loch Leven Castle** (HS; ☎ 07778 040483; adult/child incl Kinross ferry £4.50/2.25; 9.30am-5.30pm, last sailing 4.15pm Apr-Sep) served as a fortress and prison from the late 14th century. Its most famous captive was Mary, Queen of Scots, who spent almost a year incarcerated here from 1567. Her infamous charms bewitched Willie Douglas, who managed to get hold of the cell keys to release her, then rowed her across to the shore. The castle is now roofless but basically intact.

**Roxburghe Guest House** ( ☎ 862498; www.roxburghe guesthouse.co.uk; 126 High St, Kinross; s/d/tr £30/60/70) is a lovely guesthouse with cool, tastefully furnished rooms in a rickety old property; Roxburghe feels like a home away from home. Prices may be up for negotiation for small groups.

**Turfhills House B&B** ( ☎ 863881; turfhillshouse@aol .com; s/d £40/70) is a sumptuous, genteel, musty old Georgian house with grand Victorian furnishings, set in some lush gardens. It's next to the tourist office and makes an excellent overnight stop if you're whizzing up the M90 motorway. Note that no singles are available in July and August.

Scottish Citylink has bus services between Perth (30 minutes, hourly) and Kinross. In the other direction buses go to Edinburgh (1½ hours, hourly).

## PERTH

☎ 01738 / pop 44,000

Lodged snugly in a lush valley alongside the M90, Perth's biggest drawcard is historical Scone Palace, but the city's grand Georgian buildings by the banks of the River Tay possess their own splendour. This market town was once a weaving, dyeing and glove-making centre and Scotland's capital. Today it exudes a demure pride, suggesting the town walls have not forgotten their past significance. Perth is not simply quaint, though; embedded in the centuries-old architecture skirting the cobblestone streets is a cosmopolitan vibe, reflected in imaginative cuisine, welcoming pubs, historical sites and a gallery or two.

### History

Perth's rise in importance derives from Scone (pronounced scoon), 2 miles north of the town. In 838, Kenneth MacAlpin became the first king of a united Scotland and brought the Stone of Destiny (see the boxed text, p81) to Scone. An important abbey was built on the site. From this time on, all Scottish kings were invested here, even after Edward I of England stole the sacred talisman, carting it off to London's Westminster Abbey in 1296. In 1996 Prime Minister John Major persuaded the Queen to promise to return it to Scotland, but it went to Edinburgh Castle rather than back to Scone. There's actually some doubt about whether Edward I stole the real stone – he might have stolen a fake!

From the 12th century, Perth was Scotland's capital, and in 1437 James I was murdered here. There were four important monasteries in the area and the town was a target for the Reformation movement in Scotland.

### Orientation

Most of the town lies on the western bank of the River Tay; Scone Palace and some of the B&Bs are on the eastern bank. There are two large parks: North Inch, the scene of the infamous Battle of the Clans in 1396, and South Inch. The bus and train stations are close to each other, near the northwestern corner of South Inch.

### Information

**Lloyds TSB** (King Edward St) Has an ATM.
**Perth Library** (AK Bell Library; ☎ 444949; York Place; 9.30am-5pm Mon, Wed & Fri, to 8pm Tue & Thu, to 4pm Sat) Free internet access; lots of terminals.

**Perth Royal Infirmary** ( ☎ 623311; Taymount Tce) Hospital; west of the town centre.

**Tourist office** ( ☎ 450600; Lower City Mills, West Mill St; ☽ 9.30am-4.30pm Mon-Sat, 10am-2pm Sun Apr-Jun, 9.30am-6pm Mon-Sat, 11am-4pm Sun Jul & Aug, call for rest of year) An efficient tourist office that can assist with tracking down accommodation in the local area.

## Sights
### SCONE PALACE

Decadent **Scone Palace** ( ☎ 552300; adult/child £7.50/4.50; ☽ 9.30am-5.30pm Apr-Oct; ⓺ ), located 2 miles north of Perth and just off the A93 near Old Scone, was constructed in 1580 on a site intrinsic to Scottish history. It is one of Perthshire's premier tourist attractions.

The interior is a gallery of historical treasures and fine French furniture, including Marie Antoinette's writing table and a 16th-century needlework hanging, worked by Mary, Queen of Scots. Superb antique Chinese vases mingle with 18th- and 19th-century porcelain, and the walls drip with regal portraits of earls and countesses. Even the cornices, ceilings and walls are exquisite (the drawing-room wallpaper is silk!). The earl and countess of Mansfield have owned the palace for almost 400 years and the incumbents still host family functions in their sumptuous abode.

Outside, the resident peacocks unfold their splendid plumage in the magnificent grounds, which incorporate a pinetum, a wild garden, a butterfly garden and the all-important cricket

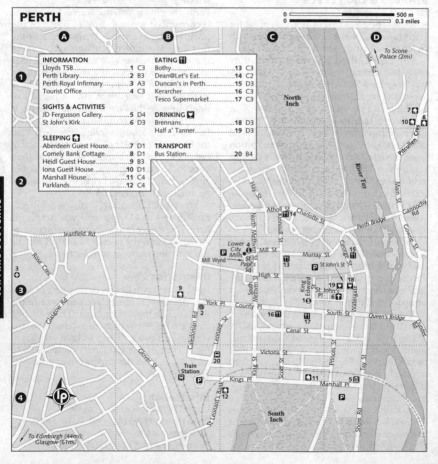

**PERTH**

0 — 500 m
0 — 0.3 miles

| INFORMATION | |
|---|---|
| Lloyds TSB | 1 C3 |
| Perth Library | 2 B3 |
| Perth Royal Infirmary | 3 A3 |
| Tourist Office | 4 C3 |

| SIGHTS & ACTIVITIES | |
|---|---|
| JD Fergusson Gallery | 5 D4 |
| St John's Kirk | 6 D3 |

| SLEEPING 🏠 | |
|---|---|
| Aberdeen Guest House | 7 D1 |
| Comely Bank Cottage | 8 D1 |
| Heidl Guest House | 9 B3 |
| Iona Guest House | 10 D1 |
| Marshall House | 11 C4 |
| Parklands | 12 C4 |

| EATING 🍴 | |
|---|---|
| Bothy | 13 C3 |
| Dean@Let's Eat | 14 C2 |
| Duncan's in Perth | 15 D3 |
| Kerarcher | 16 C3 |
| Tesco Supermarket | 17 C3 |

| DRINKING 🍷 | |
|---|---|
| Brennans | 18 D3 |
| Half a' Tanner | 19 D3 |

| TRANSPORT | |
|---|---|
| Bus Station | 20 B4 |

To Scone Palace (2mi)

North Inch

River Tay

Perth Bridge

To Edinburgh (44mi); Glasgow (61mi)

South Inch

**CENTRAL SCOTLAND**

pitch. Bus 3 from Perth comes here roughly hourly most of the day.

### ST JOHN'S KIRK

Daunting **St John's Kirk** (admission free; ☷ 10am-4pm Mon-Sat May-Sep plus 10am-1pm Sun Jun-Sep), founded in 1126, is surrounded by cobbled streets and is still the centrepiece of the town. In 1559 John Knox preached a powerful sermon here that helped begin the Reformation, inciting a frenzied destruction of Scone abbey and other religious sites.

### JD FERGUSSON GALLERY

Within the original Perth waterworks building, aptly titled the Round House, the **JD Fergusson Gallery** ( ☎ 441944; cnr Marshall Pl & Tay St; admission free; ☷ 10am-5pm Mon-Sat) contains the most extensive collection of work by notable Scottish Colourist and Perthshire local JD Fergusson. Pieces reflect heavy French (due to Fergusson's prolonged stay across the channel) and postimpressionist influences.

## Sleeping

**Comely Bank Cottage** ( ☎ 631118; comelybankcott@ hotmail.com; 19 Pitcullen Cres; s £30, d & tw per person £24-27) A bit cheaper than other places on this strip, but with no sacrifice in room quality or level of hospitality. Comely Bank has a really personal touch with lovely rooms that reveal a woman's influence. Room 1 is an excellent double.

**Heidl Guest House** ( ☎ 635031; www.heidl.co.uk; 43 York Pl; s/d from £25/50) A solid old favourite, close to the centre, the Heidl offers an excellent range of rooms and serves up a decent brekky, too. Ask for room 3 or 4 in the 'tower' at the top of the building; they share a bathroom and have lots of space. Heidl is a little lacking in atmosphere, but the friendly hosts try their best.

**Aberdeen Guest House** ( ☎ /fax 633183; buchan@a berdeenguesthouse.fsnet.co.uk; 13 Pitcullen Cres; d £55) A cheery place with terrific, spacious rooms and thoughtful hosts – if you find a friendlier guesthouse than this, take it. Rooms are well furnished and homely, and have that extra touch that comes from people who enjoy their work. French and German spoken.

**Parklands** ( ☎ 622451; www.theparklandshotel.com; 2 St Leonard's Bank; standard/superior r incl dinner £160/172; ⚐ ) The former home of lord provosts (mayors), Parklands is one of the most luxurious places to stay in Perth, and a great little hideaway. It's

a small hotel with 14 sumptuous rooms and a restaurant. There are often cheaper package deals available.

Also recommended:

**Marshall House** ( ☎ 442886; gallagher@marshall -guest-house.freeserve.co.uk; 6 Marshall Pl; s/d £30/50) One of the superior-value places along this stretch. The downstairs twin is clean as a whistle, spacious and cheerfully decorated.

**Iona Guest House** ( ☎ /fax 627261; 2 Pitcullen Cres; s/d £30/55) Room 2 is a favourite here.

## Eating

Perth has an exceptionally good dining scene and a strong café and outside-dining culture.

**Bothy** ( ☎ 449792; 33 Kinnoull St; lunch mains £5-11, dinner mains £12-15; ☷ lunch & dinner) The Bothy is a comfy leather couch and wooden wine rack affair with a certain intimacy – it attracts couples and older diners. For lunch, sandwiches like baked mozzarella and grilled aubergine with olive and natural yogurt feature. Tuck into braised beef olives with white pudding for dinner.

**Dean@Let's Eat** ( ☎ 643377; 77 Kinnoull St; starters £6-8, mains £15-18; ☷ lunch & dinner Tue-Sat) Noted for its excellent service, this award-winning bistro is the best place in town for splashing out on a special meal. Outstanding cuisine comes in the form of creative dishes such as a spicy roast cashew nut salad with couscous and chargrilled vegetables. Enjoy an apéritif on the comfy couches before indulging your palate.

**Kerarcher** ( ☎ 449777; 168 South St; 2/3 course dinner £15/19; ☷ dinner Tue-Sat) This classic seafood restaurant keeps things simple. They combine fresh seafood with ingredients that add hints of flavour to complement but not overpower the dishes; this is a recipe for success. Try the seared Skye scallops and Scottish black pudding garnished with cape gooseberry.

Also in town:

**Tesco supermarket** (South St)

**Duncan's in Perth** ( ☎ 626016; 33 George St; mains $14; ☷ lunch & dinner Mon-Sat) The cool, clean interior here is ambient and relaxed, and the food is pretty good too. Produce is sourced from around the country – how can you not be drawn to seared wood pigeon?

## Drinking

Perth has a healthy pubs-per-capita ratio and in the courtyard situated around St John's Kirk you won't have to stray far to change draughts.

**Half a' Tanner** (St John's Pl) A warm, popular and hospitable place, on fine days the crowd spills into the courtyard.

**Brennans** (St John's St) This pub is small in size but big on personality – there's live music on weekends and a happy buzz every night. It's a bit of a warren inside, with a low ceiling, but it's very friendly and there are good ales on tap.

## Getting There & Away

### BUS
Scottish Citylink operates regular buses from Perth to Glasgow (£8, 1½ hours), Edinburgh (£7.70, 1½ hours), Dundee (£5, 35 minutes), Aberdeen (£15.70, 2¼ hours) and Inverness (£14, 2¾ hours).

Stagecoach buses serve Dunkeld (30 minutes, every hour or two Monday to Saturday), Pitlochry (1¼ hours, every hour or two Monday to Saturday) and Aberfeldy (1¼ hours, roughly hourly Monday to Saturday). Citylink also serves Dunkeld and Pitlochry regularly.

Stagecoach also serves Crieff (45 minutes, at least hourly), St Fillans (1¼ hours, five daily Monday to Saturday – some services change in Crieff) via Crieff and Comrie, and Dunning (40 minutes, at least hourly Monday to Saturday) via Forteviot.

Strathtay Scottish buses travel from Perth to Blairgowrie (45 minutes, hourly Monday to Saturday) and Dundee (£3.50, 1¾ hours, hourly).

### TRAIN
There's a train service from Glasgow's Queen St (£11.60, one hour, at least hourly Monday to Saturday, every two hours Sunday), and a service from Edinburgh (£11.60, 1½ hours, at least hourly Monday to Saturday). Other rail destinations include Stirling (£9.30, 30 minutes, one or two per hour) and Pitlochry (£10, 30 minutes, two hourly, fewer on Sunday).

# STRATHEARN
West of Perth, the wide strath (valley) of the River Earn was once a great forest where medieval kings hunted. The whole area is known as Strathearn, a very attractive region of undulating farmland, hills and lochs. The Highlands begin in the western section of Strathearn.

## Dunning
☎ 01764 / pop 900
If you think you've entered spooky country around here, you may just be right. On the

way into Dunning, about a mile west of the town by the B8062, there's a strange **cross** on a pile of stones with the words 'Maggiewall burnt here 1657 as a witch'. Keep away from bonfires.

The village is dominated by the 12th-century Norman tower of **St Serfs church** ( ☎ 684497; admission free; ⏰ 9.30am-5.30pm Apr-Sep), but most of the building dates from 1810. The magnificent 9th-century **Dupplin Cross**, one of the earliest Christian stone crosses in Scotland, was originally near Forteviot (3 miles from Dunning). It's now the regal centrepiece of St Serfs Church. Historic Scotland provides a guided talk on the mysterious monolith.

A wonderful, eccentric little nook-and-cranny pub, **Kirkstyle Inn** ( ☎ 684248; Kirkstyle Sq; mains £7-16; ⏰ lunch & dinner) is an atmospheric inn with a warm glow and a local touch – the food's not half bad either. Try the Spitfire brew. Book ahead at weekends as it's very popular.

Historic Dunning is about 8 miles southwest of Perth. Stagecoach bus 17 runs from Perth to Forteviot and Dunning (40 minutes, at least hourly Monday to Saturday). Docherty's Midland Coaches runs between Dunning and Auchterarder (15 minutes, up to 10 times daily Monday to Saturday).

## Auchterarder
☎ 01764 / pop 4000
Four miles west of Dunning, the small, neat town of Auchterarder meanders along a winding High St.

There's a **tourist office** ( ☎ 0845 225 5121; 90 High St; ⏰ Mon-Sat Apr-Sep, Sun Jul & Aug) with a **heritage centre** (admission free) detailing wide-ranging aspects of local history. There are absorbing B&W pictures of the town and nearby Dunning.

Just up the road, 3 miles from Auchterarder on the A9, you'll find **Tullibardine** ( ☎ 682252; Blackford; tours £5; ⏰ 10am-5.30pm), Scotland's newest distillery. It's just off the A9 and reopened in 2004 after being closed for 10 years. Tours are short and sweet, which means 'tasting time' comes around nice and quick.

The highly rated **Gleneagles Hotel** ( ☎ 662231; www.gleneagles.com; Auchterarder; r from £370; 👶 ♿ ), just over 2 miles west of Auchterarder, is a splendid place with three championship golf courses. Room charges include full use of the extensive leisure facilities. The priciest room is the £1900 Royal Lochnagar Suite, complete with antiques, silk-lined walls and hand-woven carpets. The hotel even has its own train station, 50 minutes (£11.50) from Glasgow, and there's free transport between the station and the hotel. However, if you can afford to stay here, you can afford the limousine from Glasgow airport (£160). Gleneagles has also earned a reputation as a very child-friendly hotel, making it ideal for families. There's plenty here to keep kids entertained, including a nursery with all the latest gizmos. Check the website for special deals.

Docherty's Midland Coaches runs buses from Auchterarder to Dunning (15 minutes, up to 10 times daily Monday to Saturday), Stirling (45 minutes, three daily Monday to Friday) and Perth (40 minutes, at least hourly).

## Around Auchterarder

If you want to throw a line in and have a good chance of being rewarded for your efforts, drop by **Orchill Loch Trout Fishery** ( ☎ 01764-682287; www.orchillloch.bravehost.com; Braco; 🔥 ). The main loch (fly fishing) is regularly stocked with rainbow trout and there's bait fishing too in a separate pond, particularly good for the kids. A four-hour ticket allows three fish and costs £13.50; a full day allows five fish and is only £22. Orchill is on the backroad between Gleneagles and Braco; access is off the A822 or A823.

## Crieff & Around

☎ 01764

Scraping the edge of the Highlands, elegant Crieff (population 6579) is an old, resort-style town, as popular with tourists today as it was in Victorian times.

### INFORMATION

**Bank of Scotland** (Lodge St) Has ATM.
**Library** ( ☎ 653418; 6 Comrie St; 🕙 10am-7.30pm Mon, Wed & Fri, 10am-1pm & 2-5pm Tue, 10am-1pm Thu, 10am-12.30pm Sat) Free internet access.
**Police station** (King St)
**Post office** (High St)
**Royal Bank of Scotland** (West High St) Has ATM.
**Tourist office** ( ☎ 652578; crieffttic@visitscotland.com; Town Hall, High St; 🕙 10am-4pm Mon-Sat Apr-Jun & Sep-Oct, to 3pm Nov-Mar, 9.30am-5.30pm Mon-Sat Jul & Aug) In the clock tower.

### SIGHTS

In the basement at the tourist office, **Stones, Stocks & Stories** ( ☎ 652578; High St; admission free) is a small but interesting exhibition of the town

stocks (leg clamps used as a form of punishment), the Drummond Cross (1400–1600) and a formidable 9th-century Pictish cross slab.

The highly rated **Famous Grouse Experience** ( ☎ 656565; The Hosh; tours from £4.50; 🕙 9am-6pm), at the Glenturret Distillery, 1 mile north of town, has a range of tours of the traditional malting process. Visitors are also treated to a hi-tech bonanza that includes a virtual giant jigsaw and 'flying with the grouse'.

**Innerpeffray Library** ( ☎ 652819; Innerpeffray; adult/child incl tour £2.50/50p; 🕙 10am-12.45pm & 2-4.45pm Wed-Sat, 2-4pm Sun Mar-Oct, by appointment only Nov-Feb), about 4 miles southeast of Crieff on the B8062, is Scotland's first lending library (founded in 1680). There's a huge collection of rare, interesting and ancient books, some of them 500 years old.

### SLEEPING

**our pick** **Comrie Croft** ( ☎ 670140; www.comriecroft .com; dm/d from £13/30) A friendly, rustic place to stay with great facilities, this croft is suited to backpackers (with wheels) or families. There's mountain-bike hire, fishing, walking routes, lots of games for the kids and plenty of places to just laze about. The Croft is by Crieff, 4 miles out on the A85 towards Comrie.

**Comely Bank Guest House** ( ☎ 653409; www.comely bank.demon.co.uk; 32 Burrell St; r per person £22-26; 🔥 ) This is a top Scottish guesthouse, welcoming, homely and neat as a pin. The downstairs double is huge, frilly and velvety, while upstairs rooms have a more modern décor and are still a good size. All rooms are en suite except for one double.

**Leven House Hotel** ( ☎ 652529; Comrie Rd; r per person £23-25) Probably trading since Victorian times, the best way to describe Leven House is floral, floral, floral. The décor may not win any design awards, but this 1970s-era hotel offers good-value rooms and the friendly hosts make you feel right at home.

**Crieff Hydro** ( ☎ 655555; www.crieffhydro.com; Ferntower Rd; dinner, bed & breakfast per person £40-190; 🔥 🔥 ) An upmarket, classy hotel that's refreshingly unpretentious. It caters well for kids, including an excellent childcare facility.

### EATING

**Thai E-San Restaurant** ( ☎ 652652; Waverley Hotel, 7 James Sq; starters £3.50, mains £6-11; 🕙 lunch & dinner) Locals rave about the Thai food at this simple eatery. Check out the banquets, too – great value.

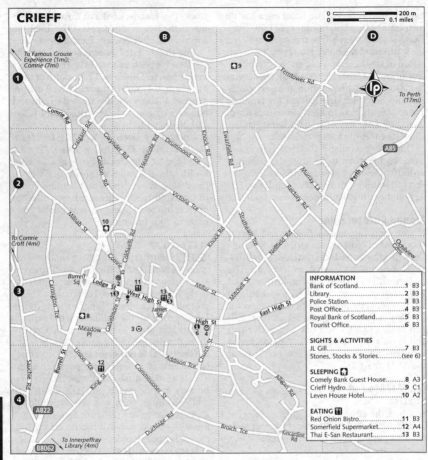

CRIEFF

**INFORMATION**
Bank of Scotland.....................1 B3
Library.....................................2 B3
Police Station..........................3 B3
Post Office...............................4 B3
Royal Bank of Scotland............5 B3
Tourist Office...........................6 B3

**SIGHTS & ACTIVITIES**
JL Gill......................................7 B3
Stones, Stocks & Stories.......(see 6)

**SLEEPING**
Comely Bank Guest House........8 A3
Crieff Hydro.............................9 C1
Leven House Hotel..................10 A2

**EATING**
Red Onion Bistro....................11 B3
Somerfield Supermarket.........12 A4
Thai E-San Restaurant............13 B3

**Red Onion Bistro** ( ☎ 654407; 1 West High St; ⏲ lunch mains £10-14; ⏲ lunch & dinner Mon-Wed, Fri & Sat) Going from strength to strength, the Red Onion has dishes showing a lot of flair. The simple, pleasing dining room is perfect for tucking into a roasted rump of lamb with caramelised red cabbage and rosemary *jus*. Vegetarian dishes are also available (such as butternut squash, chilli and ginger risotto).

For local produce, **JL Gill** ( ☎ 653011; www.scottishproduce.co.uk; 26 West High St) is an old-fashioned shop specialising in whisky and cheese. It's a good spot to pick up whisky specials, including some you may have trouble sourcing elsewhere (such as the Caol Ila Signatory Vintage). For self-catering, there's a **Somerfield supermarket** (Union Tce).

**GETTING THERE & AWAY**
Hourly Stagecoach buses link Crieff with Perth (45 minutes), less frequently on Sunday. Other buses run to Comrie (20 minutes, roughly hourly Monday to Saturday, every two hours Sunday), St Fillans (35 minutes, five daily Monday to Saturday) and Stirling (50 minutes, four to eight daily).

## Upper Strathearn
☎ 01764
The two Highland villages of **Comrie** (population 1839) and **St Fillans** (population 350), in upper Strathearn, are surrounded by forests and craggy, bare mountain tops where deer and mountain hares both live in abundance.

Comrie has a rather tattered elegance hinting at its previous heyday. St Fillans enjoys an excellent location at the eastern end of **Loch Earn**, which reflects the silhouettes of distant, towering peaks in its glittering waters.

The **Four Seasons Hotel** ( ☎ 685333; www.the fourseasonshotel.co.uk; St Fillans; standard/superior r £48/58) is a refined hotel with a touch of elegance, with two beautifully appointed sitting rooms and a small bar with loch views – great places to relax. There is a ton of activities to choose from here, including water-skiing, quad biking and pony trekking. There are also six secluded chalets nestled in the slopes behind the hotel.

Comrie is 24 miles west of Perth, and St Fillans is about 5 miles further west. Stagecoach operates daily buses from Perth, via Crieff, to Comrie and St Fillans (see opposite).

# WEST PERTHSHIRE

This remote area of Perthshire is a jewel in central Scotland's crown. It's difficult to reach via public transport – buses are usually once-a-day postal services; however, these fabulous hills and lochs are well worth making an effort to see.

## Aberfeldy

☎ 01887 / pop 1900

The happening heart of Scotland: adventure sports, art and castles all feature on the menu here. Aberfeldy is slightly shabby and rough around the edges, but with some great attractions nearby, and a spot deep in forest country, it's well worth a linger.

The helpful, knowledgeable **tourist office** ( ☎ 820276; The Square; ☺ 10am-4pm Mon-Sat Easter-Jun & Sep-Oct, 9.30am-5.30pm Mon-Sat Jul & Aug, 10am-3pm Mon-Sat Nov-Easter), in an old church, is an exceptionally efficient and friendly place. The **Royal Bank of Scotland** (8 The Square) has an ATM.

### SIGHTS

The **Watermill** ( ☎ 822896; www.aberfeldywatermill .com; Mill St; admission free; ☺ 10am-5pm Mon-Sat, noon-5pm Sun; ♿ ) is an unusual and much-needed attraction in the centre of town. Incorporating a bookshop (the largest in the Highlands) with a great Scottish collection, gallery with contemporary works of art and a coffee shop, you could while away several hours in this old mill. Bucket-loads of character are thrown in for good measure and the highlight is perhaps the working mill machinery, giving the gallery a unique space to exhibit its works of art.

### SLEEPING & EATING

**our pick** **Adventurers Escape Hostel** ( ☎ 820498; www .adventurers-escape.co.uk; Weem; beds £13-16) A top-notch hostel just outside Aberfeldy, it has a range of rooms for different size groups (starting with two). All are warm and well looked after. You can also self-cater, and if you're into kayaking, you're in the right place as the National Kayak School runs from the hostel. Best of all though, you're right next to a great pub.

**Tigh'n Eilean Guest House** ( ☎ /fax 820109; www .tighneilean.com; Taybridge Dr; s £35-40 d £55-64) Everything about this property screams comfort – it's a gorgeous place overlooking the Tay. Individually designed rooms all have a unique sense of space. For couples our fave is the Jacuzzi room (it's huge!) and for solo travellers the wood-lined twin with private bath is very snug.

**Guinach House** ( ☎ 820251; www.guinachhouse.co.uk; Urlar Rd; s/d £95/110) More like a boutique hotel, Guinach has modish rooms and a casual, laid-back ambience. Rooms have private access from the rest of the house and are individually styled – our favourite is the zebra room, although the red room with freestanding bathtub runs a close second. The whole place is set on a large estate, so there's plenty of rambling options just beyond the front doorstep.

Also recommended:

**Balnearn House** ( ☎ 820431; www.balnearnhouse .com; Crieff Rd; s/d from £40/50) A sedate, refined and quite luxurious option. Most rooms have great natural light. Rooms upstairs are better.

**Black Watch Inn** ( ☎ 820699; Bank St; mains £6-10; ☺ lunch & dinner) Good range of pub food dabbling in Thai and Scottish dishes.

### GETTING THERE & AWAY

Stagecoach runs buses from Aberfeldy to Pitlochry (45 minutes, hourly Monday to Saturday, less on Sunday), Blairgowrie (1¼ hours, two daily Monday to Friday) and Perth (1¼ hours, 10 daily Monday to Saturday).

Local bus operators run a circular route from Aberfeldy through Loch Tay (Crannog Centre), Kenmore, Fortingall and back to Aberfeldy up to five times daily Monday to Friday. There's also a service through to Killin (one hour) up to five times daily Monday to Saturday (although it only operates on a Saturday from June to September when there's a connecting service through to Oban).

## Around Aberfeldy

**Castle Menzies** ( ☎ 01887-820982; Weem; adult/child £4/2; ⊙ 10.30am-5pm Mon-Sat, 2-5pm Sun Apr–mid-Oct), 1.5 miles west of town by the B846, is the impressive restored 16th-century seat of the chief of the clan Menzies. The Z-plan tower house is magnificently located against a backdrop of Scottish forest. And inside it doesn't disappoint. The place smells just like a castle should – musty and lived in. It reeks of authenticity despite extensive restoration work and is a highly recommended ramble. Check out the fireplace in the dungeon-like kitchens and the gaudy great hall upstairs, with windows unfurling a ribbon of lush, green countryside extending into wooded hills beyond the estate.

**Glenlyon Gallery** ( ☎ 01887-820202; www.glenlyon gallery.com; Boltachan; ⊙ 10am-5pm Thu-Tue Mar-Oct, closed Tue & Thu Nov, Dec & Feb), near Aberfeldy, brings the wildlife and startling natural beauty of Perthshire to life with vivid paintings and sketches by a talented local artist. Some of Scotland's most priceless treasures are captured on canvas and, if you're interested, can be shipped anywhere in the world. The gallery is signposted off the B846, 1 mile north of Aberfeldy.

**Highland Adventure Safari** ( ☎ 01887-820071; www .highlandadventuresafaris.co.uk; B846; 🏂 ) is ideal for those wanting to spot some wildlife or simply enjoy Perthshire's magnificent countryside. Standard trips include the 2½-hour Adventure Safari for £35/13.50 per adult/child, which includes a dram in the wilderness, and the Safari Hike for £60, which includes a walk in the mountains and a picnic. Wildlife you may spot includes golden eagles, osprey and red deer. There's also gold-panning for kids at the visitor centre. It's on the B846, just past Castle Menzies.

## Loch Tay

The greater part of mighty Ben Lawers (1214m), Scotland's ninth-tallest peak, looms over Loch Tay. Traces of rock art that could date back to the Neolithic period 5000 years ago have recently been uncovered. Drop into the **visitor centre** (NTS; ☎ 01567-820397; adult/child £2/1, parking donation £2; ⊙ 10am-5pm Apr-Sep) high on the slopes of the mountain; the access road is off the A827, on the northern shore of the loch, and continues over a wild pass to Glen Lyon. A trail leads to the summit from the centre, but you should take a good map (OS

map 51). There is also a much easier nature trail from the visitor centre and ranger-guided walks in summer. Call by for the jaw-dropping views if nothing else.

A stout little water-bus, **MV Glen Lyon** ( ☎ 01567-820111) takes passengers on one-hour cruises of Loch Tay. The departure point is the Tay Forest Park car park at the eastern end of the loch, near Kenmore. Cruises depart hourly, weather permitting, and cost £7/5 per adult/child.

## Kenmore

The wealthy village of Kenmore, at the eastern end of Loch Tay, is about 6 miles west of Aberfeldy. It's a small but pretty place dominated by a church and clock tower. Don't forget the camera, as it's the perfect place for some happy snaps. Just a quarter of a mile along the south Loch Tay road from the village, the **Scottish Crannog Centre** ( ☎ 01887-830583; adult/child £5/3.50; ⊙ 10am-5.30pm mid-Mar–Oct, 10am-4pm Sat & Sun Nov) has a fascinating reconstruction of an artificial, Iron Age island-house. There are exhibits from archaeological dives of crannogs (see the boxed text, below) and artistic impressions of what they may have looked like. Tours run hourly.

**our pick** **Kenmore Hotel** ( ☎ 01887-830205; www .kenmorehotel.com; The Square; s/d £70/100), touched with a quiet sense of dignity, claims to be Scotland's oldest inn and dates from 1572. Its quaint, spacious rooms are generously furnished and full of character. On the chimneypiece in the bar look out for the romantic description of the countryside written by Robert Burns in 1787. After a few drinks in the bar, watch out for the low doorways on your way upstairs. The **Taymouth Restaurant** (starters

---

### CRANNOGS

Usually built in a loch for defensive purposes, a crannog (from the Gaelic word *crann*, meaning 'tree') consists of an artificial rock island with timber posts and struts supporting a hut above high-water level. Crannogs were used on many lochs, including Lochs Awe, Earn and Tay, from prehistoric times up to the 18th century. Some crannogs had curious underwater causeways that could zigzag or had traps, making night-time assaults without a boat extremely difficult.

£6, mains £12-16; ☽ dinner) overlooks Loch Tay and the mouthwatering menu uses Scottish produce in simple but tasty combinations; the service is first class.

See the Aberfeldy section (p223) for your public-transport options.

## Fortingall & Glen Lyon

Fortingall is one of the prettiest villages in Scotland, with 19th-century thatched cottages in a very tranquil setting. The **church** (admission free; ☽ 10am-4pm Apr-Oct) has impressive wooden beams and a 7th-century **monk's bell**. In the churchyard, there's a 5000-year-old **yew**, probably the oldest tree in Europe. This tree was already ancient when the Romans camped in the meadows by the River Lyon. It's also famous as the reputed birthplace of Pontius Pilate. Today the tree is a shell of its former self – at its zenith it had a girth of over 17m! But souvenir hunters have reduced it to two much smaller trunks.

Rickety Roman bridges, Victorian lodges, a Caledonian pine forest, and sheer peaks splashed with pink and purple heather that poke through swirling clouds mark the drive along the tiny road into the wonderful **Glen Lyon**. The longest enclosed glen in Scotland, it becomes wilder and more uninhabited as it snakes its way west towards Loch Lyon – few visitors penetrate its remote upper reaches, where capercaillie live in patches of pine forest. You'll need wheels, preferably the motorised kind, but if you're keen and you've the time, cycling through Glen Lyon would be a great way to experience this special place. Stop at the **Glenlyon Post Office, Shop & Tearoom** (Bridge of Balgie; dishes £2-5; ☽ lunch Fri-Tue) for sandwiches, soup, homemade savoury tarts and sweetie-treaties.

### SLEEPING & EATING

**Fortingall Hotel** ( ☎ 01887-830367; www.fortingall hotel.com; s/d from £85/120; ☐ ) This completely refurbished hotel is winner of the 2007 Small Scottish Hotel of the Year award. And it's easy to see why. Rooms are sumptuous, beds the sink-in-and-smile variety and the en suites fit for royalty. If you've got the coin, go for the Glen Lyon Superior room – you may have to be dragged out kicking and screaming when it's time to leave. There are special offers if you stay more than one night. Meals are available for guests and nonguests and mains cost £16 to £20.

**our pick** **Milton Eonan** ( ☎ 01887-866318; www.milton eonan.com; Bridge of Balgie; r per person £35) Tucked away just over the Bridge of Balgie from the tiny Glen Lyon hamlet is an absolute gem of a property. It was part of a much larger estate in the hands of the Wills family (Wills Tobacco), but was mostly sold off in the '70s. It's location, next to a small waterfall and surrounded by mountain views, is stunning. Inside, Milton Eonan is exceedingly comfortable, with well-furnished rooms and vintage furniture giving it a touch of class. You can also rent the property out as a private, self-catering option.

Behind Milton Eonan is **Ben Lawers Bunkhouse** (www.benlawersbunkhouse.com; bed £12.50; ☖ ), excellent for hikers or cyclists and sleeping up to six people. It's clean and very well kitted out. It would also work well for families seeking a cheaper option than Milton Eonan.

See the Aberfeldy section for public-transport options (p223).

## Lochs Tummel & Rannoch

The route along Lochs Tummel and Rannoch is worth doing any way you can – by foot, bicycle or car – just don't miss it. Hills of ancient birch and forests of spruce, pine and larch make up the **Tay Forest Park** – the king of Scotland's forests. These wooded hills roll into the glittering waters of the lochs, and while tracking along the southern side of Loch Tummel you'll be greeted by Highland cattle, grand houses and startling views – a reminder of the undeniable raw beauty of Perthshire. A visit in autumn is recommended, when the birch trees are at their finest.

**Queen's View Visitor Centre** ( ☎ 01796-473123; Strathtummel; car-park fee £1; ☽ 10am-6pm late-Mar–mid-Nov), at the eastern end of Loch Tummel, has a magnificent outlook towards Schiehallion (1083m). There are displays and audiovisual programmes about the area. The centre highlights the brilliant forward thinking of the replanting of Tay Forest 300 years ago. The results are all around.

Waterfalls, towering mountains and a shimmering loch greet visitors to the hidden treasure of **Kinloch Rannoch**. It's a great base for local walks (you can walk up Schiehallion from Braes of Foss – see www.jmt.org for more information) or cycle trips around **Loch Rannoch**. There is a Spar supermarket with an ATM in town. **Dunalastair Activity Centre** ( ☎ 07884-492920; activities@dunalastair.co.uk) has a

CENTRAL SCOTLAND

plethora of activities on offer, such as fishing, kayaking (£15), canyoning (£35) and white-water rafting (£35). You can also hire bikes for £15 a day. If you prefer an easy stroll, try the **clan trail** around the loch, which has road-side notice boards about local clans. Beyond the western end of the loch you enter bleak Rannoch Moor, which extends all the way to Glen Coe. The rivers and lochs on the moor are good for fishing.

### SLEEPING & EATING

**Garden B&B** ( ☎ 01882-632434; jimwilson@onetel.com; Kinloch Rannoch; r per person £35) Right off the beaten track between Kinloch Rannoch and Tummel Bridge, this place has just two rooms. But both come with private bathroom and private sitting room (for each room!). The double is better than the twin – much larger. If you're looking for solitude and a touch of eccentricity, this is the place.

**Bunrannoch House** ( ☎ /fax 01882-632407; www .bunrannoch.co.uk; Kinloch Rannoch; r per person with/without dinner £60/35) Grand Bunrannoch House is a former shooting lodge, set back from the edge of town. A collage of flowering purple rhododendrons and the smell of homecooking (rhubarb pie if you're lucky) greets visitors up the driveway. The two family rooms at the top are the best rooms but all have lovely views. Renovation plans include restoration of the original two-level verandah, and the opening of a bar-café. Meals are available; a set-course dinner costs £27.50.

**Post Taste** ( ☎ 01882-632333; The Square, Kinloch Rannoch; paninis £5, mains £11-15; 10am-8.30pm Mon-Sat, 10am-4pm Sun; ) The local post office, café, tourist information centre, internet and gift shop – there's not much they don't do. Open for lunch and light snacks through the afternoon and for dinner. Try the Rannoch venison casserole.

**Loch Tummel Inn** ( ☎ 01882-634272; Strathtummel; bar suppers £6, restaurant mains £10-14; lunch & dinner) This old coaching inn is a snug spot for a decent feed from a menu featuring seafood. The bar is open all day for a leisurely pint in the beer garden overlooking Loch Tummel. The inn is about 3 miles from Queen's View.

### GETTING THERE & AWAY

**Elizabeth Yule Transport** ( ☎ 01796-472290) operates a service between Kinloch Rannoch and Pitlochry (50 minutes, up to five a day Monday to Saturday) via Queen's View and Loch

Tummel Inn. The Pitlochry–Rannoch Station postbus has a once-daily service (Monday to Saturday) via Kinloch Rannoch and both sides of the loch.

ScotRail runs two to four trains daily from Rannoch station north to Fort William (£8, one hour) and Mallaig, and south to Glasgow (£18, 2¾ hours).

## PERTH TO AVIEMORE

There are a number of major sights strung along the A9 – which becomes a scenic treat after Pitlochry. It's the main route north to Aviemore (p330) and Inverness (p318) in the Highlands.

### Dunkeld & Birnam

☎ 01350 / pop 1000

Ever been to a feel-good town? Well, Dunkeld and Birnam, with their enviable location nestled in the heart of Perthshire's big-tree country, await. The towns happily throb with tourists, and so they should – there are architectural delights to enjoy here, including a magnificent cathedral. It is walkers in the surrounding area, though, who really grease the wheels of tourism, even through the winter months. Dunkeld's **tourist office** ( ☎ 727688; dunkeldtic@visitscotland.co.uk; The Cross; 9.30am-4pm Mon-Sat Apr-Jun & Sep-Oct, 9am-5.30pm Jul & Aug) has to be one of the friendliest in all of the country. Pick up its leaflet on local walks.

### SIGHTS & ACTIVITIES

Situated between open grassland between the River Tay on one side and rolling hills on the other, **Dunkeld Cathedral** (HS; ☎ 727601; High St; admission free; 9.30am-5.30pm May-Sep, to 4.30pm Oct-Apr) is one of the most beautifully sited cathedrals in Scotland. Don't miss it on a sunny day, as there are few more lovely places to be. Half the cathedral is still in use as a church; the rest is in ruins, and you can explore it all. The oldest part of the original church is the choir, completed in 1350. The 15th-century tower is still standing. The cathedral was damaged during the Reformation and burnt during the Battle of Dunkeld in 1689.

If you're looking to entertain the kids for a few hours, drop by **Going Pottie** ( ☎ 728044; www .goingpottie.com; Cathedral St; activities from £5; 10am-5pm Mon-Sat, 11am-4pm Sun; ) where kids can get a paintbrush in their hand and create colourful ceramics…and mayhem.

Across the bridge is Birnam, made famous by *Macbeth*. There's not much left of Birnam Wood, but there is a small, leafy **Beatrix Potter Park** (the children's author spent childhood holidays in the area). In the park you'll find some local history on the life of Beatrix Potter who wrote the evergreen story of *Peter Rabbit*.

**Loch of the Lowes Wildlife Centre** ( ☎ 727337; Loch of the Lowes; admission £3; ☷ 10am-5pm Apr-Sep), 2 miles east of Dunkeld off the A923, has wildlife displays mostly devoted to the majestic osprey. There's also an excellent bird-watching hide with binoculars provided, where you can see the birds nesting during breeding season.

### SLEEPING & EATING
**Taybank** ( ☎ 727340; www.thetaybank.com; Tay Tce, Dunkeld; s/d £25/50) The Taybank is a live-music bar fielding musos from around the area who specialise in late-night jamming. There are simple rooms upstairs with shared bathroom. Traditional Scottish food includes the beloved stovie; mains range from £5 to £8. It's very friendly and once you gaze out over the Tay from the breakfast room nursing your hangover, you may not want to leave at all.

**Birnam House Hotel** ( ☎ 727462; www.birnamhouse hotel.co.uk; Perth Rd, Birnam; r per person from £40) This grand-looking place with crow-stepped gables has undergone major renovations (damn, we liked it the way it was – unrenovated and proud of it). Tastefully fitted rooms differ in size and quality of furnishings, so have a look at a few. Most, fortunately, retain the character of the building. Dishes at the adjoining Tap Inn (mains £6 to £9) display a distinctive creative flair.

### GETTING THERE & AWAY
Dunkeld is 15 miles north of Perth. Scottish Citylink buses between Glasgow/Edinburgh (£10, two hours, at least three daily) and Inverness stop at Birnam House Hotel. Birnam to Perth (£5.50) or Pitlochry (£5.50) takes 20 minutes.

Strathtay Scottish has a bus between Blairgowrie (30 minutes) and Aberfeldy (40 minutes), via Dunkeld, twice daily Monday to Friday; there's no bus to Aberfeldy during school holidays.

Trains run to Glasgow (£12, 1½ hours, roughly hourly Monday to Saturday, four on Sunday) and to Inverness (£19.50, two hours, eight daily Monday to Saturday, five on Sunday).

## Pitlochry
☎ 01796 / pop 2600
Pitlochry is a tourist magnet – the place is swamped in summer. But somehow it doesn't detract from this most charming of Highland towns. It's an excellent place to base yourself if you want to explore the region, and it has good transport connections if you're long on time and short on wheels.

### INFORMATION
**Computer Services Centre** ( ☎ 473711; 67 Atholl Rd; per min 5p; ☷ 9.30am-5.30pm Mon-Fri, to 12.30pm Sat) Internet access; opposite the Royal Bank.
**Police station** (Atholl Rd)
**Post office** (Atholl Rd)
**Royal Bank of Scotland** (Atholl Rd) Has ATM.
**Tourist office** ( ☎ 472215; pitlochrytic@visitscotland .com; 22 Atholl Rd; ☷ Mon-Sat year-round) Inconsistent service when we were there; sells the useful publication *Pitlochry Walks* (50p), which lists four short and four long local walks.

### SIGHTS
If you fancy a tour of a whisky distillery, Pitlochry has two. **Bell's Blair Athol Distillery** ( ☎ 482003; Atholl Rd; tour incl voucher redeemable against purchases £5; ☷ 11am-4pm Mon-Fri Jan-Easter, Nov & Dec, 9.30am-5pm Mon-Sat Easter-Sep & noon-5pm Sun Jun-Sep, 10am-4pm Mon-Fri Oct) is at the southern end of town. The **Edradour Distillery** ( ☎ 472095; admission free; ☷ 9.30am-6pm Mon-Sat, 11.30am-5pm Sun Mar-Oct, call to confirm winter hr) is proudly Scotland's smallest distillery, 2.5 miles east of Pitlochry on the A924.

At the Pitlochry Festival Theatre, the excellent **Explorers: The Scottish Plant Hunters Garden** ( ☎ 484600; adult/child £3/1; Foss Rd; ☷ 10am-5pm Apr-Oct) commemorates 300 years of plant collecting and those who hunted down 'new' species. The new-age landscaping in the 2.5-hectare garden includes a couple of pavilions built from Scottish timber and an amphitheatre. The whole collection is based on plants brought back to Scotland by Scottish explorers. In their words: 'These men would put Indiana Jones to shame'. There is plenty of seating to drink in the views over town.

Just behind the tourist office is **Heathergems** ( ☎ 474391; 22 Atholl Rd; ☷ 9am-5.30pm May-Sep, 9am-5pm Mon-Sat Oct-Apr), the factory outlet of a most unusual and beautiful form of Scottish jewellery. The jewellery is made from natural heather stems and the Celtic designs in particular are very good. You can actually

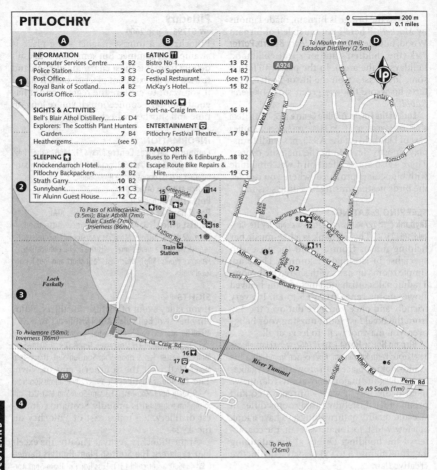

## PITLOCHRY

**INFORMATION**
Computer Services Centre......**1** B2
Police Station.........................**2** C3
Post Office............................**3** B2
Royal Bank of Scotland..........**4** B2
Tourist Office.......................**5** C3

**SIGHTS & ACTIVITIES**
Bell's Blair Athol Distillery........**6** D4
Explorers: The Scottish Plant Hunters
  Garden.............................**7** B4
Heathergems......................(see 5)

**SLEEPING**
Knockendarroch Hotel............**8** C2
Pitlochry Backpackers............**9** B2
Strath Garry........................**10** B2
Sunnybank..........................**11** C3
Tir Aluinn Guest House..........**12** C2

**EATING**
Bistro No 1.........................**13** B2
Co-op Supermarket...............**14** B2
Festival Restaurant...............(see 17)
McKay's Hotel......................**15** B2

**DRINKING**
Port-na-Craig Inn..................**16** B4

**ENTERTAINMENT**
Pitlochry Festival Theatre........**17** B4

**TRANSPORT**
Buses to Perth & Edinburgh....**18** B2
Escape Route Bike Repairs &
  Hire...............................**19** C3

---

view the jewellery being made through windows into the workshop. Definitely worth a browse.

## SLEEPING

**Pitlochry Backpackers** ( ☎ 470044; www.scotlands-top-hostels.com; 134 Atholl Rd; dm/tw/d £13.50/33/37) This is a cracking hostel smack-bang in the middle of town with three- to eight-bed dorms that are in mint condition, and there's no extra charge for linen. Couples should grab the excellent en-suite double, a real bargain. Friendly, laid-back and very comfortable.

**Sunnybank** ( ☎ 473014; thomas@tszeller.fsnet.co.uk; 19 Lower Oakfield Rd; r per person £25-35) Austrian-run Sunnybank certainly has a sunny aspect and offers fresh, good-value rooms in a large

modern house. Some rooms have that alpine thing going on.

**our pick Tir Aluinn Guest House** ( ☎ 473811; www.tiraluinn.co.uk; 10 Higher Oakfield Rd; s/d £27/54) This place is a real find – there are three extremely well-kept, bright rooms and the hosts *sooo* have the right attitude. Apart from being thoughtful and charming, they don't levy a surcharge at solo travellers because in their words 'we've too many single friends and it's not their fault'. Right on. The brilliant breakfast includes something for everyone (like healthy options and herbal teas). Highly recommended and great value for Pitlochry.

**Strath Garry** ( ☎ 472469; www.strathgarryhotel.co.uk; 113 Atholl Rd; s/d £40/60) Recently refurbished and with a top location, Strath Garry makes you

CENTRAL SCOTLAND

never want to leave. Why? Well, it's a (small) hotel-bar-café-restaurant – you'll never want for anything, and it's all done pretty well, although we'd recommend venturing further afield for dinner. En-suite rooms are very snug and have some luxurious touches – we lost a researcher who sunk into one of the beds and was never seen again.

**Knockendarroch Hotel** ( ☎ 473473; www.knocken darroch.co.uk; Higher Oakfield Rd; dinner, bed & breakfast per person £75) Geez, we like this place. Knockendarroch lures visitors with its grace, ornate grandeur and old-world charisma. Sumptuous rooms vary – room 3 is the largest and has gorgeous views, although top-floor rooms have the real stunners. Take your partner here – they won't forget it. To cap it off the restaurant is outstanding.

### EATING

**Bistro No 1** ( ☎ 472660; 100 Atholl Rd; mains £9-13; ⊙ breakfast, lunch & dinner) The new kid on the block serves up a good selection of dishes with a couple of veggie options for dinner. Inside is a comfortable set up with modern booth seating ideal for couples or families. Tuck into whole plaice stuffed with a salmon mousse, with lemon and dill oil. Gourmet sandwiches furnish the menu for lunch.

**McKay's Hotel** ( ☎ 473885; 138 Atholl Rd; mains £9; ⊙ lunch & dinner) This place is one big pub-restaurant serving basic, filling Scottish pub fare – it'll stick to ya ribs. There's a huge open fireplace, perfect for toasting the tush in winter. The boisterous barn of a bar in the rear serves the same food with more atmosphere and live bands. A pie and a pint is £6 from noon to 5pm.

**Festival Restaurant** ( ☎ 484626; Foss Rd; 2-/3-course set dinner £19.50/22.50; ⊙ lunch & dinner) Admire views from floor-to-ceiling windows and watercolour paintings of Highland scenes in this elegant restaurant at the Pitlochry Festival Theatre. Dishes such as the grilled corn-fed chicken breast on a potato cake with baby beetroot and snowpeas, followed by Scottish cheeses and oatcakes, go down a treat.

There's a **Co-op supermarket** (West Moulin Rd) if you're self-catering.

### DRINKING & ENTERTAINMENT

**Port-na-Craig Inn** ( ☎ 472777; www.portnacraig.com; Port na Craig Rd) The Fisherman's Bar, right on the water's edge, is the best place for a drink on a warm evening. In front of the Festival Theatre, you may even see local fishermen land salmon from the River Tummel.

**Pitlochry Festival Theatre** ( ☎ 484626; Foss Rd; tickets £5-30; ⊙ ) This well-known theatre stages a different play for six nights out of seven during its season from May to mid-October.

### GETTING THERE & AWAY

Scottish Citylink runs approximately hourly or two-hourly buses between Inverness and Glasgow/Edinburgh via Pitlochry. Prices and journey times to destinations from Pitlochry are: Inverness (£11, two hours), Aviemore (1¼ hours), Perth (45 minutes), Edinburgh (£11, two hours) and Glasgow (£11, 2¼ hours).

Stagecoach runs buses to Aberfeldy (30 minutes, hourly Monday to Saturday, three Sunday), Dunkeld (25 minutes, up to 10 daily Monday to Saturday) and Perth (one hour, up to 10 daily Monday to Saturday).

Pitlochry is on the main rail line from Perth to Inverness. There are nine trains a day from Perth (£10, 30 minutes), fewer on Sunday.

### GETTING AROUND

**Escape Route Bike Repairs & Hire** ( ☎ 473859; 3 Atholl Rd; half-/full day from £10/18; ⊙ 9am-5.30pm Mon-Sat, 10am-5pm Sun) rents out bikes; discounts on rentals of three or more days. For a taxi, call **Elizabeth Yule Transport** ( ☎ 472290); a taxi to Blair Castle will cost you £12.

**CENTRAL SCOTLAND**

---

### BEST PUB IN SCOTLAND?

**Moulin Inn** ( ☎ 01796-472196; Moulin; starters £3.50-6.50, mains £7-10; ⊙ lunch & dinner) Just a mile north of Pitlochry, the Moulin is a gem with plenty of great nooks and is one of our fave pubs in the country. Fireplaces, a low roof, stained glass, lots of unpolished wood – it's an atmospheric little inn that was trading here long before visitors arrived in nearby Pitlochry. It makes a great spot to escape the crowds for a meal or an afternoon drink – you could walk here from town. There's a reasonably priced menu with simple, home-cooked food served in generous portions and a specials board that changes regularly; try the seafood pancake. The hotel brews its own ales – the smooth, ruby-coloured Ale of Atholl is particularly good.

## Pass of Killiecrankie

Drop into the **Killiecrankie Visitors Centre** (NTS; ☎ 01796-473233; Killiecrankie; admission free, car-park fee £2; ⏱ 10am-5.30pm Apr-Oct; ♿ ) in this beautiful, rugged gorge, 3.5 miles north of Pitlochry. It has great interactive displays on the Jacobite rebellion, and local flora and fauna. There's plenty to touch, pull and open – great for kids. There are some stunning walks into the wooded gorge; keep an eye out for red squirrels.

Winner of a plethora of awards and almost exactly between Pitlochry and Blair Atholl, **Killiecrankie House Hotel** ( ☎ 01796-473220; www .killiecrankiehotel.co.uk; Killiecrankie; standard/superior dinner, bed & breakfast £89/99, bed & breakfast £65; 2-/3-course dinner £22/28) is brilliant for treating that someone special.

Local buses run between Pitlochry and Blair Atholl via Killiecrankie (10 minutes, three to seven daily).

## Blair Castle & Blair Atholl

☎ 01796

One of the most popular tourist attractions in Scotland, magnificent **Blair Castle** ( ☎ 481207; Blair Atholl; castle & grounds adult/child/family £7.50/4.70/19.50; ⏱ 9.30am-5.30pm Easter-Oct, call Pitlochry tourist office for winter hr) is the seat of the duke of Atholl. Set beneath forested slopes above the River Garry, this impressive whitewashed castle plays host (in May) to the parade of the Atholl Highlanders – the only private army in Europe.

Thirty rooms are open to the public, and they are packed with paintings, arms and armour, china, lace, and embroidery, presenting a near-complete picture of upper-class life in the Highlands from the 16th century to the present. One of the most impressive rooms is the ballroom. A piper plays at the entrance to the castle three times a day in summer. Blair Castle is located 7 miles north of Pitlochry, and a mile from Blair Atholl village.

For a great cycle, walk or drive, take the stunning road to **Glenfender** from Blair Atholl village. It's about 3 miles on a long, windy uphill track to a farmhouse; the views of snow-capped peaks along the way are spectacular.

The gothic **Atholl Arms Hotel** ( ☎ 481205; Blair Atholl; s/d from £50/65), a pub near the train station, is convenient for the castle and sometimes does special deals. The fussy rooms are of a high standard. Book ahead on weekends. The Bothy Bar here is very reminiscent of the Moulin Inn in Pitlochry – even the locally brewed

beers are the same. Snug with booth seating, low-slung roof, bucket-loads of character and an enormous fireplace. There's no better place to be when the rain is lashing outside.

Local buses run a service between Pitlochry and Blair Atholl (25 minutes, three to seven daily). Four buses a day (Monday to Saturday) go directly to the castle. There's a train station in the village, but not all trains stop here.

For a continuation of this route, as it moves north up the A9, see the Cairngorms section (p329).

## BLAIRGOWRIE & GLENSHEE

The route along the A93 through Glenshee is one of the most spectacular drives in the country. The meandering burns and soaring peaks, splotched with blinding-white snow, tend to dwarf open-mouthed drivers – it's surprising that there aren't more accidents along this road. Blairgowrie (population 8500) and Braemar (see p255) are the main accommodation centres for the Glenshee ski resort, although there is a small settlement 5 miles south of the ski runs at **Spittal of Glenshee**.

There's a helpful **tourist office** ( ☎ 01250-872960; blairgowrietic@visitscotland.com; 26 Wellmeadow; ⏱ daily Apr-Oct, Tue-Sat Nov-Mar) with plenty of walking information. You'll find two banks with ATMs on High St, just behind the tourist office.

### Skiing

**Glenshee ski resort** ( ☎ 01339-741320; www.ski-glenshee.co.uk), on the border of Perthshire and Aberdeenshire, has 38 pistes and is one of Scotland's largest skiing areas. After a good fall of snow and when the sun burns through the clouds, you will be in a unique position to drink in the beauty of this country; the skiing isn't half bad either. The chairlift can whisk you up to 910m, near the top of the **Cairnwell** (933m). Whenever there's enough snow in winter it opens daily (it's usually closed in summer, but check with the tourist office). A half- /one-day lift pass costs £18/24, although prices are cheaper for beginners.

### Sleeping & Eating

**Spittal of Glenshee Hotel** ( ☎ 01250-885215; www.spittalofglenshee.co.uk; Spittal of Glenshee; dm £16, r per person from £32, with en suite from £38; ♿ ) This hotel is a very 'Scottish experience' – it's a great old country lodge that has burnt down numerous times, but don't worry; the insurers have calculated that it is likely the next fire won't be until 2029. There's a good bar and a bunkhouse (without cooking facilities).

**Rosebank House** ( ☎ 01250-872912; colhotel@rosebank35.fsnet.co.uk; Balmoral Rd, Blairgowrie; s/d £25/50) This fine Georgian property is a great deal. Good-sized rooms upstairs are well kept and have small but clean en suites, and there's a large front garden. The friendly owners take good care of guests, and no surcharge is levied on solo travellers. Try to get a room overlooking the garden. Note that rooms do not have TVs as the owners like to encourage communal conversation.

**Slipstream** (Tannage St; mains £4.50; ☺ lunch) Younger folk may prefer this cool place across the road from Angus Hotel. Come here for cheap, simple lunches such as paninis, burgers and Mexican chilli. You can eat outside overlooking the river.

### Getting There & Away

Strathtay Scottish operates a service from Perth to Blairgowrie (50 minutes, three to seven daily). There's also a bus from Blairgowrie to Dundee (50 minutes, hourly, less frequent on Sunday).

The only service from Blairgowrie to the Glenshee area, about 30 miles away, is the postbus to Spittal of Glenshee (no Sunday service).

## AROUND BLAIRGOWRIE

**Alyth** is a charming little village with a small canal and some exquisite stone bridges about 5 miles east of Blairgowrie. Ask at Blairgowrie's tourist office for the *Walk Old Alyth* leaflet; there are lots of historical buildings, including church ruins dating from 1296. If you're looking to escape the rain, perusing the displays on local history at **Alyth Museum** ( ☎ 01738-632488; Commercial St; admission free; ☺ 1-5pm Wed-Sun May-Sep) is a fine way to pass an hour or so.

**Alyth Hotel** ( ☎ 01828-632447; 6 Commercial St, Alyth; s/d £45/65) is a classic town pub that has had an excellent refurbishment. Old-style rooms upstairs are better than renovated ones though, with a lot more space and a user-friendly design. Either way try and get a room overlooking the Square; room 1 is a good choice. The downstairs bar and restaurant is infinitely cosy with low-slung roof, stone walls and all manner of clutter giving it a homely feel. Mains range between £9 and £14.

Off the A94 and 8 miles east of Blairgowrie, **Meigle** is worth the trip for those with a fascination for Pictish stones. The tiny **Meigle Museum** (HS; ☎ 01828-640612; adult/child £3/1.50; ☺ 9.30am-12.30pm & 1.30-5.30pm Apr-Sep) has 26 such carved stones from the 7th to the 10th century, all found in the local area. The pieces range from the Nordic to the exotic – they include a Viking headstone and, bizarrely, a carving of a camel.

# Northeast Scotland

The northern and eastern slopes of the Grampian Mountains are draped with a broad, green mantle of fertile lowlands, fringed with forests and hemmed around with long, sandy beaches and rugged, bird-haunted cliffs, bejewelled here and there with picturesque little fishing villages.

Many visitors pass by this corner of the country in their headlong rush to the tourist honey-pots of Loch Ness and Skye. But they're missing out on a part of the country that's as beautiful and diverse as the more obvious attractions of the western Highlands and islands.

Within its bounds you will find two of Scotland's four largest cities – Dundee, the city of jute, jam and journalism, the cradle of some of Britain's favourite comic characters, and home to Captain Scott's Antarctic research ship, the *Discovery;* and Aberdeen, the granite city, an economic powerhouse fuelled by the riches of North Sea oil.

Angus, to the north of Dundee, is a region of rich farmland and scenic glens dotted with the mysterious stones left behind by the ancient Picts, while Aberdeen's rural hinterland is home to a thriving indigenous culture, where the old Scottish dialect known as the Doric still survives. Here you'll find the greatest concentration of Scottish Baronial castles anywhere in the country, and lovely little fishing villages such as Pennan and Gardenstown.

In the north is the ancient earldom of Moray, famous for the cathedral town of Elgin, the beaches of Banff and Lossiemouth, and dozens of distilleries that cluster along the banks of the River Spey.

## HIGHLIGHTS

- Hiking through the hills around beautiful **Glen Clova** (p243)
- Meditating on the meaning of the mysterious **Pictish stones** (p242) of Angus
- Tucking into the freshest of Scottish seafood at the **Harbour Restaurant** (p259) in Gardenstown
- Exploring the hills, forests, castles and pretty villages of **Royal Deeside** (p254)
- Being initiated into the mysteries of malt whisky on a Speyside **distillery tour** (p263)

★ Gardenstown
★ Speyside
Royal ★ Deeside
Glen Clova ★
★ Angus

| ■ POPULATION: 780,000 | ■ AREA: 10,979 SQ KM |
|---|---|

NORTHEAST SCOTLAND

## Getting Around

The Dundee to Aberdeen route is served by **Scottish Citylink** ( ☎ 0870 550 5050; www.citylink .co.uk) buses. **Stagecoach Strathtay** (www.stage coachbus.com/strathtay) in Dundee and Angus and **Stagecoach Bluebird** (www.stagecoachbus.com /bluebird) in Aberdeenshire and Moray are the main regional bus operators, with a range of services linking all the main towns and cities. Stagecoach Bluebird offers a Bluebird Explorer ticket (adult/child £13/6.50) that allows unlimited travel on all its services for one day.

From mid-May to September, the Speyside Stroller (bus 500) runs from Cullen, on the Banffshire coast, to the Cairngorm Mountain Railway via Buckie, Spey Bay, Fochabers, Elgin, Dufftown, Tomintoul, Grantown-on-Spey and Aviemore (3¾ hours, once daily, Saturday and Sunday only). The Heather Hopper (bus 501) links Ballater to Grantown-on-Spey via Strathdon and Tomintoul (1½ hours, twice daily mid-May to September).

**Royal Mail postbuses** ( ☎ 0845 774 0740; www.post bus.royalmail.com) run to remote communities in the Angus Glens and Deeside, charging on average £2 to £5 for single journeys.

The Dundee–Inverness railway line passes through Arbroath, Montrose, Stonehaven, Aberdeen, Huntly and Elgin.

You can pick up a public-transport map and guide from tourist offices and bus stations. For timetable information, call **Traveline** ( ☎ 0871 200 2233).

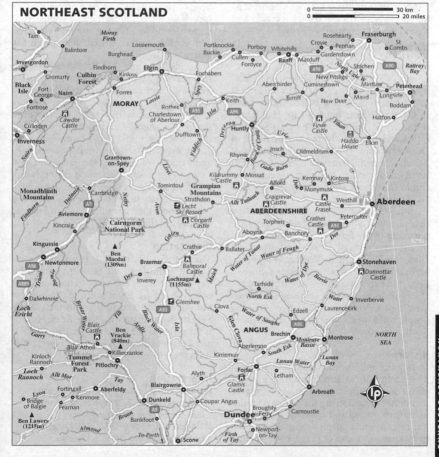

NORTHEAST SCOTLAND

# DUNDEE & ANGUS

Angus is a region of fertile farmland stretching north from Dundee – Scotland's fourth-largest city – to the Highland border. It's an attractive area of broad straths (valleys) and low, green hills contrasting with the rich, red-brown soil of freshly ploughed fields. Romantic glens finger their way into the foothills of the Grampian Mountains, while the scenic coastline ranges from the red-sandstone cliffs of Arbroath to the long, sandy beaches around Montrose. This was the Pictish heartland of the 7th and 8th centuries, and many interesting Pictish symbol stones (p242) survive here.

Apart from the crowds visiting Discovery Point in newly confident Dundee and the coach parties shuffling through Glamis Castle, Angus is a bit of a tourism backwater and a good place to escape the hordes.

## DUNDEE

☎ 01382 / pop 144,000

London's Trafalgar Sq has Nelson on his column, Edinburgh's Princes St has its monument to Sir Walter Scott and Belfast has a statue of Queen Victoria outside City Hall. Dundee's City Sq, on the other hand, is graced – rather endearingly – by the bronze figure of Desperate Dan. Familiar to generations of British school children, Dan is one of the best-loved cartoon characters from the children's comic *The Dandy,* published by Dundee firm DC Thomson since 1937.

Dundee enjoys perhaps the finest location of any Scottish city, spreading along the northern shore of the Firth of Tay, and can boast tourist attractions of national importance in Discovery Point and the Verdant Works museum. Add in the attractive seaside suburb of Broughty Ferry, some lively nightlife and the Dundonians themselves – among the friendliest, most welcoming and most entertaining people you'll meet – and Dundee is definitely worth a stopover.

## History

During the 19th century Dundee grew from its trading port origins to become a major player in the shipbuilding, whaling, textile and railway engineering industries. Dundonian firms owned and operated most of the jute mills in India (jute is a natural fibre used in making ropes and sacking), and the city's

textile industry employed as many as 43,000 people – little wonder Dundee earned the nickname 'Juteopolis'.

Dundee is often called the city of the 'Three Js' – jute, jam and journalism. According to legend, it was a Dundee woman Janet Keillor who invented marmalade in the late 18th century; her son founded the city's famous Keillor jam factory. Jute is no longer produced, and when the Keillor factory was taken over in 1988 production was transferred to England. Journalism still thrives, however, led by the family firm of DC Thomson. Best known for children's comics, such as *The Beano,* Thomson is now the city's largest employer.

In the late 19th and early 20th centuries Dundee was one of the richest cities in the country – there were more millionaires per head of population here than anywhere else in Britain – but the textile and engineering industries declined in the second half of the 20th century, leading to high unemployment and urban decay.

In the 1960s and '70s Dundee's cityscape was scarred by ugly blocks of flats, office buildings and shopping centres linked by unsightly concrete walkways – the view as you approach across the Tay Road Bridge does not look promising – and most visitors passed it by. Since the mid-1990s, however, Dundee has reinvented itself as a tourist destination, and a centre for banking, insurance and new industries, and its waterfront is currently undergoing a major redevelopment. It also has more university students – one in seven of the population – than any other town in Europe, except Heidelberg.

## Orientation

The compact city centre is focussed on City Sq, just 400m from the northern end of the Tay Road Bridge. The train station and Discovery Point are 300m south of City Sq; the bus station is 400m to the northeast along Seagate. Immediately north of the city centre is the prominent hill of Dundee Law (174m), and 4 miles to the east is Broughty Ferry, Dundee's seaside resort.

## Information

**Dundee Central Library** ( ☎ 431500; Wellgate; ⏱ 9.30am-6pm Mon, Tue & Fri, 10am-6pm Wed, 9.30am-5pm Sat) Free internet access.

**Main post office** ( ☎ 0845 722 3344; 4 Meadowside) A block north of the Overgate Shopping Centre.

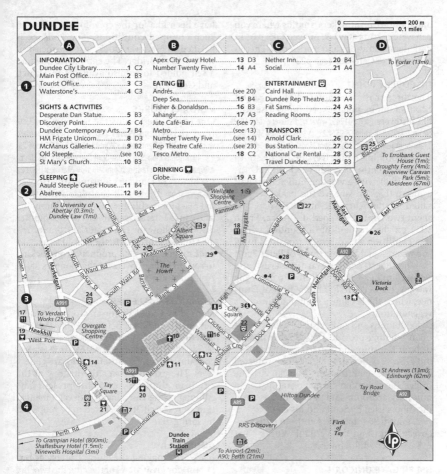

## DUNDEE

0    200 m
0    0.1 miles

**INFORMATION**
Dundee City Library.........1 C2
Main Post Office...............2 B3
Tourist Office....................3 C3
Waterstone's....................4 C3

**SIGHTS & ACTIVITIES**
Desperate Dan Statue........5 B3
Discovery Point.................6 C4
Dundee Contemporary Arts....7 B4
HM Frigate Unicorn............8 D3
McManus Galleries............9 B2
Old Steeple..................(see 10)
St Mary's Church.............10 B3

**SLEEPING**
Aauld Steeple Guest House....11 B4
Abalree..........................12 B4

Apex City Quay Hotel..........13 D3
Number Twenty Five...........14 A4

**EATING**
Andrés..........................(see 20)
Deep Sea.......................15 B4
Fisher & Donaldson............16 B3
Jahangir........................17 A3
Jute Café-Bar.................(see 7)
Metro..........................(see 13)
Number Twenty Five.........(see 14)
Rep Theatre Café............(see 23)
Tesco Metro....................18 C2

**DRINKING**
Globe...........................19 A3

Nether Inn......................20 B4
Social...........................21 A4

**ENTERTAINMENT**
Caird Hall......................22 C3
Dundee Rep Theatre........23 A4
Fat Sams........................24 A3
Reading Rooms...............25 D2

**TRANSPORT**
Arnold Clark....................26 D2
Bus Station......................27 C2
National Car Rental...........28 C3
Travel Dundee..................29 B3

**Ninewells Hospital** ( ☎ 660111; ✍ casualty 24hr)
At Menzieshill, west of the city centre.

**Tourist office** ( ☎ 527527; www.angusanddundee
.co.uk; 21 Castle St; ✍ 9am-6pm Mon-Sat, noon-4pm Sun
Jun-Sep, 9am-5pm Mon-Sat Oct-May)

**Waterstone's** ( ☎ 200322; 35 Commercial St; ✍ 9am-
6pm Mon, Tue & Thu-Sat, 9.30am-5pm Wed, 11am-5pm
Sun) Dundee's biggest bookshop.

## Sights
### CITY CENTRE
The heart of Dundee is **City Sq**, flanked to the
south by the 1930s façade of **Caird Hall**, which
was gifted to the city by a textile magnate
and is now home to the City Chambers. A
more recent addition to the square, unveiled
in 2001, is a bronze statue of **Desperate Dan**, the

lantern-jawed hero of the children's comic
*The Dandy* (he's clutching a copy in his right
hand), which has been published in Dundee
since 1937.

Pedestrianised High St leads west into
Nethergate, flanked to the north by **St Mary's
Church**. Most of the church dates from the 19th
century, but the **Old Steeple** was built around
1460.

The focus for the city's emerging Cultural
Quarter is **Dundee Contemporary Arts** ( ☎ 909900;
www.dca.org.uk; Nethergate; admission free; ✍ galleries &
shop 10.30am-5.30pm Tue, Wed, Fri & Sat, 10.30am-8.30pm
Thu, noon-5.30pm Sun; print studio 11am-9pm Tue-Thu, 11am-
6pm Fri & Sat), a centre for modern art, design
and cinema. The galleries here exhibit work by
contemporary UK and international artists,

NORTHEAST SCOTLAND

and there are printmakers' studios where you can watch artists at work, or even take part in craft demonstrations and workshops. There's also the Jute Café-Bar (see p237).

### DISCOVERY POINT

The three masts of Captain Robert Falcon Scott's famous polar expedition vessel the **RRS Discovery** ( ☎ 201245; www.rrsdiscovery.com; Discovery Quay; adult/child £6.95/4.25; ☼ 10am-6pm Mon-Sat, 11am-6pm Sun Apr-Oct, 10am-5pm Mon-Sat, 11am-5pm Sun Nov-Mar) dominate the riverside to the south of the city centre. The ship was built in Dundee in 1900, with a wooden hull at least half a metre thick to survive the pack ice, and sailed for the Antarctic in 1901 where she spent two winters trapped in the ice. From 1931 on she was laid up in London where her condition steadily deteriorated, until she was rescued by the efforts of Peter Scott (son of Robert) and the Maritime Trust, and restored to her 1925 condition. In 1986 she was given a berth in her home port of Dundee, where she became a symbol of the city's regeneration.

Exhibitions and audiovisual displays in the main building provide a fascinating history of both the ship and Antarctic exploration, but *Discovery* herself – afloat in a protected dock – is the star attraction. You can visit the bridge, the galley and the mahogany-panelled officers' wardroom, and poke your nose into the cabins used by Scott and his crew.

A joint ticket that gives entry to both Discovery Point and the Verdant Works costs £11.25/7 per adult/child.

### HM FRIGATE UNICORN

Unlike the polished and much-restored *Discovery*, Dundee's other floating tourist attraction retains the authentic atmosphere of a salty old sailing ship. Built in 1824, the 46-gun **HM Frigate Unicorn** ( ☎ 200893; Victoria Dock; adult/child £4/3; ☼ 10am-5pm Apr-Sep, noon-4pm Wed-Fri, 10am-4pm Sat & Sun Oct-Mar) is the oldest British-built ship still afloat – she was mothballed soon after launching and never saw action. By the mid-19th century sailing ships were outclassed by steam and the *Unicorn* served as a gunpowder store, then later as a training vessel. When it was proposed to break up the ship for scrap in the 1960s, a preservation society was formed.

Wandering around the four decks gives you an excellent impression of what it must have been like for the crew forced to live in such cramped conditions. The *Unicorn* is berthed in Victoria Dock, just northeast of the Tay Road Bridge. The entry price includes a self-guided tour (also available in French and German).

### VERDANT WORKS

One of the finest industrial museums in Europe, the **Verdant Works** ( ☎ 225282; www.verdant works.com; West Henderson's Wynd; adult/child £6.95/4.25; ☼ 10am-6pm Mon-Sat, 11am-6pm Sun Apr-Oct, 10.30am-4.30pm Wed-Sat, 11am-4.30pm Sun Nov-Mar) explores the history of Dundee's jute industry. Housed in a restored jute mill complete with original machinery still in working condition, the museum's interactive exhibits and computer displays follow the raw material from its origins in India through to the manufacture of a wide range of finished products, from sacking to rope to wagon covers for the pioneers of the American West.

### MCMANUS GALLERIES

Housed in a solid Victorian Gothic building designed by Gilbert Scott in 1867, **McManus Galleries** ( ☎ 432084; www.mcmanus.co.uk; Albert Sq; admission free; ☼ 10.30am-5pm Mon-Sat, 12.30-4pm Sun) contains the city's museum and art collection. The exhibits cover the history of the city from the Iron Age to the present day. Although closed for a major redevelopment at time of research, it's expected to be reopened by spring 2008.

### DUNDEE LAW

It's worth making the climb up **Dundee Law** (174m) for great views of the city, the two Tay bridges and across to Fife. The **Tay Rail Bridge** – at just over 2 miles long, it was the world's longest when it was built – was completed in 1887 and replaced an earlier bridge whose stumps can be seen alongside. The original bridge collapsed during a storm in 1879, less than two years after it was built, taking a train and 75 lives along with it. The 1.5-mile **Tay Road Bridge** was opened in 1966.

Dundee Law is a short walk northwest of the city centre, along Constitution Rd.

## Festivals & Events

If you're around in late June-early July, look out for the **Dundee Blues Bonanza** (www.dundee bluesbonanza.co.uk), a two-day festival of free blues, boogie and roots music.

## Sleeping

Most of Dundee's city-centre hotels are business oriented, and offer lower rates on weekends. The main concentrations of B&Bs are along Broughty Ferry and Arbroath Rds east of the city centre, and on Perth Rd to the west. If you don't fancy a night in the city, consider staying at nearby Broughty Ferry (p239).

Accommodation in Dundee is usually booked solid when the Open Golf tournament is staged at Carnoustie or St Andrews (as it will be in 2010) – check www.opengolf .com for future dates and venues.

### BUDGET

At the time of research there was no backpacker hostel in Dundee, but there were plans to open one in the near future – check www .hoppo.com or ask at the Edinburgh Backpackers Hostel (p99).

**Riverview Caravan Park** ( ☎ 535471; www.river view.co.uk; Marine Dr, Monifieth; tent or campervan sites £13; ☯ Apr-Oct) The nearest camping ground to Dundee is attractively sited near the beach, 5 miles east of the city centre.

**Abalree** ( ☎ 223867; 20 Union St; s/d £20/34) This is a pretty basic B&B – there are no en suites – but the owners are welcoming (don't be put off by the dark entrance) and it couldn't be more central, close to both train and bus stations. This makes it popular, so book ahead.

### MIDRANGE

**Aauld Steeple Guest House** ( ☎ 200302; www.aauld steepleguesthouse.co.uk; 94 Nethergate; s/d £25/44) Just as central as Abalree, but a bit more comfortable, the Aauld Steeple has spacious double and family rooms, some with views of St Mary's Church. Suffers a bit from street noise, though.

**Errolbank Guest House** ( ☎ 462118; 9 Dalgleish Rd; s/d £32/56; P ) A mile east of the city centre, just north of the road to Broughty Ferry, Errolbank is a lovely Victorian family home, with small, flowery en-suite rooms set in a quiet street.

**Number Twenty Five** ( ☎ 200399; www.g1group.co.uk; 25 South Tay St; r £60) Set in an elegant Georgian town house in the heart of the city's cultural quarter, upstairs from the restaurant of the same name, this place has four luxurious boutique-style bedrooms.

**Shaftesbury Hotel** ( ☎ 669216; www.shaftesbury -hotel.co.uk; 1 Hyndford St; s/d £55/69) The family-run, 12-room Shaftesbury is a Victorian mansion built for a jute baron and has many authentic period features, including a fine marble fireplace in the dining room. It's 1.5 miles west of the city centre, just off Perth Rd.

**Grampian Hotel** ( ☎ 667785; www.grampianhotel.com; 295 Perth Rd; s/d from £55/70; P ) The Grampian is a small and welcoming hotel set in a restored Victorian town house with six spacious bedrooms (all en suite), just five minutes' walk from the West End.

### TOP END

**Apex City Quay Hotel** ( ☎ 202404; www.apexhotels.co.uk; 1 West Victoria Dock Rd; s/d from £80/90; P ☯ ) Though it looks plain from the outside, the Apex overlooks the city's redeveloping waterfront and sports the sort of stylish, spacious, sofa-equipped rooms that make you want to lounge around all evening munching chocolate in front of the TV. If you can drag yourself away from your room, there are spa treatments, saunas and Japanese hot tubs to enjoy.

## Eating

**Jute Café-Bar** ( ☎ 909246; Dundee Contemporary Arts, 152 Nethergate; mains lunch £6-9, dinner £9-13; ☯ 10am-midnight Mon-Sat, noon-midnight Sun) The industrial-chic café-bar in the Dundee Contemporary Arts centre serves excellent pasta dishes, panini and salads, as well as more adventurous Mediterranean-Asian fusion cuisine; tables spill out into the sunny courtyard in summer. Early bird menu (5pm to 7pm daily) offers a two-course dinner for £11.

**our pick André's** ( ☎ 224455; 134a Nethergate; 2-course lunch £7.50, mains £8-11; ☯ noon-3pm & 5-11pm Tue-Sat, 1-11pm Sun) A quaint little corner that appears to have been fashioned out of someone's attic bedroom, André's nevertheless offers an authentic taste of France with a small, ever-changing menu of French classics ranging from onion soup to *boeuf bourguignon*.

**Number Twenty Five** ( ☎ 200399; 25 South Tay St; mains £8-11; ☯ food served noon-10pm) This elegant bar set in a Georgian town house offers a mellow, candle-lit dining room serving good-value bistro cuisine, including courgette and white bean soup, char-grilled lamb and crispy sea bass with wild mushrooms.

**Rep Theatercafé** ( ☎ 206699; Tay Sq; mains £6-12; ☯ café 10am-late, restaurant noon-3pm & 5-10pm Mon-Sat) The city's arty types hang out in this Continental-style café-bar and restaurant in the foyer at the Dundee Rep Theatre. Great sandwiches and pizza, as well as tasty steaks, fish cakes and veggie dishes.

**our pick** **Metro** ( ☎ 0845 365 0002; Apex City Quay Hotel, 1 West Victoria Dock Rd; mains £8-14; ☽ noon-2.30pm & 6-9.30pm) Sleek slate-blue banquettes, white linen napkins, black-clad staff and a view of Victoria Dock lend an air of city sophistication to this stylish hotel brasserie. The bargain lunch menu (two-/three-course for £8/10) includes tempting dishes such as gravadlax with mustard dressing, and crab linguini with sweet peppers and saffron butter.

**Jahangir** ( ☎ 202022; 1 Session St; mains £9-14; ☽ 5pm-midnight) The food is good, but it's worth going to this curry house for the décor alone – pure Hollywood Moghul, with a turbaned doorman, an over-the-top tent, and a tinkling fountain inhabited by live goldfish and carp (no, they're not on the menu).

There's an excellent tearoom in the upmarket bakery and patisserie **Fisher & Donaldson** (12 Whitehall St; ☽ 6.30am-5pm Mon-Sat), while Dundee's best fish and chips can be found at **Deep Sea** (81 Nethergate; ☽ 9.30am-6.30pm Mon-Sat).

Self-caterers can shop at **Tesco Metro** (Murraygate; ☽ 7am-midnight Mon-Fri, 7am-10pm Sat, 10am-7pm Sun).

## Drinking

There are many lively pubs, especially in the West End and along West Port. The large, stylish **Nether Inn** ( ☎ 349970; 134 Nethergate), with its comfy couches, pool table and drinks promos, is popular with students, while **Social** ( ☎ 202070; 10 South Tay St) is a lively style bar with a separate dining area. The **Globe** ( ☎ 224712; 53-57 West Port) serves good bar meals from noon to 7.30pm (6pm Sunday) and often has live music or sport on the big-screen TV.

## Entertainment

Dundee's nightlife may not be as hot as Glasgow's, but there are lots of places to go – pick up a free what's-on guide from the tourist office, or check out the What's On section of www .dundee.com. Tickets for most events are on sale at the Dundee Contemporary Arts centre.

**Caird Hall** ( ☎ 434940; www.cairdhall.co.uk; 6 City Sq; ☽ box office 9am-4.30pm Mon-Fri, 9.30am-1.30pm Sat) The Caird Hall hosts regular concerts of classical music, as well as organ recitals, rock bands, dances, fetes and fairs. Check its website for details of coming events.

**Dundee Rep Theatre** ( ☎ 223530; www.dundeerep theatre.co.uk; Tay Sq; ☽ box office 10am-6pm or start of performance) Dundee's main venue for the performing arts, the Rep is home to Scotland's only full-time repertory company and to the Scottish Dance Theatre.

**Fat Sams** ( ☎ 228181; www.fatsams.co.uk; 31 South Ward Rd; admission £5-13; ☽ 10.30pm-2.30am Tue-Sun) Fat Sams has been around for more than 20 years but is still one of the city's most popular clubs, with regular live gigs, DJs and student nights pulling in a young crowd (including lots of students from St Andrews University).

**Reading Rooms** ( ☎ 07905 353301; www.myspace.com /thereadingrooms; 57 Blackscroft; admission £3-8; ☽ 8.30pm or 10.30pm-2.30am Wed-Sat) Dundee's hippest venue is an arty, bohemian hang-out that hosts some of Scotland's best indie club nights. Live gigs have ranged from island singer-songwriter Colin MacIntyre (aka Mull Historical Society) to Glasgow guitar fiends Franz Ferdinand.

## Getting There & Away

The Tay Road Bridge linking Dundee and Fife costs 80p per car southbound, but is toll free for northbound traffic.

### AIR

Two and a half miles west of the city centre, **Dundee Airport** ( ☎ 662200; Riverside Dr) has daily scheduled services to London City airport (ScotAirways), Birmingham and Belfast (FlyWhoosh). A taxi to the airport takes five minutes and costs £3.

### BUS

**National Express** ( ☎ 08705 808080; www.nationalexpress .com) operates two direct services a day from London to Dundee (£35, 10½ hours).

**Scottish Citylink** ( ☎ 0870 550 5050; www.citylink .co.uk) has hourly buses from Dundee to Glasgow (£11, two hours), Perth (£5, 35 minutes), Aberdeen (£1, 1½ hours) and Edinburgh (£11, two hours, change at Perth); book via www .megabus.com for fares as low as £2. Some Aberdeen buses travel via Arbroath, others via Forfar. There are also direct buses to Oban (£20, 3½ hours).

Stagecoach Strathtay operates buses to Perth (one hour, hourly), Blairgowrie (one hour, hourly), Forfar (40 minutes, once or twice an hour), Kirriemuir (one hour, half-hourly), Brechin (1¼ hours, 10 daily, change at Forfar) and Arbroath (one hour, half-hourly).

Stagecoach Fife bus 99 runs to St Andrews (40 minutes, every 15 minutes Monday to Saturday, hourly on Sunday).

For timetable information, call **Traveline** ( ☎ 0871 200 2233).

## TRAIN

Trains run to Dundee from Edinburgh (£18, 1¼ hours) and Glasgow (£21, 1½ hours) at least once an hour Monday to Saturday, hourly on Sunday from Edinburgh, and every two hours on Sunday from Glasgow.

Trains from Dundee to Aberdeen (£22, 1¼ hours) travel via Arbroath and Stonehaven. There are around two trains an hour, fewer on Sunday.

## Getting Around

The city centre is compact, and is easy to get around on foot. For information on local public transport, call **Travel Dundee** ( ☎ 201121; www .traveldundee.co.uk; Forum Shopping Centre, 92 Commercial St; ☾ 9.15am-4.55pm Mon-Fri, 10am-3.55pm Sat). City bus fares cost 60p to £1.25 depending on distance; buy your ticket from the driver (exact fare only – no change given).

Phone **Discovery Taxis** ( ☎ 732111) if you need a taxi. If you'd like to drive yourself, rental companies in Dundee include **Arnold Clark** ( ☎ 225382; East Dock St) and **National Car Rental** ( ☎ 224037; 45-53 Gellatly St).

## BROUGHTY FERRY

☎ 01382

Dundee's attractive seaside suburb, known locally as 'The Ferry', lies 4 miles east of the city centre. It has a castle, a long, sandy beach, and a number of good places to eat and drink, and is handy for the golf courses at nearby Carnoustie.

## Sights

**Broughty Castle Museum** ( ☎ 436916; Castle Green; admission free; ☾ 10am-4pm Mon-Sat, 12.30-4pm Sun, closed Mon Oct-Mar) occupies a 16th-century tower house that looms imposingly over the harbour, guarding the entrance to the Firth of Tay. There's a fascinating exhibit on Dundee's whaling industry, and the chance of spotting seals and dolphins offshore.

## Sleeping

**Invermark House** ( ☎ 739430; www.invermark.co.uk; 23 Monifieth Rd; s/d £30/45; ℗ ) Invermark is a grand Victorian villa set in its own grounds, built for a jute baron in the mid-19th century, with five large en-suite bedrooms and an elegant lounge and dining room with a view of the gardens.

**Ashley House** ( ☎ 776109; www.ashleyhousebroughty ferry.co.uk; 15 Monifieth Rd; s/d from £30/50; ℗ ) This spacious and comfortable guesthouse has long

been one of Broughty Ferry's best, with four cheerfully decorated bedrooms equipped with hotel-grade beds and DVD player; one has a particularly grand bathroom.

**Fisherman's Tavern** ( ☎ 775941; www.fishermans -tavern-hotel.co.uk; 10-16 Fort St; s/d £39/64; ⓑ ) A delightful 17th-century terraced cottage just a few paces from the seafront, the Fisherman's was converted to a pub in 1827. It now has 11 stylishly modern rooms, most with en suite, and an atmospheric pub (see below).

**Hotel Broughty Ferry** ( ☎ 480027; www.hotel broughtyferry.com; 16 W Queen St; s/d £68/88; ℗ ☲ ) Doesn't look like much from the outside, but this is the Ferry's swankiest place to stay, with 16 beautifully decorated bedrooms, a sauna and solarium, and a small, heated pool. It's only a five-minute stroll from the waterfront.

## Eating & Drinking

**Fisherman's Tavern** ( ☎ 775941; 10-16 Fort St; mains £6-9; ☾ food served noon-2.30pm & 5-7.30pm) The Fisherman's – a maze of cosy nooks and open fireplaces in a 17th-century cottage – is a lively little pub where you can wash down fresh local seafood with a choice of Scottish real ales.

**Visocchi's** ( ☎ 779297; 40 Gray St; mains £7-10; ☾ 9.30am-5pm Tue, 9.30am-8pm Wed, Thu & Sun, 9.30am-1pm Fri & Sat) Visocchi's – a 70-year-old institution – is a traditional, family-run Italian café that sells delicious homemade ice cream, good coffee, and a range of burgers, pizzas and pasta dishes.

**Ship Inn** ( ☎ 779176; 121 Fisher St; mains £9-14; ☾ food served noon-2pm & 5-10.30pm Mon-Fri, noon-10.30pm Sat & Sun) On the seafront around the corner from the Fisherman's is the snug, wood-panelled, 19th-century Ship Inn, which serves topnotch dishes ranging from gourmet haddock and chips to venison steaks. It's always busy, so get in early if you want a meal.

## Getting There & Away

Buses 7 to 12 run from Dundee High St to Broughty Ferry (20 minutes) several times an hour from Monday to Saturday, and hourly on Sunday.

## GLAMIS CASTLE & VILLAGE

Looking every inch the Scottish Baronial castle, with its roofline sprouting a forest of pointed turrets and battlements, **Glamis Castle** ( ☎ 01307-840393; www.glamis-castle.co.uk; adult/child £7.50/4.30; ☾ 10am-6pm mid-Mar–Oct, 11am-5pm Nov

& Dec, closed 22 Dec–mid-Mar) was the legendary setting for Shakespeare's *Macbeth*. A royal residence since 1372, it is the family home of the earls of Strathmore and Kinghorne – the Queen Mother (born Elizabeth Bowes-Lyon; 1900–2002) spent her childhood at Glamis (pronounced glams) and Princess Margaret (the Queen's sister; 1930–2002) was born here.

The five-storey, L-shaped castle was given to the Lyon family in 1372, but was significantly altered in the 17th century. Inside, the most impressive room is the drawing room, with its vaulted plasterwork ceiling. There's a display of armour and weaponry in the haunted crypt and frescoes in the chapel (also haunted). Duncan's Hall is where King Duncan was murdered in *Macbeth*. You can also look around the royal apartments, including the Queen Mother's bedroom. The one-hour guided tours depart every 15 minutes (last tour at 4.30pm, or 3.30pm in winter).

The **Angus Folk Museum** (NTS; ☎ 01307-840288; Kirkwynd, Glamis; adult/child £5/4; ⏰ 11am-5pm Mon-Sat, 1-5pm Sun Jul & Aug, noon-5pm Sat & Sun only Easter-Jun & Sep), in a row of 18th-century cottages just off the flower-bedecked square in Glamis village, houses a fine collection of domestic and agricultural relics.

Glamis Castle is 12 miles north of Dundee. There are two to four buses a day from Dundee (35 minutes) to Glamis; some continue to Kirriemuir.

## ARBROATH
☎ 01241 / pop 22,800

Arbroath is an old-fashioned seaside resort and fishing harbour, home of the famous Arbroath smokie (a form of smoked haddock) – no visit is complete without buying a pair of smokies from one of the many fish shops and eating them with your fingers while sitting beside the harbour. Yum.

The town has a brand-new **visitor centre & tourist office** ( ☎ 872609; Fishmarket Quay; ⏰ 9.30am-5.30pm Mon-Sat, 10am-3pm Sun Jun-Aug, 9am-5pm Mon-Fri, 10am-5pm Sat Apr, May & Sep, 9am-5pm Mon-Fri, 10am-3pm Sat Oct-Mar) beside the harbour.

There's internet access at **Coldroom Computers** ( ☎ 431777; 15 Westport; per 15 min 50p; ⏰ 10am-5.30pm Mon-Fri, noon-4pm Sat).

### Sights & Activities

The magnificent, red-sandstone ruins of **Arbroath Abbey** (HS; ☎ 878756; Abbey St; adult/child

£4.50/2.25; ⏰ 9.30am-5.30pm Apr-Sep, 9.30am-4.30pm Oct-Mar), founded in 1178 by King William the Lion, dominate the town centre. It is thought that Bernard of Linton, the abbot here in the early 14th century, wrote the famous Declaration of Arbroath in 1320 asserting Scotland's right to independence from England (see the boxed text, p30). You can climb to the top of one of the towers for a grand view over the town.

The **Arbroath Museum** ( ☎ 875598; Ladyloan; admission free; ⏰ 10am-5pm Mon-Sat year-round, plus 2-5pm Sun Jul & Aug), housed in the elegant Signal Tower, covers local history, including the textile and fishing industries. The tower was originally used to communicate with the construction team working on the Bell Rock Lighthouse 12 miles offshore, which was built between 1807 and 1811 by the famous engineer Robert Stevenson (grandfather of writer Robert Louis Stevenson).

**St Vigeans Museum** (HS; ☎ 878756; admission free; ⏰ key available 9.30am-6.30pm Apr-Sep, to 4.30pm Mon-Sat Oct-Mar), about a mile north of the town centre, houses a superb collection of Pictish and medieval sculptured stones. It was closed for refurbishment at the time of research, but should re-open in 2009.

If you fancy catching your own fish, the **Marie Dawn** ( ☎ 873957) and **Girl Katherine II** ( ☎ 874510) offer three-hour sea-angling trips (usually from 2pm to 5pm) out of Arbroath harbour for £14 per person, including tackle and bait.

The coast northeast of Arbroath consists of dramatic red-sandstone cliffs riven by inlets, caves and natural arches. An excellent **walk** follows a path along the top of the cliffs for 3 miles to the quaint fishing village of **Auchmithie**, which claims to have invented the Arbroath smokie. The humble smokie achieved European Union 'Protected Geographical Indication' status in 2004 – the term 'Arbroath smokie' can be only be used legally to describe haddock smoked in the traditional manner within an 8km radius of Arbroath.

### Sleeping & Eating

**Old Vicarage** ( ☎ 430475; www.theoldvicaragebandb.co.uk; 2 Seaton Rd; s/d from £35/50; **P** ) The three five-star bedrooms in this attractive Victorian villa have a pleasantly old-fashioned atmosphere, and the extensive breakfast menu includes Arbroath smokies. The house is on a quiet street close to the start of the cliff-top walk to Auchmithie.

**Harbour Nights Guest House** ( ☎ 434343; www.harbour nights-scotland.com; 4 The Shore; s/d from £40/50) With a superb location overlooking the harbour, five stylishly decorated bedrooms and a gourmet breakfast menu, Harbour Nights is our favourite place to stay in Arbroath. Rooms 2 and 3, with harbour views, are a bit more expensive (doubles £60 to £65), but well worth asking for when booking.

**Smithie's** ( ☎ 873344; 16 Keptie St; mains £3-5; 🕙 9.30am-4.30pm Mon-Fri, 9.30am-4pm Sat) Housed in a former butcher's shop, with hand-painted tiles and meat hooks on the ceiling, Smithie's is a great little neighbourhood deli and café serving Fairtrade coffee, pancakes, wraps and freshly made pasta – butternut squash and sage tortellini make a tasty change from macaroni cheese for a vegetarian lunch.

**Sugar & Spice Tearoom** ( ☎ 437500; 9-13 High St; mains £5-8; 🕙 10am-4pm Mon-Sat, noon-4pm Sun; 🚼 ) With its flounces, frills and black-and-white uniformed waitresses, this chintzy tearoom verges on the twee. However, the place is very child-friendly – there's an indoor play area and a Wendy house out the back – and the tea and scones are sublime. You can even try an Arbroath smokie, grilled with lemon butter.

**our pick** But'n'Ben **Restaurant** ( ☎ 877223; 1 Auchmithie; mains £6-11; 🕙 noon-3pm, 4-5.30pm & 7-10pm Mon & Wed-Sat, noon-5.30pm Sun) Above the harbour in Auchmithie, this cosy, tartan-clad cottage restaurant serves the best of local seafood – the Arbroath smokie pancakes are recommended – plus great homemade cakes and desserts.

**Gordon's Restaurant** ( ☎ 830364; Main St, Inverkeillor; 3-course lunch £25, 4-course dinner £37; 🕙 noon-1.45pm Wed-Sun, 7-9pm Tue-Sun) Six miles north of Arbroath, in the tiny and unpromising-looking village of Inverkeillor, is this hidden gem – an intimate and rustic eatery serving gourmet-quality Scottish cuisine, with three comfortable bedrooms (single/double from £55/80) for those who don't want to drive back to a hotel after dinner.

## Getting There & Away

There are frequent buses from Dundee to Arbroath, but the scenic train journey along the coast (£4, 20 minutes, two per hour) is the better option. Trains continue from Arbroath to Aberdeen (£17, 50 minutes) via Montrose and Stonehaven.

Bus 140 runs from Arbroath to Auchmithie (15 minutes, six daily Monday to Friday, three daily on Saturday and Sunday).

## MONTROSE

☎ 01674 / pop 11,800

Despite its seaside setting, broad main street of Victorian buildings and reputation as a golfing resort, Montrose exudes an austere and slightly down-at-heel atmosphere. It sits at the mouth of the River South Esk, where its industrial harbour serves the North Sea oil industry; and is backed by the broad, tidal mud flats of Montrose Basin, a rich feeding ground for thousands of resident and migrant birds.

**Montrose Basin Visitor Centre** ( ☎ 676336; Rossie Braes; adult/child £3/2; 🕙 10.30am-5pm Apr-Oct, 10.30am-4pm Nov-Mar) at the southern edge of town has indoor and outdoor hides, and viewing platforms with high-powered binoculars and remote-controlled TV cameras where you can zoom in on the local wildlife. In summer you can see curlews, oystercatchers and eider ducks – and perhaps an otter if you're lucky – and in autumn the basin is invaded by huge flocks of pink-footed and greylag geese. The bird-watching is best from two hours after high tide till two hours before the next high tide – check times at any tourist office.

Prettier than Montrose's town beach, the 2-mile strand of **Lunan Bay** to the south is overlooked by the dramatic ruin of **Red Castle**.

Montrose lies on the Dundee to Aberdeen railway line.

## FORFAR

☎ 01307 / pop 13,200

Forfar, the county town of Angus, is the home of Scotland's answer to the Cornish pasty: the famous **Forfar bridie**. A shortcrust pastry turnover filled with cooked minced beef, onion and gravy, it was invented in Forfar in the early 19th century. If you fancy trying one, head for **James McLaren & Son** ( ☎ 462762; 8 The Cross; 🕙 8am-4.30pm Mon-Wed, Fri & Sat, 8am-1pm Thu), a family bakery bang in the centre of town, which has been selling tasty, home-baked bridies since 1893.

Strathtay Scottish buses from Dundee to Kirriemuir travel via Forfar.

## ABERLEMNO

Five miles northeast of Forfar, on the B9134, are the mysterious **Aberlemno stones**, some of Scotland's finest Pictish symbol stones (see boxed text, p242). By the roadside there are three 7th- to 9th-century slabs with various symbols, including the z-rod and double disc, and in the churchyard at the bottom of the hill there's a magnificent 8th-century stone displaying a Celtic cross, interlace decoration, entwined beasts and, on the reverse, scenes of the Battle of Nechtansmere (where the Picts vanquished the Northumbrians in 685). The stones are covered up from November to March; otherwise there's free access at all times.

## KIRRIEMUIR
☎ 01575 / pop 6000

Known as the Wee Red Town because of its close-packed, red-sandstone houses, Kirriemuir is famed as the birthplace of JM Barrie (1860–1937), writer and creator of the much-loved *Peter Pan*. A willowy bronze statue of the 'boy who wouldn't grow up' graces the intersection of Bank and High Sts.

The tourist office is in the Gateway to the Glens Museum (see right).

### Sights

**JM Barrie's Birthplace** (NTS; ☎ 572646; 9 Brechin Rd; adult/child £5/4; 🕙 11am-5pm Mon-Sat, 1-5pm Sun Jul & Aug, noon-5pm Sat-Wed, 1-5pm Sun Apr-Jun, Sep & Oct) is the town's big attraction, a place of pilgrimage for *Peter Pan* fans from all over the world. The

two-storey house where Barrie was born has been furnished in period style, and preserves Barrie's writing desk and the wash house at the back that served as his first 'theatre'. The ticket also gives admission to the **Camera Obscura** (adult/child £3/2 for Camera Obscura only; 🕙 11am-5pm Mon-Sat, 1-5pm Sun Jul & Aug, noon-5pm Sat-Wed Easter-Jun & Sep) on the hill top northeast of the town centre, gifted to the town by Barrie himself.

The old Town House opposite the *Peter Pan* statue dates from 1604 and houses the **Gateway to the Glens Museum** ( ☎ 575479; admission free; 🕙 10am-5pm Mon-Sat), a useful introduction to local history, geology and wildlife for those planning to explore the Angus Glens.

For generations of local school kids, the big treat when visiting Kirriemuir was a trip to the **Star Rock Shop** ( ☎ 572579; 27-29 Roods). Established in 1833, it still specialises in traditional Scottish 'sweeties' (candy), ranged in colourful jars along the walls – humbugs, tablet, cola cubes, pear drops, and the original Star Rock, still made to an 1833 recipe.

### Sleeping & Eating

**Crepto B&B** ( ☎ 572746; david@jessma.wanadoo.co.uk; Kinnordy Pl; r per person £23-26; Ⓟ ) You'll get a warm welcome at this modern B&B, tucked away

---

### PICTISH SYMBOL STONES

The mysterious carved stones that dot the landscape of eastern Scotland are the legacy of the warrior tribes who inhabited these lands 2000 years ago. The Romans occupied the southern half of Britain from AD 43 to 410, but the region to the north of the firths of Forth and Clyde – known as Caledonia – was abandoned as being too dangerous, sealed off behind the ramparts of the Antonine Wall and Hadrian's Wall.

Caledonia was the homeland of the Picts, a collection of tribes named by the Romans for their habit of painting or tattooing their bodies. In the 9th century they were culturally absorbed by the Scots, leaving behind only a few archaeological remains, a scattering of Pictish place names beginning with 'Pit', and hundreds of mysterious carved stones decorated with intricate symbols, mainly in northeast Scotland. The capital of the ancient Southern Pictish kingdom is said to have been at Forteviot in Strathearn; and Pictish symbol stones are to be found throughout this area and all the way up the eastern coast of Scotland into Sutherland and Caithness.

It is thought that the stones were set up to record Pictish lineages and alliances, but no-one is sure exactly how the system worked. They are decorated with unusual symbols, including z-rods (lightning bolt?), circles (the sun?), double discs (hand mirror?) and fantastical creatures, as well as figures of warriors on horseback, hunting scenes and (on the later stones) Christian symbols.

Local tourist offices provide a free leaflet titled the *Angus Pictish Trail*, which will guide you to the main Pictish sites in the area. The finest assemblage of stones in their natural outdoor setting is at Aberlemno (p241), and there are excellent indoor collections at St Vigeans Museum (p240) and the Meigle Museum (p231). The Pictavia interpretive centre at Brechin (p245) provides a good introduction to the Picts, and is worth a look before you visit the stones.

*The Pictish Trail* by Anthony Jackson lists 11 driving tours, while *The Symbol Stones of Scotland* by the same author provides more detail on the history and meaning of the Pictish stones.

in a quiet cul-de-sac about 10 minutes' walk from the town centre (head along Glengate and Kinnordy Rd).

**Airlie Arms Hotel** ( ☎ 572847; www.airliearms-hotel .co.uk; St Malcolm's Wynd; s/d £40/65; **P** ) This attractive old coaching inn, just a few minutes' walk from the tourist office, has luxurious en-suite rooms and a stylish, candle-lit café-bar called the Wynd (mains £6 to £9), open from noon to 3pm Friday to Sunday and 5 pm to 9pm daily.

**Visocchi's** ( ☎ 572115; 37 High St; mains £2-4) A proudly old-fashioned family café that serves Costa coffee and great homemade ice cream.

## Getting There & Away

Stagecoach Strathtay runs bus services from Dundee to Kirriemuir (£5, 1¼ hours, hourly Monday to Saturday, every two hours Sunday) via Glamis (20 minutes, two daily Monday to Saturday) and Forfar (25 minutes).

## ANGUS GLENS

The northern part of Angus is bounded by the Grampian Mountains, where five scenic glens – Isla, Prosen, Clova, Lethnot and Esk – cut into the hills along the southern edge of the Cairngorms National Park. All have attractive scenery, though each glen has its own distinct personality: Glen Clova and Glenesk are the most beautiful, while Glen Lethnot is the least frequented. You can get detailed information on walks in the Angus Glens from the tourist office in Kirriemuir and from the Glen Clova Hotel in Glen Clova.

## Glen Isla

At Bridge of Craigisla at the foot of the glen is a spectacular, 24m waterfall called **Reekie Linn**; the name Reekie (Scottish for 'smoky') comes from the billowing spray that rises from the falls.

A 5-mile walk beyond the road end at Auchavan leads into the wild and mountainous upper reaches of the glen, where the **Caenlochan National Nature Reserve** protects rare alpine flora on the high plateau.

A **Royal Mail postbus** ( ☎ 0845 774 0740) runs from Blairgowrie to Auchavan via Alyth (once daily, except Sunday).

## Glen Prosen

Near the foot of Glen Prosen, 6 miles north of Kirriemuir, there's a good forest walk up

to the **Airlie monument** on Tulloch Hill (380m); start from the eastern road, about a mile beyond Dykehead.

From Glenprosen Lodge, at the head of the glen, a 9-mile walk along the **Kilbo Path** leads over a pass between Mayar (928m) and Driesh (947m), and descends to Glendoll Lodge at the head of Glen Clova (allow five hours).

## Glen Clova

The longest and loveliest of the Angus Glens stretches north from Kirriemuir for 20 miles, broad and pastoral in its lower reaches but growing narrower and craggier as the steep, heather-clad Highland hills close in around its head.

The minor road beyond the Glen Clova Hotel ends at a Forestry Commission car park (£1.50 per car) with toilets and a picnic area, which is the trailhead for a number of strenuous walks through the hills to the north.

**Jock's Road** is an ancient footpath that was much used by cattle drovers, soldiers, smugglers and shepherds in the 18th and 19th centuries; 700 Jacobite soldiers passed this way during their retreat in 1746, en route to final defeat at Culloden. From the car park the path strikes west along Glen Doll, then north across a high plateau (900m) before descending steeply into Glen Callater and on to Braemar (15 miles, allow five to seven hours). The route is hard going and should not be attempted in winter; you'll need OS 1:50,000 maps Nos 43 and 44.

An easier, but still strenuous, circular walk starts from the Glen Clova Hotel, making a circuit of the scenic corrie (glacial hollow) that encloses **Loch Brandy** (6 miles, four hours).

our pick **Glen Clova Hotel** ( ☎ 01575-550350; www .clova.com; Glen Clova; s/d £50/80; **P** ) is a lovely old drover's inn near the head of the glen and a great place to get away from it all. As well as 10 comfortable, country-style, en-suite rooms (one with a four-poster bed), it has a bunkhouse out the back (£11 per person), a rustic, stone-floored climbers' bar with a roaring log fire, and a bay-windowed **restaurant** (mains £4-10; ⊙ noon-8.15pm Sun-Thu, noon-8.45pm Fri & Sat) with views across the glen. The menu includes steak and Guinness pie and lamb casserole with rosemary gravy, and there are separate children's and vegetarian menus.

A **Royal Mail postbus** ( ☎ 0845 774 0740) to Glen Clova departs from Kirriemuir post office at 8.30am and 3.10pm Monday to Friday,

NORTHEAST SCOTLAND

8.30am only on Saturday. The morning run goes all the way to Glendoll at the head of the glen (2½ hours), the afternoon one only as far as Glen Clova Hotel (1¾ hours).

## Glen Lethnot

This glen is noted for the **Brown & White Caterthuns** – two extraordinary Iron Age hill forts, defended by ramparts and ditches, perched on twin hill-tops at its southern end. A minor road crosses the pass between the two summits, and it's an easy walk to either fort from the parking area in the pass; both are superb viewpoints. If you don't have a car, you can walk there from Brechin (6 miles) or from Edzell (5 miles).

## Glenesk

The most easterly of the Angus Glens, Glenesk, runs for 15 miles from Edzell to lovely **Loch Lee**, surrounded by beetling cliffs and waterfalls. Ten miles up the glen from Edzell is **Glenesk Folk Museum** ( ☎ 01356-648070; The Retreat; adult/child £2/1; ☽ noon-6pm daily Jun–mid-Oct, noon-6pm Sat & Sun only Easter-May), an old shooting lodge that houses a fascinating collection of antiques and artefacts documenting the local culture of the 17th, 18th and 19th centuries. It also has a tearoom, restaurant and gift shop, and has public internet access.

Five miles further on the public road ends at **Invermark Castle**, an impressive ruined tower guarding the southern approach to the Mounth, a hill track to Deeside.

## EDZELL

☎ 01356 / pop 785

The picturesque village of Edzell, with its broad main street and grandiose monumental arch, dates from the early 19th century when Lord Panmure decided that the original medieval village, a mile to the west, spoiled the view from Edzell Castle. The old village was razed and the villagers moved to this pretty, planned settlement.

Lord Panmure's predecessors as owners of **Edzell Castle** (HS; ☎ 648631; adult/child £4/2; ☽ 9.30am-5.30pm Apr-Sep, to 4.30pm Sat-Wed Oct-Mar; ☒ ) were the Lindsay earls of Crawford, who built this 16th-century L-plan tower house. Sir David Lindsay, a cultured and well-travelled man, laid out the castle's beautiful **Pleasance** in 1604 as a place of contemplation and learning. Unique in all of Scotland, this Renaissance walled garden is lined with niches for nesting birds, and sculptured plaques illustrating the cardinal virtues, the arts and the planetary deities.

Two miles north of Edzell, the B966 to Fettercairn crosses the River North Esk at Gannochy Bridge. From the lay-by just over the bridge, a blue-painted wooden door in the stone wall gives access to a delightful footpath that leads along the wooded river gorge for 1.5 miles to a scenic spot known as the **Rocks of Solitude**.

**Alexandra Lodge** ( ☎ 648266; www.alexandralodge .co.uk; Inveriscandye Rd; s/d £45/70; P ) is an attractive Edwardian villa with comfortable bedrooms and a lovely wood-panelled lounge, while the **Panmure Arms Hotel** ( ☎ 648950; www.panmurearms hotel.co.uk; 52 High St; s/d from £50/75, bar meals; P ) is a pretty, mock-Tudor place serving excellent bar meals (£9 to £10) from noon till 2pm Monday to Friday and noon till 9pm Saturday and Sunday.

Bus 29A or 29C that runs from Brechin to Laurencekirk stops at Edzell (15 minutes, two to four a day Monday to Friday, one on Saturday).

## BRECHIN

☎ 01356 / pop 7200

The name of the local football team, Brechin City, proclaims this diminutive town's main claim to fame – as the seat of **Brechin Cathedral** (now demoted to a parish church) it has the right to call itself a city, albeit the smallest one in Scotland. Adjacent to the cathedral is a 32m-high **round tower** built around 1000 as part of a Celtic monastery. It is of a type often seen in Ireland, but one of only three that survive in Scotland. Its elevated doorway, 2m above the ground, has carvings of animals, saints and a crucifix.

Housed nearby in the 18th-century former town hall, court room and prison, **Brechin Museum** ( ☎ 622687; St Ninian's Sq; admission free; ☽ 9am-5pm Mon-Fri, 10am-noon Sat) records the history of the round tower, cathedral and town.

The town's (OK, city's) picturesque Victorian train station dates from 1897 and is now the terminus of the restored **Caledonian Railway** ( ☎ 622992; www.caledonianrailway.co.uk; 2 Park Rd), which runs steam trains (adult/child £5/3 return) along a 3.5-mile stretch of track to Bridge of Dun. Trains run on Sunday from late May to mid-September, on Saturday in July and August, and at Easter and Christmas. From Bridge of Dun it's a 15-minute signposted walk to the **House of Dun** (NTS; ☎ 810264; adult/child £8/5; ☺ 11.30am-5.30pm Jul & Aug, 12.30-5.30pm Wed-Sun Apr-Jun, Sep & Oct), a beautiful Georgian country house built in 1730.

Adjoining Brechin Castle Centre (a gardening and horse-riding centre on the A90 just west of Brechin) is **Pictavia** (☎ 626241; www .pictavia.org.uk; adult/child £3.25/2.25; ☺ 9.30am-5.30pm Mon-Sat, 10.30am-5.30pm Sun Easter–mid Oct, 9am-5pm Mon-Sat, 10am-5pm Sun mid-Oct–Easter), an interpretive centre telling the story of the Picts, and explaining current theories about the mysterious carved symbol stones they left behind. It's worth making a trip here before going to see the Pictish stones at Aberlemno.

### Getting There & Away

Scottish Citylink buses between Dundee and Aberdeen stop at Clerk St in Brechin. Stagecoach Strathtay buses depart from South Esk St heading to Forfar (30 minutes, hourly), Aberlemno (15 minutes, six a day) and Edzell.

Bus 24 links Brechin and Stonehaven (55 minutes, five daily Monday to Saturday, three on Sunday).

# ABERDEENSHIRE & MORAY

Since medieval times Aberdeenshire and its northwestern neighbour Moray have been the richest and most fertile regions of the Highlands. Aberdeenshire is famed for its Aberdeen Angus beef cattle, its many fine castles and the prosperous 'granite city' of Aberdeen. Moray's main attractions are the Speyside whisky distilleries that line the valley of the River Spey and its tributaries.

## ABERDEEN

☎ 01224 / pop 197,300

Aberdeen is the powerhouse of the northeast, fuelled by the North Sea petroleum industry. Oil money has made the city as expensive as London and Edinburgh, and there are hotels, restaurants and clubs with prices to match the depth of petroleum industry pockets. Fortunately, most of the cultural attractions, such as the excellent Maritime Museum and the Aberdeen Art Gallery, are free.

Known throughout Scotland as the granite city, much of the town was built using silvery grey granite hewn from the now abandoned

Rubislaw Quarry, at one time the biggest artificial hole in the ground in Europe. On a sunny day the granite lends an attractive glitter to the city, but when low, grey rain clouds scud in off the North Sea it can be hard to tell where the buildings stop and the sky begins.

Royal Deeside is easily accessible to the west, Dunottar Castle to the south, sandy beaches to the north and whisky country to the northwest.

### History

Aberdeen was a prosperous trading and fishing port centuries before oil became a valuable commodity. After the townspeople supported Robert the Bruce against the English at the Battle of Bannockburn in 1314, the king rewarded the town with land for which he had previously received rent. The rental income was used to establish the Common Good Fund, to be spent on town amenities, a fund that survives to this day: it helped to finance Marischal College, the Central Library, the art gallery and the hospital, and also pays for the colourful floral displays that have won the city numerous awards.

The name Aberdeen is a combination of two Pictish-Gaelic words, *aber* and *devana,* meaning 'the meeting of two waters'. The area was known to the Romans, and was raided by the Vikings when it was already an important port trading in wool, fish, hides and fur. By the 18th century paper- and rope-making, whaling and textile manufacture were the main industries, and in the 19th century it became a major herring-fishing centre.

Since the 1970s Aberdeen has been the main focus of the UK's offshore oil industry, home to oil company offices, engineering yards, a bustling harbour filled with supply ships, and the world's busiest civilian heliport. Unemployment rates, once among the highest in the country, are now among the lowest.

### Orientation

Central Aberdeen is built on an east–west ridge to the north of the River Dee. Union St, the main shopping street, runs along the crest of this ridge between Holburn Junction in the west and Castlegate in the east. The bus and train stations are next to each other, between Union St and the river. Aberdeen Beach is 800m east of the city centre. Old Aberdeen is just over a mile to the north of the city centre along King St.

## Information

### BOOKSHOPS

**Waterstone's** Union Bridge ( ☎ 592440; 3-7 Union Bridge; ☯ 9am-5.30pm Mon-Sat, 10am-4pm Sun); Union St ( ☎ 210161; 269 Union St; ☯ 9am-8pm Mon-Thu, 9am-6pm Fri & Sat, 10am-5.30pm Sun)

### INTERNET ACCESS

**Books & Beans** ( ☎ 646438; 22 Belmont St; per 15min £1; ☯ 8am-6pm Mon-Sat) Fairtrade coffee and second-hand books.

**Café LAN** ( ☎ 593054; 11 Market St; per 20min £1; ☯ 10am-9pm Mon-Sat, noon-8pm Sun)

**Central Library** ( ☎ 652500; Rosemount Viaduct; ☯ 9am-7pm Mon-Thu, 9am-5pm Fri & Sat) Free internet access in the Media Centre; sessions limited to 30 minutes.

**Tourist office** ( ☎ 288828; www.agtb.org; 23 Union St; per 10min 50p; ☯ 9am-6.30pm Mon-Sat, 10am-4pm Sun Jul & Aug, 9am-5.30pm Mon-Sat Easter-Jun, Sep & Oct, 9am-4.30pm Mon-Sat Oct-Easter)

### MEDICAL SERVICES

**Aberdeen Royal Infirmary** ( ☎ 681818; Foresterhill) About a mile northwest of the western end of Union St.

### POST

**Main post office** ( ☎ 0845 722 3344; St Nicholas Shopping Centre, Upperkirkgate; ☯ 9am-5.30pm Mon-Sat)

**Union St post office** (489 Union St)

### TOURIST INFORMATION

**Tourist office** ( ☎ 288828; www.agtb.org; 23 Union St; ☯ 9am-6.30pm Mon-Sat, 10am-4pm Sun Jul & Aug, 9am-5.30pm Mon-Sat Easter-Jun, Sep & Oct, 9am-4.30pm Mon-Sat Oct-Easter).

## Sights

### ABERDEEN HARBOUR

Aberdeen has a busy, working harbour crowded with survey vessels and supply ships servicing the offshore oil installations, and car ferries bound for Orkney and Shetland. From dawn until about 8am the colourful **fish market** on Albert Basin operates as it has done for centuries.

Overlooking all this nautical bustle is the **Maritime Museum** ( ☎ 337700; www.aagm.co.uk; Shiprow; admission free; ☯ 10am-5pm Mon-Sat, noon-3pm Sun), centred on a three-storey replica of a North Sea oil production platform, with exhibits explaining all you ever wanted to know about the petroleum industry. Other galleries, some situated in **Provost Ross's House**, the oldest building in the city, cover the shipbuilding, whaling and fishing industries. Sleek and

speedy Aberdeen clippers were a 19th-century shipyard speciality, used by British merchants for the importation of tea, wool and exotic goods (opium, for instance) to Britain, and, on the return journey, the transportation of emigrants to Australia.

### UNION ST

Union St is the city's main thoroughfare, lined with solid, Victorian granite buildings. The oldest area is **Castlegate**, at the eastern end, where the castle once stood. When it was captured from the English for Robert the Bruce, the password used by the townspeople was 'Bon Accord', which is now the city's motto.

In the centre of Castle St stands the 17th-century **Mercat Cross**, bearing a sculpted frieze of portraits of Stuart monarchs. The Baronial heap towering over the eastern end of Castle St is the **Salvation Army Citadel**, which was modelled on Balmoral Castle.

On the northern side of Union St, 300m west of Castlegate, is **St Nicholas Church**, the so-called 'Mither Kirk' (Mother Church) of Aberdeen. The granite spire dates from the 19th century, but there has been a church on this site since the 12th century; the early 15th-century **St Mary's Chapel** survives in the eastern part of the church.

Surrounded by concrete and glass office blocks in what was once the worst slum in Aberdeen is **Provost Skene's House** ( ☎ 641086; Guestrow; admission free; ☯ 10am-5pm Mon-Sat, 1-4pm Sun), a late-medieval, turreted town house occupied in the 17th century by the provost (the Scottish equivalent of a mayor) Sir George Skene. It was also occupied for six weeks by the duke of Cumberland on his way to Culloden in 1746. The tempera-painted ceiling with its religious symbolism, dating from 1622, is unusual for having survived the depredations of the Reformation. It's a period gem featuring earnest-looking angels, soldiers and St Peter with crowing cockerels.

### MARISCHAL COLLEGE

Across Broad St from Provost Skene's House is **Marischal College**, founded in 1593 by the 5th Earl Marischal, and merged with King's College (founded 1495) in 1860 to create the modern University of Aberdeen. The huge and impressive façade in Perpendicular Gothic style – unusual in having such elaborate masonry hewn from notoriously hard-to-work granite – dates from 1906 and is the

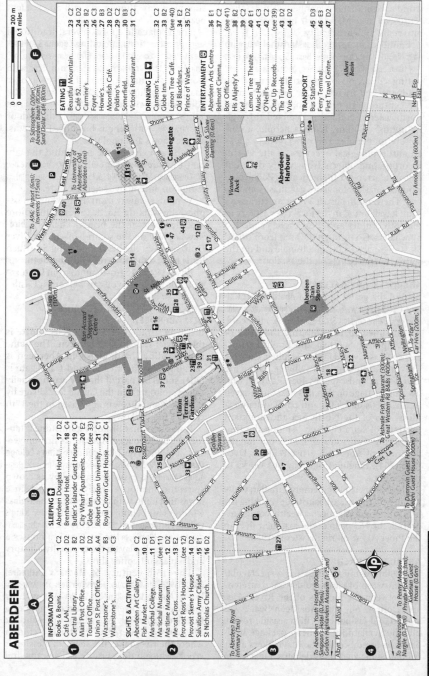

# ABERDEEN

**INFORMATION**
| | |
|---|---|
| Books & Beans | 1 C2 |
| Café LAN | 2 D2 |
| Central Library | 3 B2 |
| Main Post Office | 4 D2 |
| Tourist Office | 5 D2 |
| Union St Post Office | 6 A4 |
| Waterstone's | 7 B3 |
| Waterstone's | 8 C3 |

**SIGHTS & ACTIVITIES**
| | |
|---|---|
| Aberdeen Art Gallery | 9 C2 |
| Fish Market | 10 E3 |
| Marischal College | 11 D1 |
| Maritime Museum | 12 D2 |
| Mercat Cross | 13 E2 |
| Provost Ross's House | (see 12) |
| Provost Skene's House | 14 C2 |
| Salvation Army Citadel | 15 E1 |
| St Nicholas Church | 16 D2 |

**SLEEPING**
| | |
|---|---|
| Aberdeen Douglas Hotel | 17 D2 |
| Brentwood Hotel | 18 C4 |
| Butler's Islander Guest House | 19 C4 |
| City Wharf Apartments | 20 D2 |
| Globe Inn | (see 33) |
| Robert Gordon University | 21 C1 |
| Royal Crown Guest House | 22 C4 |

**EATING**
| | |
|---|---|
| Beautiful Mountain | 23 C2 |
| Café 52 | 24 D2 |
| Carmine's | 25 B2 |
| Foyer | 26 C3 |
| Howie's | 27 B3 |
| Moonfish Café | 28 D2 |
| Poldino's | 29 C2 |
| Somerfield | 30 B3 |
| Victoria Restaurant | 31 C2 |

**DRINKING**
| | |
|---|---|
| Cameron's | 32 C2 |
| Globe Inn | 33 B2 |
| Lemon Tree Café | (see 40) |
| Old Blackfriars | 34 E2 |
| Prince of Wales | 35 D2 |

**ENTERTAINMENT**
| | |
|---|---|
| Aberdeen Arts Centre | 36 E1 |
| Belmont Cinema | 37 C2 |
| Box Office | (see 41) |
| His Majesty's | 38 B2 |
| Kef | 39 C2 |
| Lemon Tree Theatre | 40 E1 |
| Music Hall | 41 C3 |
| O'Neill's | 42 C2 |
| One Up Records | (see 39) |
| The Tunnels | 43 D2 |
| Vue Cinema | 44 D2 |

**TRANSPORT**
| | |
|---|---|
| Bus Station | 45 D3 |
| Ferry Terminal | 46 E3 |
| First Travel Centre | 47 D2 |

world's second-largest granite structure (after L'Escorial near Madrid). It now houses the university's science faculty.

Founded in 1786, the **Marischal Museum** ( ☎ 274301; Marischal College, Broad St; admission free; ☽ 10am-5pm Mon-Fri, 2-5pm Sun) houses a fascinating collection of material donated by graduates and friends of the university over the centuries. In one room, the history of northeastern Scotland is depicted through its myths, customs, famous people, architecture and trade. The other gallery gives an anthropological overview of the world, incorporating objects from vastly different cultures, arranged thematically (Polynesian wooden masks alongside gas masks and so on). There are the usual Victorian curios, an Inuit kayak found in the local river estuary in the 18th century and Inuit objects collected by whalers. Go through the arch from Broad St, straight across the quadrangle and up the stairs; the museum is on the 1st floor.

### ABERDEEN ART GALLERY

Behind the grand façade of **Aberdeen Art Gallery** ( ☎ 523700; www.aagm.co.uk; Schoolhill; admission free; ☽ 10am-5pm Mon-Sat, 2-5pm Sun; ☒) is a cool, marble-lined space exhibiting the work of contemporary Scottish and English painters, such as Gwen Hardie, Stephen Conroy, Trevor Sutton and Tim Ollivier. There are also several landscapes by Joan Eardley, who lived in a cottage on the cliffs near Stonehaven in the 1950s and '60s, and painted tempestuous oils of the North Sea and poignant portraits of slum children. Among the Pre-Raphaelite works upstairs, look out for the paintings of Aberdeen artist William Dyce (1806–64), ranging from religious works to rural scenes.

Downstairs is a large, empty, circular, white room, with fish-scaled balustrades evoking the briny origins of Aberdeen's wealth, commemorating the 165 people who lost their lives in the Piper Alpha oil rig disaster in 1988.

### ABERDEEN BEACH

Just 800m east of Castlegate is a spectacular 2-mile sweep of clean, golden sand stretching between the mouths of the Rivers Dee and Don. At one time Aberdeen Beach was a good, old-fashioned British seaside resort, but the availability of cheap package holidays has lured Scottish holidaymakers away from its somewhat chilly delights. On a warm

summer's day, though, it's still an excellent beach.

The Esplanade sports several traditional seaside attractions, including **Codona's Amusement Park** ( ☎ 595910; Beach Blvd; admission free, pay per ride; ☽ 11am-midnight Sat & Sun), complete with stomach-churning waltzers, dodgems, a roller coaster, log flume and haunted house. The adjacent **Sunset Boulevard** ( ☎ 595910; admission free, pay per game; ☽ 10am-midnight) is the indoor alternative, with tenpin bowling, Dodgems, arcade games and pool tables.

Halfway between the beach and the city centre is **Satrosphere** ( ☎ 640340; www.satrosphere.net; 179 Constitution St; adult/child £5.75/4.50; ☽ 10am-5pm), a hands-on, interactive science centre.

You can get away from the fun fair atmosphere by walking north towards the more secluded part of the beach. There's a **bird-watching hide** on the south bank of the River Don, between the beach and King St, which leads back south towards Old Aberdeen.

Buses 14 and 15 (eastbound) from Union St go to the beach; or you can walk from Castlegate in 10 minutes.

### OLD ABERDEEN

Just over a mile north of the city centre is the district called Old Aberdeen. The name is misleading – although Old Aberdeen is certainly old, the area around Castlegate is older still. This part of the city was originally called Aulton, from the Gaelic for 'village by the pool', and this was anglicised in the 17th century to Old Town.

It was here that Bishop Elphinstone established King's College, Aberdeen's first university, in 1495. The 16th-century **King's College Chapel** ( ☎ 272137; College Bounds; admission free; ☽ 9am-4.30pm Mon-Fri) is easily recognised by its crown spire; the interior is largely unchanged since it was first built, with impressive stained-glass windows and choir stalls. The nearby **King's College Visitor Centre** ( ☎ 273702; College Bounds; admission free; ☽ 10am-5pm Mon-Sat, 2-5pm Sun) houses a multimedia display on the university's history and a pleasant coffee shop.

The 15th-century **St Machar's Cathedral** ( ☎ 485988; The Chanonry; admission free; ☽ 9am-5pm Mon-Sat Apr-Oct, 10am-4pm Mon-Sat Nov-Mar), with its massive twin towers, is a rare example of a fortified cathedral. According to legend, St Machar was ordered to establish a church where the river takes the shape of a bishop's crook, which it does just here. The cathedral is best known for its impressive heraldic ceiling, dating from 1520, which has 48 shields of kings, nobles, archbishops and bishops. Sunday services are held at 11am and 6pm.

Bus 20 from Littlejohn St (just north of Marischal College) runs to Old Aberdeen every 15 to 20 minutes.

### GORDON HIGHLANDERS MUSEUM

The excellent **Gordon Highlanders Museum** ( ☎ 311200; St Lukes, Viewfield Rd; adult/child £4/2; 10.30am-4.30pm Tue-Sat, 12.30-4.30pm Sun Apr-Oct, 10am-4pm Thu-Sat Nov, Feb & Mar) records the history of one of the British Army's most famous fighting units, described by Winston Churchill as 'the finest regiment in the world'. Originally raised in the northeast of Scotland by the 4th duke of Gordon in 1794, the regiment was amalgamated with the Seaforths and Camerons to form the Highlanders regiment in 1994. The museum is about a mile west of the western end of Union St – take bus 14 or 15 from Union St.

## Sleeping

There are clusters of B&Bs on Bon Accord St and Springbank Tce (both 400m southwest of the train station), and along Great Western Rd (the A93, a 25-minute walk southwest of the city centre). They're usually more expensive than the Scottish average and, with so many oil industry workers staying the night before flying offshore, single rooms are at a premium. Prices tend to be lower on weekends.

### BUDGET

**Aberdeen Youth Hostel** (SYHA; ☎ 0870 004 1100; 8 Queen's Rd; dm £13-15) This hostel, set in a granite Victorian villa, is a mile west of the train station. Walk west along Union St and take the right fork along Albyn Pl until you reach a roundabout; Queen's Rd continues on the western side of the roundabout.

During the university summer holidays some colleges let rooms to visitors:

**Robert Gordon University** ( ☎ 262134; www .scotland2000.com/rgu; Business & Vacation Accommodation Service, Schoolhill, Aberdeen AB10 1FR; 6 people for 2 nights £130; mid-Jun–mid-Aug) Flats comprise six to eight single rooms with shared bathroom, lounge and kitchen, close to the city centre.

**University of Aberdeen** ( ☎ 272664; www.abdn .ac.uk/confevents; Conference Office, King's College, Old Aberdeen AB24 3FX; r per person from £15, s/d £50/75) Basic self-catering flats (available mid-Jun to mid-Aug), or

plush B&B rooms at Kings Hall in the heart of Old Aberdeen (available year-round).

### MIDRANGE

**Dunrovin Guest House** ( ☎ 586081; www.dunrovinguest house.co.uk; 168 Bon Accord St; s/d from £40/60; P ) Dunrovin is a typical granite Victorian house with eight bedrooms; the upstairs rooms are bright and airy, and the friendly owners will provide a veggie breakfast if you wish.

**Butler's Islander Guest House** ( ☎ 212411; www .butlersguesthouse.com; 122 Crown St; s £33-60, d £50-70; ) Just across the street from the Royal Crown, Butler's is a cosy place with a big breakfast menu that includes fresh fruit salad, kippers and kedgeree as alternatives to the traditional fry-up.

**our pick** **Globe Inn** ( ☎ 624258; 13-15 North Silver St; s/d £48/53) This popular pub (see p251) has seven appealing and comfortable guest bedrooms upstairs, done out in dark wood with burgundy bedspreads. There's live music in the pub on weekends so it's not a place for early-to-bed types, but the price vs location factor can't be beat. No dining room, so breakfast is continental, served on a tray in your room.

**Royal Crown Guest House** ( ☎ 586461; www.royal crown.co.uk; 111 Crown St; s £35-70, d £60-80; P ) The Royal Crown has eight small but nicely furnished bedrooms, and has a top location only five minutes' walk from the train station (up a steep flight of stairs).

**Brentwood Hotel** ( ☎ 595440; www.brentwood-hotel .co.uk; 101 Crown St; s £41-86, d £62-96; P ) The friendly and flower-bedecked Brentwood, set in a granite town house, is one of the most attractive hotels in the area, comfortable and conveniently located, but often busy during the week – weekend rates are much cheaper.

Other recommendations:

**Adelphi Guest House** ( ☎ 583078; www.adelphiguest house.com; 8 Whinhill Rd; s/d from £28/50)

**Penny Meadow Private Hotel** ( ☎ 588037; frances@pennymeadow.freeserve.co.uk; 189 Great Western Rd; s/d £45/70; P )

**Kildonan Guest House** ( ☎ 316115; www.kildonan -guesthouse.com; 410 Great Western Rd; s/d £36/52)

### TOP END

**Aberdeen Douglas Hotel** ( ☎ 582255; www.aberdeen douglas.com; 43-45 Market St; s £45-85, d £60-120) You can't miss the grand Victorian façade of this historic landmark, which first opened its doors as a hotel in 1853. Recently renovated, it now offers classy modern rooms with polished woodwork and crisp white bed linen, and is barely a minute's walk from the train station.

**Simpson's Hotel** ( ☎ 327777; www.simpsonshotel.co.uk; 59 Queen's Rd; s £75-160, d £95-180; P &.) Simpson's, a mile west of Union St, is a stylish boutique hotel decorated with a Mediterranean-Italian theme in shades of sand, terracotta and aqua. It's aimed at both business and private guests, and is totally wheelchair accessible. Cheaper rates on weekends.

**City Wharf Apartments** ( ☎ 0845 094 2424; www.citywharfapartments.co.uk; 19-20 Regent Quay; d £120; &. &.) You can watch the bustle of Aberdeen's commercial harbour as you eat breakfast in one of these luxury serviced apartments, complete with stylish, fully equipped kitchen, champagne-stocked minibar and daily maid service. Available by the night or the week, with discounts for longer stays.

## Eating
### BUDGET

**Beautiful Mountain** ( ☎ 645353; 11-13 Belmont St; mains £3-6; ☽ 8am-5pm Mon-Fri, 9am-5pm Sat) This cosy café is squeezed into a couple of tiny rooms (seating upstairs), but serves all-day breakfasts and tasty sandwiches (smoked salmon, Thai chicken, pastrami) on sourdough, bagels, ciabatta and lots of other breads, along with exquisite espresso and consummate cappuccino.

**Sand Dollar Café** ( ☎ 572288; 2 Beach Esplanade; mains £4-7; ☽ 9am-5pm) This place is a cut above your usual seaside café – on sunny days you can sit at the wooden tables outside and share a bottle of chilled white wine, and there's a tempting menu that includes pancakes with maple syrup, homemade burgers and chocolate brownie with Orkney ice cream.

**Victoria Restaurant** ( ☎ 621381; 140 Union St; mains £4-8; ☽ 9am-5pm Fri-Wed, 9am-6.30pm Thu) The Victoria, above the Jamieson & Carry jewellery shop, is a traditional, posh Scottish tearoom, with delicious fresh soups, salads and sandwiches. Breakfast served till 11.30am.

**Carmine's** ( ☎ 624145; 32 Union Tce; 3-course lunch £6, pizza £5-11; ☽ 11.45am-2.30pm & 4.45-6.45pm Mon-Sat) Cosy little Carmine's is famed for good, inexpensive Italian food, including the best pizza in town; the lunch deal is available Monday to Friday only. No licence, so BYOB, and best to book; the place seats only 16 people.

For self-caterers, **Somerfield** (Union St; ☽ 7am-8pm Mon-Sat, 8am-8pm Sun) is a convenient city-centre supermarket near the Music Hall.

### MIDRANGE

**Ashvale Fish Restaurant** ( ☎ 596581; 42-48 Great Western Rd; takeaways £3-5, sit-in mains £7-10; ☽ 11.45am-11pm; &.) The Ashvale, an upmarket fish-and- chip shop, is well known outside the city, having won several awards. The Ashvale Whale – a one-pound cod fillet (£8) in batter – is a speciality; finish it off and you get a second one free (as if you'd want one by then!).

**Howie's** ( ☎ 639500; 50 Chapel St; 2-course lunch/dinner £11/18; ☽ noon-2.30pm & 6-10pm) The Aberdeen branch of the well-known Edinburgh chain of restaurants is a chic bistro dishing up great-value 'modern Scottish' cuisine accompanied by very reasonably priced house wine.

**Café 52** ( ☎ 590094; 52 The Green; mains £13; ☽ noon-9.30pm) This little haven of laid-back industrial chic – a high, narrow space lined with bare stonework, rough plaster and exposed ventilation ducts – serves some of the finest and most inventive cuisine in the northeast, from starters such as refreshing lettuce and sorrel soup or silky carpaccio of tuna with passion fruit, to mains like its signature dish – a Thai seafood stockpot served with rustic chips.

**Moonfish Café** ( ☎ 644166; 9 Correction Wynd; mains £11-17; ☽ noon-11pm) A funky little eatery tucked away on a back street, the Moonfish menu combines light snacks based on Spanish tapas and Greek *mezes* (starters) with more filling Mediterranean dinner dishes, such as chicken breast wrapped in Parma ham with garlic and rosemary.

**Foyer** ( ☎ 582277; 82a Crown St; mains £12-18; ☽ 11am-10pm) A light, airy space filled with blonde wood and bold colours, Foyer is an art gallery as well as a restaurant and is run by a charity that works against youth homelessness and unemployment. The seasonal menu is full of interesting vegetarian options such as jerusalem artichoke clafoutis with creamed green peas and leek stew, and salad of char-grilled halloumi cheese with mint, watermelon, red onion and pumpkin seed. A light lunch menu (mains £7 to £9) is available from 11am to 6pm.

**Rendezvous@Nargile** ( ☎ 323700; cnr Forest Ave; mains £13-18; ☽ noon-10pm; &.) This stylish West End venue specialises in Turkish cuisine, serving tasty spreads of *mezes*, *shakshuka* (a blend of roast peppers, tomatoes, aubergines and chilli), *djadjik* (yoghurt with garlic and cucumber) and *sigara boregi* (cheese pastries), for example – followed by delicious, melt-in-the-mouth kebabs and marinated meats, and vegetarian dishes such as *mantar guvec* (casseroled button mushrooms in creamy sauce with a cheese and couscous crust).

**Poldino's** ( ☎ 647777; 7 Little Belmont St; lunch mains £9-19; ✆ noon-2.30pm & 6-10.45pm Mon-Sat) Poldino's is a long-established Aberdeen eatery – an upmarket, Italian family restaurant that never fails to impress with the quality of its food and service.

### TOP END

**Silver Darling** ( ☎ 576229; Pocra Quay, North Pier; lunch mains £11-13, dinner mains £19-22; ✆ noon-1.45pm Mon-Fri & 7-9.30pm Mon-Sat) The Silver Darling (an old Scottish nickname for herring) is housed in a former Customs office, with picture windows overlooking the sea at the entrance to Aberdeen harbour. Here you can enjoy fresh Scottish seafood prepared by a top French chef while you watch the porpoises playing in the harbour mouth. The lunch menu offers good-value gourmet delights, such as roast monkfish with chickpea and cumin purée; bookings are recommended.

## Drinking

Aberdeen is a great city for a pub crawl – it's more a question of knowing when to stop than where to start. There are lots of pre-club bars in and around Belmont St, with more traditional pubs scattered throughout the city centre.

**Lemon Tree Café** ( ☎ 621610; 5 West North St; ✆ noon-4pm Thu-Sun; ✿ ) The bohemian café-bar at the theatre does excellent coffee, cakes and light meals, and there's live blues on Friday, jazz on Sunday and kids' activities on Saturday.

**Globe Inn** ( ☎ 624258; 13-15 North Silver St; ✆ noon-3pm & 5-11pm Mon-Thu, noon-1am Fri & Sat, 12.30pm-midnight Sun) This lovely Edwardian-style pub with wood panelling, marble-topped tables and walls hung with old musical instruments is a great place for a quiet lunchtime or afternoon drink. It serves good coffee as well as real ales and malt whiskies, and has live music in the evenings Friday to Sunday. And probably the poshest pub toilets in the country.

**Prince of Wales** ( ☎ 640597; 7 St Nicholas Lane) Tucked down an alley off Union St, Aberdeen's best-known pub boasts the longest bar in the city, and a great range of real ales and good-value pub grub. Quiet in the afternoons, but standing-room only in the evenings.

**Cameron's** ( ☎ 644487; 6 Little Belmont St) Known as Ma Cameron's, this is Aberdeen's oldest pub, established in 1789. It has a pleasantly old-fashioned atmosphere, with lots of wood, brick and stone, and a range of excellent real ales and malt whiskies.

**Old Blackfriars** ( ☎ 581922; 52 Castlegate) This is one of the most attractive traditional pubs in the city, with a lovely stone and timber interior and a relaxed atmosphere – a great place for an afternoon pint.

**Blue Lamp** ( ☎ 647472; 121 Gallowgate) A long-standing feature of the Aberdeen pub scene, the Blue Lamp is a favourite student hang-out – a dark, but not dingy, drinking den with good beer, good *craic* and a jukebox selection that has barely changed since Elvis died. There are regular sessions of live folk and acoustic music.

## Entertainment

### CINEMAS

**Vue Cinema** ( ☎ 08712 240240; 10 Shiprow; adult/child £6.65/4.15) A seven-screen multiplex, conveniently located just off Union St, that shows mainstream, first-run films.

**Belmont Cinema** ( ☎ listings 343534, bookings 343536; 49 Belmont St; adult/child £6.40/4) The Belmont is a great little art-house cinema, with a lively programme of cult classics, director's seasons, foreign films and mainstream movies. There's also a Saturday morning kids club, with a children's movie screened at 11.30am.

### NIGHTCLUBS

Check out what's happening in the club and live-music scene at local record shops – try **One Up Records** (17 Belmont St).

**Kef** ( ☎ 648000; 9 Belmont St; admission free-£5; ✆ 11pm-2am Sun-Thu, to 3am Fri & Sat) Decked out with a Moroccan theme – there are booths with lots of rugs and comfy cushions to lie around on – this is Aberdeen's most laid-back club, with DJs playing seven nights a week. The main attractions are Jungle Nation (drum n bass and jungle) and Wax (hip-hop).

**The Tunnels** ( ☎ 211121; www.thetunnels.co.uk; Carnegie's Brae; admission £3-10; ✆ from 8pm or 9pm) This cavernous club hosts regular DJ nights, from new music on Tuesday's Club NME to the Dirty Disco indie night most Fridays and Saturdays. It's also a great live music venue, with a packed programme of up-and-coming Scottish bands.

**O'Neill's** ( ☎ 621456; 9 Back Wynd; admission £2-4; ☺ to 2am Sun-Thu, 3am Fri & Sat) Upstairs at O'Neill's you're guaranteed a wild night of pounding, hardcore Irish rock, indie and alternative tunes; downstairs is a (slightly) quieter bar packed with rugby types downing large quantities of Murphy's stout.

### THEATRE & CONCERTS

**His Majesty's** ( ☎ 637788; www.hmtaberdeen.com; Rosemount Viaduct) The main theatre in Aberdeen hosts everything from ballet and opera to pantomimes and musicals.

**Aberdeen Arts Centre** ( ☎ 635208; www.aberdeen artscentre.org.uk; King St) The Arts Centre stages regular drama productions in its theatre, and changing exhibitions in its gallery.

**Lemon Tree Theatre** ( ☎ 642230; www.lemontree .org; 5 West North St) The Lemon Tree theatre has an interesting programme of dance, music and drama, and often has live rock, jazz and folk bands playing. There are also children's shows, ranging from comedy to drama to puppetry.

You can book tickets for most concerts and other events at the **Box Office** ( ☎ 641122; ☺ 9.30am-6pm Mon-Sat) next to the **Music Hall** ( ☎ 632080; Union St), the main venue for classical music concerts.

## Getting There & Away

### AIR

**Aberdeen Airport** ( ☎ 722331; www.aberdeenairport.com) is at Dyce, 6 miles northwest of the city centre. There are regular flights to numerous Scottish and UK destinations, including Orkney and Shetland, and international flights to the Netherlands, Norway, Denmark, France and the Czech Republic.

Bus 27 runs regularly from Union St to the airport (£1.80, 35 minutes). A taxi from the airport to the city centre costs £12.

### BOAT

Car ferries from Aberdeen to Orkney and Shetland are run by **Northlink Ferries** ( ☎ 0845 600 0449; www.northlinkferries.co.uk). For more details, see p405. The ferry terminal is a short walk east of the train and bus stations.

### BUS

The **bus station** (Guild St) is next to the train station.

National Express runs direct buses from London (£40, 12 hours) twice daily, one of them overnight. Scottish Citylink runs direct services to Dundee (£11, two hours), Perth (£16, 2½ hours), Edinburgh (£20, 3¼ hours) and Glasgow (£20, 4¼ hours).

Bus 10 runs hourly to Inverness (£11, 3¾ hours) via Huntly, Keith, Fochabers, Elgin (£10, two hours) and Nairn. Service 201 runs every half-hour (hourly on Sunday) to Crathes Castle gate (45 minutes), continuing once an hour (less frequently on Sunday) to Ballater (1¾ hours) and every two hours to Crathie (for Balmoral Castle) and Braemar (£8, 2¼ hours).

Other local buses serve Stonehaven, Fraserburgh, Peterhead, Banff and Buckie.

### TRAIN

There are several trains a day from London's King's Cross to Aberdeen (£112, 7½ hours); most services involve a change of train at Edinburgh.

Other destinations served from Aberdeen by rail include Edinburgh (£36, 2½ hours), Glasgow (£36, 2¾ hours), Dundee (£22, 1¼ hours) and Inverness (£23, 2¼ hours).

## Getting Around

### BUS

The main city bus operator is **First Aberdeen** ( ☎ 650065; www.firstaberdeen.com). Local fares cost from 70p to £1.80; pay the driver as you climb onboard the bus. A FirstDay ticket (adult/ child £3.50/2.50) allows unlimited travel from the time of purchase until midnight on all First Aberdeen buses. Information, route maps and tickets are available from the **First Travel Centre** (47 Union St; ☺ 8.45am-5.30pm Mon-Sat).

The most useful services for visitors are buses 18, 19 and 24 from Union St to Great Western Rd (for B&Bs); bus 27 from the bus station to the Aberdeen Youth Hostel and the airport; and bus 20 from Marischal College to Old Aberdeen.

### CAR

For rental cars try **Arnold Clark** ( ☎ 249159; www .arnoldclarkrental.com; Girdleness Rd) or **1car1 Car Hire** ( ☎ 594248; www.1car1.com; 16 South College St).

### TAXI

The main city-centre taxi ranks are at the train station and on Back Wynd, off Union St. To order a taxi, phone **ComCab** ( ☎ 353535) or **Rainbow Cabs** ( ☎ 878787).

# AROUND ABERDEEN
## Stonehaven
☎ 01569 / pop 9600

Originally a small fishing village, Stonehaven has been the county town of Kincardineshire since 1600 and is now a thriving, family-friendly seaside resort. There's a **tourist office** ( ☎ 762806; 66 Allardice St; ☺ 10am-7pm Mon-Sat, 1-5.30pm Sun Jul & Aug, 10am-1pm & 2-5.30pm Mon-Sat Jun & Sep, 10am-1pm & 2-5pm Mon-Sat Apr, May & Oct) near Market Sq in the town centre.

### SIGHTS & ACTIVITIES
From the lane beside the tourist office, a boardwalk leads south along the shoreline to the picturesque cliff-bound **harbour**, where you'll find a couple of appealing pubs and the town's oldest building, the **Tolbooth**, built about 1600 by the Earl Marischal. It now houses a small **museum** (admission free; ☺ 10am-noon & 2-5pm Mon & Thu-Sat, 2-5pm Wed & Sun) and a restaurant.

At the northern end of town is the **Open-Air Swimming Pool** ( ☎ 762134; adult/child £3.50/2; ☺ 10am-7.30pm Mon-Fri, 11am-6pm Sat & Sun Jul & Aug, 1-7.30pm Mon-Fri, 10am-6pm Sat & Sun Jun), an Olympic-size (50m), heated, sea-water pool in Art Deco style, dating from 1934. The pool is also open for 'midnight swims' from 10pm to midnight on Wednesday from the end of June to mid-August.

A pleasant, 15-minute walk along the cliff tops south of the harbour leads to the spectacular ruins of **Dunnottar Castle** ( ☎ 762173; adult/child £5/1; ☺ 9am-6pm daily Jul-Sep, 9am-6pm Mon-Sat & 2-5pm Sun Easter-Jun & Oct, 10.30am-dusk Fri-Mon Nov-Easter), spread out across a grassy promontory rising 50m above the sea. As dramatic a film set as any director could wish for, it provided the backdrop for Franco Zeffirelli's *Hamlet*, starring Mel Gibson. The original fortress was built in the 9th century; the keep is the most substantial remnant, but the drawing room (restored in 1926) is more interesting.

The **Lady Gail 2** ( ☎ 765064; adult/child £10/5) offers boat trips from the harbour to the nearby sea cliffs of Fowlsheugh nature reserve, which from May to July are home to around 160,000 nesting seabirds, including kittiwakes, guillemots, razorbills and puffins.

### FESTIVALS & EVENTS
The town hosts several special events, including the famous **Fireball Ceremony** (www.stonehaven fireballs.co.uk) at Hogmanay (31 December), when people parade along the High St at midnight swinging blazing fireballs around their heads,

and the three-day **Stonehaven Folk Festival** (www .stonehavenfolkfestival.co.uk) in mid-July.

### SLEEPING & EATING
our pick **24 Shorehead** ( ☎ 767750; www.twentyfourshore head.co.uk; 24 Shorehead; s/d £50/60) Location makes all the difference, and the location of this former cooperage offering peaceful B&B accommodation can't be beat – last house at the end of the road, overlooking the harbour, with lovely sea views – using the binoculars provided, you can even spot seals from your bedroom.

**Beachgate House** ( ☎ 763155; www.beachgate .co.uk; Beachgate Lane; s/d £55/70; P ) This luxurious modern bungalow is right on the seafront, just a few paces from the tourist office; two of its five rooms have sea views, as does the lounge/dining room.

**Marine Hotel** ( ☎ 762155; 9-10 The Shore; mains £7-12; ☺ food served noon-2.30pm & 5.30-9pm) A recent makeover with bare timber, slate and dove-grey paintwork has given this popular harbour-side pub a boutique look; the old juke box is gone, but there are still half a dozen real ales on tap, and a bar meals menu that includes fresh seafood specials.

**Carron Restaurant** ( ☎ 760460; 20 Cameron St; mains £10-16; ☺ noon-2pm & 6-9.30pm Tue-Sun) This beautiful Art Deco restaurant is a remarkable survival from the 1930s, complete with bow-fronted terrace, iron fanlights, Deco mirrors, player piano and original tiled toilets. The French- and Mediterranean-inspired menu makes the most of local produce, matching the elegance of the surroundings.

**Tolbooth Restaurant** ( ☎ 762287; Old Pier; mains £15-18; ☺ noon-2pm & 6-11pm Tue-Sun) Set in a 17th-century house overlooking the harbour, this is one of the best seafood restaurants in the region – reservations are recommended. From Tuesday to Saturday you can get a three-course lunch for £15.

You can enjoy excellent coffee and cakes with a view of the harbour at the **Boathouse Café** ( ☎ 764666; Old Pier; ☺ 9am-4.30pm Tue & Wed, 9am-10pm Thu-Sat, 10am-6.30pm Sun), while the **Bervie Chipper** ( ☎ 762658; 12 David St; ☺ noon-9pm) serves the best fish and chips in town – it's a branch of the Inverbervie chip shop that lay claims to inventing the notorious deep-fried Mars Bar (and yes, it's still on the menu!).

### GETTING THERE & AWAY
Stonehaven is 15 miles south of Aberdeen, and is served by the frequent buses travelling

NORTHEAST SCOTLAND

between Aberdeen (45 minutes, hourly) and Dundee (1½ hours). Trains to Dundee are faster (£11, 55 minutes, hourly) and offer a more scenic journey.

## Castle Fraser

The impressive 16th- to 17th-century **Castle Fraser** (NTS; ☎ 01330-833463; adult/child £8/5; ☑ 11am-5pm Jul & Aug, 11am-5pm Wed-Sun Apr-Jun, noon-5pm Wed-Sun Sep & Oct) is the ancestral home of the Fraser family. The largely Victorian interior includes the great hall (with a hidden opening where the laird could eavesdrop on his guests), the library, various bedrooms and an ancient kitchen, plus a secret room for storing valuables; Fraser family relics on display include needlework hangings and a 19th-century artificial leg. The 'Woodland Secrets' area in the castle grounds is designed as an adventure playground for kids.

The castle is 16 miles west of Aberdeen and 3 miles south of Kemnay. Buses from Aberdeen to Alford stop at Kemnay.

## Haddo House

Designed in Georgian style by William Adam in 1732, **Haddo House** (NTS; ☎ 01651-851440; Tarves; adult/child £8/5; ☑ 11am-5pm Jul & Aug, 11am-5pm Fri-Mon Apr-Jun, Sep & Oct) is best described as a classic English stately home transplanted to Scotland. Home to the Gordon family, it has sumptuous Victorian interiors with wood-panelled walls, Persian rug–scattered floors and a wealth of period antiques. The beautiful grounds and terraced gardens are open all year (9am to dusk).

Haddo is 19 miles north of Aberdeen, near Ellon. Buses run hourly Monday to Saturday from Aberdeen to Tarves/Methlick, stopping at the end of the Haddo House driveway; it's a mile-long walk from bus stop to house.

## Fyvie Castle

Though a magnificent example of Scottish Baronial architecture, **Fyvie Castle** (NTS; ☎ 01651-891266; adult/child £8/5; ☑ 11am-5pm Jul & Aug, noon-5pm Sat-Wed Apr-Jun, Sep & Oct) is probably more famous for its ghosts, which include a phantom trumpeter and the mysterious Green Lady. The castle's art collection includes portraits by Thomas Gainsborough and Sir Henry Raeburn.

The castle is 25 miles north of Aberdeen on the A947 towards Turriff. A bus runs hourly every day from Aberdeen to Banff and Elgin via Fyvie village, a mile from the castle.

## DEESIDE

The valley of the **River Dee** – often called Royal Deeside because of the royal family's long association with the area – stretches west from Aberdeen to Braemar, closely paralleled by the A93 road. From Deeside north to Strathdon is serious castle country – there are more examples of fanciful Scottish Baronial architecture here than anywhere else in Scotland.

The Dee, world-famous for its **salmon fishing**, has its source in the Cairngorm Mountains west of Braemar, the starting point for long walks into the hills. The **FishDee website** (www .fishdee.co.uk) has all you need to know about fishing on the river.

## Crathes Castle

The atmospheric, 16th-century **Crathes Castle** (NTS; ☎ 01330-844525; adult/child £10/7; ☑ 10am-5.30pm Apr-Sep, 10.30am-3.45pm Wed-Sun Nov-Mar; ☑ ) is famous for its Jacobean painted ceilings, magnificently carved canopied beds, and the 'Horn of Leys', presented to the Burnett family by Robert the Bruce in the 14th century. The beautiful formal **gardens** include 300-year-old yew hedges and colourful herbaceous borders.

The castle is on the A93, 16 miles west of Aberdeen, on the main Aberdeen to Ballater bus route.

## Ballater

☎ 01339 / pop 1450
The attractive little village of Ballater owes its 18th-century origins to the curative waters of nearby Pannanich Springs (now bottled commercially as Deeside Natural Mineral Water) and its prosperity to nearby Balmoral Castle.

The **tourist office** ( ☎ 755306; Station Sq; ☑ 9am-6pm Jul & Aug, 10am-5pm Sep-Jun) is in the Old Royal Station. For internet access, go to **Cybernaut** ( ☎ 755566; 14 Bridge St; per 15min £1.75; ☑ 9am-7pm Mon-Sat & noon-4pm Sun).

### SIGHTS & ACTIVITIES

When Queen Victoria travelled to Balmoral she would alight from the royal train at Ballater's **Old Royal Station** ( ☎ 755306; Station Sq; admission free; ☑ 9am-6pm Jul & Aug, 10am-5pm Sep-Jun). The station has been beautifully restored, and now houses a museum, a restaurant and the tourist office. (At the time of research the museum was hoping to have a Victorian royal coach on display by summer 2008.) Note the crests on the shop fronts along the main street proclaiming 'By Royal Appointment' – the village is a major supplier of provisions for Balmoral.

Also on Station Sq is **Dee Valley Confectioners** ( ☎ 755499; Station Sq; admission free; ☺ 9am-noon & 2-4.30pm Mon-Thu Apr-Oct), where you can drool over the manufacture of traditional Scottish sweeties; and **Cabin Fever** ( ☎ 754004; Station Sq), where you can rent mountain bikes (£15 per day, or £35 for a full-suspension model), or arrange to go pony-trekking, quad-biking, clay-pigeon shooting or canoeing.

As you approach Ballater from the east the hills start to close in, and there are many pleasant **walks** in the surrounding area. The steep woodland walk up **Craigendarroch** (400m) takes just over one hour. **Morven** (871m) is a more serious prospect, taking about six hours, but offers good views from the top; ask at the tourist office for more info.

### SLEEPING & EATING

Accommodation here is fairly expensive and budget travellers usually continue to Braemar.

**Celicall** ( ☎ 755699; celicall@euphony.net; 3 Braemar Rd; s/d from £35/46; **P** ) Celicall is a friendly, family-run B&B in a modern cottage right across the street from Station Sq, within easy walking distance of all attractions.

**our pick Auld Kirk** ( ☎ 755762; www.theauldkirk.com; Braemar Rd; s/d from £50/70) Here's something a little out of the ordinary – a six-bedroom 'restaurant with rooms' housed in a converted 19th-century church. A recent makeover blends original features with sleek modern décor, and the stylish restaurant (2- /3-course dinner £23/29) serves local lamb, venison and wild rabbit.

**Green Inn** ( ☎ 755701; www.green-inn.com; d £60; **P** ) A lovely old house dotted with plush armchairs and sofas, this is another 'restaurant with rooms' – three comfortable en-suite bedrooms – with the accent on fine dining: the menu includes French-influenced dishes such as roast quail with crayfish, truffle and wild mushrooms. A 2- /3-course dinner costs £31 to £37 and meals are served from 7pm till 9pm Tuesday to Saturday.

**Old Station Café** ( ☎ 755050; Station Sq; mains £7-15; ☺ 10am-5pm daily, 6.30-8.30pm Thu-Sat) The former waiting room at Queen Victoria's train station is now an attractive dining area with black-and-white floor tiles, basketwork chairs, and marble fireplace and table tops. Daily specials

make good use of local produce, from salmon to venison, and good coffee and home-baked goods are available all day.

### GETTING THERE & AWAY

Bus 201 runs from Aberdeen to Ballater (1¾ hours, hourly Monday to Saturday, six on Sunday) via Crathes Castle, and continues to Braemar (30 minutes).

## Balmoral Castle

Eight miles west of Ballater lies **Balmoral Castle** ( ☎ 01339-742334; www.balmoralcastle.com; adult/child £7/3; ☺ 10am-5pm Apr-Jul, last admission 4pm), the Queen's Highland holiday home, screened from the road by a thick curtain of trees. Built for Queen Victoria in 1855 as a private residence for the royal family, it kicked off the revival of the Scottish Baronial style of architecture that characterises so many of Scotland's 19th-century country houses.

The admission fee includes an interesting and well thought out audio guide, but the tour is very much one through garden and grounds; as for the castle itself, only the ballroom, which displays a collection of Landseer paintings and royal silver, is open to the public. Don't expect to see the Queen's private quarters! Dedicated royal-watchers will enjoy themselves; otherwise it's hard to justify braving the crowds and the admission fee just for a lot of photographs of smiling royals, a few pieces of art and some stuffed animals.

The massive, pointy-topped mountain that looms to the south of Balmoral is **Lochnagar** (1155m), immortalised in verse by Lord Byron, who spent his childhood years in Aberdeenshire:

England, thy beauties are tame and domestic
To one who has roamed o'er the mountains afar.
O! for the crags that are wild and majestic:
The steep frowning glories of dark Lochnagar.

Balmoral is beside the A93 at Crathie and can be reached on the Aberdeen to Braemar bus.

## Braemar

☎ 01339 / pop 400

Braemar is a pretty little village with a grand location on a broad plain ringed by mountains where the Dee valley and Glen Clunie meet. In winter this is one of the coldest places in the country – temperatures as low as minus 29°C have been recorded – and during spells of severe cold hungry deer wander the streets looking for a bite to eat. Braemar is an excellent base for hill walking, and there's skiing at nearby Glenshee.

The **tourist office** ( ☎ 741600; The Mews, Mar Rd; 9am-6pm Aug, 9am-5pm Jun, Jul, Sep & Oct, 10am-1.30pm & 2-5pm Mon-Sat, 2-5pm Sun Nov-May), opposite the Fife Arms Hotel, has lots of useful info on walks in the area. There's a bank with an ATM in the village centre, a couple of outdoor equipment shops and an **Alldays** ( 7.30am-9pm Mon-Sat, 9am-6pm Sun) grocery store.

## SIGHTS & ACTIVITIES
The **Braemar Highland Heritage Centre** ( ☎ 741944; Mar Rd; admission free; 9am-6.30pm Jul & Aug, 10am-6pm Jun & Sep, 10am-5.30pm Mon-Sat, noon-5pm Sun Mar-May, call for winter hr), beside the tourist office, tells the story of the area with displays and videos.

Just north of the village, turreted **Braemar Castle** dates from 1628 and served as a government garrison after the 1745 Jacobite rebellion. It was taken over by the local community in 2007 and was undergoing restoration at the time of research; it should be open to the public in 2008.

An easy walk from Braemar is up **Creag Choinnich** (538m), a hill to the east of the village above the A93. The route is waymarked and takes about 1½ hours. For a longer walk (three hours) and superb views of the Cairngorms, head for the summit of **Morrone** (859m), southwest of Braemar. Ask at the tourist office for details of these and other walks.

You can hire bikes from **Braemar Mountain Sports** ( ☎ 741242; 5 Invercauld Rd; 9am-6pm) for £10/15 per half-day/day.

## FESTIVALS & EVENTS
More than 20,000 people, including the royal family, descend on Braemar on the first Saturday in September for the annual **Braemar Gathering** ( ☎ 755377; www.braemargathering.org; adult/child £7/2), the most famous Highland games in the country. Bookings for ringside and grandstand seats (£13 to £22) are essential. See the boxed text, below, for more information.

## SLEEPING
**ourpick Rucksacks Bunkhouse** ( ☎ 741517; 15 Mar Rd; bothy £7, dm £12, tw £30; P ) A shiny new extension now houses the comfortable dorms in this appealing cottage bunkhouse, with cheaper beds in an alpine-style bothy (shared sleeping platform for 10 people). Extras including a drying room, laundry and even a sauna (£10 an hour) mean that Rucksacks is understandably popular with walkers and climbers. Nonguests are welcome to use the internet (£2 per hour, 10.30am to 4.30pm), laundry (£4) and even the showers (£2), and the friendly owner is a fount of knowledge about the local area.

**Braemar Youth Hostel** (SYHA; ☎ 0870 004 1105; 21 Glenshee Rd; dm £13-14; late Dec-Oct) This hostel is housed in a grand former shooting lodge just south of the village centre on the A93 to Perth; it has a comfy lounge with pool table, and a barbecue in the garden.

**Craiglea** ( ☎ 741641; www.craigleabraemar.com; Hillside Dr; s/d from £25/46; P ) Craiglea is a homely B&B set in a pretty stone-built cottage with three en-suite bedrooms. Vegetarian breakfasts are available and the owners can give advice on local walks.

**Clunie Lodge Guesthouse** ( ☎ 741330; www.clunie lodge.com; Cluniebank Rd; r per person from £25; P ) A spacious Victorian villa set in beautiful gardens, the Clunie is a great place to relax after a hard day's hiking, with its comfortable resi-

---

### BRAEMAR GATHERING
There are Highland games in many towns and villages throughout the summer, but the best known is the **Braemar Gathering** ( ☎ 01339-755377; www.braemargathering.org), which takes place on the first Saturday in September. It's a major occasion, organised every year since 1817 by the Braemar Royal Highland Society. Events include highland dancing, pipers, tug-of-war, a hill race up Morrone, tossing the caber, hammer- and stone-throwing and the long jump. International athletes are among those who take part.

These kinds of events took place informally in the Highlands for many centuries as tests of skill and strength, but they were formalised around 1820 as part of the rise of Highland romanticism initiated by Sir Walter Scott and King George IV. Queen Victoria attended the Braemar Gathering in 1848, starting a tradition of royal patronage that continues to this day.

dents lounge, bedrooms with views of the hills and red squirrels scampering through the neighbouring woods. There's a drying room for wet weather gear and secure storage for cycles.

**Braemar Lodge Hotel** ( ☎ 741627; www.braemarlodge .co.uk; Glenshee Rd; dm £11, s/d £60/100; **P** ) This Victorian shooting lodge on the southern outskirts of the village has bags of character, not least in the wood-panelled Malt Room bar, which is as well stocked with mounted deer heads as it is with single malt whiskies. There's a good restaurant with views of the hills, plus a 12-berth hikers' bunkhouse in the hotel grounds.

Campers will find good facilities at **Invercauld Caravan Club Site** ( ☎ 741373; tent sites £9-14; ⊙ late Dec-Oct), or you can camp wild (no facilities) along the minor road on the east bank of the Clunie Water, 3 miles south of Braemar.

### EATING
**Hungry Highlander** (14 Invercauld Rd; mains £3-7; ⊙ noon-8pm Tue, 10am-8pm Wed, Thu & Sun, 10am-10pm Fri & Sat) If you're too late for a sit-down dinner at one of the restaurants, this place serves a range of take-away meals and hot drinks.

**Taste** ( ☎ 741425; Airlie House, Mar Rd; mains £9-10; ⊙ 10am-5pm Thu-Tue, 6.30-8.30pm Fri & Sat; ⚄ ) Taste is a relaxed little café with armchairs in the window, serving soups, snacks, coffee and cakes during the day, and more substantial fare – beef and Guinness casserole, or vegetable crumble with a cheese and nut topping – in the evenings.

**our pick** **Gathering Place Bistro** ( ☎ 741234; 9 Invercauld Rd; mains £15-17; ⊙ 12.20-2.30pm Wed-Sat, 6-9pm Tue-Sat) This bright and breezy bistro is an unexpected corner of culinary excellence, with a welcoming dining room and sunny conservatory, tucked below the main road junction at the entrance to the village.

### GETTING THERE & AWAY
Bus 201 runs from Aberdeen to Braemar (2¼ hours, hourly Monday to Saturday, six on Sunday). The drive from Perth to Braemar is beautiful, but there's no public transport on this route.

## Inverey
Five miles west of Braemar is the tiny settlement of Inverey. Numerous mountain walks start from here, including the adventurous walk through the **Lairig Ghru** pass to Aviemore (see the boxed text, p334).

The **Glen Luibeg** circuit (15 miles, six hours) is a good day walk. Start from the woodland car park 250m beyond the **Linn of Dee**, a narrow gorge at the road bridge about 1.5 miles west of Inverey, and follow the footpath and track to Derry Lodge and Glen Luibeg – there are beautiful remnants of the ancient Caledonian pine forest here. Continue westwards on a pleasant path over a pass into Glen Dee, then follow the River Dee back downstream to the linn. Take OS 1:50,000 map sheet No 43.

A good short walk (3 miles, 1½ hours) begins at the **Linn of Quoich** – a waterfall that thunders through a narrow slot in the rocks. Head uphill on a footpath on the east bank of the stream, past the impressive rock scenery of the **Punch Bowl** (a giant pothole), to a modern bridge that spans the narrow gorge and return via an unsurfaced road on the far bank.

The **Inverey Youth Hostel** (SYHA; ☎ 0870 004 1126; dm £12.25; ⊙ May-Sep) provides basic digs in a cosy little cottage (only 14 beds, so book ahead).

A Royal Mail postbus runs from Braemar to Inverey Youth Hostel (15 minutes), Linn of Dee (20 minutes) and Luibeg (30 minutes), departing from Braemar post office at 1.20pm Monday to Saturday.

## STRATHDON
The valley of the River Don, home to many of Aberdeenshire's finest castles, stretches westward from Kintore, 13 miles northwest of Aberdeen, taking in the villages of Kemnay, Monymusk, Alford (*ah*-ford) and tiny Strathdon. The A944 parallels the lower valley; west of Alford, the A944, A97 and A939 follow the river's upper reaches.

Bus 220 runs from Aberdeen to Alford (1½ hours, seven a day Monday to Saturday, four on Sunday); the Strathdon A2B bus continues from Alford to Strathdon village (50 minutes, two daily Tuesday and Thursday only) via Kildrummy.

From May to September the Heather Hopper bus runs twice daily from Ballater to Grantown-on-Spey via Strathdon, Corgarff, the Lecht and Tomintoul.

## Alford
☎ 01975 / pop 1925
Alford has a **tourist office** ( ☎ 562052; Old Station Yard, Main St; ⊙ 10am-5pm Mon-Sat, 12.45-5pm Sun Jun-Aug, 10am-1pm & 2-5pm Mon-Fri, 10am-noon & 1.45-5pm Sat, 12.45-5pm Sun Apr, May & Sep), banks with ATMs and a supermarket.

The **Grampian Transport Museum** ( ☎ 562292; www.gtm.org.uk; adult/child £5.40/2.70; ☉ 10am-5pm Apr-Sep, 10am-4pm Oct) houses a fascinating collection of vintage motorbikes, cars, buses and trams, including a Triumph Bonneville in excellent nick, a couple of Model T Fords (including one used by Drambuie), a Ferrari F40 and an Aston Martin V8 Mk II. Unusual exhibits include a 19th-century horse-drawn sleigh from Russia, a 1942 Mack snowplough and the Craigievar Express, a steam-powered tricycle built in 1895 by a local postman.

Next to the museum is the terminus of the narrow-gauge **Alford Valley Steam Railway** ( ☎ 562811; www.alfordvalleyrailway.org.uk; adult/child £2.50/1; ☉ trains run daily Jun-Aug, Sat & Sun only Apr, May & Sep), a heritage line that runs from here to Haughton Country Park.

For B&B, you can't do better than **Frog Marsh** ( ☎ 571355; www.frogmarsh.com; Mossat; d/ste £70/90), a restored and extended cottage 6 miles west of Alford, which has two gorgeous doubles plus a luxury suite in the attic space.

### Craigievar Castle

The most spectacular of the Strathdon castles, **Craigievar Castle** (NTS; ☎ 01339-883280; adult/child £10/7; ☉ noon-5.30pm Jul & Aug, noon-5.30pm Fri-Tue Easter-Jun & Sep), a superb example of the original Scottish Baronial style 9 miles south of Alford, has managed to survive pretty much unchanged since its completion in the 17th century. The lower half is a plain tower house, the upper half sprouts corbelled turrets, cupolas and battlements – an extravagant statement of its builder's wealth and status.

### Kildrummy Castle

Nine miles west of Alford lie the extensive remains of the 13th-century **Kildrummy Castle** (HS; ☎ 01975-571331; adult/child £3.50/1.75; ☉ 9.30am-5.30pm Apr-Sep), former seat of the Earl of Mar and once one of Scotland's most impressive fortresses. After the 1715 Jacobite rebellion the earl was exiled to France and his castle fell into ruin.

If you're in the mood for a night of luxury, head for **Kildrummy Castle Hotel** ( ☎ 01975-571288; www.kildrummycastlehotel.co.uk; s/d £95/165; Ⓟ ) just along the road, a splendid Baronial hunting lodge complete with original oak panelling, log fires and four-poster beds.

### Corgarff Castle

In the wild upper reaches of Strathdon, near the A939 from Corgarff to Tomintoul, is the impressive fortress of **Corgarff Castle** (HS; ☎ 01975-651460; adult/child £4.50/2.25; ☉ 9.30am-6.30pm daily Apr-Sep, 9.30am-4.30pm Sat & Sun Oct-Mar). The tower house dates from the 16th century, but the star-shaped defensive curtain wall was added in 1748 when the castle was converted to a military barracks in the wake of the Jacobite rebellion.

**Jenny's Bothy** ( ☎ 01975-651449; www.jennysbothy .co.uk; dm £9) is a welcoming year-round bunkhouse set in a remote croft; look out for the sign by the main road, then follow the old military road (drivable) for 0.75 miles.

### Lecht Ski Resort

At the head of Strathdon the A939 – a magnificent rollercoaster of a road, much loved by motorcyclists – crosses the Lecht pass (637m), where there's a small skiing area with lots of short easy and intermediate runs. **Lecht 2090** ( ☎ 01975-651440; www.lecht.co.uk) hires out skis, boots and poles for £16 a day; a one-day lift pass is £23. A two-day package, including ski hire, lift pass and instruction, costs £84.

The ski centre opens in summer, too, when you can rent go-karts and quad bikes (£8.75 a session).

## NORTHERN ABERDEENSHIRE

North of Aberdeen, the Grampian Mountains fall away to rolling agricultural plains pocked with small, craggy volcanic hills. This fertile lowland corner of northeastern Scotland is known as Buchan, a region of traditional farming culture immortalised by Lewis Grassic Gibbon in his trilogy, *A Scots Quair,* based on the life of a farming community in the 1920s. The old Scots dialect called the Doric lives on in everyday use here – if you think the Glaswegian accent is difficult to understand, just try listening in to a conversation in Peterhead or Fraserburgh.

The Buchan coast alternates between rugged cliffs and long, long stretches of sand, dotted with picturesque little fishing villages such as Pennan, where parts of the film *Local Hero* were shot.

### Peterhead
☎ 01779 / pop 17,950
Peterhead's sprawling harbour stands as testimony to a once-great fishing industry. Not much more than a decade ago the high-tech trawlers operating from here were so productive that they supported a Ferrari-driving

fishing community with a large disposable income. Overfishing and EU quotas and restrictions have now led to a point where the entire industry is in danger of disappearing, and the town is turning to tourism and North Sea oil for salvation.

**Peterhead Maritime Heritage** ( ☎ 473000; The Lido, South Rd; admission free; ☒ 10.30am-5pm Mon-Sat, 11.30am-5pm Sun Jun-Sep) documents the town's involvement in the whaling and fishing industries and their replacement by North Sea oil; it overlooks a good sandy beach beside the marina. The central **Arbuthnot Museum** ( ☎ 477778; St Peter St; admission free; ☒ 11am-1pm & 2-4.30pm Mon-Sat, closes 1pm Wed) has wide-ranging displays on local history and Arctic whaling.

Buses 260 and 263 run from Aberdeen to Peterhead (1¼ hours, every 30 minutes Monday to Saturday and hourly on Sunday).

## Fraserburgh
☎ 01346 / pop 12,500
Fraserburgh, affectionately known to locals as the Broch, is Europe's largest shellfish port. Like Peterhead, Fraserburgh's fortune has been founded on the fishing industry and has suffered from its general decline. The harbour is still fairly busy, though, and is an interesting place to wander around; there are good sandy beaches east of the town. There's a **tourist office** ( ☎ 518315; Saltoun Sq; ☒ 10am-1pm & 2-5pm Mon-Sat Apr-Oct), a supermarket and banks with ATMs.

The excellent **Scottish Lighthouse Museum** ( ☎ 511022; www.lighthousemuseum.org.uk; Kinnaird Head; adult/child £5/2.20; ☒ 10am-6pm Mon-Sat, 11am-6pm Sun Jul & Aug, 11am-5pm Mon-Sat, noon-5pm Sun Apr-Jun, Sep & Oct, 11am-4pm Mon-Sat, noon-4pm Sun Nov-Mar) provides a fascinating insight into the network of lights that have safeguarded the Scottish coast for over 100 years, and the men and women who built and maintained them (plus a sobering fact – that all the world's lighthouses are to be decommissioned by 1 January 2080). A guided tour takes you to the top of the old Kinnaird Head lighthouse, built on top of a converted 16th-century castle; the engineering is so precise that the 4.5-ton light assembly can be rotated by pushing with a single finger. The anemometer here measured the strongest wind speed ever recorded in the UK, with a gust of 123 knots (142mph) on 13 February 1989.

**Maggie's Hoosie** ( ☎ 514761; 26 Shore St, Inverallochy; admission free; ☒ 2-4.30pm May-Sep), 4 miles east of

Fraserburgh, is a traditional fishwife's cottage with earthen floors and original furnishings, a timeless reminder of a bygone age.

Buses 267 and 268 run hourly to Fraserburgh from Aberdeen (1½ hours) via Ellon.

## Pennan
Pennan is a picturesque harbour village tucked beneath red-sandstone cliffs, 12 miles west of Fraserburgh. The whitewashed houses are built gable-end to the sea, and the waves break just a few metres away on the other side of the village's only street. Most of the cottages are now holiday homes – around a quarter of them were damaged when a huge mudslide caused by torrential rain hit the village in 2007.

The village featured in the 1983 film *Local Hero*, and fans of the film still come to make a call from the red telephone box that played a prominent part in the plot. However, the box in the film was just a prop, and it was only later that film buffs and locals successfully campaigned for a real one to be installed!

The interior of the village hotel, the **Pennan Inn**, also appeared in the film, though one of the houses further along the seafront to the east doubled for the exterior of the fictional hotel. The beach scenes were filmed on the other side of the country, at Camasdarach Beach in Arisaig, see p348.

Bus 273 from Fraserburgh to Banff stops at the Pennan road end (25 minutes, two a day, Saturday only), 350m south of (and a steep climb uphill from) the village.

## Gardenstown & Crovie
The fishing village of Gardenstown (or Gamrie, pronounced *game*-rey), founded by Alexander Garden in 1720, is built on a series of cramped terraces tumbling down the steep cliffs above the tiny harbour. Drivers should beware of severe gradients and hairpin bends in the village, parts of which can only be reached on foot. Crovie (pronounced crivvy), 800m to the east, is even more claustrophobically picturesque.

**ourpick** **Harbour Restaurant** ( ☎ 01261-851690; 2a Harbour St, Gardenstown; mains £13-16; ☒ noon-2.30pm Thu-Mon, 6-10pm Wed-Mon) is a hidden gem, a tiny place overlooking Gardenstown harbour serving superbly prepared seafood; if the weather's looking good book early and grab a table on the little outdoor terrace.

## Huntly

☎ 01466 / pop 4400

An impressive ruined castle and an attractive main square make this small town worth a stopover between Aberdeen and Elgin. The **tourist office** ( ☎ 792255; The Square; ✆ 10am-5.30pm Mon-Sat, 10am-3pm Sun Jul & Aug, 10am-1pm & 2-5pm Mon-Sat Apr-Jun, Sep & Oct) is on the main square, next to a bank with an ATM.

Castle St (beside the Huntly Hotel) runs north from the town square to an arched gateway and tree-lined avenue that leads to 16th-century **Huntly Castle** (HS; ☎ 793191; adult/child £4.50/2.25; ✆ 9.30am-5.30pm Apr-Sep, 9.30am-4.30pm Sat-Wed Oct-Mar), the former stronghold of the Gordons on the banks of the River Deveron. Over the main door is a superb carving that includes the royal arms and the figures of Christ and St Michael.

Just off the A96 3 miles northwest of Huntly is the **Peregrine Wild Watch Centre** ( ☎ 760790; Bin Forest; admission free; ✆ 10am-5pm Apr-Aug), a centre where you can observe rare peregrine falcons, both live from a hide and via a remote camera monitoring their nest site.

There are a couple of hotels on the main square and a handful of B&Bs in the surrounding streets; the hospitable **Hillview** ( ☎ 794870; www.hillviewbb.com; Provost St; r per person £17-23; P ) and its tasty breakfast pancakes are recommended.

If you want to spoil yourself, continue along the drive beyond the castle to the **Castle Hotel** ( ☎ 792696; www.castlehotel.uk.com; s/d from £73/103; P ), a splendid 18th-century mansion set amid acres of parkland. It's comfortably old fashioned, with a grand wooden staircase, convoluted corridors, the odd creaky floorboard and rattling sash window, but must be among the most affordable country house hotels in Scotland.

Bus 10 from Aberdeen (1½ hours, hourly) to Inverness passes through Huntly. There are also regular trains from Aberdeen to Huntly (one hour, every two hours), continuing to Inverness.

## MORAY

The old county of Moray (pronounced murray), centred on the county town of Elgin, lies at the heart of an ancient Celtic earldom and is famed for its mild climate and rich farmland – the barley fields of the 19th century once provided the raw material for the Speyside whisky distilleries, one of the region's main attractions for present-day visitors.

## Elgin

☎ 01343 / pop 21,000

Elgin's been the provincial capital of Moray for over eight centuries and was an important town in medieval times. Dominated by a hilltop monument to the 5th duke of Gordon, Elgin's main attraction is its impressive ruined cathedral, where the tombs of the duke's ancestors lie.

The **tourist office** ( ☎ 542666; 17 High St; ✆ 9am-6pm Mon-Sat, 11am-4pm Sun Jun-Aug, 9am-5pm Mon-Sat, 11am-3pm Sun Apr, May, Sep & Oct, 10am-4pm Mon-Sat Nov-Mar) is a short distance east of the pedestrianised High St. The bus station is a block north of the High St, and the train station is 900m south of the town centre. The **post office** (Batchen St; ✆ 8.30am-6pm Mon-Fri, 8.30am-4pm Sat) is just south of High St, and there's internet access at **Moray Business & Computer Centre** ( ☎ 552000; 20 Commerce St; per 15min £1; ✆ 9am-5pm Mon-Sat).

### SIGHTS

Many people think that the ruins of **Elgin Cathedral** (HS; ☎ 547171; adult/child £4.50/2.25, joint ticket with Spynie Palace £6/3; ✆ 9.30am-5.30pm Apr-Sep, 9.30am-4.30pm Sat-Wed Oct-Mar), known as the 'lantern of the north', are the most beautiful and evocative in Scotland. Consecrated in 1224, the cathedral was burned down in 1390 by the infamous Wolf of Badenoch, the illegitimate son of Robert II, following his excommunication by the Bishop of Moray. The octagonal chapter house is the finest in the country.

Palaeontologists and Pict lovers will enjoy **Elgin Museum** ( ☎ 543675; 1 High St; adult/child £3/1; ✆ 10am-5pm Mon-Fri, 11am-4pm Sat Apr-Oct), where the highlights are its collections of fossil fish and Pictish carved stones.

**Spynie Palace** (HS; ☎ 546358; adult/child £3.50/1.75; ✆ 9.30am-5.30pm Apr-Sep, 9.30am-4.30pm Sat & Sun Oct-Mar), 2 miles north of Elgin, was the residence of the medieval bishops of Moray until 1686. The massive tower house commands lovely views over Spynie Loch.

Not a sight as such, but a sight for sore eyes perhaps, **Gordon & MacPhail** ( ☎ 545110; www.gordonandmacphail.com; 58-60 South St; ✆ 9am-5pm Mon-Sat) is the world's largest specialist malt whisky dealer. Over a century old and offering around 450 different varieties, its Elgin shop is a place of pilgrimage for whisky connoisseurs, as well as housing a mouth-watering delicatessen.

### SLEEPING & EATING

**Southbank Guest House** ( ☎ 547132; www.southbank-guesthouse.co.uk; 36 Academy St; s/d from £40/50; P )

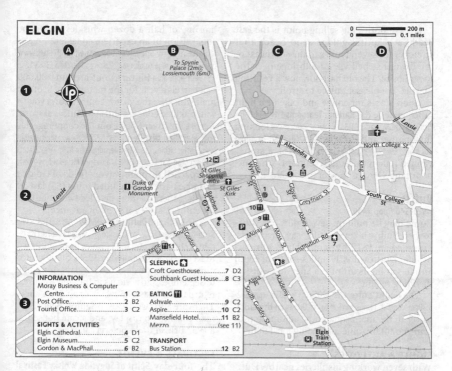

## ELGIN

To Spynie
Palace (2mi);
Lossiemouth (6mi)

| INFORMATION | |
| --- | --- |
| Moray Business & Computer | |
| Centre.....................................1 | C2 |
| Post Office................................2 | B2 |
| Tourist Office...........................3 | C2 |
| | |
| **SIGHTS & ACTIVITIES** | |
| Elgin Cathedral........................4 | D1 |
| Elgin Museum...........................5 | C2 |
| Gordon & MacPhail..................6 | B2 |

| SLEEPING | |
| --- | --- |
| Croft Guesthouse.....................7 | D2 |
| Southbank Guest House.....8 | C3 |
| | |
| **EATING** | |
| Ashvale.....................................9 | C2 |
| Aspire.....................................10 | C2 |
| Mansfield Hotel......................11 | B2 |
| Mezzo...............................(see 11) | |
| | |
| **TRANSPORT** | |
| Bus Station.............................12 | B2 |

The family-run, 12-room Southbank is set in a large Georgian town house in a quiet street south of Elgin's centre, just five minutes' walk from the cathedral and other sights.

**Croft Guesthouse** ( ☎ 546004; www.thecroftelgin .co.uk; 10 Institution Rd; s/d £45/68; **P** ) The Croft offers a taste of Victorian high society, set in a spacious mansion built for a local lawyer back in 1848. The house is filled with period features – check out the cast-iron and tile fireplaces – and the three large bedrooms are equipped with easy chairs and crisp bed linen.

**Mansfield Hotel** ( ☎ 540883; www.themansefield .com; Mayne Rd; s/d £95/125; **P** ) Centred on a 19th-century manse (minister's house), but with extensive modern additions, the Mansfield offers elegant accommodation both in sleek, modern rooms aimed at business travellers, and in more traditional rooms with four-poster beds.

**Mezzo** ( ☎ 540883; cnr Hay & South Sts; mains £7-12; ◷ noon-2.30pm & 6-9.30pm Mon-Thu, noon-9.30pm Fri & Sat, 5-9.30pm Sun) This lively bar and restaurant is part of the Mansfield Hotel complex, and serves tasty bistro fare, including pasta, pizza, burgers and various vegetarian dishes.

**Aspire** ( ☎ 540932; 9a Moss St; mains £12-19; ◷ 10am-10pm) Housed in a converted church, Aspire (geddit?) is a stylish bar and restaurant that serves everything from morning coffee to candlelit dinners, with a cosmopolitan menu that ranges from steak to seafood to vegetarian.

**Ashvale** (11 Moss St; ◷ 11.45am-10pm daily) A branch of the famous Aberdeen fish-and-chip shop.

### GETTING THERE & AWAY
There are buses from Elgin to Banff and Macduff (£8, one hour), Dufftown (£4, 30 minutes), Inverness (£8, one hour) and Aberdeen (£10, two hours). Elgin is on the Aberdeen to Inverness railway line.

## Lossiemouth
☎ 01343 / pop 9000
Lossie, as it's known locally, is the former port of Elgin, now better known as a seaside resort, yachting harbour and air force base; it's also the birthplace of James Ramsay MacDonald (1866–1937), who was the UK's first Labour prime minister (served 1923–24 and 1929–31; there's a plaque at 1 Gregory Pl, where he was born).

**NORTHEAST SCOTLAND**

Lossiemouth's big selling point is the **East Beach**, a beautiful golden-sand beach that stretches for several miles to the southeast of the town, reached via a footbridge over the River Lossie. The old harbour, now a yachting marina, is a pleasant place to stroll.

Good places for coffee and cake or a light lunch include the **Harbour Tearooms** ( ☎ 814622; 5 Pitgaveny Quay; snacks £1-3; ☺ 9am-5pm), overlooking the marina, and **La Caverna** ( ☎ 813027; 20 Clifton Rd; mains £9-12; ☺ noon-2pm & 5-9.30pm), a stone-vaulted Italian café and restaurant – the outdoor tables have a view of the beach.

## Dufftown
☎ 01340 / pop 1450

Rome may be built on seven hills, but Dufftown's built on seven stills, say the locals. Founded in 1817 by James Duff, 4th earl of Fife, Dufftown is 17 miles south of Elgin and lies at the heart of the Speyside whisky-distilling region.

The **tourist office** ( ☎ 820501; ☺ 10am-1pm & 2-5.30pm Mon-Sat, 11am-3pm Sun Easter-Oct) is in the clock tower in the main square; the adjoining museum contains some interesting local items.

### SIGHTS & ACTIVITIES

With seven working distilleries nearby, Dufftown has been dubbed Scotland's malt whisky capital. Ask at the tourist office for a **Malt Whisky Trail** (www.maltwhiskytrail.com) booklet, a self-guided tour around the seven stills plus the Speyside Cooperage.

As well as housing a selection of distillery memorabilia (try saying that after a few drams), the **Whisky Museum** ( ☎ 821097; 24 Fife St; ☺ 1-4pm Mon-Fri) holds 'nosing and tasting evenings' where you can learn what to look for in a fine single malt (£6 per person; 8.30pm Tuesdays in July and August). You can then test your new-found skills at the nearby **Whisky Shop** ( ☎ 821097; 1 Fife St), which stocks hundreds of single malts and a huge range of bottled Scottish beers.

At the northern edge of town is the **Glenfiddich Distillery Visitor Centre** ( ☎ 820373; www.glenfiddich.co.uk; admission free; ☺ 9.30am-4.30pm Mon-Sat, noon-4.30pm Sun Easter–mid-Oct, 9.30am-4.30pm Mon-Fri mid-Oct–Easter), where the guided tour includes a visit to the bottling plant – the only Highland distillery where bottling takes place on the premises. Your free dram is genuinely free, but enthusiasts can opt for the in-depth, 2½-hour Connoisseur's Tour (£20), which includes a 'nosing' of half a dozen whiskies under the supervision of an experienced taster.

The nearby **Speyside Cooperage** ( ☎ 871108; www .speysidecooperage.co.uk; Craigellachie; adult/child £3.20/1.90; ☺ 9am-4pm Mon-Fri) turns out around 100,000 oak barrels a year for the maturing of Scottish malt whiskies; the visitor centre allows you to watch skilled coopers and apprentices at work. Across the River Spey from the cooperage lies the **Macallan Distillery** ( ☎ 872280; www.themacallan .com; Easter Elchies, Craigellachie; admission free; ☺ 9.30am-4.30pm Mon-Sat Easter-Oct, 11am-3pm Mon-Fri Nov-Mar), approached through waving fields of Golden Promise barley. The guided tours (£5) last 30 minutes; there's a more detailed two-hour tour for enthusiasts (£15; book in advance).

The **Keith and Dufftown Railway** ( ☎ 821181; www .keith-dufftown-railway.co.uk; Dufftown Station) is a heritage railway line running for 11 miles from Dufftown to Keith. Trains hauled by 1950s diesel motor units run on Saturdays and Sundays from June to September, plus Fridays in July and August; a return ticket costs £9.50/4.50 for an adult/child. There are also two 1930s 'Brighton Belle' Pullman coaches on display, and a café housed in a 1957 British Rail cafeteria car.

### FESTIVALS & EVENTS

The four-day **Spirit of Speyside Whisky Festival** (www.spiritofspeyside.com), held at the end of April/ beginning of May, takes in whisky tastings, tours, locally produced food and traditional music, as does the **Autumn Speyside Whisky Festival** (www.spiritofspeyside.com), which takes place at the end of September.

### SLEEPING & EATING

**Fife Arms Hotel** ( ☎ 820220; www.fifearmsdufftown .co.uk; 2 The Square; s/d £30/50; P ) This welcoming hotel offers slightly cramped but comfortable accommodation in a modern block around the back; its bar is stocked with a wide range of single malts, and the restaurant (mains £8 to £16) dishes up sizzling steaks, homemade steak pies and locally farmed ostrich steaks.

**Davaar B&B** ( ☎ 820464; www.davaardufftown.co.uk; 17 Church St; s/d £35/50) Just along the street opposite the tourist office, Davaar is a sturdy Victorian villa with three smallish but comfily kitted out rooms; the breakfast menu is superb, offering the option of Portsoy kippers instead of the traditional fry-up (which uses eggs from the owners' own chickens).

**A Taste of Speyside** ( ☎ 820860; 10 Balvenie St; mains £14-17; ☺ noon-2pm & 6-9pm Tue-Sun) This upmarket restaurant prepares traditional Scottish dishes using fresh local produce, including a challenging platter of smoked salmon, smoked venison, brandied chicken liver paté, cured herring, a selection of Scottish cheeses and homemade bread (phew!). A two-course lunch costs £12.50.

### GETTING THERE & AWAY
Buses link Dufftown to Elgin (50 minutes, hourly), Huntly, Aberdeen and Inverness.

On summer weekends, you can take a train from Aberdeen or Inverness to Keith, and then ride the Keith and Dufftown Railway (see Sights, p262) to Dufftown.

## Tomintoul
☎ 01807 / pop 320
This high-altitude (345m) village was built by the Duke of Gordon in 1775 on the old military road that leads over the Lecht pass from Corgarff, a route now followed by the A939 (usually the first road in Scotland to be blocked by snow when winter closes in). The duke hoped that settling the dispersed population of his estates in a proper village would help to stamp out cattle stealing and illegal distilling.

Tomintoul (pronounced tom-in-*towel*) is a pretty, stone-built village with a grassy, tree-lined main square, where you'll find the **tourist office** ( ☎ 580285; The Square; ☉ 9.30am-1pm & 2-5pm Mon-Sat Easter-Oct, plus 1-5pm Sun Aug); and, next door, the **Tomintoul Museum** ( ☎ 673701; The Square; admission free; ☉ 10am-4pm Mon-Sat Jun-Sep, 10am-4pm Mon-Fri May & Oct), which has displays on a range of local topics. The surrounding Glenlivet Estate (now the property of the Crown) has lots of walking and cycling trails – the estate's **information centre** ( ☎ 580283; www.crownestate.co.uk/glenlivet; Main St)

---

### TOP 10 SINGLE MALT WHISKIES – OUR CHOICE

After a great deal of diligent research (and not a few sore heads), Lonely Planet's *Scotland* authors and editors have selected their 10 favourite single malts from across the country (with the proviso that each offers a good distillery tour).

**Bowmore** (Islay) Smoke, peat and salty sea air – a classic Islay malt. One of the few distilleries that still malts its own barley (p291).

**Bruichladdich** (Islay) Peat, peat and more peat – not for the faint-hearted! A visitor-friendly distillery with a quirky, innovative approach (p292).

**Edradour** (Highland) Smooth and sweet, with toffee, vanilla and honey notes. The country's smallest and prettiest distillery (p227).

**Glenfiddich** (Speyside) Fragrant, fruity and interesting, especially the special finishes. Distillery still in family ownership after 120 years (opposite).

**Glenmorangie** (Highland) Fruit, flowers, citrus and honey – a breath of springtime. Distillery has the tallest stills in Scotland (p356).

**Glenturret** (Highland) The backbone of the Famous Grouse blend. Pretty little distillery, with a cute resident cat called Amber (p221).

**Highland Park** (Island) Full and rounded, with heather, honey, malt and peat. Award-winning distillery tour (p409).

**Macallan** (Speyside) The king of Speyside malts, with sherry and bourbon finishes. Distillery set amid waving fields of Golden Promise barley (opposite).

**Old Pulteney** (Highland) Light and sherry scented, with a tang of salt air. The most northerly distillery on the mainland (p361).

**Springbank** (Campbeltown) Complex flavours – sherry, citrus, pear-drops, peat – with a salty tang. Entire production process from malting to bottling takes place on site (p288).

A visit to a whisky distillery should be part of any trip to Scotland – many distilleries around the country open their doors to visitors. For some, showing tourists around has become a slick marketing operation complete with promotional videos, gift shops that rival Harrods in size and glitziness, and an admission charge of around £3 to £5 (in most places this is refundable if you buy something in the shop).

See also How To Be A Malt Whisky Buff, p55.

distributes free maps of the area – and a spur of the **Speyside Way** long-distance footpath (see the boxed text, p59) runs between Tomintoul and Ballindalloch, 15 miles to the north.

Accommodation for walkers includes the **Tomintoul Youth Hostel** (SYHA; ☎ 0870 004 1152; Main St; dm £13; ☼ May-Sep), housed in the old village school. The small, family-run **Glenavon Hotel** ( ☎ 580218; www.glenavon-hotel.co.uk; The Square; r per person £20-28; **P** ) is a more comfortable alternative.

### GETTING THERE & AWAY

Buses 362 and 363 operate an infrequent service from Tomintoul to Dufftown (40 minutes, one or two daily Monday to Saturday) and to Elgin (1¼ hours, one daily Thursday only) respectively. The Speyside Stroller and Heather Hopper bus services (p233) also stop at Tomintoul.

## Banff & Macduff

☎ 01261 / combined pop 7750

The handsome Georgian town of Banff and the busy fishing port of Macduff lie on either side of Banff Bay separated only by the mouth of the River Deveron. Banff Links – 800m of clean golden sand stretching to the west – and Macduff's impressive aquarium pull in the holiday crowds.

The **tourist office** ( ☎ 812419; Collie Lodge, High St; ☼ 10am-5pm Mon-Sat, noon-5pm Sun Apr-Sep) is beside St Mary's car park in Banff.

### SIGHTS

**Duff House** ( ☎ 818181; adult/child £6/5; ☼ 11am-5pm Apr-Oct, 11am-4pm Thu-Sun Nov-Mar) is an impressive baroque mansion on the southern edge of Banff (upstream from the bridge, and across from the tourist office). Built between 1735 and 1740 as the seat of the earls of Fife, it was designed by William Adam and bears similarities to that Adam masterpiece, Hopetoun House (p115). Since being gifted to the town in 1906 it has served as a hotel, a hospital and a POW camp, but is now an art gallery. One of Scotland's hidden gems, it houses a superb collection of Scottish and European art, including important works by Raeburn and Gainsborough. Nearby **Banff Museum** ( ☎ 622906; High St; admission free; ☼ 2-4.30pm Mon-Sat Jun-Sep) has award-winning displays on local wildlife, geology and history, and Banff silver.

The centrepiece of **Macduff Marine Aquarium** ( ☎ 833369; 11 High Shore; adult/child £5.20/2.60; ☼ 10am-5pm) is a 400,000L open-air tank, complete with

kelp-coated reef and wave machine. Marine oddities on view include the brightly coloured cuckoo wrasse, the warty-skinned lumpsucker and the vicious-looking wolf fish.

### SLEEPING & EATING

**Banff Links Caravan Park** ( ☎ 812228; Banff; tent/campervan from £7/12; ☼ Apr-Oct) This camp site is beside the beach, 800m west of town.

**Bryvard Guest House** ( ☎ 818090; www.bryvardguesthouse.co.uk; Seafield St, Banff; s/d £35/60) The Bryvard is an imposing Edwardian town house close to the town centre, with four bedrooms (two with en suite). Go for the 'suite', which has a four-poster bed and a sea view; there's a minimum stay of two nights in high season.

**County Hotel** ( ☎ 815353; www.thecountyhotel.com; 32 High St, Banff; s/d £40/75; **P** ) The County occupies an elegant Georgian mansion in the town centre, and is owned by a French chef – the hotel's bistro serves light meals (mains £7 to £10), while the restaurant (L'Auberge) offers the finest French cuisine (a la carte mains £22 to £30, three-course dinner £21 to £26).

### GETTING THERE & AWAY

Bus 305 runs from Banff to Elgin (1½ hours, hourly) and Aberdeen (two hours), while bus 271/272 runs less frequently to Fraserburgh (one hour, once daily Monday to Friday).

## Portsoy

☎ 01261 / pop 1730

The pretty fishing village of Portsoy has an atmospheric 17th-century harbour and a maze of narrow streets lined with picturesque cottages. An ornamental stone known as Portsoy marble – actually a beautifully patterned green and pale pink serpentine – was quarried near Portsoy in the 17th and 18th centuries, and was reputedly used in the decoration of some rooms in the Palace of Versailles. The **Portsoy Marble Shop & Pottery** ( ☎ 842404; Shorehead; ☼ 10am-5pm Apr-Oct) beside the harbour sells hand-made stoneware and objects made from the local marble.

Each year on the last weekend in June or first weekend in July, Portsoy harbour is home to the **Scottish Traditional Boat Festival** ( ☎ 842951; www .scottishtraditionalboatfestival.co.uk), a lively gathering of historic wooden sailing boats accompanied by sailing races, live folk music, crafts demonstrations, street theatre and a food festival.

The 12-room **Boyne Hotel** ( ☎ 842242; www .boynehotel.co.uk; 2 North High St; s/d £35/65) is a cosy and atmospheric place to stay, while the **Shore**

**Inn** ( ☎ 842831; Church St) is a characterful real-ale pub overlooking the harbour.

Portsoy is 8 miles west of Banff; the hourly bus between Elgin and Banff stops here.

## Fordyce
### pop 150

This impossibly picturesque village lies about 3 miles southwest of Portsoy. The main attractions are the 13th-century **St Tarquin's Church**, with its extraordinary canopied Gothic tombs, and the impressive 16th-century tower house of **Fordyce Castle**. The castle isn't open to the public, but its whitewashed west wing provides atmospheric **self-catering accommodation** ( ☎ 01261-843722; www.fordycecastle.co.uk; per week £395-595, 3 nights in low season £295) for up to four people.

The nearby **Joiner's Workshop & Visitor Centre** ( ☎ 01771-622906; admission free; ☽ 10am-6pm Thu-Mon) has a collection of woodworking tools and machinery, and stages woodwork demonstrations by a master joiner.

## Fochabers & Around
☎ 01343 / pop 1500

Fochabers sits beside the last bridge over the River Spey before it enters the sea. The town has a pleasant square, with a church and clock tower dated 1798, and a handful of interesting antique shops.

West of the bridge over the Spey is **Baxters Highland Village** ( ☎ 820666; admission free; ☽ 9am-5.30pm Apr-Dec, 10am-4pm Jan-Mar), which charts the history of the Baxter family and their well-known brand of quality Scottish foodstuffs. The brand was founded in 1868 when they opened their first shop in Fochabers. There's a factory tour with cookery demonstrations on weekdays.

Four miles north of Fochabers, at the mouth of the River Spey, is the tiny village of **Spey Bay**, the starting point for the Speyside Way long-distance footpath (see boxed text, p59). It's also home to the **WDCS Wildlife Centre** ( ☎ 820339; www.wdcs.org; Tugnet Ice House; admission free; ☽ 10.30am-5pm Apr-Jun, Sep & Oct, to 7pm Jul & Aug) with an interesting display on the Moray Firth dolphins, which can occasionally be seen off the mouth of the river.

Fochabers is on the Aberdeen to Inverness bus route.

## Findhorn
☎ 01309 / pop 885

The attractive village of Findhorn lies at the mouth of the River Findhorn, just east of the Findhorn Bay nature reserve. It's a great place for bird-watching, seal-spotting and coastal walks.

**Findhorn Heritage Centre** ( ☎ 630349, admission free; ☽ 2-5pm daily Jun-Aug, 2-5pm Sat & Sun May & Sep), housed in a former salmon-fisher's bothy at the northern end of the village, records the history of the settlement. The beach is just over the dunes north of the heritage centre – at low tide, you can see seals hauled out on the sandbanks off the mouth of the River Findhorn.

Hippies old and new should check out the **Findhorn Foundation** ( ☎ 690311; www.findhorn.org; ☽ 10am-5pm Mon-Fri year-round, plus 1-4pm Sat Mar-Nov & 1-4pm Sun May-Sep), an international spiritual community founded in 1962. There's a small permanent population of around 150, but the community receives thousands of visitors each year. With no formal creed, the community is dedicated to cooperation with nature, 'dealing with work, relationships and our environment in new and more fulfilling ways', and fostering 'a deeper sense of the sacred in everyday life'. Projects include eco-friendly houses, a biological sewage-treatment plant and a wind-powered generator. Guided tours (£3) are available at 2pm on Monday, Wednesday, Friday and Saturday from April to October, and on Sunday as well from May to September.

The **Kimberley Inn** ( ☎ 690492; mains £6-12; ☽ food served noon-10pm) does good bar meals.

## Culbin Forest

On the western side of Findhorn Bay is Culbin Forest, a vast swathe of Scots and Corsican pine that was planted in the 1940s to stabilise the shifting sand dunes that buried the Culbin Estate in the 17th century. The forest is a unique wildlife habitat, supporting plants, birds and animals (such as the pine marten) that are normally found only in ancient natural pine woods, and is crisscrossed by a maze of walking trails.

## Forres

The tidy town of Forres, 4 miles south of Findhorn, is famous for **Sueno's Stone**, a remarkable, 6.5m-high Pictish stone. It is the tallest and most elaborately carved Pictish stone in Scotland, dating from the 9th or 10th century, and is thought to depict a battle between the Picts and invading Scots or Vikings. It's protected from the elements by a huge plate-glass box.

# Southern Highlands & Islands

From the rasping spout of a minke whale as it breaks the surface of the sea off the coast of Islay, to the mysterious 'krek-krek-krek' of a corncrake hiding amid the long summer grass of Coll, the coast and islands of southwest Scotland are filled with unusual wildlife experiences. Here you can spot otters tumbling in the kelp along a deserted shore, watch sea eagles snatch fish from a lonely loch, and thrill to the sight of dolphins riding the bow wave of your boat.

The region covered in this chapter corresponds with the old county of Argyll, whose name comes from the Gaelic *earra-ghaidheal* – the seaboard of the Gael. Though measuring only 155 miles north to south, Argyll's convoluted coastline is a staggering 2300 miles in length. This is a corner of Scotland where sea travel is as important as road and rail – a network of ferry crossings allows you to island-hop your way from the Firth of Clyde to Oban and beyond, via the whisky distilleries of Islay, the wild mountains of Jura and the scenic delights of little Colonsay.

Oban itself is the gateway to the isles – from the peaceful backwaters of Kerrera and Lismore to the dramatic coastal scenery of Mull and the wild, windswept beaches of Coll and Tiree. The waters around these islands are rich in marine wildlife, and offer some of the best whale-watching opportunities in Europe.

The region is rich in prehistoric sites and is home to important religious and political centres of the past, including Dunadd, the ancient crowning place of Scottish kings; Finlaggan, the lake-island headquarters of the medieval Lords of the Isles; and the sacred island of Iona, where St Columba based his mission to spread Christianity throughout Scotland.

---

## HIGHLIGHTS

- Staring in wonder at the magnificent marble-clad halls of **Mount Stuart** (p283)
- Walking barefoot across the strand from Colonsay to **Oronsay** (p296) to visit the medieval priory
- Riding a high-speed motorboat through the surging white water of the **Gulf of Corryvreckan** (boxed text, p294)
- Sitting by a log fire in the **Port Charlotte Hotel** (p292), sampling some of Islay's finest single malt whiskies
- Whale watching in the waters off the west coast of **Mull** (boxed text, p305)

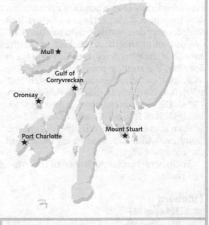

Mull ★

Gulf of Corryvreckan ★

Oronsay ★

Port Charlotte ★

Mount Stuart ★

- POPULATION: 91,300
- AREA: 227,420 SQ KM

# LOCH LOMOND & AROUND

The 'bonnie banks' and 'bonnie braes' of Loch Lomond have long been Glasgow's rural retreat – a scenic region of hills, lochs and healthy fresh air within easy reach of Scotland's largest city. Since the 1930s Glaswegians have made a regular weekend exodus to the hills, by car, by bike and on foot, and today the loch's popularity shows no sign of decreasing (Loch Lomond is within an hour's drive of 70% of Scotland's population).

The region's importance was recognised when it became the heart of **Loch Lomond &** the **Trossachs National Park** ( ☎ 01389-722600; www .lochlomond-trossachs.org) – Scotland's first national park, created in 2002.

## LOCH LOMOND

Loch Lomond is the largest lake in mainland Britain and, after Loch Ness, perhaps the most famous of Scotland's lochs. Its proximity to Glasgow (20 miles away) means that the tourist honeypots of Balloch, Loch Lomond Shores and Luss get pretty crowded in summer. The main tourist focus is on the loch's western shore, along the A82, and at the southern end, around Balloch, which can occasionally be a nightmare of jet skis and motorboats. The eastern shore, which is followed by the West Highland Way long-distance footpath, is a little quieter.

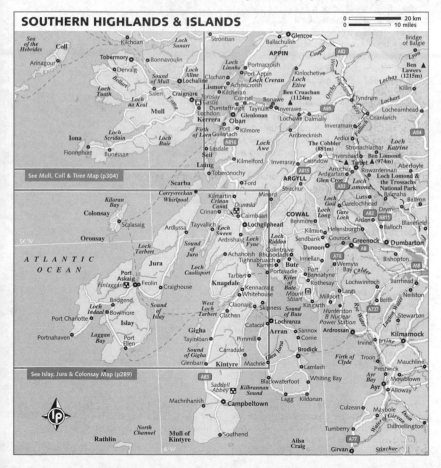

SOUTHERN HIGHLANDS & ISLANDS

## GAELIC & NORSE PLACE NAMES

Throughout the Highlands and islands of Scotland the indigenous Gaelic language has left a rich legacy of place names. They're often intermixed with Old Norse names left behind by the Viking invaders who occupied the western and northern islands between the 8th and 13th centuries. The spelling is now anglicised but the meaning is still clear once you know what to look for. Here are a few of the more common Gaelic and Norse names and their meanings.

### Gaelic Place Names

**ach, auch** – from *achadh* (field)
**ard** – from *ard* or *aird* (height, hill)
**avon** – from *abhainn* (river or stream)
**bal** – from *baile* (village or homestead)
**ban** – from *ban* (white, fair)
**beg** – from *beag* (small)
**ben** – from *beinn* (mountain)
**buie** – from *buidhe* (yellow)
**dal** – from *dail* (field or dale)
**dow, dhu** – from *dubh* (black)
**drum** – from *druim* (ridge or back)
**dun** – from *dun* or *duin* (fort or castle)
**glen** – from *gleann* (narrow valley)
**gorm** – from *gorm* (blue)
**gower, gour** – from *gabhar* (goat), eg Ardgour (height of the goats)
**inch, insh** – from *inis* (island, water-meadow or resting place for cattle)
**inver** – from *inbhir* (river mouth or meeting of two rivers)
**kil** – from *cille* (church), as in Kilmartin (Church of St Martin)
**kin, ken** – from *ceann* (head), eg Kinlochleven (head of Loch Leven)
**kyle, kyles** – from *caol* or *caolas* (narrow sea channel)
**more, vore** – from *mor* or *mhor* (big), eg Ardmore (big height), Skerryvore (big reef)
**strath** – from *srath* (broad valley)
**tarbert, tarbet** – from *tairbeart* (portage), meaning a narrow neck of land between two bodies of water, across which a boat can be dragged
**tay, ty** – from *tigh* (house), eg Tyndrum (house on the ridge)
**tober** – from *tobar* (well), eg Tobermory (Mary's well)

### Norse Place Names

**a, ay, ey** – from *ey* (island)
**bister, buster, bster** – from *bolstaor* (dwelling place, homestead)
**geo** – from *gja* (chasm)
**holm** – from *holmr* (small island)
**kirk** – from *kirkja* (church)
**pol, poll, bol** – from *bol* (farm)
**quoy** – from *kvi* (sheep fold, cattle enclosure)
**sker, skier, skerry** – from *sker* (rocky reef)
**ster, sett** – from *setr* (house)
**vig, vaig, wick** – from *vik* (bay, creek)
**voe, way** – from *vagr* (bay, creek)

Loch Lomond straddles the Highland border and its character changes as you move north. The southern part is broad and island-studded and fringed by woods and Lowland meadows. However, north of Luss the loch narrows, occupying a deep trench gouged out by glaciers during the Ice Age, with 900m mountains crowding in on either side.

*(Continued on page 277)*

# SCOTTISH EXPERIENCES

For a small country, Scotland packs a lot in. For gourmets there's a host of national dishes that have been rediscovered by modern palates, while whisky – the water of life – has never gone out of fashion. For burning off those calories and clearing the cobwebs, the country's awe-inspiring open spaces come in both easy-access and off-the-beaten-track varieties, while for the historically and culturally inclined there are many reminders of Scotland's turbulent history and world-famous traditions.

# Food & Drink

Scottish cuisine has been given a make-over during the last decade with inventive chefs adding contemporary twists to traditional favourites, using top local ingredients. Wash your meal down with a local beer and round your evening off with a mature whisky and your taste buds are in for a real treat.

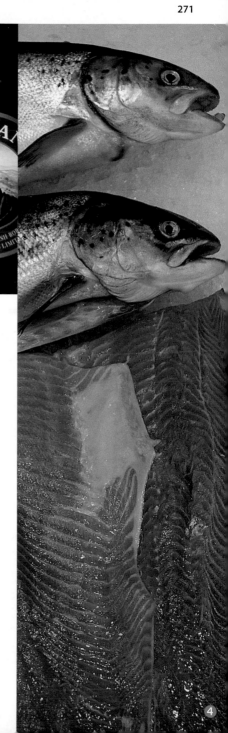

### ① Haggis
Yes, it contains things (sheep's stomach, heart and lungs) that you wouldn't normally want to even look at, never mind eat, but this most famous of Scottish dishes (p52) tastes better than it sounds.

### ② Whisky
Learning to distinguish your malts from your grains and your singles from your blendeds is one way to make a day both fun and educational (p55).

### ③ Beer
Real ale and the Scottish pub go hand in hand and while nationally produced brews are found across the country, it's worth keeping your eye (and your mouth) open for local specialities (p56).

### ④ Salmon
Scottish salmon (p53) is deservedly well known, but make sure you go for the tastier – and more expensive – wild variety to fully appreciate the wonderful flavour.

# The Great Outdoors

Whether you want to bag a Munro or two, simply sit by a river and fish, or get as far away from it all as possible, Scotland has myriad ways for the visitor to expend some energy and appreciate the country's beautiful scenery.

### 1 Bag Ben Nevis
The highest Munro of them all (p345) is within reach of anyone who's reasonably fit – treat Britain's tallest peak with respect and your reward (weather permitting) is a truly magnificent view.

### 2 Catch Your Own Supper
Hugely popular in Scotland, fishing (p59) is just about the most relaxing way to while away some hours. Pick a river, get your permit, and enjoy the views and tranquillity while waiting for something to bite.

### 3 The Cairngorms
Walking, climbing, skiing, spotting rare wild animals or just sitting back with a whisky and a fine view, the Cairngorms (p329) can be as active – or not – as you like.

### 4 North Coast Beaches
They may not have Caribbean weather, but the stunning beaches around Durness (p368; pictured), Cape Wrath (p369) and Stoer (p369) are just as beautiful and you can often have one all to yourself.

### 5 West Highland Way
Running from just north of Glasgow to Fort William, this 95-mile walk (p280) is an excellent way of seeing some of the best of the Highlands (for the lazy, the West Highland railway covers similar terrain).

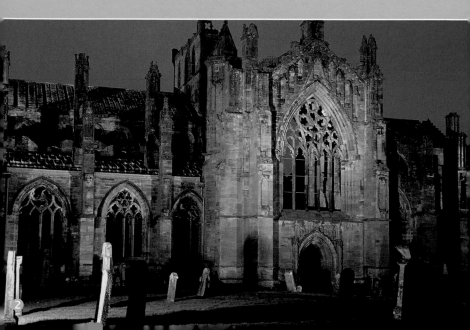

# Uncovering the Past

The legacy of Scotland's tumultuous and often violent history can be found in its extraordinary array of prehistoric sites, religious ruins and other historic attractions. Today these relics offer visitors intriguing insights into some of the defining battles, heroes and forgotten worlds of the country's rich and turbulent past.

### ❶ Callanish
These mysterious standing stones (p395) dominate their atmospheric location in the west of Lewis and have been a feature of the Hebridean landscape for nearly 5000 years.

### ❷ Border Abbeys
Rolling countryside and ruined abbeys are the big draws along the border with England. Visit Melrose (p158; pictured), Jedburgh (p160) and Kelso (p155) for a look at Scotland's religious life, pre-Reformation.

### ❸ Glen Coe
The peacefulness and beauty of this valley (p337) today belie the fact that it was the scene of a ruthless 17th-century massacre when the local MacDonalds were murdered by soldiers of the Campbell clan.

### ❹ The Lewis Chessmen
Made in Norway in the 12th century but lost in the sand on the Isle of Lewis until 1831, these exquisite chesspieces (p396) show the skill of Norwegian craftsmen of the time and the Scandinavian influence in Scotland.

### ❺ Isle of Iona
The home of Scottish Christianity, this small island (p309) can get very busy, so stay the night and enjoy the island's spiritual atmosphere without the crowds.

# Iconic Scotland

Every country has its national stereotypes but in Scotland some of these have gone from embarrassing anachronisms to cool symbols of a resurgent nation. Walter Scott may have rekindled interest in the 1800s but it's 21st-century Scots, with their new parliament and increasing confidence, that have reclaimed once-derided clichés.

### ❶ Kilts & Tartan

You won't see many worn in the streets on a daily basis, but the tartan kilt (p40) is now firmly established as the smartest way for a Scotsman to dress for special occasions.

### ❷ Bagpipes

The only musical instrument ever classified as a weapon, the bagpipe (p40) might be found in other parts of the British Isles and Europe but it's associated with nowhere as much as with Scotland.

(Continued from page 268)

## Orientation

Loch Lomond is 22 miles long and varies in width from 1 to 5 miles. The A82 along the western shore is the main road north from Glasgow to Fort William. The minor road along the eastern shore, reached from Balloch via Drymen, ends at Rowardennan; hikers can continue along this shore on the West Highland Way.

## Information

**Balloch tourist office** ( ☎ 0870 720 0607; Balloch Rd; ☟ 9.30am-6pm Jun-Aug, 10am-6pm Apr & Sep)

**Balmaha National Park Centre** ( ☎ 01389-722100; Balmaha; ☟ 10am-5pm Easter-Oct)

**National Park Gateway Centre** ( ☎ 0845 345 4978; www.lochlomondshores.com; Loch Lomond Shores, Balloch; ☟ 9.30am-6.30pm Jul & Aug, 9.30am-6pm Jun & Sep, 10am-6pm Apr & May, 10am-5pm Nov-Mar)

**Tarbet tourist office** ( ☎ 0870 720 0623; ☟ 10am-6pm Jul & Aug, 10am-5pm Easter-Jun, Sep & Oct) At the junction of the A82 and the A83.

## Activities

### WALKING

The big walk around here is the **West Highland Way** (p280), which runs along the eastern shore of the loch. There are shorter lochside walks at Firkin Point on the western shore and at several other places around the loch. You can get further information on local walks from the national park information centres at Loch Lomond Shores and Balmaha.

Rowardennan is the starting point for an ascent of **Ben Lomond** (974m), a popular and relatively easy five- to six-hour round trip. The route starts at the car park just past the Rowardennan Hotel.

### BOAT TRIPS

The main centre for boat trips is Balloch, where **Sweeney's Cruises** ( ☎ 01389-752376; www .sweeneyscruises.com; Balloch Rd) offers a range of trips including a one-hour cruise to Inchmurrin and back (adult/child £6.50/4, departs hourly), and a two-hour cruise (£12/6, departs 1pm and 3pm) around the islands. The quay is directly opposite Balloch train station, beside the tourist office. Sweeney's also runs hourly cruises from the Maid of the Loch jetty at Loch Lomond Shores.

**Cruise Loch Lomond** ( ☎ 01301-702356) is based in Tarbet and offers trips to Inversnaid and Rob Roy MacGregor's cave. You can also be dropped off at Rowardennan and picked up at Inversnaid after a 9-mile hike along the West Highland Way.

The mail boat, run by **Balmaha Boatyard** ( ☎ 01360-870214; The Boatyard, Balmaha), cruises from Balmaha to the loch's four inhabited islands, departing at 11.30am and returning at 2pm with a one-hour stop on Inchmurrin (adult/child £8/4). Trips depart daily in July and August, and Monday, Thursday and Saturday in May, June and September.

### OTHER ACTIVITIES

The mostly traffic-free **Clyde and Loch Lomond Cycle Way** links Glasgow to Balloch (20 miles), where it links with the **West Loch Lomond Cycle Path**, which continues along the loch shore to Tarbet (10 miles).

You can rent **rowing boats** at Balmaha Boatyard (above) for £10/30 per hour/day, or £20/50 for a boat with outboard motor. **Lomond Adventure** ( ☎ 01360-870218), also in Balmaha, rents out per half-/full day Canadian **canoes** (£20/25), **kayaks** (£15/20) and **sailing dinghies** (£45 a day).

At Loch Lomond Shores (below) you can hire canoes (£10/15 per half-/full hour) and bicycles (£7/10/15 per two hours/four hours/ full day), take a **guided canoe trip** on the loch or go **pony trekking** (£1 a ride).

## Western Shore

The town of **Balloch**, which straddles the River Leven where it flows from the southern end of Loch Lomond, is the loch's main population centre and transport hub. A Victorian resort once thronged by day-trippers transferring between the train station and the steamer quay, it is now a 'gateway centre' for Loch Lomond and the Trossachs National Park.

**Loch Lomond Shores** ( ☎ 01389-722406; www.loch lomondshores.com), a major tourism development a half-mile north of Balloch, sports a national park information centre plus various visitor attractions, outdoor activities and boat trips. It's home to the **Loch Lomond Aquarium** ( ☎ 01389-721500; adult/child £8.95/6.50; ☟ 10am-6pm), which has displays on the wildlife of Loch Lomond, an otter enclosure (housing short-clawed Asian otters, not Scottish ones), and a host of sealife exhibits ranging from sharks to stingrays to seahorses.

In keeping with the times, the heart of the development is a large shopping mall.

The vintage paddle steamer **Maid of the Loch** ( ☎ 01389-711865; admission free; 🕐 11am-4pm May-Oct), built in 1953, is moored here while awaiting full restoration – you can nip aboard for a look around.

Unless it's raining, give Loch Lomond Shores a miss and head for the little picture-postcard village of **Luss**. Stroll among the pretty cottages with roses around their doors (the cottages were built by the local laird in the 19th century for the workers on his estate), then pop into the **Clan Colquhoun Visitor Centre** ( ☎ 01436-671469; adult/child £1/free; 🕐 10.30am-6pm Easter-Oct) for some background history before enjoying a cuppa at the Coach House Coffee Shop.

### SLEEPING & EATING

**Loch Lomond Youth Hostel** (SYHA; ☎ 0870 004 1136; Arden; dm £15-16; 🕐 Mar-Oct) Forget about roughing it, this is one of the most impressive hostels in the country – an imposing 19th-century country house set in beautiful grounds overlooking the loch. It's 2 miles north of Balloch and very popular, so book in advance in summer. And yes, it *is* haunted.

**Ardlui Hotel** ( ☎ 01301-704243; www.ardlui.co.uk; Ardlui; s/d £55/90; P ) If the Drover's Inn (below) is a little rough for your bedtime tastes, nip down the road to the plush Ardlui Hotel, a comfy country house hotel with a great loch-side location and a view of Ben Lomond from the breakfast room.

**Coach House Coffee Shop** ( ☎ 01436-860341; Luss; mains £4-11; 🕐 10am-5pm) With its chunky pine furniture and deep, deep sofa in front of a rustic fireplace, the Coach House is one of the cosiest places to eat on Loch Lomond. The menu includes coffee and tea, home-baked cakes, scones and ciabattas, and more-substantial offerings such as haggis.

**our pick** **Drover's Inn** ( ☎ 01301-704234; www.the droversinn.co.uk; Inverarnan; bar meals £6-9; 🕐 food served 11.30am-10pm Mon-Sat, noon-9pm Sun; P ) This is one howff (drinking den) you shouldn't miss – a low-ceilinged place with smoke-blackened stone, bare wooden floors spotted with candle wax, barmen in kilts and walls festooned with moth-eaten stag's heads and stuffed birds; there's even a stuffed bear, and the dessicated husk of a basking shark. The bar serves hearty hill-walking fuel such as steak and Guinness pie with mustard mash, and hosts live folk music on Friday and Saturday nights. We recommend this inn more as a place to eat and drink than to stay – accommodation

(single/double from £35/68) varies from eccentric, old-fashioned and rather run-down rooms in the old building (including a ghost in room 6), to more comfortable rooms (with en-suite bathrooms) in the modern annexe across the road (ask to see your room before taking it, though).

## Eastern Shore

The road along the loch's eastern shore passes through the attractive village of **Balmaha**, where you can hire boats or take a cruise on the mail boat (see p277). There are several picnic areas along the lochside; the most attractive is at **Millarochy Bay** (1.5 miles north of Balmaha), which has a nice gravel beach and superb views across the loch to the Luss hills.

The road ends at **Rowardennan**, but the West Highland Way continues north along the shore of the loch. It's 7 miles to Inversnaid, which can be reached by road from the Trossachs (p199), and 15 miles to Inverarnan on the main A82 road at the northern end of the loch.

### SLEEPING & EATING

**Cashel Campsite** ( ☎ 01360-870234; Rowardennan; backpackers per person £5, tent sites per 2 people incl car £14-15; 🕐 Apr-Oct) This is the most attractive camping ground in the area and is 3 miles north of Balmaha, by the loch.

**Rowardennan Youth Hostel** ( ☎ 0870 004 1148; Rowardennan; dm £13-14; 🕐 Mar-Oct) Housed in an attractive Victorian lodge, this hostel has a superb setting right on the loch shore, beside the West Highland Way.

**Oak Tree Inn** ( ☎ 01360-870357; www.oak-tree-inn .co.uk; Balmaha; bunkroom per person £25, s/d £50/70; P 👶 ) An attractive traditional inn built in slate and timber, the child-friendly Oak Tree offers luxurious guest bedrooms for pampered hikers, and two four-bed bunkrooms for hardier souls. The rustic restaurant dishes up hearty meals (£7 to £15; noon to 9pm) such as sausage and mash, haggis, and vegetable lasagne, and cooks up an excellent bowl of *Cullen skink*.

**Passfoot Cottage** ( ☎ 01360-870324; www.passfoot .com; Balmaha; r per person from £28; 🕐 Apr-Sep) Passfoot is a pretty little whitewashed cottage decked out with colourful flower baskets, with a lovely location overlooking Balmaha Bay. The bright bedrooms have a homely feel, and there's a large lounge with a wood-burning stove and loch view.

**Rowardennan Hotel** ( ☎ 01360-870273; www.roward ennanhotel.com; Rowardennan; bar meals £7-17; ☒ food served 11am-9pm; P ) Originally an 18th-century drovers' inn, the Rowardennan has two big bars (often crowded with rain-sodden hikers) and a beer garden (often crowded with midges). Rooms are available (£47.50), but we can't really recommend it as a place to stay – overpriced and a bit run down – but it's the only place to eat and drink beyond Balmaha.

### Getting There & Away

First Glasgow buses 204 and 215 run from Argyle St in central Glasgow to Balloch and Loch Lomond Shores (1½ hours, at least two per hour).

Scottish Citylink coaches from Glasgow to Oban and Fort William stop at Luss (£6, 55 minutes, six daily), Tarbet (£7, 65 minutes) and Ardlui (£10, 1¼ hours).

There are frequent trains from Glasgow to Balloch (£4, 45 minutes, two per hour) and a less-frequent service on the West Highland line from Glasgow to Arrochar & Tarbet (one station, halfway between the two villages) and Ardlui (£12, 1½ hours, three or four daily), continuing to Oban and Fort William.

### Getting Around

#### BUS

**McColl's Coaches'** ( ☎ 01389-754321) bus 309 runs from Balloch to Balmaha (25 minutes, every two hours Monday to Saturday). An SPT Daytripper ticket (www.spt.co.uk/tickets) gives a family group unlimited travel for a day on most bus and train services in the Glasgow, Loch Lomond and Helensburgh area. Buy the ticket (£8.50 for one adult and one or two children, £15 for two adults and up to four children) from any train station or main Glasgow bus station.

#### FERRY

There are several passenger ferries on Loch Lomond, with fares ranging from £1 to £5 per person, and around £1 for a bicycle. These are mostly small motorboats that operate on demand, rather than to a set timetable – telephone, or call at the establishment listed for more information.

**Ardlui to Ardleish** ( ☎ 01307-704243; Ardlui Hotel) From 9am to 8pm on demand.

**Balmaha to Inchcailloch** ( ☎ 01360-870214; Balmaha Boatyard, Balmaha) From 9am to 8pm on demand.

**Inverbeg to Rowardennan** ( ☎ 01360-870273; Rowardennan Hotel) Three daily Easter to September.

**Inveruglas to Inversnaid** ( ☎ 01877-386223; Inversnaid Hotel) On demand.

**Tarbet to Inversnaid** ( ☎ 01301-702356; Cruise Loch Lomond, Tarbet) Once daily, May to September.

## HELENSBURGH

☎ 01436 / pop 16,500

With the coming of the railway in the mid-19th century, Helensburgh – named in the 18th century after the wife of Sir James Colquhoun of Luss – became a popular seaside retreat for wealthy Glaswegian families. Their spacious Victorian villas now populate the neat grid of streets that covers the hillside above the Firth of Clyde, but none can compare with the splendour of **Hill House** ( ☎ 673900; Upper Colquhoun St; adult/child £8/5; ☒ 1.30-5.30pm Apr-Oct). Built in 1902 for the Glasgow publisher Walter Blackie, it is perhaps architect Charles Rennie Mackintosh's finest creation – its timeless elegance feels as chic today as it no doubt did when the Blackies moved in a century ago.

Helensburgh has a ferry connection with Gourock (p148) via Kilcreggan, and a frequent train service to Glasgow (£4.60, 50 minutes, two per hour).

## ARROCHAR

☎ 01301 / pop 650

The village of Arrochar has a wonderful location, looking across the head of Loch Long to the jagged peaks of the **Cobbler** (881m). The mountain takes its name from the shape of its north peak (the one on the right), which looks like a cobbler hunched over his bench. The village has several hotels and shops, and a bank and a post office.

If you want to climb the Cobbler, start from the roadside car park at Succoth near the head of Loch Long. A steep uphill hike through the woods is followed by an easier section as you head into the valley below the triple peaks. Then it's steeply uphill again to the saddle between the north and central peaks. The central peak (to the left/south) is the highest point, but it's awkward to get to – scramble through the hole and along the ledge to reach the airy summit. The north peak (to the right/north) is an easy walk. Allow five to six hours for the 5-mile return trip.

There's good camping at **Ardgartan Caravan & Campsite** ( ☎ 702293; Ardgartan; tent sites per person £4-7; ☒ Apr-Oct) at the foot of Glen Croe.

## WEST HIGHLAND WAY

This classic hike – the country's most popular long-distance path – stretches for 95 miles through some of Scotland's most spectacular scenery, from Milngavie (pronounced mull-*guy*), on the northwestern fringes of Glasgow, to Fort William.

The route begins in the Lowlands but the greater part of the trail is among the mountains, lochs and fast-flowing rivers of the western Highlands. After following the eastern shore of Loch Lomond and passing Crianlarich and Tyndrum, the route crosses the vast wilderness of Rannoch Moor and reaches Fort William via Glen Nevis, in the shadow of Britain's highest peak, Ben Nevis.

The path is easy to follow, making use of old drovers' roads (along which Highland cattle were once driven to Lowland markets), an old military road (built by troops to help subdue the Highlands in the 18th century) and disused railway lines.

Best done from south to north, the walk takes about six or seven days (the fastest time, set during the West Highland Way Race in 2006, is 15 hours 45 minutes!). Many people round it off with an ascent of Ben Nevis (p345). You need to be properly equipped with good boots, waterproofs, maps, a compass, and food and drink for the northern part of the walk. Midge repellent is also essential.

*The West Highland Way Official Guide* by Bob Aitken and Roger Smith is the most comprehensive guidebook. The Harveys map *West Highland Way* shows the entire route in a single map sheet.

Accommodation shouldn't be too difficult to find, though between Bridge of Orchy and Kinlochleven it's limited. At peak times (May, July and August), book accommodation in advance. There are some youth hostels and bunkhouses on or near the path, and it's possible to camp in some parts. A list of accommodation is available for free from tourist offices.

For more information check out the website www.west-highland-way.co.uk.

The black-and-white, 19th-century **Village Inn** ( ☎ 702279; Arrochar; mains £8-16; ☯ food served noon-5pm & 6-9pm) is a lovely spot for lunch, or just a pint of real ale – the beer garden has a great view of the Cobbler. There are 14 en-suite bedrooms (per person £35 to £50); the ones at the top end of the price range have four-poster beds and a view over the loch.

Scottish Citylink buses from Glasgow to Inveraray and Campbeltown call at Arrochar and Ardgartan (£7, 1¼ hours, three daily). See p279 for trains to Arrochar & Tarbet station.

# SOUTH ARGYLL

## COWAL

The remote Cowal peninsula is cut off from the rest of the country by the lengthy fjords of Loch Long and Loch Fyne – it's an area more accessible by boat than by car. It's comprised of rugged hills and narrow lochs, with only a few small villages; the scenery around Loch Riddon is particularly enchanting. The only town on the mainland is the old-fashioned holiday resort of Dunoon.

From Arrochar, the A83 to Inveraray loops around the head of Loch Long and climbs up Glen Croe. The pass at the head of the glen is called the **Rest and be Thankful** – when the original military road through the glen was repaired in the 18th century, a stone was erected at the top inscribed 'Rest, and be thankful. This road was made, in 1748, by the 24th Regt…Repaired by the 93rd Regt. 1786'. A copy of the stone can be seen at the far end of the parking area at the top of the pass.

There's a Forest Enterprise **visitors centre** ( ☎ 702432; Ardgartan; admission free; ☯ 10am-5pm Apr-Oct) at the foot of the glen, with information on various walks in the Cowal peninsula.

As you descend Glen Kinglas on the far side of the Rest and be Thankful, the A815 forks to the left just before Cairndow; this is the main overland route into Cowal. From Glasgow, the most direct route is by ferry from Gourock to Dunoon (see p148 for details).

### Dunoon & Around

☎ 01369

Like Rothesay on the Isle of Bute, Dunoon (population 9100) is a Victorian seaside resort that owes its existence to the steamers that once carried thousands of Glaswegians on pleasure trips 'doon the watter' (down the water) in the 19th and 20th centuries. As with Rothesay, Dunoon's fortunes declined in recent decades when cheap foreign holidays stole its market – however, while the Bute resort appears to be recovering, Dunoon is still a bit down in the dumps.

The **tourist office** ( ☎ 0870 720 0629; 7 Alexandra Pde; ⏰ 9am-5.30pm Mon-Fri, 10am-5pm Sat & Sun Apr-Sep, 9am-5pm Mon-Thu, 10am-5pm Fri, 10am-4pm Sat & Sun Oct-Mar) is on the waterfront 100m north of the pier; there's internet access for £1 per 12 minutes.

### SIGHTS & ACTIVITIES

The town's main attraction is still, as it was in the 1950s, strolling along the **promenade**, licking an ice-cream cone and watching the yachts at play in the Firth of Clyde. On a small hill above the seafront is a statue of **Highland Mary** (1763–86), one of the great loves of Robert Burns' life. She was born near Dunoon, but died tragically young; her statue gazes longingly across the firth to Burns' home territory in Ayrshire.

The **Benmore Botanic Garden** ( ☎ 706261; Benmore; adult/child £3.50/1; ⏰ 10am-6pm Apr-Sep, to 5pm Mar & Oct), 7 miles north of Dunoon, was originally planted in the 19th and early 20th centuries. It contains the country's finest collection of flowering trees and shrubs, including Bhutanese and Chilean rainforest specimens, and is entered along a spectacular avenue of giant Californian redwoods planted in 1863. The café here (which stays open all year) is a nice place for lunch or a coffee.

### FESTIVALS & EVENTS

Dunoon hosts the annual **Cowal Highland Gathering** (www.cowalgathering.com) in mid-August; the spectacular finale traditionally features 3000 bagpipers playing en masse.

**Cowalfest** (www.cowalfest.org) is a 10-day arts and walking festival that takes in art exhibitions, film screenings, guided walks and bicycle rides throughout the Cowal peninsula.

### SLEEPING & EATING

**Dhailling Lodge** ( ☎ 701253; www.dhaillinglodge.com; 155 Alexandra Pde; s/d £37/70; 🖳 🅿 ♿ ) You can experience some of Dunoon's former elegance at this large Victorian villa overlooking the bay about 0.75 miles north of the CalMac ferry pier. The owners are the essence of Scottish hospitality, and can provide excellent evening meals (£21.50 for five courses) if you wish.

**Black of Dunoon** ( ☎ 702311; 113 George St) The local bakery, halfway along the main street, is famous for its traditional, all-butter Scottish shortbread.

**Chatters** ( ☎ 706402; 58 John St; mains £8-16; ⏰ noon-3pm & 6-10pm Wed-Sat) Chatters is a pretty little cottage restaurant serving traditional Scottish dishes, and is famous for its tempting desserts. The two-course lunch (£11) is excellent value.

### GETTING THERE & AWAY

Dunoon is served by two competing ferry services from Gourock (p148) – the CalMac ferry is better if you are travelling on foot and want to arrive in the town centre.

## Tighnabruaich

☎ 01700 / pop 200

Sleepy little Tighnabruaich (pronounced tinna-*broo*-ach), a colony of seaside villas built by wealthy Glasgow families at the turn of the 20th century, is one of the most attractive villages on the Firth of Clyde. It was once a regular stop for Clyde steamers, and the old wooden pier is still occasionally visited by the paddle steamer *Waverley* (see boxed text Getting Around on the Clyde, p125).

The link with the sea continues in the **Tighnabruaich Sailing School** ( ☎ 811717; www.tssargyll.co.uk; Carry Farm; ⏰ May-Sep), 2 miles south of Tighnabruaich. A five-day dinghy-sailing course costs £205, excluding accommodation.

The village is home to **An Lochan** ( ☎ 811239; www.anlochan-argyll.co.uk; Tighnabruaich; 2-course lunch £14, 3-course dinner £48; 🅿 ), a luxurious boutique hotel (rooms £120 to £190) that's comfortable, but in our opinion, a tad over-priced. The food is exquisite, and uses fresh, locally sourced produce – from nettle and dandelion risotto to seared scallops with a smear of smoky, caramelised shallot purée – but portions are very small.

If all you want to do is fill up with good, hearty homemade grub, go for the mussels and chips at the **Burnside Bistro** ( ☎ 811739; mains £5-13; ⏰ 9am-9pm) in the village centre, or a bar meal at the **Kames Hotel** ( ☎ 811489; mains £7-12; ⏰ food served noon-2.30pm & 6-9pm), a mile to the south.

## ISLE OF BUTE

☎ 01700 / pop 7350

The island of Bute lies pinched between the thumb and forefinger of the Cowal peninsula, separated from the mainland by a narrow, scenic strait known as the Kyles of Bute. The Highland Boundary Fault cuts through the middle of the island so that, geologically speaking, the northern half is in the Highlands and the southern half in the central Lowlands – a metal arch on Rothesay's Esplanade marks the fault line.

The **Isle of Bute Discovery Centre** ( ☎ 505156; www.visitbute.com; Esplanade, Rothesay; ☿ 10am-6pm Mon-Fri, 9.30am-5pm Sat & Sun Jul & Aug, 10am-5pm daily Apr-Jun & Sep, 10am-5pm Mon-Fri, 11am-4pm Sat & Sun Oct-Mar) in Rothesay's restored Winter Garden provides tourist information, and has internet access for £1 per 12 minutes.

The five-day **Isle of Bute Jazz Festival** (www .butejazz.com) is held over the first weekend of May, and in late July there's the **ButeLive** (www .butelive.co.uk) music and arts festival.

### SIGHTS & ACTIVITIES

In the southern part of the island you'll find the 12th-century ruin of **St Blane's Chapel**, with a 10th-century tombstone in the graveyard, and a sandy beach at **Kilchattan Bay**.

There are more good beaches on the west coast. **Scalpsie Bay** is a 400m walk across a field from the parking area, and has a fantastic outlook to the peaks of Arran. You can often spot seals basking at low tide off Ardscalpsie Point, to the west.

**Ettrick Bay** is bigger, easier to reach, and has a tearoom (not the most attractive building on the island), but is not as pretty as Scalpsie.

There are lots of easy walks on Bute, including the **West Island Way**, a waymarked 30-mile walking route from Kilchattan Bay to Port Bannatyne; map and details are available from the Isle of Bute Discovery Centre.

Cycling on Bute is excellent – the roads are well surfaced and fairly quiet. You can hire a bike from the **Bike Shed** ( ☎ 07718 023571; 23-25 East Princes St, Rothesay) for £10/15 per half-/full day.

**Kingarth Trekking Centre** ( ☎ 831673; Kilchattan Bay) offers paddock rides for kids (£5; minimum age eight years), riding lessons (£20 per hour), and pony treks (£35 for two hours).

### GETTING THERE & AWAY

CalMac ferries travel between Wemyss Bay (p148) and Rothesay (passenger/car £3.80/15.25, 35 minutes, hourly). Another CalMac ferry crosses the short stretch of water between Rhubodach in the north of the island and Colintraive (passenger/car £1.20/7.65, five minutes, every 15 to 20 minutes) in Cowal.

West Coast Motors buses run four or five times a week from Rothesay to Tighnabruaich and Dunoon via the ferry at Colintraive. On Monday and Thursday a bus goes from Rothesay to Portavadie (via the Rhubodach–Colintraive ferry), where there's a ferry to Tarbert in Kintyre (passenger/car £3.20/14.65, 25 minutes, hourly).

## Rothesay

From the mid-19th century until the 1960s, Rothesay – once dubbed the Margate of the Clyde – was one of the most popular holiday resorts in Scotland. Its Esplanade was bustling with day-trippers disembarking from the numerous steamers crowded round the pier, and its hotels were filled with elderly holiday-makers and convalescents taking advantage of the town's famously mild climate.

The fashion for foreign holidays that took off in the 1970s saw Rothesay's fortunes decline, and by the late 1990s it had become dilapidated and despondent. But in the last few years a nostalgia-fuelled resurgence of interest in Rothesay's holiday heyday has seen many of its Victorian buildings restored, the ferry terminal rebuilt, and a new feeling of optimism in the air.

### SIGHTS

Just two blocks inland from the pier are the splendid ruins of 13th-century **Rothesay Castle** ( ☎ 502691; King St; adult/child £4/2; ☿ 9.30am-5.30pm Apr-Sep, 9.30am-4.30pm Sat-Wed Oct-Mar), with seagulls

---

**THE MAIDS OF BUTE**

One of the best walks on Bute is from the ferry pier at Rhubodach to the northern tip of the island (1.5 miles), where you can watch yachts negotiate the rocky narrows at the Burnt Islands. Just around the point are the Maids of Bute, two rocks painted to look like old women. The story goes that the distinctively shaped (but then unpainted) rocks were first noticed by the skipper of a pleasure steamer in the early 20th century, who always pointed them out to the passengers on his boat. Frustrated that the tourists could never see the resemblance, he sent a deckhand ashore with a couple of tins of paint to give them some clothes and recognisable faces. No one is quite sure who now maintains the maids, but every time the paint begins to peel, it's not long before a fresh coat brightens them up.

and jackdaws nesting in the walls. Once a favourite residence of the Stuart kings, it is unique in Scotland in having a circular plan, with four massive round towers. The landscaped moat, with its manicured turf, flower gardens and lazily cruising ducks, makes a picturesque setting.

There aren't too many places where a public toilet would count as a tourist attraction, but Rothesay pier's **Victorian toilets** (adult/child 10p/free), dating from 1899, are a monument to lavatorial luxury, a disinfectant-scented temple of green marble, glistening white enamel, glass-sided cisterns and gleaming copper pipes. The attendant will escort ladies into the hallowed confines of the gents for a look around if those facilities are unoccupied.

The most interesting displays in **Bute Museum** ( ☎ 503157; 7 Stuart St; adult/child £2/1; ⊙ 10.30am-4.30pm Mon-Sat, 2.30-4.30pm Sun Apr-Sep, 2.30-4.30pm Tue-Sat Oct-Mar) are those recounting the history of the famous Clyde steamers. Other galleries cover natural history, archaeology and geology; the prize exhibit is a stunning jet necklace found in a Bronze Age burial on the island.

Gardeners will enjoy the beautifully restored **Victorian Fernery** ( ☎ 504555; Ascog; adult/child £3/free; ⊙ 10am-5pm Wed-Sun mid-Apr–mid-Oct) at Ascog Hall, on the southern edge of town.

### SLEEPING

**Ascog Farm** ( ☎ 503372; Ascog; r per person £20; P ) All four rooms at this peaceful farmhouse B&B have been laid out in accordance with the rules of feng shui. It's 3 miles from Rothesay, heading south on the A844 coastal road.

**Glendale Guest House** ( ☎ 502329; www.glendale-guest-house.com; 20 Battery Pl; s/d/f from £35/60/90; P ) Look out for the ornate, flower-bedecked façade on this beautiful Victorian villa, complete with pinnacled turret – all those windows mean superb sea views from the front-facing bedrooms, the elegant, 1st-floor lounge, and the breakfast room, where you'll find homemade smoked haddock fishcakes on the menu as well as the traditional fry-up.

**Moorings** ( ☎ 502277; www.themoorings-bute.co.uk; 7 Mountstuart Rd; s/d £35/50; P ) Another delightful Victorian lodge with good sea views, the family-friendly Moorings has an outdoor play area for kids and a high chair in the breakfast room. Vegetarian breakfasts not a problem.

**Boat House** ( ☎ 502696; www.theboathouse-bute.co.uk; 15 Battery Pl; s/d from £45/60; ♿ ) The Boat House brings a touch of class to Rothesay's guest-

house scene, with quality fabrics and furnishings and an eye for design that feels a little like a boutique hotel without the expensive price tag. Other features include sea views, a central location, and a ground-floor room kitted out for wheelchair users.

### EATING

**Musicker** ( ☎ 502287; 11 High St; mains £3-4; ⊙ 9am-5pm) This cool little café, tricked out in pale minty green, serves the best coffee on the island, alongside a range of sandwiches with imaginative fillings – haggis and cranberry, anyone? It also sells music CDs (folk, world and country) and sports an old-fashioned jukebox.

**Waterfront Bistro** ( ☎ 505166; 16 East Princes St; mains £7-13; ⊙ noon-3pm Sat & Sun, 5.30-9pm Thu-Mon) Cheerful and informal, the wood-panelled Waterfront has a bistro menu that ranges from haddock and chips to red Thai chicken curry to grilled langoustines with garlic butter; bottled real ale from the Arran complements the wine list. (Credit cards are not accepted.)

**Pier at Craigmore** ( ☎ 502867; Mount Stuart Rd; mains lunch £5-8, dinner £11-21; ⊙ 10.30am-4.30pm daily, 6.30-9.30pm Fri & Sat) Housed in the former waiting room at a Victorian pier on the eastern edge of town, the Craigmore is a neat little bistro with fantastic views. The lunch menu offers sandwiches, salads, homemade burgers and quiche, while dinner is more sophisticated with seafood, steak and lamb.

## Around Rothesay

### MOUNT STUART

The Stuart earls of Bute are direct descendants of Robert the Bruce and have lived on the island for 700 years. When a large part of the family seat was destroyed by fire in 1877, the third marquess of Bute, John Patrick Crichton-Stuart (1847–1900) – one of the greatest architecture patrons of his day, and the builder of Cardiff Castle and Castell Coch in Wales – commissioned Sir Robert Rowand Anderson to create a new one. The result – **Mount Stuart** ( ☎ 503877; www.mountstuart.com; adult/child £7.50/3.50; ⊙ 11am-5pm Sun-Fri, 10am-2pm Sat Easter & May-Sep) – became the finest neo-Gothic palace in Scotland, and the first to have electric lighting, central heating and a heated swimming pool.

The heart of the house is the stunning **Marble Hall**, a three-storey extravaganza of Italian marble that soars 25m to a dark-blue vault spangled with constellations of golden stars. Twelve stained-glass windows represent the seasons and the signs of the zodiac, with crystal stars casting rainbow-hued highlights across the marble when the sun is shining.

The design and decoration reflect the third marquess' fascination with astrology, mythology and religion, a theme carried over into the grand **Marble Staircase** beyond (where wall panels depict the six days of the Creation), and the lavishly decorated **Horoscope Bedroom**. Here the central ceiling panel records the positions of the stars and planets at the time of the marquess' birth on 12 September 1847.

Yet another highlight is the **Marble Chapel**, built entirely out of dazzling white Carrara marble. It has a dome lit to spectacular effect by a ring of ruby-red stained-glass windows – at noon on midsummer's day a shaft of blood-red sunlight shines directly onto the altar. It was here that Stella McCartney – daughter of ex-Beatle Sir Paul, and friend of the present marquess, former racing driver Johnny Dumfries – was married in 2003.

Mount Stuart is 5 miles south of Rothesay. Bus 90 runs from the bus stop outside the ferry terminal at Rothesay to Mount Stuart (15 minutes, 10 per day May to September). You can buy a special **Mount Stuart Day Trip** ticket (adult/child £18.50/9.25) that covers return train, ferry and bus travel from Glasgow (or any train station in Stratchclyde region) to Mount Stuart, as well as admission. Ask at the Glasgow tourist office or any train station.

## INVERARAY

☎ 01499 / pop 700

You can spot Inveraray long before you get here – its neat, whitewashed buildings stand out from a distance on the shores of Loch Fyne. It's a planned town, built by the duke of Argyll in Georgian style when he revamped his nearby castle in the 18th century. The **tourist office** ( ☎ 0845 225 5121; Front St; ☻ 9am-6pm Jul & Aug, 10am-5pm Mon-Sat Apr-Jun, Sep & Oct, 10am-3pm Mon-Sat Nov-Mar) is on the seafront, and has internet access for £1 per 12 minutes.

### Sights

**Inveraray Castle** ( ☎ 302203; adult/child £6.30/4.10; ☻ 10am-5.45pm Mon-Sat, 1-5.45pm Sun Apr-Oct) has been the seat of the dukes of Argyll – chiefs of Clan Campbell – since the 15th century. The 18th-century building, with its fairytale turrets and fake battlements, houses an im-

pressive armoury hall, its walls patterned with a collection of more than 1000 pole arms, dirks, muskets and Lochaber axes. The castle is 500m north of town, entered from the A819 Dalmally road.

**Inveraray Jail** ( ☎ 302381; Church Sq; adult/child £6.50/3.50; ☻ 9.30am-6pm Apr-Oct, 10am-5pm Nov-Mar), in the centre of town, is an award-winning, interactive tourist attraction. You can sit in on a trial, try out a cell, and discover the harsh torture meted out to unfortunate prisoners. The attention to detail – including a life-sized model of an inmate squatting on a 19th-century toilet – more than makes up for the sometimes tedious commentary.

The ship *Arctic Penguin*, a three-masted schooner built in 1911 and one of the world's last surviving iron sailing ships, is permanently moored in Inveraray harbour and houses the **Inveraray Maritime Museum** ( ☎ 302213; The Pier; adult/child £3.80/2.20; ☻ 10am-6pm Apr-Sep, 10am-5pm Oct-Mar). It has interesting photos and models of the old Clyde steamers and a display about Para Handy (see the boxed text Essential Scottish Reads, p44). Kids will love exploring below the decks – there's a special play area in the bowels of the ship.

### Sleeping & Eating

**Inveraray Youth Hostel** ( ☎ 0870 004 1125; Dalmally Rd; dm £13; ☻ Apr-Oct) To get to this hostel, housed in a comfortable, modern bungalow, go through the arched entrance on the seafront – it's set back on the left of the road about 100m further on.

**ourpick** **George Hotel** ( ☎ 302111; www.thegeorge hotel.co.uk; Main St East; s/d from £35/70; P ) The George Hotel boasts a magnificent choice of opulent rooms, complete with four-poster beds, period furniture, Victorian roll-top baths and private Jacuzzis (these superior rooms cost £120 to £140 a double). The cosy wood-panelled bar, with its rough stone walls, flagstone floor and peat fires, is a delightful place for a bar meal (mains £6 to £8). Food is served from noon till 9pm daily.

**Claonairigh House** ( ☎ 302160; www.claonairigh house.co.uk; Bridge of Douglas; s/d from £40/90; ☐ P ) This grand 18th-century house, built for the duke of Argyll in 1745, is set in 3 hectares of grounds on the bank of a river (salmon-fishing available). There are three homely en-suite rooms, one with a four-poster bed, and a resident menagerie of dogs, ducks, chickens and goats. It's 4 miles south of town on the A83.

**Loch Fyne Oyster Bar** ( ☎ 600236; Clachan, Cairndow; mains £10-18; ☺ 9am-9pm) Six miles northeast of Inveraray in Cairndow, this rustic-themed restaurant serves excellent seafood, though the service can be a bit hit-and-miss. It's housed in a converted byre, and the menu includes locally farmed oysters, mussels and salmon. The neighbouring shop sells packaged seafood to take away.

## Getting There & Away

Scottish Citylink buses run from Glasgow to Inveraray (£9, 1¾ hours, six daily Monday to Saturday, two Sunday). Three of these buses continue to Lochgilphead and Campbeltown (£10, 2½ hours); the others continue to Oban (£8, 1¼ hours).

## CRINAN CANAL

☎ 01546

Completed in 1801, the picturesque Crinan Canal runs for 9 miles from Ardrishaig to Crinan allowing seagoing vessels – mostly yachts, these days – to take a short cut from the Firth of Clyde and Loch Fyne to the west coast of Scotland, avoiding the long and sometimes dangerous passage around the Mull of Kintyre. You can easily walk or cycle the full length of the canal towpath in an afternoon.

**Gemini Cruises** ( ☎ 07776 082256, 07736 520099; www.gemini-crinan.co.uk), based at Crinan Harbour a half-mile west of the Crinan Hotel, runs two-hour boat trips (adult/child £20/15) to the spectacular Gulf of Corryvreckan (see boxed text The Scottish Maelstrom, p294). It will also ferry groups across to the northern end of Jura (£50 for up to 12 passengers and bicycles, 30 minutes) by prior arrangement.

The canal basin at Crinan is the focus for the annual **Crinan Classic Boat Festival** (www.isleofjura.com/crinanclassic), held over the last weekend in July, when traditional wooden yachts, motor boats and dinghies gather for a few days of racing, drinking and music.

The plush **Cairnbaan Hotel** ( ☎ 603668; www.cairnbaan.com; Cairnbaan; s/d £80/132, mains £9-16; P ), halfway along the canal, serves good food – including seafood pie topped with chive mash, and Thai-spiced butternut squash risotto – in a comfortable conservatory. The accommodation is a bit overpriced though.

The even more luxurious, and even more overpriced **Crinan Hotel** ( ☎ 830261; www.crinanhotel.com; Crinan; s/d from £135/235; P ), overlooking Loch Crinan at the northwestern end of the

canal, has one of Scotland's top seafood restaurants. Better to eat in the hotel's **Crinan Bar** (mains £10-18; ☺ food served noon-2.30pm & 6-8.30pm), though – it's better value for money.

The **coffee shop** ( ☺ 10am-5.30pm) on the western side of the canal basin at Crinan has great home-baked cakes and scones.

## KILMARTIN GLEN

☎ 01546

In the 6th century Irish settlers arrived in this part of Argyll and founded the kingdom of Dalriada, which eventually united with the Picts in 843 to create the first Scottish kingdom. Their capital was the hill fort of Dunadd, on the plain to the south of Kilmartin Glen.

This magical glen is the focus of one of the biggest concentrations of prehistoric sites in Scotland. Burial cairns, standing stones, stone circles, hill forts and cup-and-ring-marked rocks litter the countryside – within a 6-mile radius of Kilmartin village there are 25 sites with standing stones and over 100 rock carvings.

There's a shop and post office in Kilmartin village.

## Sights

Your first stop should be **Kilmartin House Museum** ( ☎ 510278; www.kilmartin.org; adult/child £4.60/1.70; ☺ 10am-5.30pm Mar-Oct), in Kilmartin village, a fascinating interpretive centre that provides a context for the ancient monuments you can go on to explore, alongside displays of artefacts recovered from various sites. The project was partly funded by midges – the curator exposed himself in Temple Wood on a warm summer's evening and was sponsored per midge bite!

The oldest monuments at Kilmartin date from 5000 years ago and comprise a linear cemetery of **burial cairns** that runs south from Kilmartin village for 1.5 miles. There are also ritual monuments (two stone circles) at **Temple Wood**, three-quarters of a mile southwest of Kilmartin. The museum bookshop sells maps and guides.

**Kilmartin Churchyard** contains some 10th-century Celtic crosses and lots of medieval grave slabs with carved effigies of knights. Some researchers have surmised that these were the tombs of Knights Templar who fled persecution in France in the 14th century.

The hill fort of **Dunadd**, 3.5 miles south of Kilmartin village, was the seat of power of the first kings of Dalriada, and may have been where the Stone of Destiny (p81) was originally located. The faint rock carvings of a wild boar and two footprints with an ogham inscription may have been used in some kind of inauguration ceremony. The prominent little hill rises straight out of the boggy plain of the Moine Mhor Nature Reserve. A slippery path leads to the summit where you can gaze out on much the same view that the kings of Dalriada enjoyed 1300 years ago.

At **Kilmichael Glassary** (a mile east of Dunadd) and **Achnabreck** (half a mile south) there are rock faces carved with elaborate designs – like ripples from a pebble dropped into a pond – known to archaeologists as cup-and-ring marks. Archaeologists have speculated that the marks may have had religious significance, or served as a record of land ownership or boundaries, but their meaning and purpose remains a mystery.

### Sleeping & Eating

**Burndale B&B** ( ☎ 510235; bbdalekilmartin@aol.com; s/d from £30/54; P ) Set in a lovely Victorian manse (minister's house), this homely and hospitable B&B is just a short walk north from the Kilmartin House Museum.

**Kilmartin Hotel** ( ☎ 510250; www.kilmartin-hotel .com; s/d £40/65; P ) Though the rooms are a bit on the small side, this attractively old-fashioned hotel is full of atmosphere and has a restaurant, and a real-ale bar where you can enjoy live folk music at weekends.

**our pick Glebe Cairn Café** ( ☎ 510278; mains £5-7; ✆ 10am-5pm, lunch noon-3pm, dinner 7-9pm Thu-Sat in summer) The café in the Kilmartin House Museum has a lovely conservatory with a view across fields to a prehistoric cairn. Daily specials include homemade soup and dishes such as smoked haddock pancakes, and red pepper and spring onion hummus with oatcakes, while the drinks menu ranges from espresso to elderflower wine by way of Fraoch heather-scented ale.

### Getting There & Away

Bus 423 between Oban and Ardrishaig (four daily Monday to Friday, two on Saturday) stops at Kilmartin (£4, one hour).

You can walk or cycle along the Crinan Canal from Ardrishaig, then turn north at Bellanoch on the minor B8025 road to reach Kilmartin (12 miles one way).

## KINTYRE

The Kintyre peninsula – 40 miles long and 8 miles wide – is almost an island, with only a narrow isthmus at Tarbert connecting it to the wooded hills of Knapdale. During the Norse occupation of the Western Isles, the Scottish king decreed that the Vikings could claim as their own any island they could circumnavigate in a longship. So in 1098 the wily Magnus Barefoot stood at the helm while his men dragged their boat across this neck of land, thus validating his claim to Kintyre.

### Tarbert

☎ 01880 / pop 1500

The attractive fishing village and yachting centre of Tarbert is the gateway to Kintyre, and well worth a stopover for lunch or dinner. There's a **tourist office** ( ☎ 820429; Harbour St; ✆ 9am-5pm Mon-Sat Apr-Oct), a Co-op supermarket and two banks with ATMs near the head of the harbour.

#### SIGHTS & ACTIVITIES

The picturesque harbour is overlooked by the crumbling, ivy-covered ruins of **Tarbert Castle**, built by Robert the Bruce in the 14th century. You can hike up to it via a signposted footpath beside the **Loch Fyne Gallery** (Harbour St; ✆ 10am-5pm daily), which showcases the work of local artists.

Tarbert is the starting point for the 103-mile **Kintyre Way** (www.kintyreway.com), a walking route that runs the length of the peninsula to Southend at the southern tip. The first section, from Tarbert to Skipness (9 miles), makes a makes a pleasant day-hike, climbing through forestry plantations to a high moorland plateau where you can soak up superb views to the Isle of Arran.

**Highland Horse Riding** ( ☎ 820333; www.high landhorseriding.com; An Tairbeart; ✆ Apr-Oct), on the western edge of the village, offers sightseeing and wildlife-spotting pony treks into the hills of Knapdale.

#### FESTIVALS & EVENTS

Tarbert is a lively little place, and never more so than during the annual **Scottish Series Yacht Race** (www.clyde.org), held over five days around the last weekend in May, when the harbour is crammed with hundreds of visiting yachts. The **Tarbert Seafood Festival** (www.seafood-festival .co.uk) is held on the first weekend in July, and the **Tarbert Music Festival** (www.auqn74.dsl.pipex.com) is on the third weekend in September.

## SLEEPING & EATING

There are plenty of B&Bs and hotels, but be sure to book ahead during festivals and major events. Contact the tourist office for details about more local accommodation options.

**Springside B&B** ( ☎ 820413; www.scotland-info.co.uk /springside; Pier Rd; r per person £25-28; **P** ) You can sit out the front of this attractive fisherman's cottage, which overlooks the entrance to the harbour, and watch the yachts and fishing boats come and go. There are four comfy rooms, three with en suite, and the house is just five minutes' walk from the village centre in one direction, and a short stroll from the Portavadie ferry in the other.

**our pick** **Corner House Bistro** ( ☎ 820263; Harbour St; mains £12-26; ☻ 6-10pm) It's worth making the trip to Tarbert just to eat at this relaxed and romantic restaurant, with its log fires, candlelight and award-winning French chef who knows exactly what to do with top-quality local seafood. The entrance is on the side street around the corner from the Corner House pub – look for the green awning.

## GETTING THERE & AWAY

Tarbert is served by five Scottish Citylink coaches a day between Campbeltown and Glasgow (Glasgow to Tarbert £13, 3¼ hours; Tarbert to Campbeltown £6, 1¼ hours).

CalMac operates a car ferry from Tarbert to Portavadie on the Cowal peninsula (passenger/car £3.20/15, 25 minutes, hourly).

Ferries to the islands of Islay (p290) and Colonsay (p296) depart from Kennacraig ferry terminal on West Loch Tarbert, 5 miles southwest of Tarbert.

## Skipness

☎ 01880 / pop 100

The tiny village of Skipness is on the east coast of Kintyre, about 13 miles south of Tarbert, in a pleasant and quiet setting with great views of Arran. There's a post office and general store in the village.

Beyond the village rise the substantial remains of 13th-century **Skipness Castle** ( ☻ 24hr), a former possession of the Lords of the Isles. It's a striking building, composed of dark-green local stone trimmed with contrasting red-brown sandstone from Arran. The tower house was added in the 16th century and was occupied until the 19th. From the top you can see the roofless, 13th-century **St Brendan's**

**Chapel** down by the shore; the kirkyard contains some excellent carved grave slabs.

**Skipness Seafood Cabin** ( ☎ 760207; sandwiches £2, mains £5-8; ☻ 11am-6pm Sun-Fri late May-Sep), in the grounds of nearby Skipness House, serves tea, coffee and home baking, as well as local fish and shellfish dishes. In fine weather you can eat at outdoor picnic tables with grand views of Arran.

Local bus 448 runs between Tarbert and Skipness (35 minutes, two daily Monday to Saturday).

At Claonaig, 2 miles southwest of Skipness, there's a daily car ferry to Lochranza on the Isle of Arran (passenger/car £4.65/21, 30 minutes, seven to nine daily).

## Isle of Gigha

☎ 01583 / pop 120

Gigha (pronounced *ghee*-a) is a low-lying island, 6 miles long by about a mile wide, that's famous for its sandy beaches and mild climate – subtropical plants thrive in the island's **Achamore Gardens** ( ☎ 505254; Achamore House; admission free, donation requested; ☻ 9am-dusk). Locally made Gigha cheese is sold in many parts of Argyll – there are several varieties produced on the island, including pasteurised goat's-milk cheese and oak-smoked cheddar.

The island's limited accommodation includes **Post Office House** ( ☎ 505251; www.gighastores .co.uk; r per person £22-25; **P** ), a Victorian house at the top of the hill above the ferry slip (it houses the island post office and shop as well as being a B&B), and the **Gigha Hotel** ( ☎ 505254; www.gigha.org.uk; r per person £35-48), 100m south of the post office, which serves up bar meals (£6 to £8), or if you're feeling peckish, four-course dinners (£30). You can also eat at the **Boat House Café Bar** ( ☎ 505123; mains £7-13; ☻ 11am-4pm & 6-11pm) near the ferry slip.

There's a range of self-catering cottages available as well (see www.gigha.org.uk for details). Camping is allowed on a grassy area beside the Boat House near the ferry slip – there's no charge but space is limited, so call the Gigha Hotel in advance to check availability, and book in at the hotel when you arrive.

CalMac runs a ferry from Tayinloan in Kintyre to Gigha (passenger/car £5.60/21 return, 20 minutes, hourly Monday to Saturday, six on Sunday) – only return fares are available. A bicycle costs an extra £2.20.

You can rent bikes from Post Office House or Gigha Hotel for £10 per day.

## Mid-Kintyre

At Glenbarr, 6 miles south of Tayinloan, is **Glenbarr Abbey Visitor Centre** ( ☎ 01583-421247; adult/child £3/2; ⊙ 10am-5pm Wed-Mon Easter-Oct), a centre for the Clan Macalister. This 18th-century house has a large collection of clothes, thimbles and china, and a pair of gloves worn by Mary, Queen of Scots. Angus Macalister, the laird of Glenbarr, will himself take you on an entertaining guided tour.

On the east coast of Kintyre is the pretty village of **Carradale**, with its mile-long sweep of golden beach on Carradale Bay. The **Network Heritage Centre** ( ☎ 01586-431296; admission free; ⊙ 10am-5pm Mon-Sat, 12.30-5pm Sun Jul & Aug, 10am-5pm Tue, Wed, Fri & Sat, 12.30-4pm Sun Easter-Jun & Sep–mid-Oct) is housed in the old school house, and has fishing, farming and forestry displays.

There are several interesting ruins in the area, including a vitrified Iron Age fort on the eastern point of Carradale Bay, and the 12th-century **Saddell Abbey** (5 miles south), founded by Somerled, Lord of the Isles.

## Campbeltown

☎ 01586 / pop 6000

Campbeltown, with its ranks of gloomy grey council houses, feels a bit like an Ayrshire mining town that's been placed incongruously on the shores of a beautiful Argyllshire harbour. It was once a thriving fishing port and whisky-making centre, but industrial decline and the closure of the former air force base at nearby Machrihanish saw Campbeltown's fortunes decline.

The town feels a very long way from anywhere else, a feeling intensified by the continuing failure to re-open the ferry link from Campbeltown to Ballycastle in Northern Ireland (every year the message from the government is, 'something will be done *next* year'). But renewal is in the air – the spruced-up seafront, with its flower beds, smart Victorian buildings and restored Art Deco cinema, lends the town a distinctly optimistic air.

The **tourist office** ( ☎ 552056; ⊙ 9am-5.30pm Mon-Sat) is beside the harbour. There are plenty of shops and banks in the nearby town centre.

### SIGHTS & ACTIVITIES

There were once no fewer than 32 distilleries in the Campbeltown area, but most closed down in the 1920s. Today, **Springbank Distillery** ( ☎ 552085; tours £3; ⊙ by arrangement 2pm Mon-Fri) is one of only three that now operate in town.

It is also one of the very few distilleries in Scotland that distils, matures and bottles all its whisky on the one site.

One of the most unusual sights in Argyll is in a cave on the southern side of the island of **Davaar**, at the mouth of Campbeltown Loch. On the wall of the cave is an eerie painting of the Crucifixion by local artist Archibald MacKinnon, dating from 1887. You can walk to the island at low tide across a shingle bar called the Dhorlinn (allow at least 1½ hours for the round trip), but make sure you're not caught by a rising tide – check tide times with the tourist office before you set off.

**Mull of Kintyre Seatours** ( ☎ 0870 720 0609; www.mull-of-kintyre.co.uk) operates two-hour high-speed boat trips (adult/child from £25/15) out of Campbeltown harbour to look for wildlife – seals, porpoises, minke whales, golden eagles and peregrine falcons – in the turbulent tidal waters beneath the spectacular sea cliffs of the Mull of Kintyre.

The **Mull of Kintyre Music Festival** ( ☎ 551053; www.mokfest.com), held in Campbeltown in late August, is a popular event featuring traditional Scottish and Irish music.

### GETTING THERE & AWAY

Scottish Citylink buses run from Campbeltown to Glasgow (£16, 4½ hours, three daily) via Tarbert, Inveraray, Arrochar and Loch Lomond. They also run to Oban (£17, four to five hours, three daily), changing buses at Inveraray.

British Airways/Loganair operates two flights daily, Monday to Friday, from Glasgow to Campbeltown (£50, 35 minutes).

## Mull of Kintyre

A narrow winding road, about 18 miles long, leads south from Campbeltown to the Mull of Kintyre, passing some good sandy beaches near Southend. The name of this remote headland was immortalised in Paul McCartney's famous song – the former Beatle owns a farmhouse in the area. A lighthouse marks the spot closest to Northern Ireland, whose coastline, only 12 miles away, is visible across the North Channel.

# ISLE OF ISLAY

☎ 01496 / pop 3400

The most southerly island of the Inner Hebrides, Islay (pronounced *isle*-a) is best known for its single malt whiskies, which have a distinctive smoky flavour. There are eight working distilleries, all of which welcome visitors and offer guided tours.

Islay's whisky industry contributes approximately £100 million a year to the government in excise duty and value-added tax (VAT); that's about £30,000 for every man, woman and child on the island. Little wonder that the islanders complain about the lack of government investment in the area.

With a list of over 250 recorded bird species, Islay also attracts bird-watchers. It's an important wintering ground for thousands of white-fronted and barnacle geese. As well as the whisky and wildfowl, there are miles of sandy beaches, pleasant walking, and good food and drink.

## ORIENTATION

There are two ferry terminals on the island, both served by ferries from Kennacraig in West Loch Tarbert – Port Askaig on the east coast and Port Ellen in the south. Islay airport lies midway between Port Ellen and Bowmore.

There's a camp site and bunkhouse at Kintra, near Port Ellen, and a camp site and youth hostel in Port Charlotte. If you want to camp elsewhere, ask permission first. Camping is prohibited on the Ardtalla and Dunlossit estates on the eastern side of Islay.

## INFORMATION

**Celtic House** ( ☎ 810304; The Square, Bowmore) Books about Islay, Jura and whisky.

**Islay Service Point** ( ☎ 810332; Jamieson St, Bowmore; ☷ 9am-12.30pm & 1.30-5pm Mon-Fri) Free internet access.

**Islay tourist office** ( ☎ 0870 720 0617; The Square, Bowmore; ☷ 9.30am-5.30pm Mon-Sat & 2-5pm Sun Jul & Aug, 10am-5pm Mon-Sat & 2-5pm Sun Apr-Jun, 10am-5pm Mon-Sat Sep & Oct)

**MacTaggart Community CyberCafé** ( ☎ 302693; 30 Mansfield Pl, Port Ellen; per 30min £1; ☷ noon-7pm) Internet access.

**MacTaggart Leisure Centre** ( ☎ 810767; School St, Bowmore; ☷ noon-9pm Mon-Fri, 10.30am-5.30pm Sat & Sun) Coin-operated laundrette (wash £3.75, dry £1.75).

## TOURS

**Islay Birding** ( ☎ 850010; www.islaybirding.co.uk) Provides full-day bird-watching tours (adult/child £40/20) of the island, and will pick you up from your accommodation.

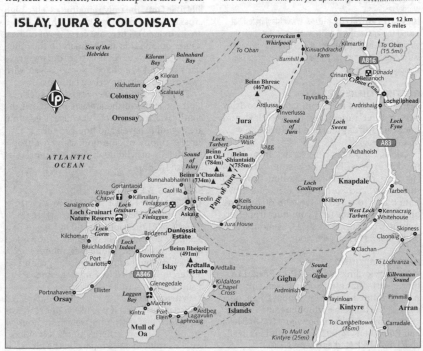

## ISLAY, JURA & COLONSAY

There are also two-hour dawn and dusk tours (£25 per person). Also offers bushcraft courses (£60 for a day) teaching outdoor survival skills.

**Islay Marine Charters** ( ☎ 850436) Based at Port Askaig, offering wildlife cruises through the Sound of Islay (adult/child £16/9) to Ardmore Island to see seals and seabirds, and to Loch Tarbert on Jura (£26/15) where you can spot red deer, wild goats, seals and possibly otters.

**Islay Sea Safaris** ( ☎ 07768 450000; www.islaysea safari.co.uk) Can arrange customised tours (£25 per person per hour) by sea from Port Ellen to visit some or all of Islay and Jura's distilleries in a single day, as well as bird-watching trips, coastal exploration, and trips to Jura's remote west coast and the Corryvreckan whirlpool.

**Islay Stalking** ( ☎ 850120; www.thegearach.co.uk) Here's your chance to stalk deer and other wildlife in the company of a gamekeeper, and shoot them not with a gun but with a camera. Morning and evening photographic tours are £20/10 per adult/child.

### FESTIVALS & EVENTS

**Feis Ile** (Islay Festival; www.islayfestival.org) Held at the end of May, this is a week-long celebration of traditional Scottish music and takes in the Islay Whisky Festival. Events include *ceilidhs* (informal entertainment and dance), pipe-band performances, distillery tours, barbecues and whisky tastings.

**Islay Jazz Festival** ( ☎ 810262; www.islayjazzfestival .co.uk) This annual three-day festival takes place over the second weekend in September. It sees a varied line-up of international talent playing at various venues across the island.

### GETTING THERE & AWAY

British Airways flies from Glasgow to Islay two or three times daily on weekdays and once on Saturday and Sunday (£90 one way, 45 minutes).

**CalMac** ( ☎ 302209) runs ferries from Kennacraig in West Loch Tarbert to Port Ellen (passenger/car £8.30/59, 2¼ hours, one to three daily) and Port Askaig (same fare, two hours, one to three daily). On Wednesday only in summer the ferry continues from Port Askaig to Colonsay (£4.40/23, 1¼ hours) and on to Oban (£12/57, 4¾ hours).

### GETTING AROUND

A bus service links Ardbeg, Port Ellen, Bowmore, Port Charlotte, Portnahaven and Port Askaig (limited service on Sunday). Pick up a copy of the timetable from the tourist office.

Taxis are available in Bowmore ( ☎ 810449) and Port Ellen ( ☎ 302155). Car hire is available from **D & N MacKenzie** ( ☎ 302300).

You can hire bikes in Bowmore and Port Charlotte.

## Port Ellen & Around

Port Ellen is the main point of entry for Islay. It has a **Co-op Food minimarket** ( ☯ 8am-8pm Mon-Sat, noon-7.30pm Sun), a pub and a bank (closed most afternoons and all day Wednesday); there's an ATM in the Spar shop around the corner from the bank. While there's nothing to see in the town itself, the coast stretching northeast from Port Ellen is one of the loveliest parts of the island.

There are three **whisky distilleries** in close succession: **Laphroaig** ( ☎ 302418; ☯ visitor centre 9am-5pm Mon-Fri, tours 10.15am & 2.15pm by appointment); **Lagavulin** ( ☎ 302400; ☯ tours 9.30am, 11.15am & 2.30pm Mon-Fri); and **Ardbeg** ( ☎ 302244; ☯ visitor centre 10am-5pm daily Jun-Aug, 10am-4pm Mon-Fri Sep-May, tours 10.30am, 11.30am, 2.30pm & 3.30pm Jun-Aug, 10.30am & 2.30pm Mon-Fri Sep-May). All guided tours are £3.

A pleasant bike ride leads past the distilleries to the atmospheric, age-haunted **Kildalton Chapel**, 8 miles northeast of Port Ellen. In the kirkyard is the exceptional late-8th-century **Kildalton Cross**, the only remaining Celtic high cross in Scotland (most surviving high crosses are in Ireland). There are carvings of biblical scenes on one side and animals on the other. There are also several extraordinary grave slabs around the chapel, some carved with swords and Celtic interlace patterns.

The kelp-fringed *skerries* (small rocky islands or reefs) of the **Ardmore Islands**, off the southeastern corner of Islay near Kildalton, are a wildlife haven and home to the second-largest colony of common seals in Europe. For details of wildlife cruises see the Tours section (p289).

### SLEEPING & EATING

**our pick** **Kintra Farm** ( ☎ 302051; www.kintrafarm .co.uk; Kintra; tent sites £3, per person £3, r per person £28-35; ☯ Apr-Sep) At the southern end of Laggan Bay, 3.5 miles northwest of Port Ellen, Kintra offers three bedrooms in a homely farmhouse B&B, and a basic but beautiful camping ground on buttercup-sprinkled turf amid the dunes with a sunset view across the beach.

**Oystercatcher B&B** ( ☎ 300409; 63 Frederick Cres, Port Ellen; r per person £25-30) If you like your breakfasts fishy, then this welcoming waterfront house is the place for you – there's smoked haddock, smoked salmon and kippers on the menu, as well as the usual stuff. Bedrooms are small but comfortable and nicely decorated.

**Glenmachrie Country Guest House** ( ☎ 305260; www .glenmachrie.com; per person from £60; **P** ) This delightful farmhouse B&B is 4 miles north of Port Ellen, set in a large landscaped garden where the kids can play safely. Dinner is a superb four-course affair using fresh local produce (veggie dishes available) with sunset views from the dining room. (Note that credit cards are not accepted – it's cash or cheque only.)

**our pick Old Kiln Café** ( ☎ 302244; Ardberg; mains £3-9; 10am-4pm daily Jun-Aug, 10am-3pm Mon-Fri Sep-Jun, lunch served from noon) Housed in the former malting kiln at Ardbeg Distillery, this well-run café serves hearty homemade soups such as sweet potato and chilli, tasty light meals (try a panini sandwich with haggis and apple chutney, or a platter of smoked Islay beef, venison and pastrami), and a range of home-baked desserts including traditional *clootie dumpling* (a rich steamed pudding filled with currants and raisins) with ice cream.

## Bowmore

The attractive Georgian village of Bowmore was built in 1768 to replace the village of Kilarrow, which just had to go – it was spoiling the view from the laird's house. Its centrepiece is the distinctive **Round Church** at the top of Main St, built in circular form to ensure that the devil had no corners to hide in.

Bowmore is in the centre of the island, 10 miles from both Port Askaig and Port Ellen, and is the island's main town. It has a **tourist office** ( ☎ 0870 720 0617; The Square), two banks with ATMs, and a **Co-op supermarket** (Main St; 8am-8pm Mon-Sat, 12.30-7pm Sun).

**Bowmore Distillery** ( ☎ 810671; School St; adult/child £2/1; visitor centre 9am-5pm daily Jul-Sep, 9am-5pm Mon-Sat Easter-Jun, 9am-5pm Mon-Fri & 9am-noon Sat Oct-Easter, tours 10am, 11am, 2pm & 3pm) is the only distillery on the island that still malts its own barley. The tour, which begins with an overblown 10-minute marketing video, is redeemed by a look at (and taste of) the germinating grain laid out in golden billows on the floor of the malting shed.

If the weather's bad, there's always the **MacTaggart Leisure Centre** ( ☎ 810767; School St; pool adult/child £2.70/1.70; pool 12.30-5pm Tue, 2-6pm Wed, 3.30-9pm Thu, 1-2pm & 3-4pm Fri, 2.30-3.30pm Sat, 10.30am-5.30pm Sun), with a 25m pool (heated using the waste energy from the distillery!), sauna and fitness centre.

**Islay House Square**, a collection of craft shops and studios 3 miles northeast of Bowmore at Bridgend, is home to **Islay Ales** ( ☎ 810014; www .islayales.com; 10.30am-5pm Mon-Sat, plus noon-4pm Sun Jun-Aug), a microbrewery that produces a range of real ales, all bottled by hand. After a tour of the premises, you can taste the ales for free, and buy a bottle or two to drink outdoors or back home (the brewery doesn't have a bar licence) – our favourite is Angus Og, a refreshing, summery pale ale.

You can hire **bikes** at the post office, near the church at the top of Main St, for £10 per day.

### SLEEPING & EATING

**Lambeth House** ( ☎ 810597; lambethguesthouse@tiscali .co.uk; Jamieson St; r per person £35-50) The Lambeth is a simple, good-value guesthouse with four bedrooms, and is a short stroll from the harbour. It also offers a two-course evening meal for £10.

**Lochside Hotel** ( ☎ 810244; www.lochsidehotel.co.uk; 19 Shore St; r per person from £45; ) The ten en-suite bedrooms at the Lochside are kitted out with chunky pine furniture, including one room adapted for wheelchair users. The conservatory dining room provides sweeping views over Loch Indaal, plus the bar boasts a range of 250 single malts.

**Harbour Inn** ( ☎ 810330; www.harbour-inn.com; The Square; s/d from £75/110) The plush seven-room Harbour Inn, smartly decorated with a nautical theme, is the poshest place in town. The restaurant (mains £16 to £24) has harbour views and serves fresh local oysters, lobster and scallops, Islay lamb and Jura venison. Food is served from noon to 2pm and 6pm to 9pm.

**Cottage Restaurant** ( ☎ 810422; 45 Main St; mains £4-7; 10am-4pm Mon-Sat) This old-fashioned, tartan-clad tearoom does a line in healthy home-cooked food, as well as some traditional artery-clogging café favourites such as sausage and chips.

## Port Charlotte

Eleven miles from Bowmore, on the opposite shore of Loch Indaal, is the attractive village of Port Charlotte. It has a **general store** ( 9am-12.30pm & 1.30-5.30pm Mon-Sat, 11.30am-1.30pm Sun) and post office, and you can hire **bikes** from the house opposite the Port Charlotte Hotel.

Islay's long history is lovingly recorded in the **Museum of Islay Life** ( ☎ 850358; adult/child £3/1; 10am-5pm Mon-Sat, 2-5pm Sun Easter-Sep, 10am-4pm Mon-Sat Oct-Easter), housed in the former Free

Church. Prize exhibits include an illicit still, 19th-century crofters' furniture, and a set of leather boots once worn by the horse that pulled the lawnmower at Islay House (so it wouldn't leave hoof-prints on the lawn!). There are also touch-screen computers displaying archive photos of Islay in the 19th and early 20th centuries.

The **Islay Natural History Visitor Centre** ( ☎ 850288; adult/child £3/1.50; ☺ 10am-4pm Mon-Sat Apr-Oct), next to the youth hostel, has displays explaining the island's natural history, with advice on where to see wildlife, and lots of interesting hands-on exhibits for kids.

The **Bruichladdich Distillery** ( ☎ 850190; www .bruichladdich.com; tours £4; ☺ 9am-5pm Mon-Fri & 10am-4pm Sat, tours 10.30am, 11.30am & 2.30pm), at the northern edge of the village, re-opened in 2001 with all its original Victorian equipment restored to working condition. Independently owned and independently minded, Bruichladdich (pronounced brook-*lah*-day) produces an intriguing range of distinctive, very peaty whiskies. It also runs a whisky 'academy', a five-day course during which you learn to malt, mash, brew, distil, cask and bottle your own whisky (£795 per person, including food and accommodation for four nights).

### SLEEPING & EATING

**Port Mor Campsite** ( ☎ 850441; tent sites per person £5) The sports field to the south of the village doubles as a camp site – there are toilets, showers, laundry and a children's play area in the main building.

**Islay Youth Hostel** (SYHA; ☎ 0870 004 1128; dm £13; ☺ Apr-Oct) This modern and comfortable hostel is housed in a former distillery building with views over the loch.

**Debbie's Minimarket** ( ☎ 850319; ☺ 9am-5.30pm Mon-Sat) The village shop and post office at Bruichladdich doubles as a deli that stocks good wine and posh picnic grub, and also serves the best coffee on Islay – sit at one of the outdoor tables and enjoy an espresso with a sea view.

**Croft Kitchen** ( ☎ 850230; mains lunch £3-7, dinner £11-14; ☺ snacks 10am-5pm, lunch noon-3pm, dinner 5.30-7.30pm) This laid-back little bistro serves as a café during the day and transforms into a restaurant serving quality meals in the evening.

**Port Charlotte Hotel** ( ☎ 850360; www.portcharlotte hotel.co.uk; bar meals £7-10, restaurant mains £15-22; ☺ restaurant 6.30-9pm, bar meals noon-2pm & 5-8pm; P ) This lovely old Victorian hotel has a stylish, candle-lit restaurant serving local seafood (seared scallops with braised leeks and truffle cream sauce), Islay beef, venison and duck. The bar is well stocked with Islay malts and real ales, and has a nook at the back with a view over the loch towards the Paps of Jura. Rooms are available (single/double £75/120).

## Portnahaven

Six miles southwest of Port Charlotte the road ends at **Portnahaven**, another pretty village that was purpose-built as a fishing harbour in the 19th century. A mile north of the village is the pretty little shell-sand beach of **Currie Sands**, with a lovely view of Orsay island.

The next inlet to the north of the beach is occupied by the world's first commercially viable, wave-powered electricity generating station, built on cliffs that are open to the Atlantic swell. The 500kW plant – known as the **Limpet** (land-installed, marine-powered energy transformer) – provides enough electricity to power 200 island homes.

## Loch Gruinart & Around

Seven miles north of Port Charlotte is **Loch Gruinart Nature Reserve**, where you can hear corncrakes in summer and see huge flocks of migrating ducks, geese and waders in spring and autumn; there's a hide with wheelchair access. The nearby **Royal Society for the Protection of Birds (RSPB) Information Centre** ( ☎ 850505; admission free; ☺ 10am-5pm Apr-Oct, 10am-4pm Nov-Mar) offers two- to three-hour guided walks around the reserve (£2 per person, 10am Thursday and 6pm Tuesday in August).

Three miles north of the reserve, at **Kilnave Chapel**, is a Celtic stone cross made from an improbably thin slab; though less elaborate than the cross at Kildalton, it is more delicate. The beach at **Killinallan**, northeast of the reserve, is one of Islay's best. You can walk for miles along the raised beaches on the coast to its north.

**Kilchoman Distillery** ( ☎ 850011; www.kilchoman distillery.com; Rockfield Farm, Kilchoman; tours £3.50; ☺ 10am-5.30pm Mon-Sat May-Sep, plus 10am-5.30pm Sun Jul & Aug, 10am-5pm Mon-Fri Apr & Oct-Dec, tours at 11am & 3pm), 5 miles southwest of Loch Gruinart, is Islay's newest, going into production in 2005. The distillery grows its own barley on Islay, and the visitor centre explores the history of farmhouse distilling on the island. But it'll be at least 2010 before we get to taste the fruits of its labours…

**ourpick** **Visitor Centre Café** (main £5-9; ☺ 10am-5pm Mon-Fri Mar-Oct, plus Sat Apr-Sep, plus Sun Jul & Aug) at Kilchoman Distillery rustles up an excellent lunch – crusty brown rolls filled with hot-smoked salmon and dill mayo, plus a bowl of rich, smoky *Cullen skink* on the side.

## Finlaggan

Lush meadows swathed in buttercups and daisies slope down to reed-fringed Loch Finlaggan, the medieval capital of the Lords of the Isles (see the boxed text, p29). This bucolic setting, 3 miles southwest of Port Askaig, was once the most important settlement in the Hebrides, the central seat of power of the Lords of the Isles from the 12th to the 16th centuries. From the little island at the northern end of the loch the descendants of Somerled administered their island territories and entertained visiting chieftains in their great hall. Little remains now except the tumbled ruins of houses and a chapel, but the setting is beautiful and the history fascinating. A wooden walkway leads over the reeds and water lilies to the island, where information boards describe the remains.

**Finlaggan Visitor Centre** ( ☎ 810629; admission free; ☺ 1-4.30pm May-Sep, 1-4.30pm Tue, Thu & Sun Apr, 1-4pm Tue & Thu Oct), in a nearby cottage, explains the site's history and archaeology. The island itself is open at all times.

Buses from Port Askaig stop at the road-end, from where it's a 15-minute walk to the loch.

## Port Askaig & Around

Port Askaig is little more than a hotel, a shop (with ATM), a petrol pump and a ferry pier, set in a picturesque nook halfway along the Sound of Islay, the strait that separates the islands of Islay and Jura.

There are two distilleries within easy reach: **Caol Ila Distillery** ( ☎ 840207; ☺ tours by appointment Mon-Fri), pronounced cull *ee*-la, a mile to the north, and **Bunnahabhain Distillery** ( ☎ 840646; www.bunnahabhain.com; ☺ 9am-4.30pm Mon-Fri Mar-Oct, by appointment Nov-Feb), pronounced boo-na-*ha*-ven, 3 miles north of Port Askaig. Both enjoy a wonderful location with great views across to Jura.

The rooms at the **Port Askaig Hotel** ( ☎ 840245; www.portaskaig.co.uk; s/d £39/90; **P** ), beside the ferry pier, seem pleasantly stuck in the 1970s, but the staff are warm and friendly, the breakfast is good and there's a great view of the Paps of Jura from the residents lounge. The beer

garden is a popular spot to sit and watch the comings and goings at the quay.

## ISLE OF JURA

☎ 01496 / pop 170

Jura lies off the coast of Argyll, long, dark and low like a vast Viking longship, its billowing sail the distinctive triple peaks of the Paps of Jura. A magnificently wild and lonely island, it's the perfect place to get away from it all – as George Orwell did in 1948. Orwell wrote his masterpiece *1984* while living at the remote farmhouse of Barnhill in the north of the island, describing it in a letter as 'a very un-get-at-able place'.

Jura takes its name from the Old Norse *dyr-a* (deer island) – an apt appellation, as the island supports a population of around 6000 red deer. The deer outnumber their human cohabitants by about 35 to one. Most of the island is occupied by deer-stalking estates, and access to the hills may be restricted during the stalking season (July to February); the Jura Hotel can provide details of areas to be avoided.

The community-run **Jura Service Point** ( ☎ 820161; Craighouse; ☺ 10am-1pm Mon-Fri), 400m north of the Jura Hotel, provides tourist information and free internet access. **Jura Stores** ( ☎ 820231; Craighouse; ☺ 9am-1pm & 2-5pm Mon-Fri, 9am-1pm & 2-4.30pm Sat) is the island's only shop. There's no bank or ATM, but you can get cashback on a debit card at the Jura Hotel.

## Sights & Activities

Apart from the superb wilderness walking and wildlife-watching, there's not a whole lot to do on the island apart from visit the **Isle of Jura Distillery** ( ☎ 820240; admission free; ☺ by appointment) or wander around the beautiful walled gardens of **Jura House** (adult/child £2.50/free; ☺ 9am-5pm year-round) at the southern end of the island. There's a lovely walk from the gardens down to a tiny white-sand beach where, if you're lucky, you might spot an otter, and in summer a **tea tent** ( ☺ 11am-5pm Mon-Fri, 11am-4pm Sun Jun-Aug) sells hot drinks, home baking, crafts and plants.

There's also the **Feolin Study Centre** (www.the isleofjura.co.uk; admission free; ☺ 9am-5pm), just south of the ferry slip at Feolin, which has a small exhibition on Jura's history and provides information on all aspects of the island's history, culture and wildlife.

There are also regular **ceilidhs** (evenings of traditional Scottish entertainment including

## THE SCOTTISH MAELSTROM

It may look innocuous on the map, but the Gulf of Corryvreckan – the 1km-wide channel between the northern end of Jura and the island of Scarba – is home to one of the three most notorious tidal whirlpools in the world (the others are the Maelstrom in Norway's Lofoten Islands, and the Old Sow in Canada's New Brunswick).

The tide doesn't just rise and fall twice a day, it flows – dragged around the earth by the gravitational attraction of the moon. On the west coast of Scotland, the rising tide – known as the flood tide – flows northwards. As the flood moves up the Sound of Jura, to the east of the island, it is forced into a narrowing bottleneck jammed with islands and builds up to a greater height than the open sea to the west of Jura. As a result, millions of gallons of sea water pour westwards through the Gulf of Corryvreckan at speeds of up to 8 knots – an average sailing yacht is going fast at 6 knots.

The Corryvreckan whirlpool forms where this mass of moving water hits an underwater pinnacle, which rises from the 200m-deep sea bed to within just 28m of the surface, and swirls over and around it. The turbulent waters create a magnificent spectacle, with white-capped breakers, standing waves, bulging boils and overfalls, and countless miniature maelstroms whirling around the main vortex.

Corryvreckan is at its most violent when a flooding spring tide, flowing west through the gulf, meets a westerly gale blowing in from the Atlantic. In these conditions, standing waves up to 5m high can form and dangerously rough seas extend more than 3 miles west of Corryvreckan, a phenomenon known as the Great Race.

You can see the whirlpool by making the long hike to the northern end of Jura (check tide times at Jura Hotel, and see Walking, below, for walk details), or by taking a boat trip from Islay (see Tours, p289), Easdale (p302) or Crinan (p285).

music, song and dance) held throughout the year where visitors are made very welcome; check the notice board outside Jura Stores for announcements.

## WALKING

There are few proper footpaths on Jura, and any off-the-beaten-path exploration will involve rough going through giant bracken, knee-deep bogs and thigh-high tussocks. The only real trail is **Evans' Walk**, a stalkers' path that leads for 6 miles from the main road through a pass in the hills to a hunting lodge above the remote sandy beach at Glenbatrick Bay. The path leaves the road 4 miles north of Craighouse (just under a mile north of the bridge over the Corran River). The first 0.75 mile is hard going along an interwoven braid of faint, squelchy trails through lumpy bog; aim at or just left of the cairn on the near horizon. The path firms up and is easier to follow after you cross a stream. On the descent on the far side of the pass look out for wild orchids and sundew, and keep an eye out for adders basking in the sun. Allow six hours for the 12-mile round trip.

Another good walk is to a viewpoint for the **Corryvreckan whirlpool** (see boxed text, above),

the great tidal race between the northern end of Jura and the island of Scarba. From the northern end of the public road at Lealt you hike along a 4WD track past Barnhill to Kinuachdrachd Farm (6 miles). About 30m before the farm buildings a footpath forks left (there's an inconspicuous wooden signpost low down) and climbs up the hill-side before traversing rough and boggy ground to a point 50m above the northern tip of the island. A rocky slab makes a natural grandstand for viewing the turbulent waters of the Gulf of Corryvreckan; if you have timed it right (check tide times at the Jura Hotel), you will see the whirlpool as a writhing mass of white water diagonally to your left and over by the Scarba shore. Allow five to six hours for the round trip (16 miles) from the road end.

Climbing the **Paps of Jura** is a truly tough hill walk over ankle-breaking scree that requires good fitness and navigational skills (you'll need eight hours for the 11 long, hard and weary miles). A good place to start is by the bridge over the Corran River, 3 miles north of Craighouse. The first peak you reach is Beinn a'Chaolais (734m), the second is Beinn an Oir (784m) and the third is Beinn Shiantaidh (755m). Most people also climb Corra

Bheinn (569m), before joining Evans' Walk to return to the road. If you succeed in bagging all four, you can reflect on the fact that the record for the annual Paps of Jura fell race is just three hours!

There are easier **short walks** (one or two hours) east along the coast from Jura House, and north along a 4WD track from Feolin. *Jura – A Guide for Walkers* by Gordon Wright (£2) is available from the tourist office in Bowmore, Islay.

## Sleeping & Eating

Places to stay on the island are very limited, so book ahead – don't rely on just turning up and hoping to find a bed. Most of Jura's accommodation is in self-catering cottages that are let by the week (see www.juradevelopment.co.uk).

You can camp for free in the field below the Jura Hotel (ask at the bar first, and pop a donation in the bottle); there are toilets and hot showers (£1 coin needed) in the block behind the hotel.

**Kinuachdrachd Farm** ( ☎ 07899 912116; joanmikekd@ hotmail.com; dm £7, d £35) There is a basic bunkhouse and more luxurious farmhouse B&B accommodation at this remote farm in the far north of the island. You can hike or bike here, or arrange for the owner to come and pick you up from the end of the public road at Lealt.

**Jura Hotel** ( ☎ 820243; www.jurahotel.co.uk; Craighouse; s/d from £47/82; **P** ) The 18-room Jura is the most comfortable place to stay on the island; ask for a room at the front with a view of the bay. The hotel also serves decent bar meals (£6 to £10) and the bar itself is a very sociable place to spend the evening. Food is served from noon to 2pm and 6.30pm to 9pm.

## Getting There & Away

A car ferry operated by **ASP Seascot** ( ☎ 840681) shuttles between Port Askaig on Islay and Feolin on Jura (passenger return £2.50, bicycle free, car and driver return £14, five minutes, hourly Monday to Saturday, every two hours Sunday). There is no direct car-ferry connection to the mainland.

**Gemini Cruises** ( ☎ 01546-830238; www.gemini-crinan .co.uk; Kilmahumaig, Crinan) operates a water-taxi service on demand and will take passengers from Crinan on the mainland to the north end of Jura (£50 one way for up to 12 passengers).

From Easter to September, **Lorn Ferry Service** ( ☎ 01951-200320; www.colonsay.org.uk/4jayne.html) runs a pedestrian- and bicycle-only ferry from Loch Tarbert on Jura to Colonsay (£15, two hours, one daily Tuesday and Friday). Prior booking is essential. (At the time of research this service was suspended, but may start up again.)

## Getting Around

**Alex Dunnachie** ( ☎ 820314) runs a minibus service between Feolin and Craighouse, timed to coincide with ferry arrivals and departures at Feolin. One or two of the runs continue north as far as Inverlussa.

**Mike Richardson** ( ☎ 07899 912116) operates a Landrover taxi service from the road end at Lealt to Kinuachdrachd Farm for those wanting to shorten the hike to the Corryvreckan whirlpool (minimum £20 for two people, plus £5 a head).

You can hire bikes from **Jura Bike Hire** ( ☎ 07092 180747) at Bramble Cottage in Keils, a mile northeast of Craighouse.

# ISLE OF COLONSAY

☎ 01951 / pop 100

Legend has it that when St Columba set out from Ireland in 563, his first landfall was Colonsay. But on climbing a hill he found he could still see the distant coast of his homeland, and pushed on further north to found his monastery in Iona, leaving behind only his name (Colonsay means 'Columba's Isle').

Colonsay is a connoisseur's island, a little jewel box of varied delights, none exceptional but each exquisite – an ancient priory, a woodland garden, a golden beach – set amid a Highland landscape in miniature: rugged, rocky hills, cliffs and sandy strands, machair and birch woods, even a trout loch. Here, hill walkers bag 'McPhies' – defined as 'eminences in excess of 300ft' (90m) – instead of Munros (see boxed text, p62). There are 22 in all; the super-competitive will bag them all in one day.

## Orientation & Information

The ferry pier is at **Scalasaig**, the main village, where you'll find a **general store** ( ☼ 9am-1pm & 2-5.30pm Mon & Wed-Fri, 9am-1pm Tue & Sat), post office, public telephone and free internet access at the **Service Point** ( ☎ 200263; ☼ 9.30am-12.30pm Mon-Fri). There's no tourist office and no bank or ATM on the island. General information is available at the CalMac waiting room beside the ferry pier, and at www.colonsay.org.uk.

The tiny **Colonsay Bookshop** ( ☎ 200232; 2-5pm Mon, Tue & Thu-Sat, 12.30-5pm Wed) at Kilchattan, on the west side of the island, has an excellent range of books on Hebridean history and culture.

## Sights & Activities

If the tides are right, don't miss the chance to walk across the half-mile of cockleshell-strewn sand that links Colonsay to the smaller island of Oronsay. Here you can explore the 14th-century ruins of **Oronsay Priory**, one of the best-preserved medieval priories in Scotland. There are two beautiful late-15th-century stone crosses in the kirkyard, but the highlight is the collection of superb 15th- and 16th-century carved grave slabs in the Prior's House; look for the ugly little devil trapped beneath the sword-tip of the knight on the right-hand side of the two horizontal slabs. The island is accessible on foot for about 1½ hours either side of low water, and it's a 45-minute walk from the road-end on Colonsay to the priory. There are tide tables posted at the ferry terminal in Scalasaig.

The **Woodland Garden** ( ☎ 200211; Kiloran; admission free; garden dawn-dusk, café 9am-5pm Wed & Fri Easter-Sep) at Colonsay House, 1.5 miles north of Scalasaig, is tucked in an unexpected fold of the landscape and is famous for its outstanding collection of hybrid rhododendrons and unusual trees. The formal walled garden around the mansion has a terrace café.

There are good sandy beaches at several points around the coast but **Kiloran Bay** in the northwest, a scimitar-shaped strand of dark golden sand, is outstanding. If there are too many people here for you, walk the 3 miles north to beautiful **Balnahard Bay**, accessible only on foot or by boat.

Back at Scalasaig, the **Colonsay Brewery** ( ☎ 200190; www.colonsaybrewery.co.uk; shop 10.30am-1pm & 2.30-5.30pm Wed, 4-7pm Fri & Sun, 10am-1pm Sat) offers you the chance to have a look at how it produces its hand-crafted ales – the Colonsay IPA is a grand pint.

**Kevin & Christa Byrne** ( ☎ 200320; byrne@colonsay .org.uk) offer guided tours on foot (£20 per hour per tour for up to eight people) or by mini-bus (£25 per hour per tour), and boat trips for fishing (£15 per person), seal- and bird-watching (£25 per person) or whale-spotting (£30 per person).

## Sleeping & Eating

Short-stay accommodation on Colonsay is limited and should be booked before coming to the island. Wild camping is allowed, as long as you abide by the provisions of the Scottish Outdoor Access Code (p57). See www.colonsay .org.uk for self-catering accommodation options.

**Keepers Backpackers Lodge** ( ☎ 200312; Kiloran; dm £12-14, tw £32) Set in a former gamekeeper's house near Colonsay House, this lodge is about 30 minutes' walk from the ferry terminal (you can arrange to be picked up at the pier). Advance bookings are essential. You can hire bikes here for £5 per day.

**our pick The Colonsay** ( ☎ 200316; www.thecolonsay .com; Scalasaig; s/d from £60/110; P ) Completely refurbished in 2007, this wonderfully laid-back hotel is set in an atmospheric old inn dating from 1750, a short walk uphill from the ferry pier. The bar is a convivial melting pot of locals, guests, hikers, cyclists and visiting yachties, and the stylish restaurant (mains £9 to £18) offers down-to-earth cooking using local produce as much as possible, from Colonsay oysters and lobsters to herbs and salad leaves from Colonsay House gardens. Food is served from noon to 2pm and 6pm to 9pm.

**Island Lodges** ( ☎ 200320; byrne@colonsay.org.uk; Scalasaig; chalets 2-night stay £150-195) These comfortable and modern self-catering holiday chalets, sleeping from two to five people, are just 10 minutes' walk from the ferry pier at Scalasaig. You can check last-minute availability at www.colonsay.org.uk.

**Pantry** ( ☎ 200325; 9am-8pm Mon-Fri, 9am-6pm Sat, 2.30-8pm Sun Apr-Sep) This tearoom, close to the ferry pier, serves up light meals, snacks and ice creams. It also opens from October to March on the days that the ferry calls.

## Getting There & Around

From April to October CalMac operates a car ferry from Oban to Colonsay (passenger/car £12/57, 2¼ hours, one daily except Saturday); from November to March the ferry runs on Monday, Wednesday and Friday only.

From April to October, on Wednesday only, the ferry from Kennacraig on the Kintyre peninsula to Islay's Port Askaig continues to Colonsay. A day trip from Kennacraig or Port Askaig to Colonsay allows you six hours on the island; a day return fare from Port Askaig to Colonsay is £7.55/40 per passenger/car.

From Easter to September, **Lorn Ferry Service** (☎ 01951-200320; www.colonsay.org.uk/4jayne.html) runs a pedestrian- and bicycle-only ferry from Colonsay to Loch Tarbert on Jura, Port Askaig on Islay and Uisken on Mull (all routes £15). Prior booking is essential. (At the time of research this service was suspended, but may start up again.)

A 90-minute **bus tour** (☎ 200320) of the island costs £7.50, available Monday and Friday, departing at 10.30am from the ferry pier. Booking is essential.

From January 2008 **Highland Airways** (www .highlandairways.co.uk) will operate flights twice daily, three days a week, from Connel Airfield (near Oban) to the islands of Colonsay, Coll and Tiree. The return fare to any of the islands will be around £65.

# OBAN & MULL

## OBAN

☎ 01631 / pop 8120

Oban is a peaceful waterfront town on a delightful bay, with sweeping views to Kerrera and Mull. OK, that first bit about peaceful is true only in winter; in summer the town centre is a heaving mass of humanity, its streets jammed with traffic and crowded with holidaymakers, day-trippers and travellers headed for the islands. But the setting is still lovely.

There's not a huge amount to see in the town itself, but it's an appealingly busy place with some excellent restaurants and lively pubs, and it's the main gateway to the islands of Mull, Iona, Colonsay, Barra, Coll and Tiree.

## Orientation

The bus, train and ferry terminals are all grouped conveniently together next to the harbour on the southern edge of the bay. The tourist office is one block east of the train station, and George St, the main drag, runs north along the promenade to North Pier. From the pier, Corran Esplanade runs round the northern edge of the bay to the youth hostel.

## Information

**Esplanade post office** (☎ 562340; Corran Esplanade)
**Fancy That** (☎ 562996; 112 George St; per hr £3; ☼ 10am-5pm) Internet access.
**Lorn & Islands District General Hospital** (☎ 567500; Glengallan Rd) Southern end of town.

**Main post office** (☎ 510450; Lochside St; ☼ 8am-6pm Mon-Sat, 10am-1pm Sun) Inside Tesco supermarket.
**Police station** (☎ 510500; Albany St)
**Tourist office** (☎ 563122; www.oban.org.uk; Argyll Sq; ☼ 9am-7pm daily Jul & Aug, 9am-5.30pm Mon-Sat & 10am-5pm Sun May, Jun & Sep, 9am-5.30pm Mon-Sat Oct-Apr) Internet access is also available for £1 per 12 minutes.
**Waterstone's** (☎ 571455; 12 George St; ☼ 9am-5.30pm Mon, Tue & Thu-Sat, 9.30am-5.30pm Wed, 11am-5pm Sun) Bookshop.

## Sights

Crowning the hill above the town centre is the Victorian folly known as **McCaig's Tower** (admission free; ☼ 24hr). Its construction was commissioned in 1890 by local worthy John Stuart McCaig, an art critic, philosophical essayist and banker, with the philanthropic intention of providing work for unemployed stonemasons. To reach it on foot, make the steep climb up Jacob's Ladder (a flight of stairs) from Argyll St and then follow the signs. The views over the bay are worth the effort. **Pulpit Hill**, to the south of the bay, is another excellent viewpoint; the footpath starts to the right of Maridon House B&B on Dunuaran Rd.

**Oban Distillery** (☎ 572004; Stafford St; guided tour £5; ☼ 9.30am-5pm Mon-Sat Easter-Oct, plus noon-5pm Sun Jul-Sep, 9.30am-5pm Mon-Fri Nov-Dec & Feb-Easter, closed Jan) has been producing Oban single malt whisky since 1794. There are guided tours available (last tour begins one hour before closing time), but even without a tour, it's still worth a look at the small exhibition in the foyer.

Military buffs should visit the little **War & Peace Museum** (☎ 570007; www.obanmuseum.org.uk; Corran Esplanade; admission free; ☼ 10am-6pm Mon-Sat & 10am-4pm Sun May-Sep, 10am-4pm daily Mar & Apr), which chronicles Oban's role in WWII as a base for Catalina seaplanes and as a marshalling area for Atlantic convoys.

The **Oban Rare Breeds Farm Park** (☎ 770608; www.obanrarebreeds.com; New Barran Farm, Glencruitten; adult/child £6/4; ☼ 10am-6pm late-Mar-Oct) is a favourite with children, who get to meet all kinds of animals at close quarters, including rabbits, goats, cows, deer and even llamas. The farm maintains rare breeds of domesticated animals, including Tamworth pigs, Shetland and Soay sheep and longhorn cattle; it is 2 miles east of the town centre.

A pleasant 1-mile north along the coast road beyond Corran Esplanade leads to **Dunollie Castle**, built by the MacDougalls of Lorn in the 13th century and unsuccessfully besieged for a year during the 1715 Jacobite rebellion. It's always open but very much a ruin. You can continue along this road to the beach at **Ganavan Sands**, 2.5 miles from Oban.

## Activities

A tourist-office leaflet lists local **bike rides**, which include a 7-mile Gallanach circular tour, a 16-mile route to the Isle of Seil and routes to Connel, Glenlonan and Kilmore. You can hire mountain bikes from **Evo Bikes** ( ☎ 566996; 29 Lochside St; ⏱ 9am-5.30pm Mon-Sat), opposite Tesco swupermarket, for £15 per day.

Based at North Connel, **sea-kayaking** coach **Rowland Woollven** ( ☎ 710417; www.rwoollven.co.uk) offers instruction for beginners and guided

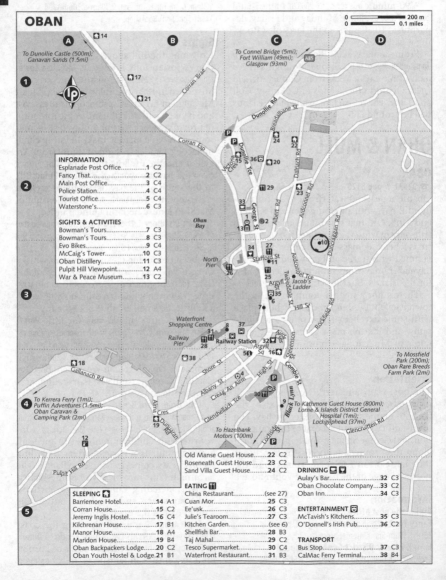

# OBAN

0 — 200 m
0 — 0.1 miles

To Dunollie Castle (500m);
Ganavan Sands (1.5mi)

To Connel Bridge (5mi);
Fort William (49mi);
Glasgow (93mi)

Corran Brae

Dunollie Rd

Breadalbane St

Corran Esp

Corran Esp

Dunollie Tce

Victoria Cres

George St

Albert Rd

Dalriach Rd

Ardconnel Rd

Duncraggan Rd

**INFORMATION**
Esplanade Post Office.............1 C2
Fancy That.............................2 C2
Main Post Office.....................3 C4
Police Station.........................4 C4
Tourist Office.........................5 C4
Waterstone's..........................6 C3

**SIGHTS & ACTIVITIES**
Bowman's Tours......................7 C3
Bowman's Tours......................8 C3
Evo Bikes...............................9 C4
McCaig's Tower.....................10 C3
Oban Distillery......................11 C3
Pulpit Hill Viewpoint.............12 A4
War & Peace Museum...........13 C2

Oban Bay

North Pier

Stafford St

Ardconnel Tce

Tweeddale St

Jacob's Ladder

Argyll St

Hill St

Rockfield Rd

Waterfront Shopping Centre

Railway Pier

Railway Station

Argyll Sq

Stevenson St

Combie St

To Mossfield Park (200m);
Oban Rare Breeds Farm Park (2mi)

Gallanach Rd

Shore St

Albany St

Creag An Airm

High St

Black Lynn

To Kathmore Guest House (800m);
Lorne & Islands District General Hospital (1mi);
Lochgilphead (37mi)

To Kerrera Ferry (1mi);
Puffin Adventures (1.5mi);
Oban Caravan & Camping Park (2mi)

Alma Cres

Dunuaran

Glenshellach Tce

To Hazelbank Motors (100m)

Lochside St

Glencruitten Rd

Pulpit Hill Rd

**SLEEPING**
Barriemore Hotel....................14 A1
Corran House........................15 C2
Jeremy Inglis Hostel...............16 C4
Kilchrenan House...................17 B1
Manor House.........................18 A4
Maridon House......................19 B4
Oban Backpackers Lodge........20 C2
Oban Youth Hostel & Lodge....21 B1

Old Manse Guest House.........22 C2
Roseneath Guest House.........23 C2
Sand Villa Guest House..........24 C2

**EATING**
China Restaurant.............(see 27)
Cuan Mor.............................25 C3
Ee'usk.................................26 C3
Julie's Tearoom.....................27 C3
Kitchen Garden.................(see 6)
Shellfish Bar.........................28 B3
Taj Mahal............................29 C3
Tesco Supermarket...............30 C4
Waterfront Restaurant...........31 B3

**DRINKING**
Aulay's Bar...........................32 C3
Oban Chocolate Company......33 C2
Oban Inn.............................34 C3

**ENTERTAINMENT**
McTavish's Kitchens...............35 C3
O'Donnell's Irish Pub.............36 C2

**TRANSPORT**
Bus Stop..............................37 C3
CalMac Ferry Terminal...........38 B4

tours (£100 for a full day) for more experienced paddlers in the waters around Oban.

If you fancy exploring the underwater world, **Puffin Adventures** ( ☎ 566088; www.puffin .org.uk; Port Gallanach) offers a 1½-hour Try-a-Dive package (£58) for complete beginners.

Various operators offer **boat trips** to spot seals and other marine wildlife, departing from the North Pier slipway (adult/child £7/5); ask for details at the tourist office.

## Tours

From April to October, **Bowman's Tours** ( ☎ 563221; www.bowmanstours.co.uk; Railway Pier & Queens Park) offers a Three Isles day trip from Oban that visits Mull, Iona and Staffa (adult/child £44/22, 10 hours, daily); the crossing to Staffa is weather dependent. A shorter day trip visits Mull and Iona only (£32/16, eight hours, daily).

Bowman's also runs a **wildlife tour** (adult/child £44/22) departing from Oban at 10am Sunday to Friday from early May to late July. The trip takes in a ferry crossing to Craignure on Mull, travel by coach to Fionnphort, and a cruise around Staffa and the Treshnish Isles, plus two hours ashore on Lunga to visit a puffin colony, returning to Oban at 8pm.

## Festivals & Events

**Argyllshire Gathering** ( ☎ 562671; www.obangames .com; adult/child £8/4) Held over two days in late August, this is one of the most important events on the Scottish Highland games calendar and includes a prestigious pipeband competition. The main games are held at Mossfield Park on the eastern edge of town.

**West Highland Yachting Week** ( ☎ 563309; www .whyw.co.uk) At the end of July/beginning of August, Oban becomes the focus of one of Scotland's biggest yachting events. Hundreds of yachts cram into the harbour and the town's bars are jammed with thirsty sailors.

## Sleeping

Despite having lots of B&B accommodation, Oban's beds can still fill up quickly in July and August so try to book ahead. If you can't find a bed in Oban, consider staying at Connel, 4 miles to the north.

### BUDGET

**Oban Caravan & Camping Park** ( ☎ 562425; www .obancaravanpark.com; Gallanachmore Farm; tent site £11.50; Apr-Oct) This camping ground has a superb location overlooking the Sound of Kerrera, 2.5 miles south of Oban. The quoted rate includes

up to two people and a car; extra people are £2 each. A one-person tent with no car is £5.

**Jeremy Inglis Hostel** ( ☎ 565065; jeremyinglis@ mctavishs.freeserve.co.uk; 21 Airds Cres; dm £9.5-10.50, tw £18) This bargain place is more of a basic B&B than a hostel – most 'dorms' have only two or three beds, and are decorated with books, flowers and cuddly toys. The kitchen is a little cramped, but the owner is friendly and knowledgeable (and makes delicious home-made jam). The price includes a continental breakfast.

**Oban Backpackers Lodge** ( ☎ 562107; www.oban backpackers.com; Breadalbane St; dm £12.50-13.50; ) This is a friendly place with a good vibe and an attractive communal area with lots of sofas and armchairs. From the train station, walk 800m north along George St, past the cinema, and veer right into Breadalbane St.

**Oban Youth Hostel & Lodge** (SYHA; ☎ 0870 004 1144; Corran Esplanade; dm £13-15, r per person £15-17; ) Oban's SYHA hostel is set in a grand Victorian villa on the Esplanade, 0.75 miles north of the train station. The metal bunks are a bit creaky, but there are good showers and the lounge has great views across Oban Bay. The neighbouring lodge has four-bedded rooms with en-suite bathrooms.

**Corran House** ( ☎ 566040; www.corranhouse.co.uk; 1 Victoria Cres; dm £15, s/d from £25/40; ) The family-friendly Corran House has a nice waterfront location and offers big comfy beds in four- and six-bed dorms, as well as twin and double rooms. Facilities include a kitchen, a laundry and bike hire.

### MIDRANGE

**Maridon House** ( ☎ 562670; maridonhse@aol.com; Dunuaran Rd; s/d £30/54) The bright blue, flower-bedecked Maridon House has eight rooms (all with private bathroom), and is only a few minutes' walk from the ferry terminal. The owners are very helpful and will provide a vegetarian breakfast if you ask.

**Kilchrenan House** ( ☎ 562663; www.kilchrenanhouse .co.uk; Corran Esplanade; r per person £32-45; ) You'll get a warm welcome at the Kilchrenan, an elegant Victorian villa built for a textile magnate in 1883. Most of the rooms have views across Oban Bay, but Nos 5 and 9 are the best – No 5 has a huge freestanding bath tub, perfect for soaking weary bones.

**Barriemore Hotel** ( ☎ 566356; www.barriemore-hotel .co.uk; Corran Esplanade; s/d from £55/80; ) The Barriemore enjoys a grand location, overlooking the entrance to Oban Bay. There are 13 spacious rooms – ask for one with a sea view – a guest lounge with magazines and newspapers, and plump Loch Fyne kippers on the breakfast menu.

**Old Manse Guest House** ( ☎ 564886; www.obanguesthouse.co.uk; Dalriach Rd; s/d from £61/72; P 🖫 ) Set on a hillside above the town, the Old Manse commands great views over to Kerrera and Mull. The sunny, brightly decorated bedrooms have some nice touches (a couple of wine glasses and a corkscrew), and kids are made welcome.

Other recommendations:

**Sand Villa Guest House** ( ☎ 562803; www.holiday oban.co.uk; Breadalbane St; r per person £25-30)

**Roseneath Guest House** ( ☎ 562929; www.rose neathoban.com; Dalriach Rd; s/d from £35/54; P )

**Kathmore Guest House** ( ☎ 562104; www.kathmore .co.uk; Soroba Rd; s £35-60, d £50-70; P )

**TOP END**

**Manor House** ( ☎ 562087; www.manorhouseoban.com; Gallanach Rd; s/d from £80/145; P ) Built in 1780 for the duke of Argyll as part of his Oban estates, the Manor House is now one of Oban's finest hotels. It has small but elegant rooms in Georgian style, a posh bar frequented by local and visiting yachties, and a fine restaurant serving Scottish and French cuisine. Children under 12 are not welcome.

## Eating

There's no shortage of places to eat in Oban. Most are strung out along the bay between the train station and North Pier, and along George St.

**BUDGET**

ourpick **Shellfish Bar** (Railway Pier; sandwiches £3; 🕑 9am- 6pm) If you want to savour superb Scottish seafood without the expense of an upmarket restaurant, head for Oban's famous seafood stall – it's the green shack on the quayside. Here you can buy fresh and cooked seafood to take away – prawn sandwiches, dressed crab, and fresh oysters for only 55p each.

**Julie's Tearooms** ( ☎ 565952; 37 Stafford St; mains £3-7; 🕑 10am-5pm Tue-Sat) Nip into Julie's neat little café for homemade soup with crusty bread, tea and a scone, or some delicious Luca's ice cream.

ourpick **Kitchen Garden** ( ☎ 566332; 14 George St; mains £3-7; 🕑 9am-5pm Mon-Sat, 10.30am-5pm Sun, 6-9pm Thu-Sat) This deli is packed with delicious

picnic food, and also has a great little café on a mezzanine floor above the shop – good coffee, scones and cakes, and homemade soups and sandwiches.

For takeaway food, try the **Taj Mahal** ( ☎ 566400; 146 George St; mains £5-9; 🕑 noon-2pm & 5pm-midnight) for Indian food, or **China Restaurant** ( ☎ 563575; 39 Stafford St; mains £7-10; 🕑 noon-2pm & 5-10.30pm) for Chinese.

Self-caterers and campers can stock up at **Tesco** (Lochside St; 🕑 8am-10pm Mon-Sat, 9am-6pm Sun).

**MIDRANGE & TOP END**

**Cuan Mor** ( ☎ 565078; 60 George St; mains £8-12; 🕑 food served noon-4pm & 6-10pm) This always-busy bar and bistro sports a no-nonsense menu of old favourites – from haddock and chips to sausage and mash with onion gravy – spiced with a few more sophisticated dishes such as scallops with black pudding and raisin vinaigrette.

ourpick **Waterfront Restaurant** ( ☎ 563110; Waterfront Centre, Railway Pier; mains £8-19; 🕑 noon-2.15pm & 5.30-9.30pm) Housed in a converted seamen's mission, the Waterfront's stylish, unfussy décor – dusky pink and carmine with pine tables and local art on the walls – does little to distract from the superb seafood freshly landed at the quay just a few metres away. The menu ranges from crispy-battered haddock and chips to pan-fried scallops with garlic butter and crab spring rolls. There's an early evening menu (5.30pm to 6.45pm) offering a choice of half-a-dozen main courses at £8 to £10, or soup followed by fish and chips for £9.75.

**Ee'usk** ( ☎ 565666; North Pier; mains £12-20; 🕑 noon-3pm & 6-10pm) Bright and modern Ee'usk (it's how you pronounce *iasg*, the Gaelic word for fish) occupies Oban's prime location on the North Pier, where floor-to-ceiling windows allow diners on two levels to enjoy views over the harbour to Kerrera and Mull, all the while sampling a seafood menu ranging from fragrant Thai fish cakes to langoustines with chilli and ginger. A little overpriced, perhaps, but both food and location are first class.

## Drinking

**Oban Chocolate Company** ( ☎ 566099; 34 Corran Esplanade; 🕑 10am-5pm Mon-Sat Apr-Sep, plus 12.30-4pm Sun Jul & Aug, 10am-5pm Tue-Sat Feb, Mar & Oct-Dec, closed Jan) This shop specialising in hand-crafted chocolates also has a café serving excellent coffee and hot chocolate, with big leather sofas in a window with a view of the bay.

**Oban Inn** ( ☎ 562484; Stafford St) The lively Oban Inn, overlooking the harbour by North Pier, is the best pub in town. It's a traditional bar with wood panelling, brass rails and stained glass, and has real ales, a wide range of single malt whiskies and good bar food (£7) – the *moules frites* (mussels and chips) are a local favourite. Food is served from noon to 8.30pm.

**Aulay's Bar** ( ☎ 562596; 8 Airds Cres) An authentic Scottish bar, Aulay's is cosy and low-ceilinged, its walls covered with old photographs of Oban ferries and other ships. It pulls in a mixed crowd of locals and visitors with its warm atmosphere and wide range of malt whiskies.

## Entertainment

**McTavish's Kitchens** ( ☎ 563064; George St; adult/child show only £4.50/2, show if dining £2.50/1; ☾ show 8pm May-Sep) The nightly 'Scottish show' here caters to the kilts-and-tartan tourist market, with Scottish country dancing, live bands, piping, fiddle music and Gaelic songs.

**O'Donnells Irish Pub** ( ☎ 564849; Breadalbane St; ☾ 2pm-1am Sun-Thu, 2pm-2am Fri & Sat) This Irish bar, opposite Oban Backpackers, has live entertainment – usually Celtic music – most nights.

## Getting There & Away
### BOAT

**CalMac** ( ☎ 566688; www.calmac.co.uk) ferries link Oban with the islands of Kerrera, Mull, Coll, Tiree, Lismore, Colonsay, Barra and Lochboisdale. See relevant island entries for details of ferry services. Information and reservations for all CalMac ferry services are available at Oban's ferry terminal. Ferries to the Isle of Kerrera depart from a separate jetty, about 2 miles southwest of Oban town centre.

### BUS

Scottish Citylink buses run to Oban from Glasgow (£15, three hours, four daily) via Inveraray; from Fort William (£10, 1½ hours, four daily), with connections to Inverness; and from Perth (£11, three hours, twice daily Friday to Monday) via Tyndrum and Killin.

**West Coast Motors** ( ☎ 0870 850 6687) bus 423 runs from Oban to Lochgilphead (£4.50, 1¾ hours, four daily Monday to Friday, two on Saturday) via Kilmartin.

The **West Highland Flyer** ( ☎ 07780 724248) is a minibus service that links Oban with Fort William (£8, 1¼ hours) and Mallaig (£16, 2½

hours, one daily Monday to Saturday), where you can connect with the Skye Flyer (p381); it operates from April to late October. Bicycles can be carried for an extra £2.

### TRAIN

Oban is at the end of a scenic route that branches off the West Highland line at Crianlarich. There are up to three trains daily from Glasgow to Oban (£18, three hours).

The train's not much use for travelling north from Oban; to reach Fort William requires a detour via Crianlarich (3¾ hours). Take the bus instead.

## Getting Around
### BUS

The main bus stop is outside the train station. West Coast Motors bus 417 runs from here to Ganavan Sands via Oban Youth Hostel (five minutes, two per hour Monday to Saturday). Bus 431 connects the train station with the Kerrera ferry and Oban Caravan & Camping Park (15 minutes, two or three daily Monday to Saturday from late May to September).

### CAR

**Hazelbank Motors** ( ☎ 566476; www.obancarhire.co.uk; Lynn Rd; ☾ 8.30am-5.30pm Mon-Sat) rents small cars from £40/225 per day/week including VAT, insurance and CDW (collision damage waiver).

### TAXI

There's a taxi rank outside the train station. Otherwise, call **Oban Taxis** ( ☎ 564666) or **Kennedy's Taxis** ( ☎ 564172).

# AROUND OBAN
## Isle of Kerrera
☎ 01631 / pop 40

Some of the best **walking** in the area is on Kerrera, which faces Oban across the bay. There's a 6-mile circuit of the island (allow three hours), which follows tracks or paths (use Ordnance Survey map 49) and offers the chance to spot wildlife such as Soay sheep, wild goats, otters, golden eagles, peregrine falcons, seals and porpoises. At **Lower Gylen**, at the southern end of the island, there's a ruined castle.

**Kerrera Bunkhouse & Tea Garden** ( ☎ 570223; www .kerrerabunkhouse.com; Lower Gylen; dm £14) is a charming seven-bed bothy (hut) in a converted 18th-century stable near Gylen Castle, a 2-mile walk south from the ferry (keep left at the fork just past the telephone box). Booking ahead is recommended. You can get snacks and light meals at the nearby Tea Garden, which is open from 10.30am to 4.30pm Wednesday to Sunday, Easter to September.

There's a daily passenger **ferry** ( ☎ 563665) to Kerrera from Gallanach, about 2 miles southwest of Oban town centre, along Gallanach Rd (adult/child return £4/2, bicycle 50p, 10 minutes). From Easter to October it runs halfhourly from 10.30am to 12.30pm and 2pm to 6pm daily, plus 8.45am Monday to Saturday. From November to Easter there are five or six crossings a day.

## Isle of Seil

☎ 01852 / pop 500

The small island of Seil, 10 miles southwest of Oban, is best known for its connection to the mainland – the so-called **Bridge over the Atlantic**, designed by Thomas Telford and opened in 1793. The graceful bridge has a single stone arch and spans the narrowest part of the tidal Clachan Sound.

On the west coast of the island is the pretty conservation village of **Ellanbeich**, with its whitewashed cottages. It was built to house workers at the local slate quarries, but the industry collapsed in 1881 when the sea broke into the main quarry pit – the flooded pit can still be seen. The **Scottish Slate Islands Heritage Trust** ( ☎ 300449; Ellanbeich; adult/child £1.50/25p; ☷ 10.30am-5pm Apr-Jun & Sep, 10.30am-6pm Jul & Aug) displays fascinating old photographs illustrating life in the village in the 19th and early 20th centuries.

Coach tours flock to the **Highland Arts Studio** ( ☎ 300273; Easdale; ☷ 9am-9pm Apr-Sep, 10am-6pm Oct-Mar), a crafts and gift shop and a shrine to the eccentric output of the late 'poet, artist and composer' C John Taylor. Please, try to keep a straight face.

Just offshore from Ellanbeich is the small island of Easdale, which has more old slate-workers' cottages and the interesting **Easdale Island Folk Museum** ( ☎ 300370; adult/child £2.25/50p; ☷ 10.30am-5.30pm Apr-Oct). The museum has displays about the slate industry and life on the islands in the 18th and 19th centuries. Climb to the top of the island (a 38m peak!) for a great view of the surrounding area.

**Sea.fari Adventures** ( ☎ 300003; www.seafari.co.uk; Easdale Harbour) runs a series of exciting boat trips in high-speed RIBs (rigid inflatable boats) to the Corryvreckan whirlpool (adult/child from £30/22.50; see boxed text, p294) and the remote Garvellach Islands (£38/27.50); there's also a three-hour whale-watching trip (£39/29).

Anyone who fancies their hand at ducks and drakes should try to attend the **World Stone-Skimming Championships** (www.stoneskimming.com), held each year in Easdale on the last Sunday in September.

### GETTING THERE & AROUND

**West Coast Motors** ( ☎ 0870 850 6687) bus 418 runs four times a day, except Sunday, from Oban to Ellanbeich and on to North Cuan for the ferry to Luing.

**Argyll & Bute Council** ( ☎ 01631-562125) operates the daily passenger-only ferry service from Ellanbeich to Easdale island (£1.50 return, bicycles free, five minutes, every 30 minutes).

## Isle of Luing

☎ 01852 / pop 180

Luing (pronounced ling), about 6 miles long and 1.5 miles wide, is separated from the southern end of Seil by the narrow Cuan Sound. There are two attractive villages – **Cullipool** at the northern end and **Toberonochy** in the east – but Luing's main pleasures are scenic.

The **slate quarries** of Cullipool were abandoned in 1965. About 1.5 miles out to sea you can see the remains of the extensively quarried slate island of **Belnahua** – workers used to live on this remote and desolate rock. You can get a closer look on a boat trip from Easdale (see Sea.fari Adventures, left).

There are two Iron Age forts, the better being **Dun Leccamore**, about a mile north of Toberonochy. In Toberonochy itself are the ruins of the late medieval **Kilchattan Church** and a graveyard with unusual slate gravestones.

You can visit both villages, the fort, the ruined chapel and the scenic west coast on a pleasant 8-mile circular walk.

### GETTING THERE & AROUND

A small **car ferry** ( ☎ 01631-562125) runs from Cuan (on Seil) to Luing (passenger/car £1.50/6 return, bicycles free, five minutes, every 30 minutes).

There's a Monday to Saturday **postbus** ( ☎ 314243) service from the ferry to Cullipool and Toberonochy.

**Sunnybrae Caravan Park** ( ☎ 314274), just 50m from the ferry slip, rents bikes for £10/15 per half-/full day.

# ISLE OF MULL

pop 2600

From the rugged ridges of Ben More and the black basalt crags of Burg to the blinding white sand, rose-pink granite and emerald waters that fringe the Ross, Mull can lay claim to some of the finest and most varied scenery in the Inner Hebrides. Add in two impressive castles, a narrow-gauge railway, the sacred island of Iona and easy access from Oban and you can see why it's sometimes impossible to find a spare bed on the island.

Despite the number of visitors who flock to the island, it seems to be large enough to absorb them all; many stick to the well-worn routes from Craignure to Iona or Tobermory, returning to Oban in the evening. Besides, there are plenty of hidden corners where you can get away from the crowds.

The waters to the west of Mull provide some of the best whale-spotting opportunities in Scotland, with several operators offering whale-watching cruises (see the boxed texts p305 and p311).

## ORIENTATION

About two-thirds of Mull's population lives in and around Tobermory, the island's capital, in the north. Craignure, at the southeastern corner, has the main ferry terminal and is where most people arrive. Fionnphort is at the far western end of the long Ross of Mull peninsula, and is where the ferry to Iona departs.

## INFORMATION

**Clydesdale Bank** ( ☎ 0345-826818; Main St, Tobermory; ☒ 9.15am-4.45pm Mon-Fri) Has a 24-hour ATM.
**Craignure tourist office** ( ☎ 01680-812377; Craignure; ☒ 8.30am-5pm Mon-Sat, 10.30am-5pm Sun)
**Dunaros Hospital** ( ☎ 01680-300392; Salen) Has a minor injuries unit; the nearest casualty department is in Oban.
**Post office** ( ☎ 01688-302058; Main St, Tobermory; ☒ 9am-1pm & 2-5.30pm Mon, Tue, Thu & Fri, 9am-1pm Wed & Sat)
**Tobermory tourist office** ( ☎ 01688-302182; The Pier, Tobermory; ☒ 9am-6pm Mon-Sat & 10am-5pm Sun Jul & Aug, 9am-5pm Mon-Sat & 11am-5pm Sun May & Jun, shorter hrs rest of year)

## TOURS

See Bowman's Tours, p299, for details of day trips from Oban to Mull, Staffa and Iona by ferry and bus.

**Gordon Grant Marine** ( ☎ 01681-700388; www
.staffatours.com) Runs boat trips from Fionnphort to Staffa (adult/child £20/10, 2½ hours, daily April to October), and to Staffa and the Treshnish Isles (£40/20, five hours, Sunday to Friday May to July).
**Mull Magic** ( ☎ 01688-301245; www.mullmagic
.com) Offers guided walking tours in the Mull countryside (£32.50 per person), as well as customised tours and four-day walking holidays.

## FESTIVALS & EVENTS

**Mishnish Music Festival** ( ☎ 01688-302383; www
.mishnish.co.uk/musicfestival.htm) Held in the last week-end of April, this festival involves three days of foot-stomping traditional Scottish and Irish folk music at Tobermory's favourite pub.
**Mendelssohn on Mull** ( ☎ 01688-301108; www
.mullfest.org.uk) A week-long festival of classical music in early July.
**Mull Highland Games** ( ☎ 01688-302001; www
.mishnish.co.uk/mhg.htm) Third Thursday in July.
**Mull & Iona Food Festival** (www.wildisles.co.uk/food) Five days of food and drink tastings, chef demonstrations, farm tours, produce markets, restaurant visits and a host of other events. Early September.
**Tour of Mull Rally** ( ☎ 01254-826564; www.2300club
.org) Part of the Scottish Rally Championship; around 150 cars are involved and public roads are closed for parts of the weekend in early October.

## GETTING THERE & AWAY

There are frequent **CalMac** ( ☎ 0870 565 0000; www
.calmac.co.uk) ferries from Oban to Craignure (passenger/car £4.15/37, 40 minutes, every two hours). There's another car-ferry link between Fishnish, on the east coast of Mull, and Lochaline (£2.55/11.15, 15 minutes, at least hourly).

A third CalMac car ferry links Tobermory to Kilchoan on the Ardnamurchan peninsula (£3.95/21, 35 minutes, seven daily Monday to Saturday); from June to August there are also five sailings on Sunday.

## GETTING AROUND
### Bicycle

You can hire bikes for about £10 to £15 a day from the following places.
**Blazing Saddles** ( ☎ 01681-700235; Seaview B&B, Fionnphort)
**Brown's Hardware Shop** ( ☎ 01688-302020; Main St, Tobermory)
**On Yer Bike** ( ☎ 01680-300501; Craignure) Has an outlet in the craft shop near the ferry terminal in Craignure.

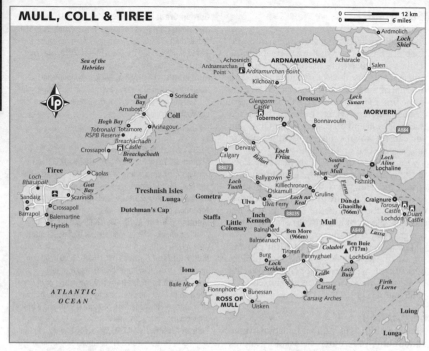

## MULL, COLL & TIREE

### Bus

Public transport on Mull is fairly limited. **Bowman's Tours** ( ☎ 01680-812313; www.bowmanstours.co.uk) is the main operator, connecting the ferry ports and the island's main villages. The routes useful for visitors are bus 495 from Craignure to Tobermory (£7 return, one hour, six daily Monday to Friday, four or five Saturday and Sunday) and bus 496 from Craignure to Fionnphort (£11 return, 1¼ hours, three or four daily Monday to Saturday, one Sunday).

On weekdays **RN Carmichael** ( ☎ 01688-302220) buses go from Tobermory to Dervaig (five daily) and Calgary (four daily); there are only two buses on Saturday and none on Sunday.

### Car

Almost all of Mull's road network consists of single-track roads. There are petrol stations at Craignure, Fionnphort, Salen and Tobermory.

**Mull Taxi** ( ☎ 07760 426351; www.mulltaxi.co.uk) is based in Tobermory, and has a vehicle that is wheelchair accessible.

## Craignure & Around
☎ 01680

There's not much to see at Craignure other than the ferry terminal and the hotel, so turn left, walk 200m and hop onto the **Mull Railway** ( ☎ 812494; Old Pier Station; adult/child return £4.50/3; ☼ Apr-Oct), a miniature steam train that will take you 1.5 miles south to Torosay Castle.

**Torosay Castle & Gardens** ( ☎ 812421; www.torosay.com; adult/child £5.50/3; ☼ house 10.30am-5pm Easter-Oct, gardens 9am-sunset year-round) is a rambling Victorian mansion in the Scottish Baronial style, stuffed with antique furniture, family portraits and hunting trophies. 'Take your time but not our spoons' advises the sign, and you're left to wander at will.

Two miles beyond Torosay is **Duart Castle** ( ☎ 812309; www.duartcastle.com; adult/child £5/2.50; ☼ 10.30am-5.30pm daily May–mid-Oct, 11am-4pm Sun-Thu Apr), a formidable fortress dominating the Sound of Mull. The seat of the Clan Maclean, this is one of the oldest inhabited castles in Scotland – the central keep was built in 1360. It was bought and restored in 1911 by war hero Sir Fitzroy Maclean and has damp dungeons, vast halls and bathrooms equipped with

---

## WATCHING WILDLIFE ON MULL

Mull's varied landscapes and habitats, from high mountains and wild moorland to wave-lashed sea cliffs, sandy beaches and seaweed-fringed skerries, offer the chance to spot some of Scotland's rarest and most dramatic wildlife, including eagles, otters, dolphins and whales.

**Mull Wildlife Expeditions** ( ☎ 01688-500121; www.torrbuan.com; Ulva Ferry) Offers full-day Land Rover tours of the island with the chance of spotting red deer, golden eagles, peregrine falcons, white-tailed sea eagles, hen harriers, otters, and perhaps dolphins and porpoises. The cost (adult/child £36/33) includes pick-up from your accommodation or from any of the ferry terminals, a picnic lunch and use of binoculars. The timing of this tour makes it possible as a day trip from Oban, with pick-up and drop-off at the Craignure ferry.

**Sea Life Surveys** ( ☎ 01688-302916; www.sealifesurveys.com) Runs whale-watching trips from Tobermory harbour to the waters north and west of Mull. An all-day whale watch (£70 per person, daily April to October) gives up to eight hours at sea (not recommended for kids under 14), and has a 95% success rate for sightings. The four-hour family whale-watch is geared more towards children and costs £40/35 per adult/child. The booking office is next to MacGochan's pub, in the big car park at the southern end of the waterfront (from summer 2008 it will be in the new harbour offices beside the pub).

**Turus Mara** ( ☎ 0800 085 8786; www.turusmara.com) Runs boat trips from Ulva Ferry in central Mull to Staffa and the Treshnish Isles (adult/child £43/23, 6½ hours, daily April to October), with an hour ashore on Staffa and two hours on Lunga, where you can see seals, puffins, kittiwakes, razorbills and many other species of seabird.

---

ancient fittings. A bus runs from Craignure to the castle at 10.45am and 12.50pm.

### SLEEPING

To camp within walking distance of the ferry, turn left and walk south for five minutes to **Shieling Holidays** ( ☎ 812496; www.shielingholidays.co.uk; tent & 2 people £13, with car £15, dm £11; ☺ late-Mar–Oct), a well-equipped camping ground with great views. Most of the permanent accommodation, including the hostel dorms and toilet block (dribbly showers), consists of 'cottage tents' made from heavy-duty tarpaulin, which gives the place a bit of a PVC-fetish feel.

Recommended B&Bs within 10 minutes' walk of the ferry include **Pennygate Lodge** ( ☎ 812333; info@pennygatelodge.co.uk; s/d from £31/56; ℗ ), next to the Shieling Holidays entrance, and **Dee-Emm B&B** ( ☎ 812440; www.dee-emm.co.uk; s/d from £50/50; ℗ ), a half-mile south of Craignure on the road towards Fionnphort.

## Tobermory

☎ 01688 / pop 750

Tobermory, the island's main town, is a picturesque little fishing port and yachting centre with brightly painted houses arranged around a sheltered harbour, with a grid-patterned 'upper town'. As the setting for the children's TV programme *Balamory*, the town swarms in summer with toddlers towing parents around looking for their favourite TV characters (frazzled parents can get a *Balamory* booklet from the tourist offices in Oban and Tobermory).

### SIGHTS & ACTIVITIES

Places to go on a rainy day include **Mull Museum** ( ☎ 302603; Main St; adult/child £1/20p; ☺ 10am-4pm Mon-Fri, 10am-1pm Sat Easter-Oct), which records the history of the island. There are also interesting exhibits on crofting, and on the 'Tobermory galleon', a ship from the Spanish Armada that sank in Tobermory Bay in 1588 and has been the object of treasure seekers ever since.

There's also **An Tobar Arts Centre** ( ☎ 302211; Argyll Tce; admission free; ☺ 10am-5pm Mon-Sat, 1-4pm Sun May-Sep, 10am-4pm Tue-Sat Oct-Apr), an art gallery and exhibition space, and the **Tobermory Distillery** ( ☎ 302645; guided tour £2.50; ☺ 10am-5pm Mon-Fri Easter-Oct), which offers guided tours. This tiny distillery, established in 1798, produces two award-winning malt whiskies – Tobermory 10-year-old and Ledaig 10-year-old.

The Hebridean Whale & Dolphin Trust's **Marine Discovery Centre** ( ☎ 302620; www.whaledolphinturst.co.uk; 28 Main St; admission free; ☺ 10am-5pm Mon-Fri, 11am-4pm Sun Apr-Oct, 11am-5pm Mon-Fri Nov-Mar) has displays, videos and interactive exhibits on whale and dolphin biology and ecology, and is a great place for kids to learn about sea mammals. It also provides information about volunteering and reporting sightings of whales and dolphins.

**Sea Life Surveys** ( ☎ 01688-302916; www.sealife surveys.com) runs whale-watching boat trips out of Tobermory harbour; for more information see the boxed text, p305.

You can hire mountain bikes from **Archibald Brown** ( ☎ 302020; 21 Main St) for £10/15 per five/24 hours.

## SLEEPING

Tobermory has dozens of B&Bs, but the place can still be booked solid in July and August, especially at weekends.

**Tobermory Campsite** ( ☎ 302624; www.tobermory campsite.co.uk; Newdale, Dervaig Rd; tent sites per adult/child £5/2; ☺ Mar-Oct; ⚒ ) The nearest place to camp is this quiet, family-friendly camping ground a mile west of town on the road to Dervaig.

**Tobermory Youth Hostel** (SYHA; ☎ 0870 004 1151; Main St; dm £14.50; ☺ Mar-Oct) This hostel has a great location, set in a Victorian house right on the waterfront. Bookings are recommended.

**2 Victoria St** ( ☎ 302263; 2 Victoria St; s/d £22/34) Set in an 18th-century stone house in the upper town, this is a traditional, old-school B&B with simple, homely bedrooms (with shared bathroom) and a very friendly and hospitable landlady.

**Baliscate Guest House** ( ☎ 302048; www.baliscate .co.uk; Salen Rd; r per person £25; P ) A handsome 18th-century house set in beautiful gardens, Baliscate has three large en-suite bedrooms, a breakfast conservatory and a comfortable lounge with library. The house is a mile south of the village centre, off the main road towards Craignure.

**Ptarmigan** ( ☎ 302863; www.bed-&-breakfast-tober mory.co.uk; The Fairways; s/d from £85/95; ☺ Mar-Nov; P ☺ ) Here's a first – a B&B with a heated, indoor 10m swimming pool! Ptarmigan is a large modern house built by the former owners of the Western Isles Hotel, and offers luxury B&B in a beautiful setting with superb views over Tobermory Bay – ask for the upper turret bedroom, with its own balcony.

**our pick Highland Cottage Hotel** ( ☎ 302030; www .highlandcottage.co.uk; Breadalbane St; d £140-175; ☺ mid-Mar-Oct; P ☺ ) Antique furniture, four-poster beds, embroidered bedspreads and fresh flowers and candlelight lend this small hotel (only six rooms) an appealingly old-fashioned cottage atmosphere, but with all mod cons including cable TV, full-size baths and room service. There's also an excellent fine-dining restaurant.

## EATING & DRINKING

**Fish & Chip Van** (mains £4-5; ☺ 12.30-9pm Mon-Sat Apr-Dec) If it's just takeaway you're after, you can tuck into some of Tobermory's best gourmet fish and chips down on the waterfront. Where else will you find a chip van selling freshly cooked prawns and scallops?

**MacGochan's** ( ☎ 302350; Ledaig; mains £7-15; ☺ food served noon-10pm) A lively pub beside the car park at the southern end of the waterfront, MacGochan's does good bar meals, and often has outdoor barbecues on summer evenings; there's a more formal restaurant upstairs, and live music in the bar at weekends.

**our pick Café Fish** ( ☎ 301253; The Pier; mains £8-18; ☺ 11am-3pm & 6-9pm) Seafood doesn't come much fresher than the stuff served at this warm and welcoming little restaurant overlooking Tobermory harbour – as their motto says, 'the only thing frozen here is the fisherman'! Langoustines and squat lobsters go straight from boat to kitchen to join rich shellfish bisque, fat scallops, seafood pie and catch of the day on the daily-changing menu, alongside freshly baked bread, homemade desserts and a range of Scottish cheeses.

**Mishnish Hotel** ( ☎ 302009; Main St; mains £9-15; ☺ food served noon-2pm & 6-9pm) You can't miss the bright yellow façade of this hotel. It's a favourite hang-out for visiting yachties and a good place for a bar meal, or dinner at the more formal restaurant upstairs. The wood-panelled and flag-draped 'Mish' is a fine traditional pub where you can listen to live folk music, toast your toes by the open fire, burrow into a booth with a book, or challenge the locals to a game of pool.

**Anchorage** ( ☎ 302313; 28 Main St; mains £14-18; ☺ 10am-4pm & 6-9pm) This nautical bistro decked out in smart navy blue and white, with bare stone walls and rope-wound pillars, is run by a French chef who turns out adventurous dishes based on local shellfish, beef and venison.

**Tobermory Chocolate Factory** ( ☎ 302526; Main St; ☺ café 9.30am-5pm Mon-Sat & 10.30am-3pm Sun, shop 9am-6pm Mon-Sat & 10am-4pm Sun) This tempting little shop not only sells exquisite handmade chocolates, but also has a café that serves excellent espresso, cappuccino and hot chocolate.

Campers can stock up on provisions at the **Co-op supermarket** (Main St; ☺ 8am-8pm Mon-Sat, 12.30-7pm Sun), and the **Island Bakery** ( ☎ 302223; Main St; ☺ 9am-5pm Mon-Sat), which sells delicious, locally baked wholegrain bread, cakes, biscuits and pastries, as well as having a great deli counter.

## ENTERTAINMENT

**Mull Theatre** ( ☎ 302673; www.mulltheatre.com; Royal Bldgs, Main St) is one of Scotland's best-known touring companies, putting on shows all over Scotland. Its long-time home in Dervaig, the Little Theatre, has closed and performances are now staged in various village halls on Mull; check the website or visit the Tobermory box office for programme details of the latest shows.

## North Mull

☎ 01688

The road from Tobermory west to Calgary cuts inland, leaving most of the north coast of Mull wild and inaccessible. Just outside Tobermory a long, single-track road leads north for 4 miles to majestic **Glengorm Castle** ( ☎ 302321; Glengorm; admission free; ✆ 10am-5pm daily Easter–mid-Oct) with views across the sea to Ardnamurchan, Rum and the Outer Hebrides. The castle houses an art gallery and pottery featuring the work of local artists, a farm shop selling local produce, and an excellent coffee shop serving meals (from noon to 4.30pm) made with fresh local ingredients.

The **Old Byre Heritage Centre** ( ☎ 400229; Dervaig; adult/child £4/2; ✆ 10.30am-6.30pm Wed-Sun Easter-Oct; ☒ ) brings Mull's heritage and natural history to life through a series of tableaux and half-hour film shows; prize for most bizarre exhibit goes to the 40cm-long model of a midge. The centre's tearoom serves good, inexpensive snacks, including homemade soup and clootie dumpling, and there's a kids outdoor play area.

Mull's best (and busiest) silver-sand beach, flanked by cliffs and with views out to Coll and Tiree, is at **Calgary**, about 12 miles west of Tobermory. And yes – this is the place from

---

### WALKING ON MULL

More information on the following walks can be obtained from the tourist offices in Oban, Craignure and Tobermory.

#### Ben More

The highest peak on the island, Ben More (966m) offers spectacular views of the surrounding islands when the weather is clear. A trail leads up the mountain from Loch na Keal, by the bridge on the B8035 over the Abhainn na h-Uamha (the river 8 miles southwest of Salen, Ordnance Survey (OS) 1:50,000 map sheet 49, grid reference 507368). Return the same way or continue down the narrow ridge to the eastern top, A'Chioch, then descend to the road via Gleann na Beinn Fhada. The glen can be rather wet and there's not much of a path. The round trip is 6.5 miles; allow five to six hours.

#### Carsaig Arches

One of the most adventurous walks on Mull is along the coast west of Carsaig Bay to the Carsaig Arches at Malcolm's Point. There's a good path below the cliffs most of the way from Carsaig, but it becomes a bit rough and exposed near the arches – the route climbs and then traverses a very steep slope above a vertical drop into the sea (not for the unfit or faint-hearted). You'll see spectacular rock formations on the way, culminating in the arches themselves. One, nicknamed the 'keyhole', is a freestanding rock stack; the other, the 'tunnel', is a huge natural arch. The western entrance is hung with curtains of columnar basalt – an impressive place. The round trip is 8 miles – allow three to four hours' walking time from Carsaig plus at least an hour at the arches.

#### Burg

At the tip of the remote Ardmeanach peninsula there is a remarkable 50-million-year-old fossil tree preserved in the basalt lava flows of the cliffs. A 4WD track leads from the car park at Tiroran to a house at Burg; the last 2.5 miles to the tree is on a very rough coastal path. About 500m before the tree, a metal ladder allows you to climb down to the foreshore, which is only accessible at low tide – check tide times at Tobermory tourist office before setting off. Allow six to seven hours for the strenuous 14-mile round trip.

which the more famous Calgary in Alberta, Canada, takes its name.

### SLEEPING & EATING

**Calgary Hotel** ( ☎ 400256; www.calgary.co.uk; Calgary; r per person from £48; P ) The Calgary provides delightfully rustic accommodation a few minutes' walk from the sandy beach at Calgary Bay. There are also two lovely self-catering loft apartments available for £440 per week (sleeping two to four people). There's also a tearoom and restaurant where you can tuck into a two- or three-course dinner (£20/25).

**Bellachroy Hotel & Pub** ( ☎ 400314; www.bellachroy hotel.co.uk; Dervaig; s/d from £60/80; P ) The six-room Bellachroy is an atmospheric 17th-century droving inn; the bar, known as the Bear Pit, is a focus for local social life and serves good-value bar meals (£6 to £9) from noon to 2.30pm and 5.30pm to 9pm.

You can camp for free at the southern end of the beach at Calgary Bay – keep to the area south of the stream. There are no facilities other than the public toilets across the road; water comes from the stream.

## Central Mull
☎ 01680

The central part of the island, between the Craignure–Fionnphort road and the narrow isthmus between Salen and Gruline, contains the island's highest peak, Ben More (966m) and some of its wildest scenery (see the boxed text, p307).

The narrow B8035 road along the southern shore of Loch na Keal squeezes past some impressive cliffs before cutting south towards Loch Scridain. About a mile along the shore from Balmeanach, where the road climbs away from the coast, is **Mackinnon's Cave**, a deep and spooky fissure in the basalt cliffs that was once used as a refuge by Celtic monks; a big, flat rock inside, known as Fingal's Table, may have been their altar.

**Balmeanach Park Caravan & Camping Site** ( ☎ 300342; tent, car & 2 people £11; ☼ Mar-Oct) is a peaceful camping ground 10 minutes' walk from the Fishnish–Lochaline ferry, on the main road between Craignure and Tobermory.

There's a very basic **camping ground** (tent/campervan sites £4/5) at Killiechronan, half a mile north of Gruline (toilets and water are a five-minute walk away), and plenty of wild camping on the south shore of Loch na Keal below Ben More.

## South Mull
☎ 01681

The road from Craignure to Fionnphort climbs through some wild and desolate scenery before reaching the southwestern part of the island, which consists of a long peninsula called the **Ross of Mull**. The Ross has a spectacular south coast lined with black basalt cliffs that give way further west to white-sand beaches and pink granite crags. The cliffs are highest at Malcolm's Point, near the superb **Carsaig Arches** (see the boxed text, p307).

The little village of **Bunessan** has a hotel, tearoom, pub and some shops, and is home to the **Ross of Mull Historical Centre** ( ☎ 700659; admission £1; ☼ 10am-4.30pm Mon-Fri Apr-Oct), a Portakabin that houses displays on local history, geology, archaeology, genealogy and wildlife.

A minor road leads south from here to the beautiful white-sand bay of **Uisken**, with views of the Paps of Jura. You can camp beside the beach here (£1 a head, ask permission at Uisken Croft), but there are no facilities.

At the western end of the Ross, 38 miles from Craignure, is **Fionnphort** (pronounced *finn*-a-fort) and the ferry to **Iona**. The coast here is a beautiful blend of pink granite rocks, white sandy beaches and vivid turquoise sea. The **Columba Centre** ( ☎ 700660; admission free; ☼ 10am-5.30pm Apr-Oct) has displays about the life of St Columba, the Celts and the history of Iona.

### SLEEPING & EATING

**Fidden Farm** ( ☎ 700427; tent sites per adult/child £4/2; ☼ Apr-Sep) There's a basic but beautifully situated camping ground here, with a view over pink granite reefs to the Iona and Erraid; it's 1.25 miles south of Fionnphort (continue on the road past the Columba Centre).

**our pick Seaview** ( ☎ 700235; www.iona-bed-breakfast -mull.com; Fionnphort; s/d from £35/56; P ) Barely a minute's walk from the Iona ferry, the five-bedroom Seaview has a breakfast conservatory with grand views across to Iona. The owner – a semiretired fisherman – is happy to take guests for a trip along the coast in his lobster boat.

**Staffa House** ( ☎ 700677; www.staffahouse.co.uk; Fionnphort; s/d from £35/60; P ) Several readers have recommended this family B&B for its charm and hospitality. The house is packed with antiques and period features, and like the Seaview offers breakfast in a conservatory with a view of Iona.

**Pennyghael Hotel** ( ☎ 704288; www.pennyghaelhotel .com; Pennyghael; s/d from £65/100; **P** ) This delightful, six-room country hotel is set in a 17th-century farmhouse near the head of Loch Scridain, about halfway between Craignure and Fionnphort, and has great views across the loch. Evening meals (four-course dinner £28) are available from 7pm to 9pm.

# ISLE OF IONA
☎ 01681 / pop 130

There are few more uplifting sights on Scotland's west coast than the view of Iona from Mull on a sunny day – an emerald island set in a sparkling turquoise sea. From the moment you step off the ferry you begin to appreciate the hushed, spiritual atmosphere that pervades this sacred island. Not surprisingly, the island attracts a lot of daytrippers, so if you want to experience the island's peace and quiet then the solution is to spend a night here. Once the crowds have gone for the day, you can wander in peace around the ancient graveyard where the early kings of Scotland are buried, attend an evening service at the abbey, or walk to the top of the hill and gaze south towards Ireland, as St Columba must have done so many centuries ago.

There's a tiny post office on the right as you head uphill from the ferry, and a **Spar** ( 9am-5.30pm Mon-Sat, noon-5pm Sun) grocery store a little further along on the left. Turn left on leaving the ferry to find **Finlay Ross Ltd** ( 10am-5.15pm Mon-Sat, 11am-5pm Sun), which sells gifts, books and maps, rents out bikes, and provides a laundry service. There are several art and craft shops on the island too.

## History
St Columba sailed from Ireland and landed on Iona in 563 before setting out to spread Christianity throughout Scotland. He established a monastery on the island and it was here that the *Book of Kells* – the prize attraction of Dublin's Trinity College – is believed to have been transcribed. It was taken to Kells in Ireland when Viking raids drove the monks from Iona.

The monks returned and the monastery prospered until its destruction during the Reformation. The ruins were given to the Church of Scotland in 1899, and by 1910 a group of enthusiasts called the **Iona Community** (www.iona .org.uk) had reconstructed the abbey. It's still

a flourishing spiritual community that holds regular courses and retreats.

## Sights & Activities
Head uphill from the ferry pier and turn right through the grounds of a ruined 13th-century **nunnery** with fine cloistered gardens, and exit at the far end. Across the road is the **Iona Heritage Centre** ( ☎ 700576; adult/child £1.90/free; 10.30am-4.30pm Mon-Sat Apr-Oct), which covers the history of Iona, crofting and lighthouses; the centre's coffee shop serves delicious home baking.

Turn right here and continue along the road to **Reilig Oran**, an ancient cemetery that holds the graves of 48 of Scotland's early kings, including Macbeth, and a tiny Romanesque chapel. Beyond rises the spiritual heart of the island – **Iona Abbey** (HS; ☎ 700512; adult/child £4.50/2.25; 9.30am-5.30pm Apr-Sep, 9.30am-4.30pm Oct-Mar; ). The spectacular nave, dominated by Romanesque and early Gothic vaults and columns, contains the elaborate, white marble tombs of the 8th duke of Argyll and his wife. A door on the left leads to the beautiful Gothic cloister, where medieval grave slabs sit alongside modern religious sculptures. A replica of the intricately carved **St John's Cross** stands just outside the abbey – the massive 8th-century original is in the **Infirmary Museum** (around the far side of the abbey) along with many other fine examples of early Christian and medieval carved stones.

Back at the ferry slip, **Alternative Boat Hire** ( ☎ 700537; www.boattripsiona.com) offers cruises in a traditional wooden sailing boat to see, well, whatever you like – go fishing, bird-watching, picnicking, or just drift along admiring the scenery. Three-hour trips cost £15/7 per adult/child.

The **MV Volante** ( ☎ 700362; www.volanteiona.com) provides four-hour sea-angling trips (£30 per person including tackle and bait), as well as 1½-hour round-the-island wildlife cruises (adult/child £14/8) and 3½-hour whale-watching trips (£30 per person).

The **MV Iolaire** ( ☎ 700358) runs three-hour boat trips to Staffa (£20/10), departing Iona pier at 9.45am and 1.45pm, and from Fionnphort at 10am and 2pm.

## Sleeping & Eating
**our pick** **Iona Hostel** ( ☎ 700781; www.ionahostel.co.uk; Lagandorain; dm £17.50; check-in 4-7pm) This hostel is set in an attractive, modern timber building on a working croft, with stunning views out to Staffa and the Treshnish Isles. Rooms are

clean and functional, and the well-equipped lounge/kitchen area has an open fire. It's at the northern end of the island – to get here, continue along the road past the abbey for 1.5 miles (a 20- to 30- minute walk).

**Iona Cottage** ( ☎ 700579; Baile Mor; r per person £25) This pretty little whitewashed cottage sits directly in front of the ferry landing, with a neat garden looking across to the Ross of Mull.

**Shore Cottage** ( ☎ 700744; www.shorecottage.co.uk; Baile Mor; s/d from £37/56) This attractive modern house is just a few minutes' walk south from the ferry. There are three bedrooms (all with en suite), and breakfast is served in a sunroom with great views across the sea to Mull.

**our pick** **Argyll Hotel** ( ☎ 700334; www.argyll hoteliona.co.uk; Baile Mor; s/d from £69/98; ☯ Feb-Nov) The terrace of cottages above the ferry slip houses this cute little hotel – it has 16 snug rooms (a sea view costs rather more – £130/150 for a single/double) and a country house restaurant with wooden fireplace and antique tables and chairs. The kitchen is supplied by a huge organic garden around the back, and the menu (mains £9 to £15) includes 'real beans on toast' (blackeye, lima and haricot beans in tomato and rosemary sauce on home-baked wholemeal toast). Food is served from 12.30pm to 2pm and 7pm to 8.30pm.

### Getting There & Away
The passenger ferry from Fionnphort to Iona (£3.85 return, five minutes, hourly) runs daily. There are also various day trips available from Oban (see Tours, p299) to Iona.

## ISLE OF ULVA
☎ 01688 / pop 16
Ulva, a privately owned island on the west coast of Mull, has good walking and off-road biking, a 9th-century Viking fort, and an old chapel with a graveyard. A short walk north of the ferry landing is **Sheila's Cottage Heritage Centre** ( ☎ 500241; admission incl with ferry ticket; ☯ 9am-5pm Mon-Fri Easter-Oct, 9am-5pm Sun Jun-Aug) a reconstruction of a traditional thatched crofter's cottage with displays about the history of the island.

At the **Boathouse tearoom** (mains £5-15), beside the ferry landing, you can savour locally harvested oysters washed down with Guinness. An interpretative centre upstairs has information on walks and natural history.

The two-minute ferry crossing (adult/child/bicycle £5/2/50p return) runs on demand during the heritage centre's opening hours.

## ISLE OF STAFFA
Felix Mendelssohn, who visited the uninhabited island of Staffa in 1829, was inspired to compose his *Hebrides Overture* after hearing waves echoing in the impressive and cathedral-like **Fingal's Cave**. The cave walls and surrounding cliffs are composed of vertical, hexagonal basalt columns that look like pillars (Staffa is Norse for 'Pillar Island'). You can land on the island and walk into the cave via a causeway. Nearby **Boat Cave** can be seen from the causeway, but you can't reach it on foot. Staffa also has a sizable puffin colony, north of the landing place.

Northwest of Staffa lies a chain of uninhabited islands called the **Treshnish Isles**. The two main islands are the curiously shaped **Dutchman's Cap** and **Lunga**. You can land on Lunga, walk to the top of the hill, and visit the shag, puffin and guillemot colonies on the west coast at **Harp Rock**.

Unless you have your own boat, the only way to reach Staffa is on an organised boat trip – see the Tours section, p299, and the boxed text, p305, for details.

## ISLE OF COLL
☎ 01879 / pop 100
Rugged and low lying, Coll is Tiree's less fertile and less populous neighbour. The northern part of the island is a mix of bare rock, bog and lochans (small lochs) – the south is swathed in golden shell-sand beaches and machair dunes up to 30m high.

**Arinagour**, a half-mile from the ferry pier, is the only village, and is home to the **Island Stores** ( ☯ 10am-5.30pm Mon & Fri, 10am-5.30pm Tue & Thu, 9am-5.30pm Wed, 9.30am-5pm Sat) grocery shop, a post office (with ATM), some craft shops and a petrol pump. For more information see www .visitcoll.co.uk.

### Sights & Activities
The island's main attraction is the peace and quiet – empty beaches, bird-haunted coastlines, and long walks along the shore. The biggest and most beautiful sandy beaches are at **Crossapol** in the south, and **Hogh Bay** and **Cliad** on the west coast.

In summer, you may be lucky enough to hear the 'krek-krek-krek' of the corncrake at the **RSPB Nature Reserve** at Totronald in the southwest of the island; there's a free **information centre** ( ☎ 230301; ☯ at all times). From Totronald a sandy 4WD track runs north past the dunes backing Hogh Bay to the road at Totamore, allowing walkers and cyclists to make a circuit back to Arinagour rather than returning the way they came.

There are two ruined castles about 6 miles southwest of Arinagour, both known as **Breachachadh Castle**, built by the Macleans in medieval times.

### Sleeping & Eating
**Garden House Camping & Caravan Site** ( ☎ 230374; Uig; tent site £2-3 plus per person £2; ☺ May-Sep) A basic camping ground with toilets and cold water only, 4.5 miles southwest of Arinagour. Dogs are not allowed.

**Coll Hotel** ( ☎ 230334; www.collhotel.com; Arinagour; r per person £35-50; ℗ ) The island's only hotel is an atmospheric old place. It has quirkily shaped rooms with white-painted, wood-panelled walls, many of which have lovely views over the manicured hotel gardens and the harbour. The hotel also has a really good restaurant (mains £8 to £16) that serves dishes ranging from crab sandwiches to venison casserole. Food is served from noon to 2pm and 6pm to 9pm.

our pick **Island Café** ( ☎ 230262; Arinagour; mains £5-7; ☺ 11am-5pm Mon, 11am-7.30pm Fri & Sat, 11am-4pm Sun, plus 11am-5pm Tue & Wed Jul & Aug) This cheerful little café serves hearty, homemade meals such as sausage and mash with onion gravy, haddock and chips, and vegetarian cottage pie, accompanied by organic beer, wine and cider.

Most accommodation on Coll is self-catering, but a few places offer B&B, including **Taigh-na-Mara** ( ☎ 230354; www.taighnamara.info; r per person £25-30) in Arinagour. You can camp

for free on the hill above the Coll Hotel (no facilities); ask at the hotel first.

### Getting There & Around
A CalMac car ferry runs from Oban to Coll (passenger/car £13/77, 2¾ hours, one daily) and continues to Tiree (one hour); the fare between Coll and Tiree is £3.40/21. On Thursdays only, you can take a ferry from Coll and Tiree to Barra in the Outer Hebrides (£10.30/46, four hours).

See the Colonsay's Getting There & Around section (p296) for details of flights to Coll.

Mountain bikes can be hired from the post office in Arinagour for £10 per day.

## ISLE OF TIREE
☎ 01879 / pop 765
Low-lying Tiree (pronounced tye-*ree*; from the Gaelic *tiriodh*, meaning 'land of corn') is a fertile sward of lush, green machair liberally sprinkled with yellow buttercups, much of it so flat that, from a distance, the houses seem to rise out of the sea. It's one of the sunniest places in Scotland, but also one of the windiest – cyclists soon find that although it's flat, heading west usually feels like going uphill. One major benefit – the constant breeze keeps away the midges.

The surf-lashed coastline is scalloped with broad, sweeping beaches of white sand, hugely popular with windsurfers and kite-surfers. Most visitors, however, come for the bird-watching, beachcombing and lonely coastal walks.

### Orientation & Information
The ferry arrives at **Gott Bay**, on the eastern side of the island. The airport is right in the centre.

---

**THAR SHE BLOWS!**

The North Atlantic Drift – a swirling tendril of the Gulf Stream – carries warm water into the cold, nutrient-rich seas off the Scottish coast, resulting in huge blooms of plankton. Small fish feed on the plankton, and bigger fish feed on the smaller fish. And this huge seafood smorgasbord attracts large numbers of marine mammals, from harbour porpoises and dolphins to minke whales and even – though sightings are rare – humpback and sperm whales.

In contrast to Iceland and Norway, Scotland has cashed in on the abundance of minke whales off its coast by embracing whale watching rather than whaling. There are now dozens of operators around the coast offering whale-watching boat trips lasting from a couple of hours to all day; some have whale-sighting success rates of 95%.

While seals, porpoises and dolphins can be seen year-round, minke whales are migratory. The best time to see them is from June to August, with August being the peak month for sightings. The website of the **Hebridean Whale & Dolphin Trust** (www.whaledolphintrust.co.uk) has lots of information on the species you are likely to see, and how to identify them.

A booklet titled *Is It a Whale?* is available from tourist offices and bookshops, and provides tips on identifying the various species of marine mammal that you're likely to see.

There's a bank (without ATM), post office and **Co-op supermarket** ( 8am-8pm Mon-Fri, 8am-6pm Sat, noon-6pm Sun) in Scarinish, the main village, a half-mile south of the ferry pier.

Tourist information and internet access are available at the **Rural Centre** ( 220677; Crossapol; 10am-4pm Mon-Sat), and An Iodhlann (see opposite), but there is no accommodation book-ing service. For more information see www .isleoftiree.com.

## Sights

In the 19th century Tiree had a population of 4500, but poverty and overcrowding – plus food shortages following the potato famine of 1846 – led the landowner, the duke of Ar-

---

### WHALE-WATCHING WISDOM: RUSSEL LEAPER

Russel Leaper works for the International Fund for Animal Welfare (IFAW), conducting scientific research to try and help reduce threats to whales around the world. He lives in Banavie, near Fort William.

**How does Scotland's west coast compare in the league of world whale-watching spots?** Rather like the weather, whale watching in Scotland is less predictable than elsewhere. There is a good chance of seeing minke whales and harbour porpoise. Bottlenose and common dolphins are also seen regularly, and there is a small chance of seeing several other species of whales and dolphin. Basking sharks are also often seen on whale-watching trips. The whale-watching season tends to run from April to September because of the weather [they're easier to spot in calm conditions] but the whales may be around longer than this.

**What was your most memorable whale sighting in Scottish waters?** In 20 years of studying whales around the world, it's Scotland that has given me some of my most memorable encounters. On a small sailing boat on a glassy calm day in the Sound of Arisaig, myself and a group of children watched for nearly an hour as a minke whale played with the boat like a dolphin. The huge body with a small, curious eye, would pass back and forth underneath us before surfacing to breathe out with a rasping blow that smelt of rotten vegetables. A special experience shared with my own children, but also with two girls from Belarus. Visiting Scotland for a month to escape a home still suffering from the effects of Chernobyl, they had never seen the sea before, let alone made eye contact with a whale.

**Are whale and dolphin numbers in Scottish waters rising, falling, staying the same?** We only have rather approximate estimates of numbers for a few species and almost no information on trends. The numbers of animals close to the coast varies from year to year but we don't really know how this relates to overall numbers. Unfortunately, Norway still kills several hundred minke whales a year from the same population that is watched around Scotland.

**Does the whale-watching industry in Scotland have any negative impact on cetacean populations?** There's certainly a risk that whale watching can disturb whales but we don't have any evidence that this is a problem on the west coast of Scotland. The quantity of boat traffic, including whale watching, is much lower than many other areas.

**How can visitors ensure that their whale-watching activity has minimal impact?** Scottish Natural Heritage has developed the Scottish Marine Wildlife Watching Code (www.marinecode.org). These are simple, common-sense measures to minimise disturbance. Feedback from customers is probably the most effective way of ensuring that operators stick to the code. You can contribute to minimising impact by knowing the code and telling the boat operator if they are not respecting it.

**Are there any organisations that people can get involved with on a voluntary basis?** IFAW is one of a number of groups campaigning on behalf of whales and dolphins at an international level. Locally, the Hebridean Whale & Dolphin Trust based in Tobermory (see p305) runs programmes with volunteers and also collates sightings.

gyll, to introduce a policy of assisted emigration. Between 1841 and 1881 more than 3600 people left the island, many of them emigrating to Canada, the USA, Australia and New Zealand.

**An Iodhlann** ( ☎ 220793; www.aniodhlann.org.uk; Scarinish; admission free; ☻ 10.30am-5pm Mon-Fri Jul-Sep, 10.30am-3.30pm Mon-Fri Oct-Jun; ⓓ ) is a historical and genealogical library and archive, where many of the estimated 38,000 descendants of Tiree emigrants come to trace their ancestry. The centre stages a **summer exhibition** (adult/child £3/free; ☻ 2-5pm Jul-Sep) on island life and history.

At **Sandaig**, in the far west of the island, is the **Island Life Museum** (admission free; ☻ 2-4pm Mon-Fri Jun-Sep), a row of quaint thatched cottages each restored as a 19th-century crofter's home.

The picturesque harbour and hamlet of **Hynish**, near the southern tip of the island, was built in the 19th century to house workers and supplies for the construction of the Skerryvore Lighthouse, which stands 10 miles offshore. **Skerryvore Lighthouse Museum** (admission free; ☻ 9am-5pm) occupies the signal tower above the harbour, which was once used to communicate by semaphore with the lighthouse site.

For the best view on the island, walk up nearby **Ben Hynish** (141m), which is capped by a conspicuous radar station known locally as the Golf Ball.

### Activities

Reliable wind and big waves have made Tiree one of Scotland's top windsurfing venues – the annual **Tiree Wave Classic** (www.tireewaveclassic.com) competition is held here in October.

**Wild Diamond Watersports** ( ☎ 220399; www.surf schoolscotland.co.uk), based at Loch Bhasapoll in the northwest of the island, runs courses in surfing, windsurfing, kitesurfing and kayaking, and rents out equipment. A day's equipment hire costs from £20, and a beginners course (five hours over two days) costs £60 including gear.

You can also try **sand-yachting** ( ☎ 220317; per hr £15) on Gott Bay beach at low tide.

### Sleeping & Eating

**Balinoe Croft Campsite** ( ☎ 220399; Balinoe; tent sites per person £6) A sheltered site in the southwest of the island, near Balemartine, with great views of Mull.

**Millhouse Hostel** ( ☎ 220435; www.tireemillhouse .co.uk; Cornaigmore; dm £13, tw £31) Housed in a converted barn next to an old water mill, this small but comfortable hostel is 5 miles west from the ferry pier.

**Ceabhar** ( ☎ 220684; www.ceabhar.com; Sandaig; r per person from £30; ⓓ ⓟ ) This snug little cottage B&B has a fantastic location at the western end of the island, looking out over the Atlantic towards the sunset. The owners are outdoor enthusiasts and can advise on kitesurfing, powerkiting and scuba diving. There's also a restaurant (mains £7 to £12) in a sunny conservatory with sea views, open 5pm to 9pm daily, and 12.30pm to 2pm Sunday).

**Kirkapol** ( ☎ 220729; www.kirkapoltiree.co.uk; Gott Bay; s/d £32/60; ⓟ ) Set in a converted 19th-century church overlooking the island's biggest beach, the Kirkapol has six homely rooms and a big lounge with a leather-studded sofa. It's 2 miles north of the ferry terminal.

**our pick Scarinish Hotel** ( ☎ 220308; www.tiree scarinishhotel.com; Scarinish; s/d from £40/70; ⓟ ) There's hospitality on tap at the Scarinish, with enthusiastic owners who go out of their way to make you feel welcome. The recently redecorated rooms are crisp and clean, and the restaurant (mains £8 to £18) and traditional lean-to bar have a cosy atmosphere. Meals are served from noon to 2pm and 6pm to 9pm.

### Getting There & Around

British Airways/Loganair flies from Glasgow to **Tiree airport** ( ☎ 220309) once daily (£80, 50 minutes) from Monday to Saturday. See also Colonsay's Getting There & Around section (p296) for additional flights to Tiree.

Ferry connections and fares are the same as for Coll (see Getting There & Around, p311).

You can rent bicycles from Millhouse Hostel and from **McLennan Motors** ( ☎ 220555; Scarinish); the latter will also rent you a car. For a taxi, call **John Kennedy** ( ☎ 220419).

# NORTH ARGYLL

## LOCH AWE

Loch Awe is one of Scotland's most beautiful lochs, with rolling forested hills around its southern end and spectacular mountains in the north. It lies between Oban and Inveraray and is the longest loch in Scotland – about 24 miles long – but is less than a mile wide for most of its length. See www.loch-awe.com for more information.

At its northern end, the loch widens out and there are several islands you can visit: **Inishail** has a ruined church and **Fraoch Eilean** has a broken-down castle. You can hire boats from **Loch Awe Boats** ( ☎ 01866-833256; The Boat House, Ardbrecknish); a rowing boat costs £5/30 per hour/day, a motor boat £10/40. Ardbrecknish is on the south shore of the loch, 8 miles southwest of Dalmally.

Also at the northern end of Loch Awe are the scenic ruins of **Kilchurn Castle** (admission free; ☉ 9am-5pm Apr-Sep), built in 1440, which enjoys one of Scotland's finest settings; you can climb to the top of the four-story castle tower. It's a half-mile walk from the A85 road, just east of the bridge over the River Orchy.

At its northern end, Loch Awe escapes to the sea through the narrow **Pass of Brander**, where Robert the Bruce defeated the MacDougalls in battle in 1309. In the pass, by the A85, you can visit **Cruachan power station** ( ☎ 01866-822618; www .visitcruachan.coo.uk; Lochawe; adult/child £5/2; ☉ 9.30am-5pm Easter-Nov, tours every 30 min). Electric buses take you more than half a mile inside Ben Cruachan, allowing you to see the pump-storage hydroelectric scheme in action.

### Getting There & Away

Scottish Citylink buses from Glasgow to Oban go via Dalmally, Lochawe village and Cruachan power station. Trains from Glasgow to Oban stop at Dalmally and Lochawe village. See p301 for details.

## LOCH ETIVE

Hemmed in by dramatic mountain scenery, Loch Etive stretches for 17 miles from Connel to Kinlochetive (accessible by road from Glencoe).

### Connel

☎ 01631 / pop 500

At Connel Bridge, 5 miles north of Oban, Loch Etive is joined to the sea by a narrow channel partly blocked by an underwater rock ledge. When the tide flows in and out – as it does twice a day – millions of tons of water pour through this bottleneck, creating spectacular white-water rapids known as the **Falls of Lora**. You can park near the north end of the bridge and walk back into the middle to have a look.

**Dunstaffnage Castle** ( ☎ 562465; Dunstaffnage; adult/child £3.50/1.75; ☉ 9.30am-5.30pm Apr-Sep, 9.30am-4.30pm Sat-Wed Oct-Mar), 2 miles west of Connel, looks like a schoolkid's drawing of what a castle

should look like – square and massive, with towers at the corners, and perched on top of a rocky outcrop. It was built around 1260 and was captured by Robert the Bruce during the Wars of Independence in 1309. The haunted ruins of the nearby 13th-century **chapel** contain lots of Campbell tombs decorated with skull and crossbone carvings.

Buses between Oban and Fort William or Glasgow, and trains between Oban and Glasgow, all stop in Connel. See p301 for details.

### Taynuilt

☎ 01866 / pop 700

One of the region's most unusual historical sights is **Bonawe Iron Furnace** ( ☎ 822432; adult/child £4/2; ☉ 9.30am-5.30pm Apr-Sep), near Taynuilt. Dating from 1753, it was built by an iron-smelting company from the English Lake District because of the abundance of birchwood in the area. The wood was made into charcoal, which was needed for smelting the iron – to produce Bonawe's annual output of 700 tons of pig iron took 10,000 acres of woodland. A fascinating self-guided tour leads you around the various parts of the site.

From the jetty opposite the entrance to Bonawe, **Loch Etive Cruises** ( ☎ 822430) runs boat trips to the head of Loch Etive and back between one and three times daily (except Saturday) from April to October. There are two-hour cruises (adult/child £10/8, depart 10am and noon) and three-hour cruises (£15/12, departs 2pm). You may spot eagles, otters, seals and deer, and at the head of the loch you can see the famous Etive slabs – dotted with rock climbers in dry weather.

Aficionados of smoked salmon should pay a visit to **Inverawe Smokehouse & Fishery** ( ☎ 822274; www.smokedsalmon.co.uk; Inverawe; admission free; ☉ 8am-5.30pm Mar-Oct), 2 miles east of Taynuilt, where local salmon (and trout, herring and venison) is smoked over split oak logs. There's also an angling school and trout fishery where you can learn to fly-fish, and a tearoom where you can sample the smokery's mouthwatering produce.

Taynuilt is 6 miles east of Connel. Scottish Citylink buses and trains to and from Oban stop here. See p301 for details.

## APPIN & AROUND

☎ 01631

The Appin region, once ruled over by the Stewarts of Appin from their stronghold at Castle

Stalker, stretches north from the rocky shores of Loch Creran to the hills of Glencoe.

The **Scottish Sea Life Sanctuary** ( ☎ 720386; www.sealsanctuary.co.uk; Barcaldine; adult/child £9.50/7.50; ☒ 10am-5pm Mar-Oct), 8 miles north of Oban on the shores of Loch Creran, provides a haven for orphaned seal pups. As well as the seal pools there are tanks with herring, rays and flatfish, touch pools for children, an otter sanctuary and displays on Scotland's marine environment.

**Glen Creran**, at the head of Loch Creran, is a scenic glen with several good walks. North of Loch Creran, at Portnacroish, there's a wonderful view of **Castle Stalker** perched on a tiny offshore island – Monty Python buffs will recognise it as the castle that appears in the final scenes of the film *Monty Python and the Holy Grail*. **Port Appin**, a couple of miles off the main road, is a pleasant spot with a passenger ferry to the island of Lismore.

The delightfully quaint **Pierhouse Hotel** ( ☎ 730302; www.pierhousehotel.co.uk; Port Appin; s £70-85, d £90-135; P ) sits on the waterfront above the ferry pier for Lismore. The restaurant enjoys a view across the water to Lismore, and specialises in local seafood and game. Meals (mains £15 to £23) are served from noon to 2pm and 6.30pm to 9pm.

You can hire bikes from **Port Appin Bike** ( ☎ 730391) at the entrance to the village for £7/10 per half-/full day.

Scottish Citylink buses between Oban and Fort William stop at the Sea Life Sanctuary and Appin village. See p301 for details.

## LISMORE

☎ 01631 / pop 170

The first thing you notice about the island of Lismore is how green it is (the Gaelic name Lios Mor means 'Great Garden') – all lush grassland sprinkled with wildflowers, with grey blades of limestone breaking through the soil. And that's the secret – limestone is rare in the Highlands, but it weathers to a very fertile soil.

Lismore is long and narrow – 10 miles long and just over a mile wide – with a road running almost its full length. **Clachan**, a scattering of houses midway between Achnacroish and Point, is the nearest the island has to a village. **Lismore Stores** ( ☎ 760272; ☒ 9am-5.30pm Mon, Tue, Thu & Fri, 9am-1pm Wed & Sat), between Achnacroish and Clachan, is a grocery store and post office, and has internet access.

**St Moluag's Centre** (Ionad Naomh Moluag; ☎ 760300; www.celm.org.uk; adult/child £3/free; ☒ 11am-5pm) houses a fascinating exhibition on Lismore's history and culture; alongside stands a reconstruction of a crofter's cottage. The **Lismore Café** (mains £3-5; ☒ 10am-5pm daily, plus 7-10.30pm Fri only Apr-Oct) here has an outdoor deck with a stunning view of the mainland mountains. The centre is in the middle of the island – if you're walking, you can take a short cut by starting along the coastal path north of the pier at Achnacroish (2 miles by road, just over 1 mile by the path).

The romantic ruins of 13th-century **Castle Coeffin** have a lovely setting on the west coast, a mile from Clachan (follow the waymarked path). **Tirefour Broch**, a defensive tower with double walls reaching 4m in height, is directly opposite on the east coast.

There is very little short-stay accommodation on Lismore. However, there are several self-catering options advertised on www.isle oflismore.com.

### Getting There & Around

A CalMac car ferry runs from Oban to Achnacroish, with two to five sailings Monday to Saturday (passenger/car £2.90/£25, 50 minutes).

**Argyll & Bute Council** ( ☎ 01546-604695) operates the passenger-only ferry from Port Appin to Point (£1.22, 10 minutes, hourly). Bicycles are carried for free.

A Royal Mail postbus runs the length of the island daily Monday to Saturday, and there's a **taxi service** ( ☎ 760220).

**Lismore Bike Hire** ( ☎ 760213) will deliver your bike to the ferry slip; rental costs £6/10 per half-/full day.

# Central & Western Highlands

From the high, subarctic plateau of the Cairngorms and the great, humpbacked hills of the Monadhliath to the more rugged, rocky peaks of Glen Coe, the Mamores and Ben Nevis, the central mountain ranges of the Scottish Highlands are testimony to the sculpting power of ice and weather. Here the Scottish scenery is at its grandest, with soaring hills of rock and heather bounded by rugged glens, rushing waterfalls and stands of Scots pine, remnants of the Caledonian forest that once covered the whole country.

Not surprisingly, this part of the country is an adventure playground for outdoor sports enthusiasts. Aviemore, Glen Coe and Fort William draw hordes of hill walkers and rock climbers in summer, and skiers, snowboarders and ice climbers in winter. There are purpose-built mountain-biking trails at Nevis Range and Laggan (near Newtonmore), the world's biggest indoor ice-climbing wall at Kinlochleven, and three of Scotland's five ski resorts at Nevis Range, Cairngorm and Glen Coe.

Inverness, the Highland capital, provides a spot of urban rest and relaxation before you strike south through the forests and lochs of the Great Glen, stopping perhaps to check Loch Ness for monsterish disturbances. The glens to the northwest of Loch Ness – Strathfarrar, Strathglass and Glen Affric – are among the most beautiful in the country, and offer a wealth of scenic low-level hiking.

From Fort William, the base camp for climbing Ben Nevis, the aptly named Road to the Isles skirts one of Europe's last great wilderness areas before reaching the gorgeous beaches of Arisaig and Morar and the ferry port of Mallaig, jumping-off point for exploring the isles of Eigg, Rum, Muck and Canna.

---

## HIGHLIGHTS

- Hiking among the hills, lochs and forests of beautiful **Glen Affric** (p324)
- Wandering through the ancient Caledonian forest at **Rothiemurchus** (p331)
- Making it to the summit of **Ben Nevis** (p345) – and being able to see the view
- Rattling your teeth loose on the championship downhill mountain-bike course at **Nevis Range** (p344)
- Taking in the stunning panorama from the summit of the **Sgurr of Eigg** (p351)

★ Glen Affric

Rothiemurchus ★

Ben Nevis Nevis Range
(1344m) ★★

★ Sgurr of Eigg (393m)

- POPULATION: 140,000
- AREA: 9660 SQ KM

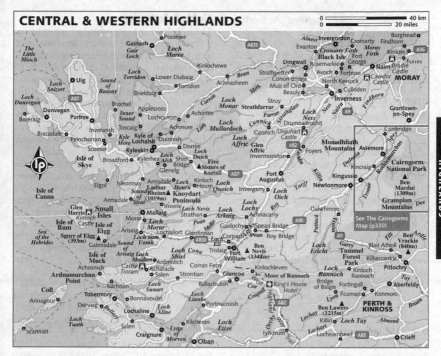

CENTRAL & WESTERN HIGHLANDS

See The Cairngorms Map (p330)

## Getting Around

**Scottish Citylink** ( ☎ 0870 550 5050; www.citylink.co.uk) runs buses from Perth to Inverness and from Glasgow to Fort William, and links Inverness to Fort William along the Great Glen. The **Nevis'n'Coe Roverbus** ( ☎ 01463-710555; www.rapsons .co.uk) is the main regional bus company, with offices in Aviemore, Inverness and Fort William. Roverbus tickets are valid for unlimited travel on Rapsons/Highland Country buses in various regions, including Inverness–Nairn (one day £9), Aviemore (one day/three days £6/15) and Fort William–Glencoe (one day/three days £6/15).

From mid-May to September, the Speyside Stroller (bus 500) runs from Cullen, on the Banffshire coast, to the Cairngorm Mountain Railway via Elgin, Dufftown, Tomintoul, Grantown-on-Spey, Carrbridge and Aviemore (3¾ hours, once daily, Saturday and Sunday only). The Heather Hopper (bus 501) links Grantown-on-Spey to Ballater via Tomintoul and Strathdon (1½ hours, twice daily mid-May to September).

Two railway lines serve the region: the Perth–Aviemore–Inverness line in the east,

and the Glasgow–Fort William–Mallaig line in the west.

For timetable information, call **Traveline** ( ☎ 0871 200 2233).

# INVERNESS & THE GREAT GLEN

Inverness, one of the fastest growing towns in Britain, is the capital of the Highlands. It's a transport hub and jumping-off point for the central, western and northern Highlands, the Moray Firth coast and the Great Glen.

The Great Glen is a geological fault running in an arrow-straight line across Scotland from Fort William to Inverness. The glaciers of the last ice age eroded a deep trough along the fault line that is now filled by a series of lochs – Linnhe, Lochy, Oich and Ness. The glen has always been an important communication route – General George Wade built a military road along the southern side of Loch Ness in the early 18th century, and in 1822 the various lochs were linked by the Caledonian Canal to create a cross-country waterway. The modern A82 road along the glen was completed in 1933 – a date that coincides neatly with the first modern sightings of the Loch Ness Monster (see the boxed text Strange Spectacle On Loch Ness, p328).

## INVERNESS
☎ 01463 / pop 55,000

Inverness, the primary city and shopping centre of the Highlands, has a great location astride the River Ness at the northern end of the Great Glen. In summer it overflows with visitors intent on monster hunting at nearby Loch Ness, but it's worth a visit in its own right for a stroll along the picturesque River Ness and a cruise on the Moray Firth in search of its famous bottlenose dolphins.

The city was probably founded by King David in the 12th century, but thanks to its often violent history few buildings of real age or historical significance have survived – much of the older part of the city dates from the period following the completion of the Caledonian Canal in 1822.

### Orientation
The broad and shallow River Ness, which flows a short 6 miles from Loch Ness into the Moray Firth, runs through the heart of the city. The city centre lies on the eastern bank, at the foot of the castle hill, with the bus and train stations next to each other a little to the north.

### Information
**Leakey's** ( ☎ 239947; Greyfriars Hall, Church St; ✆ 10am-5.30pm Mon-Sat) An excellent second-hand bookshop with a good café.
**Main post office** ( ✆ 9am-5.30pm Mon-Fri, to 6pm Sat) On Queensgate.
**New City Laundrette** ( ☎ 242507; 17 Young St; ✆ 8am-8pm Mon-Fri, to 6pm Sat, 10am-4pm Sun) Charges £3 per load, £1.40 to dry; internet access for £1 per 20 minutes.
**Tourist office** ( ☎ 234353; www.visithighlands.com; Castle Wynd; ✆ 9am-6pm Mon-Sat, 9.30am-5pm Sun Jul & Aug, 9am-5pm Mon-Sat, 10am-4pm Sun Jun, Sep & Oct, 9am-5pm Mon-Sat Apr & May, limited hr Nov-Mar) Bureau de change and accommodation booking service; also sells tickets for tours and cruises. Internet access for £1 per 20 minutes.
**Waterstone's** ( ☎ 717474; 50-52 High St; ✆ 9am-5.30pm Mon & Wed-Sat, 9.30am-5.30pm Tue, 10.30am-5pm Sun) The city's biggest bookshop.

## Sights & Activities
The hill above the city centre is topped by the picturesque Baronial turrets of **Inverness Castle**, a pink-sandstone confection dating from 1847 that replaced a medieval castle blown up by the Jacobites in 1746; it serves today as the Sheriff's Court. Between the castle and the tourist office is **Inverness Museum & Art Gallery** ( ☎ 237114; Castle Wynd; admission free; ✆ 9am-5pm Mon-Sat), with wildlife dioramas, geological displays, period rooms with historic weapons, Pictish stones and a missable art gallery.

But save the museum for a rainy day – the main attraction in Inverness is a leisurely stroll along the river to the **Ness Islands**. Planted with mature Scots pine, fir, beech and sycamore, and linked to the river banks and each other by elegant Victorian footbridges, the islands make an appealing picnic spot. They're a 20-minute walk south of the castle – head upstream on either side of the river (the start of the Great Glen Way, see p327), and return on the opposite bank. On the way you'll pass the red-sandstone towers of **St Andrew's Cathedral**, dating from 1869, and the modern Eden Court Theatre, which hosts regular art exhibits, both on the west bank.

If the rain does come down, you could opt for a spot of retail therapy in the **Victorian Market**, a shopping mall that dates from the 1890s and has rather more charm than its modern equivalents.

## Tours
### WALKING TOURS
Guided walking tours of the city (adult/child £4/2) leave from outside the tourist office and last 1¼ hours; check with the tourist office for details.

**Davy the Ghost Tours** ( ☎ 07730 831069; adult/child £7.50/5) offers 1¼-hour tours led by an '18th-century ghost' in period costume. Expect tales of the city's horrific past, including ghosts, witches, murders and hangings. Tours depart at 7pm from the blackboard outside the tourist office.

### BUS & TAXI TOURS
**City Sightseeing** ( ☎ 07765 834825; adult/child £6/3; ✆ 10am-4pm) From late May to September, 45-minute, hop-on, hop-off bus tours around Inverness, departing from Bridge St near the tourist office once an hour. The ticket is also valid on a 1¾-hour route that takes in Culloden, Cawdor Castle and Fort George (every two hours, 9.30am to 3.30pm).

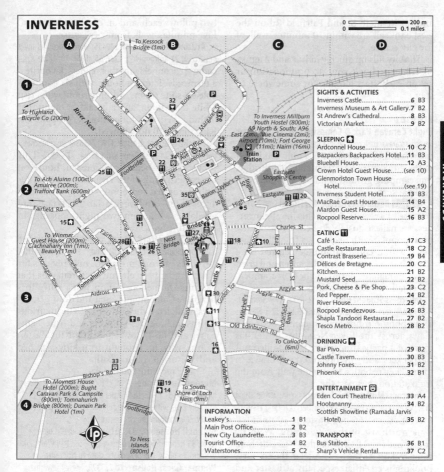

**INVERNESS**

0 ____ 200 m
0 ____ 0.1 miles

**SIGHTS & ACTIVITIES**
Inverness Castle.............................6 B3
Inverness Museum & Art Gallery.7 B2
St Andrew's Cathedral..................8 B3
Victorian Market...........................9 B2

**SLEEPING**
Ardconnel House..........................10 C2
Bazpackers Backpackers Hotel....11 B3
Bluebell House.............................12 A3
Crown Hotel Guest House.......(see 10)
Glenmoriston Town House
    Hotel...................................(see 19)
Inverness Student Hotel..............13 B3
MacRae Guest House...................14 B4
Mardon Guest House...................15 A2
Rocpool Reserve..........................16 B3

**EATING**
Café 1.........................................17 C3
Castle Restaurant........................18 C2
Contrast Brasserie.......................19 B4
Délices de Bretagne....................20 B2
Kitchen.......................................21 B2
Mustard Seed..............................22 B2
Pork, Cheese & Pie Shop.............23 C2
Red Pepper.................................24 B2
River House.................................25 A2
Rocpool Rendezvous...................26 B3
Shapla Tandoori Restaurant........27 B2
Tesco Metro................................28 B2

**DRINKING**
Bar Pivo......................................29 B2
Castle Tavern..............................30 B3
Johnny Foxes..............................31 B2
Phoenix......................................32 B1

**ENTERTAINMENT**
Eden Court Theatre.....................33 A4
Hootananny................................34 B2
Scottish Showtime (Ramada Jarvis
    Hotel)...................................35 B2

**TRANSPORT**
Bus Station.................................36 B1
Sharp's Vehicle Rental.................37 C2

**INFORMATION**
Leakey's.......................................1 B1
Main Post Office...........................2 B2
New City Laundrette.....................3 B3
Tourist Office...............................4 B2
Waterstones.................................5 C2

---

**Inverness Taxis** ( ☎ 222900; www.inverness-taxis
.co.uk) A wide range of day tours to Urquhart Castle, Loch
Ness and Culloden, and as far away as Skye. Fares per car
(with up to four people) range from £40 (two hours) to
£170 (all day).

**John O'Groats Ferries** ( ☎ 01955-611353; www.jog
ferry.co.uk; ☒ departs 7.30am) From May to September,
daily tours (lasting 13½ hours; adult/child £47/23.50) by
bus and passenger ferry from Inverness to Orkney.

## CRUISES
**Jacobite Cruises** ( ☎ 233999; www.jacobite.co.uk;
Glenurquhart Rd) Cruise boats depart at 10.35am and
1.35pm from Tomnahurich Bridge for a 3½-hour trip along
Loch Ness, including visits to Urquhart Castle and Loch
Ness 2000 Monster Exhibition (adult/child £21/15 including
admission fees). You can buy tickets at the tourist office

and catch a free minibus to the boat. Other cruises, from
one to 6½ hours, available.

**Moray Firth Cruises** ( ☎ 717900; Shore St Quay, Shore
St; ☒ 10.30am-4.30pm Mar-Oct, plus 6pm cruises Jul &
Aug) Offers 1½-hour wildlife cruises (adult/child £12.50/9)
to look for dolphins, seals and bird life. Sightings aren't
guaranteed, but the commentaries are excellent, and on
a fine day it's good just being out on the water. Follow
the signs to Shore St Quay from the far end of Chapel St or
catch the free shuttle bus that leaves from the tourist office
15 minutes before sailings (every 1½ hours).

## Sleeping
Inverness has a good range of backpacker
accommodation, and there are lots of guesthouses and B&Bs along Old Edinburgh Rd
and Ardconnel St on the east side of the river,

and on Kenneth St and Fairfield Rd on the west bank; all are within 10 minutes' walk of the city centre.

The city fills up quickly in July and August, so either prebook your accommodation or get an early start looking for somewhere to stay.

## BUDGET

**Bught Caravan Park & Campsite** ( ☎ 236920; www .invernesscaravanpark.com; Bught Lane; tent site per person £6, campervan £13; ✆ Easter–mid-Oct) A mile southwest of the city centre near Tomnahurich Bridge, this camping ground is hugely popular with backpackers.

**our pick Bazpackers Backpackers Hotel** ( ☎ 717663; 4 Culduthel Rd; dm/tw £13/35; 🖳 ) This may be Inverness's smallest hostel (30 beds), but it's the most popular with readers – a friendly, quiet place with a convivial lounge centred on a wood-burning stove, a small garden and great views, though the dorms can be a bit cramped. No email or online bookings.

**Inverness Student Hotel** ( ☎ 236556; www.scotlands -top-hostels.com; 8 Culduthel Rd; dm £13.50; 🖳 ) Set in a rambling old house with comfy beds and views across the River Ness, this hostel has more of a party atmosphere than chilled out Bazpackers, and runs organised pub crawls in town. They're both a 10-minute walk from the train station, just past the castle.

**Inverness Millburn Youth Hostel** (SYHA; ☎ 0870 004 1127; Victoria Dr; dm £14-16; ✆ Apr-Dec; 🖳 P ) Inverness' modern 166-bed hostel is 10 minutes' walk northeast of the city centre. With its comfy beds and flashy stainless-steel kitchen, some reckon it's the best hostel in the country. Booking is essential, especially at Easter and in July and August.

## MIDRANGE

**Crown Hotel Guest House** ( ☎ 231135; www.inverness -guesthouse.info; 19 Ardconnel St; s/d £35/54; ♿ P ) Similar in layout to the ever-popular Ardconnel next door, but child-friendly, the Crown has kind and helpful owners; two of the six bedrooms are family rooms (with a double, single, and folding bed in each), and there's a spacious lounge equipped with games consoles, DVDs and board games.

**Ach Aluinn** ( ☎ 230127; www.achaluinn.com; 27 Fairfield Rd; s/d £35/60; P ) This large, detached Victorian house is bright and homely, and offers all you might want from a guesthouse – private bathroom, TV, reading lights, comfy beds with

two pillows each, and an excellent breakfast. Five minutes' walk from city centre.

**Ardconnel House** ( ☎ 240455; www.ardconnel-inver ness.co.uk; 21 Ardconnel St; s £40-55, d £56-70) The six-room Ardconnel is another readers' favourite – a terraced Victorian house with six comfortable en-suite rooms, a dining room with crisp white table linen, and a breakfast menu that includes Vegemite for homesick Antipodeans. Kids under 10 not allowed.

**MacRae Guest House** ( ☎ 243658; joycemacrae@ hotmail.com; 24 Ness Bank; s/d £45/64; P ♿ ) This pretty, flower-bedecked Victorian house on the eastern bank of the river has smart, tastefully decorated bedrooms – one is wheelchair accessible – and vegetarian breakfasts are available. Minimum two-night bookings in July and August.

**our pick Trafford Bank** ( ☎ 241414; www.trafford bankguesthouse.co.uk; 96 Fairfield Rd; s £60-75, d £80-104; P ) Lots of word-of-mouth rave reviews for Trafford Bank, an elegant Victorian villa that was once home to a bishop, just a mitre-toss from the Caledonian Canal and only 10 minutes' walk from the city centre. The luxurious rooms include fresh flowers and fruit, bathrobes and fluffy towels – ask for the Tartan Room, with its wrought-iron king-size bed and Victorian roll-top bath.

Other recommendations:

**Mardon Guest House** ( ☎ 231005; www.mardonguest house.co.uk; 37 Kenneth St; r per person £26-30; P ) Friendly B&B, with six cosy rooms (all en suite), just five minutes' walk from the city centre.

**Bluebell House** ( ☎ 238201; www.bluebell-house .com; 31 Kenneth St; r per person £27-35; P ) Warm and welcoming hosts, top breakfasts, close to city centre.

**Winmar Guest House** ( ☎ 239328; www.thewinmar .co.uk; 78 Kenneth St; s/d £35/70; P ) Another readers' recommendation; spacious sandstone villa with comfortable lounge, and kippers, croissants and fry-up on the breakfast menu.

**Moyness House Hotel** ( ☎ 233836; www.moyness .co.uk; 6 Bruce Gardens; r per person £36-40; P ) Elegant Victorian villa with a beautiful garden and peaceful setting, 10 minutes' walk southwest of the city centre.

**Amulree** ( ☎ 224822; amulree@btinternet.com; 40 Fairfield Rd; s/d £36/54) Comfortable, four-bedroom Victorian B&B less than 10 minutes' walk west of the city centre.

## TOP END

**Dunain Park Hotel** ( ☎ 230512; www.dunainparkhotel .co.uk; Dunain Park; d £138-198; P 🐾 ) This sumptuous country house hotel offers more traditional décor, with its Victorian four-poster beds, Georgian-style furniture and Italian marble bathrooms, all set in beautiful wooded grounds just five minutes' stroll from the Caledonian Canal and River Ness. The hotel is a mile southwest of Inverness on the A82 to Fort William.

**ourpick** **Rocpool Reserve** ( ☎ 240089; www .rocpoolc.com; Culduthel Rd; d £140-280; P ) Boutique chic meets the Highlands in this swanky and sophisticated little hotel, where an elegant Georgian exterior conceals an oasis of contemporary cool. A gleaming white entrance hall lined with contemporary art leads to designer rooms in shades of chocolate, cream and coffee; expect lots of hi-tech gadgetry in the more expensive rooms, ranging from iPod docks to balcony hot tubs with aquavision TV.

Also recommended:

**Glenmoriston Town House Hotel** ( ☎ 223777; www.glenmoriston.com; 20 Ness Bank; d £130-170; P ) Luxurious boutique hotel on the banks of the River Ness. Can organise golfing and fishing for guests.

## Eating
### BUDGET
**Pork, Cheese & Pie Shop** ( ☎ 237776; Eastgate; pies £1.50-2; ⌚ 9am-5pm Tue-Sat, to 4pm Mon) This deli sells a wide range of quality Scottish produce, but the main event as far as we're concerned is the great selection of delicious gourmet pies (to take away) – choose from lamb and rosemary, game and blackberry or Cumberland sausage and tomato (and many others), and munch contentedly on a park bench beside the river.

**Délices de Bretagne** ( ☎ 712422; 6 Stephen's Brae; mains £5-7; ⌚ 9am-5pm Mon-Sat, 10am-5pm Sun) This café brings a little taste of France to the Highlands, with its Art-Nouveau décor and a menu of tasty *galettes* (savoury pancakes), crepes, Breton cider and excellent coffee.

**Shapla Tandoori Restaurant** ( ☎ 241919; 2 Castle Rd; mains £9-11; ⌚ noon-2.30pm & 6-11pm) Head upstairs and choose a table by the window, where you can enjoy a curry with a splendid view over the river. You can get a three-course lunch for £6 from noon to 2.30pm Monday to Saturday.

Other good places for breakfast, coffee or a snack include the café in **Leakey's** ( ☎ 239947; Greyfriars Hall, Church St; ⌚ 10am-5.30pm Mon-Sat), the **Castle Restaurant** ( ☎ 230925; 41-43 Castle St; ⌚ 9am-8.30pm) and **Red Pepper** ( ☎ 237111; 74 Church St; ⌚ 9am-5.30pm).

Self-caterers can stock up at **Tesco Metro** (King St; ⌚ 7.30am-10pm Mon-Sat, 9am-6pm Sun).

### MIDRANGE & TOP END
**Kitchen** ( ☎ 259119; 15 Huntly St; mains £8-14; ⌚ noon-10pm) Opened by the people who own the Mustard Seed, this spectacular new glass-fronted restaurant offers good-value, informal dining with a view over the river. The menu focuses on fresh local produce and covers a range of old favourites, from battered cod with chips and mushy peas, to homemade burgers, to pasta and pesto with char-grilled veggies. Two-course lunch for £7 (noon to 3pm), and two-course early evening dinner for £10 (5pm to 7pm).

**Café 1** ( ☎ 226200; 75 Castle St; mains £9-16; ⌚ noon-2pm & 6-9.30pm Mon-Sat; ♿ ) Café 1 is a friendly and appealing little bistro with candle-lit tables amid elegant blonde-wood and wrought-iron décor. There is an international menu based on quality Scottish produce, from succulent Aberdeen Angus steaks to grilled sea bass with red pesto and crispy leeks. Express menu (all mains £6) noon to 2pm daily, and 5.30pm to 6.45pm Monday to Friday; children's menu available.

**Mustard Seed** ( ☎ 220220; 16 Fraser St; mains £12-14; ⌚ noon-10pm) This bright and bustling bistro brings a dash of big-city style to Inverness. The menu changes weekly, but focuses on Scottish and French cuisine with a modern twist. Grab a table on the upstairs balcony if you can – it's the best outdoor lunch spot in Inverness, with a great view across the river. It's best to book on weekends and any day in July and August.

**Rocpool Rendezvous** ( ☎ 717274; 1 Ness Walk; mains £11-17; ⌚ noon-2.30pm & 6-10pm) Lots of polished wood, navy-blue leather and stainless-steel trim lend a nautical air to this relaxing bistro, which offers a Mediterranean-influenced menu that makes the most of quality Scottish produce, especially seafood (there's a special seafood menu on Friday). The two-course lunch (noon to 2.30pm Monday to Saturday) is £10.

**ourpick** **Contrast Brasserie** ( ☎ 227889; 22 Ness Bank; 3-course dinner £25; ⌚ noon-2.30pm & 5-10pm) Book early for what we think is the best restaurant in Inverness – a dining room that drips designer style, smiling professional staff, a jug of water brought to your table without asking, and truly delicious food – a light, crisp samosa filled with meltingly tender, spiced, shredded

CENTRAL & WESTERN HIGHLANDS

lamb with a curry dipping sauce, followed by pan-fried whitefish with buttery shredded savoy cabbage and chanterelles; 10 out of 10. And at £7 for a two-course lunch, the value is incredible.

**River House** ( ☎ 222033; 1 Greig St; main £15-19; ❂ noon-2pm & 5.30-9.30pm Tue-Sat, 6-9.30pm Sun) The River House is an elegant restaurant of the polished wood and crisp white linen variety, serving the best of British venison, beef, lamb, duck and seafood. A two-course lunch is £11.50.

## Drinking

**Phoenix** ( ☎ 233685; 108 Academy St) This is the best of the traditional pubs in the city centre, with a mahogany horseshoe bar, a comfortable, family-friendly lounge, and good food at both lunchtime and in the evening. Real ales on tap include the rich and fruity Orkney Dark Island.

**Castle Tavern** ( ☎ 718718; 1-2 View Pl) Recently taken over by the owners of the Clachnaharry Inn, who have installed a tasty selection of real ales, this pub has a wee suntrap of a terrace out the front, a great place for a pint on a summer afternoon.

**Bar Pivo** ( ☎ 713307; 38-40 Academy St) This Czech-themed pub – half of the industrial-chic bar area is made up to look like a Prague metro station – offers no fewer than three Czech beers on draught, plus another six in bottles, as well as Scottish-made Belhaven real ales. Gay friendly.

**Johnny Foxes** ( ☎ 236577; 26 Bank St) Stuck beneath the ugliest building on the riverfront, Johnny Foxes is a big and boisterous Irish bar, with a wide range of food served all day and live music nightly.

our pick **Clachnaharry Inn** ( ☎ 239806; 17-19 High St; Clachnaharry) Just over a mile northwest of the city centre, on the bank of the Caledonian Canal just off the A862, this is a delightful old coaching inn (with beer garden out back) serving an excellent range of real ales.

## Entertainment

**Eden Court Theatre** ( ☎ 234234; www.eden-court.co.uk; Bishop's Rd) Following major renovations and extensions, the Eden Court has reopened as the Highlands' main cultural venue, theatre, art-house cinema and conference venue. It stages a busy programme of drama, dance, comedy, music, film and children's events, and has a good bar and restaurant. Pick up a

programme from the foyer or check its website; there's a box office (open 11.30am to 3.30pm Monday to Saturday) in Debenham's department store in the Eastgate Shopping Centre.

**Scottish Showtime** ( ☎ 830930; www.nessie.org .uk; Ramada Jarvis Hotel, Church St; tickets £16; ❂ 8.30pm Mon-Thu) From June to early September the Inverness Suite at the Ramada Jarvis Hotel stages 'Scottish Showtime', an evening of traditional Scottish music, song and dance aimed squarely at the tourist market. Tickets available from the tourist office.

**Hootananny** ( ☎ 233651; www.hootananny.com; 67 Church St) Hootananny is the city's best live-music venue, with traditional folk and/or rock music sessions nightly, including big-name bands from all over Scotland (and, indeed, the world). The bar is well stocked with a range of beers from the local Black Isle Brewery.

**Vue Cinema** ( ☎ 08712-240240; Inverness Retail & Business Park, Eastfield Way) This is a seven-screen multiplex cinema way out on the eastern edge of the city, just south of the A96 to Nairn.

## Getting There & Away

### AIR

**Inverness airport** ( ☎ 01667-464000; www.hial.co.uk) is at Dalcross, 10 miles east of the city on the A96 towards Aberdeen. There are scheduled flights to London, Belfast, Glasgow, Edinburgh, Stornoway, Benbecula, Orkney, Shetland and several other British airports. For more information, see p452.

### BUS

**National Express** ( ☎ 0870 580 8080; www.national express.com) operates a direct overnight bus from London to Inverness (£20, 13 hours, one daily), with more frequent services requiring a change at Glasgow.

**Scottish Citylink** ( ☎ 0870 550 5050; www.citylink .co.uk) has direct connections to Glasgow (£19, four hours, hourly), Edinburgh (£19, 3½ to 4½ hours, hourly), Fort William (£10, two hours, five daily), Ullapool (£9, 1½ hours, two daily except Sunday), Portree on the Isle of Skye (£17, 3½ hours, five daily) and Thurso (£15, 3½ hours, two daily).

If you book far enough in advance, **Megabus** ( ☎ 0900 160 0900; www.megabus.com) offers fares from as little as £1.50 for buses from Inverness to Glasgow and Edinburgh, and £6 to London.

Buses to Aberdeen (3¾ hours, hourly) are operated by Stagecoach Bluebird, while Rapsons/Highland Country buses serve Aviemore (1¾ hours, three daily Monday to Friday) via Grantown-on-Spey, and also run on the Inverness–Fort William route.

### TRAIN

There is one direct train daily from London to Inverness (£139, eight hours); others require a change at Edinburgh (nine hours, five daily). There are several direct trains a day from Glasgow (£37, 3½ hours), Edinburgh (£37, 3¼ hours) and Aberdeen (£23, 2¼ hours), and three daily Monday to Saturday (one or two on Sunday) to Thurso and Wick (£15, four hours).

The line from Inverness to Kyle of Lochalsh (£17, 2½ hours, four daily Monday to Saturday, two Sunday) provides one of Britain's great scenic train journeys.

## Getting Around

### TO/FROM THE AIRPORT

**Rapsons Jet** ( ☎ 710555; www.thejet.co.uk) buses run from the airport to Queensgate in the city centre (£2.90, 20 minutes, every 30 minutes). A taxi costs around £13. There are plans for a rail link to the airport, but at the time of writing there was no scheduled opening.

### BICYCLE

Bike-rental outlets include **Highland Bicycle Co** ( ☎ 234789; 16a Telford St; ☯ 8.30am-5.30pm Mon-Sat), which charges £12 a day.

### BUS

City services and buses to places around Inverness, including Nairn, Forres, the Culloden battlefield, Beauly, Dingwall and Lairg, are operated by **Rapsons/Highland Country** ( ☎ 710555; www.rapsons.com). An Inverness Roverbus ticket costs £9 and gives unlimited travel for a day on buses serving Culloden, Cawdor Castle, Fort George and Nairn.

### CAR

The tourist office has a handy Car Hire leaflet. The big boys charge from around £40 per day, or you could try **Sharp's Vehicle Rental** ( ☎ 236694; www.sharpsreliablewrecks.co.uk; Inverness train station) for cheaper rates starting at £23 per day.

### TAXI

Call **Highland Taxis** ( ☎ 222222).

## AROUND INVERNESS
### Culloden Battlefield

The Battle of Culloden in 1746, the last pitched battle ever fought on British soil, saw the defeat of Bonnie Prince Charlie and the end of the Jacobite dream when 1200 Highlanders were slaughtered by government forces in a 68-minute rout. The duke of Cumberland, son of the reigning king George II and leader of the Hanoverian army, earned the nickname 'Butcher' for his brutal treatment of the defeated Scottish forces. The battle sounded the death knell for the old clan system, and the horrors of the Clearances soon followed. The sombre moor where the conflict took place has scarcely changed in the ensuing 260 years.

Kilted guides offer one-hour guided tours of the battlefield; an impressive new **visitor centre** (NTS; ☎ 01463-790607; www.nts.org.uk/culloden; adult/child £8/6.50 ☯ 9am-6pm Apr-Oct, 10am-4pm Nov-Mar) was under construction at the time of research, and should be open by the time you read this.

Culloden is 6 miles east of Inverness. See left for details of bus services.

### Fort George

The headland guarding the narrows in the Moray Firth opposite Fortrose is occupied by the magnificent and virtually unaltered 18th-century artillery fortification of **Fort George** (HS; ☎ 01667-462777; adult/child £6.50/3.25; ☯ 9.30am-5.30pm Apr-Sep, to 4.30pm Oct-Mar). One of the finest examples of its kind in Europe, it was established in 1748 as a base for George II's army of occupation in the Highlands – by the time of its completion in 1769 it had cost the equivalent of around £1 billion in today's money. The mile-plus walk around the ramparts offers fine views out to sea and back to the Great Glen. Given its size, you'll need at least two hours to do the place justice. The fort is off the A96 about 11 miles northeast of Inverness.

### Nairn

☎ 01667 / pop 11,000

Nairn is a popular golfing and seaside resort with a good sandy beach. The town has a **tourist office** ( ☎ 452763; 62 King St; ☯ Apr-Oct), banks with ATMs and a post office.

The most interesting part of Nairn is the old fishing village of **Fishertown**, down by the harbour. **Nairn Museum** ( ☎ 456791; Viewfield House; adult/child £3/50p; ☯ 10am-4.30pm Mon-Fri, to 1pm Sat; ☯ ), a few minutes' walk from the tourist office, has displays on the history of Fishertown, as well as on local archaeology, geology and natural history.

You can spend many pleasant hours wandering along the **East Beach**, one of the finest in Scotland.

The big event in the town's calendar is the **Nairn Highland Games** (www.nairnhighlandgames.co.uk), held in mid-August. Also in August is the week-long **Nairn International Jazz Festival** (www.nairnjazz.com). Contact the tourist office for details of both events.

### SLEEPING & EATING

**Glebe End B&B** ( ☎ 451659; www.glebe-end.co.uk; 1 Glebe Rd; r per person £25-35; **P** ) It's people as much as place that make a good B&B, and the owners here are all you could wish for – helpful and welcoming. The house is lovely too, a spacious Victorian villa with home-from-home bedrooms and a sunny conservatory where breakfast is served.

**Sunny Brae Hotel** ( ☎ 452309; www.sunnybrae hotel.com; Marine Rd; s £92, d £98-130; **P** ) Beautifully decked out with fresh flowers and pot plants, the Sunny Brae enjoys an enviable location with great views across the Moray Firth. The hotel restaurant specialises in Scottish produce cooked with continental flair, with dishes such as smoked haddock gratin, and braised shank of local lamb with ratatouille and risotto.

**Boath House Hotel** ( ☎ 454896; www.boath-house.com; Auldearn; s/d from £180/220; **P** ) This beautifully restored Regency mansion, set in private woodland gardens 2 miles east of Nairn on the A96, is one of Scotland's most luxurious country house hotels, and includes a spa offering a range of holistic treatments, and a fine dining restaurant.

### GETTING THERE & AWAY

Buses run hourly (less frequently on Sunday) from Inverness to Aberdeen via Nairn. The town also lies on the Inverness to Aberdeen railway line; there are five to seven trains a day from Inverness (£4.30, 20 minutes).

## Cawdor

The 14th-century home of the Thanes of Cawdor, **Cawdor Castle** ( ☎ 01667-404615; adult/child £7.30/4.50; ⏱ 10am-5.30pm May–mid-Oct) is reputedly the castle of Shakespeare's *Macbeth* and was the scene of Duncan's murder in the play – a bit of poetic licence from the bard, since the central tower dates from the 14th century (the wings were 17th-century additions) and

Macbeth died in 1057. The castle is 5 miles southwest of Nairn.

**Cawdor Tavern** ( ☎ 01667-404777; bar meals £6-10) in the nearby village is worth a visit, though it can be difficult deciding what to drink as it stocks over 100 varieties of whisky. There's also good pub food, with tempting daily specials.

## Brodie Castle

Set in 70 hectares of parkland, **Brodie Castle** (NTS; ☎ 01309-641371; adult/child £8/5; ⏱ 10.30am-5pm daily Apr, Jul & Aug, Sun-Thu only May, Jun, Sep & Oct) has several highlights, including a library with more than 6000 peeling, dusty volumes. There are wonderful clocks, a huge Victorian kitchen and a 17th-century dining room with wildly extravagant moulded plaster ceilings depicting mythological scenes. The Brodies have been living here since 1160, but the present structure dates mostly from 1567, with many additions over the years.

The castle is 8 miles east of Nairn. Stagecoach Bluebird bus 305 from Inverness to Aberdeen stops at Brodie (45 minutes, hourly).

# WEST OF INVERNESS
## Beauly
☎ 01463 / pop 1160

Mary, Queen of Scots is said to have given this village its name in 1564 when she exclaimed, in French: '*Quel beau lieu!*' (What a beautiful place!). Founded in 1230, the red-sandstone **Beauly Priory** is now an impressive ruin; a small information kiosk next door has information on the history of the priory.

The central **Priory Hotel** ( ☎ 782309; www.priory -hotel.com; The Square; s/d £48/90; **P** ) has bright, modern rooms and serves good bar meals. Another good place for lunch is the restaurant in the **House of Beauly** ( ☎ 784702; Station Rd; mains £5-7) shopping and visitor centre.

Buses 18 and 19 from Inverness run to Beauly (hourly Monday to Saturday, four on Sunday), and the town lies on the Inverness–Thurso railway line.

## Strathglass & Glen Affric
☎ 01456

The broad valley of **Strathglass** extends about 18 miles inland from Beauly, followed by the A831 road to **Cannich**, the only village in the area, where there's a grocery store and a post office.

Several long and narrow valleys lead west from Strathglass into an almost roadless wilderness. **Glen Affric**, one of the most beautiful glens in Scotland, extends deep into the hills beyond Cannich. The upper reaches of the glen, now designated as Glen Affric National Nature Reserve, is a scenic wonderland of shimmering lochs, rugged mountains and native Scots pine, home to pine marten, wildcat, otter, red squirrel and golden eagle.

About 4 miles southwest of Cannich is **Dog Falls**, a scenic spot where the River Affric squeezes through a narrow, rocky gorge. A waymarked walking trail leads there easily from Dog Falls car park.

From the parking area and picnic site at the eastern end of **Loch Affric** there are several short walks along the river and the loch shore. The circuit of Loch Affric (10 miles, allow five hours) follows good paths right around the loch and takes you deep into the heart of some very wild scenery. Contact Inverness tourist office for more information.

It's possible to walk all the way from Cannich to Glen Shiel on the west coast (35 miles) in two days, spending the night at the remote Glen Affric Youth Hostel (see below).

### SLEEPING & EATING
**Glen Affric Youth Hostel** (SYHA; ☎ bookings 0870 155 3255, no phone at the hostel; Allt Beithe, Glen Affric; dm £13.50; Apr-Oct) This remote and rustic hostel is set amid magnificent scenery at the halfway point of the cross-country walk from Cannich to Glen Shiel, 8 miles from the nearest road. Facilities are basic and you'll need to take all supplies with you. Book in advance.

**Kerrow House** ( ☎ 415243; www.kerrow-house .co.uk; Cannich; s £44-60, d £54-70; P ) This wonderful Georgian hunting lodge has bags of old-fashioned character – it was once the home of Highland author Neil M Gunn, and has spacious grounds with 3.5 miles of private trout fishing. It's a mile south of Cannich on the minor road along the east side of the River Glass.

**Tomich Hotel** ( ☎ 415399; www.tomichhotel.co.uk; Tomich; s/d from £68/105; P ☒ ) About 3 miles southwest of Cannich on the southern side of the river, this Victorian hunting lodge has a blazing log fire, a Victorian restaurant, eight comfortable en-suite rooms and – a bit of a surprise out here in the wilds – a small, heated indoor swimming pool.

Other recommendations:
**Cannich Caravan Park** ( ☎ 415364; www.highland camping.co.uk; Cannich; tent sites per person £4.50, plus per car £1)

**Glen Affric Backpackers** ( ☎ 415263; Charrein Lodge, Cannich; dm £11)

### GETTING THERE & AWAY
Bus 17 runs from Inverness to Cannich (one hour, three to five a day Monday to Friday, plus two on Saturday during school holidays) via Drumnadrochit.

## BLACK ISLE
The Black Isle – a peninsula rather than an island – is linked to Inverness by the Kessock Bridge.

Rapsons/Highland Country buses run from Inverness to Fortrose and Rosemarkie (30 minutes, hourly Monday to Saturday); most continue to Cromarty (55 minutes).

### Fortrose & Rosemarkie
At **Fortrose Cathedral** you'll find the vaulted crypt of a 13th-century chapter house and sacristy, and the ruinous 14th-century south aisle and chapel. **Chanonry Point**, 1.5 miles to the east, is a favourite dolphin-spotting vantage point – there are one-hour **dolphin-watching cruises** (adult/child £10/7) departing from the harbour at Avoch (pronounced auch), 3 miles southwest.

In Rosemarkie, the **Groam House Museum** ( ☎ 01381-620961; admission by donation; 10am-5pm Mon-Sat, 2-4.30pm Sun Easter & May-Sep, 2-4pm Sat & Sun Oct-Apr) has a superb collection of Pictish stones engraved with designs similar to those on Celtic Irish stones.

From the northern end of Rosemarkie's High St, a short but pleasant signposted walk leads you through the gorges and waterfalls of the **Fairy Glen**.

Once you've worked up a thirst, retire to the bar at the **Anderson Hotel** ( ☎ 01381-620236; Union St, Fortrose) to sample its range of real ales (including Belgian beers and Somerset cider) and more than 200 single malt whiskies.

### Cromarty
☎ 01381 / pop 720
The Cromarty Firth, north of the Black Isle, is often dotted with huge offshore oil rigs lying at anchor; some are mothballed, others waiting for maintenance work at the Nigg Bay shipyards before being towed out to the North Sea.

The pretty village of Cromarty at the northeastern tip of the Black Isle has lots of 18th-century stone houses, two stores, a post office and a bank with ATM.

CENTRAL & WESTERN HIGHLANDS

The 18th-century **Cromarty Courthouse** (☎ 01381-600418; Church St; adult/child £3/2; ☒ 10am-5pm Apr-Oct) details the town's history using contemporary references. Kids will love the talking mannequins.

Nearby the courthouse is **Hugh Miller's Cottage** (NTS; ☎ 01381-600245; Church St; adult/child £5/2.50; ☒ 12.30-4.30pm daily Apr-Sep & Sun-Wed Oct), the thatch-roofed birthplace of Hugh Miller (1802–56), a local stonemason and amateur

---

### ART & INSPIRATION: INSIDER TIPS FROM HIGHLAND ARTISTS

Erlend and Pamela Tait are artists who live and work near Kiltarlity, Inverness-shire. They recently moved back to the Highlands after several years living in Edinburgh. You can see their work at www.erlendtait.com and www.pamelatait.co.uk.

**Has moving back to the Highlands been good for you as artists?**
**Pam:** Moving up here has definitely been great for me as it has made me feel far more focused on my work. I think having so much open space around has really given my head the freedom and clarity it needs to create. Since moving back here my work has developed dramatically, which I think has been mainly due to focus I have been able to give, but I know that the plants, small flowers and patterns in the land have all been heavily influencing my work.
**Erlend:** Moving back up north has been invaluable. In Edinburgh I felt caged in by the buildings and the size of the city. I was concentrating on music by night (gigging and recording) and doing church window restoration throughout the country as the day job. I wanted to draw and paint again and needed to return to the Highlands to do this. I'm also designing far more stained glass now as opposed to restoring it.

**What aspects of Scotland inspire you as artists?**
**Pam:** The open landscape. What I love most about living up here is we can go anywhere in the car, even on a boring trip into town to get shopping, and I will always get blown away by the scenery. That to me is an endless supply of inspiration.
**Erlend:** I'm inspired, of course, by the rural landscape of the Highlands. However, my main inspiration comes from the folklore and fairy tales of the Black Isle where I grew up, and of Orkney where my family originates. One aspect of my work deals with where the physical landscape meets with mythology.

**You are exhibiting in various galleries around Scotland – are there other artists on show whose work you especially admire?**
**Erlend:** Michael Forbes, Kate Carruthers, Kate Leney and Paul Kershaw, among many others. I'm also a member of a small group who have a website at www.highlandartists.co.uk.
**Pam:** There's also Alex Main, Gerald Laing, Fin MacRae and Alex Dunn.

**Are there any 'hidden corners' in your region, somewhere off the tourist trail, that you would recommend visitors should go and see?**
**Erlend:** The Fairy Glen in Rosemarkie (p325) – carvings, locations and lore. And the Clootie Well near Munlochy is a magical place where you hang a piece of your clothing to cure an ailment or bring you good luck. Generally, the Black Isle, Orkney, and the area around Glen Affric are my favourite places in Scotland. Although Mull's good too, and Skye…
**Pam:** Dogs Falls over Glen Affric way (p324). It's a beautiful drive there, just stunning, and there's great walks to do there too, but when you see the falls you are just looking at time gone by, carved in the stone by the power of the water – it's amazing, makes you feel all funny…

I really like the shop called Over the Rainbow in Portree (p386). It has the most amazing selection of clothes, handbags, jewellery, postcards, cushions, socks and other stuff. That actually doesn't make it sound that amazing but it really is! And we both love the Anderson Hotel in Fortrose (p325) – it just has the most amazing selection of whiskies and beers and it's a lovely pub to be in. I know if we lived in Fortrose it wouldn't be long before we had great big red toffee noses!

geologist who later moved to Edinburgh and became a famous journalist and newspaper editor. The Georgian villa next door is home to a museum celebrating his life and achievements.

From Cromarty harbour, **Ecoventures** ( ☎ 01381-600323; www.ecoventures.co.uk) runs 2½-hour boat trips (adult/child £20/15) into the Moray Firth to see bottlenose dolphins and other wildlife.

## LOCH NESS

Deep, dark and narrow, Loch Ness stretches for 23 miles between Inverness and Fort Augustus. Its bitterly cold waters have been extensively explored in search of Nessie, the elusive Loch Ness monster, but most visitors see her only in cardboard-cutout form at the monster exhibitions. The busy A82 road runs along the northwestern shore, while the more tranquil and picturesque B862 follows the southeastern shore. A complete circuit of the loch is about 70 miles – travel anticlockwise for the best views.

### Activities

The 73-mile **Great Glen Way** (www.greatglenway .com) long-distance footpath stretches from Inverness to Fort William, where walkers can connect with the West Highland Way (see boxed text, p280). It is described in detail in *The Great Glen Way*, a guide by Jacquetta Megarry and Sandra Bardwell.

The Great Glen Way footpath shares some sections with the 80-mile **Great Glen Mountain Bike Trail**, a waymarked mountain-bike route that follows canal towpaths and gravel tracks through forests, avoiding roads where possible.

The climb to the summit of **Meallfuarvonie** (699m), on the northwestern shore of Loch Ness, makes an excellent short hill walk: the views along the Great Glen from the top are superb. It's a 6-mile round trip, so allow about three hours. Start from the car park at the end of the minor road leading south from Drumnadrochit to Bunloit.

### Drumnadrochit

☎ 01456 / pop 800
Seized by monster madness, its gift shops bulging with Nessie cuddly toys, Drumnadrochit is a hotbed of beastie fever, with two monster exhibitions battling it out for the tourist dollar.

The **Loch Ness Exhibition Centre** ( ☎ 450573; www .loch-ness-scotland.com; adult/child £5.95/4; ⏱ 9am-8pm Jul & Aug, to 6pm Jun & Sep, to 5.30pm Oct, 9.30am-5pm Easter-May, 10am-3.30pm Nov-Easter; ♿ ) is the better of the two Nessie-themed attractions, with a scientific approach that allows you to weigh the evidence for yourself, and featuring original footage of monster sightings plus exhibits of equipment used in the various underwater monster hunts.

The more homely **Original Loch Ness Monster Centre** ( ☎ 450342; www.lochness-centre.com; adult/child £5/3.50; ⏱ 9am-8pm Jul & Aug, 10am-5.30pm Apr-Jun, Sep & Oct, 10am-4pm Nov-Mar) shows a superficial 30-minute Loch Ness video (with multilingual headsets), but its main function is to sell you tacky Loch Ness monster souvenirs.

One-hour monster-hunting cruises, complete with sonar and underwater cameras, aboard the **Nessie Hunter** ( ☎ 450395; www.lochness -cruises.com), operate from Drumnadrochit. Cruises depart hourly from 9am to 6pm daily from Easter to December, and cost £10/6 for an adult/child.

### Urquhart Castle

Commanding a brilliant location with outstanding views (on a clear day), **Urquhart Castle** (HS; ☎ 450551; adult/child £6.50/3.25; ⏱ 9.30am-6pm Apr-Sep, to 5pm Oct-Mar; ♿ ) is a popular Nessie-watching hot spot. A controversial new visitor centre (most of which is beneath ground level) includes a video theatre (with a dramatic 'unveiling' of the castle at the end of the film), displays of medieval items discovered in the castle, a huge gift shop and a restaurant. The site is often very crowded in summer.

The castle was repeatedly sacked and rebuilt over the centuries, but was finally blown up in 1692 to prevent the Jacobites from using it. The five-storey tower house at the northern point is the most impressive remaining fragment and offers wonderful views across the water.

### Sleeping & Eating

**Loch Ness Backpackers Lodge** ( ☎ 450807; www.loch ness-backpackers.com; Coiltie Farmhouse, East Lewiston; dm/d/ f £12.50/30/45) This snug, friendly hostel housed in a cottage and barn has six-bed dorms, one double and a large barbecue area. It's about 0.75 miles from Drumnadrochit, along the A82 towards Fort William; turn left where you see the sign for Loch Ness Inn, just before the bridge.

CENTRAL & WESTERN
HIGHLANDS

## STRANGE SPECTACLE ON LOCH NESS

Highland folklore is filled with tales of strange creatures living in lochs and rivers, notably the kelpie (water horse) that lures unwary travellers to their doom. The use of the term 'monster', however, is a relatively recent phenomenon whose origins lie in an article published in the *Inverness Courier* on 2 May 1933, entitled 'Strange Spectacle on Loch Ness'.

The article recounted the sighting of a disturbance in the loch by Mrs Aldie Mackay and her husband: 'There the creature disported itself, rolling and plunging for fully a minute, its body resembling that of a whale, and the water cascading and churning like a simmering cauldron.'

The story was taken up by the London press and sparked off a rash of sightings that year, including a notorious on-land encounter with London tourists Mr and Mrs Spicer on 22 July 1933, again reported in the *Inverness Courier*:

It was horrible, an abomination. About 50 yards ahead, we saw an undulating sort of neck, and quickly followed by a large, ponderous body. I estimated the length to be 25 to 30 feet, its colour was dark elephant grey. It crossed the road in a series of jerks, but because of the slope we could not see its limbs. Although I accelerated quickly towards it, it had disappeared into the loch by the time I reached the spot. There was no sign of it in the water. I am a temperate man, but I am willing to take any oath that we saw this Loch Ness beast. I am certain that this creature was of a prehistoric species.

The London newspapers couldn't resist. In December 1933 the *Daily Mail* sent Marmaduke Wetherall, a film director and big-game hunter, to Loch Ness to track down the beast. Within days he found 'reptilian' footprints in the shoreline mud (soon revealed to have been made with a stuffed hippopotamus foot, possibly an umbrella stand). Then in April 1934 came the famous 'long-necked monster' photograph taken by the seemingly reputable Harley St surgeon Colonel Kenneth Wilson. The press went mad and the rest, as they say, is history.

In 1994, however, Christian Spurling – Wetherall's stepson, by then 90 years old – revealed that the most famous photo of Nessie ever taken was in fact a hoax, perpetrated by his stepfather with Wilson's help. Today, of course, there are those who claim that Spurling's confession is itself a hoax. And, ironically, the researcher who exposed the surgeon's photo as a fake still believes wholeheartedly in the monster's existence.

Hoax or not, there's no denying that the bizarre mini-industry that has grown up around Loch Ness and its mysterious monster since that eventful summer 75 years ago is the strangest spectacle of all.

**Loch Ness Youth Hostel** (SYHA; ☎ 0870 004 1138; dm £12.50-13.25; ☿ Apr-Sep) This hostel is housed in a big lodge overlooking Loch Ness, and many dorms have loch views. It's located on the A82 road, 13 miles southwest of Drumnadrochit, and 4 miles northeast of Invermoriston. Buses from Inverness to Fort William stop nearby.

**Gillyflowers** ( ☎ 450641; gillyflowers@cali.co.uk; s/d from £40/50; ☿ Mar-Oct; **P** ) This B&B is a renovated 18th-century farmhouse on the southern edge of Drumnadrochit village, with two comfortable en-suite rooms with tartan-canopied beds. Walkers and cyclists are welcome.

**Borlum Farm Caravan & Camping Park** ( ☎ 450220; tent/campervan sites per person £5; ☿ Mar-Oct) This campsite's 800m southeast of Drumnadrochit.

Near Drumnadrochit's village green are the pleasant **Glen Café Bar** ( ☎ 450282; mains £7-9) and the **Fiddler's Coffee Shop & Restaurant** ( ☎ 450678; mains £11-17). The coffee shop does cappuccino and croissants, while the restaurant serves traditional Highland fare, such as venison casserole, and a wide range of bottled Scottish beers.

## Getting There & Away

Scottish Citylink and Highland Country buses from Inverness to Fort William run along the shores of Loch Ness (six to eight daily, five on Sunday); those headed for Skye turn off at Invermoriston. There are bus stops at Drumnadrochit (£6, 30 minutes), Urquhart Castle car park (£6, 35 minutes) and Loch Ness Youth Hostel (£8, 45 minutes).

## FORT AUGUSTUS

☎ 01320 / pop 510

Fort Augustus, at the junction of four old military roads, was originally a government garrison and the headquarters of General George Wade's road-building operations in the early 18th century. Today it's a neat and picturesque little place, often overrun by tourists in summer.

There's a **tourist office** ( ☎ 366367; 🕙 9am-6pm Mon-Sat, to 5pm Sun Easter-Oct) in the central car park, and an ATM and bureau de change (in the post office) beside the canal.

### Sights & Activities

At Fort Augustus, boats using the **Caledonian Canal** are raised and lowered 13m by a 'ladder' of five consecutive locks. It's fun to watch, and the neatly landscaped canal banks are a great place to soak up the sun or compare accents with fellow tourists. The **Caledonian Canal Heritage Centre** ( ☎ 366493; admission free; 🕙 10am-5pm Apr-Oct), beside the lowest lock, showcases the history of the canal.

The **Clansman Centre** ( ☎ 366444; admission free; 🕙 10am-6pm Apr-Oct) has an exhibition on 17th-century Highland life, with live demonstrations of how to put on a plaid (the forerunner of the kilt) and how the claymore (Highland sword) was made and used. There is also a workshop where you can purchase handcrafted reproduction swords, dirks and shields.

The **Royal Scot** ( ☎ 366277; www.cruiselochness.com; 🕙 10am-4pm Mar-Oct, 2pm Sat & Sun only Nov & Dec) offers one-hour cruises (adult/child £9/5.25) on Loch Ness accompanied by the latest hi-tech sonar equipment so you can keep an underwater eye open for Nessie.

### Sleeping & Eating

**Fort Augustus Caravan & Camping Park** ( ☎ 366618; www.campinglochness.co.uk; tent/campervan sites per adult/child £5.50/2.75; 🕙 Apr-Sep; ♿ ) This campsite is just south of the village on the western side of the road to Fort William, and has a playhouse, sandpit and tree swing for the kids.

**Morag's Lodge** ( ☎ 366289; www.moragslodge.com; Bunnoich Brae; dm/tw/f £16/42/51; 🖳 P ) This large and well-run hostel is based in a big Victorian house with great views of Fort Augustus' hilly surrounds, and has a convivial bar with open fire. It's hidden away in the trees up the steep side road just north of the tourist office car park.

**Lorien House** ( ☎ 366736; www.lorien-house.co.uk; Station Rd; d £55-60) Lorien is a cut above your usual B&B – the bathrooms come with bidets and the breakfasts with smoked salmon, and there's a library of walking, cycling and climbing guides in the lounge.

**Lovat Arms Hotel** ( ☎ 0845 450 1100; www.lovatarms-hotel.com; Main Rd; d £110-270; ♿ P ) Recently given a stylish and luxurious makeover, the bedrooms in this grand old hotel are spacious and elegantly furnished, while the lounge is equipped with a log fire, comfy armchairs and grand piano. Kids are allowed in the bar-restaurant, and a children's high tea is served 5.30pm to 8.30pm.

**Lock Inn** ( ☎ 366302; bar meals £5-11; 🕙 food served noon-8pm) A superb little pub right on the canal bank, the Lock Inn has a vast range of malt whiskies and a tempting menu of bar meals that includes Orkney salmon, Highland venison and daily seafood specials; the house speciality is beer-battered haddock and chips.

### Getting There & Away

Scottish Citylink and Highland Country buses from Inverness to Fort William stop at Fort Augustus (£9, one hour, six to eight daily Monday to Saturday, five on Sunday).

# THE CAIRNGORMS

The **Cairngorms National Park** (www.cairngorms.co.uk) encompasses the highest landmass in Britain – a broad mountain plateau, riven only by the deep valleys of the Lairig Ghru and Loch Avon, with an average altitude of over 1000m and including five of the six highest summits in the UK. This wild mountain landscape of granite and heather has a sub-Arctic climate and supports rare alpine tundra vegetation and high-altitude bird species, such as snow bunting, ptarmigan and dotterel.

The harsh mountain environment gives way lower down to scenic glens softened by beautiful open forests of native Caledonian pine, home to rare animals and birds such as pine marten, wildcat, red squirrel, osprey, capercaillie and crossbill.

This is prime hill-walking territory, but even couch potatoes can enjoy a taste of the high life by taking the Cairngorm Mountain Railway (p334) up to the edge of the Cairngorm plateau.

CENTRAL & WESTERN
HIGHLANDS

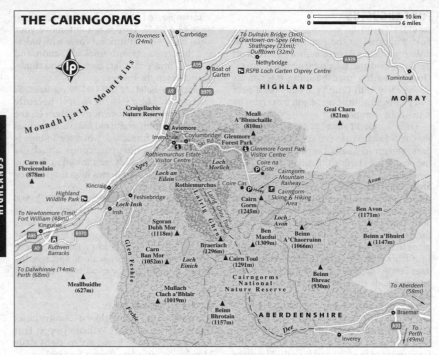

## THE CAIRNGORMS

## AVIEMORE

☎ 01479 / pop 2400

Aviemore is the gateway to the Cairngorms, the region's main centre for transport, accommodation, restaurants and shopping. It's not the prettiest town in Scotland by a long stretch – the main attractions are in the surrounding area – but when bad weather puts the hills off limits, Aviemore fills up with hikers, cyclists and climbers (plus skiers and snowboarders in winter) cruising the outdoor equipment shops or recounting their latest adventures in the cafés and bars. Add in tourists and locals and the eclectic mix makes for a lively little town.

### Orientation

Aviemore is on a loop off the A9 Perth–Inverness road; almost everything of note is to be found along the main drag, Grampian Rd. The train station and bus stop are towards the southern end.

The Cairngorm skiing area and mountain railway lie 9 miles east of Aviemore along the B970 (Ski Rd) and its continuation through Coylumbridge and Glenmore.

### Information

There are ATMs outside the Tesco supermarket, and currency exchange at the post office and the tourist office, all located on Grampian Rd.

**Old Bridge Inn** ( ☎ 811137; 23 Dalfaber Rd; per 30min £1; ⏲ 11am-11pm Sun-Thu, to midnight Fri & Sat) Internet access is available here.

**Tourist office** ( ☎ 810363; www.visitaviemore.com; The Mall, Grampian Rd; ⏲ 9am-6pm Mon-Sat, 9.30am-5pm Sun Jul & Aug, 9am-5pm Mon-Sat, 10am-4pm Sun Easter-Jun, Sep & Oct, limited hr Oct-Easter)

**Waterstone's** ( ☎ 810797; 87 Grampian Rd; ⏲ 9am-5.30pm Mon & Wed-Sat, 9.30am-5.30pm Tue, 11am-5pm Sun) For books and maps.

### Sights

Aviemore's mainline train station is also home to the **Strathspey Steam Railway** ( ☎ 810725; www.strathspeyrailway.co.uk; Station Sq), which runs steam trains on a section of restored line between Aviemore and Broomhill, 10 miles to the northeast, via Boat of Garten. There are four or five trains daily from June to September, and a more limited service in April, May, October and December; a return ticket from

Aviemore to Broomhill is £9.50/4.75 per adult/child. An extension to Grantown-on-Spey is planned; in the meantime, you can continue from Broomhill to Grantown-on-Spey by bus.

The **Aviemore Highland Resort** ( ☎ 0845 223 6217; www.aviemorehighlandresort.com) to the west of Grampian Rd is a complex of hotels, chalets, restaurants, a swimming pool, gym, spa, computer games arcade and a huge, shiny shopping mall. The **swimming pool** (adult/child £6/3; ☽ 8am-8pm) and other leisure facilities are open to nonresidents.

## Activities
### WALKING
A trail leads west from Aviemore Youth Hostel and passes under the A9 into the **Craigellachie Nature Reserve**, a great place for short hikes across steep hill sides covered in natural birch forest. Look out for birds and other wildlife, including the peregrine falcons that nest on the crags from April to July. If you're very lucky, you may even spot a capercaillie.

The **Rothiemurchus Estate Visitor Centre** ( ☎ 812345; www.rothiemurchus.net; Inverdruie; admission free; ☽ 9am-5.30pm), a mile southeast of Aviemore along the B970, has a free *Visitor Guide & Footpath Map* detailing access to 50 miles of footpaths through the estate's beautiful Caledonian pine forests, including the wheelchair-accessible 4-mile trail around **Loch an Eilein**, with its ruined castle and peaceful pine woods. See also the boxed text Mountain Walks in the Cairngorms, p334.

### FISHING
**Rothiemurchus Fishery** ( ☎ 810703; Rothiemurchus Estate, Inverdruie) at the southern end of the village has a loch where you can cast for rainbow trout; buy permits (from £10 to £30 a day, plus £3.50 for tackle hire) at the Fish Farm Shop in Inverdruie. If you're a fly-fishing virgin, there's a beginner's package, including tackle hire, one hour's instruction and one hour's fishing, for £35. For experienced anglers, there's also salmon and sea trout fishing on the River Spey – a day permit costs around £20; numbers are limited, so it's best to book in advance.

You can also fish for brown trout and pike on **Loch Morlich** – permits are available from the warden's office at Glenmore Caravan & Camping Site (p334).

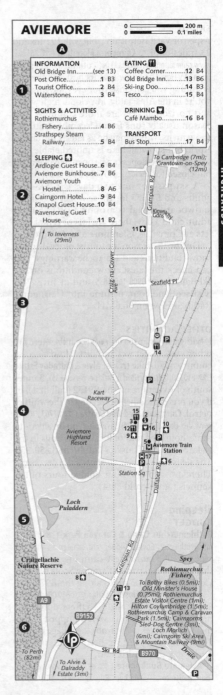

CENTRAL & WESTERN HIGHLANDS

## SKIING

Aspen or Val d'Isere it ain't, but with 19 runs and 23 miles of piste **Cairngorm Mountain** ( ☎ 861261; www.cairngormmountain.co.uk) is Scotland's biggest ski area. When the snow is at its best and the sun is shining you can close your eyes and imagine you're in the Alps; sadly, low cloud, high winds and horizontal sleet are more common. The season usually runs from December until the snow melts, which may be as late as the end of April, but snowfall here is unpredictable – in some years the slopes can be open in November, but closed for lack of snow in February.

A ski pass for one/two days is £28/54 for adults and £17/33 for those under 16. Ski or snowboard rental is around £19/13.50 per adult/child a day; there are lots of rental outlets at Coire Cas, Glenmore and Aviemore.

During the season the tourist office displays snow conditions and avalanche warnings. You can check the latest snow conditions on the **Ski Hotline** ( ☎ 0900 165 4655) and at http://ski .visitscotland.com, or tune into Cairngorm Radio Ski FM on 96.6MHz.

## OTHER ACTIVITIES

If bad weather keeps you off the hills, there are other ways to get wet and dirty. Join a cross-country quad-bike trek at **Alvie & Dalraddy Estate** ( ☎ 810330; Dalraddy Holiday Park; per person £35), 3 miles south of Aviemore on the B9152 (call first), or if you prefer the smell of wet dog to the whiff of petrol, **Cairngorm Sled-Dog Centre** ( ☎ 07767 270526; www.sled-dogs.co.uk; Ski Rd) can take you on a two- to three-hour sled tour of local forest trails in the wake of a team of huskies (adult/child £50/35). The sleds have wheels, so snow's not necessary. There are also one-hour guided tours of the kennels (adult/child £8/4).

## Sleeping

### BUDGET

**Rothiemurchus Camp & Caravan Park** ( ☎ 812800; info@rothie.net; Coylumbridge; tent/campervan sites per person £5.50) The nearest camping ground is this year-round park set among Scots pines at Coylumbridge, 1.5 miles along the B970.

**Aviemore Youth Hostel** (SYHA; ☎ 0870 004 1104; 25 Grampian Rd; dm £13-15; 🖳 P ) Offers upmarket hostelling in a spacious, well-equipped building, five minutes' walk from the village centre. There are four- and six-bed rooms, and the doors stay open until 2am.

**Aviemore Bunkhouse** ( ☎ 811181; www.aviemore -bunkhouse.com; Dalfaber Rd; dm/tw/f £14/34/48;

🖳 P 🚹 ) This independent hostel, next door to the Old Bridge Inn, provides accommodation in bright, modern six- or eight-bed dorms, each with private bathroom, and one twin/family room. There's a drying room, secure bike storage and wheelchair-accessible dorms. From the train station, cross the pedestrian bridge over the tracks, turn right and walk south on Dalfaber Rd.

**Kinapol Guest House** ( ☎ 810513; www.kinapol.co.uk; Dalfaber Rd; s/d from £30/40; P ) The Kinapol is a modern bungalow offering basic but comfortable B&B accommodation, across the tracks from the train station. All three rooms have shared bathrooms.

### MIDRANGE

**Ravenscraig Guest House** ( ☎ 810278; www.aviemore online.com; Grampian Rd; r per person £30-38; P 🚹 ) Ravenscraig is a large, flower-bedecked Victorian villa with six spacious en-suite rooms, plus another six in a modern annexe at the back (one wheelchair accessible). It serves traditional and veggie breakfasts in an attractive conservatory dining room.

**Old Minister's House** ( ☎ 812181; www.theold ministershouse.co.uk; Rothiemurchus; r per person £35-42; P ) This former manse dates from 1906 and has four rooms with a homely, country farmhouse feel. It's in a lovely setting amid Scots pines on the banks of the River Druie, just 0.75 miles southeast of Aviemore.

**Ardlogie Guest House** ( ☎ 810747; www.ardlogie .co.uk; Dalfaber Rd; s/d £35/60; P ) Handy for the train station, the five-room Ardlogie has great views over the River Spey towards the Cairngorms, there's a boules pitch in the garden, and guests get free use of the local country club's pool, spa and sauna.

**Cairngorm Hotel** ( ☎ 810233; www.cairngorm.com; Grampian Rd; s/d £50/80; 🖳 P ) Better known as the Cairn, this long-established hotel is set in the fine old granite building with the pointy turret opposite the train station. It's a welcoming place with comfortable rooms and a determinedly Scottish atmosphere, all tartan carpets and stags' antlers. There's live music on weekends, so it can get a bit noisy – not for early-to-bedders.

### TOP END

**Hilton Coylumbridge** ( ☎ 810661; www.coylumbridge .hilton.com; Coylumbridge; s/d from £85/110; 🚹 P 🚮 ) This modern, low-rise Hilton, set amid the pine woods just outside Aviemore, is a wonderfully child-friendly hotel, with bedrooms for up to two adults and two children, indoor and outdoor play areas, a crèche and a baby-sitting service.

## Eating & Drinking

**Coffee Corner** ( ☎ 810564; 85 Grampian Rd; snacks £2-5; ☺ 9am-5pm) This cosy café is a good place to relax with newspapers and a steaming mug of coffee on a rainy day. It does good breakfasts, scones and ice-cream sundaes.

**Café Mambo** ( ☎ 811670; The Mall, Grampian Rd; mains £7-9; ☺ food served noon-8.30pm Mon-Thu, noon-7.30pm Fri & Sat, 12.30-8.30pm Sun) The Mambo is popular with snowboarders – a chill-out café in the afternoon, serving burgers, steaks and Tex-Mex grub, it turns into a clubbing and live-band venue in the evenings.

**Old Bridge Inn** ( ☎ 811137; 23 Dalfaber Rd; bar meals £9, mains £11-19; ☺ food served noon-2pm & 6-9pm, to 9.30pm Fri & Sat) The Old Bridge has a snug bar, complete with roaring log fire in winter, and a cheerful, chalet-style restaurant at the back serving quality Scottish cuisine.

**Ski-ing Doo** ( ☎ 810392; 9 Grampian Rd; mains £7-10, steaks £13-15; ☺ 1pm-late Mon, Tue & Thu-Sat, 5.30pm-late Sun; ☺ ) A long-standing Aviemore institution, the child-friendly Ski-ing Doo (it's a pun…oh, ask the waiter!) is a favourite with family skiers. An informal place offering a range of hearty, homemade burgers, chilli dishes and juicy steaks.

For campers and self-caterers there's a massive **Tesco** (Grampian Rd; ☺ 8am-10pm Mon-Sat, 9am-6pm Sun) supermarket in the middle of town. Head to **Rothiemurchus Larder** ( ☎ 810858; Rothiemurchus Estate Visitor Centre, Inverdruie), a mile along Ski Rd, for smoked trout, venison, pâté and other picnic delicacies.

## Getting There & Away

### BUS

Buses stop on Grampian Rd; buy tickets at the tourist office. Scottish Citylink connects Aviemore with Inverness (£6.40, 45 minutes), Newtonmore (£6, 30 minutes), Pitlochry (£9, 1¼ hours), Perth (£13, two hours), Glasgow (£17, 3¼ hours) and Edinburgh (£17, 3¼ hours).

Buses 33 and 36 link Aviemore with Grantown-on-Spey (35 minutes, five daily weekdays, two Saturday) via Carrbridge (15 minutes), while bus 34 runs the Grantown-on-Spey–Aviemore–Cairngorm car park route (hourly, less frequent between Aviemore and Grantown-on-Spey on weekends).

### TRAIN

There are direct train services to Glasgow/ Edinburgh (£36, three hours, three daily) and Inverness (£9, 40 minutes, nine daily).

## Getting Around

### BIKE

Several places in Aviemore, Rothiemurchus Estate and Glenmore have mountain bikes for hire, including **Bothy Bikes** ( ☎ 810111; www.bothybikes.co.uk; Ski Rd), which charges £20 a day for a quality bike with front suspension and disc brakes.

### BUS

Bus 34 links Aviemore to Cairngorm car park (hourly June to September and mid-December to April, three daily Monday to Friday May and October to mid-December) via Coylumbridge.

## AROUND AVIEMORE
### Loch Morlich
☎ 01479

Six miles east of Aviemore, Loch Morlich is surrounded by some 8 sq miles of pine and spruce forest that make up the Glenmore Forest Park. Its attractions include a sandy beach (at the east end) where you'll find the popular **Loch Morlich Watersports Centre** ( ☎ 861221; Glenmore; ☺ 9am-5pm May-Oct), which rents out Canadian canoes (£15.50 an hour), kayaks (£8), windsurfers (£15.50), sailing dinghies (£20) and rowing boats (£15).

The park's **visitor centre** ( ☎ 861220) has a small exhibition on the Caledonian forest and sells the *Glen More Forest Guide Map*, detailing local walks. The circuit of Loch Morlich (one hour) makes a pleasant outing; the trail is pram- and wheelchair-friendly.

The warden at the neighbouring **Cairngorm Reindeer Centre** ( ☎ 861228; Glenmore; adult/child £8/6) will take you on a tour to see and feed Britain's only herd of reindeer, who are very tame and will even eat out of your hand. Walks take place at 11am, plus another at 2.30pm from May to September, and 3.30pm Monday to Friday in July and August.

One of Britain's leading adventure sports training centres, **Glenmore Lodge** ( ☎ 861256; www.glenmorelodge.org.uk; Glenmore; r per person £22; ☒ ) offers courses in hill walking, rock climbing, ice climbing, canoeing, mountain biking and mountaineering. The centre's comfortable B&B accommodation is available to all, even

**MOUNTAIN WALKS IN THE CAIRNGORMS**

The climb from the car park at the Coire Cas ski area to the summit of **Cairn Gorm** (1245m) takes about two hours (one way). From there, you can continue south across the high-level plateau to Ben Macdui (1309m), Britain's second-highest peak. This takes eight to 10 hours return from the car park and is a serious undertaking, for experienced and well-equipped walkers only.

The **Lairig Ghru trail**, which can take eight to 10 hours, is a demanding 24-mile walk from Aviemore through the Lairig Ghru pass (840m) to Braemar. An alternative to doing the full route is to make the six-hour return hike up to the summit of the pass and back to Aviemore. The path starts from Ski Rd, a mile east of Coylumbridge, and involves some very rough going.

Warning – the Cairngorm plateau is a sub-Arctic environment where navigation is difficult and weather conditions can be severe, even in midsummer. Hikers must have proper hill-walking equipment, and know how to use a map and compass. In winter it is a place for experienced mountaineers only.

if you're not taking a course, as is the indoor-climbing wall, gym and sauna.

**Cairngorm Lodge Youth Hostel** (SYHA; ☎ 0870 004 1137; Glenmore; dm £14; ✹ closed Nov–mid-Dec) is set in a former shooting lodge and enjoys a great location at the east end of Loch Morlich; pre-booking is essential.

**Glenmore Caravan & Camping Site** ( ☎ 861271; Glenmore; tents & campervans £8-17; ✹ closed Nov–mid-Dec) Campers can set up a base at this attractive loch-side site with pitches amid the Scots pines; rates include up to four people per tent/campervan.

## Cairngorm Mountain Railway

Aviemore's most popular attraction is the **Cairngorm Mountain Railway** ( ☎ 01479-861261; ✹ 10am-5pm May-Nov, 9am-4.30pm Dec-Apr), a funicular train that will whisk you to the edge of Cairngorm plateau (1085m) in just eight minutes (adult/child return £8.95/5.65). The bottom station is at the Coire Cas car park at the end of Ski Rd; at the top is an exhibition, a shop (of course) and a restaurant. Unfortunately, for environmental and safety reasons, you're not allowed out of the top station in summer, not even to walk down – you must return to the car park on the funicular. However, you can hike to the summit from the car park, and then go down on the railway. After 4.30pm the train only carries restaurant visitors.

The **Ptarmigan Restaurant** ( ☎ 01479-861336; 3-course dinner incl train fare £35; ✹ 6.30-10.30pm Fri & Sat Jul-Sep) in the top station is Britain's highest restaurant, and offers – weather permitting – a spectacular sunset dining experience. The menu combines traditional Scottish produce with contemporary style. Bookings essential.

## Kincraig & Glen Feshie

The **Highland Wildlife Park** ( ☎ 01540-651270; Kincraig; adult/child £10/7.50; ✹ 10am-6pm Apr-Oct, to 4pm Nov-Mar, last entry 2hr before closing) near Kincraig, 6 miles southwest of Aviemore, features a drive-through safari park and animal enclosures that offer the chance to get close to rarely seen native wildlife, such as wildcat, capercaillie, pine marten, white-tailed sea eagle and red squirrel, as well as species that once roamed the Scottish hills but have long since disappeared, including wolf, lynx, wild boar, beaver and European bison. Visitors without cars get driven around by staff (at no extra cost).

At Kincraig the Spey widens into Loch Insh, home of the **Loch Insh Watersports Centre** ( ☎ 01540-651272; www.lochinsh.com; Kincraig), which offers canoeing, windsurfing, sailing, bike hire and fishing, as well as B&B accommodation from £24 per person. The food here is good, especially after 6.30pm when the loch-side café metamorphoses into a cosy restaurant.

Beautiful, tranquil **Glen Feshie** extends south from Kincraig, deep into the Cairngorms, with Scots pine woods in its upper reaches surrounded by big, heathery hills. The 4WD track to the head of the glen makes a great mountain-bike excursion (25 mile round trip).

**Glen Feshie Hostel** ( ☎ 01540-651323; glenfeshiehostel@ totalise.co.uk; Glen Feshie; dm/tw £10/36), about 5 miles south of Kincraig, is a cosy, independent 14-bed hostel popular with hikers. Rates include bed linen and a steaming bowl of porridge to start the day.

## Carrbridge
☎ 01479 / pop 540
Carrbridge, 7 miles northeast of Aviemore, is a good alternative base for exploring the

region. It takes its name from the graceful old bridge (spotlit at night), built in 1717, over the thundering rapids of the Dulnain.

The **Landmark Forest Heritage Park** ( ☎ 841613; adult/child £9.75/7.60; ⏰ 10am-7pm mid-Jul–Aug, to 6pm Apr–mid-Jul, to 5pm Sep-Mar; ♿ ), set in a forest of Scots pines, is a theme park with a difference; the theme is timber. The main attractions are the Ropeworx highwire adventure course, the Treetops Trail (a raised walkway through the forest canopy that allows you to view red squirrels, crossbills and crested tits), and the steam-powered sawmill.

**Carrbridge Bunkhouse Hostel** ( ☎ 841250; www .carrbridge-bunkhouse.co.uk; dm £8) is a cosy, wood-panelled forest cabin, complete with hot showers, drying room and sauna. It's just off the A938 at Bogroy, on the western edge of the village.

Highland Country bus 15 runs from Inverness to Carrbridge (45 minutes, four daily Monday to Friday, two on Saturday) and onwards to Grantown-on-Spey (20 minutes).

## Boat of Garten
☎ 01479 / pop 570

Boat of Garten is known as the Osprey Village because these rare and beautiful birds of prey nest nearby at the **RSPB Loch Garten Osprey Centre** ( ☎ 831694; Tulloch, Nethybridge; adult/child 50p; ⏰ 10am-6pm Apr-Aug; ♿ ). The ospreys migrate here each spring from Africa and nest in a tall pine tree – you can watch from a hide as the birds feed their young. The centre is signposted about 2 miles east of the village.

**Fraoch Lodge** ( ☎ 831331; Deshar Rd; r per person £16-18; Ⓟ ) provides luxury hostel-style accommodation in a Victorian town house, in twin or family rooms. There's a lounge with an open fire and a self-catering kitchen; rates include a light breakfast.

The **Old Ferryman's House** ( ☎ 831370; s/d £26/52; Ⓟ ) is a charming cottage B&B on the riverbank on the far side of the bridge to the east of the village (follow the signs to Nethybridge), while the **Boat Hotel** ( ☎ 831258; www.boathotel.co.uk; s/d from £75/100; Ⓟ ) is a luxurious country hotel with a superb restaurant.

Boat of Garten is 6 miles northeast of Aviemore. The most interesting way to get here is on the Strathspey Steam Railway (p330).

## GRANTOWN-ON-SPEY
☎ 01479 / pop 2170

Grantown (pronounced granton) is an elegant Georgian town on the banks of the Spey, a favoured haunt of anglers and the tweed cap and green wellies brigade. Thronged with tourists in summer, it reverts to a quiet backwater in winter. Most hotels can kit you out for a day of fly-fishing or put you in touch with someone who can. There's a **tourist office** ( ☎ 872773; 54 High St; ⏰ 9.30am-5pm Mon-Sat & 10am-4pm Sun Apr-Sep), a bank, ATMs and a post office.

### Sleeping & Eating

**Brooklynn** ( ☎ 873113; www.woodier.com; Grant Rd; r per person £26-30; Ⓟ ) This beautiful Victorian villa features original stained glass and wood panelling, and seven spacious, luxurious rooms (all doubles have en suites). The food – dinner is available as well as breakfast – is superb, too.

**Culdearn House Hotel** ( ☎ 872106; www.culdearn .com; Woodlands Tce; r per person £55-75; Ⓟ ) Yet another plush Victorian villa (Grantown is full of them) with corniced ceilings, marble fireplaces and original wood panelling, this hotel has an excellent restaurant with a log fire and candle-lit tables. Note that children under 10 are not welcome.

**Coffee House & Ice Cream Parlour** (High St; ⏰ 9.30am-5pm Mon-Sat, 10am-4.30pm Sun) A traditional family café that sells delicious home-made ice cream.

**Craggan Mill** ( ☎ 872288; Craggan Mill; mains £12-20; ⏰ noon-2.30pm & dinner Wed-Mon) Housed in a restored 18th-century meal mill just south of town on the A95 towards Aviemore, the Craggan is strong on rustic atmosphere and friendly service. The menu doesn't disappoint either, with expertly prepared Scottish seafood, salmon, beef and venison, and desserts that include traditional clootie dumpling made to an old family recipe.

**Glass House** ( ☎ 872980; Grant Rd; mains £17-19; ⏰ noon-1.45pm Wed-Sat, 7-9pm Tue-Sat, 12.30-2pm Sun) Set a block north of the main street, and looking more like a private home than a restaurant, this elegant but unpretentious place is famous for its fresh, seasonal menus that focus on local produce with dishes such as roast loin of pork with black pudding sauce, Scottish asparagus and wild mushrooms.

### Getting There & Away

For details of buses to Aviemore, see Getting There & Away in the Aviemore section. See also Getting Around on p317 for details of summer-only bus services from Grantown to Cullen, Elgin, Dufftown, Tomintoul and Ballater.

## KINGUSSIE

☎ 01540 / pop 1410

The gracious old Spey-side town of Kingussie (pronounced kin-yewsie) sits at the foot of the great heather-clad humps known as the Monadhliath Mountains. The town is best known as the home of the excellent Highland Folk Museum.

### Sights

The open-air **Highland Folk Museum** ( ☎ 661307; www.highlandfolk.museum; Duke St; adult/child £2.50/1.50; ☽ 10am-5pm Mon-Sat Apr-Aug, to 4pm Mon-Fri Sep & Oct) comprises a collection of historical buildings and relics revealing many aspects of Highland culture and lifestyle. The museum is laid out like a village and has a traditional thatch-roofed Isle of Lewis *blackhouse* (low-walled stone cottage), a water mill and a 19th-century corrugated-iron shed for smoking salmon. Actors in period costume give demonstrations of traditional crafts. There's another section of the museum at nearby Newtonmore.

Perched dramatically on a river terrace and clearly visible from the main A9 road, the roofless **Ruthven Barracks** (admission free; ☽ 24hr) was one of four garrisons built by the British government after the first Jacobite rebellion of 1715 as part of a Hanoverian scheme to take control of the Highlands. Ironically, the barracks were last occupied by Jacobite troops awaiting the return of Bonnie Prince Charlie after the Battle of Culloden. Learning of his defeat and subsequent flight, they destroyed the barracks before taking to the glens. The ruins are spectacularly floodlit at night.

### Activities

The Monadhliath Mountains, northwest of Kingussie, attract fewer hikers than the nearby Cairngorms and make an ideal destination for walkers seeking peace and solitude. However, during the deer-stalking season (August to October), you'll need to check with the tourist office before setting out.

The recommended six-hour circular walk to the 878m summit of **Carn an Fhreiceadain**, above Kingussie, begins north of the village. It continues to Pitmain Lodge and along the Allt Mor river before climbing to the cairn on the summit. You can then follow the ridge east to the twin summits of Beinn Bhreac before returning to Kingussie via a more easterly track.

### Sleeping & Eating

**Lairds Bothy Hostel** ( ☎ 661334; www.thetipsylaird.co.uk; 68 High St; dm £10) Tucked behind the Tipsy Laird pub in the main street, this good-value hostel has several comfortable three- and four-bed rooms, but suffers a bit with noise from the bar; ah well, if you can't beat 'em, join 'em.

**Homewood Lodge** ( ☎ 661507; www.homewood-lodge-kingussie.co.uk; Newtonmore Rd; r per person £25-30; Ⓟ ) This elegant Victorian lodge on the western outskirts of town offers double rooms with exquisite views of the Cairngorms – a nice way to wake up in the mornings!

**Hermitage** ( ☎ 662137; Spey St; r per person from £26; Ⓟ ) The five-bedroom Hermitage is a lovely old house with plenty of character, filled with Victorian period features. The lounge has a log fire, and there are good views of the Cairngorms from the garden.

**Osprey Hotel** ( ☎ 661510; www.ospreyhotel.co.uk; Ruthven Rd; r per person £30-35; Ⓟ ) Overlooking the town's flower-filled memorial gardens, this cosily old-fashioned Victorian town house has eight brightly refurbished rooms, and serves tasty home cooking at breakfast and dinner.

**Cross** ( ☎ 661166; www.thecross.co.uk; Tweed Mill Brae, Ardbroilach Rd; 3-course dinner £45, ☽ 7-9pm Tue-Sat, closed Jan; Ⓟ ) Housed in a converted water mill beside the Allt Mor burn, the Cross is one of the finest restaurants in the Highlands. The intimate, low-raftered dining room has an open fire and a patio overlooking the stream, and serves a daily-changing menu of fresh Scottish produce accompanied by a superb wine list. If you want to stay the night, there are eight stylish bedrooms to choose from. Double rooms cost between £130 and £190.

### Getting There & Away

There are Scottish Citylink buses from Kingussie to Perth (£11, 1¾ hours, five daily), Aviemore (£5, 25 minutes, five to seven daily) and Inverness (£9, one hour, six to eight Monday to Saturday, three Sunday).

From the train station at the southern end of town there are trains to Edinburgh (£36, 2½ hours, seven a day Monday to Saturday, two Sunday) and Inverness (£9, one hour, eight a day Monday to Saturday, four Sunday).

## NEWTONMORE

☎ 01540 / pop 980

Three miles southwest of Kingussie lies the peaceful backwater of Newtonmore, home to the excellent **Highland Folk Museum** ( ☎ 661307;

adult/child £5/3; ⊙ 10.30am-5.30pm Apr-Aug, 11am-4.30pm Sep, 11am-4.30pm Mon-Fri Oct), a sister establishment to the museum of the same name in Kingussie. The Newtonmore site includes a reconstructed village with wattle and daub cottages, a school and a farm, and on-site demonstrations of woodcarving, spinning and peat-fire baking. You'll need two to three hours to make the most of a visit here.

Ten miles southwest of Newtonmore, on the A86 road towards Spean Bridge, is **Laggan Wolftrax** ( ☎ 01528-544786; www.basecampmtb.com; Strathmashie Forest, Laggan; admission free; ⊙ 10am-6pm Mon-Wed & Fri, 10am-9pm Thu, 9am-8pm Sat, 9am-6pm Sun), a mountain-biking centre with purpose-built trails ranging from open-country riding to black-diamond downhills. Cycle hire is available on site, from £18 a day for an ordinary mountain bike to £35 for a full-suspension downhill rig.

### Sleeping

**Eagleview Guest House** ( ☎ 673675; www.eagle viewguesthouse.co.uk; Perth Rd; r per person £25-41; P ) The family-friendly Eagleview is one of the nicest places to stay in the area, with beautifully decorated bedrooms, spacious bathrooms with power showers, and nice little touches like wall-mounted flat-screen TVs, cafetieres with real coffee on your hospitality tray and real milk rather than that yucky UHT stuff.

As a popular hill-walking base camp, Newtonmore is well endowed with budget accommodation, including the **Strathspey Mountain Hostel** ( ☎ 673694; www.newtonmore.com/strathspey; Main St; dm £12; P ), a snug 19th-century cottage with two six-bunk dorms and two triple rooms.

### Getting There & Around

The Scottish Citylink buses that serve Kingussie (see p336) also stop at Newtonmore.

You can rent bikes (from £5 a day) from Strathspey Mountain Hostel.

## DALWHINNIE

The remote village of Dalwhinnie, bypassed by the main A9 road, straggles along its single street in glorious isolation amid wild and windswept scenery. From a distance you can spot the distinctive twin pagoda-shaped roofs of the malt kiln at **Dalwhinnie Distillery** ( ☎ 01540-672219; ⊙ 9.30am-4.30pm Mon-Fri year-round, plus 9.30am-4.30pm Sat Jun-Oct, plus 12.30-4.30pm Sun Jul & Aug), which offers guided tours for £5. It is the

highest in Scotland (326m above sea level) and one of the most remote.

Three or four trains a day on the Glasgow/Edinburgh to Inverness line stop at Dalwhinnie's tiny station, 600m from the distillery.

# WEST HIGHLANDS

This area extends from the bleak blanket-bog of the Moor of Rannoch to the west coast beyond Glen Coe and Fort William, and includes the southern reaches of the Great Glen. The scenery is grand throughout, with high and wild mountains dominating the glens. Great expanses of moor alternate with lochs and patches of commercial forest. Fort William, at the inner end of Loch Linnhe, is the only sizable town in the area.

## GLEN COE

Scotland's most famous glen is also one of the grandest and, in bad weather, the grimmest. The approach to the glen from the east, watched over by the rocky pyramid of **Buachaille Etive Mor** – the Great Shepherd of Etive – leads over the Pass of Glencoe and into the narrow upper valley. The southern side is dominated by three massive, brooding spurs, known as the **Three Sisters**, while the northern side is enclosed by the continuous steep wall of the knife-edged Aonach Eagach ridge. The main road threads its lonely way through the middle of all this mountain grandeur, past deep gorges and crashing waterfalls, to the more pastoral lower reaches of the glen around Loch Achtriochtan and Glencoe village.

Glencoe was written into the history books in 1692 when the resident MacDonalds were murdered by Campbell soldiers in what became known as the Glencoe Massacre (see boxed text, p339).

### Activities

There are several short, pleasant walks around **Glencoe Lochan**, near the village. To get there, turn left off the minor road to the youth hostel, just beyond the bridge over the River Coe. There are three walks (40 minutes to an hour), all detailed on a signboard at the car park. The artificial lochan was created by Lord Strathcona in 1895 for his homesick Canadian wife Isabella and is surrounded by a North American–style forest.

A more strenuous hike, but well worth the effort on a fine day, is the climb to the **Lost Valley**, a magical mountain sanctuary still haunted by the ghosts of murdered MacDonalds (only 2.5 miles round trip, but allow three hours). A rough path from the car park at Allt na Reigh (on the A82, 6 miles east of Glencoe village) bears left down to a footbridge over the river, then climbs up the wooded valley between Beinn Fhada and Gearr Aonach (the first and second of the Three Sisters). The route leads steeply up through a maze of giant, jumbled, moss-coated boulders before emerging – quite unexpectedly – into a broad, open valley with an 800m-long meadow as flat as a football pitch. Back in the days of clan warfare, the valley – invisible from below – was used for hiding stolen cattle; its Gaelic name, Coire Gabhail, means 'corrie of capture'.

The summits of Glen Coe's mountains are for experienced mountaineers only. Details of hill-walking routes can be found in the Scottish Mountaineering Club's guidebook *Central Highlands* by Peter Hodgkiss.

### East of the Glen

A few miles east of Glencoe proper, on the south side of the A82, is the car park and base station for the **Glencoe Mountain Resort** ( ☎ 01855-851226; www.glencoemountain.com), where commercial skiing in Scotland first began back in 1956. The Lodge Café-Bar has comfy sofas where you can soak up the view through the floor-to-ceiling windows.

The **chairlift** (adult/child £8/5; ☺ 9.30am-4.30pm Thu-Mon May-Sep) continues to operate in summer – there's a grand view over the Moor of Rannoch from the top station – and provides access to a downhill mountain-biking track. In winter a lift pass costs £25 a day and equipment hire is £20 a day.

Two miles west of the ski centre, a minor road leads along peaceful and beautiful **Glen Etive**, which runs southwest for 12 miles to the head of Loch Etive. On a hot summer's day the River Etive contains many tempting pools for swimming in, and there are lots of good picnic sites.

The remote **King's House Hotel** ( ☎ 01855-851259; www.kingy.com; Glencoe; bar meals £6-10; ⓟ ) claims to be one of Scotland's oldest licensed inns, dating from the 17th century. It lies on the old military road from Stirling to Fort William (now followed by the West Highland Way; see boxed text, p280), and after the Battle of Cul-

loden it was used as a Hanoverian garrison – hence the name. The hotel serves good pub grub – it's famous for its haggis, neeps and tatties (haggis, mashed turnip and mashed potato), and has long been a meeting place for climbers, skiers and hill walkers. The lounge has a picture window with a stupendous view of Buachaille Etive Mor, a great place to sit and admire the scenery with a glass of malt whisky. Single/double rooms are available for £28/60.

### Glencoe Village

☎ 01855 / pop 360

The little village of Glencoe stands on the south shore of Loch Leven at the western end of the glen, 16 miles south of Fort William. The small, thatched **Glencoe Folk Museum** ( ☎ 811664; Glencoe; adult/child £2/free; ☺ 10am-5.30pm Mon-Sat Apr-Oct) houses a varied collection of military memorabilia, farm equipment, and tools of the woodworking, blacksmithing and slate-quarrying trades.

About 1.5 miles east of the village, towards the glen, is the **Glencoe Visitor Centre** (NTS; ☎ 811307; Inverigan; adult/child £5/4; ☺ 9.30am-5.30pm Apr-Aug, 10am-5pm Sep & Oct, 10am-4pm Thu-Sun Nov-Mar; & ). A modern facility with an ecotourism angle, the centre provides comprehensive information on the geological, environmental and cultural history of Glencoe via hitech interactive and audiovisual displays, and tells the story of the Glencoe Massacre (see boxed text, opposite) in all its gory detail.

At **Lochaber Watersports** ( ☎ 821391; www.lochaber watersports.co.uk; West Laroch; ☺ 9.30am-5pm Apr-Oct) you can hire canoes (£10 an hour), rowing boats, sailing dinghies, mountain bikes (£15 a day) and even a 10m sailing yacht complete with skipper (£150 for three hours, up to five people).

### SLEEPING & EATING

**Invercoe Caravan & Camping Park** ( ☎ 811210; www .invercoe.co.uk; Glencoe; tent sites per person £6, plus car £3, campervan £17) Our favourite official campsite in Glencoe, this place has great views of the surrounding mountains.

**Glencoe Independent Hostel** ( ☎ 811906; www.glen coehostel.co.uk; Glencoe; dm £9.50-12; ⓟ ) This handily located hostel, just 10 minutes' walk from the Clachaig Inn, is set in an old farmhouse with six- and eight-bed dorms, and a bunkhouse with another 16 bed spaces in communal, Alpine-style bunks. There's also a cute little

## THE GLENCOE MASSACRE

Glen Coe – Gleann Comhann in Gaelic – is sometimes (wrongly) said to mean 'the glen of weeping', a romantic mistranslation that gained popularity in the wake of the brutal murders that took place here in 1692.

Following the Glorious Revolution of in 1688, in which the Catholic King James VII/II (VII of Scotland, II of England) was replaced on the British throne by the Protestant King William II/III, supporters of the exiled James – known as Jacobites, most of them Highlanders – rose up against William in a series of battles. In an attempt to quash Jacobite loyalties, King William offered the Highland clans an amnesty on condition that all clan chiefs take an oath of loyalty to him before 1 January 1692.

Maclain, the elderly chief of the MacDonalds of Glencoe, had long been a thorn in the side of the authorities. Not only was he late in setting out to fulfil the king's demand, but he mistakenly went first to Fort William before travelling slowly through winter mud and rain to Inveraray, where he was three days late in taking the oath before the Sheriff of Argyll.

The secretary of state for Scotland, Sir John Dalrymple, decided to use the fact that Maclain had missed the deadline to punish the troublesome MacDonalds, and at the same time set an example to other Highland clans, some of whom had not bothered to take the oath.

A company of 120 soldiers, mainly from the Campbell territory of Argyll, were sent to the glen under cover of collecting taxes. It was a long-standing tradition for clans to provide hospitality to travellers and, since their commanding officer was related to Maclain by marriage, the troops were billeted in MacDonald homes.

After they'd been guests for 12 days, the government order came for the soldiers to 'fall upon the rebels the MacDonalds of Glencoe and put all to the sword under 70. You are to have a special care that the Old Fox and his sons do upon no account escape'. The soldiers turned on their hosts at 5am on 13 February, killing Maclain and 37 other men, women and children. Some of the soldiers alerted the MacDonalds to their intended fate, allowing them to escape; many fled into the snow-covered hills, where another 40 people died of exposure.

The ruthless brutality of the incident caused a public uproar, and after an inquiry several years later Dalrymple lost his job. There's a monument to Maclain in Glencoe village, and members of the MacDonald clan still gather here on 13 February each year to lay a wreath.

wooden cabin that sleeps up to three (£48 per night).

**Glencoe Youth Hostel** (SYHA; ☎ 0870 004 1122; Glencoe; dm £13.50-14.50; 🖳 🅿 ) The 62-bed Glencoe hostel is very popular with hikers, though the atmosphere is a little institutional. It's a 1.5-mile walk from the village along the minor road on the northern side of the river.

**Crafts & Things** ( ☎ 811325; Glencoe; mains £3-5; ⏱ 9.30am-5.30pm; 🦽 ) Just off the main road between Glencoe and Ballachulish, the coffee shop in this craft shop is a good spot for a lunch of homemade lentil soup with crusty rolls, ciabatta sandwiches, or just coffee and carrot cake. There are tables outdoors, and a box of toys to keep the little ones occupied.

our pick **Clachaig Inn** ( ☎ 811252; www.clachaig.com; Clachaig, Glencoe; bar meals £7-11; 🅿 ) The Clachaig has long been a favourite haunt of hill walkers and climbers. As well as comfortable en-suite accommodation (single/double for £70/80),

there's a smart, wood-panelled lounge bar, with lots of sofas and armchairs, mountaineering photos and climbing magazines to leaf through. Climbers usually head for the lively Boots Bar on the other side of the hotel – it has log fires, serves real ale and good pub grub, and has live Scottish, Irish and blues music every Wednesday and Saturday nights.

### GETTING THERE & AWAY

Scottish Citylink buses run between Fort William and Glencoe (£5, 30 minutes, eight daily) and from Glencoe to Glasgow (£14, 2½ hours, eight daily).

## KINLOCHLEVEN

☎ 01855 / pop 900

Kinlochleven is hemmed in by high mountains at the head of the beautiful fjord-like Loch Leven, about 7 miles east of Glencoe village. The aluminium smelter that led to the town's development in the early 20th century has now closed, and the opening of the Ballachulish Bridge in the 1970s allowed the main road to bypass the place completely. A ray of hope was provided by the opening of the West Highland Way, which now brings a steady stream of hikers through the village.

## Sights & Activities

The final section of the **West Highland Way** (see boxed text, p280) stretches for 14 miles from Kinlochleven to Fort William. The village is also the starting point for easier walks up the glen of the River Leven, through pleasant woods to the Grey Mare's Tail waterfall, and harder mountain hikes into the Mamores.

If you fancy trying your hand at ice-climbing, even in the middle of summer, head for the **Ice Factor** ( ☎ 831100; www.ice-factor.co.uk; Leven Rd; 9am-10pm Tue-Thu, 9am-7pm Fri-Mon), the world's biggest indoor ice-climbing wall; a 1½-hour beginner's course costs £55. There's also a rock-climbing wall, sauna and steam room, and a café and bar-bistro.

The **Aluminium Story Visitor Centre** ( ☎ 831663; Linnhe Rd; admission free; 10am-1pm & 2-5pm Mon-Fri Apr-Sep, 10am-1pm Mon, Wed & Fri, 10am-2pm & 6-8pm Tue & Thu Oct-Mar) tells the interesting story of the British Aluminium Company smelter (which opened in 1908) and the Blackwater Reservoir hydroelectric scheme that powered it.

## Sleeping & Eating

**Blackwater Hostel** ( ☎ 831253; www.blackwaterhostel .co.uk; Lab Rd; dm/tw £13/29, tent sites per person £5) This 40-bed hostel has spotless, pine-panelled dorms with en-suite bathrooms and TV, and a level, well-sheltered camping ground.

**Lochleven Seafood Cafe** ( ☎ 821048; Loch Leven; mains £7-14; noon-9pm Wed-Sun) An outstanding and welcome addition to the region's restaurants, this place serves superb shellfish freshly plucked live from tanks – oysters on the half shell, razor clams, scallops, lobster and crab – plus a daily fish special, and a couple of non-seafood dishes. For warm summer days, there's an outdoor terrace with a view across the loch to the Pap of Glencoe, a distinctive conical-shaped mountain.

## Getting There & Away

Highland Country bus 44 runs from Fort William to Kinlochleven (50 minutes, eight to 10 a day Monday to Saturday, three on Sunday) via Ballachulish and Glencoe village.

# FORT WILLIAM

☎ 01397 / pop 9910

Basking on the shores of Loch Linnhe amid magnificent mountain scenery, Fort William has one of the most enviable settings in the whole of Scotland. If it wasn't for the busy dual carriageway crammed between the town centre and the loch, and one of the highest rainfall records in the country, it would be almost idyllic. Even so, it's not a bad little town, and its easy access by rail and bus makes it a good place to base yourself for exploring the surrounding mountains and glens.

Magical Glen Nevis begins near the northern end of the town and wraps itself around the southern flanks of Ben Nevis (1344m) – Britain's highest mountain and a magnet for hikers and climbers. The glen is also popular with movie makers – parts of the films *Braveheart*, *Rob Roy* and *Harry Potter & the Sorcerer's Stone* were filmed here.

## History

There is little left of the original fort from which the town derives its name – it was pulled down in the 19th century to make way for the railway. The first castle here was constructed by General Monk in 1654 and called Inverlochy, but the meagre ruins by the loch are those of the fort built in the 1690s by General Mackay and named after King William II/III. In the 18th century it became part of a chain of garrisons (along with Fort Augustus and Fort George) that controlled the Great Glen in the wake of the Jacobite rebellions.

Originally a tiny fishing village called Gordonsburgh, the town took its present name with the opening of the railway in 1901, which, along with the building of the Caledonian Canal, helped it grow into a tourist centre. This has been consolidated in the last three decades by the huge increase in popularity of climbing, skiing, mountain biking and other outdoor sports.

## Orientation

The town straggles along the shore of Loch Linnhe for around 3 miles. The compact town centre is clustered around High St and Cameron Sq, 200m southwest of the train and bus stations, and is easy to get around on foot. Glen Nevis and Ben Nevis are 3 miles north of the town centre.

## Information

**Belford Hospital** ( ☎ 702481; Belford Rd) Opposite the train station.

**Lloyds TSB** ( ☎ 0845 303 0109; 6 Tweedale, High St; ⊙ 9.30am-4pm Mon & Tue, 10am-4pm Wed, 9.30am-5.30pm Thu, 9.30am-5pm Fri) Twenty-four hour ATM.

**Nevisport** ( ☎ 704921; Airds Crossing, High St; ⊙ 9am-5.30pm Mon-Sat, 9.30am-5pm Sun) Outdoor equipment, guidebooks and maps. Internet access in downstairs bar (per 10 minutes £1).

**One World Internet Café** ( ☎ 07976 961695; 123 High St; per 15min £1; ⊙ 9am-9pm Apr-Sep, 10am-5pm Oct-Mar)

**Post office** ( ☎ 0845 722 3344; 5 High St)

**Royal Bank of Scotland** ( ☎ 705191; 6 High St; ⊙ 9.15am-4.45pm Mon, Tue, Thu & Fri, 10am-4.45pm Wed) Twenty-four hour ATM.

**Tourist office** ( ☎ 703781; www.visithighlands.com; Cameron Sq; ⊙ 9am-6pm Mon-Sat, 10am-5pm Sun Apr-Sep, limited hr Oct-Mar) Internet access (per 20 minutes £1).

## Sights

The small but fascinating **West Highland Museum** ( ☎ 702169; Cameron Sq; adult/child £3/50p; ⊙ 10am-5pm Mon-Sat Jun-Sep, plus 2-5pm Sun Jul & Aug, 10am-4pm Mon-Sat Oct-May) is packed with all manner of Highland memorabilia. Look out for the secret portrait of Bonnie Prince Charlie – after the Jacobite rebellions all things Highland were banned, including pictures of the exiled leader, and this tiny painting looks like nothing more than a smear of paint until viewed in a cylindrical mirror, which reflects a credible likeness of the prince.

A tour of the **Ben Nevis Distillery** ( ☎ 702476; Lochy Bridge; ⊙ 9am-5pm Mon-Fri year-round, plus 10am-4pm Sat Easter-Sep & noon-4pm Sun Jul & Aug) makes for a warming rainy-day alternative to exploring the hills; the guided tour costs £4/2 per adult/child.

## Activities

From late May to early October, the **Jacobite Steam Train** ( ☎ 01463-239026; www.steamtrain.info) makes the scenic two-hour run from Fort William to Mallaig, departing from Fort William train station at 10.20am Monday to Friday (plus weekends in July and August), returning from Mallaig at 2.10pm (adult/child £28/16 day return). There's a brief stop at Glenfinnan station (p347), and you get 1½ hours in Mallaig (p348). Classed as one of the great railway journeys of the world, the route crosses the historic Glenfinnan Viaduct, made famous in the *Harry Potter* films – the Jacobite's owners supplied the steam locomotive and rolling stock used in the film.

The **Lochaber Leisure Centre** ( ☎ 704359; Belford Rd; pool £2.30, wall £2.70; ⊙ 7.15am-9pm Mon-Fri, 12.30-4pm Sat & Sun) has a swimming pool, indoor climbing wall, gym, sauna and other leisure facilities.

You can hike from the town centre to the summit of **Cow Hill** (287m) for a superb view of Ben Nevis, the Great Glen and Loch Linnhe. From the roundabout at the end of High St, head south along Lundavra Rd for 0.75 miles and turn left after Lochview Dr onto an unsurfaced road that leads to the TV mast at the top of the hill. Halfway to the summit another path descends on the far side of the hill into Glen Nevis, from where you can return to town along the road (6 miles total, allow 2½ hours).

For details of walking and cycling routes from Fort William to Inverness through the Great Glen, see p327.

## Tours

**Al's Tours** ( ☎ 700700; www.alstours.com) Taxi tours with driver-guide around Lochaber and Glencoe cost £80/195 for a half- /full day.

**Seal Island Cruises** ( ☎ 07766 138538) Operates 1½-hour (adult/child £10/8, three daily) and 3½-hour (adult/child £30/20, Friday only) wildlife cruises on Loch Linnhe departing from the Town Pier, visiting a seal colony and a salmon farm.

## Sleeping

It's best to book well ahead in summer, especially for hostels. See also the Glen Nevis Sleeping & Eating section (p344).

### BUDGET

**Calluna** ( ☎ 700451; www.fortwilliamholiday.co.uk; Heathercroft, Connochie Rd; dm/tw £12/28; P ) Run by well-known mountain guide Alan Kimber and wife, Sue, the Calluna offers self-catering apartments geared to groups of hikers and climbers, but also takes individual travellers prepared to share; there's a fully equipped kitchen and an excellent drying room for your soggy hiking gear.

**Fort William Backpackers** ( ☎ 700711; www.scot lands-top-hostels.com; Alma Rd; dm/tw £13.50/33; 🖳 ) A 10-minute walk from the bus and train stations, this lively and welcoming hostel is set in a grand Victorian villa, perched on a hill side with great views over Loch Linnhe.

**Bank Street Lodge** ( ☎ 700070; www.bankstreet lodge.co.uk; Bank St; dm/tw £13/45) Part of a modern

CENTRAL & WESTERN
HIGHLANDS

hotel and restaurant complex, the Bank Street Lodge offers the most central budget beds in town, only 250m from the train station. It has kitchen facilities and a drying room.

**St Andrew's Guest House** ( ☎ 703038; www.standrews guesthouse.co.uk; Fassifern Rd; r per person £20-25; **P** ) Set in a lovely 19th-century building that was once a rectory and choir school, St Andrew's retains period features, such as carved masonry, wood panelling and stained-glass windows, and has six spacious bedrooms, some with stunning views – good value at the price.

## MIDRANGE

**Glenlochy Guest House** ( ☎ 702909; www.glenlochyguest house.co.uk; Nevisbridge; r per person £35-38; **P** ) Convenient for Glen Nevis, Ben Nevis and the

end of the West Highland Way, the Glenlochy is a sprawling modern place, with 12 en-suite rooms set in a huge garden beside the River Nevis, a pleasant place to sit on summer evenings.

**Tornevis Guest House** ( ☎ 772868; www.tornevis .co.uk; Banavie; r per person £35-40; ☿ Apr-Oct; **P** ) This luxury B&B is set in a spacious modern house with a great location, enjoying an uninterrupted view of Ben Nevis. The friendly and knowledgeable owners have been in the business for many years, and can recommend local walks and attractions.

Other recommendations:

**No 6 Caberfeidh** ( ☎ 703756; www.6caberfeidh.com; 6 Caberfeidh, Fassifern Rd; r per person £20-30) Friendly B&B; vegetarian breakfast on request.

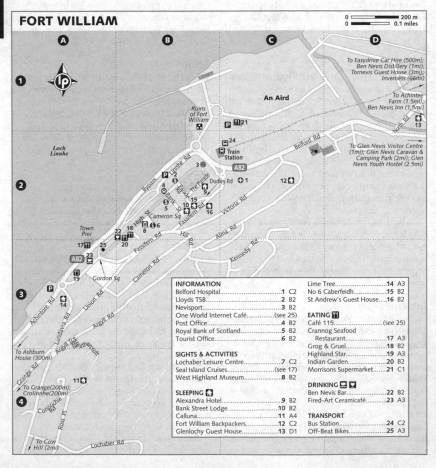

**FORT WILLIAM**

0    200 m
0    0.1 miles

**Ashburn House** ( ☎ 706000; www.highland5star.co.uk; Achintore Rd; r per person £40-50; P ) Grand Victorian villa; children under 12 not welcome.

## TOP END

**our pick** **Grange** ( ☎ 705516; www.grangefortwilliam.com; Grange Rd; r per person from £52; P ) An exceptional 19th-century villa set in its own landscaped grounds, the Grange is crammed with antiques and fitted with log fires, chaise longues and Victorian roll-top baths. The Turret Room, with its window seat in the turret overlooking Loch Linnhe, is our favourite.

**Lime Tree** ( ☎ 701806; www.limetreefortwilliam.co.uk; Achintore Rd; r per person £45-55; P ) Much more interesting than your average guesthouse, this former Victorian manse overlooking Loch Linnhe is an 'art gallery with rooms', decorated throughout with the artist-owner's atmospheric Highland landscapes; there's also a dedicated gallery space with changing exhibitions. Recently extended and upgraded, it's now a bit overpriced perhaps, and – at the time of research at least – the restaurant can't be recommended, but the staff are helpful and enthusiastic and with a bit of feedback hopefully things will improve.

**Crolinnhe** ( ☎ 702709; www.crolinnhe.co.uk; Grange Rd; r per person £55-63; P ) If you can't get into the Grange try the neighbouring Crolinnhe, another grand 19th-century villa, with loch-side location, beautiful gardens and sumptuous accommodation. A vegetarian breakfast is provided on request.

**Alexandra Hotel** ( ☎ 702241; www.strathmorehotels .com; The Parade; s/d from £59/99; P ) A large, traditional, family-oriented hotel bang in the middle of town, the Victorian-era Alexandra has been refurbished with modern, business hotel–style rooms and is a comfortable and convenient choice, despite the tourist-oriented tartan-toned décor.

## Eating

**Café 115** ( ☎ 702500; 115 High St; mains £5-10; ☼ 9am-9.30pm; ♿ ) This tidy little café covers all bases, from coffee and croissants at breakfast, to soup, sandwiches and nachos at lunchtime, to steak, seafood and vegetarian dishes at dinner. Babies and young children are made welcome.

**Grog & Gruel** ( ☎ 705078; 66 High St; mains £8-11; ☼ bar meals noon-9pm, restaurant 5-9pm) The Grog & Gruel is a traditional-style, wood-panelled pub with an excellent range of cask ales from regional Scottish and English microbreweries. Upstairs is a lively Tex-Mex restaurant, with a crowd-pleasing menu of tasty enchiladas, burritos, fajitas, burgers, steaks and pizza.

**Crannog Seafood Restaurant** ( ☎ 705589; Town Pier; mains £10-15; ☼ noon-2.30pm & 6-9.30pm) The Crannog easily wins the prize for the best location in town – it's perched on the Town Pier, giving window-table diners an uninterrupted view down Loch Linnhe. Informal and unfussy, it specialises in fresh local seafood – there are three or four daily fish specials plus the main menu – though there are beef, poultry and vegetarian dishes too.

For takeaway grub, try the **Indian Garden** ( ☎ 705011; 88 High St; mains £7-12) for curries, or the **Highland Star** ( ☎ 703905; 155 High St; mains £5-9) for Chinese food.

Self-caterers can stock up at **Morrisons Supermarket** (An Aird; ☼ 8.30am-8pm Mon-Wed, to 9pm Thu & Fri, 8am-8pm Sat, 9am-6pm Sun), next to the train station.

## Drinking

**Fired Art Ceramicafé** ( ☎ 705005; 147 High St; ☼ 10am-5pm Mon-Sat; ♿ ♿ ) Enjoy what is probably the best coffee in town at this colourful café, or go for a hot chocolate, milk shake or smoothie; the kids can be kept busy painting their own coffee mugs in the pottery studio at the back.

**Ben Nevis Bar** ( ☎ 702295; 105 High St) The Ben Nevis, whose lounge bar enjoys a good view over the loch, exudes a relaxed, jovial atmosphere where climbers and tourists can work off leftover energy jigging to live music (Thursday and Friday nights).

## Getting There & Away

Fort William lies 146 miles from Edinburgh, 104 miles from Glasgow and 66 miles from Inverness.

### BUS

Scottish Citylink buses link Fort William with Glasgow (£16, three hours, eight daily) and Edinburgh (£23, four hours, one daily direct, seven with a change at Glasgow) via Glencoe and Crianlarich, as well as Oban (£9.40, 1½ hours, four daily), Inverness (£10, two hours, five daily) and Portree on the Isle of Skye (£21, three hours, three daily).

Bus 500 runs to Mallaig (1½ hours, three daily weekdays, one on Saturday) via Glenfinnan (30 minutes) and Arisaig (one hour).

CENTRAL & WESTERN HIGHLANDS

See also p301 for details of the minibus service between Oban, Fort William and Portree.

### CAR
The tourist office has a leaflet listing car-hire companies. **Easydrive Car Hire** ( ☎ 701616; www .easydrivescotland.co.uk; Unit 36a, Ben Nevis Industrial Estate, Ben Nevis Dr) has small cars from £32/175 a day/week, including tax and unlimited mileage, but not CDW.

### TRAIN
The spectacular West Highland line runs from Glasgow to Mallaig via Fort William. There are two or three trains daily from Glasgow to Fort William (£22, 3¾ hours), and four or five daily between Fort William and Mallaig (£9, 1½ hours). Travelling from Edinburgh (£36, five hours), you have to change at Glasgow's Queen St station.

There's no direct rail connection between Oban and Fort William – you have to change at Crianlarich, so it's faster to use the bus.

The overnight Caledonian Sleeper service connects Fort William and London Euston (£135 sharing a twin-berth cabin, 13 hours).

## Getting Around
The **Nevis'n'Coe Roverbus** ( ☎ 01463-710555; www .rapsons.co.uk) ticket (adult/child £6/4) gives unlimited travel for one day on bus services in the Fort William and Glencoe area (a three-day ticket costs £15/10).

There's a **taxi rank** ( ☎ 702545, 773030) on the corner of High St and The Parade.

**Off-Beat Bikes** ( ☎ 704008; 117 High St; ☼ 9am-5.30pm) rents out mountain bikes for £15/10 for a day/half-day.

## AROUND FORT WILLIAM
### Glen Nevis
☎ 01397
You can walk the 3 miles from Fort William to scenic Glen Nevis in about an hour or so. The **Glen Nevis Visitor Centre** ( ☎ 705922; ☼ 9am-5pm Apr-Oct) is situated 1.5 miles up the glen, and provides information on walking as well as specific advice on climbing Ben Nevis.

From the car park at the far end of the road along Glen Nevis, there is an excellent 1.5-mile walk through the spectacular Nevis Gorge to **Steall Meadows**, a verdant valley dominated by a 100m-high bridal-veil waterfall. You can reach the foot of the falls by crossing the river on a wobbly, three-cable wire bridge –

one cable for your feet and one for each hand – a real test of balance!

### SLEEPING & EATING
**Glen Nevis Caravan & Camping Park** ( ☎ 702191; www .glen-nevis.co.uk; tent £6.50, tent & car £10.50, campervan £11, plus per person £2.50; ☼ mid-Mar–Oct) This big, well-equipped site is a popular base camp for Ben Nevis and the surrounding mountains.

**Achintee Farm** ( ☎ 702240; www.achinteefarm.com; Achintee; dm £12.50-14, r per person £34) This attractive farmhouse offers excellent B&B accommodation and also has a small bunkhouse attached. It's just 100m from the Ben Nevis Inn, and ideally positioned for climbing Ben Nevis.

**our pick** **Ben Nevis Inn** ( ☎ 702240; www.ben-nevis -inn.co.uk; Achintee; dm £14; ☐ P ) A good alternative to the youth hostel is this great barn of a pub (real ale and tasty bar meals available), with a comfy 24-bed hostel downstairs. It's at the Achintee start of the path up Ben Nevis, and only a mile from the end of the West Highland Way.

**Glen Nevis Youth Hostel** (SYHA; ☎ 0870 004 1120; Glen Nevis; dm £15.50; ☐ ) Large, impersonal and reminiscent of a school camp, this hostel is 3 miles from Fort William, beside one of the starting points for the tourist track up Ben Nevis.

### GETTING THERE & AWAY
From late May to late September bus 42 runs from Fort William bus station up Glen Nevis to the youth hostel (10 minutes, every 80 minutes Monday to Saturday, four daily Sunday) and on to the Lower Falls 3 miles beyond the hostel (20 minutes).

### Nevis Range
The **Nevis Range ski area** ( ☎ 01397-705825; www .nevisrange.co.uk), 6 miles north of Fort William, spreads across the northern slopes of Aonach Mor (1221m). The gondola that gives access to the bottom of the ski area at 655m operates year-round from 10am to 5pm; a return trip costs £8.50/5 for an adult/child (15 minutes each way). At the top there's a restaurant and a couple of walking routes through nearby **Leanachan Forest**. During the ski season a one-day lift pass costs £24/14 per adult/child; a one-day package, including equipment hire, lift pass and four hours' instruction, costs £44.

A world championship **downhill mountainbike trail** ( ☼ 11am-3pm mid-May–mid-Sep) – for experienced riders only – runs from the Snowgoose restaurant to the base station; bikes are carried on a rack on the gondola cabin. A single trip with your own bike costs £10.25; including bike hire it's £25 to £50 depending on the bike. There are also 25 miles of waymarked mountain-bike trails in the nearby forest.

From late May to late September bus 42 runs from Fort William bus station to Nevis Range (15 minutes, every 80 minutes Monday to Saturday, four daily Sunday).

## Corpach to Loch Lochy

Corpach lies at the southern entrance to the Caledonian Canal, 3 miles north of Fort William; there's a classic picture-postcard view of Ben Nevis from the mouth of the canal. Nearby is the award-winning **Treasures of the Earth** ( ☎ 01397-772283; Corpach; adult/child £3.50/2; ⏰ 9.30am-7pm Jul-Sep, 10am-5pm Oct-Dec & Feb-Jun) exhibition, a rainy-day diversion, with a great collection of gemstones, minerals, fossils and other geological curiosities.

A mile east of Corpach, at Banavie, is **Neptune's Staircase**, an impressive flight of eight locks that allows boats to climb 20m to the main reach of the Caledonian Canal. The B8004 road runs along the west side of the canal to Gairlochy at the south end of Loch Lochy, offering superb views of Ben Nevis; the canal towpath on the east side makes a great walk or bike ride (6.5 miles).

From Gairlochy the B8005 continues along the west side of Loch Lochy to Achnacarry and the **Clan Cameron Museum** ( ☎ 01397-712480; adult/child £3/free; ⏰ 11am-5pm Jul & Aug, 1.30-5pm Easter-Jun & Sep–mid-Oct), which records the history of the clan and its involvement with the Jacobite rebellions, including items of clothing that once belonged to Bonnie Prince Charlie.

From Achnacarry the Great Glen Way and Great Glen Mountain Bike Trail (p327) continue along the roadless western shore of Loch Lochy, and a dead-end minor road leads west along lovely **Loch Arkaig**.

There are a couple of backpacker hostels in Corpach: **Farr Cottage Lodge** ( ☎ 01397-772315; www .farrcottage.com; dm/tw £13/34; 🖳 🅿 ) and **Blacksmiths Hostel** ( ☎ 01397-772467; www.highland-mountain-guides

---

**CLIMBING BEN NEVIS**

As the highest peak in the British Isles, Ben Nevis (1344m) attracts many would-be ascensionists who would not normally think of climbing a Scottish mountain – a staggering (often literally) 100,000 people reach the summit each year.

Although anyone who is reasonably fit should have no problem climbing Ben Nevis on a fine summer's day, an ascent should not be undertaken lightly. Every year people have to be rescued from the mountain. You will need proper walking boots (the path is rough and stony, and there may be soft, wet snowfields on the summit), warm clothing, waterproofs, a map and compass, and plenty of food and water.

Here are a few facts to mull over before you go racing up the tourist track: the summit plateau is bounded by 700m-high cliffs and has a sub-Arctic climate; at the summit it can snow on any day of the year; the summit is wrapped in cloud nine days out of 10; in thick cloud, visibility at the summit can be 10m or less; and in such conditions the only safe way off the mountain requires careful use of a map and compass to avoid walking over those 700m cliffs.

The tourist track (the easiest route to the top) was originally called the Pony Track. It was built in the 19th century for the pack ponies that carried supplies to a meteorological observatory on the summit (now in ruins), which was manned continuously from 1883 to 1904.

There are three possible starting points for the tourist track ascent – Achintee Farm; the foot-bridge at Glen Nevis Youth Hostel; and, if you have a car, the car park at Glen Nevis Visitor Centre. The path climbs gradually to the shoulder at Lochan Meall an t-Suidhe (known as the Halfway Lochan), then zigzags steeply up beside the Red Burn to the summit plateau. The highest point is marked by a trig point on top of a huge cairn beside the ruins of the old observatory; the plateau is scattered with countless smaller cairns, stones arranged in the shape of people's names and, sadly, a fair bit of litter.

The total distance to the summit and back is 8 miles; allow at least four or five hours to reach the top, and another 2½ to three hours for the descent. Afterwards, as you celebrate in the pub with a pint, consider the fact that the record time for the annual Ben Nevis Hill Race is just under 1½ hours – up *and* down. Then have another pint.

.co.uk; dm £12.50; (P) ) – the latter is part of an outdoor activities centre and can organise courses in climbing, kayaking and other sports.

## Glen Spean & Glen Roy

Near Spean Bridge, at the junction of the B8004 and A82, 2.5 miles east of Gairlochy stands the **Commando Memorial**, which commemorates the WWII special forces soldiers who trained in this area.

Four miles further east, at Roy Bridge, a minor road leads north up Glen Roy, which is noted for its intriguing, so-called **parallel roads**. These prominent horizontal terraces contouring around the hill side are actually ancient shorelines formed during the last ice age by the waters of an ice-dammed glacial lake. The best viewpoint is 3 miles up Glen Roy.

## ARDGOUR & ARDNAMURCHAN

The drive from Corran Ferry, 8 miles south of Fort William, to Ardnamurchan Point, the most westerly point on the British mainland, is one of the most beautiful in the western Highlands, especially in late spring and early summer when much of the narrow, twisting road is lined with the bright pink and purple blooms of rhododendrons. A car ferry (car £5.20, passenger free, 10 minutes, two an hour) crosses from the Fort William–Glencoe road to Ardgour at Corran Ferry.

The road clings to the northern shore of Loch Sunart, going through the pretty villages of **Strontian** – which gave its name to the element strontium, first discovered in ore from nearby lead mines in 1790 – and **Salen**.

The mostly single-track road from Salen to Ardnamurchan Point is only 25 miles long, but it'll take you 1½ hours each way. It's a dipping, twisting, low-speed roller coaster of a ride through sun-dappled native woodlands draped with lichen and fern. Just when you're getting used to the views of Morvern and Mull to the south, it makes a quick detour to the north for a panorama over the islands of Rum and Eigg.

## Sights

Midway between Salen and Kilchoan is the fascinating **Ardnamurchan Natural History Centre** ( ☎ 01972-500209; Glenmore; adult/child £4/2; ☼ 10.30am-5.30pm Mon-Sat, noon-5.30pm Sun Easter-Oct). Devised by local photographer Michael MacGregor, it tries to bring you face to face with the flora and fauna of the Ardnamurchan peninsula.

The Living Building exhibit is designed to attract local wildlife, with a mammal den that is occasionally occupied by hedgehogs or pine martens, an owl nest-box, a mouse nest and a pond. If the beasties are not in residence, you can watch recorded video footage of the animals. There's also live CCTV coverage of a golden eagle feeding site.

The scattered crofting village of **Kilchoan**, the only village of any size west of Salen, is best known for the scenic ruins of 13th-century **Mingary Castle**. The village has a **tourist office** ( ☎ 01972-510222; Pier Rd; ☼ Easter-Oct), a shop and a hotel.

The final 6 miles of road ends at the 36m-high, grey granite tower of **Ardnamurchan Lighthouse**, built in 1849 by the Stevensons to guard the westernmost point of the British mainland. The **Kingdom of Light Visitor Centre** ( ☎ 01972-510210; adult/child £3/1.70; ☼ 10am-5pm Apr-Oct), by Kilchoan, will tell you more than you'll ever need to know about lighthouses, with lots of hands-on stuff for kids; the guided tour (£6) includes a trip to the top of the lighthouse. But the main attraction here is the expansive view over the ocean – this is a superb sunset viewpoint, provided you don't mind driving back in the dark.

## Sleeping & Eating

**Salen Hotel** ( ☎ 01967-431661; www.salenhotel.co.uk; Salen; r per person from £30; (P) ) A traditional Highland pub with views over Loch Sunart, the Salen Hotel has three rooms upstairs in the pub (with sea views) and another three rooms (each with en suite) in a modern chalet out the back. The cosy lounge has a roaring fire and comfy sofa, and the bar meals, including seafood, venison and other game dishes, are very good.

**Ardnamurchan Natural History Centre** ( ☎ 01972-500209; Glenmore; mains £4-8; ☼ 10.30am-5.30pm Mon-Sat, noon-5.30pm Sun Easter-Oct) The café at this wildlife centre serves delicious lunches, ranging from fresh salads and sandwiches to daily specials such as prawns and crayfish tails.

**Inn at Ardgour** ( ☎ 01855-841225; www.ardgour.biz; Ardgour; mains £8-12; (P) ) This pretty, whitewashed coaching inn, draped in colourful flower baskets, makes a great place for a lunch break or overnight stop. Single rooms cost between £45 and £65, doubles £60 to £100. The restaurant is set in the row of cottages once occupied by the Corran ferrymen, and serves traditional, homemade Scottish dishes.

You can camp at **Resipole Caravan Park** ( ☎ 01967-431235; www.resipole.co.uk; Resipole; tent sites £8, with car £13). Alternatively, the **Kilchoan House Hotel** ( ☎ 01972-510200; www.kilchoanhouse hotel.co.uk; Kilchoan; s/d £38/65, tent sites per person £3; ☷ Mar-Oct; ℗ ) will let you pitch a tent in its garden; ask at the bar first.

### Getting There & Away

Bus 500 runs from Fort William to Lochailort and Acharacle, continuing to Salen and Kilchoan on request (3¼ hours, one daily Monday to Saturday). For details of ferries between Kilchoan and Tobermory, see p303.

## SALEN TO LOCHAILORT

The A861 road from Salen to Lochailort passes through the low, wooded hills of Moidart. A minor road (signposted Dorlin) leads west from the A861 at Shiel Bridge to a picnic area looking across to the picturesque roofless ruin of 13th-century **Castle Tioram**. The castle sits on a tiny island in Loch Moidart, connected to the mainland by a narrow strand that is submerged at high tide (the castle's name, pronounced *chee*-ram, means 'dry'). It was the ancient seat of the Clanranald Macdonalds, but the Clanranald chief ordered it to be burned (to prevent it falling into the hands of Hanoverian troops) when he set off to fight for the Jacobite side in the 1715 rebellion. At the time of research it was closed to the public while the owner and Historic Scotland wrangled over plans for its future.

As the A861 curls around the north shore of Loch Moidart you will see a line of five huge beech trees between the road and the shore. Known as the **Seven Men of Moidart** (two have been blown down by gales and replaced with saplings), they were planted in the late 18th century to commemorate the seven local men who accompanied Bonnie Prince Charlie from France and acted as his bodyguards at the start of the 1745 rebellion.

## ROAD TO THE ISLES

The 46-mile A830 from Fort William to Mallaig is traditionally known as the Road to the Isles, as it leads to the jumping-off point for ferries to the Small Isles and Skye. This is a region steeped in Jacobite history, having witnessed both the beginning and the end of Bonnie Prince Charlie's doomed attempt to regain the British throne.

The final section of this scenic route, between Arisaig and Mallaig, has recently been upgraded to a fast straight road. Unless you're in a hurry, opt for the old coastal road (signposted Alternative Coastal Route).

Between the A830 and the A87 far to the north lies Scotland's 'Empty Quarter', a rugged landscape of wild mountains and lonely sea lochs roughly 20 miles by 30 miles in size, mostly uninhabited and penetrated only by two minor roads (along Lochs Arkaig and Quoich). If you want to get away from it all, this is the place to go.

### Getting Around

The Fort William to Mallaig railway line has three or four trains a day, with stops at many points along the way, including Corpach, Glenfinnan, Lochailort, Arisaig and Morar.

**Cycles2U** ( ☎ 01687-450291, 07800 956913; cycles2u@ btinternet.com) provides bicycle hire (adult/child £16/10 a day), and allows you to pick up and drop off the bikes at various points along the Fort William to Mallaig route.

### Glenfinnan

☎ 01397 / pop 100

Glenfinnan is hallowed ground for fans of Bonnie Prince Charlie, and its central shrine is the **Glenfinnan Monument**. This tall column, topped by a statue of a kilted Highlander, was erected in 1815 on the spot where the Young Pretender first raised his standard and rallied the clans on 19 August 1745, marking the start of the ill-fated campaign that would end in disaster 14 months later. The setting, at the north end of Loch Shiel, is hauntingly beautiful.

The nearby **Glenfinnan Visitor Centre** ( ☎ 722250; admission free; ☷ 9.30am-5.30pm Jul & Aug, 10am-5pm Easter-Jun, Sep & Oct; ⅋ ) recounts the story of the '45, as the Jacobite rebellion of 1745 is known, when the prince's loyal clansmen marched and fought from Glenfinnan south to Derby, then back north to final defeat at Culloden.

A half-mile west of the visitor centre is **Glenfinnan Station Museum** ( ☎ 722295; adult/child £1/50p; ☷ 9am-5pm Jun–mid-Oct), a shrine of a different kind whose object of veneration is the great days of steam on the West Highland line. The famous 21-arch **Glenfinnan Viaduct**, just east of the station, was built in 1901, and featured in the movie *Harry Potter & the Chamber of Secrets*. A pleasant walk of around 0.75 miles leads to a viewpoint for the viaduct and the loch.

The **Glenfinnan Highland Games** ( ☎ 722324) are held on the Saturday nearest to 19 August.

Two converted railway carriages at Glenfinnan Station house the 10-berth **Sleeping Car Bunkhouse** ( ☎ 722295; dm £10) and the atmospheric **Dining Car** ( ☎ 722295; snacks £1-4; ☻ 9am-5pm Jun–mid-Oct), which serves scones with cream and jam and pots of tea, with superb views of the mountains above Loch Shiel.

**Prince's House Hotel** ( ☎ 722246; www.glenfinnan .co.uk; s £65, d £85-140; ℗ ) is a delightful old coaching inn from 1658; it's a good place to pamper yourself – ask for the spacious, tartan-clad Stuart Room if you want to stay in the oldest part of the hotel. Note that only dinner, bed and breakfast rates (£160 to £195 a double) are available on weekends from Easter to October. There's no documentary evidence that Bonnie Prince Charlie actually stayed here in 1745, but then again it was the only sizable house in Glenfinnan at that time, so…

## Arisaig & Morar
☎ 01687

The 5 miles of coast between Arisaig and Morar is a fretwork of rocky islets, inlets and gorgeous silver-sand beaches backed by dunes and machair, with stunning sunset views across the sea to the silhouetted peaks of Eigg and Rum. The **Silver Sands of Morar**, as they are known, draw crowds of bucket-and-spade holidaymakers in July and August, when the many camping grounds scattered along the coast are filled to overflowing.

Fans of the movie *Local Hero* still make pilgrimages to **Camusdarach Beach**, just south of Morar, which starred in the film as Ben's beach. To find it, look for the car park 800m north of Camusdarach camp site; from here, a wooden footbridge and a 400m walk through the dunes lead to the beach. (The village that featured in the film is on the other side of the country, at Pennan; see p259.)

**Loch nan Uamh** (pronounced loch nan oo-ah, meaning the loch of the caves) washes the southern shores of Arisaig; this was where Bonnie Prince Charlie first set foot on the Scottish mainland on 11 August 1745, on the shingle beach at the mouth of the Borrodale burn. Just 2 miles to the east of this bay, on a rocky point near a parking area, the **Prince's Cairn** marks the spot where he finally departed Scottish soil, never to return, on 19 September 1746.

### SLEEPING & EATING

There are at least a half-dozen camping grounds between Arisaig and Morar; all are open in summer only, and are often full in July and August, so book ahead. Some are listed on www.road-to-the-isles.org.uk.

**Camusdarach Campsite** ( ☎ 450221; www.camusdarach .com; South Morar; tent sites £9-14; ☻ Mar-Oct) A small and beautiful site with good facilities, only three minutes' walk from the *Local Hero* beach.

**Garramore House** ( ☎ 450268; South Morar; r per person £28-35; ☝ ℗ ) Built as a hunting lodge in 1840, it served as a Special Operations Executive HQ during WWII. Today it's a wonderfully atmospheric, child- and pet-friendly guesthouse and restaurant (mains £9 to £12) set in lovely woodland gardens with great views to the Small Isles and Skye.

**Old Library Lodge & Restaurant** ( ☎ 450651; www .oldlibrary.co.uk; Arisaig; mains £10-15; ☻ food served noon-2.30pm & 6.30-9.30pm) The Old Library is a charming restaurant with rooms (£40 to £50 per person) set in converted 200-year-old stables overlooking the waterfront in Arisaig village. The lunch menu concentrates on soups and freshly made sandwiches, while dinner is a more sophisticated affair offering local seafood and lamb.

## Mallaig
☎ 01687 / pop 800

If you're travelling between Fort William and Skye, you may find yourself overnighting in the bustling fishing and ferry port of Mallaig. Indeed, it makes a good base for a series of day trips by ferry to the Small Isles and Knoydart. There's a **tourist office** ( ☎ 462170; ☻ 10am-5.30pm Mon-Fri, 10.15am-3.45pm Sat, noon-3.30pm Sun), a post office, a bank with ATM and a **Co-op supermarket** ( ☻ 8am-10pm Mon-Sat, 9am-9pm Sun).

The village's rainy-day attractions are limited to **Mallaig Heritage Centre** ( ☎ 462085; Station Rd; adult/child £1.80/free; ☻ 9.30am-4.30pm Mon-Sat, noon-4pm Sun), which covers the archaeology and history of the region, including the heart-rending tale of the Highland Clearances in Knoydart.

The **MV Grimsay Isle** ( ☎ 07780 815158) provides entertaining, customised sea-fishing trips and seal-watching tours (book at the tourist office), while the **Brightwater** ( ☎ 07747 034767; www.seaotter.co.uk) offers high-speed boat trips to Skye, the Small Isles and Mull.

### SLEEPING & EATING

**Sheena's Backpacker's Lodge** ( ☎ 462764; www.mallaig backpackers.co.uk; Harbour View; dm £13) Sheena's is a friendly, 12-bed hostel in a lovely old house overlooking the harbour. On a sunny day the hostel's Tea Garden terrace café (mains £3 to £7), with its flowers, greenery and cosmopolitan backpacker staff, feels more like the Med than Mallaig, though at busy times service can be glacially slow. The speciality of the house is a pint-glass full of Mallaig prawns with dipping sauce.

**Springbank Guest House** ( ☎ 462459; www.spring bank-mallaig.co.uk; East Bay; r per person £20; P ) A little further around the bay than the Moorings, the Springbank is a traditional West Highland house with seven homely guest bedrooms, again with superb views across the harbour to the Cuillin of Skye.

**Moorings Guest House** ( ☎ 462225; mooringsguest house@tiscali.co.uk; East Bay; r per person £22-24; ♿ ) Just beyond the tourist office, this four-bedroom B&B has grand views over the harbour, not only from the upstairs bedrooms but also from the conservatory-style breakfast room, which doubles as a tearoom open to the public from Easter to September.

**our pick** **Fish Market** ( ☎ 462299; Station Rd; mains £8-18; ☺ noon-2.30pm & 6-9pm) There are at least half-a-dozen signs in Mallaig advertising 'seafood restaurant', but this bright, modern, bistro-style place next to the harbour is our favourite, serving simply prepared scallops with garlic and fennel, grilled langoustines with garlic butter, and fresh Mallaig haddock fried in breadcrumbs, as well as the tastiest *Cullen skink* (soup made with smoked haddock, potato, onion and milk) on the west coast. Upstairs is a tearoom (mains £4 to £5) that serves delicious hot roast-beef rolls with horseradish sauce, and scones with clotted cream and jam; it's open from 11am to 5pm.

### GETTING THERE & AWAY

Bus 500 and Scottish Citylink coaches link Fort William to Mallaig (£5, 1¼ hours, one a day Monday to Friday) via Glenfinnan, Arisaig and Morar. See also Getting There & Away (p301) for details of the summer minibus service linking Portree, Mallaig, Fort William and Oban.

The beautiful West Highland railway links Mallaig to Fort William (£9, 1½ hours) and Glasgow (£25, 5¼ hours, four a day Monday to Saturday, two Sunday). In summer vintage steam trains (p341) operate between Fort William and Mallaig.

Ferries run from Mallaig to the Small Isles, the Isle of Skye and Knoydart; see the transport information of these areas for more details.

## KNOYDART PENINSULA

☎ 01687 / pop 70

The Knoydart peninsula is the only sizable area in Britain that remains inaccessible to the motor car, cut off by miles of rough country and the embracing arms of Lochs Nevis and Hourn – Gaelic for the lochs of Heaven and Hell. No road penetrates this wilderness of rugged hills – **Inverie**, its sole village, can only be reached by ferry from Mallaig, or on foot from the remote road-end at Kinloch Hourn (a tough 16-mile hike).

The main reasons for visiting are to climb the remote 1020m peak of **Ladhar Bheinn** (pronounced *laar*-ven), which affords some of the west coast's finest views, or just to enjoy the feeling of being cut off from the rest of the world. There are no shops, no TV and no mobile phone reception (although there *is* internet access); electricity is provided by a private hydroelectric scheme – truly 'off the grid' living! For more information, see www .knoydart-foundation.com.

There are a couple of walkers' bunkhouses near Inverie, including the **Knoydart Foundation Bunkhouse** ( ☎ 462242; info@knoydart.org; Inverie; dm £14; 🖳 ), 15 minutes' walk east of the ferry pier, and the atmospheric **Torrie Shieling** ( ☎ 462669; torrie@knoydart.org; Inverie; dm £15), a 20-minute walk to the west. You can camp for free on the Long Beach, a 10-minute walk east of the ferry, but there's no facilities.

The very basic **Barisdale Bothy** ( ☎ 01764-684946; www.barisdale.com; Barrisdale; dm £3, tent sites per person £1), 6 miles west of Kinloch Hourn on the footpath to Inverie, has sleeping platforms without mattresses – you'll need your own sleeping bag and foam mat.

The **Pier House** ( ☎ 462347; www.thepierhouseknoy dart.co.uk; Inverie; r per person £35) is the first place you'll see when you walk off the ferry. A guesthouse and restaurant, it offers B&B in its four homely bedrooms, and is famous for its superb seafood, venison and vegetarian dishes.

The neighbouring **Old Forge** ( ☎ 462267; Inverie; mains £8-16; ♿ ) is listed in the *Guinness Book of Records* as Britain's most remote pub. It's surprisingly sophisticated – as well as having real ale on tap, there's an Italian coffee machine for those wilderness lattes and cappuccinos, and the house special is a platter of langoustines with aïoli dipping sauce. In the evening you can sit by the fire, pint of beer in hand and join the impromptu *ceilidh* (an evening of traditional Scottish entertainment including music, song and dance) that seems to take place just about nightly.

### Getting There & Away

A passenger ferry operated by **Bruce Watt Cruises** ( ☎ 462320; www.knoydart-ferry.co.uk) links Mallaig to Inverie (£8/10 single/return, 45 minutes) twice daily Monday to Friday from mid-May to mid-September, and on Monday, Wednesday and Friday only the rest of the year (no weekend ferries). Taking the morning boat gives you four hours ashore in Knoydart before the afternoon return trip.

# SMALL ISLES

The scattered jewels of the Small Isles – Rum, Eigg, Muck and Canna – lie strewn across the silvery-blue cloth of the Cuillin Sound to the south of the Isle of Skye. Their distinctive outlines enliven the glorious views from the beaches of Arisaig and Morar.

Rum is the biggest and boldest of the four, a miniature Skye of pointed peaks and dramatic sunset silhouettes. Eigg is the most pastoral and populous, dominated by the miniature sugarloaf mountain of the Sgurr. Muck is a botanist's delight with its wildflowers and unusual alpine plants, and Canna is a craggy bird sanctuary made of magnetic rocks.

If your time is limited and you can only visit one island, choose Eigg; it has the most to offer on a day trip.

### Getting There & Away

The main ferry operator is **CalMac** ( ☎ 08705 650000; www.calmac.co.uk), which operates the passenger-only ferry from Mallaig to Eigg (£9.85 return, 1¼ hours, five a week), Muck (£15.15 return, 1½ hours, four a week), Rum (£14.55 return, 1¼ hours, five a week) and Canna (£18.30 return, two hours, four a week). You can also hop between the islands without returning to Mallaig, but the timetable is complicated and it requires a bit of planning – you would need at least five days to visit all four. A bicycle costs £2.20 extra on all routes.

From May to September **Arisaig Marine** ( ☎ 01687-450224; www.arisaig.co.uk) operates day cruises from Arisaig harbour to Eigg (£16 return, one hour, six a week), Rum (£22 return, 2½ hours, two or three a week) and Muck (£17 return, two hours, three a week). The trips include whale watching, with up to an hour for close viewing. Sailing times allow four or five hours ashore on Eigg, two or three hours on Muck or Rum.

## ISLE OF RUM

☎ 01687 / pop 30

The Isle of Rum – the biggest and most spectacular of the Small Isles – was once known as the Forbidden Island. Cleared of its crofters in the early 19th century to make way for sheep, from 1888 to 1957 it was the private sporting estate of the Bulloughs, a nouveau riche Lancashire family who made their fortune in the textile industry. Curious outsiders who ventured too close to the island were liable to find themselves staring down the wrong end of a gamekeeper's shotgun.

The island was sold to the Nature Conservancy in 1957. Since then it has been a reserve noted for its deer, wild goats, ponies, golden and white-tailed sea eagles, and a 120,000-strong nesting colony of Manx shearwaters. Its dramatic, rocky mountains – known as the Rum Cuillin for their similarity to the peaks on neighbouring Skye – draw hill walkers and climbers.

**Kinloch**, where the ferry lands, is the island's only settlement; it has a small **grocery shop** ( ⏲ 5-7.30pm), post office and public telephone. There's a **tearoom** ( ⏲ 11am-4pm Apr-Sep) in the village hall. The hall itself is open at all times for people to shelter from the rain (or the midges!). For more information see www.isleofrum.com.

### Sights & Activities

When George Bullough – a dashing, Harrow-educated cavalry officer – inherited Rum along with half his father's fortune in 1891, he became one of the wealthiest bachelors in Britain. Bullough blew half his inheritance on building his dream bachelor pad – the ostentatious **Kinloch Castle** ( ☎ 462037; adult/child £6/3; ⏲ guided tours Mon-Sat, to coincide with ferry times). The bachelor shipped in pink sandstone from Dumfriesshire and 250,000 tonnes of Ayrshire topsoil for the gardens, and paid his workers a shilling extra a day to wear tweed kilts – just so they'd look more picturesque. Hummingbirds were kept in the greenhouses and alligators in the garden, and guests were entertained with an orchestrion, the Edwardian equivalent of a Bose hifi system. Since the Bulloughs left, the castle has survived as a perfect time capsule of upper-class Edwardian eccentricity. The guided tour should not be missed.

The only part of the island that still belongs to the Bullough family is the **Bullough Mausoleum** in Glen Harris, a miniature Greek temple that wouldn't look out of place on the Acropolis; Lady Bullough was laid to rest here alongside her husband and father-in-law in 1967, having died at the age of 98.

There's some great coastal and mountain walking on the island, including a couple of easy, waymarked **nature trails** in the woods around Kinloch. Glen Harris is a 10-mile round trip from Kinloch, on a rough 4WD track – allow four to five hours' walking. The climb to the island's highest point, **Askival** (812m), is a strenuous hike and involves a bit of rock scrambling (allow six hours for the round trip from Kinloch).

## Sleeping & Eating
Accommodation on Rum is strictly limited, and if you want to stay overnight on the island, you have to contact the **reserve office** (☎ 462026) in advance.

**Kinloch Campsite** (tent sites per person £3) Near the castle, this is the only place on the island where camping is allowed. The only facilities are toilets and a water supply, and there's not much in the way of level ground! Book in advance with the reserve office. Wild camping in the rest of the island is allowed, but check with the reserve office first for advice on avoiding nesting areas and other wildlife that might suffer from disturbance.

**Kinloch Castle Hostel** (☎ 462037; dm/d £14/55; ☺ Mar-Oct) The castle has 45 hostel beds and four double bedrooms in its rear wing. There's also a small restaurant offering a cooked breakfast (£7) and dinner (£13.50) to guests and nonguests alike.

## ISLE OF EIGG
☎ 01687 / pop 70
The Isle of Eigg made history in 1997 when it became the first Highland estate to be bought out by its inhabitants. The island is now owned and managed by the **Isle of Eigg Heritage Trust** (www.isleofeigg.org), a partnership among the islanders, Highland Council and the Scottish Wildlife Trust.

The ferry landing is at Galmisdale in the south. **An Laimhrig** (☎ 482432), the building above the pier, houses a post office, grocery store, craft shop and tearoom. You can hire bikes here, too.

## Activities
The island takes its name from the Old Norse *egg* (edge), a reference to the **Sgurr of Eigg** (393m), an impressive mini-mountain that towers over Galmisdale. Ringed by vertical cliffs on three sides, it's composed of pitchstone lava with columnar jointing similar to that seen on the Isle of Staffa and at the Giant's Causeway in Northern Ireland.

The climb to the summit (4.5 miles round trip; allow three to four hours) begins on the stony road leading up from the pier, which continues uphill through the woods to a red-roofed cottage. Go through the gate to the right of the cottage and turn left; just 20m along the road a cairn on the right marks the start of a boggy footpath that leads over the eastern shoulder of the Sgurr, then traverses beneath the northern cliffs until it makes its way up onto the summit ridge.

On a fine day the views from the top are magnificent – Rum and Skye to the north, Muck and Coll to the south, Ardnamurchan Lighthouse to the southeast and Ben Nevis shouldering above the eastern horizon. Take binoculars – on a calm summer's day there's a good chance of seeing minke whales feeding down below in the Sound of Muck.

A shorter walk (2 miles; allow 1½ hours round trip, and bring a torch) leads west from the pier to the spooky and claustrophobic **Uamh Fraing** (Massacre Cave). Start as for the Sgurr of Eigg, but 800m from the pier turn left through a gate and into a field. Follow the 4WD track and fork left before a white cottage to pass below it. A footpath continues across the fields to reach a small gate in a fence; go through it and descend a ridge towards the shore.

The cave entrance is tucked inconspicuously down to the left of the ridge. The entrance is tiny – almost a hands-and-knees job – but the cave opens out inside and runs a long way back. Go right to the back, turn off your torch, and imagine the cave packed shoulder to shoulder with terrified men, women and children. Then imagine the panic as your enemies start piling firewood into the entrance. Almost the entire population of Eigg – around

400 people – sought refuge in this cave when the MacLeods of Skye raided the island in 1577. In an act of inhuman cruelty, the raiders lit a fire in the narrow entrance and everyone inside died of asphyxiation. There are more than a few ghosts floating around in here.

Other good walks are to the deserted crofts of **Grulin** on the southwest coast (5 miles, two hours round trip), and north to Laig Beach with its famous **singing sands** – the sand makes a squeaking noise when you walk on it (8 miles, three hours return). You can get more information on island walks from the craft shop in An Laimhrig.

## Sleeping & Eating

All accommodation should be booked in advance. For a full listing of self-catering accommodation, see www.iselofeigg.org.

**Glebe Barn** ( ☎ 482417; www.glebebarn.co.uk; Galmisdale; dm/tw £12/26) The Glebe has excellent bunkhouse accommodation – a smart, maple-floored lounge with central fireplace, modern kitchen, laundry, drying room, and bright, clean dorms and bedrooms.

**Sandavore Bothy** ( ☎ 482480; suehollands@talk21 .com; Sandavore; per night/week £25/150) This tiny, one-room bothy, a 15-minute walk from the pier, has space for four people in one double bed and two bunk beds. It's a real Hebridean experience – accessible only on foot, no electricity (just gaslight and candles), cold running water only and outside toilet.

**An Laimhrig** ( ☎ 482416; www.isleofeigg.org; Galmisdale) There's a good café here. The neighbouring craft shop takes fees for camping near the head of the bay at Galmisdale (£3 a tent); you can use the showers and toilets at the pier.

You can also camp at **Sue Holland's Croft** ( ☎ 482480; suehollands@talk21.com; per tent £4) at Cleadale in the north of the island.

## ISLE OF MUCK
☎ 01687 / pop 30

The tiny island of Muck, measuring just 2 miles by 1 mile, has exceptionally fertile soil, and the island is carpeted with wildflowers in spring and early summer. It takes its name from the Gaelic *muc* (pig), and pigs are still raised here.

Ferries call at the southern settlement of **Port Mor**. There's a tearoom and craft shop above the pier, which also acts as an information centre. See also www.isleofmuck.com.

It's an easy 15-minute walk along the island's only road from the pier to the sandy beach at **Gallanach** on the northern side of the island. A longer and rougher hike (1½ hours round trip) goes to the top of **Beinn Airein** (137m) for the best views. Puffins nest on the cliffs at the western end of Camas Mor, the bay to the south of the hill. On Wednesday in summer you can take a **guided tour** (£1) around the island by tractor and trailer; it departs at 1.30pm from Port Mor.

The cosy six-bed **Isle of Muck Bunkhouse** ( ☎ 462042; dm £11.50), with its oil-fired Rayburn stove, is just above the pier, as is the welcoming eight-room **Port Mor House Hotel** ( ☎ 462365; hotel@isleofmuck.com; r per person £43); rates include evening meals, which are also available to nonguests (£15, book in advance).

You can camp on the island for free – ask at the craft shop first.

## ISLE OF CANNA
☎ 01687 / pop 17

The roadless island of Canna is a moorland plateau of black basalt rock, just 5 miles long and 1.25 miles wide. **Compass Hill** (143m), at the northeastern corner, contains enough magnetite (an iron oxide mineral) to deflect the navigation compasses in passing yachts.

The ferry arrives at the hamlet of **A'Chill** at the eastern end of the island, where tourists have left extensive graffiti on the rock face south of the harbour. There's a tearoom and craft shop by the harbour, and a tiny post office in a hut.

You can walk to **An Coroghon**, just east of the ferry pier, a medieval stone tower perched atop a sea cliff, and continue to Compass Hill, or take a longer hike along the southern shore past a **Celtic cross** and the remains of the 7th-century **St Columba's Chapel**.

In 2006 the island was cleared of a plague of rats that had threatened its population of native wood mice and nesting seabirds (see boxed text Invasion of the Killer Hedgehogs, p401). In the same year the National Trust for Scotland (Canna's owner), worried about the viability of the island community, sent out an international appeal for new residents.

It received more than 400 applications for the two vacant properties available, both of which were filled by the end of 2007 – one of the new families moved into **Tighard** (www .ntsholidays.com), which should be operating as a guesthouse by spring 2008.

Contact the **warden** ( ☎ 462466) for permission to camp, or check www.ntsholidays.com for self-catering accommodation.

# Northern Highlands & Islands

The northern Highlands epitomises most visitors' romantic notion of Scotland. Vast, wild expanses punctuated by sparkling, steely blue lochs, and towering mountain ranges veined with snow, their summits often lost in swirling cloud. This is powerful country, and you can almost feel the desolation and tragedy of the Clearances – the silence can be deafening. But the romanticism of the region is inescapable too, and if you've ever heard the call of the wild, you're likely to be mesmerised here. There's something unique and Scottish in all of this – it's the ethereal light that squeezes through the clouds and tangos over Europe's northern fringe, illuminating its rugged splendour and changing its appearance by the hour, or even by the minute.

The stunning scenery extends offshore to the Isle of Skye, where the jagged peaks of the Cuillin Hills tear at the mist, and the ghosts of Bonnie Prince Charlie and Flora Macdonald haunt the hallways of Dunvegan Castle. Skye is a paradise for walkers, climbers and wildlife enthusiasts, with its dramatic mountains, lonely lochs and scenic coastlines, home to golden eagles, peregrine falcons, otters, deer and seals.

And that magical light intensifies as you head west to the Outer Hebrides – the 'isles at the edge of the sea' – with their landscapes of peat bog, lochan and bare, glaciated gneiss. These harsh landscapes are softened by glittering shell-sand beaches, wildflower-strewn machair, and buttercup meadows where the outlines of ruined crofts are visible in the turf like fossils in a stone. This necklace of remote islands is a last bastion of Gaelic culture, where the hardships of life in the old *blackhouses* still remain within living memory.

## HIGHLIGHTS

- Gorging on fresh, succulent seafood in the delightful town of **Ullapool** (p371), with its picture-perfect harbour
- Grappling with the Highlands' mighty peaks in the stunning mountainous playgrounds of **Inverpolly Nature Reserve** (p371), **Assynt** (p370) and **Glen Torridon** (p375)
- Enjoying crab sandwiches at the **Stein Inn** (p387) after touring the craft studios and workshops of Duirinish and Waternish on Skye
- Hiking up to spectacular **Coire Lagan** (p383) amid the jagged peaks of the Cuillin mountains of Skye
- Exploring the remote and beautiful beaches on the west coast of **Lewis** (p391) and **Harris** (p396) in the Outer Hebrides

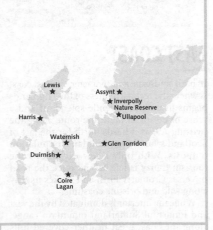

- POPULATION: 175,000
- AREA: 20,000 SQ KM

NORTHERN HIGHLANDS & ISLANDS

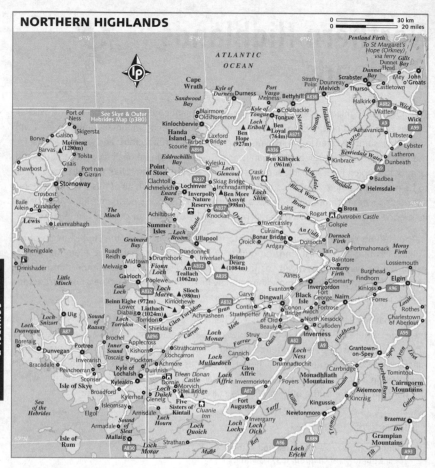

**NORTHERN HIGHLANDS**

# EAST COAST

In both landscape and character, the east coast is where the real barrenness of the Highlands begins to unfold. A gentle splendour and a sense of escapism mark the route along the twisting A9, as it heads north for the last of Scotland's far-flung, mainland population outposts. With only a few exceptions the tourism frenzy is left behind once the road traverses Cromarty Firth and snakes its way along wild and pristine coastline.

While the interior is dominated by the vast and mournful Sutherland mountain range, along the coast great heather-covered hills heave themselves out of the wild North Sea.

Dominated by miles of stone fencing crawling its way over hills and pastures, the rolling farmland drops suddenly into the icy waters, and the only interruptions en route are the small, historic towns moored precariously on the coast's edge.

## Getting Around

Call **Traveline** ( ☎ 0871 200 22 33) for public-transport information. The region is well served by buses, and trains follow the coast up to Wick then across to Thurso. **Scottish Citylink** ( ☎ 0870 550 5050) runs regular services from Inverness through to Wick, stopping at most towns on the A9 and A99 along the way, before taking the short cut inland to Thurso. **Rapsons/Highland Country** ( ☎ 01463-710555) operates buses from Wick to Thurso, via the coast and John o'Groats. **Stagecoach Inverness** (☎ 01463-239292) runs services to towns close to (including north of) Inverness.

## STRATHPEFFER
☎ 01997 / pop 950

Strathpeffer is a delightful Highland town, its creaking old pavilions and grandiose hotels dripping with Victorian charm and a faded grandeur.

The village was a fashionable spa in Victorian and Edwardian times, when chic society folk congregated here to splash about in the sulphurous waters.

The self-service **tourist office** (☎ 421415; ⌚ 10am-5pm Tue-Sat, late-May–late-Sep) is in the Pump Room and has limited info. You'll find a supermarket and a post office nearby in the town square.

## Sights

The renovated **Pump Room** (☎ 421415; adult/child £2/1.50; ⌚ 10am-5pm Tue-Sat, late-May–late-Sep) has some splendid displays showing the bizarre lengths Victorians went to in the quest for a healthy glow.

At the old Victorian train station is the **Highland Museum of Childhood** (☎ 421031; adult/child £2/1.50; ⌚ 10am-5pm Mon-Sat, 2-5pm Sun Apr-Oct; ♿). It has a wide range of social history displays about childhood in the Highlands, and also has activities for children, including a dressing-up box and a toy train.

The **Eagle Stone** (follow the signs from the main drag) is well worth a look when you're in town. It's a pre-7th century Pictish stone connected to local folklore – the Brahan Seer, who predicted many future events.

The **Strathpeffer & District Pipe Band** plays in the town square every Saturday from 8pm, May to September. There's also Highland dancing and a festive air.

## Sleeping & Eating

**Wyvis View B&B** (☎ 421053; rob@wyvisview.fsnet.co.uk; Ardival; s/d £26/44) This homely B&B provides comfy accommodation at the back of Strathpeffer (turn up the road next to Craigvar, opposite the town square) up on a hill. Terrific views are enjoyed via a mini garden conservatory. Inside, two rooms share a private bathroom. Your host is motherly and the breakfast sufficient to fast until dinner time.

**Highland Hotel** (☎ 421457; www.shearingsholidays.com; r per person £35-55) Many of the old spa hotels have fallen into neglect, but this one has been renovated. It's a magnificent, European chateau-style building overlooking the town, with a wood-panelled lobby and lounge, plus lovely wooded grounds. Book in advance for the best deals.

**Craigvar** (☎ 421622; www.craigvar.com; The Square; s/d £37/70) Luxury living with a refined touch is what you'll find in this delightful Georgian town house. All the little extras that mark out a classy place are here, such as a welcome drink, bathrobes and fresh fruit. Couples should go for the 'Blue Room' with its sensational four-poster bed – you'll need to collapse back into it after the gourmet breakfast.

**Maya** (☎ 420008; Main St; box of chocs £1.80-24; ⌚ 10am-5pm Tue-Sat) Ohh, this place is dangerous. Bringing Belgian chocolates to the Highlands, Maya is the ultimate in sweet indulgence. It also serves up hot drinks, including hot chocolate…which goes perfectly with chocolate.

---

**TOP 10 PLACES TO GET OFF THE EATEN TRACK**

Here's a selection of the best eating you'll find as you journey through the northern Highlands, often in remote, less touristed communities.

**Red Poppy Restaurant** ( ☎ 423332; dinner mains £10-15; ❧ lunch Tue-Sun, dinner Tue-Sat) In the restored historical Victorian spa pavilion is a much needed dining option in town. There's a large selection of meals including game dishes such as wild boar steaks, and dining is in elegant surrounds. We found it hard to go past the disoriented duck breast with a vodka, cranberry and orange glaze.

Also recommended:

**Strathpeffer Hotel** ( ☎ 421200; strathpeffer .hotel@virgin.net; standard/superior r per person £32/42) Solid pub rooms.

**Museum Coffeeshop** (light meals £2-4; ❧ 10am-5pm) In the old Victorian train station, a good pit stop for a toastie or panini.

### Getting There & Around

Stagecoach Inverness operates buses from Inverness to Strathpeffer (45 minutes, at least hourly Monday to Saturday, four on Sunday). The Inverness to Gairloch and Durness buses, plus some Inverness to Ullapool buses, also run via Strathpeffer.

**Square Wheels Cycles** ( ☎ 421000; The Square; ❧ 10am-6pm Thu-Mon) rents mountain bikes for £10/15 per half-/full day. Price decreases with multi-day hire.

## TAIN

☎ 01862 / pop 3600

Tain is Scotland's oldest royal burgh (town) and was an important pilgrimage centre. It has certainly retained a sense of yesteryear, and the town streets are worth a wander for the fine examples of Victorian architecture. It also has a couple of excellent attractions, making it a desirable spot to break a journey along the east coast.

**Tain Through Time** ( ☎ 894089; adult/child £3.50/2.50; ❧ 10am-5pm Mon-Sat, Apr-Jun Sep & Oct, to 6pm Jul & Aug) is a fascinating heritage centre that describes the history of Tain as a place of pilgrimage, tracing events from the time of St Duthac through to the Reformation. St Duthac was born in Tain, died in Armagh (Ireland) in 1065, and is commemorated by the 12th-century ruins of **St Duthac's Chapel**, as well as by **St Duthus Church**.

On the northern edge of town is the excellent **Glenmorangie Distillery & Visitor Centre** ( ☎ 892477; ❧ 9am-5pm Mon-Fri Sep-May, 9am-5pm Mon-Fri, 10am-4pm Sat, noon-4pm Sun Jun-Aug), which produces some of the finest single malts in the Highlands. For proof, knock back a dram

of the sherry- or Madeira-wood finish. There are also excellent tours (£3).

Rooms are of a high standard at the bustling **St Duthus Hotel** ( ☎ 894007; Tower St; s/d £35/60, without bathroom £30/50). The bathrooms are spotless and the snazzy dining area, serving treats (mains £7 to £9) such as smoked haddock and spring-onion fishcakes, has a cheery vibe.

Scottish Citylink buses from Inverness to Thurso pass through Tain (five daily). Stagecoach Inverness runs frequent express buses from Inverness (£6.30, one hour).

There are up to three trains daily to Inverness (£10.10, one hour) and Thurso (£12.30, 2½ hours).

## PORTMAHOMACK

☎ 01862 / pop 650

Portmahomack is a former fishing village in a flawless spot – right off the beaten track and gazing across the water at snowcapped peaks. The best place to enjoy the town is the grassy foreshore at the far end of Main St, near the little harbour.

The intriguing **Tarbat Discovery Centre** ( ☎ 871351; Tarbatness Rd; adult/child £3.50/1; ❧ 10am-5pm May-Sep, 2-5pm Mar, Apr & Oct; ♿ ) has some excellent carved Pictish stones. When 'crop circles' appeared a few years ago, the foundations of an Iron Age settlement were discovered around the village church. The church then became the centre of excavations – it's now the discovery centre.

There are good coastal walks at **Tarbat Ness**, 3 miles northeast of the village; the headland is marked by a tall, red-and-white-striped lighthouse.

If you're staying, try the friendly and comfortable **Caledonian Hotel** ( ☎ 871345; www.caley hotel.co.uk; Main St; d £44) overlooking the village's sandy beach. Only two rooms overlook Dornoch Firth, so book early. Seafood aficionados shouldn't miss the bright and cheerful **Oyster Catcher Restaurant** ( ☎ 871560; Main St; starters £7-10, mains £10-23; ❧ lunch & dinner Wed-Sun) – there are many delectable lobster dishes.

Stagecoach Inverness runs from Tain to Portmahomack (30 minutes, at least three daily Monday to Friday).

## BONAR BRIDGE & AROUND

The A9 crosses the Dornoch Firth, on a bridge and causeway, near Tain. An alternative route goes around the firth via the tiny settlements of **Ardgay**, where you'll find a train station,

## THE HIGHLANDS' JURASSIC PARK

In a pristine spot in the northern Highlands a revolutionary project is changing the concept of wildlife conservation in Scotland. **Alladale Wilderness Lodge & Reserve** ( ☎ 01863-755338; www .alladale.com; Ardgay), home to the country's most northerly tuft of ancient Scots pine forest, is releasing formerly extinct species to roam on its vast estate. Wildlife on the reserve now includes red deer, roe deer, wild boar, wild ponies and golden eagles. In 2007 capercailly, red squirrel, bison and moose were all due for release. Longer-term plans include former predators, once abundant in Scotland, such as grey wolves, European brown bears and Eurasian lynx.

Visitors can stay in the lodge, where accommodation is very exclusive; there are eight luxury rooms accommodating 16 guests and it's usually available to groups only. However, some dates from April through to August are reserved for couples booking a four-night stretch for £800, all-inclusive. Call the lodge or see the website for details. Activities include guided nature walks, 4WD safaris, fishing and mountain biking. There were no wildlife safaris at the time of writing, but when they are introduced day trips will be £45/18 for adults/children for six hours. This gives people not staying in the lodge the opportunity to see the reserve.

Alladale is approximately 40 miles north of Inverness. Drop into **Alladale Country Store** ( ☎ 01863-766323; Ardgay; ⏰ 9am-5pm Mon-Sat, 10am-4pm Sun) for information on the reserve including the progress of species introduction. If safaris haven't started but you're keen for a look around, they may well take you up there for a tour.

---

shop and hotel, and **Bonar Bridge**, where the A836 to Lairg branches west.

From Ardgay, a single-track road leads 10 miles up Strathcarron to **Croick**, the scene of notorious evictions during the 1845 Clearances (see the boxed text, p360). You can still see the sad messages scratched by refugee crofters from Glencalvie on the eastern windows of Croick Church.

If a youth hostel could attract a five-star rating, opulent **Carbisdale Castle Youth Hostel** (SYHA; ☎ 0870 004 1109; Culrain; dm adult/child £16/12.50; ⏰ Mar-Sep) would score six. Carbisdale Castle was built in 1914 for the dowager duchess of Sutherland – it is now Scotland's biggest and most luxurious hostel, its halls studded with statues and dripping with opulence. It's 10 minutes' walk north of Culrain train station. Advance bookings are recommended.

Trains from Inverness to Thurso stop at Ardgay and Culrain (£12.10, two or three times daily), half a mile from Carbisdale Castle.

## LAIRG

☎ 01549 / pop 900

Lairg is an attractive village, although the tranquillity can be rudely interrupted by the sound of military jets heard whining and cracking overhead. At the southern end of Loch Shin, it's the gateway to the remote mountains and loch-speckled bogs of central Sutherland. The A836 from Lairg to Tongue passes Ben Klibreck (961m) and Ben Loyal (764m).

Lairg has a seasonal **tourist office** ( ☎ 402160; Ferrycroft Countryside Centre; ⏰ 10am-5pm Mon-Sat Apr, 10am-5.30pm Mon-Sat May, Sep & Oct, 9.30am-5.30pm Mon-Sat Jun-Aug & 11.30am-5.30pm Sun Jul-Aug; 🖳 ) on the far side of the river from the village. There are also shops, a bank (with ATM) and a post office.

From June to September, just south of Lairg, you can watch salmon leaping the **Falls of Shin** on their way upstream to spawn.

**Sleeperzzz** ( ☎ 01408-641343; www.sleeperzzz.com; Rogart Station; r per person £12; ⏰ Mar–mid-Nov), nine miles east of Lairg is a charming and unique hostel. Ten compartments in two 1st-class railway carriages have been fitted with two comfortable bunks each; there's also a compartment with a little kitchen and another with a dining room.

Rooms are surprisingly modern and very good value at the solid **Nip Inn** ( ☎ 402243; www .nipinn.co.uk; Main St; r per person £27-32). The décor is bright, en suites are sparkling and the inn caters for solo travellers. The restaurant's open for lunch and dinner (£10 to £14) and bar meals are available (£8).

Stagecoach Inverness buses run from Inverness to Tain (£6.30, one hour, frequent); MacLeods then picks up the link from Tain to Lairg (30 minutes, four daily Monday to Saturday). Buses also run to Helmsdale (one hour, three daily Monday to Friday).

Trains from Inverness to Thurso stop at Lairg (£12.10, 1¾ hours) and Rogart (£12.10, two hours) two or three times daily in each direction.

# DORNOCH
☎ 01862 / pop 1200

It's difficult to believe that Scotland's last executed witch perished in a vat of boiling tar in Dornoch in 1722, because today this graceful village is all happy families. On the coast, 2 miles off the A9, this symphony in sandstone bewitches visitors with flowers, greenery and affable locals at every turn.

The **tourist office** ( ☎ 255121; Castle St; ☽ 9am-5pm Mon-Fri, 9.30am-5pm Sat, call for winter hrs; 🖳 ) is in the Highland Council Building next to Dornoch Castle Hotel and has limited information, plus internet access.

## Sights
The town is clustered around the 13th-century **Dornoch Cathedral**, which is shaped like a crucifix. The crisscross of light streaming through adjacent stained-glass windows creates a powerful effect. The original building was destroyed in 1570 during a clan feud. Despite some patching up, it wasn't completely rebuilt until 1837.

If you've struck Dornoch on a sunny day make sure you have a walk along its golden sand **beach**, which stretches for miles.

South of Dornoch, seals are often visible on the sand bars of **Dornoch Firth**.

## Sleeping & Eating
**Trevose Guest House** ( ☎ 810269; trevose@amserve.net; Cathedral Sq; s/d £25/50) A gorgeous early-19th-century stone cottage claiming primo location, spilling out onto the village green across from the cathedral. Firm mattresses and a selection of shared and en-suite bathrooms make this place a good choice, and there's a smokers' guest lounge. Watch the low roofs.

**Dornoch Castle Hotel** ( ☎ 810216; www.dornochcastle hotel.com; Castle St; garden s/tw from £50/65, castle s/d from £70/110, suite £210) Fancy a night in a castle? Then try this grand, 16th-century former bishop's palace. The stately rooms vary considerably, but you're unlikely to be disappointed no matter what you choose – ask for a room number at random! In the evening toast your toes in the cosy bar before dining in style at the first-rate restaurant (dinner mains £15 to £18) tucking into dishes such as the duo of pheasant and pigeon, and served with black and white pudding torte with a brandy onion jus.

The restaurant's open for lunch and dinner; bar meals are also available (£6 to £8).

**Eagle Hotel** ( ☎ 810008; Castle St; bar meals £8-10; ☽ lunch & dinner) Chow down at this top little boozer complete with eccentric ornamentation and man-sized meals. Look out for two- and three-course lunch specials. Wash it all down with a Dornoch Ale.

**2 Quail Restaurant** ( ☎ 811811; Castle St; 4-course dinner £37; ☽ dinner Tue-Sat Apr-Oct, Fri & Sat Nov-Mar) A tiny restaurant that excels in fine dining – one of the best in this part of the Highlands. Bookings are essential.

Also recommended:

**Rosslyn Villa** ( ☎ 810237; Castle St; r per person £19) The best B&Bs come with simplicity and a smile. No breakfast.

**Auchlea** ( ☎ 811524; www.auchlea.co.uk; B9168; r per person £22.50-30) A purpose-built lodging with three en-suite rooms; near the A9 turn-off to Dornoch, about 1.5 miles from town.

## Getting There & Away
Scottish Citylink has services to/from Inverness (£7.20, 1¼ hours, four to five daily) and Thurso (£11, 2¼ hours, four to five daily), stopping in the square at Dornoch.

# GOLSPIE
☎ 01408 / pop 1400

Golspie is an attractive town off the main drag, and would be a congenial option for a day or two (particularly if you feel like pulling on the walking boots or exploring a castle).

One mile north of town is mighty **Dunrobin Castle** ( ☎ 633177; adult/child £7/5; ☽ 10.30am-4.30pm Mon-Sat, noon-4.30pm Sun Apr, May & Sep–mid-Oct, 10.30am-5.30pm Mon-Sat, noon-5.30pm Sun Jun-Aug), the largest house in the Highlands (187 rooms). Although it dates back to around 1275, most of what you see today was built in French style between 1845 and 1850. One of the homes of the earls and dukes of Sutherland, it's richly furnished and offers an intriguing insight into their opulent lifestyle. The house also displays innumerable gifts from farm tenants (probably grateful they weren't victims of the Clearances – see the boxed text, p360).

Golspie is the starting point for some good walks. One trail leads north along the coast for 5 miles to Brora, passing the remains of the Iron Age broch (defensive tower) of **Carn Liath** about halfway along. The other trail climbs steeply above the village to the summit of **Ben Bhraggie** (394m), which is crowned by a massive monument to the duke of Sutherland that was erected in 1834 and is visible for miles around.

On the approach into town from Dornoch is **Blar Mhor** ( ☎ 633609; geordie@blarmhor.fsnet.co.uk; A9; s/d £25/40; 🖳 ), an excellent guesthouse with large beautifully kept rooms (our fave is the double opposite the lounge) in a towering Victorian mansion. There are landscaped gardens and the lounge offers a chance to relax in the evening and socialise with other guests.

Buses between Inverness and Thurso stop in Golspie. There are also trains from Inverness (£13.50, two hours, two or three daily).

# HELMSDALE

☎ 01431 / pop 900

Backed by yellow gorse-bedecked hills and set on a wide river mouth, Helmsdale has an enviable location. It's surrounded by stunning, undulating coastline and the River Helmsdale – one of the best salmon rivers in the Highlands.

For tourist information and internet access, go to the **Strath Ullie Crafts & Information Centre** ( ☎ 821402; The Harbour, Shore St; 🖳 ), which was being renovated at the time of research.

## Sights & Activities

The excellent **Timespan Heritage Centre** ( ☎ 821327; Dunrobin St) has a gallery relating the Gartymore Story – when hundreds of families were forcibly removed from their native homes by the House of Sutherland in the early 19th century. The gallery is intriguing because it's a collection of stories based on people in the area, their possessions and, importantly, their memories. The centre was closed for renovation when we passed through.

Helmsdale is known for its salmon fishing and if you feel like throwing in a line, drop into **River Helmsdale Fishing Tackle** ( ☎ 07780-861466; Dunrobin St; 🕙 9am-5pm Mon, Tue, Thu & Fri, 9am-12.45pm Wed & Sat).

## Sleeping & Eating

**Helmsdale Youth Hostel** ( ☎ 821636; cnr A9 & Old Caithness Rd; dm £15; 🕙 May-Sep; 🖳 ) This hostel has had a major refurbishment and is in very good nick – there's an open fire, excellent eight-bed dorms and en-suite family rooms. It gets busy; book well ahead for July and August.

**Belgrave Arms Hotel** ( ☎ 821242; enquiries@belgrave armshotel.com; cnr Dunrobin St & A9; s/d from £24/44) The Belgrave, a small family-run hotel, has a genuine feel to it, with a slightly musty odour and creaky floorboards. Importantly, though, the rooms are fresh and well maintained.

**Bridge Hotel** ( ☎ 821100; www.bridgehotel.net; Dunrobin St; s/d £75/105; 🔥 ) Ideally located, this early-19th-century lodging is a top place to stay. The suite (£145) is more like a mini flat and the luxurious doubles with polished-wood furniture have great hill and river views. For some, the only drawback may be the hunting theme, with numerous 'trophies' on the wall. Doggy beds are available on request. Call for discounts on tariffs listed above.

**La Mirage** ( ☎ 821615; 7 Dunrobin St; light meals £3-5, mains £8-15; 🕙 lunch & dinner) Former proprietor Nancy Sinclair has gone to great lengths to become Barbara Cartland's double (Cartland holidayed here for over 60 years). Accordingly, her restaurant's décor oozes pink kitsch, and is a drawcard in itself. The menu boasts standard grills and vegetarian options, as well as good-value fish cooked with class.

## Getting There & Away

Buses from Inverness and Thurso stop in Helmsdale, as do trains (from Thurso £12.50, 1¼ hours, four daily).

# HELMSDALE TO LATHERON

About 7 miles north of Helmsdale, a 15-minute walk east from the A9 (signposted) takes you to **Badbea**. It's here that the ruins of crofts are perched on the cliff top. The **Berriedale Braes**, 2.5 miles beyond the Badbea parking area, is a difficult section of the A9, with steep gradients and hairpin bends.

**Dunbeath** has a spectacular setting in a deep glen – it makes a good stop on the way to the northern towns. There are a couple of shops and a **heritage centre** ( ☎ 01593-731233; www.dunbeath-heritage.org.uk; The Old School; adult/child £2/free; 🕙 10am-5pm Apr-Sep, Mon-Fri Oct-Mar), with displays about the history of Caithness, including crofting and fisheries. There are also exhibitions, including one on the crash of the Sunderland flying boat near Dunbeath in 1942.

The friendly and laid-back **Kingspark Llama Farm** ( ☎ 01593-751202; Berriedale; s/d from £22/45), a working llama farm, 4 miles south of Dunbeath, has cosy rooms with low-slung ceilings and shared bathrooms. Guests are greeted with a cheery smile and sent on their way with a happy stomach.

At the **Clan Gunn Heritage Centre & Museum** ( ☎ 01593-741700; adult/child £2.50/1; ◷ 11am-1pm & 2-4pm Mon-Sat Jun & Sep, 11am-1pm & 2-4pm Mon-Sat, 2-4pm Sun Jul & Aug) in Latheron, 3 miles northeast of Dunbeath on the A9, you'll learn that a Scot, not Christopher Columbus, discovered America – but you might take this claim with a pinch of salt! Even if you don't want to go in, it's worth pulling into the car park on a fine day to admire the stunning views.

## LYBSTER

☎ 01593

Lybster is a purpose-built fishing village dating from 1810, with a stunning harbour area surrounded by grassy cliffs.

The major crowd-pleaser here is the **Waterlines Visitor Centre** ( ☎ 721520; adult/child £2.50/50p; ◷ 11am-5pm May-Sep; ♿ ♿ ). It has a heritage exhibition, a smokehouse (giving visitors a whiff of the kippering process) and CCTV beaming live pictures of nesting sea birds from nearby cliffs. After a visit you can sit on outdoor benches and munch on some home baking while admiring the views across the stunning harbour setting.

The warm and welcoming **Portland Arms Hotel** ( ☎ 721721; www.portlandarms.co.uk; s/d £75/86), on the A9 main road in town, is an atmospheric old pub with log fires and a farmhouse feel. There's a mix of older and refurbished rooms – all are pretty good.

Scottish Citylink buses between Thurso and Inverness run via Lybster (one hour, up to four daily), Latheron and Dunbeath. Rapsons/Highland Country runs four times daily from Wick to Ulbster, Lybster, Dunbeath and Berriedale.

### CROFTING & THE CLEARANCES

In many parts of the Highlands and islands you will see clusters of ruined cottages crumbling amid the bracken – all that remains of deserted farming communities. Up until the 19th century the most common form of farming settlement here was the *baile*, a group of a dozen or so families who farmed the land granted to them by the local chieftain in return for military service and a portion of the harvest. The arable land was divided into strips called *rigs*, which were allocated to different families by annual ballot so that each took turns at getting the poorer soils; this system was known as *runrig*. The families worked the land communally, and their cattle shared the grazing land.

But this lifestyle was swept away in the wake of the Highland Clearances, which took place between around 1750 and the 1880s. Following the ban on private armies, clan chiefs no longer needed military service from their tenants, and saw sheep farming as far more profitable than collecting rent from poverty-stricken farmers. Tens of thousands of tenant farmers were evicted from their homes and their land.

Those who chose not to emigrate or move to the cities to find work were forced to eke a living from narrow plots of marginal agricultural land, often close to the coast. This was a form of smallholding that became known as crofting. The small patch of land barely provided a living, and had to be supplemented by other work such as fishing and kelp-gathering. The close-knit community of the *baile* was replaced by the widely scattered cottages of the crofting settlements that you can still see today.

When economic depression hit in the late 19th century, many crofters couldn't pay their rent. This time, however, they resisted expulsion, instead forming the Highland Land Reform Association and their own political party. Their resistance led to several of their demands being acceded to by the government; the Crofters' Holdings Act of 1886 provided for security of tenure, fair rents and eventually the supply of land for new crofts.

Today the Scottish Highlands are, in many parts, a graveyard of broken communities, communities that ceased living and breathing more than 200 years ago. Evidence of the cruel evictions is everywhere and the human tragedy has scarred this majestic landscape. While economic recovery is in full swing, the human cost is irrecoverable and the desolation of the countryside is in harmony with the poor souls lost to starvation, poverty and estrangement from their ancestral lands.

Crofting tenancies still exist and complex regulations now protect the crofters. The Land Reform Act, passed in 2003, gave crofters the absolute right to buy their tenancy, and a law abolishing feudal tenure come into effect in late 2004, ending 900 years of feudalism.

## AROUND LYBSTER

At Ulbster, 5 miles north of Lybster on the A99, is **Whaligoe Steps**, a spectacular staircase cut into the cliff face. It provides access to a tiny natural harbour ringed by vertical cliffs and echoing with the cackle of nesting fulmars. The path begins at the end of the minor road beside the telephone box, opposite the road signposted 'Cairn o' Get'. The **Cairn o'Get**, a prehistoric burial cairn, is a mile northwest of Ulbster. From the car park cross the stile and follow the black-and-white marker poles for approximately 1 mile. Wear decent shoes as the ground is boggy.

There are several interesting prehistoric sites near Lybster. Five miles to the northwest of Lybster, on the minor road to Achavanich, just south of Loch Stemster, are the unsigned 30 **Achavanich Standing Stones**. In a desolate setting, these crumbling monuments of the distant past still capture the imagination with their evocative location. It's all about colours: blue skies, a steely grey loch, and the soft browns and greens of the land. The setting and absence of modern tourism makes this place special.

A mile east of Lybster on the A99, a turn-off leads north to the **Grey Cairns of Camster**. Dating from between 4000 BC and 2500 BC, these burial chambers are hidden in long, low mounds rising from an evocatively desolate stretch of moor. The Long Cairn measures 60m by 21m. You can enter the main chamber, but must first crawl into the well-preserved Round Cairn, which has a corbelled ceiling. From the site you can then continue 7 miles north on this remote road to approach Wick on the A882.

Back on the A99, the **Hill o'Many Stanes**, 2 miles beyond the Camster turn-off, is a curious, fan-shaped arrangement of 22 rows of small stones that probably date from around 2000 BC. Staggeringly, there were 600 in the original pattern. On a sunny day, the views from this hill are stunning.

## WICK

☎ 01955 / pop 7400

While we wouldn't quite say that Wick has turned a corner, the town appears to be a little less dismal than it once was. That said, take a walk around Wick Harbour or High St mall and you'll see the weird (and depressing) thing about this town – it's just too quiet for a place this size. In any case, you should spend at least a night, as it takes a wee while to dig under the town's economically depressed façade to enjoy its fascinating history, grittiness and admirable attractions.

### Information

**Bank of Scotland** (Bridge St) Has ATM.
**Royal Bank of Scotland** (Bridge St) Has ATM.
**Tourist office** (McAllans; 66 High St; ☼ 9am-5.30pm Mon-Sat) Unattended station in McAllans Clothing Store.
**Wick Carnegie Library** ( ☎ 602864; Sinclair Tce; ☼ 10am-6pm Mon & Thu, 10am-8pm Tue & Fri, 10am-1pm Wed & Sat) Free internet access.

### Sights

#### WICK HERITAGE CENTRE

The town's award-winning local **museum** ( ☎ 605393; 18-27 Bank Row; adult/child £3/50p; ☼ 10am-5pm Easter-Oct, outside these months call for hrs) deserves all the praise heaped upon it. Tracking the rise and fall of the herring industry, it displays everything from fishing equipment to complete herring fishing boats. It's a fantastic museum – without doubt one of the best in the country – and is absolutely huge inside, crammed with memorabilia and extensive displays describing the days of the mid-19th century when Wick was the largest herring port in Europe.

The Johnston photographic collection is the museum's star exhibit. From 1863 to 1977, three generations of Johnstons photographed everything that happened around Wick, and the 70,000 photographs are an amazing portrait of the town's life. Prints of the early photos are for sale.

#### CASTLES

A path leads a mile south of town to the ruins of 12th-century **Old Wick Castle**, with the spectacular cliffs of the **Brough** and the **Brig**, as well as **Gote o'Trams**, a little further south. In good weather, it's a fine coastal walk to the castle, but take care on the final approach. Three miles northeast of Wick is the magnificently located cliff-top ruin of **Castle Sinclair**.

#### DISTILLERY

**Old Pulteney** ( ☎ 602371; www.oldpulteney.com; Huddart St) is the most northerly distillery on mainland Scotland and runs excellent tours (£3.50) at 11am and 2pm from Monday to Friday (closed in July). Old Pulteney whisky has a light, earthy character with a hint of sea air and sherry. The visitors centre is free and gives an interesting, abbreviated account of the distilling process.

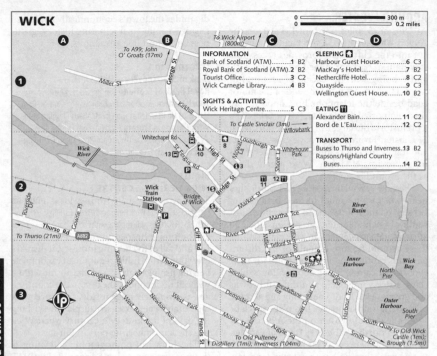

## WICK

**INFORMATION**
Bank of Scotland (ATM)...........1 B2
Royal Bank of Scotland (ATM).2 B2
Tourist Office............................3 C2
Wick Carnegie Library.............4 B3

**SIGHTS & ACTIVITIES**
Wick Heritage Centre..............5 C3

**SLEEPING**
Harbour Guest House...............6 C3
MacKay's Hotel.........................7 B2
Nethercliffe Hotel.....................8 C3
Quayside...................................9 C3
Wellington Guest House.........10 B2

**EATING**
Alexander Bain........................11 C2
Bord de L'Eau..........................12 C2

**TRANSPORT**
Buses to Thurso and Inverness.13 B2
Rapsons/Highland Country
Buses.....................................14 B2

## Sleeping & Eating

Wick has a shortage of B&B accommodation and while it's not exactly flooded with visitors during summer it can often be difficult to jag a room. Solution: book ahead.

**Quayside** ( ☎ 603229; www.quaysidewick.co.uk; 25 Harbour Quay; r per person £22-28) This place should be your first port of call for accommodation – they've been in the business for many years and know what they're doing. It overlooks the harbour, has a large range of neat rooms and is handy for the heritage centre and the chippy a couple of doors down. There's a self-catering option (£50 for two), as well. Note that the single is *very* small. Book ahead. Motorcyclists welcome.

**MacKay's Hotel** ( ☎ 602323; www.mackayshotel.co.uk; Union St; s/d £65/90; 🖳 ) The renovated MacKay's is Wick's best hotel. Rooms vary in layout and size so ask to see a few; prices drop if you're staying more than one night. The 2.75m-long Ebenezer Pl, the shortest street in Britain, runs past one end of the hotel. The bistro here is a fine-dining option for lunch or dinner. Service is friendly and the ingredients are sourced locally.

**Alexander Bain** ( ☎ 609920; Market Pl; dishes £5-8; ☯ lunch & dinner) This is the only pub in town that serves food on weeknights. It's a cavernous place in the middle of the pedestrianised High St, attracting a mix of tourists, families and ragtag locals. It's probably the best place to see a cross section of Wick in the evening. After all where else do you go? Cheap but average food includes pastas, salads, burgers, steaks and wraps. A beer and burger is £4.25 while the Sunday roast is £7.

**Bord de L'Eau** ( ☎ 604400; 2 Market St; starters £5, mains £11-13; ☯ lunch Tue-Sat, dinner Tue-Sun) This serene, upmarket French restaurant is the best place to eat in Wick. It overlooks the river and serves dishes such as *escargot*, and grilled lamb fillets with a thyme and honey jus. The menu is very meat based.

Also recommended:

**Harbour Guest House** ( ☎ 603276; harbour.guest house@supanet.com; 6 Rose St; s/d £23/46) Decent digs for a decent price.

**Wellington Guest House** ( ☎ 603287; High St; s £30-35, tw £45-55; 🅿 ) This place probably wouldn't make it in this book in other towns. But in Wick – well, choice is limited. Aged rooms are average with cramped en suites.

However, it is clean and there's a splash of colour and modern décor to brighten things up in the rooms.
**Nethercliffe Hotel** ( ☎ 602044; fax 605691; Louisburgh St; s/d £50/65; ⑤ ) A very friendly, small hotel with good-value rooms exhibiting warmth and flowery old-fashioned décor.

### Getting There & Away
Wick is a transport gateway to the surrounding area. **Logan Air** ( ☎ 602294; www.loganair.co.uk) flies between Edinburgh and Wick airport (from £120 return, one hour, one daily Monday to Saturday) and on to the Orkney Islands. **Eastern Airways** ( ☎ 01652-680600; www.easternairways.com) flies to Aberdeen (£110 return, 35 minutes, three Monday to Friday).

Scottish Citylink operates buses to/from Inverness (£15, three hours, four daily) and Thurso (£6, 40 minutes, four daily).

Rapsons/Highland Country runs the connecting service to John o'Groats (40 minutes, up to five daily Monday to Saturday) for the passenger ferry to Burwick, Orkney. Also connects up with the Gills Bay ferry to St Margaret's Hope, Orkney.

Trains service Wick from Inverness (£14.60, four hours, one or two daily).

## JOHN O'GROATS
☎ 01955 / pop 500

We've tried – we really have. Readers have written to us pointing out the error of our ways – 'you're too harsh on John o'Groats' they say. Well sorry...but we still can't find anything endearing to say about the place – it's horrible. Scotland's worst and most embarrassing tourist attraction, it's falsely believed to be the most northerly point on the British mainland (it's actually Dunnet Head; right), has been milking this geographical extremity for years. The main attraction is basically a car park surrounded by shoddy craft and souvenir shops. The only thing making a trip here remotely worthwhile is jumping on board **North Coast Marine Adventures** ( ☎ 611797; www.northcoast-marine-adventures.co.uk), which runs scenic wildlife trips. Seals, whales, dolphins and seabirds can all be spotted and these guys minimise disturbance of the environment. For accommodation, try Wick (opposite), Mey (right) or Thurso (p366), all nearby.

Two miles east of John o'Groats is the much better **Duncansby Head**, which is home to many sea birds at the start of summer. A path leads to **Duncansby Stacks**, spectacular natural rock formations soaring 60m above the sea. There is a series of narrow inlets and deep coves on this wonderful stretch of coast.

### Getting There & Away
Rapsons/Highland Country runs buses between John o'Groats and Wick (40 minutes, up to five daily Monday to Saturday). There are also up to five services Monday to Saturday to/from Thurso.

From May to September, the passenger ferry MV *Pentland Venture*, operated by **John o'Groats Ferries** ( ☎ 611353; www.jogferry.co.uk), shuttles across to Burwick in Orkney (adult/child return £26/13); a coach tour of Orkney mainland, including the ferry fare, is £38/19. Ninety-minute wildlife cruises to the island of Stroma or Duncansby Head cost £15.

## MEY
☎ 01847 / pop 200

Mey is a very small village scattered along the A836. **Castle of Mey** ( ☎ 851473; www.castleofmey.org.uk; adult/child £7.50/3; ⏱ 10.30am-4pm May–late-Jul & mid-Aug–Sep), a big crowd-puller, is about 6 miles from John o'Groats, off the A836 to Thurso. It's the former home of the late Queen Mother, and hardened royal buffs will get a kick out of items of memorabilia and pictures of the Queen Mum, but for everyone else there's not that much to see inside. Outside in the castle grounds, though, there's an unusual walled garden that's worth a stroll around, and there are lovely views over the Pentland Firth.

The nearby **Castle Arms Hotel** ( ☎ 851992; www.castlearms.co.uk; s/d £57/90), a former 19th-century coaching inn, has a friendly bar downstairs and decent (if slightly pricey) rooms upstairs. Or try **Hawthorns** ( ☎ 851710; www.thehawthornsbnb.co.uk; s/d £30/50), where rooms are huge and the owner's cheery smile is just as big.

**The Tea Cosy** ( ☎ 01955-611770; East Mey; sandwiches £4; ⏱ lunch), the most northerly tearoom on mainland Scotland, is worth popping into for some freshly prepared gourmet sandwiches, quiches or a ploughman's lunch. The owners aim to please and will make you something up on request (if they can!). There are also magnificent views out to the North Sea.

## DUNNET HEAD
Let's put a common misconception to rest. Contrary to popular belief, naff John o'Groats is not the British mainland's most northerly

point; that honour goes to Dunnet Head, 10 miles to the west. The head is marked by a lighthouse dating from 1832.

Not only is Dunnet Head the real 'most northerly point', it's also well worth coming out here for the views of the startling sea cliffs and the vista over to Orkney and beyond, all near the lighthouse. The lonely car park (with plaques about local flora and fauna and a self-guided tour of the area) is a welcome relief from the con of John o'Groats.

Just southwest of Dunnet Head there is a magnificent stretch of sandy beach, at the southern end of which lies the tiny harbour of **Castlehill**. It's here that a heritage trail explains the evolution of the local flagstone industry.

# NORTH & WEST COAST

Quintessential Highland country such as this, marked by single-track roads, breathtaking emptiness and a wild, fragile beauty, is a rarity on the modern, crowded, highly urbanised island of Britain. You could get lost up here for weeks – and that still wouldn't be enough time.

Carving its way from Thurso to Glencoul, the north and northwest coastline is a feast of deep inlets, forgotten beaches and surging peninsulas. Within the rugged confines, the deep interior is home to vast, empty spaces, enormous lochs and some of Scotland's highest peaks.

The remarkable thing about the landscape is that it makes you feel special. Whether it's blazing sunshine or a murky greyness, the character of the land is totally unique and constantly changing – for that window of time in which you glimpse it, you capture an exclusive snapshot of this ancient area in your mind (or on your camera). Park the car and gaze. This northernmost slab of the Highlands is the stuff of coastal-drive dreams.

## Getting Around

Public transport in the northwest is, well, pretty awful. There's no doubt that this region is best explored by car – you'll be able to reach the sites and towns far more easily and, doing it all in your own time, you'll get a lot more from the experience. Getting to Thurso or Kyle of Lochalsh by bus or train is easy, but following the coast between these

places, especially from October to May, is when the fun really starts. **Royal Mail postbuses** (☎ 0845 774 0740; www.postbus.royalmail.com) run year-round; fares vary, but long journeys are usually good value at around £4 or £5. See its website for details of routes, which cover most towns in this section. **Rapsons/Highland Country** (☎ 01847-893123) runs services to major towns.

To travel across the north coast, from Thurso to Durness, the Monday to Saturday postbus services are your only option.

From late April to late September, **Tim Dearman Coaches** (☎ 01349-883585; www.timdearmancoaches .co.uk) runs buses from Inverness to Durness (£17, five hours, one daily Monday to Saturday, plus Sunday in July and August) via Ullapool and Lochinver.

An alternative is to come up from Inverness via Lairg. Apart from trains, **Stagecoach Inverness** (☎ 01463-239292) operates to/from Tain (£6.30, 1¼ hours, hourly or two hourly) and **MacLeods Coaches** (☎ 01408-641354) operates a connecting service to Lairg (£3.50, 45 minutes, four daily Monday to Saturday). A postbus will then get you from Lairg through to Tongue (one daily Monday to Saturday).

There are regular Scottish Citylink buses between Inverness and Ullapool.

**Rapsons/Westerbus** (☎ 01571-84473) runs every Monday, Wednesday, Thursday and Saturday between Ullapool and Gairloch.

The once-daily (except Sunday) Westerbus service from Inverness to Gairloch, runs via Achnasheen and Kinlochewe, or via Dundonnell on Monday, Wednesday and Saturday. The route via Dundonnell provides a link between Ullapool and Gairloch (via Braemore Junction). The Achnasheen–Kinlochewe–Torridon postbus can be used in conjunction with the Westerbus, taking you from Gairloch to Kinlochewe and Torridon (at least one day after the Ullapool to Gairloch leg).

From Torridon, the **MacLennan** (☎ 01520-755239) bus service goes to Strathcarron (£3.50, once daily Monday to Saturday from June to September), or call for times for the rest of the year.

## THURSO & SCRABSTER
☎ 01847 / pop 7800
The mainland's most northerly town, Thurso can seem bleak and rather depressing, though a new tourist development called Caithness Horizons, some classy eating options and a

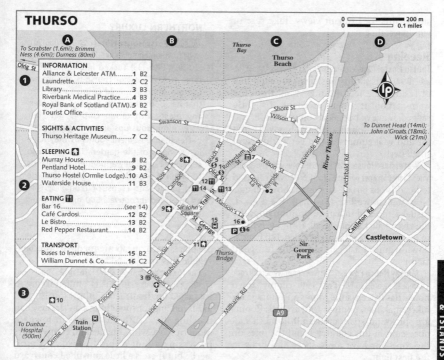

**THURSO**

**NORTHERN HIGHLANDS & ISLANDS**

wide range of accommodation are fighting against the tide. In the evening the young come out to play: note the teens doing bog laps of the centre in their little cars, music blaring.

Thurso is useful as a service centre too, and as an overnight stop en route to Orkney – the view across Pentland Firth to Hoy beckons visitors to a more appealing location. Ferries cross from Scrabster, 2.5 miles west of Thurso, to Orkney. Tiny Scrabster, little more than a collection of BP oil storage containers, revolves around its port.

## Information

**Alliance & Leicester ATM** (cnr Olrig & Rotterdam Sts)
**Dunbar Hospital** (☎ 893263; Ormlie Rd)
**Laundrette** (Riverside Pl; small wash £3; ☼ 9am-6pm Mon-Fri, 10am-5.30pm Sat)
**Library** (☎ 893237; Davidson's Lane; ☼ 10am-6pm Mon & Wed, to 8pm Tue & Fri, to 1pm Thu & Sat) Free internet access.
**Riverbank medical centre** (☎ 892027; Janet St)
**Royal Bank of Scotland** (Olrig St) ATM.
**Tourist office** (☎ 892371; Riverside Rd; ☼ Mon-Sat Apr-May & Sep-Oct, daily Jun-Aug)

## Sights & Activities

**Thurso Heritage Museum** (☎ 892459; High St), in the old Town Hall, displays Pictish and Christian fossils and carved stones, and a reconstruction of a croft interior. It was closed at the time of research for a major renovation and will reopen as Caithness Horizons in late 2008, featuring a museum, tourist office, visitor displays and a café.

Thurso is an unlikely **surfing** centre, but the nearby coast has arguably the best and most regular surf on mainland Britain. There's an excellent right-hand reef break on the eastern side of town, directly in front of Lord Thurso's castle (closed to the public), and another shallow reef break 5 miles west at Brimms Ness.

Thurso's idyllic country **riverside walk** will make you feel miles away from town. Access is near Waterside House and you can walk upstream, retracing your footsteps to come back (there was a bridge you could cross to come back on the other side, but it has been washed out). It's a beautiful walk, taking about 45 minutes at a stroll, and is a very popular local pursuit in decent weather. You can also walk all the way to Scrabster (40 minutes) along cliffs for brilliant views. Take care in windy weather.

## Sleeping

**Thurso Hostel** (Ormlie Lodge; ☎ /fax 896888; Ormlie Rd; s/d £10/17) This scruffy hostel is a students' hall of residence a few minutes' walk from the train station. It has an excellent, if slightly ragged, range of budget accommodation, and is great value. Rooms are small, but well cared for and well equipped: you get a fridge and small desk.

**Waterside House** ( ☎ 894751; www.watersidehouse.info; 3 Janet St; r per person £19-25) Not what it used to be, this old girl is starting to show her age. Nonetheless we like this B&B. It's a good, casual setup and in a great position opposite the river – just a short walk from everything in town. Not sheer luxury granted, but hands-down winner for location and the feel-good factor.

**Murray House** ( ☎ 895759; www.murrayhousebb.com; 1 Campbell St; s/d £30/60) This 19th-century town house have five en-suite rooms and storage for bikes, making it popular with cyclists. Rooms are spick-and-span, modern if floral (it's an obsession in this country!), and the ones on the top floor have more space and draw in the best light.

**Pentland Hotel** ( ☎ 893202; www.pentlandhotel.co.uk; Princes St; s £40-45, d £70-80) The business-style rooms in this place are great value. They're big enough to have a couch and a separate nook with a desk. It's a stylish place, and surprisingly tranquil inside, given its central location. There are plenty of open areas for lounging around while you wait for the ferry to Orkney.

## Eating

**Café Cardosi** ( ☎ 896212; cnr Olrig & Traill Sts; dishes £3-4; ☽ 9am-6pm Mon-Sat) Stylishly decked out in warm colours and a trendy, minimalist décor, Cardosi pumps out decent coffee, salads, light hot meals and sandwiches. The decadent home-baked cakes are a standout, but the best thing about this joint is people-watching, both inside and on the busy street outside.

**Le Bistro** ( ☎ 893737; 2 Traill St; lunch £5-8, dinner mains £10-13; ☽ lunch Tue-Sat, dinner Wed-Sat) One of our faves in northern Scotland, this bright, Mediterranean-style bistro with top-notch food wins our 'best place to eat in town' award, hands down. The kitchen whips up both traditional and exotic fare, and service comes with a smile. Seafood dishes feature on

---

> ### NORTHERN LUXURY
>
> **ourpick Forss House Hotel** ( ☎ 01847-861201; www.forsshousehotel.co.uk; Forss by Thurso; s £70-80, d £105-135) Tucked into a thicket of trees 4 miles west of Thurso is elegant accommodation in an old Georgian mansion that has both character and style. Besides, any place with tartan carpets gets our vote. Sumptuous upstairs rooms are much better than basement rooms as they have lovely views of the garden. There are also separate, beautifully appointed Woodlands suites in the garden itself, which provide both privacy and a sense of tranquillity. And as an added incentive…300 malt whiskies await.

---

the blackboard, meals are made to order and vegetarians are catered for.

**Bar 16** (The Holborn; ☎ 892771; 16 Princes St; bar meals £7-10; ☽ lunch & dinner) This is Thurso trying to get tarted up. It attracts a mix of tourists and locals looking for something a bit classier than trawling the scruffy local pubs in town. A modern space with couches and comfy chairs possessing a hint of minimalism, it's a bit sterile but there's a little sun-filled courtyard perfect for an evening drink. Steer clear of the seafood salad but try the chicken fajitas or sirloin steak baguette for a winner.

**Red Pepper Restaurant** (The Holborn; ☎ 892771; 16 Princes St; starters £5, mains £9-14; ☽ lunch & dinner) A step up again in the local dining scene. A simple dining room with lots of wood, good lighting and, most importantly, well-prepared food with generous portions and lots of local produce. Try the smoked chicken and spinach linguine followed by homemade cheesecake.

## Getting There & Around

Thurso is 130 miles from Inverness and 21 miles from Wick. From Inverness, Scottish Citylink buses operate via Wick to Thurso (£15, 3½ hours, three to five daily). Rapsons/Highland Country runs a service to Wick (45 minutes, hourly) and also to John o'Groats (one hour, five Monday to Friday, three Saturday).

There are two or three daily train services from Inverness in summer (£14.60, 3½ hours), but space for bicycles is limited so book ahead.

It's a 2-mile walk from Thurso train station to the ferry port at Scrabster, or there are buses from Olrig St. **William Dunnet & Co** ( ☎ 893101; Manson's Lane; ⊙ 8am-5.30pm Mon-Fri, 9am-1pm Sat) rents cars; a small car starts at £25 per day, plus 10p per mile – you can drop it off in Wick if you're heading that way.

## THURSO TO DURNESS
It's 80 winding and often spectacular coastal miles from Thurso to Durness.

### Dounreay & Melvich
On the coast 10 miles west of Thurso is the **Dounreay Nuclear Power Station.** The plant is being decommissioned and cleaning up the site and storing the waste safely will take until 2036; the cost will run into billions of pounds (see p66). Just beyond Dounreay, **Reay** has a shop and an interesting little harbour dating from 1830. **Melvich** overlooks a fine beach and there are great views from **Strathy Point** (a 2-mile drive from the coast road, then a 15-minute walk).

### Bettyhill (Am Blaran Odhar)
☎ 01641 / pop 550
The panorama of a sweeping, sandy beach backed by velvety green hills with bulbous, rocky outcrops makes a sharp contrast to the sad history of this area. Bettyhill is a crofting community of resettled tenant farmers kicked off their land during the Clearances (see the boxed text, p360).

Bettyhill **tourist office** ( ☎ 521244; ⊙ 10.30am-5pm Mon-Thu, to 7.30pm Fri & Sat Apr-Oct) has limited information on the area, but if you're after a bite to eat, Elizabeth's Cafe (mains £6) here serves good home-cooked food (such as local Bettyhill crab). There's also a shop and post office.

**Strathnaver Museum** ( ☎ 521418; Clachan; adult/child £2/50p; ⊙ 10am-1pm & 2-5pm Mon-Sat Apr-Oct, by arrangement at other times), in an old church, tells the sad story of the Strathnaver Clearances. The museum contains memorabilia of Clan Mackay, various items of crofting equipment and a 4000-year-old beaker.

**Bettyhill Hotel** ( ☎ /fax 521352; enquiries@bettyhill.info; s/d from £25/50; ⊙ lunch & dinner) has a range of renovated rooms with en suites – they're stylishly decorated and emit a cool summer feel. There are rip-roaring views from some (such as No 2) over the sandy beach fringing Torrisdale Bay. The restaurant (mains £9) here churns out some interesting cuisine, catering for vegetarian, vegan and gluten-free diets. It's a very friendly, down-to-earth hotel.

From Bettyhill, the B871 turns south for Helmsdale, through **Strathnaver**, where the Clearances took place.

### Coldbackie & Tongue
☎ 01847 / pop 450
Coldbackie has outstanding views over sandy beaches, turquoise waters and offshore islands. If you haven't seen that magical Scottish light at work yet, there's a good chance you'll see it here – park the car for a few minutes and watch. Only 2 miles further on is Tongue, with the evocative 14th-century ruins of **Castle Varrich**, once a Mackay stronghold. To get to the castle, take the trail next to the Royal Bank of Scotland, near Ben Loyal Hotel – it's an easy stroll. Tongue has a shop, post office, bank and petrol station.

Having just undergone a major refurbishment, **Tongue Youth Hostel** ( ☎ 01847 611 789; Tongue; adult/child £12.50/9.50; ⊙ Apr-Sep) is the top budget option in the area with two- to seven-bed dorms. Huge windows draw light and sublime views into the lounge, dining area and many of the rooms. Check out the delicious, home baking on site – drop in for a bit of choccy cake.

**our pick** **Strathtongue Old Manse** ( ☎ 01847-611252; www.strathtongue.co.uk; Tongue; r per person £25), just a half-mile east of Coldbackie and set back from the A836, is a ripper of a B&B. The host knows her business and there's a choice of an en-suite double or a double and twin sharing a private bathroom (good for families). It's a real nook-and-cranny house and there's loitering ducks on hand to greet new arrivals.

At the junction of the A836 and A838 and within stumbling distance of two pubs is charming **Tigh-nan-Ubhal** ( ☎ 611281; www.spanglefish.com/tigh-nan-ubhal; Main St; r per person £25-30; ♿ ). There are snug, loft-style rooms with plenty of natural light, but the basement double with spa is the pick of the bunch – it's the biggest en suite we've seen in northern Scotland. There's also a fixed caravan out the back sleeping up to four people – perfect for families.

**Ben Loyal Hotel** ( ☎ 611216; www.benloyal.co.uk; Main St; r per person £35-40; ⊙ lunch & dinner) has great rooms with magic views (room No 1 is a fave). In the restaurant (mains £7 to £16), try the local Kyle of Tongue oysters.

Vying for the position of best-located B&B in Scotland, **Cloisters** ( ☎ 601286; www.cloistertal.demon.co.uk; Talmine; s/d from £27.50/45; ♿ ) has three en-suite twin rooms with brilliant views over the Kyle of Tongue and offshore islands. Tastefully furnished, this place would suit older visitors or families. To get here from Tongue, cross the causeway and take the turn-off to Melness, almost immediately on your right.

## Tongue to Durness

From Tongue it's 37 miles to Durness – you can take the causeway across the **Kyle of Tongue** or the beautiful old road that goes around the head of the kyle. A detour to **Melness** and **Port Vasgo** may be rewarded with the sight of seals on the beach.

Continuing west, the road crosses a desolate moor past **Moine House** (a ruin built as a shelter for travellers in 1830) to the northern end of **Loch Hope**. A 10-mile detour south along the loch leads to **Dun Dornaigil**, a well-preserved broch in the shadow of **Ben Hope** (927m). If you'd like to bag this Munro, it's a 4.5-mile, four-hour round trip along the route from the car park, which is 2 miles before the broch, near a large barn. It's a relatively easy walk but often cold at the exposed top.

Beyond Loch Hope, on the main road, **Heilam** has stunning views out over **Loch Eriboll**, Britain's deepest sea inlet and a shelter for ships during WWII.

## DURNESS (DIURANAIS)
☎ 01971 / pop 350

The scattered village of Durness (www.durness .org) is strung out along cliffs, which rise from a series of pristine beaches. It has one of the finest locations in Scotland. When the sun shines the effects of blinding white sand, the cry of sea birds and the lime-coloured seas combine in a magical way. The only blight is the sometimes constant thumping from the Ministry of Defence (MOD) artillery range on Cape Wrath, which can shatter the tranquillity of this northern outpost.

### Orientation & Information

What's known as Durness is really two villages strung along the main road: Durness, in the west, and Smoo, a mile to the east.

Durness has two stores (Spar supermarket has an ATM).

**Durness Community Building** (1 Bard Tce; per 30min £1) Self-serve internet access, opposite MacKays Hotel.

**Health centre** ( ☎ 511273)

**Tourist office** ( ☎ 511368; durness@visitscotland.com;

( 10am-5pm Mon-Sat Apr, May & Oct, 10am-5pm Mon-Sat, to 4pm Sun Jun-Sep) Organises guided walks in summer.

## Sights & Activities

A mile east of the village centre is a path, near the SYHA hostel, down to **Smoo Cave**. The vast cave entrance stands at the end of an inlet, or geo, and a river cascades through its roof into a flooded cavern, then flows out to sea. There's evidence the cave was inhabited about 6000 years ago. You can take a **boat trip** (adult/child £3/1.50) into the floodlit cave (contact the tourist office for more info), although after heavy rain the waterfall can make it impossible to get in. The village has several beautiful **beaches**. One of the best is Sangobeg, but there's also a 'secret beach' just to the east, which can't be seen from the road. Around the coast, there are wrecks, caves, seals and whales. Inquire at the tourist office for **trout-fishing** permits.

The old radar station at **Balnakeil**, less than a mile up a minor road from Durness, has been turned into a hippy craft village, with a bookshop, restaurants and art-and-craft workshops.

## Sleeping & Eating

**Sango Sands Oasis** ( ☎ 511222; Durness; adult/child camp sites per person £5/2.50) Pitch your tent on the northern edge of the country and dangle your feet over the precipice, admiring the sweeping views over the Atlantic's twinkling waters.

**Lazy Crofter Bunkhouse** ( ☎ 511202; fiona@durness hostel.com; Durness; dm £12) This hostel has excellent clean facilities and a lofty position overlooking the water. A bothy vibe gives it a Highland feel and it's really geared for groups. Note that some mattresses are pretty average.

**Wild Orchid Guest House** ( ☎ 511280; wildorchid guesthouse@hotmail.co.uk; rd to Ullapool; r per person £30) Just up the road from MacKays is a guesthouse with cool, contemporary rooms. Doubles are much better than the twins, which are pokier and plainer. Conveniently, a tearoom is right next door.

**MacKays Hotel** ( ☎ 511202; www.visitmackays.com; Durness; s £45, d £80-90) This refurbished hotel has tastefully decorated rooms with rustic Highland furnishings and an air of sophistication. The deluxe rooms have super king-size beds and big showers – they're worth the extra 10 quid.

**Loch Croispol Bookshop & Restaurant** ( ☎ 511777; Balnakeil Craft Village; lunch & snacks £4-8; ( 10am-5pm

Mon-Sat, to 4pm Sun; ⅋ ) At this place you can feed your body and your mind. Set among books featuring all things Scottish are a few tables where you can enjoy an all-day breakfast, and sandwiches and other scrumptious fare at lunch, such as fresh Achiltibuie salmon.

Also recommended:

**Glengolly B&B** ( ☎ 511255; Durness; r per person £25-30) Quaint, cottage-style rooms. Worrying collection of ceramic dogs.

**Cocoa Mountain** ( ☎ 511233; Balnakeil Craft Village; hot choc £2.50, 9 truffles £6.50; ☽ 9am-6pm summer, 10am-5pm winter) Handmade chocolates include a chilli, lemongrass and coconut white-chocolate truffle and many more unique flavours.

**Balnakeil Bistro** ( ☎ 511335; Balnakeil Craft Village; mains £8-10; ☽ lunch & dinner; ⌨ ) Dine on rainbow trout, Lochinver pies and nut loaf. Come for the food, not the décor.

## DURNESS TO ULLAPOOL

It's 69 miles from Durness to Ullapool, with plenty of diversions along the way. The road to Ullapool has jaw-dropping scenery – dangerous on single-track roads as drivers struggle to tear their eyes away from vast, desolate plains spliced with rivulets of burns (streams), towering peaks and giant rocky outcrops.

Rugged **Cape Wrath** is crowned by a lighthouse (dating from 1827) and stands close to the sea-bird colonies on **Clo Mor Cliffs**, the highest coastal cliffs on the mainland. Getting to Cape Wrath involves a **ferry** ( ☎ 01971-511376) ride across the Kyle of Durness (£4.70 return, 10 minutes one way) and a connecting **minibus** ( ☎ 01971-511287) for the 11 miles to the cape (£7.50 return, 40 minutes one way). Contact the tourist office before setting out to make sure the ferry is running.

**Kinlochbervie** was one of Scotland's premier fish-landing ports and there's a lovely beach at **Oldshoremore**, a crofting settlement about 2 miles northwest of Kinlochbervie. South of Cape Wrath, **Sandwood Bay** boasts one of Scotland's best and most isolated beaches, guarded at one end by the spectacular rock pinnacle Am Buachaille. Sandwood Bay is about 2 miles north of the end of a track from Blairmore (approach from Kinlochbervie), or you could walk south from the cape (allow eight hours) and on to Blairmore. Sandwood House is a creepy ruin reputedly haunted by the ghost of a 17th-century shipwrecked sailor.

The outlook from the **Kinlochbervie Hotel** ( ☎ 01971-521275; www.kinlochberviehotel.com; r per

person £35-55) must be the envy of almost every hotel in Scotland. Traditionally furnished, room Nos 1 and 2 are the best with simply magnificent water views. Meals are available (mains £8 to £11).

**Braeside** ( ☎ 01971-521325; r per person £23) is a friendly, well-established B&B in a modern bungalow. There's no surcharge for solo travellers.

**Scourie** is a pretty crofting community. If you're looking to spoil yourself, **Scourie Lodge** ( ☎ 01971-502248; s/d £50/80), in a gorgeous building overlooking the bay, has three luxurious rooms and a garden with possibly the most northerly palm trees in the world. Dinner is available (£22).

Ferries (adult/child £10/5, on demand, 9.30am to 2pm Monday to Saturday, April to early September) go to the important **Handa Island** sea-bird sanctuary from Tarbet, 6 miles north of Scourie; call ☎ 07768-167786.

### Kylesku & Loch Glencoul
☎ 01971

Cruises on Loch Glencoul pass treacherous-looking mountains, seal colonies and the 213m-drop of **Eas a'Chual Aulin**, Britain's highest waterfall. In summer, the **MV Statesman** ( ☎ 502345) runs two-hour trips twice daily (except Saturday) from Kylesku Old Ferry Pier for £15/5 per adult/child to see waterfalls and baby seals. There are also trips to the lovely **Kerrachar Gardens** (www.kerrachar.co.uk; ferry £12, admission £3), which are only accessible by boat from Kylesku.

While you wait for the ferry you can toast your toes by a log fire, enjoy a pint (decent ales on tap) and tuck into a superb bar meal at the **Kylesku Hotel** ( ☎ 502231; www.kyleskuhotel.co.uk; Kylesku; mains £8-13; ☽ lunch & dinner), overlooking the pier. Seafood is the speciality including local mussels and smoked haddock and salmon fish cakes. If you fancy bunkering down for the night, rooms are available (single/double £60/90).

### Old Man of Stoer

It's roughly a 30-mile detour off the A894 to the **Point of Stoer** and the **Rhu Stoer Lighthouse** (1870) and back to the main road again. Along the coast road you need to be prepared for single-track roads, blind bends, summits and sheep. The rewards are spectacular views, pretty villages and excellent beaches. From the lighthouse, it's a good one-hour cliff walk to the Old Man of Stoer, a spectacular sea stack.

There are more good beaches between Stoer and Lochinver, including one at Achmelvich. **Achmelvich Youth Hostel** (SYHA; ☎ 0870 004 1102; dm adult/child £12.50/9.50; ☼ Apr-Sep) is about 1.5 miles from the Lochinver–Drumbeg postbus route, and 4 miles from Lochinver. Sheltered by rocky hills and found close to the beach, it's a small rustic place with basic dorms.

## Lochinver & Assynt
☎ 01571

The distinctive region of Assynt comprises a landscape of spectacular peaks rising from the moorland. Lochinver (population 639) is the main settlement. The busy little fishing port is a popular port of call for tourists, with its laid-back attitude, good facilities, striking scenery and award-winning visitor centre.

The **tourist office & visitor centre** (☎ 0845 225 5121; Main St; ☼ 10am-5pm Mon-Sat, 10am-4pm Sun Jun-Aug, 10am-5pm Apr-May & Sep-Oct) has an interpretive display on the story of Assynt, from flora and fauna to clans, conflict and controversy. There's a supermarket in town, as well as a post office, bank (with an ATM), petrol station and **doctor** (☎ 844755).

Using local landscapes as inspiration **Highland Stoneware** (☎ 844376; Lochinver) ensure that you can relive the majesty of the northwest every time you look into the bottom of your teacup. Even better are the mosaics outside, especially the car.

The Lochinver–Lairg road (A837) meets the Durness road (A894) at **Skiag Bridge**, by Loch Assynt, about 10 miles east of Lochinver. Half a mile south of here, by the loch, there's the ruin of the late 15th-century MacLeod stronghold, **Ardvreck Castle**. There are wonderful summer sunsets over the castle and the loch.

The stunningly shaped hills of Assynt are popular with walkers and include peaks such as Suilven (731m), Quinag (808m), Ben More Assynt (998m) and Canisp (846m). The tourist office has a leaflet with brief details of walks in the area called *Walks Around Assynt* (50p). For a more in-depth guide, pick up a copy of *Walks: West Sutherland* (£3).

### SLEEPING & EATING

**Ardglas** (☎ 844257; www.ardglas.co.uk; Inver, Lochinver; r per person £22) The comfortable Ardglas is a bastion in the hospitality trade with modern rooms, a decent-sized single and top views from the guests' lounge. Room No 8 is a good choice with a small couch and lovely water views. All rooms share a bathroom.

**Inchnadamph Lodge** (☎ 822218; www.inch-lodge.co.uk; Inchnadamph; dm/d £15/22; 💻) By the Lochinver–Lairg road, this place is a friendly 50-bed lodge with lots of rustic accommodation. Most rooms are spacious and clean and there's a separate music/TV lounge for late partying. The facilities are excellent and it's very popular with groups. There's also a self-catering cottage (£65 to £85 per night depending on the number of nights; sleeps up to six). Tip: don't try booking accommodation over the internet – it doesn't work.

**Culag Hotel** (☎ 844270; Lochinver; s/d £39/53) This old waterfront hotel was formerly a smokehouse for herring; less fishy these days, this sprawling mansion has gracious rooms with huge en suites. A cooked breakfast will hit your pocket to the tune of £7.

**Albannach** (☎ 844407; www.thealbannach.co.uk; Baddidarroch, Lochinver; d per person £120-165) The Albannach is sheer indulgence, on a grand scale. You'll discover roaring fireplaces, furniture found only in antique shops and a demure, sophisticated atmosphere. The restaurant menu uses organic, wild produce and is highly recommended (tariff includes dinner).

**Lochinver Larder & Riverside Bistro** (☎ 844356; 3 Main St; pies £5.75, mains £10-13; ☼ 10am-8.30pm) With an outstanding ensemble of inventive food made with local produce, Lochinver pies are a particular standout here and are famous in this part of the world: try the smoked haddock, or wild boar and apricot – very tasty. The bistro here also churns out delicious seafood dishes

---

### NAKED NO LONGER

A pleasant surprise of touring around the northern Highlands is the number of forests and woods, contrary to the perception that the northern Scottish landscape, though beautiful, is stark naked. There are fine walking trails that explore these forests, often gentle in nature, and the surrounds change character with the season. Highlights can include wildlife and ancient ruins, as well as survivors of the ancient forests that once carpeted this area. For detailed walking advice grab a copy of *The Forests of the Far North* brochure, free at tourist offices and produced by the Forestry Commission (www.forestry.gov.uk/scotland).

in the evening, including monkfish goujons. If you get addicted to the pies, don't worry – they deliver throughout Britain.

## Inverpolly Nature Reserve

The Inverpolly Nature Reserve has numerous glacial lochs and the three peaks of Cul Mor (849m), Stac Pollaidh (613m) and Cul Beag (769m). **Stac Pollaidh** provides one of the most exciting walks in the area, with some good scrambling on its narrow sandstone crest. It takes just three hours on a round trip from the car park at Loch Lurgainn.

## Achiltibuie

☎ 01854 / pop 300

With sheep nibbling the grassy roadside verges, the gorgeous Summer Isles moored just off the coast and the silhouettes of mountains skirting the bay, this town personifies idyllic Scottish beauty and is the perfect place for some serious relaxation.

**Summer Isles Cruises** ( ☎ 622200) operates boat trips to the Summer Isles from Achiltibuie – you'll see some magnificent island scenery. The 3½-hour trips cost £20/10 per adult/child, and you get one hour ashore on **Tanera Mor**, where the post office issues its own stamps.

**Summer Isles Hotel** ( ☎ 622282; www.summerisles hotel.co.uk; Achiltibuie; s £85-165, d £135-200; ☑ Easter-Oct) is the Russian caviar of country hotels, exuding class, comfort and rustic sophistication. It makes a great spot to take a break from urban dwelling. The bar has quality bar meals (£5 to £12) ranging from sandwiches to the local speciality – seafood (try the platter for a taste of everything), or you might like to tuck into the five-course dinner (£51).

The rudimentary 20-bed **Achininver Youth Hostel** (SYHA; ☎ 0870 004 1101; Achininver, Achiltibuie; dm adult/child £12.50/9.50; ☑ May-Sep) is designed for walkers and outdoor enthusiasts – you have to walk half a mile off the main road to reach it. Its remote, serene location has to be one of the best in the country.

There are buses Monday to Saturday from Reiff, Badenscallie (half a mile from the hostel) and Achiltibuie to Ullapool (1½ hours, one or two daily Monday to Friday, one Saturday).

## ULLAPOOL

☎ 01854 / pop 1400

Ullapool's harbourside façade is postcard-perfect and, on a sunny day, its surrounding rocky slopes are mirrored in the glassy veneer of the bay. A ferry service links Ullapool to Stornoway on the Isle of Lewis, churning a consistent trade of overnighters in its wake. There are few attractions, but heaps of great walking, piles of accommodation, mountains of delectable seafood and a couple of good watering holes.

## Information

**Bank of Scotland** (West Argyle St) Has an ATM.
**Laundrette** (Broomfield Holiday Park; wash £2.50)
**Library** ( ☎ 612543; Mill St; ☑ 9am-5pm Mon, Wed & Fri, 9am-5pm & 6-8pm Tue & Thu, closed Mon & Wed during holidays) Free internet access.
**Royal Bank of Scotland** (cnr Ladysmith & Argyle Sts) Has an ATM.
**Tourist office** ( ☎ 613031, 0845 225 5121; ullapool@visitscotland.com; 6 Argyle St; ☑ 9am-4.30pm Apr-May, 9am-5pm Mon-Sat, 10am-4pm Sun Jun–mid-Sep, 10am-5pm Mon-Sat mid-Sep–late-Oct, call for hours Nov-Mar) Service standards have dropped.
**Ullapool Bookshop** ( ☎ 612918; Quay St; ☑ 9am-9pm Mon-Fri, 9am-6pm Sat, 10am-6pm Sun; ☑ ) Lots of books on Scottish topics, and maps of the area. Internet access available.

## Sights

**Ullapool Museum & Visitor Centre** ( ☎ 612987; 7-8 West Argyle St; adult/child £3/50p; ☑ 10am-5pm Mon-Sat Apr-Oct) is in a converted Telford Parliamentary church. An audiovisual presentation, interactive exhibits and various other displays chart the history of Loch Broom and its people.

**Rhue Studio** ( ☎ 612460; www.rhueart.co.uk; Rhue; admission free; ☑ 10am-6pm Mon-Sat Apr-Sep, call for details Oct-Mar), 2.5 miles northwest of Ullapool, displays and sells the excellent art of contemporary landscape painter James Hawkins. The vivid and reflective works take a moment to adjust to, but they are wonderful interpretations. His work on the Outer Hebrides is breathtaking.

## Activities

Ullapool is a great centre for hill walking. A good path up **Gleann na Sguaib** heads for the top of **Beinn Dearg** from Inverlael, at the inner end of Loch Broom. Ridge-walking on the **Fannichs** is relatively straightforward and many different routes are possible. The tourist office can supply you with all the information and maps you need. Good walking books sold at the tourist office include *Walks in Wester Ross* (£2.50), or you can pick up a copy of the freebie guide to local woodland walks.

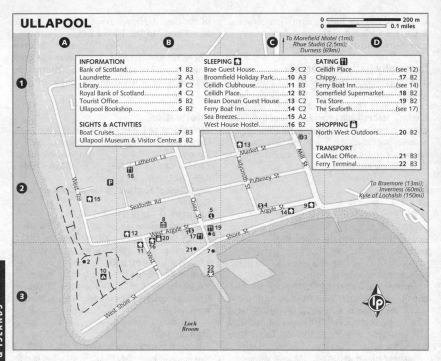

**ULLAPOOL**

| INFORMATION | |
|---|---|
| Bank of Scotland | 1 B2 |
| Laundrette | 2 A3 |
| Library | 3 C2 |
| Royal Bank of Scotland | 4 C2 |
| Tourist Office | 5 B2 |
| Ullapool Bookshop | 6 B2 |

| SIGHTS & ACTIVITIES | |
|---|---|
| Boat Cruises | 7 B3 |
| Ullapool Museum & Visitor Centre | 8 B2 |

| SLEEPING | |
|---|---|
| Brae Guest House | 9 C2 |
| Broomfield Holiday Park | 10 A3 |
| Ceilidh Clubhouse | 11 B3 |
| Ceilidh Place | 12 B2 |
| Eilean Donan Guest House | 13 C2 |
| Ferry Boat Inn | 14 C2 |
| Sea Breezes | 15 A2 |
| West House Hostel | 16 B2 |

| EATING | |
|---|---|
| Ceilidh Place | (see 12) |
| Chippy | 17 B2 |
| Ferry Boat Inn | (see 14) |
| Somerfield Supermarket | 18 B2 |
| Tea Store | 19 B2 |
| The Seaforth | (see 17) |

| SHOPPING | |
|---|---|
| North West Outdoors | 20 B2 |

| TRANSPORT | |
|---|---|
| CalMac Office | 21 B3 |
| Ferry Terminal | 22 B3 |

To Morefield Motel (1mi);
Rhue Studio (2.5mi);
Durness (69mi)

To Braemore (13mi);
Inverness (60mi);
Kyle of Lochalsh (150mi)

Loch
Broom

## Tours

There are regular **boat cruises** to the Summer Isles departing from the ferry terminal (adult/child £24/12, four hours), as well as two-hour wildlife cruises.

## Sleeping

Note that during summer Ullapool is very busy and finding accommodation can be tricky – if you're looking for a single it's virtually impossible unless you are willing to pay a high surcharge (£35 for a room) – the answer: book ahead.

**Broomfield Holiday Park** ( ☎ 612664; West Lane; camp sites £9-13; ☼ May-Oct) On an inviting verge of Loch Broom, this camping ground has pesky midges, good facilities (including a laundrette) and lawns manicured with nail scissors.

**West House Hostel** (Scotpackers; ☎ /fax 613126; www.scotpackers-hostels.co.uk; West Argyle St; dm £14/35, self-catering cottage £80; ☐ ) This is a brilliant place to stay and one of the best backpackers in northern Scotland. Small, spacious dorms (some with en suite) have comfy bunks, and doubles have TV and hot-drink facilities. It's

clean, well run and very friendly – the owner has the right attitude.

**Sea Breezes** ( ☎ 612148; 2 West Tce; s/d £18/50) The recommended Sea Breezes is a brilliant choice – you couldn't buy better views from the en-suite double room, and the single is small but very good value. It's personable, laid-back and virtually impossible to leave disappointed. Booking ahead is advisable.

**Brae Guest House** ( ☎ 612421; Shore St; r per person £22-28) This is a traditional, comfy place worth trying when things are busy in town. The location is excellent and rooms along the seafront have magnificent views as they're raised from the busy street level. You can even watch fishermen bringing in their catch.

**Eilean Donan Guest House** ( ☎ 612524; edonan@ ullapoolholidays.com; 14 Market St; s/d £30/55) This top-class guesthouse has an open fire in the sitting room for those blustery evenings, a full-blown restaurant (two-/three-course dinners £17/22) and excellent rooms with bathroom. It's in a lovely, tree-lined street a few minutes' walk from the seafront.

**Ferry Boat Inn** ( ☎ 612366; www.ferryboat-inn.com; Shore St; r per person £40) The vivacious Ferry Boat is the liveliest place in town. The stylish, tastefully furnished rooms – a contrast to the grubby corridors – get snapped up quickly in summer. Book in advance if you want a room with a view across Loch Broom (Nos 1, 3 and 4); the alternative is looking at a brick wall.

**Ceilidh Place** ( ☎ 612103; reservations@ceilidh.demon .co.uk; 14 West Argyle St; r per person £48-68; 🖳 ) Take your pick from the individually designed rooms in this nook-and-cranny hotel that exudes warmth and class. Price depends upon size, position (view), facilities and how long you stay – there are good specials in the off season. Nearby, **Ceilidh Clubhouse** ( ☎ 612103; West Lane; dm £15-20) has upmarket, pokey, rustic-style dorms with reputedly the best showers in Scotland.

## Eating & Drinking

**Chippy** (Quay St; fish & chips £4.75; 🕙 9am-9.30pm) A previous winner of a best UK takeaway award. The grub here really is a cut above your average greasy chippy – the chips are freshly sliced and the fish is freshly cooked.

**Tea Store** ( ☎ 612995; Argyle St; snacks & light meals £2-5; 🕙 8am-5pm Mon-Sat, 10am-4pm Sun) A decent coffee nook for a light meal and a read of the newspaper. It serves filled rolls, toasties, jacket spuds and is also good for breakfasts (including vegetarian options).

**The Seaforth** ( ☎ 612122; Quay St; mains £7.50-10; 🕙 lunch & dinner) Accolades for the seafood dishes at this place are growing, which include homemade fish pie, a platter of creel-caught langoustines and crayfish tails with apple salad. Eat in the bustling pub downstairs with its booth seating, or for more sedate dining venture upstairs to the bistro where a taste-fully furnished room and another bar is a good setup for families or groups.

**Ferry Boat Inn** ( ☎ 612366; Shore St; bar meals £8, mains £7-12; 🕙 lunch & dinner) This cosy pub is the best watering hole in town and *the* spot to pull up a bar stool and nurse a local ale. It usually has a great cross section of tourists and locals.

**Morefield Motel** ( ☎ 612161; North Rd; mains £8-14; 🕙 lunch & dinner) This sedate motel serves an outstanding medley of local seafood, in-cluding langoustine, salmon, swordfish and lobster, in its lounge bar. It has a deservedly fine reputation and is popular with locals and tourists alike. There's not much atmosphere, so come for the food not the buzz. If you can't decide from the extensive menu and specials board, choose the seafood sampler. The motel

is off the A835, a mile north of the harbour (follow Mill St).

**Ceilidh Place** ( ☎ 612103; 14 West Argyle St; light meals £7, mains £14-20; 🕙 breakfast, lunch & dinner) The res-taurant of this hotel serves inventive dishes catering for most palates. The mushrooms are shiitake and the sauce is vermouth. The res-taurant's soulless setting lets the place down, but it comes to life in summer, serving as Ullapool's main entertainment centre and pouring some excellent local ales.

For self-catering, you'll find a large Somer-field supermarket next to the car park north of Seaforth Rd.

## Shopping
**North West Outdoors** ( ☎ 613323; West Argyle St) Good for outdoor equipment.

## Getting There & Around
Ullapool is 215 miles from Edinburgh and 60 miles from Inverness. Scottish Citylink has three daily buses, Monday to Saturday, from Inverness to Ullapool (£9, 1½ hours), connecting with the ferry. CalMac runs a ferry service to Stornoway on the Isle of Lewis; see p390 for details. Tickets can be purchased from the CalMac office.

Bikes can be hired from West House Hostel (opposite).

## ULLAPOOL TO THE EAST COAST
The A835 goes south from Ullapool to Braemore Junction, then continues over the wild Dirrie More to the Glascarnoch dam, with great views of Beinn Dearg on the way. This section is sometimes closed by snow in winter.

Five miles south of Inchbae, there's a junc-tion where the A832 goes west to Gairloch through pleasant **Strath Braan**. The A835 con-tinues southeast, past Garve village and Loch Garve to **Contin**.

**Coul House Hotel** ( ☎ 01997-421487; www.coulhouse hotel.com; Contin; s/d £80/150) is a very fine country mansion dating from 1821. Set in its own pri-vate wilderness, this charming country hotel with blazing log fire will entice you to linger. Luxury rooms include mountain views and four-poster beds. Its restaurant is open for dinner (mains £16 to £18) and serves eclec-tic modern fusion. Interpreted: everything's delicious.

Ullapool to Inverness buses follow this route and stop off at Contin, Garve and

Aultguish. Trains from Inverness to Kyle of Lochalsh stop at Garve.

## ULLAPOOL TO KYLE OF LOCHALSH

Although it's less than 50 miles as the crow flies from Ullapool to Kyle of Lochalsh, it's more like 150 miles along the circuitous coastal road – but don't let that put you off. It's a deliciously remote region and there are fine views of beaches and bays backed by mountains all the way along.

### Falls of Measach

The A832 doubles back to the coast from the A835, 12 miles from Ullapool. Just after the junction, the Falls of Measach ('ugly' in Gaelic) spill 45m into the spectacularly deep and narrow Corrieshalloch Gorge. You can cross from side to side on a wobbly suspension bridge, built by Sir John Fowler of Braemore. The thundering falls and misty vapours rising from the gorge are very impressive – a shame about the logging in the plantation forest bordering the falls.

### Dundonnell & Around

☎ 01854 / pop 200

Dundonnell appears half-drowned after a good soaking, with a combination of imposing ridges overlooking the lowlands of this tiny settlement. **An Teallach** (1062m) is a magnificent mountain – the highest summit can be reached by a path starting less than 500m southeast of the Dundonnell Hotel (six hours return). Traversing the ridge to Sail Liath is a more serious proposition, with lots of scrambling in precarious places and difficult route-finding. Carry Ordnance Survey (OS) map No 19, food, water and waterproofs – it's amazing how quickly the weather can turn foul here.

**Badrallach Bothy** ( ☎ 633281; www.badrallach.com; Croft 9, Badrallach; bothy per person £5, camp sites per 2 people £9, r per person £30), 7 miles from the A832, has a good range of accommodation, as well as boats, bikes and fishing gear for hire. It's the perfect place to get away from it all and acquaint yourself with the rural beauty of this country.

**Dundonnell Hotel** ( ☎ 633204; www.dundonnellhotel .com; Dundonnell; r per person £40-55) provides good refuge from the elements and has elegant, traditionally furnished rooms; the loch-and mountain-facing premier rooms have great views. Adventurous menus (three-course dinner £18) and attentive service ensure an enjoyable culinary experience too. Try the clam chowder or the local mussels.

### Gairloch & Around

☎ 01445 / pop 1100

Gairloch is a group of villages (comprising Auchtercairn, Strath and Charlestown) around the inner end of a loch of the same name. The surrounding area has beautiful sandy beaches, good trout-fishing and bird-watching. Hill walkers also use Gairloch as a base for the Torridon hills and An Teallach.

The **tourist office** ( ☎ 712071; ☼ daily May-Sep) is at the car park in Auchtercairn, next to the museum, where a road branches off to the main centre at Strath.

The **Gairloch Marine Life Centre** ( ☎ 712636; Pier Rd, Charlestown; admission free; ☼ 10am-4pm Easter-Sep) has audiovisual and interactive displays, lots of charts and photos, and knowledgeable staff. **Gairloch Marine Cruises** ( ☎ 712636; www.porpoise-gairloch.co.uk; cruises per adult/child £20/10) run from the centre and sail up to three times daily (weather permitting) from Easter to October; during the two-hour trips you may see basking sharks, porpoises and minke whales.

**Rua Reidh Lighthouse Hostel** ( ☎ 771263; ruareidh@tiscali.co.uk; dm/d £10/30), by Melvaig, and 13 miles from Gairloch (at the end of the road), is an excellent hostel and will give you a taste of a lighthouse-keeper's life. Buses from Gairloch run as far as Melvaig, then it's a 3-mile walk along the road to the lighthouse. En-suite doubles, twins and family rooms are also available.

If you're looking for a place to hole up for the night in town, **Wayside Guest House** ( ☎ 712008; Strath; s/d £30/50) has water views from two cosy rooms, which share a bathroom. Another double and family room have no view but are en suite. It's right next to Strath Stores.

The rustic **Old Inn** ( ☎ 01445-712006; www.the oldinn.net; Charlestown; s/d £45/90) has a range of excellent snug rooms, some (such as No 4) with four-poster beds. Downstairs, the bar is an atmospheric nook-and-cranny affair, with the best pint of ale in town, and serves recommended bar meals (£7 to £14) of the delectable seafood variety. The inn is just opposite Gairloch Pier.

The **Mountain Coffee Company & Hillbillies Bookshop** ( ☎ 712316; Village Sq, Strath; mains £3-6; ☼ breakfast & lunch) is a shrine to all things mountaineering and has a lazy, chilled-out vibe. It sells excel-

NORTHERN HIGHLANDS & ISLANDS

lent hearty food for walkers, best consumed in the attached conservatory. Besides, how can you go past a place that sells a mars bar cappuccino, New York bagels and mountain scones?

## Loch Maree & Victoria Falls

Loch Maree is sprinkled with islands, and a series of peaks line its northern shore, culminating in 980m-high **Slioch**. The A832 runs alongside the loch.

The Victoria Falls (commemorating the visit of Queen Victoria in 1877) tumble down to the loch between Slattadale and Talladale. Look for the 'Hydro Power' signs to find it.

## Kinlochewe & Around

☎ 01445

Tiny Kinlochewe is a good base for outdoor activities. You'll find an outdoor-equipment shop, a petrol station with a tearoom and a shop/post office that runs a café in summer. Check out the **Beinn Eighe Visitor Centre** ( ☎ 760254; admission free; ☼ 10am-5pm Easter-Oct), a mile north of Kinlochewe, with interactive displays (good for kids, too) on local geography, ecology, flora and fauna, and walking routes.

There's a basic, free **camping ground** ( ☎ 760254) 1.5 miles north of the village. **Hillhaven** ( ☎ 760204; www.kinlochewe.info; Kinlochewe; s/d £35/56) is an excellent, friendly B&B that organises hawk-flying displays. The bright rooms here have lovely, contemporary furnishings, are en suite and look out over the garden.

**Kinlochewe Hotel** ( ☎ 760253; www.kinlochewehotel .co.uk; Kinlochewe; dm £10, r per person £40) has pulled up its socks and now offers big, soft, heavy-linen hotel rooms (No 8 is the best double). There's also a bunkhouse with one no-frills 12-bed dorm, a decent kitchen and clean bathrooms. Bring a towel and sleeping bag. Lunch and dinner is served daily (bar meals £6 to £13), except Monday nights.

East of Kinlochewe, the single-track A832 continues to Achnasheen, where there's a train station.

## Torridon & Around

Southwest from Kinlochewe, the A896 follows **Glen Torridon**, overlooked by multiple peaks, including Beinn Eighe (1010m) and Liathach (1055m). The drive along Glen Torridon is one of the most breathtaking in Scotland. Mighty, brooding mountains, often partly ob-scured by clumps of passing clouds, seemingly drawn to their peaks like magnets, loom over the tiny, winding, single-track road.

The road reaches the sea at Torridon, where there is a **Countryside Centre** ( ☎ 01445-791221; Torridon Mains; donation adult/child £3/2; ☼ 10am-5pm Easter-Sep) offering information on flora, fauna and walks in the rugged area. There's an unstaffed **Deer Museum** ( ☼ daylight hours year-round) nearby, which contains a collection of photos and odds and ends put together by a previous ranger.

The **camping ground** ( ☎ 01381-621252; Torridon; camp sites free) here has good showers and you get a grassy patch to pitch your tent, along with stunning views and wide-open, exhilarating space.

The modern, squat **Torridon Youth Hostel** (SYHA; ☎ 0870 004 1154; Torridon; dm adult/child £13.50/10.50; ☼ Mar-Oct) is in a magnificent location near the Countryside Centre and is used mainly by outdoor enthusiasts.

**Ferroch** ( ☎ 01445-791451; www.ferroch.co.uk; Annat, Loch Torridon; s/d £45/66), just southwest of Torridon village, is a guesthouse that, once you've woken up to the views, you'll never want to leave.

Magnificent **Loch Torridon Country House Hotel** ( ☎ 01445-791242; www.lochtorridonhotel.com; Torridon; s £160, d £300, 4-course dinner £48; ☼ ), complete with clock tower, is a class act and one of the best places to stay in Scotland. Everything about this property screams luxury…in a very quiet, refined way. Rates include dinner, but non-guests can dine here too. Check the website for special offers.

The A896 continues westwards to lovely **Shieldaig**, which boasts an attractive main street of whitewashed houses. **Tigh an Eilean Hotel** ( ☎ 01520-755251; Shieldaig; bar meals £8-13, 3-course dinner £43; ☼ lunch & dinner) dishes out locally caught seafood so fresh that it may still be squirming on your plate.

## Applecross

☎ 01520 / pop 200

A long side trip abandons the A896 to follow the coast road to the delightfully remote seaside village of Applecross. Or you can continue a bit further down the A896 to one of the best drives in the country (best in terms of the remote and incredibly rugged and spectacular scenery, not the actual road, which winds and twists and balances on sheer precipices). The road climbs steeply to the **Bealach na Ba pass**

(626m), then drops dramatically to the village. This drive is pure magic and a must if you're in the area. Note, this road can be closed in winter. Applecross itself is a delightful wooded village gazing across to the peaks of Skye.

You can pitch your tent at the **Applecross Camp Site & Flower Tunnel** ( ☎ 744268; camp sites for 2 from £12), which also has a licensed pizza restaurant (pizzas from £5) in a flower-filled conservatory.

The family-run **Applecross Inn** ( ☎ 744262; applecrossinn@globalnet.co.uk; Shore St; s/d £70/100; ♿ )

is the kind of pub you could easily spend all day in. You will find excellent food (bar meals £8 to £10), real ales (Red Cuillen on tap) and usually a decent mix of locals and tourists. You couldn't ask for a better place to hole up.

Back on the main road, the A896 runs south from Shieldaig to **Kishorn**, where there's a general store and post office, and spectacular views westwards to the steep sandstone Applecross hills.

---

## TALES FROM A CHAMPION MUNRO BAGGER: STEVEN FALLON

Steven Fallon, a hill walker, fell runner and qualified Mountain Leader who lives in Edinburgh, is the world's most prolific Munro bagger, having climbed all of Scotland's 284 Munros (peaks of 3000ft and higher) no fewer than 13 times. At the time of writing, he only had 62 more to climb to complete his 14th round, and was halfway to ticking off the Corbetts (peaks from 2500ft to 2999ft) as well.

**How long have you been bagging Munros, and what got you interested in the first place?** For Christmas 1988 my parents gave me the Scottish Mountaineering Club guidebook *The Munros* – I hadn't realised there were so many fabulous peaks in Scotland! So off I went and ticked them off one by one. This took me to so many wonderful parts of Scotland that I would never have visited otherwise, and once I'd 'completed' (ie bagged all the Munros), I started on the Corbetts with the intention of repeating only my favourite Munros. But before I knew it I was well through my second round of Munros and, well, the rest is history.

**Do you have a favourite, and/or least favourite Munro?** As to my favourites, practically anything in the northwest Highlands could feature – they tend to be pointy with great views. I'd single out Slioch by Loch Maree (p375); Beinn Alligin, Liathach and Beinn Eighe in Torridon (p375); the Five Sisters of Kintail (p378); and all of the mountains in the Cuillin of Skye (p383). However, my most-most-favourite has to be Ladhar Bheinn (p349) in the Knoydart Peninsula. It's pretty remote and to reach it requires a long walk-in along the southern shore of Loch Hourn. It's just so beautiful there. The mountain itself is complex with corries and ridges, and the summit has great views over Eigg to Skye and beyond. I'm pining just thinking about it!

My least favourite, without debate, has to be Ben Klibreck, the most northerly Munro after Ben Hope. It rises above a desolate area where the ground is wet, tussocky and tiring to move over. The last pull up to the summit builds you up to expect wonderful views, but the vista from the summit is really quite disappointing, looking over flat ground in most directions.

**Which is the easiest Munro, and which is the hardest?** With only 430m of ascent over 5km, the easiest Munros have to be the Cairnwell and Carn Aosda from the Glenshee ski resort (p230). Good paths and ski-tows make for simple navigation over these two peaks, and if you time it right, you'll be back at the café in time for something to eat. Check out my website (www .stevenfallon.co.uk) for the 10 easiest Munro walks.

The hardest peak depends entirely on your thinking. A'Mhaighdean in Wester Ross is the most remote, and most people have to backpack in over two or three days to tick this one off. Well worth it though! The most difficult technically has to be the aptly named Inaccessible Pinnacle in the Cuillin Hills on Skye. It's a clamber up a long fin of rock with sensational, tremble-inducing exposure, followed by an abseil down a short but vertical drop. Most Munro-baggers will have to enlist the help of their rock-climbing friends or hire a guide.

For more information about bagging Munros, see the boxed text, p62.

## Lochcarron

☎ 01520 / pop 950

The appealing, whitewashed village of Lochcarron is a veritable metropolis with two supermarkets, a bank (with an ATM), post office and petrol station. A long shoreline footpath at the loch's edge provides the perfect opportunity for a stroll to walk off breakfast.

**The Old Manse** ( ☎ 722208; www.theoldmanse.lochcarron.com; Church St; s/d £25/50, tw with loch view £55) is a top Scottish guesthouse beautifully appointed and in a prime lochside position. Rooms are simply gorgeous and the twin overlooking the water is larger and well worth the extra £5. The owner loves his whisky, especially Glenmorangie (Madeira-wood finish, of course). This is a refined, quite luxurious place to stay and would really suit couples: it's made for snuggling.

**Clisham Guesthouse** ( ☎ 722995; www.clishamguesthouse.co.uk; Main St; d £50, self-catering chalet per person £20) is very friendly and has a chalet with great privacy behind the guesthouse. It sleeps three comfortably (one twin and a fold-out futon). Inside there are three doubles, one with seaviews.

If you stay at the small, quiet **Rockvilla Hotel** ( ☎ 722379; rockvillahotel@btInternet.com; Main St; r £65-75) choose room Nos 1 or 2 – they are slightly cheaper, and have private facilities and dreamy views. Open for lunch and dinner (mains £8 to £13), the hotel kitchen serves some wonderful fresh seafood and is renowned for its scallops.

## Plockton

☎ 01599 / pop 450

Plockton is so idyllic that it could be designed by Hollywood, but there's nothing fake about the grandeur and beauty of this set. The place is overrun with tourists and its design around the harbour – a small, protected bay dotted with mini islands – means it gets cramped. It's especially popular with over-55s and we'd recommend a visit out of season (ie not in summer).

Cycling is a great way to explore the area and **Plockton Cycle Hire** ( ☎ 544255; Plockton Cottages, Frithard Rd) rents bikes for £9/14 per half-/full day.

**Calum's Seal Trips** ( ☎ 544306; cruises adult/child £7/4.50) runs seal-watching cruises. There are swarms of the slippery fellas just outside the harbour and the trip comes with an excellent commentary. Trips leave daily at 10am, noon, 2pm and 4pm. You may even spot an otter.

**Plockton Station Bunkhouse** ( ☎ 544235; mickcoe@btInternet.com; Nessun Dorma; dm £11-12) is in the former station building with excellent, clean facilities and comfy four- and six-bed dorms. It's modern, and very convenient for the train.

The black-painted **Plockton Hotel** ( ☎ 544274; www.plocktonhotel.co.uk; Harbour St; starters £4.50, mains £7-13; ☯ lunch & dinner) has a selection of comfy rooms (per person £35 to £50) overlooking the bay and serves up classy pub food – think rustic dining in an elegant pub setting. Bench seating grazing the loch shore makes it the best place for a drink on a warm evening.

## KYLE OF LOCHALSH

☎ 01599 / pop 750

Before the Skye Bridge opened, Kyle of Lochalsh (normally just called Kyle) was the main jumping-off point for trips to the Isle of Skye. Now, however, its many B&B owners watch most of their trade whiz past without stopping.

The **tourist office** ( ☎ 534198, 534390; ☯ 9.30am-5pm Mon-Fri, 10am-4pm Sat & Sun Easter-Oct), beside the main seafront car park, stocks information on Skye.

There's a string of B&Bs just outside of town on the road to Plockton. **Clais an Torrain** ( ☎ 530205; Church Rd; s/d £35/55) has two excellent, en-suite rooms in a rustic, down-to-earth, friendly environment. It's all very homely, unlike some of the more soulless B&Bs in this town.

For a bit more luxury, **Kyle Hotel** ( ☎ 534204; Main St; r per person from £40) has deluxe doubles with spa bath that are deliciously decadent.

The best place to eat is the **Waverley** ( ☎ 534337; Main St; starters £6, mains £12-17; ☯ dinner, closed Thu). This superb restaurant is an intimate place with excellent service; try the taste of land and sea, combining Aberdeen Angus fillet steak with fresh local prawns.

Kyle can be reached by bus from Inverness (£14, 2½ hours), and by three daily direct Scottish Citylink buses from Glasgow (£25.50, 5½ hours).

The 82-mile train ride between Inverness and Kyle of Lochalsh (£16.50, 2½ hours, up to four daily) is one of Scotland's most scenic rail routes.

## KYLE TO THE GREAT GLEN

It's 55 miles southwest via the A87 from Kyle to Invergarry, which lies between Fort William and Fort Augustus, on Loch Oich.

## Eilean Donan Castle

Photogenically sited at the entrance to Loch Duich, near Dornie village, **Eilean Donan Castle** ( ☎ 01599-555202; Dornie; adult/child £5/2; ☼ 10am-6pm mid-Mar–mid-Nov, from 9am Jul & Aug) is one of Scotland's most evocative castles, and must be represented in millions of photo albums. It's on an offshore islet, magically linked to the mainland by an elegant, stone-arched bridge. It's very much a re-creation inside with an excellent introductory exhibition. Keep an eye out for the photos of castle scenes from the movie *Highlander*. There's also a sword used at the battle of Culloden in 1746. The castle was ruined in 1719 after Spanish Jacobite forces were defeated at the Battle of Glenshiel, and it was rebuilt between 1912 and 1932.

Scottish Citylink buses from Fort William and Inverness to Portree stop opposite the castle and by the bridge at Dornie.

## Glen Shiel & Glenelg

From Eilean Donan Castle, the A87 follows Loch Duich into spectacular Glen Shiel, with 1000m-high peaks soaring up on both sides of the road. At Shiel Bridge, a narrow side road goes over the **Bealach Ratagain** (pass) to Glenelg, where there's still a ferry to Skye.

There are several good walks in the area, including the low-level route from Morvich to Glen Affric Youth Hostel (p325), via spectacular **Gleann Lichd** (17 miles). A traverse of the **Five Sisters of Kintail** is a classic and none-too-easy expedition; start a mile east of the Glen Shiel battle site and finish at Shiel Bridge (eight to 10 hours). For more information on these walks, contact the tourist office at Kyle of Lochalsh.

From the Bealach Ratagain, there are great views of the Five Sisters. Continue past Glenelg in the direction of Arnisdale to the two fine ruined Iron Age **brochs** – Dun Telve and Dun Troddan. Dun Telve still stands to a height of 10m, making it the second-best-preserved broch in Scotland, after Mousa (p430) in the Shetlands.

From Glenelg round to the road-end at **Arnisdale**, the scenery becomes even more spectacular, with great views across Loch Hourn to Knoydart.

**Ratagan Youth Hostel** (SYHA; ☎ 0870 004 1147; Shiel Bridge; dm adult/child £12.50/9.50; ☼ May-Oct; ▣ ) is a particularly good hostel. It has excellent facilities and a to-die-for spot by Loch Duich. If you want a break from Munro bagging, this is the place. There's at least one local bus a day from the Kyle of Lochalsh to the hostel (half hour).

**Kintail Lodge Hotel** ( ☎ 01599-511275; www.kintail lodgehotel.co.uk; Shiel Bridge; bunkhouse bed £13.50, r per person £40-57) has two bunkhouses, with self-catering facilities, sleeping six people each. With 10 of the 12 fine rooms facing the loch, you'd be unlucky not to get a decent outlook from a room inside the hotel. The tasty bar meals (£10), including local venison and seafood, are available for lunch and dinner.

Scottish Citylink buses between Fort William, Inverness and Skye operate along the A87. There's a postbus operating once daily, except Sunday, from Kyle to Arnisdale via Shiel Bridge and Glenelg.

## Cluanie Inn

Beyond the top of Glen Shiel, the A87 passes the remote, but welcoming, **Cluanie Inn** ( ☎ 01320-340238; www.cluanieinn.com; Glenmoriston; r per person £32-60), which has a great lived-in feel to it, providing shelter and good cheer from the elements. It's a classy lodge and very popular with outdoor enthusiasts. There's even a four-poster bed, spa and sauna in here. At lunch and dinner time there's bar meals (£7 to £15) for hungry walkers, including freshly shot haggis. From the inn, you can walk along several mountain ridges, bagging Munros to your heart's content. There's a low-level route through to Glen Affric Youth Hostel (p325), which takes three hours, but it gets very wet at certain times of year.

# ISLE OF SKYE

**pop 9900**

The Isle of Skye (an t-Eilean Sgiathanach in Gaelic) takes its name from the old Norse *sky-a*, meaning 'cloud island', a Viking reference to the often mist-enshrouded Cuillin Hills. It's the biggest of Scotland's islands, a 50-mile-long smorgasbord of velvet moors, jagged mountains, sparkling lochs and towering sea cliffs. The stunning scenery is the main attraction, but when the mist closes in there are plenty of castles, crofting museums and cosy pubs and restaurants to retire to.

Along with Edinburgh and Loch Ness, Skye is one of Scotland's top three tourist destinations. However, the hordes tend to stick to Portree, Dunvegan and Trotternish, and it's almost always possible to find peace and quiet in the island's farther-flung corners. Come prepared for changeable weather: when it's fine it's very fine indeed, but all too often it isn't.

## Information

Portree and Broadford are the main population centres on Skye.

### INTERNET ACCESS

**Columba 1400 Community Centre** ( ☎ 01478-611400; Staffin, Trotternish; per 30min £1; ⊙ 10.30am-4.30pm Mon-Sat)

**Island Outdoors** ( ☎ 01478-611073; The Green, Portree; per 15min £1; ⊙ 9am-5.30pm daily Apr-Oct, closed Sun Nov-Mar)

**Portree tourist office** ( ☎ 01478-612137; Bayfield Rd, Portree; per 20min £1; ⊙ 9am-6pm Mon-Sat & 10am-4pm Sun Jun-Aug, 9am-5pm Mon-Fri & 10am-4pm Sat Apr, May & Sep, limited opening Oct-Mar)

**Sligachan Hotel** ( ☎ 01478-650204; www.sligachan.co.uk; Sligachan; per 15min £1)

**South Skye Computers** ( ☎ 01471-898222; Old Corrie Industrial Estate, Broadford; per 15min £1.25; ⊙ 10am-5pm Mon-Fri)

### MEDICAL SERVICES

**Hospital** ( ☎ 01478-613200; Portree) There's a casualty department and dental surgery here.

### MONEY

Only Portree and Broadford have banks with ATMs. Portree's tourist office has a currency exchange desk.

### TOURIST INFORMATION

**Broadford tourist office** ( ☎ 01471-822361; The Car Park, Broadford; ⊙ 10am-5pm Mon-Fri, 11am-4pm Sat Apr-Oct)

**Dunvegan tourist office** ( ☎ 01470-521581; 2 Lochside, Dunvegan; ⊙ 10am-5pm Mon-Sat Jun-Oct, plus 10am-4pm Sun Jul & Aug, 10am-5pm Mon-Fri Apr & May, limited opening Nov-Mar)

**Portree tourist office** ( ☎ 01478-612137; Bayfield Rd, Portree; ⊙ 9am-6pm Mon-Sat & 10am-4pm Sun Jun-Aug, 9am-5pm Mon-Fri & 10am-4pm Sat Apr, May & Sep, limited opening Oct-Mar)

## Activities

### WALKING

Skye offers some of the finest – and in places the roughest and most difficult – walking in Scotland. There are many detailed guidebooks available, including a series of four walking

guides by Charles Rhodes, available from the Aros Centre and the tourist office at Portree. You'll need Ordnance Survey (OS) 1:50,000 maps 23 and 32. Don't attempt the longer walks in bad weather or in winter.

Easy, low-level routes include: through Strath Mor from Luib (on the Broadford–Sligachan road) to Torrin (on the Broadford–Elgol road, allow 1½ hours, 4 miles); from Sligachan to Kilmarie via Camasunary (four hours, 11 miles); and from Elgol to Kilmarie via Camasunary (2½ hours, 6.5 miles). The walk from Kilmarie to Coruisk via Camasunary and the 'Bad Step' (allow five hours, 11 miles round trip) is superb but slightly harder (the Bad Step is a rocky slab poised above the sea that you have to scramble across; it's easy in fine, dry weather, but some walkers find it intimidating).

**Skye Walking Holidays** ( ☎ 01470-552213; www.skyewalks.co.uk; Duntulm Castle Hotel, Trotternish) organises three-day guided walking holidays for £340 per person, including four nights of hotel accommodation.

### CLIMBING

The Cuillin Hills is a playground for rock climbers, and the two-day traverse of the Cuillin Ridge is the finest mountaineering expedition in the British Isles. There are several mountain guides who can provide instruction and safely introduce inexperienced climbers to the harder routes. Agencies include **Cuillin Guides** ( ☎ 01478-640289; www.cuillin-guides.co.uk) and **Skye Guides** ( ☎ 01471-822116; www.skyeguides.co.uk). A five-day basic rock-climbing course costs around £300, and a private mountain guide for one or two clients can be hired for around £90 a day.

### SEA-KAYAKING

The sheltered coves and sea lochs around the coast of Skye provide magnificent sea-kayaking opportunities. **Whitewave Outdoor Centre** ( ☎ 01470-542414; www.white-wave.co.uk; Linicro, Kilmuir; ⊙ Mar-Oct) and **Skyak Adventures** ( ☎ 01471-833428; www.skyakadventures.com; 13 Camuscross, Isleornsay) provide kayaking instruction, guiding and equipment hire for beginners and experts. It costs around £25 for a half-day kayak hire with instruction.

## Tours

There are several operators who offer guided tours of Skye, covering history, culture and

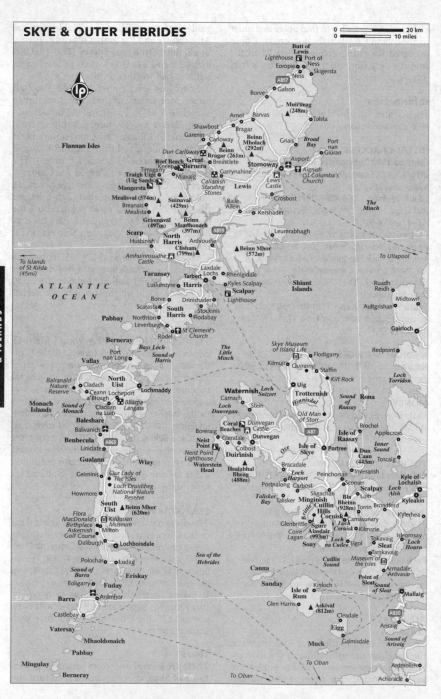

# SKYE & OUTER HEBRIDES

wildlife, including **Red Deer Travel** ( ☎ 01478-612142) and **Isle of Skye Tour Guide Co** ( ☎ 01471-844440; www.isle-of-skye-tour-guide.co.uk). Rates are around £170 for an eight-hour tour for up to six people.

## Getting There & Away
### BOAT
Despite there being a bridge, there are still a couple of ferry links between Skye and the mainland.

**CalMac** ( ☎ 01471-844248; www.calmac.co.uk) operates the Mallaig to Armadale ferry (driver or passenger £3.40, car £18.40, 30 minutes, eight daily Monday to Saturday, five to seven on Sunday). It's very popular in July and August, so book ahead if you're travelling by car.

For details of ferries from Uig on Skye to the Outer Hebrides, see p390.

**Skye Ferry** ( ☎ 01599-522273; www.skyeferry.co.uk) runs a tiny vessel (six cars only) on the short Glenelg to Kylerhea crossing (car and up to four passengers £8.50, motorcycle £5, pedestrian £1, bicycle £1.50, five minutes, every 20 minutes). The ferry operates from 9am to 7pm Monday to Saturday from Easter to October only, and 10am to 6pm Sunday from mid-May to August.

### BUS
Scottish Citylink runs direct buses from Glasgow to Portree (£29, 6¼ hours, three daily) and Uig via Crianlarich, Fort William and Kyle of Lochalsh. Buses also run from Inverness to Portree (£17, 3½ hours, twice daily).

### CAR & MOTORCYCLE
The Isle of Skye became permanently tethered to the Scottish mainland when the Skye Bridge opened in 1995. The controversial bridge tolls were abolished in 2004 and the crossing is now free.

There are petrol stations at Broadford (open 24 hours), Armadale, Portree, Dunvegan and Uig.

## Getting Around
Getting around the island by public transport can be a pain, especially if you want to explore away from the main Kyleakin–Portree–Uig road. Here, as in much of the Highlands, there are only a few buses on Saturdays, and only one Sunday service (between Kyle of Lochalsh and Portree).

**Highland Country** (www.rapsons.co.uk) operates the main bus routes on the island, linking all the main villages and towns. Its Skye Roverbus ticket gives unlimited bus travel for one/three days for £6/15. For timetable info, call **Traveline** ( ☎ 0871 200 22 33).

From May to September, the **Skye Flyer** ( ☎ 07780 724248) minibus service links Mallaig with Uig via Armadale, Broadford and Portree (£15, 1½ hours, one daily); bikes can be carried. At Mallaig, it connects with the West Highland Flyer to Fort William and Oban (p301),

You can order a taxi or rent a car from **Kyle Taxi Company** ( ☎ 01599-534323). Rentals cost from around £35 a day, and you can arrange for the car to be waiting at Kyle of Lochalsh train station.

## KYLEAKIN (CAOL ACAIN)
☎ 01599 / pop 100
Poor wee Kyleakin had the carpet pulled from under it when the Skye Bridge opened – it went from being the gateway to the island to a backwater bypassed by the main road. It's now a pleasant, peaceful little place, with a harbour used by yachts and fishing boats.

The village is something of a backpacker ghetto, with four hostels in close proximity. The homely **Dun Caan Independent Hostel** ( ☎ 534087; www.skyerover.co.uk; Castle View; dm from £13), in a fine, old, pine-panelled house overlooking the harbour, has the most attractive location.

A shuttle bus runs half-hourly between Kyle of Lochalsh and Kyleakin (five minutes), and there are eight to 10 buses daily (except Sunday) to Broadford and Portree.

## BROADFORD (AN T-ATH LEATHANN)
☎ 01471 / pop 1050
Broadford is a service centre for the scattered communities of southern Skye. The long, straggling village has a **tourist office** ( ☎ 822361; The Car Park; ✆ 10am-5pm Mon-Fri, 11am-4pm Sat Apr-Oct), a 24-hour petrol station, a large **Co-op supermarket** ( ✆ 8am-10pm Mon-Fri, 10am-4pm Sat & Sun), a laundrette, a bank with ATM, and a **hospital** ( ☎ 822137).

Ashaig Airstrip, 3 miles east of Broadford, is the venue for the annual **Skye Music Festival** (www.skyemusicfestival.co.uk), held over a weekend at the end of May. It's Scotland's most atmospheric music gig, with the sea on one side and the mountains on the other. Past line-ups have included artists such as Kasabian, Primal Scream, Echo and the Bunnymen and the Buzzcocks, as well as Skye-born DJ Mylo.

## Sleeping & Eating

There are lots of B&Bs in and around Broadford, and the village is well placed for exploring southern Skye by car. Recommended B&Bs include **Berabhaigh** ( ☎ 822372; berabhaigh@iselofskye .net; 3 Lime Park; r per person £30; ✕ closed Nov-Feb; P ) ), a lovely, old croft house with views over the bay, and neighbouring **Limestone Cottage** ( ☎ 822142; www.limestonecottage.co.uk; 4 Lime Park; r per person £37.50), a delightful, ivy-clad cottage. Both are just off the main road, near Creelers restaurant.

Broadford has several places at which to eat, but one really stands out. **Creelers** ( ☎ 822281; Lower Harrapool; mains £8-15; ✕ noon-10pm Mon-Sat) is a small, bustling, no-frills restaurant that serves some of the best seafood on Skye; the house speciality is a rich, spicy seafood gumbo. Book ahead, and if you can't get a table then nip around to the back door, where you'll find Ma Doyle's Takeaway, for fish and chips (£4.50) to go.

## SLEAT

If you cross over the sea to Skye on the ferry from Mallaig you arrive in Armadale, at the southern end of the long, low-lying peninsula known as Sleat (pronounced slate). The landscape of Sleat itself is not exceptional, but it provides a grandstand for ogling the magnificent scenery on either side – take the steep and twisting minor road that loops through **Tarskavaig** and **Tokavaig** for stunning views of the Isle of Rum, the Cuillin Hills and Bla Bheinn.

### Armadale

☎ 01471 / pop 150

Armadale, where the ferry from Mallaig arrives, is little more than a store, a post office, and a couple of houses. Just along the road is the part-ruined Armadale Castle, former seat of Lord Macdonald of Sleat and home to the **Museum of the Isles** ( ☎ 844305; adult/child £5/3.80; ✕ 9.30am-5.30pm Easter-Oct, gift shop only 11am-3pm Mon-Fri Nov-Easter). The museum will tell you all you ever wanted to know about Clan Donald, as well as providing an easily digested history of the Lordship of the Isles. Prize exhibits include rare portraits of clan chiefs, and a wine glass that was once used by Bonnie Prince Charlie. The ticket also gives admission to the lovely castle gardens.

**Sea.fari** ( ☎ 844787, 833316; www.seafari.co.uk) runs two-/three-hour boat trips in a high-speed RIB (rigid inflatable boat) for £25/35 per person. These trips have a high success rate for spotting minke whales in summer, with rarer sightings of bottlenose dolphins and basking sharks – even a humpback whale was spotted in August 2004.

**Aird Old Church Gallery** ( ☎ 844291; www.skyewater colours.co.uk; admission free; ✕ 10am-5pm Mon-Sat Easter-Sep), at the end of the narrow road that leads southwest from Armadale through Ardvasar village, exhibits the powerful landscape painting of Peter McDermott. The track beyond the gallery provides a good walk to the lighthouse and pretty little beach at **Point of Sleat** (5 miles round trip).

The no-frills **Armadale Youth Hostel** (SYHA; ☎ 0870 004 1103; dm £13; ✕ Apr-Sep) has a great location on the north side of the ferry harbour, while the rustic **Flora MacDonald Hostel** ( ☎ 844272; www.skye-hostel.co.uk; The Glebe, Kilmore; dm/tw/q £11/28/50; P ) is 3 miles north of the ferry, on a farm full of Highland cattle and Eriskay ponies.

The **Pasta Shed** ( ☎ 844264; The Pier, Armadale; mains £5-10; ✕ 9am-6pm), beside the ferry pier, is a cute little conservatory with some outdoor tables. It serves good seafood dishes, pizzas, fish and chips, crab salads and coffees – you can sit in or take away.

There are six or seven buses a day (Monday to Saturday) from Armadale to Broadford and Portree.

### Isleornsay

This pretty harbour, 8 miles north of Armadale, is opposite Sandaig Bay on the mainland, where Gavin Maxwell lived and wrote his much-loved memoir *Ring of Bright Water*. **Gallery An Talla Dearg** ( ☎ 01767-650444; admission free; ✕ 10am-6pm Mon-Fri, 10am-4pm Sat & Sun Apr-Oct) exhibits the works of artists inspired by Scottish landscape and culture.

**Hotel Eilean Iarmain** ( ☎ 01471-833266; from s/d £120/140; P ) is a charming old Victorian hotel with log fires, an excellent restaurant and 12 luxurious rooms, many with sea views. The hotel's cosy, wood-panelled An Praban bar serves delicious, gourmet-style bar meals (£6 to £9) – try the haddock in beer batter, venison burger or vegetarian lasagne.

**our pick** **Toravaig House Hotel** ( ☎ 01471-820200; www.skyehotel.co.uk; Sleat; r per person £75-85; P ), 3 miles south of Isleornsay, is one of those places where the owners know a thing or two about hospitality – as soon as you arrive you'll feel right at home, whether relaxing on the plump sofas by the log fire in the lounge, or admiring the view across the Sound of Sleat from the lawn chairs in the garden. The spacious bedrooms – ask for room No 1 (Eriskay), with its enormous sleigh bed – are luxuriously equipped, from the rich and heavy bed linen to the huge, high-pressure shower-heads, and the elegant Iona restaurant (mains £13 to £18; open for lunch and dinner) serves the best of local fish, game and lamb. After dinner, you can retire to the lounge with a single malt and flick through the yachting magazines, or try your hand at tickling the ivories on the baby grand in the corner.

## ELGOL (EALAGHOL)

On a clear day, the journey along the road from Broadford to Elgol is one of the most scenic on Skye. It takes in two classic postcard panoramas – the view of Bla Bheinn across Loch Slapin (near Torrin), and the superb view of the entire Cuillin range from Elgol pier.

**Bella Jane** ( ☎ 0800 731 3089; www.bellajane.co.uk; ☙ Easter–mid-Oct) offers a three-hour cruise (adult/child £18/6) from Elgol harbour to the remote **Loch na Cuilce**, an impressive inlet surrounded by soaring peaks and acres of bare rock slabs. On a calm day, you can clamber ashore here to make the short walk to **Loch Coruisk** in the heart of the Cuillin Hills. You get 1½ hours ashore, and visit a seal colony en route. The prettier and more traditional wooden launch **Misty Isle** ( ☎ 01471-866288; www .mistyisleboattrips.co.uk) offers similar cruises for £12.50/5 (no Sunday service).

**Aquaxplore** ( ☎ 0800 731 3089; www.aquaxplore.co.uk) runs 1½-hour high-speed boat trips from Elgol to an abandoned shark-hunting station on the island of Soay (adult/child £18/12). There are longer trips (£38/26, four hours) to Rum, Canna and Sanday to visit breeding colonies of puffins, with the chance of seeing minke whales on the way.

Bus 49 runs from Broadford to Elgol (40 minutes, three daily Monday to Friday, two Saturday).

## CUILLIN HILLS

☎ 01478

The Cuillin Hills are Britain's most spectacular mountain range. Though small in stature (**Sgurr Alasdair**, the highest summit, is only

993m), the peaks are near-alpine in character, with knife-edge ridges, jagged pinnacles, scree-filled gullies and acres of naked rock. While they are a paradise for experienced mountaineers, the higher reaches of the Cuillin are off limits to the majority of walkers.

The good news is that there are also plenty of good, low-level hikes within the ability of most walkers. One of the best (on a fine day) is the steep climb from Glenbrittle camping ground to **Coire Lagan** (6 miles round trip; allow at least three hours). The impressive upper corrie contains a lochan for bathing (for the hardy!), and the surrounding cliffs are a playground for rock climbers – bring along your binoculars.

There are two main bases for exploring the Cuillin – **Sligachan** to the north, and **Glenbrittle** to the south.

### Sleeping & Eating

**Sligachan Hotel** ( ☎ 650204; www.sligachan.co.uk; Sligachan; dm/s/d £12/65/90; **P** 🖳 ) The Slig, as it has been known to generations of climbers, is a near village in itself, encompassing an overpriced hotel, a bunkhouse, self-catering cottages, a big barn of a bar (complete with kids playroom) and an adventure playground.

**Seamus's Bar** (mains £7-10; ☙ food served 5-11pm) This place dishes up decent bar meals, including haggis, neeps and tatties, steak and ale pie, and spicy bean casserole, and serves real ales from its own microbrewery (plus a range of 200 malt whiskies), but service can be a tad indifferent.

Across the road from the hotel is a basic **camping ground** ( ☎ 650333; tent sites per person £4), but be warned – this spot is a midge magnet.

At the southern end of the Cuillin you have the choice of the Scandinavian-style, timber **Glenbrittle Youth Hostel** (SYHA; ☎ 0870 004 1121; Glenbrittle; dm £12.50; ☙ Apr-Sep), or the excellent **camping ground** ( ☎ 640404; tent sites per adult/child £5/3) down by the sea. As at Sligachan, the midges here can be diabolical.

### Getting There & Away

Sligachan, on the main Kyle–Portree road, is easily accessible by bus; Glenbrittle is harder to reach. Bus 53 runs five times a day Monday to Friday (once on Saturday) from Portree to Carbost via Sligachan (50 minutes); from there, you'll have to hitch or walk the remaining 8 miles to Glenbrittle (this can be slow, especially late in the day).

## MINGINISH
☎ 01478

Loch Harport, to the north of the Cuillin, divides the Minginish peninsula from the rest of Skye. On its southern shore lies the village of Carbost, home to the smooth, sweet and smoky Talisker malt whisky, produced at **Talisker Distillery** ( ☎ 614308; Carbost; guided tour £5; ✆ 9.30am-5pm Mon-Sat Easter-Oct, 2-5pm Mon-Fri Nov-Easter). This is the only distillery on Skye; the guided tour includes a free dram. Magnificent **Talisker Bay**, 5 miles west of Carbost, has a sandy beach, sea stack and waterfall.

The **Old Inn** ( ☎ 640205; Carbost; dm/s/d £12/34/65; **P** ) is an atmospheric wee pub, offering accommodation in bright B&B bedrooms and an appealing chalet-style bunkhouse. The bar is a favourite with walkers and climbers from Glenbrittle – there's an outdoor patio at the back with great views over Loch Harport – and between noon and 10pm, it serves excellent pub grub (£5 to £10), from French onion soup and haddock and chips, to wicked homemade cranachan (traditional Scottish dessert made with cream, whisky, raspberries and toasted oatmeal).

Three miles northwest of Carbost is the **Skyewalker Independent Hostel** ( ☎ 640250; Fiskavaig Rd, Portnalong; dm £12; 🖳 ), housed in the old village school. There's a tiny **camping ground** (tent sites per person £3) out the back.

There are five buses a day on weekdays (one on Saturday) from Portree to Carbost via Sligachan.

## PORTREE (PORT RIGH)
☎ 01478 / pop 1920

Portree is Skye's largest and liveliest town. It has a pretty harbour lined with brightly painted houses, and there are great views of the surrounding hills. Its name (from the Gaelic for King's Harbour) commemorates James V, who came here in 1540 to pacify the local clans.

### Information
**Bank of Scotland** ( ☎ 0845 720 3040; Somerled Sq; ✆ 9am-12.30pm & 1.30-5pm Mon-Fri) Has an ATM.
**Hospital** ( ☎ 01478-613200; Portree) Has casualty department and dental surgery.
**Island Outdoors** ( ☎ 01478-611073; The Green, Portree; ✆ 9am-5.30pm daily Apr-Oct, closed Sun Nov-Mar) Outdoor equipment shop with internet access for £1 per 15 minutes.
**Post office** ( ☎ 612533; Wentworth St; ✆ 9am-5.30pm Mon-Sat) Offers currency exchange.

**Royal Bank of Scotland** ( ☎ 612822; Bank St; ✆ 9.15am-4.45pm Mon, Tue, Thu & Fri, 10am-4.45pm Wed) Has ATMs.
**Tourist office** ( ☎ 612137; Bayfield Rd; ✆ 9am-6pm Mon-Sat & 10am-4pm Sun Jun-Aug, 9am-5pm Mon-Fri & 10am-4pm Sat Apr, May & Sep, limited opening Oct-Mar) Provides internet access (£1 per 20 minutes) and currency exchange.

### Sights & Activities
On the southern edge of Portree, the **Aros Experience** ( ☎ 613649; Viewfield Rd; ✆ 9am-5.30pm) is a combined visitor centre, book and gift shop, restaurant, theatre and cinema. The visitor centre (adult/child £3/2) offers a look at some fascinating, live CCTV images from local sea eagle and heron nests, and a viewing of a strangely commentary-free wide-screen video of Skye's impressive scenery (it's worth waiting for the aerial shots of the Cuillin). The centre is a useful rainy-day retreat, with an indoor, soft play area for children.

**An Tuireann Art Centre** ( ☎ 613306; www.antuireann .org.uk; Struan Rd; admission free; ✆ 10am-5pm Mon-Sat), half a mile west of town on the B885, is an appealing gallery that hosts changing exhibitions of contemporary art. It also has an excellent café.

The **Lady B Boat Trips** ( ☎ 612093; www.skyeboats .com) offers two-hour boat excursions from Portree harbour to the Isle of Raasay (adult/child £12/6, Monday to Saturday), offering the chance to see seals, porpoises and – if you're lucky – white-tailed sea eagles.

### Festivals & Events
The annual **Isle of Skye Highland Games** (www .skye-highland-games.co.uk) are held in Portree in early August.

### Sleeping
Portree is well supplied with B&Bs, but many of them are in bland, modern bungalows that, though comfortable, are often lacking in character. Accommodation fills up fast in July and August, so be sure to book ahead.

#### BUDGET
**Torvaig Camping** ( ☎ 612209; Torvaig; tent sites per person £3; ✆ Apr-Oct) This is the closest camping ground to Portree; there's no shop on site, so bring your own supplies. It's a mile north of town on the A87 to Uig.

**our pick Bayfield Backpackers** ( ☎ 612231; www .skyehostel.co.uk; Bayfield; dm £13; 🖳 🖧 ) Clean, central and modern, this hostel provides the best backpacker accommodation in town. The owner really makes you feel welcome, and is a font of advice on what to do and where to go in Skye.

**Bayview House** ( ☎ 613340; www.bayviewhouse .co.uk; Bayfield; r per person from £20; **P** ) This is a modern house with spartan but sparklingly clean rooms, some with sea and mountain views, and bathrooms with power showers. At this price and location, it's a bargain.

### MIDRANGE
**Woodlands B&B** ( ☎ 612980; jmaccallumwoodlands@ hotmail.com; Viewfield Rd; r per person £25-30) A great location, with views across the bay, and unstinting hospitality make this modern B&B,

a half-mile south of the town centre, a good choice.

**our pick Ben Tianavaig B&B** ( ☎ 612152; www .ben-tianavaig.co.uk; 5 Bosville Tce; r per person £30; 🖳 ) A warm welcome awaits from the Aussie/Brit couple who run this appealing B&B bang in the centre of town. All four bedrooms have a view across the harbour to the hill that gives the house its name.

**Peinmore House** ( ☎ 612574; www.peinmorehouse .co.uk; r per person £35-45; **P** ) Located around 2 miles south of Portree, this former manse has recently been cleverly converted into a stylish and comfortable guesthouse with a spectacular, oak-floored lounge, enormous bedrooms, excellent breakfasts and panoramic views.

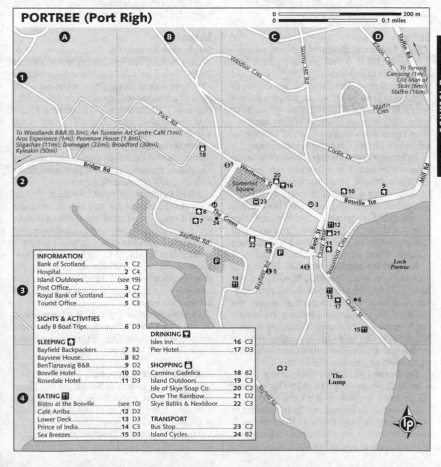

**PORTREE (Port Righ)**

| INFORMATION | |
|---|---|
| Bank of Scotland | 1 C2 |
| Hospital | 2 C4 |
| Island Outdoors | (see 19) |
| Post Office | 3 C2 |
| Royal Bank of Scotland | 4 C3 |
| Tourist Office | 5 C3 |

| SIGHTS & ACTIVITIES | |
|---|---|
| Lady B Boat Trips | 6 D3 |

| SLEEPING 🏠 | |
|---|---|
| Bayfield Backpackers | 7 B2 |
| Bayview House | 8 B2 |
| BenTianavaig B&B | 9 D2 |
| Bosville Hotel | 10 D2 |
| Rosedale Hotel | 11 D3 |

| EATING 🍴 | |
|---|---|
| Bistro at the Bosville | (see 10) |
| Café Arriba | 12 D2 |
| Lower Deck | 13 D3 |
| Prince of India | 14 C3 |
| Sea Breezes | 15 D3 |

| DRINKING 🍷 | |
|---|---|
| Isles Inn | 16 C2 |
| Pier Hotel | 17 D3 |

| SHOPPING 🛍 | |
|---|---|
| Carmina Gadelica | 18 B2 |
| Island Outdoors | 19 C3 |
| Isle of Skye Soap Co | 20 C2 |
| Over The Rainbow | 21 D2 |
| Skye Batiks & Nextdoor | 22 C3 |

| TRANSPORT | |
|---|---|
| Bus Stop | 23 C2 |
| Island Cycles | 24 B2 |

To Woodlands B&B (0.3mi); An Tuireann Art Centre Café (1mi); Aros Experience (1mi); Peinmore House (1.8mi); Sligachan (11mi); Dunvegan (22mi); Broadford (30mi); Kyleakin (50mi)

To Torvaig Camping (1mi); Old Man of Storr (6mi); Staffin (16mi)

Loch Portree

The Lump

NORTHERN HIGHLANDS & ISLANDS

**TOP END**

**Rosedale Hotel** ( ☎ 613131; www.rosedalehotelskye.co.uk; Beaumont Cres; s/d £60/110; ☒ Mar-Nov) The Rosedale is a cosy, old-fashioned hotel – you'll be welcomed with a glass of whisky or sherry when you check in – delightfully situated down by the waterfront. Its three converted fishermen's cottages are linked by a maze of narrow stairs and corridors, and the excellent restaurant has a view of the harbour.

**Bosville Hotel** ( ☎ 612846; www.bosvillehotel.co.uk; 9-11 Bosville Tce; s/d from £110/118) The Bosville brings a little bit of metropolitan style to Skye with its designer fabrics and furniture, flat-screen TVs, fluffy bathrobes and bright, spacious bathrooms. It's worth splashing out a bit for the 'premier' rooms, with leather recliner chairs from which you can lap up the view over the town and harbour.

## Eating

**our pick** **Café Arriba** ( ☎ 611830; Quay Brae; light meals £4-6, dinner mains £10-13; ☒ 7am-10pm May-Sep, 8am-5.30pm Oct-Apr) This funky little café, brightly decked out in primary colours, has the best choice of vegetarian grub on the island, ranging from a veggie breakfast fry-up to Indian-spiced bean cakes with mint yoghurt, as well as carnivorous treats such as slow-cooked haunch of venison with red wine and beetroot gravy.

**An Tuireann Art Centre Café** ( ☎ 613306; Struan Rd; mains £4-8; ☒ snacks 10am-4.30pm, lunch noon-2pm Mon-Sat) It's worth the short journey out of town (a mile west on the B885) to eat at this organic café, where you can enjoy homemade soups (such as sweet potato, parsnip, or *Cullen skink*) and imaginative vegetarian and vegan dishes, as well as a few seafood and chicken specials. There's also a good kids menu.

**Bistro at the Bosville** ( ☎ 612846; 7 Bosville Tce; mains £8-15; ☒ noon-2.30pm & 5.30-10pm) This hotel bistro sports a relaxed atmosphere, an award-winning chef, and a menu that makes the most of Skye-sourced produce including lamb, game, seafood, cheese, organic vegetables and berries, and adds an original twist to traditional dishes – how about haddock fried in a cumin and sesame seed batter?

**Sea Breezes** ( ☎ 612016; 2 Marine Buildings, Quay St; mains £12-18; ☒ noon-2.30pm & 5.30-10pm Tue-Sun, closed Nov, Jan & Feb) A good choice for seafood, Sea Breezes is an informal, no-frills restaurant specialising in local fish and shellfish fresh from the boat – try the impressive seafood platter, a small mountain of langoustines,

crab, oysters and lobster. Book early, as it's often hard to get a table.

Portree's favourite fish-and-chip shop is **Lower Deck** (Quay St; ☒ noon-2.30pm & 6-9pm) down by the harbour. For a curry (takeaway or sit-in), try **Prince of India** ( ☎ 612681; Bayfield Rd; mains £6-10; ☒ noon-midnight Jul-Sep, noon-2pm & 5-11.30pm Oct-Jun).

## Drinking

**Isles Inn** ( ☎ 612129; Somerled Sq) Portree's pubs are nothing special, but the Isles Inn is more atmospheric than most. The Jacobean bar, with its flagstone floor and open fires, pulls in a lively mix of young locals, backpackers and tourists.

**Pier Hotel** ( ☎ 612094; Quay St) You can almost guarantee a weekend sing-song at this nautical-themed waterfront bar.

## Shopping

**Skye Batiks & Nextdoor** ( ☎ 613331; The Green; ☒ 9am-6pm May, Jun & Sep, 9am-9pm Jul & Aug, 9am-5pm Mon-Sat Oct-Apr) Skye Batiks is a cut above your average gift shop, selling a range of interesting crafts such as carved wood, jewellery and batik fabrics with Celtic designs, with lighting, kitchenware and all kinds of interesting stuff in the adjoining Nextdoor.

**Over the Rainbow** ( ☎ 612555; Quay Brae) Crammed with colourful knitwear, tweeds and country and casual clothing, as well as glassware, crafts and all kinds of interesting gifts.

**Island Outdoors** ( ☎ 611073; The Green; ☒ 9am-5.30pm Apr-Oct, closed Sun Nov-Mar) This store stocks a good range of equipment, clothing, books and maps for climbing, walking, camping and kayaking; it also has public internet access.

**Isle of Skye Soap Co** ( ☎ 611350; Somerled Sq; ☒ 9am-5.30pm Mon-Fri, 9am-5pm Sat) A sweet-smelling gift shop that specialises in handmade soaps and cosmetics made using natural ingredients and aromatherapy oils.

**Carmina Gadelica** ( ☎ 612585; 4 Wentworth St; ☒ 9am-5.30pm Mon-Sat, 9am-8pm Jul & Aug) Browse the shelves here for CDs of Gaelic music and books on local subjects.

## Getting There & Around

The main bus stop is in Somerled Sq. There are six Scottish Citylink buses a day, including Sundays, from Kyle of Lochalsh to Portree (£10, one hour) and on to Uig.

Highland Country Buses services (Monday to Saturday only) run from Portree to Broadford (40 minutes, at least hourly) via Sligachan (15 minutes); to Armadale (1¼ hours, connecting with the ferries to Mallaig); to Carbost (40 minutes, four daily); to Uig (30 minutes, six daily); and to Dunvegan Castle (40 minutes, five daily Monday to Friday, three on Saturday). There are also five or six buses a day on a circular route around Trotternish (in both directions) taking in Flodigarry (20 minutes), Kilmuir (1¼ hours) and Uig (30 minutes). See p381 for details of buses from the mainland.

You can hire bikes at **Island Cycles** ( ☎ 613121; The Green; ☺ 9am-5pm Mon-Sat) for £8/12 per half-/full day.

## DUNVEGAN (DUN BHEAGAIN)

☎ 01470

Skye's most famous historic building, and one of its most popular tourist attractions, is **Dunvegan Castle** ( ☎ 521206; Dunvegan; adult/child £7/4; ☺ 10am-5pm Easter-Oct, 11am-4pm Nov-Easter), seat of the chief of Clan MacLeod. It has played host to Samuel Johnson, Sir Walter Scott and, most famously, Flora MacDonald (p388). The oldest parts are the 14th-century keep and dungeon, but most of it dates from the 17th to 19th centuries.

In addition to the usual castle stuff – swords, silver and family portraits – there are some interesting artefacts, most famous being the **Fairy Flag**, a diaphanous silk banner that dates from some time between the 4th and 7th centuries. Bonnie Prince Charlie's waistcoat and a lock of his hair, donated by Flora MacDonald's granddaughter, share a room with **Rory Mor's Drinking Horn**, a beautiful 16th-century vessel of Celtic design that could hold half a gallon of claret. Upholding the family tradition in 1956, John Macleod – the 29th chief, who died in 2007 – downed the contents in one minute and 57 seconds 'without setting down or falling down'.

From the end of the minor road beyond Dunvegan Castle entrance, an easy walk of 1 mile leads to the **Coral Beaches** – a pair of blindingly white beaches composed of the bleached exoskeletons of coralline algae known as maerl.

On the way to Dunvegan from Portree you'll pass **Edinbane Pottery** ( ☎ 582234; www.edin bane-pottery.co.uk; Edinbane; ☺ 9am-6pm, closed Sat & Sun Nov-Easter), one of the island's original craft workshops, established in 1971, where you can watch potters at work creating beautiful and colourful stoneware.

## DUIRINISH & WATERNISH

☎ 01470

The **Duirinish** peninsula to the west of Dunvegan, and **Waternish** to the north, boasts some of Skye's most atmospheric hotels and restaurants, plus an eclectic range of artists' studios and crafts workshops. Portree tourist office provides a free booklet listing them all.

It's worth making the long drive beyond Dunvegan to the west side of the Duirinish peninsula to see the spectacular sea cliffs of **Waterstein Head**, and to walk down to **Neist Point lighthouse** with its views to the Outer Hebrides.

At Stein on the Waternish peninsula is **Dandelion Designs** ( ☎ 592218; Captain's House, Stein; ☺ 11am-5pm Easter-Oct), an interesting little gallery with a good range of colour and monochrome landscape photography, lino prints by Liz Myhill, and a range of handmade arts and crafts.

A few miles north of Stein you'll find **Shilasdair Yarns** ( ☎ 592297; www.shilasdair-yarns.co.uk; Carnach; ☺ 10am-6pm Apr-Oct). The couple who run this place moved to Skye in 1971 and now raise sheep, hand-spin woollen yarn, and hand-dye a range of wools and silks using natural dyes. You can see the dyeing process in the workshop behind the studio, which sells finished knitwear as well as yarns.

### Sleeping & Eating

**our pick** **Stein Inn** ( ☎ 592362; www.steininn.co.uk; Stein, Waternish; bar meals £6-9; ☺ food served noon-4pm & 6-9.30pm Mon-Sat, 12.30-4pm & 6.30-9pm Sun Easter-Oct; **P** ) This old country inn dates from 1790 and has a handful of bedrooms (per person £26 to £36) all with sea views, a lively little bar, and a delightful beer garden – a real suntrap on summer afternoons – beside the loch. The bar serves real ales from the Isle of Skye Brewery, and does an excellent crab sandwich for lunch.

**Three Chimneys** ( ☎ 511258; www.threechimneys .co.uk; Colbost, Dunvegan; 3-course lunch/dinner £28/48; ☺ 12.30-2pm Mon-Sat Mar-Oct, 6.30-9pm daily year-round; **P** ) In Colbost, halfway between Dunvegan and Waterstein, is another superb romantic retreat combining a gourmet restaurant in a candle-lit crofter's cottage with sumptuous five-star rooms (double £255) in the modern house next door. Book well in advance, and note that young kids are not welcome in the restaurant in the evenings.

**Lochbay Seafood Restaurant** ( ☎ 592235; Stein, Waternish; mains £10-21, lobster £30-40; ☷ 11am-2pm Tue-Sat, 6.30-9pm Mon-Sat) Just along the road from the Stein Inn is one of Skye's most romantic restaurants, a cosy farmhouse kitchen with terracotta tiles and a wood-burning stove, and a menu that includes most things that either swim in the sea or live in a shell. Best to book ahead.

## TROTTERNISH
☎ 01470

The Trotternish peninsula to the north of Portree has some of Skye's most beautiful – and bizarre – scenery.

### East Coast

First up is the 50m-high, potbellied pinnacle of crumbling basalt known as the **Old Man of Storr**, prominent above the road 6 miles north of Portree. Walk up to its foot from the car park in the woods at the northern end of Loch Leathan (round trip 2 miles). This seemingly unclimbable pinnacle was first scaled in 1955 by English mountaineer Don Whillans. North again, near Staffin (Stamhain), is spectacular **Kilt Rock**, a stupendous cliff of columnar basalt whose vertical ribbing is fancifully compared to the pleats of a kilt.

Staffin Bay is dominated by the dramatic basalt escarpment of the **Quiraing**, whose impressive land-slipped cliffs and pinnacles constitute one of Skye's most remarkable landscapes. From a parking area at the highest point of the minor road between Staffin and Uig you can walk north to the Quiraing in half an hour. The adventurous (and ener-getic) can scramble up to the left of the slim pinnacle called the **Needle** to find a hidden, grass-topped plateau known as the **Table**.

### SLEEPING & EATING

**Dun Flodigarry Hostel** ( ☎ 552212; www.hostelflodigarry .co.uk; Flodigarry; dm/tw £12.50/28; ☐ ) If the local hotel is too expensive for you, this nearby hostel shares the same superb views, and you can still visit the hotel bar for afternoon tea – it's only a 100m walk away.

**Flodigarry Country House Hotel** ( ☎ 552203; www.flodigarry.co.uk; Flodigarry; d £100-190; ☐ ) Flora MacDonald (see below) lived in a farmhouse cottage at Flodigarry in northeast Trotternish from 1751 to 1759. The cottage and its pretty garden are now part of this delightful hotel – you can stay in the cottage itself (there are two bedrooms), or in the more spacious rooms in the hotel itself. The bright, modern bistro (mains £9 to £18) has great views over the Inner Sound, and serves lunch and dinner featuring local produce such as langoustines, lobster, lamb and venison.

### West Coast

The peat-reek of crofting life in the 18th and 19th centuries is preserved in thatched cottages at **Skye Museum of Island Life** ( ☎ 552206; Kilmuir; adult/child £2.50/50p; ☷ 9.30am-5pm Mon-Sat Easter-Oct). Behind the museum is Kilmuir Cemetery, where a tall Celtic cross marks the **grave of Flora MacDonald** (see below); the cross was erected in 1955 to replace the original, of which 'every fragment was removed by tourists'.

Whichever way you arrive at **Uig** (pronounced oo-ig), the picture-perfect bay,

---

### FLORA MACDONALD

Flora MacDonald, who became famous for helping Bonnie Prince Charlie escape after his defeat at the Battle of Culloden, was born in 1722 at Milton in South Uist, where a memorial cairn marks the site of one of her early childhood homes.

In 1746, she helped Bonnie Prince Charlie make his way from Benbecula to Skye disguised as her Irish maidservant. With a price on the prince's head their little boat was fired on, but they managed to land safely and Flora escorted the prince to Portree where he gave her a gold locket containing his portrait before setting sail for Raasay.

Waylaid on the way home, the boatmen admitted everything. Flora was arrested and imprisoned in the Tower of London. She never saw or heard from the prince again.

In 1747, she returned to Skye, marrying Allan MacDonald and having nine children. Dr Samuel Johnson stayed with her in 1773 during his trip to the Western Isles, but later poverty forced her family to emigrate to North Carolina. There her husband was captured by rebels. Flora returned to Kingsburgh on Skye where she died in 1790. She was buried in Kilmuir churchyard, wrapped in the sheet on which both Bonnie Prince Charlie and Dr Johnson had slept.

ringed by steep hills, rarely fails to impress. If you've time to kill while waiting for a ferry to the Outer Hebrides, visit the **Isle of Skye Brewery** ( ☎ 542477; The Pier, Uig; ⊗ 9am-5pm Mon-Fri), which sells locally brewed cask ales and bottled beers.

Just south of Uig, a minor road (signposted 'Sheader and Balnaknock') leads in a mile or so to the **Fairy Glen**, a strange and enchanting natural landscape of miniature conical hills, rocky towers, ruined cottages and a tiny roadside lochan.

There's a cluster of B&Bs in Uig, as well as the **Uig Youth Hostel** (SYHA; ☎ 0870 004 1155; Uig; dm £13.50; ⊗ late-Apr–Oct) and a lovely old coaching inn, the **Uig Hotel** ( ☎ 542205; Uig; s/d from £50/100; P ).

## ISLE OF RAASAY
☎ 01478 / pop 160
Raasay is the rugged, 10-mile-long island that lies off Skye's east coast. There are several good walks here, including one to the flat-topped conical hill of **Dun Caan** (443m). Forest Enterprise publishes a free leaflet (available from the tourist offices in Portree or Kyle of Lochalsh) with suggested walks and forest trails.

The extraordinary ruin of **Brochel Castle**, perched on a pinnacle at the northern end of Raasay, was home to Calum Garbh MacLeod, an early-16th-century pirate. At the battle of Culloden in 1746, Raasay supplied Bonnie Prince Charlie with around 100 fighting men and 26 pipers, but the people paid dearly for their Jacobite sympathies when victorious government forces arrived and proceeded to murder, rape and pillage their way across the island.

### Sleeping
Raasay House, which has been home to **Raasay Outdoor Centre** (www.raasayoutdoorcentre.co.uk) for more than 20 years, was taken into community ownership in 2007 and is undergoing a major renovation. It should reopen in spring 2009, when it will once again provide outdoor activity courses and hostel accommodation.

**Raasay Youth Hostel** (SYHA; ☎ 0870 004 1146; Creachan Cottage; dm £13.50; ⊗ May-Sep) Set in a rustic cottage high on the hill overlooking Skye, this hostel is a fair walk from the ferry pier (2.5 miles) but is a good base for exploring the island.

Other island accommodation includes the picturesquely situated **Isle of Raasay Hotel**

( ☎ 660222; www.isleofraasayhotel.co.uk; Borodale House, Inverarish; s/d £50/80; P ) just above the ferry pier, and **Churchton Guest House** ( ☎ 660260; Suisnish; r per person £35), half a mile to the north.

### Getting There & Away
A CalMac **ferry** (bicycle/passenger/car £1.10/2.75/10.70) runs from Sconser, on the road from Portree to Broadford, to the southern end of Raasay (15 minutes, hourly Monday to Saturday, twice daily Sunday). There are no petrol stations on the island.

# OUTER HEBRIDES

pop 26,500
A professor of Spanish and a professor of Gaelic met at a conference and began discussing the relative merits of their respective languages. 'Tell me,' said the Spanish professor, 'do you have a Gaelic equivalent for the Spanish phrase *mañana, mañana*?' The Hebridean professor thought for a while, then replied, 'No, I do not think that we have in Gaelic a word that conveys such a pressing sense of urgency'.

An old joke perhaps, but one that hints at the slower pace of life you can expect to find in the Gaelic-speaking communities of the Outer Hebrides, a place where the morning papers arrive in the afternoon and almost everything – in Lewis and Harris at least – closes down on Sundays.

The Outer Hebrides – also known as the Western Isles, or Na h-Eileanan an Iar in Gaelic – are a 130-mile-long string of islands lying off the northwest coast of Scotland. There are 119 islands in total, of which the five main inhabited islands are: Lewis and Harris (two parts of a single island, although often described as if they are separate islands), North Uist, Benbecula, South Uist and Barra. The middle three (often referred to simply as 'the Uists') are connected by road-bearing causeways.

The ferry crossing from Ullapool or Uig to the Western Isles marks an important cultural divide – more than a third of Scotland's registered crofts are in the Outer Hebrides, and no less than 60% of the population are Gaelic speakers. The rigours of life in the old island *blackhouses* (low-walled stone cottages with turf roofs and earthen floors) are still within living memory.

Religion still plays a prominent part in public and private life, especially in the Protestant north where shops and pubs close their doors on Sundays and some accommodation providers prefer guests not to arrive or depart on the Sabbath. The Roman Catholic south is a little more relaxed about these things.

The name Hebrides is not Gaelic, and is probably a corruption of Ebudae, the Roman name for the islands. But the alternative derivation from the Norse *havbredey* – 'isles at the edge of the sea' – has a much more poetic ring, alluding to the broad vistas of sky and sea that characterise the islands' often bleak and treeless landscapes. But there is beauty here too, in the machair (grassy, wildflower-speckled dunes) and dazzling white-sand beaches, majesty in the rugged hills and sprawling lochs, and mystery in the islands' fascinating past. It's a past signalled by Neolithic standing stones, Viking place names, deserted crofts and folk memories of the Clearances (p360).

If your time is limited, head straight for the west coast of Lewis with its prehistoric sites, preserved *blackhouses* and beautiful beaches. As with Skye, the islands are dotted with arts and crafts studios – the tourist offices can provide a list.

## Information
### INTERNET ACCESS
**Community Library** ( ☎ 01871-810471; Community School, Castlebay, Barra; ☾ 9am-4.30pm Mon & Wed, 9am-4.30pm & 6-8pm Tue & Thu, 9am-3.30pm Fri, 10am-12.30pm Sat) Free access.

**Stornoway Public Library** ( ☎ 01851-708631; 19 Cromwell St, Stornoway, Lewis; ☾ 10am-5pm Mon-Wed & Sat, 10am-6pm Thu & Fri) Free access.

**Taigh Chearsabhagh** ( ☎ 01876-500293; Lochmaddy, North Uist; per 20min 50p; ☾ 10am-5pm Mon-Sat Feb-Jun & Sep-Dec, 10am-5pm Mon-Thu & Sat, to 8pm Fri Jul & Aug)

### MEDICAL SERVICES
Both hospitals have casualty departments.
**Uist & Barra Hospital** ( ☎ 01870-603603; Balivanich, Benbecula)
**Western Isles Hospital** ( ☎ 01851-704704; MacAulay Rd, Stornoway, Lewis)

### MONEY
There are banks with ATMs in Stornoway (Lewis), Tarbert (Harris), Lochmaddy (North Uist), Balivanich (Benbecula), Lochboisdale (South Uist) and Castlebay (Barra). Elsewhere, some hotels and shops offer cashback facilities.

### TOURIST INFORMATION
**Castlebay tourist office** ( ☎ 01871-810336; Main St, Castlebay, Barra; ☾ 9am-1pm & 2-5pm Mon-Sat, noon-4pm Sun Apr-Oct)
**Lochboisdale tourist office** ( ☎ 01878-700286; Pier Rd, Lochboisdale, South Uist; ☾ 9am-1pm & 2-5pm Mon-Fri, 9.30am-5pm Sat, 9-9.30pm Tue & Thu Apr-Oct)
**Lochmaddy tourist office** ( ☎ 01876-500321; Pier Rd, Lochmaddy, North Uist; ☾ 9am-1pm & 2-5pm Mon-Fri, 9.30am-1pm & 2-5.30pm Sat, 8-9pm Mon, Wed & Fri Apr-Oct)
**Stornoway tourist office** ( ☎ 01851-703088; 26 Cromwell St, Stornoway, Lewis; ☾ 9am-6pm & 8-9pm Mon, Tue & Thu, 9am-8pm Wed & Fri, 9am-5.30pm & 8-9pm Sat year-round)
**Tarbert tourist office** ( ☎ 01859-502011; Pier Rd, Tarbert, Harris; ☾ 9am-5pm Mon-Sat, plus 8-9pm Tue, Thu & Sat Apr-Oct)

## Getting There & Away
### AIR
There are airports at Stornoway (Lewis), and on Benbecula and Barra.

There are flights to Stornoway from Edinburgh, Inverness, Glasgow and Aberdeen. There are also two flights a day (weekdays only) between Stornoway and Benbecula.

There are daily flights from Glasgow to Barra and Benbecula. At Barra, the planes land on the hard-sand beach at low tide, so the timetable depends on the tides.

Airlines serving the Western Isles:
**British Airways/Loganair** ( ☎ 0870 850 9850; www.britishairways.com)
**Eastern Airways** ( ☎ 0870 366 9100; www.easternairways.com)
**Highland Airways** ( ☎ 01851-701282; www.highlandairways.co.uk)

### BOAT
### Ferry
**CalMac** ( ☎ 0870 565 0000; www.calmac.co.uk) runs car ferries from Ullapool to Stornoway (Lewis); from Uig (Isle of Skye) to Lochmaddy (North Uist) and Tarbert (Harris); and from Oban to Castlebay (Barra) and Lochboisdale (South Uist).

| Crossing | Duration | Car | Driver/Passenger |
| --- | --- | --- | --- |
| Ullapool-Stornoway | 2¾hr | £73 | £15 |
| Uig-Lochmaddy | 1¾hr | £47 | £10 |
| Uig-Tarbert | 1½hr | £47 | £10 |
| Oban-Castlebay | 4¾hr | £79 | £22 |
| Oban-Lochboisdale | 6¾hr | £79 | £22 |

From Monday to Saturday there are two or three ferries a day to Stornoway, one or two a day to Tarbert and Lochmaddy, and one a day to Castlebay and Lochboisdale; on Sundays there are ferries (same frequency) to Castlebay, Lochboisdale and Lochmaddy, but none to Tarbert and Stornoway. You can also take the ferry from Lochboisdale to Castlebay (car/passenger £36/6, 1½ hours, one daily Monday, Tuesday and Thursday) and from Castlebay to Lochboisdale (one daily Wednesday, Friday and Sunday).

Advance booking for cars is essential in July and August; foot and bicycle passengers should have no problems. The fare for a bicycle is £2.20 on top of the passenger fare.

CalMac has 12 different Island Hopscotch tickets for set routes in the Outer Hebrides, offering a saving of around 10% (tickets are valid for one month).

## Getting Around

Despite their separate names, Lewis and Harris are actually one island. Berneray, North Uist, Benbecula, South Uist and Eriskay are all linked by road bridges and causeways. There are car ferries between Leverburgh (Harris) and Berneray, Tarbert (Harris) and Lochmaddy (North Uist), Eriskay and Castlebay (Barra), and Lochboisdale (South Uist) and Castlebay (Barra).

The local council publishes two booklets of timetables (one covering Lewis and Harris, the other the Uists and Barra) that list all bus, ferry and air services in the Outer Hebrides. Timetables can also be found online at www.cne-siar.gov.uk/travel.

### BICYCLE

Many visiting cyclists plan to cycle the length of the archipelago, but if you're one of them, remember that the wind is often strong (you may hear stories of people pedalling downhill and freewheeling uphill), and the prevailing direction is from the southwest – so south to north is usually the easier direction. There are few serious hills, except for a stiff climb on the main road just north of Tarbert.

Bikes can be hired for around £8 to £10 a day or £35 to £45 a week in Stornoway (Lewis), Leverburgh (Harris), Howmore (South Uist) and Castlebay (Barra). **Rothan Cycles** (www.rothan.com) offers a delivery and pick-up service at various points between Eriskay and Stornoway.

### BUS

The bus network covers almost every village in the islands, with around four to six buses a day on all the main routes; however, there are no buses at all on Sundays. You can pick up timetables from the tourist offices, or call **Stornoway bus station** ( ☎ 01851-704327) for information.

### CAR & MOTORCYCLE

Away from the fast, two-lane road between Tarbert and Stornoway, most roads are single-track. The main hazard is posed by sheep wandering about or sleeping on the road. Petrol stations are far apart (almost all of those on Lewis and Harris are closed on Sunday), and fuel is about 10% more expensive than on the mainland.

There are petrol stations at Stornoway, Barvas, Borve, Uig, Breacleit (Great Bernera), Ness, Tarbert and Leverburgh on Lewis and Harris; Lochmaddy and Cladach on North Uist; Balivanich on Benbecula; Howmore, Lochboisdale and Daliburgh on South Uist; and Castlebay on Barra.

Cars can be hired from around £26 per day from **Lewis Car Rentals** ( ☎ 01851-703760; www.lewis-car-rental.co.uk; 52 Bayhead St, Stornoway) and **Ask Car Hire** ( ☎ 01870-602818; enquiries@askcarhire.com; Liniclate, Benbecula).

## LEWIS (LEODHAIS)

☎ 01851 / pop 18,600

The northern part of Lewis is dominated by the desolate expanse of the Black Moor, a vast, undulating peat bog dimpled with glittering lochans, seen clearly from the Stornoway–Barvas road. But Lewis' finest scenery is on the west coast, from Barvas southwest to Mealista, where the rugged landscape of hill, loch and sandy strand is reminiscent of the northwestern Highlands. The Outer Hebrides' most evocative historic sites – Callanish Standing Stones, Dun Carloway, and Arnol Blackhouse Museum – are also to be found here.

The old *blackhouses* of this region may have been abandoned, but an increasing number are being restored as holiday homes. Most crofts still follow a traditional pattern dating back to medieval times, with narrow strips of land, designed to give all an equal share of good and bad soil, running from the foreshore (with its valuable seaweed, used as fertiliser), across the machair (the grassy sand dunes that

---

### KEEPING THE SABBATH

Religion still plays a major role in island life, especially on predominantly Protestant Lewis and Harris where the Sabbath is still widely observed by members of the 'free churches'.

The Calvinist Free Church of Scotland (known as the 'Wee Frees'), and the even more fundamentalist Free Presbyterian Church of Scotland (the 'Wee Wee Frees'), which split from the established Church of Scotland in 1843 and 1893 respectively, are deeply conservative, permitting no ornaments, organ music or choirs. Their ministers deliver uncompromising sermons (usually in Gaelic) from central pulpits, and precentors lead the congregation in unaccompanied but fervent psalm singing. Visitors are welcome to attend services, but due respect is essential.

The Protestants of the Outer Hebrides have succeeded in maintaining a distinctive fundamentalist approach to their religion, with Sunday being devoted largely to religious services, prayer and Bible reading. On Lewis and Harris, the last bastion of Sabbath observance in the UK, almost everything closes down on a Sunday. But a few cracks have begun to appear.

There was outrage when British Airways/Loganair introduced Sunday flights from Edinburgh and Inverness to Stornoway in 2002, with members of the Lord's Day Observance Society spluttering that this was the thin end of the wedge. They were probably right – in 2003 a Stornoway petrol station began to open on a Sunday, and now does a roaring trade in Sunday papers and takeaway booze. Then in 2006 the CalMac ferry from Berneray to Leverburgh in Harris started a Sunday service, despite strong opposition from the residents of Harris (ironically, they were unable to protest at the ferry's arrival, as that would have meant breaking the Sabbath).

---

provide the best arable land) to the poorer sheep-grazing land on hill or moor. Today, few crofts are economically viable, so most islanders supplement their income with fishing, tweed-weaving, and work on oil rigs and fish farms.

## Stornoway (Steornabhagh)
**pop 6000**

Stornoway is the bustling 'capital' of the Outer Hebrides and the only real town in the whole archipelago. It's a surprisingly busy little place, with cars and people swamping the centre on weekdays. Though set on a beautiful natural harbour, the town isn't going to win any prizes for beauty or atmosphere, but it's a pleasant enough introduction to this remote corner of the country.

Stornoway is the Outer Hebrides' administrative and commercial centre, home to the Western Isles Council (Comhairle nan Eilean Siar) and the islands' Gaelic TV and radio stations. It turns into a bit of a ghost town on Sundays, especially between 11am and 12.30pm when almost everyone is at church.

### INFORMATION

There are banks with ATMs near the tourist office.

**Baltic Bookshop** ( ☎ 702802; 8-10 Cromwell St; ☑ 9am-5.30pm Mon-Sat) Good for books and maps.

**Post office** ( ☎ 0845 722 3344; 16 Francis St)

**Sandwick Rd Petrol Station** ( ☎ 702304; Sandwick Rd) The only shop in town that's open on a Sunday (from 10am to 4pm); the Sunday papers arrive around 2pm.

**Stornoway Public Library** ( ☎ 708631; 19 Cromwell St; ☑ 10am-5pm Mon-Wed & Sat, 10am-6pm Thu & Fri) Free internet access.

**Tourist office** ( ☎ 703088; www.visithebrides.com; 26 Cromwell St; ☑ 9am-6pm & 8-9pm Mon, Tue & Thu, 9am-8pm Wed & Fri, 9am-5.30pm & 8-9pm Sat) A short walk from the ferry pier.

### SIGHTS

The modern, purpose-built **An Lanntair Art Centre** ( ☎ 703307; www.lanntair.com; Kenneth St; admission free; ☑ 10am-11pm Mon-Wed, 10am-midnight Thu & Sat, 10am-1am Fri), complete with art gallery, theatre, cinema and restaurant, is the centre of the town's cultural life; it hosts changing exhibitions of contemporary art, and is a good source of information on cultural events.

The **Museum nan Eilean** ( ☎ 703773; Francis St; admission free; ☑ 10am-5.30pm Mon-Sat, shorter winter hours) strings together a loose history of the Outer Hebrides from the earliest human settlements some 9000 years ago to the 20th century, exploring traditional island life and the changes inflicted by progress and technology.

The **Lewis Loom Centre** ( ☎ 704500; 3 Bayhead; adult/child £1/50p; ☑ 9am-5.30pm Mon-Sat) houses an exhibition on the history of Harris Tweed; the 40-minute guided tour (£2.50 extra) includes spinning and weaving demonstrations.

**Lews Castle**, the Baronial mansion across the harbour, was built in the 1840s for the Matheson family, then owners of Lewis. It was gifted to the community by Lord Leverhulme in 1923 and was home to the local college for 40 years, but has lain empty since 1997 (the college now occupies modern buildings in the castle grounds); it is now slated for development as a museum and hotel. The beautiful grounds are open to the public, and host the Hebridean Celtic Festival (right).

The roofless ruin of the 14th-century **St Columba's Church** (Aignish; admission free; 🕑 24hr), 4 miles east of town on the Eye peninsula, features the grave slabs of Roderick McLeod, 7th clan chief (around 1498), and his daughter (1503).

## FESTIVALS

The **Hebridean Celtic Festival** (www.hebceltfest.com) is a four-day extravaganza of folk/rock/Celtic music held in the second half of July.

## SLEEPING
### Budget

**Laxdale Holiday Park** ( ☎ 703234; www.laxdaleholiday park.com; 6 Laxdale Lane; tent £5-7 plus per person £2, dm/d £12/45; 🕑 Apr-Oct; 🅿 ) This camping ground, 1.5 miles north of town off the A857, has a sheltered woodland setting, though the tent area is mostly on a slope – get there early for a level pitch. There's also a bunkhouse that stays open year-round.

**Heb Hostel** ( ☎ 709889; www.hebhostel.co.uk; 25 Kenneth St; dm £15; 🖳 ) The recently opened Heb is a

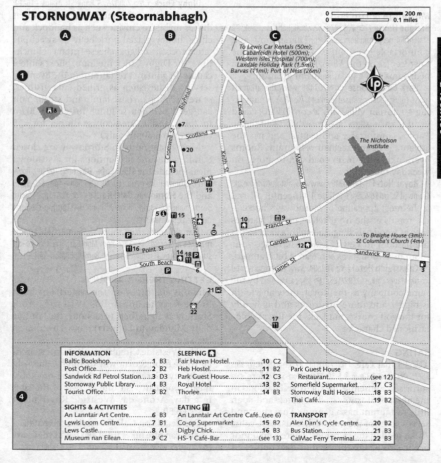

| INFORMATION | | SLEEPING 🏠 | | Park Guest House | |
|---|---|---|---|---|---|
| Baltic Bookshop | 1 B3 | Fair Haven Hostel | 10 C2 | Restaurant | (see 12) |
| Post Office | 2 B2 | Heb Hostel | 11 B2 | Somerfield Supermarket | 17 C3 |
| Sandwick Rd Petrol Station | 3 D3 | Park Guest House | 12 C3 | Stornoway Balti House | 18 B3 |
| Stornoway Public Library | 4 B3 | Royal Hotel | 13 B2 | Thai Café | 19 B2 |
| Tourist Office | 5 B2 | Thorlee | 14 B3 | | |
| | | | | TRANSPORT | |
| SIGHTS & ACTIVITIES | | EATING 🍴 | | Alex Dan's Cycle Centre | 20 B2 |
| An Lanntair Art Centre | 6 B3 | An Lanntair Art Centre Café | (see 6) | Bus Station | 21 B3 |
| Lewis Loom Centre | 7 B1 | Co-op Supermarket | 15 B2 | CalMac Ferry Terminal | 22 B3 |
| Lews Castle | 8 A1 | Digby Chick | 16 B3 | | |
| Museum nan Eilean | 9 C2 | HS-1 Café-Bar | (see 13) | | |

NORTHERN HIGHLANDS & ISLANDS

friendly, easy-going hostel close to the ferry, with comfy wooden bunks, a convivial living room with peat fire, and a welcoming owner who can provide all kinds of advice on what to do and where to go.

**Thorlee** ( ☎ 705466, 706300; www.thorlee.com; 1-3 Cromwell St; d from £35; P ) The family-oriented Thorlee has bright and cheerful rooms and a great central location with views over the harbour – an absolute bargain. If there's no answer at the guesthouse, ask at the Stag Bakery next door.

**Fair Haven Hostel** ( ☎ 705862; hebsurf@madasafish .com; 28 Francis St) This sociable and well-equipped hostel, aimed mainly at surfers, was closed for renovations at the time of research, but should be open by spring 2008.

### Midrange & Top End

**Braighe House** ( ☎ 705287; www.braighehouse.co.uk; 20 Braighe Rd; per person from £35; P ) This spacious and comfortable guesthouse, 3 miles east of the town centre on the A866, has stylish, modern bedrooms and a great seafront location.

**Park Guest House** ( ☎ 702485; www.theparkguest house.co.uk; 30 James St; s/d from £44/76; P ) A charming Victorian villa with a conservatory and eight luxurious rooms (mostly en suite), the Park is comfortable and central and has the advantage of an excellent restaurant. Rooms overlooking the main road can be noisy on weekday mornings.

**Royal Hotel** ( ☎ 702109; www.royalstornoway.co.uk; Cromwell St; s/d £69/99; P ) The 19th-century Royal is the most appealing of Stornoway's hotels – the rooms at the front retain period features such as wood panelling, and enjoy a view across the harbour to Lews Castle. Ask to see your room first, though, as some are a bit cramped.

**Cabarfeidh Hotel** ( ☎ 702604; www.cabarfeidh-hotel .co.uk; Manor Park; s/d £92/125; P & ) Owned by the same company as the Royal, the Cabarfeidh is bigger and more luxurious and is handy for the golf course, but lacks the Royal's old-fashioned character.

### EATING

our pick **Thai Café** ( ☎ 701811; 27 Church St; mains £5-7; ☷ noon-2.30pm & 5.30-11pm Mon-Sat) Here's a surprise – authentic, inexpensive Thai food in the heart of Stornoway. This spick-and-span little restaurant has a genuine Thai chef, and serves some of the most delicious, best-value Asian food in the Hebrides. There's no liquor licence, so BYOB (bring your own bottle).

**An Lanntair Art Centre Café** ( ☎ 703307; Kenneth St; snacks £2-6, mains £8-11; ☷ breakfast 10am-noon, lunch noon-2.15pm, dinner 5.30-9pm Mon-Sat) The stylish and family-friendly restaurant at the art centre serves a broad range of freshly prepared dishes, from tasty bacon rolls at breakfast, to burgers, baguettes or mince and tatties for lunch, to Thai curry, beef and Guinness pie or nut roast for dinner.

**Park Guest House Restaurant** ( ☎ 702485; 30 James St; mains £14-18; ☷ 6.30-8.30pm Tue-Sat) The restaurant at the Park Guest House specialises in Scottish seafood, beef and game (plus one or two vegetarian dishes), simply prepared, allowing the flavour of the food to speak for itself. It offers a good-value, three-course dinner for £16 between 5pm and 6.30pm.

**Digby Chick** ( ☎ 700026; 5 Bank St; mains £16-19; ☷ noon-10pm Mon-Sat) A modern restaurant that dishes up bistro cuisine such as haddock and chips, honey-glazed pork belly or sweet potato, broccoli and goat cheese frittata at lunchtime, the Digby Chick metamorphoses into a candle-lit gourmet restaurant in the evening, serving dishes such as grilled langoustines, seared scallops, roast lamb and steak. You can get a two-course lunch for £8 (11.30am to 2pm), and a three-course dinner for £15 (5.30pm to 6.30pm only).

Most restaurants in Stornoway are closed Sundays, but the few options for a sit-down meal include the **HS-1 Café-Bar** ( ☎ 702109; Royal Hotel, Cromwell St; mains £6-10; ☷ noon-4pm & 5-9pm) and the **Stornoway Balti House** ( ☎ 706116; 24 South Beach; mains £7-13; ☷ noon-2.30pm & 6-11pm), a decent curry restaurant.

For self-catering, there's a **Somerfield supermarket** (Ferry Rd; ☷ 8am-8pm Mon-Sat) and a **Co-op supermarket** (Cromwell St; ☷ 8am-8pm Mon-Sat).

### GETTING THERE & AROUND

The bus station is on the waterfront, next to the ferry terminal. Bus W10 runs from Stornoway to Tarbert (one hour, four or five daily Monday to Saturday) and Leverburgh (two hours).

The Westside Circular bus W2 runs a circular route from Stornoway through Callanish, Carloway, Garenin and Arnol; the timetable means you can visit one or two of the sites in a day. A one-day Westside Rover ticket costs £6.50.

For details on CalMac ferries, see p390.

You can hire bikes from **Alex Dan's Cycle Centre** ( ☎ 704025; www.hebrideancycles.co.uk; 67 Kenneth St).

## Butt of Lewis (Rubha Robhanais)

The Butt of Lewis (no snickering, please) – the extreme northern tip of the Hebrides – is windswept and rugged, with a very imposing lighthouse, pounding surf and large colonies of nesting fulmars on the high cliffs. There's a bleak sense of isolation here, with nothing but the grey Atlantic between you and Canada.

Just before the turn-off to the Butt at Eoropie (Eoropaidh), you'll find **St Moluag's Church** (Teampull Mholuidh), an austere, barn-like structure believed to date from the 12th century but still used by the Episcopal Church. The main settlement here is **Port of Ness** (Port Nis) with its attractive harbour. To the west of the village is the sandy beach of **Traigh**, which is popular with surfers and has a kids adventure playground nearby.

## Arnol

One of Scotland's most evocative historic buildings, the **Arnol Blackhouse** (HS; ☎ 710395; adult/child £5/2.50; ☯ 9.30am-5.30pm Mon-Sat Apr-Sep, to 4.30pm Mon-Sat Oct-Mar, last admission 30min before closing; ☖) is not so much a museum as a perfectly preserved fragment of a lost world. Built in 1885, this traditional *blackhouse* – a combined byre, barn and home – was inhabited until 1964 and has not been changed since the last inhabitant moved out. The staff faithfully rekindle the central peat fire every morning so you can experience the distinctive peat-reek; there's no chimney, and the smoke finds its own way out through the turf roof, windows and door – spend too long inside and you might feel like you've been kippered! The museum is just off the A858, about 3 miles west of Barvas.

At nearby **Bragar**, a pair of whalebones form an arch by the road, with the rusting harpoon that killed the whale dangling from the centre.

## Garenin (Na Gearrannan)

The picturesque and fascinating **Gearrannan Blackhouse Village** is a cluster of nine restored thatch-roofed *blackhouses* perched above the exposed Atlantic coast. One of the cottages is home to the **Blackhouse Museum** ( ☎ 643416; adult/child £2.20/1; ☯ 9.30am-5.30pm Mon-Sat Apr-Sep), a traditional 1955 *blackhouse* with displays on the village's history, while another houses the **Taigh an Chocair Restaurant** ( ☎ 643416, 710506; mains £3-6; ☯ 11am-5pm Mon-Sat, dinner Thu-Sat). Dinner is by booking only.

**Garenin Crofters' Hostel** (www.gatliff.org.uk; dm adult/child £9/6) occupies one of the village *blackhouses*, and is one of the most atmospheric hostels in Scotland (or anywhere else for that matter).

The other houses in the village are let out as self-catering **holiday cottages** ( ☎ 643416; www .gearrannan.co.uk; per week for 2 people £273-385) offering the chance to stay in a unique and luxurious, modernised *blackhouse* with attached kitchen and lounge. There's a minimum five-night let from June to August.

## Carloway (Carlabagh)

**Dun Carloway** (Dun Charlabhaigh) is a 2000-year-old, dry-stone broch, perched defiantly above a beautiful loch with views to the mountains of North Harris. The site is clearly signposted along a minor road off the A858, a mile southwest of Carloway village. One of the best-preserved brochs in Scotland, its double walls (with internal staircase) still stand to a height of 9m and testify to the engineering skills of its Iron Age architects.

The tiny, turf-roofed **Doune Broch Centre** ( ☎ 643338; admission free; ☯ 10am-5pm Mon-Sat late-May–mid-Sep) nearby has interpretative displays and exhibitions about the history of the broch and the life of the people who lived there.

## Callanish (Calanais)

The **Callanish Standing Stones** ( ☎ 621422; admission free), 15 miles west of Stornoway on the A858 road, form one of the most complete stone circles in Britain and are one of the most atmospheric prehistoric sites anywhere. Its ageless mystery, impressive scale and undeniable beauty leave a lasting impression. Sited on a wild and secluded promontory overlooking Loch Roag, 13 large stones of beautifully banded gneiss are arranged, as if in worship, around a 4.5m-tall central monolith. Some 40 smaller stones radiate from the circle in the shape of a cross, with the remains of a chambered tomb at the centre. Dating from 3800 to 5000 years ago, the stones are roughly contemporary with the pyramids of Egypt.

The nearby **Calanais Visitor Centre** ( ☎ 621422; admission free, exhibition £1.85; ☯ 10am-6pm Mon-Sat Apr-Sep, to 4pm Mon-Sat Oct-Mar) is a *tour de force* of discreet design. Inside is a small **exhibition** that speculates on the origins and purpose of the stones, and an excellent café (snacks £1 to £5).

If you plan to stay the night, you have a choice of **Eshcol Guest House** ( ☎ 621357; www.eshcol

**NORTHERN HIGHLANDS & ISLANDS**

.com; 21 Breascleit; r per person £37; (P)) and neighbouring **Loch Roag Guest House** (☎ 621357; www.lochroag.com; 22a Breascleit; r per person £33-44; (P)), half a mile north of Callanish. Both are modern bungalows with the same friendly owner who is very knowledgeable about the local area.

**Tigh Mealros** (☎ 621333; Garrynahine; mains £9-15; 7-9pm Mon-Sat), a private family home set in a sculpture garden, offers a tasty à la carte menu featuring seafood, steak and vegetarian dishes, including not-to-be-missed local scallops. Bookings are essential.

## Great Bernera

This rocky island is connected to Lewis by a bridge built by the local council in 1953 – the islanders had originally planned to destroy a small hill with explosives and use the material to build their own causeway. On a sunny day, it's worth making the long detour to the island's northern tip for a picnic at the perfect little sandy beach of **Bosta** (Bostadh).

In 1996 archaeologists excavated an entire Iron Age village at the head of the beach. Afterwards, the village was re-buried for protection, but a reconstruction of an **Iron Age house** (☎ 612331; Bosta; adult/child £2/50p; noon-4pm Mon-Fri May-Sep) now sits nearby. Stand around the peat fire, above which strips of mutton hang to be smoked, while the custodian explains the domestic arrangements – truly fascinating, and well worth the trip.

There are five buses a day between Stornoway and the hamlet of Breacleit (one hour, Monday to Saturday) on Great Bernera; two or three a day will continue to Bosta on request. Alternatively, there's a signposted 5-mile **coastal walk** from Breacleit to Bosta.

## Miavaig (Miabhaig) & Mealista (Mealasta)

The B8011 road (signposted Uig, on the A858 Stornoway–Callanish road) from Garrynahine to Timsgarry (Timsgearraidh) meanders through scenic wilderness to some of Scotland's most stunning beaches. At **Miavaig**, a loop road detours north through the Bhaltos Estate to the pretty, mile-long white strand of **Reef Beach**; there's a basic **camping ground** (per person £2) in the machair behind the beach.

From April to September, **Sea Trek** (☎ 672464; www.seatrek.co.uk; Miavaig Pier) runs two-hour boat trips (adult/child £30/20; Monday to Saturday) to spot seals and nesting sea birds, and more-adventurous, all-day trips (£90 per person; two per month, June and July only) in a high-speed RIB to the **Flannan Isles**, a remote group of tiny, uninhabited islands 25 miles northwest of Lewis. Puffins, seals and a ruined 7th-century chapel are the main attractions, but the isles are most famous for the mystery of the three lighthouse keepers who disappeared without trace in December 1900.

From Miavaig the road continues west through a rocky defile to Timsgarry and the vast, sandy expanse of **Traigh Uige** (Uig Sands) – the famous 12th-century Lewis chesspieces made of walrus-ivory were discovered in the sand dunes here in 1831. Of the 78 pieces, 67 are in the British Museum in London, with 11 in Edinburgh's Museum of Scotland (p86); you can buy replicas at various outlets on the island.

There's a very basic **camp site** (☎ 672248; per person £2) on the south side of the bay (signposted 'Ardroil Beach'; toilet only, no showers). If you fancy dining or staying somewhere really special, head to **Bonaventure** (☎ 672474; www.bonaventurelewis.co.uk; Aird Uig; 3-course dinner £27; 6.30-9pm daily, closed Nov & Feb), possibly the most remote French restaurant in Europe. It's housed in a converted, pine-clad military prefab that's perched above a wild, cliff-bound Atlantic cove 3 miles north of Timsgarry. The food is superb – local seafood, lamb and venison prepared by the resident French chef/owner – and the setting unique. Booking is essential. If you want to stay the night, there are three comfy double rooms (from £25 per person).

The minor road that continues south from Timsgarry to **Mealista** passes a few smaller, but still spectacular, white-sand beaches; beware, though – the surf can make swimming treacherous.

## HARRIS (NA HEARADH)
☎ 01859 / pop 2000

Harris, to the south of Lewis, is the scenic jewel in the necklace of islands that comprise the Outer Hebrides, a spectacular blend of rugged mountains, pristine beaches, flower-speckled machair and barren rocky landscapes. The isthmus at Tarbert splits Harris neatly in two – North Harris is dominated by mountains that rise forbiddingly above the peat moors to the south of Stornoway – Clisham (799m) is the highest point; South Harris is lower-lying, fringed by beautiful white-sand beaches on the west, and a convoluted rocky coastline to the east.

---

### FOR PEAT'S SAKE

In the Outer Hebrides, where trees are few and far between and coal is absent, peat has been the main source of domestic fuel for many centuries. Although oil-fired central heating is now the norm, many houses have held on to their peat fires for nostalgia's sake.

Peat in its raw state is extremely wet and can take a couple of months to dry out. It is cut from roadside bogs, where the cuttings are at least a metre deep. Rectangular blocks of peat are cut using a long-handled tool called a *tairsgeir* (peat-iron); this is extremely hard work and can cause blisters even on hands that are used to manual labour.

The peat blocks are carefully assembled into a *cruach-mhonach* (peat stack), each balanced on top of the other in a grid pattern thus creating maximum air space. Once the peat has dried out it is stored in a shed.

Peat burns much more slowly than wood or coal and produces a not unpleasant smell, but in the old *blackhouses* (which had no chimney) it permeated every corner of the dwelling, not to mention the inhabitants' clothes and hair, hence the expression 'peat-reek' – the ever-present smell of peat smoke that was long associated with island life.

---

Harris is famous for Harris Tweed, a high-quality woollen cloth still hand-woven in islanders' homes. The industry employs around 400 weavers; staff at Tarbert tourist office can tell you about weavers and workshops that you can visit.

## Tarbert (An Tairbeart)
### pop 480

Tarbert is a harbour village with a spectacular location, tucked into the narrow neck of land that links North and South Harris. It has ferry connections to Uig on Skye.

The **tourist office** ( ☎ 502011; Pier Rd; ☼ 9am-5pm Mon-Sat, plus 8-9pm Tue, Thu & Sat Apr-Oct) is in the car park just uphill from the ferry terminal. Village facilities include a petrol station, bank, ATM and two general stores. The **Harris Tweed Shop** ( ☎ 502493; Main St; ☼ 9.15am-5.30pm May-Sep) stocks a wide range of books on the Hebrides and sells gifts, crafts and the famous cloth itself.

### SLEEPING & EATING

**Rockview Bunkhouse** ( ☎ 502081; imacaskill@aol.com; Main St; dm £10) This hostel on the street above the harbour is a bit cell-like with its cramped dorms and air of neglect, but it's close to the ferry; if there's no answer, ask at the post office. The Rhenigidale hostel (right) is a better bet for a longer stay.

**Harris Hotel** ( ☎ 502154; www.harrishotel.com; s/d £60/110; P ) Run since 1903 by four generations of the Cameron family, Harris Hotel is a 19th-century sporting hotel, originally built for deer-stalkers visiting the North Harris Estates. It has spacious, comfy rooms and a good restaurant; look out for JM Barrie's initials scratched on the dining-room window (the author of *Peter Pan* visited in the 1920s). The hotel is on the way out of the village, on the road north towards Stornoway.

**Firstfruits** ( ☎ 502439; Pier Rd; mains £3-10; ☼ 10am-4.30pm Mon-Sat Apr-Sep, 7-9pm Tue-Sat May-Aug) This is a cosy little cottage tearoom near the tourist office – handy while you wait for a ferry.

## North Harris

Magnificent North Harris is the most mountainous region of the Outer Hebrides. There are few roads, but many opportunities for climbing, walking and bird-watching.

The B887 leads west to **Hushinish**, where there's a lovely silver-sand beach, passing the impressive shooting lodge of **Amhuinnsuidhe Castle**, now an exclusive hotel. Just northwest of Hushinish is the uninhabited island of **Scarp**, the scene of bizarre attempts to send mail by rocket in 1934, a story recounted in the movie *The Rocket Post* (2001), which was shot in Harris.

**Rhenigidale Crofters' Hostel** (www.gatliff.org.uk; dm adult/child £9/6) can be reached on foot from Tarbert (6 miles, allow three hours). It's an excellent walk, but take all the necessary supplies for a mountain hike (map, compass, protective clothing etc). Take the road towards Kyles Scalpay for 2 miles and, at a bend in the road just beyond Laxdale Lochs, veer off to the left on a signposted track across the hills (marked on Ordnance Survey maps). The hostel is a white building standing above the road on the eastern side of the glen; the warden lives in the house closest to the shore.

The remote hamlet of Rhenigidale can also be reached by road; bus W11 will take you there from Tarbert (30 minutes, two a day Monday to Saturday), but you'll have to book in advance ( ☎ 502250).

## South Harris

If you think Scotland has no decent beaches, wait till you see the **west coast** of South Harris. The blinding white sands and turquoise waters of **Luskentyre** and **Scarasta** would be major holiday resorts if they were transported to somewhere with a warm climate; as it is, they're usually deserted.

The culture and landscape of the Hebrides are celebrated in the fascinating exhibition at **Seallam! Visitor Centre** ( ☎ 520258; Northton; adult/child £2.50/2; ☿ 10am-5pm Mon-Sat). *Seallam* is Gaelic for 'Let me show you'. The centre, which is in Northton, just south of Scarasta, also has a genealogical research centre for people who want to trace their Hebridean ancestry.

The **east coast** is a complete contrast to the west – a strange, rocky moonscape of naked gneiss pocked with tiny lochans, the bleakness lightened by the occasional splash of green around the few crofting communities. Film buffs will know that the psychedelic sequences depicting the surface of Jupiter in *2001: A Space Odyssey* were shot from an aircraft flying low over the east coast of Harris.

The narrow, twisting road that winds its way along this coast is known locally as the **Golden Road**, because of the vast amount of money it cost per mile. It was built in the 1930s to link all the tiny communities known as 'The Bays'. The **MV Lady Catherine** ( ☎ 530310; www.scenic-cruises.co.uk), based at Flodabay harbour halfway down the east coast, offers three-hour wildlife cruises (adult/child £12/6) from May to September.

At the southernmost tip of this coastline stands the impressive 16th-century **St Clement's Church** (Rodel/Roghadal; admission free), which was abandoned in 1560 after the Reformation. Inside the echoing nave is the impressive tomb of Alexander MacLeod, the man responsible for the church's construction. Crude carvings show hunting scenes, a castle, a galleon, and various saints, including St Clement clutching a skull.

The village of **Leverburgh** (An t-Ob; www.lever burgh.co.uk) is named after Lord Leverhulme (the creator of Sunlight soap, and the founder of Unilever), who bought Lewis and Harris in 1918. He had grand plans for the islands, and for Obbe, as Leverburgh was then known. It was to be a major fishing port with a population of 10,000, but the plans died with Lord Leverhulme in 1925 and the village reverted to a sleepy backwater. There is a post office with an ATM, a general store and a petrol station.

### SLEEPING & EATING

**Am Bothan** ( ☎ 520251; www.ambothan.com; Leverburgh; dm £15; P ⑤ ) This attractive, chalet-style hostel has small, neat dorms and a great porch where you can enjoy morning coffee with views over the creek.

**Sorrel Cottage** ( ☎ 520319; www.sorrelcottage.co.uk; 2 Glen, Leverburgh; r per person from £23) Sorrel Cottage is a pretty crofter's house, about 1.5 miles west of the ferry at Leverburgh. Evening meals can be provided (£16 a head), and vegetarians and vegans are happily catered for.

**Carminish Guest House** ( ☎ 520400; www.carminish .com; 1a Strond, Leverburgh; s/d £45/58; P ) One of the few B&Bs in Harris that is open all year, the welcoming Carminish is a modern house with three comfy guest bedrooms. There's a view of the ferry from the dining room, and lots of nice little touches such as handmade soaps, a tin of chocolate biscuits in the bedroom, and the latest weather forecast posted on the breakfast table.

**Rodel Hotel** ( ☎ 520210; www.rodelhotel.co.uk; Rodel; s/d from £70/100; P ) Don't be put off by the rather grey and grim exterior of this remote hotel – the interior has been refurbished to a high standard and offers four large, luxurious bedrooms; the one called Iona has the best view, across the little harbour. Open for dinner from 5.30pm to 9pm, the hotel restaurant (mains £14 to £16) serves delicious local seafood and game, with dishes such as local mussels steamed in white wine with a fennel and cream sauce.

**Skoon Art Café** ( ☎ 530268; 4 Geocrab; mains £3-7; ☿ 10am-5pm Tue-Sat Mar-Oct, noon-4pm Wed-Sat Nov-22 Dec, lunch served 11am-4pm) Set halfway along the Golden Road, this neat little art gallery doubles as an excellent café serving delicious homemade soups (broccoli and roast almond is a favourite), sandwiches, cakes and desserts (try the marmalade and ginger cake).

### GETTING THERE & AROUND

A CalMac car ferry zigzags through the reefs of the Sound of Harris from Leverburgh to

Berneray (pedestrian/car £5.60/25.50, 1¼ hours, three or four daily Monday to Saturday). You can hire bicycles from Sorrel Cottage for £10 a day.

## BERNERAY (BEARNARAIGH)
☎ 01876 / pop 140

Berneray (www.isleofberneray.com) was linked to North Uist by a causeway in October 1998, but that hasn't altered the peace and beauty of the island. The beaches on its west coast are some of the most beautiful and unspoilt in Britain, and seals and otters can be seen in Bays Loch on the east coast.

The basic but atmospheric **Gatliff Hostel** (www.gatliff.org.uk; Baile; dm adult/child £9/6, camping per person £5), housed in a pair of restored *blackhouses* right by the sea, is the place to stay.

In summer, snacks are available at the **Lobster Pot** (☺ Mon-Sat), the tearoom attached to Ardmarree Stores (a grocery shop near the causeway; closed Sunday). The **Nurses Cottage** (☺ 11am-3pm Mon-Fri Jun-Aug) provides tourist information.

Bus W19 runs from Berneray (Gatliff Hostel and Harris ferry) to Lochmaddy (30 minutes, six daily Monday to Saturday). For details of ferries to Leverburgh (Harris), see opposite.

## NORTH UIST (UIBHIST A TUATH)
☎ 01876 / pop 1550

North Uist, an island half-drowned by lochs, is famed for its fishing but also has some magnificent beaches on its north and west coasts. For bird-watchers this is an earthly paradise, with regular sightings of waders and wildfowl ranging from redshank to red-throated diver to red-necked phalarope. The landscape is less wild and mountainous than Harris, but it has a sleepy, subtle appeal.

## Lochmaddy (Loch nam Madadh)
Little Lochmaddy is the first village you hit after arriving on the ferry from Skye. There's a **tourist office** (☎ 500321; Pier Rd; ☺ 9am-1pm & 2-5pm Mon-Fri, 9.30am-1pm & 2-5.30pm Sat, 8-9pm Mon, Wed & Fri Apr-Oct), a couple of stores, a bank with ATM, a petrol station, a post office and a pub.

**Taigh Chearsabhagh** (☎ 500293; admission free, donation requested for museum; ☺ 10am-5pm Mon-Sat Feb-Jun & Sep-Dec, 10am-5pm Mon-Thu & Sat, to 8pm Fri Jul & Aug) is a museum and arts centre that preserves and displays the history and culture of the Uists, and is also a thriving community centre, post office and meeting place. The centre's lively

café (mains £2 to £5) dishes up lovely homemade soups, sandwiches and cakes, and provides internet access at 50p for 20 minutes.

Buses from Lochmaddy to Berneray, Langass, Clachan na Luib, Benbecula and Lochboisdale run five or six times a day Monday to Saturday.

### SLEEPING & EATING
**Uist Outdoor Centre** (☎ 500480; www.uistoutdoorcentre.co.uk; Cearn Dusgaidh; dm £12; ⌨ P ) This shoreside activity centre has a smart bunkhouse with four-bed dorms and offers a range of activities including sea-kayaking, rock climbing and diving.

**Old Courthouse** (☎ 500358; oldcourthouse@tiscali.co.uk; Lochmaddy; r per person from £25; P ) This charming, Georgian-style villa has four guest rooms and is within walking distance of the ferry, on the road that leads to Uist Outdoor Centre. Excellent porridge for breakfast, and kippers are on the menu too.

**Lochmaddy Hotel** (☎ 500331; www.lochmaddyhotel.co.uk; s/d £51/95; P ) This is a traditional anglers' hotel (you can buy fishing permits here) with comfy, recently refurbished rooms, many with harbour views. The lively hotel bar pulls in anglers, locals and tourists, and serves excellent pub grub (mains £7 to £12) including seafood, venison and king-size steaks.

Taigh Chearsabhagh (see left) is also a good place to eat.

### Bharpa Langass & Pobull Fhinn
A waymarked circular path beside the Langass Lodge Hotel (just off the A867, 6 miles southwest of Lochmaddy) leads to the chambered Neolithic burial tomb of **Bharpa Langass** and the stone circle of **Pobull Fhinn** (Finn's People); both are reckoned to be around 5000 years old. There are lovely views over the loch, where you may be able to spot seals and otters.

The delightful **Langass Lodge Hotel** (☎ 580285; www.langasslodge.co.uk; Locheport; s/d from £50/90; P ⑤ ) is a former shooting lodge set in splendid isolation overlooking Loch Langais. Recently refurbished and extended, it now offers a dozen appealing rooms, many with sea views, and one of the Hebrides' best restaurants (two-/three-course dinner £24/29), noted for its fine seafood and game.

### Balranald Nature Reserve
Bird-watchers flock to this Royal Society for the Protection of Birds (RSPB) nature reserve,

18 miles west of Lochmaddy, in the hope of spotting the rare red-necked phalarope or hearing the distinctive call of the corncrake. There's a **visitors centre** ( ☎ 510372; admission free; ⚕ Apr-Sep; ☻ ) with a resident warden who offers 1½-hour guided walks (£3, depart visitor centre 10am on Tuesdays, May to August).

## BENBECULA (BEINN NA FAOGHLA)
☎ 01870 / pop 1200

Benbecula is a low-lying island whose flat, lochan-studded landscape is best appreciated from the summit of **Rueval** (124m), the island's highest point. There's a path around the south side of the hill (signposted from the main road; park beside the landfill site) that is said to be the route taken to the coast by Bonnie Prince Charlie and Flora MacDonald during the prince's escape in 1746.

The control centre for the British army's Hebrides Missile Range (located on the northwestern tip of South Uist) is the island's main source of employment, and **Balivanich** (Baile a'Mhanaich) – looking like a corner of a Glasgow housing estate planted incongruously on the machair – is the commercial centre serving the troops and their families. The village has a bank with an ATM, a post office and a large **Co-op supermarket** ( ☻ 8am-8pm Mon-Sat, 12.30-6pm Sun).

## SOUTH UIST (UIBHIST A DEAS)
pop 1900

South Uist is the second-largest island in the Outer Hebrides, and saves its choicest corners for those who explore away from the main north–south road. The low-lying west coast is an almost unbroken stretch of white-sand beach and flower-flecked machair, while the multitude of inland lochs provide excellent trout fishing. The east coast, riven by four large sea lochs, is hilly and remote, with spectacular **Beinn Mhor** (620m) the highest point.

As you drive south from Benbecula you cross from the predominantly Protestant northern half of the Outer Hebrides into the mostly Roman Catholic south, a religious transition marked by the granite statue of **Our Lady of the Isles** on the slopes of Rueval (the hill with the military radomes on its summit), and the presence of many roadside shrines.

### The North
The northern part of the island is mostly occupied by the watery expanses of Loch Bee and

Loch Druidibeg. **Loch Druidibeg National Nature Reserve** is an important breeding ground for birds such as dunlin, redshank, ringed plover, greylag goose and corncrake; you can take a 5-mile self-guided walk through the reserve (pick up a leaflet from the Scottish Natural Heritage office on the main road beside the loch).

Two miles south of Loch Druidibeg is the attractive hamlet of **Howmore** (Tobha Mor), with several restored, thatched *blackhouses*, one of which houses the **Tobha Mor Crofters' Hostel** (www.gatliff.org.uk; dm adult/child £9/6).

You can rent bikes from **Rothan Cycles** ( ☎ 01870-620283; www.rothan.com; 9 Howmore; per day/week from £8/35) where the road to the hostel leaves the main road.

### The South
Six miles south of Howmore, **Kildonan Museum** ( ☎ 01878-710343; Kildonan; adult/child £1.50/free; ☻ 10am-5pm Mon-Fri, 2-5pm Sun Easter-Oct) explores the lives of local crofters through its collection of artefacts – an absorbing exhibition of black-and-white photography and first-hand accounts of harsh Hebridean conditions. There's also an excellent tea room and craft shop.

Amid the ruined *blackhouses* of Milton, half a mile south of the museum, a cairn marks the site of **Flora MacDonald's birthplace**.

**Askernish Golf Course**, originally laid out by the legendary Tom Morris in 1891, was recently rediscovered among the dunes on South Uist. At the time of research it was being restored, and this classic, old-fashioned links course should be open for play once again in summer 2008.

### LOCHBOISDALE (LOCH BAGHASDAIL)
☎ 01878

The ferry port of Lochboisdale is the island's largest settlement, with a **tourist office** ( ☎ 700286; ☻ 9am-1pm & 2-5pm Mon-Fri, 9.30am-5pm Sat, 9am-9.30pm Tue & Thu Apr-Oct), a bank with ATM, a grocery store and a petrol station. There's a **Co-op supermarket** ( ☻ 8am-8pm Mon-Sat, 12.30-6pm Sun) at Daliburgh, 3 miles west of the village.

For details of ferries from Lochboisdale to Oban, see p390.

### Sleeping & Eating
**Lochside Cottage** ( ☎ 700472; loch-side_cottage@tiscali .co.uk; r per person £25; **P** ) This friendly B&B, 1.5 miles south of the ferry, has rooms with a view and a sun lounge barely a fishing-rod's length from its own trout loch.

## INVASION OF THE KILLER HEDGEHOGS

In 1974, a couple of hedgehogs were introduced to South Uist by a local gardener in an attempt to control the slugs in his garden. Hedgehogs had never been native to the islands, and the incomers waddled innocently into a vacant ecological niche. They spread like wildfire, and by 2002, it was estimated that there were around 5000 of the spiny slug-munchers in the Uists. But what's more, they were posing a mortal threat to important colonies of rare ground-nesting birds – eggs are a favourite hedgehog food.

In 2002, Scottish Natural Heritage (SNH) announced that a cull was the only way to preserve the bird population, and for the next few years each summer saw a battle between the SNH culling teams and animal rights organisations. While SNH combed the fields at night with flashlights, hog-spotters and lethal injections, the British Hedgehog Preservation Society and other campaign groups were offering £20 a head for live hedgehogs, which they transported to the mainland for release into the wild. The cull was ended in 2007 in favour of transporting live hedgehogs to the mainland.

If the Uist invaders had been rats rather than cute Mrs Tiggywinkles, the public reaction might have been different, as the inhabitants of Canna, in the Small Isles, will confirm. Rats were accidentally introduced to the tiny island (population 14) by a ship a century ago – by 2005 the rodent raiders numbered more than 10,000, forcing out native species including wood mice and birds – the island's population of burrow-nesting Manx shearwaters had ceased to nest there.

Canna's owner, the National Trust for Scotland, called in a crack team of rat-trappers from New Zealand, who trapped all the native wood mice and sent them for a nice holiday on the mainland, before wiping out the rats with poison bait. The plan seems to have worked. The woodmice were returned to their island home in 2006, and by summer 2007 the Manx shearwaters were nesting on Canna once more. Any public outcry? Not a squeak.

**NORTHERN HIGHLANDS & ISLANDS**

**ourpick** **Polochar Inn** ( ☎ 700215; www.polocharinn
.co.uk; Polochar; s/d £45/70; **P** ) Recently taken over by local sisters Morag McKinnon and Margaret Campbell, this 18th-century inn has been transformed into a stylish and welcoming hotel with a stunning location looking out across the sea to Barra. There's an excellent restaurant and bar menu (mains £7 to £13), that includes fish chowder, haddock and chips, local salmon and Uist lamb. Polochar is 7 miles southwest of Lochboisdale, on the way to Eriskay.

**Lochboisdale Hotel** ( ☎ 700332; www.lochboisdale
.com; s/d £50/90; **P** ) This old-fashioned huntin'-and-fishin' hotel has spacious, modernised rooms, many of which have stunning views across the Minch. The lounge bar has a roaring fire in winter, and hosts regular traditional music sessions; it also serves decent bar meals (£8 to £12).

## ERISKAY (EIRIOSGAIGH)
☎ 01878 / pop 170
In 1745, Bonnie Prince Charlie first set foot in Scotland on the west coast of Eriskay, on the sandy beach (immediately north of the ferry terminal) still known as **Prince's Strand** (Coilleag a'Phrionnsa).

More recently, the SS *Politician* sank just off the island in 1941. The islanders salvaged much of its cargo of around 250,000 bottles of whisky and, after a binge of dramatic proportions, the police intervened and a number of the islanders landed in jail. The story was immortalised by Sir Compton Mackenzie in his comic novel *Whisky Galore*, later made into a famous film.

A CalMac car ferry links Eriskay with Ardmhor at the northern end of Barra (pedestrian/car £6/18, 40 minutes, four or five daily).

## BARRA (BARRAIGH)
☎ 01871 / pop 1150
With its beautiful beaches, wildflower-clad dunes, rugged little hills and strong sense of community, diminutive Barra – just 14 miles in circumference – is the Outer Hebrides in miniature. For a great view of the island, walk up to the top of **Heaval** (383m), a mile northeast of Castlebay.

**Castlebay** (Bagh a'Chaisteil), in the south, is the largest village. There's a **tourist office** ( ☎ 810336; Main St; ☷ 9am-1pm & 2-5pm Mon Sat, noon-4pm Sun Apr-Oct), a bank with ATM, a post office and two grocery stores. There's free internet access at the **Community Library** ( ☎ 810471; Community School, Castlebay; ☯ 9am-4.30pm Mon & Wed, 9am-4.30pm & 6-8pm Tue & Thu, 9am-3.30pm Fri, 10am-12.30pm Sat).

## Sights & Activities

Castlebay takes its name from **Kisimul Castle** (HS; ☎ 810313; Castlebay; adult/child incl ferry £4.50/2.25; ☯ 9.30am-5.30pm Apr-Sep), first built by the Mac-Neil clan in the 11th century. It was sold in the 19th century and restored in the 20th by American architect Robert MacNeil, who be-came the 45th clan chief; he gifted the castle to Historic Scotland in 2000 for an annual rent of £1 and a bottle of whisky (Talisker single malt, if you're interested).

The **Barra Heritage Centre** ( ☎ 810413; www.barra heritage.com; Castlebay; adult/child £2/1; ☯ 11am-4pm Mon-Sat May-Aug, 11am-4pm Mon, Wed & Fri Mar, Apr & Sep) has Gaelic-themed displays about the island, local art exhibitions and a tearoom. The centre also manages a restored 19th-century thatched

cottage, the **Black Shieling** (adult/child £2/75p; ☯ 1-4pm Mon-Fri May-Sep), 3 miles north of Castlebay on the west side of the island.

**Traigh Mor** (the Big Strand), in the north of the island, is a vast expanse of firm golden sand that serves as Barra's airport (a mile across at low tide, and big enough for three 'runways'), the only beach airport in the world that handles scheduled flights. Watching the little Twin Otter aircraft come and go is a popular spectator sport.

## Sleeping & Eating

Accommodation on Barra is limited, so make a reservation before committing to a night on the island.

**Dunard Hostel** ( ☎ 810443; www.dunardhostel .co.uk; Castlebay; dm/d from £11/30; ℗ ) Dunard is a friendly, family-run hostel just five minutes' walk from the ferry terminal. The owners can organise sea-kayaking tours for £25/40 a half-/full day.

---

### THE EVEN FURTHER OUTER HEBRIDES

St Kilda (www.kilda.org.uk) is a collection of spectacular sea stacks and cliff-bound islands about 45 miles west of North Uist. The largest island, Hirta, measures only 2 miles by 1 mile, with huge cliffs along most of its coastline. Owned by National Trust for Scotland (NTS), the islands are a Unesco World Heritage site and are the biggest sea-bird nesting site in the North Atlantic, home to more than a million birds.

#### History

Hirta was inhabited by a Gaelic-speaking population of around 200 until the 19th century, when the arrival of church missionaries and tourists began the gradual breakdown of St Kilda's tradi-tional way of life. By the 1920s, disease and emigration had seen the islands' economy collapse, and the 35 remaining islanders were evacuated, at their own request, in 1930. The people had survived here by keeping sheep, fishing, growing a few basic crops such as barley, and climbing the cliffs barefoot to catch sea birds and collect their eggs. Over the centuries, this resulted in a genetic peculiarity – St Kilda men had unusually long big toes.

#### Visiting St Kilda

Boat tours to St Kilda are a major undertaking. For a full listing of tour operators, check out the website www.kilda.org.uk. **Western Edge Charters** ( ☎ 01506-387633; www.westernedge.co.uk) oper-ates leisurely, six-day expeditions on a 12m sailing yacht departing from Berneray (North Uist) for around £600 per person.

The only way to spend any time in the islands is to join one of the two-week NTS work parties that visit St Kilda from mid-May to August. The NTS charges volunteers for doing archaeologi-cal and conservation work in and around the village ruins – you have to be physically fit and prepared to work for up to 36 hours per week. And you have to pay for the privilege – from £555 to £645 (including transport from Oban in a converted lifeboat and full board in dorm accommodation). To get an application form, send a stamped, self-addressed envelope to St Kilda Work Parties, NTS, Balnain House, 40 Huntly St, Inverness IV3 5HR. The closing date for applications is 31 January.

**Faire Mhaoldonaich** ( ☎ 810441; www.fairemhaol donaich.com; Nasg; r per person £23-25; ⏱ Mar-Oct; Ⓟ ) This B&B is a modern house with spacious, comfortable rooms and great views over Bagh Beag to the isle of Mhaoldonaich; it's a mile west of Castlebay on the road to Vatersay.

**Craigard Hotel** ( ☎ 810200; www.isleofbarra.com/craigard .html; Castlebay; s/d £55/80; Ⓟ ) The Craigard has snug rooms and a conservatory restaurant (mains £7 to £11) with grand views across the harbour to the islands south of Barra; the house speciality is cockles gathered from the airport beach.

### Getting There & Around

See p390 for details of CalMac ferries from Castlebay to Oban and Lochboisdale (South Uist) and flights to the Scottish mainland; see p401 for the ferry from Ardmhor, at the northern end of Barra, to Eriskay.

Bus W32 makes a regular circuit of the island, and also connects with flights at the airport.

You can hire bikes from **Barra Cycle Hire** ( ☎ 810284; 29 St Brendan's Rd, Castlebay).

## PABBAY (PABAIDH), MINGULAY (MIUGHALAIGH) & BERNERAY (BEARNARAIGH)

These three uninhabited islands, gifted to the National Trust for Scotland (NTS) in 2000, are important breeding sites for sea-bird species such as fulmar, black guillemot, common and Arctic tern, great skua, puffin and storm petrel. There are boat trips to the islands from Castlebay, Barra, in settled weather for around £15 per person; ask at Barra tourist office for details. The puffin season lasts from June to early August.

**NORTHERN HIGHLANDS & ISLANDS**

# Orkney & Shetland Islands

Floating off Scotland's remote northeast coast, the Orkney and Shetland Islands are captivating archipelagos forming an antithesis to modern urban grit. Life has always been different in this part of the country. Things move a bit slower and local folk appreciate a smile and a wave more than most. And, importantly, the march of progress hasn't undermined a sense of community, or a sense of place. Globalisation may have delivered the internet into many Orcadian and Shetland homes, but it hasn't interrupted a traditional way of life where separations between cultural heritage and island myth and legend are distinctly hazy.

Devolution came to these islands long before the rest of Scotland. Their geographical isolation, Norse roots and distinctive geography gives each group its own identity. This character is accentuated by echoes of the past; the islands are a living, breathing museum, with our distant ancestors leaving behind an extraordinary diary of human development. It's this sort of fusion that makes a trip to Scotland's far-flung northern outposts a highlight of any visit.

Breathtaking scenery means walking and cycling are both popular and (with sometimes ferocious headwinds) challenging island pursuits. The wildlife spectacle here is unparalleled in the British Isles, and visitors may spot porpoises, elusive otters and seal colonies – but it is the thriving bird population that is a real draw card, with millions of sea birds breathing life into forbidding coastal areas. And who can resist sitting among colonies of comical puffins as they totter about their daily business?

## HIGHLIGHTS

- Shaking your head in astonishment at extraordinary **Skara Brae** (p417) and **Maes Howe** (p416), prehistoric perfection that predates the pyramids
- Blowing away the cobwebs amid the raw, desolate and beautiful landscapes of **Unst** (p434) and **Yell** (p433)
- Island hopping the magical **Northern Islands** (p419) of Orkney, where crystal azure waters lap against glittering white-sand beaches
- Checking out Shetland's absorbing brand-new **museum** (p426), which details 5000 years worth of history and landscapes
- Scuba diving in Europe's premier underwater museum of sunken warships in **Scapa Flow** (p412)

★Unst

★Yell

★ Shetland Museum, Lerwick

★ Northern Islands

Skara Brae ★
Maes Howe ★

★ Scapa Flow

| | |
|---|---|
| ■ POPULATION: ORKNEY 19,500; SHETLAND 22,000 | ■ AREA: ORKNEY 990 SQ KM; SHETLAND 1466 SQ KM |

# ORKNEY ISLANDS

Orkney captures the imagination and the eye, its balding turf reflective of constantly changing shades of light as clouds scurry across windswept skies. In summer the days are lengthy and the sunniest moments are often long into the evening – a great time to be out exploring. Orcadians are a friendly bunch, seemingly immune to the unpredictable climate, and are fiercely independent of mainland Scotland, even though their magical archipelago is situated a mere 6 miles off the north coast.

Only 17 of Orkney's 70 islands are inhabited and some of the most dramatic scenery is along the coast where 300m cliffs plunge into white, sandy beaches. The archipelago contains a sliver of mankind's ancient existence that's found nowhere else. Prehistoric sites are sprinkled throughout the islands – Europe's greatest concentration – their stone walls immune to 5000 years of climatic onslaught. The Flinstonesque furniture of Skara Brae, the tomb of Maes Howe and numerous standing stones weave a mystical milieu while providing a snapshot of the way people have worshipped, lived and perished since ancient times.

Today's animated contemporary culture, its roots firmly embedded in traditional island life, is best experienced among the smaller islands and in the larger towns of Kirkwall and Stromness on Mainland, with their Norse roots, inviting drinking holes, chatty locals and vibrant festivals.

## Tours

**Orkney Island Holidays** ( ☎ 01856-711 373; www .orkneyislandholidays.com; Furrowend, Shapinsay) offers holidays based on Shapinsay, with guided tours of archaeological sites, bird-watching trips, wildlife trips and excursions to other islands. One-week, all-inclusive packages cost £950.

**Wildabout Orkney** ( ☎ /fax 01856-851 011; www.wild aboutorkney.com) operates tours covering Orkney's history, ecology, folklore and wildlife. Day trips operate year-round and cost £45. The minibus tours pick you up at Stromness ferry terminal, and at Palace Rd and Kirkwall Youth Hostel in Kirkwall.

**Discover Orkney** ( ☎ /fax 01856-872 865; 44 Clay Loan, Kirkwall, Mainland) caters to individuals and small groups, offering guided tours and walks throughout the islands in the company of a qualified guide. Specific tours are tailored to your interests and your guide comes from a long line of Orcadians.

## Getting There & Away
### AIR
**British Airways/Loganair** ( ☎ 0845 773 3377; www .loganair.co.uk) flies at least twice daily (except Sunday) from Kirkwall airport to Aberdeen (one hour), Edinburgh (1¾ hours), Glasgow (1¾ hours) and Inverness (45 minutes), with connections to London Heathrow, Birmingham, Manchester and Belfast. There are two daily flights (Monday to Friday, one each on Saturday and Sunday) from Kirkwall to Sumburgh airport on Shetland (35 minutes). You can book on the website; fares fluctuate depending on date and time of departure.

### BOAT
Car ferries to and from Orkney can be very busy in July and August – it's best to book ahead at these times.

### From Scrabster, Shetlands & Aberdeen
**Northlink Ferries** ( ☎ 0845 600 0449; www.northlink ferries.co.uk) operates ferries from Scrabster to Stromness (passenger return £26 to £30, car return £82 to £90, 1½ hours, three daily Monday to Friday, two on weekends). Northlink also sails from Aberdeen to Kirkwall (passenger return £32 to £50, car return £126 to £172, up to 7¼ hours, three or four weekly) and on to Lerwick (passenger return £27 to £40, car return £100 to £160, up to 7½ hours, one daily) on the Shetland Islands. Note that there are only two or three services weekly from Lerwick to Kirkwall, but daily services from Lerwick to Aberdeen.

Fares vary according to low-, mid- and peak-season trips (we've provided low and peak fares), and travel times vary due to winds.

### From Gills Bay
**Pentland Ferries** ( ☎ 01856-831 226; www.pentlandferries .co.uk) offers a shorter and less expensive car-ferry crossing than the Northlink trip. Boats leave from Gills Bay, about 3 miles west of John o'Groats, and head to St Margaret's Hope in Orkney (passenger/car £12/28, one hour). There are three to four crossings daily in summer and usually three in winter.

# ORKNEY ISLANDS

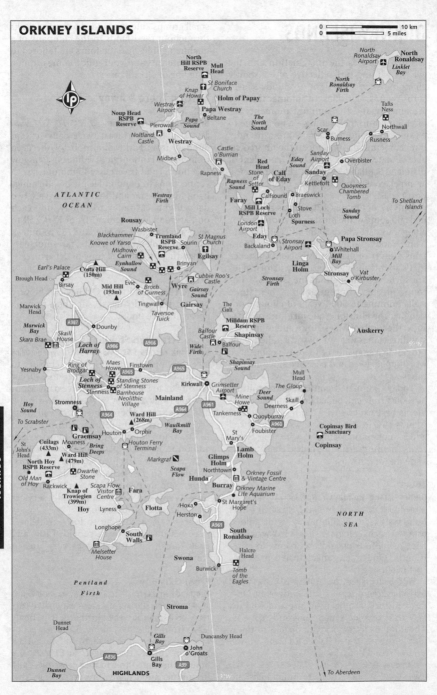

0                    10 km
0              5 miles

North Hill RSPB Reserve
Mull Head
St Boniface Church
Knap of Howar
Holm of Papay
North Ronaldsay Airport
North Ronaldsay
Linklet Bay
North Ronaldsay Firth
Tafts Ness
Westray Airport
Papa Westray
Beltane
Papa Sound
Northwall
Scar
Burness
Rusness
Noup Head RSPB Reserve
Pierowall
Noltland Castle
Westray
Midbea
Castle o'Burrian
Rapness
Red Head
Stone of Setter
Eday Sound
Sanday Airport
Overbister
Sanday
Kettletoft
Quoyness Chambered Tomb
Rapness Sound
Call of Eday
Calfsound
Braeswick
Faray
Mill Loch RSPB Reserve
Stove
Loth
Spurness
Sanday Sound
To Shetland Islands

ATLANTIC OCEAN

Westray Firth
Rousay
Wasbister
Blackhammer
Trumland RSPB Reserve
Knowe of Yarso
Midhowe Cairn
Sourin
St Magnus Church
Egilsay
London Airport
Eday
Backaland
Stronsay Airport
Papa Stronsay
Whitehall
Mill Bay
Linga Holm
Stronsay
Vat o'Kirbuster
Earl's Palace
Costa Hill (150m)
Brinyan
Cubbie Roo's Castle
Wyre
Gairsay Sound
Stronsay Firth
Brough Head
Birsay
Mid Hill (193m)
Evie
Broch of Gurness
Gairsay
The Galt
Marwick Head
Tingwall
Taversoe Tuick
Milldam RSPB Reserve
Auskerry
Marwick Bay
Skaill House
Dounby
Balfour Castle
Shapinsay
Skara Brae
Loch of Harray
Wide Firth
Balfour
Yesnaby
Ring of Brodgar
Maes Howe
Finstown
Shapinsay Sound
Mull Head
The Gloup
Loch of Stenness
Standing Stones of Stenness
Stenness
Barnhouse Neolithic Village
Kirkwall
Grimsetter Airport
Deer Sound
Skaill
Deerness
Hoy Sound
Stromness
Mainland
Mine Howe
Tankerness
Quoyburray
Copinsay Bird Sanctuary
To Scrabster
Ward Hill (268m)
Waulkmill Bay
St Mary's
Foubister
Copinsay
Graemsay
Houton
Orphir
Houton Ferry Terminal
Lamb Holm
Cuilags (433m)
Moaness
Bring Deeps
Markgraf
Scapa Flow
Glimps Holm
North Hoy RSPB Reserve
Ward Hill (479m)
Dwarfie Stone
Northtown
Orkney Fossil & Vintage Centre
St John's Head
Old Man of Hoy
Rackwick
Scapa Flow Visitor Centre
Fara
Hunda
Burray
Orkney Marine Life Aquarium
Knap of Trowieglen (399m)
Hoy
Lyness
Flotta
Hoxa
St Margaret's Hope
NORTH SEA
Longhope
South Walls
Herston
Melsetter House
Swona
South Ronaldsay
Halcro Head
Tomb of the Eagles
Burwick
Pentland Firth
Stroma
Dunnet Head
Gills Bay
Duncansby Head
Gills Bay
John o'Groats
Dunnet Bay
HIGHLANDS
To Aberdeen

ORKNEY & SHETLAND ISLANDS

### From John o'Groats
During the summer period, **John o'Groats Ferries** ( ☎ 01955-611 353; www.jogferry.co.uk) operates a passenger-only ferry (p363) from John o'Groats to Burwick, on the southern tip of South Ronaldsay.

### BUS
**Scottish Citylink** ( ☎ 0870 550 5050; www.citylink.co.uk) has daily coaches from Inverness to Scrabster (£16, three hours), connecting with the ferries to Stromness. Early-morning departures from Glasgow or Edinburgh, and overnighters from London, connect with the Scrabster bus at Inverness.

**John o'Groats Ferries** ( ☎ 01955-611 353; www.jogferry.co.uk) operates the summer-only Orkney bus service from Inverness to Kirkwall. Tickets (one way/return £30/42, five hours) include bus travel from Inverness to John o'Groats, passenger ferry to Burwick and another bus from Burwick to Kirkwall. There's one bus daily in May and two daily from June to early September.

## Getting Around
**Orkney Islands Council** ( ☎ 01856-873 535) publishes the *Orkney Public Transport Timetable*, a detailed schedule of all bus, ferry and air services around and to/from Orkney. The timetable is available free from tourist offices.

The largest island, Mainland, is joined by road-bearing causeways to Burray and South Ronaldsay. The other islands can be reached by air and ferry services.

### TO/FROM THE AIRPORT
**British Airways/Loganair** ( ☎ 01856-873 457; www.loganair.co.uk) operates interisland flights between Kirkwall airport and North Ronaldsay, Westray, Papa Westray, Stronsay, Sanday and Eday. For details, see each island's entry in this chapter.

### BICYCLE
You can hire bikes from various locations on Mainland, including **Cycle Orkney** ( ☎ 01856-875 777; Tankerness Lane, Kirkwall; adult/child bikes per day from £10/6; ⏰ 9am-5.30pm Mon-Sat) and **Orkney Cycle Hire** ( ☎ 01856-850 255; 54 Dundas St, Stromness; per day £6-10).

### BOAT
**Orkney Ferries** ( ☎ 01856-872 044; www.orkneyferries.co.uk; Shore St, Kirkwall) operates car ferries from Mainland to Hoy, Flotta and the northern Orkney islands; for details see each island's section later in the chapter.

### CAR
There are several car-hire companies on Mainland, including **Orkney Car Hire** ( ☎ 01856-872 866; www.orkneycarhire.co.uk; Junction Rd, Kirkwall) and **Norman Brass Car Hire** ( ☎ 01856-850 850; Blue Star Filling Station, North End Rd, Stromness). Small-car rates begin at around £34/164 per day/week, although there are specials for as low as £25 per day.

To hire a camper van, contact **Orkney Motorhome Hire** ( ☎ 01856-874 391; www.orkney-motor home-hire.co.uk). The vans sleep two adults comfortably, but two adults and three kids at a pinch. Weekly rates are £390 from November to March, £490 in July and August, and £440 all other months.

### PUBLIC TRANSPORT
**Orkney Coaches** ( ☎ 01856-870 555) runs bus services on Mainland and South Ronaldsay. Most buses don't operate on Sunday. Day Rover (£6) and 3-Day Rover (£15) tickets will save you money, allowing unlimited travel on Orkney Coaches' bus routes. **Causeway Coaches** ( ☎ 01856-831 444) runs to St Margaret's Hope on South Ronaldsay.

## KIRKWALL
☎ 01856 / pop 6200
With its roads pounded by the footsteps of tourists on their summer Orcadian pilgrimage, Kirkwall has an energy that ebbs and flows along its busy streets. It's set back from a wide bay, and its vigour, combined with the atmospheric paved streets and twisting wynds (lanes), gives Orkney's capital a distinctive character. Magnificent St Magnus Cathedral takes pride of place in the centre of town, and the nearby Earl's and Bishop's Palaces are also worth a ramble. Founded in the early 11th century, the original part of Kirkwall is one of the best examples of an ancient Norse town.

## Information
There are banks with ATMs on Broad St and Albert St.

**Balfour Hospital** ( ☎ 888000; New Scapa Rd)
**Launderama** ( ☎ 872982; 47 Albert St; ⏰ 8.30am-5.30pm Mon-Fri, 9am-5pm Sat) Service wash and dry £7.50.
**Orcadian Bookshop** ( ☎ 878888; www.orcadian.co.uk; 50 Albert St) Great selection of local books and newspapers.

ORKNEY & SHETLAND ISLANDS

**Orkney Library** ( ☎ 873166; 44 Junction Rd; ☒ 9am-7pm Mon-Thu, 9am-5pm Fri, Sat; ▢ ) Fast and free internet access (one-hour maximum).

**Post office** (Junction Rd)

**Support Training** ( ☎ 873582; cnr Junction Rd & West Tankerness Lane; per hr £5; ☒ 8.30am-5.30pm Mon-Fri, 10am-5pm Sat) Internet access.

**Tourist office** ( ☎ 872856; www.visitorkney.com; 6 Broad St; ☒ 9am-5pm Mon-Fri, 10am-4pm Sat Oct-Apr, 9am-6pm May & Sep, 8.30am-8pm Jun-Aug) Very helpful. Has a good range of publications on Orkney.

## Sights
### ST MAGNUS CATHEDRAL
Founded in 1137 and constructed from local red sandstone and yellow Eday stone, fabulous **St Magnus Cathedral** ( ☎ 874894; Broad St; admission

free; ☒ 9am-6pm Mon-Sat, 1-6pm Sun Apr-Sep, 9am-1pm & 2-5pm Mon-Sat Oct-Mar) should not be missed. The powerful atmosphere of an ancient faith pervades the impressive interior. Lyrical and melodramatic epitaphs of the dead line the walls inside and emphasise the serious business of 17th- and 18th-century bereavement.

Earl Rognvald Brusason commissioned the cathedral in the name of his martyred uncle, Magnus Erlendsson, who was killed by Earl Hakon Paulsson on Egilsay in 1117. Work began in 1137, but the building is actually the result of 300 years of construction and alteration, and includes Romanesque, transitional and Gothic styles.

During summer only, 40-minute tours of the cathedral's upper levels start at 11am and

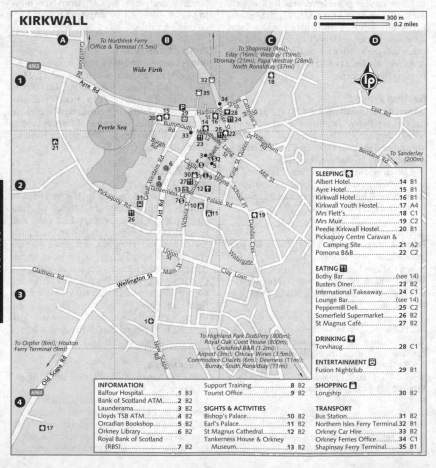

**KIRKWALL**

**INFORMATION**
| | | |
|---|---|---|
| Balfour Hospital | 1 | B3 |
| Bank of Scotland ATM | 2 | B2 |
| Launderama | 3 | B2 |
| Lloyds TSB ATM | 4 | B2 |
| Orcadian Bookshop | 5 | B2 |
| Orkney Library | 6 | B2 |
| Royal Bank of Scotland (RBS) | 7 | B2 |
| Support Training | 8 | B2 |
| Tourist Office | 9 | B2 |

**SIGHTS & ACTIVITIES**
| | | |
|---|---|---|
| Bishop's Palace | 10 | B2 |
| Earl's Palace | 11 | B2 |
| St Magnus Cathedral | 12 | B2 |
| Tankerness House & Orkney Museum | 13 | B2 |

**SLEEPING**
| | | |
|---|---|---|
| Albert Hotel | 14 | B1 |
| Ayre Hotel | 15 | B1 |
| Kirkwall Hotel | 16 | B1 |
| Kirkwall Youth Hostel | 17 | A4 |
| Mrs Flett's | 18 | C1 |
| Mrs Muir | 19 | C2 |
| Peedie Kirkwall Hostel | 20 | B1 |
| Pickaquoy Centre Caravan & Camping Site | 21 | A2 |
| Pomona B&B | 22 | C2 |

**EATING**
| | | |
|---|---|---|
| Bothy Bar | (see 14) | |
| Busters Diner | 23 | B2 |
| International Takeaway | 24 | C1 |
| Lounge Bar | (see 14) | |
| Peppermill Deli | 25 | C2 |
| Somerfield Supermarket | 26 | B2 |
| St Magnus Café | 27 | B2 |

**DRINKING**
| | | |
|---|---|---|
| Torvhaug | 28 | C1 |

**ENTERTAINMENT**
| | | |
|---|---|---|
| Fusion Nightclub | 29 | B1 |

**SHOPPING**
| | | |
|---|---|---|
| Longship | 30 | B2 |

**TRANSPORT**
| | | |
|---|---|---|
| Bus Station | 31 | B2 |
| Northern Isles Ferry Terminal | 32 | B1 |
| Orkney Car Hire | 33 | B2 |
| Orkney Ferries Office | 34 | C1 |
| Shapinsay Ferry Terminal | 35 | B1 |

2pm on Tuesday and Thursday and cost £5.50 per person.

### EARL'S PALACE & BISHOP'S PALACE
Near the cathedral, and on opposite sides of the street, these two ruined Historic Scotland (HS) **palaces** ( ☎ 871918; Watergate; adult/child £2.20/75p; ⏰ 9.30am-6.30pm Apr-Sep) are worth poking around. The Earl's Palace was once known as the finest example of French Renaissance architecture in Scotland. It's the better of the two palaces, with many lower rooms still intact. One room features an interesting history of its builder, Earl Patrick Stewart, who was executed in Edinburgh for treason. He started construction in about 1600, but he ran out of money and it was never completed.

The Bishop's Palace was built in the mid-12th century to provide comfortable lodgings for Bishop William the Old. There's a good view of the cathedral from the tower, and a plaque showing the different phases of the cathedral's construction.

### TANKERNESS HOUSE & ORKNEY MUSEUM
This fine restored **merchant's house** ( ☎ 873191; Broad St; admission free; ⏰ 10.30am-5pm Mon-Sat & 2-5pm Sun Apr-Sep, 10.30am-5pm Mon-Sat Oct-Mar) gives an intriguing glimpse into Orkney's archaeological treasure chest, starting from the first settlers, who arrived over 5000 years ago. Exhibits include Pictish stones, 'bone' pins and Iron Age jewellery. The highlight is the photo archive downstairs, which offers snapshots of a technologically distant past. Keep an eye out for the temporary exhibitions.

### HIGHLAND PARK DISTILLERY
Not only is Highland Park a very fine single malt, but the tour (£5) of the world's most northerly **whisky distillery** ( ☎ 874619; Holm Rd; ⏰ 10am-5pm Mon-Fri Apr, Sep & Oct, 10am-5pm Mon-Sat & noon-5pm Sun May-Aug, 1-5pm Mon-Fri Nov-Mar) is also one of the best. You'll see the whole whisky-making process – this is one of the few distilleries that still does its own barley malting, known as floor malting. Tours are run half-hourly.

### ORKNEY WINE COMPANY
About 2 miles south of Kirkwall off the A961, **Orkney Wine Company** ( ☎ 878700; www.orkneywine .co.uk; Operahalla, St Ola) produce handmade wines made from berries, flowers and vegetables, all naturally fermented. Get stuck into some

gooseberry or gorse-flower plonk – not everyone's cup of tea but surprisingly addictive.

## Festivals & Events
The **St Magnus Festival** ( ☎ 871445; www.stmagnus festival.com) takes place in June and is a colourful celebration of music and the arts.

Kirkwall is transformed into a seething swell of islanders and tourists on New Year's Day and Christmas Day, when the boisterous and chaotic (read: frankly crazy) ball game known as the **Ba'** takes place. The streets become a heaving mass of people, striking this way and that as the ba' moves through the throng.

## Sleeping
### BUDGET
**Peedie Kirkwall Hostel** ( ☎ 875477; kirkwallpeedie hostel@talk21.com; 1 Ayre Houses, Ayre Rd; dm from £10) This clean, compact, independent hostel has small dorms with comfy wooden bunks (two or four beds to a room), washbasin and TV in each room. It's on the waterfront next to Ayre Hotel, five minutes' walk west of the town centre.

**Kirkwall Youth Hostel** (SYIIA; ☎ 0870 004 1133; Old Scapa Rd; dm adult/child £13.50/10; ⏰ Mar-Oct) Kirkwall's well-equipped hostel is a 10-minute walk south of the bus station. Though no architectural gem, it's large (with plenty of four-bed dorms), has decent facilities and is very friendly. You'll probably get a room to yourself.

Also recommended:

**Pickaquoy Centre Caravan & Camping Site** ( ☎ 879900; Pickaquoy Rd; camp site per 2 people & tent £6.60) Plenty of grass and decent facilities.

**Mrs Flett's** ( ☎ 873160; Cumliebank, Cromwell Rd; r per person from £19) Small, traditional and very friendly B&B.

### MIDRANGE
**Pomona B&B** ( ☎ 872325; cjsmuir@btinternet.com; 9 Albert St; r per person £20) We rubbed our hands with glee when we found this old-fashioned B&B at the back of the café with the same name. With six en suite rooms it's not the roomiest lodging in Orkney, but it is a bargain and possibly the best located, just off the main drag in the heart of town. Singles note: no surcharge – yippee!!

**ourpick Crossford** ( ☎ 876142; crossford@bushinternet .com; Heatherly Loan, St Ola; r per person £30) Situated in St Ola, just up the road from Highland Park Distillery, is this excellent, homely little B&B.

**ORKNEY & SHETLAND ISLANDS**

There's just one double en-suite room (with a lovely outlook), a small dining/sitting area and lots of privacy. There's also a small single the owner will probably let out if there's three of you (but you have to share the en suite). Very convenient to Kirkwall, but with a rural setting, you get the best of both worlds. Look for the sign just after Highland Park, heading south from Kirkwall.

**Mrs Muir** ( ☎ 874805; 2 Dundas Cres; s/d £30/44) This highly recommended mansion, the old manse for the church, has some of the best accommodation in town. Cavernous rooms have huge windows that flood the place with light. Bathrooms are shared, but these lodgings are something special.

**Kirkwall Hotel** ( ☎ 872232; www.kirkwallhotel.com; Harbour St; s/d from £60/90; ☐ ) A grand old bastion of Orcadian hospitality, this hotel sits in a prime location gazing proudly over the harbour. Executive rooms face the front, have magnificent views and enough room to park your car next to your bed – they're huge! You're paying for the grandeur, but once you're snuggled into the downstairs bar, you won't care. Room size and bed quality is variable in standard rooms.

Also recommended:

**Commodore Chalets** ( ☎ 781319; www.commodore chalets.co.uk; St Marys; s/d £25/50) An excellent alternative to staying in Kirkwall. Austere B&B and self-catering options. Just before the first Churchill Barrier heading south, 6 miles from Kirkwall.

**Royal Oak Guest House** ( ☎ /fax 877177; www.royal oakhouse.co.uk; Holm Rd; s/d £35/50) Has modern rooms that would suit business travellers or families.

**Sanderlay** ( ☎ 875587; www.sanderlay.co.uk; 2 Viewfield Drive; s/d £35/56; ♿ ) Sombre Sanderlay is a classy guesthouse in a family home, with understated and first-rate rooms.

### TOP END

**Ayre Hotel** ( ☎ 873001; www.ayrehotel.co.uk; Ayre Rd; £75/100, seaview supplement £10) The Ayre Hotel is a very busy 200-year-old town-house hotel. The service can be surly, sure, but this four-star affair is the classiest joint in town. Modern bedrooms are formally furnished with dark polished wood, huge beds and low ceilings. Try to get a room with sea views, it's worth the extra.

**Albert Hotel** ( ☎ 876000; www.alberthotel.co.uk; Mounthoolie Lane; s/d £110/150) Central, child-friendly Albert Hotel has a pleasant, traditional feel to it. Functional, tidy rooms have

king-size beds and you'll get a discount if you stay more than three nights. Excellent meals are served downstairs, and one of the best bars in town is also here. Major refurbishments were ongoing at the time of research as a fire ripped through the place in 2005.

## Eating

**Peppermill Deli** ( ☎ 878878; 21 Albert St; lunch £3; ☺ 8.30am-6pm Mon-Fri, 9am-5.30pm Sat, 11am-4pm Sun) The best place in town to grab a takeaway lunch; the selection of fillings for paninis, baguettes, wraps and toasties is almost limitless. It's also numero uno for coffee and you can grab smoked seafoods and cheeses here for picnics.

**Busters Diner** ( ☎ 876717; 1 Mounthoolie Lane; mains £5.50-11.50; ☺ lunch Tue-Sat, dinner Tue-Sun) A perpetually busy, American-style diner churning out generous portions of hot dogs, pizza and burgers, and Tex-Mex such as enchiladas and tacos. Busters is popular with the younger crowd.

**Albert Hotel** ( ☎ 876000; Mounthoolie Lane; bar suppers £7, Stables Restaurant mains £12; ☺ lunch & dinner) The Albert has the lively, friendly Bothy Bar and the more sedate Lounge Bar dishing out scrumptious bar suppers using lots of local produce, such as Orcadian beef and cheeses.

**Kirkwall Hotel** ( ☎ 872232; Harbour St; mains £10-14; ☺ lunch & dinner) Although catering for most diners, with a mix of beef, lamb, game and veggie dishes, the seafood is the highlight at this hotel restaurant, with sauces that bring out the flavour of the sea. Locals reckon it's the best tucker in town. Dining here is a sedate experience, not for those with food fights on their minds.

**Somerfield supermarket** (Pickaquoy Rd) is the best place to stock up on provisions.

Also recommended:

**International Takeaway** ( ☎ 874773; Bridge St; fish supper £4; ☺ lunch & dinner Mon-Sat) Fires out some kicking kebabs and decent fish and chips.

**St Magnus Café** ( ☎ 873354; Broad St; light meals under £2; ☺ 9.30am-6pm & 7-10pm Mon-Fri, 9.30am-4pm Sat) Old-fashioned food hall serving cheap, honest food such as toasties and bacon rolls.

## Drinking & Entertainment

**Bothy Bar** ( ☎ 876000; Mounthoolie Lane) Found in the Albert Hotel, this cosy nook was the best bar in town. It was closed at the time of research due to fire damage but was expected to reopen soon. Matchmakers, in the same building, is more sedate and, with its comfy horseshoe seating, is good for groups.

**Torvhaug** (cnr Bridge & Shore Sts) Style cats slink into the ultracool Torvhaug with its sleek, dark leather and moody red lighting in the bar downstairs and club with DJs upstairs. Shadowy nooks are good on a stormy night – it has a real nightspot feel about it.

**Fusion Nightclub** ( ☎ 879489; Ayre Rd; admission club nights £3-7; ⊗ from 10pm Thu-Sat, last entry 11.45pm) A rocking club catering to most musical tastes – from retro and cheesy chart numbers to soul, funk and hip-hop. Local DJs also spin the latest dance tunes and the club sometimes hosts live gigs. The dress code is smart casual.

## Shopping

Kirkwall has some gorgeous jewellery and crafts in shops along Albert St. Try **Longship** ( ☎ 888790; 7 Broad St; ⊗ 9am-5.30pm Mon-Sat) for Orkney-made crafts and gifts, and especially for exquisite designer jewellery.

## Getting There & Away

The **airport** ( ☎ 886210) is 2.5 miles east of the town centre. For information on flying into Orkney, see p405. For flights and ferries from Kirkwall to the northern islands, see the island sections.

Bus 1 runs direct from Kirkwall to Stromness (40 minutes, hourly, four Sunday); bus 2 runs to Orphir and Houton (20 minutes, four or five Monday to Saturday); and there are also buses from Kirkwall to Stromness via Birsay (one hour).

Bus 6 runs from Kirkwall to Tingwall (30 minutes, three to five daily Monday to Saturday) and the ferry to Rousay, and on to Evie (40 minutes, four daily Monday to Saturday).

From May to September, bus 10A runs between Kirkwall and the John o'Groats ferry at Burwick (40 minutes, two to five daily). From May to September, a special tourist service (bus 8A) runs twice daily Monday to Friday between Kirkwall and Stromness via Stenness standing stones, the Ring of Brodgar and Skara Brae.

## EAST MAINLAND TO SOUTH RONALDSAY

☎ 01856

The sinking of the battleship HMS *Royal Oak* in 1939 – torpedoed by a German U-boat that snuck through Kirk Sound into Scapa Flow – prompted Winston Churchill to commis-

sion better defences for this important naval harbour. Causeways made of concrete blocks were laid across the channels on the eastern side of Scapa Flow, linking Mainland to the islands of Lamb Holm, Glimps Holm, Burray and South Ronaldsay. The **Churchill Barriers**, flanked by the rusting wrecks of the old blockships that once guarded the channels, now carry the main road from Kirkwall to Burwick. There are good sandy beaches by barrier Nos 3 and 4.

### GETTING THERE & AWAY

Orkney Coaches bus 94 from Kirkwall runs to Deerness in East Mainland (30 minutes, four daily Monday to Saturday), with one bus calling at Tankerness. From May to September, bus 10A runs from Kirkwall to Burwick (40 minutes, two to five daily).

Causeway Coaches travels from Kirkwall to South Ronaldsay's St Margaret's Hope (30 minutes, six daily Monday to Friday, three on Saturday, one on Sunday).

### East Mainland

On a farm at Tankerness is the mysterious Iron Age site of **Mine Howe** ( ☎ 861234; adult/child £2.50/1.50; ⊗ 10am-3pm Wed, Fri & Sun May, 10am-5pm daily Jun-Aug, 11am-4pm daily early Sep, 10am-2pm Wed, Fri & Sun late Sep), discovered in 1946 but reopened by farmer Douglas Paterson in September 1999. The Howe is an eerie underground chamber whose function is unknown – staff from the Channel 4 TV series *Time Team* carried out an archaeological dig here in 2000 and concluded that it may have had some ritual significance, perhaps as an oracle or shrine. Be careful as you climb down – the stairs are narrow and wet. There are other archaeological works situated in the area and, presumably, many historical mysteries yet to be uncovered.

On the far eastern shore of Mainland, a mile north of Skaill, is the **Gloup**, a spectacular natural arch and sea cave. There are large colonies of nesting sea birds at **Mull Head**, and the shores of **Deer Sound** attract wildfowl.

### Lamb Holm

On the tiny island of Lamb Holm, the **Italian Chapel** ( ☎ 781268; admission free; ⊗ 9am-10pm Apr-Sep, 9am-4.30pm Oct-Mar) is all that remains of a POW camp that housed the Italian soldiers who worked on the Churchill Barriers. They built the chapel in their spare time, using two Nissen huts, scrap metal and their considerable

## DIVING SCAPA FLOW'S WRECKS

The many wrecks that litter the floor of Scapa Flow make it one of the most popular diving locations in Europe. Enclosed by Mainland, Hoy and South Ronaldsay, this is one of the world's largest natural harbours and has been used by vessels as diverse as King Hakon's Viking ships in the 13th century and members of today's NATO fleet.

It was from Scapa Flow that the British Home Fleet sailed to meet the German High Seas Fleet at the Battle of Jutland on 31 May 1916. After the war, 74 German ships were interned in Scapa. Conditions for the German sailors were poor, and there were several mutinies as the negotiations for the fate of the ships dragged on. When the terms of the armistice were agreed on 6 May 1919, with the announcement of a severely reduced German navy, Admiral von Reuter (who was in charge of the German fleet in Scapa Flow) decided to take matters into his own hands. On 21 June, a secret signal to scuttle the ships was passed from vessel to vessel, and the British watched incredulously as every German ship began to sink.

Most of the ships were salvaged but seven remain on the sea floor, attracting divers from all over the world. There are three battleships – the *König*, the *Kronprinz Wilhelm* and the *Markgraf* – which are all over 25,000 tonnes. The first two were subjected to blasting for scrap metal, but the *Markgraf* is undamaged and considered one of the best dives in the area. Four light cruisers (4400 to 5600 tonnes) – the *Karlsruhe, Dresden, Brummer* and *Köln* – are particularly interesting, as they lie on their sides and are very accessible to divers. The *Karlsruhe,* though severely damaged, is only 10m below the surface. Its twisted superstructure has now become a huge metal reef encrusted with diverse sea life.

As well as the German wrecks, numerous other ships rest on the sea bed in Scapa Flow. HMS *Royal Oak*, which was sunk by a German U-boat in October 1939, with the loss of 833 crew, is an official war grave.

Recommended contacts for diving in Scapa Flow:

**Diving Cellar** ( ☎ 01856-850 055; www.divescapaflow.co.uk; 4 Victoria St, Stromness)
**Scapa Scuba** ( ☎ /fax 01856-851 218; www.scapascuba.co.uk; Lifeboat House, Dundas St, Stromness)

---

artistic and decorative skills. One of the artists returned in 1960 to restore the paintwork. It's quite extraordinary inside and definitely worth seeing.

## Burray

Sleepy Burray village, on the southern side of this island, has a general store, a post office and a couple of places to stay.

Nearby, **Orkney Fossil & Vintage Centre** ( ☎ 731255; Viewforth; adult/child £3.50/2; ☼ 10am-6pm Apr-Sep) has a quirky collection of household and farming relics and 360-million-year-old fish fossils. The fossils are from the Devonian period, which predates the dinosaurs (Jurassic period) by about 200 million years. There are also galleries devoted to the world wars.

**Ankersted** ( ☎ 731217; www.ankersted.co.uk; r per person £22) is a great place to stay, with fine rooms, all with private bathroom. The upstairs lounge and balcony area overlook Watersound Bay and barrier No 4, and are exclusively for guests' use. Stay a week and you get a free night.

**Sands Hotel** ( ☎ 731298; www.thesandshotel.co.uk; Burray; s/d £65/80) is a spiffy, refurbished 19th-century herring station, right on the pier. Very modern rooms have stylish furnishings, some with superb water views. The restaurant (mains £15, bar meals £7.50), with its genteel, nautical feel, dishes out decent nosh, and tables in the sunlit conservatory migrate outside in sunny weather. It's open for lunch and dinner.

## South Ronaldsay

The main village on South Ronaldsay is **St Margaret's Hope**, named after Margaret, the Maid of Norway, who died here in 1290 on the way from her homeland to marry the future Edward II of England.

### SIGHTS
### Tomb of the Eagles

This 5000-year-old chambered **tomb** ( ☎ 831339; Liddle Farm; adult/child £6/3; ☼ 9.30am-5.30pm Apr-Sep, by arrangement Oct-Mar), at the southern tip of South Ronaldsay, is run as a visitor attraction by local farmers. Their entertaining and informative tour is a real draw-card and an excellent way to experience this relic. It's possible that sky burials occurred here; there's evidence that the bodies of people had been stripped of their flesh before being put in the tomb, possibly by being placed on top of wooden platforms just outside the tomb entrance and providing the eagles with a feast. You'll also see a **burnt mound**, an impressive Bronze Age kitchen. The tomb is a 20-minute walk east of Burwick.

### Orkney Marine Life Aquarium
This **aquarium** ( ☎ 831700; B9044, Grimness; adult/child £5.50/4; 🕙 10am-6pm; ♿ ) showcases the fascinating and diverse collection of marine animals found in Scapa Flow and Orcadian coastal waters. Giant shellfish such as lobsters are a feature, and there's a rock pool that allows up-close and personal inspections of local creatures – great for everyone, especially kids. Injured seals that have been nursed back to health can be viewed in open-air pools, and there's also an old creel boat to clamber about on.

#### SLEEPING & EATING
**St Margaret's Hope Backpackers** ( ☎ 831225; St Margaret's Hope; dm £11) The backpackers, next to the Murray Arms, is a lovely stone cottage and has one single, two twins and a six-bed dorm with comfy bunks. There's a great lounge, a kitchen and good hot showers. It's an excellent setup, particularly as the pub is right outside the front door. Book ahead for weekends. Enquiries at the Trading Post shop next door.

**Murray Arms Hotel** ( ☎ 831205; murrayarms@freeuk .com; St Margaret's Hope; hotel s/d £35/70) This bastion of hospitality is a good accommodation choice. It has been restored over the years and offers quality, if slightly frumpy, rooms. The bar is popular with locals and a great spot to have a chinwag with some Orcadians.

**our pick** **Bankburn House** ( ☎ 831310; St Margaret's Hope; standard/en suite r £44/60; 🖳 ) On the A961, just outside town, this place has four smashing upstairs rooms in a large rustic house. Two rooms have en suite, all are a brilliant size, and a lot of thought has been put into guests' comfort. There's also a huge stretch of lawn out the front, which overlooks the town and bay – perfect for sunbathing on those shimmering, summery Orkney days.

**The Creel** ( ☎ 831311; Front Rd, St Margaret's Hope; starters £7, mains £18.50; 🕙 dinner Tue-Sun) Arguably the best restaurant in Orkney, the Creel serves fresh local produce – simply prepared, but delicious. Try the roasted haddock with mussels, razor clams and squid stew. There are also

three first-class rooms (single/double £60/100) with panoramic views of the small harbour.

## SOUTH MAINLAND
☎ 01856
With its gently rolling landscape, South Mainland may not have the archaeological treasures of the north, but it does have its share of the island's history. There are a few things to see at **Orphir**, a scattered community with no shop, about 9 miles west of Kirkwall. The town's **Orkneyinga Saga Centre** (admission free; 🕙 9am-5pm) has displays relating to the Orkneyinga Saga (see the boxed text, below), and a wide-screen video show.

Just behind the centre is the **Earl's Bu** (admission free; 🕙 24hr), the foundations of a 12th-century manor house belonging to the Norse earls of Orkney. There are also the remains of **St Nicholas' Church**, a unique circular building that was originally 9m in diameter. Built before 1136 and modelled on the rotunda of the Church of the Holy Sepulchre in Jerusalem, it was popular with pilgrims after the capture of the Holy Land during the First Crusade.

If it's sunny and you're thinking about a picnic, head to **Waulkmill Bay**, between Kirkwall and Orphir. The huge sandy beach is perfect for strolling and there is bench seating with impressive views.

**Roving Eye Enterprises** ( ☎ 811309; adult/child £28/14) offers terrific boat trips, with the opportunity to view some of the rusting hulks of the German High Seas Fleet at the bottom of Scapa Flow – and you don't even get your feet wet! The boat uses a video camera

---

### ORKNEYINGA SAGA
Written around 1200 this Saga is a rich tale of sorcery, political intrigue, and cunning and unscrupulous acts among the Viking Earls of Orkney. The Saga roughly covers the period between 900 and 1200. Part myth and part historical fact, it begins with the capture of the islands by the king of Norway and then recounts the next 300 tumultuous years until they become part of Scotland. Characters of Orcadian folklore such as Sigurd the Powerful and Magnus the Martyr regularly crop up – it's a wonderful piece of medieval literature and the Orkneyinga Saga Centre is well worth a couple of hours.

**ORKNEY & SHETLAND ISLANDS**

attached to a ROV (remotely operated vehicle). The trips, which must be booked in advance, depart from Houton Pier at 1.20pm from May to September, last around three hours and include a visit to the Scapa Flow Visitor Centre (p418) at Lyness.

## Sleeping

**Foinhaven** ( ☎ 811249; foinhavenbandb@orphir1.free serve.co.uk; Germiston Rd, Orphir; s/d £40/60) For a farm stay, old-fashioned hospitality and one of the best breakfasts around, try the solitude at this place, 1.5 miles from Orphir, overlooking Waulkmill Bay. Rooms are traditional and bathrooms modern – a speck of dirt would feel lonely in here. The rate comes down if you stay more than one night.

**Houton Bay Lodge** ( ☎ 811320; www.houtonbaylodge .com; Houton; s/d from £50/75; ☐ ) Particularly good for families or business folk, this old seaplane base has been extensively refurbished, and the cool, stylish, contemporary rooms decked out with pine furniture are top notch (No 5 is a fave). Slick leather chairs, comfy beds and en suites complete the happy picture. The lodge is right behind the ferry terminal with departures for Flotta and Hoy.

## Getting There & Away

Bus 2 runs from Kirkwall to Houton (25 minutes, three to five daily Monday to Saturday) via Orphir. For details of ferries from Houton to Hoy, see p418.

## STROMNESS

☎ 01856 / pop 1600

An elongated little port, Stromness lacks Kirkwall's size and punch but makes up for that with bucket loads of character. The rambling, winding streets flanking the town have changed little since the 18th century and the flagstone-paved main street curves along the waterfront, amid attractive stone cottages. Guesthouses, pubs and eateries interrupt traditional trade along the main street, where cars and pedestrians move at the same pace as each other.

## Information

**Bank of Scotland** (Dundas St) Has an ATM.
**Royal Bank of Scotland** (Victoria St) Near the pier; has an ATM.
**Stromness Library** ( ☎ 850907; Alfred St; ⓨ 2-7pm Mon-Thu, 2-5pm Fri, 10am-5pm Sat) Free internet access.
**Sutherlands Pharmacy** ( ☎ 876399; 31 Victoria St)

**Tourist office** ( ☎ 850716; ⓨ 9am-5pm May-Sep, 9.30am-3.30pm Mon-Fri & 8.30am-2.30pm Sat Oct-Apr) Small and friendly office in the ferry terminal building.

## Sights

The main recreation in Stromness is simply strolling back and forth along the narrow, atmospheric main street. The **Pier Arts Centre**

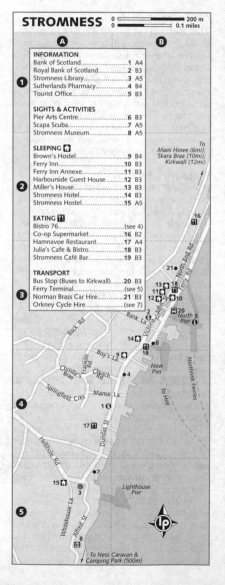

**STROMNESS**    0    200 m
              0    0.1 miles

**INFORMATION**
Bank of Scotland..................1 A4
Royal Bank of Scotland..........2 B3
Stromness Library................3 A5
Sutherlands Pharmacy...........4 B4
Tourist Office....................5 B3

**SIGHTS & ACTIVITIES**
Pier Arts Centre..................6 B3
Scapa Scuba.......................7 A5
Stromness Museum................8 A5

**SLEEPING** ⌂
Brown's Hostel....................9 B4
Ferry Inn.........................10 B3
Ferry Inn Annexe..................11 B3
Harbourside Guest House..........12 B3
Miller's House....................13 B3
Stromness Hotel..................14 B3
Stromness Hostel.................15 A5

**EATING** ⊞
Bistro 76....................(see 4)
Co-op Supermarket...............16 B2
Hamnavoe Restaurant.............17 A4
Julia's Cafe & Bistro............18 B3
Stromness Café Bar..............19 B3

**TRANSPORT**
Bus Stop (Buses to Kirkwall).....20 B3
Ferry Terminal................(see 5)
Norman Brass Car Hire...........21 B3
Orkney Cycle Hire............(see 7)

To Maes Howe (6mi); Skara Brae (10mi); Kirkwall (12mi)

To Ness Caravan & Camping Park (500m)

( ☎ 850209; 30 Victoria St) is an exquisite gallery that has now reopened following a major extension and refurbishment.

The superb **Stromness Museum** ( ☎ 850025; 52 Alfred St; adult/child £3/50p; ☼ 10am-5pm May-Sep, 11am-3.30pm Mon-Sat Oct-Apr) is full of knick-knacks from maritime and natural-history exhibitions covering whaling, the Hudsons Bay Company and the sunk German fleet. You can happily nose around the place for a couple of hours. Across the street from the museum is the house where local poet and novelist George Mackay Brown (see the boxed text, right) lived.

## Festivals & Events

The annual **Orkney Folk Festival** ( ☎ 851331; www .orkneyfolkfestival.com) is a four-day event based in Stromness in the third week of May, with a programme of folk concerts, *ceilidhs* (evenings of traditional Scottish entertainment including music, song and dance) and casual pub sessions.

## Sleeping

**Ness Caravan & Camping Park** ( ☎ 873535; camp site per tent & 2 people £6.60) This breezy, fenced-in camping ground overlooks the bay at the southern end of town and is as neat as a pin.

**Stromness Hostel** ( ☎ 850589; office@stromnesshostel .co.uk; 6 Hellihole Rd; dm adult/child from £10.50/8.50; ☼ May-Sep) This sedate hostel is a 10-minute walk from the ferry terminal and is a comfortable spot, but it's not for party animals. Facilities have been spruced up in a recent overhaul and now feature en-suite dorms.

**Brown's Hostel** ( ☎ 850661; www.brownshostel.co.uk; 45 Victoria St; dm £11) Brown's is a popular 14-bed independent hostel, just five minutes' walk from the ferry. It opens year-round and there's no curfew. There are single, double and family rooms, all clean but small. The location is excellent for getting around town.

**Miller's House** ( ☎ 851969; millershouse@orkney.com; 7 John St; s £35-40, d £46-50) Miller's House also runs Harbourside Guest House, a couple of doors down at 13 John St (same prices). They're both lovely historical houses that have been extensively renovated inside to fully exploit their light and space. The rooms in Harbourside are better, but all are quite luxurious. Expect a cracking breakfast in the morning. Over summer you'll need to book in advance.

**our pick** **Ferry Inn** ( ☎ 850280; www.ferryinn.com; John St; s/d £35/70) The Ferry Inn is a great pub to stay in. Rooms are cutesy, except No 9, which is spacious and has good views. The lively bar downstairs pulls locals and tourists alike, and there are often bands in summer. The Ferry Inn also runs the annexe (15 John St) across the road, which has cheaper rooms (£25 for a single, no surcharge).

**Stromness Hotel** ( ☎ 850298; www.stromnesshotel .com; Victoria St; r per person £48) The grandest place in town, 19th-century Stromness lords it over the harbour. Everything seems on a very imposing scale – the rooms are a bit old-fashioned, but stupendous views from the almost floor-to-ceiling windows more than compensate for the building's faded splendour. Room No 2 is a beauty, with brilliant harbour vistas.

## Eating

**Stromness Café-Bar** (Victoria St; mains £2.50-7; ☼ breakfast, lunch & dinner) This quirky little space, with attached shop, is good for a snack or something more substantial. Orkney beer is available and best enjoyed on the back terrace overlooking the water.

**Julia's Café & Bistro** ( ☎ 850904; 20 Ferry Rd; mains lunch £5-8; ☼ 9am-5pm Mon-Sat, 10am-5pm Sun) A light and airy eatery, Julia's can get frantic when the tour buses converge. Featuring local produce wherever possible, meals are not sophisticated affairs but they are tasty, filling and reasonably priced. For lunch, chow down on melts, open crab or salmon sandwiches, crisp salads and a homemade nut roast for vegetarians. Follow up with Orkney fudge cheesecake.

### GEORGE MACKAY BROWN (1921–96)

One of Scotland's finest 20th-century poets, George Mackay Brown was born in Stromness and spent most of his life drawing inspiration for poems, stories and books from his native islands. Many of his writings are about protecting Orkney's culture from the relentless progress he saw unfolding in Scotland. One of his best-known works, a novel called *Greenvoe,* published in 1972, is about Orcadian life being threatened by a mystifying nuclear development called Black Star. His last novel, *Beside the Ocean of Time,* published in 1994, was shortlisted for the Booker Prize. If you're interested in learning more about the great man, pick up a copy of *George Mackay Brown: The Life* by Maggie Fergusson, published in 2006.

**Bistro 76** ( ☎ 851803; 76 Victoria St; starters £4, mains £8.50; ☽ dinner Mon-Sat) This is an intimate cellar restaurant with a standout menu that will entice most palates through the door (from steak lovers to vegetarians). It's located under the Orca Hotel.

**Stromness Hotel** (bar meals £7, restaurant mains £8-15; ☽ lunch & dinner) The Stromness Hotel does excellent seafood dishes fused with tastes of the Orient (try the seafood chow mein), and there are vegetarian options. You can toast the toes in the Flattie Bar downstairs.

**Hamnavoe Restaurant** ( ☎ 850606; 35 Graham Pl; starters £7, mains £13-16; ☽ dinner Tue-Sat Apr-Sep) Taking itself pretty seriously, Stromness' gourmet restaurant uses local Orcadian produce and is especially good for seafood. Dining takes place among the crisp linen of its elegant dining room.

Self-caterers can stock up at the **Co-op supermarket** (North End Rd).

## Getting There & Away

For information on ferries to Scrabster, Lerwick and Aberdeen, see p405. For bus services, see p407.

## WEST & NORTH MAINLAND

☎ 01856

This part of Orkney is sprinkled with outstanding prehistoric monuments, many of them in the care of HS.

## Stenness

The scattered village of Stenness, about 4 miles northeast of Stromness, consists of little more than some houses, a petrol station and a hotel. Around it, however, are some of the most captivating prehistoric monuments on Orkney, easily accessible using the regular bus service between Stromness and Kirkwall (p411). For an idea of the wealth of Orkney's prehistoric past, keep an eye out for single standing stones in pastureland around Stenness and Brodgar – weird sentrylike figures whose past relevance has been long forgotten.

Just 500m north of the Stenness crossroads, on the B9055, are the **Standing Stones of Stenness**. Only four of the original 12 mighty slabs of this prehistoric stone circle remain erect. Fenced off from the world outside, just like the sheep in the next field, the stones are impressive for their sheer size (one is over 5m high) and, of course, age – they were erected around 2500 BC.

A short walk to the east are the excavated remains of **Barnhouse Neolithic Village**, thought to have been inhabited by the builders of Maes Howe.

## Maes Howe

Egypt has the pyramids, Scotland has **Maes Howe** (HS; ☎ 761606; adult/child £5/2.50; ☽ 9.30am-5pm Apr-Sep, 9.30am-4pm Oct-Mar). Constructed about 5000 years ago, it's the finest chambered tomb in Western Europe. A long, low stone passage leads into a chamber in the centre of an earth-covered mound, which is over 6.7m high and 35m across. The size of the local sandstone slabs used, and the skill with which they were laid, is mind-boggling. During the winter solstice, Maes Howe takes on Indiana Jones–esque qualities as blood-red sunsets align themselves with the passage, striking a cairn entrance at the rear of the chamber with alarming precision. These sunsets are recorded live at www.maeshowe.co.uk in December and January.

In the 12th century, Vikings returning from the Crusades broke into the tomb, searching for treasure. They found none but left a wonderfully earthy collection of graffiti, carved in runes on the walls of the tomb, including 'Thorni bedded Helgi' – some things never change. There's also some Viking artwork here, including a crusader cross, a lion, a walrus and a knotted serpent.

Entry is through a timed ticketing system (due to the popularity of the site) and includes an excellent 45-minute guided tour, filling your mind with both awe and questions about this astonishing place. Buy your ticket across the road at Tormiston Mill. Maes Howe is about 10 minutes' walk east of the Stenness crossroads.

## Ring of Brodgar

Situated about a mile north of Stenness, along the road towards Skara Brae, is this wide circle of **standing stones** (admission free; ☽ 24hr), some over 5m tall. Twenty-two of the original 60 stones still stand among the heather. These mysterious giants, their curious shapes mutilated by years of climatic onslaught, fire the imagination – what were they for? On a grey day with dark clouds thudding low across the sky, the stones look secretive and seem to be almost sneering at the jostling summer crowds. Raised skyward 4500 years ago, the stones still attract the forces of nature – on 5 June 1980 one was struck by lightning.

## Skara Brae & Skaill House

A visit to extraordinary **Skara Brae** (HS; ☎ 841815; Bay of Skaill; adult/child £5.50/2.75, joint ticket with Skaill House £6.50/3.25; ☒ 9.30am-5.30pm Apr-Sep, 9.30am-4.30pm Oct-Mar) offers the best opportunity in Scotland for a glimpse of Stone Age life. Idyllically situated by a sandy bay 8 miles north of Stromness, and predating the pyramids of Giza and Stonehenge, Skara Brae is northern Europe's best-preserved prehistoric village.

Even the stone furniture – beds, boxes and dressers – has survived the 5000 years since a community lived and breathed here. It was hidden until 1850, when waves whipped up by a severe storm eroded the sand and grass above the beach, exposing the houses underneath. There's an excellent interactive exhibit and short video, arming visitors with facts and theory, which will enhance the impact of the site. The official guidebook, available from the visitors centre, includes a good self-guided tour.

The joint ticket will also get you into **Skaill House** ( ☒ Apr-Sep), an early-17th-century mansion and the former home of the laird of Breckness, who discovered Skara Brae. The library here has secret shelves behind the book shelves – straight out of a spy movie! The porthole window exemplifies just how thick the outer walls are and the property is built on the site of a Pictish graveyard. Upstairs rooms afford lovely views.

Buses run to Skara Brae from Kirkwall and Stromness (May to September only). It's possible to walk along the coast from Stromness to Skara Brae via Yesnaby and the Broch of Borwick (9 miles).

## Yesnaby Sea Stacks

Six miles north of Stromness are some spectacular but easy coastal walks (the Stromness tourist office has details). Less than half a mile south of the car park at Yesnaby is the Yesnaby Castle sea stack. Watch out during the nesting season in early summer when dive-bombing sea birds determinedly protect their nests.

## Birsay

The small village of Birsay, with a shop and a post office, is 6 miles north of Skara Brae. The ruins of the **Earl's Palace** (admission free; ☒ 24hr), built in the 16th century by the despotic Robert Stewart, earl of Orkney, dominate the village centre. Today it's a mass of half walls and crumbling columns, the latter climbing like dilapidated chimney stacks. Nevertheless, the size of the palace is impressive, matching the reputed ego and tyranny of its former inhabitant.

At low tide (check tide times at the shop in Earl's Palace) you can walk out to the **Brough of Birsay** (HS; ☎ 841815; adult/child £3/1.50; ☒ 9.30am-5.30pm mid-Jun–Sep), about 0.75 miles northwest of the Earl's Palace. On the island, you'll find the extensive ruins of a Norse settlement and the 12th-century St Peter's Church.

**Links House** ( ☎ 721221; www.ewaf.co.uk; The Palace; s/d £35/60), a doting old property right in the village of Birsay, has bright, character-filled rooms (mind your head), some with en suite. There's a guest lounge and light-flooded conservatory for reflecting over the day's events.

Or try the family-run **Barony Hotel** ( ☎ 721327; www.baronyhotel.com; Birsay; r per person £35; ☒ May-Sep), overlooking the Loch of Boardhouse, about half a mile south of Birsay. This groaning old place has seen better days, but it's a lot better on the inside than it looks. It also has a beautiful, tranquil, loch-side location – recommended for anglers.

## Evie

On an exposed headland at Aikerness, a 1.5-mile walk northeast from the straggling village of Evie, you'll find the **Broch of Gurness** (HS; ☎ 751414; adult/child £4.50/2.25; ☒ 9.30am-5.30pm Apr-Sep). Built around 100 BC, it's the best-preserved example of a fortified stone tower in Orkney. Surrounding it are the shells of houses, discernable by the hearths in the centre of each. The small visitors' centre helps unravel the mysteries of this ancient culture.

**Eviedale Cottages & Campsite** ( ☎ /fax 751270; eviedale@orkney.com; Dyke Farm, Evie; camp sites £4.50-8.50, self-catering cottages per week £280-320; ☒ camping ground Apr-Sep), at the northern end of the village, has a good grassed area for camping, with picnic tables. This would suit people looking to avoid the larger municipal sites – no laundry, dogs or caravans. Next door is self-catering accommodation in excellent, renovated farm cottages.

**Woodwick House** ( ☎ 751330; www.woodwickhouse .co.uk; Evie; s £32, d £64-96) has large, stark rooms in a relaxed country house. The building is set in gorgeous gardens, where guests can catch glimpses of the sea. When you're feeling peckish, there are three-course homemade dinners (£28) using Orcadian produce, and an à la carte menu offering delights such as Orkney sirloin steak with a grilled stilton and caramelised-onion topping. It's a top place to treat yourself and that someone special.

## HOY
☎ 01856

Orkney's second-largest island, Hoy (the name means 'High Island'), got the lion's share of this archipelago's scenic beauty. Shallow turquoise bays lace the perimeter, while peat and moorland cover Orkney's highest hills. The highest point is Ward Hill (479m), in the north of Hoy. This dramatic landscape can be accessed on foot or by wheels, and will tempt hands to cameras. Note that the ferry service from Mainland gets very busy over summer – book ahead.

### Sights
The northern part of the island boasts spectacular coastal scenery, including some of Britain's highest vertical cliffs – St John's Head on the northwest coast rises 346m. Hoy is probably best known for the **Old Man of Hoy**, a 137m-high rock stack that can be seen from the Scrabster-Stromness ferry. The northern part of Hoy has been maintained as a nature reserve by the Royal Society for the Protection of Birds (RSPB) since 1983.

**Lyness**, on the eastern side of Hoy, was an important naval base during both world wars, when the British Grand Fleet was based in Scapa Flow. With the dilapidated remains of buildings and an uninspiring outlook towards the oil terminal on Flotta Island, this isn't a pretty place. However, the **Scapa Flow Visitor Centre** (Lyness Interpretation Centre; ☎ 791300; admission by donation; ⊙ 9am-4.30pm Mon-Fri & 10.30am-4pm Sun) is a fascinating naval museum and photographic display, located in an old pumphouse that once fed fuel to the ships.

### Activities
First scaled in 1966, the **Old Man of Hoy** is a rock-climber's delight. The easiest approach to the Old Man is from Rackwick Bay, a two- to three-hour walk by road from Moaness Pier (in Hoy village on the east coast, where the ferries dock) through the beautiful **Rackwick Glen**. You'll pass the 5000-year-old **Dwarfie Stone**, the only example of a rock-cut tomb in Scotland and, according to Sir Walter Scott, the favourite residence of Trolld, a dwarf from

Norse legend. On your return you can take the path via the **Glens of Kinnaird** and **Berriedale Wood**, Scotland's most northerly tuft of native forest.

The most popular walk climbs steeply westwards from Rackwick Bay, then curves northwards, descending gradually to the edge of the cliffs opposite the Old Man of Hoy. Allow seven hours for the return trip from Moaness Pier, or three hours from Rackwick, a village on the west coast – there's a hostel here from where the walk begins.

### Sleeping & Eating
**Rackwick Youth Hostel** ( ☎ 873535 ext 2404 office hours only; Rackwick; dm adult/child £10/8.70; ⊙ Apr-Sep) The Rackwick, 6 miles from the ferry at Moaness, is a snug (two four-bed dorms), clean place, popular with walkers. You'll need your own sleeping bag and supplies. The warden wanders in to collect your dosh in the evening.

**Hoy Youth Hostel** ( ☎ 873535 ext 2404 office hours only; Moaness; dm adult/child £12.60/9.70) This is a pretty schmick place with an enviable location, around 15 minutes' walk from Moaness Pier, at the base of the rugged Cuilags. Rooms come with twin beds and a bunk bed, or there are family rooms, all with en suite. Good special offers from April to June.

**Old Hall Cottage** ( ☎ 701213; www.oldhallcottage.co.uk; Longhope; B&B from £20, cottage per wk £315) If you're after a self-catering option, check out this old renovated hall with impeccable facilities, gorgeous gardens and lovely views. It's a good spot for a zen moment.

**Quoydale** ( ☎ 791315; www.orkneyaccommodation.co.uk; s/d from £20/36) There are several B&Bs on the island, including the welcoming Quoydale, nestled at the base of Ward Hill on a working farm one mile from the ferry terminal. It has spectacular views over Scapa Flow and offers tours and a taxi service.

**Stromabank Hotel** ( ☎ 701494; www.stromabank.co.uk; Longhope; bar meals £6-10; ⊙ lunch Sat & Sun, dinner Fri-Wed) The small, atmospheric Stromabank offers tasty home-cooked meals using lots of local produce, from its small menu.

Groceries can be bought at the shops in Lyness and Longhope.

### Getting There & Away
**Orkney Ferries** ( ☎ 850624) runs passenger ferries between Stromness and Moaness Pier (£3.50, 30 minutes, two to five daily May to September). There's a reduced schedule from October

to April. In the other direction, the service departs 30 minutes after its arrival on Hoy.

There's also a frequent **car ferry** ( ☎ 811397) to Lyness (Hoy) from Houton on Mainland (passenger/car £3.50/10, 40 minutes, up to six daily Monday to Friday, two or three Saturday and Sunday). The more limited Sunday service runs from May to September.

### Getting Around

Transport on Hoy is very limited. **North Hoy Transport** ( ☎ 791315) runs a minibus service between Rackwick and Moaness, meeting the 10am weekday ferry from Stromness. Otherwise, call the same number for a taxi service.

You can hire mountain bikes at **Moaness pier** ( ☎ 791225; per day £8). Hitching is possible, but on this island there are more sheep than cars.

## NORTHERN ISLANDS

The group of windswept islands north of Mainland provides a refuge for migrating birds and a nesting ground for sea birds; there are several RSPB reserves. Some of the islands are also rich in archaeological sites, but it's the beautiful scenery, with wonderful white-sand beaches and lime-green to azure seas, that is the main attraction.

The tourist offices in Kirkwall and Stromness have the useful *Islands of Orkney* brochure with maps and details of these islands. Note that the 'ay' at the end of each island name (from the Old Norse for 'island') is pronounced 'ee' (Shapinsay is pronounced *shap*-in-see).

**Orkney Ferries** ( ☎ 01856-872044) enables you to make day trips to many of the islands from Kirkwall on most days of the week (Friday only to North Ronaldsay), but it's really worth staying for at least a few nights.

### Shapinsay

☎ 01856 / pop 300

Just 20 minutes by ferry from Kirkwall, Shapinsay is a low-lying, intensively cultivated island with a superb castle. There are two general stores and a post office.

**Balfour Castle** ( ☎ 711282; www.balfourcastle.com; Balfour Village; adult/child £18/9), completed in 1848 in the turreted Scottish Baronial style, is Shapinsay's most impressive draw-card. Guided tours (2.15pm Sunday from May to September) must be booked in advance; the price includes the ferry, admission to the castle and afternoon tea.

It's also possible to stay at **Balfour Castle** ( ☎ 711282; www.balfourcastle.com; Balfour Village; B&B incl dinner per person from £100), in the grand, old-fashioned Victorian rooms, with the added attraction that you are, of course, spending the night in a castle. A boat is available for guests for island trips, bird-watching and sea fishing.

About 4 miles from the pier, at the far northeastern corner of the island, is the Iron Age **Burroughston Broch** (admission free; ☽ 24hr), one of the best-preserved brochs (defensive towers) in Orkney.

**Girnigoe** ( ☎ 711256; jean@girnigoe.net; Girnigoe; r per person £25) is a friendly, traditional farmhouse at the northern end of the island. The breakfasts (with Mrs Wallace's homemade bread and jam) and local kippers are excellent and dinner is also available.

Orkney Ferries operates a ferry from Kirkwall (passenger/car £3.50/10, 25 minutes, six daily Monday to Friday, four or five Saturday and Sunday May to September). Services are limited in winter.

### Rousay

☎ 01856 / pop 200

History buffs will adore this hilly island. Lying close to Mainland's northeast, it's known as 'the Egypt of the North' for its numerous archaeological sites. Most of the island is classed as a Site of Special Scientific Interest (SSSI), but it also has the important **Trumland RSPB Reserve** and three trout-fishing lochs. Cycling around the island's one road gives you magnificent views of seacliffs, Egilsay and especially Mainland, where green velvet-clad hills heave themselves out of the icy North Sea.

Marion's shop, and a post office that looks like a hen coop, are at Sourin, 2.5 miles north of the pier.

#### SIGHTS

West of the pier are the prehistoric burial cairns (piles of stones to mark a path or junction) of **Taversoe Tuick**, **Blackhammer**, **Knowe of Yarso** and Midhowe Cairn.

**Midhowe Cairn** is an extraordinary burial cairn, containing the remains of 25 people. Dating from the 3rd millennium BC, the 'Great Ship of Death', as it's called, is the longest chambered cairn in Orkney. Bird and animal bones accompany the human remains, perhaps meant as food for the deceased. It's housed inside a modern barnlike building, about 5.5 miles west of the pier, and a half-mile walk down from the road.

Nearby **Midhowe Broch** (admission free; ☼ 24hr) is the best example of a broch in Orkney. The tourist offices on Mainland have the useful *Westness Walk* leaflet describing the mile-long walk from Midhowe Cairn to Westness Farm. It outlines 5000 years of Orkney history and includes Viking and Pictish burial sites.

**Trumland House** (gardens £1.50; ☼ 10am-5pm Mon-Fri May-Sep) is probably the largest private house in Orkney and is currently undergoing extensive restoration. The grounds, with their thicket of native trees, are worth a stroll – you enter the walled garden through a medieval gate.

### SLEEPING & EATING

**Trumland Farm Hostel** ( ☎ 821252; Trumland Farm; camp sites £5, dm £10, bedding extra £2) On an organic farm half a mile west of the ferry, this hostel offers great views and accommodation in two tidy but cramped six-bed dormitories (and one single room). Excellent self-catering facilities are also available. It's private from the rest of the farm.

**Taversoe Hotel** ( ☎ 821325; www.taversoehotel .co.uk; s/d £35/60) This hotel is about 2 miles southwest of the pier. There's one twin with en suite but no view, or two doubles with shared bathroom and each with brilliant views; all are being refurbished. There are panoramic views from the dining room – the perfect place to munch on a home-cooked pizza. Mains cost £4 to £7 and takeaway food is also available. The restaurant is closed Mondays.

**Pier Restaurant** ( ☎ 821359; snacks £3, mains £7; ☼ 11am-11pm Mon, Tue & Thu, 11am-6.30pm Wed & Sun, 11am-1am Fri & Sat) By the pier, this is an ideal spot for a bar meal, snack or dram of whisky to warm the insides while you wait for the ferry.

### GETTING THERE & AROUND

A small **car ferry** ( ☎ 751360) connects Tingwall on Mainland with Rousay (passenger/car £3.50/10, 30 minutes, up to six daily) and the nearby islands of Egilsay and Wyre.

**Rousay Transport** ( ☎ 821234) offers a taxi tour of the island for £21 (up to four people). There's also a minibus tour, which includes guided visits to the historic sites on Tuesday and Thursday (£16 for adults, £35 for a family).

Bikes can be rented for £7 per day from Trumland Farm.

## Egilsay & Wyre

These two small islands lie east of Rousay. On **Egilsay** (population 37), a cenotaph marks the spot where Earl Magnus was murdered in 1117. After his martyrdom, pilgrims flocked to the island, and **St Magnus Church**, now roofless, was built. Today it provides a rare example of a round-towered Viking church. Much of Egilsay is an RSPB reserve; listen for the corncrakes at the southern end of the island.

**Wyre** (population 18) is even smaller than Egilsay. It was the domain of the Viking baron Kolbein Hruga ('Cubbie Roo'); the ruins of his castle, built around 1145, and the nearby 12th-century **St Mary's Chapel**, can be visited free. Seal sightings at the beach on Wyre's western sliver are virtually guaranteed. These two islands are reached on the Rousay–Tingwall ferry (see left).

## Stronsay

☎ 01857 / pop 350

A peaceful and attractive island, Stronsay draws seals, migratory birds and tourists, the latter coming to walk or pedal over its beautiful landscapes and four curving bays. In the 19th century, Whitehall harbour became one of Scotland's major herring ports, but then the fisheries collapsed in the 1930s.

### SIGHTS & ACTIVITIES

The old **Stronsay Fish Mart** ( ☎ 616386; Whitehall; admission free; ☼ 11am-6pm Mon & Wed, 11am-7pm Thu-Sat & 10am-7pm Sun May-Sep) now houses a herring industry interpretation centre, designed to take visitors back to the herring boom days. There's also a hostel and café here.

Just across the harbour from Whitehall is the small island of **Papa Stronsay**, where Earl Rognvald Brusason was murdered in 1046. The island is owned by a monastic order, the Transalpine Redemptorists; the monks will provide **boat trips** ( ☎ 616389) to the island by prior arrangement.

There are good coastal walks on the island and, in the east, the **Vat o'Kirbuster** is the best example of a *gloup* (natural arch) in Orkney.

At the southern end of the island, you can visit the **seal-watch hide** on the beach. There's also a chance to see otters at nearby **Loch Lea-shun**.

### SLEEPING & EATING

**Stronsay Fish Mart** ( ☎ 616386; Whitehall; dm £11) Part of the island's former herring station has been converted into a 10-bed hostel with shower and kitchen. It's clean and well run, but pretty basic. Bedding is an extra £3 if you don't have a sleeping bag. The neighbouring café serves takeaways, snacks and meals all day.

**Stronsay Bird Reserve** ( ☎ 616363; Castle, Mill Bay; full board/B&B per person £28/20) Birders in particular will enjoy staying at the friendly, comfortable Stronsay Bird Reserve, a 40-minute walk south from the ferry pier. Rates include all the tea and coffee you can drink and ensure hours of conversation with the chatty owners.

**Stronsay Hotel** ( ☎ 616213; www.stronsayhotel.co.uk; Whitehall; s/d from £38/76; ☽ lunch & dinner; ☕ ) The island's watering hole has immaculate refurbished rooms. There's also recommended pub grub (meals from £7) in the bar, with excellent seafood (including paella and lobster) in particular. There are good deals for multinight stays. Dogs welcome

### GETTING THERE & AWAY
**British Airways/Loganair** ( ☎ 01856-872 494) flies from Kirkwall to Stronsay (one way/return £31/62, 20 minutes, two daily Monday to Saturday).

A **car ferry** ( ☎ 01856-872 044) links Kirkwall with Stronsay (passenger/car £6.50/15, 1½ hours, two to three daily) and Eday.

## Eday
☎ 01857 / pop 120

Eday has a hilly centre, with cultivated fields situated around the coast. There is the impressive standing **Stone of Setter** and close by, the chambered cairns of **Braeside**, **Huntersquoy** and **Vinquoy**. Huntersquoy is a two-storey cairn, like Taversoe Tuick (p419) on Rousay. Keep an eye out for the Eday Heritage visitor centre, which should be open by the time you read this. The early-17th-century **Carrick House** ( ☎ 622260; adult/child £2.50/1; ☽ by appointment), with its floor bloodstained from a pirate skirmish, is worth a visit; tours of the house run in summer with advance notice.

It's worth getting hold of the *Eday Heritage Walk* leaflet from the Kirkwall tourist office, which details an interesting four-hour ramble from the Community Enterprises shop up to the cliffs of Red Head in the north of the island.

**Eday Minibus Tour** ( ☎ 622206) offers 2¼-hour guided tours (£9) from the ferry pier on Monday, Wednesday and Friday from May to August. Tickets don't include lunch, and Friday is the best day, as you get more time on the island.

### SLEEPING & EATING
**Eday Hostel** (SYHA; ☎ 622206; Bay of London; dm adult/child £9.50/8.50) Four miles north of the ferry pier, this simple, renovated, 24-bed hostel is like a cross between an army barracks and a church hall. You'll need your own sleeping bag, although cotton bags are provided.

**Mrs Popplewell's** ( ☎ 622248; Blett, Carrick Bay; B&B incl dinner per person £30, croft house per person £25) Mrs Popplewell has a charming cottage opposite the Calf of Eday. There's also a couple of fully equipped, self-catering croft houses nearby sleeping three people each. Mrs Popplewell bakes fresh bread daily, and she serves snacks and meals at her craft shop.

**The Red House** ( ☎ 622282; mains £3-10 ☽ 11am-9pm Wed, Fri, Sat & Sun Jun-Sep; ☐ ) Drop into this group of 19th-century croft buildings for home-cooked lunches, evening meals, local history, internet access and even battery charging!

### GETTING THERE & AROUND
There are two flights from Kirkwall (one way/return £31/62, 30 minutes) to London airport – that's London, Eday – on Wednesday only. The ferry service from Kirkwall usually sails via Stronsay (passenger/car £6.50/15, 1¼ to two hours, two to three daily), but occasionally it's direct. There's also a link between Sanday and Eday (20 minutes).

**Alan Stewart** ( ☎ 622206) runs the local minibus and taxi service. He charges around £5 for a trip along the length of Eday.

## Sanday
☎ 01857

Aptly named, blissfully quiet Sanday is ringed by Orkney's best beaches – with dazzling white sand of the sort you'd expect in the Caribbean. The island is almost entirely flat apart from a colossal sand dune and the cliffs at Spurness; the dunes are 12 miles long and growing, due to sand build-up.

There are several archaeological sites here, the most impressive being the **Quoyness chambered tomb** (admission free; ☽ 24hr), similar to Maes Howe (see p416) and dating from the 3rd millennium BC. It has triple walls, a main chamber and six smaller cells. At the northeastern tip of Sanday, there's **Tafts Ness**, with around 500 prehistoric burial mounds.

### SLEEPING & EATING
With permission, you can camp anywhere on the island.

**Ayre's Rock Hostel** ( ☎ 600410; diane@ayresrock.fsnet
.co.uk; bed £12, with breakfast £16, with breakfast & dinner £22,
camping £4) This place is well appointed, and offers
self-catering or B&B accommodation in the
form of two twins and an en suite family room.
Also onsite is a craft shop and a chippie.

**Kettletoft Hotel** ( ☎ /fax 600217; www.kettletofthotel
.co.uk; Kettletoft; r per person £25-30) The welcoming and
family-friendly Kettletoft is a refurbished elderly
statesman located near the centre of the island.
The pub here serves tasty bar meals for around
£8, leaning towards the seaward side of things,
with lobster even scuttling onto some dishes.

**Belsair** ( ☎ 600206; info@belsairsanday.co.uk; Kettletoft; r per person £25-30) The Belsair overlooks the
harbour and has tidy en suite rooms that are
good value. Its bar meals and evening dinner
feature Orcadian produce, and staff will even
do you a packed lunch.

### GETTING THERE & AROUND
There are flights from Kirkwall to Sanday
(one way/return £31/62, 20 minutes, twice
daily Monday to Saturday). There are ferries
between Kirkwall and Sanday (passenger/car
£6.50/15, 1½ hours, two daily May to September), and a link to Eday.

**Bernie Flett** ( ☎ 600284) hires out bicycles for
£8 per day.

## Westray
☎ 01857 / pop 700
The largest of the northern islands, Westray
is a jewel in the archipelago's crown. With
prehistoric sites, sandy beaches and lovely cliff
scenery, this island is a favourite. The friendly
locals, great places to stay and fresh seafood
entice visitors to linger. The ferry docks at
Rapness in the south of the island, but Pierowall, seven miles to the northwest, is the main
village. It has grocery shops, a post office and
a hotel. For information about island facilities,
call the **Westray & Papa Westray Tourist Association**
( ☎ 677404; www.westraypapawestray.com).

### SIGHTS
Pierowall has one of the best natural harbours
in Orkney – it was once an important Viking
base. The **Westray Heritage Centre** ( ☎ 677414; Pierowall; adult/child £2/50p; ◷ 10am-noon & 2-5pm Tue-Sat
& 11.30am-5pm Sun & Mon May-Sep) has interesting
displays on local history and nature and has
recently added a new wing.

Believe in fairies? You may change your mind
if you swing by **Orkney Faerie Museum & Gallery**

( ☎ 677320; www.orkneyfaeriemuseum.com; admission free,
storytelling 50p; ◷ 10am-5.30pm Mon-Sat, 2pm-4.30pm Sun
mid-Apr–Sep), where a converted old crofthouse
showcases Orcadian folklore and legend with
tales of faeries, wee folk, trows and mermaids.

A half-mile west of Pierowall lie the ruins of
creepy **Noltland Castle** (HS; admission free; ◷ 9.30am-
6.30pm mid-Jun–Sep), a 16th-century fortified Z-plan
tower house. The RSPB reserve at **Noup Head**
coastal cliffs, in the northwest of the island, attracts vast numbers of breeding sea birds from
April to July. There are big puffin colonies here
and at **Castle o'Burrian**, a mile north of Rapness.

### SLEEPING & EATING
With permission, you can set up camp almost
anywhere.

**The Barn** ( ☎ 677214; www.thebarnwestray.co.uk;
Chalmersquoy, Pierowall; dm adult/child £13/9.50, camp
sites from £4; ♿ ) This excellent, intimate, modern, 13-bed hostel is an Orcadian gem. It's
heated throughout and has an inviting lounge,
complete with DVD collection for when the
weather turns foul. The price includes bed
linen, shower and pristine kitchen facilities.
Local advice comes free.

**ourpick Bis Geos Hostel** ( ☎ 677420; www.bisgeos
.co.uk; Bis Geos; dm £11; ◷ Apr-Oct; ⌨ ) Hands down
Orkney's best hostel, it's worth the trek out
here just to stay at Bis Geos. The hostel is
decked out in a nautical theme with old sails
and whalebones and furnished with modern
stuff to keep you comfy. Bunks are individually curtained with rustic hessian. The spectacular surrounds are best enjoyed from the
conservatory. It's about 2 miles west of Pierowall and 30 minutes' hike from Noup Head.
Ask about self-catering cottages too.

**Mrs Groat** ( ☎ 677374; Sand o'Gill; B&B/self-catering per
person £22/32) Friendly Mrs Groat, at the northern end of Pierowall, has two properties that
she lets out as B&B or self-catering accommodation. Each property has a double plus a
two-bunk bedroom – good for families.

**Pierowall Hotel** ( ☎ 677472; www.orknet.co.uk/piero
wall; Pierowall; s/d £24/44, with bathroom £28/60) The comfortable, eight-room Pierowall Hotel is famous
throughout Orkney for its popular fish and
chips – the fish is caught fresh by the hotel's
boats and is available to eat in or takeaway.
Toast your toes by the coal fire in the lounge.

### GETTING THERE & AWAY
There are flights from Kirkwall to Westray (one
way/return £31/62, 20 minutes, one or two

daily Monday to Saturday). A ferry links Kirkwall with Rapness (passenger/car £6.50/15, 1½ hours, two to three daily May to September). There are one to two ferries daily in winter.

There's also a passenger-only ferry from Pierowall to Papa Westray (£6.50, 25 minutes, three to six daily in summer); the crossing is free if you travel direct from the Rapness ferry. From October to April the boat sails by arrangement; phone ☎ 677216.

## Papa Westray

Known locally as Papay (*pa*-pee), this exquisitely peaceful, tiny island (4 miles long by a mile wide) attracts superlatives. It is home to Europe's oldest domestic building, the **Knap of Howar** (built about 5500 years ago), and to Europe's largest colony of arctic terns (about 6000 birds) at North Hill. Even the two-minute hop from Westray airfield is featured in *Guinness World Records* as the world's shortest scheduled air service. The island was also the cradle of Christianity in Orkney – **St Boniface's Church** was founded in the 8th century, though most of the recently restored structure is from the 12th century.

From May to September, **Jim Davidson** ( ☎ 644259) runs boat trips to the **Holm of Papay**, a small island about a half-mile east of Papa Westray, for £5 per person. The main reason for a visit is to see the huge **chambered cairn**, with 16 beehive cells, and wall carvings. You enter through the roof – there's a torch so you can light your way as you crawl around in the gloomy interior.

**Beltane Guest House & Hostel** ( ☎ 644321; papay beltane2@hotmail.com; dm £10, s/d £27/50; ⌣ lunch & dinner), owned by the local community co-op, is the best place to stay on the island. It comprises a 16-bed Scottish Youth Hostel Association (SYHA) approved hostel and a guesthouse with four simple and immaculate rooms with en suite. There is also a small shop and generous lunches and dinners (meals from £7) on offer using Orkney beef, seafood, lamb and veggies. The hotel is just over a mile north of the ferry.

B&B or full board is available at the friendly **School Place** ( ☎ 644268; sonofhewitj@aol.com; s/d £20/38). The conservatory is good for quiet reflection and the owners are happy to impart information about their beloved island community.

### GETTING THERE & AWAY

There are two or three daily flights to Papa Westray (£15, 15 minutes) from Kirkwall,

Monday to Saturday; it's an amazing deal compared with other flights in Orkney – about twice the distance for a fraction of the price (taxes not included). For ferry details, see opposite.

## North Ronaldsay

☎ 01857 / pop 50

All of 3 miles long and almost completely flat, North Ronaldsay is a real outpost surrounded by rolling seas and big skies. The delicious peace and quiet and excellent bird-watching lures visitors here; the island is home to cormorant and seal colonies and is an important stopover for migratory birds. There's also a piteous colony of sheep, kept off the rich farmland by a 13-mile-long wall all around the island and forced to feed only on seaweed, which is said to give their meat a unique flavour.

Powered by wind and solar energy, **Observatory Guest House** ( ☎ 633200; alison@nrbo.prestel.co.uk; dm £11, s £31-35, d £50-60) is a working croft next to the ferry pier, and offers first-rate accommodation and ornithological activities. Note that under-15s are half-price, and under-fours are free. The attached **Obscafe** (meals £4-8; ⌣ lunch & dinner) has piping hot meals and much-needed caffeine injections.

**Garso Guest House** ( ☎ /fax 633244; christine@garso .fsnet.co.uk; B&B per person £35, cottage per person per night £30) is a comfortable B&B and self-catering cottage sleeping five, with open fire and all your mod cons. It's at the northern end of the island, about 3 miles from the pier. Mrs Muir, one of the owners, also offers a taxi and minibus service.

There are two or three daily flights to North Ronaldsay (£15, 20 minutes) from Kirkwall, Monday to Saturday. There's a weekly ferry from Kirkwall on Friday (passenger/car £6.50/15, 2½ hours).

# SHETLAND ISLANDS

The rugged and remote Shetland Islands – a collection of mighty, wind-ravaged clumps of brown and green earth rising from the frigid waters of the North Sea – are Scotland's northerly outpost and feel miles away from anywhere. Mainland is the biggest island with over 100 windswept and virtually treeless islands making up the archipelago.

Far more desolate and cut off than Orkney, the light here is even more changeable than

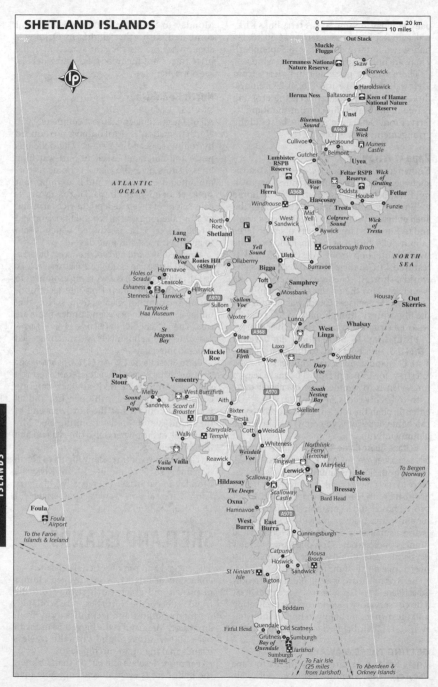

# SHETLAND ISLANDS

0 —————————— 20 km
0 —————————— 10 miles

Out Stack

Muckle Flugga

Skaw

Norwick

Hermaness National Nature Reserve

Haroldswick

Herma Ness

Baltasound

Keen of Hamar National Nature Reserve

Unst

Bluemull Sound

Sand Wick

A968

Cullivoe

Uyeasound

Muness Castle

Gutcher

Belmont

Lumbister RSPB Reserve

Uyea

Feltar RSPB Reserve

Wick of Gruting

The Herra

Basta Voe

A968

Oddsta

Houbie

Fetlar

Windhouse

Hascosay

Tresta

Funzie

West Sandwick

Mid Yell

Colgrave Sound

Wick of Tresta

ATLANTIC OCEAN

North Roe

Shetland

Yell

Aywick

Lang Ayre

Yell Sound

NORTH SEA

Ronas Voe

Ronies Hill (450m)

Ollaberrry

Ulsta

Grossabrough Broch

Hamnavoe

Bigga

Burravoe

Holes of Scrada

Leascole

Hillswick

Toft

Samphrey

Housay

Out Skerries

Eshaness

Tanwick

A970

Stenness

Sullom

Mossbank

Tangwick Haa Museum

Sullom Voe

Voxter

Lunna

West Linga

Whalsay

St Magnus Bay

Brae

A968

Laxo

Vidlin

Muckle Roe

Olna Firth

Voe

Dury Voe

Symbister

Papa Stour

Vementry

West Burrafirth

South Nesting Bay

Melby

Aith

Sound of Papa

Sandness

Scord of Brouster

Bixter

A971

Tresta

Skellister

Walls

Stanydale Temple

Cott

Weisdale

Whiteness

Northlink Ferry Terminal

Vaila Sound

Vaila

Reawick

Weisdale Voe

Tingwall

Maryfield

Isle of Noss

Hildassay

Scalloway

Lerwick

The Deeps

Scalloway Castle

Bressay

Oxna

Hamnavoe

Bard Head

West Burra

East Burra

A970

Cunningsburgh

To Bergen (Norway)

Foula

Foula Airport

Catpund

Hoswick

Mousa Broch

To the Faroe Islands & Iceland

Sandwick

St Ninian's Isle

Bigton

Boddam

Quendale

Old Scatness

Fitful Head

Grutness

Sumburgh

Bay of Quendale

Jarlshof

Sumburgh Head

To Fair Isle (25 miles from Jarlshof)

To Aberdeen & Orkney Islands

on mainland Scotland. Different parts of the island are variously illuminated at any given hour – the window for that perfect photo can be short. The setting is still uniquely Scottish, though, with deep, naked glens flanked by steep hills, twinkling, sky-blue lochs and, of course, sheep with no comprehension of the 'right of way' on roads.

The islands' far-flung location is belied by the activity and charisma of the capital, Lerwick, causing you to forget the 60-plus oceanic miles between you and the mainland. But once you're outside the humming capital, the isolation sweeps you off your feet – frequent thundering gales thrash across the raw landscape and mother nature whips up the wild Atlantic into white-cap frenzies that smash into imposing coastal cliffs.

## Getting There & Away
Unlike Orkney, Shetland is relatively expensive to get to from mainland Scotland.

### AIR
The oil industry ensures that air connections are good. The main airport is at Sumburgh, 25 miles south of Lerwick. There are three to five flights daily between Sumburgh and Aberdeen (one hour) with **British Airways (BA)/Loganair** ( ☎ 0845 773 3377; www.loganair.co.uk). BA flies daily between Orkney and Shetland (35 minutes). You can also fly direct from London (Stansted), Inverness, Glasgow and Edinburgh.

### BOAT
**Northlink Ferries** ( ☎ 0845 600 0449; www.northlink ferries.co.uk) runs car ferries between Lerwick and Kirkwall in Orkney (see p405).

Northlink also runs overnight car ferries from Aberdeen to Lerwick (passenger return £42 to £64, car return £170 to £230, 12 to 14 hours, daily) leaving Aberdeen at 5pm or 7pm.

For details of the ferry link between Lerwick, Torshavn (Faroe Islands) and Bergen (Norway), see the Transport chapter, p452.

## Getting Around
The *Shetland Transport Timetable*, an invaluable publication listing all local air, sea and bus services, costs £1 and is available from the Lerwick tourist office (p426).

### BICYCLE
If it's fine, cycling on the islands' excellent roads can be an exhilarating way to experience the stark beauty of Shetland. It can, however, be very windy (wind speeds up to 194mph have been recorded!) and there are few spots to shelter. Hire bikes from **Grantfield Garage** ( ☎ 01595-692 709; North Rd, Lerwick; per day/week £7.50/45).

### CAR & MOTORCYCLE
The wide roads seem more like motorways after Orkney's tiny, winding lanes. Remember the golden rule when driving: give passing cars a wave. Car rental is cheaper in Lerwick than at the airport.

**Bolts Car Hire** ( ☎ 01595-693636; 26 North Rd, Lerwick) Small cars start from £22 per day for a weekly rental; £25 daily for two or three days.

**John Leask & Son** ( ☎ 01595-693162; www.leasks travel.co.uk/car-hire; Esplanade, Lerwick)

**Star Rent-a-Car** ( ☎ 01595-692075; www.starrentacar .co.uk; 22 Commercial Rd, Lerwick) Opposite the bus station; offers pick-up and drop off at airport and ferry points throughout the Shetland Islands.

### PUBLIC TRANSPORT
There are several **bus operators** ( ☎ 01595-694 100). Call for detailed information on services.

For interisland ferry services, see the relevant Getting There & Away sections.

## LERWICK
☎ 01595 / pop 6900
The capital of the Shetlands stubbornly defies its seclusion from the rest of Scotland with a vitality that's surprising for such an isolated town. The constant influx of tourists and oil workers provides vibrancy and energy, breathing life into the grand Victorian housing that abounds here. Lerwick is the only place of any size in this island group.

Although the Shetland Islands have been occupied for several thousand years, Lerwick was only established in the 17th century. In the late 19th century it was the largest herring town in northern Europe. Today, it's the main port of entry into the Shetlands and a transit point to the North Sea oil rigs.

## Information
**Bank of Scotland** (Commercial St) Has an ATM.
**Gilbert Bain Hospital** ( ☎ 743000; South Rd)
**Lerwick Health Centre** ( ☎ 693201; South Rd)
**Manson's Dry Cleaners** ( ☎ 695335; Kantersted Rd) Charges £9 for a wash and dry.
**Shetland Library** ( ☎ 693868; Lower Hillhead; ☼ 10am-7pm Mon, Wed & Fri, 10am-5pm Tue, Thu & Sat; ▣ ) Free internet access.

**Shetland Times Bookshop** (☎ 695531; 71 Commercial St; ⏲ 9am-6pm Mon-Fri, 9am-5pm Sat) Has every book you could possibly want to read about the Shetlands, with topics from the famous WWII Shetland Bus to how to spot adorable puffins around the islands.

**Support Training** (☎ 695026; 6a Mounthooly St; per hr £2; ⏲ 9am-1pm & 2-5pm Mon-Fri; ⌨ ) Internet access.

**Tourist office** (☎ 693434; www.visitshetland.com; Market Cross; ⏲ 8am-6pm Mon-Fri, 8am-4pm Sat & Sun Apr-Oct, 9am-5pm Mon-Fri Nov-Mar) This friendly office has a good range of books and maps, and a comprehensive selection of brochures detailing Shetlands' activities. *Walks on Shetland* (£6.99), by Mary Welsh, is a good walking guide. There's also a bureau de change here.

## Sights

Above the town, there are excellent views from the battlements of **Fort Charlotte** (Charlotte St; admission free; ⏲ 9.30am-sunset), built in 1665 to protect the harbour from the Dutch navy.

**Shetland Museum** (☎ 695057; Hay's Dock; admission free; ⏲ 10am-5pm Mon, Wed, Fri & Sat, 10am-7pm Thu, noon-5pm Sun) is an impressive recollection of 5000 years worth of culture and people, and their interaction with this ancient landscape. There's a smorgasbord of Shetland treasures, including hanging boats, and you can even pop into the underground home of a 'trowie knowe' (a Shetland mythical creature).

There's a lot of memorabilia and an authentic feel to the **Böd of Gremista** (☎ 695057; Gremista; admission free; ⏲ 10am-1pm & 2-5pm Wed-Sun May–mid-Sep), a restored 18th-century fishing booth located 1 mile north of the centre; the highlight is the chatty old salt who shows visitors around.

The fortified site of **Clickimin Broch** (admission free; ⏲ 24hr), just under a mile southwest of the town centre, was occupied from the 7th century BC to the 6th century AD. It's impressively large and its setting on a small loch gives it a feeling of being removed from the present day – unusual given the surrounding urban encroachment.

The **Up-Helly-Aa Exhibition** (St Sunniva St; adult/child £3/1; ⏲ 2-4pm & 7-9pm Tue, 7-9pm Fri, 2-4pm Sat mid-May–mid-Sep) explains the truly bizarre, annual Viking fire festival (see the boxed text, right).

## Festivals & Events

It's well worth being here for the **Folk Festival** (www.shetlandfolkfestival.com) in the last week of April, or the **Fiddle & Accordion Festival** in mid-October. See the boxed text, right, for

---

**VIKING MAYHEM**

Given the connections with their Scandinavian neighbours, it's not surprising that islanders wish to honour their Norse heritage. And what better way to do it than by burning a replica Viking longship? The **Up-Helly-Aa festival**, which takes place on the last Tuesday in January, is all about fancy dress and pageantry: costumed revellers with flaming torches lug a wooden galley through Lerwick to the designated torching site. Leading the charge is a horde of Vikings wearing sheepskins and winged helmets and armed with axes and shields. This festival dates back to Norse times, when Vikings celebrated the rebirth of the sun at yule by torching a longship in the bay.

---

a description of the wacky **Up-Helly-Aa** festival, which takes place on the last Tuesday in January.

## Sleeping

### BUDGET

**Clickimin Caravan & Camp Site** (☎ 741000; Lochside; camp sites per small/large tent £7/11; ⏲ May-Sep) By the loch on the western edge of town, Clickimin is a small and tidy park with good grassy sites. Rates include the use of the ablutions facility in the adjacent Clickimin Leisure Centre.

**ourpick** **Lerwick Youth Hostel** (SYHA; ☎ 692114; King Harald St; dm adult/child £15.50/12.50; ⏲ Apr-Sep; ♿ ) This hostel, in a grand building with modern facilities, has spacious dorms and is clean and well maintained. Although the kitchen is small, there's a café on site. It's very popular with groups, so book ahead.

### MIDRANGE

**Fort Charlotte Guesthouse** (☎ 692140; www.fortchar lotte.co.uk; 1 Charlotte St; s £20-35, d from £55) This place is like *Dr Who*'s tardis – much bigger inside than it looks from the outside. In a quiet, central part of Lerwick, it has bright and cheery rooms and the best single accommodation in town. Book ahead, as it's very popular. The family room is particularly good value for three people (£55).

**Carradale Guest House** (☎ 692251; carradale@ btinternet.com; 36 King Harald St; s £22-35, d £46-60) It's very friendly at Carradale and perpetually busy. The rooms, although a mix of old and new, are large and well furnished and provide a concoction of comforts for visitors. Couples should ask for the huge family room, which is traditionally decked out and has a private bathroom.

**ourpick Alderlodge** ( ☎ 695705; 6 Clairmount Pl; s/d £37/£54) This large stone building, a former bank, is a delightful place to stay. Imbued with a sense of space and light, common in these gracious old buildings, the rooms are large and, in this particular case, well furnished. The friendly hosts, who are flexible with checking-out and breakfast times, make the place special.

**Glen Orchy House** ( ☎ 692031; www.guesthouse lerwick.com; 20 Knab Rd, Breiwick Bay; s/d £47/74) In a great spot close to the centre but also within a stone's throw of coastal walks, this huge place would be a great spot to treat that someone special. It's a lovely guesthouse and the large conservatory, complete with stunning coastal views, makes a good cuddle spot. Yep, it used to be a convent…put it out of your mind.

### TOP END
**Grand Hotel** ( ☎ 692826; www.kgqhotels.co.uk; Commercial St; s £73, d from £100) With its air of faded grandeur, this bastion of hospitality is 'grand' indeed. Rooms are mostly twins and singles, but there are four double rooms – couples should go straight for No 330, which is an enormous room (refurbished with four-poster bed) with dazzling harbour views. You'll feel like royalty.

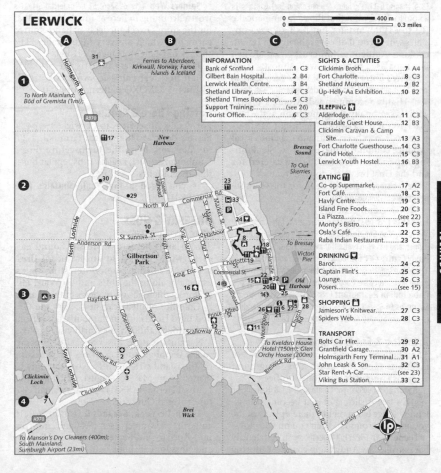

**LERWICK**

0 ——— 400 m
0 ——— 0.3 miles

| INFORMATION | |
|---|---|
| Bank of Scotland | 1 C3 |
| Gilbert Bain Hospital | 2 B4 |
| Lerwick Health Centre | 3 B4 |
| Shetland Library | 4 C3 |
| Shetland Times Bookshop | 5 C3 |
| Support Training | (see 26) |
| Tourist Office | 6 C3 |

| SIGHTS & ACTIVITIES | |
|---|---|
| Clickimin Broch | 7 A4 |
| Fort Charlotte | 8 C3 |
| Shetland Museum | 9 B2 |
| Up-Helly-Aa Exhibition | 10 B2 |

| SLEEPING | |
|---|---|
| Alderlodge | 11 C3 |
| Carradale Guest House | 12 B3 |
| Clickimin Caravan & Camp Site | 13 A3 |
| Fort Charlotte Guesthouse | 14 C3 |
| Grand Hotel | 15 C3 |
| Lerwick Youth Hostel | 16 B3 |

| EATING | |
|---|---|
| Co-op Supermarket | 17 A2 |
| Fort Café | 18 C3 |
| Havly Centre | 19 C3 |
| Island Fine Foods | 20 C3 |
| La Piazza | (see 22) |
| Monty's Bistro | 21 C3 |
| Osla's Café | 22 C3 |
| Raba Indian Restaurant | 23 C2 |

| DRINKING | |
|---|---|
| Baroc | 24 C2 |
| Captain Flint's | 25 C3 |
| Lounge | 26 C3 |
| Posers | (see 15) |

| SHOPPING | |
|---|---|
| Jamieson's Knitwear | 27 C3 |
| Spiders Web | 28 C3 |

| TRANSPORT | |
|---|---|
| Bolts Car Hire | 29 B2 |
| Grantfield Garage | 30 A2 |
| Holmsgarth Ferry Terminal | 31 A1 |
| John Leask & Son | 32 C3 |
| Star Rent-A-Car | (see 23) |
| Viking Bus Station | 33 C2 |

Ferries to Aberdeen, Kirkwall, Norway, Faroe Islands & Iceland

To North Mainland; Böd of Gremista (1mi)

Holmsgarth Rd

A970

New Harbour

Lower Hillhead

North Rd

Commercial Rd

St Magnus St

Market St

Bressay Sound

To Out Skerries

Gilbertson Park

St Sunniva St

Burgh Rd

King Harald St

St Olaf St

Harbour St

Charlotte St

Commercial St

Hillhead

Bressay

Victoria Pier

Old Harbour

King Erik St

Hayfield La

Gilbertson Rd

Bell's Rd

Union St

Prince Alfred St

Church Rd

South Rd

Cairnfield Rd

South Lochside

North Lochside

Anderson Rd

Scalloway Rd

To Kveldsro House Hotel (150m); Glen Orchy House (200m)

Breiwick Rd

Clickimin Loch

Clickimin Rd

A970

Brei Wick

Knab Rd

Cressy Loan

To Manson's Dry Cleaners (400m); South Mainland; Sumburgh Airport (23mi)

**Kveldsro House Hotel** (☎ 692195; reception@ kveldsrohotel.co.uk; Greenfield Pl; s/d £90/112) Shetland's most luxurious hotel overlooks the harbour. It's a dignified small hotel that will appeal to older visitors or couples looking for a treat. Room Nos 415 and 417 are doubles with striking views over the harbour, or if after a twin, try No 413, which has two walls of windows and Shetland views.

## Eating

**Island Fine Foods** (☎ 690606; Harrison Sq; light meals £3; ☺ 9am-4pm Mon-Sat) This clean, modern place is the best spot in town for a freshly roasted coffee. It also does paninis, bagels, tasty pita breads, and wraps with a variety of fillings.

**Osla's Café** (☎ 696005; 88 Commercial St; pancakes £3-4, mains £6-11; ☺ lunch & dinner Mon-Sat) Osla's is a sparky little joint that flips a mean pancake (£3 to £4) downstairs, but it's La Piazza upstairs where you'll discover the joys of Italian cooking. Authentic, thin-crust pizzas are just like Papa used to make…well, almost.

**Monty's Bistro** (☎ 696555; 5 Mounthooly St; mains lunch £5-8, dinner £11-17; ☺ lunch & dinner Tue-Sat, dinner Mon) Highly recommended, Monty's Bistro, with its seasonally changing menu, is the best place to eat in Lerwick. The bright Mediterranean décor, cheery staff and delicious local produce combine to make it an excellent dining experience. Vegetarians are catered for and the Unst brews go down a treat.

Self-caterers should head for the **Co-op supermarket** (Holmsgarth Rd).

Also recommended:

**Fort Café** (☎ 693125; 2 Commercial Rd; fish supper £4; ☺ lunch Mon-Sat, dinner daily) Reliable place for a fish supper, and has won praise from vegetarians.

**Havly Centre** (☎ 692100; 9 Charlotte St; light meals £3-5; ☺ 10am-3pm Mon- Fri, 10am-4.45pm Sat) Mug-a-chino mums and carrot cake. Good spot for a read of the newspaper.

**Raba Indian Restaurant** (☎ 695585; 26 Commercial Rd; mains £6-9; ☺ lunch & dinner) Highly recommended curry house; Sunday buffet is a bargain at £8.50.

## Drinking & Entertainment

The Shetland Fiddlers play at a number of locations, and it's worth attending their sessions – inquire at the tourist office.

**Baroc** (☎ 690995; cnr Commercial Rd & Harbour St; ☺ 11am-1am) A slick spot that becomes the island's lounge bar at nights, there's plenty of the younger set around to keep you on your toes.

**Lounge** (☎ 692231; 4 Mounthooly St) A friendly bar patrolled by Andy Capp characters during the day, Lounge features a variety of live music performances several nights a week, including informal jam sessions.

**Captain Flint's** (☎ 692249; 2 Commercial Rd) This lively bar throbs with happy conversation and has a distinctly nautical, creaky-wooden feel. There's a cross-section of young 'uns, tourists and older locals. There's live music some nights.

**Posers** (☎ 692826; 24 Commercial St; admission £5) At the Grand Hotel, Posers is Lerwick's only nightclub. Show the locals your latest moves to the booming, dated dance music.

## Shopping

Best buys are the woollen jerseys, cardigans and sweaters for which Shetland is world-famous.

**Spiders Web** (☎ 695246; 51 Commercial St) It's worth dropping in here as much for a chat as for the store's excellent array of hand-knitted garments, which are very high quality. The shop is opposite the Queen's Hotel.

**Jamieson's Knitwear** (☎ 693114; 93 Commercial St) You'll find real Fair Isle sweaters with the distinctive OXOXO pattern, from £50.

## Getting There & Around

For details of services to Lerwick, see p425. Ferries dock at Holmsgarth terminal, a 20-minute walk from the town centre. From Sumburgh airport, Leask's runs regular buses that meet flights.

If you need a taxi, call **Sinclair's Taxis** (☎ 694617).

## BRESSAY & NOSS
☎ 01595 / pop 350

Two islands lie across Bressay Sound east of Lerwick. The 34-sq-km island of Bressay (bress-ah) has some interesting walks, especially along the cliffs and up Ward Hill (226m), which has good views of the island.

Colonies of birds can be seen at the Ord and Bard Head cliffs in the south. For serious **bird-watching**, though, it's worth visiting Noss, a National Nature Reserve east of Bressay, to see the huge number of sea birds nesting on the island's 183m cliffs. Noss can only be visited from May to August, when Scottish Natural Heritage (SNH) operates a small visitor centre at Gungstie.

From Lerwick, **Seabirds & Seals** (☎ 693434) runs three-hour cruises (9.30am and 2pm mid-April to mid-September) around Bressay and Noss for £35; book with the tourist office.

It also runs the Shetland Submarine, which is a remote-controlled minisub bringing live colour feeds of underwater wildlife from the caves of Bressay.

**Maryfield House Hotel** ( ☎ 820207; mains £8-11), by the ferry quay, offers bar meals with seafood specialities.

### Getting There & Away

From Lerwick there are daily ferries (passenger/car return £3.20/7.60, seven minutes, frequent) to Bressay. It's then 2.5 miles across the island (some people bring rented bikes from Lerwick) to take the inflatable dinghy to Noss (adult/child £3/1.50, 10am to 5pm Tuesday, Wednesday and Friday to Sunday May to August) – but check with the **SNH** ( ☎ 0800 107 7818) before leaving Lerwick, as the dinghy doesn't operate in bad weather.

## CENTRAL & WEST MAINLAND
### Scalloway

☎ 01595 / pop 820

The former capital of Shetland, Scalloway (scall-o-wah), on the west coast 6 miles from Lerwick, is now a busy fishing village set around bare, rolling hills. It's a little shabby but has an air of authenticity away from the tourist hordes.

During WWII, the Norwegian resistance movement operated the Shetland Bus from here. The trips were very successful, carrying agents, wireless operators and military supplies for the resistance movement and returning with refugees, recruits for the Free Norwegian Forces and, in December, Christmas trees for the treeless Shetlands! The **Shetland Bus Memorial** in Scalloway is a moving tribute on the waterfront, built of stones from both countries. The Norwegian stones are sourced from the home areas of 44 Norwegian men who died running the gauntlet between Norway and the Shetland Islands.

The small, volunteer-run **Scalloway Museum** ( ☎ 880675; Main St; donation requested; ☺ 9.30-11.30am & 2-4.30pm Mon & 10am-noon & 2-4.30pm Tue-Sat May-Sep) is best visited for its Shetland Bus displays, and a peek at Scalloway's glory days.

Down in the village close to the waterfront, the **Scalloway Hotel** ( ☎ 880444; Main St; s/d £55/85) has modern, spotless rooms with small en suites. Some rooms have good views over the harbour and the Scalloway may be a decent option if everything in Lerwick is full.

Being in the North Atlantic Fisheries College, it's no surprise that the **Da Haaf Restau-**

rant ( ☎ 880747; Port Arthur; fish dishes £9-12; ☺ lunch & dinner) specialises in seafood – excellent local seafood at that. It's easily the best place to eat in town.

Buses run from Lerwick (25 minutes, roughly hourly Monday to Saturday) to Scalloway.

### Weisdale

☎ 01595

It's worth dropping into the Bonhoga Gallery in the restored **Weisdale Mill** ( ☎ 830400; Weisdale; admission free; ☺ 10.30am-4.30pm Tue-Sat, noon-4.30pm Sun). The first purpose-built gallery in the Shetlands, it has monthly, changing exhibitions, and everything – jewellery, crafts and paintings – is on sale. It's an excellent place to visit, very friendly, and you're likely to meet some resident artists. There's also a café that's ideal for tucking into Orcadian produce, in a sunlit conservatory overlooking the burn (stream).

On the western shore of Weisdale Voe, south of the mill, are the ruins of the house where John Clunies Ross (1786–1853) was born. In 1827 he settled in the Indian Ocean's Cocos Islands, where he proclaimed himself king.

### Western Side

☎ 01595

The western side of Mainland is notable for its varied scenery: bleak moors, sheer cliffs, rolling green hills, and numerous cobalt-blue lochs and inlets. It's ideal for walking, cycling and fishing.

Out in the Atlantic Ocean, about 15 miles southwest of Walls, is the 8-sq-km island of **Foula** (Bird Island), which competes with Fair Isle for the title of Scotland's most isolated inhabited island. Foula supports 42 people, 1500 sheep and 500,000 sea birds, including the rare Leach's petrel and Scotland's largest colony of great skuas. It's all amid dramatic cliff scenery, particularly the awesome, sheer Kame (372m). There isn't a shop on the island, but centrally located **Mrs Taylor's** ( ☎ /fax 753226; Leraback; B&B incl dinner per person £35) offers accommodation and good food.

Foula is reached by thrice-weekly **ferries** ( ☎ 753226, 743976) from Walls or Scalloway (passenger return £6, car and driver return £14, four hours) and **flights** ( ☎ 840246) from Tingwall (return £50 to £60).

Northwest from Walls, the road crosses desolate moorland and then descends through green fields before arriving at the small crofting community of **Sandness**. Visible about a mile offshore is the island of **Papa Stour**, home to huge colonies of auks, terns and skuas. It's mostly made up of volcanic rock that has eroded to form sea caves, underground passages, arches and columns. Access to the island is by ferry from West Burrafirth (passenger return £6, car and driver return £8, 40 minutes, daily except Tuesday and Thursday), east of Sandness; book with **W Clark** ( ☎ 810460).

## SOUTH MAINLAND

From Lerwick, the main road south winds 25 miles down the eastern side of this long, narrow, hilly tail of land that ends at Sumburgh Head. The waters lapping against the cliffs are an inviting turquoise in many places. If it weren't for the raging Arctic gales, you may almost be tempted to have a dip.

### Sandwick & Around
☎ 01950 / pop 1350

Opposite the small, scattered village of Sandwick is the **Isle of Mousa**, an RSPB reserve. The impressive double-walled **Mousa Broch** (13m) stands on the island – this well-preserved broch was built from local sandstone between 100 BC and AD 100 and features in two Viking sagas as a hide-out for eloping couples! The island is also home to many sea birds and waders; around 6000 storm petrels nest on Mousa, but they're only on the island at night. Common and grey seals can be seen on the beach and among the rocks at West Voe.

From mid-April to mid-September, **Tom Jamieson** ( ☎ 431367; www.mousaboattrips.co.uk) runs daily boat trips (adult/child return £10/5, 15 minutes) from Leebitton harbour in Sandwick, allowing two hours on Mousa. He also conducts night trips to view the petrels.

Back on Mainland, **Hoswick Visitor Centre** ( ☎ 431406; Hoswick; admission free; ⏰ 10am-5pm Mon-Sat & 11am-5pm Sun May-Aug) has a great collection of old wirelesses (including the daddy of them all – the Murphy-type wireless). There are displays on fishing, whaling, weaving and peat casting.

The old-style rooms with shared bathroom are pretty average at the friendly **Barclay Arms Hotel** ( ☎ 431226; fax 431262; Hoswick; s/d £25/50), but you come here for the *craic* (conversation, gossip, fun), not the comforts – there's traditional live music at night in a great bar overlooking the water, and there are real ales on tap.

If you'd prefer a cosy B&B, try **Solbrekke** ( ☎ 431410; Park Rd, Sandwick; r per person £22), which overlooks Mousa Broch.

There are buses between Lerwick and Sandwick (25 minutes, three to seven daily).

### Bigton & Around

Buses from Lerwick stop twice daily (Monday to Saturday) in Bigton on the west coast, but it's another couple of miles to the **tombolo** (a narrow isthmus) that connects Mainland with St Ninian's Isle. This geologically important site is the largest shell-and-sand tombolo in Britain and is an SSSI.

Across the tombolo is **St Ninian's Isle**, where you'll find the ruins of a 12th- century church, beneath which are traces of an earlier Pictish church. During excavations in 1958, Pictish treasure, probably dating from AD 800 and consisting of 27 silver objects, was found beneath a broken sandstone slab. They're now kept in the Museum of Scotland (p86) in Edinburgh.

### Boddam

From this small village there's a side road that leads to the **Shetland Crofthouse Museum** ( ☎ 01595-695057; South Voe; admission free; ⏰ 10am-1pm & 2-5pm mid-Apr–Sep). The years clunk by the wayside when you enter, as you step back into a primitive existence. Built in 1870, it has been restored, thatched and furnished with 19th-century furniture and utensils. The Lerwick–Sumburgh bus stops right outside.

### Quendale
☎ 01950

South of Boddam, a minor road runs southwest to Quendale. Here you'll find the small but excellent, restored and fully operational 19th-century **Quendale Watermill** ( ☎ 460969; adult/child £2/50p; ⏰ 10am-5pm mid-Apr–mid-Sep), the last of Shetland's water mills.

The village overlooks a long, sandy beach to the south in the Bay of Quendale. West of the bay there's dramatic cliff scenery and **diving** in the waters between Garth's Ness and Fitful Head and to the wreck of the oil tanker *Braer* off Garth's Ness.

From Lerwick there are two buses daily to Quendale from Monday to Saturday.

### Sumburgh
☎ 01950

With its clear waters, sea cliffs, and grassy headlands jutting out into sparkling blue waters, Sumburgh is one of the most scenic places to stay on the island. The sandy beach fringed with turquoise waters makes this place seem more like an idyllic Pacific holiday destination…when the sun shines.

## SIGHTS

At the southern tip of Mainland, this village is home to the international airport and **Jarlshof** (HS; ☎ 460112; adult/child £4.50/2.25; 🕑 9.30am-5.30pm Apr-Sep), Shetland's most impressive archaeological attraction. This large settlement, with buildings from prehistory through Norse times to the 16th century, was hidden under the sand until it was exposed by a gale at the end of the 19th century. It's a thought-provoking place, mainly in ruins, but with a fascinating, intact wheelhouse that defies time. You should buy the short guide, which interprets the ruins from a number of vantage points (otherwise a fair bit of imagination is required).

Near Jarlshof you can visit **Sumburgh Head**, an RSPB reserve. The lighthouse here isn't open to the public, but you can view the many birds that inhabit the cliffs below. At various times there are puffins (over 2000 pairs), kittiwakes (1000 pairs), fulmars, guillemots (over 13,000 breed here), razorbills and cormorants. The other important bird-watching area is the **Pool of Virkie**, the bay just east of the airport.

The best thing about a visit to the remarkable excavation at **Old Scatness** ( ☎ 461869; Dunrossness; adult/child £4/2; 🕑 10am-5.30pm Sun-Thu May-Oct, call for winter hr; 🔧 ) is that it's very much a work in progress. A broch from around 300 BC is the centrepiece of the site, which is surrounded by wheelhouses and evidence of later Viking occupation. It's all compelling stuff and ideal for kids. Guides dressed in period costume take visitors into reconstructions of Iron Age houses and divulge all kinds of fascinating facts about life a couple of thousand years ago.

## SLEEPING & EATING

**Betty Mouat's Cottage** ( ☎ 460249; Old Scatness, Dunrossness; beds £10) This is a simple 10-bed camping *böd* (basic accommodation for walkers) affair with potbelly stove, fuel for sale and coin-operated showers. It's by Old Scatness – book at Lerwick tourist office and pay the warden on site.

**Sumburgh Hotel** ( ☎ 460201; www.sumburgh-hotel .zetnet.co.uk; Sumburgh; s/d from £55/70) Next to Jarlshof is an upmarket, country-style hotel with a high standard of accommodation. For a treat go for the St Ninian room with its four-poster bed and stunning views. The bar

meals here (£8; open lunch and dinner) are delicious – pub faves such as steak-and-Guinness pie feature alongside seafood dishes and vegetarians are catered for.

## GETTING THERE & AWAY

To get to Sumburgh from Lerwick, take the airport bus (45 minutes, five daily Monday to Saturday, three on Sunday) and get off at the second-last stop.

# FAIR ISLE

☎ 01595 / pop 70

It's a stomach-churning ferry ride to Fair Isle but worth it for the stunning cliff scenery, isolation and hoards of winged creatures. About halfway to Orkney, Fair Isle is one of Scotland's most remote inhabited islands. It's only 3 miles by 1.5 miles in size and is probably best known for its patterned knitwear, still produced in the island's co-operative, Fair Isle Crafts.

It's also a paradise for bird-watchers, who form the bulk of the island's visitors. Fair Isle is in the flight path of migrating birds, and thousands breed here. They're monitored by the **Bird Observatory**, which collects and analyses information year-round; visitors are more than welcome to participate.

The small **George Waterston Memorial Centre** ( ☎ 760244; Taft; donations welcome; 🕑 2-4pm Mon, 10.30am-noon Wed & 2-4pm Fri May-Sep) has photos and exhibits on the island's natural history, crofting, fishing, archaeology and knitwear.

**Fair Isle Lodge & Bird Observatory** ( ☎ /fax 760258; www.fairislebirdobs.co.uk; full-board dm/s/d £30/44/78) offers home cooking and free guided walks; it's located about 400m from the ferry terminal.

## Getting There & Away

There are **flights** ( ☎ 840246) to Fair Isle from Tingwall (£62 return, 25 minutes, twice daily Monday, Wednesday and Friday). There's also a return flight from Sumburgh on Saturday.

From May to September, the *Good Shepherd IV* ferry sails from Grutness (near Sumburgh) to Fair Isle (£6 return, three hours) on Tuesday, Saturday and alternate Thursdays, and from Lerwick (£6 return, 4½ hours) on alternate Thursdays. In winter, there's one return trip on Tuesday. Book with **JW Stout** ( ☎ 760222).

# NORTH MAINLAND

The north of Mainland is very photogenic – jumbles of cracked, peaty, brown hills blend with grassy pastureland and extend like bony fingers of land into numerous lochs and out into the wider, icy, grey waters of the North Sea. Different shades of light give it a variety of characters. Get the camera primed.

## Voe
☎ 01806

Lower Voe is a pretty collection of buildings beside a tranquil bay on the southern shore of Olna Firth.

In previous incarnations, red-painted **Sail Loft** ( ☎ 588392, 588708; Lower Voe; beds £9), by the pier, was a fishing shed and knitwear factory, but it's now a camping *böd*, with coin-operated showers and fuel for sale. Book at the Lerwick tourist office and pay the warden on site.

How do mussels and a pint sound? Try the excellent seafood, including local salmon, in the appealing, wood-panelled **Pierhead Restaurant & Bar** ( ☎ 588332; Lower Voe; starters £6, mains £10-15; ☼ lunch & dinner), opposite Sail Loft. Eat in the restaurant or go for the cheaper bar meals.

There are buses from Lerwick to Voe (35 minutes, up to six daily Monday to Saturday and two on Sunday during school terms).

## Whalsay & Out Skerries
☎ 01806 / pop 1050

South of Voe, the B9071 branches east to Laxo, the ferry terminal for the island of **Whalsay**. This is one of the most prosperous of Shetland's islands, due to its large fishing industry whose fleet is based at the modern harbour of **Symbister**.

Whalsay is popular for sea angling, and for trout fishing in its lochs. There are also scenic walks in the south and east where colonies of sea birds breed and where you may catch sight of seals.

**Grieve House** ( ☎ 566341; Sodom; beds £7), the former home of famous poet Hugh MacDiarmid, is now a simple camping *böd*. There's no electricity or shower, but there is fuel for sale. Book through the Lerwick tourist office.

There are regular **ferries** ( ☎ 566259) between Laxo and Symbister (£3.20 return, 30 minutes, daily).

Northeast of Whalsay, another thriving fishing community occupies the 2 sq miles of **Out Skerries** (or just Skerries). It's made up of the three main islands of Housay, Bruray (these two connected by a road bridge) and Grunay, plus a number of islets. Their rugged cliffs teem with bird life.

There are **ferries** ( ☎ 515226) between Out Skerries and Lerwick on Tuesday and Thursday (passenger return £5.60, car and driver return £8, 2½ hours), and Friday to Monday to Vidlin (passenger return £5.60, car and driver return £8, 1½ hours), about 3 miles northeast of Laxo.

## Brae & Around
☎ 01806

Accommodation is the reason to stop in the tiny township of Brae. However, you should book in advance – guesthouses are often full, as they mainly cater to oil workers (the upside for solo travellers is that there are plenty of single beds). Pack a bottle of your favourite single malt to keep you company on those stormy nights.

There's fine **walking** on the peninsula west of Brae, and to the south on the red-granite island of **Muckle Roe**, which is connected to the peninsula by a bridge. Muckle Roe also offers good **diving** off its west and north coasts.

**Drumquin Guest House** ( ☎ 522621; Brae; r per person £45-50) is a large, laid-back place with good

---

**BIRD-WATCHING IN SHETLAND**

For bird-watchers, Shetland is paradise. This island group is internationally famous for its bird life. As well as being a stopover for migrating Arctic species, there are huge sea-bird breeding colonies.

Out of the 24 sea-bird species that nest in the British Isles, 21 are found here; June is the height of the breeding season. The **Royal Society for the Protection of Birds** (RSPB; www.rspb .org.uk) maintains several reserves on south Mainland and on the island of Fetlar. There are National Nature Reserves at **Hermaness** (where you can't fail to be entertained by the clownish antics of the almost tame puffins) and on the **Isle of Noss**. **Fair Isle** also supports large sea-bird populations.

A useful website is www.nature-shetland.co.uk. Take care when bird-watching as the cliff-edge sites can be dangerous.

rooms (mix of en suite and shared bathrooms) and chilled hosts. Breakfast is served in a light-flooded conservatory.

Just outside Brae and built in 1588, luxurious, genteel **Busta House Hotel** ( ☎ 522506; www .bustahouse.com; s/d from £75/100, 4-course dinner extra £27.50) has a fine restaurant that's open for dinner and is a gem – it would make a great place to splash out. Refurbished rooms are tastefully decked out, and retain a classy but homely charm. They're all individually designed and named after places in Shetland. Linga and Foula, the former with four-poster bed, are both delightful rooms.

The town's only restaurant, **Brae Indian Takeaway** ( ☎ 522500; A970; dishes £6-9; ☒ dinner Tue-Sun), is an offshoot of the Raba Indian Restaurant (p428) in Lerwick. The chefs' considerable culinary skills give diners a choice of excellent curries. You will need somewhere to chow down as there's no dining on site.

Brae Stores, near the junction in the village centre, is a supermarket and post office.

Buses from Lerwick to Eshaness and North Roe stop in Brae (35 minutes, up to seven daily Monday to Saturday).

### Eshaness & Hillswick
☎ 01806

About 11 miles northwest of Brae the road ends at the red basalt cliffs of Eshaness, which form some of the most impressive, wild, coastal scenery in Shetland. Howling Atlantic gales whip the ocean into a white-cap frenzy before it crashes into the base of the cliffs. When the wind subsides there is superb **walking** and panoramic views from the lighthouse (closed to the public) on the headland.

A mile east of Eshaness, a side road leads south to the **Tangwick Haa Museum** ( ☎ 503389; Tangwick Haa; admission free; ☒ 11am-5pm mid-April–Sep), located in a restored 17th-century house. The wonderful collection of ancient black-and-white photos capture the sense of community here.

At **Hamnavoe**, which you reach from another side road heading north, about 3.5 miles east of Eshaness, is the basic (no showers or electricity), stone **Johnny Notions Camping Böd** ( ☎ 503362; beds £7); book through the Lerwick tourist office. This was the birthplace of Johnny 'Notions' Williamson, an 18th-century blacksmith who inoculated several thousand people against smallpox using a serum and method he had devised himself.

Decent camping sites, light meals (£5 to £8) and shelter from the roaring gales are available at **Braewick Café & Campsite** ( ☎ 503345; Braewick, Eshaness; camp site £6.50; ☒ 10am-5pm Mon-Fri, 10am-6pm Sat & Sun), a stunning spot overlooking St Magnus Bay.

**Almara B&B** ( ☎ /fax 503261; www.almara.shetland .co.uk; Urafirth; r per person £25), just before Hillswick, is a friendly family home with spiffy rooms decked out in wood furnishings. The elevation of the property provides the real draw and the views are just stunning. The single and one of the doubles share a bathroom that has a long, deep tub – perfect for soothing weary bones.

Down on the quay, **Booth** ( ☎ 503348; Hillswick; suggested donation per dish £3-8; ☒ May-Sep) serves vegetarian food in a hippy crofters' house – actually a 300-year-old former Hanseatic trading-post house and one of Shetland's oldest buildings. All proceeds go to the local wildlife sanctuary.

Buses from Lerwick run (evenings only) to Hillswick (1¼ hours) and Eshaness (1½ hours).

## THE NORTH ISLES

Yell, Unst and Fetlar make up the three islands of the North Isles, all connected to each other by ferry.

### Yell
☎ 01957 / pop 1100

Yell is all about colours: the browns and vivid, lush greens of the peaty moor, grey clouds thudding through the skies and the steely blue waters of the North Atlantic, which are never far away. The peat makes the ground look cracked and parched, although it's swimming most of the year. It's a desolate island with some good coastal and hill walks, especially around the **Herra peninsula**, about halfway up the west coast.

Across Whale Firth from the peninsula is **Lumbister RSPB Reserve**, where red-throated divers (called rain geese in Shetland), merlins, bonxies, Arctic skuas and other bird species breed. The area is home to a large otter population, too. The otters are best viewed near the shores of Whale Firth, where you may also spot common and grey seals.

South of Lumbister, on the hill side above the main road, stand the reputedly haunted ruins of **Windhouse**, dating from 1707. About a mile east of here is **Mid Yell**, the island's largest village and a natural harbour. The road north

**ORKNEY & SHETLAND ISLANDS**

to Gutcher passes **Basta Voe**, where many otters inhabit the shores. In the north, around the village of **Cullivoe**, there's more good walking along the attractive coastline.

From Ulsta ferry terminal, the road leads 5 miles east to Burravoe. The **Old Haa Museum** (☎ 722339; Burravoe; admission free; 🕑 10am-4pm Tue-Thu & Sat, 2-5pm Sun Apr-Sep) has a fascinating exhibition on local flora, fauna and military history, and there's a small gallery. It's given authenticity by the musty old stone building (Yell's oldest building, built in 1672) in which it's housed, and there's a genealogy centre for those whose ancestors came from these parts. Yell Crafts is here too, selling Fair Isle woollen garments and some vivid (and reasonably priced) paintings of Shetland scenery.

### SLEEPING & EATING

**Windhouse Lodge** (☎ 702231; Mid Yell; beds £9) Below the haunted ruins of Windhouse, and on the A968, you'll find this well-kept, clean, snug camping *böd* with a pot-belly stove to warm your toes. You can book beds at Lerwick tourist office.

**Gutcher Post Office** (☎ 744201; margaret.tulloch@btopenworld.com; Gutcher; r per person £22.50) This friendly place has cosy rooms and is a stone's throw from the ferry pier. The owner has a definite piggy fetish! It's very cheerful but note that the singles are *very* small. Dinner costs £12.

**Wind Dog Café** (☎ 744321; Gutcher; snacks & light meals £3-4; 🕑 9am-5pm Mon-Fri, 10am-5pm Sat & Sun, dinner May-Sep; 💻) While you're waiting for the ferry to Unst, you can snack at this warm, eclectic little café. It serves up paninis, burgers and hot drinks. There's also a small library inside, ideal if the rain is pelting outside.

**Hilltop Restaurant & Bar** (☎ 702333, Mid Yell; bar meals £6; 🕑 lunch & dinner) An inviting spot to hunker down, simple bar meals (of the fish and chip variety) are served, although the puller is the wonderful views. The bar is a good spot to meet chatty locals.



### GETTING THERE & AWAY

Yell is connected with Mainland by **ferry** (☎ 722259) between Toft and Ulsta (passenger return £3.20, car and driver return £7.60, 20 minutes, frequent). Although you don't need to book, traffic is constant from May to September so it's wise to do so during those months.

Buses leave Lerwick for Toft ferry pier (one hour, two to five daily, Sunday during school terms only). There are connecting buses at Ulsta for other parts of the island.

## Unst

**☎ 01957 / pop 1100**

Unst is a lot smaller but prettier than Yell with bare, velvety-smooth hills and clusters of settlements that cling to their waterside locations, fiercely resisting the buffeting winds. It also feels less isolated and has more of a community. With an area of 45 sq miles it's Scotland's northernmost inhabited island. There's a wide variety of vegetation – over 400 different plant species. Some of the most unusual examples can be seen at the 30-hectare **Keen of Hamar National Nature Reserve** northeast of Baltasound.

In the northwest is the wonderfully wild and windy National Nature Reserve of **Hermaness**. Here you can sit on the high cliffs, commune with the thousands of sea birds and Shetland's largest colony of puffins (best seen in May and June), and gaze across the sea towards the Arctic Circle. The more energetic should take on the superb **cliff-top walk** along the west coast.

The **Hermaness Visitor Centre** (☎ 711278; Shore Station, Burrafirth; admission free; 🕑 9am-5pm mid-Apr–mid-Sep), near the reserve's entrance, has an interactive sea-bird exhibit and provides information on the island's wildlife.

Robert Louis Stevenson wrote *Treasure Island* while living on Unst and the map in the novel is reputedly based on the island. Stevenson's uncle built the lighthouse on **Muckle Flugga**, one of the group of rocks off Hermaness; another of the rocks is **Out Stack**, Scotland's most northerly point.

**Unst Heritage Centre** (☎ 711528; Haroldswick; adult/child £2/free, joint Unst Boat Haven ticket £3; 🕑 May-Sep) houses a modern museum with a history of the Shetland pony, and a nostalgic look at the past. There's a re-creation of a croft house complete with box bed and, for weather-obsessed Brits, a summary of the last 170 years of weather in the Shetlands.

**Unst Boat Haven** (☎ 711528; Haroldswick; adult/child £2/free, joint Unst Heritage Centre ticket £3; 🕑 May-Sep) is housed in a large shed and is every boaty's delight, with rowing and sailing boats, photographs of more boats, and maritime artefacts.

For a swig of the most northerly beer in Britain, drop into **Valhalla Brewery** (☎ 711658; Baltasound; tours £3.50; 🕑 9am-5pm Mon-Fri).

Scotland's oddest **bus shelter**, complete with sofa, TV, books, flower box and decorative ornaments, is at Baltasound – it looks as though someone just got kicked out of home. It even has its own website (www.unstbusshelter.shetland.co.uk). If this was a few hundred miles further south it would be ripped off and graffitied within hours – it speaks volumes of the community spirit that still exists throughout these islands.

### SLEEPING & EATING

**our pick** **Gardiesfauld Hostel** ( ☎ 755279; www.gardiesfauld.shetland.co.uk; Uyeasound; dm adult/child £11/8, tent & 2 people £6; 🕑 Apr-Sep) This 35-bed hostel is very clean, has excellent kitchen facilities and sun-drenched common areas for relaxing. There are dorms with a maximum of 10 beds, a twin and a family room with en suite. Nonresidents are welcome to use common areas. It's always open and is the place to go if you miss the ferry. The bus stops right outside.

**Saxa Vord** ( ☎ 711711; www.saxavord.com; Haroldswick; dm £15, self-catering house per week £250-450) This former RAF base has grand plans, including a natural and cultural heritage centre due to open in 2008. At the moment the well-equipped bunkhouse (seven rooms with one two-bed bunk in each) is open and so are the holiday houses, which would really suit families or groups who want to be in close proximity to each other. There's a restaurant on site that dishes out local produce and pours Unst's Valhalla beer.

**Clingera Guest House** ( ☎ 711579; clingera@btopenworld.com; Baltasound; r per person £18-25) This is one of the best places to stay on the island. It has affable hosts and huge, immaculate rooms with en suites. The twin has a separate sitting room and is terrific value. The owners also rent out a couple of self-catering croft houses.

**Baltasound Hotel** ( ☎ 711334; www.baltasound-hotel.shetland.co.uk; Baltasound; s/d £49/78) The cottage-style rooms inside this solid place are better than the rooms in the nearby chalets, which are a bit cramped. It's also a decent watering hole with a lovely country outlook, and it's popular with tourist buses. Try the local real ale White Wife, named after a ghostly figure seen by the A968, just south of Baltasound.

Self-caterers can stock up at Skibhoul Store & Bakery (Baltasound) or at Haroldswick Shop, where you can heat up and eat your purchase (eg pie or pizza) in its little kitchen.

### GETTING THERE & AWAY

Unst is connected with Yell by a small car **ferry** ( ☎ 722395) between Gutcher and Belmont (free, 10 minutes, frequent).

Haroldswick is 55 miles from Lerwick and, if you don't have a car, you must spend the night on Unst as buses only run once daily.

## Fetlar

☎ 01957 / pop 90

Fetlar is the smallest (five miles by two miles) but most fertile of the North Isles. Much of the island is designated an SSSI. There's great bird-watching here, and the 705 hectares of grassy moorland around Vord Hill (159m) in the north form the **Fetlar RSPB Reserve**. Common and grey seals can also be seen on the shores. The reserve is closed during the breeding season from May to August; contact the **warden** ( ☎ 733246) at Baelans.

Scenic **walking** is possible on much of the island, especially around the bay near Tresta, at Urie and Gruting in the north, and Funzie in the east.

There's no petrol on Fetlar, but there's a shop and a post office in Houbie, the main village. The excellent **Fetlar Interpretive Centre** ( ☎ 733206; Houbie; adult/child £2/free; 🕑 1-5pm Mon-Fri & 2-5pm Sat & Sun May-Sep), near the post office, has photos, audio recordings and videos on the island and its history.

The **Garths Campsite** ( ☎ 733227; Gord; camp sites £4-7.40), 2.5 miles from the ferry, overlooks the beach at Tresta and has great facilities. Nearby is the friendly **Gord B&B** ( ☎ 733227; nicboxall@btinternet.com; Gord; r per person £25, B&B incl dinner £37), with terrific sea views and two twin rooms and one double, all with en suite.

The shop-café in Houbie serves homemade food.

Regular ferries from Oddsta in the island's northwest connect with Gutcher on Yell and Belmont on Unst.

ORKNEY & SHETLAND ISLANDS

DIRECTORY

# Directory

## CONTENTS

## ACCOMMODATION

For a peaceful night's slumber, Scotland provides a comprehensive choice of accommodation to suit all visitors. For budget travel (less than £25 per person a night), the options are camping grounds, bothies or *böds* (see Something Different, p438), hostels and cheap B&Bs. Midrange-budget travellers will find a plethora of comfortable B&Bs and guesthouses (£25 to £50 per person a night). For top-end lodgings (£50-plus per person a night) there are some superb hotels, the most interesting being converted castles and mansions. In Glasgow, midrange and top-end travellers can experience unique, cutting-edge design accommodation – even in some pubs!

Almost all B&Bs, guesthouses and hotels (and even some hostels) provide breakfast; if this is not the case, then it is mentioned in individual reviews throughout the guide.

Prices tend to increase over the peak tourist season (June to September) and are at their highest in July and August. Outside of these months, and particularly in winter, special deals are often available at guesthouses and hotels. Smaller establishments will often close from around November to March, particularly in more remote areas. If you're going to be in Edinburgh in the festival month of August or at Hogmanay (New Year), book as far in advance as you can – a year if possible – as the

---

### PRACTICALITIES

- Leaf through Edinburgh's *Scotsman* newspaper or Glasgow's *Herald,* the oldest daily in the English-speaking world.
- Have a giggle at the popular Labour tabloid, the *Daily Record,* or try the *Sunday Post* for rose-tinted nostalgia.
- BBC Radio Scotland (AM 810kHz, FM 92.4-94.7MHz) provides a Scottish point of view.
- Zone out in front of the box to BBC1 and BBC2 and three commercial channels (ITV1, Channel Four and Channel Five). Regional ITV channels, Scottish Television and Grampian TV, give a Scottish perspective.
- Buy or watch videos on the PAL system.
- Plug into a square three-pin adaptor (different from the Australian three pin) before plugging into the electricity supply (240V, 50Hz AC).
- Use the metric system for weights and measures, with the exception of road distances (in miles) and beer (in pints).

city will be packed. If travelling by yourself, see p445 for more accommodation-related information.

Tourist offices have an accommodation booking service (£2 to £3, local and national), which can be handy over summer. However, note that they can only book places that are registered with **VisitScotland** (www.visitscotland.com/accommodation); there are many other fine accommodation options which, for one reason or another, choose not to register with the tourist board.

## B&Bs & Guesthouses

B&Bs are a Scottish institution. At the bottom end you get a bedroom in a private house, a shared bathroom and a fry-up (juice, coffee or tea, cereal and cooked breakfast – bacon, eggs, sausage, baked beans and toast). Midrange B&Bs have en-suite bathrooms, TVs in each room and more variety (and healthier options) for breakfast. Almost all B&Bs provide hospitality trays (tea- and coffee-making facilities) in bedrooms. An excellent option are farm B&Bs, which offer traditional Scottish hospitality, huge breakfasts and a quiet rural setting – good for discharging urban grit. Pubs may also offer cheap (and sometimes noisy) B&B and can be good fun.

Guesthouses, often large converted private houses, are an extension of the B&B concept. They are normally more upmarket than B&Bs, offering quality food and more luxurious accommodation.

## Camping & Caravan Parks

Free 'wild' camping became a legal right under the Land Reform Bill. However, campers are obligated to camp on unenclosed land, in small numbers and away from buildings and roads (see the boxed text, p57).

Commercial camping grounds are geared to caravans and vary widely in quality. A tent site is £5 to £12. If using a tent regularly, buy *Scotland: Caravan & Camping*, available from most tourist offices. VisitScotland has a free map showing caravan and camping parks around Scotland, also available at tourist offices.

## Homestays

A convenient and increasingly popular holiday option is to join an international house-exchange organisation. You sign up for a year and place your home on a website giving de-

tails of what you're looking for, where and for how long. You organise the house swap yourself with people in other countries and arrange to swap homes, rent free, for an agreed period. Shop around, as registration costs vary between organisations. Check out **Home Base Holidays** (www.homebase-hols.com) and **Home Link International** (www.homelink.org.uk).

## Hostels

If you're on a budget, numerous hostels offer cheap accommodation and are great centres for meeting fellow travellers – in Scotland the standard of facilities is generally very good. The more upmarket hostels have en-suite bathrooms in their dorms, and all manner of luxuries giving them the feel of hotels if it weren't for the bunk beds.

Hostels have facilities for self-catering, and many provide internet access and can usually arrange activities and tours.

From May to September and on public holidays, hostels can be booked out, sometimes by large groups, so phone in advance.

### INDEPENDENT & STUDENT HOSTELS

There are a large number of independent hostels, most with prices around £10 to £16. Facilities vary considerably, but some of the best are listed in this guide and because they are aimed at young backpackers, they can often be great places to party. The free *Independent Backpackers Hostels Scotland* guide (www.hostel-scotland.co.uk), available from tourist offices, lists over 100 hostels in Scotland.

### SCOTTISH YOUTH HOSTEL ASSOCIATION

The **Scottish Youth Hostel Association** (SYHA; ☎ 0870 155 3255; www.syha.org.uk; 7 Glebe Cres, Stirling FK8 2JA) has a network of decent, reasonably priced hostels and produces a free booklet available from SYHA hostels and tourist offices. Although there were some closures in 2006 and other hostels closed for extended periods for

---

**BOOK ACCOMMODATION ONLINE**

For more accommodation reviews and recommendations by Lonely Planet authors, check out the online booking service at www.lonelyplanet.com. You'll find the true, insider lowdown on the best places to stay. Reviews are thorough and independent. Best of all, you can book online.

refurbishment, there are still more than 60 to choose from around the country. Some such as Loch Lomond and Carbisdale Castle are fabulous, with extravagant interiors and a touch of grandeur. Average prices are about £13 an adult, £10 a child, more in summer.

### Hotels

Hotels normally service the top end of the scale and there are some wonderfully luxurious places, including rustic country house hotels in fabulous settings, and castles complete with crenellated battlements, grand staircases and the obligatory rows of stags' heads. Expect all the perks at these places, often including a gym, sauna, pool and first-class service.

Interestingly, midrange hotels, independent or chain, have not really caught on in Scotland and apart from the bigger cities, midrange-budget travellers will often have to splurge if they want a night away from a B&B or guesthouse. The exception is Glasgow, which has many chic, stylish city hotels that fall into the upper midrange and top-end class – these are listed in detail in the Glasgow chapter.

### Rental Accommodation

Self-catering accommodation is very popular in Scotland and staying in a house in a city or cottage in the country gives you an opportunity to get a feel for a region and its community. The minimum stay is usually one week in the summer peak season, three days or less at other times. Details are in the regional accommodation guides available from tourist offices. Alternatively, buy a copy of VisitScotland's *Scotland: Self-Catering*. Expect a week's rent for a two-bedroom cottage to cost from £150 in winter, £175 April to June and £250 July to September. Places in the city range from £175 to over £700 per week.

The following are good places to start your search:

**CKD Galbraith** ( ☎ 0131-556 4422; www.ckdgalbraith .co.uk; 17 Dublin St, Edinburgh EH1 3PG) Offers a wide range of self-catering accommodation, from cottages to castles.

**Ecosse Unique** ( ☎ 01835-822277; www.uniquescot land.com; Lilliesleaf, Melrose, Roxburghshire TD6 9JD) Offers furnished holiday homes all over the country.

**Landmark Trust** ( ☎ 01628-825925; www.landmark trust.org.uk; Shottesbrooke, Maidenhead, Berkshire SL6 3SW England) A building-preservation charity that restores historic buildings and lets them out as accommodation.

### Something Different

Scotland offers a surprising diversity of accommodation and it's possible to bunk down on a cruise around the Hebrides (a good way to see remote St Kilda) or the Caledonian Canal; in converted churches (spooky!); in a *blackhouse* (primitive 19th-century living); and in an art gallery, wigwam or lighthouse. Information on specific establishments is littered throughout this guide and can also be found on the website of **VisitScotland** (www .visitscotland.com/accommodation).

Simple, alternative accommodation can be found at bothies – basic shelters, often in remote places. They're not locked, there's no charge and you can't book. A camping barn (*böd* in Shetland) – usually a converted farm building – is where walkers can stay for around £7 to £10 per night. Take your own cooking equipment, sleeping bag and mat. We have listed many bothies and *böds* in this guide; tourist offices also have lists.

### University Accommodation

Many Scottish universities offer their student accommodation to visitors during the holidays. Most rooms are comfy, functional, single bedrooms, some with shared bathroom, but there are also twin and family units, self-contained flats and shared houses. Full-board, half-board, B&B and self-catering options are often available. Rooms are usually let out late June to late September. B&B costs around £25 to £35 per person. Details are provided throughout regional chapters.

## BUSINESS HOURS

Shops open at least 9am to 5.30pm Monday to Friday and most open Saturday too; with late night shopping usually until 8pm Thursday in the cities. A growing number also open Sunday, typically 11am to 5pm. Even in small towns, supermarkets stay open to 8pm daily and a few city supermarkets open 24 hours. In country towns, some shops have an early-closing day – usually Tuesday, Wednesday or Thursday.

In the Highlands and islands followers of the Free Church of Scotland and the Free Presbyterian Church often observe the Sabbath strictly, and in some areas, notably Harris and Lewis, all shops (apart from one busy petrol station) are closed Sundays, and there are no mainland ferries.

Approximate standard opening hours:
**Banks** 9.30am to 4pm Monday to Friday, plus some are
open 9.30am to 12.30pm Saturday.
**Cafés** 10am to 5pm; in large towns and cities some open
for breakfast from about 7am. If licensed, they may stay
open for dinner too.
**Post offices** 9am to 5.30pm Monday to Friday, 9am–
12.30pm Saturday.
**Pubs & Bars** 11am to 11pm Monday to Thursday, 11am
to 1pm Friday and Saturday, 12.30pm to 11pm Sunday;
lunch is served noon to 2.30pm, dinner 6pm to 9pm daily.
**Restaurants** Lunch noon to 2.30pm, dinner 6pm to 9pm or
10pm; in small towns and villages the chippy (fish and chip
shop) is often the only place to buy cooked food after 8pm.

## CHILDREN

Throughout this book we have listed child-
friendly accommodation and recommended
places and activities suitable for families. Reviews of venues that are child friendly are
indicated by the use of this icon: ⑤.

It's well worth asking in tourist offices
for local family-based publications. The
*List* magazine (available at newsagents and
bookshops) has a section on children's activities and events in and around Glasgow and
Edinburgh; also check local newspapers. If
going to Orkney, pick up a copy of the excellent *Child Friendly Orkney* book (free) from
Kirkwall tourist office, which is jam-packed
with activities, sightseeing and accommodation suggestions.

Children are well received around Scotland, particularly in more traditional areas
such as the Highlands and islands. Another
great destination for families is Dumfries &
Galloway in southern Scotland (see p181),
which has many child-friendly attractions
and B&Bs.

A lot of pubs are family friendly and some
have great beer gardens where kids can run
around and exhaust themselves while you
have a quiet pint. However, be aware that
most Scottish pubs, even those that serve bar
meals, are forbidden by law to admit children
under 14; even in family-friendly pubs (ie
those in possession of a Children's Certificate), under-14s are only admitted between
11am and 8pm, and only when accompanied
by an adult aged 18 or over.

Children under a certain age can often stay
free with their parents in hotels, but be prepared for hotels and B&Bs that won't accept
children; call ahead to get the lowdown. More
hotels and guesthouses these days provide
child-friendly facilities, including cots. Many
restaurants (especially the larger ones) have
highchairs available. Nappy-changing facilities can be found in shopping centres.

The larger car-hire companies can provide
safety seats for children – ask when booking.
Note that attitudes towards breast-feeding in
public are generally a little conservative.

See Edinburgh for Children, p93, and Glasgow for Children, p133, for more on travel in
those two cities with the kids. See also Lonely
Planet's *Travelling with Children*, by Cathy
Lanigan.

## CLIMATE CHARTS

'Variable' is a vague but appropriate way to
describe the many moods of Scotland's cool,
temperate climate. Considering how far north
the country lies you might expect a colder
climate, but the winds from the Atlantic are
warmed by the Gulf Stream.

The climate charts (p440), provide an indication of temperature and rainfall around
the country. See also the When to Go section,
p18, in the Getting Started chapter.

## COURSES

With the remarkable revival of Scottish Gaelic
since the 1980s, a number of courses on the
language and culture are available:
**Cothrom na Fèinne** ( ☎ 01599-566240; Balmacara
Mains, Kyle IV40 8DN) Residential language courses take
place during the first week of the month, year-round. Individually tailored weekends are £100; courses start at £250.
**Royal Scottish Country Dance Society** ( ☎ 0131-225
3854; www.rscds.org) In July and August, this society holds
a summer school in St Andrews; fees from £133 a week.
**Sabhal Mór Ostaig** ( ☎ 01471-888000; www.smo.uhi
.ac.uk; Sleat, Isle of Skye IV44 8RQ) Offers courses in Gaelic
language, song, piping and the fiddle. Courses cost from
£140 per week plus accommodation.

## CUSTOMS

Travellers arriving in the UK from other EU
countries don't have to pay tax or duty on goods
for personal use, and can bring back as much
EU duty-paid alcohol and tobacco as they like.
However, if you bring in more than the following, you'll probably be asked some questions:
3200 cigarettes, 400 cigarillos, 200 cigars, 3kg of
smoking tobacco, 10L of spirits, 20L of fortified
wine (eg port or sherry), 90L of wine and 110L
of beer. Those under 17 cannot import any
alcohol or tobacco. There are different allow-
ances for tobacco products from the newer EU

DIRECTORY

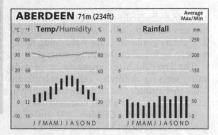

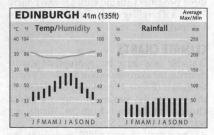

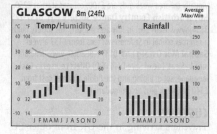

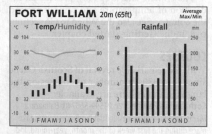

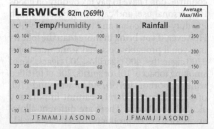

member countries, though (such as Estonia, Poland, Hungary, Latvia, Lithuania, Slovakia, the Czech Republic and Slovenia) – check the website following for further details.

Travellers from outside the EU can bring in, duty-free, a maximum of 200 cigarettes *or* 100 cigarillos *or* 50 cigars *or* 250g of tobacco; 2L of still table wine; 1L of spirits *or* 2L of fortified wine, sparkling wine or liqueurs; 60mL of perfume; and £145 worth of all other goods, including gifts and souvenirs. Anything over this limit must be declared to customs officers on arrival.

For details of restrictions and quarantine regulations, see the website of **HM Customs and Excise** (www.hmrc.gov.uk).

## DANGERS & ANNOYANCES

Scotland has the usual big-city crimes (often alcohol and/or drug related), mainly in Edinburgh and Glasgow, so normal caution is advised. Don't wander unlit city streets at night, and be aware of who is around you late at night anywhere on the streets. Pickpockets and bag snatchers operate in crowded places, but this isn't a common problem.

Never leave valuables in a car, and remove all luggage overnight. Report thefts to the police and ask for a statement, or your travel insurance won't pay out; bear in mind that thefts from cars may be excluded.

One of the most annoying and frightening aspects of touring the Highlands is the sudden appearance and sound of military jets. It's something you never get used to.

Midges and clegs can be annoying problems in the Scottish Highlands and islands; see p458.

## DISCOUNT CARDS
### Hostel Cards

If travelling on a budget, membership of the **Scottish Youth Hostel Association/Hostelling International** (SYHA/HI; ☎ 01786-891400; www.syha.org.uk) is a must (annual membership over/under 16 is £8/free, life membership is £80).

### Senior Cards

Discount cards for those over 60 are available for train travel (see p456).

### Student & Youth Cards

The most useful card is the International Student Identity Card (ISIC), which displays your photo. This can perform wonders, including producing discounts on entry to attractions and on many forms of transport.

There's a global industry in fake student cards, and many places now stipulate a maximum age for student discounts or substitute a 'youth discount' for 'student discount'. If under 26 but not a student, you can apply for the Euro/26 card, which goes by various names in different countries, or an International Youth Travel Card (IYTC) issued by the **International Student Travel Confederation** (ISTC; www.istc.org). These cards are available through student unions, hostelling organisations or youth travel agencies.

## EMBASSIES & CONSULATES
### Consulates in Scotland

Most foreign diplomatic missions are in London, but many countries also have consulates in or near Edinburgh:

**Australia** (Map pp76-7; ☎ 0131-243 2589; Honorary Consul, Mr William Roxburgh, Forsyth House, 93 George St, Edinburgh EH2 3ES) Edinburgh Office does not provide notarial services. Contact the Australian High Commission in London ( ☎ 020-7379 4334).

**Canada** (Map pp76-7; ☎ 0131-473 6320; Festival Sq, 50 Lothian Rd, EH3 9WJ)

**Denmark** (Map p71; ☎ 0131-220 0300; 48 Melville St, EH3 7HF)

**France** (Map pp72-3; ☎ 0131-225 7954; 11 Randolph Cres, EH3 7TT)

**Germany** (Map pp72–3; ☎ 0131-337 2323; 16 Eglinton Cres, EH12 5DG)

**Ireland** (Map pp72-3; ☎ 0131-226 7711; 16 Randolph Cres, EH3 7TT)

**Japan** (Map pp72-3; ☎ 0131-225 4777; 2 Melville Cres, EH3 7HW)

**Netherlands** (Map pp76-7; ☎ 0131-220 3226; Thistle Ct, 1-2 Thistle St, EH2 1DD)

**USA** (Map pp72-3; ☎ 0131-556 8315; 3 Regent Tce, EH7 5BW)

Eight countries have consulates in Lerwick, Shetland Islands. Denmark, Iceland, Netherlands and Sweden are based at **Hay & Co** ( ☎ 01595-692533; 66 Commercial Rd) and Finland, France, Germany and Norway at **Shearer Shipping Services** ( ☎ 01595-692556; off Commercial Rd).

## FESTIVALS & EVENTS

Countless diverse events are held around the country all year. Even small villages have weekly markets, and many still enact traditional customs and ceremonies, some dating back hundreds of years.

VisitScotland publishes a comprehensive list, *Events in Scotland*, twice a year.

The **Traditional Music & Song Association** ( ☎ 0131-667 5587; www.tmsa.info) publishes an excellent annual listing of music, dance and cultural festivals around Scotland.

Highlights of Scotland's many festivals and events are listed here. There's more on these and other events in the Edinburgh chapter (p96) and the regional chapters throughout the book.

### JANUARY
**Burns Night** Suppers all over the country (and the world for that matter) are held on 25 January to celebrate Robbie Burns.
**Celtic Connections** (www.grch.com) A celebration of Celtic music and culture, held mid- to late January in Glasgow.
**The Ba'** A seething swell of islanders and tourists take part in this boisterous and chaotic ball game, held on New Year's Day in Kirkwall, Orkney.
**Up-Helly-Aa** Re-enactment of a Viking fire festival; held last Tuesday in January in Lerwick, Shetland.

### FEBRUARY
**Six Nations Rugby Tournament** (www.6nations .co.uk) Between Scotland, England, Wales, Ireland, France and Italy, held February to March; home games played at Murrayfield, Edinburgh.

### MARCH
**Whuppity Scourie** Residents in Lanark stage traditional events to chase away the winter blues; held 1 March.

### APRIL
**Rugby Sevens** Seven-a-side rugby tournament, held April and May in various towns throughout the Borders region – the first is in Galashiels and Melrose in early April.

### MAY
**Beltane Fire Festival** (www.beltane.org) An incredibly popular, wild and wacky pagan fire festival celebrating the end of winter; 10,000 people descend upon Calton Hill, Edinburgh on 30 April.
**Shetland Folk Festival** (www.shetlandfolkfestival.com) Folk music festival featuring local and international acts, held in early May.
**Burns an' a' That** (www.burnsfestival.com) Celebrations of the great bard have really taken off over the last few years in Ayrshire.
**Spirit of Speyside Whisky Festival** (www.spiritof speyside.com) Five days of distillery tours, knocking back the 'water of life', food, art and outdoor activities; held late April to early May in Moray and Speyside.
**Orkney Folk Festival** (www.orkneyfolkfestival.com) A brilliant time to be in these islands, with concerts, *ceilidhs*

**DIRECTORY**

(evenings of traditional Scottish entertainment), impromptu music sessions and workshops; held in late May.
**Scottish FA Cup Final** (www.scottishfa.co.uk) Deciding match in Scotland's premier football tournament; held at Glasgow's Hampden Park.

## JUNE
**Glasgow Jazz Festival** (www.jazzfest.co.uk) A growing event with big-name jazz acts in venues all over the city – George Sq is particularly good for free jazz; held late-June in Glasgow.
**Riding of the Marches** Horse riding, with parades, brass bands etc, commemorating conflict with England; held in various Border towns, Selkirk is one of the biggest and best.
**Royal Highland Show** (www.royalhighlandshow.org) Scotland's national agricultural show; held late June in Edinburgh.
**St Magnus Festival** (www.stmagnusfestival.com) A midsummer celebration of the arts; music, literature and visual arts; held mid- to late June in Orkney.
**West End Festival** (www.westendfestival.co.uk) Two-week festival of music and the arts; Glasgow's biggest festival.

## JULY
**T in the Park** (www.tinthepark.com) Music festival in the footsteps of Glastonbury; held over a mid-July weekend at Balado, by Kinross.

## AUGUST
**Edinburgh International Book Festival** (www.ed bookfest.co.uk) A celebration of literature held in Charlotte Sq featuring talks from various literary people and local authors; held mid- to late August.
**Edinburgh International and Fringe Festivals** (www.eif.co.uk, www.edfringe.com) Premier international arts festivals, running for three weeks; the city's largest annual event attracting millions each year; held mid-August to early September.
**Edinburgh International Film Festival** (www .edfilmfest.org.uk) A truly international selection of films; from West Africa, to Iran to Peru; held mid- to late August.
**Edinburgh Military Tattoo** Pageantry and military displays running for three weeks – an impressive spectacle and an unforgettable night if you like the bagpipes.
**World Pipe Band Championships** Gathering of over 100 pipe bands in Glasgow.

## SEPTEMBER
**Braemar Gathering** (www.braemargathering.org) Kilts, cabers and bagpipes, attended by the Queen; held early September in Deeside.

## OCTOBER
**Royal National Mod** (www.the-mod.co.uk) Gaelic music festival competition; held mid-October in various locations.

## NOVEMBER
**St Andrew's Week** Held around Saint Andrew's Day (30 November), the feast day of Scotland's patron saint. Includes Scottish food and drink, music and a kite festival on the West Sands.

## DECEMBER
**Hogmanay** Celebrations to greet the New Year, including a huge street party – Edinburgh is the biggest (it's heaving), but there are festivities all over the country on 31 December.
**Stonehaven Fireball Festival** Large procession of fireball-swinging locals who fling their flaming orbs into the sea; 31 December, Stonehaven.

# FOOD
In larger towns and cities we have organised places to eat in this guide by neighbourhood, then price, based on the average cost of a main course on the dinner menu: budget up to £7; midrange £7 to £15, top end above £15. In smaller places, eating reviews are listed in ascending order of cost. Note though that lunch mains are often cheaper than dinner mains, and many places offer an 'early bird' special with lower prices (usually available between 5pm and 7pm). See p438 for restaurant opening hours, and the Food & Drink chapter (p52) for information about tucking into Scottish cuisine.

# GAY & LESBIAN TRAVELLERS
Although many Scots are fairly tolerant of homosexuality, overt displays of affection aren't wise if conducted away from acknowledged 'gay' venues or districts – hostility may be encountered. The age of homosexual consent is 16.

Edinburgh and Glasgow have small but flourishing gay scenes. The website www .gayscotland.com and the monthly magazine *Scotsgay* (www.scotsgay.com) keep gays, lesbians and bisexuals informed about gay-scene issues. Another good info source is the **GLGBT Centre** ( ☎ 0141-552 4958; www.glgbt.org.uk; 84 Bell St, Glasgow); otherwise, contact the **Gay & Lesbian Switchboard** ( ☎ 0141-332 8372; info@lgls.org). See also the boxed texts in the Glasgow (p144) and Edinburgh (p111) chapters.

# HOLIDAYS
## Public Holidays
Although bank holidays are general public holidays in the rest of the UK, in Scotland they only apply to banks and some other commer-

cial offices. Bank holidays occur at the start of January, the first weekend in March, the first and last weekend in May, the first weekend in August, and Christmas Day and Boxing Day. Christmas Day, New Year's Day, 2 January, Good Friday and Easter Monday are also general public holidays. Scottish towns normally have their own spring and autumn holiday; dates vary from year to year and from town to town.

## School Holidays

School holidays (two weeks at Easter, early July to late August, one week in October and two or three weeks at Christmas) are always a busy time, particularly in summer when families often go on their annual break to the countryside. As this coincides with peak tourist season, accommodation is harder to come by and it's often worth booking ahead.

## INSURANCE

This not only covers you for medical expenses, theft or loss, but also for cancellation of, or delays in, any of your travel arrangements. There's a variety of policies and your travel agent can give recommendations. The international student travel policies handled by STA Travel and other reputable student travel organisations are usually good value.

Make sure the policy includes health care and medication in the countries you may visit on your way to/from Scotland. See p457 for advice on health insurance.

Always read the small print carefully. Some policies specifically exclude 'dangerous activities', such as scuba diving, motorcycling, skiing, mountaineering and even trekking.

You may prefer a policy that pays doctors or hospitals directly rather than forcing you to pay on the spot and claim the money back later. If you have to claim later, make sure you keep all documentation. Some policies ask you to call back (reverse charges) to a centre in your home country where an immediate assessment of your problem is made.

Not all policies cover ambulances, helicopter rescue or emergency flights home. Most policies exclude cover for pre-existing illnesses.

Worldwide travel insurance is available at www.lonelyplanet.com/travel_services. You can buy, extend and claim online anytime – even if you're already on the road.

## INTERNET ACCESS

If you're travelling in Scotland with a laptop, you should be able to connect to the internet via a hotel room phone socket for the cost of a local call by registering with an internet roaming service such as **MaGlobe** (www.maglobe.com). Many upmarket hotels offer in-room internet connections via RJ-11 Ethernet sockets or wi-fi. For help and information on getting online from hotel rooms see www.kropla.com.

There is a growing number of wi-fi hot spots around Scotland where you can access the internet with a wi-fi–enabled laptop, including McDonald's restaurants, Starbucks coffee shops and anywhere within 50m of blue-topped BT internet payphones; search for wi-fi hot spots on www.jiwire.com.

If you don't have a laptop, the best places to check email and surf the internet in Scotland are public libraries – almost every town and village in the country has at least a couple of computer terminals devoted to the internet, and they are free to use. In bigger towns and cities the libraries may well have cyber centres, which mean fast connections and lots of terminals – details are given under destination headings throughout this guidebook. In some regions (such as the Highlands) you will be given a user name and password so you can access the internet easily at any library in the area.

Internet cafés also exist in the cities and larger towns and are generally good value, charging approximately £2 to £5 per hour. Always check the minimum charge, though, before you settle in – sometimes it's not worth the 10 minutes it takes to check your emails. Keep in mind that many of the larger tourist offices across the country also have internet access.

## LEGAL MATTERS

The 1707 Act of Union preserved the Scottish legal system as separate from the law in England and Wales.

Police have the power to detain anyone suspected of having committed an offence punishable by imprisonment (including drugs offences) for up to six hours. They can search you, take photos and fingerprints, and question you. You are legally required to provide your correct name and address – not doing so, or giving false details, is an offence – but you are not obliged to answer any other questions. After six hours, the police must either formally charge you or let you go. If you are detained and/or arrested, you have the right to inform a solicitor and one other person, though you have no right to actually see the solicitor or to make a telephone call. If you don't know a solicitor, the police will inform the duty solicitor for you.

In the wake of September 11, the UK parliament passed several pieces of legislation to crack down on terrorist activity, the latest being the Terrorism Act 2006. The result is a curtailment of civil liberties and the government can now detain foreigners suspected of terrorist activities, without charge, for a period of 28 days, and an extension of this period is being pushed by the government.

If you need legal assistance, contact the **Scottish Legal Aid Board** ( ☎ 0131-226 7061; www.slab.org .uk; 44 Drumsheugh Gardens, Edinburgh).

Possession of a small amount of cannabis is an offence punishable by a fine, but possession of a larger amount of cannabis, or any amount of harder drugs, is much more serious, with a sentence of up to 14 years in prison. Police have the right to search anyone they suspect of possessing drugs.

You're allowed to have a maximum blood-alcohol level of 35mg/100mL when driving. Traffic offences (illegal parking, speeding etc) usually incur a fine for which you're allowed 30 to 60 days to pay. In Glasgow and Edinburgh the parking inspectors are numerous and without mercy – NEVER leave your car around the city centres without a valid parking ticket, or you risk a hefty fine – upwards of £30.

## MAPS

Most bookshops stock a range of decent road atlases. If you plan to go off the beaten track, you'll need one that shows at least 3 miles to the inch (1.9km to 1cm).

Alternatively, tourist offices have free maps at a scale of about 10 miles to one inch (6.4km to 1cm), which are adequate for most purposes. For general touring, the clear *Collins Touring Map of Scotland* shows most tourist attractions.

If you're about to tackle Munros, you'll require maps with far greater detail than the maps in this guide, or the ones supplied by tourist offices. Look out for the Collins map of the *Munros*. The Ordnance Survey (OS) caters to walkers, with a wide variety of maps at different scales. Alternatively, look out for the excellent walkers' maps published by Harveys; they're at scales of 1:40,000 and 1:25,000.

## MONEY

The British currency is the pound sterling (£), with 100 pence (p) to a pound. 'Quid' is the slang term for pound.

Several Scottish banks issue their own banknotes. You shouldn't have trouble changing them in shops etc immediately south of the Scotland–England border, but elsewhere it may be difficult. All UK banks will accept them, but foreign banks will not.

Euros are accepted in Scotland only at some major tourist attractions and a few upmarket hotels – it's always better to have sterling cash. For exchange rates see the inside front cover of this book. For information on costs, see p19.

### ATMs

Automatic teller machines (ATMs – called cashpoints in Scotland) are widespread and you'll usually find at least one in small towns and villages. You can use Visa, MasterCard, Amex, Cirrus, Plus and Maestro to withdraw cash from ATMs belonging to most banks and building societies in Scotland.

Cash withdrawals from some ATMs may be subject to a small charge (about £1.50), but most are free.

### Cash

Nothing beats cash for convenience – or risk. It's still a good idea, though, to travel with some local currency in cash, if only to tide you over until you get to an exchange facility. There's no problem if you arrive at Edinburgh, Glasgow, Glasgow Prestwick or Aberdeen airports; all have good-value exchange counters open for incoming flights.

## Credit Cards

Visa, MasterCard, Amex and Diners Club cards are widely recognised, although some places will charge for accepting them (generally for small transactions). Charge cards such as Amex and Diners Club may not be accepted in smaller establishments. Credit and credit/debit cards like Visa and MasterCard are more widely accepted. Combine plastic and travellers cheques so you have something to fall back on if an ATM swallows your card or the local banks don't accept it.

## International Transfers

Money sent by telegraphic transfer (usually at a cost of about £15) should reach you within a week; by mail, allow at least two weeks. When it arrives, it'll most likely be converted into local currency. You can also transfer money by either Moneygram or Thomas Cook. US travellers can also use **Western Union** ( ☎ 0800 833833; www.westernunion.com).

## Moneychangers

Be careful using bureaus de change; they may offer good exchange rates but frequently levy outrageous commissions and fees. The bureaus de change at international airports are exceptions to the rule. They charge less than most high-street banks, and cash sterling travellers cheques for free.

US dollars are probably the best currency to carry (especially if you intend further travel outside Europe), although the euro is an attractive alternative.

## Travellers Cheques

Amex or Thomas Cook cheques are widely accepted and have efficient replacement policies. Bring pounds sterling to avoid changing currencies twice. In Scotland, travellers cheques are usually only accepted by banks.

Take most cheques in large denominations, say £100; commission is usually charged per cheque.

## PHOTOGRAPHY & VIDEO

There are plenty of places in the cities to transfer digital images onto CD; see the Information sections of towns for listings of internet cafés. Both print and slide film are widely available; if there's no specialist photographic shop around, Boots, the chemist chain, is the most likely stockist. The cost for a roll of 36-exposure print film starts from £4.50, excluding processing; processing print films ranges from £4.50 to £9, depending on how quickly you want it back. A 36-exposure slide film costs from £8 (excluding processing) to £11 (including processing). A three-pack of 90-minute Digital 8/Hi8 video cassettes costs around £16; a three-pack of 30-minute DV-Mini cassettes costs £10.

**Mathers** ( ☎ 01204-522186) offers bulk-buy mail-order film at very good prices. A 10-pack of 24-exposure print film is £12, plus £3 postage. Most towns have several shops where you can get print films processed in as little as one hour.

With dull, overcast conditions common throughout the whole of Scotland, high-speed film (ISO 200 or ISO 400) is useful. In summer, the best times of day for photography are usually early in the morning and late in the afternoon when the glare of the sun has passed. For expert guidance pick up a copy of Lonely Planet's *Travel Photography*.

Many tourist attractions either charge for taking photos or ban photography altogether. Use of a flash is often forbidden to protect delicate pictures and fabrics. Video cameras are often not allowed because of the inconvenience they can cause to other visitors.

## POST

Mail sent within the UK can go either 1st or 2nd class. First-class mail is faster (normally next-day delivery) and more expensive (34p for up to 100g) than 2nd-class mail (24p). An airmail letter (60g) to European countries costs 90p, to South Africa, the USA and Canada £1.58, and Australia and New Zealand £1.74. An airmail letter generally takes five days to get to the USA or Canada and around a week to Australia or New Zealand.

If you don't have a permanent address, mail can be sent to poste restante in the town or city where you're staying. Amex offices also hold card-holders' mail for free.

## SOLO TRAVELLERS

Travelling solo in Scotland is quite easy and relatively common. The biggest nuisance for solo travellers on a midrange budget is finding single rooms in B&Bs and guesthouses. Many accommodation owners are reluctant to let a double room (even when it's quiet) to one person without charging a supplement, particularly in the peak season when a solo traveller may be asked to pay double rates. To avoid difficulties, book ahead when you

**DIRECTORY**

can and seek out places with single rooms. We've made many such recommendations throughout this guide.

The easiest place to meet other people, be it locals or tourists, is in the many pubs around the country. In small towns and villages they're usually the centre of social interaction. Although most Scots are not extroverts, they are generally very friendly and welcoming to foreign visitors (especially after a few beers). For budget travellers, hostels are an excellent way to meet other travellers.

Women travelling by themselves should encounter no extra difficulties, as long as sensible precautions observed in most Western countries are adhered to – see Women Travellers, p448, for more information.

## TELEPHONE

The famous red telephone boxes are a dying breed now, surviving mainly in conservation areas.

To call Scotland from abroad dial your country's international access code then ☎ 44 (the UK country code), then the area code (dropping the first 0) followed by the telephone number.

You'll mainly see two types of phone booths in Scotland: one takes money (and doesn't give change), while the other uses prepaid phone cards and credit cards. Some phones accept both coins and cards. The minimum charge is 40p for the first 20 minutes.

All phones come with reasonably clear instructions in several languages. British Telecom (BT) offers phonecards for £3, £5, £10 and £20; they're widely available from retailers, including post offices and newsagents.

Some codes worth knowing:

- ☎ 0345 – local call rate
- ☎ 0800 – toll-free call
- ☎ 0845 – local call rate
- ☎ 0870 – national call rate
- ☎ 0871 – national call rate
- ☎ 0891 – premium rate
- ☎ 9064 – premium call rate

### International Calls

Dial ☎ 155 for the international operator. To get an international line (for international direct dialling) dial ☎ 00, then the country code, area code (drop the first zero if there is one) and number. Direct dialling is cheaper, but some budget travellers prefer operator-connected reverse-charge (collect) calls.

You can also use the Home Country Direct service to make a reverse-charge or credit-card call via an operator in your home country.

### Local & National Calls

Local calls are charged by time; national calls are charged by time and distance. Daytime rates are from 8am to 6pm Monday to Friday; cheaper rates are from 6pm to 8am Monday to Friday, and the cheap weekend rate is from midnight Friday to midnight Sunday. The last two rates offer substantial savings.

For directory inquiries call ☎ 118500 (free from public telephones but 42p per minute from a private phone). To get the operator call ☎ 100. The *Yellow Pages* business directory (with maps) is at www.yell.co.uk.

### Mobile Phones

Codes for mobile phones usually begin with ☎ 07. The UK uses the GSM 900/1800 network, which covers the rest of Europe, Australia and New Zealand, but isn't compatible with the North American GSM 1900 (though some North Americans have GSM 1900/900 phones that work in Scotland). If you have a GSM phone, check with your service provider about using it in the UK, and beware of calls being routed internationally (very expensive for a 'local' call). You can rent a mobile phone – ask a tourist office for details – or buy a 'pay-as-you-go' phone for as little as £20.

## TOURIST INFORMATION

The Scottish Tourist Board, known as **VisitScotland** ( ☎ 0845 225 5121; www.visitscotland.com; Ocean Point One, 94 Ocean Dr, Leith, Edinburgh EH6 6HJ), deals with inquiries made by post and telephone only.

Most larger towns have tourist offices that open 9am or 10am to 5pm Monday to Friday, and on weekends in summer. In small places, particularly in the Highlands, tourist offices only open from Easter to September.

VisitScotland now controls all tourist offices in Scotland (previously they were independently managed through regional tourist boards). This won't affect visitors dropping in on tourist offices to pick up local information (the same cheery staff work in them), although note that many now have a central telephone number. This means that like banks and many other large organisations, tourist offices are now afflicted with that 21st-century disease: if you call a local office, you'll be connected to a central call centre instead to deal with your query.

# TRAVELLERS WITH DISABILITIES

For many travellers with disabilities, Scotland is a strange mix of user-friendliness and un-friendliness. Most new buildings are accessible to wheelchair users, so large, new hotels and modern tourist attractions are usually fine. However, most B&Bs and guesthouses are in hard-to-adapt older buildings. This means that travellers with mobility problems may pay more for accommodation than their more able-bodied fellows.

It's a similar story with public transport. Newer buses sometimes have steps that lower for easier access, as do trains, but it's wise to check before setting out. Tourist attractions sometimes reserve parking spaces near the entrance for disabled drivers.

Many ticket offices, banks etc are fitted with hearing loops to assist the hearing-impaired; look for the symbol of a large ear.

A few tourist attractions, such as Glasgow Cathedral, have Braille guides or scented gardens for the visually impaired.

VisitScotland produces the guide *Accessible Scotland* for wheelchair-bound travellers, and many tourist offices have leaflets with accessibility details for their area. Perthshire tourist offices have the *Access For All* brochure that provides info on transport, parking, activities and accommodation in the Perthshire region.

Many regions have organisations that hire wheelchairs – contact the local tourist office for details. There are many countryside rambles in Perthshire that have been adapted for wheelchair users – see www.perthshire .co.uk.

**Historic Scotland** (HS; ☎ 0131-668 8600; www.historic -scotland.gov.uk; Longmore House, Salisbury Pl, Edinburgh EH9 1SH) has a free leaflet outlining access and facilities for the disabled to HS properties, and also produces a large-print version of HS's promotional brochure.

The **Royal Association for Disability & Rehabilitation** (RADAR; ☎ 020-7250 3222; www.radar.org.uk; Information Dept, 12 City Forum, 250 City Rd, London EC1V 8AF) publishes a guide (£13.50 including postage) on travelling in the UK and has an accommodation website.

**Holiday Care Service** ( ☎ 0845 124 9971; www.holiday care.org.uk; Holiday Care Information Unit, 7th fl, Sunley House, 4 Bedford Park, Croydon, Surrey CR0 2AP) publishes regional information guides (£5) to Scotland and can offer general advice.

Rail companies offer a Disabled Persons Railcard (see p456).

Note that we have used the wheelchair icon ⑤ throughout this guide to indicate attractions and hotels that are wheelchair accessible – see the destination chapters.

## USEFUL ORGANISATIONS

Membership of Historic Scotland (HS) and the National Trust for Scotland (NTS) is worth considering, especially if you're going to be in Scotland for a while. Both are non-profit organisations dedicated to the preservation of the environment, and both care for hundreds of spectacular sites. Throughout this guide the abbreviations HS and NTS are used to indicate places that are under the care of these organisations.

**Historic Scotland** (HS; ☎ 0131 668 8600; www .historic-scotland.gov.uk; Longmore House, Salisbury Pl, Edinburgh EH9 1SH) A year's membership costs from £37/70 for an adult/family, and gives free entry to HS sites (half-price entry to sites in England and Wales). Also offers short-term 'Explorer' membership – three/seven/10 days for £19/27/32. Standard HS property opening times are 9.30am to 5.30pm daily April to September, closing one hour earlier October to March. (Note, some properties have extended hours in October.)

**National Trust for Scotland** (NTS; Map pp76-7; ☎ 0131-243 9300; www.nts.org.uk; 28 Charlotte Sq, Edinburgh EH2 4ET) A year's membership of the NTS, costing £50 (£15 for those aged under 25, £29 for seniors), offers free access to all NTS and National Trust properties (in the rest of the UK).

## VISAS

Visa regulations are always subject to change, so it's essential to check with your local British embassy, high commission or consulate before leaving home. Currently, if you're a citizen of Australia, Canada, New Zealand, South Africa or the USA, you can stay for up to six months (no visa required), but are not allowed to work. The Working Holidaymaker scheme, for Commonwealth citizens aged 17 to 30 inclusive, allows visits of up to two years, but arrangements must be made in advance through a British embassy.

Commonwealth citizens with a UK-born parent may be eligible for a Certificate of Entitlement to the Right of Abode, which entitles them to live and work in the UK. Commonwealth citizens with a UK-born grandparent could qualify for a UK Ancestry-Employment Certificate, allowing them to work full time for up to four years in the UK. EU citizens can live and work in Britain free of

**DIRECTORY**

immigration control and don't need a visa to enter the country.

All other nationalities should contact their nearest British diplomatic mission to obtain a visa. Six month multiple-entry visas cost from £63.

British immigration authorities have always been tough; dress neatly and carry proof that you have sufficient funds with which to support yourself. A credit card and/or an onward ticket will help.

No visas are required for Scotland if you arrive from England or Northern Ireland. For more info, see www.ukvisas.gov.uk or the **Lonely Planet** (www.lonelyplanet.com) website.

### Visa Extensions

To inquire about extending your stay in the UK, contact the **Home Office, Immigration & Nationality Directorate** ( ☎ 0870 606 7766; Lunar House, 40 Wellesley Rd, Croydon, London CR9 2BY) *before* your existing permit expires.

## WOMEN TRAVELLERS

Women are unlikely to have problems in Scotland, but common-sense caution should be observed, especially in towns and cities. Women can enter most pubs alone, but there are still a few places where this may attract unwanted attention. Cosmopolitan city pubs and most rural pubs are fine – you'll get a pretty good idea when you walk in. Sticking to pubs frequented by tourists is a safe bet.

Many parts of central Edinburgh and Glasgow are best avoided late at night. Be aware of red-light districts in both cities – between Salamander St and Leith Links (Leith, Edinburgh) and Anderston/Blythswood Sq (Glasgow).

The National Office of **Rape Crisis** ( ☎ Glasgow 0141 552 3200, Edinburgh 0131 556 9437; www.rapecrisis scotland.org.uk) has a website with details of local offices around the country.

The contraceptive pill is available only on prescription; however, the 'morning-after' pill (effective against conception for up to 72 hours after unprotected sexual intercourse) is available over-the-counter at chemists.

For general advice on health issues, contraception and pregnancy, visit a Well Woman clinic – ask at local libraries or doctors' surgeries. In Edinburgh, contact **Well Woman Services** ( ☎ 0131 332 7941; 18 Dean Tce, Stockbridge).

## WORK

Whatever your skills, it's worth registering with a number of temporary employment agencies – there are plenty in the cities.

Hostel notice boards sometimes advertise casual work. Without skills, it's difficult to find a job that pays enough to save money. Pick up the free *TNT* (www.tntmagazine .co.uk), found in larger cities – it lists jobs and employment agencies aimed at travellers.

Low-paid seasonal work is available in the tourist industry, usually in restaurants and pubs. This was once the domain of Australian, South African and New Zealand travellers but the recent membership enlargement of the EU has seen many Eastern Europeans also travel to Scotland for these jobs. In particular, you'll probably meet Poles, Slovakians and Slovenians working in pubs, hotels and restaurants in the Highlands.

EU citizens don't need a work permit – see also Visas (p447) for details about the Working Holidaymaker scheme for Commonwealth citizens. Students from the USA who are at least 18 years old and studying full time at a college or university can get a Blue Card permit allowing them to work for six months in the UK. It's available through the **British Universities North America Club** (BUNAC; www .bunac.org.uk). The club also runs programmes for Australians, Canadians and New Zealanders. For more details, check out the website.

# Transport

## CONTENTS

# GETTING THERE & AWAY

## AIR

There are direct flights to Scottish airports from England, Wales, Ireland, the USA, Canada, Scandinavia and several countries in western and central Europe. From elsewhere, you'll probably have to fly into a European hub and catch a connecting flight to a Scottish airport – London, Amsterdam, Frankfurt and Paris have the best connections. If flying from North America, it's worth looking at Icelandair, which often has good deals to Glasgow via Reykjavik.

### Airports & Airlines

Scotland has four main international airports of its own. London is the main UK gateway for long-haul flights.

---

**THINGS CHANGE...**

The information in this chapter is particularly vulnerable to change. Check directly with the airline or a travel agent to make sure you understand how a fare (and ticket you may buy) works and be aware of the security requirements for international travel. Shop carefully. The details given in this chapter should be regarded as pointers and are not a substitute for your own careful, up-to-date research.

---

**Aberdeen** (ABZ; ☎ 0870 040 0006; www.aberdeen airport.com)
**Edinburgh** (EDI; ☎ 0870 040 0007; www.edinburgh airport.com)
**Glasgow** (GLA; ☎ 0870 040 0008; www.glasgowairport .com)
**Glasgow Prestwick** (PIK; ☎ 0871 223 0700; www.gpia .co.uk)
**London Gatwick** (LGW; ☎ 0870 000 2468; www.gat wickairport.com)
**London Heathrow** (LHR; ☎ 0870 000 0123; www .heathrowairport.com)

A few short-haul international flights land at **Dundee** (DND; ☎ 01382-662200; www.dundeecity.gov.uk/airport), **Inverness** (INV; ☎ 01667-464000; www.hial.co.uk) and **Sumburgh** (LSI; ☎ 01950-461000; www.hial.co.uk).

There are many airlines serving Scottish airports. The main ones:

**Aer Arann** (RE; ☎ 0800 587 2324; www.aerarann.com)
**Aer Lingus** (EI; ☎ 0870 876 5000; www.aerlingus.com)
**Air France/Cityjet** (AF; ☎ 0870 142 4343; www.air france.co.uk)
**Air Malta** (KM; ☎ 0845 607 3710; www.airmalta.com)
**Air Transat** (TS; ☎ 020-7616 9187; www.airtransat.com)
**Atlantic Airways** (RC; ☎ 08701 999 440; www .flyshetland.com)
**bmi** (BD; ☎ 0870 607 0555; www.flybmi.com)
**bmibaby** (WW; ☎ 0870 264 2229; www.bmibaby.com)
**British Airways** (BA; ☎ 0870 850 9850; www.british airways.co.uk)
**Centralwings** (C0; ☎ +48 22 558 0045; www.central wings.com)
**Continental Airlines** (CO; ☎ 0845 607 6760; www .continental.com)
**Eastern Airways** (T3; ☎ 0870 366 9100; www.eastern airways.com)
**easyJet** (U2; www.easyjet.com)
**FlyBe** (BE; ☎ 0871 700 0123; www.flybe.com)
**FlyGlobespan** (GSM; ☎ 0870 556 1522; www.flyglobe span.com)
**FlyWhoosh** (WEA; ☎ 0871 282 6767; www.flywhoosh.com)
**Germanwings** (4U; ☎ 020-8321 7255; www.german wings.com)
**Highland Airways** (HS; ☎ 0845 450 2245; www.high landairways.co.uk)
**Icelandair** (FI; ☎ 0870 787 4020; www.icelandair.com)
**Jet2.com** (LS; ☎ 0871 226 1737; www.jet2.com)
**KLM Cityhopper** (UK; ☎ 0870 507 4074; www.klmuk.com)

**Lufthansa** (LH; ☎ 0870 8737 747; www.lufthansa
.co.uk)
**Ryanair** (FR; www.ryanair.com)
**Scandinavian Airlines** (SK; ☎ 0870 60 727 727; www
.flysas.com)
**US Airways** (US; ☎ 0845 600 3300; www.usairways.com)
**Wideroe** (WF; ☎ +47 8100 1200; www.wideroe.no)
**Zoom Airlines** (OOM; ☎ 0870 240 0055; www.fly
zoom.com)

## Australia & New Zealand

Many airlines compete on flights between
Australia and New Zealand and the UK and
there is a wide range of fares. Round-the-
world (RTW) tickets are often real bargains
and can sometimes work out cheaper than a
straightforward return ticket.

Expect to pay anything from A$2000 to
A$3000. Adding a connecting flight from
London to Edinburgh should only add around
A$100 to the cost of the ticket.

### AUSTRALIA
**Flight Centre** ( ☎ 133 133; www.flightcentre.com.au)
**STA Travel** ( ☎ 134 782; www.statravel.com.au)

### NEW ZEALAND
**Flight Centre** ( ☎ 0800 243 544; www.flightcentre
.co.nz)
**STA Travel** ( ☎ 0800 474 400; www.statravel.co.nz)

## Canada

Zoom Airlines flies direct to Glasgow from
Vancouver, Toronto and Ottawa (up to five
a week, year-round), and from Calgary and
Halifax (once or twice a week, May to October
only). Charter operator Air Transat has one
direct flight a week from Toronto to Edinburgh (May to October) and Glasgow (April to
October), and weekly flights to Glasgow from
Calgary and Vancouver (May to October).

**Travel CUTS** ( ☎ 1-866 246 9762; www.travelcuts.com)
is Canada's national student travel agency and
has offices in all major cities.

## Continental Europe

There are several direct flights a day into Edinburgh and/or Glasgow from Amsterdam,
Brussels, Frankfurt, Geneva, Hamburg, Madrid, Moscow, Paris, Prague, Warsaw, Rome
and many other European cities.

## England & Wales

There are more than a hundred flights a day
between London and Edinburgh and Glasgow,
and several daily from other UK airports. BA
has flights to Glasgow and Edinburgh from
London, Birmingham and Manchester, and to
Aberdeen and Inverness from London.

EasyJet flies from London to Edinburgh,
Glasgow, Inverness and Aberdeen, and

---

### CLIMATE CHANGE & TRAVEL

Climate change is a serious threat to the ecosystems that humans rely upon, and air travel is the
fastest-growing contributor to the problem. Lonely Planet regards travel, overall, as a global benefit, but believes we all have a responsibility to limit our personal impact on global warming.

#### Flying & Climate Change

Pretty much every form of motor travel generates $CO_2$ (the main cause of human-induced climate
change) but planes are far and away the worst offenders, not just because of the sheer distances
they allow us to travel, but because they release greenhouse gases high into the atmosphere.
The statistics are frightening: two people taking a return flight between Europe and the US will
contribute as much to climate change as an average household's gas and electricity consumption over a whole year.

#### Carbon Offset Schemes

Climatecare.org and other websites use 'carbon calculators' that allow jetsetters to offset the
greenhouse gases they are responsible for with contributions to energy-saving projects and
other climate-friendly initiatives in the developing world – including projects in India, Honduras,
Kazakhstan and Uganda.

Lonely Planet, together with Rough Guides and other concerned partners in the travel industry,
supports the carbon offset scheme run by climatecare.org. Lonely Planet offsets all of its staff
and author travel.

For more information, check out our website: lonelyplanet.com.

from Bristol to Edinburgh and Glasgow. Air France/Cityjet flies from London City to Edinburgh and Dundee; bmibaby has flights from Birmingham, East Midlands and Cardiff to Edinburgh and Glasgow, and from Birmingham to Aberdeen. Eastern Airways flies from various English airports to Aberdeen and Inverness. Prices vary a lot. A standard economy return ticket from London to Edinburgh or Glasgow is around £250, while budget airlines offer flights for as little as £20 one way, travelling midweek and booking a month or two in advance.

Dependable UK travel agencies include **STA Travel** ( ☎ 08712 300 040; www.statravel.co.uk) and **Trailfinders** ( ☎ 08450 585 858; www.trailfinders.com).

## Ireland

BA flies from Londonderry to Glasgow. EasyJet has direct flights from Belfast to Glasgow and Edinburgh. There are daily flights from Dublin to Edinburgh and Glasgow with Aer Lingus. Ryanair flies from Dublin to Glasgow Prestwick, Edinburgh and Aberdeen. FlyBe flies from Belfast to Glasgow, Edinburgh Aberdeen and Inverness.

The Irish youth and student travel agency **usitNOW** ( ☎ 01-602 1904; www.usitnow.ie) has offices in most major cities in Ireland.

## Scandinavia

SAS flies from Copenhagen and Stavanger to Aberdeen, and from Stockholm to Edinburgh and Glasgow; and Wideroe has flights to Aberdeen from Bergen and Stavanger. Ryanair flies from Oslo and Gothenburg to Glasgow Prestwick.

Icelandair has daily flights between Reykjavik and Glasgow, and Atlantic Airways links Shetland to the Faroe Islands and London.

## USA

Continental flies daily from New York (Newark) to Glasgow and Edinburgh, while FlyGlobespan flights operate four times a week between Boston and Glasgow.

**STA Travel** ( ☎ 800 781 4040; www.statravel.com) has offices in major cities.

## LAND
### Bus

Buses are usually the cheapest way to get to Scotland from other parts of the UK. The main operators are **National Express** ( ☎ 0870 580 8080; www.gobycoach.com) and its subsidiary **Scottish**

**Citylink** ( ☎ 0870 550 5050; www.citylink.co.uk), with regular services from London and other cities in England, Wales and Northern Ireland.

**Silver Choice Travel** ( ☎ 01355-249499; www.silverchoicetravel.co.uk) operates a daily overnight service from London to Glasgow/Edinburgh, charging from £24 for an Apex (advanced purchase) return. **Megabus** ( ☎ 0900 160 0900; www.megabus.com) has one-way fares from London to Glasgow from as little as £1.50 if you book well in advance. For info on bus passes and discount cards, see p453.

Scottish Citylink runs a daily bus service to Edinburgh from Belfast (£23, seven hours) and Dublin (£31, 10½ hours).

### Car & Motorcycle

Drivers of EU-registered vehicles will find bringing a car or motorcycle into Scotland fairly easy. The vehicle must have registration papers and a nationality plate, and you must have insurance. The International Insurance Certificate (Green Card) isn't compulsory, but it is excellent proof that you're covered. If driving from mainland Europe via the Channel Tunnel or ferry ports, head for London and follow the M25 orbital road to the M1 motorway, then follow the M1 and M6 north.

### Train

Travelling to Scotland by train is usually faster and more comfortable than the bus, but more expensive. Taking into account check-ins and travel time between city centre and airport, the train is a competitive alternative, time wise, to air travel on the London to Edinburgh route. You can get timetable and fares info for all UK trains from the **National Rail Enquiry Service** ( ☎ 08457 484 950; www.nationalrail.co.uk).

#### CHANNEL TUNNEL SERVICES

With the opening of a high-speed rail link to the new St Pancras International station, it is possible to travel from Paris or Brussels to London in around two hours on the **Eurostar** ( ☎ in UK 08705 186 186, in France 0892 35 35 39; www.eurostar.com) service. From St Pancras it's a quick and easy change to Kings Cross or Euston for trains to Edinburgh or Glasgow. Total journey time from Paris to Edinburgh is about eight hours.

#### UK

There is a fast and frequent rail service between London Kings Cross and Edinburgh

**TRANSPORT**

(four hours, every half-hour). A standard open return costs around £240 but special offers sometimes have single fares as low as £16. The train between London Euston and Glasgow is slower at 5½ hours.

**First ScotRail** ( ☎ 0845 755 0033; www.firstscotrail .com) runs the Caledonian Sleeper, an overnight service connecting London Euston with Edinburgh, Glasgow, Stirling, Perth, Dundee, Aberdeen, Fort William and Inverness. A standard sleeper berth (sharing a twin cabin) from London to Edinburgh is £110/155 for a single/return, and to Inverness, Aberdeen or Fort William is £135/180. Services to Edinburgh from other parts of England and Wales usually mean changing trains at some point. First ScotRail also has Rail & Sail deals between Edinburgh and Glasgow and Belfast via the ferry crossings at Stranraer and Troon.

## SEA
### Continental Europe
**Superfast Ferries** ( ☎ in UK 0870 234 0870, in Belgium 050 252 252; www.superfast.com) runs a car ferry between Rosyth, 12 miles northwest of Edinburgh, and Zeebrugge in Belgium (17½ hours, one daily). Return passenger fares in high season (July and August) range from €170 in an aircraft-style seat to €566 in a luxury cabin. A car is €239 return.

### Northern Ireland
Car ferry links between Northern Ireland and Scotland are run by **Stena Line** ( ☎ 08705 707 070; www.stenaline.co.uk) and **P&O Irish Sea** ( ☎ 0870 242 4777; www.poirishsea.com). Stena Line travels the Belfast–Stranraer route and P&O Irish Sea the Larne–Troon and Larne–Cairnryan routes. There's a choice of standard and high-speed ferries on the Stranraer and Cairnryan routes, high speed only on the Troon route.

The following prices are advance purchase one-way fares for a foot passenger/car with driver, in high season; fares vary with time and day of departure, and are often less than quoted here.

| Crossing | Duration | Frequency | Fare (£) |
| --- | --- | --- | --- |
| Belfast-Stranraer | 3¼hr | 2-4 daily | 23/100 |
| Belfast-Stranraer | 1¾hr | 4 daily | 23/120 |
| Larne-Cairnryan | 1¾hr | 8 daily | 20/94 |
| Larne-Cairnryan | 1hr | 2 daily (Mar-Sep) | 20/84 |
| Larne-Troon | 1¾hr | 2 daily (Mar-Sep) | 20/104 |

### Scandinavia
From May to early September, **Smyril Line** ( ☎ +298 345900; www.smyril-line.com) operates a weekly car ferry between Shetland (Lerwick), the Faroe Islands (Torshavn), Iceland (Seydisfjordur), Norway (Bergen) and Denmark (Hantsholm). It leaves from Lerwick on Monday for Bergen, and on Wednesday for Torshavn and Seydisfjordur. The Lerwick to Bergen crossing takes 13½ hours, Lerwick to Torshavn is 13 hours and Torshavn to Seydisfjordur is 15 hours.

# GETTING AROUND

Public transport in Scotland is generally good, but it can be costly compared with other European countries. Buses are usually the cheapest way to get around, but also the slowest. With a discount pass, trains can be competitive; they're also quicker and often take you through beautiful scenery.

**Traveline** ( ☎ 0871 200 2233; www.travelinescotland .com) provides timetable info for all public transport services in Scotland, but can't provide fare information or book tickets.

## AIR
Most domestic air services are geared to business needs, or are lifelines for remote island communities. Flying is a pricey way to cover relatively short distances, and only worth considering if you're short of time and want to visit the Hebrides, Orkney or Shetland.

### Airlines in Scotland
**British Airways/Loganair** ( ☎ 0870 850 9850; www .loganair.co.uk)
**Eastern Airways** ( ☎ 0870 366 9100; www.easternair ways.com)
**Highland Airways** ( ☎ 0845 450 2245; www.highland airways.co.uk)

British Airways/Loganair is the main domestic airline in Scotland, with flights from Glasgow to Barra, Benbecula, Campbeltown, Islay, Kirkwall, Sumburgh, Stornoway and Tiree; from Edinburgh to Inverness, Kirkwall, Sumburgh, Stornoway and Wick; from Aberdeen to Kirkwall and Sumburgh; and from Inverness to Kirkwall, Stornoway and Sumburgh. They also operate interisland flights in Orkney and Shetland, and from Barra to Benbecula.

**TRANSPORT**

Eastern Airways flies from Aberdeen to Stornoway and Wick. Highland Airways has flights from Inverness to Sumburgh and Stornoway, and from Stornoway to Benbecula.

## BICYCLE

Scotland is a compact country, and travelling around by bicycle is a perfectly feasible proposition if you have the time. Indeed, for touring the islands a bicycle is both cheaper (in terms of ferry fares) and more suited to their small size and more leisurely pace of life. For more information, see p59.

## BOAT

The main ferry operators are **Caledonian Mac-Brayne** (CalMac; ☎ 0870 565 0000; www.calmac.co.uk) for the west coast and islands, and **Northlink Ferries** ( ☎ 0845 600 0449; www.northlinkferries.co.uk) for Orkney and Shetland. CalMac's Island Rover ticket gives unlimited travel on its ferry services, and costs £52/75 for a foot passenger for eight/15 days, plus £249/372 for a car, or £124/187 for a motorbike. Bicycles travel free with a foot passenger's Island Rover ticket. There are also more than two dozen Island Hopscotch tickets, which give lower fares for various combinations of crossings; these are listed on the website and in the CalMac timetables booklet available from tourist offices throughout Scotland. Northlink ferries sail from Aberdeen and Scrabster (near Thurso) to Orkney, from Orkney to Shetland and from Aberdeen to Shetland. See the relevant destinations for full details of ferry services and fares.

## BUS

The national network is operated by **Scottish Citylink** ( ☎ 0870 550 5050; www.citylink.co.uk), with comfy, reliable buses serving all main towns. Off the main roads, you'll have to switch to local serv-ices. If planning a journey off the main routes, phone **Traveline** ( ☎ 0871 600 2233; www.traveline scotland.com) for up-to-date timetables.

Many remote villages can only be reached by **Royal Mail postbuses** ( ☎ 0845 774 0740; www.postbus.royalmail.com). These are minibuses, or sometimes four-seater cars, driven by postal workers delivering and collecting the mail. They follow circuitous routes through some of the loveliest areas of Scotland, and are useful for walkers – there are no official stops, and you can hail a postbus anywhere on its route. Fares are usually £2 to £5 one way.

From April to September, **Macbackpackers** ( ☎ 0131-558 9900; www.macbackpackers.com) offers a jump-on, jump-off minibus tour running from Edinburgh to Inverness, Skye, Fort William, Glencoe, Oban and Stirling. A ticket, valid for up to three months, costs £75. It also offers one- to seven-day guided minibus tours of the Highlands, as do the following outfits: **Celtic Adventures** ( ☎ 0131-225 3330; www.celtic adventures.com) Combined tours of Scotland and Ireland. **Haggis Adventures** ( ☎ 0131-557 9393; www.haggis adventures.com) **Wild in Scotland** ( ☎ 0131-478 6500; www.wild-in -scotland.com)

### Bus Passes

The Scottish Citylink Explorer Pass can be bought in the UK by both UK and overseas citizens. It offers unlimited travel on all Scottish Citylink services within Scotland for any three days out of five (£35), for any five days out of 10 (£59), or any eight days out of 16 (£79). It also gives discounts on various regional bus services, on Northlink and CalMac ferries, and in SYHA hostels. It is not valid on National Express coaches.

Scottish Citylink offers discounts to students, SYHA members, and holders of the **Young Scot card** ( ☎ 0808 801 0338; www.youngscot.org), which gives discounts all over Scotland and Europe. Holders of a National Entitlement Card, available to seniors and disabled people who are UK citizens, gives free bus travel throughout the country.

## CAR & MOTORCYCLE

Travel by car or motorcycle allows you to get to remote places and to travel quickly, independently and flexibly. Scotland's roads are generally good and far less busy than in England, so driving's more enjoyable. However, cars are nearly always inconvenient in city centres.

Motorways (designated 'M') are toll-free dual carriageways, limited mainly to central Scotland. Main roads ('A') are dual or single carriageways and are sometimes clogged with slow-moving trucks or caravans; the A9 from Perth to Inverness is notoriously busy.

Life on the road is more relaxed and interesting on the secondary roads (designated 'B') and minor roads (undesignated). These wind through the countryside from village to village. You can't travel fast, but you won't want to. In many country areas, and especially in the Highlands and islands, roads are only single track with passing places. Remember that passing places are not only for allowing oncoming traffic to pass, but also for overtaking – check your rear-view mirror often, and pull over to let faster vehicles pass if necessary. It's illegal to park in passing places. In the Highlands and islands there's the added hazard of suicidal sheep wandering onto the road (be particularly wary of lambs in spring).

At around 98p per litre (equivalent to more than US$7 per US gallon), petrol's expensive by American or Australian standards; diesel is about 1p per litre cheaper. Distances, however, aren't as great. Prices tend to rise as you get further from the main centres and are over 10% higher in the Outer Hebrides (around £1.09 a litre). In remote areas petrol stations are widely spaced and sometimes closed on Sunday.

### Driving Licence

A non-EU licence is valid in Britain for up to 12 months from time of entry into the country. If bringing a car from Europe, make sure you're adequately insured.

### Hire

Car rental is relatively costly and often you'll be better off making arrangements in your home country for a fly/drive deal. The international rental companies charge from around £140 a week for a small car (Ford Fiesta, Peugeot 106); local companies, such as **Arnold Clark** ( ☎ 0845 607 4500; www.arnoldclarkrental .co.uk), start from £23 a day or £110 a week.

The main international hire companies:
**Avis** ( ☎ 0870 606 0100; www.avis.co.uk)
**Budget** ( ☎ 0870 153 9170; www.budget.co.uk)
**Europcar** ( ☎ 0870 607 5000; www.europcar.co.uk)
**Hertz** ( ☎ 0870 844 8844; www.hertz.co.uk)
**Thrifty Car Rental** ( ☎ 0808 234 7642; www.thrifty .co.uk)

Tourist offices have lists of local car-hire companies.

To rent a car, drivers must usually be aged 23 to 65 – outside these limits special conditions or insurance requirements may apply.

If planning to visit the Outer Hebrides, Orkney or Shetland, it'll often prove cheaper to hire a car on the islands, rather than pay to take a rental car across on the ferry.

### Road Rules

Anyone using the roads a lot should get the *Highway Code,* which is widely available in bookshops. Vehicles drive on the left; front-seat belts are compulsory and if belts are fitted

## ROAD DISTANCES (MILES)

| | Aberdeen | Dundee | Edinburgh | Fort William | Glasgow | Inverness | Kyle of Lochalsh | Mallaig | Oban | Scrabster | Stranraer |
|---|---|---|---|---|---|---|---|---|---|---|---|
| Dundee | 70 | | | | | | | | | | |
| Edinburgh | 129 | 62 | | | | | | | | | |
| Fort William | 165 | 121 | 146 | | | | | | | | |
| Glasgow | 145 | 84 | 42 | 104 | | | | | | | |
| Inverness | 105 | 131 | 155 | 66 | 166 | | | | | | |
| Kyle of Lochalsh | 188 | 177 | 206 | 76 | 181 | 82 | | | | | |
| Mallaig | 189 | 161 | 180 | 44 | 150 | 106 | 34 | | | | |
| Oban | 180 | 118 | 123 | 45 | 94 | 110 | 120 | 85 | | | |
| Scrabster | 218 | 250 | 279 | 185 | 286 | 119 | 214 | 238 | 230 | | |
| Stranraer | 233 | 171 | 120 | 184 | 80 | 250 | 265 | 232 | 178 | 374 | |
| Ullapool | 150 | 189 | 215 | 90 | 225 | 135 | 88 | 166 | 161 | 125 | 158 |

in the back seat, then they must be worn too; the speed limit is 30mph in built-up areas, 60mph on single carriageways and 70mph on dual carriageways; you give way to your right at roundabouts (traffic already on the roundabout has right of way). Motorcyclists must wear helmets.

It is a criminal offence to use a hand-held mobile phone or similar device while driving; this includes while you are stopped at traffic lights, or stuck in traffic, when you can expect to be moving again at any moment.

See also p443 for information on drinking and driving and other legal matters.

## HITCHING

Hitching is never entirely safe in any country and we don't recommend it. Travellers who hitch take a small but potentially serious risk. However, many people choose to hitch, and the advice that follows should help to make their journeys as fast and safe as possible.

Hitching is fairly easy in Scotland, except around big cities and built-up areas, where you'll need to use public transport. Although the northwest is more difficult because there's less traffic, waits of over two hours are unusual (except on Sunday in 'Sabbath' areas). On some islands, where public transport is infrequent, hitching is so much a part of getting around that local drivers may stop and offer you lifts without you even asking.

It's against the law to hitch on motorways or their immediate slip roads; make a sign and use approach roads, nearby roundabouts or service stations.

## TOURS

There are lots of companies in Scotland offering all kinds of tours, including historical, activity-based and backpacker tours. It's a question of picking the tour that suits your requirements and budget. More companies are listed in destination chapters under Tours.

**Classique Tours** ( ☎ 0141-889 4050; www.classique tours.co.uk; 8 Underwood Rd, Paisley PA3 1TD) Bus tours of the western isles in vintage 1950s coaches, departing from Glasgow and staying in atmospheric country hotels.
**Heart of Scotland Tours** ( ☎ 01828-627799; www .heartofscotlandtours.co.uk) Specialises in minicoach day tours of central Scotland and the Highlands, departing from Edinburgh.
**Hebridean Princess** ( ☎ 01756-704704; www.hebridean .co.uk) Luxury cruises around the west coast of Scotland, the Outer Hebrides, and the Orkney and Shetland islands.

**Mountain Innovations** ( ☎ 01479-831331; www .scotmountain.co.uk; Fraoch Lodge, Deshar Rd, Boat of Garten PH24 3BN) Good-value guided activity holidays and courses in the Highlands; walking, mountain biking, kayaking, skiing and horse riding.
**Rabbie's Trail Burners** ( ☎ 0131-226 3133; www.rab bies.com; 207 High St, Edinburgh EH1 1PE) One- to five-day tours of the Highlands in 16-seat minibuses.
**Scot-Trek** ( ☎ 0141-334 9232; www.scot-trek.co.uk; 9 Lawrence St, Glasgow G11 5HH) Guided walks for all levels; ideal for solo travellers wanting to link up with others.

## TRAIN

Scotland's rail network extends to all major cities and towns, but the railway map has a lot of large, blank areas in the Highlands and the Southern Uplands where you'll need to switch to bus or car. The West Highland line from Glasgow to Fort William and Mallaig, and the Inverness to Kyle of Lochalsh line are two of the world's most scenic rail journeys.

For info on train timetables call the **National Rail Enquiry Service** ( ☎ 08457-484950; www.nationalrail .co.uk) or download timetables from www.first scotrail.com.

Bikes are carried free on all First ScotRail trains, but space is sometimes limited. Reservations are compulsory on certain rail routes, including the Glasgow–Oban–Fort William–Mallaig line and the Inverness–Kyle of Lochalsh line; they are recommended on many others. You can make reservations for your bicycle from eight weeks to two hours in advance at main train stations, or when booking tickets by phone ( ☎ 0845 755 0033).

There are two classes of train travel: 1st and standard. First class is 30% to 50% more than standard but, except on very crowded trains, isn't really worth the extra money.

### Costs & Reservations

Rail travel is more expensive than the bus: a standard return from Edinburgh to Inverness is about £50 compared with £33 on the bus.

**First ScotRail** ( ☎ 0845 755 0033; www.firstscotrail .com) operates most train services in Scotland. Reservations are recommended for intercity trips, especially on Fridays and public holidays; for shorter journeys, just buy a ticket at the station before you go. On certain routes, including the Glasgow–Edinburgh express, and in places where there's no ticket office at the station, you can buy tickets on the train.

Children under five travel free; those five to 15 usually pay half-fare. On weekends

TRANSPORT

on some intercity routes you can upgrade a standard-class ticket to 1st class for £3 to £5 per single journey – ask the conductor on the train.

There's a bewildering array of ticket types.

**Single** Valid for a single (ie one-way) journey at any time on the particular day specified; expensive.

**Day Return** Valid for a return journey at any time on the particular day specified; relatively expensive.

**Cheap Day Return** Valid for a return journey on the day specified on the ticket, but there are time restrictions (you're not usually allowed to travel on a train that leaves before 9.15am); relatively cheap.

**Open Return** For outward travel on a stated day and return on any day within a month.

**SuperSaver** The cheapest ticket where advance purchase isn't necessary; can't be used on Friday, and travel must be after 9.15am Monday to Thursday; the return must be within a calendar month.

**Saver** Higher priced than the SuperSaver, but can be used any day; travel must be after 9.15am on weekdays.

**Value Advance** Similarly priced to SuperSaver but with fewer time/day restrictions; however, you must buy tickets before 6pm on the day before travel and specify both outward and return journey times; limited availability so book early.

## Discount Cards

Discount **railcards** (www.railcard.co.uk) are available for people aged 60 and over, for people aged 16 to 25 (or mature full-time students), and for those with a disability ( ☎ 0845 605 0525, text-phone 0845 601 0132). The Senior Railcard (£20), Young Persons Railcard (£20) and Disabled Persons Railcard (£18) are each valid for one year and give one-third off most train fares in Scotland, England and Wales. Fill in an application at any major train station. You'll need proof of age (birth certificate, passport or driving licence) for the Young Persons and Seniors railcards (proof of enrolment for mature-age students) and proof of entitlement for the Disabled Persons Railcard.

## Train Passes

First ScotRail has a range of good-value passes for train travel. You can buy them at BritRail outlets in the USA, Canada and Europe, at the British Travel Centre in Regent St, London, at train stations throughout Britain, at certain UK travel agents and from **First ScotRail Telesales** ( ☎ 0845 755 0033; www.firstscotrail.com).

The Freedom of Scotland Travelpass gives unlimited travel on all ScotRail and Strathclyde Passenger Transport trains, all CalMac ferry services and on certain Scottish Citylink coach services (on routes not covered by rail). It's available for four days' travel out of eight (£100) or eight days out of 15 (£135).

The Highland Rover pass allows travel from Glasgow to Oban, Fort William and Mallaig, and from Inverness to Kyle of Lochalsh, Aviemore, Aberdeen and Thurso; it also gives free travel on the Oban/Fort William to Inverness bus, on the Oban–Mull and Mallaig–Skye ferries, and on buses on Mull and Skye. It's valid for four days' travel out of eight (£65). The Central Scotland Rover covers train travel between Glasgow, Edinburgh, North Berwick, Stirling and Fife. It's £37 for three days' travel out of seven.

Note that Travelpass and Rover tickets are not valid for travel on certain (mainly commuter) services before 9.15am weekdays.

# Health

## CONTENTS

## BEFORE YOU GO

While Scotland has excellent health care, prevention is the key to staying healthy while travelling in the country. A little planning before departure, particularly for pre-existing illnesses, will save trouble later. Bring medications in their original, clearly labelled containers. A signed, dated letter from your physician describing your medical conditions and medications, including generic names, is also a good idea. If carrying syringes or needles, be sure to have a physician's letter documenting their medical necessity. Carry a spare pair of contact lenses and glasses, and take your optical prescription with you.

### INSURANCE

If you're an EU citizen, a European Health Insurance Card (EHIC), available from health centres or, in the UK, post offices, covers you for most medical care. EHIC will not cover you for nonemergencies, or emergency repatriation. Citizens from non-EU countries should find out if there is a reciprocal arrangement for free medical care between their country and the UK. If you do need health insurance, make sure you get a policy that covers you for the worst possible case, such as an accident requiring an emergency flight home. Find out in advance if your insurance plan will make payments directly to providers or reimburse you later for overseas health expenditures.

### RECOMMENDED VACCINATIONS

No jabs are required to travel to Scotland. The World Health Organization, however, recommends that all travellers should be covered for diphtheria, tetanus, measles, mumps, rubella, polio and Hepatitis B, regardless of their destination.

## IN TRANSIT

### DEEP VEIN THROMBOSIS (DVT)

Blood clots may form in the legs during plane flights, chiefly because of prolonged immobility. The longer the flight, the greater the risk. The chief symptom of deep vein thrombosis is swelling or pain in the foot, ankle or calf, usually but not always on just one side. When a blood clot travels to the lungs, it may cause chest pain and difficulty breathing. Travellers with any of these symptoms should immediately seek medical attention.

To prevent the development of DVT on long flights you should walk about the cabin, contract the leg muscles while sitting, drink plenty of fluids, and avoid alcohol and tobacco.

### JET LAG & MOTION SICKNESS

To avoid jet lag (common when crossing more than five time zones) try drinking plenty of nonalcoholic fluids and eating light meals. Upon arrival, get exposure to natural sunlight and readjust your schedule (for meals, sleep etc) as soon as possible.

Antihistamines such as dimenhydrinate (Dramamine) and meclizine (Antivert, Bonine) are usually the first choice for treating motion sickness. A herbal alternative is ginger.

## IN SCOTLAND

### AVAILABILITY & COST OF HEALTH CARE

Excellent health care is readily available and for minor self-limiting illnesses pharmacists can give valuable advice and sell over-the-counter medication. They can also advise when more specialised help is required and point you in the right direction.

## TRAVELLER'S DIARRHOEA

If you develop diarrhoea, be sure to drink plenty of fluids, preferably in the form of an oral rehydration solution such as dioralyte. If diarrhoea is bloody, persists for more than 72 hours or is accompanied by fever, shaking, chills or severe abdominal pain, you should seek medical attention.

## ENVIRONMENTAL HAZARDS
### Heat Stroke

Heat exhaustion (yes, it can happen in Scotland!) occurs following excessive fluid loss with inadequate replacement of fluids and salt. Symptoms to look out for include headache, dizziness and tiredness. Dehydration is already happening by the time you actually feel thirsty – aim to drink sufficient water to produce pale, diluted urine. To treat heat exhaustion drink water and/or fruit juice, and cool the body with cold water and fans.

### Hypothermia

Hypothermia occurs when the body loses heat faster than it can produce it. As ever, proper preparation will reduce the risks of getting it. Even on a hot day in the mountains, the weather can change rapidly, so carry waterproof garments, warm layers and a hat, and inform others of your route.

Hypothermia starts with shivering, loss of judgment and clumsiness. Unless rewarming occurs, the sufferer deteriorates into apathy, confusion and coma. Prevent further heat loss by seeking shelter, warm dry clothing, hot sweet drinks and shared body warmth.

### Midges & Clegs

The most painful problems facing visitors to the Highlands and islands are midges and clegs. The midge is a tiny, 2mm-long bloodsucking fly. Midges are at their worst during the twilight hours, and on still, overcast days. They proliferate from late May to mid-September, but especially mid-June to mid-August – which unfortunately coincides with the main tourist season. Cover up, particularly in the evening, wear light-coloured clothing (midges are attracted to dark colours) and, most importantly, use a reliable insect repellent containing DEET or DMP.

The cleg, or horse fly, is 13mm long and slate grey in colour. A master of stealth, it loves to land unnoticed on neck or ankle, and can give a painful bite. It can even bite through hair or light clothing. Unlike midges, they are most active on warm, sunny days, and are most common in July and August.

## TRAVELLING WITH CHILDREN

Make sure the children are up to date with routine vaccinations, and discuss possible travel vaccines well before departure as some vaccines are not suitable for children under a year old. See also Lonely Planet's *Travelling with Children* by Cathy Lanigan.

# Language

## CONTENTS

Scottish Gaelic (*Gàidhlig* – pronounced *gallic* in Scotland) is spoken by about 80,000 people in Scotland, mainly in the Highlands and islands, and by many native speakers and learners overseas. It is a member of the Celtic branch of the Indo-European family of languages, which has given us Gaelic, Irish, Manx, Welsh, Cornish and Breton.

Although Scottish Gaelic is the Celtic language most closely associated with Scotland it was quite a latecomer to those shores. Other Celtic languages in the form of Pictish and Brittonic had existed prior to the arrival and settlement by Gaelic-speaking Celts (Gaels) from Ireland from the 4th to the 6th centuries AD. These Irish settlers, known to the Romans as Scotti, were eventually to give their name to the entire country. Initially they settled in the area on the west coast of Scotland in which their name is perpetuated, Earra Ghaidheal (Argyll). As their territorial influence extended so did their language, and from the 9th to the 11th centuries Gaelic was spoken throughout the country. For many centuries the language was the same as the language of Ireland; there is little evidence of much divergence before the 13th century. Even up to the 18th century the bards adhered to the strict literary standards of Old Irish.

The Viking invasions from AD 800 brought linguistic influences which are evident in many of the coastal place names of the Highlands.

Gaelic culture flourished in the Highlands until the 18th century and the Jacobite rebellions. After the Battle of Culloden in 1746 many Gaelic speakers were forced from their ancestral lands; this 'ethnic cleansing' by landlords and governments culminated in the Highland Clearances of the 19th century. Although still studied at academic level, the spoken language declined, being regarded as little more than a mere 'peasant' language of no modern significance.

It was only in the 1970s that Gaelic began to make a comeback with a new generation of young enthusiasts who were determined that it should not be allowed to die. People from all over Scotland, and indeed worldwide, are beginning to appreciate their Gaelic heritage.

After two centuries of decline, the language is now being encouraged through financial help from government agencies and the EU. Gaelic education is flourishing from playgroups to tertiary levels. This renaissance flows out into the field of music, literature, cultural events and broadcasting.

The Gaelic language has a vital role to play in the life of modern Scotland. If you'd like a witty insight into the quirks of Scottish Gaelic and Britain's other regional dialects and languages, get a copy of Lonely Planet's pocket-sized *British Language & Culture*. It includes a comprehensive list of useful Gaelic words and phrases.

## MAKING CONVERSATION

**Good morning.**
   *Madainn mhath.*      madding va
**Good afternoon/Good evening.**
   *Feasgar math.*      fesskurr ma
**Good night.**
   *Oidhche mhath.*      uh eech uh va
**How are you?**
   *Ciamar a tha thu?*      kimmer uh ha oo?
**Very well, thank you.**
   *Glè mhath, tapadh leat.*      gley va, tappuh let
**I'm well, thank you.**
   *Tha mi gu math,*      ha mee goo ma,
   *tapadh leat.*      tappuh let
**That's good.**
   *'S math sin.*      sma shin
**Please.**
   *Mas e do thoil e.*      mahs eh doh hawl eh
**Thank you.**
   *Tapadh leat.*      tappuh let
**Many thanks.**
   *Mòran taing.*      moe ran ta eeng
**You're welcome.**
   *'Se do bheatha.*      sheh doh veh huh
**I beg your pardon.**
   *B'àill leibh.*      baaluv

**Excuse me.**
*Gabh mo leisgeul.*    gav mo lishk yal
**I'm sorry.**
*Tha mi duilich.*    ha mee dooleech
**Do you speak (have) Gaelic?**
*A bheil Gàidhlig agad?*    uh vil ga lick ackut?
**Yes, a little.**
*Tha, beagan.*    ha, beg an
**Not much.**
*Chan eil mòran.*    chan yil moe ran
**What's your name?**
*De an t ainm a tha ort?*    jae an tannam uh ha orsht?
**I'm...**
*Is mise...*    is meeshuh...
**Good health/Cheers!**
*Slàinte mhath!*    slahntchuh va!
**Goodbye.** (lit: Blessings go with you)
*Beannachd leat.*    b yan achd let
**Goodbye.** (The same with you)
*Mar sin leat.*    mar shin let

## FOOD & DRINK
**I'm hungry.**
*Tha an t-acras orm.*    ha an tac russ orrom
**I'm thirsty.**
*Tha am pathadh orm.*    ha am pah ugh orrom
**I'd like...**
*Bu toigh leam...*    boo tawl lehum
**I don't like...**
*Cha toigh leam...*    chah tawl lehum
**That was good.**
*Bha siud math.*    va shood ma

**Very good.**
*Glè mhath.*    gley va

| a biscuit | *brioscaid* | briskatch |
|---|---|---|
| bread | *aran* | aran |
| broth/soup | *brot* | broht |
| butter | *ìm* | eem |
| cheese | *càise* | kashuh |
| cream | *bàrr* | baahrr |
| dessert | *mìlsean* | meehlshuhn |
| fish | *iasg* | eeusk |
| meat | *feòil* | fehyawl |
| oatcakes | *aran coirce* | aran korkuh |
| peas | *peasair* | pessir |
| porridge | *lee lite* | chuh |
| potatoes | *buntàta* | boontahtuh |
| salmon | *bradan* | brahdan |
| vegetables | *glasraich* | glasreech |

| a cup of coffee | *cupa cofaidh* | coopa cawfee |
|---|---|---|
| a cup of tea | *cupa tì* | coopa tee |
| black coffee | *cofaidh dubh* | cawfee dooh |
| black tea | *tì dhubh* | tee dhooh |
| with milk | *le bainne* | leh bahnyuh |
| with sugar | leh *le siùcar* | shooh car |
| a glass of water | *glainne uisge* | glahnyuh ooshkuy |
| a glass of wine | *glainne fìon* | glahnyuh feeuhn |
| beer | *leann* | lyawn |
| red wine | *fìon dearg* | feeuhn jerrack |
| white wine | *fìon geal* | feeuhn gyahl |
| whisky | *uisge beatha* | ooshkuy beh huh |

Also available from Lonely Planet:
*British Language & Culture*

# Glossary

**bag** – reach the top of (as in to 'bag a couple of peaks' or 'Munro bagging')
**bailey** – the space enclosed by castle walls
**ben** – mountain
**birlinn** – Hebridean galley
**blackhouse** – low-walled stone cottage with thatch or turf roof and earth floors; shared by both humans and cattle and typical of the Outer Hebrides until the early 20th century
**böd** – once a simple trading booth used by fishing communities, today it refers to basic accommodation for walkers etc
**bothy** – hut or mountain shelter
**brae** – hill
**broch** – defensive tower
**burgh** – town
**burn** – stream
**buttie** – sandwich

**cairn** – pile of stones to mark path or junction, also peak
**ceilidh** – pronounced *kay*-lay; evening of traditional Scottish entertainment including music, song and dance
**Celtic High Cross** – a large, elaborately carved stone cross decorated with biblical scenes and Celtic interlace designs dating from the 8th to 10th centuries
**chippy** – fish and chip shop
**close** – entrance to an alley
**corrie** – circular hollow on a hill side
**craic** – lively conversation
**craig** – exposed rock
**crannog** – artificial island in a loch built for defensive purposes
**cratur** – whisky
**crofting** – smallholding in marginal agricultural areas following the Clearances
**Cullen skink** – soup made with smoked haddock, potato, onion and milk

**dene** – valley
**dirk** – dagger
**dram** – a measure of whisky
**dun** – fort

**firth** – estuary

**glen** – valley
**gloup** – natural arch

**Hogmanay** – New Year's Eve
**howff** – pub or shelter
**HS** – Historic Scotland

**kirk** – church
**kyle** – narrow strait of water

**law** – round hill
**linn** – waterfall
**lochan** – small loch

**machair** – grass- and wildflower-covered dunes
**Mercat Cross** – a symbol of the trading rights of a market town or village, usually found in the centre of town and usually a focal point for the community
**motte** – early Norman fortification consisting of a raised, flattened mound with a keep on top; when attached to a *bailey* it is known as a motte-and-bailey
**Munro** – mountain of 3000ft (914m) or higher
**Munro bagger** – a hill walker who tries to climb all the Munros in Scotland

**ness** – headland
**neuk** – corner
**NNR** – National Nature Reserve, managed by the SNH
**NTS** – National Trust for Scotland
**nyvaig** – Hebridean galley

**pap** – breast-shaped hill
**pend** – arched gateway
**Picts** – early inhabitants of north and east Scotland (from Latin *pictus*, or 'painted', after their body paint decorations)
**provost** – mayor

**rhinn** or **rhin** – headland
**RIB** – rigid inflatable boat
**rood** – an old Scots word for a cross
**RSPB** – Royal Society for the Protection of Birds

**Sassenach** – from Gaelic *Sasannach*, meaning anyone who is not a Highlander (including Lowland Scots)
**sett** – tartan pattern, or cobblestone
**shinty** – fast and physical ball-and-stick sport similar to Ireland's hurling
**SMC** – Scottish Mountaineering Club
**SNH** – Scottish Natural Heritage, a government organisation directly responsible for safeguarding and improving Scotland's natural heritage
**sporran** – purse worn around waist with the kilt
**SSSI** – Site of Special Scientific Interest
**strath** – valley
**SYHA** – Scottish Youth Hostel Association

**wynd** – lane

THE AUTHORS

# The Authors

## NEIL WILSON
**Coordinating Author**

Neil was born in Scotland and, save for a few years spent in England and Australia, has lived there for most of his life. When he was 14 he relieved the boredom of a rainy school holiday by leafing through a book about the Scottish mountains. The photographs of mist-veiled ridges, yawning cliffs and distant sea lochs opened the door to a lifelong enthusiasm for the great outdoors, and since then he has hiked, biked, climbed, sailed or snowboarded in almost every corner of the country. Neil has been a full-time writer and photographer since 1988 and has written around 45 guidebooks for various publishers, including Lonely Planet's guide to his home town of Edinburgh.

Neil wrote the introductory chapters (except History and Environment), Edinburgh, Northeast Scotland, Southern Highlands & Islands, Central & Western Highlands, the Skye & Outer Hebrides section of Northern Highlands & Islands, and the Transport chapter.

## ALAN MURPHY

Alan discovered Scotland sometime in the mid-1990s when he lived and worked in Edinburgh for two years. Since then he has returned on numerous occasions and this is the third time he has co-authored the *Scotland* book. With a journalistic background, and a love for all things Scottish (except deep-fried Mars Bars), Alan considers it a privilege to write about this country. For him Scotland is inspiring, almost indescribably beautiful and simply like coming home. This time around Alan wrote the Environment, History and Directory chapters, Southern Scotland, Glasgow, Central Scotland, Orkney & Shetland Islands, plus the Northern Highlands section of Northern Highlands & Islands. Alan's favourite part of Scotland is a slice of big tree country somewhere in Perthshire, among the glens and misty covered peaks of the Scottish heartland.

# Behind the Scenes

## THIS BOOK

This book is the 5th edition of Lonely Planet's *Scotland* and was updated by Neil Wilson and Alan Murphy. The 1st edition was written by Tom Smallman and Graeme Cornwallis. Neil coordinated the 2nd edition, with contributions from Graeme, and the 3rd and 4th editions were written by Neil and Alan. This guidebook was commissioned in Lonely Planet's London office and was produced by the following people:

**Commissioning Editor** Clifton Wilkinson
**Coordinating Editor** Rosie Nicholson
**Coordinating Cartographer** Csanad Csutoros
**Coordinating Layout Designer** Margaret Jung
**Managing Editor** Bruce Evans
**Managing Cartographer** Mark Griffiths
**Managing Layout Designer** Adam McCrow
**Assisting Editors** David Andrew, Gennifer Ciavarra, Anna Metcalfe, Kristin Odijk, Tom Smallman
**Assisting Cartographer** Chris Lee Ack
**Cover Designer** Brendan Dempsey
**Project Managers** Bronwyn Hicks, Glenn van der Knijff
**Language Content Coordinator** Quentin Frayne

**Thanks to** David Connolly, Ryan Evans, James Hardy, Jim Hsu, Indra Kilfoyle, Yvonne Kirk, Lisa Knights, Wayne Murphy, Naomi Parker, Cara Smith, Celia Wood

## THANKS
### NEIL WILSON

Many thanks to all the helpful and enthusiastic staff at tourist offices throughout the country, and to the many travellers I met on the road who chipped in with advice and recommendations. Thanks also to Carol Downie for keeping me company on a soggy camping trip to Skye and the Outer Hebrides, and for providing advice on shopping (never my strong point), and to Andrew Henderson, Steven Fallon, Russell Leaper, Erlend Tait and Pamela Tait. Finally, thanks to co-author Alan and to the ever-helpful and patient editors and cartographers at Lonely Planet.

### ALAN MURPHY

Scotland is a project I love working on and every trip is a treat as I not only get to travel around one of the best countries in the world, but also get to catch up with some of my best friends in the world. The support of my family and friends was as usual rock solid, and the cornerstone of this project. In Edinburgh thanks to Bryan McRitchie foremost a friend, but also musician and adviser on all things musical. Still in Edinburgh, Nial Briggs provided conversation, laughs and pints down at the Baillie. Tourist offices around the country were, as usual, incredibly helpful and I am indebted to them. The

---

### THE LONELY PLANET STORY

Fresh from an epic journey across Europe, Asia and Australia in 1972, Tony and Maureen Wheeler sat at their kitchen table stapling together notes. The first Lonely Planet guidebook, *Across Asia on the Cheap*, was born.

Travellers snapped up the guides. Inspired by their success, the Wheelers began publishing books to Southeast Asia, India and beyond. Demand was prodigious, and the Wheelers expanded the business rapidly to keep up. Over the years, Lonely Planet extended its coverage to every country and into the virtual world via lonelyplanet.com and the Thorn Tree message board.

As Lonely Planet became a globally loved brand, Tony and Maureen received several offers for the company. But it wasn't until 2007 that they found a partner whom they trusted to remain true to the company's principles of travelling widely, treading lightly and giving sustainably. In October of that year, BBC Worldwide acquired a 75% share in the company, pledging to uphold Lonely Planet's commitment to independent travel, trustworthy advice and editorial independence.

Today, Lonely Planet has offices in Melbourne, London and Oakland, with over 500 staff members and 300 authors. Tony and Maureen are still actively involved with Lonely Planet. They're travelling more often than ever, and they're devoting their spare time to charitable projects. And the company is still driven by the philosophy of *Across Asia on the Cheap*: 'All you've got to do is decide to go and the hardest part is over. So go!'

BEHIND THE SCENES

special thing about travelling around Scotland is its people – and once again my appreciation for their friendly patter and hospitality. Lastly, thanks to my co-author Neil – a fantastic author to work with and a great resource on Scotland. I'm constantly amazed at the nooks and crannies of Edinburgh he drags me along to, forcing me of course to down a few pints in the capital's pubs before sending me off researching...his generous welcome is always much appreciated.

## OUR READERS

Many thanks to the travellers who used the last edition and wrote to us with helpful hints, useful advice and interesting anecdotes:

Louise Austen, Shannon Bartlett, Fraser Bell, Maria Belyaeva, Keith Blackburn, Douglas Bowers, Linda Breeze, Stephen Broomfield, Susan Brunning, Benny Cahan, Linda Cahill, Emmanuel Cazelles, Bjørn Clasen, Steve Copland, Kathryn Entner, Kantara Farms, G Ferguson, Ane Forsmo, Georgia Frank, Gerardina Fuhrmann, Liz Gammie, Richard Gammie, Becka Gardner, Ryan Gee, Fiona Gilchrist, Michael Girard, Sophia Gkioka, Jean Govenlock, Jonathan Grafton, Anna Grigson, Rebecca Hay, Jens Hogel, Thomas Ihly, Lorraine Jelley, Rhys & Kylie Johnston, Tessa De Jong, Lauren Kangars, James Kearney, Peter Kilpatrick, Andrew P Kirk, Paul Lally, Sam Lawn, Vincent Ling, Sandra Little, Carrie Lubitz, Trevor Mazzucchelli, Robert Mccandless, David Mcintosh, Shona Mcroberts, Katharina Menzel, Shane Morkin, Josh Nakaya, Kars Neven, B J Newale, Gerald Olsen, Amy Paterson, Giel Ramaekers, Stewart Robertson, Peter Rosieur, Mary Sheppard, John Sifling, Carole Simkins, Christine Steen, Sarah Stolz, Claudia Sumler, Tim Taels, Loredano Tessitore, Bobby Thomson, Jamie Umaña, Barry Der van Woude, Anna Vitenbergs, Ann Warden, Robert Watson, Simon Whittaker

### SEND US YOUR FEEDBACK

We love to hear from travellers – your comments keep us on our toes and help make our books better. Our well-travelled team reads every word on what you loved or loathed about this book. Although we cannot reply individually to postal submissions, we always guarantee that your feedback goes straight to the appropriate authors, in time for the next edition. Each person who sends us information is thanked in the next edition – and the most useful submissions are rewarded with a free book.

To send us your updates – and find out about Lonely Planet events, newsletters and travel news – visit our award-winning website: **www.lonelyplanet.com/contact**.

Note: we may edit, reproduce and incorporate your comments in Lonely Planet products such as guidebooks, websites and digital products, so let us know if you don't want your comments reproduced or your name acknowledged. For a copy of our privacy policy visit www.lonelyplanet.com/privacy.

## ACKNOWLEDGMENTS

Many thanks to the following for the use of their content:

Globe on title page ©Mountain High Maps 1993 Digital Wisdom, Inc.

# Index

INDEX

INDEX

INDEX

INDEX

**000** Map pages
**000** Photograph pages

INDEX

**000** Map pages
**000** Photograph pages

**INDEX**

**INDEX**

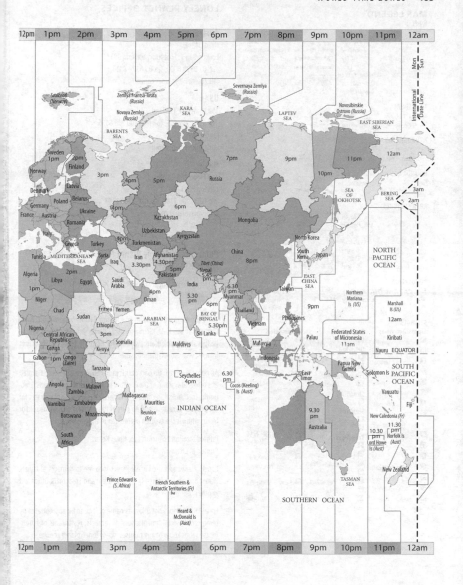

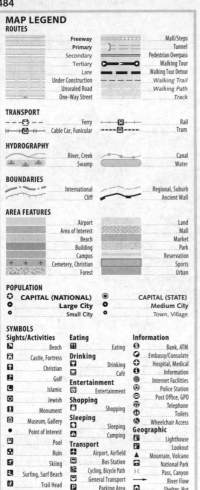

## MAP LEGEND

**ROUTES**

| | |
|---|---|
| Freeway | Mall/Steps |
| Primary | Tunnel |
| Secondary | Pedestrian Overpass |
| Tertiary | Walking Tour |
| Lane | Walking Tour Detour |
| Under Construction | Walking Trail |
| Unsealed Road | Walking Path |
| One-Way Street | Track |

**TRANSPORT**

| | |
|---|---|
| Ferry | Rail |
| Cable Car, Funicular | Tram |

**HYDROGRAPHY**

| | |
|---|---|
| River, Creek | Canal |
| Swamp | Water |

**BOUNDARIES**

| | |
|---|---|
| International | Regional, Suburb |
| Cliff | Ancient Wall |

**AREA FEATURES**

| | |
|---|---|
| Airport | Land |
| Area of Interest | Mall |
| Beach | Market |
| Building | Park |
| Campus | Reservation |
| Cemetery, Christian | Sports |
| Forest | Urban |

**POPULATION**

| | |
|---|---|
| CAPITAL (NATIONAL) | CAPITAL (STATE) |
| Large City | Medium City |
| Small City | Town, Village |

**SYMBOLS**

**Sights/Activities**
- Beach
- Castle, Fortress
- Christian
- Golf
- Islamic
- Jewish
- Monument
- Museum, Gallery
- Point of Interest
- Pool
- Ruin
- Skiing
- Surfing, Surf Beach
- Trail Head
- Winery, Vineyard
- Zoo, Bird Sanctuary

**Eating**
- Eating

**Drinking**
- Drinking
- Café

**Entertainment**
- Entertainment

**Shopping**
- Shopping

**Sleeping**
- Sleeping
- Camping

**Transport**
- Airport, Airfield
- Bus Station
- Cycling, Bicycle Path
- General Transport
- Parking Area
- Petrol Station
- Taxi Rank

**Information**
- Bank, ATM
- Embassy/Consulate
- Hospital, Medical
- Information
- Internet Facilities
- Police Station
- Post Office, GPO
- Telephone
- Toilets
- Wheelchair Access

**Geographic**
- Lighthouse
- Lookout
- Mountain, Volcano
- National Park
- Pass, Canyon
- River Flow
- Shelter, Hut
- Spot Height
- Waterfall

## LONELY PLANET OFFICES

**Australia**
Head Office
Locked Bag 1, Footscray, Victoria 3011
☎ 03 8379 8000, fax 03 8379 8111
talk2us@lonelyplanet.com.au

**USA**
150 Linden St, Oakland, CA 94607
☎ 510 893 8555, toll free 800 275 8555
fax 510 893 8572
info@lonelyplanet.com

**UK**
2nd Floor, 186 City Road,
London EC1V 2NT
☎ 020 7106 2100, fax 020 7106 2101
go@lonelyplanet.co.uk

**Published by Lonely Planet Publications Pty Ltd**
ABN 36 005 607 983

Cover photograph: The ruins of Kilchurn Castle overlook Loch Awe, Cladich, Strathclyde, Scotland, ABEL/Getty Images. Many of the images in this guide are available for licensing from Lonely Planet Images: www.lonelyplanetimages.com.

Printed through Colorcraft Ltd, Hong Kong.
Printed in China.